HAYTON AND MITCHELL COMMENTARY AND CASES ON THE LAW OF TRUSTS AND EQUITABLE REMEDIES

HAYTON AND MITCHELL COMMENTARY AND CASES ON THE LAW OF TRUSTS AND EQUITABLE REMEDIES

THIRTEENTH EDITION

By

CHARLES MITCHELL
Fellow and Tutor in Law, Jesus College, Oxford and
Professor of Law, University of Oxford

SWEET & MAXWELL
LONDON • 2010

THOMSON REUTERS

First Edition 1939 by J.A. Nathan
Second Edition 1951 by O.R. Marshall
Third Edition 1955 by O.R. Marshall
Fourth Edition 1961 by O.R. Marshall
Second Impression 1966 by O.R. Marshall
Fifth edition 1967 by O.R. Marshall
Second impression 1971 by O.R. Marshall
Sixth edition 1975 by D.J. Hayton
Seventh edition 1980 by D.J. Hayton
Eighth edition 1986 by D.J. Hayton
Second impression 1988 by D.J. Hayton
Third impression 1989 by D.J. Hayton
Ninth edition 1991 by D.J. Hayton
Second impression 1994 by D.J. Hayton
Tenth edition 1996 by D.J. Hayton
Second impression 1997 by D.J. Hayton
Third impression 1999 by D.J. Hayton
Fourth impression 2000 by D.J. Hayton
Eleventh edition 2001 by D.J. Hayton
Second impression 2001 by D.J. Hayton
Third impression 2003 by D.J. Hayton
Twelfth edition 2005 by D.J. Hayton and C.C.J. Mitchell

Published in 2010 by Thomson Reuters (Legal) Limited
(Registered in England & Wales, Company No 1679046.
Registered Office and address for service: 100 Avenue Road, London NW3 3PF)
trading as Sweet & Maxwell

For further information on our products and services, visit
www.sweetandmaxwell.co.uk

Typeset by LBJ Typesetting Ltd of Kingsclere
Printed in Great Britain by Ashford Colour Press, Gosport, Hants

No natural forests were destroyed to make this product;
only farmed timber was used and re-planted.

A CIP catalogue record for this book is available from the British Library.

ISBN-13 978-1-84703-730-5

ACKNOWLEDGMENTS

The Publishers and Author wish to thank the following for permission to reprint material from publications in which they have copyright:

The Charity Commission

The Charity Commission's Annual Reports

James Kessler QC

The Modern Trust Precedent from James Kessler, *Drafting Trusts and Will Trusts*, 7th edn (2004)

PREFACE

This book was edited by David Hayton for 30 years, between 1975 and 2005. During this time he took the book through six editions, and transformed it from an annotated collection of case extracts into a combined textbook and case-book, with extensive in-depth discussion that contextualises and illuminates selected passages from the case law. For the last (12th) edition of the book David invited me to join him as co-editor, and following his appointment as a Justice of the Caribbean Court of Justice in 2005, I have now taken over as sole editor of this (13th) edition. I am very grateful to David for entrusting me with this responsibility, and for his continued input into parts of the text, particularly Chapter 16, on trusts and the conflict of laws, which he has once more updated.

For this edition I have made some changes to the structure of the book and revised parts of the discussion to account for new developments over the past five years. I have found space for sections of the Charities Act 2006 and the Perpetuities and Accumulations Act 2009, excerpts from two Charity Commission documents, *Charities and Public Benefit* (January 2008 version) and *Public Benefit and Fee-Charging* (December 2008 version), and extracts from these cases: *BCCI (Overseas) Ltd v Akindele* [2001] Ch. 437; *Barlow Clowes International Ltd v Eurotrust International Ltd* [2006] 1 W.L.R. 1476; *Breakspear v Ackland* [2009] Ch. 32; *Chartbrook Ltd v Persimmon Homes Ltd* [2009] Bus. L.R. 1200; *Chopra v Bindra* [2009] 2 F.L.R. 786; *Re Griffiths (deceased)* [2009] Ch. 162; *Hanchett-Stamford v Att.-Gen.* [2009] Ch. 173; *HMRC v Trustees of the Peter Clay Discretionary Trust* [2009] Ch. 296; *Sieff v Fox* [2005] 1 W.L.R. 3811; *Stack v Dowden* [2007] 2 A.C. 432; *Re Walters (deceased)* [2009] Ch. 212; and *Wyndham v Egremont* [2009] W.T.L.R. 1473.

To make way for this new material, I have deleted extracts from these cases: *Abacus Trust Co (Isle of Man) Ltd v Barr* [2003] Ch. 409; *Re Burroughs-Fowler* [1916] 2 Ch. 251; *Cannon v Hartley* [1949] Ch. 213; *Chan v Zacharia* (1984) 154 C.L.R. 178; *Chellaram v Chellaram* [1985] Ch. 409; *Re Cleaver (deceased)* [1981] 1 W.L.R. 939; *Re Cook's ST* [1965] Ch. 902; *Re EVTR* [1987] B.C.L.C. 646; *Grant v Edwards* [1986] Ch. 638; *Huntingford v Hobbs* [1993] 1 F.L.R. 736; *Knocker v Youle* [1986] 1 W.L.R. 934; *Re Montagu's S.T.* [1987] Ch. 264; *National Anti-Vivisection Society v IRC* [1948] A.C. 31; *Oxley v Hiscock* [2004] 2 F.L.R. 669; *Pilkington v IRC* [1964] A.C. 612; *R. v District Auditor, ex parte West Yorkshire CC* [2001] W.T.L.R. 785; and *Vacuum Oil Co Pty Ltd v Wiltshire* (1945) 72 C.L.R. 319.

I could not have undertaken the task of editing this book if I had not had the benefit of many enlightening conversations about trusts and equity with generations of students at King's College London and Oxford. I have also learnt much from the friends and colleagues with whom I have taught this fascinating subject. Besides David Hayton, I should also therefore like to thank Rob Chambers, Catriona Cook, Christian Daly, Ray Davern, Adam Doyle, Jamie Edelman, Emma Ford, Simon Gardner, Jon Garton, Josh Getzler, Jamie Glister, Ben McFarlane, Mike Macnair, Paul Matthews, Peter Oliver, James Penner, Irit Samet-Porat, Bill Swadling, Leslie Turano, and Theresa Villiers. For their insights and their enthusiasm, I owe them all a great debt.

Charles Mitchell
1 January 2010

CONTENTS

TABLE OF CASES

South Place Ethical Society, Re; sub nom. Barralet v Attorney General [1980] 1 W.L.R. 1565; [1980] 3 All E.R. 918, Ch D 6–44, 6–166, 6–224, 6–283
Southwood v Attorney General [2000] W.T.L.R. 1199; (2000–01) 3 I.T.E.L.R. 94, CA (Civ Div) 6–25, 6–116, 6–170
Space Investments Ltd v Canadian Imperial Bank of Commerce Trust Co (Bahamas) Ltd [1986] 1 W.L.R. 1072; [1986] 3 All E.R. 75, PC (Bah) 11–07, 13–30, 13–31, 13–34
Spafax (1965) v Dommett (1972) 116 S.J. 711, CA (Civ Div) 4–113
Special Commissioners of Income Tax v Pemsel; sub nom. R. v Income Tax Commissioners [1891] A.C. 531, HL 6–33, 6–49, 6–163, 6–185
Specialist Plant Services Ltd v Braithwaite Ltd (1987) 3 B.C.C. 119; [1987] B.C.L.C. 1, CA (Civ Div) 4–40
Speight, Re. *See* Speight v Gaunt
Speight v Gaunt; sub nom. Speight, Re (1883–84) L.R. 9 App. Cas. 1, HL 9–191, 11–14, 11–55
Spellson v George (1987) 11 N.S.W.L.R. 300 . . . . 9–28, 11–07
Spence, Re; sub nom. Quick v Ackner [1949] W.N. 237 . . . . 3–141, 3–163
Spence (Deceased), Re; sub nom. Ogden v Shackleton [1979] Ch. 483; [1978] 3 W.L.R. 483, Ch D 6–314, **6–330**
Spence v Brown [1988] Fam. Law 291, CA (Civ Div) 4–38
Spence v Crawford [1939] 3 All E.R. 271; 1939 S.C. (H.L.) 52, HL 17–258
Spence v Union Marine Insurance Co Ltd (1867–68) L.R. 3 C.P. 427, CCP 13–13, 13–15
Spencer's Will, Re (1887) 57 L.T. 519 3–142
Sphere Drake Insurance Ltd v Euro International Underwriting Ltd [2003] EWHC 1636 (Comm); [2003] Lloyd's Rep. I.R. 525 15–72
Spiliada Maritime Corp v Cansulex Ltd (The Spiliada) [1987] A.C. 460; [1986] 3 W.L.R. 972, HL 16–02
Spiliada, The. *See* Spiliada Maritime Corp v Cansulex Ltd
Spiro v Glencrown Properties Ltd [1991] Ch. 537; [1991] 2 W.L.R. 931, Ch d 3–19
Sporle v Barnaby (1864) 10 Jur. 1142 9–169
Sports Network Ltd v Calzaghe [2008] EWHC 2566 (QB) 4–45
Sprague, Re (1880) 43 L.T. 236 4–90
Springette v Defoe [1992] 2 F.L.R. 388; [1992] 2 F.C.R. 561, CA (Civ Div) 14–91, 14–92, 14–95, 14–163, 15–22, 15–64
Sproule v Bouch. *See* Bouch, Re
Stacey v Elph (1883) 1 My. & K. 195 . . . . 8–05, 9–21
Stack v Dowden; sub nom. Dowden v Stack [2007] UKHL 17; [2007] 2 A.C. 432; [2007] 2 W.L.R. 831 . . . . 14–93, 14–94, 14–95, 14–163, 15–16, 15–17, 15–26, 15–27, 15–28, 15–30, 15–32, 15–34, 15–36, **15–49**
Standing v Bowring (1886) L.R. 31 Ch. D. 282, CA 8–06, 14–98, 14–124, 14–139
Staniar v Evans; Evans v Staniar (1887) L.R. 34 Ch. D. 470, Ch D 1–45
Staniland v Willott (1850) 3 Mac. & G. 664 2–114
Stanley v IRC [1944] K.B. 255, CA 1–91, 9–177
Stannard v Fisons Pension Trust Ltd [1992] I.R.L.R. 27, CA (Civ Div) 10–88, 10–93, 10–94
Stapleton, Re [1946] 1 All E.R. 323 9–181
Stapylton Fletcher Ltd (In Administrative Receivership), Re; Ellis Son & Vidler Ltd (In Administrative Receivership), Re [1994] 1 W.L.R. 1181; [1995] 1 All E.R. 192, Ch D 4–100
Star Sea, The. *See* Manifest Shipping Co Ltd v Uni-Polaris Insurance Co Ltd
Starglade Properties Ltd v Nash [2010] EWHC 99 (Ch) 12–76
State Bank of India v Sood [1997] Ch. 276; [1997] 2 W.L.R. 421, CA (Civ Div) 3–85, 13–105
Statek Corp v Alford [2008] EWHC 32 (Ch); [2008] B.C.C. 266; [2008] Lloyd's Rep. F.C. 127 . . . . 11–145, 12–76
Statoil ASA v Louis Dreyfus Energy Services LP (The Harriette N) [2008] EWHC 2257 (Comm); [2009] 1 All E.R. (Comm) 1035; [2008] 2 Lloyd's Rep. 685 17–255
Stead, Re; sub nom. Witham v Andrew [1900] 1 Ch. 237, Ch D 3–163
Steadman v Steadman [1976] A.C. 536; [1974] 3 W.L.R. 56, HL 3–20, 3–25, 3–26
Steed's Will Trusts, Re; sub nom. Sandford v Stevenson [1960] Ch. 407; [1960] 2 W.L.R. 474, CA 7–25, 7–29, 7–37

TABLE OF STATUTES

[References to paragraphs in **bold** *indicate that the text is reproduced in full]*

TABLE OF STATUTORY INSTRUMENTS

1912 Public Trustee Rules (SI 1912/348)
r.30 8–35
1991 County Court Remedies Regulations (SI 1991/1222)
reg.2 17–10
1998 Civil Procedure Rules (SI 1998/3132) 17–25, 17–36
r.6.33 16–44
r.6.36 . . . . 16–03, 16–44
Pt 6 PD6B 16–03
para.3.1 16–44
Pt 8 7–33
Pt 31 9–36
r.31.16 9–36
Pt 31 PD 9–36
Pt 40 PD para.15 . . . . 9–179, 9–182
Pt 64 . . . . 2–56, 15–91
2001 Uncertificated Securities Regulations (SI 2001/3755) 3–90
reg.38(5) 4–104
Civil Jurisdiction and Judgments Order (SI 2001/3929) 16–44
art.3 16–44
Sch.1 para.9 . . . . 16–43, 16–44
para.12 16–43
2007 Civil Jurisdiction and Judgments Regulations (SI 2007/1655) 16–44
2009 Family Provision (Intestate Succession) Order (SI 2009/135) . . 1–131

TABLE OF EU, INTERNATIONAL AND FOREIGN LEGISLATION

References to paragraphs in **bold** *indicate that the text is reproduced in full*

Guernsey

1989 Trusts (Guernsey) Law

art.34(7) 9–217

Jersey

1984 Trusts (Jersey) Law

art.9 16–24

art.12 16–71

art.15 16–71

art.30(10) 9–217

art.32(1) 16–29

PART I

INTRODUCTION

1 INTRODUCTION

1. What is a Trust?

1–01 A trust arises when the owner of property declares himself a trustee of it, or transfers it to someone else to be a trustee of it, for the benefit of one or more beneficiaries, or for a charitable purpose. Trustees have two roles: first, to hold and administer the trust assets; and, second, in the case of a trust for beneficiaries, to distribute the income from the trust assets (and ultimately the assets themselves) to appropriate beneficiaries or, in the case of a charitable trust, to apply the income from the trust assets (or the assets themselves) to the charitable purpose.

1–02 The fundamental primary obligations of trustees are to keep within the terms of the trust and loyally to further the interests of the beneficiaries, prioritising these over their own personal interests, save to the extent that the trust instrument permits them to benefit themselves. To show that they are performing these core duties, trustees must provide the beneficiaries with accounts explaining the current state of the trust assets and the history of the trustees' dealings with them.

1–03 A trust fund consists of all the assets held on trust by a trustee. These are owned by the trustee (or by a nominee or custodian to his order), but they never become part of his personal estate. Hence the trust assets are not available to satisfy any claims of the trustee's personal creditors, heirs or divorcing spouse. The assets must only be used to benefit the beneficiaries or to further the trust's charitable purpose.

1–04 The priority of the beneficiaries' interests over the trustee's private creditors is achieved by giving the beneficiaries an equitable proprietary interest in the trust fund. Their equitable proprietary interest binds anyone coming to own the trust property unless he is protected as a bona fide purchaser of the legal title without notice of the beneficiaries' equitable interest, or else by special statutory provisions.[1]

1–05 The beneficiaries' equitable interests in the trust fund are, however, subordinated to an equitable lien (or charge) in favour of the trustee to secure payment of trustee remuneration. The trustee's lien also secures his claim to recover the amount of liabilities which he incurs towards third parties with whom he has dealings while acting as trustee. A trust, unlike a company incorporated under the Companies Act 2006, is not a legal person that is capable of suing and being sued. Instead the trustee personally acquires rights against, and incurs liabilities to, third parties with whom he deals while managing the trust affairs. If he incurs a personal liability to a third party while acting as trustee, then he can claim an indemnity out of the trust fund.

1–06 The concept of a trust fund is special, whether or not this is spelt out in the definition section of the trust instrument. It covers the original assets (often of small value) that are transferred to the trustee by the settlor of the trust when it is first created, assets that are subsequently transferred to the

---

[1] e.g. the overreaching provisions in the Law of Property Act 1925 ss.2 and 27 which simplify the sale of land in which beneficiaries have equitable interests by conferring a good title on a purchaser free from such interests if the purchase moneys are paid to a trust corporation or to two trustees, so that the beneficiaries' interests are detached from the land and attached to the proceeds of the sale.

trustee to form part of the trust fund, and assets that are subsequently acquired by the trustee in exchange for the assets that were settled on trust.

1–07 So far as subsequent transfers to the trustee are concerned, if these are made by the settlor to the trustee as trustee of the settlor's subsisting trust, then no new trust of the property is created: the trustee is trustee of one trust for the beneficiaries, the property from time to time owned by him as trustee being held *en masse* as a fund.[2] If, however, a third party transfers his property to a trustee of a settlor's subsisting trust, then the third party will be viewed as the settlor of the proportion of the trust fund represented by the value of his addition unless he intended the added property to be held as a separate trust fund but on the same terms as provided by the earlier trust.[3]

1–08 So far as subsequent acquisitions by the trustee are concerned, the trust fund extends beyond new assets that are acquired by the trustee in authorised transactions. The beneficiaries can also claim new assets acquired by the trustee in unauthorised transactions (e.g. because the trust instrument does not empower him to acquire the relevant type of investment), and also assets that he has wrongfully sought to acquire for himself by using trust funds or money which he has obtained by abusing his office (e.g. by accepting a bribe). By ratifying the trustee's actions, the beneficiaries can turn such wrongfully acquired assets into assets that form part of the trust fund and belong to them in equity.

1–09 Suppose, for example, that a trustee sells trust assets and in breach of trust uses the proceeds to buy a house for himself. The beneficiaries can trace the value that was represented by the trust assets into the value represented by the house, and adopt the house purchase as an authorised transaction, with the result that the house forms part of the trust fund and is held by the trustee as part of the property held on trust for the beneficiaries.[4]

1–10 Furthermore, if the trustee makes a gift of trust property to a third party who is not a beneficiary and this person uses it to buy a house, for example, then again the beneficiaries can claim that the money, and subsequently the house, became part of the trust fund held on trust for them. The third party, as a donee with a derivatively flawed title who gave no value in exchange for the money, only owns the money, and the house, subject to the beneficiaries' equitable proprietary interests.

1–11 Moreover, from the moment that he becomes aware of the beneficiaries' equitable proprietary interests, the third party is placed under a personal duty to return the money or house. He must return the property to the original (or a replacement) trustee so that the trust fund can be reconstituted, and the property held for the beneficiaries on the terms of the original trust. Alternatively, if the beneficiaries have absolute interests under the trust (and not limited or discretionary interests), then it may be appropriate for the third party to transfer the property to the beneficiaries outright.

1–12 What happens if a third party recipient of misdirected trust property does not retransfer the property after he knows of the beneficiaries' equitable proprietary interests, and instead spends it all on an expensive holiday, so that it becomes impossible for him to restore the property because he no longer has it? The answer is that he must compensate the beneficiaries by paying them the current value of the property instead, as a monetised form of performing his obligation to return the property in its original form. Trustees are also liable to pay compensation calculated in this way where they have lost or misapplied trust assets in unauthorised transactions.

---

[2] *Kennon v Spry* (2008) 238 C.L.R. 366 at [183].

[3] *CIR v Dick* (2001) 4 I.T.E.L.R. 317 at [40].

[4] "That which is the fruit of the trust property or the trusteeship is itself trust property": *Swain v Law Society* [1982] 1 W.L.R. 17 at 36, per Oliver L.J. See too *Re Hallett's Estate* (1880) 13 Ch.D. 696 at 709; *Att.-Gen. of Hong Kong v Reid* [1994] 1 A.C. 324 at 338.

The law of trusts is concerned with the utilisation and preservation of wealth, whether in the form of family funds, pension funds, unit trusts, charitable funds, union funds, club funds, employee share ownership trusts, or in the form of rights (whether secured or unsecured) against a borrower intended as a commercial security device to be held by trustees for the benefit of a collection of lenders. It is also about settling property on trustees so as to minimise liability to various taxes. **1–13**

Historically, much of trusts law emerged out of the desire of settlors to preserve family wealth, tying up property so that it could be enjoyed by successive generations, protecting the family from the depredations of creditors and of particular relatives with extravagant reckless dispositions, or providing secretly for people with whom an open association was not desired. More recently, much trusts law has been generated by disputes in respect of pension funds; in respect of secured commercial lending; in respect of shared home ownership; in respect of assets that are allegedly the traceable proceeds of property subject to a trust or other fiduciary relationship; and in respect of the personal liabilities of those who receive misdirected trust property or who dishonestly assist in a breach of trust or other fiduciary duty. **1–14**

The trust concept is extremely flexible. In English law trusts can be used until the end of a perpetuity period to achieve almost any lawful end, except that problems arise where it is sought to use trusts to provide directly for the furtherance of non-charitable purposes. Maitland quite rightly characterised the trust concept as "the greatest and most distinctive achievement performed by Englishmen in the field of jurisprudence."[5] No lawyer can claim to provide a proper service for his private or corporate clients without a thorough grasp of trust law and its potentialities. **1–15**

What then is a trust? It is impossible to define such a flexible concept precisely. However, three quasi-definitions are now set out to provide a rough and ready introduction to trust law. **1–16**

Austin W. Scott and William F. Fratcher, *The Law of Trusts* 4th edn (1989), para.2.3

Even if it were possible to frame an exact definition of a legal concept, the definition would not be of great practical value. A definition cannot properly be used as though it were a major premise so that rules governing conduct can be deduced from it. Our law, at least, has not grown in that way. When the rules have been arrived at from other sources, it may be possible to attempt to frame a definition. But the definition results from the rules, and not the rules from the definition. **1–17**

All that one can properly attempt to do is to give such a description of a legal concept that others will know in a general way what one is talking about. It is possible to state the principal distinguishing characteristics of the concept so that others will have a general idea of what the writer means. With this in mind, those responsible for the *Restatement of Trusts* proposed the following definition or description of an express trust. It is **1–18**

> "a fiduciary relationship with respect to property, subjecting the person by whom the title to property is held to equitable duties to deal with the property for the benefit of another person, which arises as a result of a manifestation of an intention to create it."

In this definition or description the following characteristics are to be noticed: (1) a trust is a relationship; (2) it is a relationship of a fiduciary character; (3) it is a relationship with respect to property, not one involving merely personal duties; (4) it involves the existence of equitable duties imposed upon the holder of the title to the property to deal with it for the benefit of another; and (5) it arises as a result of a manifestation of an intention to create the relationship.

[5] F.W. Maitland *Selected Essays* (1963), p.129.

Hague Convention on the Law Applicable to Trusts and on their Recognition (1985)[6]

Article 2

1–19 For the purposes of this Convention, the term "trust" refers to the legal relationships created—inter vivos or on death—by a person, the settlor, when assets have been placed under the control of a trustee for the benefit of a beneficiary or for a specified purpose.

1–20 A trust has the following characteristics—

(a) the assets constitute a separate fund and are not a part of the trustee's own estate;

(b) title to the trust assets stands in the name of the trustee or in the name of another person on behalf of the trustee;

(c) the trustee has the power and the duty, in respect of which he is accountable, to manage, employ or dispose of the assets in accordance with the terms of the trust and the special duties imposed upon him by law.

1–21 The reservation by the settlor of certain rights and powers, and the fact that the trustee may himself have rights as a beneficiary, are not necessarily inconsistent with the existence of a trust.

D. Hayton, S. Kortmann and R. Verhagen (eds), *Principles of European Trust Law* (1999)[7]

Article 1

1–22 (1) In a trust, a person called the "trustee" owns assets segregated from his private patrimony and must deal with those assets (the "trust fund") for the benefit of another person called the "beneficiary" or for the furtherance of a purpose.

(2) There can be more than one trustee and more than one beneficiary; a trustee may himself be one of the beneficiaries.

(3) The separate existence of the trust fund entails its immunity from claims by the trustee's spouse, heirs and personal creditors.

(4) In respect of the separate trust fund a beneficiary has personal rights and may also have ["and also has" for common law countries] proprietary rights against the trustee and against third parties to whom any part of the trust fund has been wrongfully transferred.

Article 2

1–23 The general rule is that in order to create a trust a person called the "settlor" in his lifetime or on death must, with the intention of creating a segregated trust fund, transfer assets to the trustee. However, it may also be ["it is also" for common law countries] possible to create a trust by making it clear that he is to be trustee of particular assets of his.

Article 3

1–24 (1) The trust fund consists not only of the original assets and those subsequently added, but also of those assets from time to time representing the original or added assets.

[6] The Convention was signed on July 1, 1985, and came into force on January 1, 1992.

[7] The Principles of European Trust Law were prepared by an international working group so as to assist countries interested in implementing The Hague Trusts Convention.

It will be seen that the last two definitions or descriptions do not refer to beneficiaries having equitable property interests (as opposed to the legal property interests of the trustees). This distinction originated in English law (where the Chancery courts operating an equitable jurisdiction developed separately from other courts which applied the common law) and was perpetuated in many British colonies (e.g. America, Australia, Bahamas, Barbados, Bermuda, Cayman Islands). However it does not appear in the trust laws of India, Japan, Liechtenstein, Quebec, Scotland or South Africa.[8] The historical development of equity and the trust is discussed in the next section. **1–25**

2. The Historical Development of Equity and the Trust

A. Equity and the Court of Chancery

The trust is a creature of Equity and not of the common law. So what is "Equity"? In this context Equity can only be described as the body of rules which evolved from the rules applied and administered by the Court of Chancery before the Judicature Act 1873. Since that Act came into force on November 1, 1875, the rules of Equity and the rules of common law have been concurrently applied and administered in all courts.[9] **1–26**

The Court of Chancery grew out of the residuum of justice left in the King where his common law courts for some special reason brought about an unjust result, e.g. because they provided no remedy owing to the rigidity of the writ system or only an inadequate remedy or because a party could not succeed due to the power or wealth of the other party.[10] An aggrieved person would petition the King who would refer it to his Chancellor as his right-hand man. The Chancellor, who was an ecclesiastic, with some knowledge of Roman law and canon law, first advised the King and his Council, but towards the end of the fifteenth century began making decrees on his own authority. He was concerned with affording relief in hard cases and acted in personam against defendants who were imprisoned for contempt if they did not observe his decrees. At first, Equity varied according to the Chancellor's conscience—or the size of the Chancellor's foot, as Selden remarked.[11] The work of hearing petitions led to increasing judicial activity of the Chancellor in what came to be known as the Court of Chancery. Lawyers, like Lord Nottingham at the end of the seventeenth century, instead of ecclesiastics, became Chancellors and began systematically developing a body of rules of equity. **1–27**

It is crucial to appreciate that Equity is only a gloss on, or supplement to,[12] the common law that is a self-sufficient system whose rigour needed mitigating in the interests of justice and of social and economic change. To give some examples, Equity's trust concept has been used to enable landowners in their lifetimes in effect to devise land (i.e. pass land on by will), something which they could not do at common law; again, the trust was used to enable married women in effect to have separate property from their husbands, something which the common law did not permit; and again, it was used to enable merchant venturers to do business under deeds of settlement almost as if they had formed a limited company with separate legal personality, something which the common law did not enable them to do until some time later. Equity developed a modern law of mortgages (including tacking, marshalling, consolidation, and the crucial doctrine of the equity of redemption) and of restrictive **1–28**

---

[8] D. Hayton, "The Development of the Trust Concept in Civil Law Jurisdictions" [2000] 8 Journal of International Trust & Corporate Practice 159; J. Glasson and G. Thomas (eds), *The International Trust* 2nd edn (2006).

[9] Supreme Court of Judicature Act 1873 ss. 24, 25, now the Senior Courts Act 1981 s.49.

[10] For fuller accounts see W.S. Holdsworth, *History of English Law*, Vol.1 (1903) at pp.395 ff.; A. Kiralfy (ed.), *Potter's Historical Introduction to English Law* 4th edn (1958) at pp.152 ff.; S.F.C. Milsom, *Historical Foundations of the Common Law* 2nd edn (1981) at pp.82 ff.; J. H. Baker, *Introduction to English Legal History* 4th edn (2002), Chs 6, 14, 15, 16.

[11] F. Pollock (ed.), *Table Talk of John Selden* (1927), at p.43.

[12] F. W. Maitland, *Equity* (2nd edn) pp.18–19.

covenants, when the common law had closed the category of negative easements. Equity also gave effect to interests in land created for value without satisfying formal common law requirements.

1–29 Equity developed the remedies of injunction and specific performance which are hugely popular with claimants in cases where the common law remedy of damages is ill-suited to solve their problems, e.g. cases of repeated wrongdoing where the claimant wants the defendant to desist from his wrongful actions rather than continue and pay damages for the privilege, and cases where the claimant wants the defendant to render a promised performance rather than paying its financial value as damages for breach of contract. In its auxiliary jurisdiction, Equity has also been able to assist proceedings at common law by interrogatories, disclosure (formerly termed "discovery"), set-off, and the taking of accounts.

B. The Relationship between Equity and the Common Law

1–30 The draftsman of the Judicature Acts 1873–75, Sir Arthur Wilson, identified three aspects to the relationship between Equity and the common law.[13]

i. The First Aspect

1–31 First, Equity recognises and enforces rights and duties known to the common law but then goes further in recognising and enforcing other rights and duties. The classic example is the trust, e.g. where property is vested in trustees for A for life, remainder to B absolutely. The common law protects the trustees' legal title to the property and facilitates their dealing with third parties, but if A or B wishes to enforce his rights then it is equity that governs the position. In other words the trustees' rights are legal rights and the beneficiaries' rights are equitable rights.

1–32 The trust derives from the mediaeval practice of a "feoffor" conveying a legal estate in land to a "feoffee to uses" to hold it to the use of a "cestui que use". This was done to enable a knight to go off to the Crusades, leaving someone to safeguard his land for himself and his family,[14] or to enable some body to benefit as a "cestui que use" which could not directly benefit as a feoffee owing to the Mortmain Statutes[15] or to vows of poverty.[16] Lifetime "uses" could also be exploited to enable land to be devised in effect and as a tax avoidance device to avoid burdensome feudal incidents. The number of trustees could be kept up so that there was never a death of a sole individual to provoke the levy of feudal dues on death of the estate owner.

1–33 To defeat this method of avoiding feudal incidents, the Statute of Uses 1535 was enacted. This "executed" the use so that the legal estate vested automatically in the cestui que use and not the feoffee to uses.[17] Hence the person who had all along been intended to get the benefit of the property became the legal owner with all the undesirable fiscal consequences that this entailed. Draftsman then hit on a further device to circumvent the Statute of Uses 1535, namely for a legal estate to be conveyed to A to the use of B to the use of C. At first, the courts responded to this by holding that B

---

13 See (1875) 19 Sol. Jo. at pp.633–634.

14 To protect the land a "real" action to recover the land (the "*rem*", meaning "thing" in Latin) had to be brought by an adult male "seised" of the land by virtue of feoffment with livery of seisin and present in court.

15 The Mortmain Statutes prevented land being conveyed without a royal licence into the "dead hand" of a corporation (not liable to the feudal dues payable on marriage, death or the heir being under age).

16 e.g. the Order of Franciscan Friars.

17 This soon led to a rebellion as it prevented land being indirectly devised: hence the Statute of Wills 1540 was enacted to enable land to be directly devised, with anti-tax-avoidance provisions in the Statute of Explanation of Wills 1542 treating certain lifetime dispositions as if devices by will.

held the legal estate as his own property, the first use being executed by the statute and the second use being void as repugnant to the first use. However, by the middle of the seventeenth century the courts had come to enforce the second use as a matter of course (not just to prevent fraud or remedy a mistake) and it came to be known as a "trust" to distinguish it from the first use. The drafting formula became "Unto and to the use of B and his heirs in trust for C and his heirs" and C came to be known as the cestui que trust. After the repeal of the Statute of Uses in 1925, land was conveyed "to B in fee simple on trust for C in fee simple".

Over the years C's equitable interest came to be enforced in the Court of Chancery not just against the trustee or a donee of the legal estate from the trustee, but against anyone having the legal estate, other than a bona fide purchaser for value of the legal estate without notice ("Equity's darling"). Notice comprised actual knowledge and knowledge which a person should have had if he had made reasonable inquiries and inspections ("constructive notice"); such actual or constructive notice of a purchaser's agent will be imputed to the purchaser ("imputed notice") unless the agent was acting in fraud of his principal and the matter of which he had notice was relevant to the fraud. **1–34**

ii. The Second Aspect

The second aspect is that common law and equity may each provide different remedies but leave the claimant free to enjoy whatever remedy was allowed by the other. For example, the common law affords the "bad man" the freedom to break his contract with another person, or misappropriate another person's property, and pay damages; but if special circumstances justify the intervention of Equity, then Equity insists that he must be a "good man", and decrees specific performance of the contract, or grants an injunction ordering him to desist from his wrongdoing. Again, a contract relating to land, before becoming void at law for lack of writing required by the Law of Property (Miscellaneous Provisions) Act 1989, was not enforceable in court if written evidence was lacking, although the deposit could be forfeited or recovered for failure of consideration. But in Equity specific performance could be ordered if there was an act of part performance. Conversely, a voluntary (i.e. gratuitous) covenant under seal enables the covenantee to obtain common law damages for breach,[18] but Equity will not decree specific performance because it holds that "Equity will not assist a volunteer," i.e. an intended donee. **1–35**

iii. The Third Aspect

The third aspect of the relationship between Equity and the common law is that there are rare cases where the rules of Equity and of common law conflict. In 1616 it was held that Equity prevailed because the Court of Chancery could effectively issue common injunctions restraining parties who were successful in common law courts from enforcing their judgments, or restraining parties from continuing with a common law action.[19] Now the Senior Courts Act 1981 s.49 states that:[20] **1–36**

> "Every Court exercising jurisdiction in England or Wales in any civil cause or matter shall continue to administer law and equity on the basis that, wherever there is any conflict or variance between the rules of equity and the rules of common law with reference to the same matter, the rules of equity shall prevail."

---

[18] *Cannon v Hartley* [1949] Ch. 213.

[19] *Earl of Oxford's Case* (1615) 1 Rep. Ch. 1.

[20] Replacing the Judicature Act 1873 s.25(11), and the Judicature Act 1925 s.44. The Senior Courts Act 1981 was previously known as the Supreme Court Act 1981, but was renamed by the Constitutional Reform Act 2005 Sch.11 para.1.

1–37 Examples of conflict are as follows. In an action on a deed at law it was no defence for a defendant to plead a written variation for value not in a deed, but such a defendant could obtain a common injunction in equity.[21] Similarly, if a legal estate owner purportedly granted a lease exceeding three years in writing, instead of by deed, and the document contained a term enabling the landlord to claim a year's rent in advance, then at law the landlord (only being entitled to rent in arrear at law) could not sue for such rent or levy distress for such rent, so he could be liable to the tenant for illegal distress. Since Equity would be prepared to decree specific performance so as to have a legal lease by deed executed and before then look on as done that which ought to be done, the landlord could obtain a common injunction in respect of the tenant's action for legal distress.[22] An example of variance arises where a claimant seeks contribution from sureties where one of them is insolvent. At law if A, B, and C are sureties for £30,000 and A becomes insolvent then B and C are only liable for £10,000 each.[23] In Equity B and C are liable for £15,000 each.[24] The claimant receives less at law than in Equity, and so no question arose before 1875 of a defendant seeking a common injunction as happened in cases of conflict.

1–38 The argument has often been made that if one were creating a legal system from scratch, then one would not design a set of rules, and then design a second set of rules which overlays the first set, making it necessary to have a third set of rules to determine whether the first or the second set governs cases where the two sets produce different outcomes.[25] Why create such a complex system, which must inevitably be hard to understand and tend towards injustice because similar situations will not readily be recognised and will be treated in different ways? On occasion these concerns have led the judiciary to eliminate some of the differences between equity and the common law that have built up over time. For example, in *Great Peace Shipping Ltd v Tsavlisis Salvage (International) Ltd*[26] the Court of Appeal held that there is no equitable jurisdiction to grant rescission of a contract on the ground of common mistake where the contract is valid at common law; and in *Halpern v Halpern (Nos 1 and 2)*[27] Carnwath L.J. suggested that the "counter-restitution impossible" bar to rescission should operate in substantially the same way whether the claim rests on duress (at common law) or undue influence (in equity).[28]

1–39 In contrast, those who support the maintenance (and indeed, the continuing development) of the equitable jurisdiction say that it enables the courts to deliver a more nuanced and thus fairer form of justice than might be achieved by a simpler, single set of rules.[29] Moreover, the bifurcation of property ownership into legal and equitable interests comprises the essential conceptual basis for one of English law's greatest inventions, the trust. To this we shall now return.

---

[21] *Berry v Berry* [1929] 2 K.B. 316.

[22] *Walsh v Lonsdale* (1882) 21 Ch.D. 9, on which see *Chan v Cresdon Pty Ltd* (1989) 168 C.L.R. 242.

[23] *Batard v Hawes* (1853) 2 E & B 287.

[24] *Lowe & Sons v Dixon & Sons* (1885) 16 Q.B.D. 455.

[25] e.g. S. Worthington, *Equity* 2nd edn (2006), Ch.2. Cf. A. Burrows, *Fusing Common Law and Equity: Remedies, Restitution and Reform* (Hochelaga Lecture, 2002) at pp.1–26; A. Burrows, "We Do This at Common Law But That in Equity" (2002) 22 O.J.L.S. 1; K. Mason, "Fusion: Fallacy, Future or Finished?" in S. Degeling and J. Edelman (eds), *Equity and Commercial Law* (2005).

[26] [2003] Q.B. 679, disapproving *Solle v Butcher* [1950] 1 K.B. 671.

[27] [2008] Q.B. 195 at [70] ff.

[28] See too *Harris v Digital Pulse Pty Ltd* (2003) 56 N.S.W.L.R. 298, where the differing views of the members of the NSWCA about the relationship between equitable and legal doctrine led them to draw different conclusions about the viability of ordering a defendant to pay exemplary damages for breach of fiduciary duty.

[29] See e.g. D. O'Sullivan, S. Elliott, and R. Zakrzewski, *The Law of Rescission* (2008) Ch.10, arguing that it is a strength of English law that it currently gives claimants an automatic common law right to rescind a contract on strong facts, and an equitable right to rescission that is available at the discretion of the court on weaker facts where a more sensitive balancing of interests is required.

3. The Rights and Duties of Trustees and Beneficiaries

A. The Trustees' Position

1–40 Ownership of trust property is vested in the trustees (or their nominees, although the trustees technically then own an interest in the property owned by the nominees), to be managed and dealt with wholly for the benefit of the beneficiaries. As James L.J. stated in *Smith v Anderson*:[30]

> "A trustee is a man who is the owner of the property and deals with it as principal, as owner and as master, subject only to an equitable obligation to account to some persons to whom he stands in the relation of trustee."

1–41 Because they are the owners of the trust property, trustees have many opportunities to abuse their position and, as a prophylactic measure, Equity has therefore imposed very strict rigorous duties upon them. Indeed, so onerous have these duties become that properly drawn trust instruments greatly relax the standards that Equity would otherwise demand: were it not for such relaxation few individuals or companies would be prepared to act as trustees. As long as illegality or public policy or uncertainty does not intervene, the draftsmen of trust instruments have a free hand to vary or negative trust law doctrines provided that the irreducible core content of the trust concept remains.

1–42 This irreducible core consists of a duty to act in good faith for the beneficiaries' interest in preference to the trustee's own interests: without this, it could not be said that there existed a trust at all, since the trustees could simply take the property for themselves with impunity.[31] Provided that this core duty is in place, however, the trustees have an independent, unfettered discretion when managing the trust fund, although, of course, this must be held according to the terms of the trust for the relevant beneficiaries, and a trust deed may also provide that the consent of someone other than the trustees (e.g. an individual or a committee or a company, usually designated as a "protector") is required before certain things can be done.

1–43 The interests of the beneficiaries are paramount and the trustees must do their best to hold the balance fairly between those beneficiaries (with life interests) interested in income and those beneficiaries (with absolute interests in remainder) interested in capital. Indeed, the trustees have a paternalistic function of protecting each beneficiary against himself. Even if all the beneficiaries interested in a particular trust are each of full capacity and wish the trustees to do a certain thing the trustees can refuse if they consider that some of the beneficiaries are not objectively acting in their own best interests.[32] However, if all the beneficiaries are between them absolutely entitled to the trust property and are each of full capacity, then under the *Saunders v Vautier*[33] principle, the beneficiaries have a fundamental proprietary power to call for the trust property to be vested in them (or their nominees) by the trustees, so terminating the trust.

1–44 Since the beneficiaries' interests are paramount, the trustees cannot (in the absence of authorisation in the trust instrument) invest trust moneys as they might invest their own: they must "play safe" and invest only in investments authorised under the Trustee Act 2000. Even if they have a broad express power of investment they cannot speculate because (in the absence of a contrary provision in the trust instrument) they have to exercise as much care as a prudent man of business would exercise if investing for other persons for whom he felt morally obliged to provide.

---

[30] (1880) 15 Ch.D. 247 at 275.

[31] *Armitage v Nurse* [1998] Ch. 241.

[32] *Re Brockbank* [1949] Ch. 206, subject to the beneficiaries' power to direct the trustees to retire and appoint other designated persons to become trustees in their place, under the Trusts of Land and Appointment of Trustees Act 1996 s.19.

[33] *Saunders v Vautier* (1841) 4 Beav. 115.

1–45 A trustee has no distinct legal personality in his representative capacity separate from himself in his personal capacity.[34] Thus, he is personally liable to the extent of his whole personal fortune for debts contracted in managing the trust fund,[35] whether contracting in his own name or as trustee,[36] unless he makes it clear to the third parties with whom he deals that he is to be liable only to the extent that the trust fund is available to him to satisfy the liability.[37] To discharge liabilities properly incurred by him as trustee he has a right of indemnity against the trust fund[38] (but only after discharging any liability for any breaches of trust[39]), and the third parties with whom he has dealt may be subrogated to this right and thus obtain repayment out of the trust fund in the event that the trustee becomes bankrupt and cannot satisfy their claims personally.[40]

1–46 If a third party commits a tort or a breach of contract in the course of his dealings with the trustee, while the trustee is acting as such, then it is generally only the trustee who has standing to sue the third party for his wrongdoing. Only in exceptional cases, where in breach of trust the trustee has refused to sue a third party, will the beneficiaries be permitted to sue the third party themselves, joining the trustee as co-defendant, so that all interested parties are bound by the court's judgment.[41] In such cases a beneficiary sues not in his own right but "in right of the trust and in the room of the trustee",[42] the trustee, before the Judicature Acts 1873–75, being compelled by the Court of Chancery to let the beneficiary use the trustee's name to sue the third party in the common law court.

B. The Beneficiaries' Position

1–47 There has been much controversy over the nature of a beneficiary's interest under a trust, based upon the differences between *in personam* rights against trustees and in rem rights against trust property.[43] However, much depends on the meaning in context of in personam and in rem, and on whether one is dealing with a bare trust (A holds on trust for X absolutely) or a fixed trust (A holds on trust for X for life, remainder to Y for life, remainder to Z absolutely) or a discretionary trust (A holds on trust to distribute the income and capital between such of X Y or Z or their spouses and issue as he sees fit).

---

[34] However, for some taxation purposes trustees are considered a single continuing body of persons distinct from the actual individuals who are from time to time trustees: Taxation of Chargeable Gains Act 1992 s.69; *Bond v Pickford* [1983] S.T.C. 517; *Jasmine Trustees Ltd v Wells & Hind (a firm)* [2008] Ch. 194.

[35] *Fraser v Murdoch* (1881) 6 App. Cas. 855 at 874; *Staniar v Evans* (1886) 34 Ch.D. 470 at 477.

[36] *Watling v Lewis* [1911] 1 Ch. 414 at 423–424; *Burt, Boulton & Hayward v Bull* [1895] 1 Q.B. 276 at 285.

[37] *Lumsden v Buchanan* (1865) 4 Macq. 950 at 955; *Muir v City of Glasgow Bank* (1879) 4 App. Cas. 337 at 355 and 388.

[38] *Re Blundell* (1888) 40 Ch. D. 370 at 377; *Re Exhall Coal Co Ltd* (1886) 35 Beav. 449 at 453.

[39] *Jacubs v Rylance* (1874) L.R. 17 Eq. 341; *Doering v Doering* (1889) 42 Ch.D. 203.

[40] C. Mitchell and S. Watterson, *Subrogation: Law and Practice* (2006) Ch.12.

[41] *Hayim v Citibank* [1987] A.C. 730 at 748; *Parker-Tweedale v Dunbar Bank Plc* [1991] Ch. 12 at 19, 23 and 25; *Roberts v Gill* [2009] 1 W.L.R. 331; and cf. *shell UK Ltd v Total UK Ltd* [2010] EWCA Civ. 180 at [111] ff. but not where T has the benefit of a non-assignable contract with X and, T having declared a trust of the contract for B, B tries to sue X as if B were an assignee of T which is the very thing forbidden by the contract: *Don King Productions Inc v Warren* [2000] Ch. 291; *Barbados Trust Co Ltd v Bank of Zambia* [2007] 1 Lloyd's Rep. 495 at [133]–[136], per Hooper L.J., with Waller and Rix L.JJ. in the context of an acknowledged commercial debt differing at [47] and [119].

[42] *Parker-Tweedale v Dunbar Bank Plc* [1991] Ch. 12 at 19, per Nourse L.J.

[43] W.G. Hart, "What is a Trust?" (1899) 15 L.Q.R. 294; A.W. Scott, "The Nature of the Rights of the *Cestui Que Trust*" (1917) 17 Col. L.R. 269; H. Stone, "The Nature of the Rights of the *Cestui Que Trust*" (1917) 17 Col. L.R. 467; H.C. Hanbury, "The Field of Modern Equity" (1929) 45 L.Q.R. 196; V. Latham, "The Right of the Beneficiary to Specific Items of the Trust Fund" (1954) 32 Can. B.R. 520; D.M. Waters, "The Nature of the Trust Beneficiary's Interest" (1967) 45 Can. B.R. 219; P. Parkinson, "Reconceptualising the Express Trust" [2002] C.L.J. 657; D.J. Hayton, "Developing the Obligation Characteristic of the Trust" (2001) 117 L.Q.R. 97; P. Matthews, "From Obligation to Property, and Back Again?" in D.J. Hayton (ed.) *Extending the Boundaries of Trusts and Similar Ring-Fenced Funds* (2002); A.M. Honoré, "Trusts: The Inessentials" in J. Getzler (ed.), *Rationalizing Property, Equity and Trusts* (2003); R. Nolan, "Equitable Property" (2006) 122 L.Q.R. 232; L.D. Smith, "Trust and Patrimony" (2008) 38 Revue Générale de Droit 379.

In all cases X has an equitable chose in action, a right in personam against the trustee, to inspect the trust accounts and affirm or repudiate the trustee's actions, and to demand that the trustee reconstitute the trust fund in the event that anything is found missing, either by returning the missing assets themselves, or by paying in their current value, as a form of monetised substitute performance of his duty to deliver the assets *in specie*. Where the trustee causes X loss by breaching his duties, e.g. by negligently investing the trust funds in a losing investment, then X will also have a personal right to insist that the trustee pays the amount of the loss caused by his breach of duty into the trust fund. **1–48**

Where X is a beneficiary under a bare trust he also may demand transfer of the legal title from the trustee and so obtain the trust property in rem for himself as legal and beneficial owner;[44] he may assign, or declare a sub-trust of, his equitable interest in the trust property; he may follow misdirected trust property into the hands of third-party recipients from the trustee and assert a proprietary claim to this property unless the third party is a bona fide purchaser of the legal title for value without notice of X's equitable interest,[45] or else is a purchaser who complies with the overreaching requirements of the Law of Property Act 1925 s.27. Thus X also has proprietary in rem rights in the trust assets. **1–49**

If X is a beneficiary with a limited interest under a fixed trust, then he has a disposable equitable proprietary interest, but he cannot claim the trust capital unless the other beneficiaries, Y and Z, are each of full capacity and join in demanding it from the trustees so that they can then divide it between themselves as they agree. X has a right to the income produced by the trust assets and is regarded as having part of the equitable ownership of the assets themselves.[46] Hence if they are situate in New York State he is treated for tax purposes as interested in foreign assets, namely New York assets,[47] it being immaterial that the trustees reside in and administer the trust in England so that his equitable chose in action is English. **1–50**

If X is a beneficiary under a discretionary trust, then he merely has a hope of receiving something. He cannot compel the trustees to pay him anything (so that the source of any entitlement is the exercise of the trustees' discretion) and he cannot substitute another person for himself as a potential recipient of discretionary sums, although he can release his rights,[48] and he has sufficient in rem standing to trace misdirected trust assets and claim their return for the benefit of all those interested under the trust.[49] **1–51**

To conclude, in order to understand the working operation of a trust it is best to regard the interest of a beneficiary as an in personam right to compel the trustees to perform the trust, i.e. as an equitable chose in action situated where the trustees reside and administer the trust. But where the trustee has become insolvent or things have gone wrong and trust property reaches the hands of a third party (other than equity's darling), then it is appropriate to regard the interest of a beneficiary as an equitable in rem right,[50] as a result of his having an interest in a fund throughout.[51] **1–52**

---

44 *Saunders v Vautier* (1841) 4 Beav. 115.
45 *Re Diplock* [1948] Ch. 465.
46 *New Zealand Insurance Co Ltd v CPD (Victoria)* [1973] V.R. 659.
47 *Baker v Archer-Shee* [1927] A.C. 844; *Hamilton-Russell's Executors v IRC* (1943) 25 T.C. 200 at 207–208; *IRC v Berrill* [1981] 1 W.L.R. 1449 at 1460.
48 *Re Gulbenkian's Settlement (No.2)* [1970] Ch. 408.
49 A residuary beneficiary under an unadministered estate can assert "the estate's right of property": *Commissioner for Stamp Duties v Livingston* [1965] A.C. 694 at 714.
50 Unless the *lex situs* governing transfer of the relevant property was a foreign one having no concept of equitable proprietary right in its code of property principles.
51 R.C. Nolan, "Property in a Fund" (2004) 120 L.Q.R. 108.

4. The Utility, Versatility and Vitality of the Trust Concept

A. Historical Uses of the Trust

1–53 In the past, the trust was used in a wide variety of ways, as a property-holding arrangement which could be tailored to the differing needs of property owners according to the economic and social circumstances of the time. For example:

- It enabled land indirectly to be left on death to someone other than the owner's legal heir until Parliament made it possible to do this directly in 1540.
- It enabled members of an unincorporated association to trade via trustees with the apparent benefit of limited liability until the courts after 80 years or so held the members to be personally liable, thereby compelling Parliament to enact legislation permitting limited liability corporations in the mid-nineteenth century.
- When married women would otherwise have had no property rights, the father of a married woman could transfer property to trustees to hold to her "separate use", so that she had some financial independence before legislation conferred independence on wives in the late nineteenth century.

1–54 Where the King or Parliament considered that the trust device was being abused, legislation was enacted to block such abuse. For example:

- Transfers to trustees with intent to avoid creditors were first blocked in 1376, while transfers to trustees to the use of a corporation (to whom transfers could not be made directly due to the Statute of Mortmain) were blocked in 1391.
- Transfers to trustees to avoid wardship rights of feudal lords were blocked in 1490, while the general device of using "uses" to avoid feudal incidents was blocked in 1535.
- More recently, transfers made within six years of death to trustees (or others) with intent to defeat claims of the transferor's dependants under the Inheritance (Provision for Family & Dependants) Act 1975 can be set aside as far as necessary, as can dispositions to trustees (or others) with intent to defeat the claims of the transferor's spouse or children under the Matrimonial Causes Act 1973.
- On the tax front, legislation now ensures that settlors cannot make transfers to trustees so as to obtain unfair tax advantages, e.g. settlors are taxed on trust income if creating a trust for their infant children or a trust under which the settlor or his spouse can receive any benefit, while taxes on death in respect of property are not avoided by a settlor who is not entirely excluded from benefiting for such property under his lifetime trust.

B. Modern Uses of the Trust

i. Conveyancing

1–55 The trust concept has proved particularly useful in conveyancing. If two or more persons wish to own land jointly they cannot be the absolute and beneficial legal owners, as although up to four people can be the legal owners of land, all beneficial interests must take effect behind a trust. Where land is owned by two or more persons, the Law of Property Act 1925 ss.34–36 formerly imposed a trust for sale with power to postpone sale. Under the Trusts of Land and Appointment of Trustees Act 1996 the trust for sale was replaced by a trust to hold land with power to sell or otherwise dispose of it as an absolute owner can. Trustees hold property as joint tenants so that on the death of one trustee the property automatically passes to the surviving trustees by virtue of the *ius accrescendi*. On the death of the last surviving trustee his personal representatives take over his function until they appoint new trustees.[52]

ii. The Family Context

Tax considerations often make it desirable for wealthy people to create trusts in order to mitigate their family taxation liabilities, and the basic principles of taxation which affect trusts are considered below, in Section 5. Trusts are also used to provide for the management of the affairs of beneficiaries who are mentally or physically handicapped or who are spendthrift or who are young or who are old. They are also used to prevent the law of succession operating to vest the deceased's property absolutely in his adult children who could then dissipate the property. Thus a settlor's trust can preserve and generate family assets for three or four generations, successive family members benefiting from avoiding division of the assets into smaller and smaller shares each generation and from economies of scale in the management of the large pool of family assets. **1–56**

Examples of family trusts are: **1–57**

- a grandparent's fixed trust for such of the grandchildren who attain 25 years in equal shares;
- a testator's fixed trust for the surviving spouse for life, remainder to their children equally, but with power for the spouse by will or by deed to appoint the capital unequally between such of the children and the children's children as may be seen fit in the spouse's absolute discretion;
- a testator's fixed trust for the surviving spouse for life, remainder equally to each of their children for the life of each respective child, with the capital of such child's share to pass equally to such child's children, subject to an overriding power for the surviving spouse to appoint as in the previous example and after the death of such spouse for the trustees to have such power of appointment;
- a discretionary trust for such of the descendants of the settlor/testator as the trustees shall see fit in their absolute discretion from time to time to pay income or capital to, before expiry of an 80-year perpetuity period.

The settlor can provide a legally significant (but not legally binding) letter of wishes to guide the trustees in the exercise of their discretions, while family members can be trustees and employ professional discretionary portfolio managers to manage investments and other professionals for other tasks. Often a professional trust corporation is trustee, while family input can be preserved via the trust instrument providing for a "protector" with arrangements for the appointment of successor protectors. The protector may be the settlor or his surviving spouse or a specified child or a committee or board or, even, a company whose shares are owned by family members. The protector may have powers of vetoing trustees' proposed distributions of capital or proposed sales of particular assets **1–58**

[52] Trustee Act 1925 ss.18 and 36.

and power to replace the trustees, even with foreign trustees to be subjected to a new foreign trust law replacing English law as the law governing the trust. The protector will generally be subject to similar fiduciary duties as trustees in exercising his powers unless the trust instrument or special circumstances indicate otherwise.

1–59 Lifetime trusts are more useful than testamentary trusts because the probate process on death is a public one revealing the terms of the will and the taxable size of the deceased's estate. Moreover, if a settlor has assets in many jurisdictions then he does not want those assets to pass on death subject to different succession laws and a variety of forced heirship regimes, forcing different fractions of his estate to pass to his children and treating gifts made within differing periods before death as part of such estate. To avoid such complex situations, well-advised wealthy persons with valuable assets in a variety of countries put most of their assets into a lifetime trust so as to escape the application of laws governing succession to a deceased's estate.

1–60 If a person dies intestate then his administrators hold his estate on a statutory trust with a power of sale. A similar trust arises whenever land is co-owned if an express trust is not created in the co-ownership documentation.

1–61 Finally, under this heading, note that the trust has been used by the courts with increasing frequency over the past 40 years to resolve property-ownership disputes between unmarried cohabitants. Suppose that an unmarried couple have lived together for many years in a home, legal title to which is only vested in one of them, although the other has contributed, financially or in some other way, to the ongoing upkeep of the property and/or their shared family life. If they separate and the question arises whether the property should be divided between them, the divorce legislation has no application, and the courts have turned instead to the constructive trust as a mechanism for allocating property rights in the home.

iii. The Commercial Context

1–62 Trusts developed in the context of preserving and developing family wealth and of furthering charitable purposes. Private client lawyers specialise in these areas, thereby helping their clients in generating family wealth and using any surplus to advance philanthropic purposes. In the twentieth and twenty-first centuries, the trust structure has also been used in a wide variety of ingenious ways by commercial and financial lawyers. As a result, it has been estimated that no more than 10 per cent of trust assets are now comprised in family and charitable trusts, and the most important dimension of the trust concept has become its utility as an instrument of commerce. Common uses of the trust in this context are as follows.[53]

1–63 *Pensions for employees*. To ensure funding of pensions for retired employees, money is paid (pursuant to the contract of employment) to trustees to manage as a segregated fund. The retired employee then receives thereout either a percentage of his final salary or a lump sum that must be used to purchase an annuity.

1–64 *Collective investment schemes*. A trust is used as an open ended collective investment vehicle (with no fixed or irreducible capital base) in which the value of units in the unit trust held for a particular

---

[53] For detailed discussion of the commercial and financial uses of trusts see C. Duffet, "Using Trusts in International Financial and Commercial Transactions" (1992) 1 Jo. Int. T. Corp. P. 23; J.H. Langbein, "The Secret Life of the Trust: The Trust as an Instrument of Commerce" (1997) 107 Yale L.J. 165; D.J. Hayton (ed.), *Extending the Boundaries of Trusts and Similar Ring-Fenced Funds* (2002), chapters by D.J. Hayton and S. Worthington; D.J. Hayton, *English Trusts and Their Commercial Counterparts in Continental Europe: A Report for the Association of Corporate Trustees* (2002); M. Graziadei, V. Mattei and L. Smith (eds), *Commercial Trusts in European Private Law* (2005); P. Rawlings, "The Changing Role of the Trustee in International Bond Issues" [2007] J.B.L. 43.

unit-holder investor is directly related to the value of the assets held by the custodian trustee to the order of the managing trustee. Investors can sell their units back to the manager whenever they wish, whereupon a charge to capital gains tax will arise (but no such charge arises against the trustees or the unit holders on the disposal and reinvestment of underlying trust assets).

"Unit trusts" (known as "mutual funds" in North America) differ from "investment trusts" (as featured in share price pages of newspapers) because the latter actually are companies so that the investor owns shares in the company, the value of which will depend not just on the value of the assets owned by the company but also upon the dividend policy of the company, so that the share price will stand at a discount to the net asset value. Open-ended investment companies (OEICs)—as open-ended as unit trusts—can now be created with share prices directly reflecting the value of underlying assets. Unit trusts can quote one price for acquisition of units and another for redemption of units, while OEICs have a single pricing system, leading many unit trusts to move to a single pricing system. A unit trust can only issue "income" or "accumulation" units while an OEIC can issue different classes of share intended for different types of investment or investor. **1–65**

Collective security trusts for holders of bonds or debenture stock. The trustee has the benefit of the borrower's promise to repay the loan collectively provided by a group of lenders and often also has assets of the borrower as security for repayment. The trustee is an independent professional person (not the agent of either the lenders or the borrower) who can be relied upon confidentially to monitor matters and to decide the proper response to any default or even to modify the terms of the loan without the expense and trouble of a meeting with the lenders except in defined special circumstances. The rights of the trustee and any fruits of such rights (e.g. proceeds of sale of a security) are held as a separate fund for the lenders (of whom there are too many to be co-owners of the security interest, four being the maximum for co-ownership of interests in land), so protecting them against the insolvency of the trustee whose office as trustee will then be filled by another trustee. **1–66**

Syndicated loan trusts. Where slices of capital will be provided at differing times and may be from lenders different from the original lenders, trustees of collective security trusts can have overriding powers to afford subsequent lenders the same priority as earlier lenders or even a higher priority but, perhaps, only if a specified proportion of the earlier lenders agree. Indeed, to deal with the case where all the lenders are repaid but further loans are needed (e.g. in financing the Channel Tunnel) matters can be arranged so that the trustee continues to hold the security but for the new lenders without the need for anything further to be done (like registration of a new charge if the old charge were considered to have ceased when all the old lenders had been paid). **1–67**

Subordination trusts. Subordination of a creditor occurs where one creditor, the "subordinated" or "junior" creditor, agrees not to be paid by a debtor until another creditor, the "senior" creditor, of the common debtor has been paid. To avoid the insolvency rule that requires rateable distributions to creditors from an insolvent debtor, a trust deed is executed under which the junior debt is payable by the debtor to a trustee, who is to hold any payment made in respect of the junior debt on trust first for the benefit of the senior creditor to the amount of the senior debt, and then, if any money remains, for the junior creditor. The senior creditor is thus protected against the insolvency of both the junior creditor and the debtor.[54] **1–68**

Securitisation trusts of special purpose vehicles (SPVs). For the purposes of enabling a complex portfolio of assets (e.g. secured or unsecured debts, credit card receivables) to be available as security to **1–69**

---

[54] Subordination trusts do not contravene the fundamental pari passu rule for treatment of creditors in insolvency: *Re British and Commonwealth Holdings Plc (No.3)* [1992] 1 W.L.R. 672; *Re Maxwell Communications Corp Plc (No 2)* [1993] 1 W.L.R. 1402; *Perpetual Trustee Co Ltd v BNY Corporate Trustee Services Ltd* [2010] B.C.C. 59.

investors, a company, known as an SPV, purchases the portfolio, borrowing the money via a collective security bond issue. The shares in the SPV and the portfolio are held on trust to repay the bondholders with any (small) surplus held on trust for the bondholders or for charitable purposes (or for non-charitable purposes where expressly permitted by foreign laws, e.g. of Bermuda, Cayman Islands, Isle of Man, Jersey). This avoids the original owner of the portfolio beneficially owning shares in the SPV, and so avoids the SPV's debt appearing on such owner's consolidated balance sheet. Where there is a shortage in the financial markets of AAA rated bonds or of high yielding bonds it is possible to use this securitisation trust device to put together a "ring-fenced" package of corporate bonds to help satisfy the shortage.

1–70 *Project financing and future income streams*. If L contracts to lend £50 million to B and actually pays over the money to B on the basis that B will hold on trust for L all the money that B expects to acquire from a particular source once B acquires it, then as soon as B does acquire it B holds it on trust for L.[55] This enables B to acquire money now in respect of a future income stream expected from a particular project, e.g. a tunnel, a mine, an oil well. Such income will be used to service the debt interest and to repay capital.

1–71 *Temporary purpose trusts of money until a debtor–creditor relationship arises (Quistclose trusts)*.[56] C can transfer money to D on trust for C, but give D the power to apply the money to a particular purpose which the parties have agreed. Until the money is used for this specified purpose it belongs to C in equity, but after D has exercised his power by applying the money to the specified purpose, he simply owes C a personal obligation to repay the money on such terms as the parties have agreed. This arrangement protects C against the risk that D will become insolvent before he has spent the money on the agreed purpose, and that his other creditors will then make claims against the money.

1–72 *Client accounts, e.g. of solicitors*. If X, involved in a profession or business, has an office (or private) account with a bank and a separate client account for clients' money, then the client account money is held on trust for the clients, who are thus safe if X becomes insolvent. It is a fundamental feature of the trust concept that anyone can open in his own name an account designated as a trust account for the benefit of others, who are then protected against the insolvency of the account holder. In such event they are entitled to the balance in the account and to assets wrongfully purchased by the account holder in his own name with money drawn from the account or wrongfully given away to a third party.

1–73 *Trusts affecting personal accounts of agents or purchasers so as to protect interests of principals or vendors*. P Co may sell its fleet of cars or its airline tickets through the agency of A Co which will merely be in a debtor–creditor relationship with P Co, having to pay it an amount corresponding to the proceeds of sale less A Co's commission. Purchasers from A Co will not make out one cheque in favour of A Co for its commission and a second cheque in favour of P Co for the balance, but just a cheque for the whole amount in favour of A Co, which will pay the cheque into its personal account. P Co then runs the risk of A Co's insolvency.

1–74 To avoid this risk,[57] P Co can negotiate an arrangement whereby A Co contractually agrees that it will hold a specified (fractional or percentage) part of the proceeds of sale that represents the whole

---

[55] *Re Lind* [1915] 2 Ch. 345; *Palette Shoes Pty Ltd v Krohn* (1937) 58 C.L.R. 1 at 26–27.

[56] Named for *Barclays Bank Ltd v Quistclose Investment Ltd* [1970] A.C. 567, as explained in *Twinsectra Ltd v Yardley* [2002] 2 A.C. 164.

[57] *Re Fleet Disposal Services Ltd* [1995] 1 B.C.L.C. 345; *Re Lewis's of Leicester Ltd* [1995] 1 B.C.L.C. 428; *Re ILG Travel Ltd (in admin.)* [1995] 2 B.C.L.C. 128; *Air Canada v M & L Travel Ltd* [1993] 3 S.C.R. 787; background position to *Royal Brunei Airlines v Tan* [1995] 2 A.C. 378.

proceeds less its commission on trust for P Co, that it will pay an amount of money corresponding to such part to P Co within a specified period of, say, five working days (such payment to discharge the relevant indebtedness of A Co to P Co), and that it will not let the balance in the account within such period fall below the amount due to P Co.[58]

1–75 V Co may sell raw materials to W Co which W Co uses to produce manufactured products belonging wholly to W Co and which W Co then sells. To avoid the insolvency risk arising from W Co only being a debtor of V Co, V Co can negotiate in its contract of sale with W Co, that W Co will be trustee of such a (fractional or percentage) part of the proceeds of sale of the newly manufactured products as is equivalent to the amount owing to V Co by W Co at the time W Co received such proceeds,[59] W Co will pay to V Co such amount within a specified period of, say, five working days, and will not let the balance in its account within such period fall below such amount due to V Co.

1–76 In both these instances of principal–agent and vendor–purchaser the principal or vendor will be able to assert an equitable lien or charge for the amount of its money over the personal bank account of the agent or purchaser and an equitable proprietary interest in any traceable product purchased with its money. Note, however, that if the agent or purchaser breaches its contract by paying the money into an overdrawn account with the result that it is irredeemably lost (the bank being a bona fide purchaser for value), then the principal or vendor cannot retrieve the situation by asserting a proprietary claim against some other property in the agent or purchaser's hands.[60] Moreover, the principal or vendor will not have any equitable proprietary rights if the alleged trust was a sham (both parties from the outset agreeing on irregular payments under a debtor–creditor relationship to help the cash-flow of the agent or purchaser), nor will it have such rights if the parties expressly or impliedly agree to ouster of the trust relationship by a debtor–creditor relationship.

1–77 *Building contracts: retention trusts*. Standard form building construction contracts have a clause for the employer of the management contractor, which employs various works contractors, to set up a retention trust fund of a percentage (e.g., 3 or 5 per cent) of each amount certified by the architect as due to the management contractor for itself and the works contractors. Half of this fund is payable when the architect issues the certificate of practical completion and the final half upon issue of the certificate of completion of making good defects. Thus, the employer has a measure of security to ensure the building is properly completed and the management contractor and works contractors have some protection against the insolvency of the employer.

1–78 *Sinking fund trusts*. Where major expenditure will be needed after a number of years, money can be paid regularly to a trustee so that an adequate amount will certainly be available to carry out a particular purpose, for example major repairs or renewals for blocks of flats, for old heritage property, or for good environmental land reclamation after working out of a mine.

1–79 *Employee share ownership trusts*. A company can arrange for some of its shares to be held on trust for allocation to particular employees in due course (who then receive favoured tax treatment if they do not sell their shares for three years). Thus its employees are encouraged to work hard (so helping it and the economy to develop). The trust also provides a market for shares in the employer company. "All employee" trusts of shares are particularly encouraged by provisions in the Finance Act 2000, the Inland Revenue even publishing model trust deeds.

---

[58] One cannot trace beyond the lowest intermediate balance (*Roscoe v Winder* [1915] 1 Ch. 62); this clause is not vital but serves to emphasise the trust relationship.

[59] *Associated Alloys Pty Ltd v ACN 001 452 106 Pty Ltd (in liq.)* (2000) 202 C.L.R. 588 at [28]: "There being value [provided by V Co], and equity regarding as done that which ought to be done, a completely constituted trust would arise in respect of those proceeds as they were received by the Buyer [P Co]".

[60] *Re BA Peters Plc (in admin.)* [2009] B.P.I.R. 248.

1–80 *Trusts of shares to separate control from ownership of the company*. It may be useful to have voting rights vested in independent trustees rather than in those owning the economic value. Thus, where A and B are 60:40 shareholders in a joint venture company they can transfer their shares to T on the basis T must vote 75 per cent as B directs, which provides B with greater protection than if A merely contracted with B to vote 35 of his 60 as B directs, in which case A could break his contract and harm B's interests.

1–81 Independent trustees may be controlling directors of a company so that those owning the economic value do not have control which would contravene public interest laws, e.g. for the conduct of banking business or for regulating fair competition (where the regulatory authority may require the shares to be sold but afford the trustees a reasonable time for this, so avoiding a forced sale at a depressed price that would have had to occur if the beneficiary controlled the company).

1–82 *Custodian trusts in the financial or securities markets*. To facilitate speedy inexpensive dealings in stocks and shares, many of such securities are held by a corporate custodian, often for a sub-custodian, which holds for a broker who holds for a client. Because there can be no bailment or custody of intangibles, intangibles must be owned by the custodian as trustee, with sub-custodians, brokers and their clients having only a proportionate equitable co-ownership interest in the fungible pool of securities legally owned by the custodian as trustee.

1–83 This trust of a pool of assets for persons entitled to proportionate shares therein as equitable co-owners provides purchasers of securities with a proprietary interest and avoids technical certainty problems concerning which specific securities belong to whom. Thus, if Nominee Plc is registered shareholder of ten million shares in Bigg Plc, and Subcustodian Plc is interested in two million shares out of which it sold 100,000 to P, P does not actually own a specific 100,000 shareholding. Rather, P owns a one twentieth share of Subcustodian's one fifth share of Nominee's shareholding.

1–84 *Pledges of bills of lading*. Pledging the bill of lading with the other shipping documents requires delivery to the lender, but the buyer-borrower needs these documents to obtain the goods from the shipping company. If the lender parts with the documents unconditionally the pledge will be extinguished. Thus, the buyer provides the lender with a trust letter or receipt in which, in return for the release of the documents, the buyer undertakes he will hold the documents and then the goods and any proceeds of sale on trust for the lender, who is thereby deemed to continue in constructive possession of the documents, so that the pledge remains valid.

5. Taxation Aspects of Trusts

1–85 In the family context, settlors often create trusts in order to mitigate their family taxation liabilities, and once such trusts are up and running, tax considerations are also likely to influence the trustees' decision-making, for example, when deciding whether to invest the trust fund for capital growth or income maximisation, and whether to distribute income or appoint capital to the beneficiaries. To understand the creation and operation of many trusts, it is therefore essential to understand the basic principles of taxation which affect them. The following account will give an outline of this subject, but it is no more than an outline of some highly complex and technical material, especially as regards those anti-avoidance provisions which are designed to prevent the versatile flexibility of the trust from being manipulated to obtain tax advantages.[61]

---

[61] For a more detailed introduction, see A.J. Oakley, *Parker and Mellows: The Modern Law of Trusts* (9th edn, 2008) Ch.15. Specialist works are E. Chamberlain and C. Whitehouse, *Trust Taxation* (2007); J. Tiley, *Revenue Law* (6th edn, 2008).

A. Income Tax

The settlor's position. An individual's taxable income is taxed progressively at rates laid down annually in the Finance Act. In the tax year 2009–2010 there was a starting rate of 10 per cent (up to £2,230), then a 22 per cent basic rate (up to £37,400) and a 40 per cent higher rate (over £37,400). In the past, progressively higher slices of taxable income were taxed at progressively higher rates (up to a top rate as high as 83 per cent). For dividend income the rate in 2009/2010 was 10 per cent for those below the higher rate limit, and 32.5 per cent for those above it. For other savings income there was a starting rate of 10 per cent (up to £2,320), a basic rate of 20 per cent (up to £34,800) and then a higher rate of 40 per cent (above £34,800). **1–86**

The progressive nature of income tax is such that, in circumstances not covered by anti-avoidance provisions, a tax saving can be achieved by a wealthy person hiving off some of his income to trustees or an individual or a charity not taxable at the higher rates or at all. He can do this either by covenanting to pay income to them or by transferring the income-producing capital itself. If capital taxes have lower rates than income tax (as was the case until 1988), or have the advantage that the first £10,100 of gains each year are exempt from capital gains tax (as was the case in the tax year 2009/2010), then further tax savings can be achieved by using trustees' powers of accumulation of income to convert income into capital and eventually to pass it over to beneficiaries as capital. However, there has been less scope for this since April 6, 2004, when the maximum rate of tax on accumulated trust income was raised to 40 per cent from 34 per cent. Tax-efficient benefits in kind (e.g. free loans of cash, chattels, houses) may also be conferred on beneficiaries. **1–87**

Anti-avoidance provisions, however, reduce the opportunities for settlements to be used to avoid income tax. In considering whether such provisions apply one must ask three questions: **1–88**

- Do the settlor and his spouse retain any possibility of benefiting from the settled property other than in very limited contingencies? If so, then the trust income is treated as wholly his.[62] If a settlor receives a capital sum by way of loan from the trust or repayment of his loan to the trust, then he is treated as receiving taxed net income (to the extent of available undistributed income for that year and the next 10 years) equal to such sum.[63]
- If the settlor is not caught by the foregoing rules, but income is actually paid by the trustees to or for the benefit of the settlor's minor unmarried children (or allocated on a bare trust to pay the income therefrom to such children), then such income ranks as the settlor's. If income is accumulated, then any capital payment to or for the benefit of the unmarried minor is deemed to be a payment of income, ranking as the settlor's income, to the extent that there is accumulated income available to cover the payment.[64]
- Was a covenanted payment of income either a maintenance payment for an ex-spouse or a separated spouse or an annual payment made for bona fide commercial reasons in connection with his trade profession or vocation or a covenant for charity capable of lasting for more than three years? If so, then it is deductible from the settlor's income.[65]

The trustees' position. Obviously trustees cannot take the trust income for themselves, but for the purposes of the income tax regime as it applies to trusts, trustees are "entitled" to the trust income **1–89**

[62] Income Tax (Trading and Other Income) Act 2005 ss.624 ff.
[63] Income Tax (Trading and Other Income) Act 2005 ss.633 ff.
[64] Income Tax (Trading and Other Income) Act 2005 ss.629 ff.
[65] Income Tax (Trading and Other Income) Act 2005 ss.626–628.

in the sense that they are able to claim receipt of the income. The trust income is quite separate from the trustees' own personal income and their personal tax circumstances are irrelevant. They are "together treated as if they were a single person (distinct from the persons who are trustees of the settlement from time to time)",[66] but they are not technically "individuals" for income tax purposes, and so they are not liable to higher rate tax which is applicable to individuals only. Instead they are liable to basic rate tax of 20 per cent, or 20 per cent lower rate tax on savings (except for dividends taxed at 10 per cent), under the appropriate income tax schedules on all the income produced by the trust fund. Trust income can have no deduction against it for personal allowances or for expenses incurred in administering the trust.[67] Much income will be received by the trustees after deduction of tax (e.g. dividends or building society interest) but in other cases (e.g. profits of carrying on a trade[68]) the trustees will need to pay the basic rate tax.

1–90 There is one important exception to the foregoing rules, namely that if no one such as a life tenant has an interest in possession in the trust,[69] entitling him as of right to the income, then the trustees must pay tax at the "trust rate",[70] which was 40 per cent in the tax year 2009/2010, but which rose to 50 per cent on April 6, 2010, except for dividend income which is taxed at the "dividend trust rate",[71] which was 32.5 per cent in the tax year 2009/2010, but which rose to 42.5 per cent on April 6, 2010. In such cases there would otherwise be too much scope for minimising liability to tax by exercising powers of accumulation or by delaying exercising discretionary powers over income until a tax-efficient beneficiary has materialised. However, in the case of these accumulation and maintenance trusts and discretionary trusts the expenses incurred in administering the trust which are properly chargeable to income can be deducted from the income liable to the additional rate charge.[72]

1–91 *The beneficiary's position.* A beneficiary who is currently entitled to trust income as it arises (i.e. who has an interest in possession like a life tenant) is liable to income tax for the year of assessment in which that income arises, even if none of the income is actually paid to him in that year.[73] One should note that the effect of Trustee Act 1925 s.31[74] (which may be excluded by the trust instrument) is to convert a minor's apparent entitlement to income under a trust for him for life into a contingent interest, since it imposes a duty upon the trustees to accumulate income (so far as not needed for his maintenance, education or benefit) until his majority, and if he dies before attaining his majority then the accumulated income passes with the capital, to which it has accrued, to the person entitled to capital after his death.[75]

1–92 The beneficiary will be entitled to the balance after the trustees have paid basic rate tax or lower rate or the 10 per cent dividend tax and their administration expenses. This net sum (e.g. £7,000 where gross income of £10,000 has borne £2,200 basic rate tax and £800 expenses) is then grossed up by the relevant rate of tax (£7,000 × 100 – 22 = £8,974) to find the taxable sum to rank as part of the beneficiary's total taxable income. He is given a tax credit for the difference (£8,974 – £7,000 = £1,974) (except for the 10 per cent dividend tax) so that if his total income is such that he bears basic

---

[66] Income Tax Act 2007 s.474(1).
[67] *Aikin v Macdonald's Trustees* (1894) 3 T.C. 306.
[68] Of course, expenses incurred in earning the profits may be deducted and loss relief may be claimed.
[69] For the meaning of interest in possession see *Pearson v IRC* [1981] A.C. 75, discussed in n.102 below.
[70] Income Tax Act 2007 s.479(4).
[71] Income Tax Act 2007 s.479(3).
[72] Income Tax Act 2007 s.484; *Carver v Duncan* [1985] A.C. 1082; *HMRC v Trustees of the Peter Clay Discretionary Trust* [2009] Ch. 296.
[73] *Baker v Archer-Shee* [1927] A.C. 844; *Hamilton-Russell's Executors v IRC* (1943) 25 T.C. 200.
[74] Reproduced at para.9–179. One should also note that a person with a contingent right, e.g. upon attaining 30 years of age, obtains a vested right to income on attaining majority: Trustee Act 1925 s.31(1)(ii).
[75] *Stanley v IRC* [1944] K.B. 255.

rate tax, only then does this credit satisfy his liability.[76] If he is not liable to tax then he can reclaim the amount of the tax credit from the Revenue (£1,974 rather than the £2,200 actually paid by the trustees); if he is liable to higher rate tax then he only has to pay the difference between the amount of such liability and the amount of the tax credit.

A beneficiary not entitled to trust income as it arises (i.e. who does not have an interest in possession, but who depends upon the discretion of the trustees) is charged on what he receives. He will receive the income net of the trust rate tax deducted by the trustees, and will obtain a tax credit for this deduction and will be able to reclaim some of this sum if his total income is such that he is assessable at some lower rate than 50 per cent. The imposition of tax at 50 per cent on the trustees is thus not a worrying factor where they distribute the income to beneficiaries who are liable to basic rate tax or no tax at all. **1–93**

Once income has been accumulated it loses its character as income and accrues to the capital fund (i.e. it becomes capitalised), and so payments of accumulated income will be payments of capital and will normally be receipts of capital in the beneficiary's hands and so will not liable to income tax. However, if a beneficiary is given £x per annum and the trustees have a duty or a power to make up that sum out of capital if the trust income is less than £x, then such "topping up" payments of capital will be taxed as income in the beneficiary's hands.[77] Moreover, regular payments out of capital may be characterised as income receipts of the beneficiary if paid to enable him to keep up his standard of living.[78] However, a disposition of capital in exercise of a power over capital will normally not rank as income in the beneficiary's hands even if the money is used for what might be termed as an income purpose.[79] **1–94**

B. *Inheritance Tax*

Inheritance tax ("IHT") is imposed on that part of a person's estate that exceeds his lifetime allowance (which in the tax year 2009/2010 was £325,000). The tax focuses on transfers of value which may either be exempt, potentially exempt, or chargeable.[80] On death the deceased is treated as having made a transfer of value of the whole of his estate immediately before his death,[81] but for IHT purposes, his estate includes any property that he disposed of other than for value during the seven years immediately prior to his death. The value of this property is taken to be the amount by which the transfer reduced the value of the transferor's estate, rather than the amount by which it increased the value of the recipient's estate (which will not necessarily be the same).[82] **1–95**

To understand the IHT treatment of gifts into trusts it must be appreciated that prior to March 22, 2006, the legislation distinguished between three types of trusts—discretionary trusts, accumulation and maintenance ("A & M") trusts, and interest in possession trusts. A gift into a discretionary trust was a chargeable transfer, attracting an immediate "entry charge", periodic 10-year charges, and an "exit charge" when property came out of the trust again. In contrast, gifts into the other two types of trust were potentially exempt transfers, ripening into exempt transfers with the passing of time, and so they were attractive devices from a tax planning perspective. However, the tax planning landscape **1–96**

---

[76] Where the trustees deduct their administration expenses the beneficiary is only entitled to gross up his net receipt after tax and these expenses, and so his grossed-up income will be less than the trustees' gross income: *Macfarlane v IRC* 1929 S.C. 453; 14 T.C. 532. If the trustees had paid him the gross £10,000 less £2,200 tax then if he were below the tax threshold he would reclaim the £2,200 and then pay the trustees their £800 expenses, so leaving him with £9,200 instead of £8,974 where the trustees first paid their expenses before paying him.

[77] *Brodies's Will Trustees v IRC* (1933) 17 T.C. 432; *Lindus & Horton v IRC* (1933) 17 T.C. 442.

[78] *Cunard's Trustees v IRC* [1962] 1 All E.R. 159.

[79] *Stevenson v Wishart* [1987] 1 W.L.R. 1204.

[80] Inheritance Tax Act 1984 ("IHTA") s.3A.

[81] IHTA s.4.

[82] IHTA s.3.

was radically changed by the Finance Act 2006, which brought many A & M trusts and interest in possession trusts into the IHT regime that formerly applied to discretionary trusts only. The purpose of these changes was partly to align the IHT treatment of different trusts, and partly to prevent A & M trusts and interest in possession trusts from being used as tax avoidance devices. The following account will describe the IHT regime applying to settlements prior to March 22, 2006, and then explain the regime applying to settlements after this date.

1–97 *The settlor's position.* Prior to March 22, 2006, if a settlor transferred assets to trustees or declared himself trustee of specific assets then this amounted to a transfer of value. However, if he made a gift on trusts but reserved any benefit to himself, then the gifted property was treated as still belonging to him so as to be taxable on his death with the rest of his estate at 40 per cent,[83] e.g. if he was one of the beneficiaries of his discretionary trust or a remunerated trustee or, not being a beneficiary, retained the de facto use of the gifted property.

1–98 A gift into a discretionary trust (other than an A & M trust) was a chargeable transfer (so that IHT was immediately payable),[84] while transferring property into an interest in possession trust or an A & M trust was a potentially exempt transfer,[85] ripening into an exempt transfer if the settlor survived for seven years. IHT was charged at 40 per cent for death transfers and transfers within three years of death, and half that for lifetime transfers, unless the transferor died within seven years, a sliding scale operating between three and seven years of the transfer.[86]

1–99 If the settlor paid the IHT inter vivos in respect of his discretionary settlement, so diminishing his estate further, then he was treated as having made a transfer of value of such amount as after payment of IHT thereon left the value of the settled property, i.e. his gift was grossed up.[87] However this did not happen if the trustees paid the IHT out of the trust fund.[88]

1–100 The 2006 Act has assimilated gifts into interest in possession trusts and A & M trusts with gifts into discretionary trusts for IHT purposes. Hence the only types of gift into a trust that are now potentially exempt transfers are gifts into a disabled trust, and gifts into a bereaved minor's trust.[89]

1–101 *Taxation of settlements before March 22, 2006.* Prior to March 22, 2006, trusts with no interest in possession (e.g. discretionary trusts), other than A & M trusts, were liable to a periodic charge to IHT every 10th anniversary,[90] and it was up to the trustees to pay this out of the trust fund.[91] If during a 10-year period capital ceased to be subject to such trusts (e.g. because it was distributed to a beneficiary or because it was resettled or sub-settled on interest in possession trusts or privileged trusts (discussed below)), then there was an exit charge in respect of such capital.[92] Basically, the exit charge represented a proportion of the periodic charge payable on the next 10-year anniversary of the trust and depended on the time elapsed since the last such anniversary.

1–102 Calculation of the tax actually payable was complex, involving a hypothetical transfer of value by a hypothetical transferor with a cumulative total including that of the settlor in the seven years before creating the trust.[93] The rate of IHT was calculated at 30 per cent of the lifetime rates applicable to

---

[83] Finance Act 1986 s.102.
[84] IHTA s.2.
[85] IHTA s.3A(2).
[86] IHTA s.7.
[87] IHTA ss.3(1), 162(3), 164.
[88] IHTA ss.3(1), 162(3), 164 and 199(1)(c).
[89] Finance Act 2006, Sch.20, para.9, amending IHTA s.3A. See further para.1–108.
[90] IHTA ss.61, 64.
[91] IHTA ss.201(1)(a), 212.
[92] IHTA s.65.
[93] IHTA ss.66, 68, 69. The exit charge rate necessarily had to be calculated as a proportion of the effective rate of the last periodic charge.

the hypothetical transfer,[94] so that the maximum rate was 6 per cent (30 per cent of 20 per cent). Thus discretionary trusts could still be useful propositions, especially if they were kept just below the £263,000 threshold (as it was in the tax year 2005/2006) and were made by settlors with small cumulative totals of chargeable transfers. Additions of property by the original settlor to his trust had to be avoided, however, since these often caused more IHT to be charged (at the next 10-year anniversary) than would have been the case if he had created a new separate settlement.[95]

If the trustees paid IHT in respect of the exit charge out of property remaining in the discretionary settlement then the chargeable amount had to be grossed up,[96] but this did not happen if the recipient of the capital ceasing to be subject to the discretionary trust paid the IHT.[97] **1–103**

For policy reasons some trusts which would otherwise have fallen to be taxed as trusts with no interest in possession received privileged treatment prior to March 22, 2006. Accumulation and maintenance trusts for minors were the most significant privileged trusts for private tax planning.[98] Such trusts were privileged so as not to discriminate between gifts to minors or to adults contingent upon attaining 25 years of age (which must take effect behind trusts) and outright gifts to adults of 25 years or more. No periodic or exit charges were payable and no charge arose when a beneficiary became entitled to the settled property.[99] **1–104**

Such privileged treatment was accorded to settled property if:[100] **1–105**

(1) one or more persons ("beneficiaries") would, on or before attaining a specified age not exceeding 25,[101] become beneficially entitled to it or to an interest in possession in it; and

(2) no interest in possession subsisted in it, and the income from it was to be accumulated so far as not applied for the maintenance education or benefit of a beneficiary; and

(3) either (a) all the persons who were or had been beneficiaries were or had been either (i) grandchildren of a common grandparent, or (ii) children, widows or widowers of such grandchildren who had themselves been beneficiaries but had died before the time when, had they survived, they would have become entitled as in (1) above, or (b) not more than 25 years had elapsed since the commencement of the settlement or, if it was later, since the time when the conditions in (1) and (2) had become satisfied with respect to the property.

Prior to March 22, 2006, a different IHT regime also applied to interest in possession trusts.[102] The person beneficially entitled to the interest in possession (e.g. a life interest) was deemed to own the **1–106**

---

94 IHTA s.66(1).
95 IHTA s.67.
96 IHTA s.65(2)(b).
97 IHTA s.65(2)(a).
98 There were other privileged trusts which also received special treatment, e.g. charitable trusts and protective trusts: IHTA ss.72–77, 86–89.
99 IHTA ss.58(1)(b), 71(4).
100 IHTA s.71(1), (2).
101 No age had to be specified in the settlement or an age greater than 25 could be specified for entitlement to capital so long as Trustee Act 1925 s.31(1)(ii) applied to confer a vested right to income on a beneficiary attaining majority.
102 On the meaning of "interest in possession", see *Pearson v IRC* [1981] A.C. 753, where a 3:2 majority of the House of Lords rejected the traditional Chancery view that the mere existence of a power to accumulate or otherwise divert income from a life tenant, L, did not prevent L having an interest in possession, L being entitled to income unless the trustees positively diverted it. Thus, a beneficiary does not have an interest in possession if the trustees have power to divert the income away from him (e.g. by accumulating it, so that it accrues to capital to which he has no certainty of succeeding, or by paying it or applying it for the benefit of another beneficiary). A power to terminate an interest in possession (e.g. a power to appoint or advance some or all the capital to X) does not prevent the interest being an interest in possession so long as the power is not exercised.

whole settled capital so that if he disposed of his interest (e.g. gave it away or sold it) or his interest came to an end[103] (other than upon his becoming absolutely entitled to the capital[104]) then there was deemed to be a transfer of value equal to that of the whole settled capital. Where he sold his interest the amount of the transfer of value was reduced by the proceeds of sale.[105] His lifetime transfer of value was potentially exempt but if he died within seven years or died owning the interest then the amount of IHT payable depended upon his cumulative total in the preceding seven years.[106] It was, however, the trustees who were primarily liable to pay the IHT out of the trust property.[107]

1–107 *Taxation of settlements after March 22, 2006*. The Finance Act 2006 brought interest in possession trusts and A & M trusts created after March 22, 2006 into the discretionary trust regime.[108] Hence lifetime transfers into either type of settlement are now subject to an "entry charge" of 20 per cent if the value of the transfer exceeds the nil rate band, and there is also a periodic charge of 6 per cent on the value of the assets every 10 years from the start of the settlement. There is also an exit charge of 6 per cent on the value of assets leaving the trust.

1–108 However these rules are modified in the case of trusts for the disabled, trusts for bereaved minors, and "18-to-25 trusts". Transfers of assets into a trust for someone with a mental or physical disability are potentially exempt transfers so that no IHT will be payable if the person making the transfer survives for seven years after making the transfer; nor are such trusts subject to a 10-yearly charge; nor are exit charges a consideration so long as the asset stays in the trust and remains the "interest" of the beneficiary.[109] Trusts for the benefit of a bereaved minor (i.e. a person aged under 18 who has lost at least one parent or step-parent) are not subject to 10-yearly or exit charges, provided that (a) the assets in the trust are set aside for the exclusive benefit of the bereaved minor, and (b) the beneficiary becomes fully entitled to the assets in the trust at the age of 18 at the latest.[110] "18-to-25 trusts" resemble trusts for bereaved minors insofar as they can be created only on the death of the parent of a beneficiary, or under the Criminal Injuries Compensation Scheme. Despite the name, the beneficiary can be any age under 25, provided that he becomes fully entitled to the assets in the trust by the age of 25 (and in practice after the age of 18); until he reaches that age, any income must either be accumulated or used for his benefit as must any capital payment. Again, the 10-yearly charge does not apply; however, exit charges will apply to assets leaving the trust during the time that the beneficiary is aged between 18 and 25.[111]

1–109 The effect of the 2006 changes on estate planning can be illustrated by an example. Suppose that a settlor has young children with no immediate income needs and he wishes to put money into a trust for their future benefit with a view to reducing possible IHT liability, while preserving some flexibility for the trustees to decide which of them to benefit in due course. Before 2006 he would most probably have been advised to create an A & M trust with appropriate powers of selection. Now he would most probably be advised to create a discretionary trust. This would give greater flexibility either to

103 IHTA s.52(1). If the interest terminated on his death then the settled capital was aggregated with his estate: ss.4(1), 49(1).

104 IHTA s.53(2) or if the capital reverted to the settlor or passes to the beneficiary's spouse: s.53(3), (4).

105 IHTA s.52(2).

106 IHTA ss.51(1), 52(2), 7.

107 IHTA ss.201(1)(a), 212(1). A new beneficiary with an interest in possession could also be liable though he had power to recoup the tax: ss.201(1)(b), 212(1), (2).

108 Assets put into an interest in possession trust before March 22, 2006 are not affected by the changes, and are not subject to the 10-yearly charge. Nor are there any exit charges so long as the assets stay in the trust and remain the "interest" of the beneficiary. However, if new assets are put into the settlement on or after March 22, 2006, then these are potentially liable to the 10-yearly charges.

109 Finance Act 2006 Sch.20 para.6, inserting new IHTA ss.89A–89B.

110 Finance Act 2006 Sch.20 para.1, inserting new IHTA ss.71A–71C.

111 Finance Act 2006 Sch.20 para.1, inserting new IHTA ss.71D–71G.

roll up income inside the trust or to distribute it, and would also give greater flexibility to choose who can be benefited under the trust and the terms on which they can be benefited in the future. No advantage would be gained from an estate planning perspective if he created an A & M trust, since A & M trusts and discretionary trusts are now taxed in the same way.

C. Capital Gains Tax

The settlor's position. On settling capital assets *inter vivos*[112] (other than sterling currency or his principal private residence[113]) a settlor will be chargeable to capital gains tax ("CGT") on this disposal even if he (or his spouse) is a trustee or sole trustee or life tenant or if the settlement is revocable.[114] It was formerly possible to hold over the payment of CGT until the settled property was eventually sold,[115] but this ceased to be possible unless the property was business property,[116] or the creation of the trust involved a chargeable transfer for the purposes of IHT.[117] Since March 22, 2006, however, the *inter vivos* creation of any trust except a trust for a disabled person has constituted a chargeable transfer for IHT purposes. Hence with the exception of a trust for a disabled person it is once more possible to elect for CGT holdover relief whenever a trust is created inter vivos. **1–110**

Actual disposals by trustees. Until April 5, 2008, CGT was payable by trustees on actual disposals of trust assets at the trusts' rate of 40 per cent; since then, the CGT payable has been 18 per cent, the rate which applies to all disposals of assets which realise a chargeable capital gain.[118] Trustees have an annual exemption of half that of individuals (hence £5,050 in the tax year 2009/2010),[119] and from a tax planning perspective, it is desirable for trustees to use up their full exemption each year by selling trust assets in order to realise accrued capital gains and prevent unnecessary CGT liability arising in future. They can also set off gains against losses in the same year or previous years.[120] Any unrelieved losses when the trust ends, and a beneficiary becomes absolutely entitled to the settled property, will enure for the benefit of the beneficiary.[121] **1–111**

Actual disposals of beneficiaries' equitable interests. To prevent double taxation there is no CGT charge when a beneficiary disposes of his underlying equitable interest in settled property so long as that interest has not at any time been acquired for money or money's worth (other than another interest under the settlement).[122] **1–112**

Life interest in possession trusts. On the death of a life tenant in possession where the settlement continues the trustees are deemed to dispose of and re-acquire the settled property at its then market value, but CGT will not be charged.[123] After all, IHT will be charged on the settled property.[124] **1–113**

---

112 No charge to CGT arises where a testator's will creates a trust since his estate is already liable to IHT: the trustees (and then the legatees) take over the value of the property at the testator's death as their base value: Taxation of Chargeable Gains Act 1992 (TCGA) s.62.

113 TCGA s.21(1)(b) and ss.222–226 as amended by Finance Act 2004 s.117.

114 TCGA s.70. However, if the settlor or his spouse retains any interest in the settled property subsequent capital gains of the trustees are charged to the settlor: *Billingham v Cooper* [2001] S.T.C. 1177.

115 Finance Act 1980 s.79, which was repealed in 1989.

116 TCGA s.165.

117 TCGA s.260.

118 Finance Act 2008 s.8, replacing TCGA s.4.

119 Finance Act 1998 s.118; TCGA Sch.1: the fraction dwindles to one-tenth if the settlor creates 10 or more settlements. Gains of £8,500 are exempt in 2005–2006 for individuals.

120 TCGA s.2.

121 TCGA s.71.

122 TCGA s.76. If the trust is non-resident there will be a charge: TCGA s.85(1).

123 TCGA s.72.

124 IHTA ss.4, 49(1).

Thus the property's base value gets a CGT-free uplift. However, any held-over gain on the creation of the settlement will be chargeable, and payable by the trustees.[125]

1–114 If the life interest terminates other than on the life tenant's death but the settlement continues (e.g. to A for life or until remarriage, then B for life, then C absolutely and A remarries or releases her interest) there is no charge to CGT.[126] The original base value of the property in the trustees' hands remains unaltered.

1–115 If the life tenant dies and the settlement ends because a person becomes absolutely entitled to the settled property, the trustees are deemed to dispose of and re-acquire the settled property at its then market value, but CGT will not be charged.[127] After all, IHT will be charged on the property that has now become nominee property.[128] The absolutely entitled beneficiary will take over the property with its base value as at the life tenant's death. However, any held-over gain on the creation of the settlement will be chargeable at the beneficiary's expense.

1–116 If the life interest terminates other than on the life tenant's death and the settlement ends in respect of particular property because a person becomes absolutely entitled to the settled property, such property is deemed to have been disposed of by the trustees and CGT is chargeable at 18 per cent.[129] The position is as set out in the next paragraph, except that no hold-over relief is available because the disposition will be a potentially exempt transfer for IHT purposes.[130] If the trustees do not pay the tax within six months then the absolutely entitled person becomes liable.[131]

1–117 *Trusts with no life interest in possession*. When a person becomes absolutely entitled to any settled property as against the trustees, the assets comprised in the part to which he has become entitled are deemed to have been disposed of by the trustees for market value and CGT is chargeable.[132] The rate of CGT is 18 per cent. However, because the absolute entitlement occasions an exit charge to IHT an election can be made to hold over the gain and this can extend to any held-over gain on the creation of the settlement.[133]

1–118 The charge to CGT arises whether the person becoming absolutely entitled does so in his personal capacity as beneficiary, or in a fiduciary capacity as trustee of another trust.[134] If trust assets wholly cease to be subject to the trusts, powers and provisions of one settlement and become subject to the trusts, powers and provisions of another settlement, there is a deemed disposal of the assets even if the trustees of the two settlements happen to be the same persons.[135] The trustees of a settlement are treated as a single continuing body of persons distinct from the actual persons who may from time to time be the trustees,[136] so that a change of trustees occasions no charge to CGT or IHT.

1–119 Difficult questions arise where trustees of a settlement containing a power of appointment or of allocation or of appropriation or of advancement exercise such power so that part of the settled property falls to be held by them on trusts other than those to which it was subject immediately beforehand. Does the exercise of the power create a new trust, whose trustees are absolutely entitled against the old trustees, so that there has been a deemed disposal, or does it merely create a sub-trust under the

---

125 TCGA ss.74, 65.

126 The event falls outside the charging provisions, TCGA ss.71, 72. However, IHT will be payable: IHTA ss.51, 52.

127 TCGA ss.71, 73.

128 IHTA ss.4, 49(1).

129 TCGA s.71.

130 Except where discretionary trustees become absolutely entitled against interest in possession trustees (not a potentially exempt transfer) when hold-over relief will be available: TCGA s.260.

131 TCGA s.69(4).

132 TCGA s.7.

133 TCGA s.260. However, if the gain on an asset is held over then on a subsequent sale taper relief is only available for the seller's period of ownership.

134 *Hoare Trustees v Gardner* [1979] Ch. 10 at 13–14.

135 *Hart v Briscoe* [1979] Ch. 1 at 5; *Bond v Pickford* [1983] S.T.C. 517; cf. *Swires v Renton* [1991] S.T.C. 490.

136 *Roome v Edwards* [1982] A.C. 279; *Bond v Pickford* [1983] S.T.C. 517; *Jasmine Trustees Ltd v Wells & Hind (a firm)* [2008] Ch. 194; TCGA s.69(1).

umbrella of the old original trust so that there has been no deemed disposal? If the power is in a wide form authorising an application of the trust fund freed and released from the original trusts of the settlement, so that the original trusts are replaced by other exhaustive trusts, then such an application of the trust fund will be a deemed disposal.[137] If the power is in a narrow form, e.g. a special power to appoint the trust fund on trusts for a class of beneficiaries, their spouses and children (but with no unusual provision allowing the trustees to delegate their duties to other persons or otherwise contemplating the creation of an entirely new trust) then any appointed property will be regarded as a sub-trust within the original trust, even if the sub-trusts are exhaustive, so there will be no deemed disposal.[138]

Since April 6, 2006, when trust property has been resettled, the settlor of the resettled property **1–120** has been treated as the settlor of the new settlement from the time of the disposal.[139]

6. Aspects of Wills and Intestacy Law

In a study of trust law there are many occasions when points relating to wills or intestacies crop up. **1–121** Hence a general outline knowledge of the law of wills and intestacy is useful before embarking on a detailed study of trust law.

First, one needs to distinguish the position of personal representatives ("PRs") winding up a **1–122** deceased person's estate from the position of trustees holding the trust property. The PRs' function is to collect in the deceased's assets, pay off all debts, taxes and expenses and, then, to distribute the assets to those entitled under the will or intestacy. Their duty is owed to the estate as a whole, and they are under no duty to consider the effect of the exercise of their administrative powers so as to keep an even hand between those interested in income and those interested in capital.[140] Until they agree to the assets passing to the legatees or devisees the legal and beneficial title to the assets is vested in the PRs.[141] The legatees or devisees have no equitable interest in such assets: they merely have an equitable right to compel due administration of the estate, although this chose in action (unlike the right of a beneficiary under a discretionary trust) can be assigned or bequeathed.[142]

To assist them in their functions PRs have a statutory power to appropriate assets to legatees or **1–123** devisees,[143] and if only a sole PR has been appointed, then while he is acting as such he can give a valid receipt for capital moneys arising on a sale of a trust of land.[144] PRs can only be appointed by will or by the court.[145] Finally, one of several PRs has full power to deal with the deceased's pure personalty.[146] However, in respect of freehold or leasehold land the concurrence of all the PRs is required to enter into any contract and then to convey the land.[147]

---

137 Hold-over relief will be available in respect of business or agricultural assets or if an IHT charge arises because interest in possession trusts are the new trusts.

138 See *Bond v Pickford* [1983] S.T.C. 517. Trusts are exhaustive if the beneficial interest is fully disposed of so that there is no need to refer elsewhere to discover what happens after someone dies or fails to obtain a vested interest.

139 TCGA s.68A, inserted by Finance Act 2006 Sch.12 para.1(2).

140 *Re Hayes's WT* [1971] 1 W.L.R. 758. Trustees have such a duty.

141 "Whatever property comes to the executor *virtute officii* comes to him in full ownership without distinction between legal and equitable interests: the whole property in his": *Commissioner for Stamp Duties v Livingston* [1965] A.C. 694 at 701. Thus "no legatee, devisee or next of kin has any beneficial interest in the assets being administered": *Re Hayes's WT* [1971] 1 W.L.R. 758 at 764.

142 *Re Leigh's WT* [1970] Ch. 277 at 281–282; *Crowden v Aldridge* [1993] 1 W.L.R. 433; *Marshall v Kerr* [1995] 1 A.C. 148 at 157–158; *Re Maye* [2008] 1 W.L.R. 115 at [16]; *Re Hemming, deceased* [2009] Ch. 313.

143 Administration of Estates Act 1925 s.41. Trustees only have such power if expressly conferred upon them.

144 Law of Property Act 1925 s.27(2).

145 Trustees can be appointed under Trustee Act 1925 s.36.

146 *Attenborough v Solomon* [1913] A.C. 76 where a PR, three years after he had become a trustee of the deceased's silver, pledged it and this was invalid since trustees must act jointly.

147 Law of Property (Miscellaneous Provisions) Act 1994 s.16.

1–124 When PRs have completed administration of the deceased's estate they become trustees of the residuary estate,[148] and their conduct will be sufficient to imply an assent of personalty to themselves as trustees.[149] As trustees they can exercise the statutory power that trustees have to appoint new or additional trustees.[150] Such an appointment makes the new or additional trustees trustees of the trusts of the residuary estate but it does not obtain the benefit of Trustee Act 1925 s.40;[151] thus, to the extent that the residuary estate consists of land, the legal estate therein remains outstanding in the PRs until a written assent is executed by them (or their successors in title) in favour of such trustees,[152] no earlier implied assent from conduct being possible for legal estates in land.[153] Thus, personal representatives need to execute a written assent in favour of themselves as trustees so that subsequent appointments by them are effective under s.40.

1–125 Basically, a will (unless made by a privileged military testator) must be in writing signed at the end by the testator (or by some other person in his presence and by his direction).[154] The testator's signature has to be made or acknowledged by him in the presence of two witnesses both with the testator at the same time. The witnesses must then sign their names in the testator's presence. The document must be intended to take effect only on the testator's death.[155] Thus, if S by deed settles £50,000 upon trust for himself for life and then for R absolutely, the formalities for a will are not applicable since S's settlement takes effect immediately, giving R a present vested interest in remainder, and entitling S only to the income from the £50,000 for the rest of his life. If S instead had made a will bequeathing £50,000 to R absolutely, S could use in his lifetime not only the income from the £50,000 but also the whole £50,000: he could also revoke his will and bequeath the £50,000 to X instead.

1–126 Gifts by will may fail to take effect for various reasons, including ademption, abatement, lapse, the beneficiary being an attesting witness or the spouse or civil partner thereof,[156] the beneficiary disclaiming the gift, or the beneficiary's marriage to the testator having been dissolved or annulled unless a contrary intention appears in the will.[157] Ademption occurs if T specifically leaves some property such as "my Ming dynasty vase" or "my house Blackacre" but no longer has the property when he dies: the legacy or devise is adeemed and the legatee or devisee receives nothing.[158] Abatement is a little less drastic: if T's debts are such that the Ming vase and Blackacre forming part of T's estate at T's death have to be sold but that a surplus remains after using the proceeds to pay off the debts then a rateable proportion will pass to the legatee and devisee. General legacies such as "I bequeath £5,000 to A, £3,000 to B and £1,000 to C" must first abate to their entire extent before resort can be had to specific gifts.[159]

1–127 Lapse occurs if a legatee or devisee predeceases the testator unless the legatee or devisee was a child (or other issue) of the testator and left issue alive at the testator's death: in such an exceptional

---

148 *Eaton v Daines* [1894] W.N. 32; *Re Ponder* [1921] 2 Ch. 59; *Re Cockburn's W.T.* [1957] 1 Ch. 438.
149 *Attenborough v Solomon* [1913] A.C. 76; C. Stebbings [1984] Conv. 423.
150 *Re Cockburn's W.T.* [1957] 1 Ch. 438.
151 See para.8–32.
152 *Re King's WT* [1964] Ch. 542.
153 An implied informal assent is possible for equitable interests if the PR is also beneficially entitled: *Re Edwards's WT* [1982] Ch. 30.
154 Wills Act 1837 s.9. See para.3–129.
155 *Att.-Gen. v Jones* (1817) 3 Price 368; *Governors of Foundling Hospital v Crane* [1911] 2 K.B. 367.
156 Wills Act 1837 s.15, as restricted by Wills Act 1968, and extended by Civil Partnership Act 2004 Sch.4 para.3.
157 Law Reform (Succession) Act 1995 s.3, substituting Wills Act 1837 s.18A.
158 See, e.g. *Banks v National Westminster Bank Plc* [2006] W.T.L.R. 1693.
159 The order in which property has to be resorted to in order to pay debts, etc. is laid down in Pt II, 1st Sch. to the Administration of Estates Act 1925.

case the gift is effective in favour of the surviving issue *per stirpes*.[160] Where lapse occurs the gift fails and will fall into any residuary gift of the testator (e.g. "I leave all the residue of my property not otherwise hereinbefore disposed of to R"). Necessarily, if it is the residuary legatee, R, who has predeceased the testator and occasioned the lapse, then the gifted property must be undisposed of and so pass to the next-of-kin under the intestacy rules applicable on the partial intestacy of the testator. Similarly, if a trust in a will fails, the property purportedly subject to the trust will pass under the residuary gift unless the trust was of the residuary property when the property will pass to the next-of-kin under the intestacy rules.

If it is uncertain whether or not a beneficiary predeceased the testator (e.g. where they are both killed by a bomb or in a car or plane crash), then the younger is presumed to have survived the elder under the *commorientes* rule in the Law of Property Act 1925 s.184. **1–128**

A beneficiary under a will or intestacy may disclaim the gift to him.[161] The gift then falls back into the deceased's estate and passes to whomsoever would have been entitled if the disclaiming beneficiary had predeceased the deceased.[162] Once a beneficiary has accepted the gift he cannot disclaim it,[163] but he can assign it on to whomsoever he wants. **1–129**

This leaves us with the intestacy rules, but first it should be noted that, while a testator in his will can appoint "executors" to administer the testator's estate and who will obtain "probate" of the will, where a person dies intestate his closest relatives normally have to take out "letters of administration" and act as "administrators": the phrase "personal representatives" covers both executors and administrators. A testator's will, if professionally drafted, will, after specific gifts, usually give everything to the executors on a trust for sale and, on an intestacy, statute directs the administrators to hold the intestate's property on a trust with a power of sale.[164] **1–130**

Where an intestate is survived by a spouse and issue,[165] the spouse takes the intestate's personal chattels absolutely and the net sum of £250,000 free of death duties and costs.[166] The residue is held on "the statutory trusts" for the issue subject to the spouse having a life interest[167] in half the residue. If the intestate is survived by a spouse and one or more of the following, that is to say, a parent, a brother or sister of the whole blood, or issue of such a brother or sister, but leaves no issue, then the spouse takes the personal chattels absolutely and the net sum of £450,000 free of death duties and costs: half of any residue is held for the surviving spouse absolutely and the other half is held for the surviving parents or parent or, if there is no surviving parent, it is held on "the statutory trusts" for the **1–131**

---

[160] Wills Act 1837 s.33, as substituted by Administration of Justice Act 1982 s.19. Illegitimate issue count: Family Law Reform Act 1969 s.16. "*Per stirpes*" means through their stocks of descent so that children of a deceased child take the share their parent would have taken had he survived.

[161] *Townson v Tickell* (1819) 3 B. & Ald. 31; *Re Scott* [1975] 1 W.L.R. 1260. A gift of a single whole (e.g. residue) must be wholly accepted or wholly disclaimed, partial acceptance amounting to whole acceptance: *Guthrie v Walrond* (1882) 22 Ch.D. 573; *Re Joel* [1943] Ch. 311.

[162] *Re Backhouse* [1931] W.N. 168.

[163] *Re Hodge* [1940] Ch. 260.

[164] Administration of Estates Act 1925 s.33, as amended by Trusts of Land and Appointment of Trustees Act 1996 Sch.2.

[165] "Issue" includes illegitimate issue: Family Law Reform Act 1987 s.1. Indeed, unless s.1 of that Act is excluded any disposition (by will or deed) referring to various relatives (e.g. child, nephew) covers both legitimate and illegitimate relatives. Civil partners now have the same rights as spouses: Civil Partnership Act 2004 Sch.4 paras 7 et seq.

[166] The rules are in the Administration of Estates Act 1925 s.46 and the current amount of the statutory legacies in Family Provision (Intestate Succession) Order 2009/135. Interest of 4 per cent is payable on unpaid statutory legacies. The spouse must survive the intestate by 28 days to take the legacy: Law Reform (Succession) Act 1995 s.1, inserting new AEA s.46(2A).

[167] The surviving spouse has a right to have the personal representatives purchase or redeem the life interest by paying over its capital value: Administration of Estates Act 1925 s.47A. She also has a right to compel the personal representatives to appropriate the matrimonial home at a proper valuation towards satisfaction of her interest under the intestacy: Intestates' Estate Act 1952 s.5; *Re Phelps* [1980] Ch. 275.

brothers and sisters of the whole blood. If the intestate leaves a spouse and no issue and no parent or brother or sister of the whole blood and no issue of such brother or sister then the surviving spouse takes everything.

1–132 If the intestate leaves issue, but no surviving spouse, then everything is held on "the statutory trusts" for the issue. If the intestate leaves no spouse and no issue any surviving parent or parents of the intestate take the assets absolutely. If, in such circumstances, there is no such surviving parent the intestate's relatives are entitled in the following order so that if any member of one class takes a vested interest he excludes all members of subsequent classes:

(i) the brothers and sisters of the whole blood on "the statutory trusts",

(ii) brothers and sisters of the half blood on "the statutory trusts",

(iii) grandparents,

(iv) uncles and aunts of the whole blood on "the statutory trusts",

(v) uncles and aunts of the half blood on "the statutory trusts".

In default the Crown (or the Duchy of Lancaster or of Cornwall) takes everything as bona vacantia.

1–133 If property is held on the statutory trusts, e.g. for issue, this means that the property is held upon trust equally for all the intestate's children living at his death who have attained or subsequently attain 18 years of age or who marry under that age: if a child predeceased the intestate, but left issue living or conceived at the death of the intestate, then such issue stand in the parent's shoes and take his share if they go on to attain 18 years of age or marry thereunder.[168] Thus, if an intestate widower dies leaving a 40-year-old son (with two daughters of his own) and two grandchildren aged 20 and 15, being the children of a deceased son of the intestate, then the 40-year-old son takes one-half of the intestate's property, and the two grandchildren acquire interests in the other half. The elder grandchild takes one-quarter of the property absolutely while the other quarter is held for the younger grandchild contingent upon his attaining 18 or marrying thereunder: if he should die before then his elder brother would then obtain the whole half share that would have passed to his father had he not predeceased the intestate.

1–134 Finally, mention may be made of the fact that if a testator's will or the intestacy rules fail to make reasonable financial provision for the testator's or intestate's dependants then an application under the Inheritance (Provision for Family and Dependants) Act 1975 can be made for the court to order reasonable provision to be made. Sections 10 and 11 have special provisions to deal with dispositions within six years of death intended to defeat applications for financial provision and with contracts to leave property by will.

7. Classification of Trusts and Powers

A. Express Trusts and Trusts Imposed by Law

1–135 Trusts are either express trusts or trusts imposed by law. Express trusts are created when a settlor positively expresses his intention to create a trust of specific property and subsequent substituted property from time to time comprised within the trust fund, whether using the word "trust" or other informal words expressing the same idea.[169] All other trusts are imposed by law: by statute, or by the

[168] Administration of Estates Act 1925 s.47(1).
[169] *Comiskey v Bowring-Hanbury* [1905] A.C. 84; *Paul v Constance* [1977] 1 W.L.R. 527.

rules of equity. Laying statutory trusts to one side,[170] only two types of trust are imposed by law: resulting trusts and constructive trusts. Under English law, these trusts arise because the rules of equity stipulate that they are imposed in particular circumstances. These rules give the courts no general discretion to bring trusts into being, or to refuse to do so, according to their assessment of the equities of a case.[171] The generic term "implied trusts" is also sometimes used to describe resulting and constructive trusts,[172] but confusingly this term has also been used in several other ways, and to avoid such confusion it is best avoided altogether.

The word "resulting" derives from the Latin word "*resalire*": "to jump back". Hence a resulting trust is literally a trust which returns beneficial ownership of the trust property to a person who owned the property before it reached the trustee's hands: in equity, the beneficial interest "jumps back" to its previous owner. Using the term "resulting trust" in a literal sense, we could therefore meaningfully say that an "express resulting trust" would be created if X transferred £500 to Y with the instruction that Y should hold the money on trust for X. However, trust lawyers rarely use the term "resulting trust" to describe an express trust which carries the beneficial interest back to its previous owner.[173] They almost always use it to describe a trust which conforms to this pattern, and which is imposed by law.[174] **1–136**

The verb "to construe" means "to interpret". Hence the word "constructive" is used to denote the fact that the law interprets—or, effectively, deems—a party's actions or words to have had some effect in law, even though they may not actually have had this effect in fact.[175] For example, a person with "constructive notice" is deemed to know the answers to questions that a reasonable person in his position would have asked, even if he does not actually know the answers because he has not actually asked the questions. In the case of a "constructive trust", the law deems a defendant to have conferred the same proprietary rights on a claimant as he would have acquired, had the defendant validly declared an express trust in his favour, even though no such valid declaration has actually been made.[176] Thus a "constructive trust" is literally a trust which is not an express trust, and which is imposed by law. **1–137**

Why are resulting and constructive trusts imposed, and what (if any) are the differences between them? Unfortunately, these questions are difficult to answer. We can list the situations in which the courts have imposed resulting and constructive trusts, but establishing a more rigorous taxonomy of these situations is a challenging task. One problem is that the classifications "resulting trust" and "constructive trust" seem to cut across one another. If a constructive trust is a trust imposed by law in circumstances where no express trust has been validly declared, and a resulting trust is a trust which returns beneficial ownership of the trust property to a previous owner, then it seems to follow that some trusts can be both resulting trusts and constructive trusts. **1–138**

Different judges have drawn different conclusions from this. On one view, all trusts imposed by law are constructive trusts, and resulting trusts are a sub-set of constructive trusts which conform to a **1–139**

---

170 Statutory trusts are not discussed at any length in this book, but see e.g. Law of Property Act 1925 ss.19, 34–36 (as amended by Trusts of Land and Appointment of Trustees Act 1996) imposing trusts on legal estates conveyed to minors and co-owned legal estates; Administration of Estates Act 1925 s.33 imposing trusts on the estate of a deceased intestate (discussed at paras 1–130 ff.).

171 *Re Goldcorp Exchange Ltd* [1995] 1 A.C. 74 at 104; *Westdeutsche Landesbank Girozentrale v Islington LBC* [1996] A.C. 669 at 714–716; *Re Polly Peck International Ltd (No.2)* [1998] 3 All E.R. 812 at 827 and 831.

172 *Cowcher v Cowcher* [1972] 1 W.L.R. 425 at 430, though the Trustee Act 1925 s.68(17) in speaking of "implied and constructive trusts" means "resulting and constructive trusts".

173 But see, e.g. *Latimer v CIR* [2004] 1 W.L.R. 1466 at [41], per Lord Millett.

174 e.g. *Lane v Dighton* (1762) Amb. 409 at 411; *Barton v Muir* (1874) L.R. 6 P.C. 134 at 145; *Churcher v Martin* (1889) 42 Ch.D. 312 at 319; *Re English & American Insurance Co Ltd* [1994] 1 B.C.L.C. 649 at 651; *Air Jamaica Ltd v Charlton* [1999] 1 W.L.R. 1399 at 1412.

175 Sir R. Megarry, "Historical Development" in *Special Lectures of the Law Society of Upper Canada 1990—Fiduciary Duties* (1991) at p.5: " 'Constructive' seems to mean 'It isn't, but has to be treated as if it were'."

176 L.D. Smith, "Constructive Trusts and Constructive Trustees" [1999] C.L.J. 294, pp. 294–298.

particular fact-pattern,[177] so that the two are effectively interchangeable whenever these facts are encountered.[178] On another view, resulting trusts and constructive trusts are distinct categories of trust, imposed by the courts for different reasons.[179] We cannot decide which of these views is correct unless we know why constructive and resulting trusts are imposed. If they are imposed for the same reasons, then they are identical and it does not matter which label we use, although it would make life easier if we only used one label. If they are imposed for different reasons, then we can say that one type of trust is used in one set of circumstances, and the other in another set of circumstances, although we must stay alert to the possibility that these sets of circumstances may sometimes coincide. Possible reasons for the imposition of resulting and constructive trusts are discussed in Chapters 14 and 15.

B. Fixed Trusts and Discretionary Trusts

1–140 Returning to express trusts, we find that a fixed trust is a trust in which a beneficiary has a current fixed entitlement to an ascertainable part of the net income, if any, of the trust fund after deduction of sums paid by the trustees in the exercise of their administrative powers of management: the beneficiary has an interest in possession under the trust. A discretionary trust, in contrast, is a trust in which a beneficiary has no such absolute current right to direct the trustees to pay him an ascertainable part of the net income. Typically, this is the case where a beneficiary will receive income only if the trustees positively decide to carry out their duty to distribute income by favouring him rather than another member of the class of beneficiaries. There is also the atypical case where a beneficiary must receive the income unless the trustees exercise powers to divert the income elsewhere (e.g. under a power to appoint income within six months of receiving it to charity) or to withhold it (e.g. a power to accumulate income by adding it to the capital where there is no certainty that accumulations will ultimately pass to the beneficiary or his personal representatives). In such cases, the discretion-conferring powers vested in the trustees prevent an interest in possession arising (e.g. where B is a life tenant subject to dispositive powers).[180]

1–141 If a settlor wishes to provide for B by creating a trust for the benefit of B (e.g. conferring a life interest upon B) then he ought to consider whether his intention will best be carried out by conferring a distinct fixed interest upon B. For if B becomes bankrupt his life interest, like his other property, will pass to his trustee in bankruptcy for the benefit of his creditors. Moreover, B himself could sell his life interest and lose the proceeds with the result that he will then be unprovided for.

1–142 If, however, B were merely a beneficiary of a discretionary trust[181] of income, then he would have no right to any of the trust income: he would merely have a hope that the trustees' discretion would be exercised in his favour. The essence of a discretionary trust is, of course, the complete discretion of the trustees as to the amount of income, if any, to be paid to the various beneficiaries of the trust. If the trustees have no power to retain income for accumulation, then the whole income[182] has to be

---

177 *Re Llanover Settled Estates* [1926] Ch. 626 at 637, per Astbury J., approving the statement to this effect in A. Underhill, *The Law Relating to Trusts and Trustees* (8th edn, 1926), p.9.

178 *Gissing v Gissing* [1971] A.C. 886 at 905; *Cowcher v Cowcher* [1972] 1 W.L.R. 425 at 431; *Hussey v Palmer* [1972] 1 W.L.R. 1286 at 1289; *Collings v Lee* [2001] 2 All E.R. 332 at 336.

179 *Allen v Snyder* (1977) 2 N.S.W.L.R. 685 at 698; *Drake v Whipp* [1996] 1 F.L.R. 826 at 829–830; *Westdeutsche Landesbank Girozentrale v Islington LBC* [1996] A.C. 669 at 715; *Air Jamaica Ltd v Charlton* [1999] 1 W.L.R. 1399 at 1412; *Abbott v Abbott* [2008] 1 F.L.R. 1451 at [4].

180 *Gartside v IRC* [1968] A.C. 553; *Pearson v IRC* [1981] A.C. 753; *Re Trafford's Settlement* [1985] Ch. 32; *Miller v IRC* [1987] S.T.C. 108.

181 For the nature of an interest under a discretionary trust see *Gartside v IRC* [1968] A.C. 553; *Re Weir's Settlement* [1969] 1 Ch. 657 (reversed [1971] Ch. 145 on grounds not affecting these principles); *Schmidt v Rosewood Trust Ltd* [2003] 2 A.C. 709.

182 An "exhaustive" discretionary trust: *Sainsbury v IRC* [1970] 1 Ch. 712.

distributed though only among such of the beneficiaries and in such proportions as the trustees see fit.[183] Only if all the beneficiaries of the discretionary trust are each of full capacity and between themselves absolutely entitled to either the income or the income and capital of the trust and call for the trustees to transfer the income or the trust property (as the case may be) to them (or to their nominee) do the trustees' discretions determine.[184] Till then neither individually nor collectively do the beneficiaries have an interest in possession.[185]

If B is beneficiary of a discretionary trust and then sells his interest or becomes bankrupt, then his assignee or trustee in bankruptcy has no more right than he to demand payment from the trustees. If the trustees do exercise their discretion in favour of B by paying money to him or delivering goods to him then B's assignee or trustee in bankruptcy is entitled to the money or goods.[186] Indeed, where the trustees have had notice of the assignment or bankruptcy but have still paid money to B they have been held liable to his assignee or trustee in bankruptcy for the money so paid.[187] It seems, however, that if the trustees spend trust money on the maintenance of B by paying third parties for food, clothes or accommodation for B then the assignee or trustee in bankruptcy will have no claim.[188] **1–143**

Discretionary trusts thus have the advantage of protecting beneficiaries from themselves besides the obvious advantages of flexibility. However, there is the corresponding disadvantage that such trusts create uncertainty for a beneficiary since he has no fixed entitlement as he would have, say, if he had a life interest. **1–144**

C. Protective Trusts

To tackle this disadvantage, there arose the protective trust[189] conferring upon B a life (or lesser) interest determinable upon the bankruptcy of B, or upon any other event which would deprive B of the right to receive all the income of the trust, whereupon a discretionary trust springs up in favour of B and his spouse and issue. It has long been established that, while a condition or proviso for forfeiture of an interest on bankruptcy or attempted alienation of the interest is void, a determinable limitation of an interest to last until bankruptcy or attempted alienation is valid,[190] except that where a settlor purports to create such a protective trust for himself the determining event will be void against his trustee in bankruptcy for reasons of public policy.[191] **1–145**

The justification for such a distinction is that a limitation merely sets a natural limit to an interest while a condition or proviso cuts down an interest before it reaches its natural limit: if such a condition or proviso is void for being contrary to a course of devolution prescribed by law, in cutting down the natural length of an interest to prevent creditors obtaining the benefit of the interest, or for being repugnant to the nature of the alienable interest granted, then the whole natural interest is available for creditors and for alienation. A limitation, however, creates a determinable interest lasting until the limiting event happens and such interest itself is the whole natural interest. The conceptual difference **1–146**

---

[183] *Re Gourju's WT* [1943] Ch. 24; *Re Gulbenkian's Settlements (No.2)* [1970] Ch. 408; *Re Allen Meyrick's WT* [1966] 1 W.L.R. 499.

[184] *Re Smith* [1928] Ch. 915; *Schmidt v Rosewood Trust Ltd* [2003] 2 A.C. 709.

[185] *Re Trafford* [1984] 1 All E.R. 1108; *Vestey v IRC (No.2)* [1979] 2 All E.R. 225 at 235–236.

[186] *Re Coleman* (1888) 39 Ch.D. 443.

[187] *Re Neil* (1890) 62 L.T. 649; *Re Bullock* (1891) 60 L.J. Ch. 341 though *Re Ashby* [1892] 1 Q.B. 872 has created some uncertainty by indicating that an assignee or a trustee in bankruptcy can only claim to the extent to which sums paid are in excess of the amount necessary for B's maintenance.

[188] *Re Coleman* (1888) 39 Ch.D. 443 at 451; *Re Allan-Meyrick's WT*. [1966] 1 W.L.R. 499.

[189] See the statutory form invoked by use of the phrase "protective trusts" set out in the Trustee Act 1925 s.33.

[190] *Brandon v Robinson* (1811) 18 Ves. 429; *Re Leach* [1912] 2 Ch. 422; *Re Scientific Investment Pension Plan Trusts* [1999] Ch. 53 at 59.

[191] *Re Burroughs-Fowler* [1916] 2 Ch. 251; *Money Markets International Stockbrokers Ltd (in liq.) v London Stock Exchange Ltd* [2002] 1 W.L.R. 1150 at [47]–[49].

between conditional and determinable interests may be stated as the difference between giving someone a 12-inch ruler subject to being cut down to a 6-inch ruler in certain conditions and giving someone a 6-inch ruler in the first place.

1–147 Protective trusts are now normally created by use of the shorthand phrase "protective trusts" which invokes the detailed trusts set out in s.33 of the Trustee Act 1925. As will be seen upon examining this section, a protective trust contains three parts: (1) a life or lesser interest determinable on certain events; (2) a forfeiture clause specifying the determining events; (3) a discretionary trust which arises after forfeiture.

TRUSTEE ACT 1925 SECTION 33

1–148 (1) Where any income, including an annuity or other periodical income payment, is directed to be held on protective trusts for the benefit of any person (in this section called "the principal beneficiary") for the period of his life or for any less period, then, during that period (in this section called the "trust period") the said income shall, without prejudice to any prior interest, be held on the following trusts, namely:

(i) Upon trust for the principal beneficiary during the trust period or until he, whether before or after the termination of any prior interest, does or attempts to do or suffers any act or thing, or until any event happens, other than an advance under any statutory or express power,[192] whereby, if the said income were payable during the trust period to the principal beneficiary absolutely during that period, he would be deprived of the right to receive the same or any part thereof, in any of which cases, as well as on the termination of the trust period, whichever first happens, this trust of the said income shall fail or determine.

(ii) If the trust aforesaid fails or determines during the subsistence of the trust period, then, during the residue of that period, the said income shall be held upon trust for the application thereof[193] for the maintenance or support, or otherwise for the benefit, of all or any one or more exclusively of the other or others of the following persons (that is to say)—

(a) the principal beneficiary and his or her wife or husband, if any, and his or her children or more remote issue, if any; or

(b) if there is no wife or husband or issue of the principal beneficiary in existence, the principal beneficiary and the persons who would, if he were actually dead, be entitled to the trust property or the income thereof or to the annuity fund, if any, or arrears of the annuity, as the case may be; as the trustees in their absolute discretion, without being liable to account for the exercise of such discretion, think fit.

(2) This section does not apply to trusts coming into operation before the commencement of this Act, and has effect subject to any variation[194] of the implied trusts aforesaid contained in the instrument creating the trust.

(3) Nothing in this section operates to validate any trust which would, if contained in the instrument creating the trust, be liable to be set aside.[195]

---

192 See *Re Hodgson* [1913] 1 Ch. 34; *Re Shaw's Settlement* [1951] Ch. 833; *Re Rees* [1954] Ch. 202.

193 The income must be distributed: *Re Gourju's WT* [1934] Ch. 24.

194 See, e.g. *Re Wittke* [1944] Ch. 166: bequest of residue upon protective trusts for testatrix's sister, no period being specified, but trustees being given a power to pay capital to the sister from time to time. Held by Vaisey J. that a protected life interest had been created, for, had an absolute interest been given, it would have been open to the sister to call for an immediate transfer of the capital, which would have been inconsistent with the power given to the trustees.

195 This preserves inter alia the rule that although a settlor may validly create in favour of another person a life interest determinable by bankruptcy, such a limitation in favour of himself is void against his trustee in bankruptcy. See *Re Burroughs-Fowler* [1916] 2 Ch. 251; *Re Detmoid* (1889) 40 Ch.D. 585 (where a determining event, other than bankruptcy, occurred, and it was held that the life interest determined).

Whether the interest of the beneficiary is determined in the events which have happened is a question of construction of the forfeiture clause in each particular case. It is sometimes said that forfeiture clauses should be construed in favour of the principal beneficiary, but it must be remembered that he is not the sole object of the testator's bounty, and that there are other persons upon whom the testator intended to confer a benefit.[196] It is only if a doubt remains after construing the clause that this should be resolved in favour of the principal beneficiary, for "the burden is upon those who allege a forfeiture to satisfy the court that a forfeiture has occurred."[197] **1–149**

The forfeiture clause contained in s.33 is very wide, for it includes not only the acts and omissions of the principal beneficiary, but also the happening of any event which deprives him of his right to receive the income or any part thereof. So, for example, the following events have been held to cause a forfeiture: **1–150**

- the impounding by the trustees of part of the income of the principal beneficiary to repair a breach of trust committed by them in paying part of the trust fund to him at his own instigation;[198]
- the bankruptcy of the principal beneficiary, even if this had occurred before the trust first came into operation;[199]
- an order of sequestration of the income for contempt of court, even though the contempt is subsequently purged;[200] and
- the execution by the principal beneficiary of a deed of variation relinquishing his right to part of the income in certain events.[201]

On the other hand the following events were held not to cause a forfeiture: **1–151**

- the appointment by the principal beneficiary of an attorney to receive the income, even though the attorney's expenses are to be deducted from the income, and the balance paid over to the principal beneficiary;[202]
- the making by the court of an order under the Trustee Act 1925 s.57, authorising capital moneys to be raised to enable the principal beneficiary to pay certain pressing liabilities;[203]
- the charge of a lunacy percentage upon the estate of a lunatic under s.148(3) of the Lunacy Act 1890 (replaced by Mental Health Act 1983 s.106(6));[204] and

---

[196] *Re Sartoris's Estate* [1892] 1 Ch. 11 at 16.
[197] *Re Baring's ST* [1940] Ch. 737.
[198] *Re Balfour's Settlement* [1938] Ch. 928.
[199] *Re Walker* [1939] Ch. 974.
[200] *Re Baring's ST* [1940] Ch. 737.
[201] *Re Dennis's ST* [1942] Ch. 283.
[202] *Re Tancred's Settlement* [1903] 1 Ch. 715.
[203] *Re Mair* [1935] Ch. 562. Section 57 is an overriding section whose provisions are read into every settlement. Cf. *Re Salting* [1932] 2 Ch. 57. where the scheme sanctioned by the court under s.57 involved the doing of certain acts by the principal beneficiary—and his omission to do them caused a forfeiture. The scheme provided for the life tenant to pay premiums on insurance policies with a proviso that the trustees were to pay the premiums out of his income if the premiums were not duly paid: his failure to pay was held to create a forfeiture.
[204] *Re Westby's Settlement* [1950] Ch. 296. The fees payable were to be regarded as management expenses, and, even if a charge was created by the section, it was not such an incumbrance as was contemplated by the forfeiture clause. See also *Re Oppenheim's WT* [1950] Ch. 633 (appointment of receiver of person of unsound mind did not effect a forfeiture). The same result was later achieved, independently of the cases, by the Law Reform (Miscellaneous Provisions) Act 1949 s.8.

- an order of the Divorce court diverting income from husband to wife and taking effect in priority to the protective trusts.[205]

1–152 The effect of the forfeiture is to determine the principal beneficiary's life interest and to bring the discretionary trusts into operation.[206] Note, however, that an order of the court may sometimes do more than cause a forfeiture: it may destroy the protected life interest and discretionary trusts altogether. This happened in *Re Allsopp's Marriage Settlement Trusts*,[207] where an express protective trust was created by a marriage settlement in 1916 with discretionary trusts after forfeiture. In 1928 on the dissolution of the marriage the court made an order varying the marriage settlement by extinguishing the rights of the husband as if he were already dead. Vaisey J. held that the husband's protected life interest was extinguished for all purposes and the discretionary trusts were so closely connected with the life interest that they also were destroyed.

D. Powers of Appointment

1–153 A power, which is the authority to deal with property which one does not own, may be legal where it is a statutory power of attorney[208] or a mortgagee's statutory power of sale.[209] For present purposes, however, we are more interested in the power to choose who are to be the beneficial recipients of property, an equitable power that is known as a power of appointment.[210] A power of appointment is vested in the donee of the power to appoint property out of a fund to such objects of the power as he may select. A donee of a power may be able to appoint property to recipients absolutely. Alternatively, powers of appointment can be used to alter the dispositive provisions in a settlement and thus the entitlements of beneficiaries. For example, a trust might be created for such of X's children and remoter issue as the trustees shall appoint, and until and in default of appointment for X's children equally. By exercising a power of appointment, e.g. in favour of two of X's grandchildren for life, remainder to their children, the trustees can completely alter disposition of the beneficial interests under the trust, but the effect of their doing this would simply be to vary the terms of original trust, rather than to create a new trust.

1–154 Powers of appointment may be *special*, i.e. exercisable in favour only of a limited class of objects; or *general*, i.e. exercisable in favour of the whole world;[211] or *hybrid*, i.e. exercisable in favour of the whole world subject to exceptions, or exercisable in favour of a limited class only, but with a power to add further members to the class.[212] The validity of a trust depends upon the existence of a person with locus standi positively to enforce it,[213] but this does not appear necessary for the validity of a power.[214]

1–155 Powers of appointment can be conferred on the basis that the donee holds the power purely in a personal capacity, and is to be wholly unaccountable in the courts in respect of the power's exercise or non-exercise, so long as upon any exercise of the power only objects of the power are to benefit.[215]

---

205 *General Accident Fire and Life Assurance Corp Ltd v IRC* [1963] 1 W.L.R. 1207.
206 *Re Gourju's WT* [1943] Ch. 24.
207 [1959] Ch. 81.
208 Powers of Attorney Act 1971; Trustee Delegation Act 1999.
209 Law of Property Act 1925 ss.88, 101, 104.
210 LPA 1925 s.1(7).
211 *Re Penrose* [1933] Ch. 793.
212 *Re Park* [1932] 1 Ch. 580; *Re Hay's Settlement* [1982] 1 W.L.R. 202; *Re Beatty, deceased* [1990] 1 W.L.R. 1503.
213 See Ch.5.
214 *Re Shaw* [1957] 1 All E.R. 745 at 759, endorsed by *Re Wooton's WT* [1968] 2 All E.R. 618 at 624.
215 *Re Gulbenkian's Settlement* [1970] A.C. 508 at 518; *Re Hay's Settlement Trusts* [1982] 1 W.L.R. 202; *Re Wills' Trust Deed* [1964] Ch. 219; *Re Somes* [1896] 1 Ch. 250.

Such powers are known as personal powers. It would be a fraud upon the power (actionable by the beneficiaries entitled in default of a proper exercise of the power) if the donee were to exercise it so as to benefit persons who are not objects of the power.[216] Otherwise, the donee of the power is under no duty to consider exercising it and "is entitled to prefer one object to another from any motive he pleases, and however capriciously he exercises the power the court will uphold it".[217]

Trustees and other holders of fiduciary office, like executors, are also frequently given powers of appointment, and because these are conferred by virtue of the donee's fiduciary office, they are known as fiduciary powers. The donee of a fiduciary power must independently consciously consider from time to time whether or not to exercise it in a fully informed fashion (taking account of relevant factors while ignoring irrelevant factors), and he must exercise the power fairly and responsibly according to the purpose for which it was conferred, and not perversely to any sensible expectation of the settlor, e.g. by exercising it capriciously or arbitrarily or in bad faith. In exercising his discretion he must avoid any conflict between his personal interest and his fiduciary duty and he cannot fetter the future exercise of his discretion nor release his discretionary power unless this is authorised by the trust instrument (unlike the donee of a personal power who is free to release it if he wishes to do so).[218] **1–156**

The court has an inherent jurisdiction to ensure that fiduciary powers are properly exercised, pursuant to which it can order the donees to provide information to the objects of the power.[219] Where the donee of the power refuses to act, has died or disappeared, or is otherwise unsuitable to exercise the power, the court can also appoint a fit and proper person to exercise the power in his place.[220] **1–157**

The objects of a fiduciary power held by trustees and beneficiaries under a discretionary trust have some common rights.[221] Both have a right to retain any sums properly paid by the trustees in exercise of their discretion; both have a right to be considered by the trustees with a view to a distribution in their favour, although the trustees' duty of inquiry of possible recipients is higher where they have to carry out discretionary trusts than where they merely have to consider whether or not to exercise a power.[222] However, where under discretionary trusts income has to be distributed year by year among a discretionary class then if all members of such class are ascertained and of full capacity they can, if unanimous, call for the income and so have a collectively enforceable right: they can have a similar right if also similarly interested in capital.[223] The collective objects of a special power can have no such right. **1–158**

Furthermore, discretionary trusts over income remain exercisable despite the passing of time, though only in favour of such persons as would have been possible beneficiaries if the discretion had been exercised within a reasonable time, while if powers over income are not exercised within a reasonable time the discretion is extinguished and the default beneficiaries are entitled.[224] Finally, trustees are under a core duty, so far as practicable, to inform beneficiaries of full capacity and objects **1–159**

---

216 *Palmer v Locke* (1880) 15 Ch.D. 294; *Vatcher v Paull* [1915] A.C. 372; *Re Dick* [1953] Ch. 343; *Mettoy Pension Trustees Ltd v Evans* [1990] 1 W.L.R. 1587 at 1613.

217 *Re Wright* [1920] 1 Ch. 108 at 118, per Lawrence J. See too *C v C* [2009] W.T.L.R. 1419 at [15] and [19], per Munby J.

218 *Re Skeats Settlement* (1889) 42 Ch.D. 522; *Re Manisty's Settlement* [1974] Ch. 17; *Re Hay's Settlement Trusts* [1982] 1 W.L.R. 202; *Turner v Turner* [1984] Ch. 100 at 111; *Re Broadbent, deceased* [2001] W.T.L.R. 967 at [51]. Cf. *Re Wills's Trust Deeds* [1964] Ch. 219.

219 *Schmidt v Rosewood Trust Ltd* [2003] 2 A.C. 709.

220 *Mettoy Pension Trustees Ltd v Evans* [1990] 1 W.L.R. 1587; *Bridge Trustees Ltd v Noel Penny (Turbines) Ltd* [2008] Pens. L.R. 345.

221 *Vestey v IRC* [1979] 2 All E.R. 225 at 235–236.

222 *McPhail v Doulton* [1971] A.C. 424.

223 *Re Smith* [1928] Ch. 915; *Saunders v Vautier* (1841) Cr. & Ph. 240. Rights to capital are often contingent upon being alive at the "closing date" of the trust, so preventing a *Saunders v Vautier* right arising.

224 *Re Locker's ST* [1977] 1 W.L.R. 1323; *Re Allen-Meyrick's WT* [1966] 1 W.L.R. 499.

of fiduciary powers of full capacity who are primary objects of the settlor's bounty that they are beneficiaries or objects, so as to give substance to their core right to make the trustees account for the stewardship of the trust fund.[225] Indeed, the settlor can be forced to tell them the name and address of the trustees.[226] However, it is open to a settlor by expressly creating only a personal power to exclude any rights of objects of powers other than the first right mentioned at the beginning of the paragraph.[227]

8. A Discretionary Trust Precedent (Modern and Traditional)

1–160 As seeing something for yourself is much better than any description there now follows a discretionary trust precedent. Read it now, read it after reading Chapter 4, section 2, and read it after reading later chapters when the significance of its administrative clauses will be more apparent. The trust in question where no interest in possession exists usefully reveals the flexibility of a trust and common administrative clauses. It is worthwhile considering how you would explain to a lay person the effect of clauses 3 and 4 and how accountable (or free from accountability) are the trustees. Trust instruments are normally drafted so as drastically to lighten the otherwise onerous duties of trustees.

TRADITIONAL TRUST PRECEDENT

1–161 THIS SETTLEMENT is made the ________ day of ________ 20 ________ BETWEEN ________ of ________ (hereinafter called "the Settlor") of the one part and ________ of ________ and ________ of ________ (hereinafter called "the Original Trustees")[228] of the other part

WHEREAS:

(A) The Settlor is desirous of making irrevocable provision for the Specified Class as herein defined [and for charity[229]] in manner hereinafter appearing

(B) With the intention of making such provision the Settlor has prior to the execution hereof transferred to the Original Trustees the assets specified in the Second Schedule hereto and is desirous of declaring such trusts thereof as hereinafter appear

(C) The Settlor may hereafter pay or transfer further assets to or into the control of the Trustees hereof to be held by them on the trusts of this Settlement

1–162 NOW THIS DEED WITNESSETH AS FOLLOWS

1.—(1) The perpetuity period applicable to this Settlement under the rule against perpetuities shall be the period of eighty years from the execution of this deed

(2) In this Settlement and the Schedules hereto the following expressions shall have the following meanings that is to say:

(a) "the Trustees" means the Original Trustees or other trustees or trustee for the time being of this Settlement and "Trustee" has a corresponding meaning;

---

225 *Schmidt v Rosewood Trust Ltd* [2003] 2 A.C. 709.
226 *Re Murphy's Settlements* [1999] 1 W.L.R. 282.
227 *Re Manisty's ST* [1974] Ch. 17 at 25 and 27–28; *Steele v Paz Ltd* [1993–1995] Manx L.R. 426.
228 As to the identity of the Trustees see cl.8(a).
229 Delete reference to charity if settlor does not wish to benefit charity.

(b) subject to any and every exercise of the powers conferred by Clause 5 hereof "the Specified Class" has the meaning attributed to it in the First Schedule hereto;
(c) "the Appointed Day" means the day on which shall expire the period of eighty years less three days from the execution of this Deed;
(d) "The Trust Fund" means and includes:
   (i) the said assets specified in the Second Schedule hereto;
   (ii) all assets paid or transferred to or into the control of and accepted by the Trustees as additions to the Trust Fund; and
   (iii) the assets from time to time representing the said assets specified in the Second Schedule hereto and the said additions to the Trust Fund or any part or parts thereof respectively
(e) "Spouse" means a party to a marriage which is for the time being subsisting and does not include a party to a former marriage which has terminated by death or divorce or otherwise
[(f)[230] "charity" means any institution whether corporate or not (including a trust) which is established for exclusively charitable purposes and "charities" bears a corresponding meaning]
(g) "the Nominating Beneficiaries" means such of the persons referred to in the First Schedule hereto as are for the time being members of the Specified Class and *sui juris*

2. THE Trustees shall stand possessed of the Trust Fund UPON TRUST at their discretion to retain the same (so far as not consisting of cash) in its existing form of investment or to sell the same or any part or parts thereof and to invest or apply the net proceeds of any sale and any other capital moneys in or upon any kind of investment or for any of the purposes hereinafter authorised with power at any time and from time to time to vary such investments or applications for others of any nature hereby authorised. **1–163**

3.—(1)[231] THE Trustees shall stand possessed of the Trust Fund and the income thereof UPON TRUST for all or such one or more exclusively of the others or other of the members of the Specified Class if more than one in such shares and either absolutely or at such age or time or respective ages or times upon and with such limitations conditions and restrictions and such trusts and powers (including discretionary trusts and powers over income and capital exercisable by any person or persons other than the Settlor or any Spouse of the Settlor whether similar to the discretionary trusts and powers herein contained or otherwise) and with such provisions (including provisions for maintenance and advancement and the accumulation of income for any period or periods authorised by law and provisions for investment and management of any nature whatsoever and provisions for the appointment of separate trustees of any appointed fund) and generally in such manner as the Trustees (being not less than two in number or being a corporate trustee) shall in their absolute discretion from time to time by any deed or deeds revocable or irrevocable appoint PROVIDED THAT: **1–164**

(i) no such appointment shall invalidate any payment or application of capital or income previously made under the trusts or powers herein elsewhere contained; and
(ii) every appointment shall be made and every interest limited thereunder shall vest in interest (if at all) not later than the Appointed Day and no appointment shall be revoked later than the Appointed Day

[(2)[232] Subject to any appointment previously made by the Trustees under the powers hereinbefore contained the Trustees may in their absolute discretion and without prejudice to the generality of the said powers at any time and from time to time before the Appointed Day:

(a) pay or transfer the whole or any part or parts of the income or capital of the Trust Fund to any charity or charities or apply the same for any exclusively charitable purpose or purposes;

[230] Delete subcl.(f) if charities are not intended to benefit.
[231] Delete numeral (1) if subcl.(2) deleted.
[232] Delete subcl.(2) if charities are not intended to benefit.

(b) revocably or irrevocably in writing appoint that the whole or any part or share of the income of the Trust Fund or any annual or other periodic sum out of the same income shall during any period or periods ending before the Appointed Day be paid to any charity or charities;

(c) enter into any covenant or other arrangement with any charity or charities to enable or facilitate the recovery of any tax by such charity or charities in respect of any such payment transfer or appointment (as aforesaid)

PROVIDED ALWAYS that the receipt of the person purporting or appearing to be the treasurer or other proper officer of any charity or (in the case of a charitable trust) of the persons purporting or appearing to be the trustees thereof shall be a good discharge to the Trustees for any capital or income paid or transferred to such charity without the necessity for the Trustees to see further to the application thereof]

1–165 4.—(1) IN default of and subject to and until any or every exercise of the powers conferred on the Trustees by the preceding clause hereof the Trustees shall until the Appointed Day hold the income of the Trust Fund upon the trusts and with and subject to the powers and provisions following namely:

(a) During the period of twenty-one years from the execution of this Deed the Trustees shall have power to pay or apply the whole or any part or parts of such income as it arises to or for the maintenance and support or otherwise for the benefit of all or such one or more exclusively of the others or other of the persons who shall for the time being be living and members of the Specified Class if more than one in such shares and in such manner as the Trustees shall in their absolute discretion without being liable to account for the exercise of such discretion think fit.

(b) Subject to any and every exercise of the last-mentioned power the Trustees shall during the said period of twenty-one years accumulate the whole or the balance (as the case may be) of the said income by investing the same in any manner hereby authorised and shall hold the accumulations so made as an accretion to the capital of the Trust Fund for all purposes.

(c) After the expiration of the same period of twenty-one years the Trustees shall until the Appointed Day pay or apply the whole of the annual income of the Trust Fund as it arises to or for the maintenance and support or otherwise for the benefit of all or such one or more exclusively of the others or other of the persons who shall for the time being be living and members of the Specified Class if more than one in such shares and in such manner as the Trustees shall in their absolute discretion without being liable to account for the exercise of such discretion think fit

(2) In default of and subject to any or every exercise of the said powers conferred on the Trustees by the preceding clause hereof the Trustees shall stand possessed of the Trust Fund on the Appointed Day upon trust for such persons as shall be then living and members of the Specified Class if more than one in equal shares *per capita* absolutely

(3) Any income or capital of the Trust Fund which but for this present sub-clause would be undisposed of by this Deed shall be held by the Trustees upon Trust for [[233] ________ and his/her executors administrators and assigns absolutely][234] [________ and ________ and their respective executors administrators and assigns in equal shares absolutely][235] [________ (as a registered charity) absolutely and in the event of the failure of this present trust then for charitable purposes generally][236]

---

[233] The beneficiaries under this ultimate trust should not be the settlor or his spouse or anyone whom he might marry or detrimental tax consequences follow.

[234] These are alternatives, so delete as appropriate.

[235] ibid.

[236] ibid.

5. THE Trustees (being not less than two in number or being a corporate trustee) may from time to time and at any time before the Appointed Day by any deed or deeds: **1–166**

(a) declare that any person or class or description of person shall cease to be a member or members of the Specified Class and thereupon such person or class or description of person shall cease to be a member or members of the Specified Class in the same manner as if he she or they had originally been expressly excluded therefrom but without prejudice to any previous payment of capital or income to such person or any member of such class or description of person or application thereof for his her or their benefit provided that the removal of any such person or class or description of person as aforesaid shall not prejudice modify or affect any appointment of capital or income then already made [AND PROVIDED ALSO[237] that the removal of any such person or class or description of person as aforesaid shall not prejudice modify or affect the trust in favour of [________ and his/her executors administrators and assigns][238] [________ and ________ and their executors administrators and assigns][239] contained in sub-clause (3) of the last preceding clause hereof]

(b) declare that any person or persons (not being the Settlor or a Spouse of the Settlor or one of the Trustees) previously nominated in writing in that behalf by any one or more of the Nominating Beneficiaries shall thenceforth be included in the Specified Class and thereupon such person or persons shall become a member or members of the Specified Class for all the purposes hereof PROVIDED that (subject to obtaining any necessary Exchange Control consents) the Trustees shall have an absolute discretion whether or not to make any such declaration in relation to any person or persons nominated as aforesaid and PROVIDED FURTHER that any addition of any such person or persons to the Specified Class shall not prejudice modify or affect any appointment of capital or income then already made

(c) wholly or partially release or restrict all or any of the powers and discretions conferred upon them (including this present power) whether in relation to the whole Trust Fund or any part or parts thereof or the income thereof respectively

6. WHENEVER the Trustees shall determine to apply any income for the benefit of an infant the Trustees may either themselves so apply that income or for that purpose may pay the same to any parent guardian or other person for the time being having the care or custody of such infant (other than the Settlor or any Spouse of the Settlor) without being responsible for seeing to the further application thereof **1–167**

7.—(1) MONEYS to be invested under this Settlement may be invested or otherwise applied on the security of or in the purchase or acquisition of real or personal property (including the purchase or acquisition of chattels and the effecting or maintaining of policies of insurance or assurance) rights or interests of whatsoever kind and wheresoever situate including any stocks funds shares securities or other investments of whatsoever nature and wheresoever (but including derivatives for the purpose only of controlling or limiting risk) whether producing income or not and whether involving liability or not or on personal loan with or without interest and with or without security to any person (other than the Settlor or any Spouse of the Settlor) anywhere in the world including loans to any member of the Specified Class and the Trustees may grant indulgence to or release any debtor (other than as aforesaid) with or without consideration and may enter into profit sharing agreements and give and take options with or without consideration and accept substitution of any security for other security or of one debtor for another debtor to the intent that the Trustees (subject as herein provided) shall have the same unrestricted powers of investing and using moneys and transposing investments and altering the user of moneys arising under these presents as if they were absolutely entitled thereto beneficially **1–168**

237 This proviso is not required if the ultimate trust in cl.4(3) is in favour of charity.

238 Delete as appropriate, for these are alternatives.

239 ibid.

(2) It is HEREBY EXPRESSLY DECLARED that without prejudice to the generality of the foregoing sub-clause and without prejudice to any powers conferred by law the Trustees shall (subject to the terms of any appointment made under the powers hereinbefore contained) have the following additional powers-exercisable until the Appointed Day namely:

(a) The Trustees may:

(i) at any time or times lay out any part or parts of the Trust Fund in the purchase or acquisition of and paying the expenses of purchasing or acquiring and making improvements in or repairs to or on any land and buildings of freehold leasehold or of any other tenure or interest of whatsoever description situate in any part of the world whether or not in the occupation of or intended for occupation by any member or members of the Specified Class;

(ii) at any time or times lay out any part or parts of the Trust Fund in the purchase of household furniture plate linen china cutlery and articles of household use ornament or equipment or any other chattels whatsoever for the use or enjoyment of any member or members of the Specified Class whether occupying a building purchased as aforesaid or otherwise

(b) (i) any land purchased by the Trustees shall if situate in England or Wales be assured to the Trustees upon trust for sale with power to postpone sale and if situate elsewhere be assured to the Trustees either with or without any trust for sale as the Trustees shall think fit but nevertheless with power to sell the same;

(ii) in relation to any land situate outside England and Wales the powers and indemnities given to the Trustees in relation to land in England by English law shall apply as if expressed in this Deed and the net rents and profits thereof shall be applicable in like manner as if they arose from land in England;

(iii) the Trustees shall stand possessed of any land so purchased and the net proceeds of sale thereof and other capital moneys arising under this Settlement upon the trusts and with and subject to the powers and provisions (including power to purchase land) upon with and subject to which the money laid out in the purchase of such land would have been held if the same had not been so laid out;

(iv) until the sale of any land purchased as aforesaid the Trustees may permit any member or members of the Specified Class to occupy the same upon such terms (if any) as to payment or non-payment of rent rates taxes and other expenses and outgoings and as to repair and decoration and for such period or periods before the Appointed Day as the Trustees may think fit;

(v) the Trustees shall be indemnified out of the Trust Fund against all costs rents covenants obligations and outgoings relating to any land purchased as aforesaid or for which the Trustees may be liable in respect of the said premises or the said purchase

(c) Any household furniture or other chattels purchased by the Trustees as aforesaid may be handed over to any member or members of the Specified Class for his or her or their use or enjoyment for any period before the Appointed Day upon and subject to such terms and conditions (if any) as to maintaining such inventory or inventories (if any) and as to insurance and preservation as the Trustees shall think fit

(d) (i) The Trustees shall be at liberty to borrow money (otherwise than from the Settlor or any Spouse of the Settlor) for any of the purposes of this Settlement (including the provision of money to give effect to any appointment authorised hereunder or for the purpose of effecting or maintaining any policies or purchasing or subscribing for any shares or stocks securities properties options rights or interests or other property of whatsoever description) and they may pledge or mortgage the whole or any part of the Trust Fund or the future income thereof by way of security for any such loan and no lender shall be obliged to inquire as to the purpose for which any loan is required or whether the money borrowed exceeds any such requirement

(ii) The Trustees may pledge or mortgage the whole or any part of the Trust Fund by way of principal collateral or other security or by way of guarantee to secure any bank overdraft or other moneys borrowed by any member or members of the Specified Class Provided that neither the Settlor nor any Spouse of the Settlor is the lender or one of the lenders in respect of or has any interest in such overdraft or other moneys and PROVIDED FURTHER that no person other than a member or members of the Specified Class is liable for the repayment thereof

(e) The Trustees may at any time or times enter into any compromise or arrangement with respect to or may release all or any of their rights as shareholders stockholders or debenture stockholders or creditors of any company and whether in connection with a scheme of reconstruction or amalgamation or otherwise and may accept in or towards satisfaction of all or any of such rights such consideration as they shall in their discretion think fit whether in the form of shares stock debenture stock cash obligations or securities of the same or of any other company or companies or in any other form whatsoever

(f) (i) The Trustees may effect purchase or acquire any policy or policies assuring payment to the Trustees in the event of the death of any person of such sum as the Trustees in their absolute discretion (having regard to any prospective liability for tax that may arise in respect of the Trust Fund or any part thereof on the death of such person) may think fit or any endowment or sinking fund policy or policies of whatsoever nature and may pay any premium or premiums thereon out of income or capital

(ii) Without prejudice to the last-mentioned powers or to any powers vested in them under the general law the Trustees may from time to time apply any part or parts of the income or capital of the Trust Fund in or towards payment of the premium or premiums on any policy or policies in which any one or more of the members of the Specified Class shall (whether under this Settlement or any other deed or otherwise) have any beneficial interest whether vested or contingent and whether indefeasible or defeasible provided always that no person except one or more of the members of the Specified Class shall have any beneficial interest whatsoever in the said policy or policies and so that (subject to the said proviso) the Trustees shall have power if they think fit to effect any such policy or policies on any life or lives in which any one or more of the members of the Specified Class shall have an insurable interest

(iii) provided always that no income shall be paid or applied under the foregoing powers after the expiration of twenty-one years from the execution hereof if such payment or application would involve an accumulation of the said income

(iv) In relation to any policy held by them hereunder the Trustees shall have all the powers of a beneficial owner including (without prejudice to the generality of such powers) power to surrender any such policy or to convert the same into a paid up policy or into any other form of assurance or otherwise or to exercise any option thereunder or to sell mortgage charge or otherwise realise or dispose of the same

(g) The Trustees may exercise all voting rights appertaining to any investments comprised in the Trust Fund in as full free and absolute a manner as if they were absolute owners of such investments and in particular but without prejudice to the generality of the foregoing provisions shall be at liberty to exercise such voting rights either by voting or by abstaining from voting so as to ensure or further the appointment or reappointment of any one or more of their number to be directors secretaries or employees of any company in which any part of the Trust Fund may for the time being be invested or of any subsidiary of any such company and any Trustee receiving from any such company or subsidiary any fees salary bonuses or commissions for services rendered to such company or subsidiary shall be entitled to retain the same for his own benefit and shall not be required to account therefor to any person interested hereunder

(h) The Trustees shall not be bound or required to interfere in the management or conduct of the affairs or business of any company in which the Trust Fund may be invested (whether or not the

Trustees have the control of such company) and so long as no Trustee has actual knowledge of any fraud dishonesty recklessness or negligence on the part of the directors having the management of such company they may leave the same (including the payment or non-payment of dividends) wholly to such directors without being liable for any loss thereby arising

(i) The Trustees shall have the powers of appropriation and other incidental powers conferred on a personal representative by Section 41 of the Administration of Estates Act 1925 but without the necessity of obtaining the consent of any person to the exercise thereof

(j) The Trustees may apportion as they think fit any funds subject to different trusts which may have become blended and (without prejudice to the jurisdiction of the Court) may determine as they shall consider just whether any money is to be considered as capital or income and whether any expense ought to be paid out of capital or income and all other questions and matters of doubt of whatsoever description arising in the execution of the trusts of these presents and none of the Trustees and no person having formerly been one of the Trustees and no estate of any deceased Trustee shall be liable for or for the consequences of any act done or omitted to be done or for any payment made or omitted to be made in pursuance of any such determination notwithstanding that such determination shall subsequently be held to have been wrongly made

(k) The Trustees may in addition and without prejudice to any powers to employ agents or attorneys conferred by law employ and remunerate on such terms and conditions as they shall think fit any Solicitors Brokers or other agents or advisers (being in each case a person firm or corporation other than and excluding the Settlor and any Spouse of the Settlor) for the purpose of transacting all or any business of whatever nature or doing any act or giving any advice requiring to be transacted done or given in relation to the trusts hereof including any business act or advice which a trustee not being in any profession or business could have transacted done or given personally and any such Solicitor Broker or other agent or adviser shall be entitled to retain any such remuneration or his share thereof notwithstanding that he or any partner of his is a trustee or the sole trustee hereof or is a member officer or employee of or is otherwise interested in any body corporate which is a trustee or the sole trustee hereof and notwithstanding that such agent or adviser is a body corporate of which one or more of the trustees is a member officer or employee or in which one or more of the Trustees is otherwise interested. And the Trustees shall not be responsible for the default of any such Solicitor Broker or other agent or adviser or for any loss occasioned by the employment thereof in good faith

(l) The Trustees may employ and remunerate as they see fit an investment manager (who may be one of themselves or any person associated with any of themselves) so as to delegate to him full discretion to manage the Trust Fund or any part thereof within the limits and for the period stipulated by the Trustees providing his investment activities are subject to review by the Trustees no less than every six months and providing he is reasonably believed by the Trustees to be someone qualified and authorised to engage in the business of managing investments for others and the Trustees shall have authority to enter into an agreement with such investment manager on the same terms (including, for example, terms as to self-dealing and sub-delegation) as a prudent man of business can agree for the management of his own funds and the Trustees shall not be liable for any loss resulting from the exercise of the powers herein conferred so long as they act in good faith nor for any profit made by the investment manager if a Trustee or associated with a Trustee so long as management fees and commissions do not exceed those paid by an unassociated client with a portfolio of investments of similar value to that of the Trust Fund

(m) The Trustees may deposit any moneys deed securities or investments (including shares and securities to bearer) held by them as trustees with any banker or any person firm or corporation (other than and excluding the Settlor and any Spouse of the Settlor) whether in the United Kingdom or abroad for safe custody or receipt of dividends and may pay out of the income or capital of such part of the Trust Fund as they shall think proper any sum payable for such deposit and custody

(n) Assets of the Trust may be held in the names of any two or more of the Trustees and the Trustees may vest such assets in a stakeholder or in a nominee or nominees anywhere in the world (other than the Settlor or any Spouse of the Settlor) on behalf of the Trustees and entrust or concur in entrusting the realisation and reinvestment of such assets to such stakeholder nominee or nominees upon such terms as the Trustees may deem reasonable

(o) The Trustees may (at the expense of the Trust Fund) incorporate or register or procure the incorporation or registration of any company (with limited or unlimited liability) in any part of the world for any purpose including the acquisition of the Trust Fund or any part thereof and so that (if thought fit) the consideration on the sale of the Trust Fund to any such company may consist wholly or partly of fully paid shares debentures debenture stock or other securities of the company credited as fully paid which shall be allotted to or otherwise vested in the Trustees and be capital moneys in the Trustees' hands

(p) The trustees may embark upon or carry on whether alone or in partnership or as a joint venture with any other person or persons (except the Settlor or any Spouse of the Settlor) or corporation or corporations at the expense of the Trust Fund and the income thereof any trade or business whatsoever including (without prejudice to the generality of the foregoing) any forestry timber farming development insurance banking or other agricultural commercial industrial financial or professional trade or business whatsoever and may assist or finance to any extent the commencement or carrying on of any trade or business by any other or others (except as aforesaid)

(q) The trustees may effect any transaction relating to the management administration or disposition of property within the Trust Fund which falls within the jurisdiction of a court to authorise under section 57 of the Trustee Act 1925 without the necessity of obtaining an order of the court authorising such transactions

8. THE following provisions shall apply to the trusts and trusteeship hereof: **1–169**

(a) The statutory powers of appointing trustees shall apply hereto and shall be exercisable by [the Settlor][240] during [his/her][241] life PROVIDED that neither the Settlor nor any Spouse of the Settlor shall be appointed a trustee of these presents

(b) Any person whether an individual or a body corporate may be appointed as a trustee of this settlement whether or not he or it shall be resident domiciled or incorporated in the United Kingdom and the appointment as sole trustee of a body corporate ranking as a trust corporation under the law governing its incorporation shall validly discharge the trustees from all the trusts of this settlement except those if any relating to English or Welsh land then comprised in this settlement

(c) The Trustees shall have power to carry on the administration of the trusts of this settlement in any part of the world whether inside or outside the United Kingdom and power to that end to appoint and pay agents and investment managers with general discretion as to investment and disinvestment of the whole or a specified part of the trust fund upon such terms (including, for example, terms as to self-dealing and sub-delegation) as a prudent man of business can agree for the management of his own funds

(d) No Trustee shall be capable of being removed or replaced on the grounds that he has remained out of the United Kingdom for more than 12 months

(e) Subject to subclause (b) hereof the law according to which the trusts powers and provisions of this settlement shall for the time being be governed and administered shall be the law of England and Wales

(f) The Trustees shall have power exercisable at any time or time by deed or deeds executed before the Perpetuity Day in their absolute discretion (but during the lifetime of the Settlor not without his prior consent in writing) to declare that the law governing the validity of this

[240] Amend as appropriate.
[241] ibid.

settlement or the law governing the administration of this settlement shall from the date of such deed or from some later date specified therein and subject to any further exercise of this power be the law of some other State specified therein provided that such State has its own internal law of trusts and recognises the effectiveness of the exercise of this power and providing always that this power shall not be exercisable so as to render this settlement revocable or unenforceable in whole or in part or otherwise to affect the beneficial trusts and powers thereof other than the powers incorporated by Trustee Act 1925 sections 31 and 32 and analogous powers in other States and "administration" matters shall include all matters other than those governing the validity of the beneficial interests created or capable of being created under this settlement

(g) Any Trustee engaged in any profession or business shall be entitled to charge and be paid all professional or other charges made by him or his firm for business done by him or his firm in relation to the execution of the trusts hereof whether or not in the ordinary course of his profession or business and whether or not of a nature requiring the employment of a professional or business person

(h) Any corporation appointed to be a trustee hereof shall have the powers rights and benefits as to remuneration or otherwise as at or prior to its appointment may be agreed in writing between such corporation and the person or persons (or corporation or corporations) making such appointment

1–170 9. THE following provisions shall apply to the powers and discretions of the Trustees hereunder:

(1) Any Trustee may concur in exercising any such power or discretion notwithstanding that he may have a direct or other personal interest in the mode or result of exercising the same Provided that at least one of the Trustees has no such direct or other personal interest

(2) The Trustees shall not be concerned to see to the insurance preservation repair or renewal of any freehold leasehold or other property household furniture or other chattels occupied used or enjoyed by any member of the Specified Class and in the professed execution of the trusts and powers hereof no Trustee shall be liable for any loss to the trust premises arising by reason of any improper investment or application of the Trust Fund or any part thereof made in good faith

(3) The Trustees may institute and defend any legal proceedings and proceed to the final determination thereof or compromise the same as they shall in their absolute discretion think fit and shall be entitled to payment out of the Trust Fund of any costs requiring to be paid as a result of those proceedings so long as not unreasonable or incurred in bad faith

(4) Every discretion hereby conferred upon the Trustees shall be an absolute and unfettered discretion and the Trustees shall not be required to furnish to any beneficiary hereunder any reason or justification for the manner in which any such discretion may be exercised

(5) No power or discretion hereunder to which the rule against perpetuities applies shall be exercisable after the Appointed Day

1–171 10. NOTWITHSTANDING anything hereinbefore or in the schedules hereto contained:

(a) the Trust Fund and the income thereof shall be possessed and enjoyed to the entire exclusion of the Settlor and of any benefit to the Settlor by contract or otherwise;

(b) no part of the Trust Fund or the income thereof shall be paid lent or applied for the benefit of the Settlor or any Spouse of the Settlor nor shall any power or discretion hereunder be exercised so as to confer any benefit on the Settlor or any Spouse of the Settlor in any circumstances whatsoever

1–172 11. THIS Settlement and the dispositions hereby made are intended to be and are irrevocable

IN WITNESS whereof the parties hereto have hereunto set their respective hands or seals the day and year first before written

The FIRST SCHEDULE[242] hereinbefore referred to **1–173**

The Specified Class consists (subject to any exercise of the powers contained in Clause 5 of the foregoing Deed) of the following persons namely:

[(1) the children and remoter issue of the Settlor whether living at the date hereof or born hereafter;
(2) any person (other than a Trustee) who shall (whether before or after the date hereof) have married any of such children or remoter issue of the Settlor as aforesaid (whether or not such marriage shall for the time being be subsisting);
(3) A.B. (the brother of the Settlor);
(4) the children and remoter issue of the said A.B. whether living at the date hereof or born hereafter;
(5) any person (other than a Trustee) who shall (whether before or after the date hereof) have married any of such children or remoter issue of the said A.B. as aforesaid (whether or not such marriage shall for the time being be subsisting);
(6) any adopted child of the Settlor or of any of such children or remoter issue of the Settlor as aforesaid and the children and remoter issue of any such adopted child;
(7) any person (other than a Trustee) who shall (whether before or after the date hereof) have married any such adopted child or any child or remoter issue of any such adopted child as aforesaid (whether or not such marriage shall for the time being be subsisting)

Provided that for the purposes of this present definition a person shall be deemed to be the adopted child of another person only if he or she shall be recognised as the adopted child of such other person by the Law of England for the time being in force.]

THE SECOND SCHEDULE hereinbefore referred to **1–174**

MODERN TRUST SETTLEMENT

(From J. Kessler, *Drafting Trusts and Will Trusts*, 7th edn (2004))

This settlement is made [date] between: **1–175**

1 [Name of settlor] of [address] ("the Settlor") of the one part and

2 2.1 [Name of first trustee] of [address] and
2.2 [Name of second trustee] of [address]

("the Original Trustees") of the other part.

Whereas:

1 The Settlor has [two] children:

1.1 [Adam Smith] ("[Adam]") who was born on [date] and
1.2 [Mary Smith] ("[Mary]") who was born on [date].

2 This Settlement shall be known as the [Name-of-settlor Settlement 2000].

Now this deed witnesses as follows:

1. Definitions

In this settlement: **1–176**

1.1 **"The Trustees"** means the Original Trustees or the trustees of the settlement for the time being.

[242] This schedule has been completed by way of example.

1.2 **"The Trust Fund"** means:

1.2.1 property transferred to the Trustees to hold on the terms of this Settlement; and
1.2.2 all property from time to time representing the above.

1.3 **"Trust Property"** means any property comprised in the Trust Fund.

1.4 **"The Trust Period"** means the period of 80 years beginning with the date of this Settlement. That is the perpetuity period applicable to this Settlement under the rule against perpetuities.

1.5 **"The Accumulation Period"** means the period of 21 years beginning with the date of this Settlement.

1.6 **"The Beneficiaries"** means:

1.6.1 The children and descendants of the Settlor.
1.6.2 The spouses, widows and widowers (whether or not remarried) of paragraph .1 of this sub-clause:
1.6.3 The [widow] (whether or not remarried) of the Settlor.
1.6.4 Any Person or class of Persons nominated to the Trustees by:

1.6.4.1 the Settlor or
1.6.4.2 two Beneficiaries (after the death of the Settlor)

and whose nomination is accepted in writing by the Trustees.
1.6.5 At any time during which there are no Beneficiaries within paragraph .1 of this sub-clause

1.6.5.1 [specify "fall back" beneficiaries if desired, e.g. nieces and nephews and their families].
1.6.5.2 [any company, body or trust established for charitable purposes only].

1.7 "**Person**" includes a person anywhere in the world and includes a Trustee.

1–177 **2. Trust Income**

Subject to the Overriding Powers below:

2.1 The Trustees may accumulate the whole or part of the income of the Trust Fund during the Accumulation Period. That income shall be added to the Trust Fund.

2.2 The Trustees shall pay or apply the remainder of the income to or for the benefit of any Beneficiaries, as the Trustees think fit, during the Trust Period.

1–178 **3. Overriding Powers**

The Trustees shall have the following powers ("Overriding Powers"):

3.1 Power of appointment

3.1.1 The Trustees may appoint that they shall hold the Trust Fund for the benefit of any Beneficiaries, on such terms as the Trustees think fit.
3.1.2 An appointment may create any provisions and in particular:

3.1.2.1 discretionary trusts;
3.1.2.2 dispositive or administrative powers;

exercisable by any Person.
3.1.3 An appointment shall be made by deed and may be revocable or irrevocable.

3.2 *Transfer of Trust Property to new settlement*
The Trustees may by deed declare that they hold any Trust Property on trust to transfer it to trustees of a Qualifying Settlement, to hold on the terms of that Qualifying Settlement, freed and released from the terms of this Settlement.

"**A Qualifying Settlement**" here means any settlement, wherever established, under which every Person who may benefit is (or would if living be) a Beneficiary of this Settlement.

3.3 *Power of advancement*

The Trustees may pay or apply any Trust Property for the advancement or benefit of any Beneficiary.

3.4 The Overriding Powers shall be exercisable only:

3.4.1 during the Trust Period; and

3.4.2 at a time when there are at least two Trustees, or the Trustee is a company carrying on a business which consists of or includes the management of trusts.

4. Default Clause

Subject to that, the Trust Fund shall be held on trust for [Adam and Mary in equal shares–or specify default trusts as appropriate] absolutely. **1–179**

5. Appointment of Trustees

The power of appointing trustees is exercisable by the Settlor during [his] life and by will. **1–180**

6. Further Provisions

The provisions set out in the schedule below shall have effect [For a shorter form, say instead of the above: **1–181**

> "The standard provisions of the Society of Trust and Estate Practitioners (1st Edition) shall apply with the deletion of paragraph 5. Section 11 Trusts of Land & Appointment of Trustees Act 1996 (consultation with beneficiaries) shall not apply."

And omit the schedule.]

7. Exclusion of Settlor and Spouse

Notwithstanding anything else in this Settlement, no power conferred by this settlement shall be exercisable, and no provision shall operate so as to allow Trust Property or its income to become payable to or applicable for the benefit of the Settlor or the spouse of the Settlor in any circumstances whatsoever. **1–182**

In witness, [etc.]

THE SCHEDULE: FURTHER PROVISIONS

1. Additional Powers

The Trustees have the following additional powers: **1–183**

1.1 *Investment*

1.1.1 The Trustees may make any kind of investment that they could make if they were absolutely entitled to the Trust Fund. In particular the Trustees may invest in land in any part of the world and unsecured loans.

1.1.2 The Trustees are under no obligation to diversify the Trust Fund.

1.1.3 The Trustees may invest in speculative or hazardous investments but this power may only be exercised at the time when there are at least two Trustees, or the Trustee is a company carrying on a business which consists of or includes the management of trusts.

1.2 *Joint property*

The Trustees may acquire property jointly with any Person and may blend Trust Property with other property.

1.3 *General power of management and disposition*

The Trustees may effect any transaction relating to the management or disposition of Trust Property as if they were absolutely entitled to it.

1.4 Improvement

The Trustees may develop or improve Trust Property in any way. Capital expenses need not be repaid out of income under section 84(2) of the Settled Land Act 1925, if the Trustees think fit.

1.5 Income and capital

1.5.1 The Trustees may acquire:

1.5.1.1 wasting assets and
1.5.1.2 assets which yield little or no income

for investment or any other purpose.

1.5.2 The Trustees are under no duty to procure distributions from a company in which they are interested.

1.5.3 The Trustees may pay taxes and other expenses out of income although they would otherwise be paid out of capital

1.5.4 Generally, the Trustees are under no duty to hold a balance between conflicting interests of Beneficiaries.

1.5.5 The Trustees may (subject to the jurisdiction of the Court) determine whether receipts and liabilities are to be considered as capital or income, and whether expenses ought to be paid out of capital or income. The Trustees shall not be liable for any act done in pursuance of such determination (in the absence of fraud or negligence) even though it shall subsequently be held to have been wrongly made.

1.5.6 Income may be set aside and invested to answer any liabilities which in the opinion of the Trustees ought to be borne out of income or to meet depreciation of the capital value of any Trust Property. In particular, income may be applied for a leasehold sinking fund policy.

1.6 Application of trust capital as income

The Trustees may apply Trust Property as if it were income arising in the current year. In particular, the Trustees may pay such income to a Beneficiary as his income, for the purpose of augmenting his income.

1.7 Use of trust property

1.7.1 The Trustees may acquire any interest in property anywhere in the world for occupation or use by a Beneficiary.

1.7.2 The Trustees may permit a Beneficiary to occupy or enjoy the use of Trust Property on such terms as they think fit.

1.7.3 The Trustees may lend trust money to a Beneficiary. The loan may be interest free and unsecured, or on such terms as the Trustees think fit. The Trustees may charge Trust Property as security for any debts or obligations of a Beneficiary.

1.8 Trade

The Trustees may carry on a trade, in any part of the world, alone or in partnership.

1.9 Borrowing

The Trustees may borrow money for investment or any other purpose. Money borrowed shall be treated as Trust Property.

1.10 Delegation

A Trustee or the Trustees jointly (or other Person in a fiduciary position) may authorise any person to exercise all or any functions on such terms as to remuneration and other matters as they think fit. A Trustee shall not be responsible for the default of that Person (even if the delegation was not strictly necessary or convenient) provided he took reasonable care in his selection and supervision.

1.11 Nominees and custodians

1.11.1 The Trustees may appoint a person to act as their nominee in relation to such of the assets of the trust as they may determine. They may take such steps as are necessary to secure that those assets are vested in the nominee.

1.11.2 The Trustees may appoint a person to act as custodian in relation to such of the assets of the trust as they may determine. The Trustees may give the custodian custody of the assets and any documents or records concerning the assets. The Trustees are not obliged to appoint a custodian of securities payable to bearer.

1.11.3 The Trustees may appoint a person to act as nominee or custodian on such terms as to remuneration and other matters as they may think fit.

1.12 Offshore administration

The Trustees may carry on the administration of this Settlement anywhere they think fit.

1.13 Indemnities

The Trustees may indemnify any Person for any liability relating to the Settlement.

1.14 Security

The Trustees may mortgage or charge Trust Property as security for any liability incurred by them as Trustees (and may grant a floating charge so far as the law allows).

1.15 Supervision of company

The Trustees are under no duty to enquire into the conduct of a company in which they are interested, unless they have knowledge of circumstances which call for inquiry.

1.16 Appropriation

The Trustees may appropriate Trust Property to any Person or class of Persons in or towards the satisfaction of their interest in the Trust Fund.

1.17 Receipt by charities

Where Trust Property is to be paid or transferred to a charity, the receipt of the treasurer or appropriate officer of the charity shall be a complete discharge to the Trustees.

1.18 Release of powers

The Trustees (or other persons in a fiduciary position) may by deed release wholly or in part any of their rights or functions and (if applicable) so as to bind their successors.

1.19 Ancillary powers

The Trustees may do anything which is incidental or conducive to the exercise of their functions.

1.20 Insurance policies

The trustees may pay premiums of any insurance policy out of income.

2. Minors

2.1 Where the Trustees may apply income for the benefit of a minor, they may do so by paying the income to the minor's parent or guardian on behalf of the minor, or to the minor if he has attained the age of 16. The Trustees are under no duty to inquire into the use of the income unless they have knowledge of circumstances which call for inquiry. **1–184**

2.2 Where the Trustees may apply income for the benefit of a minor, they may do so by resolving that they hold that income on trust for the minor absolutely and:

2.2.1 The Trustees may apply that income for the benefit of the minor during his minority.

2.2.2 The Trustees shall transfer the residue of that income to the minor on attaining the age of 18.

2.2.3 For investment and other administrative purposes that income shall be treated as Trust Property.

3. Mentally handicapped beneficiary

1–185 Where income or capital is payable to a Beneficiary who does not have the mental capacity to appoint an attorney with an enduring general power, the Trustees may (subject to the directions of the Court or his Receiver) apply that income or capital for his benefit.

4. Disclaimer

1–186 A Person may disclaim his interest in this Settlement wholly or in part.

5. Apportionment

1–187 Income and expenditure shall be treated as arising when payable, and not from day to day, so that no apportionment shall take place.

6. Conflicts of Interest

1–188 6.1 In this paragraph:

6.1.1 "A Fiduciary" means a Person subject to fiduciary duties under the Settlement.
6.1.2 "An Independent Trustee", in relation to a Person, means a Trustee who is not:

6.1.2.1 a brother, sister, ancestor, descendant or dependent of the Person;
6.1.2.2 a spouse of paragraph .1.2.1 above, or a spouse of the Person;
6.1.2.3 a company controlled by one or more of any of the above.

6.1.3 Subject to the next sub-clause a Fiduciary may:

6.1.3.1 enter into a transaction with the Trustees, or
6.1.3.2 be interested in an arrangement in which the Trustees are or might have been interested, or
6.1.3.3 act (or not act) in any other circumstances;

even though his fiduciary duty under the Settlement conflicts with other duties or with his personal interest;
6.1.4 The above sub-clause only has effect if:

6.1.4.1 the Fiduciary first discloses to the Trustees the nature and extent of any material interest conflicting with his fiduciary duties, and
6.1.4.2 there is an Independent Trustee in respect of whom there is no conflict of interest, and he considers that the transaction arrangement or action is not contrary to the general interest of the Settlement.

6.1.5 The powers of the Trustees may be used to benefit a Trustee (to the same extent as if he were not a Trustee) provided that there is an Independent Trustee in respect of whom there is no conflict of interest.

7. Absolute Discretion Clause

1–189 7.1 The Powers of the Trustees may be exercised:

7.1.1 at their absolute discretion; and
7.1.2 from time to time as occasion requires.

7.2 The Trustees are not under any duty to consult with any Beneficiaries or to give effect to the wishes of any Beneficiaries.

8. Trustee Remuneration

8.1 A Trustee acting in a professional capacity is entitled to receive reasonable remuneration out of the Trust Fund for any services that he provides on behalf of the Trust **1–190**

8.2 For this purpose, a trustee acts in a professional capacity if he acts in the course of a profession or business which consists of or includes the provision of services in connection with:

8.2.1 the management or administration of trusts generally or a particular kind of trust, or

8.2.2 any particular aspect of the management or administration of trusts generally or a particular kind of trust.

8.3 The Trustees may make arrangements to remunerate themselves for work done for a company connected with the Trust Fund.

9. Commissions and Bank Charges

9.1 A Person may retain any reasonable commission or profit in respect of any transaction relating to this Settlement even though that commission or profit was procured by an exercise of fiduciary powers (by that Person or some other Person) provided that: **1–191**

9.1.1 The Person would in the normal course of business receive and retain the commission or profit on such transaction.

9.1.2 The receipt of the commission or profit shall be disclosed to the Trustees.

9.2 A bank may make loans to the Trustees and generally provide banking services upon its usual terms and shall not be liable to account for any profit so made even though the receipt of such profit was procured by an exercise of fiduciary powers (by the bank or some other Person).

10. Liability of Trustees

10.1 The duty of reasonable care (set out in s. 1, Trustee Act 2000) applies to all the functions of the Trustees. **1–192**

10.2 A Trustee shall not be liable for a loss to the Trust Fund unless that loss was caused by his own fraud or negligence.

10.3 A Trustee shall not be liable for acting in accordance with the advice of Counsel, of at least five years' standing, with respect to the settlement. A Trustee may recover from the Trust Fund any expenses where he has acted in accordance with such advice. The Trustees may in particular conduct legal proceedings in accordance with such advice without obtaining a court order.

10.4 The above paragraph does not apply if:

10.4.1 the Trustee knows or has reasonable cause to suspect that the advice was given in ignorance of material facts; or

10.4.2 proceedings are pending to obtain the decision of the court on the matter.

10.5 The Trustees may distribute Trust Property or income in accordance with this Settlement but without having ascertained that there is no Person who is or may be entitled to any interest therein by virtue of any illegitimate relationship. The Trustees shall not be liable to such a Person unless they have notice of his claim at the time of the distribution.

10.6 This paragraph does not prejudice any right of any Person to follow property or income into the hands of any Person, other than a purchaser, who may have received it.

11. Appointment and retirement of trustees

1–193 11.1 A Person may be appointed Trustee of the Settlement even though he has no connection with the United Kingdom.

11.2 A Trustee who has reached the age of 65 shall retire if:

11.2.1 he is requested to do so by his co-trustees, or by a Person interested in Trust Property; and

11.2.2 he is effectually indemnified against liabilities properly incurred as Trustee.

On that retirement a new Trustee shall be appointed if necessary to ensure that there will be at least two Trustees. This sub-paragraph does not apply to a Trustee who is the Settlor or the spouse or widow of the Settlor.

11.3 A Trustee may be discharged even though there is neither a trust corporation nor two Persons to act as trustees provided that there remains at least one trustee.

Questions

1–194 1. How come beneficiaries have "equitable" interests? If property is held on trust for A for life, remainder to B, would you prefer to be A or B? If they are of full capacity can they require the property to be divided between them in agreed shares?

1–195 2. If T becomes insolvent why is B better off if he is not a creditor of T but a beneficiary under a trust of which T is trustee? Explain the significance of sending a £99.99 cheque to Wonderwatches Co Ltd to buy a watch with a letter asking such company to hold the £99.99 on trust for you until delivery to you of title to the watch.

1–196 3. Would you prefer to be A, B or C in the following instances?

(a) A lends X £50,000 at 15 per cent interest;
(b) B lends Y £50,000 at 7 per cent interest secured by a mortgage on Y's house worth £100,000;
(c) C provides Z with £50,000 to enable Z to buy a £100,000 house in Z's name for the benefit of C and Z equally. Z sells the house for £140,000 and with this £140,000 buys a new house, now worth £200,000.

1–197 4. "Significantly, a trust, unlike a corporation, has no legal personality." **Discuss**.

PART II

CREATION OF EXPRESS TRUSTS

2 CONSTITUTION OF TRUSTS

1. Introduction

2–01 In this chapter and the four chapters that follow, we consider various rules governing the creation of express trusts. In this chapter we discuss the different ways of constituting a trust by ensuring that the relevant property is in the hands of the person whom the settlor intends to act as trustee, and we also look at situations where this is not accomplished with the result that the trust is incompletely constituted. In Chapter 3 we examine the rules which govern the form in which declarations of trust must be made (and the form in which dispositions of equitable interests under a trust must be made). In Chapter 4 we look at the rules which hold that three things must be certain before it can be said that a valid trust has been created, namely the settlor's intention to create the trust, the subject-matter of the trust, and the objects of the trust. In Chapter 5 we consider the principle that a valid trust must have a beneficiary. Consistently with this principle, trusts for private purposes are not generally valid under English law; exceptionally, however, trusts for charitable purposes are valid, and these are discussed in Chapter 6.

2. Constitution of Trusts

2–02 In the case of testamentary trusts, there is a perfect gift of the legal beneficial ownership to the settlor's executors, or the administrators of his estate, by virtue of his death.[1] Once they have paid all the debts owed by the deceased, relevant taxes and expenses of administering the estate, they are placed under equitable obligations[2] to transfer the relevant property to legatees or devisees entitled in their own right, or as trustees for others. So long as the three certainties are present,[3] and debts, taxes and expenses do not exhaust the relevant property, a testamentary trust will be constituted. This will be so even if the named trustee disclaims or is unable to take the property through incapacity or predeceasing the testator.[4] In such a case, whoever succeeds to the legal title will take subject to the trust, for equity will not allow a trust to fail for want of a trustee.[5]

2–03 Broadly speaking, there are two ways of constituting an inter vivos trust: (1) by the settlor transferring the property intended to be the subject-matter of the trust to persons as trustees upon trusts declared by him; or (2) by the settlor declaring that he himself will hold certain of his property as trustee upon certain trusts.

2–04 Where the settlor intends that someone else should be the trustee, he must ensure that he complies with all formality rules governing transfers of the relevant type of property. So, for example, if the subject matter of the trust is legal title to land, then the conveyance to the trustees must take the form

---

1 Administration of Estates Act 1925 ss. 1, 9, 25, and 32.
2 *Commissioner of Stamp Duties v Livingston* [1965] A.C. 694; *Marshall v Kerr* [1995] 1 A.C. 148.
3 See Ch.4.
4 *Sonley v Clock Makers' Co* (1780) 1 Bro. C.C. 81; *Re Smirthwaite's Trusts* (1871) L.R. 11 Eq. 251.
5 *Re Armitage* [1972] Ch. 438 at 445 (where it is pointed out that very exceptionally the trust can fail if the personality of the named trustee is vital to the carrying out of the trust).

of a deed,[6] and if it is registered land then the transfer must be entered onto the Land Register.[7] Legal title to chattels must be transferred by delivery or by deed of gift. A bill of exchange must be transferred by endorsement[8] and copyright by writing.[9] If the intended trust property is an equitable interest under another trust, then again the transfer must be in writing.[10]

2–05 Where a settlor declares himself to be trustee of property that is already in his hands, the court must be satisfied that the subject matter of the trust has been clearly identified or segregated from the settlor's other assets,[11] and that a present binding declaration of trust has been made complying with the requisite formalities,[12] although the trust interest may be defeasible upon exercise of a power of appointment or a power of revocation.[13]

2–06 A declaration of trust, to be effectual, need not be literal. It is unnecessary for the settlor to say "I declare myself a trustee." What is necessary is some form of expression which in the circumstances shows that he intended to constitute himself trustee and another person a beneficiary, even if he did not know that the obligation he was creating amounted to a trust.

2–07 For example, in *T Choithram International SA v Pagarani*,[14] Pagarani was a wealthy businessman who was dying of cancer. A month before he died, he organised an elaborate ceremony at his London bedside to establish a philanthropic foundation in the form of a Jersey trust of which he was settlor and one of the trustees. He executed the trust deed in the presence of three (of the other six) trustees and of his accountant and the First Secretary of the Indian High Commission. They recollected him as orally making an immediate absolute gift to "the Foundation" of all his wealth in his shareholdings and credit balances with four British Virgin Island companies. However, English law does not recognise foundations as legal persons like companies, and legal title to the property was not vested in the other trustees before Pagarani died. On his death some of his children therefore sought to establish that the gift was an imperfect gift.

2–08 Lord Browne-Wilkinson for the Privy Council held that in the context of the case "the words 'I give to the Foundation' can only mean 'I give to the Trustees of the Foundation trust deed to be held by them on the trusts of the Foundation trust deed'. Although the words are apparently words of outright gift they are essentially words of gift on trust."[15] In substance, therefore, it seems that Pagarani was regarded as having said: "As sole legal beneficial owner of the assets and as legal trustee of the Foundation I now give my beneficial interest on trust for the charitable purposes of the Foundation and so as trustee now holding such interest on the trusts of the Foundation deed".

2–09 What of the fact that he had not actually transferred title to the gifted assets to all seven trustees, including himself in his capacity as one of the trustees? Lord Browne-Wilkinson held that where trust property is vested in one of a body of trustees (as was effectively the case here), "he is bound by the trust and must give effect to it by transferring the trust property into the name of all the trustees".[16] As it happened, the four companies had altered their share registers after Pagarani's death so that

---

[6] Law of Property Act 1925 s.52.
[7] Land Registration Act 2002 ss. 29 and 30.
[8] Bills of Exchange Act 1882 s.31; Cheques Act 1957 ss. 1, 2.
[9] Copyright Designs and Patents Act 1988 s.90(3).
[10] Law of Property Act 1925 s.53(1)(c), discussed at paras 3-80 ff.
[11] See paras 4–100 ff.
[12] *Re Cozens* [1913] 2 Ch. 478 at 486, per Neville J.; *Grant v Grant* (1865) 34 Beav. 623 at 626, per Romilly M.R.
[13] *Copp v Wood* [1962] 2 D.L.R. 224; *Beecher v Major* (1865) 2 Drew & Son 431 at 437; *Young v Sealey* [1949] Ch. 278 at 284 and 294; *T Choithram International SA v Pagarani* [2001] 1 W.L.R. 1 at 11. A transfer or declaration of trust of property is presumed irrevocable: *Newton v Askew* (1848) 11 Beav. 145; *Miller v Harrison* (1871) L.R. 5 Eq. 324.
[14] [2001] 1 W.L.R. 1. See too *Paul v Constance* [1977] 1 W.L.R. 527, reproduced at paras 4–14 ff.
[15] *Choithram* at 12.
[16] *Choithram* at 12.

legal title to the shares was actually vested in the remaining six trustees. Hence the Privy Council concluded that the administrators of Pagarani's intestate estate could not claim the shares or the deposit balances with the companies.

Another interesting example of a declaration of trust occurred in *Re Ralli's WT*,[17] which is reproduced below.[18] H was the owner of a reversionary interest (after her mother's life interest) under the will of her deceased father. She covenanted with the trustees of her marriage settlement to settle, as soon as circumstances would admit, all her existing and after-acquired property (thinking particularly of the future actual assets she would become entitled to on her mother's death) upon certain trusts (which failed) and ultimately upon trusts for the benefit of the children of H's sister. A declaration of trust clause in the marriage settlement declared that all property comprised within the terms of the covenant should be subject in equity to the trusts of the settlement pending transfer to the trustees. H never assigned the reversionary interest to the trustees before she died. Buckley J. held that the reversionary interest being existing property of H at the time of her declaration of trust, there was a valid trust of the interest so that the actual assets materialising on the death of H's mother years after H's death passed (not under H's will or intestacy but) under her settlement to her sister's children. It would appear that if her reversionary interest had only been acquired by her subsequently to her settlement so as to be after-acquired property then no trust of the interest would have arisen in favour of the volunteer nieces and nephews as declarations of trust in respect of after-acquired property are ineffective at law and in equity where volunteers are concerned.[19] **2–10**

3. Equity Will Not Assist a Volunteer

A. *Ineffectual Transfers Will Not Be Reinterpreted as Effectual Declarations*

Once a trust has been completely constituted it is axiomatic that the courts will assist the beneficiaries by enforcing their rights under the trust, regardless of whether they have given any value in exchange for these rights.[20] "Once a trust relationship is established between trustee and beneficiary, the fact that a beneficiary has given no value is irrelevant",[21] and unless he expressly reserved a power to revoke the trust at the time when he created it, the settlor cannot "undo" a completely constituted trust or revoke it on the basis that the beneficiaries are only volunteers.[22] **2–11**

Before a trust has been completely constituted, however, the position is different. *Milroy v Lord*,[23] parts of which are reproduced below,[24] shows us that no matter how clearly there may have been an intention to create a voluntary trust by transferring property to trustees, if the intending "settlor" has used an ineffectual method of transfer, then the transaction will not be reinterpreted by the court as an effectual declaration of trust with the "settlor" as trustee. In such cases of incompletely constituted trusts, the courts invoke the maxim that "Equity will not assist a volunteer" to explain why they will not help the intended beneficiaries: because the "settlor" can only be treated as having promised to make a gift on trust, and because the "beneficiary" is only a volunteer, no consideration having been supplied for the promise, the "beneficiary" cannot enforce the promise.[25] **2–12**

---

17 [1964] Ch. 288.
18 At paras 2-68 ff.
19 *Williams v CIR* [1965] N.Z.L.R. 395.
20 *Paul v Paul* (1882) 20 Ch.D. 742.
21 *T Choithram International SA v Pagarani* [2001] 1 W.L.R. 1 at 12, per Lord Browne-Wilkinson.
22 *Re Bowden* [1936] Ch. 71; *Re Adlard* [1954] Ch. 29.
23 (1862) 4 De G. F. & J. 264
24 At paras 2-14 ff.
25 *Re Plumptre's Marriage Settlement* [1910] 1 Ch. 609; *Re D'Angibau* (1880) 15 Ch.D. 228.

2–13 This rule is subject to various exceptions that are considered in Section 4, below. Moreover, an intended beneficiary who is not a volunteer can enforce the settlor's promise because he simply does not fall within the scope of the rule. *Pullan v Koe*,[26] which is also reproduced below,[27] establishes that a person is not a volunteer if he provided value or can bring himself within a marriage consideration, and that Equity will help him by treating the settlor as having done that which ought to have been done, and imposing a constructive trust on the relevant assets in the settlor's hands. A promise to create a trust made before and in consideration of marriage is regarded as having been made for value. If the trust is created after marriage and contains a true recital that it was made in pursuance of an ante-nuptial promise to create the trust it will be treated as having been made for value.[28] Within the scope of marriage consideration are the parties to the marriage, their children and remoter issue.[29] Old cases allowing children of a former marriage or a possible later remarriage or illegitimate children to be within the scope of marriage consideration and to enforce trust deed covenants to settle after-acquired property, can now only be supported on the basis that such children's interests were so closely interwoven with the interests of the children of the marriage that the latter could only benefit on terms allowing the former to benefit.[30]

MILROY v LORD

Court of Appeal in Chancery (1862) 4 De G. F. & J. 264; (1862) 31 L.J. Ch. 798; (1862) 7 L.T. 178; (1862) 8 Jur. 806

2–14 Thomas Medley executed what was treated as a voluntary deed,[31] which purported to assign 50 shares in the Louisiana Bank to Samuel Lord upon trust for the benefit of the plaintiffs. The shares were transferable only by entry in the books of the bank; but no such transfer was ever made. At the relevant time Samuel Lord held a general power of attorney authorising him to transfer Thomas Medley's shares, and Thomas Medley, after the execution of the settlement, gave him a further power of attorney authorising him to receive the dividends on the bank shares. Thomas Medley lived for three years after the execution of the deed, during which period the dividends were received by Samuel Lord and remitted by him to the plaintiffs, sometimes directly and sometimes through Thomas Medley. There was thus a perfect gift of the dividends. Shortly after the execution of the deed, the settlor had delivered to Samuel Lord the certificates for the shares; and on the death of the settlor, Samuel Lord gave up the certificates to the settlor's executor. The shares stood in the settlor's name before and at the time of his death. At first instance Stuart V.C. held that a trust had been created for the plaintiffs but this decision was reversed on an appeal by the executor.

2–15 TURNER L.J. (with whom KNIGHT-BRUCE L.J. agreed): Under the circumstances of this case, it would be difficult not to feel a strong disposition to give effect to this settlement to the fullest extent, and

[26] [1913] 1 Ch. 9. See too *Re Lind* [1915] 2 Ch. 345; *Re Gillott's Settlements* [1934] Ch. 97; *Palette Shoes Pty Ltd v Krohn* (1937) C.L.R. 1 at 27.

[27] At paras 2-18 ff.

[28] *Re Holland* [1902] 2 Ch. 360.

[29] *Att.-Gen. v Jacobs-Smith* [1895] 2 Q.B. 341; *Re Cook's ST* [1965] Ch. 902.

[30] *Mackie v Herbertson* (1884) 9 App. Cas. 303 at 337; *De Mestre v West* [1891] A.C. 264 at 270; *Rennell v IRC* [1962] Ch. 329 at 341; *Re Cook's ST* [1965] Ch. 902 at 914.

[31] The deed (apparently executed in Louisiana) was expressed to be made in consideration of one dollar. In *Mountford v Scott* [1975] Ch. 258, the Court of Appeal treated £1 as valuable consideration enabling specific performance to be ordered. If a transfer or grant of a legal title for consideration fails (e.g. a purported legal lease is not granted by deed) equity will treat this as a contract to transfer or grant the legal title properly, and if the contract is specifically enforceable (complying with the requisite formalities in the Law of Property Miscellaneous Provisions Act 1989 s.2) equity will treat it as having been carried out, so that the transfer or grant is effective to create an equitable interest: *Walsh v Lonsdale* (1882) 21 Ch.D. 9.

certainly I have spared no pains to find the means of doing so, consistently with what I apprehend to be the law of the court; but, after full and anxious consideration, I find myself unable to do so. I take the law of this court to be well settled, that, in order to render a voluntary settlement valid and effectual, the settlor must have done everything which, according to the nature of the property comprised in the settlement, was necessary to be done in order to transfer the property and render the settlement binding upon him. He may, of course, do this by actually transferring the property to the persons for whom he intends to provide, and the provision will then be effectual, and it will be equally effectual if he transfers the property to a trustee for the purposes of the settlement, or declares that he himself holds it in trust for those purposes; and if the property be personal, the trust may, as I apprehend, be declared either in writing or by parol; but, in order to render the settlement binding, one or other of these modes must, as I understand the law of this court, be resorted to, for there is no equity in this court to perfect an imperfect gift. The cases, I think, go further to this extent: that if the settlement is intended to be effectuated by one of the modes to which I have referred, the court will not give effect to it by applying another of those modes. If it is intended to take effect by transfer, the court will not hold the intended transfer to operate as a declaration of trust, for then every imperfect instrument would be made effectual by being converted into a perfect trust. These are the principles by which, as I conceive, this case must be tried.

Applying, then, these principles to the case, there is not here any transfer either of the one class of shares or of the other to the objects of the settlement, and the question therefore must be whether a valid and effectual trust in favour of those objects was created in the defendant Samuel Lord or in the settlor himself as to all or any of these shares. Now it is plain that it was not the purpose of this settlement, or the intention of the settlor, to constitute himself a trustee of the bank shares. The intention was that the trust should be vested in the defendant Samuel Lord, and I think therefore that we should not be justified in holding that by the settlement, or by any parol declaration made by the settlor, he himself became a trustee of these shares for the purposes of the settlement. By doing so we should be converting the settlement or the parol declaration to a purpose wholly different from that which was intended to be effected by it and, as I have said, creating a perfect trust out of an imperfect transaction. . . . **2–16**

The more difficult question is whether the defendant Samuel Lord did not become a trustee of these shares. Upon this question I have felt considerable doubt; but in the result, I have come to the conclusion that no perfect trust was ever created in him. The shares, it is clear, were never legally vested in him; and the only ground on which he can be held to have become a trustee of them is that he held a power of attorney under which he might have transferred them into his own name; but he held that power of attorney as the agent of the settlor; and if he had been sued by the plaintiffs as trustee of the settlement for an account under the trust, and to compel him to transfer the shares into his own name as trustee, I think he might well have said: "These shares are not vested in me; I have no power over them except as the agent of the settlor, and without his express directions I cannot be justified in making the proposed transfer, in converting an intended into an actual settlement." A court of equity could not, I think, decree the agent of the settlor to make the transfer, unless it could decree the settlor himself to do so, and it is plain that no such decree could have been made against the settlor. In my opinion, therefore, this decree cannot be maintained as to the fifty Louisiana Bank shares. . . . **2–17**

PULLAN v KOE

Chancery Division [1913] 1 Ch. 9, (1913) 82 L.J. Ch. 37

A marriage settlement of 1859 contained a covenant by the husband and wife to settle the wife's after-acquired property of the value of £100 or upwards. In 1879 the wife received £285 and paid it into her husband's banking account, on which she had power to draw. Shortly afterwards part of the money was invested in two bearer bonds which remained at the bank until the husband's death in 1909. The bonds then passed into the hands of his executors. The court held that from the moment when the wife received the £285 it was specifically bound by the covenant and was consequently subject in equity to a trust enforceable in favour of all persons within the marriage consideration. Hence the trustees were entitled to claim the bonds as trust property, although their legal remedy on the covenant was statute-barred. **2–18**

2–19 SWINFEN EADY J.: The defence of laches and acquiescence was given up by the defendants, but they insisted that, although they still retained the bonds, they were under no liability to the plaintiffs. They put their case in this way—that the plaintiff trustees could not follow the bonds into their hands, that the only liability of the husband was upon his covenant, and the claim of the trustees was for damages only, and that as this claim accrued in 1879 it was long since barred by the Statutes of Limitation. . . .

2–20 [The husband] received the bonds, purchased with his wife's money, with full notice of the trusts of the settlement, and knowing that the £285 and the bonds purchased with part of it were bound by the covenant. The trustees having traced the property into his hands are entitled to claim it from his executors.

2–21 It was contended that the bonds never in fact became trust property, as both the wife and husband were only liable in damages for breach of covenant, and that the case was different from cases where property which has once admittedly become subject to the trusts of an instrument has been improperly dealt with, and is sought to be recovered. In my opinion as soon as the £285 was paid to the wife it became in equity bound by and subject to the trusts of the settlement. The trustees could have claimed that particular sum, could have obtained at once the appointment of a receiver of it, if they could have shown a case of jeopardy, and, if it had been invested and the investment could be traced, could have followed the money and claimed the investment.

2–22 This point was dealt with by Jessel M.R. in *Smith v Lucas*,[32] where he said:

> "What is the effect of such a covenant in equity? It has been said that the effect in equity of the covenant of the wife, as far as she is concerned, is that it does not affect her personally, but that it binds the property: that is to say, it binds the property under the doctrine of equity that that is to be considered as done which ought to be done. That is in the nature of specific performance of the contract no doubt. If therefore, this is a covenant to settle the future-acquired property of the wife, and nothing more is done by her, the covenant will bind the property."

Again in *Collyer v Isaacs*[33] Jessel M.R. said:

> "A man can contract to assign property which is to come into existence in the future, and when it has come into existence, equity, treating as done that which ought to be done, fastens upon that property, and the contract to assign thus becomes a complete assignment. If a person contract for value, e.g. in this marriage settlement, to settle all such real estate as his father shall leave him by will, or purports actually to convey by the deed all such real estate, the effect is the same. It is a contract for value which will bind the property if the father leaves any property to his son."

2–23 Again the trustees are entitled to come into a Court of Equity to enforce a contract to create a trust, contained in a marriage settlement, for the benefit of the wife and the issue of the marriage, all of whom are within the marriage consideration. The husband covenanted that he and his heirs, executors, and administrators should, as soon as circumstances would admit, convey, assign, and surrender to the trustees the real or personal property to which his wife should become beneficially entitled. The trustees are entitled to have that covenant specifically enforced by a Court of Equity. In *Re D'Angibau*[34] and in *Re Plumptre's Marriage Settlement*[35] it was held that the Court would not interfere in favour of volunteers, not within the marriage consideration, but here the plaintiffs are the contracting parties and the object of the proceeding is to benefit the wife and issue of the marriage.

B. Covenants to Settle or Transfer Property

2–24 If A covenants (i.e. promises in a deed) to pay £11,000 or transfer 1,000 ICI ordinary shares or transfer his unique fifth dynasty Ming vase to B, a volunteer, then B has a chose in action enforceable at law

[32] (1881) 18 Ch.D. 531 at 543.
[33] (1882) 19 Ch.D. 342 at 351.
[34] (1880) 15 Ch.D. 228 at 242.
[35] [1910] 1 Ch. 609 at 616.

against A, the deed's formalities supplying the consideration.[36] However, equity does not regard the deed's formalities as consideration and so treats B as a volunteer and "equity will not assist a volunteer". Thus B cannot obtain specific performance of the Ming vase covenant but will have to be satisfied with common law damages, as for the £11,000 covenant or the 1,000 ICI shares covenant, specific performance never being available in such cases where money compensation is itself adequate.[37] Equity, however, will not frustrate a volunteer suing at law[38] and so B may recover as damages £11,000, or the money equivalent of the shares or the Ming vase.

Fletcher v Fletcher,[39] which is reproduced below,[40] establishes that if A covenants with B to transfer £60,000 to B as trustee with express or implied intent that B shall hold the benefit of the covenant upon trust for C and D if they attain 21 years of age, then A has created a completely constituted trust of the benefit of the covenant held by B as trustee, so that this may be enforced by C and D, although they are volunteers, just as trusts are ordinarily enforceable by beneficiaries, whether they are volunteers or not. **2–25**

If A merely covenants with B to pay money or transfer property to B on trust for C and D if they attain 21, then the question arises whether A intended to create a trust of the covenant for C and D (an immediate equitable gift of the covenant) or intended only to create a trust of the subject-matter of the covenant if or when transferred to B (a future equitable gift of such subject-matter). Though volunteers, C and D will be able to enforce their claims if there is a completely constituted trust of the benefit of the covenant,[41] but they will fail if A is treated as merely promising to make a gift to B of the property to which the covenant relates, for a trust will only arise when the property is effectively given to B.[42] **2–26**

Originally, the courts were quite sympathetic to the claims of the likes of C and D but, during the twentieth century, they became reluctant to find an intention to create a completely constituted trust of the benefit of a covenant. This seems quite justifiable. Where in the context of a lengthy trust deed, typically a marriage settlement (wholly enforceable by the issue within the marriage consideration but not by the next-of-kin beneficiaries in default of issue so far as not completely constituted) there is a covenant by the settlor to transfer after-acquired property to the trustees, surely the settlor is only promising to make a gift of such property to the trustees, so that a completely constituted trust enforceable by next-of-kin volunteers will only arise upon the property being gifted to the trustees.[43] It would be most unusual for the settlor to intend to create a trust of the covenant **2–27**

---

[36] *Cannon v Hartley* [1949] Ch. 213, seals being required for deeds until August 1990.

[37] *Harnett v Yielding* (1805) 2 Sch. & Lef. 549 at 552; *Beswick v Beswick* [1968] A.C. 58.

[38] *Cannon v Hartley* [1949] Ch. 213, unless fraud, undue influence or oppressive unconscionable behaviour were involved. To succeed at law the volunteer, if not a covenantee under a deed poll, will have to be a party to the inter partes deed as well as a covenantee, LPA 1925 s.56, covering only land: *Beswick v Beswick* [1968] A.C. 58 at 76, 81, 87, 94, 105 (3:2 majority view).

[39] (1844) 4 Hare 67, where the intention was not express but implied in rather special circumstances at a time when courts were more ready to find an intent to create a trust than they now are. Other examples are *Williamson v Codrington* (1750) 1 Ves. Sen. 511; *Cox v Barnard* (1850) 8 Hare 310; *Watson v Parker* (1843) 6 Beav. 283; *Dowling v Dowling* [1917] Victoria L.R. 208.

[40] At paras 2-32 ff.

[41] *Fletcher v Fletcher* (1844) 4 Hare 67; *Cox v Barnard* (1850) 8 Hare 310 at 312 and 313; *Milroy v Lord* (1862) 4 De G.F. & J. 264 at 278; and *Re Cavendish-Browne* [1916] W.N. 341. These all indicate that a covenant for further assurance may assist the court to find an intent to create a trust of a covenant to transfer property or of the covenant for further assurance itself. After all, the benefit of the covenant for further assurance can hardly be held on a resulting trust for the settlor without making the covenant futile and meaningless.

[42] *Re Plumptre's Marriage Settlement* [1910] 1 Ch. 609.

[43] *Re Plumptre's MS* [1910] 1 Ch. 609; *Re Pryce* [1917] 1 Ch. 234. Really the settlor intends the covenant to be for the enforceable benefit of his spouse and issue and not the next-of-kin, while any actual transfer is to be for the benefit of all the beneficiaries. On this basis the position should not be affected by the Contracts (Rights of Third Parties) Act 1999: see s.1(2) preventing a third party suing "if on a proper construction of the contract it appears that the parties did not intend the term to be enforceable by the third party". It appears from s.7(3) that promises in a deed, known as specialties, are treated as contracts under s.1.

forthwith enforceable by next-of-kin volunteers, and so a clear express intention should be required for this, e.g. "to the intent that the benefit of this covenant shall be held by my trustees upon trust for."

2–28 If a deed merely contains one covenant, e.g. "A covenants with B to transfer £10,000 to him on C's twenty-fifth birthday to hold on trust for C if C attains twenty-five", then since A has constituted himself debtor of B in his capacity as trustee for C and the deed would otherwise be futile[44] it seems that it should be treated as creating a trust of the covenant as if it read "A covenants with B to transfer £10,000 to him on C's twenty-fifth birthday to the intent that B shall hold the benefit of this covenant on trust for C if he attains twenty-five." This would be the position, anyhow, following the enactment of the Contracts (Rights of Third Parties) Act 1999, if the covenant were created after May 10, 2000.

2–29 It has been suggested[45] that since four[46] of the cases where there was held to be no trust of the benefit of the covenant concerned covenants to settle after-acquired property or analogous covenants, such covenants are never capable of being the subject-matter of a trust, just as a *spes* or future property cannot be the subject of a trust or of an assignment. While one can contract to transfer not-yet-existing property, one cannot give or transfer or declare a trust of not-yet-existing property. This calls for a digression which will show that future property is non-existent property so that there is nothing for a trust to "bite" on, while a covenant relating to future property is an existing chose in action[47] which a trust can "bite" on. "A chose in action is no less a chose in action because it is not immediately recoverable by action" as Lord Oliver has made clear.[48]

2–30 Future property must be distinguished from existing vested or contingent rights to obtain property at some future time.[49] While a contingent equitable interest in remainder under a trust (e.g. to A for life, remainder to B if he attains 30 and is alive on A's death, where B has an assignable, saleable interest) is existing property, examples of future property are the hope of inheriting upon the death of some live person or of receiving property under the exercise of a power of appointment or of acquiring book-debts arising in a business or of acquiring royalties arising on a book. At law an assignment of future property is void as an assignment of nothing,[50] though, if the assignee gave valuable consideration equity will treat the assignment as a contract to assign the property when received if received,[51] the assignment being wholly inoperative if no value was given.[52] Just as an assignment of future property to trustees is void at law and inoperative in equity unless for value, a declaration of trust by S that he holds future property on trust is inoperative unless for value. This is the ratio of a New Zealand case, *Williams v CIR*,[53] which is reproduced below.[54] If S covenants to assign future property, when received if received, then equity will not enforce this in favour of volunteers but only in favour of someone who provided value or is within a marriage consideration.[55] However, at common law a covenantee can obtain full damages under a deed poll or, if also a party, where the deed is inter partes. Thus, if S in a deed with

---

[44] Cf. *Fletcher v Fletcher* (1844) 6 Hare 67. *Ex hypothesi* if B does not hold the benefit of the covenant on trust for C, he must hold it on resulting trust for A, and so cannot sue A for damages for breach of covenant.

[45] W.A. Lee (1969) 85 L.Q.R. 313.

[46] *Re Plumptre's MS* [1910] 1 Ch. 609; *Re Pryce* [1917] 1 Ch. 234; *Re Kay's Settlement* [1939] Ch. 329; *Re Cook's ST* [1965] Ch. 902.

[47] LPA 1925 s.205(1)(xx) defines property as including any thing in action.

[48] *Kwok Chi Leung Karl v Commissioner of Estate Duty* [1988] 1 W.L.R. 1035 at 1040, applied in *Re Landau* [1997] 3 All E.R. 322 at 328.

[49] See *Re Earl of Midleton's WT* [1969] 1 Ch. 600 at 607.

[50] *Holroyd v Marshall* (1862) 10 H.L.Cas. 191 at 220; *Re Tilt* (1896) 74 L.T. 163.

[51] *Holroyd* at 220.

[52] *Re Ellenborough* [1903] 1 Ch. 697.

[53] [1965] N.Z.L.R. 395.

[54] At paras 2-42 ff.

[55] *Re Ellenborough* [1903] 1 Ch. 697; *Re Lind* [1915] 2 Ch. 345; *Palette Shoes Pty Ltd v Krohn* (1937) C.L.R. 1 at 27; *Re Brooks's ST* [1939] Ch. 993.

B covenants to assign to B, a volunteer, any property that S may acquire under S's father's will or intestacy, then B may obtain full damages at common law if S breaks the covenant.[56]

2–31 In this case since B has the beneficial ownership of a presently existing covenant it seems that B may declare himself trustee of the covenant for C. It follows that S when entering into the after-acquired property covenant with B should be able intentionally to create a trust of the covenant for C, e.g. "I, S, hereby covenant to assign to B any property that I may inherit under my father's will or intestacy to the intent that B shall immediately hold the benefit of this covenant as trustee on trust for C." Since there is a completely constituted trust of the covenant it is then enforceable by C though a volunteer. In *Davenport v Bishopp*[57] Knight-Bruce V.C. indicated there could be a completely constituted trust of a covenant to settle after-acquired property, viz. relating to an indefinite amount at an indefinite future time. Further, in *Lloyd's v Harper*[58] the Court of Appeal held there was a trust of the benefit of a contractual promise to pay an uncertain amount on an uncertain future date, which is similar to a promise to assign an expectancy, and in *Royal Exchange Assurance v Hope*[59] Tomlin J. upheld a trust of a contractual promise to pay a sum arising only on a person's death before a certain date which might or might not occur. Thus, a covenant to settle after-acquired property or an analogous covenant can itself be the subject-matter of a completely constituted trust, though where the covenant relates to future property there should be a rebuttable presumption that the settlor intended not to create a trust of the covenant (an immediate equitable gift) but only a trust of the property when acquired and transferred to trustees (a future equitable gift of future property).[60]

FLETCHER v FLETCHER

Vice-Chancellor (1844) 4 Hare 67; (1844) 14 L.J. Ch. 66; (1844) 8 Jur. (O.S.) 1040

2–32 The bill was filed by Jacob, a natural son of the testator, Ellis Fletcher, demanding payment by the defendants, who were the testator's executors of the sum of £60,000 from the assets (and interest calculated from a date 12 months after the death of the testator). The claim was founded upon a voluntary deed executed by the testator some years before his death and discovered for the first time some years after his death. The deed had been retained by the testator in his own possession and, so far as appeared, he had not communicated its contents either to the trustees or to the beneficiaries. The deed was made on September 1, 1829, between Ellis Fletcher and five trustees therein named; it recited that Ellis Fletcher, being desirous of making provision for his two natural sons, John and Jacob, thereby covenanted for himself, his heirs, executors and administrators, with the said trustees, their heirs, executors, administrators and assigns, that if either or both of the sons should survive the testator, the latter's heirs, etc., would pay to the trustee, their heirs, etc., the sum of £60,000 within twelve months of the death of the testator to be held upon the following trusts: if both sons were alive at the testator's death and attained the age of twenty-one the trustees were to hold the money on trust for them both in equal shares as tenants in common; if only one son fulfilled these conditions the money was to be held on trust for him alone. In the event of either or both of the sons surviving the testator but neither attaining the age of twenty-one, the money was to fall back into residue. Both sons survived the testator but John died without attaining twenty-one. Jacob accordingly claimed that he had become solely entitled to the £60,000 and interest under the indenture of covenant. The executors admitted assets. The surviving trustees said that they had not accepted or acted in the trusts of the indenture; and they declined to accept or act in such trusts.

---

[56] *Cannon v Hartley* [1949] Ch. 213.
[57] (1843) 2 Y. & C.C.C. 451 at 460.
[58] (1880) 16 Ch.D. 290.
[59] [1928] Ch. 179.
[60] See *Re Plumptre's MS* [1910] 1 Ch. 609.

2–33 WIGRAM V.C.: It is not denied that, if the plaintiff in this case had brought an action in the name of the trustees, he might have recovered the money; and it is not suggested that, if the trustees had simply allowed their name to be used in the action, their conduct could have been impeached. There are two classes of cases, one of which is in favour of, and the other, if applicable, against, the plaintiff's claim. The question is to which of the two classes it belongs.

2–34 In trying the equitable question I shall assume the validity of the instrument at law. If there was any doubt of that it would be reasonable to allow the plaintiff to try the right by suing in the name of the surviving trustee. The first proposition relied upon against the claim in equity was that equity will not interfere in favour of a volunteer. That proposition, though true in many cases, has been too largely stated. A court of equity, for example, will not, in favour of a volunteer, enforce the performance of a contract in specie. That it will, however, sometimes act in favour of a volunteer is proved by the common case of a volunteer on a bond who may prove his bond against the assets. Again, where the relation of trustee and cestui que trust is constituted, as where property is transferred from the author of the trust into the name of a trustee, so that he has lost all power of disposition over it, and the transaction is complete as regards him, the trustee, having accepted the trust, cannot say he holds it, except for the purposes of the trust; and the court will enforce the trust at the suit of a volunteer. According to the authorities I cannot, I admit, do anything to perfect the liability of the author of the trust if it is not already perfect. The covenant, however, is already perfect. The covenantor is liable at law, and the court is not called upon to do any act to perfect it. One question made in argument has been whether there can be a trust of a covenant the benefit of which shall belong to a third party; but I cannot think there is any difficulty in that. Suppose, in the case of a personal covenant to pay a certain annual sum for the benefit of a third person, the trustee were to bring an action against the covenantor; would he be afterwards allowed to say he was not a trustee? If he cannot do so after once acknowledging the trust, then there is a case in which there is a trust of a covenant for another. In the case of *Clough v Lambert*[61] the question arose; the point does not appear to have been taken during the argument, but the Vice-Chancellor was of opinion that the covenant bound the party; that the cestui que trust was entitled to the benefit of it; and that the mere intervention of a trustee made no difference. The proposition, therefore, that in no case can there be a trust of a covenant is clearly too large, and the real question is whether the relation of trustee and cestui que trust is established in the present case.

2–35 . . . The objections made to the relief sought by the plaintiff under the covenant were three: first, that the covenant was voluntary; secondly, that it was executory; and, thirdly, that it was testamentary, and had not been proved as a will. For the purpose of considering these objections I shall first assume that the surviving trustee of the deed of September 1829 might recover upon the covenant at law; and upon that assumption the only questions will be, first, whether I shall assist the plaintiff in this suit so far as to allow him the use of the name of the surviving trustee, upon the latter being indemnified, a course which the trustee does not object to if the court shall direct it; and, secondly, whether I shall further facilitate the plaintiff's proceeding at law by ordering the production of the deed of covenant for the purposes of the trial.

2–36 Now, with regard to the first objection, for the reasons which I mentioned at the close of the argument, I think the proposition insisted upon, that because the covenant was voluntary therefore the plaintiff could not recover in equity, was too broadly stated. I referred to the case of a volunteer by specialty claiming payment out of assets, and to the case of one claiming under a voluntary trust, where a fund has been transferred. The rule against relief to volunteers cannot, I conceive, in a case like that before me, be stated higher than this, that a court of equity will not, in favour of a volunteer, give to a deed any effect beyond what the law will give to it. But if the author of the deed has subjected himself to a liability at law, and the legal liability comes regularly to be enforced in equity, as in the cases before referred to, the observation that the claimant is a volunteer is of no value in favour of those who represent the author of the deed. If, therefore, the plaintiff himself were the covenantee, so that he could bring the action in his own name, if follows, from what I have said, that in my opinion he might enforce payment out of the assets of the covenantor in this case. Then, does the interposition of the trustee of this covenant make any difference? I think it does not. Upon this part of the case I have asked myself the question, proposed by Vice-Chancellor Knight-Bruce in *Davenport v Bishopp*,[62] whether, if the surviving trustee chose to sue, there would be any equity on the part of the estate to restrain him from doing so, or, which is the same question, in principle, whether in a case in

[61] (1839) 10 Sim. 174.
[62] (1843) 2 Y. & C.C.C. 451.

which the author of the deed has conferred no discretion on the trustees (upon which supposition the estate is liable at law) the right of the plaintiff is to depend upon the caprice of the trustee, and to be kept in suspense until the Statute of Limitations might become a bar to an action by the trustee.

Or, in the case of new trustees being appointed (perhaps by the plaintiff himself, there being a power to appoint new trustees), supposing his own nominees to be willing to sue, the other trustees might refuse to sue. I think the answer to these and like questions must be in the negative. The testator has bound himself absolutely. There is a debt created and existing. I give no assistance against the testator. I only deal with him as he has dealt by himself, and, if in such a case the trustee will not sue without the sanction of the court, I think it is right to allow the cestui que trust to sue for himself, in the name of the trustee, either at law, or in this court, as the case may require. The rights of the parties cannot depend upon mere accident and caprice. Having come to this conclusion upon abstract reasoning, it was satisfactory to me to find that this view of the case is not only consistent with, but is supported by, the cases of *Clough v Lambert*[63] and *Williamson v Codrington*.[64] If the case, therefore, depended simply upon the covenant being voluntary my opinion is that the plaintiff would be entitled to use the name of the trustee at law, or to recover the money in this court, if it were unnecessary to have the right decided at law, and, where the legal right is clear, to have the use of the deed, if that use is material. **2–37**

The second question is whether, taking the covenant to be executory, the title of the plaintiff to relief is affected by that circumstance. The question is answered by what I have already said. Its being executory makes no difference, whether the party seeks to recover at law in the name of the trustee, or against the assets in this court. **2–38**

The third question is whether the plaintiff is precluded from relief in this court, on the ground suggested that this is a testamentary paper. . . . There is, therefore, no ground for the argument that the interest is testamentary. **2–39**

The only other question arises from the circumstances of the instrument having been kept in the possession of the party—does that affect its legal validity? In the case of *Dillon v Coppin*[65] I had occasion to consider that subject, and I took pains to collect the cases upon it. The case of *Doe v Knight*[66] shows that, if an instrument is sealed and delivered, the retainer of it by the party in his possession does not prevent it from taking effect. No doubt the intention of the parties is often disappointed by holding them to be bound by deeds which they have kept back, but such unquestionably is the law . . . **2–40**

Declare that the deed of September 1, 1829, constitutes a debt at law, and decree payment of the principal and interest on the same to the plaintiff. **2–41**

WILLIAMS v COMMISSIONERS OF INLAND REVENUE

New Zealand Court of Appeal [1965] N.Z.L.R. 395

Williams, who had a life interest under a trust, executed a voluntary deed, in which "the assignor by way of gift hereby assigns to the assignee for the religious purposes of the Parish of the Holy Trinity Gisborne for the four years commencing on June 30, 1960 the first £500 of the net income which shall accrue to the assignor personally while he lives in each of the said four years from the Trust. . . . And the assignor hereby declares that he is trustee for the sole use and benefit of the assignee for the purpose aforesaid of so much (if any) of the said income as may not be capable of assignment (or may come to his hands)." The question arose whether Williams had effectively divested himself of his interest in the £500 so as not to be liable for income tax on it. The New Zealand Court of Appeal held that he had not. **2–42**

TURNER J. (delivering the judgment of NORTH P. and himself): Mr Thorp, for the appellant, submitted that what was assigned by this document was a defined share in the existing life estate of the assignor in the trust property, and hence that the deed of assignment took effect, as at its date, to divest the assignor of the annual sums of £500 so that he did not thereafter derive them for taxation purposes in the years **2–43**

[63] (1839) 10 Sim. 174.
[64] (1750) 1 Ves.Sen. 511.
[65] (1839) 4 Myl. & Cr. 647 at 660.
[66] (1826) 5 B. & C. 671.

under consideration. For the respondent Commissioner it was contended that the deed was ineffective to divest the assignor of the sums, and that its effect was no more than that of an order upon the trustees still revocable by the assignor until payment.

2–44 The life interest of the appellant in the trust was at the date of the execution of the deed an existing equitable interest. Being an existing interest, it was capable in equity of immediate effective assignment. Such an assignment could be made without consideration, if it immediately passed the equitable estate: *Kekewich v Manning*.[67] There is no doubt that if the deed before us had purported to assign, not "the first £500", but the whole of the appellant's life interest under the trust, such an assignment would have been good in equity.

2–45 But while equity will recognise a voluntary assignment of an existing equitable interest, it will refuse to recognise in favour of a volunteer an assignment of an interest, either legal or equitable, not existing at the date of the assignment, but to arise in the future. Not yet existing, such property cannot be owned, and what may not be owned may not be effectively assigned: *Holroyd v Marshall*.[68] If, not effectively assigned, it is made the subject of an agreement to assign it, such an agreement may be good in equity, and become effective upon the property coming into existence but if, and only if, the agreement is made for con sideration (as in *Spratt v Commissioner of Inland Revenue*[69]), for equity will not assist a volunteer: *In Re Ellenborough*.[70]

2–46 The deed on which this appeal is founded was not made for consideration. The simple question is therefore—was that which it purported to assign (viz. "the first five hundred pounds of the net income which shall accrue") an existing property right, or was it a mere expectancy, a future right not yet in existence? If the former, counsel agree that the deed was effective as an immediate assignment: if the latter, it is conceded by Mr Thorp that it could not in the circumstances of this case have effect.

2–47 What then was it that the assignor purported to assign? What he had was the life interest of a cestui que trust in a property or partnership adventure vested in or carried on by trustees for his benefit. Such a life interest exists in equity as soon as the deed of trust creating it is executed and delivered. Existing, it is capable of immediate assignment. We do not doubt that where it is possible to assign a right completely it is possible to assign an undivided interest in it. The learned Solicitor-General was therefore right, in our opinion, in conceding that if here, instead of purporting to assign "the first £500 of the income", the assignor had purported to assign (say) an undivided one-fourth share in his life estate, then he would have assigned an existing right, and in the circumstances effectively.

2–48 But in our view, as soon as he quantified the sum in the way here attempted, the assignment became one not of a share or a part of his right, but of moneys which should arise from it. Whether the sums mentioned were ever to come into existence in whole or in part could not at the date of assignment be certain. In any or all of the years designated the net income might conceivably be less than five hundred pounds; in some or all of them the operations of the trust might indeed result in a loss. The first £500 of the net income, then, might or might not (judging the matter on the date of execution of the deed) in fact have any existence.

2–49 We accordingly reject Mr Thorp's argument that what was here assigned was a part or share of the existing equitable right of the assignor. He did not assign part of his right to income; he assigned a right to a part of the income, a different thing. The £500 which was the subject of the purported assignment was five hundred pounds out of the net income. There could be no such income for any year until the operations of that year were complete, and it became apparent what debits were to be set off against the gross receipts. For these reasons we are of opinion that what was assigned here was money; and that was something which was not presently owned by the assignor. He had no more than an expectation of it, to arise, it is true, from an existing equitable interest—but that interest he did not purport to assign. . . .

2–50 It was argued in the alternative by Mr Thorp, but somewhat faintly that if the document were not effective as an assignment it was effective as a declaration of trust, and that this result was sufficient to divest the appellant of the enjoyment of the annual sums so that he did not derive them as income. It will

[67] (1851) 1 De G.M. & G. 176; 42 E.R. 519.
[68] (1862) 10 H.L.C. 191, 210; 11 E.R. 999 at 1006, per Lord Westbury L.C.
[69] [1964] N.Z.L.R. 272.
[70] [1903] 1 Ch. 697.

be recalled in this regard that the text of the deed includes an express declaration of trust. Mr Thorp's submission was that this express declaration is effective even if the assignment fails. We agree that there may be circumstances in which a purported assignment, ineffective for insufficiency of form or perhaps through lack of notice, may yet perhaps be given effect by equity by reason of the assignor having declared himself to be a trustee; but it is useless to seek to use this device in the circumstances of the present case. Property which is not presently owned cannot presently be impressed with a trust any more than it can be effectively assigned; property which is not yet in existence may be the subject of a present agreement to impress it with a trust when it comes into the hands of the donor; but equity will not enforce such an agreement at the instance of the cestui que trust in the absence of consideration: *Ellison v Ellison*.[71] For the same reasons therefore as apply in this case to the argument on assignment Mr Thorp's second alternative submission must also fail.

C. Can the Covenantee Sue?

If A enters into a deed with B and gratuitously covenants with B to transfer existing or after-acquired property to B, but breaks the covenant, then equity will not assist B as a volunteer but it will not frustrate B from obtaining damages at common law.[72] Similarly, if A covenants with X that he will transfer £20,000 to B on trust for C then A is liable at law only to X if he fails to transfer the money.[73] **2–51**

If A covenants with B to transfer property to B on trust for C to the intent that B as trustee will hold the benefit of the covenant on trust for C, then there is a completely constituted trust of the benefit of the covenant.[74] As with all trusts B as trustee is under a duty to get in the trust property and so enforce the covenant so as to benefit C. If B breaks his duty then C can sue A and join B as co-defendant.[75] **2–52**

If A covenants with B to transfer property to B on trust for C in circumstances where there is no intention to create a trust of the covenant then A is treated as voluntarily promising to make a gift of the property referred to in the covenant, so that C will only have enforceable rights as a volunteer if A actually carries out his promise and transfers the property to B.[76] **2–53**

However, cannot B sue A for damages for breach of the covenant with B[77] and recover full damages[78] to be held on trust for C? The difficulty is that *ex hypothesi* B does not hold the covenant on trust for C so that he must either hold the covenant for his own benefit or by way of resulting trust for A, and it is clear that he is not intended to hold the covenant beneficially. If, therefore, the covenant and the right to damages for breach of covenant are held on resulting trust for the settlor, A, then surely so must any damages for breach of covenant.[79] Since A is, under the resulting trust, an absolutely entitled beneficiary of full capacity he must under the *Saunders v Vautier* principle[80] be **2–54**

---

[71] (1802) 6 Ves. Jun. 656 at 662, per Lord Eldon.
[72] *Cannon v Hartley* [1949] Ch. 213.
[73] *Colyear v Lady Mulgrave* (1836) 2 Keen 81.
[74] *Fletcher v Fletcher* (1844) 4 Hare 67.
[75] *Vandepitte v Preferred Accident Insurance Co* [1933] A.C. 70 at 79; *Wills v Cooke* (1979) 76 Law Soc. Gaz. 706; *Parker-Tweedale v Dunbar Bank Plc (No.1)* [1991] Ch. 26.
[76] *Re Plumptre's MS* [1910] 1 Ch. 609; *Re Pryce* [1917] 1 Ch. 234.
[77] Old cases tend to assume that B could be left to pursue his common law remedy without considering for whom such damages should be held: *Davenport v Bishopp* (1843) 2 Y. & C.C.C. 451 at 460; *Milroy v Lord* (1862) 4 De G.F. & J. 264 at 278; *Re Flavell* (1883) 25 Ch.D. 89 at 99; *Re Plumptre's MS* [1910] 1 Ch. 609 (damages claim statute-barred).
[78] *Robertson v Wait* (1853) 8 Exch. 299; *Lamb v Vice* (1840) 6 M. & W. 862.
[79] Cf. the resulting trust of £500 in *Re Tilt* (1896) 74 L.T. 163.
[80] See paras 7–03 ff.

able to terminate such trust and prevent the trustees from launching upon such a pointless exercise as a suit against himself for damages.[81]

2–55 A further difficulty is that if B could choose to sue and so constitute a trust of the damages this would contravene the principle in *Re Brook's ST*,[82] reproduced below.[83] This case holds that only a settlor (or his authorised agent) can completely constitute his trust, just as only a donor or his agent can complete a gift. Moreover, for the matter to be at the whim of B whether he sues or not, not only puts B in an invidious position, it contravenes the principle that the acts, neglects or defaults of the trustees cannot be allowed to affect the rights of their beneficiaries.[84]

2–56 In practice, if a trustee like B were considering suing A to benefit C he would seek to obtain the leave of the court for, otherwise, he would be at personal risk as to costs if he sued and could not prove his costs were properly incurred.[85] It is plain that the court will direct B that he must not sue for common law damages for breach of covenant where A did not create a completely constituted trust of the benefit of the covenant.[86] Equity thus goes beyond passively not assisting volunteers by positively intervening (which can only be justified on the grounds set out in the foregoing paragraphs rather than the basis mouthed by the courts that "equity will not assist a volunteer"). This negative direction is so well-established that there is no need for trustees like B to bother the court: there is a complete defence if any beneficiary like C brings a breach of trust action against B for failing to sue the covenantor for damages.[87]

2–57 If a bold trustee like B did sue (e.g. because married to the beneficiary or fully indemnified as to costs by the beneficiary), then it is submitted that such action would fail on the basis that since the settlor had not created a trust of the voluntary covenant he must *ex hypothesi* have reserved to himself the right, if he chooses, at a later date to constitute a trust of the property referred to in his covenant, having lined up the trustee as his agent to receive the property, but who meanwhile is to hold the covenant on a resulting trust for the settlor, making any action against the settlor groundless.

D. Only the Settlor (or His Authorised Agent) Can Constitute a Trust

2–58 Like the donor of a gift, the settlor must be responsible for the trust property becoming duly vested in the trustees whether he or his duly authorised agent is directly responsible.[88] This is obvious where S has created the "S" settlement and a trustee, Y, whose daughter is life tenant, steals from S a painting (that S has talked about transferring to the trust but as to which S is still undecided) so that it will grace his daughter's lounge very nicely. Equity respects the common law rule that only a donor or his

---

[81] *Hirachand Punamchand v Temple* [1911] 2 K.B. 330, where plaintiff money-lenders accepted a lesser sum from the defendant's father in satisfaction of a debt and then sued the defendant for the balance. Vaughan Williams L.J. (at 337) and Fletcher-Moulton L.J. (at 342) held that any moneys recovered would be held on trust for the father: "a court of equity would have regarded the plaintiffs as disentitled to sue except as trustees for the father and would have restrained them from suing" (at 342).

[82] [1939] 1 Ch. 993.

[83] At paras 2–62 ff.

[84] *Fletcher v Fletcher* (1844) 4 Hare 67 at 78; *Re Richerson* [1892] 1 Ch. 379.

[85] *Re Beddoe* [1893] 1 Ch. 547; *Re Yorke* [1911] 1 Ch. 370. Wherever trustees have reasonable doubts they may obtain directions from the court (and recoup their costs out of the trust funds): Civil Procedure Rules Pt 64.

[86] *Re Pryce* [1917] 1 Ch. 234 (though Eve J.'s reasoning is fallacious in that the Judicature Act fusion did not make defences available to a defendant in Chancery also available to a defendant at law); *Re Kay's Settlement* [1939] Ch. 329; *Re Cook's ST* [1965] Ch. 902.

[87] *Re Ralli's WT* [1964] Ch. 288 at 301–302.

[88] *Re Brooks's ST* [1939] 1 Ch. 993 (there could hardly be a clearer case for allowing a trustee to constitute the trust if the law were to allow this); *Re Adlard* [1954] Ch. 29.

agent can make an effective gift, and so there is no trust of the painting. The position would be the same if S mistakenly left the painting behind at Y's house, having taken it there merely to show it to Y and his daughter.

Suppose that S in his 2005 voluntary settlement has covenanted to transfer to the trustees of his settlement after-acquired property appointed to S under a special power in the 1985 "T" trust or devolving upon S under T's will or intestacy, and property is appointed to S in 2009 or bequeathed to S on T's death in 2009. What happens if, fortuitously, the "S" trustees happen also to be trustees of the "T" trust or of T's will (not so unlikely if the "S" trustees happen to be a trust corporation)? Can the trustees of the "T" trust or of T's will claim to hold the appointed or bequeathed property as trustees of the "S" settlement, thereby completely constituting a trust of such property in the "S" settlement, even though S is himself demanding the appointed or bequeathed property? *Re Brooks' ST*,[89] reproduced below,[90] holds that they cannot, and that S is entitled to the property free from any trusts since his voluntary obligation is unenforceable and he is in no way responsible for vesting title to the property in the "S" trustees. **2–59**

However, if S in 2009 had authorised the trustees of the "T" trust or of T's will to hold the appointed or bequeathed property qua trustees of the "S" settlement, the "S" settlement of such property would be completely constituted and so S would not be able to claim the property for himself.[91] Similarly, if S in his 2005 settlement had inserted a clause authorising the "S" trustees to receive property appointed or bequeathed to him and the "S" trustees had received such property from the trustees of the "T" trust or of T's will then the "S" settlement of such property would be completely constituted,[92] then so long as the authority had not been revoked before such receipt, such authority being voluntary[93] and therefore unenforceable and revocable.[94] **2–60**

In *Re Ralli's WT*,[95] reproduced below,[96] Buckley J. took an obiter view that appears to have been inconsistent with *Re Brooks's*, that case not having been cited to him. In *Re Ralli's*, S voluntarily covenanted in her 1924 settlement to assign her interest in remainder under the "T" trust of 1899 to the "S" trustees as soon as circumstances might admit, but did not do so before she died in 1956. Her interest in remainder fell into possession in 1961 by which time it so happened that X, the sole surviving trustee of S's 1924 settlement (and one of the original trustees thereof) had been appointed by a third party to be a trustee of the 1899 "T" trust and was, in fact, sole surviving trustee of the "T" trust. Buckley J. considered that since X had the title to the covenanted property as sole[97] trustee of the 1899 "T" trust and was also trustee of S's 1924 settlement containing the covenant, this completely constituted S's voluntary settlement of the assets in question. However, S was in no way responsible **2–61**

---

[89] [1939] 1 Ch. 993.

[90] At paras 2–62 ff.

[91] *Re Adlard* [1954] Ch. 29. If S had been deliberately misled by the trustees telling him he was bound to authorise them he might have a claim if he acted promptly after finding out.

[92] *Re Bowden* [1936] Ch. 71. By LPA s.53(1)(c) writing is required for the assignment of S's interest under the "T" trust or T's will to the trustees of S's settlement: *Grey v IRC* [1960] A.C. 1, as discussed at paras 3–80 ff.

[93] Or not otherwise binding as an irrevocable power of attorney or to give effect to a condition contained in a will: *Re Burton's Settlements* [1955] Ch. 82.

[94] *Re Bowden* [1936] Ch. 71, though cf. dicta in *Re Burton's Settlements* [1955] Ch. 82 at 104.

[95] [1964] Ch. 288.

[96] At paras 2–68 ff.

[97] If there had been another trustee, Y, then Y would need to seek the directions of the court. Trustees hold property jointly and must act unanimously. Since Y is not a trustee-covenantee under the 1924 settlement does not Y hold the assets on trust for S's estate so that he will be liable for breach of trust if he co-operates with X to transfer the assets to X to be held on the trusts of the 1924 settlement? If this is so then X will need to co-operate with Y to transfer the assets to S's estate and X will not be liable to the 1924 settlement beneficiaries since he was never able himself to obtain the assets for the 1924 settlement.

for the assets becoming vested in X so that according to *Re Brooks's ST*, no trust of the assets within the 1924 settlement should have arisen. Perhaps one can reconcile the cases on the basis that *Re Brooks's* concerned a live settlor who had changed his mind while in *Re Ralli's WT* the settlor had died happy without having changed her mind. Nevertheless, the view of Buckley J. should be rejected as making life impossibly difficult for trust companies managing thousands of different settlements.

RE BROOKS' SETTLEMENT TRUSTS

Chancery Division [1939] 1 Ch. 993

2–62 By the terms of a marriage settlement the income of the settled fund was directed to be paid to the wife during her life and the fund was to be held in trust for such of her issue as she might by deed or will appoint; in default of any appointment the fund was to be held in trust for all her children who being sons should attain the age of twenty-one years or being daughters should attain that age or marry in equal shares. In 1929 one of her children. A.T., executed a voluntary settlement whereby he assigned to Lloyds Bank as trustees "all the part or share, parts or shares and other interest whether vested or contingent to which the settlor is now or may hereafter become entitled whether in default of appointment, or under any appointment hereafter to be made or on failure of any such appointment of and in the trust property" subject to the marriage settlement. By an appointment in pursuance of the power executed in 1939, his mother appointed him a sum of £3,517 and released her life interest. Thereupon Lloyds Bank Ltd, who had by then become trustees of the marriage settlement as well as the voluntary settlement took out a summons asking whether they should pay A.T. the £3,517. Farwell J. held that A.T. was entitled to require payment of the sum appointed, and could not be compelled to permit the bank to retain the £3,517.

2–63 FARWELL J.: When one looks at the voluntary settlement, at first sight the answer would seem to be quite clearly that the trustees' duty was to retain the sum of £3,517 as part of the funds which the son had voluntarily settled, and the language of the voluntary settlement would seem to leave no doubt on that score, because the settlor assigned to the bank "all the part or share parts or shares and other interest whether vested or contingent to which the settlor is now or may hereafter become entitled whether in default of appointment or under any appointment hereafter to be made or on failure of any such appointment of and in the trust property which is now or may at any time hereafter become subject to the trusts of the wife's settlement." One would say, looking at the language of the settlement, that it would be difficult to find words more apt to embrace in the voluntary settlement all the interests which the son had then or might thereafter have under the marriage settlement and that accordingly the answer should be that it is the duty of the trustees to retain this as part of the voluntary settlement fund. But, when one considers the legal position in this matter, a different aspect seems to appear. If the matter could be tested simply as one of construction, the answer would appear to be in favour of the trustees of the voluntary settlement; but the question is not one of construction only, and I have to consider whether the attempt to assign that which the son has now become entitled to by virtue of the exercise of the power is enforceable against him.

2–64 The legal position in the case of a special power of appointment is not in any doubt at all. Referring to *Farwell on Powers*,[98] I find this statement of principle, which will be found in exactly the same language in earlier editions of the book, and therefore is not in any way the creation of the editor:

> "The exercise of a power of appointment divests (either wholly or partially according to the terms of the appointment) the estates limited in default of appointment and creates a new estate, and that, too, whether the property be real or personal."

The effect of this is that in the case of a special power the property is vested in the persons who take in default of appointment, subject, of course, to any prior life interest, but liable to be divested at any time by a valid exercise of the power, and the effect of such an exercise of the power is to defeat wholly or pro tanto the interests

[98] 3rd edn, p.310.

which up to then were vested in the persons entitled in default of appointment and to create new estates in those persons in whose favour the appointment had been made. That being so, it is, in my judgment, impossible to say that until an appointment has been made in favour of this son the son had any interest under his mother's settlement other than an interest as one of the people entitled in default of appointment; he had an interest in that; but that interest was liable to be divested, and, if an appointment was made in favour of the son, then to that extent the persons entitled in default were defeated and he was given an interest in the funds which he had never had before and which came into being for the first time when the power was exercised. No doubt it is quite true to say that the appointment has to be read in to the marriage settlement, but, in my judgment, that is not sufficient ground for saying that at the time when this voluntary settlement was made the son had any interest at all in the fund other than his vested interest in default of appointment; for the rest, he had nothing more than a mere expectancy, the hope that at some date his mother might think fit to exercise the power of appointment in his favour, but, until she did so choose, he had nothing other than his interest in default of appointment to which he could point and say: "That is a fund to which I shall become entitled in future or to which I am contingently entitled." Apart from this he was not contingently entitled at all; he had no interest whatever in the fund until the appointment had been executed.

If that be the true view, as I believe it to be, the result must be that, whatever the language of the settlement may be, the settlor under the voluntary settlement was purporting to assign to the trustees something to which he might in certain circumstances become entitled in the future, but to which he was not then entitled in any sense at all, and if that be so, then it is plain on the authorities that the son cannot be compelled to hand over or to permit the trustees to retain this sum and that he is himself entitled to call upon them to pay it over to him. **2–65**

There are two cases to which I have been referred. One of them is a decision of Buckley J. (as he then was) in a case of *In re Ellenborough*.[99] What Buckley J. said was this: **2–66**

> "The question is whether a volunteer can enforce a contract made by deed to dispose of an expectancy. It cannot be and is not disputed that if the deed had been for value the trustees could have enforced it. If value be given, it is immaterial what is the form of assurance by which the disposition is made, or whether the subject of the disposition is capable of being thereby disposed of or not. An assignment for value binds the conscience of the assignor. A Court of Equity as against him will compel him to do that which *ex hypothesi* he has not yet effectually done. Future property, possibilities, and expectancies are all assignable in equity for value: *Tailby v Official Receiver*.[100] But when the assurance is not for value, a Court of Equity will not assist a volunteer, the reason for that being, that, since it is merely a voluntary act and not an act for consideration at all, the conscience of the assignor is not affected so as in equity to prevent him from saying: 'I am not going to hand over this property to which now for the first time I have become entitled.' "

If that be the true view, it must follow that this particular interest, which for the first time came into being when the appointment was made, is not caught by the settlement.

Notwithstanding the fact that the language of this voluntary settlement as a matter of construction is wide enough to comprise this interest, the principle of law which I have stated makes it impossible to enforce the settlement to that extent and prevents the settlor from being compelled by this Court to transfer or permit the trustees to retain this money as part of the funds subject thereto. **2–67**

RE RALLI'S WILL TRUSTS

Chancery Division [1964] Ch. 288; [1964] 2 W.L.R. 144; [1963] 3 All E.R. 940

From 1899 Helen was entitled to one-half of her father's residuary estate subject to her mother's life interest. **2–68**
The mother died in 1961 so Helen's reversionary interest then fell into possession. In 1924 Helen in her mar-

[99] [1903] 1 Ch. 697 at 700.
[100] (1888) 13 App.Cas. 523.

riage settlement had covenanted to assign to the trustees thereof as soon as circumstances would admit all her existing and after-acquired property upon certain trusts for her children which failed (Helen dying a childless widow) and ultimately upon trusts for the benefit of the children of Helen's sister, Irene, who were volunteers. A subsequent clause in the marriage settlement was held on its proper construction to declare that all property comprised within the terms of the covenant should be subject in equity to the trusts of the settlement pending assignment to the trustees. Helen never assigned the reversionary interest before dying in 1956. The plaintiff was one of the three original trustees of the 1924 marriage settlement and was sole surviving trustee thereof. It so happened that in 1946 he had also become a trustee of Helen's father's will and was indeed sole surviving trustee. He claimed that Helen's reversion in half the residue was held on the trusts of the marriage settlement whilst the defendants, Helen's personal representatives, claimed her estate was entitled.

2–69 BUCKLEY J. held that the vested reversionary interest, being existing property of Helen at the time she made what he construed as an independent declaration of trust pending assignment to the trustees of her marriage settlement, was held on the trusts of the marriage settlement. He then continued:

2–70 If this view is right, this disposes of the case, but I think I should go on to state what would be my view, if I were mistaken in the view I have expressed. The investments representing the share of residue in question stand in the name of the plaintiff. This is because he is now the sole surviving trustee of the testator's will. Therefore, say the defendants, he holds these investments primarily on the trusts of the will, that is to say, in trust for them as part of Helen's estate. The plaintiff is, however, also the sole surviving covenantee under clause 7 of the settlement, as well as the sole surviving trustee of that settlement. This, however, affords him no answer, say the defendants, to their claim under the will unless the plaintiff, having transferred the property to them in pursuance of the trusts of the will, could compel them to return it in pursuance of their obligation under the covenant, and this, they say, he could not do. In support of this last contention they rely on *Re Plumptre's Marriage Settlement*,[101] *Re Pryce*,[102] and *Re Kay's Settlement*.[103]

2–71 The plaintiff, on the other hand, contends that, as he already holds the investments, no question of his having to enforce the covenant arises. The fund having come without impropriety into his hands is now, he says, impressed in his hands with the trusts on which he ought to hold it under the settlement; and because of the covenant it does not lie in the mouth of the defendants to say that he should hold it in trust for Helen's estate. He relies on *Re Bowden*[104] in which case a lady by a voluntary settlement purported to assign to trustees inter alia such property as she should become entitled to under the will of her father, who was still alive, and authorised the trustees to receive the property and give receipts for it. In due course her father died and the property to which the lady became entitled under his will was transferred to the trustees of the settlement. Many years later the lady claimed that the property belonged to her absolutely. Bennett, J. [held] that she was not entitled to the property.

2–72 Counsel for the defendants says that *Re Bowden* and *Re Adlard's Settlement Trust*[105] are distinguishable from the present case because in each of those cases the fund had reached the hands of the trustees of the relevant settlement and was held by them in that capacity, whereas in the present case the fund is, as he maintains, in the hands of the plaintiff in the capacity of trustee of the will and not in the capacity of trustee of the settlement. He says that *Re Burton's Settlements*,[106] the complicated facts of which I forbear to set out here, should be distinguished on the ground that, when the settlement there in question was made, the trustee of that settlement and the trustee of the settlement under which the settlor had expectations was the same, so that the settlor by her settlement gave directions to the trustee of the settlement under which she had expectations, who then already held the relevant fund.

2–73 Counsel for the plaintiff says that the capacity in which the trustee has become possessed of the fund is irrelevant. Thus in *Strong v Bird*,[107] an imperfect gift was held to be completed by the donee obtaining probate of the donor's will of which he was executor, notwithstanding that the donor died intestate as to

---

101 [1910] 1 Ch. 609.
102 [1917] 1 Ch. 234.
103 [1939] Ch. 329.
104 [1936] Ch. 71.
105 [1954] Ch. 29.
106 [1955] Ch. 82.
107 (1874) L.R. 18 Eq. 315.

her residue and that the donee was not a person entitled as on her intestacy. Similarly in *Re James*,[108] a grant of administration to two administrators was held to perfect an imperfect gift by the intestate to one of them, who had no beneficial interest in the intestate's estate.

In my judgment the circumstance that the plaintiff holds the fund because he was appointed a trustee of the will is irrelevant. He is at law the owner of the fund and the means by which he became so have no effect on the quality of his legal ownership. The question is: for whom, if any one, does he hold the fund in equity? In other words, who can successfully assert an equity against him disentitling him to stand on his legal right? It seems to me to be indisputable that Helen, if she were alive, could not do so, for she has solemnly covenanted under seal to assign the fund to the plaintiff and the defendants can stand in no better position. It is, of course, true that the object of the covenant was not that the plaintiff should retain the property for his own benefit, but that he should hold it on the trusts of the settlement. It is also true that, if it were necessary to enforce performance of the covenant, equity would not assist the beneficiaries under the settlement, because they are mere volunteers; and that for the same reason the plaintiff, as trustee of the settlement, would not be bound to enforce the covenant and would not be constrained by the court to do so, and indeed, it seems, might be constrained by the court not to do so. As matters stand, however, there is no occasion to invoke the assistance of equity to enforce the performance of the covenant. It is for the defendants to invoke the assistance of equity to make good their claim to the fund. To do so successfully they must show that the plaintiff cannot conscientiously withhold it from them. When they seek to do this, he can point to the covenant which, in my judgment, relieves him from any fiduciary obligation that he would otherwise owe to the defendants as Helen's representatives. In so doing the plaintiff is not seeking to enforce an equitable remedy against the defendants on behalf of persons who could not enforce such a remedy themselves: he is relying on the combined effect of his legal ownership of the fund and his legal right to enforce the covenant. That an action on the covenant might be statute-barred is irrelevant, for there is no occasion for such an action. **2–74**

Had someone other than the plaintiff been the trustee of the will and held the fund, the result of this part of the case would, in my judgment, have been different; and it may seem strange that the rights of the parties should depend on the appointment of the plaintiff as a trustee of the will in 1946, which for present purposes may have been a quite fortuitous event. The result, however, in my judgment, flows—and flows, I think, quite rationally—from the consideration that the rules of equity derive from the tenderness of a court of equity for the consciences of the parties. There would have been nothing unconscientious in Helen or her personal representatives asserting her equitable interests under trusts of the will against a trustee who was not a covenantee under clause 7 of the settlement, and it would have been unconscientious for such a trustee to disregard those interests. Having obtained a transfer of the fund, it would not have been unconscientious in Helen to refuse to honour her covenant, because the beneficiaries under her settlement were mere volunteers: nor seemingly would the court have regarded it as unconscientious in the plaintiff to have abstained from enforcing the covenant either specifically or in damages, for the reason, apparently, that he would have been under no obligation to obtain for the volunteers indirectly what they could not obtain directly. In such circumstances Helen or her personal representatives could have got and retained the fund. In the circumstances of the present case, on the other hand, it is not unconscientious in the plaintiff to withhold from Helen's estate the fund which Helen covenanted that he should receive: on the contrary, it would have been unconscientious in Helen to seek to deprive the plaintiff of that fund, and her personal representatives can be in no better position. The inadequacy of the volunteers' equity against Helen and her estate consequently is irrelevant, for that equity does not come into play; but they have a good equity as against the plaintiff, because it would be unconscientious in him to retain as against them any property which he holds in consequence of the provisions of the settlement. **2–75**

For these reasons I am of opinion that in the events which have happened the plaintiff now holds the fund in question on the trusts of the marriage settlement, and I will so declare. **2–76**

[108] [1935] Ch. 449.

4. Exceptions to the Rule that Equity Will Not Assist a Volunteer

2–77 There are four main exceptions to the rule that Equity will not assist a volunteer by perfecting an imperfect voluntary transfer of legal title:[109] the doctrine of proprietary estoppel; the rule in *Re Rose;*[110] the rule in *Strong v Bird;*[111] and the doctrine of *donatio mortis causa*.

A. Proprietary Estoppel

2–78 In some circumstances equity will prevent an owner of land, who has made an imperfect gift of some estate or interest in it, from asserting his title against the donee. The equity of the donee exists where he has spent money on the land in the mistaken belief that he has or will acquire an interest in it and the owner, knowing of the mistake, has stood by and allowed the expenditure to be incurred. This type of equity has a wider sphere of operation than an estoppel of the ordinary kind, and in some cases nothing short of a conveyance of the owner's estate or interest to the donee will be sufficient to satisfy the equity.

2–79 In *Thorner v Major,*[112] the House of Lords confirmed that a claimant seeking to establish a proprietary estoppel claim must prove three things: (1) that the defendant's assurances or conduct in relation to identified property were sufficiently clear and unambiguous in all the circumstances; (2) to lead the claimant reasonably to rely on those assurances or conduct; (3) by acting significantly to his detriment, so that it would be unconscionable for the defendant to deny him any remedy. Where these three things can be shown, the claimant may be awarded a sum of money,[113] possibly supported by an equitable lien on the defendant's property for the claimant's expenditure[114] or the value of his improvements[115] or lost expected occupancy rights.[116] Alternatively the court may perfect the defendant's imperfect gift by ordering the defendant to convey[117] or lease[118] land to the claimant, or to grant the claimant an easement[119] or a licence to use the premises for as long as the claimant permanently resides there[120] or until the claimant receives compensation from the defendant.[121] Where alternative

---

109 See too the Trusts of Land and Appointment of Trustees Act 1996 Sch.1 para.1: although an infant cannot hold a legal estate in land, an attempt to transfer a legal estate to him is not wholly ineffective as it operates as a declaration of trust by the grantor in favour of the minor.

110 [1952] Ch. 449.

111 (1874) L.R. 18 Eq. 315.

112 [2009] 1 W.L.R. 776.

113 *Jennings v Rice* [2002] W.T.L.R. 367 (assurance that house and contents would be left by will to claimant satisfied by award of £200,000); *Harris v Kent* [2007] EWHC 463 (Ch).

114 *Unity Joint Stock Mutual Banking Association v King* (1858) 25 Beav. 72; *Lee-Parker v Izzet (No.2)* [1972] 2 All E.R. 800 at 804–805; *Morris v Morris* [1982] 1 N.S.W.L.R. 61; *Burrows v Sharp* (1989) 23 H.L.R. 82; *Baker v Baker* (1993) 25 H.L.R. 408; *McGuane v Welch* [2008] 2 P. & C.R. 24.

115 *Raffaele v Raffaele* [1962] W.A.R. 29; *Cobbe v Yeomans Row Management Limited* [2005] W.T.L.R. 625 (where the C.A. gave a lien for an amount equal to half the increase in the value of the property as a result of the grant of planning permission obtained by the claimant's efforts and money; on appeal the H.L. held that no case of proprietary estoppel was made out, and that the claimant was merely entitled by the law of unjust enrichment to a personal claim for the value of his services: [2008] 1 W.L.R. 1752).

116 *Campbell v Griffin* [2001] W.T.L.R. 981.

117 *Pascoe v Turner* [1979] 1 W.L.R. 431; *Dillwyn v Llewelyn* (1862) 4 De G. F. & J. 517; *Re Basham* [1987] 1 All E.R. 405; *Voyce v Voyce* (1991) 62 P. & C.R. 290.

118 *Taylor Fashions Ltd v Liverpool Victoria Trustees Co Ltd* [1982] Q.B. 133n.

119 *Ward v Kirkland* [1967] Ch. 194; *Ives Investments Ltd v High* [1967] 2 Q.B. 379; *Crabb v Arun D.C.* [1976] Ch. 179.

120 *Inwards v Baker* [1965] 2 Q.B. 29; *Greasley v Cooke* [1980] 1 W.L.R. 1306; *Makaraj v Chand* [1986] A.C. 898; *Matharu v Matharu* [1994] 2 F.L.R. 597; *Holman v Howes* [2008] 1 F.L.R. 1217.

121 *Hussey v Palmer* [1972] 1 W.L.R. 1286; *Re Sharpe (a bankrupt)* [1980] 1 W.L.R. 219.

ways of satisfying the claimant's equitable rights would be equally effective, the court can give the defendant the option to choose between them.[122]

2–80 The starting point for proprietary estoppel claims used to be the five *probanda* of Fry J. in *Willmott v Barber*:[123]

> "In the first place the plaintiff must have made a mistake as to his legal rights. Secondly, the plaintiff must have expended some money or must have done some act (not necessarily upon the defendant's land) on the faith of his mistaken belief. Thirdly, the defendant, the possessor of the legal right, must know of the existence of his own right which is inconsistent with the right claimed by the plaintiff. If he does not know of it he is in the same position as the plaintiff, and the doctrine of acquiescence is founded upon conduct with a knowledge of your legal rights. Fourthly, the defendant, the possessor of the legal right, must know of the plaintiff's mistaken belief of his rights. If he does not, there is nothing which calls upon him to assert his own rights. Lastly, the defendant must have encouraged the plaintiff in his expenditure of money or in the other acts which he has done, either directly or by abstaining from asserting his legal right. . . . Nothing short of this will do."

2–81 The courts originally considered matters from the viewpoint of the defendant, the possessor of the legal right, so that he had to be at fault in some way before the claimant could claim an equity. Thus, if the defendant did not know the true position and so did not know of his right to object when he either acquiesced in or encouraged the claimant's belief then he was not estopped from subsequently asserting his rights against the claimant.[124] This still seems the case where he has merely acquiesced while his rights were being infringed at a time when he did not realise he had such rights.[125]

2–82 In cases of encouragement, however, the court now seems to regard matters from the claimant's viewpoint. It is not fault on the defendant's part that is significant: attention is directed at how unconscionable it would be if the claimant were to suffer from the defendant asserting his strict legal rights. The court adopts a broad approach "directed at ascertaining whether in particular circumstances it would be unconscionable for a party to be permitted to deny that which, knowingly or unknowingly, he has allowed or encouraged another to assume to his detriment."[126] The defendant's ignorance is merely one of the relevant factors in the overall inquiry. The court's inquiry focuses upon unconscionability at the date when it deals with the case so that events occurring well after particular encouragement are taken into account.[127] As Hoffmann L.J. has stated,[128] "Equitable estoppel . . . looks backwards from the moment when the promise falls to be performed and asks whether, in the circumstances which have actually happened, it would be unconscionable for the promise not to be kept."

2–83 In some cases there will be a clear and unequivocal express assurance that the defendant is to have a precise interest in or over particular property.[129] Alternatively, the acquiescence or standing-by of a

---

122 *Hopper v Hopper* [2009] W.T.L.R. 805 at [124] (not considered on appeal: [2008] EWCA Civ 1417).

123 (1880) 15 Ch.D. 96 at 105–106.

124 *Willmott v Barber* (1880) 15 Ch.D. 96; *Falcke v Scottish Imperial Insurance Co* (1886) 34 Ch.D. 234 at 243 and 253; *Re Vandervell's Trusts (No.2)* [1974] Ch. 269 at 300–301.

125 *Taylor Fashions Ltd v Liverpool Victoria Trustees Co Ltd* [1982] Q.B. 133n. at 147; *Amalgamated Investment and Property Co Ltd v Texas Commerce International Bank Ltd* [1982] Q.B. 84 at 204; *Sinclair v Sinclair* [2009] EWHC 926 (Ch) at [71]–[72].

126 *Taylor Fashions Ltd v Liverpool Victoria Trustees Co Ltd* [1982] Q.B. 133n. at 151, approved in *Habib Bank Ltd v Habib Bank AG Zurich* [1981] 2 All E.R. 650 at 666; *Att.-Gen. of Hong Kong v Humphreys Estate Ltd* [1987] 2 All E.R. 387 at 392; *Jones v Stones* [1999] 1 W.L.R. 1739; *Blue Haven Enterprises Ltd v Tully* [2006] W.I.R. 334 at [23].

127 *Sledmore v Dalby* (1996) 72 P. & C.R. 196; *Uglow v Uglow* [2004] W.T.L.R. 1183.

128 *Walton v Walton* (CA, 14 April 1994) endorsed in *Thorner v Major* [2009] 1 W.L.R. 776 at [62] and [101].

129 e.g. *Crabb v Arun DC* [1976] Ch. 179. Notwithstanding *Re Basham* [1896] 1 W.L.R. 1498, an assurance must be given in relation to *identified* property, and so assurances about inheriting a residuary estate may be insufficient: *Macdonald v Frost* (2010) 12 I.T.E.L.R. 577 at [19]–[21], following *Thorner v Major* [2009] 1 W.L.R. at [61].

landowner allowing the claimant to build on his land may be regarded as an implied assurance that the claimant is entitled so to build.[130] Equity, however, does not require the degree of certainty required for a valid contract or for a valid express trust when it is concerned with proprietary estoppels to prevent a defendant from escaping with unconscionable behaviour by taking refuge in an allegedly uncertain situation that he himself had deliberately created. This is particularly significant where in unique factual backgrounds testators give oral assurances to the claimant about inheriting a particular house or a particular farm and farming business. Equity requires the judge to be able to find as a fact that, in the particular circumstances, the oral statement was sufficiently clear to the particular claimant[131] so that he could reasonably understand that he was to inherit adequately identified property, thereby encouraging him to act in some detrimental fashion, and that the testator was making a commitment, not merely stating his current intention, being an intention that could change with the passage of time, with or without changes of circumstances.

2–84 In *Thorner v Major* the subject matter of the testator's 1990 commitment was his farm and ancillary business as existing at his death which occurred in 2005 and some land had been sold off and some more bought in the 1990s. Lord Walker therefore pointed out it was "unprofitable, in view of the retrospective nature of the assessment which the doctrine of proprietary estoppel requires, to speculate on what might have been."[132] *Gillett v Holt*,[133] however, shows that if the testator had reneged on his commitment (e.g. selling up and using the proceeds to buy a penthouse in which to live with a new wife) then the claimant who had worked without pay and deprived himself of the opportunity to better himself, would have been able to establish a proprietary claim in equity and consequential relief.

2–85 If the defendant gave no assurance indicating that the claimant had or would have an interest in identified property then no proprietary estoppel claim will lie, e.g. if the defendant assured the claimant that he would always provide a roof over her head or that he would see that she was financially secure both before and after his death.[134] Moreover, in the commercial context, where parties are dealing with each other at arms' length, one would expect the parties to property ventures to enter into proper contractual arrangements, and if they fail to do so then greater significance attaches to this failure than in a family or domestic context.[135] Thus in *Cobbe v Yeoman's Row Management Ltd*[136] no proprietary estoppel was established although the claimant spent time, effort and expertise in obtaining planning permission for land owned by the defendant, because he took a commercial risk in speculatively proceeding without any contract, in reliance on vague assurances of further negotiations down the line. As Lord Scott stated, an "expectation dependent upon the conclusion of a successful negotiation is not an expectation of an interest having [sufficient] certainty."[137]

2–86 The claimant must prove that he acted to his detriment in the belief that he had or would have an interest in the defendant's property.[138] A broad approach is taken to the question of detrimental reliance,[139] and the detrimental acts need not be expenditure of money or be inherently referable to

---

130 e.g *Ramsden v Dyson* (1866) L.R. 1 H.L. 129; *Thorner v Major* [2009] 1 W.L.R. 776 at [55].
131 *Thorner* at [15], [26], [56] and [85].
132 *Thorner* at [65].
133 [2001] Ch. 210 (claimant, assured of the testator's farming business, was awarded one of testator's three farms and £100,000 after being unjustifiably dismissed and excluded from the will under which he had been residuary beneficiary).
134 e.g. *Layton v Martin* [1986] 2 F.L.R. 227; *Coombes v Smith* [1986] 1 W.L.R. 808; *Lissimore v Downing* [2003] 2 F.L.R. 308; *Negus v Bahouse* [2008] 1 F.L.R. 381; *James v Thomas* [2008] 1 F.L.R. 1598; *Macdonald v Frost* [2009] W.T.L.R. 1815.
135 Lord Neuberger, "The Stuffing of Minerva's Owl? Taxonomy and Taxidermy in Equity" (2009) 68 C.L.J. 537, pp. 541–544.
136 [2008] 1 W.L.R. 1752.
137 *Cobbe* at [18].
138 *Greasley v Cooke* [1980] 1 W.L.R. 1306 at 1313–1314; *Grant v Edwards* [1986] 2 All E.R. 426 at 439; *Midland Bank v Dobson* [1986] 1 F.L.R. 171; *Holmes v South Yorkshire Police Authority* [2008] H.L.R. 33 at [28].
139 *Gillett v Holt* [2001] Ch. 210 at 232, applied in *Evans v HSBC Trust Co (UK) Limited* [2005] W.T.L.R. 1289.

the property.[140] Once the claimant shows that the defendant assured the claimant he was to have an interest in the property and that the claimant suffered detriment it will be presumed that the claimant acted to his detriment in reliance on the assurance: the onus of rebutting this presumption of reliance will then be on the defendant.[141]

B. The Rule in Re Rose

As we have discussed already, *Milroy v Lord*[142] establishes that an intended voluntary transfer of legal title is ineffectual both at law and in equity where something remains to be done in order to render the transfer effectual. However, *Re Rose*[143] establishes an exception to this principle. When a transferor has done everything which it is obligatory for him alone to do, in order to render the transfer of legal title effectual, and yet something remains to be done by a third party, then the transfer, although it is invalid at law, is nevertheless valid in equity, so that the relevant property is impressed with a constructive trust in favour of the intended transferee. In *Pennington v Waine*,[144] which is reproduced immediately below, the Court of Appeal made it clear that either the settlor must have put it out of his power to stop the transfer proceeding, for example because he has irrevocably put the transferee or his agent in a position to complete the gift (e.g. by registration of the transferee as owner of shares or land), or else circumstances akin to proprietary estoppel must make it unconscionable for him to insist on ownership of the relevant property. **2–87**

PENNINGTON v WAINE

Court of Appeal [2002] 1 W.L.R. 2075, [2002] 4 All E.R. 215

Ada owned 1,500 out of 2,000 shares in C Ltd which had custody of her share certificate. She told her nephew, Harold, who was company secretary, that she was giving him 400 shares and wanted him to become a director. She then instructed a partner in the firm of accountants which acted as the company auditors to prepare a transfer form, which she executed and returned to him. He then put the form in the file relating to the company which he kept in his office, rather than the file relating to Ada's affairs, which he also kept there. He subsequently told Harold of Ada's gift, saying that Harold need take no further action, and he asked Harold to sign the necessary form of consent to act as director now that he had qualifying shares. Harold signed the form and Ada as director countersigned it. Ada then made a will bequeathing 620 shares to Harold so that after her death he would have 1,020 of the 2,000 shares. A month later she died. Judge Howarth held there had been a valid gift of the 400 shares. **2–88**

ARDEN L.J. (with whom SCHIEMANN L.J. concurred): . . . Counsel have taken the court through the authorities in detail and it will thus be unnecessary for me to cite from the authorities at length. To reduce confusion, I will refer to the decision of Jenkins J. in *Re Rose* [1949] Ch. 78 as *Re Rose, Midland Bank v Rose* and to the decision of this court in the (unconnected) case of *Re Rose* [1952] Ch. 449 as *Re Rose, Rose v IRC*. **2–89**

---

[140] *Grant v Edwards* [1986] 2 All E.R. 426 at 439; *Jones v Jones* [1977] 2 All E.R. 231; *Greasley v Cooke* [1980] 1 W.L.R. 1306; *Re Basham* [1986] 1 W.L.R. 1498.

[141] *Greasley v Cooke* [1980] 1 W.L.R. 1306; *Coombes v Smith* [1986] 1 W.L.R. 808 at 821; *Wayling v Jones* (1993) 69 P. & C.R. 170; *Evans v HSBC Trust Company (UK) Limited* [2005] W.T.L.R. 1289 at [71].

[142] (1862) 4 De G. F. & J. 264.

[143] [1952] Ch. 449. See too *Mascall v Mascall* [1985] 49 P. & C.R. 119; *Corin v Patton* (1990) 169 C.L.R. 540; *Zeital v Kaye* [2010] EWCA Civ. 159 at [38]–[43] (where the rule did not apply on the facts). And for discussion see J. Garton, "The Role of the Trust Mechanism in the Rule in *Re Rose*" [2003] Conv. 364.

[144] [2002] 1 W.L.R. 2075.

2–90 The legal title to a share may today be conveyed by the execution and registration of an instrument of transfer (section 182(1) of the Companies Act 1985). However, the equitable interest in a share may pass under a contract of sale even if the contract is not completed by registration.[145] In addition, a share may also be the subject of a valid equitable assignment: see for example *Re Rose, Rose v IRC*.

2–91 This appeal raises the question of what is necessary for the purposes of a valid equitable assignment of shares by way of gift. If the transaction had been for value, a contract to assign the share would have been sufficient: neither the execution nor the delivery of an instrument of transfer would have been required. However, where the transaction was purely voluntary, the principle that equity will not assist a volunteer must be applied and respected. This principle is to be found in *Milroy v Lord* and other cases. . . . Accordingly the gift must be perfected, or "completely constituted".

2–92 The principle that equity will not assist a volunteer has been lucidly explained in Maitland's *Lectures on Equity*:[146]

> "I have a son called Thomas. I write a letter to him saying 'I give you my Blackacre estate, my leasehold house in the High Street, the sum of £1000 Consols standing in my name, the wine in my cellar.' This is ineffectual—I have given nothing—a letter will not convey freehold or leasehold land, it will not transfer Government stock, it will not pass the ownership in goods. Even if, instead of writing a letter, I had executed a deed of covenant—saying not I do convey Blackacre, I do assign the leasehold house and the wine, but I covenant to convey and assign—even this would not have been a perfect gift. It would be an imperfect gift, and being an imperfect gift the Court will not regard it as a declaration of trust. I have made quite clear that I do not intend to make myself a trustee, I meant to give. The two intentions are very different—the giver means to get rid of his rights, the man who is intending to make himself a trustee intends to retain his rights but to come under an onerous obligation. The latter intention is far rarer than the former. Men often mean to give things to their kinsfolk, they do not often mean to constitute themselves trustees. An imperfect gift is no declaration of trust. This is well illustrated by the cases of *Richards v Delbridge*[147] and *Heartley v Nicholson*.[148]"

2–93 Thus explained, the principle that equity will not assist a volunteer at first sight looks like a hard-edged rule of law not permitting much argument or exception. Historically the emergence of the principle may have been due to the need for equity to follow the law rather than an intuitive development of equity. The principle against imperfectly constituted gifts led to harsh and seemingly paradoxical results. Before long, equity had tempered the wind to the shorn lamb (i.e. the donee). It did so on more than one occasion and in more than one way.

2–94 Firstly it was held that an incompletely constituted gift could be upheld if the gift had been completed to such an extent that the donee could enforce his right to the shares as against third parties without forcing the donor to take any further step. Accordingly, if a share transfer has been executed by the donor and duly presented to the company for registration, the donee would be entitled, if necessary, to apply to the court for an order for rectification of the share register under section 359 of the Companies Act 1985. Such an order would not, of course, be granted if for example the directors had a discretion to refuse to register the transfer and had timeously passed a valid resolution to decline to register the transfer.[149]

2–95 That exception was extended in *Re Rose, Rose v IRC* and other cases by holding that for this exception to apply it was not necessary that the donor should have done all that it was necessary to be done to complete the gift, short of registration of the transfer. On the contrary it was sufficient if the donor had done all that it was necessary for him or her to do. . . .

2–96 [Reference was then made to the exceptional circumstances in *T Choithram International SA v Pagarani*:[150]] In that case the donor signed the trust deed setting up the foundation and then simply made an oral declaration of gift of all his wealth to the foundation. The Privy Council held that the gift to "the foundation" could only properly be construed as a gift to the purposes declared by the trust deed and

---

145 *Hawks v McArthur* [1951] 1 All E.R. 22.
146 (1932), p.73.
147 (1874) L.R. 18 Eq. 11.
148 (1875) L.R. 19 Eq. 233.
149 See *Buckley on the Companies Acts* 15th edn (2000) para.[359.277].
150 [2001] 1 W.L.R. 1.

administered by the trustees. Lord Browne-Wilkinson giving the judgment of the Privy Council referred to the arguments that the courts below had accepted, namely that:[151]

> ". . . the court will not give a benevolent construction so as to treat ineffective words of outright gift as taking effect as if the donor had declared himself a trustee for the donee (see *Milroy v Lord*). So, it is said, in this case TCP used words of gift to the foundation (not words declaring himself a trustee): unless he transferred the shares and deposits so as to vest title in all the trustees, he had not done all that he could in order to effect the gift. It therefore fails. Further it is said that it is not possible to treat TCP's words of gift as a declaration of trust because they make no reference to trusts. Therefore the case does not fall within either of the possible methods by which a complete gift can be made and the gift fails."

Lord Browne-Wilkinson disagreed with this conclusion:

> "Although equity will not aid a volunteer, it will not strive officiously to defeat a gift. This case falls between the two common-form situations mentioned above. Although the words used by TCP [the donor] are those normally appropriate to an outright gift—'I give to X'—in the present context there is no breach of the principle in *Milroy v Lord* if the words of TCP's gift (i.e. to the foundation) are given their only possible meaning in this context. The foundation has no legal existence apart from the trust declared by the foundation trust deed. Therefore the words 'I give to the foundation' can only mean 'I give to the trustees of the foundation trust deed to be held by them on the trusts of the foundation trust deed'. Although the words are apparently words of outright gift they are essentially words of gift on trust.
>
> But, it is said, TCP vested the properties not in all the trustees of the foundation but only in one, i.e. TCP. Since equity will not aid a volunteer, how can a court order be obtained vesting the gifted property in the whole body of trustees on the trusts of the foundation? . . . In their Lordships' view there should be no question. TCP has, in the most solemn circumstances, declared that he is giving (and later that he has given) property to a trust which he himself has established and of which he has appointed himself to be a trustee. All this occurs at one composite transaction taking place on 17 February. There can in principle be no distinction between the case where the donor declares himself to be sole trustee for a donee or a purpose and the case where he declares himself to be one of the trustees for that donee or purpose. In both cases his conscience is affected and it would be unconscionable and contrary to the principles of equity to allow such a donor to resile from his gift."

Accordingly the principle that, where a gift is imperfectly constituted, the court will not hold it to operate as a declaration of trust, does not prevent the court from construing it to be a trust if that interpretation is permissible as a matter of construction, which may be a benevolent construction. The same must apply to words of gift. An equity to perfect a gift would not be invoked by giving a benevolent construction to words of gift or, it follows, words which the donor used to communicate or give effect to his gift. **2–97**

The cases to which counsel have referred us do not reveal any, or any consistent single policy consideration behind the rule that the court will not perfect an imperfect gift. The objectives of the rule obviously include ensuring that donors do not by acting voluntarily act unwisely in a way that they may subsequently regret. This objective is furthered by permitting donors to change their minds at any time before it becomes completely constituted. This is a paternalistic objective, which can outweigh the respect to be given to the donor's original intention as gifts are often held by the courts to be incompletely constituted despite the clearest intention of the donor to make the gift. Another valid objective would be to safeguard the position of the donor: suppose, for instance, that (contrary to the fact) it had been discovered after Ada's death that her estate was insolvent, the court would be concerned to ensure that the gift did not defeat the rights of creditors. But, while this may well be a relevant consideration, for my own part I do not consider that this need concern the court to the exclusion of other considerations as in the event of insolvency there are other potent remedies available to creditors where insolvents have made gifts to defeat their claims.[152] There must also be, in the interests of legal certainty, a clearly ascertainable point in time at which it can be said that the gift was completed, and this point in time must be arrived at on a principled basis. **2–98**

---

[151] At 11–12.

[152] See for example ss.339 and 423 of the Insolvency Act 1986.

2–99 There are countervailing policy considerations which would militate in favour of holding a gift to be completely constituted. These would include effectuating, rather than frustrating, the clear and continuing intention of the donor, and preventing the donor from acting in a manner which is unconscionable. . . .

2–100 If one proceeds on the basis that a principle which animates the answer to the question whether an apparently incomplete gift is to be treated as completely constituted is that a donor will not be permitted to change his or her mind if it would be unconscionable, in the eyes of equity, vis à vis the donee to do so, what is the position here? There can be no comprehensive list of factors which makes it unconscionable for the donor to change his or her mind: it must depend on the court's evaluation of all the relevant considerations. What then are the relevant facts here? Ada made the gift of her own free will: there is no finding that she was not competent to do this. She not only told Harold about the gift and signed a form of transfer which she delivered to Mr Pennington for him to secure registration: her agent also told Harold that he need take no action. In addition Harold agreed to become a director of the company without limit of time, which he could not do without shares being transferred to him. If Ada had changed her mind on (say) 10 November 1998, in my judgment the court could properly have concluded that it was too late for her to do this as by that date Harold signed the form 288A, the last of the events identified above, to occur.

2–101 There is next the pure question of law: was it necessary for Ada deliver the form of transfer to Harold? I have referred above to the difference of view between Evershed M.R. and Jenkins L.J. In *Re Rose, Rose v IRC* the issue was whether the gift was perfected by 10 April 1943, by which date the donor had executed the declarations of gift and delivered the share transfers to reflect the gifts to the transferees. Argument was not therefore directed to the question whether a beneficial interest in the shares passed on the dates of the declarations of trust or on the date on which the share transfers were handed over. For my own part I do not consider that it was necessary to the conclusions of Evershed M.R. that the gift should have taken effect before the transfers were delivered to the transferees. Indeed for him so to hold would not in my view be consistent with the second sentence cited from the relevant part of his judgment (set out above) or with the fact that he went on to approve as a correct statement of the law the decision of Jenkins J. in *Re Rose, Midland Bank v Rose* (where, the share transfers having been delivered to the donee, the gift was held to be perfect because there was nothing else the donor could do) or with the fact that Morris L.J. agreed with both judgments. . . . The conclusion of Jenkins L.J. was predicated on the basis that delivery of the transfer to the donee was necessary and had occurred. Likewise the decision of this court in *Mascall v Mascall*[153] and of the Privy Council in *Pehrsson v von Greyerz*,[154] were predicated on the same basis. I have summarised those cases earlier in this judgment. Accordingly the ratio of *Re Rose, Rose v IRC* was as I read it that the gifts of shares in that case were completely constituted when the donor executed share transfers and delivered them to the transferees even though they were not registered in the register of members of the company until a later date.

2–102 However, that conclusion as to the ratio in *Re Rose, Rose v IRC* does not mean that this appeal must be decided in the appellants' favour. Even if I am correct in my view that the Court of Appeal took the view in *Re Rose, Rose v IRC* that delivery of the share transfers was there required, it does not follow that delivery cannot in some circumstances be dispensed with. Here, there was a clear finding that Ada intended to make an immediate gift. Harold was informed of it. Moreover, I have already expressed the view that a stage was reached when it would have been unconscionable for Ada to recall the gift. It follows that it would also have been unconscionable for her personal representatives to refuse to hand over the share transfer to Harold after her death. In those circumstances, in my judgment, delivery of the share transfer before her death was unnecessary so far as perfection of the gift was concerned.

2–103 It is not necessary to decide the case simply on that basis. After the share transfers were executed Mr Pennington wrote to Harold on Ada's instructions informing him of the gift and stating that there was no action that he needed to take. I would also decide this appeal in favour of the respondent on this further basis. If I am wrong in the view that delivery of the share transfers to the company or the donee is required and is not dispensed with by reason of the fact that it would be unconscionable for Ada's personal representatives to refuse to hand the transfers over to Harold, the words used by Mr Pennington should be construed as meaning that Ada and, through her, Mr Pennington became agents for Harold for the purpose of submitting the share transfer to the Company. This is an application of the principle of benevolent

[153] (1984) 50 P. & C.R. 199.

[154] 16 June 1999, unreported.

construction to give effect to Ada's clear wishes. Only in that way could the result "This requires no action on your part" and an effective gift be achieved. Harold did not question this assurance and must be taken to have proceeded to act on the basis that it would be honoured.

Accordingly in my judgment the judge was right in the conclusion that he reached. **2–104**

[CLARKE L.J. gave a separate judgment holding that mere execution of the signed share transfer form on its own amounted to a valid equitable assignment, but, if he were wrong on that, then he agreed with ARDEN L.J.'s reasons.] **2–105**

C. *The Rule in Strong v Bird*

Strong v Bird[155] decides that in certain circumstances equity should allow the common law position to prevail where a deceased creditor had appointed his debtor as his executor, and the executor could not sue himself. The common law treated the appointment[156] as extinguishing or releasing the debt on the basis:[157] **2–106**

> ". . . that a debt was no more than the right to sue for the money owing to the creditor and that a personal action was discharged when it was suspended by the voluntary act of the person entitled to bring it . . . [the true basis of the common law rule] lay in the significance attributed to the voluntary act [of appointing the executor] on the part of the testator. Once this is recognised the true character of the rule is perceived. It reflected the presumed intention of the party having the right to bring the action and was not absolute in its operation."

Since administrators are not chosen by the testator the common law did not treat the court appointment of the administrator as the release of any debt due to the deceased from the administrator.[158] In equity the debtor (whether the deceased creditor's executor or administrator) had to account for the debt to the estate so that such moneys were available to pay off creditors of the estate or to be distributed among the estate beneficiaries.[159] In *Strong v Bird* the court of equity decided that the common law should prevail, and thus the executor did not have to account for the debt, if the testator had manifested an intent to forgive the debt in his lifetime and this intent had continued till death.

Where a donor intends to make an immediate gift of specific property but fails to satisfy the legal formalities for vesting legal title in the intended donee and goes on to appoint the donee his executor and then dies, the appointment itself is no perfect gift at law of the specific property although it is in the case of a release of a debt due from an imperfectly released debtor. However, Neville J. in *Re Stewart*[160] extended *Strong v Bird*, which negatively left the situation as it was at law, since he positively treated a gift as effective though the law did not, so perfecting an imperfect gift made by the testator in his lifetime to his wife who was one of his appointed executors. He said:[161] **2–107**

---

155 (1874) L.R. 18 Eq. 315.

156 Taking out the grant of probate or becoming an executor de son tort by intermeddling sufficed and, it seems, the appointment itself, though the executor died before taking out probate or intermeddling; *Wankford v Wankford* (1704) 1 Salk. 299; *Re Applebee* [1891] 3 Ch. 422; *Re Bourne* [1906] 1 Ch. 697; *Jenkins v Jenkins* [1928] 2 K.B. 501; *Bone v Stamp Duties Commissioner* (1974) 132 C.L.R. 38.

157 *Bone* at 53, per Mason J.

158 *Wankford v Wankford* (1704) 1 Salk. 299; *Seagram v Knight* (1867) 2 Ch. App. 628; *Re Gonin* [1977] 2 All E.R. 720 at 734. Now see Administration of Estates Act 1925 s.21A added by Limitation Amendment Act 1980 s.10.

159 *Berry v Usher* (1805) 11 Ves. 87; *Jenkins v Jenkins* [1928] 2 K.B. 501.

160 [1908] 2 Ch. 251.

161 *Re Stewart* at 254.

"Where a testator has expressed the intention of making a gift of personal estate to one who upon his death becomes his executor, the intention continuing unchanged, the executor is entitled to hold the property for his own benefit. The reasoning is first that the vesting of the property in the executor at the testator's death completes the imperfect gift made in the lifetime and secondly that the intention of the testator to give the beneficial interest to the executor is sufficient to countervail the equity of beneficiaries under the will, the testator having vested the legal estate in the executor."

2–108 *Re Stewart* has been followed many times at first instance[162] and treated as good law by the Court of Appeal.[163] In *Re James*[164] Farwell J. extended *Re Stewart* to perfect an imperfect gift of real property made by a donor to his housekeeper who, on the donor's intestacy, had herself appointed by the court one of two administratrices of the deceased donor's estate, thereby obtaining legal title to the house. This extension has been doubted by Walton J. in *Re Gonin*[165] and rejected by the British Virgin Islands' Court of Appeal in *Re Pagarini*:[166] after all, it is the voluntary act of the testator in appointing his debtor as his executor that extinguishes the debt at law, so that the fortuitous appointment by the court of an administrator who was a debtor of the intestate did not extinguish the debt, and so *Strong v Bird* would have been differently decided if the defendant had been an administrator and not an executor. However, the reasoning in the above-cited dicta of Neville J. suggests that, what, perhaps, should more aptly be known as the rule in *Re Stewart* is only concerned with the acquisition of legal title like the *tabula in naufragio* "plank in the shipwreck" doctrine.[167]

2–109 What is traditionally known as the rule in *Strong v Bird* has now developed into the principle that an imperfect immediate[168] gift of specific[169] existing[170] real or personal property[171] will be perfected if the intended donee is appointed the testator's executor or administrator alone or with others so long as the intention to make the gift continues unchanged till the testator's death.[172] The gift is perfected vis-à-vis those beneficially entitled to the deceased's estate but probably not vis-à-vis creditors since a common law extinguishment of a debt by appointment of the debtor as executor did not avail against creditors.[173]

2–110 Where the imperfect gift is to trustees and one (or more) of them is appointed the donor's executor this should perfect the trust, the equity of the beneficiaries under the intended trust of the property being sufficient to countervail the equity of the testamentary residuary beneficiaries.[174]

---

162 *Re Comberback* (1929) 73 Sol. Jo. 403; *Re James* [1935] Ch. 449; *Re Nelson* (1967) 91 Sol. Jo. 533: see also *Re Ralli's WT* [1964] Ch. 288; *Re Gonin* [1979] Ch. 16.

163 *Re Freeland* [1952] Ch. 110, counsel unreservedly accepting *Re Stewart*.

164 [1935] Ch. 449.

165 [1979] Ch. 16.

166 (1999) 2 O.F.L.R. 1.

167 This doctrine confers priority upon later equitable interests whose owners somehow manage to obtain the legal estate: it was particularly significant before 1926 and still can have some effect: *McCarthy & Stone Ltd v Hodge* [1971] 1 W.L.R. 1547; *MacMillan v Bishopsgate Investment Management Plc (No.3)* [1995] 1 W.L.R. 978 at 1002–1003.

168 *Re Innes* [1910] 1 Ch. 188; *Re Freeland* [1952] Ch. 110; *Re Gonin* [1979] Ch. 16; *Re Pink* [1912] 2 Ch. 528 at 536–539; *Simpson v Simpson* [1992] 1 F.L.R. 423. *Re Goff* (1914) 111 L.T. 34 is out of line since the donor only intended to forgive the debt if the donor predeceased the donee.

169 *Re Innes* [1910] 1 Ch. 188 at 193.

170 *Morton v Brighouse* [1927] 1 D.L.R. 1009.

171 *Re James* [1935] Ch. 449.

172 It seems contrary expressions before death may be ignored if the intent to make the imperfect gift is confirmed in the will: *Re Stoneham* [1919] 1 Ch. 149 at 158. For cases on contrary intention see *Re Freeland* [1952] Ch. 110; *Re Eiser's WT* [1937] 1 All E.R. 244; *Re Wale* [1956] 1 W.L.R. 1346; *Morton v Brighouse* [1927] 1 D.L.R. 1009 (property imperfectly given to X subsequently specifically bequeathed to Y).

173 *Bone v Stamp Duties Comr.* (1974) 132 C.L.R. 38.

174 *Re Ralli's WT* [1964] Ch. 288.

With voluntary covenants, where there is no completely constituted trust of such covenants, difficulties arise in applying the rule in *Strong v Bird* where one of the trustee-covenantees is appointed executor of the deceased settlor. First, the rule requires separate specific identifiable property[175] so as to be incapable of applying where S has voluntarily covenanted to pay £20,000 or transfer shares to the value of £20,000. Second, *ex hypothesi* S has neither transferred the property nor completely constituted a trust of the covenant itself and so does not have "a present intention to make an immediate gift"[176] of the subject-matter, if indeed the covenant does not expressly refer to transferring the subject-matter at a future date. The covenant is thus "an announcement of what a man intends to do in the future and is not intended by him as a gift in the present"[177] so as not to comply with the requirement of a present intention to make an immediate gift. It may be that this requirement is unjustifiable since once the pass has been sold by equity assisting a volunteer and perfecting an imperfect immediate gift, it seems inconsistent for equity to refrain from assisting a volunteer under an imperfect gift of specific property to be made at a future time (other than the donor's death when testamentary formalities must be complied with[178]) once that time has arrived.[179] Third, it may be difficult to show that the settlor's intention continued unchanged till death. **2–111**

If S makes an imperfect gift to trustees of his settlement and dies, his intention to make the gift continuing unchanged till his death, and his executor, mistakenly believing himself legally bound to perfect the gift, does so, Astbury J. opined[180] this would be effective against the beneficiaries entitled under S's will. Can this really be so when an executor does not have as much freedom as the deceased to release debts and perfect gifts since the executor holds the estate under fiduciary obligations owed to the will beneficiaries and not as absolute owner like the deceased?[181] Would *Strong v Bird* not have been decided differently (and the debtor remain accountable in equity if the executor could not personally satisfy all creditors' claims) if the debtor had not been appointed executor but whoever was the executor had released the debt? **2–112**

D. *Donatio Mortis Causa*

Cases of *donationes mortis causa* sometimes provide an exception to the rule that equity will not perfect an imperfect gift. A *donatio mortis causa* (dmc) must comply with the following essential requirements: **2–113**

- The donor must have made the gift in contemplation, though not necessarily in expectation, of death.
- He must have delivered the subject-matter of the gift to the donee or transferred to him the means or part of the means of getting at that subject-matter, e.g. delivering a key, like car keys[182] or a key to a box containing essential indicia of title,[183] intending to part with dominion over the property to which the key relates.

---

175 *Re Innes* [1910] 1 Ch. 188.
176 *Re Freeland* [1952] Ch. 110 at 118, the Court of Appeal assuming this to be good law since counsel did not argue that *Re Innes* was wrong on this point.
177 *Re Innes* [1910] 1 Ch. 188 at 193.
178 *Re Pink* [1912] 2 Ch. 528 at 536, 538–539.
179 In *Re Ralli's WT* [1964] Ch. 288, Buckley J. assumed a covenant to transfer property as soon as circumstances would admit could come within the rule in *Strong v Bird*. See also *Re Goff* (1914) 111 L.T. 34.
180 *Carter v Hungerford* [1917] 1 Ch. 260 at 273. Astbury J.'s ratio was based on the false assumption that the settlor held the benefit of the covenant on trust for beneficiaries: but see *Re Pryce* [1917] 1 Ch. 234; *Re Kay's S.T.* [1939] Ch. 329.
181 *Stamp Duties Comr. v Livingstone* [1965] A.C. 694; *Re Diplock* [1948] Ch. 465.
182 *Woodard v Woodard* (1991) 21 Fam. Law 470 (not necessary to hand over log book).
183 *Re Lillingston* [1952] 2 All E.R. 184, *Sen v Headley* [1991] Ch. 425.

- The circumstances must have been such as to establish that the gift was to be absolute and complete only on the donor's death so as to be revocable before then. A condition to this effect need not be expressed and will normally be implied from the fact that the gift was made when the donor was ill.[184]

2–114 Since, in the case of a chose in action, physical delivery is impossible, it follows that the title of the donee will not be completely vested at the death of the donor. The question is, therefore, whether the donee can, as a volunteer, compel the personal representatives of the donor to complete the gift. Equity will not grant its assistance to the donee in every such case; it will do so only in those cases in which the donor has delivered to the donee a document which is necessary to prove title to the chose in action, i.e. a document the possession or production of which is necessary in order to entitle the possessor or producer to payment of the money as property purported to be given.[185] It is not necessary that the document should contain all the terms on which the subject-matter of the chose in action is held.[186] In the case of a bank deposit book, delivery of the book is sufficient to pass the money in the deposit account if the bank insists on production of the book before paying out. Delivery of title deeds to land or of share certificates is capable of amounting to a dmc of the land[187] or of the shares.[188] Delivery of a donor's own cheque cannot amount to a dmc of the sum represented by the cheque,[189] although delivery of a cheque payable to the donor can amount to a dmc.[190]

Questions

2–115 1. Sam is freehold owner of some unregistered land in Wales, registered shareholder of 10,000 OK Ltd shares, a depositor of £12,000 with Bigg Bank and of £14,000 with Great Bank, and is entitled to XYZ Ltd shares held for him by Eric, executor of his father's will.

Sam gives the title deed to the Welsh land to Dawn, signing a hand-written endorsement on the conveyance to himself, "Dawn, this is now yours." He orally tells Frances he is holding 4,000 of his OK shares on trust for her, tells George he is holding his Bigg account on trust for him, has Great Bank write a letter to Harriet informing her that at Sam's telephoned request it is now holding his £14,000 on trust for her, tells Ian he is holding one half of his remaining 6,000 OK shares on trust for him, and tells Eric to transfer the XYZ shares to Jennifer. Eric signs a duly completed share transfer form and encloses it with the relevant share certificate in an envelope which he gives to Jennifer, who accidentally throws it out with some old newspapers and empty envelopes.

One month later a financial disaster strikes Sam, who seeks to recover the above property if at all possible. Advise him. Would your answer be different in respect of the OK shares if he had made a further declaration of trust of 3,000 OK shares in favour of Keith?

2–116 2. Under A's father's will trusts property is settled on trust for W for life, remainder to his sons A and B equally, but W has express power to appoint the capital between A and B as she sees fit. A

184 See *Re Mustapha* (1891) 8 T.L.R. 160; *Re Lillingston* [1952] 2 All E.R. 184.

185 *Moore v Darton* (1851) 4 De G. & Sm. 517; *Re Dillon* (1890) 44 Ch.D. 76; *Birch v Treasury Solicitor* [1951] Ch. 298.

186 *Birch v Treasury Solicitor* [1951] Ch. 298; disapproving dicta in *Re Weston* [1902] 1 Ch. 680 and *Delgoffe v Fader* [1939] Ch. 922.

187 *Sen v Headley* [1991] Ch. 425 (appeal to H.L. settled).

188 *Duffícy v Mollica* [1968] 3 N.S.W.L.R. 751 at 759. This clearly should be the position if a share transfer form is properly executed and handed over: *Staniland v Willott* (1850) 3 Mac. & G. 664; *Re Craven's Estate* [1937] Ch. 423; or if land is actually conveyed: *Cooper v Seversen* (1955) 1 D.L.R. (2d) 161.

189 *Re Beaumont* [1902] 1 Ch. 889; *Re Leaper* [1916] 1 Ch. 579.

190 *Re Mead* (1880) 15 Ch.D. 651.

assigns inter alia "All my interest under my father's will trusts to Bigg Bank on trust for X for life, remainder to Y".

Advise the bank if W dies either (i) without having made an appointment so that A receives £450,000, or (ii) having appointed £500,000 to A a month before her death, so that A's half share on her death brings him assets worth £200,000.

Would your advice differ if, instead, A had assigned to the Bank inter alia "all such assets whatsoever as shall come into my possession on my mother's death under the terms of my father's will trusts"? Would it matter if these words were followed by "but pending transfer of such assets I shall hold all my interest under my father's will trusts on the trusts applicable to such assets"?

Would any of your advice to the bank differ if unknown to A the bank happened to be trustee of his father's will trusts?

3. Five years ago, 26-year-old Sheila executed a voluntary settlement of certain property and further assigned to Barclays Bank as her trustee all property to which she might become entitled under anybody's will or intestacy and she covenanted with the bank to transfer to it upon the trusts of the settlement the sum of £30,000 to which she would become entitled under another trust if she attained 30. **2–117**

   Last year Sheila's mother died, by her will appointing Barclays Bank her executor and leaving £20,000 to Sheila. After receiving the £30,000 on attaining 30 Sheila, who then banked with Lloyds Bank, sent off her cheque for that sum in favour of Barclays Bank but stopped the cheque before it was met and sent off a cheque for £12,000 in its place. This cheque was cashed.

   Sheila now claims to be entitled to recover this £12,000 and to be under no obligation to pay the £18,000 balance. She further demands that Barclays Bank pay her the £20,000 due to her under her mother's will.

   Advise the bank. Would it make any difference if Sheila had died last month having appointed Barclays Bank executor of her will and having left everything to her husband, Barry, whom she had married last year and who persisted with her claims and demands?

4. "When it comes to Chancery judges directing trustees not to sue on covenants, that are not themselves the subject-matter of a trust, the judges cannot justify their directions simply on the negative basis that 'Equity will not assist a volunteer' because Equity is positively intervening to prevent trustees exercising their common law rights." **Discuss.** **2–118**

5. On Albert's 100th birthday he asked his three children Maud, George and Emma, to visit him. To Maud he said, "Here is a large envelope for you but don't open it till you've left me." To George he said, "Here is my share certificate for 4,000 ordinary shares in PQ Ltd, together with a transfer in your favour which I've signed. You can also have my car." To Emma he said, "I feel awful. If I die I want you to have everything else including this house and all my furniture. All the necessary papers are in this deed box underneath my bed. Here is the only key." Albert died in his sleep that very night. His will appointed George his executor and left everything equally among his children. **2–119**

   In Maud's envelope were a cheque for £2,000 and the deeds of some freehold land and on the last conveyance to Albert he had written and signed, "I hold this for Maud." In the deed box Emma found several share certificates, Albert's Trustee Savings Bank passbook showing a balance of £1,000, and a receipt acknowledging that the bank had the safe custody of the title deeds to the house. George was unable to get himself registered in respect of the 4,000 shares as the directors refused to register him and were entitled to do so under the company's articles.

Advise Albert's executor on the distribution of Albert's estate.

2–120 6. Is the following approach to completely and incompletely constituted trusts a sound one?

(a) Ask whether a trust has been completely constituted by a declaration of trust by S himself or by property having been effectively given by him to trustees, bearing in mind that the strict rules as to gifts have been attenuated by *Strong v Bird* principles and *donatio mortis causa* principles and that if the intent is clear there may be a completely constituted trust of a covenant?

(b) If a trust is incompletely constituted, ask whether the beneficiary seeking to enforce the trust is (i) a convenanting party, (ii) someone who gave consideration for the settlor's covenant, or (iii) someone within the marriage consideration if the settlement was made in consideration of marriage?

(c) If a beneficiary cannot enforce the trust, ask whether the trustees as convenantees can sue at common law and hold the damages on trust, and if so, for whom?

3 FORMAL REQUIREMENTS

1. Introduction

The law provides that certain transactions, such as the creation or transfer of property rights, must take a particular form, e.g. they must be carried out in writing. The underlying purposes of such rules are, first, to ensure that an owner of property seriously considers what he is doing before transferring beneficial ownership of the property to another person, and, second, to ensure that documentary evidence exists that will make fraud more difficult and forestall problems that might otherwise arise in determining who is entitled to what, especially after many years have elapsed, when memories have faded and the main actors may even have died.[1] This chapter will consider the content and scope of the formality rules governing the creation and transfer of equitable property interests under a trust, and the consequences of non-compliance with these rules. **3–01**

2. Lifetime and Testamentary Dispositions Distinguished

A lifetime disposition is a disposition of property that takes effect during the lifetime of the disponor, i.e. the person disposing of the property. A testamentary disposition is a disposition that takes effect after his death, and must be in the form of a will. A will is "an instrument by which a person makes a disposition of his property to take effect after his decease and which is in its own nature ambulatory and revocable during his life."[2] Such a person is named a testator or testatrix. **3–02**

There are various reasons why it might matter whether a disposition is testamentary in character. One is that a testamentary disposition can always be revoked during the lifetime of the testator, but a disposition which is not testamentary may or may not be revocable, depending on its terms. Another reason is that a disposition will be void if it is testamentary and the disponor fails to comply with the formality rules contained in the Wills Act 1837. This lay behind the (unsuccessful) attempts to characterise dispositions as testamentary in *Baird v Baird*[3] and also in *Chopra v Bindra*,[4] parts of which are reproduced below. **3–03**

In *Baird*, the deceased was employed by a company that provided a pension scheme, the rules of which stated that a member could (revocably) nominate a beneficiary to receive a "death benefit" if the member died while he was in employment; if no valid nomination was made then the death benefit would go to his spouse. The deceased nominated his brother, married, and then died without altering his nomination. His brother claimed the death benefit, but his widow argued that the nomination constituted a testamentary disposition, and was void for non-compliance with statutory formality rules applying to wills. The Privy Council held that the nomination was not a testamentary disposition because this can only be a disposition of property that belongs to the testator in his lifetime, and the deceased had not owned any of the death benefit, but had merely had the contractual right to require **3–04**

[1] Cf. L. Fuller, "Consideration and Form" (1941) 41 Columbia L.R. 799, which makes similar points in connection with the formality rules governing the creation of contracts.
[2] *Baird v Baird* [1990] 2 A.C. 548 at 556, adopting *Jarman on Wills* 8th edn (1951), p.26.
[3] [1990] 2 A.C. 548.
[4] [2009] 2 F.L.R. 786.

the trustees to pay it to his nominee after his death.[5] Lord Oliver observed that "an essential characteristic of a will is that, during the lifetime of the testator, it is a mere declaration of his present intention and may be freely revoked or altered"; but it did not follow that "every document intended to operate on death and containing a power of revocation is necessarily testamentary in character."[6]

CHOPRA v BINDRA

Court of Appeal [2009] 2 F.L.R. 786

3–05 The deceased ("Akash") lived in a house with his sister ("Angela"), which they jointly owned as tenants in common upon a trust deed. Clause 1 of the deed stated that "upon the sale of the property", they would hold the net proceeds of sale on trust for themselves as tenants in common, Akash being entitled to 75 per cent of the balance of the net proceeds and Angela being entitled to the rest. Clause 4 stated that upon either of their deaths, the survivor would be entitled to the whole proceeds of sale absolutely. Akash later married and lived in the property with his wife ("Jennifer"), who was the sole beneficiary under his will. On Akash's death, Angela claimed that as the house was unsold at the time of his death she became absolutely entitled to it and its proceeds of sale under clause 4. Jennifer argued unsuccessfully that clause 4 was repugnant to the absolute interest in the proceeds given to the deceased by clause 1, and that his interest in such proceeds devolved on her under his will. She also failed to persuade the court that clause 4 was a testamentary disposition that was void for non-compliance with the Wills Act 1837. The part of Rimer L.J.'s judgment dealing with the latter point is reproduced here.

3–06 RIMER L.J. (with whom ARDEN and RICHARDS L.JJ. agreed): . . . Ms Hayes's alternative submission was that clause 4 was a purported testamentary disposition by Akash to Angela of his absolute interest, but one that was void for want of compliance with section 9 of the Wills Act 1837 (the execution of the deed had only one witness). If Ms Hayes is right that clause 1 gave Akash an absolute interest, then since clause 4 was admittedly void she did not need to invoke this further argument and there is no need to consider it.

3–07 If, however, the judge was right to hold that clause 1 gave Akash and Angela mere joint lives interests until an actual sale and that clause 4 operated as a remainder to the survivor, that remainder cannot, I consider, be regarded as a testamentary disposition. It is the essence of a testamentary disposition that it is only intended to take effect after the testator's death and is revocable during the testator's lifetime. The deed in the present case disposed of the proceeds of the unsold house with immediate effect and was irrevocable. Ms Hayes nevertheless maintained her alternative submission as an answer to the judge's upholding of clause 4 as a valid remainder.

3–08 Ms Hayes sought to make good her submission by reference to authority. She relied on two cases in particular. Neither supported her submission and, with respect, both appeared to me to illustrate its error. *Re Pfrimmer*[7] was a decision of the Manitoba Court of Appeal. Mr Pfrimmer made a will in 1930 which disposed of a house on various trusts. Following his death, the will was admitted to probate when the question arose as to whether the carrying into effect of the testamentary trusts was prevented by two documents (one called a "Declaration of Trust") that he had executed five years before he made his will. The documents related to the same house and, if they created a valid trust in respect of it, the provisions in the will could not take effect. The question was whether they did create such a trust, or whether they took effect only as a testamentary disposition. The court's conclusion was that the documents showed that the land subject to them was to remain in Mr Pfrimmer's disposition to do with what he liked and that it was not until his death that they were intended to become operative; and that they were intended to take the place of a testamentary disposition in order to avoid probate expense and succession duties "and not to create an irrevocable trust by a binding transfer of the properties." Trueman J.A., giving the judgment of the court, said:[8]

[5] Applying *Re Danish Bacon Co Ltd Staff Pension Fund Trusts* [1971] 1 W.L.R. 248.
[6] *Baird* at 557.
[7] [1936] 2 D.L.R. 460.
[8] At 464.

> "The law is clear that to give validity to a declaration of trust of property, it is necessary that the donor or grantor should have absolutely parted with his interest in the property, and have effectually put such interest beyond his own reach. . . . Whatever may be the form of an instrument, if the person executing it intends that it shall not take effect until after his death, and it is dependent upon the death for its vigour and effect, it is not a trust.
>
> "Thus, in *Malim v Keighley*,[9] the Master of the Rolls said:— 'I will lay down the rule as broad as this; wherever any person gives property, and points out the object, the property and the way in which it shall go, that does create a trust, unless he shews clearly, that his desire expressed is to be controlled by the party; and that he shall have an option to defeat it.' "

In the present case, if the judge's interpretation of the deed was correct, Akash's execution of it disposed of his interest in the unsold house; and upon its execution, it was beyond his power to recall that disposition. Clause 4 was not a disposition intended to take effect only upon Akash's death. It took effect immediately and irrevocably gave Angela a contingent remainder in his interest in the house so long as it remained unsold.

3–09 Ms Hayes also relied on *Re White*,[10] a decision of the Ontario High Court. Three sisters, Charlotte, Frances and Sarah, executed a deed with two schedules. Schedule 1 listed property jointly owned by Charlotte and Frances; and Schedule 2 listed property jointly owned by Charlotte and Sarah. The deed provided for the income of all listed properties to be payable to Charlotte and Sarah during their joint lives and the life of the survivor; and on the death of the survivor, the scheduled properties were to become the property of Frances. The trusts were akin to the joint lives interests and cross-remainders that the judge derived from the deed in the present case save for the (I consider) irrelevant distinction that, whereas Frances's interest in remainder was vested, the cross-remainders were contingent.

3–10 There was no suggestion in *White* that the ultimate gift in favour of Frances was a testamentary disposition, although it was one that Frances was only to enjoy upon the death of Charlotte and Sarah. That suggestion arose only in relation to a further provision in the deed by which, upon Charlotte's death, any property that was unlisted in either Schedule and was jointly owned by Charlotte and Frances was to be sold and its proceeds distributed in a particular way. The deed did not identify any such properties, it imposed no trusts in relation to them during Charlotte's lifetime and such properties could (as it was claimed they did) include after-acquired properties. The court's conclusion was that (i) as the properties to which this provision applied could not be identified until Charlotte's death, and (ii) they were not the subject of any dispositive provision by the deed save for the purported gift of capital after Charlotte's death, (iii) this further provision was therefore intended to operate only after Charlotte's death and so was a testamentary disposition, and (iv) it was revoked by Charlotte's later will.

3–11 There is no need to labour the obvious distinction between *White* and the present case. *White* would only be in point if, for example, there had been a further provision in the deed whereby Akash purported to give to Angela upon his death an interest he had in other property. That might well have been a purported testamentary disposition. Clause 4, however, was nothing of the sort. It is either void for repugnancy or else was a valid disposition in remainder of Akash's interest in the unsold house. It is not an invalid testamentary disposition.

3. Lifetime or Inter Vivos Trusts

A. The Statutory Provisions

3–12 Formality rules affecting the creation of inter vivos settlements and inter vivos transfers of equitable interests under a trust are set down in the Law of Property Act 1925 and the Law of Property (Miscellaneous Provisions) Act 1989.

---

[9] (1794) 2 Ves. Jun. 333 at 335.
[10] (1987) 38 D.L.R. (4th) 631.

LAW OF PROPERTY ACT 1925

3–13 Section 52(1): All conveyances of land or of any interest therein are void for the purpose of conveying or creating a legal estate unless made by deed.

3–14 Section 53(1): Subject to the provisions hereinafter contained with respect to the creation of interests in land by parol:

(a) No interest in land can be created or disposed of except by writing signed by the person creating or conveying the same, or by his agent thereunto lawfully authorised in writing, or by will, or by operation of law;
(b) A declaration of trust respecting any land or any interest therein must be manifested and proved by some writing signed by some person who is able to declare such trust or by his will;
(c) A disposition of an equitable interest or trust subsisting at the time of the disposition, must be in writing signed by the person disposing of the same, or by his agent thereunto lawfully authorised in writing or by will.

(2) This section does not affect the creation or operation of resulting, implied or constructive trusts.

3–15 Section 54(1): All interests in land created by parol and not put in writing and signed by the persons so creating the same, or by their agents thereunto lawfully authorised in writing, have, notwithstanding any consideration having been given for the same, the force and effect of interests at will only.

(2) Nothing in the foregoing provisions . . . shall affect the creation by parol of leases taking effect in possession for a term not exceeding three years at the best rent which can reasonably be obtained without taking a fine.

3–16 Section 55: Nothing in the last two foregoing sections shall—

(a) Invalidate dispositions by will . . .
(d) Affect the operation of the law relating to part performance.

3–17 Section 205(1): In this Act unless the context otherwise requires, the following expressions have the meanings hereby assigned to them—

(ii) "Conveyance" includes a mortgage, charge, lease, assent, vesting declaration, vesting instrument, disclaimer, release and every other assurance of property or of an interest therein by any instrument, except a will; "convey" has a corresponding meaning; and "disposition" includes a conveyance and also a devise, bequest, or an appointment of property contained in a will; and "dispose of" has a corresponding meaning . . .
(ix) "Land" includes land of any tenure, and mines and minerals, whether or not held apart from the surface, buildings or parts of buildings . . . and other corporeal hereditaments; also a manor, an advowson, and a rent and other incorporeal hereditaments, and an easement, right, privilege, or benefit in, over, or derived from land; but not an undivided share in land . . .
(x) "Legal estates" mean the estates, interests and charges, in or over land (subsisting or created at law) which are by this Act authorised to subsist or be created as legal estates; "equitable interests" mean all the other interests and charges in or over land or in the proceeds of sale thereof.

LAW OF PROPERTY (MISCELLANEOUS PROVISIONS) ACT 1989

3–18 Section 2(1): A contract for the sale or other disposition of an interest in land can only be made in writing and only by incorporating all the terms which the parties have expressly agreed in one document or, where contracts are exchanged, in each.

(2) The terms may be incorporated in a document either by being set out in it or by reference to some other document.

(3) The document incorporating the terms or, where contracts are exchanged, one of the documents incorporating them (but not necessarily the same one) must be signed by or on behalf of each party to the contract.

(4) Where a contract for the sale or other disposition of an interest in land satisfies the conditions of this section by reason only of the rectification of one or more documents in pursuance of an order of a court, the contract shall come into being, or be deemed to have come into being, at such time as may be specified in the order.

(5) This section does not apply in relation to—

(a) a contract to grant such a lease as is mentioned in section 54(2) of the Law of Property Act 1925 (short leases);
(b) a contract made in the course of a public auction; or
(c) a contract regulated under the Financial Services Act 1986;

and nothing in this section affects the creation or operation of resulting, implied or constructive trusts.

(6) In this section—

"disposition" has the same meaning as in the Law of Property Act 1925; "interest in land" means any estate, interest or charge in or over land or in or over the proceeds of sale of land.

(7) Nothing in this section shall apply in relation to contracts made before this section comes into force.

(8) Section 40 of the Law of Property Act 1925 (which is superseded by this section) shall cease to have effect.

B. Contracts to Create Trusts or to Dispose of Equitable Interests and the Law of Property (Miscellaneous Provisions) Act 1989 Section 2

i. The Effect of Section 2

A contract to create a trust of pure personalty need satisfy no special formalities, as also seems to be the case for a contract to dispose of an equitable interest in pure personalty.[11] But contracts to create a trust of any interest in land, and contracts to dispose of an equitable interest in land, e.g. a life interest or a co-owner's equitable interest under a trust of land, are governed by the Law of Property (Miscellaneous Provisions) Act 1989 s.2.[12] The section provides that the contract is void unless all the terms are in one document signed by both parties or in exchanged documents signed by each exchanger (or on his behalf),[13] although it is possible to incorporate terms set out in another document by referring to that document. **3–19**

[11] *Chinn v Collins* [1981] A.C. 533 at 548. See too the discussion of *Oughtred v IRC* [1960] A.C. 206 at paras 3–87 to 3–88.

[12] The 1989 Act does not apply to the exercise of an option to purchase an interest in land (*Spiro v Glencrown Properties Ltd* [1991] Ch. 537) nor to a lock-out agreement not to consider any further offers if the purchaser exchanges contracts within two weeks (*Pitt v PHH Asset Management Ltd* [1994] 1 W.L.R. 327) nor to a collateral contract (*Record v Bell* [1991] 1 W.L.R. 853) nor to an agreement supplemental to a completed contract (*Tootal Clothing Ltd v Guinea Properties Management Ltd* (1992) 64 P. & C.R. 452). However it does apply to variations: *McCausland v Duncan Lawrie Ltd* [1997] 1 W.L.R. 38. If the parties omit an agreed term (of the sale contract, rather than some collateral agreement: *North Eastern Properties Ltd v Coleman* [2010] EWCA Civ. 277) then rectification can sometimes (but not always) be obtained so that the rectified document complies with the 1989 Act: *Wright v Robert Leonard (Developments) Ltd* [1994] E.G.C.S. 69; cf. *Oun v Ahmad* [2008] EWHC 545 (Ch).

[13] Old, liberal authorities on what constituted a sufficient signature for the Statute of Frauds 1677 and the Law of Property Act 1925 are no longer relevant: the 1989 Act has a different philosophy, and a signature for the purposes of the 1989 Act must be a handwritten signature: *Firstpost Homes Ltd v Johnson* [1995] 1 W.L.R. 1567.

ii. The Consequences of Non-Compliance

3–20 Section 2 repealed and replaced the Law of Property Act 1925 s.40, which replaced part of the Statute of Frauds 1677 s.4, and also incorporated the equitable doctrine of part performance, which was specifically mentioned in s.40(2). Section 40 stated that the contract did not need to have been created by signed writing, and only needed to have been evidenced by writing signed by or on behalf of the defendant by the time that a court action was brought. Non-compliance with s.40 did not render the contract void, but merely rendered the contract unenforceable by action until the requisite signed written evidence materialised or part performance of the contract occurred. If a claimant wanted to rely on the doctrine of part performance in order to obtain specific performance of the contract, then he had to show that he had acted to his detriment in reliance on the validity of the inadequately evidenced contract.[14]

3–21 The doctrine of part performance was abolished in this context when s.40 was repealed by the 1989 Act. Since then, however, claimants have successfully argued in a series of cases starting with *Yaxley v Gotts*,[15] reproduced immediately below, that because they relied to their detriment on the validity of a contract that was void for non-compliance with s.2, the land which they expected to acquire should be impressed with a constructive trust for them, by operation of the doctrine of proprietary estoppel. The courts considered that this outcome did not undermine the purpose of the section because s.2(5) expressly provides that "nothing in this section affects the creation or operation of resulting, implied or constructive trusts."

3–22 This analysis was obviously premised on the assumption that a constructive trust for the claimant can be generated in such situations by the doctrine of proprietary estoppel. In *Cobbe v Yeomans Row Management Ltd*,[16] however, Lord Scott said that it would be "unacceptable" to hold that "an owner of land can be estopped from asserting that an agreement is void for want of compliance with requirements of section 2". In his Lordship's view, this would undermine the policy of the statute. These comments are difficult to reconcile with the earlier cases,[17] but perhaps it might be said that a proprietary estoppel claim can generate a constructive trust, but that it does not always do so, and that the s.2(5) argument can still be made where the doctrine leads to the imposition of a constructive trust, although not where it leads to the award of some other remedy.[18] Alternatively, it may be that Lord Scott's objection was not to *all* proprietary estoppel claims (other than those generating a constructive trust), but to those which are sufficiently precise for the parties' arrangement to be in or near contractual territory. However this would produce the perverse outcome that "the clearer and more precise the defendant's indication or promise, and therefore the stronger the claimant's case in principle, the more likely it is that section 2 will scotch any proprietary estoppel claim."[19] The doctrine of proprietary estoppel and its relationship with constructive trusts are discussed further in Chapters 2 and 15.[20]

---

[14] *Steadman v Steadman* [1976] A.C. 536 as narrowly interpreted in *Re Gonin* [1979] Ch. 16.
[15] [2000] Ch. 162. See too *Banner Homes Group Plc v Luff Developments Ltd* [2000] Ch. 372; *London & Regional Investments Ltd v TBI Plc* [2002] EWCA Civ 355; *Kinane v Mackie-Conteh* [2005] W.T.L.R. 345; *Kilcarne Holdings Ltd v Targetfollow (Birmingham) Ltd* [2005] 2 P. & C.R. 105; *Oates v Stimson* [2006] EWCA Civ 548; *Brightlingsea Haven Ltd v Morris* [2009] 2 P. & C.R. 11.
[16] [2008] 1 W.L.R. 1752 at [29].
[17] As observed in *Brightlingsea* at [47], per Jack J.
[18] Cf. *Kinane* at [51], per Neuberger L.J.
[19] Lord Neuberger, "The Stuffing of Minerva's Owl? Taxonomy and Taxidermy in Equity" (2009) 68 C.L.J. 537, p.546, concluding (in disagreement with Lord Scott) that in principle s.2 should offer no bar to a claim in proprietary estoppel.
[20] See paras 2–78 ff. and 15–34 ff.

YAXLEY v GOTTS

Court of Appeal [2000] Ch. 162, [1999] 3 W.L.R. 1217, [2000] 1 All E.R. 711

3–23 The claimant builder and the second defendant orally agreed that the second defendant would buy a house and give the ground floor to the claimant, in exchange for which the claimant would convert the house into flats and manage the property on his behalf. The house was actually purchased by the first defendant, who was the second defendant's son. Believing the second defendant to be the owner, the claimant performed his side of the bargain, but the parties then fell out and the first defendant refused to grant the claimant an interest in the property. The judge found there was an oral agreement with the second defendant, and that it had been adopted by the first defendant. He held that the claimant was entitled to ownership of the ground floor by virtue of the doctrine of proprietary estoppel and ordered the first defendant to grant him a 99-year lease. The defendants appealed, arguing that the oral agreement was void by virtue of the Law of Property (Miscellaneous Provisions) Act 1989 s.2, and that the doctrine of proprietary estoppel could not operate to give effect to such an agreement. The appeal was dismissed, the Court of Appeal holding that the parties' oral agreement was void and unenforceable under s.2, but that the first defendant held the property on constructive trust by operation of the doctrine of proprietary estoppel, an outcome that was permitted by s.2(5).

ROBERT WALKER L.J. (with whom CLARKE and BELDAM LJJ. agreed) set out the facts and continued:

The Historical Background

3–24 Section 2 of the Act of 1989 has repealed and replaced section 40 of the Law of Property Act 1925, which itself replaced part of section 4 of the Statute of Frauds 1677 (29 Car.2, c.3). It is not in dispute that section 2 of the Act of 1989 is an entirely new provision which marks a radical change in the law.[21] Section 40 of the Law of Property Act 1925, by contrast, largely re-enacted the relevant provisions of section 4 of the Statute of Frauds 1677, but in such a way as to incorporate and confirm a volume of case law on that section, including in particular the equitable doctrine of part performance, which was specifically mentioned in section 40(2). Section 40 was in the following terms:

> "(1) No action may be brought upon any contract for the sale or other disposition of land, or any interest in land, unless the agreement upon which such action is brought, or some memorandum or note thereof, is in writing, and signed by the party to be charged or by some other person thereunto by him lawfully authorised. (2) This section applies to contracts whether made before or after the commencement of this Act and does not affect the law relating to part performance, or sales by the court."

3–25 The development of the law was clearly summarised by Lord Reid in *Steadman v Steadman*:[22]

> "This matter has a very long history. Section 40 replaced a part of section 4 of the Statute of Frauds 1677 (29 Car.2, c.3), and very soon after the passing of that Act authorities on this matter began to accumulate. It is now very difficult to find from them any clear guidance of any general application. But it is not difficult to see at least one principle behind them. If one party to an agreement stands by and lets the other party incur expense or prejudice his position on the faith of the agreement being valid he will not then be allowed to turn round and assert that the agreement is unenforceable. Using fraud in its other and less precise sense, that would be fraudulent on his part and it has become proverbial that courts of equity will not permit the statute to be made an instrument of fraud. It must be remembered that this legislation did not and does not make oral contracts relating to land void: it only makes them unenforceable. And the statutory provision must be pleaded; otherwise the court does not apply it. So it is in keeping with equitable principles that in proper circumstances a person will not be allowed 'fraudulently' to take advantage of a defence of this kind. There is nothing about part performance in the Statute of

[21] *Firstpost Homes Ltd v Johnson* [1995] 1 W.L.R. 1567 at 1571, per Peter Gibson L.J.; *McCausland v Duncan Lawrie Ltd* [1997] 1 W.L.R. 38 at 44, per Neill L.J.

[22] [1976] A.C. 536 at 540.

> Frauds. It is an invention of the Court of Chancery and in deciding any case not clearly covered by authority I think that the equitable nature of the remedy must be kept in mind."

3–26 The decision of the House of Lords in *Steadman v Steadman* shows that the doctrine of part performance often gave rise to difficulty, even though it had been established by a decision of the House of Lords as early as *Lester v Foxcroft*.[23] The development of the doctrine during the 18th and 19th centuries was fully considered by the House of Lords in *Maddison v Alderson*,[24] especially in the speeches of the Earl of Selborne L.C. and Lord Blackburn. For present purposes it is sufficient to note that the doctrine relied strongly on the effect of the statute in making an oral contract for the disposition of land merely unenforceable, and not void; that it was essential that there should be a clearly-proved oral contract susceptible of specific performance; and that the claimant should have done acts unequivocally referable to performance of the contract on his part. The principle underlying the doctrine was expressed as follows by Lord Selborne:[25]

> "In a suit founded on such part performance, the defendant is really 'charged' upon the equities resulting from the acts done in execution of the contract, and not (within the meaning of the statute) upon the contract itself. If such equities were excluded, injustice of a kind which the statute cannot be thought to have had in contemplation would follow."

3–27 It was also of central importance to the doctrine that an oral contract was under the old law not void, but merely unenforceable.[26]

The Public Policy Principle

3–28 Mr Allston has not contended that the doctrine of part performance, as such, has survived the repeal of section 40 of the Law of Property Act 1925 and its replacement by section 2 of the Act of 1989. It is clear that it has not survived. But he has contended that a comparable equitable doctrine can and in this case should operate despite section 2, that is the species of equitable estoppel, generally referred as proprietary estoppel, on which the judge relied. Mr. Allston has also (although only after some prompting by the court) asserted the existence of a constructive trust and has relied on the exception at the end of section 2(5).

3–29 Mr Laurence, appearing with Miss Davies for the defendants (neither appeared below), did not go so far as to contend that no form of estoppel could operate in relation to an oral or documentary consensus not amounting to a contract because of non-compliance with section 2. Nor did he submit that a plaintiff was in such a situation unable to obtain any restitutionary remedy: on the contrary, the defendants' notice of appeal concedes that Mr Yaxley is entitled to claim on a quantum meruit basis. But the defendants rely on the general principle, stated in *Halsbury's Laws of England*:[27]

> "The doctrine of estoppel may not be invoked to render valid a transaction which the legislature has, on grounds of general public policy, enacted is to be invalid."

3–30 The principal authorities supporting this principle, which I will call the public policy principle, are collected in the speech of Viscount Radcliffe delivering the opinion of the Privy Council in *Kok Hoong v Leong Cheong Kweng Mines Ltd*.[28] In *Westdeutsche Landesbank Girozentrale v Islington London Borough Council*,[29] Hobhouse J. expressed the same principle in the context of unjust enrichment under an ultra vires rate swap transaction:

> "The application of the principle is subject to the requirement that the courts should not grant a remedy which amounts to the direct or indirect enforcement of a contract which the law requires to be treated as ineffective."

---

[23] (1700) Colles 108.
[24] (1883) 8 App. Cas. 467.
[25] At 475.
[26] *Britain v Rossiter* (1879) 11 Q.B.D. 123 at 130; *Maddison v Alderson* (1883) 8 App. Cas. 467 at 474–475.
[27] 4th edn, reissue, vol.16 (1992), pp. 849–850, para.962.
[28] [1964] A.C. 993 at 1015–1018.
[29] [1994] 4 All E.R. 890 at 929.

The defendants also contend that the saving at the end of section 2(5) has a narrower effect than may at first appear. **3–31**

[He considered various cases in which the Court of Appeal had made some reference to estoppel in connection with section 2 of the Act of 1989,[30] and then continued:] I have no hesitation in agreeing with what I take to be the views of Peter Gibson L.J., Neill L.J., and Morritt L.J., that the doctrine of estoppel may operate to modify (and sometimes perhaps even counteract) the effect of section 2 of the Act of 1989. The circumstances in which section 2 has to be complied with are so various, and the scope of the doctrine of estoppel is so flexible, that any general assertion of section 2 as a "no-go area" for estoppel would be unsustainable. Nevertheless the impact of the public policy principle to which Sir John Balcombe drew attention in *Godden v Merthyr Tydfil Housing Association* does call for serious consideration. It is not concerned with illegality . . . but with what Viscount Radcliffe in *Kok Hoong v Leong Cheong Kweng Mines Ltd* called a principle of general social policy:[31] **3–32**

> "to ask whether the law that confronts the estoppel can be seen to represent a social policy to which the court must give effect in the interests of the public generally or some section of the public, despite any rules of evidence as between themselves that the parties may have created by their conduct or otherwise."

In this case that principle must of course be applied consistently with the terms in which section 2 of the Act of 1989 has been enacted, including the saving at the end of section 2(5). **3–33**

Parliament's requirement that any contract for the disposition of an interest in land must be made in a particular documentary form, and will otherwise be void, does not have such an obviously social aim as statutory provisions relating to contracts by or with moneylenders, infants, or protected tenants. Nevertheless it can be seen as embodying Parliament's conclusion, in the general public interest, that the need for certainty as to the formation of contracts of this type must in general outweigh the disappointment of those who make informal bargains in ignorance of the statutory requirement. If an estoppel would have the effect of enforcing a void contract and subverting Parliament's purpose it may have to yield to the statutory law which confronts it, except so far as the statute's saving for a constructive trust provides a means of reconciliation of the apparent conflict. **3–34**

Goff & Jones, *The Law of Restitution*,[32] a textbook of high authority, reaches the tentative conclusion that **3–35**

> "even if the purchaser can demonstrate that the vendor's conduct was so unconscionable that it would be inequitable for him to rely on the absence of writing, to order the conveyance of, or to declare him trustee of, the property is an inappropriate remedy in that it frustrates the policy underlying section 2(1) of the Act of 1989."

In inquiring whether the parliamentary purpose is frustrated it is necessary to note the wide range of relief which may be granted where a claim to proprietary estoppel is established. Just how wide that range is, appears, for instance, from *Snell's Equity*.[33] The general aim is to "look at the circumstances in each case to decide in what way the equity can be satisfied"[34] and to achieve "the minimum equity to do justice to the plaintiff".[35] Sometimes the equity is given effect to simply by dismissing an adverse claim. But in other cases more positive action is needed, extending both to giving the claimant an equitable lien on the disputed property for his expenditure, and to the positive conferment of title on the claimant.[36] That is the sort of relief referred to in the Law Commission's report as going to the extent of an order for land to be transferred.[37] **3–36**

---

30 *United Bank of Kuwait Plc v Sahib* [1997] Ch. 107; *McCausland v Duncan Lawrie Ltd* [1997] 1 W.L.R. 38; *Godden v Merthyr Tydfil Housing Association* [1997] N.P.C. 1; *Bankers Trust Co v Namdar* (unreported), C.A., February 14, 1997; *King v Jackson* [1998] 1 E.G.L.R. 30.

31 [1964] A.C. 993 at 1016.

32 5th edn (1998), p.580.

33 29th edn (1990), p.577.

34 *Plimmer v Mayor of Wellington* (1884) 9 App. Cas. 699 at 714, per Sir Arthur Hobhouse.

35 *Crabb v Arun District Council* [1976] Ch. 179 at 198, per Scarman L.J.

36 As *Snell* notes at p.578, with numerous examples.

37 Law Com. No.164, pp. 18–20, para.5.5.

3–37 None of the recent authorities referred to by counsel is determinative of this appeal. The defendants can derive some assistance from the recognition of the public policy principle in *Godden v Merthyr Tydfil Housing Association*, and the respondent can derive some comfort from general remarks in *McCausland v Duncan Lawrie Ltd* and *King v Jackson*, but in all three cases the observations were directed to a very different factual context. Nor can anything in the Law Commission's report (or its earlier working paper) be decisive. The report and the working paper are invaluable guides to the old law and to the problems which constituted the "mischief" at which section 2 of the Act of 1989 is directed, but they cannot be conclusive as to how section 2, as enacted, is to be construed and applied.

Proprietary Estoppel and Constructive Trusts

3–38 At a high level of generality, there is much common ground between the doctrines of proprietary estoppel and the constructive trust, just as there is between proprietary estoppel and part performance. All are concerned with equity's intervention to provide relief against unconscionable conduct, whether as between neighbouring landowners, or vendor and purchaser, or relatives who make informal arrangements for sharing a home, or a fiduciary and the beneficiary or client to whom he owes a fiduciary obligation. The overlap between estoppel and part performance has been thoroughly examined in the defendants' written submissions, with a survey of authorities from *Gregory v Mighell*[38] to *Take Harvest Ltd v Liu*.[39]

3–39 The overlap between estoppel and the constructive trust was less fully covered in counsel's submissions but seems to me to be of central importance to the determination of this appeal. Plainly there are large areas where the two concepts do not overlap: when a landowner stands by while his neighbour mistakenly builds on the former's land the situation is far removed (except for the element of unconscionable conduct) from that of a fiduciary who derives an improper advantage from his client. But in the area of a joint enterprise for the acquisition of land (which may be, but is not necessarily, the matrimonial home) the two concepts coincide. Lord Diplock's very well known statement in *Gissing v Gissing* brings this out:[40]

> "A resulting, implied or constructive trust—and it is unnecessary for present purposes to distinguish between these three classes of trust—is created by a transaction between the trustee and the cestui que trust in connection with the acquisition by the trustee of a legal estate in land, whenever the trustee has so conducted himself that it would be inequitable to allow him to deny to the cestui que trust a beneficial interest in the land acquired. And he will be held so to have conducted himself if by his words or conduct he has induced the cestui que trust to act to his own detriment in the reasonable belief that by so acting he was acquiring a beneficial interest in the land."

3–40 Similarly Lord Bridge of Harwich said in *Lloyds Bank Plc v Rosset*:[41]

> "The first and fundamental question which must always be resolved is whether, independently of any inference to be drawn from the conduct of the parties in the course of sharing the house as their home and managing their joint affairs, there has at any time prior to acquisition, or exceptionally at some later date, been any agreement, arrangement or understanding reached between them that the property is to be shared beneficially. The finding of an agreement or arrangement to share in this sense can only, I think, be based on evidence of express discussions between the partners, however imperfectly remembered and however imprecise their terms may have been. Once a finding to this effect is made it will only be necessary for the partner asserting the claim to a beneficial interest against the partner entitled to the legal estate to show that he or she has acted to his or her detriment or significantly altered his or her position in reliance on the agreement in order to give rise to a constructive trust or a proprietary estoppel."

3–41 It is unnecessary to trace the vicissitudes in the development of the constructive trust between these two landmark authorities, except to note the important observations made by Sir Nicolas Browne-Wilkinson V.C. in *Grant v Edwards* where he said:[42]

---

[38] (1811) 18 Ves. 328.
[39] [1993] A.C. 552.
[40] [1971] A.C. 886 at 905.
[41] [1991] 1 A.C. 107 at 132.
[42] [1986] Ch. 638 at 656.

"I suggest that in other cases of this kind, useful guidance may in the future be obtained from the principles underlying the law of proprietary estoppel which in my judgment are closely akin to those laid down in *Gissing v Gissing*.[43] In both, the claimant must to the knowledge of the legal owner have acted in the belief that the claimant has or will obtain an interest in the property. In both, the claimant must have acted to his or her detriment in reliance on such belief. In both, equity acts on the conscience of the legal owner to prevent him from acting in an unconscionable manner by defeating the common intention. The two principles have been developed separately without cross-fertilisation between them: but they rest on the same foundation and have on all other matters reached the same conclusions."

In this case the judge did not make any finding as to the existence of a constructive trust. He was not asked to do so, because it was not then seen as an issue in the case. But on the findings of fact which the judge did make it was not disputed that a proprietary estoppel arose, and that the appropriate remedy was the grant to Mr Yaxley, in satisfaction of his equitable entitlement, of a long leasehold interest, rent free, of the ground floor of the property. Those findings do in my judgment equally provide the basis for the conclusion that Mr Yaxley was entitled to such an interest under a constructive trust. The oral bargain which the judge found to have been made between Mr Yaxley and Mr Brownie Gotts, and to have been adopted by Mr Alan Gotts, was definite enough to meet the test stated by Lord Bridge in *Lloyds Bank Plc v Rosset*.[44] **3–42**

The Judge's Findings Revisited

Mr Laurence's arguments, although skilfully developed in different directions, were all based on the central submission that Mr Yaxley was attempting, in defiance of the legislative policy, to enforce a supposed contract which Parliament has declared to be void (and not merely unenforceable, as under the old law). **3–43**

Mr Allston did not accept the factual basis of this central submission. He said that his case below had been that Mr Yaxley's agreement with Mr Brownie Gotts was only a "gentleman's agreement" because there was never any intention to create legal relations. I have had great difficulty in trying to reconcile that with Mr Yaxley's pleaded case, which refers to Mr Alan Gotts being a party to an oral agreement between Mr Yaxley and Mr Brownie Gotts (it also pleads, in the alternative, that Mr Alan Gotts was well aware of representations made by his father to Mr Yaxley). I have also had great difficulty in reconciling what is now said on Mr Yaxley's behalf with the judge's findings of fact, in which he said that he "was satisfied that" Alan Gotts "adopted and knew full well about the original agreement made by Brownie Gotts" and that there had been, on the part of Mr Alan Gotts "very significant adoption and encouragement of the original agreement." **3–44**

It is to my mind very difficult to be sure whether the judge found that Mr Alan Gotts orally adopted an oral consensus reached between his father and Mr Yaxley, which all three of them intended to be binding, but which could not subsist as a valid contract solely because of section 2 of the Act of 1989. If the presence or absence of such a finding were of critical importance to the disposal of this appeal, I would be inclined to remit the matter to the County Court for further findings, despite the delay and expense which would be involved. I have, however, come to the conclusion that that course is not necessary, and that the appeal should be dismissed even if the parties did arrive at an oral consensus which they believed to be binding, but which was invalidated by section 2. **3–45**

The Saving in Section 2(5)

The true scope of the judge's findings became increasingly important during the hearing of the appeal as Mr Laurence developed his submissions as to the significance of the saving in section 2(5) for "the creation or operation of . . . constructive trusts." He submitted that the saving applies so as to preserve a constructive trust in a factual situation in which such a trust would have arisen under the old law; but that it does not raise or permit a constructive trust in a factual situation in which, under the old law, a purchaser under an oral contract might have relied on the doctrine of part performance. A purchaser under a supposed contract void for non-compliance with section 2 was therefore, he said, worse off than a claimant who could plead standing-by or encouragement on the defendant's part, and reliance and expenditure on his own part, but who could not and did not plead any oral offer and acceptance. Mr Laurence accepted that **3–46**

[43] [1971] A.C. 886.
[44] [1991] 1 A.C. 107, 132.

that result might appear surprising at first glance, but said that it necessarily followed from the policy to which section 2 gives effect.

3–47 On this point Mr Laurence relied by analogy on the decision of this court in *Lloyds Bank Plc v Carrick*.[45] Mrs Carrick was a widow who orally agreed with her brother-in-law, a builder, to sell her house and pay him the proceeds, for which he would provide her with a new house. She did so and moved into the new house, which remained in the brother-in-law's name; later he mortgaged it to the bank. Mrs Carrick's rights were postponed to the bank because they had not been registered as an estate contract. Morritt L.J., with whom Beldam L.J. and Sir Ralph Gibson agreed, said:[46]

> "In this case there was a trust of the maisonette for the benefit of Mrs Carrick precisely because there had been an agreement between her and Mr Carrick which, for her part, she had substantially if not wholly performed. As between her and Mr Carrick such trust subsisted at all times after November 1982. I agree with counsel for the bank that there is no room in those circumstances for the implication or imposition of any further trust of the maisonette for the benefit of Mrs Carrick. In *Lloyds Bank Plc v Rosset* there was no contract which conferred any interest in the house on the wife. As with all statements of principle the speech of Lord Bridge of Harwich must be read by reference to the facts of the case. So read there is nothing in it to suggest that where there is a specifically enforceable contract the court is entitled to superimpose a further constructive trust on the vendor in favour of the purchaser over that which already exists in consequence of the contractual relationship. It is true that on this footing the ultimate position of Mrs Carrick with the benefit of a specifically enforceable contract may be worse than it would have been if there had been no contract. But that is because she failed to do that which Parliament has ordained must be done if her interest is to prevail over that of the bank, namely to register the estate contract. Her failure in that respect cannot, in my view, justify the implication or imposition of a trust after the execution of the charge when the dealings between Mr Carrick and Mrs Carrick before such execution did not."

3–48 I do not consider that this passage assists Mr Laurence. *Lloyds Bank Plc v Carrick* was decided under the old law and, as Morritt L.J. observed, Mrs Carrick had the benefit of a specifically enforceable contract.[47] The specifically enforceable contract itself made Mrs Carrick's brother-in-law a trustee for her, and that left no room for the imposition of a further constructive trust. In this case, by contrast, Mr Yaxley did not have a specifically enforceable contract, and there is room for a constructive trust to operate so as to avoid injustice.

3–49 Moreover it is important to note that *Lloyds Bank Plc v Carrick* was concerned with land not registered under the Land Registration Act 1925, and with the protection of Mrs Carrick's rights against third parties, and whether they fell within some category of interest registerable under the Land Charges Act 1972. Mrs Carrick's counsel conceded that her rights constituted an estate contract. But in informal negotiations between persons who are not lawyers, the distinction between an agreement to sell property and an agreement to subject property to a trust may be far from clear (compare, for instance, *Hodgson v Marks*[48]). In the present case there was evidence that Mr Brownie Gotts said to Mr Yaxley that the ground floor would be his "for ever". There is no evidence that the parties discussed whether the objective was to be achieved by a conveyance which left the rest of the property as a "flying freehold", or by the grant of a long lease, or by a declaration of trust. It was only after judgment that those technicalities were addressed.

3–50 *Hodgson v Marks* was not cited in the course of argument, but it is well known to property lawyers. It was concerned partly with overriding interests under section 70(1)(g) of the Land Registration Act 1925 and partly with section 53 of the Law of Property Act 1925, to which Mr Laurence did refer briefly in the course of his argument. Section 53(1)(b) requires a trust of land to be created or evidenced in writing, but section 53(2) is in terms very similar to the saving at the end of section 2(5): "This section does not affect the creation or operation of resulting, implied or constructive trusts."

---

[45] [1996] 4 All E.R. 630.
[46] At 639.
[47] See also what Morritt L.J. said at 637.
[48] [1971] Ch. 892.

3–51 To recapitulate briefly: the species of constructive trust based on "common intention" is established by what Lord Bridge in *Lloyds Bank Plc v Rosset*,[49] called an "agreement, arrangement or understanding" actually reached between the parties, and relied on and acted on by the claimant. A constructive trust of that sort is closely akin to, if not indistinguishable from, proprietary estoppel. Equity enforces it because it would be unconscionable for the other party to disregard the claimant's rights. Section 2(5) expressly saves the creation and operation of a constructive trust.

3–52 I cannot accept that the saving should be construed and applied as narrowly as Mr Laurence contends. To give it what I take to be its natural meaning, comparable to that of section 53(2) of the Law of Property Act 1925 in relation to section 53(1), would not create a huge and unexpected gap in section 2. It would allow a limited exception, expressly contemplated by Parliament, for those cases in which a supposed bargain has been so fully performed by one side, and the general circumstances of the matter are such, that it would be inequitable to disregard the claimant's expectations, and insufficient to grant him no more than a restitutionary remedy.

3–53 To give the saving a narrow construction would not to my mind be a natural reading of its language. Moreover it would often require the court to embark on minute inquiries into informal negotiations, between parties acting without legal advice, in order to decide whether or not the parties' "agreement, arrangement or understanding" would have amounted to a complete and legally binding contract but for the single fatal defect of non-compliance with section 2. The course which this case has taken vividly illustrates the problems involved.

C. *The Creation of Trusts and the Law of Property Act 1925 Section 53(1)(b)*

i. The Effect of Section 53(1)(b)

3–54 The Law of Property Act 1925 s.53(1)(b) replaced the Statute of Frauds 1677 s.7 with fresh wording. Transactions within s.53(1)(b), unlike those within s.53(1)(a) or s.53(1)(c), need only be evidenced at some time by signed writing and they do not actually have to be carried out by signed writing if they are to be effective. It would seem that s.53(1)(a) needs to be construed as covering the creation of equitable interests in land other than equitable interests under a trust (e.g. equitable charges, restrictive covenants), leaving s.53(1)(b) to cover the creation of equitable interests in land under a trust.[50] This protects a landowner and his heirs from the perils of oral evidence and enables purchasers to know whether or not to pay the purchase money to at least two trustees.

3–55 A settlor may create a trust of land either by declaring that he himself will henceforth hold the land on specified trusts, or by conveying the land to trustees and declaring specified trusts on which the trustees are to hold the land. In both cases the declaration of the trusts must be in writing specifying the beneficiaries, the trust property, and the nature of the trusts,[51] but the writing may be comprised in linked documents.[52] Note that the trust is unenforceable, but not void, until the requisite written evidence is present,[53] or part performance of the trust occurs.[54]

---

[49] [1991] 1 A.C. 107 at 132.

[50] In view of LPA 1925 s.52(1), s.53(1)(a) cannot be restricted to legal interests and in order to prevent s.53(1)(a) from making s.53(1)(b) otiose, para.(b) should be construed in line with the maxim *generalia specialibus non derogant* (i.e. general clauses cannot derogate from special clauses), so that declarations of trust of land fall outside the scope of s.53(1)(a): *Hagan v Waterhouse* (1991) 34 N.S.W.L.R. 308 at 385–386.

[51] *Smith v Matthews* (1861) 3 De G. F. & J. 139; *Morton v Tewart* (1842) 2 Y. & C.Ch. Case 67.

[52] *Forster v Hale* (1798) 3 Ves. 696.

[53] *Rochefoucauld v Boustead* [1897] 1 Ch. 192 at 206; *Gardner v Rowe* (1828) 5 Russ. 258.

[54] LPA 1925 s.55(d).

3–56 The signed writing must be "by some person who is able to declare such trust." So, for example, the sub-section would be satisfied if A conveyed Blackacre to B and at the same time declared signed written trusts for C. Again, if T1 and T2 held property on trust for A for life, remainder to B, but with power for the trustees to declare new trusts in favour of C or his issue, then the sub-section would be satisfied if T1 and T2 exercised this power in signed writing. It has been assumed that the absence from s.53(1)(b), unlike s.53(1)(a) or (c), of an express reference to an agent precludes the settlor's agent from being "some person who is able to declare" a trust on the settlor's behalf (even if the settlor has authorised him, in writing, to do so). However this assumption may yet prove to be unfounded because the duly authorised agent may be regarded as "some person who is able to declare such trust."

3–57 The signatory should be the person who, at the time of the signature, would be the beneficial owner (or, perhaps, his agent) if no declaration of trust had been made.[55] So, if A declares himself trustee of land for B, then the relevant person would be A; and if, subsequently, B declares that he holds his equitable interest on trust for C, then the relevant person would be B.[56] However, if A conveys land to B and orally declares a trust for C, then subsequent written evidence of the trust signed by B satisfies s.53(1)(b).[57] It may well be, however, that until B signs such writing (or an act of part performance occurs) the land will be held on resulting or constructive trust for A,[58] and that A can dispose of his interest under this trust as he wishes (unless C has earlier acted to his detriment, e.g. by building on the land, with the result that A is estopped from denying C's equitable title).

3–58 If A conveys land or transfers other property to B to hold to A's order and on some later date A then tells B to hold on trust for C, then this amounts to A disposing of his subsisting equitable interest to C, a disposition that would be void under s.53(1)(c) unless in writing signed by A or his agent.[59]

3–59 Declarations of trust of property other than land or interests in land can be made orally since no special evidential or other requirements exist.[60] But care must be taken where A has an equitable interest in any property, of which he purports to declare himself trustee for X absolutely where X is of full capacity. In substance this apparent sub-trust is a disposition of A's subsisting equitable interest within s. 53(1)(c) because the head trustee, whom X can directly sue, is now holding on trust for X and not for A, who has no active duties to perform and so drops out of the picture.[61]

ii. The Consequences of Non-Compliance

3–60 If A either transfers land to B, or buys land in B's name, on an oral understanding with B that B will hold the land on trust for A, then case law assumes that A cannot subsequently prove the express trust by bringing signed writing into existence to satisfy s.53(1)(b),[62] and that this is something which must be done by B.[63] It would be monstrous if instead B fraudulently decided to keep the land for himself and relied on the statute to deny A's equitable interest, particularly given that the statute was

---

[55] T. G. Youdan, "Formalities for Trusts of Land and the Doctrine in *Rochefoucauld v Boustead*" [1984] C.L.J. 306 at pp. 316–320.
[56] *Tierney v Wood* (1854) 19 Beav. 330; *Kronheim v Johnson* (1877) 7 Ch.D. 60.
[57] *Gardner v Rowe* (1828) 5 Russ. 258; *Smith v Matthews* (1861) 3 De G. F. & J. 139; *Mountain v Styak* [1922] N.Z.L.R. 131. If the oral trusts had been for A himself then he would have an equitable interest under a constructive trust which he could then sub-settle: *Tierney v Wood* (1854) 19 Beav. 330.
[58] See para.3–64.
[59] *Grey v IRC* [1960] A.C. 1.
[60] *Paul v Constance* [1977] 1 W.L.R. 527 (a bank account, being a chose in action); *Rowe v Prance* [2000] W.T.L.R. 249 (boat).
[61] See para.3–86.
[62] *Hutchins v Lee* (1737) 1 Atk. 447; *Young v Peachy* (1741) 2 Atk. 255; *Re Duke of Marlborough* [1894] 2 Ch. 133.
[63] *Ambrose v Ambrose* (1716) 1 P. Wms. 321; *Smith v Matthews* (1861) 3 De G.F. & J. 139; *Gardner v Rowe* (1828) 5 Russ. 258; *Mountain v Styak* [1922] N.Z.L.R. 131.

enacted with the express purpose of preventing fraud. However, it seems that there are three possible ways that A can have his claim to the land recognised in such a case.

On one view,[64] A can accept that s.53(1)(b) prevents proof of the express trust, but he can then rely on s.53(2), on the basis that an equitable interest arises in his favour by operation of law, either under a resulting trust[65] (imposed in response to the fact that the land was conveyed gratuitously in circumstances where A did not intend to transfer any beneficial interest) or a constructive trust[66] (imposed because it would be unconscionable for B to keep the land for himself). **3–61**

Alternatively,[67] there is a valid trust, although it is unenforceable by virtue of s.53(1)(b), and A can rely on equity estopping B from raising the issue of unenforceability under s.53(1)(b), because otherwise B would be using statute as an instrument of fraud; hence the court will enforce the express trust notwithstanding A's failure to comply with the sub-section. This is the basis upon which the Court of Appeal decided *Rochefoucauld v Boustead*,[68] which is reproduced below.[69] **3–62**

In *Rochefoucauld*, Lindley L.J. invoked the equitable maxim "Equity will not allow a statute to be used as an instrument of fraud", but this maxim is not confined to cases in which the conveyance was itself fraudulently obtained. If A sells her two adjoining cottages to B for below market value, B orally agreeing to let her live in one cottage for the rest of her days, then B will be compelled to hold that cottage on trust for A for life if he subsequently changes his mind and tries to defeat her interest by relying on s.53(1)(b): "The fraud which brings the principle into play arises as soon as the absolute character of the conveyance is set up for the purpose of defeating the beneficial interest."[70] **3–63**

Where A's oral understanding with B is that B will hold the land on trust for C, B clearly cannot keep the land for himself. But what happens if A repents of his intention to benefit C? Can A claim that B holds the land for him, by arguing that his failure to satisfy s.53(1)(b) means that there is no completely constituted trust for C? If C can make no special proprietary estoppel claim by virtue of detrimental reliance,[71] then it seems that B does indeed hold the land on resulting trust for A,[72] if indeed, a constructive trust for A is not imposed on the land as a mechanism to prevent B from unconscionably taking the land for himself.[73] While B would be estopped from pleading s.53(1)(b) against A or C, A can argue that nothing should stop A from pleading s.53(1)(b) against C. It is true that A previously intended to make a gift of the beneficial interest to C but if A failed to comply with the requisite formalities then he cannot be forced to make good on his previous intention by perfecting his imperfect gift.[74] **3–64**

C might try to argue that the oral trust of land is valid, though unenforceable due to s.53(1)(b),[75] suggesting that if B wished to do so, then B could carry out the trust and sign the necessary writing.[76] **3–65**

---

[64] See, e.g. R. Chambers, *Resulting Trusts* (1997), pp. 25 and 34; P.J. Millett, "Restitution and Constructive Trusts" (1998) 114 L.Q.R. 399, p.402.
[65] *Hodgson v Marks* [1971] Ch. 892; *Davies v Otty (No.2)* (1865) 35 Beav. 208; *Haigh v Kaye* (1872) L.R. 7 Ch. 469.
[66] *Scheuerman v Scheuerman* (1916) 28 D.L.R. 223; *Bannister v Bannister* [1948] 2 All E.R. 133; *Binions v Evans* [1972] Ch. 359; *British Railways Board v Pickin* [1974] A.C. 765 at 795–796.
[67] W. Swadling, "A Hard Look at *Hodgson v Marks*" in P. Birks and F. Rose (eds), *Restitution and Equity: Resulting Trusts and Equitable Compensation* (2000); W. Swadling, "The Nature of the Trust in *Rochefoucauld v Boustead*" in C. Mitchell (ed.), *Constructive and Resulting Trusts* (2010).
[68] [1897] 1 Ch. 196 at 206, esp. at 208.
[69] At paras 3–68 ff.
[70] *Bannister v Bannister* [1948] 2 All E.R. 133 at 136; *Ungurian v Lesnoff* [1990] Ch. 206.
[71] See paras 2–78 ff.
[72] *Hodgson v Marks* [1971] Ch. 892.
[73] *Bannister v Bannister* [1948] 2 All E.R. 133; *Last v Rosenfeld* [1972] 2 N.S.W.L.R. 923 at 937.
[74] *Re Brooks' ST* [1939] 1 Ch. 993 at 999.
[75] *Gardner v Rowe* (1828) 5 Russ. 258; *Rochefoucauld v Boustead* [1897] 1 Ch. 196 at 206.
[76] *Ambrose v Ambrose* (1716) 1 P. Wms. 321; *Smith v Matthews* (1861) 3 De G.F. & J. 139; *Mountain v Styak* [1922] N.Z.L.R. 131.

However, A can reply that B's authority to sign the required writing can be revoked by A's notification to him or by A's death.[77] Once A has so notified B then it would fly in the face of the statute to allow C to adduce oral evidence to establish his interest. Thus, C cannot prove any unjust deprivation to justify the imposition of a constructive trust. After all, if A had orally declared himself trustee of the land for C, then C could not adduce oral evidence to establish his interest.[78] It should make no difference that A transferred the land to B and declared oral trusts for C, for if this did affect the outcome then there would hardly be any scope for the application of s.53(1)(b).[79]

3–66 It can be argued[80] that there should be no difference between (1) A simply conveying land to B with intent manifested by oral evidence to make an outright gift to B (effective in B's favour) and (2) A conveying land to B with intent manifested by oral evidence for B to hold on trust for C as intended donee of an equitable gift. However, s.53(1)(b) deliberately creates a difference in expressly requiring written evidence of trusts of land where legal title is in one person (B) and equitable title is in another (C), so that A's claim should prevail over C's claim. This evidence provides a paper trail to enable C to enforce his interest against B's executors after B's death.

3–67 So far, we have been concerned with a gratuitous conveyance by A to B for C. However, if A sells and conveys land to B at an undervalue (so losing all interest therein) on the express understanding that B will hold the land on trust to give effect to an equitable interest of C or to a licence conferred by A on C, then C has enforceable rights against B.[81] B is not allowed to claim that C's rights are unenforceable against him because this would be fraudulent.

ROCHEFOUCAULD v BOUSTEAD

Court of Appeal [1897] 1 Ch. 196

3–68 In 1868, the plaintiff owned coffee plantations in Ceylon, the Delmar Estates, that were managed for her by the defendant. The property was mortgaged and she was worried that her ex-husband might buy up the mortgage and foreclose. Hence she agreed with the defendant that he would buy the titles from the mortgagee at a price sufficient to cover the mortgage debt and expenses, and hold these for her on trust, subject to a lien for his expenditure. In 1873, the defendant bought the titles from the mortgagee, with the conveyance saying nothing of the trust for the plaintiff. Without her knowledge, however, he then mortgaged titles to the estates to secure his own borrowings. In 1894, the plaintiff sought a declaration that he had bought the titles as trustee for her, for an account of his dealings as trustee with the estates, and for payment of the amount found to be due. By then, the titles had already been sold, but the plaintiff alleged that the proceeds of sale were sufficient to repay the defendant all she owed him, and that a surplus remained, which he should pay her.

3–69 The defendant denied that he had bought the titles as trustee for the plaintiff, and said that in any case the alleged trusts could not be proved by any writing signed by him, and that the Statute of Frauds 1677 s.7, precluded the admission of oral evidence to make good the plaintiff's allegation. Kekewich J. heard the plaintiff's oral testimony but did not admit it into evidence, on the ground that he was precluded from doing so by section 7. Hence he found that the plaintiff had not proved that the defendant had agreed to hold the titles on trust for her, and dismissed the claim. The Court of Appeal held that Kekewich J. had been wrong to use section 7 to keep out the claimant's evidence. Admitting that evidence, the court held

---

77 *Rudkin v Dolman* (1876) 35 L.T. 791; *Scheurman v Scheurman* (1916) 52 S.C.R. 625 at 636.
78 *Wratten v Hunter* [1978] 2 N.S.W.L.R. 367; *Midland Bank v Dobson* [1986] 1 F.L.R. 171; *Gissing v Gissing* [1971] A.C. 886 at 905.
79 J.D. Feltham, "Informal Trusts and Third Parties" [1987] Conv. 246.
80 T.G. Youdan, "Informal Trusts and Third Parties: A Response" [1988] Conv. 267.
81 *Ashburn Anstalt v Arnold* [1989] Ch. 1; *Lyus v Prowsa Developments Ltd* [1982] 1 W.L.R. 1044. Since the enactment of the Contracts (Rights of Third Parties) Act 1999, C can also rely on the statute.

that it proved the plaintiff's case. The defendant also sought to rely on the six-year limitation period in the Trustee Act 1888 s.8(1)(b), which governed claims for breach of trust against constructive trustees, but the court held that the trust was express, so that no limitation period applied. Hence the court granted the relief sought.

LINDLEY L.J. delivered the judgment of the court (which consisted of LORD HALSBURY L.C., LINDLEY and A.L. SMITH L.JJ.): The question raised by this appeal is whether the plaintiff is entitled to an account from the defendant of the proceeds of sale of certain coffee estates in Ceylon. The estates in question are known as the Delmar estates. They formerly belonged to the plaintiff; they were mortgaged first to Barings and then to a Dutch company, and on May 27, 1873, they were sold and conveyed to the defendant. In form the conveyance was to him absolutely, but the plaintiff insists that the estates were conveyed to the defendant as a trustee for the plaintiff, subject, however, to the repayment to the defendant of the amount which he paid for them and of the expenses which he has incurred in managing the estates. The estates were sold by the defendant or his mortgagees many years ago without the knowledge of the plaintiff, and she says that the proceeds of sale were more than sufficient to repay to the defendant all his advances, and that a considerable surplus remained which the defendant ought to have paid over to her. The defendant, in answer to this claim, says (1.) the estates were conveyed to him, not as a trustee for the plaintiff, but as beneficial owner; (2.) the trusts alleged by the plaintiff cannot be proved by any writing signed by the defendant, and the Statute of Frauds affords a defence to the action; (3.) the plaintiff's claim, even if proved, is barred (a) by the defendant's bankruptcy, (b) by the Statute of Limitations, (c) by the plaintiff's laches, an the equitable doctrines applicable to delay independently of the statute. **3–70**

Kekewich J. decided against the plaintiff on the first ground—namely, that there was no trust in favour of the plaintiff. This view of the case rendered it unnecessary for him to consider the other defences. The plaintiff has appealed from this decision; and, as we have been unable to take the same view as the learned judge of the effect of the evidence, it will be necessary for us to deal with all the other defences relied upon by the defendant. **3–71**

The circumstances under which the Delmar estates were conveyed to the defendant are to be gathered from the verbal testimony of the plaintiff, the defendant, and Mr Duff, and a mass of correspondence both before and after the conveyance. The correspondence after the conveyance is relied upon by the plaintiff as being inconsistent with the defendant's contention that he acquired the estates for himself beneficially, free from any trust in favour of the plaintiff. **3–72**

[The Court then stated the leading facts in the history of the case, and examined the parties' correspondence, and summed up as follows:] We come, therefore, to the conclusion that the plaintiff has proved that the estates in question were conveyed to the defendant on May 27, 1873, upon trust for her, but subject to a charge in his favour in respect of all sums advanced by him in order to obtain the estates from the Dutch company in the first instance, and of all sums advanced by him in order to work them as coffee plantations after he had acquired them. **3–73**

This conclusion renders it necessary to consider whether the Statute of Frauds affords a defence to the plaintiff's claim. The section relied upon is s.7, which has been judicially interpreted in *Forster v Hale*[82] and *Smith v Matthews*.[83] According to these authorities, it is necessary to prove by some writing or writings signed by the defendant, not only that the conveyance to him was subject to some trust, but also what that trust was. But it is not necessary that the trust should have been declared by such a writing in the first instance; it is sufficient if the trust can be proved by some writing signed by the defendant, and the date of the writing is immaterial. It is further established by a series of cases, the propriety of which cannot now be questioned, that the Statute of Frauds does not prevent the proof of a fraud; and that it is a fraud on the part of a person to whom land is conveyed as a trustee, and who knows it was so conveyed, to deny the trust and claim the land himself. Consequently, notwithstanding the statute, it is competent for a person claiming land conveyed to another to prove by parol evidence that it was so conveyed upon trust for the claimant, and that the grantee, knowing the facts, is denying the trust and relying upon the form of conveyance and the statute, in order to keep the land himself. This doctrine was not established until some **3–74**

---

[82] (1798) 3 Ves. 696.
[83] (1861) 3 D. F. & J. 139.

time after the statute was passed. In *Bartlett v Pickersgill*[84] the trust was proved, and the defendant, who denied it, was tried for perjury and convicted, and yet it was held that the statute prevented the Court from affording relief to the plaintiff. But this case cannot be regarded as law at the present day. The case was referred to in *James v Smith*,[85] and was treated as still law by Kekewich J.; but his attention does not appear to have been called to *Booth v Turle*,[86] nor to *Davies v Otty (No.2)*,[87] both of which are quite opposed to *Bartlett v Pickersgill*. So is *Haigh v Kaye*.[88] The late Giffard L.J., one of the best lawyers of modern times, speaking of *Bartlett v Pickersgill*, said: "It seems to be inconsistent with all the authorities of this Court which proceed on the footing that it will not allow the Statute of Frauds to be made an instrument of fraud".[89] The case not only seems to be, but is, inconsistent with all modern decisions on the subject. See, in addition to those already mentioned, *Lincoln v Wright*,[90] where a conveyance absolute in form was held to be a mortgage only. See also *In re Duke of Marlborough*,[91] in which Stirling J. examined the authorities, and held that an assignment absolute in form was subject to a trust for the plaintiff.

3–75 The defence, based on the Statute of Frauds, is met by the plaintiff in two ways. First, she says that the documents signed by the defendant prove the existence of the trust alleged; secondly, she says that if those documents do not prove what the trust is with sufficient fulness and precision, the case is one of fraud which lets in other evidence, and that with the aid of other evidence the plaintiff's case is established. In our opinion the plaintiff is correct in this contention. We are by no means satisfied that the letters signed by the defendant do not contain enough to satisfy the Statute of Frauds. Whether this is so or not, the other evidence is admissible in order to prevent the statute from being used in order to commit a fraud; and such other evidence proves the plaintiff's case completely.

3–76 Counsel for the plaintiff contended that the Statute of Frauds had no application to lands in Ceylon. But, having regard to *Leroux v Brown*,[92] and to the language of s.7 of the Statute of Frauds, we are unable to see why the defendant should not be able to rely on that statute as a defence to any proceedings in this country having for their object the proof and enforcing of a trust, even of lands abroad. The statute relates to the kind of proof required in this country to enable a plaintiff suing here to establish his case here. It does not relate to lands abroad in any other way than this: it regulates procedure here, not titles to land in other countries. If, therefore, the statute afforded the defendant a defence, he would be entitled to the benefit of it. But, for the reasons above given, the statute affords him no protection.

3–77 Having come to the conclusion that the plaintiff has proved her case by evidence admissible by our law, it is necessary to consider the other defences raised. The first is bankruptcy. The defendant became bankrupt in 1879, and he obtained his discharge in May, 1880. The Bankruptcy Act then in force was the Act of 1869, and by s.49 of that Act bankrupt trustees were not discharged from the claims of their cestuis que trust. This defence, therefore, fails.

3–78 The next defence is the Statute of Limitations. The trust which the plaintiff has established is clearly an express trust within the meaning of that expression as explained in *Soar v Ashwell*.[93] The trust is one which both plaintiff and defendant intended to create. This case is not one in which an equitable obligation arises although there may have been no intention to create a trust. The intention to create a trust existed from the first. The defendant is not able in this case to claim the benefit of s.8 of the Trustee Act, 1888, and the statute which is applicable is the Judicature Act 1873 s.25, subs. 2, which enacts as follows: "No claim of a cestui que trust against his trustee for any property held on an express trust, or in respect of any breach of such trust, shall be held to be barred by any Statute of Limitations." The Statutes of Limitations, therefore, afford no defence if the plaintiff's action is to be regarded as one brought by a cestui que trust against his trustee seeking for an account of trust property. It was, however, urged by the defendant's counsel that this action was

---

[84] (1760) 1 Eden 515.
[85] [1891] 1 Ch. 384.
[86] (1873) L. R. 16 Eq. 182.
[87] (1865) 35 Beav. 208.
[88] (1871–1872) L. R. 7 Ch. 469.
[89] See *Heard v Pilley* (1868–1869) L. R. 4 Ch. 548 at 553.
[90] (1859) 4 De G. & J. 16.
[91] [1894] 2 Ch. 133.
[92] (1852) 12 C. B. 801.
[93] [1893] 2 Q. B. 390.

really one for an account by a mortgagor against a mortgagee in possession, and that so regarded one of the Statutes of Limitations was a bar to it. In support of this contention counsel cited *Locking v Parker*;[94] *In re Alison*.[95] These cases undoubtedly shew that a conveyance upon trust for sale to secure a sum advanced is regarded as a mortgage, and that although there may be a trust declared of the surplus in favour of the mortgagor the Statute of Limitations is a bar to an action brought by him for the surplus if his title to the land is barred before a sale by the mortgagee. The ground of these decisions is that the trusts were such that the mortgagor could not enforce them and compel a sale, but could only redeem. Those cases, however, shew that the mortgagor can as cestui que trust enforce the trust of the surplus after a sale if his title to the land is not barred before the sale takes place, as it was in *In re Alison*. *Banner v Berridge*,[96] which was also cited to support the view we are considering, merely shews that a mortgagee selling under a power of sale is not an express trustee of the surplus for the mortgagor in the absence of words creating a trust for him. The mortgagee in that case was a mortgagee of a ship, and he sold as such under his statutory power. The real transactions in those cases were mortgages, and were very different from the real transaction in this case. The real transaction here was a purchase by the defendant for the plaintiff; she claims relief, not as mortgagor, but as the defendant's cestui que trust, although she admits his lien on the property for his advances; she claims an account of his dealings and transactions with her property, and in particular an account of the money which he has obtained from it. This being the real nature of her claim, the cases to which we have alluded are not applicable to it, and the Statutes of Limitations are no bar to the action.

[The court also rejected the defence of laches, and concluded:] The appeal must be allowed and the judgment be reversed. It must be declared that the defendant purchased the Delmar estates as a trustee for the plaintiff, but subject to a charge for the amount paid to the Dutch company. An account must then be directed of the defendant's dealings and transactions with the Delmar estates. The account will be an account as between a trustee and his cestui que trust, not an account as between mortgagor and mortgagee, and there must be no account on the footing of wilful default. The defendant must be allowed all his advances and outlays, with colonial interest; but he ought only to be charged simple interest at 4 per cent on balances in his hands, unless it appears that he has made more. Minutes had better be prepared and signed, and, if necessary, they can be mentioned to the Court. The defendant must pay the costs of the action up to the hearing and the costs of the appeal. **3–79**

D. Dispositions of Equitable Interests and the Law of Property Act 1925 Section 53(1)(c)

For the purposes of s.53(1)(c), "equitable interest" comprises an interest in land or in personalty.[97] The sub-section was enacted to replace the Statute of Frauds 1677 s.9, which referred to "grants and assignments" rather than "dispositions" of equitable interests, but while "disposition" undoubtedly includes "grants and assignments",[98] its meaning is wider than this, and it takes in other types of transaction as well, as established in *Grey v IRC*,[99] which is reproduced below.[100] **3–80**

The sub-section provides that any transaction which amounts to a disposition must be in signed writing or it is void. In contrast to declarations of trusts of land under s.53(1)(b), written evidence of oral dealings with equitable interests that is created after the event will not rescue a disposition from the effects of non-compliance with s.53(1)(c), unless a signed document is executed that is itself capable **3–81**

[94] (1872–1873) L.R. 8 Ch. App. 30.
[95] (1879) 11 Ch.D. 284.
[96] (1881) 18 Ch.D. 254.
[97] Assumed in *Grey v IRC* [1960] A.C. 1; *Oughtred v IRC* [1960] A.C. 206; *Vandervell v IRC* [1967] 2 A.C. 291; and treated as well established in *Re Tyler's Fund Trusts* [1967] 1 W.L.R. 1269 at 1274. The context must oust LPA 1925 s.205(1)(ii), (x).
[98] *Halley v Law Society* [2003] W.T.L.R. 845 at [69] ff.
[99] [1960] A.C. 1.
[100] At paras 000.

of making a disposition: in this case, earlier oral attempts to dispose of the equitable interest will be void, but the document will itself take effect as a valid disposition as at the date when it is executed.[101] The signed writing may comprise linked documents.[102] If the assignee of an equitable interest is himself to hold the assigned equitable interest as a trustee, then the writing need not contain the particulars of the trust which may thus be communicated orally,[103] although if the interest is in land then some subsequent written evidence will be necessary to satisfy s.53(1)(b). If no communication of the particulars of the trust is made to the assignee taking as trustee, then the assigned interest will be held on resulting trust for the assignor, and any subsequent disposition by the assignor to a new beneficiary will fall within s.53(1)(c).

3–82 There is no disposition of a subsisting equitable interest when a legal owner with full beneficial ownership makes a declaration of trust. He does not have two estates, one legal and the other equitable, one of which he transfers to the beneficiary of the new trust; rather, his declaration of trust brings a new equitable interest into existence which did not exist before.[104] Hence s.53(1)(c) does not apply, and no evidential or other writing is needed except in the case of trusts of land which fall within s.53(1)(b).

3–83 In *Grey v IRC*,[105] the House of Lords held that a beneficiary's direction to his trustees to cease holding the trust property for him, and to hold it instead for a third party, is a disposition for the purposes of s.53(1)(c), so that it must be in signed writing or it will be void. However, it seems that where trustees hold property on a bare trust for B and, pursuant to B's direction, they transfer the property to a third party absolutely, then B's interest is extinguished and the third party obtains full legal and beneficial ownership so that there is no separate disposition by B of his equitable interest that requires compliance with s.53(1)(c). This is the ratio of *Vandervell v IRC*,[106] which is also reproduced below.[107]

3–84 It is hard to reconcile *Vandervell* and *Grey*. *Grey* holds that when B directs his trustees to hold for X, so that B no longer has his equitable interest and X acquires this equitable interest, B's direction must be in writing as it is a disposition for the purposes of s.53(1)(c). Yet *Vandervell* holds that when B directs his trustees to transfer a full beneficial interest to X, so that B no longer has his equitable interest and X acquires the legal and equitable interest together, this need not be in writing as it is not a disposition for the purposes of the sub-section. The situations are different in that X receives beneficial legal ownership rather than equitable ownership in the latter case, but from B's point of view the result is the same: he no longer has the equitable interest that he had before, and the value of this has moved to X. Hence one might have thought that beneficiaries in both cases need protection from the mischief at which the rule embodied by s.53(1)(c) is aimed.[108]

---

101 *Grey v IRC* [1958] Ch. 690 at 706–707. See too B. Green, "*Grey, Oughtred* and *Vandervell*—A Contextual Reappraisal" (1984) 47 M.L.R. 385 at 391–392.

102 *Re Danish Bacon Co Ltd Staff Pension Fund* [1971] 1 W.L.R. 248.

103 *Re Tyler's Fund Trusts* [1967] 1 W.L.R. 1269.

104 *Westdeutsche Landesbank v Islington LBC* [1996] A.C. 669 at 706. A person cannot hold property on trust for himself: *Re Cook* [1948] Ch. 212.

105 [1960] A.C. 1.

106 [1967] 2 A.C. 291.

107 At paras 3–100 ff.

108 In fact the two cases are even closer than this because in *Grey* the beneficiary directed his trustees to stop holding legal title to the shares in one capacity (trustees for him) and to start holding it in a different capacity (trustees for his grandchildren), so that it was as though the trustees transferred merged legal and equitable title from one hand to another. In other words, the beneficiary's direction in *Grey* did effectively move equitable and legal title at the same time, as in *Vandervell*. Cf. *Hoare Trustees v Gardner* [1979] Ch. 10: where a trustee stops holding property for one beneficiary and starts holding it for another, this ranks as a CGT disposal by one trustee to another even if the same individual is concerned.

It may be, however, that *Vandervell* should be understood as a case of overreaching. Looking at matters from B's viewpoint, he is not seeking to replace himself as beneficiary owning an equitable interest with someone else as owner of his subsisting equitable interest. Rather, he is authorising T to transfer legal beneficial ownership of the trust property to X freed and discharged from B's rights. In the case of an authorised sale of trust property to X, it is clear that B's equitable interest would be overreached, being detached from the trust property and attached to the proceeds of sale.[109] Where, instead, T holds property on trust for B or as B directs as absolute beneficial owner, then arguably a transfer by T to X of particular assets as directed by B should similarly overreach B's equitable interest in those assets.[110] **3–85**

Where property is held on trust for B, and he declares a sub-trust of his own equitable interest, most cases distinguish the situation where B remains in the picture as a trustee for X with active duties, and the situation where he is merely a bare trustee for a sui juris Y and accordingly "drops out out of the picture", leaving Y to enforce his equitable interest directly against T. So, for example, if B declares that he will hold his equitable interest on trust for such of J to Q as he may appoint, B remains in the picture with active trust duties, and this is viewed as a declaration of trust rather than a disposition of B's equitable interest. Hence s.53(1)(c) does not apply.[111] Conversely, if B declares himself trustee of his interest for a sui juris Y absolutely, then it has been said that this is a disposition of A's entire equitable interest which must therefore be in writing within s.53(1)(c).[112] However, the Court of Appeal has now cast doubt on the latter proposition in *Nelson v Greening & Sykes (Builders) Ltd*, Lawrence Collins L.J. holding that that even though "the practical effect" of declaring a sub-trust with no active trustee duties "would seem to amount to . . . 'getting rid' of the trust of the equitable interest then subsisting", this is "not the same as saying that as a matter of law it does get rid of the intermediate trust."[113] On this view s.53(1)(c) should never apply in cases where a sub-trust is declared. In principle, however, there are good reasons for thinking that the law should hold exactly the opposite, by focusing its attention on valuable disposals of beneficial interest, rather than disposals of equitable interest regardless of their value, and that whenever B carves a subsidiary equitable interest out of his own entitlement by declaring a sub-trust, this should always fall within s.53(1)(c) if it effects a transfer of beneficial ownership, regardless of whether it can also be said that B has disposed of his equitable interest by "dropping out of the picture".[114] **3–86**

What if a beneficiary B contracts with G to transfer his equitable interest to G? If B's equitable interest is in land, whether or not held on trust for sale, then all the terms of the contract must be in writing as required by s.2 of Law of Property (Miscellaneous Provisions) Act 1989. Otherwise, it seems writing is not required. Certainly, a contract to make a disposition of an equitable interest does not seem itself to be a disposition. However, it can be said that the constructive trusteeship imposed upon **3–87**

---

109 *State Bank of India v Sood* [1997] Ch. 276. See too C. Harpum, "Overreaching, Trustees' Powers, and the Reform of the 1925 Property Legislation" [1990] C.L.J. 277; D. Fox, "Overreaching" in P. Birks and A. Pretto (eds) *Breach of Trust* (2002); R.C. Nolan "Property in a Fund" (2004) 120 L.Q.R. 108, pp. 111–117; R.C. Nolan, "Understanding the Limits of Equitable Property" (2006) 1 Journal of Equity 18, pp. 24–28.

110 R. Nolan, "*Vandervell v IRC*: A Case of Overreaching" [2002] C.L.J. 169.

111 *Onslow v Wallis* (1849) 1 Mac. & G. 506 approved in *Re Lashmar* [1891] 1 Ch. 253. It seems that if B declares himself trustee for D for life, remainder to E, then if B's duty is as bare trustee to transfer actual income to D and then the actual capital assets to E, B will be regarded as a passive trustee: *Re Lashmar* [1891] 1 Ch. 258 at 269.

112 *Grainge v Wilberforce* (1889) 5 T.L.R. 436 at 437; *Re Lashmar* [1891] 1 Ch. 253; *Grey v IRC* [1958] Ch. 375 at 382, per Upjohn J., and [1958] Ch. 690 at 715, per Evershed M.R.; *Corin v Patton* (1990) 169 C.L.R. 540 at 579, per Deane J.; *ISPT Nominees Pty Ltd v Chief Commissioner of State Revenue* (2003) 53 A.T.R. 527 at [243]–[270].

113 [2008] 1 E.G.L.R. 59 at [57].

114 B. Green, "*Grey, Oughtred* and *Vandervell*—A Contextual Reappraisal" (1984) 47 M.L.R. 385, pp. 396–399; cf. P. Matthews, "All About Bare Trusts—Part 2" [2005] P.C.B. 336, pp. 336–340.

B when he enters into a specifically enforceable contract[115] to sell his equitable interest to G means that the trustees hold on trust for B who holds on constructive trust for G, so that if B is or becomes (after receipt of the purchase price) a simple bare trustee with no active duties to perform he disappears from the picture, leaving the trustees holding on trust for G. Thus B has effectively disposed of his equitable interest and this requires writing within s.53(1)(c).[116]

3–88 Against this, however, it can be said that s.53(2) states that s.53(1) is not to affect the creation or operation of constructive trusts, and that for this reason G can become owner of the equitable interest due to the constructive trust in his favour without the need for any s.53(1)(c) writing. This view has been taken by Upjohn J.,[117] Lord Radcliffe,[118] Megarry J.[119] and Goff and Shaw L.JJ.,[120] and it was held to be correct by the Court of Appeal in *Neville v Wilson*,[121] which is reproduced below.[122] In any event, as Lord Cohen has indicated,[123] once G has paid the purchase price to B, B cannot make any claim to the equitable interest; and similarly, in *Chinn v Collins* the House of Lords thought that the availability of specific performance and the creation of a constructive trust was immaterial in a case concerned with non-specifically enforceable contractual dealings relating to an equitable interest in shares, Lord Wilberforce asserting that:[124]

> "Dealings related to the equitable interest in these [shares] required no formality. As soon as there was an agreement for their sale accompanied or followed by payment of the price, the equitable title passed at once to the purchaser and all that was needed to perfect his title was notice to the trustee or the nominee."

3–89 It seems that there is a disposition for the purposes of the sub-section where there is a release or a surrender of a subsisting equitable interest[125] but not where there is a disclaimer.[126] Where a trustee or some third party has a power to declare that funds held on trust for B are henceforth to be held on trust for X, then surprisingly it seems that his exercise of this power does not constitute a disposition of B's interest for the purposes of s.53(1)(c), even though the effect is to strip B of his equitable interest and to move it to X.[127] Variations of trusts under the Variation of Trusts Act 1958 escape s.53(1)(c) either by implication under the 1958 Act, or by virtue of a constructive trust within s.53(2).[128] Also escaping s.53(1)(c) (and the Wills Act 1837) is the exercise of an employee's contractual right to nominate a person to receive moneys payable under a pension trust fund in the event of the employee's death in service, the reason being that there is no subsisting interest in property to dispose of.[129] Similarly, if L takes out a policy on his life where rights to a money payment only crystallise

---

115 See para.15–04 ff.
116 *Oughtred v IRC* [1960] A.C. 206 at 233, per Lord Denning.
117 *Oughtred v IRC* [1958] Ch. 383.
118 *Oughtred v IRC* [1960] A.C. 206 at 227–228.
119 *Re Holt's Settlement* [1969] 1 Ch. 100.
120 *DHN Food Distributors Ltd v Tower Hamlets LBC* [1976] 1 W.L.R. 852 at 865 and 867.
121 [1997] Ch. 144, followed in *Singh v Anand* [2007] EWHC 3346 (Ch).
122 At paras 3–108 ff.
123 *Oughtred v IRC* [1960] A.C. 206 at 230.
124 [1981] A.C. 533 at 548.
125 LPA 1925 s.205(1)(ii).
126 *Re Paradise Motor Co Ltd* [1968] 1 W.L.R. 1125: disclaimer "operates by way of avoidance and not by way of disposition". See also *Allied Dunbar Assurance Plc v Fowler* [1994] 25 Est. Gaz. 149 and LPA 1925 s.52(2)(b).
127 *Re Vandervell's Trusts (No.2)* [1974] Ch. 269
128 *Re Holt's ST* [1969] 1 Ch. 100.
129 *Re Danish Bacon Co Ltd Staff Pension Fund* [1971] 1 W.L.R. 248; *Baird v Baird* [1990] 2 A.C. 548.

on his death, there is no disposition of a subsisting equitable interest if he nominates X to receive the money and hold it on trust for Y and Z, and so he does not have to do this in writing.[130]

Section 53(1)(c) is also disapplied by reg.38(5) of the Uncertificated Securities Regulations 2001.[131] **3–90** The reason for this is that most shares in public companies are now dematerialised securities that are transferred through CREST.[132] This is an electronic share trading system owned and operated by CREST Co Ltd (which is owned by Euroclear Bank). While a public company may have a register of shareholders with certificates relating to their shares, the CREST records constitute a register of title. Thus an electronic transfer from one CREST member account to another operates to transfer legal title, e.g. from Cazenove & Co to Barclays Bank Trust Co, each of whose clients' interests are pooled in a single account, each client being given an equitable interest in the whole. If written documents were needed to effect the disposition of the clients' equitable interests each time a transfer was made, the practical utility of CREST would be seriously compromised, and so the 2001 Regulations have disapplied the sub-section in this situation.

GREY v INLAND REVENUE COMMISSIONERS

House of Lords [1960] A.C. 1; [1959] 3 W.L.R. 759; [1959] 3 All E.R. 603

On February 1, 1955, Hunter, as settlor, transferred 18,000 shares of £1 each to the appellants as nominees **3–91** for himself. The appellants were the trustees of six settlements, which Hunter had previously created. On February 18, 1955, Hunter orally directed the trustees to divide the 18,000 shares into six parcels of 3,000 shares each and to appropriate the parcels to the trusts of the six settlements, one parcel to each settlement. On March 25, 1955, the trustees executed six deeds of declaration of trust (which Hunter also executed in order to testify to the oral direction previously given by him) declaring that since February 18, 1955, they held each of the parcels of 3,000 shares on the trusts of the relevant settlement. The Commissioners of Inland Revenue assessed the deeds of declaration of trust to ad valorem stamp duty on the basis that the oral declaration did not effectively create trusts of the shares, so that it was the subsequent deeds that created trusts of the shares and were stampable as instruments transferring an interest in property: they were not exempt as merely confirming an earlier effective transfer. A majority of the Court of Appeal upheld this view, and the trustees' appeal was unanimously dismissed by the House of Lords.

VISCOUNT SIMONDS (with whom LORD REID agreed, stated the facts, continued): These facts give rise **3–92** to the plain question whether the oral directions given by Mr Hunter, which are recited in each of the instruments, were effective or were, having regard to section 53(1)(c) of the Law of Property Act, 1925, wholly ineffective. In the former event the instruments would not, and in the latter would, be chargeable with ad valorem duty. . . .

Briefly, then, were the several oral directions given by Mr Hunter dispositions by him of the equitable **3–93** interest in the shares held by the appellants as nominees for him?

If the word "disposition" is given its natural meaning, it cannot, I think, be denied that a direction given **3–94** by Mr Hunter, whereby the beneficial interest in the shares theretofore vested in him became vested in another or others, is a disposition. But it is contended by the appellants that the word "disposition" is to be given a narrower meaning and (so far as relates to inter vivos transactions) be read as if it were synonymous with "grants and assignments" and that, given this meaning, it does not cover such a direction as was given in this case. As I am clearly of the opinion, which I understand to be shared by your Lordships, that there is no justification for giving the word "disposition" a narrower meaning than it ordinarily bears, it will be unnecessary to discuss the interesting problem that would otherwise arise. It was for this reason

[130] *Gold v Hill* [1999] 1 F.L.R. 54.
[131] S.I. 2001/3755.
[132] J. Benjamin and M. Yates, *The Law of Global Custody* (2nd edn, 2002), Ch.9.

that your Lordships did not think it necessary to hear learned counsel for the appellants in reply on this part of the case.

3–95 My Lords, the argument for narrowing the meaning of "disposition" was that the Law of Property Act 1925, was a consolidating Act, that among the Acts which it consolidated was the Statute of Frauds (29 Car.2, c.3) s.9, that that section enacted that "all grants and assignments of any trust or confidence shall likewise be in writing, signed by the party granting or assigning the same, or by such last will or devise, or else shall likewise be utterly void and of none effect," and that therefore the word "disposition" in section 53(1)(c) of the Act of 1925 is to be given the same meaning as would be given to "grants and assignments" in section 9 of the Statute of Frauds.

3–96 My Lords, the principles applicable to the construction of a consolidating Act are not in doubt. The presumption is that such an Act is not intended to alter the law, but this prima facie view must yield to plain words to the contrary.[133] If the Law of Property Act 1925 was a typical consolidating Act, the question would be whether the alteration from "grants and assignments" to "disposition" changed the law by enlarging the area of void transactions—a question that might not be easy to answer. But the Act of 1925 cannot be thus regarded . . .

3–97 LORD RADCLIFFE (with whom LORD COHEN and LORD KEITH agreed): My Lords, if there is nothing more in this appeal than the short question whether the oral direction that Mr Hunter gave to his trustees on February 18, 1955, amounted in any ordinary sense of the words to a "disposition of an equitable interest or trust subsisting at the time of the disposition", I do not feel any doubt as to my answer. I think that it did. Whether we describe what happened in technical or in more general terms, the full equitable interest in the eighteen thousand shares concerned, which at that time was his, was (subject to any statutory invalidity) diverted by his direction from his ownership into the beneficial ownership of the various equitable owners, present and future, entitled under his six existing settlements . . .

3–98 In my opinion, it is a very nice question whether a parol declaration of trust of this kind was or was not within the mischief of section 9 of the Statute of Frauds. The point has never, I believe, been decided and perhaps it never will be. Certainly it was long established as law that while a declaration of trust respecting land or any interest therein required writing to be effective a declaration of trust respecting personalty did not. Moreover, there is warrant for saying that a direction to his trustee by the equitable owner of trust property prescribing new trusts of that property was a declaration of trust. But it does not necessarily follow from that that such a direction, if the effect of it was to determine completely or pro tanto the subsisting equitable interest of the maker of the direction, was not also a grant or assignment for the purposes of section 9 and therefore required writing for its validity. Something had to happen to that equitable interest in order to displace it in favour of the new interests created by the direction: and it would be at any rate logical to treat the direction as being an assignment of the subsisting interest to the new beneficiary or beneficiaries or, in other cases, a release or surrender of it to the trustee.

3–99 I do not think, however, that that question has to be answered for the purposes of this appeal. It can only be relevant if section 53(1) of the Law of Property Act 1925 is treated as a true consolidation of the three sections of the Statute of Frauds concerned and as governed, therefore, by the general principle, with which I am entirely in agreement, that a consolidating Act is not to be read as effecting changes in the existing law unless the words it employs are too clear in their effect to admit of any other construction. But, in my opinion, it is impossible to regard section 53 of the Law of Property Act 1925 as a consolidating enactment in this sense.

VANDERVELL v INLAND REVENUE COMMISSIONERS

House of Lords [1967] 2 A.C. 291; [1967] 2 W.L.R. 97; [1967] 1 All ER 1

3–100 In 1958 Vandervell decided to make a gift to the Royal College of Surgeons to found a chair of pharmacology. At that time 100,000 shares in a private company which he controlled were held by a bank as trustee by way of security for annual payments made to his former wife. On November 5, 1958, a deed of variation

[133] See *Gilbert v Gilbert* [1928] P. 1 at 8, per Scrutton L.J.

was executed and, on the substitution of other securities, the shares in question were released and held by the bank in trust for Vandervell. He then decided to use the shares as a vehicle for making his gift to RCS: the shares would be transferred to the college and dividends sufficient to provide the gift would then be declared on the shares. The reason was that if Vandervell had instead caused the company to pay the dividends to him directly, so that he could pay the money to RCS himself, then he would have been assessed to surtax on the dividend income. Once the dividends had been declared, however, Vandervell wanted the RCS to release the shares to a trustee company which acted as trustee of a settlement he had made in favour of his children. Hence it was arranged that the shares would be transferred to RCS subject to an option to purchase them for £5,000 vested in the trustee company.

Vandervell orally directed the bank to transfer full legal and beneficial ownership of the shares to RCS, and during the tax years 1958–59 and 1959–60 dividends on the shares, amounting to £162,500 and £87,500, respectively, were paid. In October, 1961, the trustee company then exercised its option and paid RCS £5,000 for the shares. Vandervell was then assessed to surtax on the dividends on the basis that the transaction amounted to a settlement of property of which he had not absolutely divested himself, so that the dividends fell to be treated for surtax purposes as his income and not that of any other person. The special commissioners confirmed the assessments, and their decision was affirmed by Plowman J. and the Court of Appeal. On appeal, a majority of the House of Lords (Lord Pearce, Lord Upjohn, and Lord Wilberforce; Lord Reid and Lord Donovan dissenting) held that Vandervell was liable to pay surtax. His direction to the bank to transfer full beneficial ownership of the shares to the RCS had not been a disposition for the purposes of the Law of Property Act 1925 s.53(1)(c), and so this direction had been effective to divest Vandervell of his equitable interest even though it had been made orally. However, the IRC successfully made the alternative argument that Vandervell had continued to have an equitable interest in the shares during the relevant period because the option to purchase the shares that was vested in the trustee company had been held on a resulting trust for Vandervell. **3–101**

The following extracts from the speeches in the House of Lords concern the s.53(1)(c) point only, i.e. whether the transfer by the bank of the legal title to shares carried with it Vandervell's equitable interest although his direction had not been put in writing. **3–102**

LORD UPJOHN: . . . the object of the section, as was the object of the old Statute of Frauds, is to prevent hidden oral transactions in equitable interests in fraud of those truly entitled, and making it difficult, if not impossible, for the trustees to ascertain who are in truth the beneficiaries. When the beneficial owner, however, owns the whole beneficial estate and is in a position to give directions to his bare trustee with regard to the legal as well as the equitable estate there can be no possible ground for invoking the section where the beneficial owner wants to deal with the legal estate as well as the equitable estate. **3–103**

I cannot agree with Diplock L.J. that prima facie a transfer of the legal estate carries with it the absolute beneficial interest in the property transferred; this plainly is not so, e.g. the transfer may be on a change of trustee; it is a matter of intention in each case. If, however, the intention of the beneficial owner in directing the trustee to transfer the legal estate to X is that X should be the beneficial owner, I can see no reason for any further document or further words in the document assigning the legal estate also expressly transferring the beneficial interest; the greater includes the less. X may be wise to secure some evidence that the beneficial owner intended him to take the beneficial interest in case his beneficial title is challenged at a later date but it certainly cannot, in my opinion, be a statutory requirement that to effect its passing there must be some writing under section 53(1)(c). **3–104**

Counsel for the Crown admitted that where the legal and beneficial estate was vested in the legal owner and he desired to transfer the whole legal and beneficial estate to another he did not have to do more than transfer the legal estate and he did not have to comply with section 53(1)(c); and I can see no difference between that case and this. **3–105**

As I have said, that section is, in my opinion, directed to cases where dealings with the equitable estate are divorced from the legal estate and I do not think any of their Lordships in *Grey v IRC*[134] and *Oughtred v IRC*[135] had in mind the case before your Lordships. To hold the contrary would make assignments unnecessarily **3–106**

[134] [1960] A.C. 1.
[135] [1960] A.C. 206.

complicated; if there had to be assignments in express terms of both legal and equitable interests that would make the section more productive of injustice than the supposed evils it was intended to prevent . . .

3–107 LORD WILBERFORCE: On November 14, 1958, the taxpayer's solicitor received from the bank a blank transfer of the shares, executed by the bank, and the share certificate. So at this stage the taxpayer was the absolute master of the shares and only needed to insert his name as transferee in the transfer and to register it to become the full legal owner. He was also the owner in equity. On November 19, 1958, the solicitor . . . on behalf of the taxpayer, who intended to make a gift, handed the transfer to the College, which in due course, sealed it and obtained registration of the shares in the College's name. The case should then be regarded as one in which the taxpayer himself has, with the intention to make a gift, put the College in a position to become the legal owner of the shares, which the College in fact became. If the taxpayer had died before the College had obtained registration, it is clear on the principle of *Re Rose*[136] that the gift would have been complete, on the basis that he had done everything in his power to transfer the legal interest, with an intention to give, to the College. No separate transfer, therefore, of the equitable interest ever came to or needed to be made and there is no room for the operation of the subsection. What the position would have been had there simply been an oral direction to the legal owner (viz. the bank) to transfer the shares to the College, followed by such a transfer, but without any document in writing signed by the taxpayer as equitable owner, is not a matter which calls for consideration here . . .

NEVILLE v WILSON

Court of Appeal [1997] Ch. 144, [1996] 3 W.L.R. 460, [1996] 3 All E.R. 171

3–108 NOURSE L.J. (giving the judgment of the court to which NOURSE, ROSE and ALDOUS L.JJ. all contributed): . . . in about April 1969 the shareholders of JEN entered into an agreement with one another for the informal liquidation of JEN as contended for by Mr Jacob and thus, as part of it, for the division of JEN's equitable interest in the 120 ordinary shares in UEC registered in the names of the widow and Mr Wilson amongst themselves, as Mr Hyde put it, "on a shareholding basis"; in other words, in proportions corresponding to their existing shareholdings. . . . In consequence, JEN's equitable interest in the shares would, as the plaintiffs now claim, be divided amongst the shareholders in the proportions: 104 for the trustees of the will of the testator, and 4 each for the widow, Mr Neville, Mrs Hill and Mrs Wilson.

3–109 The effect of the agreement, more closely analysed, was that each shareholder agreed to assign his interest in the other shares of JEN's equitable interest in exchange for the assignment by the other shareholders of their interests in his own aliquot share. Each individual agreement having been a disposition of a subsisting equitable interest not made in writing, there then arises the question whether it was rendered ineffectual by s.53 of the Law of Property Act 1925 . . .

3–110 The simple view of the present case is that the effect of each individual agreement was to constitute the shareholder an implied or constructive trustee for the other shareholders, so that the requirement for writing contained in sub-s.(1)(c) of s.53 was dispensed with by sub-s.(2). That was the view taken by Upjohn J. at first instance and by Lord Radcliffe in the House of Lords in *Oughtred v IRC*. In order to see whether it is open to us to adopt it in this court, we must give careful consideration to those views and to the other speeches in the House of Lords.

In *Oughtred v IRC*[137] a mother and son were the tenant for life and absolute reversioner respectively
3–111 under a settlement of shares in a private company. By an oral agreement made on 18 June 1956 they agreed that on 26 June the son would exchange his reversionary interest under the settlement for shares in the same company owned by the mother absolutely, to the intent that her life interest in the settled shares should be enlarged into an absolute interest. On 26 June the mother and the son released the

[136] [1949] Ch. 78. [Note, however, that in *Re Rose* the taxpayer was entitled legally and equitably to the shares and did all he could to transfer them by executing a share transfer and delivering the transfer and the share certificate to the donee. Vandervell was only equitably entitled and to say that he had done all he could to vest the shares in the College was to beg the s. 53(1)(c) question of what was required of an owner of a subsisting equitable interest to achieve a disposition of that interest in the first place.]

[137] [1960] A.C. 206.

trustees by a deed which recited, amongst other things, that the settled shares were "accordingly now held in trust for [the mother] absolutely", and that it was intended to transfer them to her. On the same day the trustees transferred the settled shares to the mother by deed, the consideration being expressed to be ten shillings. It was held by Lord Keith of Avonholm, Lord Denning and Lord Jenkins, (Lord Radcliffe and Lord Cohen dissenting), that the transfer was assessable to ad valorem stamp duty. The basis of decision adopted by the majority was that, even if the oral agreement was effective to pass the equitable interest in the settled shares to the mother, the transfer, as the instrument by which the transaction was completed, was none the less a conveyance on sale within s.54 of the Stamp Act 1891.

Upjohn J., having said that s.53(2) of the 1925 Act was a complete answer to the argument that s.53(1)(c) applied, continued:[138] **3–112**

> "This was an oral agreement for value, and, accordingly, on the making thereof Peter the vendor became a constructive trustee of his equitable reversionary interest in the trust funds for the appellant. No writing to achieve that result was necessary, for an agreement of sale and purchase of an equitable interest in personalty (other than chattels real) may be made orally, and s.53 has no application to a trust arising by construction of law."

Lord Radcliffe, having expressed the view that the judgment of Upjohn J. was correct and agreeing with his reasons, said:[139] **3–113**

> "The reasoning of the whole matter, as I see it, is as follows: On June 18, 1956, the son owned an equitable reversionary interest in the settled shares; by his oral agreement of that date he created in his mother an equitable interest in his reversion, since the subject-matter of the agreement was property of which specific performance would normally be decreed by the court. He thus became a trustee for her of that interest *sub modo;* having regard to sub-s.(2) of s.53 of the Law of Property Act, 1925, sub-s.(1) of that section did not operate to prevent that trusteeship arising by operation of law."

Lord Cohen, the other member of the minority, said:[140] **3–114**

> "Before your Lordships, counsel for the Crown was prepared to agree that, on the making of the oral agreement, Peter became a constructive trustee of his equitable reversionary interest in the settled funds for the appellant, but he submitted that, none the less, s. 53(1)(c) applied and, accordingly, Peter could not assign that equitable interest to the appellant except by a disposition in writing. My Lords, with that I agree, but it does not follow that the transfer was a conveyance of that equitable interest on which ad valorem stamp duty was payable under the Stamp Act, 1891."

Having held that the transfer was not such a conveyance, he dissented on that ground.

Lord Denning said:[141] **3–115**

> "I do not think it necessary to embark on a disquisition on constructive trusts; because I take the view that, even if the oral agreement of June 18, 1956, was effective to transfer Peter's reversionary interest to his mother, nevertheless, when that oral agreement was subsequently implemented by the transfer, then the transfer became liable to stamp duty. But I may say that I do not think the oral agreement was effective to transfer Peter's reversionary interest to his mother. I should have thought that the wording of s.53(1)(c) of the Law of Property Act 1925 clearly made a writing necessary to effect a transfer, and s.53(2) does not do away with that necessity."

---

138 [1958] Ch. 383 at 390.
139 [1960] A.C. 206 at 227.
140 [1960] A.C. 206 at 230.
141 [1960] A.C. 206 at 233.

3–116 The views of their Lordships as to the effect of s.53 can be summarised as follows. Lord Radcliffe, agreeing with Upjohn J., thought that sub-s.(2) applied. He gave reasons for that view. Lord Cohen and Lord Denning thought that it did not. Although neither of them gave reasons, they may be taken to have accepted the submissions of Mr. Wilberforce QC.[142] Lord Keith and Lord Jenkins expressed no view either way. We should add that when the case was in this court, Lord Evershed M.R., in delivering the judgment of himself, Morris and Ormerod L.JJ., said:[143]

> "In this court the case for the Crown has, we think, been somewhat differently presented, and in the end of all, the question under s.53 of the Law of Property Act [1925] does not, in our judgment, strictly call for a decision. We are not, however, with all respect to the learned judge, prepared to accept, as we understand it, his conclusion on the effect of s.53 of the Law of Property Act."

The basis of this court's decision was the same as that adopted by the majority of the House of Lords.

3–117 We do not think that there is anything in the speeches in the House of Lords which prevents us from holding that the effect of each individual agreement was to constitute the shareholder an implied or constructive trustee for the other shareholders. In this respect we are of the opinion that the analysis of Lord Radcliffe, based on the proposition that a specifically enforceable agreement to assign an interest in property creates an equitable interest in the assignee, was unquestionably correct.[144] A greater difficulty is caused by Lord Denning's outright rejection of the application of s.53(2), with which Lord Cohen appears to have agreed.

3–118 So far as it is material to the present case, what sub-s.(2) says is that sub-s.(1)(c) does not affect the creation or operation of implied or constructive trusts. Just as in *Oughtred v IRC* the son's oral agreement created a constructive trust in favour of the mother, so here each shareholder's oral or implied agreement created an implied or constructive trust in favour of the other shareholders. Why then should sub-s.(2) not apply? No convincing reason was suggested in argument and none has occurred to us since. Moreover, to deny its application in this case would be to restrict the effect of general words when no restriction is called for, and to lay the ground for fine distinctions in the future. With all the respect which is due to those who have thought to the contrary, we hold that sub-s.(2) applies to an agreement such as we have in this case.

3–119 For these reasons, we have come to the conclusion that the agreement entered into by the shareholders of JEN in about April 1969 was not rendered ineffectual by s.53 of the 1925 Act.

4. Post Mortem Trusts: Secret Trusts

A. General

3–120 The doctrine of secret trusts developed as a product of equity not allowing statutes to be used as an instrument of fraud.[145] It has already been seen that statutes prescribe certain formalities for declarations of trust respecting land and for dispositions of equitable interests.[146] In addition, s.9 of the Wills Act 1837, set out below,[147] prescribes special formalities for the validity of testamentary dispositions, while the Administration of Estates Act 1925 lays down rules of intestate succession. Where a person has been induced to die intestate leaving X as his intestate successor,[148] or to leave property by will to X, on the secret oral understanding that X will hold the property on trust for B, it would allow

---

142 See [1960] A.C. 206 at 220–222.
143 [1958] Ch. 678 at 687.
144 Cf. *London and South Western Rly Co v Gomm* (1882) 20 Ch.D. 562 at 581, per Jessel M.R.
145 *Jones v Badley* (1868) 3 Ch. App.3 62 at 364; *McCormick v Grogan* (1869) L.R. 4 H.L. 82 at 88–89; *Blackwell v Blackwell* [1929] A.C. 318 at 336–337.
146 Law of Property Act 1925 s.53.
147 At para.3–129.
148 *Sellack v Harris* (1708) 2 Eq.Ca.Ab. 46.

statute to be used as an instrument of fraud by X if X were permitted to retain the property beneficially, instead of taking merely as trustee. Accordingly, equity treats X as a trustee despite the absence of the requisite formalities.

Secret trusts most commonly concern trusts engrafted on wills and in this context it is most important to distinguish between (1) fully secret trusts, (2) half-secret trusts, and (3) cases where the probate doctrine of incorporation by reference arises. Examples of each, where X has agreed to hold on trust for B, are (1) "I devise Blackacre to X absolutely"; (2) "I devise Blackacre to X upon trusts which I have communicated to him"; and (3) "I devise Blackacre to X upon trusts which I have communicated to him by letter dated November 11, 2008." **3–121**

In this last example, since the will refers to a written instrument, already existing at the date of the will, in such terms that the written instrument can be ascertained, the requirements of the doctrine of incorporation are satisfied.[149] Consequently the incorporated document will be admitted to public probate as part of the testator's will, the will's compliance with the requirements of s.9 of the Wills Act being sufficient to cover the unattested written instrument referred to in the will. It will be seen that the application of the doctrine of incorporation renders the imposition of a secret trust unnecessary as the requisite formalities for an express trust are present, preventing any possibility of fraud upon X's part. **3–122**

Testators, today, who do not want their testamentary wishes to become public by admission to probate as part of their will, can take advantage of the doctrine of secret trusts to make provision for people or organisations that they do not wish to appear to be helping. Indecisive, aged testators can also leave everything by will absolutely to their solicitors, from time to time calling upon or phoning their solicitors with their latest wishes. It is often assumed by legal writers that secret trusts are no longer much used in practice, but an empirical survey of private client practitioners carried out in 2001 showed that in fact they are still used quite frequently.[150] **3–123**

Proving secret trusts can be a problem, though the standard of proof is the ordinary civil standard on a balance of probabilities unless fraud is involved when a higher standard is required.[151] A good practical precaution is for the testator to have a document signed by the intended trustee put into the possession of the secret beneficiaries. **3–124**

The obligation on the secret trustee, T, may be a simple obligation to transfer the bequeathed property to X, or to hold the property on trusts (whether of a fixed interest or discretionary nature) for specified beneficiaries, or to pass the property by will on to Z after T has had the income or use of the property during T's lifetime,[152] or to pass by will to Z whatever remains of the property after bona fide resort to it by T in his lifetime.[153] **3–125**

B. *Fully Secret Trusts*

A fully secret trust is one where neither the existence of the trust nor its terms are disclosed by the will.[154] **3–126**

Suppose that a testator makes a valid will bequeathing or devising property to X, apparently beneficially, but communicates to X his intention that X is to hold the property on certain trusts or subject to certain conditions or charges, and X accepts this, either expressly by promise or impliedly by silence. In these circumstances, oral evidence is admissible to prove both the existence and the terms of the **3–127**

149 *In the Goods of Smart* [1902] P. 238; *Re Jones* [1942] Ch. 328, restricted by *Re Edwards WT* [1948] Ch. 440.
150 R. Meager, "Secret Trusts: Do They Have a Future?" [2003] Conv. 203.
151 *Re Snowden, deceased* [1979] Ch. 528 at 537 (disagreeing with *Ottaway v Norman* [1972] Ch. 698 at 712).
152 *Howell v Hyde* (2003) 47 ACSR 230, so if T does not retain shares in a company as required but sells them and buys new shares the beneficiaries can claim the new shares.
153 *Ottaway v Norman* [1972] Ch. 698.
154 It can also arise in cases of intestacy: *Sellack v Harris* (1708) 2 Eq. Ca. Ab. 46.

trust or conditions or charges which, if clearly proved, X will be compelled to carry out. This is the ratio of *Ottaway v Norman*,[155] which is reproduced below.[156]

3–128 Nothing short of an express or implied acceptance by X will raise a trust.[157] Communication and acceptance must be of a definite legally binding obligation of X, not of a mere hope or confidence expressed by the testator.[158] Communication and acceptance[159] may be effected at any time during the life of the testator, whether before or after the execution of the will and communication may be made through an agent.[160] *Re Keen*,[161] reproduced below,[162] shows that communication may also be made by handing to X a sealed envelope containing the terms of the trust, and requiring X not to open it until after the testator's death. Meanwhile *Re Boyes*[163] shows that if X is told in the testator's lifetime that he is to hold the property on trust, but is not informed of the terms of the trust, he holds the property on a resulting trust for the testator's residuary legatee or devisee, or if there is no such person, or the property is residuary property, then for the testator's intestate successors.[164] If X is not so told then he takes the property beneficially for himself, as is also the case if X is told that he is to take the property subject to a condition or charge but is not informed of the terms of the condition or charge.

WILLS ACT 1837 SECTION 9[165]

3–129 No will shall be valid unless—

(a) it is in writing, and signed by the testator, or by some other person in his presence and by his direction; and

(b) it appears that the testator intended by his signature to give effect to the will; and

(c) the signature is made or acknowledged by the testator in the presence of two or more witnesses present at the same time; and

(d) each witness either—

  (i) attests and signs the will; or
  (ii) acknowledges his signature, in the presence of the testator (but not necessarily in the presence of any other witness), but no form of attestation shall be necessary.

---

155 [1972] Ch. 698.

156 At paras 3–130 ff.

157 *Wallgrave v Tebbs* (1855) 2 K. & J. 313.

158 See *Att.-Gen. v Chamberlain* (1904) 90 L.T. 581; *Re Snowden, deceased* [1979] Ch. 528 at 534; *Kasperbauer v Griffith* [2000] W.T.L.R. 333 at 343.

159 The full extent of the property to be covered by the obligation must be communicated and accepted so that where a secret trust for a £5,000 legacy has been communicated to and accepted by the trustee, and the legacy is increased by £5,000 in a further codicil but nothing is said to the trustee, then the further £5,000 is not caught by the secret trust: *Re Colin Cooper, deceased* [1939] Ch. 580 at 811. The further £5,000 is taken beneficially by the fully secret "trustee".

160 *Moss v Cooper* (1861) 1 J. & H. 352. If the agent were unauthorised but the legatee did not approach the testator to clarify the matter would this amount to acquiescence?

161 [1937] Ch. 236.

162 At paras 3–149 ff.

163 (1884) 26 Ch.D. 531.

164 If X himself is the residuary beneficiary or next-of-kin then it seems the court should not impose an arbitrary salutary rule removing all temptation to make self-serving statements by prohibiting X from taking qua residuary beneficiary or next-of-kin. Only if X appeared to be lying and it was impossible to ascertain the trust terms should public policy prevent X from obtaining any advantage from his own wrong and pass the property to the person who would have taken under the intestacy rules if X had not survived the testator. Cf. *Re Sigsworth* [1935] Ch. 89.

165 Superseding the Statute of Frauds 1677 s.5, and itself substituted by the Administration of Justice Act 1982 s.17.

OTTAWAY v NORMAN

Chancery Division [1972] Ch. 698; [1972] 2 W.L.R. 50; [1971] 3 All E.R. 1325

A testator, Harry Ottaway, by will devised his bungalow (with fixtures, fittings and furniture) to his housekeeper Miss Hodges in fee simple, and gave her a legacy of £1,500 and half the residue of his estate. It was alleged that Miss Hodges had orally agreed with the testator to leave the bungalow, etc., by her will to the claimants, who were the testator's son and daughter-in-law, Mr and Mrs William Ottaway. Further, it was alleged that she had orally agreed to leave them whatever money was left at her death. By her will Miss Hodges left all her property away from the claimants, who therefore brought an action against Miss Hodges' executor, Mr Norman, for a declaration that he held the appropriate parts of Miss Hodges' estate on trust for them. Brightman J. upheld the claim except in respect of the money. **3–130**

BRIGHTMAN J.: . . . It will be convenient to call the person on whom such a trust is imposed the "primary donee" and the beneficiary under that trust the "secondary donee". The essential elements which must be proved are: (i) the intention of the testator to subject the primary donee to an obligation in favour of the secondary donee; (ii) communication of that intention to the primary donee; and (iii) the acceptance of that obligation by the primary donee either expressly or by acquiescence. It is immaterial whether these elements precede or succeed the will of the donor. I am informed that there is no recent reported case where the obligation imposed on the primary donee is an obligation to make a will in favour of the secondary donee as distinct from some form of inter vivos transfer. But it does not seem to me that that can really be a distinction which can validly be drawn on behalf of the defendant in the present case. The basis of the doctrine of a secret trust is the obligation imposed on the conscience of the primary donee and it does not seem to me that there is any materiality in the machinery by which the donor intends that that obligation shall be carried out . . . **3–131**

I find as a fact that Harry Ottaway intended that Miss Hodges should be obliged to dispose of the bungalow in favour of the plaintiffs at her death, that he communicated that intention to Miss Hodges and that Miss Hodges accepted the obligation. I find the same facts in relation to the furniture, fixtures and fittings which passed to Miss Hodges under clause 4 of Harry Ottaway's will. I am not satisfied that any similar obligation was imposed and accepted as regards any contents of the bungalow which had not devolved on Miss Hodges under clause 4 of Harry Ottaway's will. **3–132**

I turn to the question of money. In cross-examination William Ottaway said the trust extended to the house, furniture and money: **3–133**

> "Everything my father left to Miss Hodges was to be in the trust. The trust comprised the lot. She could use the money as she liked. She had to leave my wife and me whatever money was left."

In cross-examination Mrs Ottaway said that her understanding was that Miss Hodges was bound to make a will giving her and her husband the bungalow, contents and any money she had left. "She could please herself about the money. She did not have to save it for us. She was free to spend it." It seems to me that two questions arise. First as a matter of fact what did the parties intend should be comprised in Miss Hodges's obligation? All money which Miss Hodges had at her death, including money which she had acquired before Harry's death and money she acquired after his death from all sources? Or, only money acquired under Harry's will? Secondly, if such an obligation existed would it as a matter of law create a valid trust? On the second question I am content to assume for present purposes but without so deciding that if property is given to the primary donee on the understanding that the primary donee will dispose by his will of such assets, if any, as he may have at his command at his death in favour of the secondary donee, a valid trust is created in favour of the secondary donee which is in suspense during the lifetime of the primary donee, but attaches to the estate of the primary donee at the moment of the latter's death. There would seem to be at least some support for this proposition in an Australian case to which I was referred: *Birmingham v Renfrew*.[166] I do not, **3–134**

[166] (1937) 57 C.L.R. 666.

however, find sufficient evidence that it was Harry Ottaway's intention that Miss Hodges should be compelled to leave all her money, from whatever source derived, to the plaintiffs. This would seem to preclude her giving even a small pecuniary legacy to any friend or relative. I do no think it is clear that Harry Ottaway intended to extract any such far-reaching undertaking from Miss Hodges or that she intended to accept such a wide obligation herself. Therefore the obligation, if any, is in my view to be confined to money derived under Harry Ottaway's will. If the obligation is confined to money derived under Harry Ottaway's will, the obligation is meaningless and unworkable unless it includes the requirement that she shall keep such money separate and distinct from her own money. I am certain that no such requirement was ever discussed or intended. If she had the right to mingle her own money with that derived from Harry, there would be no ascertainable property on which the trust could bite at her death.[167]

3–135 There is another difficulty. Does money in this context include only cash or cash and investments, or all moveable property of any description? The evidence is quite inconclusive. In my judgment the plaintiff's claim succeeds in relation to the bungalow and in relation to the furniture, fixtures and fittings which devolved under clause 4 of Harry Ottaway's will subject, of course, to normal wastage and fair wear and tear, but not to any other assets.

C. *Half-Secret Trusts*

3–136 A half-secret trust is one where the existence of the trust is disclosed by the will but the terms are not.

3–137 Suppose, for example, that a testator makes a valid will bequeathing or devising property to X on trust, that he does not specify the objects of the trust in the will, but that he does communicate the objects to X before or at the time of the will's execution, and that the will states that the objects have been communicated to X. *Blackwell v Blackwell*,[168] which is reproduced below,[169] shows that if X accepts the trust in such a case, then he will be compelled to carry it out for the specified objects.[170] However, *Re Keen*,[171] which is also reproduced below,[172] shows that if the testator communicates the objects to X after the execution of the will, then X will hold the property on trust, because the will has created a trust, but because the objects have not been effectively specified, the beneficial interest will belong to the testator's residuary legatee or devisee, or if there is no such person, or if the property is residuary property, to the testator's intestate successors.[173]

---

167 On this principle see *Henry v Hammond* [1913] 2 K.B. 515 at 521; endorsed in *Re Chelsea Cloisters Ltd* (1980) 41 P. & C.R. 98 at 101, and followed in *Azam v Iqbal* [2008] Bus. L.R. 168.

168 [1929] A.C. 318.

169 At para.3–144 ff.

170 The full extent of the property to be covered by the obligation must be communicated so that if £5,000 is bequeathed on a half-secret trust accepted by the trustee and then a codicil increases that sum to £15,000 but the trustee is not informed of this increase, the surplus £10,000 will not be held on the half-secret trust but on trust for the residuary legatee or next-of-kin: cf. *Re Colin Cooper, deceased* [1939] Ch. 580 and 811. If the trustee had undertaken to hold the original legacy and anything extra that the testator might subsequently bequeath, then the trustee would be bound to hold everything bequeathed on the half-secret trust.

171 [1937] Ch. 236; followed in *Re Bateman's WT* [1970] 1 W.L.R. 1463, where a testator had directed his trustees to set aside £24,000 and pay the income thereof "to such persons and in such proportions as shall be stated by me in a sealed letter to my trustees". At 1468, Pennycuick V.C. stated that: "[The direction] clearly imports that the testator may, in the future after the date of the will, give a sealed letter to his trustees. It is impossible to confine the words to a sealed letter already so given. If that be the true construction of the wording it is not in dispute that the direction is invalid".

172 At paras 3–149 ff.

173 If a testator, having created a valid half-secret trust, subsequently tells the trustee not to hold for the old beneficiaries but to hold for new beneficiaries, then the trust for the new beneficiaries will fail by *Re Keen*, and it is possible that the revocation of the old trusts will fall on the basis that it was conditional on the creation of valid new trusts: it will succeed if construed as unconditional (cf. conditional revocation of wills, e.g. *Re Finnemore* [1992] 1 W.L.R. 793) so the property will pass to the residuary legatee (or the statutory next-of-kin).

The supposed justification of this is that a testator cannot, through the medium of a valid will which imposes a trust but does not create the beneficial interests of that trust, reserve to himself a power to create the beneficial interests in an informal non-testamentary manner, so giving the go-by to the requirements of the Wills Act 1837. After all, as we have seen, in the case of the probate doctrine of incorporation of documents by reference the documents must exist prior to or contemporaneously with the execution of the will, for to allow otherwise would be to give the go-by to the Wills Act. **3–138**

However, the doctrine of incorporation by reference operates within the ambit of the statutory formalities, while the whole justification for secret trusts is to impose them just where the statutory formalities have not been satisfied: they operate outside the will and independently of the Wills Act.[174] Fully secret trusts, allowing communication of the trusts between execution of the will and the testator's death, allow the go-by to be given to the Wills Act, and since a will is ambulatory, being of no effect till death, there is logically no difference between declarations of trusts before and after the will. After all, in the case of both fully and half-secret trusts communicated after the will it is fraudulent for X to deprive B of his beneficial interest which but for the testator relying on X's promise would have been secured to B by the testator altering his will, so choosing a compliant legatee as trustee. Logically, half-secret trusts in this respect should be assimilated to fully secret trusts, as in Ireland,[175] New South Wales[176] and most American jurisdictions,[177] rather than have a different rule based upon a misplaced analogy with the doctrine of incorporation by reference. **3–139**

At present, there are the following differences between half-secret trusts and the probate doctrine of incorporation: **3–140**

- In half-secret trusts the will need not specify the type of communication with any precision; in incorporation by reference the will must refer to the document to be incorporated with sufficient precision to enable it to be identified.[178]
- In half-secret trusts the communication may be oral; in incorporation by reference the document to be incorporated must be in writing.
- In half-secret trusts the testator must take the intended trustee into his confidence; in incorporation by reference the intended trustee need not be told of the document to be incorporated. Indeed, incorporation by reference may be effected in cases of absolute gift as well as in cases of trust.
- In half-secret trusts the names of the beneficiaries are not made public; in incorporation by reference the incorporated document is admitted to probate and so made public.
- A beneficiary under a half-secret trust who witnesses the will does not forfeit his beneficial interest, whereas a beneficiary named in an incorporated document who witnesses the will does.[179]

---

174 *Re Young, deceased* [1951] Ch. 344; *Re Gardner (No.2)* [1923] 2 Ch. 230; *Cullen v Att.-Gen. for Ireland* (1866) L.R. 1 H.L. 190 at 198 (in the tax context); *Blackwell v Blackwell* [1929] A.C. 318 at 340 and 342; *Re Snowden, deceased* [1979] Ch. 528 at 535. However, as P. Critchley in (1999) 115 LQR 631 at p.641 correctly states, "the mistake is to confuse 'outside the will' with 'outside the Wills Act' ": a disposition by way of secret trust is a testamentary disposition, being revocable and ambulatory, as made clear in Section 2 of this chapter, so as to fall within the Wills Act. It is the harmful effect of the secret trustee's wrongful conduct that justifies Equity's intervention.

175 *Re Browne* [1944] Ir. R. 90; *Re Prendiville* (unreported, but noted [1992] Conv. 202 by J. Mee).

176 *Ledgerwood v Petpetual Trustee Co Ltd* (1997) 41 N.S.W.L.R. 532.

177 American Law Institute, *Restatement of Trusts*, para.55(c)(h).

178 *Re Edwards' WT* [1948] Ch. 440.

179 *Re Young, deceased* [1951] Ch. 344.

- The interest of a beneficiary under a half-secret trust who predeceases the testator does not lapse: in like circumstances that of a beneficiary named in an incorporated document does.[180]

3–141 One special requirement for half-secret trusts which is inapposite for fully secret trusts and is probably derived from the false analogy with the probate doctrine of incorporation, is that the communication of the trusts and the terms of the trust must not conflict with the wording of the will, for to allow otherwise would be to allow oral evidence to contradict the express words of the will.[181] Thus, leaving property to four persons "to be dealt with in accordance with my wishes which I have made known to them" is ineffective to create a half-secret trust unless the wishes were communicated to all four:[182] communication to fewer than four would only be effective if the words "or any one or more of them" had been added.[183] Furthermore, if property is left by will to X as trustee, evidence is not admissible to show that X was meant to have some part of that property beneficially.[184]

3–142 By way of contrast, if the wording of the will gives property "to X absolutely" or "to X relying on him, but not by way of trust, to carry out my wishes . . ." then oral evidence is admissible to prove a fully-secret trust, contradicting the express words of the will, for to allow otherwise would be to allow the possibility of the perpetration of fraud.[185]

3–143 Should there really be such distinctions between fully- and half-secret trusts if their basis is that while the will must first operate to vest the property in the secret trustee, thereafter the secret trusts themselves arise outside the will?[186] Is it not illogical in the case of half-secret trusts for the court to concern itself so strictly with the wording of the will and to require communication of the trust in accordance therewith before or at the time of the will?

BLACKWELL v BLACKWELL

House of Lords [1929] A.C. 318

3–144 A testator by a codicil bequeathed £12,000 to five persons upon trust to invest according to their discretion and "to apply the income . . . for the purposes indicated by me to them." Before the execution of the codicil the objects of the trust were communicated in outline to four of the legatees and in detail to the fifth, and the trust was accepted by all of them. The fifth legatee also made a memorandum of the testator's instructions, on the same day as (though a few hours after) the execution of the codicil. The plaintiffs (the residuary legatees) now claimed a declaration that no valid trust in favour of the objects so communicated had been created, on the ground principally that parol evidence was inadmissible to establish the purposes indicated by the testator. Eve J. and the Court of Appeal held that the evidence was admissible,

---

180 *Re Gardner (No.2)* [1923] 2 Ch. 230; *Bizzey v Flight* (1876) 3 Ch.D. 269.
181 *Re Keen* [1937] Ch. 236.
182 *Re Spence* [1949] W.N. 237 following *Re Keen*.
183 The phrase "to them or either of them" was used in *Re Keen*.
184 *Re Rees* [1950] Ch. 204; *Re Tyler* [1967] 1 W.L.R. 1269; *Re Pugh's WT* [1967] 1 W.L.R. 1262; *Re Baillie* (1886) 2 T.L.R. 660; *Re Marsten* [1953] N.Z.L.R. 456. *Aliter* if property given under a fully secret trust when the possibilities of trust, conditional gift and equitable charge have to be examined: *Irvine v Sullivan* (1869) L.R. 8 Eq. 673; *Re Foord* [1922] 2 Ch. 519.
185 *Re Spencer's Will* (1887) 57 L.T. 519; *Re Williams* [1933] 1 Ch. 244; *Irvine v Sullivan*, above; cf. *Re Falkiner* [1924] 1 Ch. 88; *Re Stirling, deceased* [1954] 1 W.L.R. 763.
186 *Blackwell v Blackwell* [1929] A.C. 318 at 335: equity makes the trustee "do what the will in itself has nothing to do with; it lets him take what the will gives him and then makes him apply it as the court of conscience directs, and it does so in order to give effect to the wishes of the testator which would not otherwise be effectual." See too *Re Young, deceased* [1951] Ch. 344; *Re Snowden, deceased* [1979] Ch. 528 at 535.

and here proved a valid secret trust for the persons named by the testator in his instructions to the legatees. The plaintiffs' appeal to the House of Lords was unsuccessful.

VISCOUNT SUMNER (with whom LORD HAILSHAM L.C., LORD BUCKMASTER, LORD CARSON, and LORD WARRINGTON agreed): . . . In itself the doctrine of equity, by which parol evidence is admissible to prove what is called "fraud" in connection with secret trusts, and effect is given to such trusts when established, would not seem to conflict with any of the Acts under which from time to time the legislature has regulated the right of testamentary disposition. A court of conscience finds a man in the position of an absolute legal owner of a sum of money, which has been bequeathed to him under a valid will, and it declares that, on proof of certain facts relating to the motives and actions of the testator, it will not allow the legal owner to exercise his legal right to do what he will with his own. This seems to be a perfectly normal exercise of general equitable jurisdiction. The facts commonly, but not necessarily, involve some immoral and selfish conduct on the part of the legal owner. The necessary elements, on which the question turns, are intention, communication and acquiescence. The testator intends his absolute gift to be employed as he and not as the donee desires; he tells the proposed donee of this intention and, either by express promise or by the tacit promise, which is satisfied by acquiescence, the proposed donee encourages him to bequeath the money in the faith that his intentions will be carried out. For the prevention of fraud equity fastens on the conscience of the legatee a trust, a trust, that is, which otherwise would be inoperative; in other words it makes him do what the will in itself has nothing to do with; it lets him take what the will gives him and then makes him apply it as the court of conscience directs, and it does so in order to give effect to wishes of the testator which would not otherwise be effectual. **3–145**

To this, two circumstances must be added to bring the present case to the test of the general doctrine, first, that the will states on its face that the legacy is given on trust but does not state what the trusts are, and further contains a residuary bequest, and, second, that the legatees are acting with perfect honesty, seek no advantage to themselves, and only desire, if the court will permit them, to do what in other circumstances the court would have fastened it on their conscience to perform. **3–146**

Since the current of decisions down to *Re Fleetwood*[187] and *Re Huxtable*[188] has established that the principles of equity apply equally when these circumstances are present as in cases where they are not, the material question is whether and how the Wills Act affects this case. It seems to me that, apart from legislation, the application of the principle of equity which was made in *Fleetwood's case* and *Huxtable's case* was logical, and was justified by the same considerations as in the cases of fraud and absolute gifts. Why should equity forbid an honest trustee to give effect to his promise, made to a deceased testator, and compel him to pay another legatee, about whom it is quite certain that the testator did not mean to make him the object of his bounty? In both cases the testator's wishes are incompletely expressed in his will. Why should equity, over a mere matter of words, give effect to them in one case and frustrate them in the other? No doubt the words "in trust" prevent the legatee from taking beneficially, whether they have simply been declared in conversation or written in the will, but the fraud, when the trustee, so called in the will, is also the residuary legatee, is the same as when he is only declared a trustee by word of mouth accepted by him. I recoil from interfering with decisions of long standing, which reject this anomaly, unless constrained by statute . . . **3–147**

The limits, beyond which the rules as to unspecified trusts must not be carried, have often been discussed. A testator cannot reserve to himself a power of making future unwitnessed dispositions by merely naming a trustee and leaving the purposes of the trust to be supplied afterwards, nor can a legatee give testamentary validity to an unexecuted codicil by accepting an indefinite trust, never communicated to him in the testator's lifetime: *Johnson v Ball*,[189] *Re Boyes*,[190] *Riordan v Banon*,[191] *Re Hetley*.[192] To hold otherwise **3–148**

---

[187] (1880) 15 Ch.D. 594, where a testatrix by a codicil bequeathed to X all her personalty "to be applied as I have requested him to do." Before the execution of the codicil she had stated to X the trusts on which she intended the property to be held, and X made a memorandum of the details in her presence. Hall V.C. held that external evidence was admissible to prove the terms of the understanding between X and the testatrix.

[188] [1902] 2 Ch. 793.

[189] (1851) 5 De G. & Son 85.

[190] (1884) 26 Ch.D. 531.

[191] (1876) 10 I.R.Eq. 469.

[192] [1902] 2 Ch. 866.

would indeed be to enable the testator to "give the go-by" to the requirements of the Wills Act, because he did not choose to comply with them. It is communication of the purpose to the legatee, coupled with acquiescence or promise on his part, that removes the matter from the provision of the Wills Act and brings it within the law of trusts, as applied in this instance to trustees, who happen also to be legatees. . . .

RE KEEN, EVERSHED v GRIFFITHS

Court of Appeal [1937] Ch. 236, [1937] 1 All E.R. 452

3–149 The testator by clause 5 of his will, dated August 11, 1932, gave to his executors and trustees, Captain Hazelhurst and Mr Evershed, the sum of £10,000 free of duty "to be held upon trust and disposed of by them among such person, persons or charities as may be notified by me to them or either of them during my lifetime, and in default of such notification and so far as such notification shall not extend I declare that the said sum of £10,000 or such part thereof as shall not be disposed of in manner aforesaid shall fall into and form part of my residuary estate." Earlier, on March 31, 1932, the testator had made a will containing an identical gift. He had on that date handed to Mr Evershed a sealed envelope containing the name of the intended beneficiary, but he had not disclosed its contents to Mr Evershed, having directed that it was not to be opened until after his death. Mr Evershed regarded himself as having undertaken to hold the £10,000 in accordance with the directions contained in the sealed envelope. A new will was executed on August 11, 1932, but no fresh directions were given. Mr Evershed still regarded himself as being bound by the previous communication. On the testator's death the question arose whether the £10,000 was held by Captain Hazelhurst and Mr Evershed on trust for the intended beneficiary or whether it fell into residue. It was held by Farwell J. and the Court of Appeal that it fell into residue.

3–150 LORD WRIGHT M.R. (with whom GREENE and ROMER L.JJ. agreed): Farwell J. . . . decided adversely to the claims of the lady [the intended beneficiary] on the short ground that she could not prove that she was a person notified to the trustees by the testator during his lifetime within the words of clause 5 [of the will]. His opinion seems to be that the clause required the name and identity of the lady to be expressly disclosed to the trustees during the testator's lifetime, so that it was not sufficient to place these particulars in the physical possession of the trustees, or one of them, in the form of a memorandum which they were not to read till the testator's death.

3–151 I am unable to accept this conclusion, which appears to me to put too narrow a construction on the word "notified" as used in clause 5 in all the circumstances of the case. To take a parallel, a ship which sails under sealed orders is sailing under orders though the exact terms are not ascertained by the captain till later. I note that the case of a trust, put into writing, which is placed in the trustees' hands in a sealed envelope, was hypothetically treated by Kay J. as possibly constituting a communication in a case of this nature.[193] This, so far as it goes seems to support my conclusion. The trustees had the means of knowledge available whenever it became necessary and proper to open the envelope. I think Mr Evershed was right in understanding that the giving of the sealed envelope was a notification within clause 5.

3–152 This makes it necessary to examine the matter on a wider basis . . . The principles of law or equity relevant in a question of this nature have now been authoritatively settled or discussed by the House of Lords in *Blackwell v Blackwell*[194] [in the case of half-secret trusts and *McCormick v Grogan*[195] in the case of fully secret trusts. The Master of the Rolls then analysed the facts and decisions in those cases, and continued:] As, in my judgment, clause 5 should be considered as contemplating future dispositions, and as reserving to the testator the power of making such dispositions without a duly attested codicil, simply by notifying them during his lifetime, the principles laid down by Lord Sumner [in *Blackwell v Blackwell*] must be fatal to the appellant's claim. Indeed, they would be equally fatal even on the construction for which Mr Roxburgh contended, that the clause covered both anterior or contemporaneous notifications and future notifications. The clause would be equally invalid, but as already explained I cannot accept that construction.

---

193 *Re Boyes* (1884) 26 Ch.D. 531 at 536.
194 [1929] A.C. 318.
195 (1869) L.R. 4 H.L. 82.

In *Blackwell v Blackwell*[196] *Re Fleetwood*[197] and *Re Huxtable*[198] the trusts had been specifically declared to some or all of the trustees, at or before the execution of the will, and the language of the will was consistent with that fact. There was, in these cases, no reservation of a future power to change the trusts, in whole or in part. Such a power would involve a power to change a testamentary disposition by an unexecuted codicil, and would violate section 9 of the Wills Act. This was so held in *Re Hetley*.[199] *Johnson v Balt*[200] is, again, a somewhat different example of the rule against dispositions made subsequently to the date of the will in cases where the will in terms leaves the property on trust, and shows that the position may be different from the position where the will in terms leaves the gift absolutely. The trusts referred to, but undefined in the will, must be described in the will as established prior to, or at least contemporaneously with, its execution.

But there is a still further objection which, in the present case, renders the appellant's claim unenforceable: **3–153** the trusts which it is sought to establish by parol evidence would be inconsistent with the express terms of the will. That such an objection is fatal appears from the cases already cited, such as *Re Huxtable*. In that case, an undefined trust of money for charitable purposes was declared in the will, as in respect of the whole corpus and, accordingly, evidence was held inadmissible that the charitable trust was limited to the legatee's life, so that he was free to dispose of the corpus after his death. Similarly in *Johnson v Ball* the testator by the will left the property to trustees, upon the uses contained in a letter signed "by them and myself": it was held that that evidence was not admissible to show that, though no such letter was in existence at the date of the will, the testator had made a subsequent declaration of trust; the court held that these trusts could not be enforced. Lord Buckmaster in *Blackwell's case*[201] described *Johnson v Ball* as an authority pointing "to a case where the actual trusts were left over after the date of the will to be subsequently determined by the testator." That, in his opinion, would be a contravention of the Wills Act. I know of no authority which would justify such a contravention. Lord Buckmaster also quotes[202] the grounds on which Parker V.C. based his decision as being both "that the letter referred to in the will had no existence at the time when the will was made and that, supposing it referred to a letter afterwards signed, it is impossible to give effect to it as a declaration of the trusts since it would admit the document as part of the will and it was unattested."

In the present case, while clause 5 refers solely to a future definition, or to future definitions, of the trust, **3–154** subsequent to the date of the will, the sealed letter relied on as notifying the trust was communicated (as I find the facts) before the date of the will. That it was communicated to one trustee only, and not to both, would not, I think, be an objection (see Lord Warrington's observation in the *Blackwell* case).[203] But the objection remains that the notification sought to be put in evidence was anterior to the will, and hence not within the language of clause 5, and inadmissible simply on that ground, as being inconsistent with what the will prescribes. . . .

D. The Basis of Secret Trusts

Before dealing with the basis of secret trusts we shall consider some unusual secret trust situations **3–155** since they will help us to understand the whole phenomenon.

i. Attestation of Will by Secret Beneficiary

What happens if property is left to T on the understanding that he will hold it on a secret trust for B, **3–156** under a will that is attested by B? Potential problems arise here as a result of the Wills Act 1837 s.15, which provides that:

---

196 [1929] A.C. 318.
197 (1880) 15 Ch.D. 594.
198 [1902] 2 Ch. 793.
199 [1902] 2 Ch. 866.
200 (1851) 5 De G. & Sm. 85.
201 [1929] A.C. 318 at 331.
202 ibid. at 330.
203 ibid. at 341.

> "If any person shall attest the execution of any will to whom or to whose wife or husband any beneficial devise, legacy, estate, interest, gift, or appointment, of or affecting any real or personal estate (other than and except charges and directions for the payment of any debt or debts), shall be thereby given or made, such devise, legacy, estate, interest, gift, or appointment shall, so far only as concerns such person attesting the execution of such will, or the wife or husband of such person, or any person claiming under such person or wife or husband, be utterly null and void, and such person so attesting shall be admitted as a witness to prove the execution of such will, or to prove the validity or invalidity thereof, notwithstanding such devise, legacy, estate, interest, gift, or appointment mentioned in such will."

However, the Wills Act 1968 s.1 stipulates that:

> "For the purposes of section 15 of the Wills Act 1837 the attestation of a will by a person to whom or to whose spouse there is given or made any such disposition as is described in that section shall be disregarded if the will is duly executed without his attestation and without that of any other such person."

3–157 In *Re Young, deceased*[204] there was a bequest by a testator to his wife with a direction that on her death she should leave the property for the purposes which he had communicated to her (i.e. on a half-secret trust). Before execution of his will, a direction was given by him, and accepted by his wife, that she would leave a legacy of £2,000 to the testator's chauffeur. The chauffeur had witnessed the testator's will. Danckwerts J. held that the chauffeur had not forfeited his legacy under the Wills Act 1837 s.15, for "the whole theory of the formulation of a secret trust is that the Wills Act has nothing to do with the matter because the forms required by the Wills Act are entirely disregarded, since the persons do not take by virtue of the gift in the will, but by virtue of the secret trusts imposed upon the beneficiary who does in fact take under the will." However it is hard to see why an attesting secret beneficiary should be allowed to benefit, given that the function of s.15 is to ensure there is an impartial witness with nothing to gain or lose by his testimony. He may know he is a beneficiary at the time of attestation. He could be lying if he said he did not know: for this reason a beneficiary taking on the face of a will is subject to s.15 even if, in fact, he just witnessed the signature at the end of the will and so did not know of its contents.

ii. Trustee Predeceasing Testator

3–158 Generally, a gift by will to X is said to lapse if X predeceases the testator and the gift fails.[205] If, however, the gift is to X on trust for B and B survives the testator, then despite X's predecease the gift will not lapse, because equity will not allow a trust to fail for want of a trustee: the testator's personal representative will take over as trustee.[206] According to dicta of Cozens-Hardy L.J. in *Re Maddock*,[207] a case concerning a fully secret trust, "if the legatee renounces and disclaims, or dies in the lifetime of the testator, the persons claiming under the memorandum [i.e. the secret trusts] can take nothing." This is based on the view that the secret trusts only arise when the property that is intended to be the

---

204 [1951] Ch. 344.

205 Exceptionally, if issue predecease a testator leaving issue of their own surviving the testator, the gift takes effect in favour of the surviving issue: Wills Act 1837 s.33. The persons benefiting from this exception will not be able to disregard the deceased legatee-trustee's undertaking: cf. *Huguenin v Baseley* (1807) 14 Ves. 273.

206 *Sonley v Clock Makers' Company* (1780) 1 Bro. C.C. 81; *Mallott v Wilson* [1903] 2 Ch. 494; *Re Smirthwaite's Trusts* (1871) L.R. 11 Eq. 251; *Re Armitage, deceased* [1972] Ch. 438.

207 [1902] 2 Ch. 220 at 231.

subject-matter of the trust vests in someone under the terms of the will.[208] It follows that if the property does not so vest because of the fully secret trustee's death then no trust can arise.

iii. Trustee Disclaiming after Testator's Death

A beneficiary under a will after the testator's death can always disclaim a legacy or devise before acceptance and a person can always disclaim the office of trustee before acceptance.[209] If a person named as a half-secret trustee disclaimed the office then it would seem clear that the testator's personal representative would hold on the trusts for the secret beneficiaries. Where disclaimer by fully secret trustees is concerned, Lord Buckmaster in *Blackwell v Blackwell* thought that: "In the case where no trusts are mentioned the legatee might defeat the whole purpose by renouncing the legacy and the breach of trust would not in that case inure to his own benefit, but I entertain no doubt that the court having once admitted the evidence of the trust, would interfere to prevent its defeat."[210] Lord Buckmaster's dicta presuppose the existence of a trust whereof the legatee is in breach and apply the maxim that equity will not allow a trust to fail for want of a trustee. Whether the trusts arose on the testator's death or at an earlier time is not stated by Lord Buckmaster. By analogy with mutual wills the testator's death should be the appropriate time, it being immaterial whether or not gifts are disclaimed.[211] Disclaimer would, however, be material if the testator's orally communicated intentions to the legatee were construed not as imposing trusts but as conferring a gift subject to a personal condition. **3–159**

iv. Trustee Revoking Acceptance before the Testator's Death

Compare the three following examples: **3–160**

(a) Testator, T, bequeaths £10,000 to X absolutely, having told X that he wants X to hold the money on trust for Y. A year later X tells T that he is no longer prepared to hold the money on trust for anyone. Five years later T dies without having changed his will;

(b) the bequest as before but X tells T that he is no longer prepared to hold the money on trust for anyone only three days before T dies of a week-long illness; and

(c) the bequest as before but T is incurably insane when informed by X as before and T remains so till his death five years later.

Does X take the £10,000 beneficially only in case (a)? Is X under any obligations before T's death? What if the trust had been half secret?

---

[208] *Re Gardner* [1923] 2 Ch. 230 at 232, per Romer J.: "The obligation can be enforced if the donee becomes entitled." *Blackwell v Blackwell* [1929] A.C. 318 at 334, per Viscount Sumner: "The doctrine must, in principle, rest on the assumption that the will has first operated according to its terms." *Re Snowden, deceased* [1979] Ch. 528 at 535, per Megarry V.C.: "The whole basis of secret trusts . . . is that they operate outside the will, changing nothing that is written in it and allowing it to operate according to its tenor, but then fastening a trust on to the property in the hands of the recipient."

[209] *Re Sharman's WT* [1942] Ch. 311; *Smith v Smith* [2001] 1 W.L.R. 1937;

[210] [1929] A.C. 318 at 328.

[211] *Re Dale, deceased* [1994] Ch. 31. See also *Blackwell v Blackwell* [1929] A.C. 318 at 341, per Lord Warrington: "It has long been settled that if a gift be made to a person in terms absolutely but in fact upon a trust communicated to the legatee and accepted by him, the legatee, would be bound to give effect to the trust, on the principle that the gift may be presumed to have been made on the faith of his acceptance of the trust, and a refusal after the death of the testator to give effect to it would be a fraud on the part of the legatee."

v. Secret Beneficiary Predeceasing Testator

3–161 If T by will left property to X on trust expressly for B, and B predeceased T, then the gift to B would lapse just as an inter vivos trust for B fails if B is not alive when the trust is created.[212] One would have imagined that the result would be the same if T, having asked X to hold on trust for B, left property "to X absolutely" or "to X upon trusts that I have communicated to him". However, in *Re Gardner (No.2)*[213] Romer J. held that B's interest did not lapse as B obtained an interest as soon as T communicated the terms of the trust to X and X accepted the trust. B's interest derived not from T's will (to which the rules regarding lapse would have applied) but under the agreement between T and X. "The rights of the parties appear to me to be exactly the same as though the husband (X), after the memorandum had been communicated to him by the testatrix (T) in the year 1909 had executed a declaration of trust binding himself to hold any property that should come to him upon his wife's (T's) partial intestacy upon trust as specified in the memorandum."[214]

3–162 Such a declaration, however, does not create a properly constituted trust since the subject-matter is future property.[215] It may be that Romer J. considered that the vesting of the property in X on T's death in 1919 completely constituted the trust[216] but on the terms of the memorandum. However, the interests of those taking under the memorandum only became vested proprietary interests after T's death: until then the so-called interests only amounted to mere hope that T would not change her mind and make a different testamentary disposition or die insolvent and that X would not revoke his acceptance, so that ultimately X would receive property to hold on trust for them. Just as an inter vivos trust constituted by X in 1919 declaring himself trustee of certain property for the benefit of A, B and C equally would give B no interest, if at that date B were dead and so no longer an existing legal entity, so the trust arising in *Re Gardner (No.2)* after T's death in 1919 could give B no interest, B being dead by that date. It makes no difference that while B was alive he might have had some sort of hope that if he lived long enough a trust might come into existence for his benefit at a later date. The authority of *Re Gardner (No.2)* is thus very weak indeed.

vi. Bequest to Two on a Promise by One

3–163 The orthodox position is laid down in *Re Stead* by Farwell J.:[217]

> "If A induced B either to make, or to leave unrevoked, a will leaving property to A and C as tenants in common, by expressly promising or tacitly consenting, that he and C will carry out the testator's wishes and C knows nothing of the matter until after the testator's death, A is bound, but C is not bound: *Tee v Ferris;*[218] the reason stated being, that to hold otherwise would be to enable one

---

[212] *Re Corbishley's Trusts* (1880) 14 Ch.D. 846; *Re Tilt* (1896) 74 L.T. 163, both concerned with personalty where a gift to B gave B an absolute interest: for realty a gift by will after 1837 to B gave an absolute interest whilst till 1925 a gift by deed to B gave B only a life interest in the absence of proper words of limitation.

[213] [1923] 2 Ch. 230.

[214] *Re Gardner (No.2)* at 233. Here Romer J. may have been thinking that if B had an absolute vested interest in a 1909 settlement then funds accruing under a will taking effect in 1919 would be treated as an accretion to the 1909 settlement rather than as comprised in a separate 1919 referential settlement: see *Re Playfair, deceased* [1951] Ch. 4.

[215] *Re Ellenborough* [1903] 1 Ch. 697; *Re Northcliffe* [1925] Ch. 651; *Williams v CIR* [1965] N.Z.L.R. 395.

[216] cf. *Re Ralli's WT* [1964] Ch. 288; *Re Adlard* [1954] Ch. 29.

[217] [1900] 1 Ch. 231 at 247. The principles here discussed apply only to fully secret trusts. In the case of half-secret trusts, if the will permits communication to be made to one only of several trustees, a communication made before or at the time of the execution of the will to one only of the trustees binds all of them, the trust being a joint office: *Blackwell v Blackwell* [1929] A.C. 318; *Re Spence* [1949] W.N. 237; *Ward v Duncombe* [1893] A.C. 369; *Re Gardom* [1914] 1 Ch. 662 at 673.

[218] (1856) 2 K. & J. 357.

beneficiary to deprive the rest of their benefits by setting up a secret trust. If, however, the gift were to A and C as joint tenants, the authorities have established a distinction between those cases in which the will is made on the faith of an antecedent promise by A and those in which the will is left unrevoked on the faith of a subsequent promise. In the former case the trust binds both A and C: *Russell v Jackson*;[219] *Jones v Bradley*,[220] the reason stated being that no person can claim an interest under a fraud committed by another; in the latter case A and not C is bound: *Burney v Macdonald*[221] and *Moss v Cooper*,[222] the reason stated being that the gift is not tainted with any fraud in procuring the execution of the will. Personally, I am unable to see any difference between a gift made on the faith of an antecedent promise and a gift left unrevoked on the faith of a subsequent promise to carry out the testator's wishes; but apparently a distinction has been made by the various judges who have had to consider the question. I am bound, therefore, to decide in accordance with these authorities . . ."

However, Bryn Perrins has examined these authorities to different effect, persuasively concluding that the only question to be asked is: was the gift to C induced by A's promise? If yes, then C is bound; if no, then he is not. Thus, he writes that:[223] **3–164**

"The 'reasons stated' by Farwell J. in *Re Stead* are at first sight contradictory. One consideration is that a person must not be allowed, by falsely setting up a secret trust, to deprive another of his benefits under the will. Apparently this is decisive if the parties are tenants in common but not if they are joint tenants. On the other hand one person must not profit by the fraud of another. Apparently this is decisive only if the parties are joint tenants and not if they are tenants in common. Yet again it is apparently only fraud in procuring the execution of a will that is relevant, and not fraud in inducing a testator not to revoke a will already made. All very confusing, but add *Huguenin v Baseley*[224] and the whole picture springs into focus and the confusion disappears. Returning to A and C, whether they are tenants in common or joint tenants, C is not bound if his gift was not induced by the promise of A because to hold otherwise would be to enable A to deprive C of his benefit by setting up a secret trust; but C is bound if his gift was induced by the promise of A because he cannot profit by the fraud of another; and if the trust was communicated to A after the will was made, then C takes free if this gift was not induced by the promise of A because if there is no inducement there is no fraud affecting C."

In the light of the foregoing discussion of unusual secret trust situations it will be seen that the title of a beneficiary under a fully secret and a half-secret trust arises outside the will and is regarded by many judges[225] as arising outside the Wills Act and so not by virtue of a testamentary disposition. But even then, it seems that, except in the case of disclaimer by a fully secret trustee after the testator's **3–165**

[219] (1852) 10 Hare 204.
[220] (1868) L.R. 3 Ch. 362.
[221] (1845) 15 Sim. 6.
[222] (1861) 1 J. & H. 352.
[223] B. Perrins, "Can You Keep Half a Secret?" (1972) 88 L.Q.R. 225, p.228.
[224] (1807) 14 Ves. 273. This is authority for the principle that "No man may profit by the fraud of another". A widow was persuaded by Rev. Baseley, who managed her property, to settle some of it on him and his family. Later, she married Mr Huguenin and sought to set aside the conveyance for undue influence. She succeeded, for Lord Eldon held that the Rev. Baseley's wife and children, though innocent, were not purchasers but volunteers who could not profit from Baseley's fraud and retain their vested interests.
[225] *Re Snowden, deceased* [1979] Ch. 528 at 535; *Re Young, deceased* [1951] Ch. 344; *Re Gardner (No.2)* [1923] 2 Ch. 230; *Blackwell v Blackwell* [1929] 2 A.C. 318 at 340 and 342.

death, such a trust is conditional and dependent upon the gift by will taking effect according to its terms. Section 9 of the Wills Act 1837 should, however, be relevant because the intended secret trust property belongs absolutely and indefeasibly to the testator who is free to deal with it howsoever he pleases before he dies,[226] so that his disposition of the property outside his will is a testamentary disposition.[227] How, then, does there arise an equitable obligation binding the trustee's conscience?

3–166 The equitable principle that equity will not allow a statute to be used as an instrument of fraud was the basis for not allowing the Statute of Frauds 1677 to be invoked by persons intended to be secret trustees of testamentary gifts or to be trustees of inter vivos trusts of land.[228] The provisions of the 1677 Statute are now to be found in the Wills Act 1837 and the Law of Property Act 1925. The equitable principle should apply since there would be fraud if the secret trustee attempted to rely on the statute, whether dishonestly to try to retain a beneficial interest or to defeat a beneficial interest which he had led the testator to believe would belong to another. There would be not just a fraud on the testator in betraying the testator's confidence;[229] there would also be a harmful fraud on the secret beneficiary who would be deprived of the benefit which, but for the trustee agreeing to carry out the testator's wishes, would surely have been secured for him by other means. Thus, in a fully secret trust and also in a half-secret trust the trustee holds the testator's property not on resulting or constructive trust for the testator's residuary legatee (or next of kin as the case may be) but on the express trust for the beneficiary: it would be unconscionable for the trustee to hold the property otherwise by invoking the Wills Act for that would enable statute to be used as an instrument of fraud. Thus, C can enforce his interest where A devises land by will to B on an oral trust for C.[230]

3–167 Alternatively, the same result can be achieved if one treats such trusts as constructive trusts, exempted from the Law of Property Act 1925 s.53(1) by s.53(2), on the ground that such trusts, unlike ordinary express trusts which can be created unilaterally, depend crucially upon the trustee's express or tacit promise to honour the trust in favour of the secret beneficiary.[231] As Robert Walker L.J. stated in *Gillett v Holt*, "There must be an agreement between A and B conferring a benefit on C because it is the agreement which would make it unconscionable for B to resile from his agreement."[232] This was his view of secret trusts as well as mutual wills: "both doctrines show equity intervening to prevent unconscionable conduct".[233]

5. Post Mortem Trusts: Mutual Wills

3–168 The term "mutual wills" is used to describe documents of a testamentary character made as the result of a contract between husband and wife, or other persons, to create irrevocable interests in

---

[226] *Kasperbauer v Griffith* [2000] W.T.L.R. 333 at 343.

[227] Since secret trusts operate outside the will it is illogical in the case of a half-secret trust not to allow communication after the date of the will but before the testator's death and claim that otherwise the Wills Act would be avoided: see above, paras 3–138 to 3–139.

[228] *McCormick v Grogan* (1868) L.R. 4 H.L. 82 at 88–89; *Jones v Badley* (1868) 3 Ch. App. 362 at 364; *Rochefoucauld v Boustead* [1897] 1 Ch. 196.

[229] As stated in *Re Dale, deceased* [1994] Ch. 31 at 48, in relation to mutual wills made by two testators, T1 and T2, where T1 dies and T2 makes a will departing from what was agreed, "I am unable to see why it should be any the less a fraud on T1 if the agreement was that each testator should leave his or her property to particular beneficiaries, e.g. their children, rather than to each other."

[230] *Ottaway v Norman* [1972] Ch. 698. In *Re Baillie* (1886) 2 T.L.R. 660, 661 a half-secret trust of land failing for one reason also failed for not complying with written formalities: this seems erroneous.

[231] In *Re Cleaver, deceased* [1981] 1 W.L.R. 931 at 947, Nourse J. categorised secret trusts as constructive trusts, and Peter Gibson L.J. endorsed this in *Kasperbauer v Griffith* [2000] W.T.L.R. 333 at 342.

[232] [2001] Ch. 210 at 228.

[233] *Gillett* at 228.

favour of ascertainable beneficiaries. The revocable nature of the wills under which the interests are created is fully recognised by the court of probate,[234] but, in certain circumstances, the court of equity will protect and enforce the interests created by the agreement despite the revocation of the will by one party after the death of the other without having revoked his will.

3–169 A typical case of mutual wills arises in the following circumstances: H(usband) and W(ife) agree to execute mutual wills (or a joint will) leaving their respective properties to the survivor of them for life, with remainder to the same ultimate beneficiary (B). H dies and W makes a fresh will leaving her property away from B to her second husband (S). In these circumstances, H's will (or the joint will) is admitted to probate on his death and, under it, W gets a life interest and B an interest in remainder. On W's death, her second will is admitted to probate. Under it her property vests in her personal representatives upon a trust, not for S, but to give effect to the terms of the agreement upon which the mutual wills were made, i.e. upon trust for B.

3–170 It is clear from *Re Walters, deceased*,[235] which is reproduced below,[236] that B's interest in W's property arises under a constructive trust,[237] and that this interest arises as soon as H dies.[238] It prevails over S's interest in W's property by virtue of the maxim that "where the equities are equal the first in time prevails." Indeed, if B survives H but predeceases W then his interest in W's property does not lapse but is payable to his personal representatives, and forms part of his estate.[239] B's interest arises irrespective of whether W disclaims her benefit under H's will[240] and even if H and W left no property to each other, leaving everything to B.[241] It is the death of H, no longer having the opportunity to revoke his own will, which concludes performance of the contract and renders the will of W irrevocable in equity, although it is always revocable at law.

3–171 The courts will not impose a constructive trust merely because mutual wills are made in almost identical terms. There must be evidence of an agreement to create interests under the mutual wills which are intended to be irrevocable after the death of the first to die. As Leggatt L.J. stated in *Re Goodchild, deceased*:[242]

> "A key feature of mutual wills is the irrevocability of the mutual intentions. Not only must they be [contractually] binding when made, but the testators must have undertaken, and so must be bound, not to change their intentions after the death of the first testator."

Where there is no such evidence, the fact that the survivor takes an absolute interest is a factor against the implication of an agreement.[243] Where, however, the evidence is clear, as, for example, where it is contained in recitals in the wills themselves, the fact that each testator gave the other an absolute

---

234 *Re Heys, deceased* [1914] P. 192.
235 [2009] Ch. 212.
236 At paras 3–177 ff.
237 See too *Birmingham v Renfrew* (1937) 57 C.L.R. 666 at 680, where Latham C.J. described the trust as "a trust which is declared by the law to affect the conscience of [the survivor's] executor and of the volunteers who are devisees or legatees under his will".
238 *Thomas and Agnes Carvel Foundation v Carvel* [2008] Ch. 395 at [27], per Lewison J.: "the trust does not arise under the will of the surviving testator. Nor does it arise under any previous will of the surviving testator. It arises out of the agreement between the two testators not to revoke their wills, and the trust arises when the first of the two dies without having revoked his will". See too *Barns v Barns* (2003) 214 C.L.R. 169 at [85].
239 *Re Hagger* [1930] 2 Ch. 190.
240 *Dufour v Pereira* (1769) 1 Dick. 419 at 421; *Stone v Hoskins* [1905] P. 194 at 197; *Re Hagger* [1930] 2 Ch. 190.
241 *Re Dale, deceased* [1994] Ch. 31.
242 [1997] 1 W.L.R. 1216 at 1225. See too *Birch v Curtis* [2002] 2 F.L.R. 847 at [64] ff.
243 *Re Oldham* [1925] Ch. 75.

interest with a substitutional gift in the event of the other's prior death does not prevent a trust from arising.[244]

3–172 The requirement for mutual wills that is sometimes expressed as the need for "an agreement not to revoke" the wills is more aptly expressed as the need for "acceptance of an obligation imposed by the other party", since the obligation may well allow the will of the survivor to be revoked so long as a new will is made giving effect to the agreed arrangements.[245] The acceptance of an obligation may be difficult to prove in husband and wife situations where there is less likely to be an intention to impose legal relationships, neither party making the gifts by will on the faith of a promise by the other to accept legal obligations, but instead, making the gifts without any strings attached, confidently assuming the other party will do as asked.[246]

3–173 The principle is that the survivor becomes a trustee for the performance of the mutual agreement after the death of the first to die. Accordingly there will be no trust if the agreement is too vague to be enforced.[247] Subject to this, however, the agreement can define the property, which is to be subject to the trust, in any way that the parties to the agreement please. The trust may give the survivor nothing[248] or just give the survivor a life interest in all or a specific part of the deceased's property or it may also provide for the survivor to have a life interest in all or a specific part of his own property at the date of death of the deceased.[249] Sometimes, it may appear that the survivor is to be absolute owner of the deceased's property passing to him under the will and of his own existing and subsequently acquired property, but that he is supposed to be under some binding obligation to bequeath whatever he has left at his death to the agreed beneficiaries.[250] If the parties fail to make it clear which property is subject to the trust then this uncertainty may make it impossible for the survivor to know what dispositions he is entitled to make during his lifetime, in which it case it may be that he will have to apply to the court for directions.[251]

3–174 Before the death of the first to die the agreement is a contractual one made in consideration of the mutual promises of H and W for the benefit of B, who neither is a party to the contract nor supplies consideration.[252] Whether H would be in breach of the contract if he told W that he no longer intended to give effect to their arrangement, or if his will was automatically revoked by remarriage to someone else after divorcing W, or if he revoked his will without informing W but predeceased W, depends on the construction of the contract. Prima facie it seems that the contract will be presumed revocable upon notice to the other party or upon the will automatically being revoked by marriage so as not to be broken if such circumstances occur.[253] However, if H makes a new will containing new arrangements without informing W, but predeceases W, it seems that W can sue H's executors for damages for losses flowing from the breach of contract (though W will be released from her obligations under contract) or for specific performance if willing to fulfil her obligations.

3–175 If H dies first, by his will carrying into effect the mutual arrangement, then, in order to protect B and to prevent W repudiating her obligations, a constructive trust is imposed since B is unable to bring an

---

244 *Re Green, deceased* [1951] Ch. 148.
245 *Lewis v Cotton* [2001] W.T.L.R. 1117 at 1129.
246 *Gray v Perpetual Trustee Ltd* [1928] A.C. 391; *Re Oldham* [1925] Ch 75; *Re Goodchild, deceased* [1997] 1 W.L.R. 1216.
247 *Re Walters, deceased* [2009] Ch. 212 at [36].
248 *Re Dale, deceased* [1994] Ch. 31.
249 *Re Hagger* [1930] 2 Ch. 190.
250 Such beneficiaries may well not have vested interests liable to be divested: the parties probably intend them to benefit only if alive on the survivor's death so that if they all predecease the survivor his fiduciary obligation will cease.
251 As in *Edell v Sitzer* (2001) 4 I.T.E.L.R. 149, where the court declined to make an order as the parties had not made mutual wills. For further discussion, see P. Luxton [2009] Conv. 498.
252 *Dufour v Pereira* (1769) 1 Dick. 419 at 421; *Lord Walpole v Lord Oxford* (1797) 3 Ves. 402; *Gray v Perpetual Trustee Co* [1928] A.C. 391; *Birmingham v Renfrew* (1937) 57 C.L.R. 666; *Re Walters, deceased* [2009] Ch. 212.
253 *Dufour* at 420; *Stone v Hoskins* [1905] P. 194 at 197; *Re Marsland* [1939] Ch. 820; *Lewis v Cotton* [2001] W.T.L.R. 1117 at 1129.

action for specific performance[254] of the express terms of the contract—or was unable until advantage could be taken of the Contracts (Rights of Third Parties) Act 1999. If the contract relates not just to whatever assets might be owned at death, but also to interests in land, then equity will not allow the Law of Property (Miscellaneous Provisions) Act 1989 s.2 to be pleaded since this would be to use the statute as an instrument of fraud.[255]

It seems that the principles underlying mutual wills extend to an agreement subsequent to the making of the wills[256] and to an agreement between joint tenants not to sever their interest on terms that the survivor will dispose of the asset in an agreed manner.[257] **3–176**

RE WALTERS, DECEASED; OLINS v WALTERS

Court of Appeal [2009] Ch. 212; [2009] 2 W.L.R. 1

MUMMERY L.J. (with whom DYSON and MAURICE KAY L.JJ. agreed): Norris J. held that in 1998 Mr Harold Walters and his late wife, Freda ("the deceased") made a mutual wills contract pursuant to which they executed similar codicils amending their wills. The deceased died in 2006 leaving her will and codicil unrevoked. Mr Walters inherited her estate, but disputed the application of the mutual wills doctrine to him or to the deceased's estate in his hands. **3–177**

The judge applied the principles summarised by Dixon J. in *Birmingham v Renfrew*:[258] **3–178**

> "It has long been established that a contract between persons to make corresponding wills gives rise to equitable obligations when one acts on the faith of such an agreement and dies leaving his will unrevoked so that the other takes property under its dispositions. It operates to impose upon the survivor an obligation regarded as specifically enforceable. It is true that he cannot be compelled to make and leave unrevoked a testamentary document and if he dies leaving a last will containing provisions inconsistent with his agreement it is nevertheless valid as a testamentary act. But the doctrines of equity attach the obligation to the property. The effect is, I think, that the survivor becomes a constructive trustee and the terms of the trust are those of the will he undertook would be his last will."

This appeal is about (1) the sufficiency of the evidence for the finding of a mutual wills contract between Mr Walters and the deceased, and (2) the sufficiency in law of its terms. The litigation is regrettable. A family apparently united around the grandparents is now divided on the question whether they made a mutual wills contract. The decision on this appeal may not bring the dispute to an end. If the appeal fails, further issues may arise about the effect of the mutual wills on the ability of Mr Walters to deal with the assets derived from the deceased's estate. As recent cases have shown this equitable doctrine dating from the 18th century[259] continues to be a source of contention for the families of those who have invoked it. The likelihood is that in future even fewer people will opt for such an arrangement and even more will be warned against the risks involved. **3–179**

In its *22nd Report on the Making and Revocation of Wills* the Law Reform Committee noted particular problems with the mutual wills doctrine. It recommended that the difficulties would "be better clarified by judicial development than by legislation".[260] The novel aspect of this case is that the survivor of the alleged **3–180**

---

254 *Birmingham v Renfrew* (1937) 57 C.L.R. 666; *Re Dale, deceased* [1994] Ch. 31.
255 *Birmingham* at 690; *Lewis v Cotton* [2001] W.T.L.R. 1117 at 1131. These dicta should be preferred to the contrary finding in *Healey v Brown* [2002] W.T.L.R. 849.
256 *Re Fox* [1951] Ontario R. 378.
257 *Re Newey* [1994] 2 N.Z.L.R. 590, *Manitoba University v Sandeman* (1998) 155 D.L.R. (4th) 40.
258 (1937) 57 C.L.R. 666 at 683.
259 Lord Camden L.C.'s judgment in *Dufour v Pereira* (1769) 1 Dick. 419.
260 (Cmnd 7902, 1980) p.26, para.3.52.

contract is alive and gave evidence denying the alleged contract and disputing the application of the doctrine and its consequences. This feature was absent from all the authorities cited to the court.[261]

3–181 The declaration made by Norris J. on 18 January 2008 was that the codicils executed by Mr Walters and the deceased on 18 May 1998 take effect as mutual wills so as to bind the deceased's estate "in the hands of the defendant" and of his personal representatives. The judge made another order which has not been challenged on this appeal. He pronounced in solemn form of law for the deceased's last will dated 11 March 1988 and for its codicil dated 18 May 1998.

3–182 Ward L.J. granted permission to appeal on 19 March 2008. There are two grounds of appeal. The first is one of law: that the judge wrongly granted a declaration as to the existence of mutual wills binding the deceased's estate in the hands of Mr Walters without determining with sufficient particularity the terms of the contract. The second is one of fact: that the evidence of a mutual wills contract was not as "clear and satisfactory" as the case law requires and that the judge should have concluded on the evidence that no such contract was in fact ever made.

3–183 Mr Steinfeld, who appeared for Mr Walters, sometimes treated the two grounds as one. They are, however, distinct and require separate consideration.

Factual Background

3–184 Mr Walters was born in 1912. He is now aged 96. In 1934 he and the deceased got married. They have two daughters and five grandchildren. On 11 March 1988 they each made a will in almost identical terms replacing wills made by them in February 1953. Each appointed the other and the claimant, Mr Andrew Olins ("Andrew"), who is a solicitor and one of their grandsons, as executors. After a settled legacy each left the other their entire residuary estate absolutely, subject to surviving by 30 days. On 18 May 1998, by which time the deceased's health was failing, they made codicils in similar terms. They were drafted by Andrew.

3–185 Andrew has a younger brother, Edward. He was present at a meeting in the morning of Saturday 21 February 1998, when the grandparents executed enduring powers of attorney drafted for them by Andrew. Following the meeting Andrew also drafted two codicils and sent them to his grandparents under cover of a letter.

3–186 Clause 2 of the deceased's draft codicil was in the following terms: "This codicil is made pursuant to an agreement made between my husband and me for the disposal of our property in a similar way by mutual testamentary dispositions."

3–187 Clause 2 of Mr. Walters's draft codicil was in similar terms.

3–188 Andrew's evidence was that instructions for the codicils drafted by him had been given at the meeting on 21 February. On 31 March 1998 he wrote to his grandparents enclosing draft codicils to their wills. In the covering letter he drew their attention to clause 2 of the codicil explaining it in the following terms:

> "The other main change to your wills is at clause 2 of your codicils. By clause 2 you agree that neither of you will, at any time in the future, seek to make any further changes to the testamentary arrangements for distributing your estates without the consent of the other. Obviously after one of you dies no changes at all will be possible. You told me that you wanted this agreement in place so that the survivor of you, especially if it is grandma, does not come under any pressure from family members to change the testamentary arrangements."

3–189 In the event of one of them failing to survive the other, the codicils reduced the provision in the 1988 wills for their two daughters from gifts of capital of two thirds of the estate to life interests in the two thirds, subject to which the capital was to be divided equally amongst the grandchildren, who also took, free of any life interest, the remaining one third. The codicils were returned to Andrew at a meeting on 23 May 1998. He wrote to them on 28 May informing them that the codicils were to be placed with their wills for safekeeping.

[261] *Re Oldham* [1925] Ch. 75; *Birmingham v Renfrew* (1937) 57 C.L.R. 666; *Re Cleaver, deceased* [1981] 1 W.L.R. 939; *Re Dale, deceased* [1994] Ch. 31; *Re Goodchild, deceased* [1996] 1 W.L.R. 694, affirmed [1997] 1 W.L.R. 1216; and *Birch v Curtis* [2002] 2 F.L.R. 847.

By the time that the deceased died on 20 May 2006 at the age of 93, relations between Mr Walters and Andrew had deteriorated. The main asset in the deceased's estate is the house in Mill Hill, in which they lived and which was in her name. We were told that it is estimated to be worth about £1.5m. **3–190**

Andrew produced the codicils and contended that there was a mutual wills agreement. Mr Walters said that he had no recollection of the meeting on 21 February 1998, or of the codicils, or of the agreement referred to in clause 2 of the codicils. He also denied that the deceased's codicil and her 1988 will were validly witnessed. **3–191**

The Proceedings and the Judgment

On 16 March 2007 Andrew began these proceedings to have the deceased's 1988 will and the 1998 codicil proved in solemn form and for a declaration that the deceased's codicil takes effect as a valid and effective mutual will. Mr Walters counterclaimed for the deceased's 1953 will to be proved in solemn form and also claimed damages from the claimant for breach of duty. The judge dismissed the counterclaim. Mr Walters has not appealed against that. **3–192**

[Mummery L.J. summarised the judge's findings of fact, and continued:] The judge considered the effect of the agreement made between Mr Walters and the deceased. He held that a valid mutual will was made. He rejected submissions on behalf of Mr Walters that the agreement was not intended to be a binding agreement and that it did not satisfy the requirements for mutual wills, because it did not record any express agreement not to revoke the wills so made. He held that, as a matter of construction, the agreement described in clause 2 of the codicil was a reference to an agreement to dispose of property in a particular way and by a particular method. He did not regard the absence of any explicit mention of revocation as rendering "the mutual testamentary dispositions" incapable of enforcement as mutual wills, a reading which was reinforced by a consideration of the surrounding circumstances, in particular the covering letter of explanation. **3–193**

As for the form of the relief to be granted on the mutual wills aspect of the case, the judge held that the declaration should be that the codicils executed by the deceased and Mr Walters on 18 May 1998 "take effect as valid and effective mutual wills *so as to bind the deceased's estate*."[262] He explained the italicised words by the fact that he had made no findings or holdings as to the scope of the agreement relating to mutual wills, which he regarded as a question of construction of the agreement embodied in clause 2 of the codicil. He confirmed that, as reflected in the form of declaration, the deceased's estate was bound by the agreement "when in due course it passes to Mr Walters or his executors". He added that he regarded the issue of Mr Walters's own estate as simply not before him. The declaration was made as to the deceased's estate, but nothing else. **3–194**

Defendant's Submissions

On the first ground of appeal—the insufficiency of the terms of the contract—Mr Steinfeld submitted that it was vital to know all the terms of the contract for mutual wills. How else could the subject matter and terms of the constructive trust arising from it be determined? The judge had erred in failing to decide with sufficient particularity the scope and terms of the contract. The survivor was entitled to know exactly what he could or could not do with the assets that he acquired on the death of the deceased, or, indeed, with his own assets. **3–195**

On the judge's findings it was unclear what property was affected by the supposed constructive trust and what Mr Walters was entitled to do with the deceased's property, which had been left to him absolutely under the 1988 will, and even what he was entitled to do with his own property during the rest of his life. There was a range of possibilities as to the scope of the contract which the judge had failed to determine. Was Mr Walters prevented from dealing with the deceased's estate at all in his lifetime? Or did the constructive trust only extend to the part of the deceased's estate left when he died? Did it extend to his estate at the date of the deceased's death? Or as at the date of his death? What was the position in relation to the Mill Hill house? What, if anything, could be done in relation to it? **3–196**

The problem arising from lack of contractual certainty was, Mr Steinfeld submitted, well illustrated in two ways: first, by the form of the *quia timet* injunction originally sought in the claim form, but later **3–197**

[262] At [41].

abandoned because of the difficulty of formulating it; and secondly, and more immediately, by a very recent exchange between the parties about whether, if Mr Walters lost his appeal and was ordered to pay the costs, he would be entitled to use property coming to him absolutely from the deceased's estate to pay those costs. It was said on behalf of Andrew that Mr Walters would not be entitled to make that use of the deceased's property or make any other disposition of it inter vivos that would subvert the purpose for which the constructive trust was imposed to give effect to the contract.

3–198 It was also submitted by Mr Steinfeld that the terms of the declaration made by the judge were incorrect. The constructive trust did not affect the deceased's property in the hands of Mr Walters at all. The estate was expressly left to him absolutely. The trust would only bind his personal representatives as regards any property left by him on his death. The words "of the defendant" should be omitted from the declaration to make it clear that the constructive trust did not affect the assets of the deceased's estate in his hands.

3–199 On the second ground—the insufficiency of the evidence for a contract—it was submitted that the judge was not entitled to make a finding of a mutual wills contract . . .

Discussion and Conclusions

3–200 [Mummery L.J. held that there was "ample evidence to entitle [the judge] to find as a fact that the grandparents made the contract referred to in clause 2 of their codicils", and continued:] I turn to the legal submission that the contract found by the judge is not in law a valid and binding contract for mutual wills and that the judge was accordingly wrong in law to make the declaration in the form that he did, or at all.

3–201 In my judgment, Mr Steinfeld's submissions on insufficiency of the terms of the contract between Mr Walters and the deceased do not accurately reflect the fundamental principles of mutual wills.

3–202 It is a legally necessary condition of mutual wills that there is clear and satisfactory evidence of a contract between two testators. However, the argument resting on the alleged insufficiency or uncertainty of the terms of this contract is misconceived. The case for the existence of mutual wills does not involve making a contractual claim for specific performance or other relief. The claimant in a mutual wills case is not even a party to the contract and does not have to establish that he was.

3–203 The obligation on the surviving testator is equitable. It is in the nature of a trust of the property affected, so the constructive trust label is attached to it. The equitable obligation is imposed for the benefit of third parties, who were intended by the parties to benefit from it. It arises by operation of law on the death of the first testator to die so as to bind the conscience of the surviving testator in relation to the property affected.

3–204 It is a legally sufficient condition to establish what the judge described as "its irreducible core", which he analysed as a contract between two testators, T1 and T2:[263]

> "that in return for T1 agreeing to make a will in form X and not to revoke it without notice to T2, then T2 will make a will in form Y and agree not to revoke it without notice to T1. If such facts are established then upon the death of T1 equity will impose upon T2 a form of constructive trust (shaped by the exact terms of the contract that T1 and T2 have made). The constructive trust is imposed because T1 has made a disposition of property on the faith of T2's promise to make a will in form Y, and with the object of preventing T1 from being defrauded."

3–205 In my judgment, that is an accurate and clear statement of the equitable principles. Mr Steinfeld accepted that. He agreed that Mr Walters would be bound by a constructive trust, but only if sufficient terms of the contract were established to raise one.

3–206 The answer to the sufficiency point is, I think, summed up in a single sentence in *Snell's Equity*:[264]

> "Mutual wills provide an instance of a trust arising by operation of law to give effect to an express intention of the two testators."

[263] At [9].
[264] 31st edn (2005), para.22–31.

The intentions of Mr Walters and the deceased were sufficiently expressed in the contract to lay the foundations for the equitable obligations that bind the conscience of Mr Walters, as the survivor, in relation to the deceased's estate. The judge found all that he needed to find in order to hold that, contrary to the contentions of Mr Walters, mutual wills existed. Possible, and as yet unexplored, legal consequences of the application of the equitable principles do not negative the existence of the foundation contract or prevent a constructive trust from arising by operation of law on the death of the deceased. **3–207**

It had been accepted on behalf of Mr Walters in submissions to Norris J. that, if there was a valid contract for mutual wills, the doctrine operated by imposing a constructive trust on him as the survivor, because the deceased had performed her promise to leave her estate to him. In my judgment, the trust is immediately binding on him in relation to the deceased's property left to him on the basis of the contract. It is not postponed to take effect only after the death of Mr Walters when the property, or what may be left of it, comes into the hands of his personal representatives. **3–208**

Disputes about the actual operation of the trust in practice usually turn on construction of the contract in all the relevant circumstances. Of course, the disagreements can be resolved without litigation, if all the beneficiaries are agreed and have legal capacity to do so. If not, the disputes can be determined on an application to the court by Mr Walters in proceedings to which those interested are made parties. **3–209**

In this case the issues before the judge were the validity of the codicil and the existence of the mutual wills contract, both of which were unsuccessfully contested by Mr Walters. The judge determined those issues against him for sound reasons in an excellent judgment. He was not asked to rule on the possible legal consequences of the declaration for Mr Walters or for the beneficiaries arising on the death of the deceased. The judge prudently declined to be drawn into determining matters, such as the scope or extent of the constructive trust, which were neither raised in the pleadings nor in the submissions of the parties. As Bowen L.J. said in *Cooke v New River Co*,[265] the teaching of experience is that judgments should be given on points that the judge is bound to decide. Deciding more than is necessary could, "like the proverbial chickens of destiny", come home to roost sooner or later. Unnecessary opinions can be a source of future embarrassment, or even worse when, as here, no other points have been pleaded, investigated or argued. **3–210**

Questions

1. T1 and T2 hold property on trust for X. What formalities are required in the following situations? **3–211**
   (a) X assigns his equitable interest to Y, or to A and B on trust for Y;
   (b) X directs T1 and T2 to hold the property on trust for Y;
   (c) X contracts with Y to transfer his equitable interest to him;
   (d) X declares himself a trustee of his interest for Y;
   (e) X declares himself trustee of his interest for himself for life, remainder for Y absolutely;
   (f) X directs T1 and T2 to transfer the property to P and Q on trust for Y;
   (g) X directs T1 and T2 that they henceforth have power to appoint the property to such of Y, his spouse and issue as they may see fit, and a month later T1 and T2 declare that they therefore hold the property on trust for Y for life, remainder to his children equally.
2. Two years ago Brian transferred his cottage to Tom, orally telling Tom to hold it for Brian for life and then for Clarissa absolutely. He also transferred 10,000 ICI Plc shares, 8,000 Hanson Plc shares and 6,000 British Gas shares to his sister, Susan, orally telling her to hold them for himself or for such of their relatives as she might select. He soon told her to hold the ICI shares for Clarissa absolutely. Susan complied but said that she was now going to hold the Hanson shares for her cousin, Joy. Brian then told her to transfer the British Gas shares to Tom, who had already **3–212**

[265] (1888) 38 Ch. D. 56 at 71.

orally agreed to hold them on the same trusts as he held the cottage. Susan did so transfer the shares. A year ago Brian had a row with Clarissa and so told Tom, "Hold the cottage and the shares for me absolutely until I decide what to do about them." Last month he wrote a letter to Tom, "When I die I want you to transfer the cottage and the shares to Joy." A fortnight ago Brian died, having, by will, left everything to Eric. **Advise Eric.**

3–213 3. Is this a sound approach to gifts by will where secret trusts or mutual wills may be involved?

(a) Consider if there appears to be (i) incorporation by reference, (ii) a half-secret trust, (iii) a fully secret trust, or (iv) mutual wills.

(b) If (i) ask whether the will refers to an ascertainable already existing document or attempts to incorporate a future document or an assortment of present and future documents.

(c) If (ii) ask whether the terms of the obligation were communicated before or after the will and, if before, ask if they were communicated in accordance with the will, to a person who accepted them, who does not take beneficially under the trust if the obligation was a trust (rather than a gift upon condition).

(d) If (iii) ask whether there was an intention outside of the will to create a binding obligation, and whether the terms of the obligation were communicated in the testator's lifetime to a person who accepted the obligation.

(e) If (iv) ask whether the parties accepted that the survivor would be legally obliged to carry out the arrangements.

3–214 4. In 2006 Alan made his will as follows: "Whatever I die possessed of I give to my wife Brenda." The will was witnessed by two of Alan's daughters, Diana and Edwina. Shortly afterwards, Alan asked Brenda if she would hold half the property she received under his will for their three daughters, Diana, Edwina and Freda equally. Brenda assented to this. In 2010 Freda ran away with a merchant seaman, Wayne. As a result Alan told Brenda to keep Freda's share for herself. A year ago Diana died, childless, and a week later Alan died after a long illness. **How should his £150,000 estate be distributed? Would it make any difference if Brenda disclaimed all benefits due to pass to her under the will and relied, instead, upon her rights under the intestacy rules?**

3–215 5. H and W make wills in identical terms mutatis mutandis in pursuance of an agreement that they were each to leave their estates upon trust for sale for the survivor absolutely, the survivor being obliged to leave half of the property he owned at his death to their nephews, A and B, equally. Each agreed not to withdraw from the arrangement without giving notice to the other. W died childless having left all her estate upon trust for sale for H absolutely.

H later married S and made a second will leaving half his property to A and B equally, one quarter to S absolutely and one quarter to S "upon trusts which have been communicated to her." In a sealed envelope given to S shortly before H made his second will there were directions that S was to hold the quarter share given to her as trustee on trust for X for life remainder to Y absolutely, while one month before his death H asked S to hold her absolute quarter share upon trust for Z and she agreed. H and S were involved in a bad car crash resulting in S predeceasing H by one day.

How should H's estate be distributed if the property received by H under W's will was worth £150,000 while the property passing under H's will was worth £100,000? Would it make any difference if two years after W's death and seven years before his own death H had created a settlement of £40,000 on trust for X for life, remainder to Y absolutely? Would the position be any different if W's estate had been worth £500,000 and she had died intestate owing to her will failing to comply with the formalities required by the Wills Act 1837?

4 THE THREE CERTAINTIES

1. Introduction

4–01 To create a trust, the relevant property must be vested in the trustees (i.e. the trust must be completely constituted),[1] all requisite formalities must be complied with,[2] and the "three certainties" must be present: certainty of intention to create a trust, certainty of subject matter of the trust, and certainty of beneficiaries. These are mechanisms to ensure that there are obligations that are administratively workable and capable of being "policed" by the court. In the discussion which follows, each of the "three certainties" is considered in turn.

4–02 If it is uncertain that a property-owner has intended to create a trust then he or his estate will retain the beneficial interest in the relevant property. If there is uncertainty of subject-matter, then the alleged trust will be ineffective because it will be impossible to tell which property it should "bite" on. If certainty of intention and of subject-matter are both present, but there is uncertainty of beneficiaries, then the intended trustee will hold the property on a resulting trust for the owner or his estate as the case may be.[3] If property is given by will or other instrument to someone absolutely and subsequently in that instrument trusts are imposed on that absolute interest then if these trusts fail for uncertainty the donee will take the property for himself absolutely.[4]

2. Certainty of Intention

4–03 It must be certain that a settlor intended to create a trust because the key event that gives rise to a trust is the settlor's unilateral decision to bring the trust into being. The intended trustee's decision to accept the trust property and act as trustee then makes that trustee the trustee of the trust. If he decided against it, however, the trust would still subsist, and the beneficiaries would still have equitable interests, albeit with the settlor or the settlor's personal representative as trustee until new trustees were appointed. In the vast majority of cases the trustees know that they are trustees, having agreed with the settlor to be trustees, and the beneficiaries know that they are beneficiaries. However a trust can be created unilaterally by a settlor in circumstances where the trustees do not know that they are trustees[5] and/or the beneficiaries do not know that they are beneficiaries.[6]

4–04 Take the case of a trust created by will where the testator before he dies does not tell the trustees or the beneficiaries about his testamentary trust, which arises as soon as he dies. Equity does not allow a trust to fail for want of a trustee,[7] and so if the trustees refuse to act and disclaim the intended

---

1 See Chapter 2.
2 See Chapter 3.
3 For further discussion, see paras 14–31 ff.
4 *Hancock v Watson* [1902] A.C. 14; *Re Burton's ST* [1955] Ch. 348.
5 *Fletcher v Fletcher* (1844) 4 Hare 67; *Childers v Childers* (1857) 1 De G. & J. 482.
6 *Fletcher v Fletcher* (1844) 4 Hare 67; *Re Lewis* [1904] 2 Ch. 656; *Rose v Rose* (1986) 7 N.S.W.L.R. 679 at 686; *Re Kayford* [1975] 1 W.L.R. 279. Indeed, there may be no beneficiaries for a period while income is being accumulated and the ultimate contingent beneficiary may not be born or otherwise ascertained for some time, especially for jurisdictions other than England where the accumulation period can be as long as the perpetuity period.
7 *Mallott v Wilson* [1903] 2 Ch. 494; *Harris v Sharp* [2003] W.T.L.R. 1541; *Kynnersley v Wolverhampton C.C.* [2008] W.T.L.R. 65. See too paras 8–05 to 8–06.

trust property, the property falls to be held on trust by the person in whom the deceased's estate is vested, the executor or the administrator of the estate. This person holds the trust property (to the extent that it is not properly used for the payment of the deceased's debts and expenses) on trust for the beneficiaries until he exercises his power to appoint new trustees.[8]

4–05 The following matters are discussed in this section: (a) the language that a property owner must have used before a court will hold that he intended to create a trust; (b) the circumstances in which an arrangement that appears on its face to be a trust will be disregarded on the ground that it is a sham; (c) the types of arrangement other than a trust that a property owner might make when disposing of his property; and (d) the factors which determine whether a property owner intended to create a trust or a power.

A. *The Language Needed to Reveal Intent to Create a Trust*

4–06 No technical expressions are needed to create a trust, provided that some imperative formula is used to indicate that the person owning the relevant property is intended to be subject to a legally binding obligation to hold and manage the property for others (or himself and others). As Jessel M.R. said in *Richards v Delbridge*,[9] a settlor who intends to declare himself trustee "need not use the words 'I declare myself trustee', but he must do something which is equivalent to it, and use expressions which have that meaning". However, he added that the court "is not at liberty to construe the words otherwise than according to their proper meaning", and held that where a property-owner clearly intends to make a gift of legal title, but fails to carry out his intention, e.g. because he fails to comply with relevant formalities, then the court will not perfect his imperfect gift of legal title by reinterpreting his words as a declaration of trust. One reason is that the court does not generally assist volunteers by perfecting imperfect gifts;[10] another is that trusteeship is an onerous fiduciary office and that a person who means to get rid of all his rights to property might very well not intend to retain his rights but to come under an onerous fiduciary obligation.[11]

4–07 It may be questioned whether the court in *Paul v Constance*,[12] reproduced below,[13] was fully alive to the dangers of discovering an intention to declare a trust where a gift of legal title is a more plausible interpretation of the words used by the "settlor". Nevertheless there is much to be said for the proposition that not every property-owner understands the legal niceties, and that an owner who truly intends to create a trust should not have to use the word "trust", and should not be required to know that it is technically a trust that he is creating.[14]

4–08 An intention to create a trust of property normally requires indications that the alleged trustee must keep the specific trust property separate from his own.[15] After all if a recipient of money:[16]

---

8 This power is conferred by the Trustee Act 1925 s.36; for discussion see paras 8–09 ff.

9 (1874) L.R. 18 Eq. 11 at 14, reaffirmed in *Clarence House Ltd v National Westminster Bank Plc* [2009] EWCA Civ 1311 at [43], per Ward L.J.

10 See paras 2–11 ff.

11 F.W. Maitland, *Lectures on Equity* (1932), p.73.

12 [1977] 1 W.L.R. 177; followed in *Rowe v Prance* [1999] 2 F.L.R. 787 and *Wallbank v Price* [2008] 2 F.L.R. 501 at [50].

13 At paras 4–14 ff.

14 See also Buckley L.J. on the creation of an equitable charge in *Swiss Bank Corporation v Lloyds Bank* [1980] 2 All E.R. 419 at 426: "notwithstanding that the matter depends on the intention of the parties, if on the true construction of the relevant documents in the light of any admissible evidence as to surrounding circumstances the parties have entered into a transaction the legal effect of which is to give rise to an equitable charge, the fact that they may not have realised this consequence will not mean that there is no charge. They must be presumed to intend the consequences of their acts."

15 *Paragon Finance Plc v Thakerar & Co* [1999] 1 All E.R. 400 at 416; *Re Goldcorp Exchange Ltd* [1995] 1 A.C. 74; *Re English & American Insurance Co Ltd* [1994] 1 B.C.L.C. 345.

16 *Henry v Hammond* [1913] 2 K.B. 515 at 521; *R. v Clowes (No.2)* [1994] 2 All E.R. 316 at 325; *Commissioners of Customs & Excise v Richmond Theatre Management Ltd* [1995] S.T.C. 257.

> "is not bound to keep the money separate, but is entitled to mix it with his own money and deal with it as he pleases, and when called upon to hand over an equivalent sum of money, then he is not a trustee of the money but merely a debtor."

This principle was applied in *Azam v Iqbal*,[17] where the defendant operated a "hawala", or money transfer facility, taking sterling payments from customers in the UK, and crediting their relatives in Pakistan with rupees at an agreed exchange rate. The claimant paid him £12,000, but before the claimant's sister was paid a corresponding amount in rupees in Pakistan, a receiver was appointed over the defendant's assets. The claimant asserted that the £12,000 had been held on trust for him, but this was rejected, the judge holding that the defendant had never been required to segregate the money from his other funds, and that the parties' relationship, like that between a banker and customer,[18] had simply been that of debtor and creditor.

However, mingling of funds will not be fatal to the finding of a trust where T receives funds from A, B and C for such funds or investments purchased therewith to be held separately from T's own assets, on a trust for A, B and C in their proportionate shares[19] or where T adds funds of A, B and C to funds of his in a separate account so that such funds or investments purchased therewith are held separately from T's own assets on trust for A, B and C and T in proportionate shares.[20] T can also contract with X that if he receives proceeds of sale materialising from some specified future property, he will hold all or a specified part on trust for X, such trust then affecting the certain whole or part of the ascertained proceeds when received by T. Thus, even if they are mingled with T's funds in T's general bank account X has a right to trace such amount until properly placed in a separate account for X.[21] **4–09**

Wills often create problems where a testator expresses his confidence, wish, hope or request that a particular legatee should use the legacy in a certain way. Originally, the courts were only too ready to treat such precatory words as creating a trust,[22] and as James L.J. said in *Lamb v Eames*,[23] "the officious kindness of the Court of Chancery in interposing trusts where in many cases the father of the family never meant to create trusts, must have been a very cruel kindness indeed." Since the 1870s, however, the courts have not allowed precatory words to create a trust unless on consideration of the will as a whole it was clearly the testator's intention to create a trust.[24] **4–10**

By the Administration of Justice Act 1982 s.21, extrinsic evidence, including evidence of the testator's intention, may be admitted to assist in its interpretation (a) in so far as any part of the will is meaningless (b) in so far as the language used in any part of it is ambiguous on the face of it and (c) in so far as evidence, other than evidence of the testator's intention, shows that the language used in any part of it is ambiguous in the light of the surrounding circumstances. **4–11**

The following testamentary clauses have been held, in context, not to create a trust: "feeling confident that she will act justly to our children in dividing the same when no longer required by her,"[25] "it is my desire that she allows A.G. an annuity of £25 during her life,"[26] "I wish them to bequeath the **4–12**

---

[17] [2008] Bus. L.R. 168.
[18] *Foley v Hill* (1848) 2 H.L. Cas. 28.
[19] *R. v Clowes (No.2)*, above; *Re Goldcorp Exchange Ltd*, above.
[20] *Re Lewis's of Leicester Ltd* [1995] 1 B.C.L.C. 428.
[21] *Re Fleet Disposal Services Ltd* [1995] 1 B.C.L.C. 345; cf. *Re ILG Travel* [1995] 2 B.C.L.C. 128; *Pullan v Koe* [1913] 1 Ch. 9; *Palette Shoes Pty Ltd v Krohn* (1937) 58 C.L.R. 1 at 27.
[22] *Eade v Eade* (1820) 5 Madd. 118 at 121; *Palmer v Simmonds* (1854) 2 Drew 221; *Gutty v Cregoe* (1857) 24 Beav 185.
[23] (1871) 6 Ch.App. 597.
[24] *Lamb v Eames* (1871) 6 Ch. App. 597; *Re Adams and Kensington Vestry* (1884) 27 Ch.D. 394.
[25] *Mussoorie Bank Ltd v Raynor* (1882) 7 App. Cas. 221.
[26] *Re Diggles* (1888) 39 Ch.D. 253.

same equally between the families of O and P,"[27] "in the fullest trust and confidence that she will carry out my wishes in the following particulars,"[28] "I request that C on her death leave her property to my four sisters."[29]

4–13 The Administration of Justice Act 1982 s.22, states that:

> "Except where a contrary intent is shown, it shall be presumed that if a testator devises or bequeaths property to his spouse in terms which in themselves would give an absolute interest to the spouse but by the same instrument purports to give his issue an interest in the same property, the gift to the spouse is absolute notwithstanding the purported gift to the issue."

So, for example, if a testator leaves "all my property to my wife and after her death to our children", the wife will take the property absolutely and is under no obligation to hold it on trust for the children.[30]

PAUL v CONSTANCE

Court of Appeal [1977] 1 W.L.R. 527; [1977] 1 All E.R. 195

4–14 SCARMAN L.J. (with whom BRIDGE and CAIRNS L.J. agreed): Mr Dennis Albert Constance was a wage earner living in Cheltenham until he died on March 9, 1974. He was married to Bridget Frances Constance, the defendant in this action. But they parted in June 1965. In 1967 Mr Constance met Mrs Doreen Grace Paul, who is the plaintiff in this action. The two of them set up house together in December of that year, and they lived to all appearances as man and wife up to the date of Mr Constance's death. The house in which they lived was the property of the plaintiff.

4–15 In August 1969 Mr Constance was injured at his work. He claimed damages against his employers . . . his claim was disposed of by the payment to him of a sum of £950. This money he received by cheque early in 1973. He discussed with the plaintiff what to do with the money, and the evidence is clear that they decided it was to go into a bank account. The two of them went to see the manager of the St George's Square branch of Lloyds Bank in Cheltenham, and there they had a discussion about opening a bank account. According to the notes of evidence which the trial judge made, the two of them had a discussion with the bank manager. He explained to them the different sorts of accounts which they could open, and the decision was taken to open a deposit account. At that stage Mr Constance revealed that they were not married. It is perhaps of some significance in understanding this interview if one recalls the evidence that was given by a Mr Thomas, a fellow employee of Mr Constance's, who said that he knew that they were not married but most people did not. After Mr Constance had told the manager that they were not married the manager said: "Well, it will be in your name only then?" Mr Constance said: "Yes." Then Mr Constance asked the manager what was to happen if the plaintiff wanted to draw on the account, or if he wanted the plaintiff to draw on it, and the manager said that that could be done if she used a note with Mr Constance's signature on it authorising her to draw on the account.

4–16 The account that was opened on that day in February 1973 is at the very heart of this case. The account was maintained in Mr Constance's name from that date until the date of his death. Over the period between 1973 and his death, some 13 months later in 1974, further sums were paid into the account including, in particular, some sums which represented "bingo" winnings. It is clear from the evidence that

---

[27] *Re Hamilton* (1895) 2 Ch. 370.
[28] *Re Williams* [1897] 2 Ch. 12.
[29] *Re Johnson* [1939] 2 All E.R. 458.
[30] cf. *Re Harrison, deceased* [2006] 1 W.L.R. 1212, where the testator had expressed a sufficient contrary intention to displace the statutory presumption contained in s.22, with the result that his widow had a life interest in the relevant property which was held on trust for the children in equal shares.

Mr Constance and the plaintiff did play "bingo", and they played it really as a joint venture. They did have winnings from time to time, and at any rate three of such winnings—none of them very great—were paid into the account. It is clear from the plaintiff's evidence that they thought of those winnings as "their winnings": neither hers nor his alone, but theirs. Nevertheless, when the account was closed on the death of Mr Constance the ultimate balance, after the addition of interest, consisted largely of the initial sum of £950 representing Mr Constance's damages as a result of his injury at work. There was one withdrawal during this period, a sum of £150, and the evidence was that that money was divided between the two of them after part of it had been used for buying Christmas presents and some food.

The plaintiff began her action after the death of Mr Constance against his lawful wife, the defendant, who took out letters of administration for his estate since he died intestate. The plaintiff claims that the bank account in his name, to which I have referred, was held by him on trust for the benefit of himself and the plaintiff jointly. She claims that it was an express trust declared orally by him on numerous occasions. The defendant maintains that the whole fund contained in the account was the beneficial property of the deceased at the time of his death, and, as such, became part of his estate after death. **4–17**

The matter came on for trial and on August 12 the Judge found in favour of the plaintiff. He found the existence of an express trust, a trust for the benefit of the plaintiff and the deceased jointly, and he ordered that the sum of £499.21 be paid to the plaintiff as representing one half share of the fund to which she was beneficially entitled. **4–18**

The only point taken by the defendant on her appeal to this court goes to the question whether or not there was, in the circumstances of this case, an express declaration of trust. **4–19**

Counsel for the defendant drew the attention of the court to the so-called three certainties that have to be established before the court can infer the creation of a trust. We are concerned only with one of the three certainties, and it is this:[31] **4–20**

> "The words [that is the words of the declaration relied on] must be so used that on the whole they ought to be construed as imperative. [A little later on the learned author says:] No particular form of expression is necessary for the creation of a trust, if on the whole it can be gathered that a trust was intended. A trust may well be created, although there may be an absence of any expression in terms imposing confidence. A trust may thus be created without using the word 'trust' for what the court regards is the substance and effect of the words used."

Counsel for the defendant has taken the court through the detailed evidence and submits that one cannot find anywhere in the history of events a declaration of trust in the sense of finding the deceased man, Mr Constance, saying: "I am now disposing of my interest in this fund so that you, Mrs Paul, now have a beneficial interest in it." Of course, the words which I have just used are stilted lawyers' language, and counsel for the plaintiff was right to remind the court that we are dealing with simple people, unaware of the subtleties of equity, but understanding very well indeed their own domestic situation. It is right that one should consider the various things that were said and done by the plaintiff and Mr Constance during their time together against their own background and in their own circumstances. **4–21**

Counsel for the defendant drew our attention to two cases [*Jones v Lock*[32] and *Richards v Delbridge*[33]], and he relies on them as showing that, though a man may say in clear and unmistakable terms that he intends to make a gift to some other person, for instance his child or some other member of his family, yet that does not necessarily disclose a declaration of trust; and, indeed, in the two cases to which we have been referred the court held that, though there was a plain intention to make a gift, it was not right to infer any intention to create a trust . . . **4–22**

There is no suggestion of a gift by transfer in this case. The facts of those cases do not, therefore, very much help the submission of counsel for the defendant, but he was able to extract from them this principle: that there must be a clear declaration of trust, and that means there must be clear evidence from what is said or done of an intention to create a trust, or as counsel for the defendant put it, "an intention to dispose of a **4–23**

[31] *Snell's Equity* 27th edn, at p.111.
[32] (1865) 1 Ch.App. 25.
[33] (1874) L.R. 18 Eq. 11.

property or a fund so that somebody else to the exclusion of the disponent acquires the beneficial interest in it." He submitted that there was no such evidence.

4–24 When one looks to the detailed evidence to see whether it goes as far as that—and I think that the evidence does have to go as far as that—one finds that from the time that Mr Constance received his damages right up to his death he was saying, on occasions, that the money was as much the plaintiff's as his. When they discussed the damages, how to invest them or what to do with them, when they discussed the bank account, he would say to her: "The money is as much yours as mine." The judge, rightly treating the basic problem in the case as a question of fact, reached this conclusion. He said:

> "I have read through my notes, and I am quite satisfied that it was the intention of [the plaintiff] and Mr Constance to create a trust in which both of them were interested."

4–25 In this court the issue becomes: was there sufficient evidence to justify the judge reaching that conclusion of fact? In submitting that there was, counsel for the plaintiff draws attention first and foremost to the words used. When one bears in mind the unsophisticated character of Mr Constance and his relationship with the plaintiff during the last few years of his life, counsel for the plaintiff submits that the words that he did use on more than one occasion namely: "This money is as much yours as mine", convey clearly a present declaration that the existing fund was as much the plaintiff's as his own. The judge accepted that conclusion. I think he was well justified in doing so and, indeed, I think he was right to do so. There are, as counsel for the plaintiff reminded us, other features in the history of the relationship between the plaintiff and Mr Constance which support the interpretation of those words as an express declaration of trust. I have already described the interview with the bank manager when the account was opened. I have mentioned also the putting of the "bingo" winnings into the account, and the one withdrawal for the benefit of both of them.

4–26 The question, therefore, is whether in all the circumstances the use of those words on numerous occasions as between Mr. Constance and the plaintiff constituted an express declaration of trust. The judge found that they did. For myself, I think he was right so to find. I therefore would dismiss the appeal.

Questions

4–27 Why was Mrs Paul not entitled to the whole £998.42 as surviving joint tenant?[34] Should it not be possible to identify a declaration of trust at a particular time, e.g. to know when Mrs Paul's right commenced for limitation purposes, or for tax purposes, or for entitlement to interest?

B. Shams

4–28 If language is used that would clearly suffice to create a trust for beneficiaries, it will be strongly presumed to create a proper trust.[35] But what if the rights and obligations apparently created by the trust instrument were always intended to disguise the fact that beneficial ownership actually remains vested in the settlor? In such a case the court can treat the supposed "trust" as a nullity on the ground that the arrangements made are a sham.[36] In drawing such a conclusion the court would take account of the subjective intentions of the settlor, S, and his trustee, T, and of any conduct subsequent to the creation of the trust that shows that it was really a sham from the outset.[37]

---

34 cf. *Re Osoba* [1979] 2 All E.R. 393.

35 *A v A* [2007] 2 F.L.R. 467 at [53]. Indeed, the settlor will generally not be allowed to deny the existence of a proper trust so as to recover the property for himself: *Official Assignee in Bankruptcy v Wilson* [2008] W.T.L.R. 1235.

36 See generally M. Conaglen, "Sham Trusts" (2008) 67 C.L.J. 176.

37 *Hitch v Stone* [2001] S.T.C. 214 at [65]; *Minwalla v Minwalla* [2005] 1 F.L.R. 771.

4–29 The classic sham is where the real subjective intention of the "settlor", S, and the "trustee", T, was for T to hold the trust property to S's order, with the terms of the trust instrument to be ineffective or only effective after S's death as a testamentary disposition (if complying with the formalities for wills). If S has unilaterally declared himself trustee of particular property, then it is his subjective intention that counts.[38] If, as is more usual, S has transferred property to T for a trust to be created, then it is their subjective common intention to create a false impression that counts.[39] A degree of dishonesty is involved in a sham,[40] so that S and T must have been aware that rights and obligations appear to have been created that are different from the rights and obligations that they meant to be created.

4–30 The law recognises that the concept of a sham or pretence can relate either to the whole of a document or to some of its provisions,[41] or just to some of the trust property, e.g. property added to a proper trust some period after its creation.[42] A sham trust can become a proper trust at a later date by mutual agreement of the settlor and the original or, more likely, a new trustee,[43] but once a proper trust is created it remains a proper trust, so that if the trustee commences doing as directed by the settlor without exercising his independent discretion this will be a breach of trust.[44]

4–31 The onus of proving that a document which appears to create a proper trust is actually a sham is on the person making the allegation.[45] Factors which might support such an allegation include:[46] unusually low fees for the value of the trust fund; lack of paperwork to reveal the trustee exercising an independent discretion; letters or emails indicating the trustee feels bound to do whatever the settlor wants; and keeping the trust secret from the beneficiaries. It is clearly open to third parties such as a supposed settlor's divorcing spouse or HMRC to claim that a document purporting to create a trust is a sham,[47] but it is not open to a purported settlor to deny the objective effect of his own acts by relying on his secret dishonest intention to produce a different outcome. In *Re Reynolds*[48] the New Zealand Court of Appeal concluded from this that a "settlor's" trustee in bankruptcy could not allege the existence of a sham either, as he could be in no better position than the "settlor" himself. However, it seems strongly arguable that the trustee in bankruptcy acts on behalf of the "settlor's" creditors, and that their ability to have a transaction declared a sham should not be compromised by the "settlor's" want of probity.

C. *Trusts Distinguished from Other Relationships*

4–32 A property owner may deal with his property in a variety of ways. His expressed wishes must be examined in the context of the surrounding circumstances to identify the consequences he expects to flow

---

38 *Painter v Hutchison* [2008] B.P.I.R. 170 at [111]–[112], [115].

39 *Shalson v Russo* [2005] Ch. 281 at [188] and [190]; *A v A* [2007] 2 F.L.R. 467 at [34] and also at [50] explaining *Midland Bank v Wyatt* [1995] 1 F.L.R. 697; *Re Reynolds* [2008] 3 N.Z.L.R. 45 at [29] ff.

40 *National Westminster Bank Plc v Jones* [2001] 1 B.C.L.C. 98 at [46] and [59], endorsed in *A v A* [2007] 2 F.L.R. 467 at [53]; *MacKinnon v Regent Trust Co Ltd* [2005] W.T.L.R 1367 at [19]–[20].

41 *National Westminster Bank Plc v Jones* [2001] 1 B.C.L.C. 98 at [42], [45], and [59]; *Hill v Spread Trustee Co Ltd* [2005] B.P.I.R. 842.

42 *Re Esteem Settlement* [2004] W.T.L.R. 1 at [60]; *Hill v Spread Trustee Co Ltd* [2005] B.P.I.R. 842.

43 *A v A* [2007] 2 F.L.R. 467 at [45] and [50].

44 *Shalson v Russo* [2005] Ch. 281; *A v A* [2007] 2 F.L.R. 467 at [42].

45 *A v A* [2007] 2 F.L.R. 467 at [69]; *National Westminster Bank Plc v Jones* [2001] 1 B.C.L.C. 98 at [68]. It is a serious allegation involving dishonesty, and "the more serious the allegation the less likely it is that he event occurred and, hence, the stronger should be the evidence before the court concludes that the allegation is established on the balance of probability": *Re H (Minors)* [1996] A.C. 563 at 586.

46 See e.g. *Rahman v Chase Bank (CI) Trust Co Ltd* [1991] J.L.R. 103; *Midland Bank Trust Co v Wyatt* [1995] 1 F.L.R. 696; *Minwalla v Minwalla* [2005] 1 F.L.R. 771.

47 As in e.g. *Rahman v Chase Bank (CI) Trust Co Ltd* [1991] J.L.R. 103; *Hitch v Stone* [2001] S.T.C. 214.

48 [2008] 3 N.Z.L.R. 45.

from his actions. These indicia may then be seen as appropriate to the creation of a trust relationship or some other relationship.[49] As we have discussed already, a person can create a trust without knowing it;[50] but on the other hand, he cannot succeed in creating a trust, no matter how clear his intention to do so, if the essence of the obligation he has created is that of a debt[51] or a charge,[52] rather than that of a trust.

i. Bailment

4–33 A bailment will be created if an owner delivers possession (as opposed to ownership) of his goods to another on the condition that they will be redelivered to the owner or according to the owner's directions when the purpose of delivering the goods has been carried out (e.g. goods delivered for cleaning or for use for a year or for safe custody or as security for a loan).[53] Bailment is a common law relationship where the bailee receives a special property in the goods, the general property in which remains in the bailor.

4–34 Note that bailment of intangibles cannot exist because intangibles (e.g. copyrights, shares in companies, debts) cannot be possessed without being owned. Note, too, that "notes and coins, although property in the nature of a chattel and capable of being owned, are fungibles; and have the particular feature that, in a case where the transferor was himself the full legal and beneficial owner, ownership (or title) to the notes of coins passes with possession—save, perhaps, where there is some clear intention to treat the notes and coins as non-fungible. . . . [Hence, cash] deposited with another as banker is neither the subject of a bailment at law nor of a trust in equity."[54]

ii. Agency

4–35 If an owner transfers ownership or possession of property to another to enable him to do things on his behalf then an agency relationship will arise. The principal can direct the agent and can terminate the agency (except in certain limited circumstances[55]). The agent (unlike a trustee vis-à-vis the settlor or beneficiaries) has power to subject his principal to liability in contract and in tort. The agency normally arises as a result of a contract between principal and agent. Thus, an agency normally creates a debtor–creditor relationship. However, if a principal sells his cars via an agent obliged to pay the proceeds of each sale into a designated account and to remit to the principal by separate cheques the proceeds of such sales less commission and costs within five days then a trust arises.[56] This is crucial where the agent goes into liquidation.

4–36 In *Clarence House Ltd v National Westminster Bank Plc*,[57] a tenant of premises entered a "virtual assignment" of the economic benefits and burdens of the lease, and the question arose whether this

---

[49] *Bahr v Nicolay (No.2)* (1988) 164 C.L.R. 604 at 618–619; *Re Australian Elizabethan Theatre Trust* (1991) 30 FCR 491 at 503.

[50] e.g. *Paul v Constance* [1977] 1 W.L.R. 54; *Re Vandervell's Trusts (No.2)* [1974] Ch. 269; *Re Chelsea Cloisters Ltd* (1980) 41 P. & C.R. 98.

[51] *Commissioners of Customs & Excise v Richmond Theatre Management Ltd* [1995] S.T.C. 257; *Azam v Iqbal* [2008] Bus. L.R. 168.

[52] *Re Bond Worth Ltd* [1980] Ch. 228; *Clough Mill Ltd v Martin* [1985] 1 W.L.R. 111.

[53] There can be sufficient fiduciary relationship between bailor and bailee to give the bailor the equitable right to trace the bailed goods and their product: *Aluminium Industries Vaasen v Romalpa* [1976] 1 W.L.R. 676, but this has been much restricted as a special case: *Clough Mill Ltd v Martin* [1985] 1 W.L.R. 111

[54] *Duggan v Governor of Full Sutton Prison* [2004] 1 W.L.R. 1010 at [30].

[55] Neither the settlor nor beneficiaries of a trust (unless between them absolutely entitled and sui juris when they can terminate the trust) have such rights. A person can be a trustee but not an agent for unborn or unascertained persons: *Swain v Law Society* [1981] 3 All E.R. 797 at 822.

[56] *Re Fleet Disposal Services Ltd* [1995] 1 B.C.L.C. 345; and for sales of airline tickets: *Royal Brunei Airlines v Tan* [1995] 2 A.C. 376.

[57] [2010] L. & T.R. 1.

amounted to a declaration of trust, contrary to a term in the lease prohibiting any such declaration. The court held that it did not: because the "virtual assignee" took not only the benefits but also assumed responsibility for managing the property, "the proper meaning and cornerstone of the arrangement [was] agency", i.e. the "virtual assignee" was appointed the agent of the lessee, and this was inconsistent with a declaration of trust.[58]

iii. Loans

If A transfers to B £50,000 not by way of gift but as part of the purchase price of Blackacre for £150,000 in B's name, then A will have one-third of the equitable interest in Blackacre (under a resulting trust) which will obviously appreciate or depreciate with the value of Blackacre.[59] However, if A had merely lent B the £50,000 to help B acquire the whole beneficial interest in Blackacre, then A would merely have a personal claim against B for the debt. If the £50,000 loan had been secured by a charge on Blackacre then A would have the right to sell Blackacre to repay himself the debt out of the proceeds of sale. **4–37**

A single arrangement cannot usually be both a loan and a trust since the concepts are mutually exclusive.[60] However, it is possible for money to be lent for a particular purpose, on the basis that the money will be held on trust for the lender from the outset, subject to a power vested in the borrower to apply the money to the purpose, the exercise of which power will terminate the trust and turn the parties' relationship into one of creditor and debtor.[61] **4–38**

iv. Equitable Charges and Reservation of Title Clauses

To protect his financial interests as much as possible against insolvencies, S, a supplier of materials to a manufacturer, M Ltd, may seek to obtain[62] an equitable interest in (a) the materials; (b) any products produced using his materials; and (c) any proceeds of sale of the materials or the products either until the price of the particular materials is paid, or even until the price of all the materials supplied by S to M Ltd is paid. If M Ltd did hold (a), (b), and (c) on trust for S, then S would be entitled to these on M Ltd's insolvency, in priority to M Ltd's creditors. However, if S only had a charge then this would be void against M Ltd's liquidator unless it were registered in accordance with the Companies Act 2006 s.874. **4–39**

In *Re Bond Worth Ltd*[63] it was held that if S transfers legal title in fibre to M Ltd, purporting to reserve equitable ownership of the fibre until resale, and to become equitable owner of the proceeds of sale, and of any products produced using the fibre, and of the proceeds of sale thereof, until full **4–40**

---

[58] *Clarence House* at [44]. At [45]–[46] Ward L.J. also held that there could be no trust because the "virtual assignee" had no right under the rule in *Saunders v Vautier* (1841) Cr. & Ph. 240 (see paras 7–03 ff.) to call for a transfer of legal title, as this would have required the landlord's consent. However, it does not follow from the fact that a "beneficiary" cannot invoke the rule in *Saunders v Vautier* that there is no trust: cf. *Re Brockbank* [1948] Ch. 206, considered in *Don King Productions Inc v Warren* [2000] Ch. 291 at 321, where Lightman J. (affirmed on appeal) held that a non-assignable contract can form the subject-matter of a trust.

[59] See paras 14–97 ff.

[60] *Re Sharpe* [1980] 1 W.L.R. 219; *Spence v Browne* (1988) 18 Fam. Law 291.

[61] *Twinsectra Ltd v Yardley* [2002] 2 A.C. 164, interpreting *Barclays Bank Ltd v Quistclose Investments Ltd* [1970] A.C. 567. These cases are discussed further at paras 5–33 ff.

[62] Because S is legal and beneficial owner he cannot obtain a separate equitable interest until full ownership is vested in another party: *DKLR Holding Co (No.2) Pty Ltd v Commissioner of Stamp Duties* (1982) 149 C.L.R. 431; *Westdeutsche Landesbank Girozentrale v Islington LBC* [1996] A.C. 669 at 706 at 714.

[63] [1980] Ch. 228. See also *Specialist Plant Services Ltd v Braithwaite Ltd* [1987] B.C.L.C. 1, where the Court of Appeal held that a repairer's attempt to become part owner of any article for which it supplied parts pending payment actually created an equitable charge; *ICI New Zealand Ltd v Agnew* [1998] 2 N.Z.L.R. 129 is to similar effect.

payment be made for the relevant fibre, then this amounts to the creation of an equitable charge by M Ltd by way of security. This charge needs to be registered, and if it is not, it will be void against creditors and the liquidator.

4–41 The alternative effective approach for S to adopt is to retain full legal beneficial ownership in the materials supplied until full payment to S of money due from M Ltd.[64] *Clough Mill Ltd v Martin*,[65] reproduced below,[66] establishes that in this case, there can be no question of M Ltd granting a registrable charge over the materials because they continue to belong to S, and so M Ltd owns nothing out of which a grant can be made. Thus S can recover such raw materials in the event of M Ltd's insolvency.[67] However, if S goes further and claims to obtain legal ownership of products produced using his materials with others supplied by M Ltd or a third party until paid the money due from M Ltd, then this will normally be construed as giving rise to a charge on the products in S's favour.[68] Similarly, any clause purporting to make S owner of the proceeds of sale of such products until paid the money due from M Ltd will be construed as creating a charge.[69]

4–42 The substance of the matter is that M Ltd is intended to be entitled to the new products or the proceeds of sale thereof once it has paid the debt due to S, so that, really, S has a charge over property subject to M Ltd's equity of redemption. What, however, if M Ltd expressly contracted that it will be trustee of re-sale proceeds received by it, holding one fifth for S and four fifths for itself (so as to cover S's input and profit), or, better still, holding on trust for S such fractional part of such proceeds then received as is equivalent to the amount then owing by M Ltd to S and the rest on trust for itself? According to the High Court of Australia in *Associated Alloys Pty Ltd v ACN 001 452 106 Pty Ltd*,[70] reproduced below,[71] no charge arises here. On receipt of the proceeds "Equity looks on that as done which ought to be done", and because of this, "even if the proceeds were paid into a general bank account there could be a tracing remedy where the recipient was obliged to hold a particular portion of the proceeds on trust".[72] To reinforce S's position, M Ltd should be expressly placed under an obligation to transfer the relevant amount of money into M Ltd's account within a short period (between five to 10 working days) and under an obligation in that period not to permit the amount credited in the general account to fall below the relevant amount held on trust for S.

4–43 Where M Ltd is simply selling goods supplied by S then the contract can contain a provision that M Ltd is to hold proceeds of sale of the goods forthwith as trustee thereof for S to the extent of the fraction thereof representing the amounts then due to S by M Ltd in respect of such goods, providing that moneys subject to such trust may be paid into M Ltd's general bank account subject to being transferred into S's own account within ten working days (but without liability to pay interest thereon for such ten days) and providing that the money to the credit of M Ltd in its general bank account shall never fall below the amount held on trust for S. S should then have an equitable entitlement to such money.[73]

---

64 *Armour v Thyssen Edelstahlwerke AG* [1991] 2 A.C. 339.

65 [1985] 1 W.L.R. 111. See too *Re Highway Foods International Ltd* [1995] 1 B.C.L.C. 209.

66 At paras 4–52 ff.

67 It is a question of fact whether S's raw materials have lost their original identity through any blending process undertaken by M Ltd: *Re CKE Engineering Ltd (in admin.)* [2007] B.C.C. 975.

68 *Clough Mill Ltd v Martin* [1985] 1 W.L.R. 111; *Modelboard Ltd v Outer Box Ltd* [1993] B.C.L.C. 623.

69 *Pfeiffer v Arbuthnot Factors* [1988] 1 W.L.R. 150; *Company Computer Ltd v Abercorn Group* [1993] B.C.L.C. 603; *Re Highway Foods International Ltd* [1995] 1 B.C.L.C. 209.

70 (2000) 202 C.L.R. 588; distinguished in *Rondo Building Services Pty Ltd v Casaron Pty Ltd* [2003] 2 Qd R. 558. If the contract related not to a trust of a specific fraction or percentage but only to a trust of an amount of money then owed by M Ltd to S, then a problem arises as to certainty of subject matter because such amount is not segregated from the remaining amount of M Ltd's money, so that no more than a contractual charge can arise, requiring registration.

71 At paras 4–66 ff.

72 *Associated Alloys* at [31].

73 *Re Fleet Disposal Services Ltd* [1995] 1 B.C.L.C. 345; *Re Lewis's of Leicester Ltd* [1995] 1 B.C.L.C. 428; *Royal Trust Bank v National Westminster Bank* [1996] 2 B.C.L.C. 128; *Associated Alloys Pty Ltd v ACN 001 452 106 Pty Ltd* (2000) 202 C.L.R. 588.

v. Prepayments

4–44 When a company goes into liquidation (or an individual becomes bankrupt) it will be crucial whether a claimant has merely a personal claim, or has a proprietary claim under a trust or a charge. If a customer sent money to a company for goods and the company went into liquidation before supplying the goods the customer with his personal claim will be a mere unsecured creditor. If the customer in his letter had stipulated that his money was to be held in trust for him till he received title to the goods, then he will have an equitable interest giving him priority over the company's creditors in so far as it is possible to trace such money. If the company, fearful of liquidation, had expressly opened a trust bank account in which it had deposited customers' payments then, again, such a customer will have an equitable interest.[74] However, it is vital that the customer's money is paid into a separate account of the company to be held on trust for the customer. If the money is merely paid into the company's current account which was in debit so as to reduce the company's liability to the bank, then the money effectively disappears, so that there is never any trust fund in respect of which a proprietary claim could operate.[75]

4–45 One could take the view[76] that the company's unilateral declaration of trust is a voidable preference of the customers as creditors. The customer would expect to be a mere creditor, having done nothing to prevent his payment going into the ordinary bank account of the company to be available to creditors generally. The company's voluntary act preferred the customers' interests above those of ordinary creditors, and this is a voidable preference resulting in the customers being relegated to the position of ordinary creditors. However, the courts[77] have taken the view that the company's unilateral declaration of trust prevents the customers from becoming creditors by making them beneficiaries under a trust, just as if the customers themselves had created the trust, or does not result from the requisite subjective desire to prefer the customers. Indeed, even where there is no clear declaration of trust by the company the courts have become quite ready to infer the requisite intent to create a trust where a separate bank account has been opened when the company was in a parlous financial situation.[78]

4–46 The most extreme case is *Neste Oy v Lloyd's Bank Plc*[79] where Bingham J. held that a firm of ships' chandlers became trustees of money received as an advance payment for services, at a time when the firm knew that these services would not be performed. This principle was subsequently applied in *Re Japan Leasing (Europe) Plc*[80] and again in *Re Farepak Food and Gifts Ltd*.[81] The latter case concerned a company that operated a Christmas savings scheme under which customers could spread their Christmas savings over the year. Small contributions could be made month by month so that enough had accumulated by the beginning of November to buy Christmas goods and vouchers. In October

---

74 *Re Kayford Ltd* [1975] 1 W.L.R. 279; *Re Chelsea Cloisters Ltd* (1980) 41 P. & C.R. 98; *O.T.C. Computers Ltd (in admin.) v First National Tricity Finance Ltd* [2007] W.T.L.R. 165; *Brazzill v Willoughby* [2009] EWHC 1633 (Ch).

75 *Re BA Peters Plc (in admin.)* [2009] B.P.I.R. 248.

76 Goodhart and Jones (1980) 43 M.L.R. 489, pp. 496–498 querying whether Kayford's unilateral voluntary declaration of trust contravened the Companies Act 1948 ss. 302, 320, now Insolvency Act 1986 ss. 238, 239, but because Kayford could have declined the order and returned the prepayment could it not also accept the order only on the basis the prepayment was trust money?

77 *Re Kayford Ltd* [1975] 1 W.L.R. 279; *Re Chelsea Cloisters Ltd* (1980) 41 P. & C.R. 989; *Re Lewis's of Leicester Ltd* [1995] 1 B.C.L.C. 428 applying *Re MC Bacon* [1991] 1 Ch. 127.

78 *Re Chelsea Cloisters Ltd*, above; *Re Lewis's of Leicester Ltd*, above; and cf. *Sports Network Ltd v Calzaghe* [2008] EWHC 2566 (QB). See too M. Bridge (1992) 12 O.J.L.S. 333, pp. 335–357.

79 [1983] 2 Lloyds Rep. 658.

80 [2000] W.T.L.R. 301 at 316.

81 [2007] 2 B.C.L.C. 1; subsequent proceedings [2009] EWHC 2580 (Ch).

2006 the directors decided to cease trading and instructed their agents to stop collecting payments, but money kept coming in for a while after the directors' decision. The administrators sought directions as to how they should distribute these sums. Mann J. was willing to impose a trust on moneys in the company's hands "in so far as it could be established that [these] were paid to Farepak by customers at a time when Farepak had decided that it had ceased trading".[82]

4–47 Unfortunately, the scope and status of the *Neste Oy* principle are uncertain as a result of the Court of Appeal's decision in *Triffit Nurseries (a firm) v Salads Etcetera Ltd*.[83] The claimants grew vegetables that were distributed by an agent company, which billed customers and remitted the proceeds to the claimants, deducting commission. The company was free to mix the sums collected with its own funds and use them for its own purposes, and did not hold them on an express trust for the claimants. The company went into administrative receivership at a time when there were amounts outstanding in respect of sales of the claimants' produce. The receivers collected the outstanding sums and the question arose whether this money should go to the claimants or to the company's bank, which held a charge over its book debts. Consistently with the foregoing cases, one might have expected the court to impose a trust because the company could not conscionably have received the customers' money, knowing that it would not perform its contractual duty to account for an equivalent sum to the claimants. However, the Court of Appeal held that this was an insufficient degree of improbity to convert the company into a trustee. It is hard to understand what distinguishes the recipients in *Neste Oy* and *Farepak* from the recipient in *Triffit Nurseries*. In the first two cases the relevant funds came from the claimants, while in the latter they came from third parties, but there is no obvious reason why this should have made a difference.

vi. Privity of Contract

4–48 The well-established common law rule is that only a party to a contract can sue on it, so that if A contracts with B for the benefit of C, C cannot enforce the contract or prevent A and B from varying its terms.[84] B alone can enforce the contract: normally he can only claim nominal damages for his own loss,[85] though sometimes the equitable remedy of specific performance may be available.[86] However, statutory rules in the Contracts (Rights of Third Parties) Act 1999 now permit A and B if they wish, to enable C to enforce A's contract with B.

4–49 In contrast, if A transfers property to B on trust for C, then Equity has always held that only C can enforce the trust and compel restitution to the trust fund of any losses or profits because A drops out of the picture as a donor who has made an irrevocable gift.[87] Exceptionally, however, where A contracted with B, if it is positively provided[88] that they both[89] intended B to be the trustee of the benefit of A's promise for C (a chose in action capable of being the subject matter of a trust), then C can enforce the trust, subject to joining B as a necessary party to be bound by any judgment in the action.[90] In such

---

[82] *Re Farepak* at [40].
[83] [2000] 1 All E.R. (Comm.) 737.
[84] *Dunlop Pneumatic Tyre Co Ltd v Selfridge & Co Ltd* [1915] A.C. 847; *Scruttons Ltd v Midland Silicones Ltd* [1962] A.C. 440.
[85] *Panatown Ltd v Alfred McAlpine Construction Ltd* [2001] 1 A.C. 518.
[86] *Beswick v Beswick* [1968] A.C. 58.
[87] *Paul v Paul* (1882) 20 Ch.D. 742; *Re Astor's ST* [1952] Ch. 534 at 542; *Bradshaw v University College of Wales (Aberystwyth)* [1988] 1 W.L.R. 190 at 193–194; *Goulding v James* [1997] 2 All E.R. 239 at 247.
[88] *West v Houghton* (1879) L.R. 4 C.P.D. 197 at 203.
[89] *Re Schebsman* [1994] Ch. 83 at 89 and 104: B cannot unilaterally increase the measure of A's liability.
[90] *Vandepitte v Preferred Accident Insurance Co* [1933] A.C. 70 at 79; *Parker-Tweedale v Dunbar Bank Plc* [1991] Ch. 26. See too *Barbados Trust Co v Bank of Zambia* [2007] 1 Lloyd's Rep. 495 at [99], per Rix L.J., noting that the *Vandepitte* procedure "can operate where a contract is from the very beginning entered into by a contracting party as a trustee for a third party, as in the familiar case of a charterer under a charterparty taking the shipowner's promise to pay commission to the ship broker: *Les Affréteurs Réunis Société Anonyme v Leopold Walford (London) Ltd* [1919] A.C. 801" and adding that in such a case the procedure "operated as an exception to the rule of privity of contracts."

circumstances A and B will not be able to vary their contract without C's consent, unless such a power was expressly or by necessary implication reserved at the creation of the contract in circumstances where the power is a personal one for the benefit of A or B and not a fiduciary power for the benefit of C.

In the absence of clear trust language it is difficult to forecast exactly what are the circumstances when a court will find that a trust has been affirmatively established.[91] The courts are reluctant[92] to find an intent to create a trust, suspecting that such a claim is normally a transparent device to avoid the privity of contract doctrine. Where there is a contract between A and B for the benefit of C, B cannot unilaterally[93] improve C's position (and worsen A's position) by declaring himself trustee for C or assigning his rights to C where B's rights are inherently for nominal damages only. However, if both A and B contracted on the footing that B would be able to enforce contractual rights for the benefit of those who suffered from defective performance but who could not acquire any rights to hold A liable for breach, then B may assign such rights[94] and be regarded as trustee of such rights.[95] Such an exception to the general rule that refuses to recognise a *ius quaesitum tertio* may be regarded as "a judicial subterfuge"[96] providing "a remedy where no other would be available to a person sustaining loss which under a national legal system ought to be compensated by the person who has caused it."[97] However, the "legal position in cases such as these is now fundamentally affected by the Contracts (Rights of Third Parties) Act 1999"[98] which enables rights to be expressly enforceable by a third party like C if the contracting parties so wish. **4–50**

vii. Possibilities of Construction for Testamentary Gifts

If a testator by will leaves property to B and requires B to make some payment to C or perform some obligation in favour of C, there are five possible constructions open to a court. The testator's words may be treated as: **4–51**

- Merely indicating his motive, so that B takes an absolute beneficial interest, e.g. "to my wife, B, so that she may support herself and the children according to their needs" or "to my daughter B, on condition she provides a home for my handicapped daughter, C."[99]
- Creating a charge on the property given to B, so that B takes the property beneficially subject to the charge for securing payment of money to C,[100] e.g. "my office block, Demeter House, to my son, B, subject to paying thereout £10,000 p.a. to my widow, C."

---

91 See *Trident General Insurance Co v McNeice Bros* (1988) 165 C.L.R. 107, pointing out that *Re Foster* [1938] 4 All E.R. 357 and *Re Sinclair's Life Policy* [1938] Ch. 799 cannot logically be distinguished from *Royal Exchange Assurance v Hope* [1928] Ch. 179 and *Re Webb* [1941] Ch. 225.

92 *Re Schebsman* [1944] Ch. 538; *Green v Russell* [1959] 2 Q.B. 220; *Beswick v Beswick* [1966] Ch. 538; *Swain v Law Society* [1983] 1 A.C. 598.

93 *Re Schebsman*, above; *Darlington BC v Wiltshier Northern Ltd* [1995] 1 W.L.R. 68.

94 *Dunlop v Lambert* (1839) 6 Cl. & F. 600; *The Albazero* [1977] A.C. 774; *St Martin's Property Corp Ltd v Sir Robert McAlpine Ltd* [1994] 1 A.C. 85; *Darlington BC v Wiltshier Northern Ltd*, above.

95 *Darlington BC v Wiltshier Northern Ltd*, above; *Panatown Ltd v Alfred McAlpine Construction Ltd* [2001] 1 A.C. 518; *Rolls Royce Power Engineering Plc v Ricardo Consulting Engineers Ltd* [2004] 2 All E.R. (Comm.) 129 at [104]–[117].

96 *Swain v Law Society* [1983] 1 A.C. 598 at 611.

97 *St Martin's Property Corporation Ltd v Sir Robert McAlpine Ltd* [1994] A.C. 85 at 115.

98 *Panatown Ltd v Alfred McAlpine Construction Ltd* [2001] 1 A.C. 518 at 575.

99 *Re Brace* [1954] 1 W.L.R. 955; cf. *Re Frame* [1939] Ch. 700 and *Re Lipinski* [1976] Ch. 235. Further see Administration of Justice Act 1982 s.22.

100 *Re Oliver* (1890) 62 L.T. 533. B is under no personal obligation to make up any deficiency caused by insufficiency of the property charged.

- Creating a trust in favour of C,[101] e.g. "my office block, Demeter House, to B absolutely but so that he must pay an amount equal to the income therefrom to my widow C for the rest of her life."
- Creating a personal obligation binding B to C so that if B accepts the property he must perform the obligation in C's favour[102] (even if it costs him more than the value of the property[103]), e.g. "my leasehold cottage currently subleased to X I hereby devise to B absolutely on condition that he agrees to pay my widow C £15,000 p.a. for the rest of her life."
- Creating a condition subsequent that affects the property in B's hands making B liable to forfeit the property if the condition is broken,[104] e.g. "my 500,000 £1 shares ICI Plc to B Charity Co on condition that it pays my widow, C, an annuity of £10,000 for her life and properly maintains my family burial vault, and upon any failure to observe this condition then the RSPCA shall become entitled to the shares."

CLOUGH MILL LTD v MARTIN

Court of Appeal [1985] 1 W.L.R. 111; [1984] 3 All E.R. 982

4–52 ROBERT GOFF L.J. (with whom SIR JOHN DONALDSON M.R. and OLIVER L.J. agreed): This appeal is concerned with what is sometimes called "a retention of title clause", but more frequently nowadays a "Romalpa clause". The appellants, Clough Mills Ltd, carry on business as spinners of yarn. Under four contracts entered into between December 1979 and March 1980 they contracted to supply yarn to a company called Heatherdale Fabrics Ltd (which I shall refer to as "the buyers"), which carried on business as manufacturers of fabric. When the appellants entered into these contracts, they knew that the yarn to be supplied under them was to be used by the buyers for such manufacture. Each of the contracts incorporated the appellants' standard conditions. These included a condition (condition 12) entitled "Passing of title"; this is the Romalpa clause, with the construction and effect of which this case is concerned. . . .

4–53 [The clause] reads as follows:

> "However the ownership of the material shall remain with the Seller, which reserves the right to dispose of the material until payment in full for all the material has been received by it in accordance with the terms of this contract or until such time as the Buyer sells the material to its customers by way of bona-fide sale at full market value.
>
> If such payment is overdue in whole or in part the Seller may (without prejudice to any of its other rights) recover or re-sell the material or any of it and may enter upon the Buyer's premises by its servants or agents for that purpose.
>
> Such payments shall become due immediately upon the commencement of any act or proceeding in which the Buyer's solvency is involved.
>
> If any of the material is incorporated in or used as material for other goods before such payment the property in the whole of such goods shall be and remain with the Seller until such payment has been made, or the other goods have been sold as aforesaid, and all the Seller's rights hereunder in the material shall extend to those other goods."

4–54 On March 11, 1980 the respondent, Geoffrey Martin, was appointed receiver of the buyers. On that date the buyers still retained at their premises 375 kg of unused yarn supplied under contracts and still unpaid for.

---

101 e.g. *Irvine v Sullivan* (1869) L.R. 8 Eq. 673.
102 *Re Lester* [1942] Ch. 324.
103 *Re Hodge* [1940] Ch. 260.
104 *Att.-Gen. v Cordwainers' Company* (1833) 3 My. & K. 534; *Re Oliver* (1890) 62 L.T. 533; *Re Tyler* [1891] 3 Ch. 252; *Ellis v Chief Adjudication Officer* [1998] 1 F.L.R. 184.

So on March 11, 1980 the appellants wrote to the receiver expressing their intention to repossess the unused yarn . . . the solicitors acting for the receiver replied that the appellants' retention of title clause was invalid for, inter alia, non-registration under section 95 of the Companies Act 1948 and that the receiver would therefore continue to allow the yarn to be used and would refuse the appellants admission to collect it. The appellants therefore commenced proceedings, claiming damages from the receiver for conversion of the yarn. His Honour Judge O'Donoghue, sitting as a judge of the High Court, dismissed the claim, holding that, on its true construction, condition 12 created a charge on the yarn and that such charge was void for non-registration under section 95. It is against that decision that the appellants now appeal to this court . . .

The submission of counsel for the appellants as to the nature of the appellants' retention of title under the first sentence of the condition was extremely simple. Under the Sale of Goods Act 1979 a seller of goods is fully entitled, after delivery of the goods to the buyer, to retain title in the goods until he has been paid: see section 19(1) of that Act. That is precisely what the appellants have done by condition 12. The appellants' title did not derive from the contract; on the contrary, it was simply retained by them, though under the contract power was conferred on the buyers both to sell the goods and to use them in manufacturing other goods. As the buyers never acquired any title to the unused yarn in question, they could not charge the yarn to the appellants. So the appellants were, quite simply, the owners of the yarn; and there was no question of there being any charge on the yarn in their favour, which was void if unregistered. **4–55**

This attractively simple approach was challenged by counsel for the receiver. He submitted, first of all, that, if the first sentence of condition 12 is read literally, as counsel for the appellants suggested it should be read, the buyers can only have had possession of the yarn in a fiduciary capacity, whether as bailees or as fiduciary agents. But, he said, the power conferred on the buyers under the contract, not merely to sell the material but also to mix it with other materials in the manufacture of goods, was inconsistent with the existence of any fiduciary capacity in the buyers, or indeed with the appellants' unqualified ownership of the yarn. **4–56**

Now this is a submission which I am unable to accept. In every case, we have to look at the relevant documents and other communications which have passed between the parties, and to consider them in the light of the relevant surrounding circumstances, in order to ascertain the rights and duties of the parties *inter se*, always paying particular regard to the practical effect of any conclusion concerning the nature of those rights and duties. In performing this task, concepts such as bailment and fiduciary duty must not be allowed to be our masters, but must rather be regarded as the tools of our trade. I for my part can see nothing objectionable in an agreement between parties under which A, the owner of goods, gives possession of those goods to B, at the same time conferring on B a power of sale and a power to consume the goods in manufacture, though A will remain the owner of the goods until they are either sold or consumed. I do not see why the relationship between A and B, pending sale or consumption, should not be the relationship of bailor and bailee, even though A has no right to trace the property in his goods into the proceeds of sale. If that is what the parties have agreed should happen, I can see no reason why the law should not give effect to that intention. I am happy to find that both Staughton and Peter Gibson JJ. have adopted a similar approach in *Hendy Lennox (Industrial Engines) Ltd v Grahame Puttick Ltd*[105] and *Re Andrabell Ltd*.[106] **4–57**

Even so, it is necessary to examine counsel for the appellants' construction in a little more detail. If, under this condition, retention of title applied only to goods not yet paid for, I can see that his construction could be given effect to without any problem. But the difficulty with the present condition is that the retention of title applies to material, delivered and retained by the buyer, until payment in full for all the material delivered under the contract has been received by the seller. The effect is therefore that the seller may retain his title in material still held by the buyer, even if part of that material has been paid for. Furthermore, if in such circumstances the seller decides to exercise his rights and resell the material, questions can arise concerning (1) whether account must be taken of the part payment already received in deciding how much the seller should be entitled to sell and (2) whether, if he does resell, he is accountable to the buyer either in respect of the part payment already received, or in respect of any profit made on the resale by reason of a rise in the market value of the material . . . **4–58**

[105] [1984] 1 W.L.R. 485.
[106] [1984] 3 All E.R. 407.

4–59 To me, the answer to these questions lies in giving effect to the condition in accordance with its terms, and on that approach I can discern no intention to create a trust. The condition provides that the seller retains his ownership in the material. He therefore remains owner; but, during the subsistence of the contract, he can only exercise his powers as owner consistently with the terms, express and implied, of the contract. On that basis, in my judgment, he can during the subsistence of the contract only resell such amount of the material as is needed to discharge the balance of the outstanding purchase price; and, if he sells more, he is accountable to the buyer for the surplus. However, once the contract has been determined, as it will be if the buyer repudiates the contract and the seller accepts the repudiation, the seller will have his rights as owner (including, of course, his right to sell the goods) uninhibited by any contractual restrictions; though any part of the purchase price received by him and attributable to the material so resold will be recoverable by the buyer on the ground of failure of consideration, subject to any set-off arising from a crossclaim by the seller for damages for the buyer's repudiation.

4–60 . . . If this approach is right, I can see no reason why the retention of title in the first sentence of condition 12 should be construed as giving rise to a charge on the unused material in favour of the seller. In the course of his argument counsel for the receiver prayed in aid another proposition culled from the judgment of Slade J. in *Re Bond Worth Ltd* when he said:[107]

> "In my judgment, any contract which, by way of security for payment of a debt, confers an interest in property defeasible or destructible on payment of such debt, or appropriates such property for the discharge of the debt, must necessarily be regarded as creating a mortgage or charge, as the case may be. The existence of the equity of redemption is quite inconsistent with the existence of a bare trustee-beneficiary relationship."

4–61 However, so far as the retention of title in unused materials is concerned, I see no difficulty in distinguishing the present case from that envisaged by Slade J. Under the first sentence of the condition, the buyer does not, by way of security, confer on the seller an interest in property defeasible on the payment of the debt so secured. On the contrary, the seller retains the legal property in the material.

4–62 There is however one further point which I must consider. Counsel for the receiver relied, in support of his argument, on the fourth sentence of the condition. It will be remembered that this reads as follows:

> "If any of the material is incorporated in or used as material for other goods before such payment the property in the whole of such goods shall be and remain with the Seller until such payment has been made, or the other goods have been sold as aforesaid, and all the Seller's rights hereunder in the material shall extend to those other goods."

4–63 The submission of counsel for the receiver was that the effect of this provision is to confer on the seller an interest in the buyer's property and so must have been to create a charge; and he further submitted that, having regard to the evident intention that the seller's rights in goods in which the material provided by him has been incorporated shall be the same as his rights in unused material, the seller's rights in unused material should likewise be construed as creating a charge.

4–64 Now it is no doubt true that, where A's material is lawfully used by B to create new goods, whether or not B incorporates other material of his own, the property in the new goods will generally vest in B, at least where the goods are not reducible to the original materials.[108] But it is difficult to see why, if the parties agree that the property in the goods shall vest in A, that agreement should not be given effect to. On this analysis, under the fourth sentence of the condition as under the first, the buyer does not confer on the seller an interest in property defeasible on the payment of the debt; on the contrary, when the new goods come into existence the property in them ipso facto vests in the seller, and he thereafter retains his ownership in them, in the same way and on the same terms as he retains his ownership in the unused material. However, in considering the fourth sentence, we have to take into account not only the possibility that the buyer may have paid part of the price for the material, but also that he will have borne the cost of

[107] [1980] Ch. 228 at 248.
[108] See Bl. Com. (14th edn) pp.404–405.

manufacture of the new goods, and may also have provided other materials for incorporation into those goods; and the condition is silent, not only about repaying such part of the price for the material as has already been paid by the buyer, but also about any allowance to be made by the seller to the buyer for the cost of manufacture of the new goods, or for any other material incorporated by the buyer into the new goods. Now, no injustice need arise from the exercise of the seller's power to resell such goods provided that, having applied the price received from the resale in satisfaction of the outstanding balance of the price owed to him by the buyer, he is bound to account for the remainder to the buyer. But the difficulty of construing the fourth sentence as simply giving rise to a retention by the seller of title to the new goods is that it would lead to the result that, on the determination of the contract under which the original material was sold to the buyer, the ownership of the seller in the new goods would be retained by the seller uninhibited by any terms of the contract, which had then ceased to apply; and I find it impossible to believe that it was the intention of the parties that the seller would thereby gain the windfall of the full value of the new product, deriving as it may well do not merely from the labour of the buyer but also from materials that were his, without any duty to account to him for any surplus of the proceeds of sale above the outstanding balance of the price due by him to the seller. It follows that the fourth sentence must be read as creating either a trust or a charge. In my judgment, however, it cannot have been intended to create a trust. Those who insert Romalpa clauses in their contracts of sale must be aware that other suppliers might do the same; and the prospect of two lots of material, supplied by different sellers, each subject to a Romalpa clause which vests in the seller the legal title in a product manufactured from both lots of material, is not at all sensible. Accordingly, consistent with the approach to a similar provision in *Re Peachdart Ltd*,[109] I have come to the conclusion that, although it does indeed do violence to the language of the fourth sentence of the condition, that sentence must be read as giving rise to a charge on the new goods in favour of the seller.

Even so, I do not see why the presence of the last sentence in the condition should prevent us from giving effect to the first sentence in accordance with its terms . . . I recognise that, on the view which I have formed of the retention of title in the first sentence of condition 12 in this case, its effect is very similar to that of a charge on goods created by the buyer in favour of the seller. But the simple fact is that under the first sentence of the condition the buyer does not in fact confer a charge on his goods in favour of the seller: on the contrary, the seller retains his title in his goods, for the purpose of providing himself with security. I can see no reason in law why a seller of goods should not adopt this course, and, if the relevant contractual term is effective to achieve that result, I can see no reason why the law should not give effect to it in accordance with its terms. **4–65**

ASSOCIATED ALLOYS PTY LIMITED v ACN 001 452 106 PTY LIMITED (IN LIQUIDATION)

High Court of Australia (2000) 202 C.L.R. 588

GAUDRON, McHUGH, GUMMOW AND HAYNE JJ. (in a joint judgment): . . . The appellant, Associated Alloys Pty Ltd ("the Seller"), sold steel to the first respondent, ACN 001 452 106 Pty Limited (In Liquidation) (formerly Metropolitan Engineering and Fabrications Pty Ltd) ("the Buyer"), between 1981 and 1996. In about 1987 or 1988, the Seller began to issue invoices to the Buyer with the registration of title clause, the subject-matter of this appeal, printed on the reverse side. **4–66**

Invoices were issued by the Seller to the Buyer on August 31, September 26 and October 26, 1995. Each individually numbered invoice recorded the details of the supply and shipment of steel by the Seller, in accordance with an individually numbered order of the Buyer. Each invoice also recorded a particular United States dollar sum owed by the Buyer to the Seller in respect of the particular shipment of steel supplied thereunder. On the front of the Invoices was recorded, under the heading "PAYMENT TERMS", "PAYMENT DUE APPROX MID/END NOVEMBER '95". The bottom of the front of the Invoices was marked "Romalpa Clause set forth on the reverse side hereof applies" . . . **4–67**

[109] [1984] Ch. 131.

4–68 The clause provided:

"Reservation of Title

"[1] It is expressly agreed and declared that the title of the subject goods/product shall not pass to the [Buyer] until payment in full of the purchase price. The [Buyer] shall in the meantime take custody of the goods/product and retain them as the fiduciary agent and bailee of the [Seller].

"[2] The [Buyer] may resell but only as a fiduciary agent of the [Seller]. Any right to bind the [Seller] to any liability to any third party by contract or otherwise is however expressly negatived. Any such resale is to be at arms length and on market terms and pending resale or utilisation in any manufacturing or construction process, is to be kept separate from its own, properly stored, protected and insured.

"[3] The [Buyer] will receive all proceeds whether tangible or intangible, direct or indirect of any dealing with such goods/product in trust for the [Seller] and will keep such proceeds in a separate account until the liability to the [Seller] shall have been discharged.

"[4] The [Seller] is to have power to appropriate payments to such goods and accounts as it thinks fit notwithstanding any appropriation by the [Buyer] to the contrary.

"[5] *In the event that the [Buyer] uses the goods/product in some manufacturing or construction process of its own or some third party, then the [Buyer] shall hold such part of the proceeds of such manufacturing or construction process as relates to the goods/product in trust for the [Seller]. Such part shall be deemed to equal in dollar terms the amount owing by the [Buyer] to the [Seller] at the time of the receipt of such proceeds.*" (paragraph numbers and emphasis added)

4–69 It is the operation of the fifth paragraph of the clause ("the Proceeds Subclause") which is of prime importance for this appeal . . .

4–70 The Proceeds Subclause operates, conditionally, "[i]n the event that the [Buyer] uses the goods/product in some manufacturing or construction process of its own or some third party". This event occurred on each occasion the Buyer used the steel supplied by the Seller to manufacture the Steel Products. No question arises as to the Seller retaining any proprietary interest in the steel it supplied under the Invoices to the Buyer. This is because the steel supplied by the Seller was no longer capable of being ascertained in the Steel Products manufactured by the Buyer. This loss of ascertainability may be contrasted with the circumstances in which the first paragraph of the reservation of title clause applies. This paragraph has an operation where the steel supplied by the Seller remains intact in the hands of the Buyer or is otherwise dealt with by the Buyer in such a way that the steel supplied does not lose its ascertainability. In such a case, the goods would remain the property of the Seller and an action in trover or detinue would lie against the Buyer[110] and, in support of such an action, injunctive relief might be available in an appropriate case.[111]

4–71 The remainder of the Proceeds Subclause is divisible into two parts. The first part describes a subject-matter of commercial value. The second part operates to confer an interest in equity in that subject-matter . . .

4–72 The proper construction of the phrase "the proceeds" is revealed by a consideration of the Proceeds Subclause as a whole. The phrase has the meaning employed by Sir George Jessel M.R. in his ex tempore judgment in *Re Hallett's Estate*,[112] where the Master of the Rolls eloquently states the principles of tracing in equity. The phrase "the proceeds" is to be construed as referring to moneys received by the Buyer and not debts which may be set out in the Buyer's books (or computer records) from time to time.[113] The concluding sentence of the Proceeds Subclause would be strained if the phrase "the proceeds" were to include book debts. In the event that a debt were subject to conditions, it may prove to be difficult to determine when the Buyer is in "receipt" of that intangible obligation. Moreover, to attempt to equate a chose in action, "in

110 *Penfolds Wines Pty Ltd v Elliott* (1946) 74 C.L.R. 204 at 229; *Gollan v Nugent* (1988) 166 C.L.R. 18 at 25.

111 As was sought in *Penfolds Wines Pty Ltd v Elliott* (1946) 74 C.L.R. 204, and see *Puma Australia Pty Ltd v Sportsman's Australia Limited (No.2)* [1994] 2 Qd R. 159 at 166–169, 171–173.

112 (1880) 13 Ch.D. 696 at 708–709.

113 Questions as to the application of moneys received, which it is unnecessary now to answer, may arise where a running account exists between a supplier (e.g. the Seller) and purchaser (e.g. the Buyer).

dollar terms", to a sum of money, namely "the amount owing by the [Buyer] to the [Seller] at the time of the receipt of such proceeds", is, at the very least, conceptually problematic. In contrast, limiting the phrase "the proceeds" to refer to payments made to the Buyer results in this equation operating with certainty.

It is necessary to determine the equitable rights, liabilities and remedies which arise from the purported **4–73**
operation of the Proceeds Subclause. A pendent question also arises as to the manner in which the Buyer's contractual rights and obligations are affected by equitable considerations . . .

The contracts, in respect of each of the Invoices, spoke for the future and provided the attachment of a **4–74**
trust for "the proceeds" received from time to time. There being value, and equity regarding as done that which ought to be done, a completely constituted trust would arise in respect of those "proceeds" (giving that word the meaning considered above) as they were received by the Buyer.[114]

In their joint judgment in *Kauter v Hilton*, Dixon C.J., Williams and Fullagar JJ. identified[115]: **4–75**

> "the established rule that in order to constitute a trust the intention to do so must be clear and that it must also be clear what property is subject to the trust and reasonably certain who are the beneficiaries".

. . . In the present case, it is no objection to the effective creation of a trust that the property to be **4–76**
subjected to it is identified to be a proportion of the proceeds received by the Buyer; a proportion referable to moneys from time to time due and owing but unpaid by the Buyer to the Seller.

In respect of those proceeds from time to time bound by the trust, there is nothing in the terms of the **4–77**
trust to negative the ordinary consequence that the trustee (the Buyer) is bound to apply that sum by accounting to or at the direction of a beneficiary (the Seller). It is convenient to identify the condition which limits the beneficiary's entitlement to call upon the trust property later in this judgment. As Professor Hayton points out,[116] with reference to authority,[117] because equity treats as done that which ought to be done, even if the proceeds were paid into a general bank account of the Buyer there could be a tracing remedy where the recipient was obliged to hold a particular portion of the proceeds on trust.

In the situation just considered, where the trust is performed and discharged by appropriation of the pro- **4–78**
ceeds by the Seller, the relevant trust relationship between the Buyer and the Seller is brought to an end. A question may then arise whether, despite the Seller having been funded in this way, it might retain a good claim for that amount by an action in debt against the Buyer. The answer to that will be found not in trust law but in the terms, express or implied, of the contract between the Buyer and the Seller. In the formulation of those terms, particularly any implied terms, there is, to adapt the words of Lord Wilberforce, "surely no difficulty in recognising the co-existence in one transaction of legal and equitable rights and remedies"[118] and the giving of effect to "practical arrangements" by "the flexible interplay of law and equity" . . .[119]

The contractual agreements of the Buyer and Seller, in respect of each of the Invoices, included the **4–79**
amount to be paid by the Buyer for the steel supplied under each Invoice and stated "PAYMENT DUE APPROX MID/END NOVEMBER '95". This latter term operated as a period of credit, commercially benefiting the Buyer. The question that arises is whether this term is inconsistent with the intention to constitute a trust in the manner described above. That is, whether the purported liberty of the Buyer not to pay the Seller is consistent with the obligation to create a trust of "proceeds" which might be received by the Buyer during the period of credit. This question is resolved by reference to the contract as a whole, including the implied terms that arise.

---

114 *Palette Shoes Pty Ltd v Krohn* (1937) 58 C.L.R. 1 at 26–27; *Federal Commissioner of Taxation v Everett* (1980) 143 C.L.R. 440 at 450. See also the United States authorities considered under the heading "Debtor Declaring Himself Trustee for Creditor" in Bogert, *The Law of Trusts and Trustees*, 2nd edn rev (1984), p.19.

115 (1953) 90 C.L.R. 86 at 97.

116 Underhill and Hayton, *Law Relating to Trusts and Trustees*, 15th edn (1995) at 12(n); cf. D. Hayton, "The Uses of Trusts in the Commercial Context", in D. Hayton (ed.), *Modern International Developments in Trust Law* (1999), p.145 and p.168.

117 Including that of the Supreme Court of Canada in *Air Canada v M & L Travel Ltd* [1993] 3 S.C.R. 787 at 804–805 in which reliance was placed upon the judgment of Hope J.A. in *Stephens Travel Service International Pty Ltd (Receivers and Managers Appointed) v Qantas Airways Ltd* (1988) 13 N.S.W.L.R. 331 at 348–349, with which Kirby P. and Priestley J.A. agreed.

118 *Quistclose Investments Ltd v Rolls Razor Ltd* [1970] A.C. 567 at 581.

119 *Quistclose Investments Ltd v Rolls Razor Ltd* [1970] A.C. 567 at 582.

4-80 The rules governing the implication of an implied term as a matter of fact were stated by the Privy Council in *BP Refinery (Westernport) Pty Ltd v Shire of Hastings* . . .[120]

4-81 The implication of an implied term operates to align, or give congruence to, the rights and obligations of the Buyer and Seller in contract and the intention of these parties to create a trust in the manner described above. An implied contractual term arises, as a matter of business efficacy, that upon the receipt by the Buyer of the relevant "proceeds" (and thus the constitution of a trust of part of those proceeds), the obligation in debt is discharged. The express term in the agreement (referred to above) which provides for a period of credit within which the debt need not be paid by the Buyer is, in turn, incorporated as an express term of the trust. This term thereby prescribes the period within which the Seller, as beneficiary, cannot call upon the trust property (if the trust is constituted during the credit period). The implied term thus provides one means of discharging the debt by performance. No relevant inconsistency arises between this implied term and the express term in the agreement providing for a period of credit for the Buyer . . .

4-82 Further, no inconsistency arises between the contractual agreement and the creation of a trust of property "equal in dollar terms [to] the amount owing by the [Buyer] to the [Seller] at the time of the receipt" of the proceeds.[121] Manifestly, this term did not operate to constitute a trust in respect of the whole of the proceeds received by the Buyer except, perhaps, coincidentally.

4-83 The Proceeds Subclause is an agreement to constitute a trust of future-acquired property. It is therefore not a "charge" within the meaning of s.9 of the Law and the detailed provisions of the Law governing charges thus do not apply to it. The Proceeds Subclause is not a "registrable charge" within s.262 and the Seller had no obligation to lodge a notice under s.263 within the prescribed period (s.266(1)(c)). In turn, the Proceeds Subclause is not void as against the administrators or liquidator of the Buyer (see s.266(1)).

D. Trusts and Powers

4-84 Special attention must be paid to the distinction between trusts and powers, which has already been discussed in Chapter 1.[122] This distinction is complicated by the fact that in many cases the trustees will not just have trusts which they must carry out (e.g. "on trust to distribute the income between such of my descendants as they see fit from time to time") but also powers to distribute income or capital which they may or may not exercise (e.g. "but so that my trustees may instead distribute the income between such charities as they may see fit from time to time").

4-85 Furthermore, in construing a clause in a trust deed there may be a fine (and perhaps artificial) distinction between (a) a power of distribution of income coupled with a trust to dispose of the undistributed surplus, and (b) a trust for distribution coupled with a power to withhold a portion and accumulate it or otherwise dispose of it. Examples of these are: (a) "on trust to pay or apply the income to or for the benefit of such of my family company's employees, ex-employees and their relatives and dependants as my trustees may see fit but so that my trustees shall pay or apply any income not so paid or applied within three months of receipt by my trustees to or for the benefit of such of my issue as my trustees shall see fit"; and (b) "on trust to pay or apply the income to or for the benefit of such of my family company's employees, ex-employees and their relatives and dependants as my trustees shall see fit but so that my trustees may pay or apply any income within three months of receiving it to or for the benefit of such of my issue as my trustees may see fit".

---

[120] (1977) 180 C.L.R. 266 at 283.

[121] See Underhill and Hayton, *Law Relating to Trusts and Trustees*, 15th edn (1995), pp.11–12.

[122] At paras 1–153 ff.

Problems can arise in ascertaining the intentions of a testator. He may intend to leave property to his executors and trustees on trust for his wife W for life with: **4–86**

- a mere power for her to appoint the capital among such of their children as she may see fit, so that if the power is not exercised the capital is held on a resulting trust for the testator's estate[123]; or
- a mere power for her to appoint the capital among such of their children as she may see fit, but in default of appointment remainder for their children equally[124] (a fixed trust); or
- a mere power for her to appoint the capital among such of their children as she may see fit, but in default of appointment for such of their children and in such shares as his executors and trustees shall select in their absolute discretion[125] (a discretionary trust); or
- a "trust" power whereby she must exercise her power to appoint the capital (vested in the executors and trustees) among such of their children as she sees fit.[126] If this discretionary trust is unexercised at her death then the court will order equal division on the basis that equality is equity unless some other basis for distribution appears more appropriate[127] (which may well be the case if the class of objects is broader, e.g., my children and my nephews and nieces and the children of such persons).

Where the class of objects is so large that they cannot all be listed then, obviously, there can be no question of equal division under an implied gift in default of appointment. Thus, in welfare trusts for employees, ex-employees and their relations and dependants where the trustees are empowered to make grants to such persons, the question that arises is whether the relevant clause in the trust deed is a mere power or a "trust" power.[128] Where the person with the "trust" power has the trust property vested in him it has become the modern usage simply to say that he holds the property on discretionary trust.[129] **4–87**

The similarities between discretionary trusts and powers have led to the certainty test being the same for both: both are valid if it can be said with certainty of any given beneficiary or object that he is or is not a member of the class of beneficiaries or objects.[130] For a fixed trust for equal division, however, since it is necessary to know the exact number of beneficiaries to arrange for equal arithmetical division, the trust will only be valid if a comprehensive list of all the beneficiaries can be drawn up. **4–88**

---

[123] *Re Weekes's Settlement* [1897] 1 Ch. 289; *Re Combe* [1925] 1 Ch. 210 (after life interest, "in trust for such persons as my said son shall by will appoint but such appointment must be confined to relations of mine of the whole blood": held resulting trust when no appointment made); *Re Poulton's WT* [1987] 1 All E.R. 1068.

[124] *Wilson v Duguid* (1883) 24 Ch.D. 244 (trust for A for life, remainder to such of his children as he should by any writing appoint: held children had vested interests, liable to be divested by exercise of power, since there was an implied gift to the children equally in default of appointment). If A's power had only been exercisable by will then the implied gift in default of appointment would have been only to those children alive at A's death, since any appointment could only have been in favour of those children: *Walsh v Wallinger* (1830) 2 Russ. & M. 78 at 81. One should note that "to W for life, remainder to our children equally, but so that W may instead appoint the capital between our children in such shares as she may see fit" is equivalent to "to W for life, with power for her to appoint the capital among our children as she sees fit, but in default of appointment for our children equally": the children in both cases have immediate vested interests liable to be divested. See *Re Llewellyn's Settlement* [1921] 2 Ch. 281; *Re Arnold* [1947] Ch. 131.

[125] This gift on discretionary trust in default of appointment will need to be express, whereas a gift to beneficiaries equally in default of appointment may well be implied. If the trustees do not select beneficiaries then new trustees can be appointed or the court may order equal distribution in the absence of a more appropriate basis for distribution: *McPhail v Doulton* [1971] A.C. 424 at 457.

[126] *Brown v Higgs* (1803) 8 Ves. 561.

[127] *McPhail v Doulton* [1971] A.C. 424.

[128] *McPhail v Doulton* [1971] A.C. 424.

[129] e.g. *Re Baden's Deed Trusts (No.2)* [1973] Ch. 9; *Re Hay's ST* [1982] 1 W.L.R. 202.

[130] *McPhail v Doulton* [1971] A.C. 424.

4–89 In reading cases and textbooks it is necessary to be aware of the fact that discretionary trusts are sometimes referred to as trust powers or powers in the nature of a trust, and that the situation where, after a power, there is implied a trust in default for persons equally, is sometimes referred to as a trust power or a power in the nature of a trust or a power coupled with a trust.

4–90 In ascertaining whether or not only a mere power and no more is intended the following propositions[131] can be stated:

- If there is a gift over in default of appointment, the power is a mere power,[132] even where the gift over is void for some reason.[133]
- A residuary gift in favour of the donee of the power is not a gift over for this purpose.[134]
- To cause a power to be treated as a mere power only, the gift over must be in default of appointment, and not for any other event. Thus in the absence of a gift in default of appointment, a gift over on the failure of the appointees or any of them to reach a specified age will not necessarily prevent the power from being treated as a discretionary trust or prevent the implication of a trust for the objects equalty in default of appointment.[135]
- Where there is no gift over in default of appointment, the power may be only a mere power, or a power coupled with an implied trust in default of appointment, or a trust power or discretionary trust, according to the true intention of the settlor. This last proposition is borne out by *Re Weekes' Settlement*,[136] which is reproduced immediately below.

RE WEEKES' SETTLEMENT

Chancery Division [1897] 1 Ch. 289; (1897) 66 L.J.Ch. 179; (1897) 76 L.T. 112.

4–91 A testatrix gave a life interest in property to her husband with a "power to dispose of all such property by will amongst our children in accordance with the power granted to him as regards the other property which I have under my marriage settlements."[137] There was in her will no gift over in default of appointment, and the husband died intestate without having exercised the power. The surviving children of the marriage claimed the property in equal shares, on the ground that there was an implied gift to them in default of appointment.

4–92 ROMER J.: . . . The husband did not exercise the power of appointment, and the question is whether the children take in default of appointment.

4–93 Now, apart from the authorities, I should gather from the terms of the will that it was a mere power that was conferred on the husband, and not one coupled with a trust that he was bound to exercise. I see no words in the will to justify me in holding that the testatrix intended that the children should take if her husband did not execute the power.

4–94 This is not a case of a gift to the children with power to the husband to select, or to such of the children as the husband should select by exercising the power.

---

131 It should be noted that general powers of appointment are never considered to be in the nature of trusts, since there is no class of persons in whose favour the trust could operate. The question, therefore, arises only in connection with special powers of appointment.

132 e.g. *Re Mills* [1930] 1 Ch. 654.

133 *Re Sprague* (1880) 43 L.T. 236; *Re Sayer* [1957] Ch. 423.

134 *Re Brierley* [1894] 43 W.R. 36.

135 *Re Llewellyn's Settlement* [1921] 2 Ch. 281.

136 [1897] 1 Ch. 291. See too *Burrough v Philcox* (1840) 5 My. & Cr. 72; *Re Combe* [1925] Ch. 210; *Re Perowne* [1951] Ch. 785; *Re Scarisbrick* [1951] Ch. 622; *Re Arnold's Trusts* [1947] Ch. 131; *McPhail v Doulton* [1971] A.C. 424.

137 There were gifts over in default of appointment in those settlements.

If in this case the testatrix really intended to give a life interest to her husband and a mere power to appoint if he chose, and intended if he did not think fit to appoint that the property should go as in default of appointment according to the settlement, why should she be bound to say more than she has said in this will? **4–95**

I come to the conclusion on the words of this will that the testatrix only intended to give a life interest and a power to her husband—certainly she has not said more than that. **4–96**

Am I then bound by the authorities to hold otherwise? I think I am not. The authorities do not show, in my opinion, that there is a hard-and-fast rule that a gift to A for life with a power to A to appoint among a class and nothing more must, if there is no gift over in the will, be held a gift by implication to the class in default of the power being exercised. In my opinion the cases show (though there may be found here and there certain remarks of a few learned judges which, if not interpreted by the facts of the particular case before them, might seem to have a more extended operation) that you must find in the will an indication that the testatrix did intend the class or some of the class to take—intended in fact that the power should be regarded in the nature of a trust, only a power of selection being given, as, for example, a gift to A for life with a gift over to such of a class as A shall appoint . . . **4–97**

Held, the power was a mere power only so the children were therefore not entitled in default of appointment. **4–98**

3. Certainty of Subject-Matter

To create a valid trust, the settlor must make it certain exactly which property is to be held on trust for otherwise there will be nothing specific to which the trust can attach.[138] The beneficial interests to be taken by the beneficiaries must also be certain.[139] **4–99**

In cases where property is transferred to a trustee to hold separately from the rest of his assets, the identity of the trust property will necessarily be certain by virtue of the transfer. However, identifiability problems can arise in cases where a settlor purports to declare himself trustee of some of his property without making it clear which of his property he means. For example, if T gratuitously purports to declare himself trustee for B of 20 cases of Chateau Latour 1982 when he has 80 cases, or 20 of his 80 gold bars, then the law holds that B acquires no equitable interest until 20 cases or 20 bars have been segregated and appropriated for B.[140] **4–100**

One might have thought that it would similarly follow from the very nature of things (viz. that it is impossible to have title to specific assets when nobody knows to what assets the title relates) that if T gratuitously declares himself trustee for B of 50 of his Wonder Ltd shares when he has 950 of them, or £50 in his building society account containing £950, then B acquires no equitable interest until such shares or moneys have been segregated from T's so as to be separately held for B.[141] Most surprisingly, however, in *Hunter v Moss*,[142] the Court of Appeal upheld a gratuitous trust of 50 of T's 950 shares in a private company on the basis that:[143] **4–101**

---

138 *Palmer v Simmonds* (1854) 2 Drew. 221 at 227 ("the bulk of my residuary estate" cannot satisfy the certainty requirement though "my residuary estate" can); *Re London Wine Co (Shippers) Ltd* [1986] P.C.C. 121 (settlor cannot declare itself trustee of unascertained 20 out of 80 bottles of Ch. Lafite 1970 in its cellar though it could declare it held its holding of 80 bottles on trust as for three-quarters for itself and one-quarter for X).

139 *Boyce v Boyce* (1849) 16 Sim. 476 where T devised four houses on trust to convey whichever one she chose to Maria and to convey the others to Charlotte; and upon Maria predeceasing T so that she could not choose any house it was held the trust in favour of Charlotte was void for uncertainty. However in *Re Golay's WT* [1965] 1 W.L.R. a trust for B to receive an objectively reasonable income was upheld.

140 *Re London Wine Co Shippers Ltd* [1986] P.C.C. 121; *Re Stapylton Fletcher Ltd* [1995] 1 All E.R. 192; *Re Goldcorp Exchange* [1995] 1 A.C. 74. These problems in the sale of goods context have now been remedied by Sale of Goods Amendment Act 1995.

141 *MacJordan Construction Ltd v Brookmount Erostin* [1992] B.C.L.C. 350. cf. *Re Innes* [1910] 1 Ch. 188 at 193.

142 [1994] 1 W.L.R. 452; criticised in D.J. Hayton (1994) 110 L.Q.R. 335; followed in an undefended case as applicable to intangibles but not tangibles: *Re Harvard Securities Ltd* [1997] 2 B.C.L.C. 369; and applied in Hong Kong: *Re CA Pacific Finance Ltd* [2000] 1 B.C.L.C. 494 at 509.

143 *Hunter* at 459.

> "just as a person can give by will a specified number of his shares in a certain company, so equally he can declare himself a trustee of 50 of his shares in [a private company] and that is effective to give a beneficial proprietary interest to the beneficiary under the trust".

This overlooks a crucial difference between inter vivos and testamentary dispositions. By his death a testator does everything necessary to divest himself of all his legal and beneficial title in all his assets in favour of his executor, who is then obliged to implement his wishes subject to payment of debts, expenses and taxes. In his lifetime a donor-settlor only divests himself of his beneficial entitlement to his assets when he has done everything necessary to identify those assets to which he has relinquished entitlement, i.e. when he has separated 50 shares from the remaining 900 shares which he retains. Until then, he has simply made an imperfect gift with the result that he remains free to dispose of all or any of the property as he wishes.

4–102 Note that there is no uncertainty of subject matter problem in a case where T declares himself trustee of specified assets in proportionate undivided shares for himself and B. Thus, T can validly declare that he holds the chose in action representing his 950 shares on trust as to eighteen nineteenths for himself and one nineteenth for B: it is then clear that the subject matter of the trust is the entire shareholding, and that T and B have eighteen nineteenths and one nineteenth undivided shares in the chose.

4–103 What of the much more common situation where T is not the legal owner, but the equitable owner of shares in a public company? Suppose that legal ownership of the 5 million shares issued by Mega Plc is registered in the name of Custodian Plc, whose computer records it as holding 1 million shares for Cazenove & Co, whose computer records it in turn as holding 20,000 shares for T? Here, T is not the legal owner of 20,000 shares in Mega Plc. Rather, T owns a fiftieth equitable interest in Cazenove's one fifth equitable interest in the pool of 5 million shares legally owned by Custodian. Hence if T purports to declare a trust for B of some or all of "his" 20,000 shares, the court should not construe this as impossible and nonsensical but as reflecting an intention to declare a trust of his one fiftieth interest in Cazenove's interest in the shares owned by Custodian Plc. It seems to follow that if T happened to declare himself trustee of a notional 5,000 of his 20,000 shares, then, because he does not own any shares, he should be treated as intending to declare himself trustee of a quarter of the one fiftieth interest he does own in Cazenove's interest in the shares owned by Custodian Plc.[144] Thus certainty of subject matter of the trust is present.[145]

4. Certainty of Beneficiaries

A. *The Comprehensive List Test*

4–104 Prior to the decision in *McPhail v Doulton*,[146] reproduced below,[147] a distinction had to be drawn between trusts and powers for certainty purposes. Since trusts, even if discretionary, must be carried out, it must be possible for the courts positively to enforce and control them in the event that the trustees fail to perform their duties. For this reason there must be no linguistic or semantic uncertainty, otherwise known as conceptual uncertainty, in the description of trust beneficiaries. Nor can the class of beneficiaries be described

---

[144] Sir Roy Goode in "Are Intangible Assets Fungibles?" [2003] L.M.C.L.Q. 309 argues that this should be the case even for shares in a private company on the basis that shares in a company are merely notional units of co-ownership of a single legally indivisible asset, but this is disputed by Guy Morton in S. Worthington (ed.) *Commercial Law and Commercial Practice* (2003), pp. 296–302.

[145] As discussed in para.3–90, the LPA 1925 s.53(1)(c) formality rule governing dispositions of subsisting equitable interests does not apply in this situation because of the Uncertificated Securities Regulations 2001 reg.38(5).

[146] [1971] A.C. 424.

[147] At paras 4–138 ff.

in such a way that the trust is administratively unworkable. It used to be thought that if trustees failed to carry out a discretionary trust then it would be individious for the court to choose between the possible beneficiaries, and so the court would have to intervene instead by acting on the maxim "Equality is equity" to distribute the trust assets equally. Since no equal division could made without a comprehensive list of all the beneficiaries, it followed that discretionary trusts would fail for uncertainty unless the class of beneficiaries was described in such a way that a comprehensive list could be drawn up.[148] This must still be the position for "fixed" trusts which require equal division among the beneficiaries.

B. *The "Is or Is Not" Test*

4–105 On the other hand, where trustees are given powers of appointment, the court will not positively intervene to compel exercise of the power (except in very exceptional circumstances[149]). Provided that the trustees consider whether or not to exercise the powers and do not go beyond the scope of the powers the courts cannot intervene in a negative fashion unless the trustees can be shown to have acted *mala fide* or capriciously, i.e. for reasons which are irrational, perverse, or irrelevant to any sensible expectation of the settlor. It is entirely up to the trustees whether or not they exercise the powers, and so all that is required is that they are in a proper position to consider whether to exercise the powers or not.[150] Hence the test to determine whether the objects of the power have been defined with sufficient certainty is whether the trustees can say of anyone that he is or is not within the scope of the power. This is the ratio of the House of Lords' decision in *Re Gulbenkian's ST*,[151] reproduced below,[152] rejecting the view expressed in the Court of Appeal that it suffices if the trustees can say of a particular person or a few particular persons that he or they are within the scope of the power, although uncertainty exists in respect of many other persons.

4–106 In *McPhail v Doulton*, also known as *Re Baden's Deed Trusts (No.1)*, the House of Lords were faced with a discretionary trust that was created for benevolent (though not legally charitable) purposes, making it unsatisfactory on social policy grounds to hold the trust void when it would have been valid if it had been drafted as a power. They thus held by a 3:2 majority that the *Gulbenkian* test for powers is also the appropriate test for discretionary trusts, reasoning that in the event of trustee default it would be possible for the court to carry out a discretionary trust by distributing the trust assets not equally among all possible beneficiaries (surely the last thing the settlor ever intended on the facts of *McPhail*), but in such proportions as appropriate in the circumstances "so as to give effect to the settlor's or testator's intentions. It may do so by appointing new trustees or authorising or directing representative persons of the classes of beneficiaries to prepare a scheme of distribution, or even, should the proper basis for distribution appear, by itself directing the trustees so to distribute."[153]

C. *Application of the "Is or Is Not" Test*

4–107 Having determined in *McPhail v Doulton* that the "is or is not" test for powers would also apply to discretionary trusts the House of Lords then remitted the case to the High Court to apply this test to determine whether the trust in the case was valid or void for uncertainty. This question was therefore litigated in *Re Baden's Deed Trusts (No.2)*.[154] At first instance, Brightman J. held the trust to be valid,

---

148 *IRC v Broadway Cottages Trust* [1955] Ch. 20.
149 *Schmidt v Rosewood Trust Ltd* [2003] 2 A.C. 709 at [42] and [51]. And see para.10–05.
150 *R. v Charity Commissioners, ex parte Baldwin* [2001] W.T.L.R. 137 at 148–149.
151 [1970] A.C. 508.
152 At paras 4–133 ff.
153 [1971] A.C. 424 at 457, such methods seemingly also being available for powers of appointment to be exercised: *Schmidt v Rosewood Trust Ltd* [2003] 2 A.C. 709.
154 [1972] Ch. 607, affirmed [1973] Ch. 9.

reasoning that the potentially tricky word "relatives" passed the test because the onus of proof was on those people seeking money from the trustees to prove that they belonged to the class of beneficiaries. This decision was upheld on appeal. Stamp L.J. considered the court must be able to say of any given postulant that he definitely is a member of the beneficiary class or he definitely is not such a member, i.e. the name of a postulant must be capable of being put either in a "Yes" box or a "No" box. Thus a discretionary trust would be void if some postulants' names had to go into a "Don't know" box: if "relatives" meant descendants of a common ancestor then there would be a very large number of persons (in those pre-DNA testing days), neither known to be relatives nor known to be non-relatives, needing to be placed within the "Don't know" box, so invalidating a discretionary trust for relatives. However, Stamp L.J. was prepared to treat relatives as meaning "next-of-kin" in which case any postulant would fall within the "Yes" box or the "No" box, so validating the trust.

4–108 Sachs and Megaw L.JJ., however, held the trust valid with "relatives" bearing its broadest meaning as descendants of a common ancestor. Sachs L.J. took the robust practical view that if a postulant could not prove that his name should go into the "Yes" box then it went into the "No" box. Megaw L.J. treated Stamp L.J.'s view that a discretionary trust will fail if it cannot be shown of any individual that he definitely is or definitely is not a member of the class is to contend "in substance and reality that it does fail simply because it is impossible to ascertain every member of the class"[155] and draw up a comprehensive list thereof, a contention that had previously been rejected by *McPhail v Doulton*. However, in ascertaining whether any (as opposed to every) individual is or is not a class member it is surely not necessary to ascertain every class member and draw up a comprehensive list: to determine whether a person is "at least six feet tall" one does not need a list of all the six-footers in the world. Be that as it may, Megaw L.J. considered the "is or is not" test satisfied if "as regards a substantial number of objects it can be said with certainty that they fall within the trust, even though as regards a substantial number of other persons the answer would have to be not 'they are outside the trust' but 'it is not proven whether they are in or out.' What is a substantial number may well be a question of common sense and of some degree in relation to the particular trust."[156]

4–109 It may be questioned whether it was so wrong for Stamp L.J. to emphasise the need to ascertain those who are not class members when a person alleging a breach of trust will need to prove that the trustees distributed to an individual who was not a class member. There is also obvious uncertainty in the word "substantial". What if a class like that in *McPhail v Doulton* were enlarged by there being added a conceptually uncertain clause such as "or any of my company's customers or any of my old friends." Surely the whole trust would be void just as a discretionary trust for "my descendants and my friends" would be void, though the concept of "descendant" is clear enough.[157] Moreover, there is no real difference between Sachs and Megaw L.JJ.'s view that a trust will be valid if there is a "substantial" core of people who are clearly beneficiaries, and the view rejected by the Lords in *Re Gulbenkian* in relation to powers, namely the view expressed in that case by the Court of Appeal[158] that a power is valid if it can be said with certainty of any one or a few persons[159] that he or they are within the scope of the power although uncertainty exists as to whether other persons are within or without the power.

---

155 [1973] Ch. 9 at 23.
156 [1973] Ch. 9 at 24.
157 Is there scope for the court to develop a power to strike out an offending concept and sever it from the valid concepts within the class or classes of beneficiaries, as mooted in *Re Leek* [1969] 1 Ch. 563 at 586, and *Re Gulbenkian's Settlement* [1968] Ch. 126 at 138? It seems not: see *Tatham v Huxtable* (1950) 81 C.L.R. 639 at 652; *Re Gulbenkian's Settlement* [1970] A.C. 508 at 524; *McPhail v Doulton* [1971] A.C. 424 at 456. These all say that a trust for a large group is wholly valid or wholly void.
158 [1968] Ch. 126.
159 Megaw L.J. in *Re Baden (No.2)* [1973] Ch. 9 at 24, treats the rejected view as concerning one person but Lord Upjohn in *Re Gulbenkian's Settlement* [1970] A.C. 508 at 524, in his example of two or three individuals being clearly "old friends" treats the rejected view as concerning one or a few persons.

The crux of the matter is how the court will deal with an allegation by a beneficiary B that the trustees have committed a breach of trust by paying income to X, where, for example, the trust is for "relatives" of the settlor, and X is alleged to be not a relative. Suppose that there is no evidence capable of proving that X is or is not a relative. Does this mean that, since B has not discharged the burden of proving that X is not a relative, B's action fails? If so, then the trustees can pay income to X and, indeed, to anyone else, because anyone might well be the settlor's relative if we could go back far enough, e.g. to 4,000 B.C. It may be, however, that although the legal burden of proving a breach of trust lies on B, the evidential burden lies on the trustees once B has provided prima facie evidence that the payee is not a beneficiary. If so, then the trustees will be under an enforceable duty to pay only those who can produce evidence to prove relationship. Sachs and Megaw L.JJ. agreed with the pragmatic view taken by Brightman J. at first instance, who said:[160] **4–110**

> "In practice, the use of the expression 'relatives' cannot cause the slightest difficulty. A supposed relative to whom a grant is contemplated would, in strictness, be bound to produce the relevant birth and marriage certificates or other sufficient evidence to prove his or her relationship. If the relationship is sufficiently proved the trustees will be entitled to make the grant. If no sufficient evidence can be produced the trustees would have no option but to decline to make a grant."

D. Conceptual Certainty, Evidential Certainty, Ascertainability and Administrative Workability

As Carl Emery has emphasised,[161] questions concerning "certainty" of beneficiaries of trusts or objects of powers may relate to one or more of the following: **4–111**

> "(a) 'Conceptual uncertainty': this refers to the precision of language used by the settlor to define the classes of persons whom he intends to benefit.
> "(b) 'Evidential uncertainty': this refers to the extent to which the evidence available in a particular case enables specific persons to be identified as members of those classes—and so as beneficiaries or potential beneficiaries.
> "(c) 'Ascertainability': this refers to the extent to which 'the whereabouts or continued existence' of persons identified as beneficiaries or potential beneficiaries can be ascertained.
> "(d) 'Administrative workability': this refers to the extent to which it is practicable for trustees to discharge the duties laid upon them by the settlor towards beneficiaries or potential beneficiaries."

Evidential uncertainty does not invalidate a discretionary trust or a power since if a person is not proved to be within the beneficial class then he is outside it.[162] Nor do ascertainability problems (e.g. over the whereabouts or continued existence of a relative, A, or an ex-employee, B), because such problems are valid reasons for trustees deciding not to exercise their discretions or powers, and because, in the case of a trust, the court may give leave to distribute the trust fund on the basis that X is dead[163] or may direct a scheme for distribution amongst ascertained beneficiaries.[164] **4–112**

---

160 [1972] Ch. 607 at 626.
161 (1982) 98 L.Q.R. 551, p.552.
162 *Re Baden's Deed Trust (No.2)* [1973] Ch. 9 at 20, per Sachs L.J. The minority view of Stamp L.J. was that the evidential uncertainty (which he thought could not be resolved so simplistically) converted the apparent black and white certainty of concept into an uncertain grey concept.
163 *Re Benjamin* [1902] 1 Ch. 723.
164 *McPhail v Doulton* [1971] A.C. 424 at 457; *Re Hain* [1961] 1 W.L.R. 440 and *Muir v IRC* [1966] 3 All E.R. 38 at 44 show that a trust will not be invalidated because some of the class of beneficiaries may have disappeared or become impossible to find or it has been forgotten who they were.

4–113 If a trust is not conceptually certain then it cannot be administratively workable, e.g. a discretionary trust "for such persons as have moral claims upon me,"[165] "for my old friends[166] and business associates," "for worthy causes,"[167] "for my customers"[168] (because uncertain when they become ex-customers), "for my fans" (unless restricted to members of a particular fan club), "for Cambridge students" (unless restricted to students from time to time studying as junior members of the University of Cambridge). In rare cases a discretionary trust may alternatively be conceptually certain but administratively unworkable nonetheless, e.g. "for everyone in the world except the settlor, his spouse and past and present trustees",[169] "for the benefit of any or all or some of the inhabitants of the County of West Yorkshire",[170] or "for the black community of Hackney, Haringey, Islington and Tower Hamlets."[171] Such a "trust" would not be capable of being effectively "policed" by the court when a default beneficiary complains of the trustee's exercise of a power in favour of an object. A court must act according to some criteria, expressly or impliedly provided by the trust instrument or by extrinsic admissible evidence, so that it may control or execute the trusts: it cannot resort to pure guesswork.

4–114 However, trustees' powers to add anyone in the world (excepting the settlor, his spouse, past and present trustees) to the class of discretionary trust beneficiaries[172] and trustees' powers to appoint capital or income to anyone in the world (excepting the above small class) have been upheld by judges of first instance as not capable of being invalidated by the test of administrative workability which has been restricted to trusts. An example is *Re Hay's ST*,[173] which is reproduced below.[174] The basis for this distinction is that in the case of a discretionary trust a trustee is under more extensive obligations which the beneficiaries can positively enforce because they may lead to the court seeing to the carrying out of the trusts. In the case of powers vested in a trustee, the trustee only need consider periodically whether or not he should exercise the power, taking into account the range of objects of the power and the appropriateness of possible individual appointments; the only control exercisable by the court, in the words of Templeman J.,[175] "is the removal of the trustees and the only 'due administration' which can be 'directed' is an order requiring the trustees to consider the exercise of the power, and, in particular a request from a person within the ambit of the power." He contemplated[176] that it would be possible for objects to have no right to be informed they were objects and no right to go through the trust accounts. However, he accepted[177] that the court must be able to intervene if a wide power is exercised capriciously, i.e. for reasons which are irrational, perverse or irrelevant to any sensible expectation of the settlor.

---

165 *Re Leek* [1969] 1 Ch. 563.
166 *Brown v Gould* [1972] 53 at 57; *Re Barlow's WT* [1979] 1 All E.R. 296.
167 *Re Atkinson* [1978] 1 All E.R. 1275.
168 *Sparfax (1965) Ltd v Dommett* [1972] *The Times*, July 14.
169 *Re Hay's ST* [1982] 1 W.L.R. 202; *Yeap Cheo Neo v Ong Chen Neo* (1875) L.R. 6 P.C. 381; *Blausten v IRC* [1972] Ch. 256 at 266, 271, 272. The question of conceptual certainty and of administrative workability must be determined at the date of creation of the trust: *Re Baden's Deed Trust (No.2)* [1972] Ch. 607.
170 *R. v District Auditor, ex parte West Yorkshire CC* [2001] W.T.L.R. 795, where there were about 2,500,000 potential beneficiaries.
171 *Re Harding, deceased* [2008] Ch. 235 at [15].
172 *Re Manisty's Settlement* [1974] Ch. 17. In this case, as held by Templeman J., it is easier to discern the intention of the settlor than in the case of a power to appoint to anyone but four specified persons—unless a settlor's letter of wishes is available.
173 [1982] 1 W.L.R. 202. See too *Re Beatty's WT* [1990] 3 All E.R. 844.
174 At paras 4–156 ff.
175 [1974] Ch. 17 at 27–28. Also see *Re Gulbenkian's ST* [1970] A.C. 508 at 525.
176 [1974] Ch. 17 at 24–25.
177 [1974] Ch. 17 at 26.

But if this is the case, then for the trustees' power to be justiciable the settlor's expectations must somehow be discerned.[178] If they cannot be discerned so that the power is not justiciable then it cannot be a fiduciary power, yet a power exercisable *virtute officii* can only be a fiduciary power unless it is expressly stated not to be fiduciary but only personal.[179] The object of a fiduciary power has, like a beneficiary in default of exercise of the power, a right to seek the court's removal of the trustees for exercising the power for reasons which are irrational, perverse or irrelevant to any sensible expectation of the settlor. But if it is impossible to discern such an expectation then the court cannot adjudicate on the matter and cannot determine rights and duties. Thus, Buckley L.J. considered obiter[180] that a power to add anyone in the world to a class of beneficiaries (and, presumably, by parity of reasoning a power to appoint to anyone in the world) would be void. However, Templeman J.[181] and Megarry V.C.[182] have rejected this, considering[183] that "dispositions ought, if possible, to be upheld and the court ought not to be astute to find grounds on which a power can be invalidated." **4–115**

The need for justiciability underlies the requirement of administrative workability, and yet the High Court has created a distinction between trusts where there is positive and negative justiciability, on the one hand, and fiduciary powers where there is allegedly only negative justiciability, on the other hand. This distinction may well be disputed in an appellate court. After all, in *McPhail v Doulton*[184] the House of Lords regarded discretionary trusts ("trust powers" in the terminology of Lord Wilberforce) and powers of appointment as so similar in substance that the same certainty test should apply to both, so why only have the test of administrative workability apply to discretionary trusts? **4–116**

Furthermore, despite the views of Templeman J. in *Re Manisty*, the court may positively intervene in an extreme case where there is an improper refusal to consider exercising a power so as to direct the exercise of the power in an obviously proper way (albeit a power to benefit a beneficiary as opposed to an object of a power of appointment).[185] This has recently taken on particular significance in the context of pension fund trusts in favour of beneficiaries who have earned their interests and have legitimate expectations that powers of augmenting pensions will be exercised in their favour.[186] Indeed, in *Mettoy Pension Trustees Ltd v Evans*,[187] reproduced below,[188] Warner J. regarded Lord Wilberforce's remarks on how the court can positively see to the carrying out of discretionary trusts as equally applicable to fiduciary powers though in the context of a power to benefit beneficiaries (not objects of a power) who had earned their pension rights and expectations. Moreover, Lord Walker has **4–117**

178 In *Re Manisty's Settlement* [1974] Ch. 17 at 24–25 Templeman J. significantly stated, "In the present case if the settlement is read as a whole the expectations of the settlor are not difficult to discern."

179 *Re Gulbenkian's ST* [1970] A.C. 508 at 518, per Lord Reid, unless the trust instrument expressly makes clear that the powers are to be regarded as personal and not fiduciary.

180 *Blausten v IRC* [1972] Ch. 256 at 273; Orr and Salmon L.JJ. agreed with him at 274 and 275. The moral is to couch the power as a power for the trustees to add to the class of beneficiaries anyone from a list submitted to them by any existing beneficiary.

181 *Re Manisty's ST* [1974] Ch. 17.

182 *Re Hay's ST* [1982] 1 W.L.R. 202, applied in *IRC v Schroder* [1983] S.T.C. 480.

183 *Re Hay's* at 212. So long as conceptual certainty is present it does not matter that in substance the testator is effectively delegating his function of choosing legatees to another: *Re Abraham's WT* [1969] 1 Ch. 463; *Re Park* [1932] 1 Ch. 580; *Re Nicholls* (1987) 34 D.L.R. (4th) 321; *Re Beatty's WT* [1990] 3 All E.R. 844.

184 [1971] A.C. 424.

185 *Klug v Klug* [1918] 2 Ch. 67; *White v Grane* (1854) 18 Beav 571; *Re Lofthouse* (1885) 29 Ch.D. 921.

186 *Mettoy Pension Trustees Ltd v Evans* [1991] 2 All E.R. 513; *Thrells Ltd v Lomas* [1993] 1 W.L.R. 456; *Bridge Trustees Ltd v Noel Penny (Turbines) Ltd* [2008] Pens. L.R. 345 (where the court appointed a new trustee following the principal employer's refusal to exercise a power to distribute surplus assets to the members). And note that the Pensions Act 1995 s.25(2) avoids the need for court intervention where a liquidator is conflicted out of exercising a company's power, his power being vested in an independent person as trustee.

187 *Mettoy* at 549.

188 At paras 4–176 ff.

apparently accepted that Lord Wilberforce's remarks are applicable for the court to implement powers as well as discretionary trusts,[189] as has Lord Collins.[190]

4–118 On the safety-first principle a fiduciary power of appointment should be restricted to a workable ascertainable class of persons and a power to add persons to a beneficial class should be restricted, for example, to persons nominated in writing by existing members of the class who shall give written reasons why such an addition would have been likely to have met with the settlor's approval. Otherwise, a memorandum of wishes expressed to be of no binding legal effect, but merely indicative of the settlor's purposes in creating the trust, will probably be held by the courts to set workable parameters for the exercise of the trustee's discretion under a power (or even a trust). The power should clearly be upheld if the trust instrument expressly states that it is to be a personal power such that its exercise is to be unchallengeable unless providing the trustee with a tangible benefit so as to be a fraud on the power.

E. Personal Powers

4–119 There seems no reason why a personal power, which need not be administratively workable,[191] should have to satisfy the test for conceptual certainty of fiduciary powers.[192] Thus, there should be no need for a personal power to be defined with sufficient certainty to enable the court to say of any given postulant that he definitely is or is not an object of the power; it should suffice that the court can say of one or more persons that they are within the "core" meaning of the concept (e.g. "friends"[193]) even if the "penumbra" may be so uncertain that the court cannot say of many persons whether they qualify or not.[194] Thus, for example, a widow's personal power should be valid where her husband leaves his residuary estate to trustees upon particular discretionary trusts, but gives his widow a power to appoint up to 10 separate sums of £2,000 out of the fund to up to 10 of his "friends" not otherwise benefited by his will.

F. Conditions Subsequent and Conditions Precedent

4–120 Trusts may contain conditions subsequent or conditions precedent. If property is held subject to a condition subsequent, so that the beneficiary's vested interest will be liable to forfeiture on the happening of an event, this condition must be described in such a way that the court can see from the outset precisely and distinctly upon the happening of what event the interest is to be forfeited.[195] The circumstances involving forfeiture must be clearly known in advance so that the beneficiary knows precisely where he stands and the condition must not be void for public policy[196] for being repugnant to the essential alienability of the interest given.[197]

4–121 Where property is held on trust for persons subject to the fulfilment of a condition, so that it is up to them positively to show that they satisfy this condition precedent, a less strict standard of certainty

---

[189] *Schmidt v Rosewood Trust Ltd* [2003] 2 A.C. 309 at [42] and [51].
[190] *Scully v Coley* [2009] UKPC 29 at [29].
[191] *Re Hay's Settlement* [1982] 1 W.L.R. 202.
[192] On the distinction between personal and fiduciary powers, see paras 1–155 ff.
[193] See Browne-Wilkinson J. on "friends" in *Re Barlow's WT* [1979] 1 W.L.R. 278.
[194] See C.T. Emery (1982) 98 L.Q.R. 551, p.582 where he uses the expression "bare power" to distinguish a personal power from a fiduciary power. Exercise of the personal power would be effective so long as confined to those within the "core" meaning of the concept. Query whether it should be ineffective only when in favour of some person clearly outside the penumbra of meaning, e.g. where the alleged old friend had never met or corresponded with the testator.
[195] *Clavering v Ellison* (1859) 7 H.L.Cas.707; *Blathwayt v Lord Cawley* [1976] A.C. 397 at 429 ("being or becoming a Catholic" valid).
[196] *Church Property Trustees of Newcastle Diocese v Ebbeck* (1960) 104 C.L.R. 394: "profess Protestant faith" certain but void for public policy as designed by testator to encourage his three sons to divorce their Catholic wives.
[197] *Re Scientific Investment Pension Plan Trusts* [1999] Ch. 53 at 59.

is usually required, except where the trust is a fixed trust for equal division among all those who can satisfy a particular condition: in this case, the condition must be sufficiently certain to enable a complete list to be drawn up of those who satisfy the condition.[198] However, if instead of a fixed trust for a class there is a discretionary trust or a fiduciary power for a class of people who can satisfy a particular condition, then the condition must contain conceptually clear criteria so that it can be said of any given postulant that he is or is not a member of the class.[199]

Where, instead of a fixed amount being is held on trust for distribution between qualifying members of a class there is a trust to enable qualifying individuals to benefit to a specified extent (i.e. not "£100,000 to be distributed between such of my relatives as marry persons of the Jewish faith and of Jewish parentage as my trustees may see fit"[200] but "£5,000 to each of my relatives as marry persons of the Jewish faith and of Jewish parentage" or "£25,000 to my daughter Naomi if she marries a person of the Jewish faith and of Jewish parentage") Browne-Wilkinson J. has held in *Re Barlow's WT*[201] that the qualifying condition is valid if it is possible to say of one or more persons that he or they undoubtedly qualify, even though it may be impossible to say of others whether or not they qualify. However, while this is fine where someone like Naomi is named, it will otherwise create problems. **4–122**

In *Re Barlow's* Browne-Wilkinson J. was faced with a testatrix who directed her executor "to allow any member of my family and any friends of mine who may wish to do so to purchase" particular paintings in the testatrix's estate at a low 1970 valuation. He held that the disposition was properly to be regarded as a series of individual gifts to persons answering the description friends or blood relations of the testatrix, since the effect of the disposition was to confer on such persons a series of options to purchase. It was not necessary to discover who all the friends or relations were: all that was required was for the executors to be able to say of any individual coming forward that he had proved that he was a friend or relation on which qualifications he provided guidance.[202] He justified this on the basis of *Re Allen*[203] where the Court of Appeal had upheld a devise "to the eldest of the sons of A who shall be a member of the Church of England and an adherent to the doctrine of that Church," so allowing the eldest son to seek to establish that he qualified, even if the conditions were conceptually uncertain so that it would be impossible to say of others whether or not they qualified. He considered *Re Allen* still to be good law after *McPhail v Doulton* since the Court of Appeal in *Re Tuck's ST*[204] had mentioned it approvingly (but only in the context of revealing a distinction between conditions precedent and conditions subsequent, which he overlooked). **4–123**

He was much impressed by Lord Evershed's dictum[205] that a gift to A if he is a tall man will be valid, enabling A if he is 6ft 6ins to claim the gift. Where there is one ascertained individual, who is the only possible beneficiary, then one can accept his entitlement if he can prove he comes within the "core" **4–124**

---

198 e.g. the case of a trust for my relatives "within three degrees of consanguinity", to create certainty in equal shares as envisaged in *Re Barlow's WT* [1979] 1 W.L.R. 278.
199 *McPhail v Doulton* [1971] A.C. 424.
200 Void for uncertainty: *Clayton v Ramsden* [1943] A.C. 320.
201 [1979] 1 W.L.R. 278. This was the test suggested by Lord Denning in *Re Gulbenkian's ST* [1968] Ch. 126 at 134 for judging certainty of powers and rejected by the House of Lords on appeal. "Jewish faith and parentage" was held void for uncertainty in *Clayton v Ramsden* [1943] A.C. 320 but in *Re Tepper's WT* [1987] Ch. 358 Scott J. was reluctant to find "Jewish faith" uncertain and so adjourned the case to see if evidence of the Jewish faith as practised by the testator would clarify the matter. Both cases involved conditions subsequent.
202 *Re Baden's Deed Trusts (No.2)* [1973] Ch. 9 enables relations to be ascertained on the basis that he who does not prove he is a relation is not a relation, the concept of descendant of a common ancestor being clear. The concept of friendship is not clear. If one picture was particularly good and available at a particularly low price, so that everyone wanted this best bargain, would the purchaser have to be found by putting all possible names into a hat and drawing out one name? But would not this be impossible since the uncertain penumbra of meaning of friendship would make it impossible for the executor or the court to decide whether many persons were friends or not?
203 [1953] Ch. 810.
204 [1978] Ch. 49.
205 [1953] Ch. 810 at 817.

meaning of the qualifying condition, even if the penumbra is so conceptually uncertain that it may often be impossible to judge whether the condition is satisfied.[206] This exception will cover several ascertained beneficiaries where each is the only possible beneficiary, e.g. "£15,000 to each of my sons A, B, C and D if he is tall."

4–125 However, one ought not to extend the exception beyond individuals whose identity is ascertained from the outset to individuals whose identity can only be ascertained after deciding whether or not others have satisfied a particular condition which is conceptually uncertain, e.g. £20,000 to my first daughter to marry (or to the eldest of my daughters who shall marry) a tall adherent to the doctrine of the Church of England. If the eldest daughter, A, marries someone within the penumbra of the conceptually uncertain condition so that it is impossible to say whether she qualifies or not then it cannot help B, the second eldest, if she is within the "core" of the condition by marrying a 6ft 6ins Church of England vicar. Whether B satisfies the condition depends on the *ex hypothesi* insoluble question whether or not A has satisfied the condition.[207] The condition would fail more clearly if the gift had been to "my first female friend to marry a tall adherent to Church of England doctrine" since "friend" is a highly imprecise concept.

4–126 Browne-Wilkinson J. considered that "a gift of £10,000 to each of my friends" was valid, while accepting that a discretionary trust or power for "my friends" would be void.[208] Such a relaxed approach is anomalous and illogical. After all, a trustee or executor directed to make specific payments to qualifying beneficiaries has a duty to make such payments which may be enforced by each qualifying beneficiary, unlike the weaker position of beneficiaries or objects under discretionary trusts or powers. Furthermore, the person entitled to the fund after payment thereout of the sums to the "friends" must have a clear right to sue the trustee or executor for paying sums out to persons not ranking as "friends", so that it needs to be possible to draw up a comprehensive fixed list of friends. To protect themselves the trustees or executors (caught between the claims of the alleged friend and the residuary beneficiary) must have a right to obtain the court's directions as to the comprehensive list of persons to whom to make the payments. "Friends" gives rise not just to evidential uncertainty but to conceptual uncertainty having an uncertain penumbra making it impossible in many instances for the court to say whether a person is or is not a friend. If, pragmatically, one is to have Browne-Wilkinson J.'s exception for persons within the "core" meaning of friend why not allow discretionary trusts and powers to be validly exercised in favour of persons within the "core" meaning of friend, though House of Lords authority[209] is against this?

G. *Resolution of Uncertainty*

4–127 Questions of evidential uncertainty can be resolved by the court in the last resort, though it is possible for the trust instrument to contain a clause empowering someone like the trustees[210] or the testator's widow, or the testator's business partner to resolve any evidential uncertainty.

4–128 Apparent conceptual uncertainty may not be such if the court restrictively construes the concept, e.g. restricts "Cambridge students" to students from time to time studying as junior members of the University of Cambridge, or restricts "fans of Elvis Presley" to members of Elvis Presley fan clubs, or restricts a residuary bequest to "those beneficiaries who have only received small amounts" to those

---

206 L. McKay [1980] Conv 263 at 277; C.T. Emery (1982) 98 L.Q.R. 551 at 564.

207 C.T. Emery (1982) 98 L.Q.R. 551 at 564–565. The Court of Appeal in *Re Allen* [1953] Ch. 810 did not face up to this when dealing with a claim by the eldest son (or rather, his executor).

208 *Re Barlow's WT* [1979] 1 W.L.R. 278 at 281.

209 *Re Gulbenkian's ST* [1970] A.C. 508; *McPhail v Doulton* [1971] A.C. 424.

210 *Dundee General Hospital Board v Walker* [1952] 1 All E.R. 896.

who had received legacies of £25, £50 and £100 where other legatees had received legacies of £200 and £250.[211] A proviso that in cases of doubt the decision of the Registrar of the University of Cambridge or of the secretaries of official Elvis Presley fan clubs shall be conclusive may assist the court by restricting the concept so that it is actually certain.

However, actual conceptual uncertainty cannot be resolved by such provisos,[212] except, it seems, where a person acting as an expert (as opposed to acting as an arbitrator) is given power to resolve the matter e.g. the Chief Rabbi is to determine whether or not beneficiaries are of the Jewish faith. If the concept is "my tall relations" or "my old friends" or "my good business associates," and the testator's trustees are given power to resolve any doubts as to whether any persons qualify or not then since *ex hypothesi* the court cannot resolve the uncertainty caused by the conceptual uncertainty it is difficult to see how the trustees can. There are no clear conceptual criteria to guide them or, indeed, the court if their exercise of the power is challenged. An inherently irresolvable issue is just that; it cannot be resolved, whether by a judge or anyone else. **4–129**

If the concept is "persons whom my trustees consider to be my tall relatives or my old friends or my good business associates" the concept still seems uncertain. As Jenkins J. said in *Re Coxen*:[213] **4–130**

> "If the testator had insufficiently defined the state of affairs on which the trustees were to form their opinion he would not have saved the condition from invalidity on the ground of uncertainty merely by making their opinion the criterion, although the declaration by the trustees of this or that opinion would be an event about which in itself there could be no uncertainty."

This view was followed in *Re Jones*[214] and then in *Re Wright's WT*[215] where a gift of property to trustees "to use the same at their absolute discretion for such people and institutions as they think have helped me or my late husband" failed for conceptual uncertainty. How can the trustees consider someone to have helped a testatrix or to be a tall relative or old friend or good business associate without knowing what exactly they are supposed to consider as criteria justifying their conclusion? If their conclusion is challenged how can the court adjudicate upon the matter?[216] **4–131**

If a power to resolve conceptual uncertainty is given not as a fiduciary power but as a personal power, for example, to the testator's widow, might this validate a prima facie uncertain trust? What if a testator left his residuary estate to his executors and trustees on discretionary trust for his old friends but stated that if any doubts or disputes arose as to membership of such class then his widow's decision was to be final unless it was unreasonable, as rejecting a person clearly within the "core" meaning of "old friends" or admitting a person clearly outside the "penumbra" of meaning of "old friend," like someone whom the testator had never met or corresponded with?[217] It would seem unreasonable for a court not to accept the validity of such a personal power with the above express or implied limitation that it may not be exercised unreasonably. But if one concedes the validity of such power of the widow why should one not concede the validity of such power if vested in trustees in such terms indicating it is to be regarded not as a **4–132**

---

211 *Re Steel* [1978] 2 All E.R. 1026 at 1032; also see *O'Rourke v Bicks* [1992] S.T.C. 703.

212 *Re Coxen* [1948] Ch. 747 at 761–762; *Re Jones* [1953] Ch. 125; *Re Wright's WT* [1981] L.S. Gaz. 841. Lord Denning's dicta to the contrary in *Re Tuck's ST* [1978] Ch. 49 at 60, 62 are out of line and seem based on a misinterpretation of *Dundee General Hospital Board*, above as Eveleigh L.J. indicates [1978] Ch. 49 at 66.

213 [1948] Ch. 747 at 761–762.

214 [1953] Ch. 125: "if at any time B shall in the uncontrolled opinion of the trustee have social or other relationship with C."

215 [1981] L.S. Gaz. 841. Also see *Tatham v Huxtable* (1950) 81 C.L.R. 639, 653.

216 The jurisdiction of the court cannot be ousted: *Re Raven* [1915] 1 Ch. 673: *Re Wynn's WT* [1952] Ch. 271.

217 This is narrower than taking advantage of *Re Hay's ST* [1982] 1 W.L.R. 202 to give the widow power to add to the class of beneficiaries anyone else (apart from herself or past or present trustees) but particularly anyone she considers to be an old friend of the testator. Also see *Re Coates* [1955] Ch. 495 for the court's liberal approach before establishment of the "is or is not" test.

fiduciary power.[218] If such power was expressly limited as above the court might well accept it as conferring dispositive leeway on the trustees, just as much as on the widow, but the court would be reluctant to find such validating implied limitation on the power vested in the trustees as such.

RE GULBENKIAN'S SETTLEMENT TRUSTS

House of Lords [1970] A.C. 508; [1968] 3 W.L.R. 1127; [1968] 3 All E.R. 785

4–133 Settlements were made including a special power for trustees to appoint in favour of Nubar Gulbenkian "and any wife and his children or remoter issue . . . and any person . . . in whose house or apartment or in whose company or under whose care or control or by or with whom [he] may from time to time be employed or residing," and with trusts in default of appointment. The House of Lords unanimously upheld the power and (Lord Donovan reserving his opinion though "inclined to share" Lord Upjohn's views) rejected obiter the broad view that a power was valid if any one person clearly fell within the scope of the power. The House construed the clause as meaning "and any person or persons by whom Nubar may from time to time be employed and any person or persons with whom Nubar from time to time is residing whether in the house or apartments of such person or persons or whether in the company or under the care and control of such person or persons" and held that it could be said with certainty whether any given individual was or was not a member of that class so that the power was valid.

4–134 LORD UPJOHN (with whom LORD GUEST and LORD HODSON concurred): My lords, that is sufficient to dispose of the appeal, but the reasons of two members of the Court of Appeal went further and so must be examined.

4–135 Lord Denning M.R.[219] propounded a test in the case of powers collateral, namely, that if you can say of one particular person meaning thereby, apparently, any one person only that he is clearly within the category the whole power is good though it may be difficult to say in other cases whether a person is or is not within the category, and he supported that view by reference to authority. Winn L.J. said[220] that where there was not a complete failure by reason of ambiguity and uncertainty the court would give effect to the power as valid rather than hold it defeated since it will not have wholly failed, which put—though more broadly—the view expressed by Lord Denning M.R. Counsel for the respondents in his second line of argument relied on these observations as a matter of principle but he candidly admitted that he could not rely on any authority. Moreover, Lord Denning M.R. expressed the view[221] that the different doctrine with regard to trust powers should be brought into line with the rule with regard to conditions precedent and powers collateral . . .

4–136 [After pointing out that a fixed trust for equal division among my old friends would be void even if two or three individuals plainly were old friends, he continued:] Suppose the donor does not direct an equal division but gives a power of selection to his trustees among the class: exactly the same principles apply. The trustees have a duty to select the donees of the donor's bounty from among the class designated by the donor; he has not entrusted them with any power to select the donees merely from among known claimants within the class, for that is constituting a narrower class and the donor has given them no power to do this . . .

4–137 But with respect to mere powers,[222] while the court cannot compel the trustees to exercise their powers, yet those entitled to the fund in default must clearly be entitled to restrain the trustees from exercising it save among those within the power. So the trustees, or the court, must be able to say with certainty who is within and who is without the power. It is for this reason that I find myself unable to accept the broader position advanced by Lord Denning M.R. and Winn L.J., mentioned earlier.

---

218 Perhaps this may have been at the back of Harman L.J.'s mind in *Re Leek* [1969] 1 Ch. 563 at 579 when, whilst accepting that a discretionary trust for such persons as have moral claims on the settlor would be void for conceptual uncertainty, he uttered unorthodox dicta to the effect that if the trustees were arbiters of the class of beneficiaries, being such persons as the trustees considered to have a moral claim on the settlor, the trust would be valid.

219 [1968] Ch. 126 at 133, 134.

220 [1968] Ch. 126 at 138.

221 ibid.

222 He had just pointed out that in the case of trust powers (viz. discretionary trusts) "the trustees must exercise their power of selection and in default the court will", so he could not "see how it is possible to apply to the execution of a trust power the principles applicable to the permissible exercise by the donees, even if trustees, of mere powers."

MCPHAIL v DOULTON

House of Lords [1971] A.C. 424; [1970] 2 W.L.R. 1110; [1970] 2 All E.R. 228

The facts and the issues appear clearly in the following speech of Lord Wilberforce with which Lord Reid and Viscount Dilhorne concurred, although dissenting speeches were delivered by Lords Hodson and Guest. **4–138**

LORD WILBERFORCE: My Lords, this appeal is concerned with the validity of a trust deed dated July 17, 1941, by which Mr. Bertram Baden established a fund for the benefit, broadly, of the staff of the respondent company Matthew Hall & Co Ltd. **4–139**

The critical clauses are as follows: **4–140**

> "9. (a) The Trustees shall apply the net income of the Fund in making at their absolute discretion grants to or for benefit of any of the officers and employees or ex-officers or ex-employees of the Company or any relatives or dependants of any such persons in such amounts at such times and on such conditions (if any) as they think fit and any such grant may at their discretion be made by payment to the beneficiary or to any institution or person to be applied for his or her benefit and in the latter case the Trustees shall be under no obligation to see to the application of the money.
>
> "(b) The Trustees shall not be bound to exhaust the income of any year or other period in making such grants as aforesaid and any income not so applied shall be dealt with as provided by clause 6(a) hereof enabling moneys to be placed with any Bank or to be invested.
>
> "(c) The Trustees may realise any investments representing accumulations of income and apply the proceeds as though the same were income of the Fund and may also (but only with the consent of all the Trustees) at any time prior to the liquidation of the Fund realise any other part of the capital of the Fund which in the opinion of the Trustees it is desirable to realise in order to provide benefits for which the current income of the Fund is insufficient.
>
> "10. All benefits being at the absolute discretion of the Trustees, no person shall have any right title or interest in the Fund otherwise than pursuant to the exercise of such discretion, and nothing herein contained shall prejudice the right of the Company to determine the employment of any officer or employee."

Clause 11 defines a perpetuity period within which the trusts are, in any event, to come to an end and clause 12 provides for the termination of the fund. On this event the trustees are directed to apply the fund in their discretion in one or more of certain specified ways of which one is in making grants as if they were grants under clause 9(a) . . . **4–141**

In this House, the appellants contended that the provisions of clause 9(a) constitute a trust and not a power. If that is held to be the correct result both sides agree that the case must return to the Chancery Division for consideration, on this footing, whether this trust is valid. But here comes a complication. In the present state of authority, the decision as to validity would turn on the question whether a complete list (or on another view a list complete for practical purposes) can be drawn up of all possible beneficiaries. This follows from the Court of Appeal's decision in *Inland Revenue Comrs v Broadway Cottages Trust*[223] as applied in later cases by which, unless this House decides otherwise, the Court of Chancery would be bound. The respondents invite your Lordships to review this decision and challenge its correctness. So the second issue which arises, if clause 9(a) amounts to a trust, is whether the existing test for its validity is right in law and if not, what the test ought to be. **4–142**

Before dealing with these two questions some general observations, or reflections, may be permissible. It is striking how narrow and in a sense artificial is the distinction, in cases such as the present, between trusts or as the particular type of trust is called, trust powers, and powers. It is only necessary to read the learned judgments in the Court of Appeal[224] to see that what to one mind may appear as a power of distribution coupled with a trust to dispose of the undistributed surplus, by accumulation or otherwise, may to another appear as a trust for distribution coupled with a power to withhold a portion and accumulate or otherwise dispose of it. A layman and, I suspect, also a logician, would find it hard to understand what difference there is. **4–143**

---

[223] [1955] Ch. 20.

[224] [1969] 2 Ch. 388.

4–144 It does not seem satisfactory that the entire validity of a disposition should depend on such delicate shading. And if one considers how in practice reasonable and competent trustees would act, and ought to act, in the two cases, surely a matter very relevant to the question of validity, the distinction appears even less significant. To say that there is no obligation to exercise a mere power and that no court will intervene to compel it, whereas a trust is mandatory and its execution must be compelled, may be legally correct enough, but the proposition does not contain an exhaustive comparison of the duties of persons who are trustees in the two cases. A trustee of an employees' benefit fund, whether given a power or a trust power, is still a trustee and he would surely consider in either case that he has a fiduciary duty; he is most likely to have been selected as a suitable person to administer it from his knowledge and experience, and would consider he has a responsibility to do so according to its purpose. It would be a complete misdescription of his position to say that, if what he has is a power unaccompanied by an imperative trust to distribute, he cannot be controlled by the court if he exercised it capriciously, or outside the field permitted by the trust (cf. *Farwell on Powers*[225]). Any trustee would surely make it his duty to know what is the permissible area of selection and then consider responsibly, in individual cases, whether a contemplated beneficiary was within the power and whether, in relation to other possible claimants, a particular grant was appropriate.

4–145 Correspondingly a trustee with a duty to distribute, particularly among a potentially very large class, would surely never require the preparation of a complete list of names, which anyhow would tell him little that he needs to know. He would examine the field, by class and category; might indeed make diligent and careful enquiries, depending on how much money he had to give away and the means at his disposal, as to the composition and needs of particular categories and of individuals within them; decide on certain priorities or proportions, and then select individuals according to their needs or qualifications. If he acts in this manner, can it really be said that he is not carrying out the trust?

4–146 Differences there certainly are between trusts (trust powers) and powers, but as regards validity should they be so great as that in one case complete, or practically complete ascertainment is needed, but not in the other? Such distinction as there is would seem to lie in the extent of the survey which the trustee is required to carry out; if he has to distribute the whole of a fund's income, he must necessarily make a wider and more systematic survey than if his duty is expressed in terms of a power to make grants. But just as, in the case of a power, it is possible to underestimate the fiduciary obligation of the trustee to whom it is given, so, in the case of a trust (trust power), the danger lies in overstating what the trustee requires to know or to enquire into before he can properly execute his trust. The difference may be one of degree rather than of principle; in the well-known words of Sir George Farwell (*Farwell on Powers*[226]) trusts and powers are often blended, and the mixture may vary in its ingredients.

4–147 I now consider whether the provisions of clause 9(a) constitute a trust or a power. Naturally read, the intention of the deed seems to me clear: clause 9(a), whose language is mandatory ("shall"), creates, together with a power of selection, a trust for distribution of the income, the strictness of which is qualified by clause 9(b) which allows the income of any one year to be held up and (under clause 6(a)) either placed, for the time, with a bank, or, if thought fit, invested. Whether there is, in any technical sense an accumulation, seems to me in the present context a jejune enquiry; what is relevant is that clause 9(c) marks the difference between "accumulations" of income and the capital of the fund: the former can be distributed by a majority of the trustees, the latter cannot. As to clause 10, I do not find in it any decisive indication. If anything it seems to point in favour of a trust, but both this and other points of detail are insignificant in the face of the clearly expressed scheme of clause 9. I therefore declare that the provisions of clause 9(a) constitute a trust and remit the case to the Chancery Division for determination whether on this basis clause 9 is (subject to the effects of section 164 of the Law of Property Act 1925) valid or void for uncertainty.

4–148 This makes it necessary to consider whether, in so doing, the court should proceed on the basis that the relevant test is that laid down in the *Broadway Cottages* case[227] or some other test. That decision gave the authority of the Court of Appeal to the distinction between cases where trustees are given a power of selection and those where they are bound by a trust for selection. In the former case the position, as decided by this House, is that the power is valid if it can be said with certainty whether any given individual is or is not a member of the

225 (3rd edn, 1916), p.524.
226 ibid. at 10.
227 [1955] Ch. 20.

class and does not fail simply because it is impossible to ascertain every member of the class. (The *Gulbenkian* case.[228]) But in the latter case it is said to be necessary, for the trust to be valid, that the whole range of objects (I use the language of the Court of Appeal) should be ascertained or capable of ascertainment.

4–149 The respondents invited your Lordships to assimilate the validity test for trusts to that which applies to powers. Alternatively, they contended that in any event the test laid down in the *Broadway Cottages* case was too rigid, and that a trust should be upheld if there is sufficient practical certainty in its definition for it to be carried out, if necessary with the administrative assistance of the court, according to the expressed intention of the settlor. I would agree with this, but this does not dispense from examination of the wider argument. The basis for the *Broadway Cottages* case principle is stated to be that a trust cannot be valid unless, if need be, it can be executed by the court, and that the court can only execute it by ordering an equal distribution in which every beneficiary shares. So it is necessary to examine the authority and reason for this supposed rule as to the execution of trusts by the court.

4–150 Assuming, as I am prepared to do for present purposes, that the test of validity is whether the trust can be executed by the court, it does not follow that execution is impossible unless there can be equal division. As a matter of reason, to hold that a principle of equal division applies to trusts such as the present is certainly paradoxical. Equal division is surely the last thing the settlor ever intended; equal division among all may, probably would, produce a result beneficial to none. Why suppose that the court would lend itself to a whimsical execution? And as regards authority, I do not find that the nature of the trust, and of the court's powers over trusts, calls for any such rigid rule. Equal division may be sensible and has been decreed, in cases of family trusts for a limited class, here there is life in the maxim "equality is equity," but the cases provide numerous examples where this has not been so, and a different type of execution has been ordered, appropriate to the circumstances. . . .

4–151 So I come to *Inland Revenue Comrs v Broadway Cottage Trusts*.[229] This was certainly a case of trust, and it proceeded on the basis of an admission, in the words of the judgment, "that the class of 'beneficiaries' is incapable of ascertainment." In addition to the discretionary trust of income, there was a trust of capital for all the beneficiaries living or existing at the terminal date. This necessarily involved equal division and it seems to have been accepted that it was void for uncertainty since there cannot be equal division among a class unless all the members of the class are known. The Court of Appeal[230] applied this proposition to the discretionary trust of income, on the basis that execution by the court was only possible on the same basis of equal division. They rejected the argument that the trust could be executed by changing the trusteeship, and found the relations cases of no assistance as being in a class by themselves. The court could not create an arbitrarily restricted trust to take effect in default of distribution by the trustees. Finally they rejected the submission that the trust could take effect as a power, a valid power could not be spelt out of an invalid trust.

4–152 So I think we are free to review the *Broadway Cottages* case. The conclusion which I would reach, implicit in the previous discussion, is that the wide distinction between the validity test for powers and that for trust powers, is unfortunate and wrong, that the rule recently fastened on the courts by the *Broadway Cottages* case ought to be discarded, and that the test for the validity of trust powers ought to be similar to that accepted by this House in *Re Gulbenkian's Settlement Trusts* for powers, namely that the trust is valid if it can be said with certainty that any given individual is or is not a member of the class.

4–153 Assimilation of the validity test does not involve the complete assimilation of trust powers with powers. As to powers, I agree with my noble and learned friend Lord Upjohn in *Re Gulbenkian's Settlement* that although the trustees may, and normally will, be under a fiduciary duty to consider whether or in what way they should exercise their power, the court will not normally compel its exercise. It will intervene if the trustees exceed their powers, and possibly if they are proved to have exercised it capriciously. But in the case of a trust power, if the trustees do not exercise it, the court will; I respectfully adopt as to this the statement in Lord Upjohn's opinion.[231] I would venture to amplify this by saying that the court, if called on to execute the trust power, will do so in the manner best calculated to give effect to the settlor's or testator's intentions. It may do so by appointing new trustees, or authorising or directing representative persons of the

---

[228] [1970] A.C. 508.
[229] [1955] Ch. 20.
[230] [1968] Ch. 126.
[231] [1970] A.C. 508 at 525.

classes of beneficiaries to prepare a scheme of distribution, or even, should the proper basis for distribution appear, by itself directing the trustees so to distribute. The books give many instances where this has been done and I see no reason in principle why they should not do so in the modern field of discretionary trusts (see *Brunsden v Woolredge*,[232] *Supple v Lowson*,[233] *Liley v Hey*[234] and *Lewin on Trusts*[235]). Then, as to the trustees' duty of enquiry or ascertainment, in each case the trustees ought to make such a survey of the range of objects or possible beneficiaries as will enable them to carry out their fiduciary duty (cf. *Liley v Hey*). A wider and more comprehensive range of enquiry is called for in the case of trust powers than in the case of powers.

4–154 Two final points: first, as to the question of certainty, I desire to emphasise the distinction clearly made and explained by Lord Upjohn,[236] between linguistic or semantic uncertainty which, if unresolved by the court, renders the gift void, and the difficulty of ascertaining the existence or whereabouts of members of the class, a matter with which the court can appropriately deal on an application for directions. There may be a third case where the meaning of the words used is clear but the definition of beneficiaries is so hopelessly wide as not to form "anything like a class" so that the trust is administratively unworkable or in Lord Eldon L.C.'s words one that cannot be executed (*Morice v Bishop of Durham*[237]). I hesitate to give examples for they may prejudice future cases, but perhaps "all the residents of Greater London" will serve. I do not think that a discretionary trust for "relatives" even of a living person falls within this category . . .

4–155 Appeal allowed. Declaration that the provisions of clause 9(a) constituted a trust. Case remitted for determination whether on this basis clause 9 was (subject to the effects of section 164 of the Law of Property Act 1925) valid or void for uncertainty.

RE HAY'S SETTLEMENT TRUSTS

Chancery Division [1982] 1 W.L.R. 202; [1981] 3 All E.R. 786

4–156 By clause 4 of Lady Hay's settlement made in 1958, trustees held the trust fund "on trust for such persons or purposes for such interests and with such gifts over and (if for persons) with such provisions for their respective maintenance or advancement at the discretion of the Trustees or of any other persons as the Trustees shall by any deed or deeds revocable or irrevocable (but if revocable not after the expiration of 21 years from the date hereof) executed within 21 years from the date hereof appoint . . . and in default of such appointment in trust for the nieces and nephews of the Settlor now living in equal shares." A proviso precluded any appointment being made to the settlor, any husband of her, and any trustee or past trustee. For the first five years income was to be accumulated and then the income was to be held on discretionary trusts for the nieces and nephews or charities until the clause 4 power of appointment was exercised or ceased to be exercisable (by expiry of the 21 years). In 1969 a deed of appointment was executed, clause 1 conferring a power of appointment on the trustees (exercisable till expiry of the 21-year period in the 1958 settlement) to hold "the trust fund and the income thereof on trust for such persons and such persons as shall be appointed." Clause 2 directed that the undisposed-of income (until full exercise of the clause 1 power) be held on discretionary trusts for the benefit of any persons whatsoever (the settlor, any husband of her, any existing or former trustee excepted) or for any charity. The questions arose, whether or not the vast power of appointment in the 1958 settlement was valid; and if it was valid then whether its exercise was void in creating a vast discretionary trust that could be said to infringe the rule "*delegatus non potest delegare*" or the rule that a trust must be administratively workable?

4–157 MEGARRY V.C.: . . . The starting point must be to consider whether the power created by the first limb of clause 4 of the settlement is valid . . . The essential point is whether a power for trustees to appoint to

[232] (1765) Amb. 507.
[233] (1773) Amb. 729.
[234] (1842) 1 Hare 580.
[235] (16th edn, 1964), p.630.
[236] [1970] A.C. 508 at 524.
[237] (1805) 10 Ves. at 527.

anyone in the world except a handful of specified persons is valid. Such a power will be perfectly valid if given to a person who is not in a fiduciary position: the difficulty arises when it is given to trustees, for they are under certain fiduciary duties in relation to the power, and to a limited degree they are subject to the control of the courts. At the centre of the dispute there are *Re Manisty's Settlement Trusts*[238] (in which Templeman J. differed from part of what was said in the Court of Appeal in *Blausten v Inland Revenue Comrs*[239]); *McPhail v Doulton*,[240] which I shall call *Re Baden (No.1)*; and *Re Baden's Deed Trusts (No.2)*,[241] which I shall call *Re Baden (No.2)*. Counsel for the defendants, I may say, strongly contended that *Re Manisty's Settlement* was wrongly decided.

In *Re Manisty's Settlement* a settlement gave trustees a discretionary power to apply the trust fund for the benefit of a small class of the settlor's near relations, save that any member of a smaller "excepted class" was to be excluded from the class of beneficiaries. The trustees were also given power at their absolute discretion to declare that any person, corporation or charity (except a member of the excepted class or a trustee) should be included in the class of beneficiaries. Templeman J. held that this power to extend the class of beneficiaries was valid. In *Blausten v Inland Revenue Comrs* which had been decided some eighteen months earlier, the settlement created a discretionary trust of income for members of a "specified class" and a power to pay or apply capital to or for the benefit of members of that class, or to appoint capital to be held on trust for them. The settlement also gave the trustees power "with the previous consent in writing of the settlor" to appoint any other person or persons (except the settlor) to be included in the "specified class." The Court of Appeal decided the case on a point of construction; but Buckley L.J.[242] also considered a contention that the trustees' power to add to the "specified class" was so wide that it was bad for uncertainty, since the power would enable anyone in the world save the settlor to be included. He rejected this contention on the ground that the settlor's prior written consent was requisite to any addition to the "specified class"; but for this, it seems plain that he would have held the power void for uncertainty. Orr L.J. simply concurred, but Salmon L.J. expressly confined himself to the point of construction, and said nothing about the power to add to the "specified class". In *Re Manisty's Settlement*,[243] Templeman J. rejected the view of Buckley L.J. on this point on the ground that *Re Gestetner, deceased*,[244] *Re Gulbenkian's Settlement Trusts*[245] and the two *Baden* cases did not appear to have been fully explored in the *Blausten* case, and the case did not involve any final pronouncement on the point. In general, I respectfully agree with Templeman J. **4–158**

I propose to approach the matter by stages. First, it is plain that if a power of appointment is given to a person who is not in a fiduciary position, there is nothing in the width of the power which invalidates it per se. The power may be a special power with a large class of persons as objects; the power may be what is called a "hybrid" power, or an "intermediate" power, authorising appointment to anyone save a specified number or class of persons; or the power may be a general power. Whichever it is, there is nothing in the number of persons to whom an appointment may be made which will invalidate it. The difficulty comes when the power is given to trustees as such, in that the number of objects may interact with the fiduciary duties of the trustees and their control by the court. The argument of counsel for the defendants carried him to the extent of asserting that no valid intermediate or general power could be vested in trustees. **4–159**

That brings me to the second point, namely, the extent of the fiduciary obligations of trustees who have a mere power vested in them, and how far the court exercises control over them in relation to that power. In the case of a trust, of course, the trustee is bound to execute it, and if he does not, the court will see to its execution. A mere power is very different. Normally the trustee is not bound to exercise it, and the court will not compel him to do so. That, however, does not mean that he can simply fold his hands and ignore it, for normally he must from time to time consider whether or not to exercise the power, and the court may direct him to do this. **4–160**

When he does exercise the power, he must, of course (as in the case of all trusts and powers) confine himself to what is authorised, and not go beyond it. But that is not the only restriction. Whereas a person who **4–161**

238 [1974] Ch. 17.
239 [1972] Ch. 256.
240 [1971] A.C. 424.
241 [1973] Ch. 9.
242 [1972] Ch. 256 at 271.
243 [1974] Ch. 17 at 29.
244 [1953] Ch. 672.
245 [1970] A.C. 508.

is not in a fiduciary position is free to exercise the power in any way that he wishes, unhampered by any fiduciary duties, a trustee to whom, as such, a power is given is bound by the duties of his office in exercising that power to do so in a responsible manner according to its purpose. It is not enough for him to refrain from acting capriciously; he must do more. He must "make such a survey of the range of objects or possible beneficiaries" as will enable him to carry out his fiduciary duty. He must find out "the permissible area of selection and then consider responsibly, in individual cases, whether a contemplated beneficiary was within the power and whether, in relation to the possible claimants, a particular grant was appropriate"[246] . . .

4–162 That brings me to the third point. How is the duty of making a responsible survey and selection to be carried out in the absence of any complete list of objects? This question was considered by the Court of Appeal in *Re Baden (No.2)*. That case was concerned with what, after some divergences of judicial opinion, was held to be a discretionary trust and not a mere power; but plainly the requirements for a mere power cannot be more stringent than those for a discretionary trust. The duty, I think, may be expressed along the following lines. The trustee must not simply proceed to exercise the power in favour of such of the objects as happen to be at hand or claim his attention. He must first consider what persons or classes of persons are objects of the power within the definition in the settlement or will. In doing this, there is no need to compile a complete list of the objects, or even to make an accurate assessment of the number of them: what is needed is an appreciation of the width of the field, and thus whether a selection is to be made merely from a dozen or, instead, from thousands or millions . . . Only when the trustee has applied his mind to "the size of the problem" should he then consider in individual cases whether, in relation to other possible claimants, a particular grant is appropriate. In doing this, no doubt he should not prefer the undeserving to the deserving; but he is not required to make an exact calculation whether, as between deserving claimants, A is more deserving than B.[247]

4–163 If I am right in these views, the duties of a trustee which are specific to a mere power seem to be threefold. Apart from the obvious duty of obeying the trust instrument, and in particular of making no appointment that is not authorised by it, the trustee must, first, consider periodically whether or not he should exercise the power; second, consider the range of objects of the power; and third, consider the appropriateness of individual appointments. I do not assert that this list is exhaustive; but as the authorities stand it seems to me to include the essentials, so far as relevant to the case before me.

4–164 On this footing, the question is thus whether there is something in the nature of an intermediate power which conflicts with these duties in such a way as to invalidate the power if it is vested in a trustee. The case that there is rests in the main on *Blausten v Inland Revenue Comrs* which I have already summarised. The power there was plainly a mere power; and it authorised the trustees, with the settlor's previous consent in writing, to add any other person or persons (except the settlor) to the specified class.

4–165 After referring to *Re Park*,[248] Buckley L.J. went on:[249]

> ". . . this is not a power which suffers from the sort of uncertainty which results from the trustees being given a power of so wide an extent that it would be impossible for the court to say whether or not they were properly exercising it and so wide that it would be impossible for the trustees to consider in any sensible manner how they should exercise it, if at all, from time to time. The trustees would no doubt take into consideration the possible claims of anyone having any claim in the beneficence of the [settlor]. That is not a class of persons so wide or so indefinite that the trustees would not be able rationally to exercise their duty to consider from time to time whether or not they should exercise the power."

4–166 It seems quite plain that Buckley L.J. considered that the power was saved from invalidity only by the requirement for the consent of the settlor. The reason for saying that in the absence of such a requirement the power would have been invalid seems to be twofold. First, the class of persons to whose possible claims the trustees would be duty-bound to give consideration was so wide as not to form a true class, and this would make it impossible for the trustees to perform their duty of considering from time to time whether to exercise the power.

---

[246] *Re Baden (No.1)* [1971] A.C. 424 at 449, 457, per Lord Wilberforce.
[247] See *Re Gestetner, deceased* [1953] Ch. 672 at 688, approved in *Re Baden (No.1)* [1971] A.C. 424 at 453.
[248] [1932] 1 Ch. 581 at 583.
[249] [1972] Ch. 256 at 273.

I feel considerable difficulty in accepting this view. First, I do not see how mere numbers can inhibit the trustees from considering whether or not to exercise the power, as distinct from deciding in whose favour to exercise it. Second, I cannot see how the requirement of the settlor's consent will result in any "class" being narrowed from one that is too wide to one that is small enough. Such a requirement makes no difference whatever to the number of persons potentially included: the only exclusion is still the settlor. Third, in any case I cannot see how the requirement of the settlor's consent could make it possible to treat "anyone in the world save X" as constituting any real sort of a "class", as that term is usually understood. **4–167**

The second ground of invalidity if there is no requirement for the settlor's consent seems to be that the power is so wide that it would be impossible for the trustees to consider in any sensible manner how to exercise it, and also impossible for the court to say whether or not they were properly exercising it. With respect, I do not see how that follows. If I have correctly stated the extent of the duties of trustees in whom a mere power is vested, I do not see what there is to prevent the trustees from performing these duties. It must be remembered that Buckley L.J., though speaking after *Re Gulbenkian's Settlement* and *Re Baden (No.1)* had been decided, lacked the advantage of considering *Re Baden (No.2)*, which was not decided until some five months later. He thus did not have before him the explanation in that case of how the trustees should make a survey and consider individual appointments in cases where no complete list of objects could be compiled. I also have in mind that the settlor in the present case is still alive, though I do not rest my decision on that. **4–168**

From what I have said it will be seen that I cannot see any ground on which the power in question can be said to be void. Certainly it is not void for linguistic or semantic uncertainty; there is no room for doubt in the definition of those who are or are not objects of the power. Nor can I see that the power is administratively unworkable. The words of Lord Wilberforce in *Re Baden (No.1)*[250] are directed to discretionary trusts, not powers. Nor do I think that the power is void as being capricious. In *Re Manisty's Settlement*[251] Templeman J. appears to be suggesting that a power to benefit "residents in Greater London" is void as being capricious "because the terms of the power negative any sensible intention on the part of the settlor". In saying that, I do not think that the judge had in mind a case in which the settlor was, for instance, a former chairman of the Greater London Council, as subsequent words of his on that page indicate. In any case, as he pointed out earlier, this consideration does not apply to intermediate powers, where no class which could be regarded as capricious has been laid down. Nor do I see how the power in the present case could be invalidated as being too vague, a possible ground of invalidity considered in *Re Manisty's Settlement*.[252] Of course, if there is some real vice in a power, and there are real problems of administration or execution, the court may have to hold the power invalid: but I think that the court should be slow to do this. Dispositions ought if possible to be upheld, and the court ought not to be astute to find grounds on which a power can be invalidated. Naturally, if it is shown that a power offends against some rule of law or equity, then it will be held to be void: but a power should not be held void on a peradventure. In my judgment, the power conferred by clause 4 of the settlement is valid. **4–169**

With that, I turn to the discretionary trust of income under clause 2 of the deed of appointment. Apart from questions of the validity of the trust per se, there is the prior question whether the settlement enabled the trustees to create such a trust, or, for that matter, the power set out in clause 1 of the deed of appointment. The power conferred by clause 4 of the settlement provides that the trustees are to hold the trust fund on trust "for such persons or purposes for such interests and with such gifts over and (if for persons) with such provision for their respective maintenance or advancement at the discretion of the Trustees or any other persons as the trustees shall appoint". Clause 2 of the deed of appointment provides that the trustees are to hold the trust fund on trust to pay the income "to or for the benefit of any person or persons whatsoever . . . or to any charity" in such manner and shares and proportions as the trustees think fit". I need say nothing about purposes or charities as no question on them has arisen. The basic question is whether the appointment has designated the "persons" to whom the appointment is made. **4–170**

[250] [1971] A.C. 424 at 457.
[251] [1974] Ch. 17 at 27.
[252] [1974] Ch. 17 at 24.

4–171 Looked at as a matter of principle, my answer would be "No". There is no such person to be found in clause 2 of the deed of appointment. That seems to me to be a plain case of delegation.

4–172 Counsel for the defendants relied on *Re Hunter's Will Trusts*[253] [and *Re Morris' ST*[254]] as supporting his contention that clause 2 of the deed of appointment was void.

4–173 Now it is clear that in these authorities the rule *delegatus non potest delegare* was in issue. Does this rule apply to intermediate powers? This was not explored in argument, but I think that it is clear from *Re Triffitt's Settlement*[255] that the rule does not apply to an intermediate power vested in a person beneficially. Here, of course, the power is an intermediate power, but it is vested in trustees as such, and not in any person beneficially; and the rule is that "trustees cannot delegate unless they have authority to do so".[256] Accordingly, I do not think that the fact that the power is an intermediate power excludes it from the rule against delegation. On the contrary, the fact that the power is vested in trustees subjects it to that rule unless there is something in the settlement to exclude it. I can see nothing in the settlement which purports to authorise any such appointment or to exclude the normal rule against delegation. In my judgment, both on principle and on authority clause 2 of the deed of appointment is void as being an excessive execution of the power.

4–174 That, I think, suffices to dispose of the case. I have not dealt with the submission which counsel for the defendants put in the forefront of his argument. This was that even if the power had been wide enough to authorise the creation of the discretionary trust, that trust was nevertheless as bad as being a trust in favour of "so hopelessly wide" a definition of beneficiaries "as not to form anything like a class so that the trust is administratively unworkable".[257] I do not propose to go into the authorities on this point. I consider that the duties of trustees under a discretionary trust are more stringent than those of trustees under a power of appointment,[258] and as at present advised I think that I would, if necessary, hold that an intermediate trust such as that in the present case is void as being administratively unworkable. In my view there is a difference between a power and a trust in this respect. The essence of that difference, I think, is that beneficiaries under a trust have rights of enforcement which mere objects of a power lack.

4–175 [He then held that the nieces and nephews living at the date of the settlement had become entitled to the trust fund on the expiration of 21 years from the date of the settlement by virtue of the gift over in default of any valid appointment within the 21 years.]

METTOY PENSION TRUSTEES LTD v EVANS

Chancery Division [1990] 1 W.L.R. 1587; [1991] 2 All E.R. 515

4–176 On the liquidation of a company, which was sole trustee of its company pension fund, it became impossible for it to exercise its fiduciary power as trustee to apply surplus trust funds to benefit the beneficiaries; nor could the liquidator exercise the power because of his conflicting duties to the creditors of the company otherwise entitled to the surplus and to the beneficiary. Could the court exercise the power in the same way that the court can give effect to discretionary trusts? The answer was "Yes".

4–177 WARNER J.: The question then arises, if the discretion is a fiduciary power which cannot be exercised either by the receivers or by the liquidator, who is to exercise it? I heard submissions on that point. The discretion cannot be exercised by the directors of the company, because on the appointment of the liquidator all the powers of the directors ceased. I was referred to a number of authorities on the circumstances in which the court may interfere with or give directions as to the exercise of discretions vested

---

[253] [1963] Ch. 372.
[254] [1951] 2 All E.R. 528.
[255] [1958] Ch. 852.
[256] *Re Pilkington's Will Trusts* [1964] A.C. 612 at 639, per Viscount Radcliffe.
[257] *Re Baden (No.1)* [1971] A.C. 424 at 457, per Lord Wilberforce.
[258] See *Re Baden (No.1)* [1971] A.C. 424 at 457.

in trustees.[259] None of those cases deals directly with a situation in which a fiduciary power is left with no one to exercise it. They point however to the conclusion that in that situation the court must step in. Mr Inglis-Jones and Mr Walker urge me to say that in this case the court should step in by giving directions to the trustees as to the distribution of the surplus in the pension fund. They relied in particular on this passage in the speech of Lord Wilberforce in *McPhail v Doulton*:[260]

> "As to powers, I agree with my noble and learned friend Lord Upjohn in *Re Gulbenkian's Settlement*[261] that although the trustees may, and formally will, be under a fiduciary duty to consider whether or in what way they should exercise their power, the court will not normally compel its exercise. It will intervene if the trustees exceed their powers, and possibly if they are proved to have exercised it capriciously. But in the case of a trust power, if the trustees do not exercise it, the court will; I respectfully adopt as to this the statement in Lord Upjohn's opinion.[262] I would venture to amplify this by saying that the court, if called upon to execute the trust power, will do so in the manner best calculated to give effect to the settlor's or testator's intentions. It may do so by appointing new trustees, or by authorising or directing representative persons of the classes of beneficiaries to prepare a scheme of distribution, or even, should the proper basis for distribution appear, by itself directing the trustees so to distribute. The books give many instances where this has been done and I see no reason in principle why they should not do so in the modern field of discretionary trusts . . ."

Clearly, in the first two sentences of that passage Lord Wilberforce was referring to a discretion in category 2[263] and in the following part of it to a discretion in category 4. In that latter part he was indicating how the court might give effect to a discretionary trust when called upon to execute it. It seems to me however that the methods he indicated could be equally appropriate in a case where the court was called upon to intervene in the exercise of a discretion in category 2. In saying that I do not overlook that in *Re Manisty's Settlement*[264] Templeman J. expressed the view that the only right and the only remedy of an object of the power who was aggrieved by the trustees' conduct would be to apply to the court to remove the trustees and appoint others in their place. However, the earlier authorities to which I was referred, such as *Re Hodges* and *Klug v Klug*, had not been cited to Templeman J. I conclude that, in a situation such as this, it is open to the court to adopt whichever of the methods indicated by Lord Wilberforce appears most appropriate in the circumstances. **4–178**

Questions

1. A testator who died a month ago by his will made the following bequests: **4–179**

    (i) £10,000 to Alan and at his death the remaining part of what is left that he does not want for his own use to be divided equally between Xerxes and Yorick;

---

259 Namely *Gisborne v Gisborne* (1877) 2 App.Cas. 300; *Re Hodges, Dovey v Ward* (1878) 7 Ch.D. 754; *Tabor v Brooks* (1878) 10 Ch.D 273; *Klug v Klug* [1918] 2 Ch. 67; *Re Allen-Meyrick's Will Trusts; Mangnall v Allen-Meyrick* [1966] 1 W.L.R. 499; *McPhail v Doulton* [1971] A.C. 424; *Re Manisty's Settlement* [1974] Ch. 17 at 25–26; and *Re Locker's Settlement Trusts; Meachem v Sachs* [1977] 1 W.L.R. 1323.

260 [1971] A.C. 424 at 456–457.

261 [1970] A.C. 508.

262 See [1970] A.C. 508 at 525.

263 Note that in Warner J.'s classification, category 1 comprises any power given to a person to determine the destination of trust properly without that person being under any obligation to exercise the power or to preserve it (a personal power); category 2 comprises any power conferred on the trustees of the property or on any other person as a trustee of the power itself (a fiduciary power); category 3 comprises any discretion which is really a duty to form a judgment as to the existence or otherwise of particular circumstances giving rise to particular consequences; and category 4 comprises discretionary trusts where someone, usually the trustees, is under a duty to select from among a class of beneficiaries those who are to receive amounts of income or capital of the trust fund.

264 [1974] Ch. 17 at 25.

(ii) £50,000 to my trustees Tom and Tim to distribute among such of the inhabitants of Cambridge as they shall in their unfettered discretion think fit;

(iii) £100,000 to my said trustees to distribute among Brian, Charles, David, Ellen, Oswald, Peter, Quentin and Roger and such of my other business associates and old friends as they shall see fit;

(iv) £100,000 to my said trustees to use the income for 80 years from my death as the applicable perpetuity period or such other period as the law allows if less for providing holidays for employees and ex-employees their spouses and relatives of ICI Plc and of companies on whose boards of directors, directors of ICI Plc sit, and thereafter to use the income for the education of my relatives;

(v) residue to my son Simon trusting that he will see to it that my old friends shall have the contents of my wine cellar; and in case of any doubts he shall have power to designate who are my business associates and old friends.

Consider the validity of these bequests, the testator having lived in Cambridge all his life.

4–180 2. "If the practical distinctions between discretionary trusts and fiduciary powers are so slight as to justify the decisions in *McPhail v Doulton* and *Schmidt v Rosewood Trust Ltd*, it cannot be right to have one but not the other subject to the test of administrative workability; nor, in light of *McPhail v Doulton*, can *Re Barlow's WT* be justified." **Discuss.**

4–181 3. Simon Small, who was only 4 feet 11 inches tall, has just died. In his home-made will, he directed his executors:

(a) to pay £2,000 to each of my small relatives;

(b) to distribute £8,000 as they see fit among such persons as they consider to be friends of mine;

(c) to hold my residuary estate on trust to pay the income therefrom to my four daughters equally in their respective lifetimes but if a daughter marries a supporter of Watford Football Club the share of such daughter shall accrue to the other daughters, as shall also be the case on the death of a daughter, but on the death of my last surviving daughter they shall distribute the capital within one year among such persons connected with me who have been benefited by me in my lifetime as they shall see fit.

Advise on the validity of the above bequests.

5 THE BENEFICIARY PRINCIPLE

1. THE BASIC RULE

To underpin the binding obligation inherent in the trust concept, the trust must be directly or indirectly for the benefit of persons so that some person has locus standi to apply to the court to enforce the trust and make the trustees liable to account. Hence the court will not uphold any alleged trust that cannot be effectively supervised and sanctioned by the court at the behest of someone in whose favour performance can be decreed.[1] As Lord Evershed M.R. said in *Re Endacott*,[2] a trust "to be effective must have ascertained or ascertainable beneficiaries"; and as Viscount Simonds said in *Leahy v Att.-Gen. for New South Wales*:[3] **5–01**

> "a trust may be created for the benefit of persons as cestuis que trust but not for a purpose or object unless the purpose or object be charitable, for a purpose or object cannot sue . . .".

Must the person at whose behest the court can enforce the trust be a beneficiary with an equitable proprietary interest in the trust assets, or may he alternatively be an "enforcer" who has the right to hold the trustees to account, divorced from beneficial ownership of the property? This question is considered in Section 2. If the law insists on beneficiaries, and does not permit purpose trusts to be saved from invalidity by the appointment of an enforcer, then trusts for charitable purposes are clearly an exception to the basic rule, since they are valid despite their lack of beneficiaries, although they would not be an exception to a wider "enforcer principle" since they are enforceable in the public interest by the Attorney-General or the Charity Commission. Charitable trusts are considered separately in Chapter 6. In Section 3, below, we also discuss various cases in which the courts appear to have acknowledged some other exceptions to the basic rule against trusts for purposes, and conclude that most of these turn out not to be exceptions, since they can be reconciled with the basic rule. **5–02**

2. AN ENFORCER PRINCIPLE?

The orthodox view, that non-charitable purpose trusts are void and that settlors have no rights per se to enforce their trusts, has led to offshore jurisdictions filling a gap in the trusts "market" by enacting legislation validating non-charitable purpose trusts so long as the trust instrument appoints an enforcer (who could be the settlor or an independent or related third party) with provision for further enforcers after his death or retirement. The question arises, what would happen under the rules of English private international law if the English court were faced with a non-charitable purpose trust **5–03**

---

1 *Morice v Bishop of Durham* (1804) 9 Ves. 399 at 405; (1805) 10 Ves. 521 at 539. See too *Re Astor's ST* [1952] Ch. 534 at 549, per Roxburgh J.: "A court of equity does not recognise as valid a trust which it cannot both enforce and control."

2 [1960] Ch. 232 at 246.

3 [1959] A.C. 457 at 479; reproduced below at 5–89 ff. See too *Re Astor's S.T.* [1952] Ch. 534; *Re Shaw* [1957] 1 W.L.R. 729; *Re Denley's Trust Deed* [1969] 1 Ch. 373 at 382–383; *Re Recher's WT* [1972] Ch. 526 at 538; *Re Grant's WT* [1979] 3 All E.R. 359; *Bradshaw v University College of Wales* [1987] 3 All E.R. 200 at 203; *Re Horley Town FC* [2006] W.T.L.R. 1817 at [89]. A power to carry out abstract impersonal purposes can be valid: *Re Douglas* [1887] 35 Ch.D. 472; *Goff v Nairne* (1876) 3 Ch.D. 278; *Re Shaw* [1957] 1 W.L.R. 729; *Re Wooton's WT* [1968] 2 All E.R. 618 at 623–624.

of English assets governed by a foreign law (such as that of Jersey or the Isle of Man or Bermuda or the British Virgin Islands or the Cayman Islands) that treats such a trust as valid where the terms of the trust appoint an enforcer?

5–04 If such a foreign trust concept were either repugnant to the core of the trust concept or contrary to English public policy then the English court could only hold the trust to be void for infringing the beneficiary principle, so that a resulting trust would arise for the settlor, whose creditors, heirs or divorcing spouse could then enforce their claims against the trust assets.[4] However, English law is not so insular as to refuse to recognise any aspect of foreign law that is different from English law,[5] and on one view, the English court should recognise the validity of trusts whenever they clearly supply a mechanism for the positive enforcement of the trust so that the trustees are under an obligation to account to someone in whose favour the court can positively decree performance, whether this person is a beneficiary with a proprietary interest in the trust assets or an enforcer with no such proprietary interest.[6]

5–05 On this view, English law could accept that a trust simply needs an enforcer, whether a beneficiary or the Attorney-General or Charity Commission for charitable purpose trusts or some person expressly appointed by the trust instrument to be enforcer with locus standi[7] positively[8] to enforce the trust. After all, as Lord Walker made clear in *Schmidt v Rosewood Trust Ltd*,[9] rights to disclosure of trust documents and supporting information are not based on beneficiaries' proprietary interests but on the court's inherent jurisdiction to supervise matters and make the trustees account for their trusteeship at the behest of sufficiently interested persons, e.g. objects of powers[10] or new trustees[11] or protectors.[12]

5–06 Thus, the English courts should not hold the above Jersey trusts to be void so that the settlor is entitled from the outset to the beneficial interest under a resulting trust. Where then is the beneficial interest? Should a non-charitable purpose trust be treated like a charitable purpose trust where the trustees are the legal beneficial owners[13] but are under fiduciary and equitable duties owed to the Attorney-General and the Charity Commission or any "interested person"[14] having the permission of the Commission to hold them to account? The trustees of a non-charitable purpose trust can similarly owe fiduciary and equitable duties to the enforcer, but what if the enforcer does not enforce the trusts or, worse still, what if the trustee and the enforcer appropriate the property for themselves?[15] Under

---

4 Note that the Recognition of Trusts Act 1987 gives the right to choose any foreign trust law to govern a trust so long as not "manifestly incompatible with public policy"; and cf. the approach taken to wide exemption clauses in *Armitage v Nurse* [1998] Ch. 241 at 253.

5 The inalienability of an alimentary life interest under Scots law was accepted by the Court of Appeal in *Re Fitzgerald* [1904] 1 Ch. 573 though English life interests cannot be inalienable.

6 D.J. Hayton, "Developing the Obligation Characteristic of the Trust" (2001) 117 L.Q.R. 96. cf. P. Matthews "From Obligation to Property, and Back Again" in D.J. Hayton (ed.), *Extending the Boundaries of Trusts and Similar Ring-Fenced Funds* (2002), who argues that arrangements of the latter sort may be valid under English law on contract law principles, but cannot be trusts because these necessarily entail equitable property ownership.

7 See the emphasis on locus standi to enforce in *Re Denley's Trust Deed* [1969] 1 Ch. 373 at 382–383; *Re Astor's ST* [1952] Ch. 534 at 542; *Re Shaw* [1957] 1 W.L.R. 729 at 745.

8 The fact that the residuary legatees or the next-of-kin will take property in default of specific purposes being carried out does not indicate that the settlor-testator intended such "negatively" interested persons to be enforcers, and so the presence of such persons will not save a trust for non-charitable purposes: *Re Shaw* [1957] 1 W.L.R. 729 at 745; *Re Davidson* [1909] 1 Ch. 567 at 571.

9 [2003] 2 A.C. 709.

10 *Schmidt v Rosewood Trust Ltd* [2003] 2 A.C. 709.

11 *Young v Murphy* [1996] 1 V.R. 279.

12 *Re Hare Trust* (2001) 4 I.T.E.L.R. 288; *Von Knierem v Bermuda Trust Co Ltd* [1994] S.C.B. 154.

13 Just like executors of a testator: *Commissioners of Stamp Duty v Livingston* [1965] A.C. 694.

14 Charities Act 1993 s.33.

15 An individual enforcer cannot bind his *ex officio* successors not to enforce the trustee's duties.

the rule in *Saunders v Vautier*[16] they are not entitled to take the trust property for themselves unless they are the persons exclusively beneficially entitled to the trust property. This cannot be the case where another person becomes beneficially entitled at the end of the trust period with the right to make the trustee account for its trusteeship.

The key issue, then, is whether until the end of this trust period it is correct that the beneficial interest is not vested in the settlor under a resulting trust subject to the trustee having a valid power to carry out the non-charitable purposes,[17] and the enforcer having a valid power to ensure that the trustee exercises its power: such powers seem to be valid even under English domestic law because the approach of the courts is to facilitate settlor's intentions unless illegal or otherwise contrary to public policy. Surely, by expressly using language imposing a duty to the enforcer upon the trustee to use all the trust property exclusively to carry out the non-charitable purposes (and so not to benefit the settlor), the settlor by necessary implication has abandoned any beneficial interest in the trust property so as to oust any resulting trust.[18] Thus, the trustee must have legal beneficial ownership of the trust property but subject to fiduciary and equitable duties owed to the enforcer. **5–07**

This position achieved by foreign trust legislation does not appear to be so out of line as to be repugnant to the core trust concept or contrary to English public policy. Indeed, if in an English trust deed, a settlor abandoned all beneficial interest in the trust property to the intent that the trustee must use its legal beneficial ownership of the trust property to carry out workable non-charitable purposes for a royal lives and 21 years perpetuity period and appointed an enforcer expressly required to ensure that the trustee carries out the trusts and expressly given sufficient enforcement rights against the trustee, there seems plenty of scope for the House of Lords or a bold Court of Appeal to accept the validity of such a non-charitable purpose trust where, crucially, there is a designated enforcer to whom the trustee owes duties in respect of its legal beneficial ownership of all the trust property. **5–08**

It does not matter that the enforcer only has a power and not a duty to enforce the trustee's obligations: a beneficiary is in exactly the same position. A beneficiary has much self-interest in enforcing the trust, but so will often be the case for the person appointed to be enforcer who may, indeed, have something to lose if not enforcing the trust, e.g. removal by the members of his body from the office that led him to be the enforcer or censure at an extraordinary general meeting. Moreover, a reputable trustee duly performs trusteeship duties because he is good at them, enjoying doing them and getting paid for them, while any successor trustee is under a duty to make the old trustee remedy any breaches of duty that are discovered.[19] **5–09**

BERMUDA TRUSTS (SPECIAL PROVISIONS) ACT 1989 SECTIONS 12A AND 12B[20]

Purpose Trusts

12A—(1) A trust may be created for a non-charitable purpose or purposes provided that the conditions set out in subsection (2) are satisfied; and in this Part such a trust is referred to as a "purpose trust". **5–10**

---

16 (1841) 4 Beav. 115; discussed at paras 7–03 ff.

17 *Re Shaw* [1957] 1 All E.R. 745 at 759; endorsed in *Re Wooton's WT* [1968] 1 W.L.R. 681 at 688.

18 "If the settlor has expressly, or by necessary implication, abandoned any beneficial interest in the trust property, there is in my view no resulting trust": *Westdeutsche Landesbank v Islington LBC* [1966] A.C. 669 at 708, per Lord Browne-Wilkinson.

19 *Young v Murphy* [1996] 1 V.R. 279.

20 Inserted by the Bermuda Trusts (Special Provisions) Amendment Act 1998.

(2) The conditions are that the purpose or purposes are—

(a) sufficiently certain to allow the trust to be carried out,
(b) lawful, and
(c) not contrary to public policy.

(3) A purpose trust may only be created in writing.

(4) The rule of law (known as the rule against excessive duration or the rule against perpetual trusts) which limits the time during which the capital of a trust may remain unexpendable to the perpetuity period under the rule against perpetuities shall not apply to a purpose trust.

(5) The rule against perpetuities (also known as the rule against remoteness of vesting) as modified by the Perpetuties and Accumulations Act 1989 shall apply to a purpose trust.

Enforcement and Variation of Purpose Trust by the Court

5–11 12B—(1) The Supreme Court may make such order as it considers expedient for the enforcement of a purpose trust on the application of any of the following persons—

(a) any person appointed by or under the trust for the purposes of this subsection;
(b) the settlor, unless the trust instrument provides otherwise;
(c) a trustee of the trust;
(d) any other person whom the court considers has sufficient interest in the enforcement of the trust;

and where the Attorney-General satisfies the court that there is no such person who is able and willing to make an application under this subsection, the Attorney-General may make an application for enforcement of the trust.

(2) On an application in relation to a purpose trust by any of the following persons—

(a) any person appointed by or under the trust for the purposes of this subsection;
(b) the settlor, unless the trust instrument provides otherwise;
(c) a trustee of the trust,

the court may if it thinks fit approve a scheme to vary any of the purposes of the trust, or to enlarge or otherwise vary any of the powers of the trustees of the trust.

(3) Where any costs are incurred in connection with any application under this section, the Supreme Court may make such order as it considers just as to payment of those costs (including payment out of the property of the trust).

3. Exceptions?

A. "Anomalous" Testamentary Purpose Trusts

5–12 The Court of Appeal[21] has held that there are some anomalous cases, not to be extended, where testamentary trusts infringing the beneficiary (or enforcer) principle have been held valid as concessions to human sentiment. These anomalous cases are:

[21] *Re Endacott* [1960] Ch. 232 (residuary gift to a parish council "for the purpose of providing some useful memorial to" the testator held void for uncertainty and for infringing the beneficiary principle).

- trusts for the maintenance of particular animals;[22]
- trusts for the erection or maintenance of graves and sepulchral monuments;[23]
- trusts for the saying of masses in private;[24] and
- trusts for the promotion and furtherance of fox-hunting.[25]

5–13 These trusts are sometimes referred to as trusts of imperfect obligation since the trustees are not obliged to carry out the trusts in the absence of anyone able to apply to the court to enforce the trust. The trusts are subject to the rule against inalienability and so must be restricted directly or indirectly[26] to the common law perpetuity period. If the trustees do not take advantage of what, in substance, amounts to a power to carry out a purpose, then the person otherwise entitled to the trust property will be able to claim it. The courts here have created an exception to the principle[27] that they will not treat words creating a trust as if only creating a power.

5–14 However, it may be questioned how anomalous these trusts really are.[28] As discussed immediately below, some other "purpose" trusts have effectively been reinterpreted as trusts for persons because the performance of the purpose enures to the benefit of specific individuals, and trusts for the maintenance of particular animals can also be characterised as trusts for persons on this basis, since animals are chattels that belong to particular people. The maintenance of private graves for 99 years may be possible in any case under the Parish Councils and Burial Authorities (Miscellaneous Provisions) Act 1970 s.1, and if the construction is part of the fabric of a church then the trust will be charitable and valid on that ground.[29] Gifts for the saying of masses in private are very close to gifts for the saying of masses in public, which are charitable, and it is only the dubious rule in *Re Hetherington*[30] that divides the two—this holds that the saying of prayers can only be for the public benefit (and thus legally charitable) if persons other than the clergyman can hear them being said and are thereby benefited by his edifying example. Trusts for the promotion of fox-hunting are irreducibly anomalous, but the relevant case—*Re Thompson*—is very weakly reasoned since Romer J. erroneously based his judgment on negative enforceability by the default beneficiary when positive enforceability is necessary.[31] Moreover, fox-hunting has now been made illegal by the Hunting Act 2004.

---

22 *Pettingall v Pettingall* (1842) 11 L.J. Ch. 176; *Re Dean* (1889) 41 Ch.D. 552. Many trusts for animals generally are charitable: *Re Wedgwood* [1915] 1 Ch. 113; and see paras 6–278 and 6–281 ff.

23 *Re Hooper* [1932] Ch. 38; *Mussett v Bingle* [1876] W.N. 170; *Pirbright v Salwey* [1896] W.N. 86; *Trimmer v Danby* (1856) 25 L.J. Ch. 424.

24 *Bourne v Keane* [1919] A.C. 815 at 874–875. In Malaysia and Singapore trusts for ancestor worship (Sin Chew or Chin Shong ceremonies) have been held valid anomalous non-charitable purpose gifts if restricted to the perpetuity period: *Tan v Tan* (1946) 12 M.L.J. 159; *Hong Kong Bank Trustee Co v Farrer Tan* [1988] 1 M.L.J. 485.

25 *Re Thompson* [1934] Ch. 342, but the default beneficiary, a charity, only objected *pro forma*.

26 *Pedulla v Nasti* (1990) 20 N.S.W.L.R. 720. If a will restricts a bequest expressly "so far as the law allows" this is construed as restricting the period to 21 years so satisfying the rule against inalienability: *Re Hooper* [1932] Ch. 38. The court will not imply such a term: *Re Compton* [1946] 1 All E.R. 117. If the legacy does not have to be kept intact as endowment capital but can be spent as soon as practicable on the purpose then the rule against inalienability has no application: *Trimmer v Danby* (1856) 25 L.J. Ch. 424; *Mussett v Bingle* [1876] W.N. 170.

27 *IRC v Broadway Cottage Trust* [1955] Ch. 20 at 36; *Re Shaw* [1957] 1 W.L.R. 729 at 746.

28 As argued in P. Matthews "The New Trust: Obligations Without Rights?" in A.J. Oakley (ed.) *Trends in Contemporary Trust Law* (1996).

29 *Hoare v Osborne* (1866) L.R. 1 Eq. 585.

30 [1990] Ch. 1.

31 *Re Davidson* [1909] 1 Ch. 567 at 571; *Re Shaw* [1957] 1 W.L.R. 729 at 745.

B. "Purpose Trusts", the Performance of which Enures to the Benefit of Persons

5–15 In *Re Denley's Trust Deed*,[32] reproduced below,[33] Goff J. upheld a trust of a corporate settlor's land "to be maintained and used as and for the purposes of a recreation or sports ground primarily for the benefit of the employees of the company and secondarily for the benefit of such other persons (if any) as the trustees may allow to use the same." He considered that the attainment of these trust purposes was sufficiently for the benefit of certain individuals that the settlor should be taken to have intended that they should have locus standi to enforce the trust positively in their favour.[34] In effect, the trust was primarily for the benefit of particular people (the employees), with the specified way in which they were to be benefited being a secondary consideration. As trusts which are in effect for the benefit of people and thus similar to discretionary trusts, *Re Denley*-type purpose trusts have the benefit of the liberal Perpetuities and Accumulations Act 2009 and are not subject to the strict rule against inalienability.[35]

5–16 *Re Denley*-type purpose trusts typically involve a large fluctuating class of beneficiaries never intended to have, and never capable of having,[36] absolute ownership of the trust property, and only having a positive right to the performance of the trustee's duties in the form prescribed by the settlor. What of the cases, however, where there is a small class of identified beneficiaries who could be intended to have absolute ownership of the trust property, though the settlor purportedly qualifies this by requiring the property to be used for a specified purpose?

5–17 Take the case of a trust fund set up for the education of the seven children of a deceased clergyman. Once their formal education was over, Kekewich J.[37] held this to be an absolute gift with the reference to education expressing merely the motive of the gift. He applied the well-established, and difficult to rebut,[38] presumption of construction,[39] "If a gross sum be given, or if the whole income of property be given, and a special purpose be assigned for this gift this court regards the gift as absolute and the purpose merely as the motive of the gift, and therefore holds that the gift takes effect as to the whole sum or the whole income as the case may be."

5–18 This was applied by the Court of Appeal in *Re Osoba*[40] where a bequest to the testator's widow upon trust "for her maintenance and for the training of my daughter, Abiola, up to university grade and for the maintenance of my aged mother" was held to be a trust for the three females absolutely as joint tenants. Similarly in *Re Bowes*[41] a trust to spend £5,000 on planting trees for shelter on the

---

[32] [1969] 1 Ch. 373.

[33] At paras 5–19 ff.

[34] See too *Re Saxone Shoe Co's Trust Deed* [1962] 1 W.L.R. 934 (which would now be valid under the *McPhail v Doulton* [1971] A.C. 424 test for discretionary trusts); *Wicks v Firth* [1983] A.C. 214; *Grender v Dresden* [2009] W.T.L.R. 379 at [18]. Persons named in a trust deed and benefiting directly or indirectly (e.g. as employees) but not intended to have a right to enforce the trust have no locus standi to apply to the court: *Shaw v Lawless* (1838) 5 Cl. & Fin. 129 at 153; *Gandy v Gandy* (1885) 30 Ch.D. 57 at 69–70.

[35] *Grender v Dresden* [2009] W.T.L.R. 379 at [18]. For discussion of the perpetuity rules affecting trusts, see paras 7–62 ff.

[36] A fluctuating class can never exercise *Saunders v Vautier* rights to make the trust property their own: *Re Levy* [1960] Ch. 346 at 363; *Re Westphal* [1972] N.Z.L.R. 792 at 764–765. Exceptionally, where the beneficial class consists of members from time to time of a club who, on dissolution of the club, are entitled to divide the assets between them, the beneficiaries will be able to acquire absolute ownership: see paras 5–72 and 14–48 ff.

[37] *Re Andrew's Trust* [1905] 2 Ch. 48.

[38] *Re Abbott Fund Trust* [1900] 2 Ch. 326: fund subscribed for maintenance of two deaf and dumb ladies (so not of normal capacity) held after their deaths to pass to subscribers under resulting trust and not to survivor's estate. For other cases where the beneficiary was only entitled to claim what was necessary for the specified purpose see *Re Sanderson's Trusts* (1857) 3 K. & J. 497; *Re Gillingham Bus Disaster Fund* [1958] Ch. 300.

[39] *Re Sanderson's Trusts* (1857) 3 K. & J. 497, and see *Re Skinner* (1860) 1 J. & H. 102 at 105.

[40] [1979] 2 All E.R. 393.

[41] [1896] 1 Ch. 507.

Wemmergill Estate was held to be a trust for the estate owners absolutely with the motive of having trees planted, and so the owners could have the £5,000 to spend as they wished.

RE DENLEY'S TRUST DEED

Chancery Division [1969] 1 Ch. 373; [1968] 3 W.L.R. 457; [1968] 3 All E.R. 65

In 1936 land was conveyed by a company to trustees so that until the expiration of 21 years from the death of the last survivor of certain specified persons the land should under clause 2(c) of a trust deed "be maintained and used as and for the purpose of a recreation or sports ground primarily for the benefit of the employees of the company and secondarily for the benefit of such other person or persons (if any) as the trustees may allow to use the same." The main question was dealt with as follows in a reserved judgment: **5–19**

GOFF J.: It was decided in *Re Astor's Settlement Trusts*,[42] that a trust for a number of non-charitable purposes was not merely unenforceable but void on two grounds; first that they were not trusts for the benefit of individuals, which I refer to as "the beneficiary principle", and, secondly, for uncertainty. **5–20**

Counsel for the first defendant has argued that the trust in clause 2(c) in the present case is either a trust for the benefit of individuals, in which case he argues that they are an unascertainable class and therefore the trust is void for uncertainty, or it is a purpose trust, that is a trust for providing recreation, which he submits is void on the beneficiary principle, or alternatively it is something of a hybrid having the vices of both kinds. **5–21**

I think that there may be a purpose or object trust, the carrying out of which would benefit an individual or individuals, where that benefit is so indirect or intangible or which is otherwise so framed as not to give those persons any locus standi to apply to the court to enforce the trust, in which case the beneficiary principle would, as it seems to me, apply to invalidate the trust, quite apart from any question of uncertainty or perpetuity. Such cases can be considered if and when they arise. The present is not, in my judgment, of that character, and it will be seen that clause 2(d) of the trust deed expressly states that, subject to any rules and regulations made by the trustees, the employees of the company shall be entitled to the use and enjoyment of the land. **5–22**

Apart from this possible exception, in my judgment the beneficiary principle of *Re Astor*,[43] which was approved in *Re Endacott (decd.)*,[44] see particularly by Harman L.J.,[45] is confined to purpose or object trusts which are abstract or impersonal. The objection is not that the trust is for a purpose or object per se, but that there is no beneficiary or cestui que trust. The rule is so expressed in *Lewin on Trusts*,[46] and, in my judgment, with the possible exception which I have mentioned, rightly so. In *Re Wood*[47] Harman J. said: **5–23**

> "There has been an interesting argument on the question of perpetuity, but it seems to me, with all respect to that argument, that there is an earlier obstacle which is fatal to the validity of this bequest, namely, that a gift on trust must have a cestui que trust, and there being here no cestui que trust the gift must fail."

Again, in *Leahy v Att.-Gen. of New South Wales*[48] Viscount Simonds, delivering the judgment of the Privy Council, said: **5–24**

> "A gift can be made to persons (including a corporation) but it cannot be made to a purpose or to an object: so, also [and these are the important words] a trust may be created for the benefit of persons as cestuis que trust but not for a purpose or object unless the purpose or object be charitable. For a purpose or object cannot sue, but, if it be charitable, the Attorney-General can sue to enforce it."

---

[42] [1952] Ch. 534.
[43] [1952] Ch. 534.
[44] [1960] Ch. 232.
[45] [1960] Ch. 232 at 250.
[46] 16th edn, p.17.
[47] [1949] Ch. 498 at 501.
[48] [1959] A.C. 457 at 478.

5–25 Where, then, the trust, though expressed as a purpose, is directly or indirectly for the benefit of an individual or individuals, it seems to me that it is in general outside the mischief of the beneficiary principle.

5–26 I am fortified in this conclusion by the dicta of Lord Evershed M.R. and Harman L.J. in *Re Harpur's Will Trusts, Haller v Att.-Gen.*[49]

5–27 Some further support for my conclusion is, I think, to be found in *Re Aberconway's Settlement Trusts*[50] where it was assumed that a trust for the upkeep and development of certain gardens which were part of a settled estate was valid.

5–28 I also derive assistance from what was said by North J. in *Re Bowes*.[51] That was a bequest of a sum of money on trust to expend the same in planting trees for shelter on certain settled estates. It happened that there was a father and a son of full age, tenant for life in possession and tenant in tail in remainder respectively; so that, subject to the son disentailing, they were together absolutely entitled, and the actual decision was that they could claim the money, but North J. said[52]:

> "If it were necessary to uphold it, the trees can be planted upon the whole of it until the fund is exhausted. Therefore, there is nothing illegal in the gift itself . . .";

and:[53]

> "I think there clearly is a valid trust to lay out money for the benefit of the persons entitled to the estate."

5–29 The trust in the present case is limited in point of time so as to avoid any infringement of the rule against perpetuities and, for the reasons which I have given, it does not offend against the beneficiary principle; and unless, therefore, it be void for uncertainty, it is a valid trust.

5–30 There is, however, one other aspect of uncertainty which has caused me some concern; that is, whether this is in its nature a trust which the court can control, for, as Lord Eldon L.C. said in *Morice v Bishop of Durham*:[54]

> "As it is a maxim that the execution of a trust shall be under the control of the court, it must be of such a nature that it can be under that control; so that the administration of it can be reviewed by the court; or, if the trustee dies, the court itself can execute the trust: a trust, therefore, which, in case of maladministration could be reformed; and a due administration directed; and then, unless the subject and the objects can be ascertained upon principles familiar in other cases, it must be decided that the court can neither reform maladministration nor direct a due administration."

5–31 In my judgment, however, it would not be right to hold the trust void on this ground. The court can, as it seems to me, execute the trust both negatively by restraining any improper disposition or use of the land, and positively by ordering the trustees to allow the employees and such other persons (if any) as they may admit to use the land for the purpose of a recreation or sports ground. Any difficulty there might be in practice in the beneficial enjoyment of the land by those entitled to use it is, I think, really beside the point. The same kind of problem is equally capable of arising in the case of a trust to permit a number of persons—for example, all the unmarried children of a testator or settlor—to use or occupy a house or to have the use of certain chattels; yet no one would suggest, I fancy, that such a trust would be void.

5–32 In my judgment, therefore, the provisions of clause 2(c) are valid.

---

[49] [1962] Ch. 78 at 91, 96.
[50] [1953] Ch. 647.
[51] [1896] 1 Ch. 507.
[52] [1896] 1 Ch. 507 at 510.
[53] [1896] 1 Ch. 507 at 511.
[54] (1805) 10 Ves. 522 at 539.

C. *Quistclose Trusts*

In *Barclays Bank Ltd v Quistclose Investments Ltd*[55] a company lent money to another company in the same corporate group for the purpose of paying a dividend to the shareholders of the second company, and the second company became insolvent before the dividend was paid. The House of Lords held that the money was held for the first company on a resulting trust which arose on the failure of a primary express trust to pay the dividend. However, this analysis was difficult to reconcile with the beneficiary principle which suggested that if the primary trust was a trust for a private purpose then it should have been void.[56] Building on his extra-judicial criticisms of the reasoning in *Quistclose* and subsequent cases applying the principle,[57] Lord Millett therefore reinterpreted all these authorities in *Twinsectra Ltd v Yardley*,[58] parts of which are reproduced immediately below. **5–33**

In essence, Lord Millett held that where X lends money to Y on the condition that Y applies the money to a specific purpose in circumstances such as those which obtained in the *Quistclose* case, a trust of the money immediately arises in X's favour, but this trust is defeasible by the exercise of a power vested in Y to apply the money to the specified purpose.[59] It seems from his extra-judicial writings that Lord Millett formerly thought that the trust for X would always be an express trust, but his speech in *Twinsectra* suggests that he was persuaded by Professor Chambers' general work on resulting trusts to modify this opinion,[60] and to hold that in cases where the transferor does not declare an express trust for himself when he lends the money to the transferee, a resulting trust can arise in his favour.[61] **5–34**

TWINSECTRA LTD v YARDLEY

House of Lords [2002] 2 A.C. 164; [2002] 2 W.L.R. 802; [2002] 2 All E.R. 377

The claimant lent £1 million to Yardley for the purpose of buying property. It paid the money to Sims, a solicitor who was associated with Yardley, but who was not acting for him in the matter. Sims undertook not to release the money to Yardley except in accordance with the loan conditions. In breach of this undertaking Sims released the money to Yardley's solicitor, Leach, who released it to Yardley, who used part of the money to pay off a debt (in breach of his contract with the claimant). When Yardley failed to repay the loan the claimant sued various parties, claiming, among other things, that the money had been impressed with a *Quistclose* trust, that Sims had breached this trust when he released the money, and that Leach had dishonestly assisted in Sims' breach. The House of Lords held unanimously that the loan money had indeed been impressed with a *Quistclose* trust, and the parts of Lord Millett's speech dealing with this issue are reproduced here. Their **5–35**

---

55 [1970] A.C. 567. See too *Re ETVR* [1987] B.C.L.C. 646.

56 R. Chambers, *Resulting Trusts* (1997), pp.68–89; W.J. Swadling, "Orthodoxy" in W.J. Swadling (ed.) *The Quistclose Trust: Critical Essays* (2004).

57 P. J. Millett QC, "The *Quistclose* Trust: Who Can Enforce It?" (1985) 101 L.Q.R. 269.

58 [2002] A.C. 164; followed in *Templeton Insurance Ltd v Penningtons Solicitors* [2007] W.T.L.R. 1103 and distinguished in *Shalson v Russo* [2005] Ch. 281 at [128]–[130] and *Re Farepak Food and Gifts Ltd (in admin.)* [2007] 2 B.C.L.C. 1. In *Cooper v PRG Powerhouse Ltd* [2008] 2 All E.R. (Comm) 964, Evans-Lombe J. also purports to follow *Twinsectra*, but he does not seem to have fully assimilated Lord Millett's analysis, as he refers throughout his judgment to "the purpose trust".

59 The nature of this power is discussed in L. Smith "Understanding the Power" in Swadling, above.

60 Although not his analysis of the *Quistclose* case, which his Lordship thought vulnerable to the criticisms made in L. Ho and P. St.J. Smart "Reinterpreting the *Quistclose* Trust: A Critique of Chambers' Analysis" (2001) 21 O.J.L.S. 267. Professor Chambers answers these criticisms, and restates his position on *Quistclose*, in "Restrictions on the Use of Money" in Swadling, above; see too J. Glister, "The Nature of *Quistclose* Trusts: Classification and Reconciliation" [2004] C.L.J. 632.

61 As noted in J. Penner, "Lord Millett's Analysis" in Swadling, above, pp.50–56. See also Lord Millett's own comments in the foreword at p.ix. Whether he is an express trustee or a resulting trustee with knowledge of X's equitable interest, Y must account to X for the money from the moment of receipt, and must disgorge any profit obtained through misapplication of the money: *Abraaj Investment Management Ltd v Bregawn Jersey Ltd* [2010] EWHC 630 (Comm) at [28]–[32].

Lordships also held by a majority (Lord Millett dissenting) that Leach had not acted with the requisite degree of dishonesty for accessory liability, a controversial finding that was later revisited by the Privy Council in *Barlow Clowes International Ltd v Eurotrust International Ltd*[62] (as discussed at paras 12–70 to 12–76).

5–36 LORD MILLETT (with whom LORD SLYNN, LORD STEYN, LORD HOFFMANN and LORD HUTTON agreed on this issue): Money advanced by way of loan normally becomes the property of the borrower. He is free to apply the money as he chooses, and save to the extent to which he may have taken security for repayment the lender takes the risk of the borrower's insolvency. But it is well established that a loan to a borrower for a specific purpose where the borrower is not free to apply the money for any other purpose gives rise to fiduciary obligations on the part of the borrower which a court of equity will enforce. In the earlier cases the purpose was to enable the borrower to pay his creditors or some of them, but the principle is not limited to such cases.

5–37 Such arrangements are commonly described as creating "a *Quistclose* trust", after the well known decision of the House in *Barclays Bank Ltd v Quistclose Investments Ltd*[63] in which Lord Wilberforce confirmed the validity of such arrangements and explained their legal consequences. When the money is advanced, the lender acquires a right, enforceable in equity, to see that it is applied for the stated purpose, or more accurately to prevent its application for any other purpose. This prevents the borrower from obtaining any beneficial interest in the money, at least while the designated purpose is still capable of being carried out. Once the purpose has been carried out, the lender has his normal remedy in debt. If for any reason the purpose cannot be carried out, the question arises whether the money falls within the general fund of the borrower's assets, in which case it passes to his trustee in bankruptcy in the event of his insolvency and the lender is merely a loan creditor; or whether it is held on a resulting trust for the lender. This depends on the intention of the parties collected from the terms of the arrangement and the circumstances of the case.

5–38 In the present case Twinsectra contends that paragraphs 1 and 2 of the undertaking which Mr Sims signed on 24 December created a *Quistclose* trust. Mr Leach denies this and advances a number of objections to the existence of a trust. He says that Twinsectra lacked the necessary intention to create a trust, and relies on evidence that Twinsectra looked exclusively to Mr Sims' personal undertaking to repay the loan as its security for repayment. He says that commercial life would be impossible if trusts were lightly inferred from slight material, and that it is not enough to agree that a loan is to be made for a particular purpose. There must be something more, for example, a requirement that the money be paid into a segregated account, before it is appropriate to infer that a trust has been created. In the present case the money was paid into Mr Sims' client account, but that is sufficiently explained by the fact that it was not Mr Sims' money but his client's; it provides no basis for an inference that the money was held in trust for anyone other than Mr Yardley. Then it is said that a trust requires certainty of objects and this was lacking, for the stated purpose "to be applied in the purchase of property" is too uncertain to be enforced. Finally it is said that no trust in favour of Twinsectra could arise prior to the failure of the stated purpose, and this did not occur until the money was misapplied by Mr Yardley's companies.

Intention

5–39 The first two objections are soon disposed of. A settlor must, of course, possess the necessary intention to create a trust, but his subjective intentions are irrelevant. If he enters into arrangements which have the effect of creating a trust, it is not necessary that he should appreciate that they do so; it is sufficient that he intends to enter into them. Whether paragraphs 1 and 2 of the undertaking created a *Quistclose* trust turns on the true construction of those paragraphs.

5–40 The fact that Twinsectra relied for its security exclusively on Mr Sims's personal liability to repay goes to Twinsectra's subjective intention and is not relevant to the construction of the undertaking, but it is in any case not inconsistent with the trust alleged. Arrangements of this kind are not intended to provide security for repayment of the loan, but to prevent the money from being applied otherwise than in accordance with the lender's wishes. If the money is properly applied the loan is unsecured. This was true of all the decided cases, including the *Quistclose* case itself.

[62] [2006] 1 W.L.R. 1476.
[63] [1970] A.C. 567.

The Effect of the Undertaking

A *Quistclose* trust does not necessarily arise merely because money is paid for a particular purpose. A lender will often inquire into the purpose for which a loan is sought in order to decide whether he would be justified in making it. He may be said to lend the money for the purpose in question, but this is not enough to create a trust; once lent the money is at the free disposal of the borrower. Similarly payments in advance for goods or services are paid for a particular purpose, but such payments do not ordinarily create a trust. The money is intended to be at the free disposal of the supplier and may be used as part of his cashflow. Commercial life would be impossible if this were not the case. **5–41**

The question in every case is whether the parties intended the money to be at the free disposal of the recipient.[64] His freedom to dispose of the money is necessarily excluded by an arrangement that the money shall be used exclusively for the stated purpose, for as Lord Wilberforce observed in the *Quistclose* case:[65] **5–42**

> "A necessary consequence from this, by a process simply of interpretation, must be that if, for any reason, [the purpose could not be carried out,] the money was to be returned to [the lender]: the word 'only' or 'exclusively' can have no other meaning or effect."

In the *Quistclose* case a public quoted company in financial difficulties had declared a final dividend. Failure to pay the dividend, which had been approved by the shareholders, would cause a loss of confidence and almost certainly drive the company into liquidation. Accordingly the company arranged to borrow a sum of money "on condition that it is used to pay the forthcoming dividend". The money was paid into a special account at the company's bank, with which the company had an overdraft. The bank confirmed that the money "will only be used for the purpose of paying the dividend due on 24 July 1964". The House held that the circumstances were sufficient to create a trust of which the bank had notice, and that when the company went into liquidation without having paid the dividend the money was repayable to the lender.

In the present case paragraphs 1 and 2 of the undertaking are crystal clear. Mr Sims undertook that the money would be used solely for the acquisition of property and for no other purpose; and was to be retained by his firm until so applied. It would not be held by Mr Sims simply to Mr Yardley's order; and it would not be at Mr Yardley's free disposition. Any payment by Mr Sims of the money, whether to Mr Yardley or anyone else, otherwise than for the acquisition of property would constitute a breach of trust. **5–43**

Mr Leach insisted that such a payment would, no doubt, constitute a breach of contract, but there was no reason to invoke equitable principles merely because Mr Sims was a solicitor. But Mr Sims's status as a solicitor has nothing to do with it. Equity's intervention is more principled than this. It is unconscionable for a man to obtain money on terms as to its application and then disregard the terms on which he received it. Such conduct goes beyond a mere breach of contract. As North J. explained in *Gibert v Gonard*:[66] **5–44**

> "It is very well known law that if one person makes a payment to another for a certain purpose, and that person takes the money knowing that it is for that purpose, he must apply it to the purpose for which it was given. He may decline to take it if he likes; but if he chooses to accept the money tendered for a particular purpose, it is his duty, and there is a legal obligation on him, to apply it for that purpose."

The duty is not contractual but fiduciary. It may exist despite the absence of any contract at all between the parties, as in *Rose v Rose*;[67] and it binds third parties as in the *Quistclose* case itself. The duty is fiduciary in character because a person who makes money available on terms that it is to be used for a particular purpose only and not for any other purpose thereby places his trust and confidence in the recipient to ensure that it is properly applied. This is a classic situation in which a fiduciary relationship arises, and since it arises in respect of a specific fund it gives rise to a trust.

---

64 *Re Goldcorp Exchange Ltd* [1995] 1 A.C. 74 at 100, per Lord Mustill.
65 [1970] A.C. 567 at 580.
66 (1884) 54 L.J. Ch. 439 at 440.
67 (1986) 7 N.S.W.L.R. 679.

The Nature of the Trust

5–45 The latter two objections cannot be so easily disposed of. They call for an exploration of the true nature of the *Quistclose* trust, and in particular the location of the beneficial interest while the purpose is still capable of being carried out.

5–46 This has been the subject of much academic debate. The starting point is provided by two passages in Lord Wilberforce's speech in the *Quistclose* case. He said:[68]

> "That arrangements of this character for the payment of a person's creditors by a third person, give rise to a relationship of a fiduciary character or trust, in favour, as a primary trust, of the creditors, and secondarily, if the primary trust fails, of the third person, has been recognised in a series of cases over some 150 years."

Later, he said:[69]

> "when the money is advanced, the lender acquires an equitable right to see that it is applied for the primary designated purpose (see *In re Rogers*[70] where both Lindley L.J. and Kay L.J. recognised this) . . .".

5–47 These passages suggest that there are two successive trusts, a primary trust for payment to identifiable beneficiaries, such as creditors or shareholders, and a secondary trust in favour of the lender arising on the failure of the primary trust. But there are formidable difficulties in this analysis, which has little academic support. What if the primary trust is not for identifiable persons, but as in the present case to carry out an abstract purpose? Where in such a case is the beneficial interest pending the application of the money for the stated purpose or the failure of the purpose? There are four possibilities: (i) in the lender; (ii) in the borrower; (iii) in the contemplated beneficiary; or (iv) in suspense.

5–48 *(i) The lender*. In "The *Quistclose* Trust: Who Can Enforce It?",[71] I argued that the beneficial interest remained throughout in the lender. This analysis has received considerable though not universal academic support.[72] It was adopted by the New Zealand Court of Appeal in *General Communications Ltd v Development Finance Corp of New Zealand Ltd*[73] and referred to with apparent approval by Gummow J. in *In re Australian Elizabethan Theatre Trust*.[74] Gummow J. saw nothing special in the *Quistclose* trust, regarding it as essentially a security device to protect the lender against other creditors of the borrower pending the application of the money for the stated purpose.

5–49 On this analysis, the *Quistclose* trust is a simple commercial arrangement akin (as Professor Bridge observes) to a retention of title clause (though with a different object) which enables the borrower to have recourse to the lender's money for a particular purpose without entrenching on the lender's property rights more than necessary to enable the purpose to be achieved. The money remains the property of the lender unless and until it is applied in accordance with his directions, and insofar as it is not so applied it must be returned to him. I am disposed, perhaps pre-disposed, to think that this is the only analysis which is consistent both with orthodox trust law and with commercial reality. Before reaching a concluded view that it should be adopted, however, I must consider the alternatives.

5–50 *(ii) The borrower*. It is plain that the beneficial interest is not vested unconditionally in the borrower so as to leave the money at his free disposal. That would defeat the whole purpose of the arrangements, which is to prevent the money from passing to the borrower's trustee in bankruptcy in the event of his insolvency. It would also be inconsistent with all the decided cases where the contest was between the lender and the borrower's trustee in bankruptcy, as well as with the *Quistclose* case itself.[75]

---

68 [1970] A.C. 567 at 580.

69 At 581.

70 (1891) 8 Morr. 243.

71 (1985) 101 L.Q.R. 269.

72 See for example Priestley L.J. "The *Romalpa* Clause and the *Quistclose* Trust" in *Equity and Commercial Relationships*, edited by P. D. Finn (1987), pp. 217, 237; and Professor Michael Bridge "The *Quistclose* Trust in a World of Secured Transactions" (1992) 12 O.J.L.S. 333, 352; and others.

73 [1990] 3 N.Z.L.R. 406.

74 (1991) 102 A.L.R. 681.

75 See in particular *Toovey v Milne* (1819) 2 B. & Ald. 683; *In re Rogers, Ex p. Holland & Hannen* (1891) 8 Morr. 243.

The borrower's interest pending the application of the money for the stated purpose or its return to the lender is minimal. He must keep the money separate; he cannot apply it except for the stated purpose; unless the terms of the loan otherwise provide he must return it to the lender if demanded; he cannot refuse to return it if the stated purpose cannot be achieved; and if he becomes bankrupt it does not vest in his trustee in bankruptcy. If there is any content to beneficial ownership at all, the lender is the beneficial owner and the borrower is not. **5–51**

In the present case the Court of Appeal adopted a variant, locating the beneficial interest in the borrower but subject to restrictions. I shall have to return to this analysis later. **5–52**

(iii) In the contemplated beneficiary. In the *Quistclose* case itself, as in all the reported cases which preceded it, either the primary purpose had been carried out and the contest was between the borrower's trustee in bankruptcy or liquidator and the person or persons to whom the borrower had paid the money; or it was treated as having failed, and the contest was between the borrower's trustee-in-bankruptcy and the lender. It was not necessary to explore the position while the primary purpose was still capable of being carried out and Lord Wilberforce's observations must be read in that light. **5–53**

The question whether the primary trust is accurately described as a trust for the creditors first arose in *In re Northern Developments (Holdings) Ltd*,[76] where the contest was between the lender and the creditors. The borrower, which was not in liquidation and made no claim to the money, was the parent company of a group one of whose subsidiaries was in financial difficulty. There was a danger that if it were wound up or ceased trading it would bring down the whole group. A consortium of the group's banks agreed to put up a fund of more than £500,000 in an attempt to rescue the subsidiary. They paid the money into a special account in the name of the parent company for the express purpose of "providing money for the subsidiary's unsecured creditors over the ensuing weeks" and for no other purpose. The banks' object was to enable the subsidiary to continue trading, though on a reduced scale; it failed when the subsidiary was put into receivership at a time when some £350,000 remained unexpended. Relying on Lord Wilberforce's observations in the passages cited above, Sir Robert Megarry V.C. held that the primary trust was a purpose trust enforceable (inter alios) by the subsidiaries' creditors as the persons for whose benefit the trust was created. **5–54**

There are several difficulties with this analysis. In the first place, Lord Wilberforce's reference to *In re Rogers* makes it plain that the equitable right he had in mind was not a mandatory order to compel performance, but a negative injunction to restrain improper application of the money; for neither Lindley L.J. nor Kay L.J. recognised more than this. In the second place, the object of the arrangements was to enable the subsidiary to continue trading, and this would necessarily involve it in incurring further liabilities to trade creditors. Accordingly the application of the fund was not confined to existing creditors at the date when the fund was established. The company secretary was given to understand that the purpose of the arrangements was to keep the subsidiary trading, and that the fund was "as good as share capital". Thus the purpose of the arrangements was not, as in other cases, to enable the debtor to avoid bankruptcy by paying off existing creditors, but to enable the debtor to continue trading by providing it with working capital with which to incur fresh liabilities. There is a powerful argument for saying that the result of the arrangements was to vest a beneficial interest in the subsidiary from the start. If so, then this was not a *Quistclose* trust at all. **5–55**

In the third place, it seems unlikely that the banks' object was to benefit the creditors (who included the Inland Revenue) except indirectly. The banks had their own commercial interests to protect by enabling the subsidiary to trade out of its difficulties. If so, then the primary trust cannot be supported as a valid non-charitable purpose trust.[77] **5–56**

The most serious objection to this approach is exemplified by the facts of the present case. In several of the cases the primary trust was for an abstract purpose with no one but the lender to enforce performance or restrain misapplication of the money. In *Edwards v Glyn*[78] the money was advanced to a bank to enable the bank to meet a run. In *In re EVTR*,[79] it was advanced "for the sole purpose of buying new equipment". **5–57**

[76] Unreported, October 6, 1978.
[77] See *Re Grant's Will Trusts* [1980] 1 W.L.R. 360 and cf. *Re Denley's Trust Deed* [1969] 1 Ch. 373.
[78] (1859) 2 E. & E. 29.
[79] [1987] B.C.L.C. 646.

In *General Communications Ltd v Development Finance Corp of New Zealand Ltd*[80] the money was paid to the borrower's solicitors for the express purpose of purchasing new equipment. The present case is another example. It is simply not possible to hold money on trust to acquire unspecified property from an unspecified vendor at an unspecified time. There is no reason to make an arbitrary distinction between money paid for an abstract purpose and money paid for a purpose which can be said to benefit an ascertained class of beneficiaries, and the cases rightly draw no such distinction. Any analysis of the *Quistclose* trust must be able to accommodate gifts and loans for an abstract purpose.

5–58 *(iv) In suspense*. As Peter Gibson J. pointed out in *Carreras Rothmans Ltd v Freeman Matthews Treasure Ltd*[81] the effect of adopting Sir Robert Megarry V.C.'s analysis is to leave the beneficial interest in suspense until the stated purpose is carried out or fails. The difficulty with this (apart from its unorthodoxy) is that it fails to have regard to the role which the resulting trust plays in equity's scheme of things, or to explain why the money is not simply held on a resulting trust for the lender.

5–59 Lord Browne-Wilkinson gave an authoritative explanation of the resulting trust in *Westdeutsche Landesbank Girpcentrale v Islington Borough Council*[82] and its basis has been further illuminated by Dr Robert Chambers in his book *Resulting Trusts* published in 1997. Lord Browne-Wilkinson explained that a resulting trust arises in two sets of circumstances. He described the second as follows: "Where A transfers property to B on express trusts, but the trusts declared do not exhaust the whole beneficial interest." The *Quistclose* case was among the cases he cited as examples. He rejected the argument that there was a resulting trust in the case before him because, unlike the situation in the present case, there was no transfer of money on express trusts. But he also rejected the argument on a wider and, in my respectful opinion, surer ground that the money was paid and received with the intention that it should become the absolute property of the recipient.

5–60 The central thesis of Dr Chambers's book is that a resulting trust arises whenever there is a transfer of property in circumstances in which the transferor (or more accurately the person at whose expense the property was provided) did not intend to benefit the recipient. It responds to the absence of an intention on the part of the transferor to pass the entire beneficial interest, not to a positive intention to retain it. Insofar as the transfer does not exhaust the entire beneficial interest, the resulting trust is a default trust which fills the gap and leaves no room for any part to be in suspense. An analysis of the *Quistclose* trust as a resulting trust for the transferor with a mandate to the transferee to apply the money for the stated purpose sits comfortably with Dr Chambers' thesis, and it might be thought surprising that he does not adopt it.

5–61 *(v) The Court of Appeal's analysis*. The Court of Appeal were content to treat the beneficial interest as in suspense, or (following Dr Chambers's analysis) to hold that it was in the borrower, the lender having merely a contractual right enforceable by injunction to prevent misapplication. Potter L.J. put it in these terms:[83]

> "The purpose imposed at the time of the advance creates an enforceable restriction on the borrower's use of the money. Although the lender's right to enforce the restriction is treated as arising on the basis of a 'trust', the use of that word does not enlarge the lender's interest in the fund. The borrower is entitled to the beneficial use of the money, subject to the lender's right to prevent its misuse; the lender's limited interest in the fund is sufficient to prevent its use for other than the special purpose for which it was advanced."

This analysis, with respect, is difficult to reconcile with the court's actual decision in so far as it granted Twinsectra a proprietary remedy against Mr Yardley's companies as recipients of the misapplied funds. Unless the money belonged to Twinsectra immediately before its misapplication, there is no basis on which a proprietary remedy against third party recipients can be justified.

5–62 Dr Chambers's "novel view" (as it has been described) is that the arrangements do not create a trust at all; the borrower receives the entire beneficial ownership in the money subject only to a contractual right in the lender to prevent the money being used otherwise than for the stated purpose. If the purpose fails,

---

80 [1990] 3 N.Z.L.R. 406.
81 [1985] Ch. 207 at 223.
82 [1996] A.C. 669 at 708.
83 [1999] Lloyd's Rep. Bank. 438 at 456.

a resulting trust in the lender springs into being. In fact, he argues for a kind of restrictive covenant enforceable by negative injunction yet creating property rights in the money. But restrictive covenants, which began life as negative easements, are part of our land law. Contractual obligations do not run with money or a chose in action like money in a bank account.

Dr Chambers's analysis has attracted academic comment, both favourable and unfavourable. For my own part, I do not think that it can survive the criticism levelled against it by Lusina Ho and P. St. J. Smart [in their article] "Reinterpreting the *Quistclose* Trust: A Critique of Chambers' Analysis".[84] It provides no solution to cases of non-contractual payment; is inconsistent with Lord Wilberforce's description of the borrower's obligation as fiduciary and not merely contractual; fails to explain the evidential significance of a requirement that the money should be kept in a separate account; cannot easily be reconciled with the availability of proprietary remedies against third parties; and while the existence of a mere equity to prevent misapplication would be sufficient to prevent the money from being available for distribution to the creditors on the borrower's insolvency (because the trustee in bankruptcy has no greater rights than his bankrupt) it would not prevail over secured creditors. If the bank in the *Quistclose* case had held a floating charge (as it probably did) and had appointed a receiver, the adoption of Dr. Chambers's analysis should have led to a different outcome. **5–63**

Thus all the alternative solutions have their difficulties. But there are two problems which they fail to solve, but which are easily solved if the beneficial interest remains throughout in the lender. One arises from the fact, well established by the authorities, that the primary trust is enforceable by the lender. But on what basis can he enforce it? He cannot do so as the beneficiary under the secondary trust, for if the primary purpose is fulfilled there is no secondary trust: the precondition of his claim is destructive of his standing to make it. He cannot do so as settlor, for a settlor who retains no beneficial interest cannot enforce the trust which he has created. **5–64**

Dr Chambers insists that the lender has merely a right to prevent the misapplication of the money, and attributes this to his contractual right to specific performance of a condition of the contract of loan. As I have already pointed out, this provides no solution where the arrangement is non-contractual. But Lord Wilberforce clearly based the borrower's obligation on an equitable or fiduciary basis and not a contractual one. He was concerned to justify the co-existence of equity's exclusive jurisdiction with the common law action for debt. Basing equity's intervention on its auxiliary jurisdiction to restrain a breach of contract would not have enabled the lender to succeed against the bank, which was a third party to the contract. There is only one explanation of the lender's fiduciary right to enforce the primary trust which can be reconciled with basic principle: he can do so because he is the beneficiary. **5–65**

The other problem is concerned with the basis on which the primary trust is said to have failed in several of the cases, particularly *Toovey v Milne* and the *Quistclose* case itself. Given that the money did not belong to the borrower in either case, the borrower's insolvency should not have prevented the money from being paid in the manner contemplated. A man cannot pay some only of his creditors once he has been adjudicated bankrupt, but a third party can. A company cannot pay a dividend once it has gone into liquidation, but there is nothing to stop a third party from paying the disappointed shareholders. The reason why the purpose failed in each case must be because the lender's object in making the money available was to save the borrower from bankruptcy in the one case and collapse in the other. But this in itself is not enough. A trust does not fail merely because the settlor's purpose in creating it has been frustrated: the trust must become illegal or impossible to perform. The settlor's motives must not be confused with the purpose of the trust; the frustration of the former does not by itself cause the failure of the latter. But if the borrower is treated as holding the money on a resulting trust for the lender but with power (or in some cases a duty) to carry out the lender's revocable mandate, and the lender's object in giving the mandate is frustrated, he is entitled to revoke the mandate and demand the return of money which never ceased to be his beneficially. . . . **5–66**

As Sherlock Holmes reminded Dr Watson, when you have eliminated the impossible, whatever remains, however improbable, must be the truth. I would reject all the alternative analyses, which I find unconvincing for the reasons I have endeavoured to explain, and hold the *Quistclose* trust to be an entirely orthodox example of the kind of default trust known as a resulting trust. The lender pays the money to the borrower **5–67**

[84] (2001) 21 O.J.L.S. 267.

by way of loan, but he does not part with the entire beneficial interest in the money, and in so far as he does not it is held on a resulting trust for the lender from the outset. Contrary to the opinion of the Court of Appeal, it is the borrower who has a very limited use of the money, being obliged to apply it for the stated purpose or return it. He has no beneficial interest in the money, which remains throughout in the lender subject only to the borrower's power or duty to apply the money in accordance with the lender's instructions. When the purpose fails, the money is returnable to the lender, not under some new trust in his favour which only comes into being on the failure of the purpose, but because the resulting trust in his favour is no longer subject to any power on the part of the borrower to make use of the money. Whether the borrower is obliged to apply the money for the stated purpose or merely at liberty to do so, and whether the lender can countermand the borrower's mandate while it is still capable of being carried out, must depend on the circumstances of the particular case.

Certainty

5–68 After this over-long exposition, it is possible to dispose of the remaining objections to the creation of a *Quistclose* trust very shortly. A trust must have certainty of objects. But the only trust is the resulting trust for the lender. The borrower is authorised (or directed) to apply the money for a stated purpose, but this is a mere power and does not constitute a purpose trust. Provided the power is stated with sufficient clarity for the court to be able to determine whether it is still capable of being carried out or whether the money has been misapplied, it is sufficiently certain to be enforced. If it is uncertain, however, then the borrower has no authority to make any use of the money at all and must return it to the lender under the resulting trust. Uncertainty works in favour of the lender, not the borrower; it cannot help a person in the position of Mr Leach.

When the Trust in Favour of the Lender Arises

5–69 Like all resulting trusts, the trust in favour of the lender arises when the lender parts with the money on terms which do not exhaust the beneficial interest. It is not a contingent reversionary or future interest. It does not suddenly come into being like an 18th century use only when the stated purpose fails. It is a default trust which fills the gap when some part of the beneficial interest is undisposed of and prevents it from being "in suspense".

Conclusion

5–70 In my opinion the Court of Appeal were correct to find that the terms of paragraphs 1 and 2 of the undertaking created a *Quistclose* trust. The money was never at Mr Yardley's free disposal. It was never held to his order by Mr Sims. The money belonged throughout to Twinsectra, subject only to Mr Yardley's right to apply it for the acquisition of property. Twinsectra parted with the money to Mr Sims, relying on him to ensure that the money was properly applied or returned to it. Mr Sims act in paying the money over to Mr Leach was a breach of trust, but it did not in itself render the money incapable of being applied for the stated purpose. In so far as Mr Leach applied the money in the acquisition of property, the purpose was achieved.

D. Gifts for the Purposes of Unincorporated Bodies

5–71 Unincorporated bodies, whether called associations, clubs or societies, raise special problems since an unincorporated body, unlike a corporate body, is not a legal person capable of owning property or entering into contracts or floating charges or of being the subject of legal rights and duties.[85] For this reason clubs often incorporate themselves by registration as an Industrial and Provident Society under the 1965 Act of that title (which is considerably cheaper than converting the club into a limited

[85] Trade unions are unincorporated associations (if not incorporated as a special register body) but by the Trade Union and Labour Relations Consolidation Act 1992 s.10 they can make contracts in their own names, may sue or be sued in their own names, judgments can be enforced against them as if they were bodies corporate, and property may be vested in trustees on trust "for the union".

company under the Companies Act 2006 and which enables the structure of the club for most practical purposes to remain fundamentally the same, so that the club is run by a committee elected by the member-shareholders).

The body's property will be vested in trustees under a bare trust for the members of the body (except to the extent that statute may prevent members of certain bodies from winding up the body and dividing its property between themselves[86]). The trustees or other organ under the body's constitution may enter into contracts, thereby putting the body's property at risk vis-à-vis the claims of creditors, and may even be authorised to declare trusts binding the body's property.[87] To the extent that such valid trusts have not been declared the body's property belongs to the members, subject to their contract made between themselves under the body's constitution and subject to any claims that third parties may have resulting from contracts made by the trustees.[88] **5–72**

A member or his spouse (or anyone) may give property in their lifetime by will to the officers of the body as trustees upon certain trusts that are germane to the purpose of the body. Such trusts may be to use the property as soon as convenient in payment of everyday expenses so that the property is treated as part of the body's general assets. However, such trust property may not be intended to become the body's property to be spent as part of its general assets. The trust property may be intended to be held under a separate endowment account (so that income but not capital is spent) and managed separately from the body's general assets: neither the body's constitution nor the agreement of its members can then change the trustees' obligations as trustees of the trust property. **5–73**

An unincorporated body has the following features: **5–74**

- it is composed of two or more persons bound together for a common purpose;
- these persons have mutual rights and duties arising from a contract between them;
- the body has rules to determine (a) who controls the body and its funds and (b) the terms on which such control is exercisable;
- the body can be joined or left at will.

For lack of the second and third features the Conservative Party was held not to be an unincorporated association liable to corporation tax.[89] The Revenue had argued that the party was an unincorporated association since members' contributions surely took effect as an accretion to the funds which were the subject-matter of a contract which such members had made between themselves. How else could there be a legal relationship between a contributor and the recipient of the contribution so as to safeguard the contributor's interest?

Vinelott J.[90] suggested that the answer is that the contributor enters into a contract with the treasurer whereby in consideration of payment of the subscription the treasurer undertakes to apply the subscription towards the association's purposes: breach of this undertaking can be enjoined on normal contractual principles at the suit of the contributor. On appeal, Brightman L.J. thought that the contributor, by **5–75**

---

[86] e.g. Literary and Scientific Institutions Act 1854 s.30; *Re Bristol Athenaeum* (1899) 43 Ch.D. 236.

[87] Anything they do may be ratified by the membership since unincorporated associations have no capacity to be limited and so unlike companies cannot act ultra vires, though the ultra vires doctrine for companies has been abolished where outsiders dealing with the company are concerned: Companies Act 2006 s.39.

[88] *Re Bucks Constabulary Fund Friendly Society (No.2)* [1979] 1 W.L.R. 936.

[89] *Conservative Central Office v Burrell* [1982] 1 W.L.R. 522. The fourth feature was not in issue but it seems too restrictive since an association may well have restrictions on new membership or rules curtailing the freedom of members to leave at will.

[90] *Conservative Central Office v Burrell* [1980] 3 All E.R. 42. He appears to suggest as an alternative that the treasurer by accepting the subscription comes under a special equitable obligation similar to an executor.

way of mandate or agency, gives his contribution to the treasurer to add it to the general funds of the association. Once that has been done the mandate becomes irrevocable but the contributor will have a remedy to restrain or have made good a misapplication of the mixed fund, unless it appears on ordinary accounting principles that his own contribution has already been properly expended.

5–76 A transfer of assets for purposes (whether of an unincorporated body or otherwise[91]) may thus take effect by way of contract or of mandate (which may be gratuitous) if the donor is to retain some measure of control. Effect cannot be given to a testator's bequests in such a fashion since one cannot imply a contract or mandate between a deceased person and another,[92] though a deceased may authorise or direct his personal representatives to enter into a contract or mandate. A deceased may also in his lifetime contract to leave property by will to someone for a purpose, and if he does die, leaving such a will, then his rights and duties under the contract will vest in his personal representatives who will be able to enforce the contractual undertakings given to him.

5–77 Before the 1964 Perpetuities and Accumulations Act there were particular legal obstacles confronting gifts to unincorporated bodies. The gift could not be an absolute gift to such a body because such a body has no legal personality. It could not be a valid gift if construed as a gift to the present and future members of the body because the intent to ensure benefiting future members required the capital to be kept intact and held on trust for only the income to be used, so that the capital would remain available for the benefit of future members.[93] This rendered the gift void for infringing the rule against remoteness, though since the 1964 Act such a gift would be valid for the statutory perpetuity period.[94] If the gift were construed as a gift to the body on trust for carrying out purposes, with the gift being an endowment fund to be used for those purposes only, and not to be used without distinction between capital and income nor to be capable (on dissolution of the body) for sharing out between the then members, then such a purpose trust was void for infringing the rule against inalienability, unless it was a charitable purpose trust. Neither the 1964 Act nor the Perpetuities and Accumulations Act 2009 has affected this.[95]

5–78 The gift would be valid if construed as an absolute gift to the persons happening to be current members of the body, so that any such person could claim his proportionate share. This might not be quite what the deceased donor wished but, at least, his gift was not void. There thus developed a sophisticated construction, more likely to give effect to a testator's intention to benefit future members, but without imposing a trust to benefit future members with the attendant void for remoteness problem before the 1964 Act. This construes the gift as an absolute gift to the current members beneficially, but as an accretion to the body's property held subject to the terms of the contract which the members are subjected to by virtue of their membership of the body.[96] This contract determines how the body's assets are to be enjoyed and what are the rights of the members in respect of such assets, while the treasurer or other worthy members will hold the assets on a bare trust for current members to be dealt with according to the contract (the constitution of the body).

5–79 It follows from all the foregoing discussion that there are a number of possible constructions to consider where a gift is made to an unincorporated association.

5–80 (i) *Absolute gift of legal title to current members*. If the gift is a valid absolute gift[97] of legal title to the persons who are currently members of the unincorporated body, then any such person can claim

---

[91] e.g. a disaster appeal committee in a situation like that in *Re Gillingham Bus Disaster Fund* [1958] Ch. 300.
[92] As accepted by Vinelott J. and Brightman L.J. in the *Conservative Central Office* case, also *Re Wilson* [1908] 1 Ch. 839.
[93] *Leahy v Att.-Gen. for New South Wales* [1959] A.C. 457.
[94] See para.7–65.
[95] See s.15(4) of 1964 Act, and s.18 of the 2009 Act.
[96] *Neville Estates Ltd v Madden* [1962] Ch. 832; *Re Recher's WT* [1972] Ch. 526.
[97] If the gift is testamentary, then the testator's executors will be under a fiduciary duty to give effect to the intended absolute gift after paying debts, etc.

his proportionate share.[98] The donor-testator is not providing endowment capital, but giving his property so that each donee can deal with his share as he wishes. Exceptionally, if the contract between the donees as members of the body requires gifts to members in their capacity, or under their description, as members to be treated as an accretion to the body's fund to be dealt with according to the body's rules[99] then the donor's property will have to be so treated.[100]

(ii) *Absolute gift of legal title to the current members, taking effect as an accretion to the body's funds which are to be dealt with (under a bare trust) according to the rules of the body by which the members are all contractually bound*. This construction follows the court's analysis in *Re Recher's WT*[101] and *Re Lipinski's WT*[102] both of which are reproduced below.[103] The donor/testator is not providing endowment capital but giving his property to be freely spent[104] on day-to-day expenses or something of a more lasting nature, or to be divided up and pocketed by the members if the contractual rules allow this on dissolution or otherwise. It ought not to matter that because of some statute or subordination to some outside legal entity the members are unable to wind up the body and pocket its assets.[105] The gift in augmentation of the body's general assets is freely alienable other than directly to members: it can be totally consumed in supporting the body's purposes directly or indirectly benefiting the members who all have locus standi to sue. The gift does not have to be kept intact as endowment capital, so no trust rules concerning remoteness or inalienability can be applicable. However, if the testator knew that it was impossible or very difficult in practice for members to wind up the body and pocket its assets, so that the body was designed to carry on indefinitely, his bequest could well be construed as intending to set up endowment capital so that the income would benefit members from time to time indefinitely.[106] **5–81**

(iii) *Trust for present and future members*. On this construction the gift is intended to ensure that present and future members are either directly benefited or indirectly benefited (sufficiently to have locus standi to sue under *Re Denley's Trust Deed*) by the carrying out of the purposes of the body to which they belong. Thus, the gift is of endowment capital to be held upon trust (separate from the body's general assets available to be spent like current income) so that the income will always be available for the members from time to time or for purposes benefiting such members. **5–82**

One can have an obvious example like £100,000 left on trust "to the Club Treasurer to apply the income for the benefit qua members of those from time to time members of the Club" or a less **5–83**

---

98 *Cocks v Manners* (1871) L.R. 12 Eq. 574; *Re Smith* [1916] 1 Ch. 937; *Re Ogden* [1933] Ch. 678; *Re Clarke* [1901] 2 Ch. 110 (revealing that an expression of the purpose of the gift may merely be regarded as motive).

99 Like property caught by a donee's covenant to settle after-acquired property: *Pullan v Koe* [1913] 1 Ch. 9.

100 *Leahy v Att.-Gen. for New South Wales* [1959] A.C. 457 at 478, per Viscount Simonds: "If it is a gift to individuals, each of them is entitled to his distributive share (unless he has previously bound himself by the rules of the society that it should be devoted to some other purpose)".

101 [1972] Ch. 526. See too *Neville Estates Ltd v Madden* [1962] Ch. 832; *Universe Tankships Inc of Monrovia v International Transport Workers Federation* [1983] A.C. 366; *News Group Ltd v SOGAT* [1986] I.C.R. 716; *Bacon v O'Dea* (1989) 88 A.L.R. 486; *Re Bucks Constabulary Fund (No.2)* [1979] 1 W.L.R. 936; *Re Horley Town FC* [2006] W.T.L.R. 1817; *Hanchett-Stamford v Att.-Gen.* [2009] Ch. 173 at [28] ff.

102 [1976] Ch. 235.

103 At paras 5–101 and 5–107 ff.

104 *Re Macaulay's Estate* [1943] Ch. 435; *Re Price* [1943] Ch. 422; *Re Lipinski* [1976] Ch. 235; *Re Drummond* [1914] 2 Ch. 90 at 97–98; *Re Prevost* [1930] 2 Ch. 383.

105 The suggestion of Vinelott J. in *Re Grant's WT* [1979] 3 All E.R. 359 that a "necessary characteristic" of any gift within this second construction is the members' power to alter the rules and divide the assets between them seems unsound. It surely suffices that the gifted property is not endowment capital but can be freely spent on purposes benefiting the members. The members' contractual rights to enforce spending the property for their benefit suffices even if they cannot personally "pocket" the property: their position is similar to that of beneficiaries with locus standi to enforce purpose trusts directly benefiting them even if they have no *Saunders v Vautier* right to "pocket" the trust property.

106 *Carne v Long* (1860) 2 De G.F. & J. 75; *Bacon v Pianta* (1966) 114 C.L.R. 634 (to the Communist Party of Australia "for its sole use and benefit"); *Re Grant's WT* [1979] 3 All E.R. 359.

obvious example like "to the Club Treasurer to apply the income for the general purposes of the Club" or for a particular purpose within its various purposes. Another example would be if a testator left £1 million to the Club Treasurer "for the benefit of members from time to time of the Club" or "for the lasting benefit of the Club". Here, by necessary implication the capital needs to be set aside as an endowment so that the income can be used indefinitely for the benefit of the members directly or indirectly. Such endowment gifts before the 1964 Perpetuities and Accumulation Act would have been void for infringing the rule against remoteness. Nowadays, the trend is to stretch matters to hold that there is no endowment capital, so that there is an absolute gift accruing to the body's assets under the second construction above.

5–84 If the court cannot so hold then what is to happen if the members wind up the body, wanting to make its assets their own, or if the body is continuing its functions at expiry of the perpetuity period? In the former case, it seems likely the courts will construe the trust as a discretionary trust for members[107] until the winding up resolution, whereupon a fixed trust arises for the members equally[108] in accordance with the body's constitution. Thus the trust property passes to the members. In the latter case, the courts could take the strict view that on expiry of the perpetuity period the discretionary trust terminates[109] and there is a resulting trust in favour of the settlor's estate. However, to avoid practical problems in tracing the devolution of such estate and to achieve a more just outcome, it seems likely that the courts will be prepared to interpret the Perpetuities and Accumulations Act 2009 s.8 liberally so as to treat the settlor's gift as a class gift within the subsection. Thus, the class of members will close so as to exclude persons becoming members outside the perpetuity period. The current members at the end of that period should between them be absolutely entitled to the gifted capital. No doubt, in practice, they will be happy to transfer it to trustees as an accretion to the club's funds but a member could claim his proportionate share (at the risk of not having his membership renewed) unless the club rules expressly provided that any assets passing to a member by virtue of the membership must accrue to the club's funds.

5–85 Where the members cannot make the club assets their own because statute prohibits this, or because on dissolution the assets must pass to another body, then the trust will be construed as a purpose trust under constructions (iv) or (v).

5–86 (iv) *Trust for the charitable purposes of the association*. If the gift is intended to be of endowment capital to be held on trust for the income to be applied to a charitable purpose, then the beneficiary principle and the rule against inalienability do not apply. The funds will need to be kept separate from the non-charitable funds of the body and will remain subject to the charitable purpose, even after dissolution of the body.[110]

5–87 (v) *Trust for the non-charitable purposes of the association*. If the gift is intended to be of endowment capital to be held on trust for the income to be applied for the club's abstract non-charitable purposes then this trust will be void for infringing the beneficiary principle. This problem was considered by the Privy Council in *Leahy v Att.-Gen. for New South Wales*, which is reproduced immediately below. Likewise, in *Re Grant's WT*,[111] a testator left his estate "to the Labour Party Property Committee for the

107 See *Re Grant's WT* [1979] 3 All E.R. 359 at 368 on *Re Denley* purpose trusts.
108 Or otherwise as provided in the body's constitution, e.g. country members only receiving half that of town members.
109 Perpetuities and Accumulations Act 2009 s.7(4).
110 *Brooks v Richardson* [1986] 1 All E.R. 952; *Re Finger's WT* [1972] Ch. 300 revealing the predisposition of the court to treat a gift to an unincorporated charitable body as a trust for purposes, so as to prevent the gift lapsing if the body had been earlier dissolved and the second construction had been applied.
111 [1979] 3 All E.R. 359. Obiter dicta overlook the impact of the Perpetuities and Accumulations Act 1964 and the significance of *Re Lipinski's WT* [1976] Ch. 235. In *News Group Newspapers Ltd v SOGAT* [1986] I.C.R. 716 Lloyd L.J. seems to accept that the NLP's power to obtain CLP assets for its own needs justified Vinelott J.'s conclusions.

benefit of the Chertsey Headquarters of the Chertsey and Walton Constituency Labour Party" ("CLP") providing that if the headquarters ceased to be in the Chertsey UDC area (1972) his estate should pass to the National Labour Party ("NLP") absolutely. The CLP constitution subordinated it to the NLP, who could direct changes in the constitution and prevent the CLP changing its constitution without NLP approval. Vinelott J. held that the estate was meant to be kept intact as endowment capital on trust for Labour Party purposes and so was void for infringing the beneficiary principle and the rule against inalienability.

To escape this outcome it would have to be argued that the fulfilment of the association's non-charitable purpose enures to the benefit of a sufficiently certain class of individuals for them to have locus standi to apply for enforcement of the trust, as in *Re Denley's Trust Deeds*. Alternatively, it might be argued that a trust for the association's non-charitable purposes could be rescued by the appointment of an enforcer, e.g. the chairman from time to time of the club. If this argument were to be accepted, then the trust would need to be restricted from the outset to a common law perpetuity period so as not to infringe the rule against inalienability, and the purposes would need to be certain enough to enable the restrictions on the use of the income to be identified and enforced.[112] **5–88**

LEAHY v ATTORNEY-GENERAL FOR NEW SOUTH WALES

Privy Council [1959] A.C. 457; [1959] 2 W.L.R. 722; [1959] 2 All E.R. 300

By clause 3 of his will the testator provided as follows: "As to my property known as 'Elmslea' situated at Bungendore aforesaid and the whole of the land comprising the same and the whole of the furniture contained in the homestead thereon upon trust for such order of nuns of the Catholic Church or the Christian Brothers as my executors and trustees shall select." Counsel for the trustees argued that the disposition made thereby was good as it stood. Once the trustees selected the recipient of the gift, whether an order of nuns or the Christian Brothers, the selected body became absolutely entitled to the gift. No question of uncertainty or perpetuity was therefore involved and the gift was valid. If successful, this argument would have enabled the trustees to select as the recipient an order of nuns which was not charitable in the legal sense of that term. The phrase "order of nuns" included "contemplative" as well as "active" orders, the former of which were not charitable.[113] Hence counsel argued, in the alternative, that, if the disposition was not valid as it stood, it was nevertheless saved from invalidity by the NSW Conveyancing Act 1919–54 s.37D, which would at least have enabled active (though not contemplative) orders to be selected. **5–89**

VISCOUNT SIMONDS (with whom LORD MORTON, LORD COHEN, LORD SOMERVELL and LORD DENNING agreed): The disposition made by clause 3 must now be considered. As has already been pointed out, it will in any case be saved by the section so far as orders other than contemplative orders are concerned, but the trustees are anxious to preserve their right to select such orders. They can only do so if the gift is what is called an absolute gift to the selected order, an expression which may require examination. **5–90**

The difficulty arises out of the artificial and anomalous conception of an unincorporated society which, though it is not a separate entity in law, is yet for many purposes regarded as a continuing entity and, however inaccurately, as something other than an aggregate of its members. In law a gift to such a society simpliciter (i.e., where, to use the words of Lord Parker in *Bowman v Secular Society Ltd*,[114] neither the circumstances of the gift nor the directions given nor the objects expressed impose on the donee the character of a trustee) is nothing else than a gift to its members at the date of the gift as joint tenants or **5–91**

---

112 Cf. *Twinsectra Ltd v Yardley* [2000] W.T.L.R. 527 at 560 (reversed on other grounds [2002] 2 A.C. 164) on the certainty of analogous *Quistclose*-type trust restrictions: where the purposes are spelled out in certain workable fashion one could have all the club members as enforcers.

113 See *Gilmour v Coats* [1949] A.C. 426.

114 [1917] A.C. 406 at 437.

tenants in common. It is for this reason that the prudent conveyancer provides that a receipt by the treasurer or other proper officer of the recipient society for a legacy to the society shall be a sufficient discharge to executors. If it were not so, the executors could only get a valid discharge by obtaining a receipt from every member. This must be qualified by saying that by their rules the members might have authorised one of themselves to receive a gift on behalf of them all.

5–92 It is in the light of this fundamental proposition that the statements, to which reference has been made, must be examined. What is meant when it is said that a gift is made to the individuals comprising the community and the words are added "it is given to them for the benefit of the community?" If it is a gift to individuals, each of them is entitled to his distributive share (unless he has previously bound himself by the rules of the society that it shall be devoted to some other purpose). It is difficult to see what is added by the words "for the benefit of the community." If they are intended to import a trust, who are the beneficiaries? If the present members are the beneficiaries, the words add nothing and are meaningless. If some other persons or purposes are intended, the conclusion cannot be avoided that the gift is void. For it is uncertain and beyond doubt tends to a perpetuity.

5–93 The question then appears to be whether, even if the gift to a selected order of nuns is prima facie a gift to the individual members of that order, there are other considerations arising out of the terms of the will, or the nature of the society, its organisation and rules, or the subject-matter of the gift, which should lead the court to conclude that though prima facie the gift is an absolute one (absolute both in quality of estate and in freedom from restriction) to individual nuns, yet it is invalid because it is in the nature of an endowment and tends to a perpetuity or for any other reason.

5–94 The prima facie validity of such a gift (by which term their Lordships intend a bequest or devise) is a convenient starting-point for the examination of the relevant law. For, as Lord Tomlin (sitting at first instance in the Chancery Division) said in *Re Ogden*,[115] a gift to a voluntary association of persons for the general purposes of the association is an absolute gift and prima facie a good gift. He was echoing the words of Lord Parker in *Bowman's case*[116] that a gift to an unincorporated association for the attainment of its purposes "may . . . be upheld as an absolute gift to its members." These words must receive careful consideration, for it is to be noted that it is because the gift can be upheld as a gift to the individual members that it is valid, even though it is given for the general purpose of the association. If the words "for the general purposes of the association" were held to import a trust, the question would have to be asked, what is the trust and who are the beneficiaries? A gift can be made to persons (including a corporation) but it cannot be made to a purpose or to an object: so, also, a trust may be created for the benefit of persons as cestuis que trust but not for a purpose or object unless the purpose or object be charitable. For a purpose or object cannot sue, but, if it be charitable, the Attorney-General can sue to enforce it . . .

5–95 [He then considered a series of cases,[117] and continued:] The cases that have been referred to are all cases in which gifts have been upheld as valid either on the ground that, where a society has been named as legatee, its members could demand that the gift should be dealt with as they should together think fit; or on the ground that a trust has been established (as in *Re Drummond*) which did not create a perpetuity . . .

5–96 Their Lordships must now turn to the recent case of *Re Macaulay's Estate*,[118] which appears to be reported only in a footnote to *Re Price*.[119] There the gift was to the Folkestone Lodge of the Theosophical Society absolutely for the maintenance and improvement of the Theosophical Lodge at Folkestone. It was assumed that the donee "the Lodge" was a body of persons. The decision of the House of Lords in July 1933, to which both Lord Buckner and Lord Tomlin were parties, were that the gift was invalid. A portion of Lord Buckmaster's speech may well be quoted. He had previously referred to *Re Drummond* and *Carne v Long*. "A group of people," he said, "defined and bound together by rules and called by a distinctive name can be the subject of gift as well as any individual or incorporated body. The real question is what is the actual purpose for which the gift is made. There is no perpetuity if the gift is for the individual members for

115 [1933] Ch. 678 at 681.
116 [1917] A.C. 406 at 442.
117 *Cocks v Manners* (1871) L.R. 12 Eq. 574; *Re Smith* [1914] 1 Ch. 937; *Re Clarke* [1901] 2 Ch. 110; *Re Drummond* [1914] 2 Ch. 90; *Re Taylor* [1940] Ch. 481; *Re Price* [1943] Ch. 422; *Re Prevost* [1930] 2 Ch. 383; *Re Ray's WT* [1936] Ch. 520.
118 [1943] Ch. 435n.
119 [1943] Ch. 422.

their own benefit, but that, I think, is clearly not the meaning of this gift. Nor again is there a perpetuity if the society is at liberty in accordance with the terms of the gift to spend both capital and income as they think fit . . . If the gift is to be for the endowment of the society to be held as an endowment and the society is according to its form perpetual, the gift is bad: but, if the gift is an immediate beneficial legacy, it is good." In the result he held the gift for the maintenance and improvement of the Theosophical Lodge at Folkestone to be invalid. Their Lordships respectfully doubt whether the passage in Lord Buckmaster's speech in which he suggests the alternative ground of validity, viz., that the society is at liberty in accordance with the terms of the gift to spend both capital and income as they think fit, presents a true alternative. It is only because the society, i.e., the individuals constituting it, are the beneficiaries that they can dispose of the gift. Lord Tomlin came to the same conclusion. He found in the words of the will "for the maintenance and improvement" a sufficient indication that it was the permanence of the Lodge at Folkestone that the testatrix was seeking to secure and this, he thought, necessarily involved endowment. Therefore a perpetuity was created. A passage from the judgment of Lord Hanworth M.R. (which has been obtained from the records) may usefully be cited. He said: "The problem may be stated in this way. If the gift is in truth to the present members of the society described by their society name so that they have the beneficial use of the property and can, if they please, alienate and put the proceeds in their own pocket, then there is a present gift to individuals which is good: but if the gift is intended for the good not only of the present but of future members so that the present members are in the position of trustees and have no right to appropriate the property or its proceeds for their personal benefit, then the gift is invalid. It may be invalid by reason of there being a trust created, or it may be by reason of the terms that the period allowed by the rule against perpetuities would be exceeded."

It is not very clear what is intended by the dichotomy suggested in the last sentence of the citation, but **5–97**
the penultimate sentence goes to the root of the matter. At the risk of repetition their Lordships would point out that if a gift is made to individuals, whether under their own names or in the name of their society, and the conclusion is reached that they are not intended to take beneficially, then they take as trustees. If so, it must be ascertained who are the beneficiaries. If, at the death of the testator, the class of beneficiaries is fixed and ascertained or ascertainable within the limit of the rule against perpetuities, all is well. If it is not so fixed and not so ascertainable, the trust must fail.

It must now be asked, then, whether in the present case there are sufficient indications to displace the **5–98**
prima facie conclusion that the gift made by clause 3 of the will is to the individual members of the selected order of nuns at the date of the testator's death so that they can together dispose of it as they think fit. It appears to their Lordships that such indications are ample.

In the first place, it is not altogether irrelevant that the gift is in terms upon trust for a selected order. It **5–99**
is true that this can in law be regarded as a trust in favour of each and every member of the order. But at least the form of the gift is not to the members, and it may be questioned whether the testator understood the niceties of the law. In the second place, the members of the selected order may be numerous, very numerous perhaps, and they may be spread over the world. If the gift is to the individuals it is to all the members who were living at the death of the testator, but only to them. It is not easy to believe that the testator intended an "immediate beneficial legacy" (to use the words of Lord Buckmaster) to such a body of beneficiaries. In the third place, the subject-matter of the gift cannot be ignored. It appears from the evidence filed in the suit that Elmslea is a grazing property of about 730 acres, with a furnished homestead containing twenty rooms and a number of outbuildings. With the greatest respect to those judges who have taken a different view, their Lordships do not find it possible to regard all the individual members of an order as intended to become the beneficial owners of such a property. Little or no evidence has been given about the organisation and rules of the several orders, but it is at least permissible to doubt whether it is a common feature of them that all their members regard themselves or are to be regarded as having the capacity of (say) the Corps of Commissionaires (see *Re Clarke*) to put an end to their association and distribute its assets. On the contrary it seems reasonably clear that, however little the testator understood the effect in law of a gift to an unincorporated body of persons by their society name, his intention was to create a trust not merely for the benefit of the existing members of the selected order but for its benefit as a continuing society and for the furtherance of its work.

. . . Their Lordships, therefore, humbly advise Her Majesty that the appeal should be dismissed, but **5–100**
that the gift made by clause 3 of the will is valid by reason only of the provisions of section 37D of the

Conveyancing Act 1919–54, and that the power of selection thereby given to the trustees does not extend to contemplative orders of nuns.

RE RECHER'S WILL TRUSTS

Chancery Division [1972] Ch. 526; [1971] 3 W.L.R. 321; [1971] 3 All E.R. 401

5–101 By will dated May 23, 1957, a testator gave a share of her residue to what the judge interpreted as "the London and Provincial Anti-Vivisection Society" which had ceased to exist on January 1, 1957. The testator died in 1962. In a reserved judgment consideration was first given to the question whether the gift would have been valid if the unincorporated society had existed at the time of her death, as follows.

5–102 BRIGHTMAN J.: Having reached the conclusion that the gift in question is not a gift to the members of the London and Provincial Society at the date of death, as joint tenants or tenants in common so as to entitle a member as of right to a distributive share, nor an attempted gift to present and future members beneficially, and is not a gift in trust for the purpose of the society, I must now consider how otherwise, if at all, it is capable of taking effect.

5–103 As I have already mentioned, the rules of the London and Provincial Society do not purport to create any trusts except insofar as the honorary trustees are not beneficial owners of the assets of the society, but are trustees on trust to deal with such assets according to the directions of the committee.

5–104 A trust for non-charitable purposes, as distinct from a trust for individuals, is clearly void because there is no beneficiary. It does not, however, follow that persons cannot band themselves together as an association or society, pay subscriptions and validly devote their funds in pursuit of some lawful non-charitable purpose. An obvious example is a members' social club. But it is not essential that the members should only intend to secure direct personal advantages to themselves. The association may be one in which personal advantages to the members are combined with the pursuit of some outside purpose. Or the association may be one which offers no personal benefit at all to the members, the funds of the association being applied exclusively to the pursuit of some outside purpose. Such an association of persons is bound, I would think, to have some sort of constitution; i.e. the rights and liabilities of the members of the association will inevitably depend on some form of contract inter se, usually evidenced by a set of rules. In the present case it appears to me clear that the life members, the ordinary members and the associate members of the London Provincial Society were bound together by a contract inter se. Any such member was entitled to the rights and subject to the liabilities defined by the rules. If the committee acted contrary to the rules, an individual member would be entitled to take proceedings in the courts to compel observance of the rules or to recover damages for any loss he had suffered as a result of the breach of contract. As and when a member paid his subscription to the association, he would be subjecting his money to the disposition and expenditure thereof laid down by the rules. That is to say, the member would be bound to permit, and entitled to require, the honorary trustees and other members of the society to deal with that subscription in accordance with the lawful directions of the committee. Those directions would include the expenditure of that subscription, as part of the general funds of the association, in furthering the objects of the association. The resultant situation, on analysis, is that the London and Provincial Society represented an organisation of individuals bound together by a contract under which their subscriptions became, as it were, mandated towards a certain type of expenditure as adumbrated in rule 1. Just as the two parties to a bipartite bargain can vary or terminate their contract by mutual assent, so it must follow that the life members, ordinary members and associate members of the London and Provincial Society could, at any moment of time, by unanimous agreement (or by majority vote if the rules so prescribe), vary or terminate their multipartite contract. There would be no limit to the type of variation or termination to which all might agree. There is no private trust or trust for charitable purposes or other trust to hinder the process. It follows that if all members agreed, they could decide to wind up the London and Provincial Society and divide the net assets among themselves beneficially. No one would have any locus standi to stop them so doing. The contract is the same as any other contract and concerns only those who are parties to it, that is to say, the members of the society.

5–105 The funds of such an association may, of course, be derived not only from the subscriptions of the contracting parties but also from donations from non-contracting parties and legacies from persons who have died. In the case of a donation which is not accompanied by any words which purport to impose a trust, it seems to me that the gift takes effect in favour of the existing members of the association as an accretion to the funds which are the subject-matter of the contract which such members have made inter se, and falls to be dealt with in precisely the same way as the funds which the members themselves have subscribed. So, in the case of a legacy. In the absence of words which purport to impose a trust, the legacy is a gift to the members beneficially, not as joint tenants or as tenants in common so as to entitle each member to an immediate distributive share, but as an accretion to the funds which are the subject-matter of the contract which the members have made inter se.

In my judgment the legacy in the present case to the London and Provincial Society ought to be construed as a legacy of that type, that is to say, a legacy to the members beneficially as an accretion to the funds subject to the contract which they had made inter se. Of course, the testatrix did not intend the members of the society to divide their bounty between themselves, and doubtless she was ignorant of that remote but theoretical possibility. Her knowledge or absence of knowledge of the true legal analysis of the gift is irrelevant. The legacy is accordingly in my view valid, subject only to the effect of the events of January 1, 1957. **5–106**

RE LIPINSKI'S WILL TRUSTS

Chancery Division [1976] Ch. 235; [1976] 3 W.L.R. 522; [1977] 1 All E.R. 33

The testator bequeathed his residuary estate to trustees on trust "as to one half thereof for the Hull Judeans (Maccabi) Association in memory of my late wife to be used solely in the work of constructing the new buildings for the association and/or improvements to the said buildings." The question at issue was the validity of this bequest. **5–107**

OLIVER J.: I approach question 1 of the summons, therefore, on the footing that this is a gift to an unincorporated non-charitable association. Such a gift, if it is an absolute and beneficial one, is of course perfectly good: see, for instance, the gift to the Corps of Commissionaires in *Re Clarke*.[120] What I have to consider, however, is the effect of the specification by the testator of the purposes for which the legacy was to be applied. The principles applicable to this type of case were stated by Cross J. in *Neville Estates Ltd v Madden*[121] and they are conveniently summarised in *Tudor on Charities*, where it is said[122]: **5–108**

> "In *Neville Estates Ltd v Madden* Cross J. expressed the opinion (which is respectfully accepted as correct) that every such gift might, according to the actual words used, be construed in one of three quite different ways: (a) As a gift to the members of the association at the date of the gift as joint tenants so that any member could sever his share and claim it whether or not he continues to be a member. (b) As a gift to the members of the association at the date of the gift not as joint tenants, but subject to their contractual rights and liabilities towards one another as members of the association. In such a case a member cannot sever his share. It will accrue to the other members on his death or resignation, even though such members include persons who become members after the gift took effect. If this is the effect of the gift, it will not be open to objection on the score of perpetuity or uncertainty unless there is something in its terms or circumstances or in the rules of the association which precludes the members at any given time from dividing the subject of the gift between them on the footing that they are solely entitled to it in equity. (c) The terms or circumstances of the gift or the rules of the association may show that the property in question—i.e. the subject of the gift—is not to be at the disposal of the members for the time being but is to be held in trust for or applied for the purposes of the association as a quasi-corporate entity. In this case the gift will fail unless the association is a charitable body."

That summary may require, I think, a certain amount of qualification in the light of subsequent authority, but for the present purposes I can adopt it as a working guide. Counsel for the next-of-kin argues that **5–109**

120 [1901] 2 Ch. 110.
121 [1962] Ch. 832.
122 6th edn, 1967, p.150.

the gift in the present case clearly does not fall within the first category, and that the addition of the specific direction as to its employment by the association prevents it from falling into the second category. This is, therefore, he says, a purpose trust and fails both for that reason and because the purpose is perpetuitous . . .

5–110 Counsel for the next-of-kin points out, first, that the gift is in memory of the testator's late wife (which, he says, suggests an intention to create a permanent memorial or endowment); secondly, that the gift is solely for a particular purpose (which would militate strongly against any suggestion that the donees could wind up and pocket the money themselves, even though their constitution may enable them to do so); and, thirdly, that the gift contemplates expenditure on "improvements", which connotes a degree of continuity or permanence. All this, he says, shows that what the testator had in mind was a permanent endowment in memory of his late wife.

5–111 For my part, I think that very little turns on the testator's having expressed the gift as being in memory of his late wife. I see nothing in this expression which suggests any intention to create a permanent endowment. It indicates merely, I think, a tribute which the testator wished to pay, and it is not without significance that this self-same tribute appeared in the earlier will in which he made an absolute and outright gift to the association. The evidential value of this in the context of a construction summons may be open to doubt, and I place no reliance on it. It does, however, seem to me that nothing is to be derived from these words beyond the fact that the testator wished the association to know that his bounty was a tribute to his late wife.

5–112 I accept, however, the submission of counsel for the next-of-kin that the designation of the sole purpose of the gift makes it impossible to construe the gift as one falling into the first of Cross J.'s categories, even if that were otherwise possible. But I am not impressed by the argument that the gift shows an intention of continuity. Counsel prays in aid *Re Macaulay*[123] where the gift was for the "maintenance and improvement of the Theosophical Lodge at Folkestone". The House of Lords held that it failed for perpetuity, the donee being a non-charitable body. But it is clear from the speeches of both Lord Buckmaster and Lord Tomlin that their Lordships derived the intention of continuity from the reference to "maintenance". Here it is quite evident that the association was to be free to spend the capital of the legacy.

5–113 *Re Price*[124] itself is authority for the proposition that a gift to an unincorporated non-charitable association for objects on which the association is at liberty to spend both capital and income will not fail for perpetuity, although the actual conclusion in that case has been criticised, the point that the trust there (the carrying on of the teachings of Rudolf Steiner) was a "purpose trust" and thus unenforceable on that ground was not argued. It does not seem to me, therefore, that in the present case there is a valid ground for saying that the gift fails for perpetuity.

5–114 But that is not the end of the matter. If the gift were to the association simpliciter, it would, I think, clearly fall within the second category of Cross J.'s categories. At first sight, however, there appears to be a difficulty in arguing that the gift is to members of the association subject to their contractual rights inter se when there is a specific direction or limitation sought to be imposed on those contractual rights as to the manner in which the subject-matter of the gift is to be dealt with. This, says counsel for the next-of-kin, is a pure "purpose trust" and is invalid on that ground, quite apart from any question of perpetuity. I am not sure, however, that it is sufficient merely to demonstrate that a trust is a "purpose" trust . . .

5–115 There would seem to me to be, as a matter of common sense, a clear distinction between the case where a purpose is described which is clearly intended for the benefit of ascertained or ascertainable beneficiaries, particularly where those beneficiaries have the power to make the capital their own, and the case where no beneficiary at all is intended (for instance, a memorial to a favourite pet) or where the beneficiaries are unascertainable (as for instance in *Re Price*[125]). If a valid gift may be made to an unincorporated body as a simple accretion to the funds which are the subject-matter of the contract which the members have made inter se, and *Neville Estates v Madden*[126] and *Re Recher's Will Trusts*[127] show that it may, I do not really see why such a gift,

[123] [1943] Ch. 435.
[124] [1943] Ch. 422.
[125] [1943] Ch. 422.
[126] [1962] Ch. 832.
[127] [1972] Ch. 526.

which specifies a purpose which is within the powers of the unincorporated body and of which the members of that body are the beneficiaries, should fail. Why are not the beneficiaries able to enforce the trust or, indeed, in the exercise of their contractual rights, to terminate the trust for their own benefit? Where the donee body is itself the beneficiary of the prescribed purpose, there seems to me to be the strongest argument in common sense for saying that the gift should be construed as an absolute one within the second category, the more so where, if the purpose is carried out, the members can by appropriate action vest the resulting property in themselves, for here the trustees and the beneficiaries are the same persons. . . .

A striking case which seems to be not far from the present is *Re Turkington*,[128] where the gift was to a masonic lodge "as a fund to build a suitable temple in Stafford." The members of the lodge being both the trustees and the beneficiaries of the temple, Luxmoore J. construed the gift as an absolute one to the members of the lodge for the time being. Directly in point is the more recent decision of Goff J. in *Re Denley's Trust Deed*,[129] where the question arose as to the validity of a deed under which land was held by trustees as a sports ground: **5–116**

> ". . . primarily for the benefit of the employees of [a particular] company and secondarily for the benefit of such other person or persons . . . as the trustees may allow to use the same."

The latter provision was construed by Goff J. as a power and not a trust. The same deed conferred on the employees a right to use and enjoy the land subject to regulations made by the trustees. Goff J. held that the rule against enforceability of non-charitable "purpose or object" trusts was confined to those which were abstract or impersonal in nature where there was no beneficiary or cestui que trust. A trust which, though expressed as a purpose, was directly or indirectly for the benefit of an individual or individuals was valid provided that those individuals were ascertainable at any one time and the trust was not otherwise void for uncertainty.

I respectfully adopt the view of Goff J. as it seems to me to accord both with authority and with common sense. **5–117**

If this is the right principle, then on each side of the line does the present case fall? Counsel for the Attorney-General has submitted in the course of his argument in favour of charity that the testator's express purpose "solely in the work of constructing the new buildings for the association" referred and could only refer to the youth centre project, which was the only project for the erection of buildings which was under consideration at the material time. If this is right, then the trust must, I think, fail, for it is quite clear that that project is ultimately conceived embraced not only the members of the association, but the whole Jewish community in Hull, and it would be difficult to argue that there was any ascertainable beneficiary. I do not, however, so construe the testator's intention. The evidence is that the testator knew the association's position and that he took a keen interest in it. I infer that he was kept informed of its current plans. The one thing that is quite clear from the minutes is that from 1965 right up to the testator's death there was great uncertainty about what was going to be done. There was a specific project for the purchase of a house in 1965. By early 1966 the youth centre was back in favour. By October 1966 it was being suggested that the association should stay where it was in its rented premises. The meeting of March 21, is, I think, very significant because it shows that it was again thinking in terms of its own exclusive building and that the patrons (of whom the testator was one) would donate the money when it was needed. At the date of the will, the association had rejected the youth centre plans and was contemplating again the purchase of premises of its own; and thereafter interest shifted to the community centre. I am unable to conclude that the testator had any specific building in mind; and, in my judgment, the reference to "the . . . buildings for the association" means no more than whatever buildings the association may have or may choose to erect or acquire. The reference to improvements reflects, I think, the testator's contemplation that the association might purchase or might, at his death, already have purchased an existing structure which might require improvement or conversion or even that it might, as had at one time been suggested, expend money in improving the premises which it rented from the Jewish Institute. The association was to have the legacy to spend in this way for the benefit of its members. **5–118**

[128] [1937] 4 All E.R. 501.
[129] [1969] 1 Ch. 373 at 375.

5–119 I have already said that, in my judgment, no question of perpetuity arises here, and accordingly the case appears to me to be one of the specification of a particular purpose for the benefit of ascertained beneficiaries, the members of the association for the time being. There is an additional factor. This is a case in which, under the constitution of the association, the members could, by the appropriate majority, alter their constitution so as to provide, if they wished, for the division of the association's assets among themselves. This has, I think, a significance. I have considered whether anything turns in this case on the testator's direction that the legacy shall be used "solely" for one or other of the specified purposes. Counsel for the association has referred me to a number of cases where legacies have been bequeathed for particular purposes and in which the beneficiaries have been held entitled to override the purpose, even though expressed in mandatory terms.

5–120 Perhaps the most striking in the present context is the case of *Re Bowes*,[130] where money was directed to be laid out in the planting of trees on a settled estate. That was a "purpose" trust, but there were ascertainable beneficiaries, the owners for the time being of the estate; and North J. held that the persons entitled to the settled estate were entitled to have the money whether or not it was laid out as directed by the testator. He said:[131]

> "The owners of the estate now say 'It is a very disadvantageous way of spending this money; the money is to be spent for our benefit, and that of no one else; it was not intended for any purpose other than our benefit and that of the estate. That is no reason why it should be thrown away by doing what is not for our benefit, instead of being given to us, who want to have the enjoyment of it.' I think their contention is right. I think the fund is devoted to improving the estate, and improving the estate for the benefit of the persons who are absolutely entitled to it."

5–121 I can see no reason why the same reasoning should not apply in the present case simply because the beneficiary is an unincorporated non-charitable association. I do not think the fact that the testator has directed the application "solely" for the specified purpose adds any legal force to the direction. The beneficiaries, as members of the association for the time being, are the persons who could enforce the purpose and they must, as it seems to me, be entitled not to enforce it or, indeed, to vary it.

5–122 Thus, it seems to me that whether one treats the gift as a "purpose" trust or as an absolute gift with a superadded direction or, on the analogy of *Re Turkington*,[132] as a gift where the trustees and the beneficiaries are the same persons, all roads lead to the same conclusion.

5–123 In my judgment, the gift is a valid gift.

Questions

5–124 1. By his will Tony left:

(a) "£1,000,000 to my executor and trustee Eric to use the income to further the purposes of the UK Socialist Party so far as the law allows, such trust to be enforceable by the Leader from time to time of such Party";

(b) "£50,000 to the Treasurer of the Cambridge University Law Society to deal with it as the Society wishes";

(c) "£50,000 to the Treasurer of the Manchester Literary and Philosophical Society on trust to apply the income for the benefit of its members";

(d) "£150,000 to be used at the discretion of the chairman and executive council of the Anthroposophical Society of Great Britain to further the teachings of Rudolph Steiner";

130 [1896] 1 Ch. 507.
131 [1896] 1 Ch. 507 at 511.
132 [1937] 4 All E.R. 501.

(e) "the proceeds of sale of my residuary estate to the Treasurer of the Manchester Mavericks Darts Club to apply half the income for the purposes of the Club and half the income for providing educational assistance to the children of Club members."

Statute prevents the members of the "Lit. and Phil." Society from winding up the Society and dividing its assets between themselves, while this is possible in the case of the Darts Club only if membership falls below five, although the rules can be changed by a 90 per cent majority vote.

Advise on the validity of the above bequests.

2. How satisfactory are the reforms enacted in sections 12A and 12B of the Bermudan Trusts (Special Provisions) Act 1989 (as substituted by the Trusts Special Provisions Amendment Act 1998) when under the old law enforcement was possible only where there was an expressly appointed enforcer? Where is the beneficial equitable ownership if a settlor transfers £500,000 and all the shares in Wonder Co Ltd to trustees to the intent that he be forthwith divested of all interest in the assets which are to be used exclusively for the purpose of developing Wonder Co Ltd? How does the position differ if the trustees are under a duty to accumulate the income for the full 100-year period allowed by Bermudan law and on the expiry thereof in their discretion to distribute the trust property between such of the settlor's relatives then alive as they see fit, but with the power at any earlier time to appoint capital or income to the settlor or any of his relatives as they may see fit or to any other person nominated in writing to them by the settlor? **5–125**

3. Do you have any anxieties over a structure where a £20 million portfolio of shares, land and paintings is owned by a company, all of whose shares are held by a private trust company holding the shares on trust for the purpose of developing the value of the shares, and where the shares in the trust company are held by individuals on trust for the purpose of running the business of the trust company as trustee of only one trust? **5–126**

6 CHARITABLE TRUSTS

1. Legal Forms Used by Charities

6–01 Charities often take the legal form of a charitable trust,[1] i.e. a trust for purposes that are legally deemed to be charitable. The law that determines whether particular purposes are legally charitable forms the main subject matter of this chapter.

6–02 Charities may also take other legal forms. They may take the form of an unincorporated association,[2] of a chartered corporation,[3] of a friendly society,[4] of an industrial and provident society,[5] or of a registered company limited by guarantee (as opposed to a registered company limited by shares, the form which is used by commercial organisations intending to distribute profits to their shareholders).[6]

6–03 Since 2010, the promoters of a charity have also been able to create a Charitable Incorporated Organisation, a legal form that enables charities to acquire the benefits of incorporation without attracting the disadvantage of dual regulation by Companies House as well as the Charity Commission.[7]

6–04 All of these bodies typically have written provisions detailing their purposes and the rules governing their administration, and for the purposes of the charities legislation these provisions count as "trusts" whether or not they take effect by way of trust.[8] By the same token, charity officers are referred to as "trustees" in the legislation and in the Charity Commission literature, whether or not they are actually trustees of a charitable trust. The Charities Act 2006 s.1(1) defines a charity as "an institution which (a) is established for charitable purposes only, and (b) falls to be subject to the control of the High Court in the exercise of its jurisdiction with respect to charities".

---

1 A model trust deed for a charitable trust has been published by the Charity Commission at *http://www.charitycommission.gov.uk/Library/publications/pdfs/gd2text.pdf*. Note that under the Charities Act 1993 ss. 50–52, a group of individual trustees of a charitable trust may collectively become a corporate body (e.g. to make title holding easier by avoiding the need to transfer title to individuals becoming new trustees). However they will continue to owe duties as trustees as though no incorporation had been effected: see s.54 of the 1993 Act. See further Charity Commission, *CC 43: Incorporation of Charity Trustees* (July 2002 version).

2 The Charity Commission has published a model constitution for a charitable unincorporated association at *http://www.charity-commission.gov.uk/Library/publications/pdfs/gd3text.pdf*.

3 There are only a few of these, and they are all very well-established charities with large funds, e.g. the older universities, the Church Commissioners, and the British Museum. On the latter, see *Att.-Gen. v British Museum Trustees* [2005] Ch. 397 (museum trustees have no statutory power to return stolen art to previous owners).

4 Friendly societies are incorporated mutual assurance associations providing social or financial benefits (e.g. life assurance, funeral benefits). They are governed by the Friendly Societies Act 1992, and they are charitable only if their purpose is the relief of poverty.

5 A form generally used by housing associations. An industrial and provident society is a corporate body with members whose purpose is to carry on industry or conduct business, either as a co-operative (in which case it will not be charitable and will fall within the scope of the Industrial and Provident Societies Acts 1965 to 2002) or for the benefit of the community (in which case it will be charitable and will be governed by the Co-operatives and Community Benefit Societies Act 2003).

6 J. Gray, "Guarantee Companies in the Voluntary Sector" in A. Dunn (ed.), *The Voluntary Sector, the State and the Law* (2000) 75. The Charity Commission has published a model memorandum and articles of association of a charitable company limited by guarantee at *http://www.charitycommission.gov.uk/Library/publications/pdfs/gd1text.pdf*.

7 Charities Act 2006 s.34 and Sch.7, inserting new Charities Act 1993 Pt 8A and Sch.5B. See too Charity Commission, *Charitable Incorporated Organisation (CIO)* (March 2009 version); S.R. Cross, "New Legal Forms for Charities in the United Kingdom" [2008] J.B.L. 662.

8 Charities Act 1993 s.97(1).

2. The Advantages of Charitable Status

Whatever legal form they take, charitable trusts and organisations enjoy various fiscal and legal advantages over trusts and organisations formed for private and/or commercial purposes, reflecting the fact that their purposes enure to the public good. **6–05**

A. *Tax Advantages*

United Kingdom[9] charities do not pay income or corporation tax on their property income and investment income which is applicable to charitable purposes only and is in fact applied solely for those purposes.[10] Nor do they pay capital gains tax in respect of gains made upon disposals by them, again provided that the gain is applied solely to charitable purposes.[11] Charities can obtain 80 per cent relief as of right in respect of non-domestic rates for premises wholly or mainly used for charitable purposes and some discretionary relief in respect of the rest.[12] Charities are also exempt from stamp duty.[13] However they only have a very few reliefs from value added tax in prescribed circumstances, e.g. relating to medical supplies.[14] **6–06**

Charities are only exempt from tax on their trading income if the profits are used solely for charitable purposes, and either the trade is exercised in the course of the actual carrying out of a primary purpose of the charity,[15] or the work in connection with the trade is mainly carried out by beneficiaries of the charity,[16] or the charity can bring itself within a small scale trading exemption because its annual turnover falls below £5000.[17] Charities are also able to avoid paying tax on trading that is not within any of these exemptions, by incorporating subsidiary trading companies and causing them to donate all their profits to the charities, with the result that their taxable profits are effectively kept at zero.[18] **6–07**

No inheritance tax is payable on gifts to charities,[19] nor does a charge to capital gains tax arise on disposals of property to charities.[20] Individuals who make gifts of shares, securities and real property to charities are given relief from income tax by deducting a corresponding amount when calculating their net income for the tax year in which the gift is made.[21] Charities can also recover basic rate tax in respect of any gifts made to them under the gift aid scheme.[22] **6–08**

In the tax year 2008/9, there were around 190,000 registered charities in England and Wales, and their total incoming resources were nearly £51 billion.[23] The cost of tax reliefs to charities in the UK **6–09**

---

9 *Camille and Henry Dreyfus Foundation Inc v IRC* [1956] A.C. 39; *Civil Engineer v IRC* [2002] STC (SCD) 72. But note that under EC law, charities established in one Member State may be entitled to the benefit of tax advantages in another, as in, e.g. *Commission v Spain* (Case C-153/08) [2010] 1 C.M.L.R. 30.

10 Income and Corporation Tax Act 1988 s.505(1); Income Tax Act 2007 ss.531 and 532. See *IRC v Educational Grants Association Ltd* [1967] Ch. 123.

11 Taxation of Chargeable Gains Act 1992 s.256.

12 Local Government Finance Act 1988 ss. 43(5) and (6), 47, and 64(10).

13 Finance Act 1982 s.129.

14 Value Added Tax Act 1994 Sch.8, Groups 4, 5, 6, 8, 12, and 15 and Sch.9, Groups 6, 7, 10, 12, and 13.

15 Income Tax Act 2007 s.525(1)(a).

16 Income Tax Act 2007 s.525(1)(b).

17 Income Tax Act 2007 s.526.

18 Income and Corporation Taxes Act 1988 s.339. See too Charity Commission, *CC 35: Trustees, Trading and Tax* (April 2007 version); HMRC *Charities—Trading and Business Activities* published online at *http://www.hmrc.gov.uk/charities/guidance-notes/annex4/sectiona.htm*.

19 Inheritance Tax Act 1984 s.23.

20 Taxation of Chargeable Gains Act 1992 s.257.

21 Income Tax Act 2007 ss.431 ff. The amount of the deduction is calculated by a complex formula set out in s.434.

22 Income Tax Act 2007 ss.413 ff.

23 Charity Commission, *Annual Report for 2008/9* (2009) 14.

during this period in terms of tax payments lost to the Treasury was around £2.4 billion, and the cost of tax reliefs to individual donors was around £750 million.[24]

B. Trust Law Advantages

6–10 Charitable trusts have further advantages in that they are not subject to the rule against inalienability[25] that applies exclusively to pure purpose trusts and, to the extent that a charity might instead be a company or regarded as a trust for purposes benefiting individuals with locus standi to sue,[26] it enjoys one limited exemption from the rule against remoteness. At common law a gift over from one person to another that might possibly take effect outside the perpetuity period was void.[27] However, a gift over from one charity to another charity was valid, the property being treated as belonging to charity throughout so as not to be caught by the rule against remoteness,[28] if that rule were applicable as opposed to the rule against inalienability from which charities are in any event exempt.[29] If the gift were a gift over from a charity to a non-charity[30] or from a non-charity to a charity[31] then the rule against remoteness applied. Since the Perpetuities and Accumulations Act 1964 came into force, it has been possible in these two latter instances to wait and see when the gift over takes effect:[32] if it takes effect within the perpetuity period then it is good; if not then it is bad and the first gift becomes absolute, no longer subject to defeasance or determination. Of course, the validity of gifts over from one charity to another is unaffected by the perpetuities legislation.

6–11 Under the Perpetuities and Accumulations Act 2009 s.13, the former statutory restrictions on accumulating income were abolished for private trusts.[33] Under s.14, however, where the trustees of a charitable trust are given a duty or power to accumulate income for a period of more than 21 years, this duty or power ceases to have effect. This section was introduced on the recommendation of the Law Commission, which feared that otherwise charitable trustees might accumulate income indefinitely, although one might have thought that this would almost invariably constitute a breach of trust in any case.[34] The result of the 2009 legislation is that the privilege of indefinite duration accorded to charitable trusts continues to apply only to their endowment capital.

6–12 A charitable trust is valid although it is a pure purpose trust because the Attorney-General can enforce it, taking action against defaulting trustees where necessary. It is also the Attorney-General's responsibility (in practice now delegated to the Solicitor General) to represent charities in disputes over the construction or validity of wills and of trust deeds where there is a charitable interest at stake, to intervene where necessary in disputes over the use or sale of charitable property, to direct schemes for the administration of charities where necessary, and to direct charitable bequests in cases where a charity has not been identified or no longer exists.[35]

---

24 HMRC Statistics 2009, Table 10.2: Costs of Tax Relief; published online at *http://www.hmrc.gov.uk/stats/charities/table10–2.pdf*. This table does not include tax relief given to charities and corporate donors under the Income and Corporation Taxes Act 1988 ss. 339 and 505, or the Taxation of Chargeable Gains Act 1992 s.256.

25 e.g. *Re Banfield* [1968] 1 W.L.R. 846 compared with *Re Warre's WT* [1953] 1 W.L.R. 725 or *Re Gwyon* [1930] 1 Ch. 255.

26 Cf. *Re Denley's Trust Deed* [1969] 1 Ch. 373.

27 *Re Frost* (1889) 43 Ch.D. 246.

28 *Christ's Hospital v Grainger* (1849) 1 Mac. & G. 460; *Re Tyler* [1891] 3 Ch. 252.

29 The two rules are mutually exclusive, and so the Perpetuities and Accumulations Acts 1964 and 2009 have not needed to deal also with the rule against inalienability to save trusts for persons.

30 *Re Bowen* [1893] 2 Ch. 491.

31 *Re Peel's Release* [1921] 2 Ch. 218; *Re Dalziel* [1943] Ch. 277.

32 Perpetuities and Accumulations Act 1964 s.3. See now the Perpetuities and Accumulations Act 2009 s.7.

33 See para.7–74.

34 Law Commission, *The Rules against Perpetuities and Excessive Accumulations* (Law Com. No.251, 1998) para.10.19.

35 Attorney-General's Office, *Annual Review 2008–9* at 14.

In the case of a charitable trust, the requirement of certainty of objects is satisfied so long as the settlor manifested a general charitable intention to enable a *cy-près* scheme to be formulated for giving effect to his intention as nearly as possible.[36] Thus a trust "for world-wide charitable purposes" or "for poor persons" or "for the following charitable religious societies" without specifying any is valid, while a discretionary trust for everyone in the United Kingdom is void. The *cy-près* doctrine is peculiar to charitable trusts and will be dealt with at the end of this chapter.[37] Finally, note that charitable trustees can act by a majority instead of unanimously, which is the position for private trusts unless they are pensions trusts,[38] or the trust deed authorises majority decisions.[39] **6–13**

C. *Gifts to Charitable Companies*

A gift to a registered company whose property is held for charitable purposes (without distinguishing between capital and income) without the intervention of trusts, is usually treated as intended to be held as an addition to the company's general property and not upon trusts unless the donor uses express words importing a trust.[40] Although a company can always change its objects clause in its memorandum, a charitable company cannot do so without the prior written consent of the Charity Commission.[41] Of course, where property has been gifted upon express (endowment or non-endowment) trusts the company must always give effect to those trusts unless and until a *cy-près* scheme is finalised. A charitable company's own general property is also subject to the court's *cy-près* jurisdiction, e.g. on its winding up.[42] In the rare case where the Commission may allow a company to change its objects so as to cease to be a charity this cannot affect the application of any property acquired other than for full consideration or any property representing property so acquired or the income from any such property.[43] **6–14**

D. *Policing and Advice*

Concerns over the negligent or fraudulent mismanagement of charitable funds led to the establishment of the Charity Commission under the Charitable Trusts Acts 1853, 1855 and 1860,[44] the body **6–15**

---

[36] *Morice v Bishop of Durham* (1804) 9 Ves. Jun. 399 at 405; *Harwood v Harwood* [2005] EWHC 3019 (Ch); *Re Harding, deceased* [2008] Ch. 235 at [21]–[22]. The court has inherent jurisdiction to resolve any problems of administrative unworkability so long as the settlor has manifested a general charitable intention. If the trust is one the administration of which the court could not undertake and control and no exclusively charitable intent appears so as to found a *cy-près* scheme then the trust fails: *Re Hummultenberg* [1923] 1 Ch. 237 (legacy to the treasurer of the London Spiritualistic Alliance for the purpose of establishing a college for the training of suitable persons as mediums); *Re Koeppler's WT* [1984] Ch. 243 (legacy to trustees for the formation of an informed international public opinion and the promotion of greater co-operation in Europe and the West, though held charitable in the Court of Appeal [1986] Ch. 423); *Att.-Gen. of Cayman Islands v Wahr-Hansen* [2001] 1 A.C. 75 (trust for organisations operating for the public good held void by Privy Council).

[37] See paras 6–307 ff.

[38] Pensions Act 1995 s.32.

[39] *Re Whiteley* [1910] 1 Ch. 600 at 608. Yet another distinction is that the six-year limitation period in the Limitation Act 1980 s.21(3) applies to an action by a beneficiary under a trust but not to an action by the Attorney-General to enforce a charitable trust for the benefit of the public at large: *Att.-Gen. v Cocke* [1988] Ch. 414—although the limitation period may apply to an action to enforce a charitable trust for the benefit of a defined class, even if the Attorney-General is the claimant: *President and Scholars of the College of St Mary Magdalen, Oxford v Att.-Gen.* (1857) 6 H.L. Cas. 189.

[40] *Re Finger's WT* [1972] 1 Ch. 286 and see Charity Commissioners' *Report for 1971*, paras 22–30.

[41] Charities Act 1993 s.64(2); also see s.66.

[42] *Liverpool and District Hospital v Att.-Gen.* [1981] Ch. 193.

[43] Charities Act 1993 s.64(1).

[44] R. Tompson, *The Charity Commission and the Age of Reform* (1979). The Commissioners are given collective status as a body corporate by the Charities Act 1993 s.1A and Sch.1A.

which is still charged with the regulation of charities today. Similar concerns over the past 50 years have led to the enactment of the Charities Acts 1960, 1992, 1993 and 2006, statutes which have progressively expanded and strengthened the Charity Commission's powers. In theory, the Commission is an independent regulator, a non-ministerial government department which is accountable to the Home Secretary for its efficiency, but not for the manner in which it pursues its objectives.[45] In practice, the Commission has come under political pressure at various times, from those who believe that the voluntary sector should be more heavily regulated,[46] for example, and from those who believe that the Commission should pursue a systematic programme of wealth-redistribution by forcing charitable bodies to widen access to their facilities and services on pain of losing their charitable status.[47]

6–16 Most, though not all, charities are required by statute to register with the Charity Commission,[48] and those registered charities with a gross annual income exceeding £250,000 must submit annual accounts and returns to the Commission,[49] which is responsible for ensuring that they have been prepared accurately and honestly. All charities are also selectively targeted by the HM Revenue and Customs to ensure that their accounts are in proper order, and that they are eligible for the tax exemptions to which they lay claim. The Charity Commission has wide powers to institute inquiries into the administration of charities,[50] to require that people furnish them with information relevant to these inquiries,[51] and to obtain information relating to charities from the police and other public bodies.[52] In the event that misconduct or mismanagement in a charity's administration is discovered, the Commission can suspend or remove any of the charity's officers and appoint new ones as necessary.[53] It also has powers, corresponding to and concurrent with those possessed by the Attorney-General, to go directly to the courts for the enforcement of obligations against defaulting charity trustees and others.[54] Appeals can be made from decisions, directions, and orders made pursuant to the Commission's various powers to the First-tier Tribunal (Charity), an independent judicial body that was established in 2008.[55] The purpose of the tribunal is to provide charities and their officers with a cheaper and swifter mechanism for reviewing the Commission's decisions than is offered by the High Court. The tribunal's website is at: *www.charity.tribunals.gov.uk*. Whether there is much demand for the tribunal's services remains to be seen, but in its first 18 months of operation only three appeals were made.

6–17 As well as investigating possible misconduct and abuse of charitable funds with a view to taking remedial action, the Commission also provides charities with information and advice. It provides much useful guidance in publications that can be accessed on its website at: *http://www.charity-commission.gov.uk*. It is empowered to give advice to charity trustees to make the administration of their charity more effective,[56] and a charity trustee acting on such advice is deemed to have

---

[45] For the Commission's regulatory objectives, general functions, general duties, and incidental powers, see Charities Act 1993 ss.1B–1E.
[46] See, e.g. Select Committee on Public Accounts, *28th Report: Charity Commission—Regulation and Support of Charities* (1998), discussed in C. Mitchell, "Reviewing the Register" in C. Mitchell and S. Moody (eds), *Foundations of Charity* (2000) at pp. 188–190.
[47] e.g. House of Lords and House of Commons Joint Committee on the Draft Charities Bill, *The Draft Charities Bill* (HL 167 and HC 660, 2004), at pp.19–33.
[48] Charities Act 1993 s.3.
[49] Charities Act 1993 s.42
[50] Charities Act 1993 s.8.
[51] Charities Act 1993 s.9.
[52] Charities Act 1993 s.10.
[53] Charities Act 1993 s.18.
[54] Charities Act 1993 s.32.
[55] Under the Charities Act 1993 ss.2A–2D, inserted by Charities Act 2006 s.8. The decisions which can be challenged are set out in the Charities Act 1993 Sch.1C, added by Charities Act 2006 Sch.4.
[56] Charities Act 1993 s.29.

acted in accordance with the terms of the trust, provided that no court decision has been obtained on the matter, and that the trustee has not withheld material facts when seeking the Commission's directions.[57] The Commission will not advise on policy matters or legal questions concerning the charity's relationship with third parties,[58] and in practice it most often advises charities on how to simplify their administration, alter their trusts, amend their governing documents, transfer property and appoint new trustees.[59] The Commission can also make schemes and orders to modernise the purposes and administrative machinery of charities, and to give the trustees additional powers.[60]

3. Determining Charitable Status

A. Decision-Making Bodies

6–18 It will be seen from the foregoing discussion that trusts and organisations with charitable status enjoy various advantages which cost the state large sums of money, in the form of foregone tax revenues and the costs of charity regulation.[61] This suggests that decisions on entitlement to charitable status should be taken by a body with a democratic mandate, charged with deciding the question by undertaking a cost–benefit analysis of the proposed purposes of a trust or organisation to determine whether they merit the advantages flowing from charitable status.[62] However, no such body has ever been appointed, and decisions on charitable status are instead taken by various unelected bodies, whose basic approach is to decide the question as though it were a "pure" question of law divorced from fiscal considerations.

6–19 Thus, the courts are asked from time to time to decide whether testamentary purpose trusts are charitable; HM Revenue and Customs must frequently decide whether an institution is a "charity" for the purposes of determining its entitlement to tax reliefs; local government rating departments must decide whether institutions are entitled to rates relief; and most significantly, the Charity Commission must entertain applications by bodies to be included on the Register of Charities which it is the Commission's statutory responsibility to maintain. The effect of registration by the Commission is that for all purposes other than rectification of the Register, a body is conclusively presumed to be or to have been a charity at any time when it is or was registered.[63] Appeals from decisions by the tax authorities and the Charity Commission can be made to the courts, but in practice these have been very rare as very few voluntary bodies have the resources or the inclination to incur the costs of mounting an appeal to the courts. Concern that this has effectively left the development of the legal rules in this area entirely to the Charity Commission has led to the establishment of the First-tier Tribunal (Charity), to which appeals can be made from the Commission's decisions on charitable status (among other things).

---

[57] Charities Act 1993 s.29(2).
[58] Charity Commission, *Report for 1982*, paras 24–26.
[59] Charity Commission, *Report for 1996*, paras 123–125.
[60] Charities Act 1993 s.17.
[61] The Charity Commission's costs for the year 2008/9 were around £30 million: Charity Commission, *Resource Accounts 2008–09* (HC 444, 2009).
[62] See further C. Mitchell, "Redefining Charity in English Law" (1999) 13 Tru L.I. 21, pp. 39–41.
[63] Charities Act 1993 s.4(1). The courts are bound by this provision when considering the validity of a gift to a body which has attained or subsequently attains registration: *Re Murawski's WT* [1971] 1 W.L.R. 707. It also binds rating authorities: *Wynn v Skegness UDC* [1967] 1 W.L.R. 52. But tax relief may be refused to registered charities who spend their money on non-charitable purposes: *IRC v Educational Grants Assoc Ltd* [1967] Ch. 123.

B. Methodology

i. Analogising with Existing Charitable Purposes

6–20 When deciding the question whether the purposes of a trust or organisation are charitable, the courts and the Charity Commission first consider whether such purposes have previously been held to be legally charitable. If they have not, then they move on to ask whether an analogy can be drawn between the purposes under consideration and other purposes which have previously been held to be legally charitable. This process of analogising from one purpose to another is described in the Charity Commission's document, *RR1a: Recognising New Charitable Purposes* (October 2001 version), parts of which are reproduced below.[64] As an approach to determining charitable status, it has been strongly criticised as a charade which disguises the value judgments made by the courts and the Charity Commission as to the desirability of using public money to underwrite the pursuit of particular activities.[65] A vivid example of this artificiality is the Canadian Federal Court of Appeal's decision in *Vancouver Regional FreeNet Assoc v MNR*,[66] that the provision of free public access to the "information super-highway", including the internet, is a charitable purpose by way of analogy to the charitable purpose of repairing bridges, ports, causeways and highways.

6–21 A further peculiarity of charity law is that the precedental value of previous decisions on charitable status is not diminished by the fact that the consequences of charitable status have changed over time. Several well-known cases extending charitable status to various purposes were decided during the currency of the Mortmain and Charitable Uses Act 1736, which invalidated gifts of land to charitable purposes (unless the recipient was an exempted university or school). Examples are *Trustees of the British Museum v White*[67] and *Thornton v Howe*.[68] The expansive view taken in these cases of (respectively) education and religion now works to the advantage of analogous voluntary bodies seeking charitable status, although it worked to their disadvantage at the time when the cases were decided.

ii. Changing Social and Economic Circumstances

6–22 In recent years, the Commission has laid more stress in its decisions on the question whether changes in social and economic circumstances have made it more (or less) desirable for particular purposes to be pursued[69]—although it still does not purport to decide whether one purpose is a better use of public money than another, nor does it attempt to co-ordinate charitable activity with government

---

[64] At paras 6–31 ff.

[65] e.g. G.W. Keeton, "The Charity Muddle" (1949) 2 C.L.P. 86; N.P. Gravells, "Public Purpose Trusts" (1977) 40 M.L.R. 397: F. Quint, "The Rationale of Charity Law" (1994) 2 C.L.&P.R. 211.

[66] [1996] 3 F.C. 880.

[67] (1826) 2 Sim. & St. 594.

[68] (1862) 31 Beav. 14.

[69] See e.g. (1993) 1 Ch. Com. Dec. 4 where the Commission departed from *Re Stephens* (1892) 8 T.L.R. 792, when deciding that rifle clubs were no longer charitable; in 2001 it also departed from *GMC v IRC* [1928] All E.R. 252 in finding the General Medical Council to be a charity: *http://www.charitycommission.gov.uk/Library/registration/pdfs/gmc.pdf*. But cf. the Commission's decision on the application for registration of Good News for Israel, February 5, 2004 (establishment of the state of Israel did not justify departing from *Keren Kayemeth Le Jisroel Ltd v IRC* [1931] 2 K.B. 465 to hold that settlement of Jewish people in the Holy Land can now be accepted as furthering a religious purpose when previously it could not). The Commission considers itself justified in departing from previous court decisions on the grounds of changed social and economic circumstances because the courts have done the same thing: e.g. *National Anti-Vivisection Soc v IRC* [1948] A.C. 31, where the HL departed from *Re Foveaux* [1895] 2 Ch. 501, in holding that anti-vivisection was not a charitable purpose.

activity, save to the extent that it invariably holds that purposes which are explicitly adopted as government policy are for the public benefit.[70]

To the extent that the Commission's approach reveals something of its policy calculations about public resource allocation, it does at least bring some transparency to the decision-making process. But the question remains, whether it is desirable for the Commission and the courts to formulate policy in this area at all? In *Dingle v Turner*, Lord Cross held that "in answering the question whether any given trust is a charitable trust the courts . . . cannot avoid having regard to the fiscal privileges accorded to charities",[71] but three other law lords in the case disassociated themselves from these remarks, considering that questions of public resource allocation are unsuited for judicial determination.[72] However, ignoring the issue does not make it go away: like it or not, the courts and the Charity Commission have effectively been left to decide such questions because successive governments have not wished to take responsibility for doing so. **6–23**

iii. Construction of Trust Documents

Where the purposes of a trust or body are clearly set out in a document, the question whether these purposes are charitable must be decided by sole reference to the document, and it is irrelevant how the settlor or founders of the organisation contemplated that the purposes should be pursued.[73] The Charity Commission currently refuses to register some charities whose objects clauses use descriptions that have been lifted directly from the list in the Charities Act 2006 s.2(2), on the ground that although some of the descriptions in this list have clear meanings in law, others are ambiguous and could be interpreted as including purposes that the law has not recognised as charitable. It seems unlikely that this is a tenable position, given that s.2(5) expressly preserves the old common law meanings of the terms used in s.2(2).[74] **6–24**

If the trustees of a charity are given powers which are expressed to be incidental, but the court finds that the exercise of these powers is in substance a non-charitable purpose of the trust, then the trust will not be wholly or exclusively charitable.[75] Where a document is ambiguous, so that it is unclear whether the purposes expressed in the document are charitable, extrinsic evidence may be admitted of the manner in which the purposes have been or are capable of being carried out.[76] Some of the circumstances in which this may be needed are discussed in the Charity Commission's *Annual Report for 1966*, set out immediately below. **6–25**

---

[70] See, e.g. Charity Commission, *RR 12: The Promotion of Human Rights* (January 2005 version), noting that the UK government has incorporated the European Convention for the Protection of Human Rights into domestic law, in the course of holding that the promotion of human rights is a charitable purpose.

[71] [1972] A.C. 601 at 624.

[72] *Dingle* at 614.

[73] *Keren Kayemeth Le Jisroel Ltd v IRC* [1931] 2 K.B. 465 at 484; *IRC v Oldham Training and Enterprise Council* [1996] S.T.C. 1218 at 1234.

[74] For further discussion, see R. Holmes, "Purposes, Descriptions of Purposes and Drafting an Objects Clause" [2009] P.C.B. 295.

[75] *The Cowan Charitable Trust* [1976] Ch. Com. Rep. paras 45–49; *Vancouver Society of Immigrant and Visible Minority Women v MNR* [1999] 1 S.C.R. 10.

[76] *Incorporated Council of Law Reporting for England and Wales v Att.-Gen.* [1972] Ch. 73 at 91; *Southwood v Att.-Gen. The Times* 26 October 1998, not considered on appeal; Charity Commission, *Decision on Application for Registration by General Medical Council* (April 2, 2001), para.8; Charity Commission, *RR1a: Recognising New Charitable Purposes* (October 2001 version), para.39; Charity Commission, *Decision on Application for Registration by Crawley Model Railway Society* (12 August 2003), para.5.

CHARITY COMMISSION, *ANNUAL REPORT FOR 1966*

6–26 36. Some of our non-legal correspondents have questioned the justification for the importance which the law attaches to the words used rather than to the institution's activities. It is felt by such correspondents that it should be enough to examine the activities of the institution to decide whether it is a charity and that two organisations both doing the same things should be equally qualified for registration. But this fails to take account of the fact that the law must be concerned principally with the obligation imposed on the institution to pursue certain objects. It is this obligation which established it as a charity; and so long as an institution is free to pursue any activities it wishes it cannot be treated as an established charity however much its current activities may resemble those of other recognised charities.

6–27 37. The problem of interpreting words presents a somewhat different aspect when we are asked to consider draft documents intended to set up proposed charities. It is not unusual to find an attempt to dress up the purposes of the proposed institution in words which it is hoped will be accepted as charitable even though the purposes, so phrased, are quite remote from the true intentions of the promoters. We are convinced that this is a highly unsatisfactory course and that the governing instrument of every institution should show unequivocally what the institution really sets out to achieve. Three particular devices call for comment.

6–28 38. The first is the over-working of the word "education". Ingenious draftsmen have found it possible to embrace within this word a vast variety of activities, mainly propagandist, which do not come within the meaning of the "advancement of education" as it is used in charity law. A purpose which is not charitable cannot be made charitable merely by representing it to be a form of education.

6–29 39. The second device is the use of very wide general terms. It is of course true that there are some founders of charities, particularly those who are settling part of their own personal fortune, who genuinely expect to apply the settled property for all manner of charitable purposes; in such a case the general words are not intended to conceal a more limited true purpose. But, nonetheless, they may be difficult to interpret and it is undesirable that they should be used in any case where the proposed charity has a more limited purpose, particularly if the charity is intending to appeal to the public and not be merely the vehicle for the founder's own benevolence.

6–30 40. The third device is that of enumerating a number of objects, some perhaps charitable and others less obviously so, and then declaring that the institution is to be confined to carrying out such of the listed objects as are charitable. . . . This approach begs the question, prevents the real purpose of the institution from being readily recognised and quite unnecessarily introduces difficulty in construing and acting upon the documents in which it is used. If a proposed charity shows us a draft instrument incorporating such a phrase we consider ourselves entitled to enquire what are intended to be its activities, with a view to seeing whether those activities can be authorised in terms of clearly defined charitable purposes.

CHARITY COMMISSION, *RR.1A: RECOGNISING NEW CHARITABLE PURPOSES* (October 2001 version)

6–31 1. This publication sets out briefly the legal principles that govern charitable status and the scope which the Commission has for recognising new charitable purposes. . . .

6–32 3. In order to determine which purposes are charitable the law uses a process of precedent and analogy. The courts have decided that those purposes are charitable which fall within the objects set out in the Preamble to the Charitable Uses Act 1601 or have been held to be analogous to those objects. The Preamble contains a list of purposes which were regarded as charitable in Elizabethan times.

6–33 4. The courts added to the list of purposes which were accepted as charitable over the years and in 1891 Lord McNaghten in the *Pemsel* case[77] classified charitable purposes under four heads:

- the relief of poverty (1st head)
- the advancement of education (2nd head)

[77] *Commissioners for Special Purposes of Income Tax v Pemsel* [1891] A.C. 531.

- the advancement of religion (3rd head)
- other purposes beneficial to the community.[78]

The classification has been used since as a matter of convenience but it is not a definition.

5. Although the courts still use the Preamble as a touchstone and refer to the *Pemsel* classification, they have long recognised that what is accepted as a charitable purpose must change to reflect current social and economic circumstances. So a purpose will be charitable not only if it is within the list in the Preamble but also if it is analogous to any purpose either within it or since held to be charitable. Nowadays many charities are set up for purposes that are not mentioned in the Preamble. **6–34**

6. In this way charitable purposes have been extended and developed, by decisions of the courts and of the Charity Commissioners, so that the development of the law has reflected changes in social and economic circumstances. **6–35**

The Commission's Powers to Recognise New Charitable Purposes

7. Under section 3(1) of the Charities Act 1993, the Charity Commission has an obligation to keep a Register of institutions that are charities. In fulfilling this obligation we have the power to recognise a new purpose as charitable in circumstances where we believe the court would do so. **6–36**

8. We have the same powers as the court when determining whether an organisation has charitable status and the same powers to take into account changing social and economic circumstances—whether to recognise a purpose as charitable for the first time or to recognise that a purpose has ceased to be charitable. We interpret and apply the law as to charitable status in accordance with the principles laid down by the courts. Faced with conflicting approaches by the courts, we take a constructive approach in adapting the concept of charity to meeting the constantly evolving needs of society. The Register of Charities is therefore a reflection of the decisions made by the courts and our decisions following the example of the courts. **6–37**

9. The courts are increasingly setting out the underlying principles when deciding cases on charitable status and providing guidelines for future cases. The analysis by Slade J. in *McGovern v Att.-Gen.*[79] of the rules relating to political purposes is an example of this approach. In the same way, where appropriate, we will clarify the underlying principles raised by a particular application for registration in order to provide guidance for future applications. For example, the Commissioners, in reaching a decision on the charitable status of the Church of Scientology (England and Wales), considered and set out the underlying principles raised by that particular application for registration as a charity in order to reach their decision and so provide guidance for future applications.[80] **6–38**

Need for a flexible legal framework

10. The courts recognise that there is a need for a flexible legal framework by which new charitable purposes can be recognised in the light of changing social and economic circumstances. Lord Simonds, for example, said in the case of *National Anti-Vivisection Society v IRC.*[81] that purposes regarded as beneficial to the public and charitable in one age may not be so regarded in a later age, and vice versa. As the courts have power, in limited circumstances, not to follow previous court decisions, so do we. **6–39**

11. The courts have stressed that the law is not static and, as Lord Hailsham pointed out in *IRC v McMullen*,[82] the law must change as ideas about social values change. This has two implications: first, new objects and purposes not previously considered charitable may be held to be so; secondly, objects and purposes previously regarded as charitable may no longer be held to be charitable. Lord Wilberforce summarised the principle to be applied in *Scottish Burial Reform and Cremation Society v Glasgow Corporation*[83] when he said that the court's decisions "have to keep the law as to charities moving according as new ideas arise or old ones become obsolete or satisfied." **6–40**

---

78 Editor's note: the Charities Act 2006 s.2(2), now divides this fourth head into ten: see paras 6–47 to 6–50.

79 [1982] Ch. 321.

80 See report of the decision of the Commissioners on the application for registration by the Church of Scientology (England and Wales) which can be found on our website (*www.charitycommission.gov.uk*).

81 [1948] Ch. 31 at 74.

82 [1981] A.C. 1 at 15.

83 [1968] A.C. 138 at 154.

6–41 12. The courts have clearly indicated that they will not be rigidly bound by precedent and that a particular purpose may cease to be charitable as social circumstances change. Thus, in *National Anti-Vivisection Society v IRC*, Lord Wright said that:[84]

> ". . . trusts [providing particular remedies thought to relieve the distress caused by advanced age, sickness, disability or poverty] may, as economic ideas and conditions and ideas of social service change, cease to be regarded as being for the benefit of the community. And trusts for the advancement of learning or education may fail to secure a place as charities, if it is seen that the learning or education is not of public value."

Changing Social Circumstances

6–42 13. We also recognise the need to apply the law in changing social circumstances, although we are only able to determine which purposes are charitable in the way that the courts have done or in a way that we anticipate the courts would do. In deciding whether novel purposes are charitable or not, we seek to predict the decision the court would reach if it were to consider the matter.

6–43 14. The Commission is the first level at which an organisation may obtain a decision as to whether or not it is charitable in law. Given our predictive role in assessing whether an organisation may be charitable in anticipation of what a court itself might decide when faced with a novel charitable purpose, we may be able to recognise a new charitable purpose where the legal framework permits. It may be the case that we could also depart from previous contrary legal precedent where there has been a significant change in circumstances from when those court decisions were taken . . .

The Need for an Analogy to an Existing Purpose

6–44 23. In 1985 we reviewed our policy for deciding whether novel purposes are charitable.[85] Having examined the legal authorities, the Commissioners concluded that they must follow the courts' approach in seeking an analogy.[86] An up to date interpretation of that policy is as follows:

> "The Commission will take a constructive approach in adapting the concept of charity to meet constantly evolving social needs and new ideas through which those needs can be met. Acting within the legal framework which governs the recognition of new charitable purposes, we would aim to act constructively and imaginatively.
>
> "In considering new purposes as charitable we will look closely at those purposes which have already been recognised as charitable either under the Preamble or in subsequent decisions of the court or the Commission. We will also look at contemporary needs of society and relevant legislation passed by Parliament and, where Convention rights are in issue, to the European Convention on Human Rights and decisions of the European Court of Human Rights and the European Commission of Human Rights.
>
> "In identifying a new purpose as charitable we will, following the legal framework, need to be clear that there exists a sufficient correlation between those new purposes and purposes already accepted as charitable. While in most cases a sufficiently close analogy may be found, in others an analogy may be found by following the broad principles which may be derived from the scope of the Preamble or from decided cases of the court or the Commission.
>
> "In addition we will need to be clear that the purpose is not a political purpose as understood in charity law and that the purposes are expressed with clarity and certainty to facilitate monitoring by us and any subsequent control by the court should that be necessary."

6–45 24. In effect, our view is that we will look for a suitable analogy in order to confirm whether or not the way in which a purpose will benefit the public is charitable. We also believe it will nearly always be possible to find an analogy, if the nature of the benefit is really of a kind that ought to be recognised as charitable.

---

[84] [1948] A.C. 31 at 42.
[85] See Commissioners' *Annual Report for 1985*, paras 24–27.
[86] *Barralet v Att.-Gen.* [1980] All E.R. 918 at 926–927, per Dillon J.

> 25. Other legal authorities suggest that analogy with specific purposes already accepted as charitable is not strictly needed but that a broader analogy with the kinds of purposes already accepted as charitable is sufficient . . . We will adopt this approach where there is clear benefit to the public . . . **6–46**

4. Charitable Purposes and Public Benefit

A. *Charitable Purposes*

6–47 Before the Statute of Charitable Uses 1601, the Court of Chancery exercised jurisdiction in matters relating to charity (although in administering deceased persons' estates of personalty the ecclesiastical courts exercised a significant jurisdiction sanctioned by fines and excommunication), but notions of what was a charity were imprecise. The preamble to that statute contained a list of charitable objects which the courts used as "an index or chart" for the decision of particular cases, with the result that, in addition to the objects enumerated in the preamble, other objects analogous to them or within the spirit and intendment of the preamble came to be regarded as charitable. So, for example, in *Scottish Burial Reform and Cremation Society v Glasgow Corporation* the House of Lords held the provision of crematoria charitable by analogy with the provision of burial grounds by analogy with the upkeep of churchyards by analogy with the repair of churches.[87] This enables the courts to avoid direct assessment of the social worth of putative charitable trusts and to avoid overt value judgments.

6–48 The 1601 statute was enacted as part of a comprehensive poor law code and provided for commissioners to be appointed to investigate misappropriations of charity property. Its preamble commenced:

> "Whereas lands, chattels, money have been given by sundry well disposed persons: some for the relief of aged, impotent and poor people; the maintenance of sick and maimed soldiers and mariners, schools of learning, free schools, and scholars in universities; the repair of bridges, ports, havens, causeways, churches, sea banks and highways; the education and preferment of orphans; the relief, stock, or maintenance for houses of correction; the marriage of poor maids; the supportation aid and help of young tradesmen, handicraftsmen and persons decayed; the relief or redemption of prisoners or captives; the aid or ease of any poor inhabitants concerning payment of fifteens, setting out of soldiers and other taxes; which lands, chattels and money have not been employed according to the charitable intent of the givers by reason of frauds, breaches of trust and negligence."

6–49 The Statute of Charitable Uses 1601 was repealed by the Mortmain and Charitable Uses Act 1888, but s.13(2) of the latter Act expressly preserved the preamble to the former statute, and on the basis of its continued existence Lord Macnaghten in *Commissioners of Income Tax v Pemsel* enunciated a famous fourfold classification of charity:[88]

> " 'Charity' in its legal sense comprises four principal divisions: trusts for the relief of poverty; trusts for the advancement of education; trusts for the advancement of religion; and trusts for other purposes beneficial to the community, not falling under any of the preceding heads."

[87] [1968] A.C. 138.
[88] [1891] A.C. 531 at 583.

6–50 The Mortmain and Charitable Uses Act 1888, and with it the preamble to the Statute of Charitable Uses 1601, were repealed by the Charities Act 1960 s.38(4). Nevertheless the classification to which the Preamble gave rise continued to form the starting-point for the courts and the Charity Commission until the enactment of the Charities Act 2006. Section 2 of the 2006 Act contains a list of 13 charitable purposes, retaining the first three *Pemsel* heads, and sub-dividing the fourth into ten new heads, including a residual category of purposes which sweeps in all the existing charitable purposes which do not fall under any of the other 12 heads, and also allows for the recognition of new charitable purposes by a statutory version of the analogising process familiar from the case-law.

6–51 Note that the terms in which the statutory heads are expressed, such as "the advancement of religion", for example, are to be read in line with their meanings at common law under s.2(5). This is consistent with the Government's stated intention when putting the legislation before Parliament, which was simply to codify the existing common law rules. In some respects, however, s.2 appears to have gone further than that, and to have changed the law, in part owing to changes to the wording of the legislation as it passed through Parliament. Changes have been effected by s.2(2)(a) which recognises the prevention of poverty as a stand-alone charitable purpose; s.2(3)(a) which defines "religion" to include "a religion which does not involve belief in a god"; and s.2(3)(d) which defines "sport" to include "sports or games which promote health by involving . . . mental skill or exertion". These are all discussed further in section 5 below, when we examine each of the purposes listed in s.2 in turn.

6–52 Note, too, that some of the categories in s. 2(2) overlap, so that some purposes might fit within two or more of the descriptions of purposes listed there. Examples are trusts for the relief of those suffering from financial hardship, which could fall within s.2(2)(a) and (j); trusts for the promotion of the arts, which could fall within s.2(2)(b) and (f); and trusts for the advancement of health and care of the sick, which could fall within s.2(2)(d), (g), (j) and (l). Since the Government's main purpose in enacting s.2 was to make the law simpler and more accessible, this is unfortunate.

CHARITIES ACT 2006 SECTION 2

Meaning of "Charitable Purpose"

6–53 (1) For the purposes of the law of England and Wales, a charitable purpose is a purpose which—

(a) falls within subsection (2), and
(b) is for the public benefit (see section 3).

(2) A purpose falls within this subsection if it falls within any of the following descriptions of purposes—

(a) the prevention or relief of poverty;
(b) the advancement of education;
(c) the advancement of religion;
(d) the advancement of health or the saving of lives;
(e) the advancement of citizenship or community development;
(f) the advancement of the arts, culture, heritage or science;
(g) the advancement of amateur sport;
(h) the advancement of human rights, conflict resolution or reconciliation or the promotion of religious or racial harmony or equality and diversity;

(i) the advancement of environmental protection or improvement;
(j) the relief of those in need by reason of youth, age, ill-health, disability, financial hardship or other disadvantage;
(k) the advancement of animal welfare;
(l) the promotion of the efficiency of the armed forces of the Crown, or of the efficiency of the police, fire and rescue services or ambulance services;
(m) any other purposes within subsection (4).

(3) In subsection (2)—

(a) in paragraph (c) "religion" includes—

(i) a religion which involves belief in more than one god, and
(ii) a religion which does not involve belief in a god;

(b) in paragraph (d) "the advancement of health" includes the prevention or relief of sickness, disease or human suffering;
(c) paragraph (e) includes—

(i) rural or urban regeneration, and
(ii) the promotion of civic responsibility, volunteering, the voluntary sector or the effectiveness or efficiency of charities;

(d) in paragraph (g) "sport" means sports or games which promote health by involving physical or mental skill or exertion;
(e) paragraph (j) includes relief given by the provision of accommodation or care to the persons mentioned in that paragraph; and
(f) in paragraph (l) "fire and rescue services" means services provided by fire and rescue authorities under Part 2 of the Fire and Rescue Services Act 2004 (c.21).

(4) The purposes within this subsection (see subsection (2)(m)) are—

(a) any purposes not within paragraphs (a) to (l) of subsection (2) but recognised as charitable purposes under existing charity law or by virtue of section 1 of the Recreational Charities Act 1958 (c.17);
(b) any purposes that may reasonably be regarded as analogous to, or within the spirit of, any purposes falling within any of those paragraphs or paragraph (a) above; and
(c) any purposes that may reasonably be regarded as analogous to, or within the spirit of, any purposes which have been recognised under charity law as falling within paragraph (b) above or this paragraph.

(5) Where any of the terms used in any of paragraphs (a) to (l) of subsection (2), or in subsection (3), has a particular meaning under charity law, the term is to be taken as having the same meaning where it appears in that provision.

(6) Any reference in any enactment or document (in whatever terms)—

(a) to charitable purposes, or
(b) to institutions having purposes that are charitable under charity law,

is to be construed in accordance with subsection (1).

(7) Subsection (6)—

(a) applies whether the enactment or document was passed or made before or after the passing of this Act, but
(b) does not apply where the context otherwise requires.

(8) In this section—

"charity law" means the law relating to charities in England and Wales; and
"existing charity law" means charity law as in force immediately before the day on which this section comes into force.

B. Public Benefit

6–54 The common law has long held that a valid charitable trust must provide some identifiable and definable benefit[89] directly or indirectly for at least a section of the public, as opposed to a private class of individuals. It is clear that a trust need not benefit every person in the country to be charitable, but the courts have struggled to articulate a clear test to distinguish between charitable trusts which benefit a group of people qua members of the public, from private trusts which benefit a group of people qua private individuals.

6–55 The House of Lords in *Oppenheim v Tobacco Securities Trust Co Ltd*[90] used the personal nexus test put forward in *Re Compton* to distinguish between charitable trusts and private trusts: they held that except in "poverty" cases no class of beneficiaries can constitute a section of the public if the distinguishing quality which links them together is a relationship to a particular person either through a common ancestor or a common employer. Thus a trust for the education of the children of employees of British American Tobacco Co Ltd or any of its subsidiary or allied companies was not a valid charitable trust although there were over 110,000 current employees. If the trust had been for the education of those employed or formerly employed in the tobacco industry, however, it would have been valid as it would if it had been confined to children of those engaged in the tobacco industry in a particular county or town.

6–56 The weaknesses of the personal nexus test are revealed in the dissenting speech of Lord MacDermott in *Oppenheim*, with whose broad approach the House of Lords were in obiter agreement in *Dingle v Turner*.[91] There, Lord Cross indicated that whether or not the potential beneficiaries of a trust can fairly be said to constitute a section of the public is a question of degree in all the circumstances of the case, and that much must depend on the purposes of the trusts. If that is correct, then it means that there can be no universal test of public benefit because the question whether a purpose is charitable, and the question whether the pursuit of the purpose is for the public benefit, are not separate but interrelated questions.

6–57 Owing to the conflicting views expressed in the Lords in *Oppenheim* and *Dingle*, the lower courts and the Charity Commission have faced a dilemma in cases that compel a choice between the two views. The narrow personal nexus approach, though conducive to certainty, also leads to artificial manipulation of the legal forms so as to obtain fiscal advantages, e.g. in the case of a trust for the education of children of inhabitants of Bourneville, which might be invalidated under the broad approach as being in substance a trust benefiting employees of Cadbury Schweppes Plc. The broad approach, though less predictable in outcome, at least concerns itself with the substance of the matter and is not unduly preoccupied with form.

[89] *Gilmour v Coats* [1949] A.C. 426; *Re Pinion* [1965] Ch. 85.
[90] [1951] A.C. 297.
[91] [1972] A.C. 601.

6–58 The common law in this area has now been overtaken by the Charities Act 2006. In s.3, which concerns the public benefit requirement, the common law rules have been kept in play by subs.(3), save to the extent that subs.(2) eliminates the presumption that was formerly made in favour of charities relieving poverty, advancing education, and advancing religion, that they are for the public benefit.[92] Bodies falling under any of these heads must now affirmatively prove public benefit like everyone else.

6–59 A second, more significant change to the law was wrought by s.4, which places the Charity Commission under a duty to issue guidance "to promote awareness and understanding" of the public benefit requirement, to which guidance charity trustees are bound to "have regard" when exercising relevant powers and duties. This measure represents a compromise between MPs who pressed for a statutory definition of public benefit to be included in the legislation, essentially because they wished to use this as a stick with which to beat fee-charging charities, especially independent schools, and the Government, which preferred to skirt around the politically divisive issue of whether independent schools should continue to enjoy charitable status in the UK. As a result the Charity Commission now has the task of developing the law on public benefit, and has come under political pressure to take a more proactive line on this issue, notwithstanding its supposed status as an independent regulator. This it has now started to do. Following a consultation process with the charity sector, it has developed a set of principles that will underpin its decisions on public benefit, and it has published these in a series of guidance documents. These comprise a generic guidance document,[93] part of which is reproduced below to give a flavour of the Commission's overall approach, and a series of more focused supplementary guidance documents which consider issues specific to different charitable purposes.[94] They have also issued a document on the contentious issue of fee charging, part of which is also reproduced below.[95]

CHARITIES ACT 2006 SECTIONS 3 AND 4

3. The "Public Benefit" Test

6–60 (1) This section applies in connection with the requirement in section 2(1)(b) that a purpose falling within section 2(2) must be for the public benefit if it is to be a charitable purpose.

(2) In determining whether that requirement is satisfied in relation to any such purpose, it is not to be presumed that a purpose of a particular description is for the public benefit.

(3) In this Part any reference to the public benefit is a reference to the public benefit as that term is understood for the purposes of the law relating to charities in England and Wales.

(4) Subsection (3) applies subject to subsection (2).

4. Guidance as to Operation of Public Benefit Requirement

6–61 (1) The Charity Commission for England and Wales (see section 6 of this Act) must issue guidance in pursuance of its public benefit objective.

---

92 *National Anti-Vivisection Society v IRC* [1948] A.C. 31 at 42.

93 Charity Commission, *Charities and Public Benefit* (January 2008 version). See too Charity Commission, *Analysis of the Law Underpinning Charities and Public Benefit* (December 2008 version).

94 Charity Commission, *The Prevention or Relief of Poverty for the Public Benefit* (December 2008 version); *The Advancement of Religion for the Public Benefit* (December 2008 version); *The Advancement of Education for the Public Benefit* (December 2008 version).

95 *Public Benefit and Fee-Charging* (December 2008 version).

(2) That objective is to promote awareness and understanding of the operation of the requirement mentioned in section 3(1) (see section 1B(3) and (4) of the Charities Act 1993 (c.10), as inserted by section 7 of this Act).

(3) The Commission may from time to time revise any guidance issued under this section.

(4) The Commission must carry out such public and other consultation as it considers appropriate—

(a) before issuing any guidance under this section, or
(b) (unless it considers that it is unnecessary to do so) before revising any such guidance.

(5) The Commission must publish any guidance issued or revised under this section in such manner as it considers appropriate.

(6) The charity trustees of a charity must have regard to any such guidance when exercising any powers or duties to which the guidance is relevant.

CHARITY COMMISSION, *CHARITIES AND PUBLIC BENEFIT* (January 2008 version)

THE PRINCIPLES OF PUBLIC BENEFIT

E. Principle 1: There must be an Identifiable Benefit or Benefits

E1. Important Factors to Consider

6–62 The following are important factors to consider when deciding whether an organisation's aims meet the "benefit" principle of the public benefit requirement:

Principle 1a It must be clear what the benefits are

Principle 1b The benefits must be related to the aims

Principle 1c Benefits must be balanced against any detriment or harm

E2. Principle 1a It Must be Clear what the Benefits Are

6–63 It must be clear what benefits to the public arise from carrying out a charity's aims. Different charitable aims will involve different sorts of benefits. . . .

6–64 In assessing the public benefit of an individual organisation we are concerned only with the benefits that arise from that organisation carrying out its particular aims. The fact that it may be argued there are benefits to the public generally from specific types of charity carrying out particular charitable purposes does not mean that those benefits can simply be claimed by any organisation having those charitable purposes in its objects.

6–65 For example, there is undoubtedly an overall benefit to society from having charities that undertake cancer research. But that general benefit cannot necessarily be claimed by every organisation undertaking that sort of research. What matters is what research the particular organisation is doing, how it does it and what it does with the results. A cancer research charity that undertakes properly conducted research into finding a cure or new treatment for a particular form of cancer, and that publishes the useful results of that research from which others can learn, will provide significant benefits to the public. But, whatever overall benefit there is to society from cancer research in general, that benefit would count for very little in assessing the public benefit of an organisation conducting cancer research if the methods it used were not scientifically rigorous for example.

6–66 The benefits to the public should be capable of being recognised, identified, defined or described but that does not mean that they also have to be capable of being quantified or measured. For example, the benefits of an appreciation of a beautiful landscape, or of viewing works of art or the performing arts, spiritual contemplation, or the positive feelings we have when we help sick animals, can still be identified and experienced even though they are not touched or seen and cannot be quantified or measured.

Benefits that can be quantified and measured may be easier to identify, but we also take non-quantifiable benefits into consideration, provided it is clear what the benefits are. The benefits may or may not be physically experienced. Indeed, some benefits can seem quite remote or difficult to quantify, such as the benefits to the public generally from conserving the environment. **6–67**

In some cases an organisation's aims may be so clearly beneficial to the public that there will be no need for the organisation to provide evidence to demonstrate that there is a benefit. For example, providing emergency aid to the victims of a natural disaster would not normally require special evidence to show that it is beneficial. **6–68**

In other cases, the element of benefit to the public may be more debatable, or may depend on the circumstances, and will need to be shown by evidence. For example, it may be necessary to show the architectural or historical merit of a building that is to be preserved, or the artistic merit of an art collection, where that is not obvious. **6–69**

The nature of any evidence would depend upon the nature of the benefit. In some cases we may ask for evidence of independent, expert opinion from someone qualified in a particular field. In some cases, we may take a general consensus of objective and informed opinion into consideration. It will usually be for an organisation's founders or trustees to provide evidence which shows that their organisation's aims are for the public benefit. In some cases, we may also seek evidence from others outside the organisation where that is necessary to either confirm or refute the evidence provided by the organisation. **6–70**

In considering whether a benefit is clear, the courts have taken the view that they are not in a position to judge whether or not a political purpose is for the public benefit. Nor, by analogy, is the Charity Commission or the Charity Tribunal. A "political purpose" means any purpose directed at furthering the interests of any political party; or securing, or opposing, any change in the law or in the policy or decisions of central government or local authorities, whether in this country or abroad. This means that a political purpose cannot meet the public benefit requirement and so cannot be a charitable purpose. However, charities do have a great deal of freedom and flexibility to undertake political activities and campaigning as a way of carrying out their charitable aims. . . . **6–71**

E3. Principle 1b The Benefits must be Related to the Aims

All charities must act within their charitable aims. In assessing public benefit we will take into account any benefits that arise from carrying out those aims. **6–72**

The Charities Act provides that, to be a charity, an organisation must have charitable aims only and that, for an aim to be charitable, it must be for the public benefit. This means that, when assessing whether an organisation meets the public benefit requirement, the benefits that are relevant for us to take into consideration are those that arise as a result of the organisation pursuing its charitable aims. **6–73**

Where an organisation has more than one aim, each of those aims must be for the public benefit. The public benefit shown by one or more of its aims cannot be used to "off-set" any lack of public benefit of its other aims. For example, an arts charity promotes the arts by staging high-class operatic performances in a building which is of historic and architectural importance. It has two aims. The first aim is to advance the art of opera. The second is to preserve an important national building. It would not be sufficient, for example, if the second aim was for the public benefit but not the first. . . . **6–74**

Some charities carry out incidental activities that are not related to achieving their charitable aims. Such activities may be permitted, on the basis that they are a small or incidental part of what the charity does, but any benefit arising from such activities would not count towards any public benefit assessment of the charity's aims. For example, an amateur sport charity might take a collection for the victims of a disaster. This may be a permitted incidental activity. But the public benefit arising from the relief of need of the disaster victims does not have a sufficient connection with their charitable aim of advancing amateur sport to count in the public benefit assessment of that aim. **6–75**

Sometimes benefits arise from what a charity does that are accidental or unplanned and that are not related to its aims. For example, a charity concerned with the preservation of a particular historical building provides a skating rink in the courtyard to attract visitors and enhance their appreciation of the neighbouring building. The enhanced appreciation of the building and its surroundings will count towards the public benefit assessment. However, the health benefits some people may derive from the physical exercise of skating will not count in the public benefit assessment because it does not have sufficient connection with the building preservation aims of the charity. **6–76**

6–77 Benefits to the public that are not related to an organisation's aims cannot be used as a way of demonstrating that the aims are for the public benefit. They are not therefore taken into account when assessing public benefit.

6–78 For this reason, it is important for organisations to be able to identify what they believe is covered by their aims, as set out in their stated objects, and articulate that clearly. This is so that we (or the Charity Tribunal or the courts) can make informed decisions about whether the scope of those aims is charitable, and which benefits are related to those aims. Where an organisation's work gives rise to significant benefits that we consider are unrelated to its aims, as expressed in its stated objects, this may indicate that:

> the organisation's objects do not adequately reflect its aims or the full range of its activities; or
>
> the organisation is carrying out activities that fall outside its stated objects and which may indicate it is acting in breach of its trusts.

This might result in either our:

> asking the charity trustees to widen, or restate, the organisation's objects to better reflect its aims, the benefits of which would then count in a public benefit assessment;
>
> asking the charity trustees to stop those activities that are not in accordance with its aims, where it is clearly inappropriate for such activities to continue; or
>
> allowing the activities to continue, where that is appropriate, but explaining that the benefits of such activities will not count in any public benefit assessment of the charity.

E4. Principle 1c Benefits must be Balanced against any Detriment or Harm

6–79 "Benefit" means the overall or net benefit to the public. It is not simply a question of showing that some benefit may result.

6–80 The achievement of a particular aim may be of some benefit to the public but, in achieving that benefit, may also have detrimental or harmful effects. In assessing the public benefit of individual organisations, we will consider any evidence of significant detrimental or harmful effects of that organisation carrying out its aims in its particular circumstances. There would need to be some real evidence of detriment or harm; it cannot just be supposed.

6–81 The existence of detriment or harm does not necessarily mean that the organisation cannot be charitable. It is a question of balancing the benefits against the detriment or harm. If the detrimental or harmful consequences are greater than the benefits, the overall result is that the organisation would not be charitable.

6–82 Examples of things that might be evidenced to be detrimental or harmful might include:

> something that is damaging to the environment;
>
> something that is dangerous or damaging to mental or physical health;
>
> something that encourages or promotes violence or hatred towards others;
>
> unlawfully restricting a person's freedom.

6–83 No organisation that has aims that are illegal, or that intentionally deceives or misrepresents its aims and so is a sham, can be a charity. Where that sort of detriment or harm is present then there is no balancing to be done as, notwithstanding any benefits that might arise from carrying out the organisation's aims, it cannot be recognised as charitable. . . .

F. Principle 2: Benefit must be to the Public, or a Section of the Public

F1. Important Factors to Consider

6–84 The following are important factors to consider when deciding whether an organisation's aims meet the "public" principle of the public benefit requirement:

Principle 2a The beneficiaries must be appropriate to the aims (see section F2)

Principle 2b Where benefit is to a section of the public, the opportunity to benefit must not be unreasonably restricted (see section F3)

by geographical or other restrictions (see sections F4–F9) or

by ability to pay any fees charged (see section F10)

Principle 2c People in poverty must not be excluded from the opportunity to benefit (see section F11)

Principle 2d Any private benefits must be incidental (see section F12) F2.

Principle 2a The Beneficiaries must be Appropriate to the Aims

Who constitutes "the public, or a section of the public" for any organisation is based on those whom the organisation's aims are primarily intended to benefit. **6–85**

Sometimes the aims are intended to benefit the public generally and sometimes a section of the public. Who benefits, and in what way, will vary depending on the organisation's aims. For example, in the case of a charity providing a local village hall or community centre, the aims might be intended to benefit people living in a particular town or village. In the case of a medical research charity, the aims might be intended to benefit the sufferers of a particular disease. In the case of a charity concerned with conserving an endangered species, the aims might be intended to benefit humanity. **6–86**

Who constitutes "the public, or a section of the public" is not a simple matter of numbers, but the number of people who can potentially benefit (now or in the future) must not be negligible. What is important is who could benefit, as well as who is benefiting. The class of people who can benefit must be a public class. In general, the public class must be sufficiently large or open in nature given the charitable aim that is to be carried out. The actual number of people who can benefit at one time can be quite small provided that anyone who qualifies as a beneficiary is eligible to be considered. A charity is for the public benefit if the benefits it offers are made widely available, even though in practice only a few people from time to time are able to benefit. For example, a charity with a legitimately small number of beneficiaries might be one that offers only a small number of places for the services it provides, such as a small number of available rooms in an almshouse or care home. What is important is that anyone who is eligible to apply can be considered for those places. **6–87**

"The public, or a section of the public" can include members of future generations as well as today's generation. However, in general, benefiting future generations should not come entirely at the expense of today's. There is a balance to be struck between providing for future generations and benefiting people today. For example, in order to ensure the sustainability of the planet for future generations, it may be necessary for today's generation to make certain lifestyle changes or accommodate short-term restrictions or limitations in order to secure longer-term environmental benefits for the future. Similarly, it may be necessary to restrict or deny access to an important archaeological site or conservation area to today's generation in order to preserve it for the future. But equally, the benefit, for example, of providing for the relief of hunger of future generations needs to be balanced against the need to provide for people who are starving today. **6–88**

If the aims are intended to benefit the general public then that clearly constitutes a public class of people. Where the aims are intended to benefit a section of the public, the people who can benefit must be a sufficiently "public" class of people for it to be said that the aims are for the "public" benefit. That means making sure that the opportunity for people to benefit is not unreasonably restricted given the nature of the charitable aims to be carried out and the resources available to the organisation. **6–89**

If the class of people whom the aims are intended to benefit is unreasonably restricted then they are not "a section of the public". Where that is the case, the organisation would have to widen the class of people who can benefit, or it would not meet the public benefit requirement. . . . **6–90**

CHARITY COMMISSION *PUBLIC BENEFIT AND FEE-CHARGING* (December 2008 version)

C. Fee-charging as a public benefit issue

6–91 . . . Fee-charging is likely to be a public benefit issue where:

> the service or facility that is charged for forms a significant part of the charity's aims, or the way it carries out those aims; and/or
>
> the fees that are charged for that service or facility are high.

6–92 *A significant part of the charity's aims:* where a charity's sole or main aim, or way it carries out its aims, is to provide a service or facility for which it charges, the level of fees it charges is significant when assessing whether the organisation is carrying out those aims for the public benefit. This is because it has a bearing on who has the opportunity to benefit from that service or facility and, in particular, the extent to which the charity can show that its aims meet public benefit principles 2b and 2c.

6–93 Where the service or facility that is charged for is an insignificant aspect of what the charity does, or is just one of many ways in which the charity carries out its aims, many of which are not charged for, then fee-charging is generally less of a public benefit issue. . . .

6–94 *Charities charging low fees:* where a charity charges low fees that most people can afford, then the fee-charging is unlikely to give rise to public benefit difficulties. In most cases it will not be necessary for those charities to demonstrate any further opportunities to benefit since the low fees do not prevent people from having the opportunity to benefit from the charity's services or facilities. . . .

6–95 *Charities charging high fees:* where a charity charges high fees that many people could not afford, the trustees must ensure that:

> the benefits are not unreasonably restricted by a person's ability to pay; and that
>
> people in poverty are not excluded from the opportunity to benefit.

The charity trustees must therefore demonstrate that there is sufficient opportunity for people who cannot afford those fees to benefit in a material way that is related to the charity's aims. . . .

6–96 *Opportunities to benefit*: there must be sufficient *opportunity* to benefit for people who cannot afford to pay the fees charged for the services or facilities provided by the charity. It does not mean that people who cannot afford the fees must actually benefit. What is important is that they must not be excluded from the opportunity to benefit, whether or not they actually choose to do so. However, the opportunity to benefit should be genuine and meaningful. If the opportunity to benefit that is provided is not genuine, or is meaningless or trivial, then it would count for very little in a public benefit assessment.

6–97 . . . Some fee-charging charity trustees might wish to argue that there are wider or remote benefits to the public at large that arise from carrying out their charity's aims and that these benefits should be regarded as opportunities to benefit for people who cannot afford the fees.

6–98 For example, this might include wider or remote benefits such as:

> the general relief of public expenditure from a charity doing something that the state would otherwise have to provide, such as relieving the exchequer of the cost of educating children at state schools or treating patients at NHS hospitals; or
>
> benefits to the nation from educating students who go on to become, for example, successful entrepreneurs or scientists; or
>
> other sorts of wider or remote benefits to the public that might be claimed by any charity carrying out a charitable aim, such as encouraging charitable giving or volunteering.

6–99 In cases where such public benefits are clear and related to the charity's aims, they might be relevant when considering the public benefit of a fee-charging charity in relation to public benefit principle 1a. . . .

However, we do not consider that they are opportunities to benefit in a "material way" for people who cannot afford the fees. For that reason we do not consider they are relevant when considering the extent to which a charity meets public benefit principles 2b and 2c. . . .

Fee-charging charities must ensure that there are sufficient opportunities to benefit for people who cannot afford the fees. There are many different ways of doing this. **6–100**

This might be by: **6–101**

> *offering free or subsidised access*: enabling people who cannot afford the fees to access the service or facility by offering it at a reduced rate or for no fee, or via schemes or arrangements which offer financial assistance to help meet the cost of the fees;
>
> *providing other significant opportunities to benefit*: providing other significant opportunities to benefit that do not involve free or subsidised access to the service or facility that is charged for.

Trustees' discretion: it is for the charity's trustees to decide what sorts of opportunities to benefit they wish, and are able, to provide for people who cannot afford the fees, taking into consideration what is appropriate in their charity's circumstances. However, what is provided must be sufficient to satisfy principles 2b and 2c. **6–102**

Satisfying Principles 2b and 2c: **6–103**

> where a charity provides a sufficient amount of free or subsidised access (in the context of the charity's circumstances) to people who cannot afford the fees, this will satisfy principles 2b and 2c;
>
> where a charity provides a combination of free or subsidised access and other significant opportunities to benefit, we can take into account the totality of the opportunities to benefit it provides;
>
> where a charity provides other significant opportunities to benefit, but offers no free or subsidised access, the trustees must be able to demonstrate in what other ways the opportunities to benefit that the charity provides clearly satisfy principles 2b and 2c.

We will look at each case on its own merits and in the context of the individual charity's circumstances.

Totality of benefits: in assessing whether a charity provides sufficient opportunity to benefit for people who cannot afford the fees, we will consider the totality of the opportunities to benefit that the charity provides. . . . **6–104**

Percentage of free or subsidised access: there is no "one-size-fits-all" amount, or percentage, of free or subsidised access that fee-charging charities must offer. **6–105**

We cannot specify how many concessionary tickets a theatre should offer, or suggest a percentage of bursaries that all independent schools should offer, or say how many free beds should be available at a hospital. **6–106**

It is primarily for the trustees of the charity to decide for themselves the extent to which they offer free or subsidised access, and how much to offer to how many people, provided they can show that people who cannot afford the fees have sufficient opportunity to benefit in a material way that is related to the charity's aims. **6–107**

We have to consider what is reasonable and appropriate in each particular charity's circumstances. Offering free or subsidised access costs money and so can clearly impact on the financial situation of a charity. What is appropriate and sufficient will vary from charity to charity, depending upon, amongst other things: its charitable aims; the level of the fees charged; any relevant local needs or factors; and the resources available to the charity. **6–108**

It is unusual for a charity that charges high fees to offer no free or subsidised access. Typically, most such charities offer concessions on fees, or assistance with fees, and might also provide other significant opportunities to benefit alongside offering some free or subsidised access. . . . **6–109**

Measures aimed at people who cannot afford the fees: measures that are designed specifically, and exclusively, to assist people who cannot afford the fees are likely to provide greater opportunity to benefit than other measures. **6–110**

6–111 For example, in the context of charitable independent schools, it means that bursaries (which are usually specifically aimed at assisting children from poorer families) are likely to provide a greater opportunity to benefit to people who cannot afford the fees than would be the case with scholarships (which are usually open to anyone to apply for and which are awarded solely on academic merit).

6–112 Bursaries usually still require the applicant to show academic merit (e.g. to meet entrance requirements) but should guarantee that children, whose parents or guardians are unable to pay the fees, are given sufficient opportunity to benefit. . . .

6–113 *Providing other significant opportunities to benefit that meet local needs:* it is possible that, in looking to ensure that the public benefit requirement is met, trustees will seek opportunities to work with other service and facility providers. We do not want charities, as a result of the public benefit requirement, to provide opportunities to benefit that are not desired or valued. Charity trustees should have regard to whether the way in which they propose providing other significant opportunities to benefit are relevant and desired.

6–114 If trustees decide to explore providing other significant opportunities to benefit to meet local needs, we recommend that they engage with their partners and local communities. This is so that they can properly and sufficiently discuss and evaluate local needs when deciding what sort of services, facilities or collaboration to provide. Trustees might want to use peer review or other forms of quality assessment to assist them.

6–115 Examples of other significant opportunities to benefit that are not wanted or required, because they do not meet the needs of the intended beneficiaries, might include:

> a charitable hospital that argues that it offered the local NHS hospital the use of a consultant specialising in children's illnesses but the NHS hospital refused the offer. Where the local NHS hospital caters only for elderly patients, or if it already has sufficient medical staff, the opportunity offered by the charity would have no effect in showing that it provides other significant opportunities to benefit. In this case, the charitable hospital might provide more significant opportunities to benefit if it consults the local NHS hospital about what it could offer that would be of more assistance to the NHS hospital and to benefit people locally;
>
> a charitable independent school that offers to provide teaching staff to the local state school for certain subjects but the subject areas offered are not required by the local state school. In this case, it would be more beneficial for the trustees of the independent school to consult other education providers locally about how to achieve the maximum impact from sharing resources. It could then target the charity's assistance to state schools and other educational establishments most in need of help in ways that are likely to make most difference to their students.

C. Political Purposes

6–116 Trusts for political purposes are non-charitable on the basis that the courts have no means of judging whether a proposed change in the law would or would not be for the public benefit,[96] and the law could not stultify itself by holding that it was for the public benefit that the law itself should be changed.[97] Political purposes comprise not only attempts to change the law by legislation or to oppose proposed changes but also attempts to influence local or national government home or foreign policy.[98]

---

[96] *Bowman v Secular Society* [1917] A.C. 406 at 442, per Lord Parker.

[97] *National Anti-Vivisection Society v IRC* [1948] A.C. 31 at 49 and 62. See also *Bonar Law Memorial Trust v IRC* (1933) 49 T.L.R. 220 (Conservative); *Re Ogden* [1933] Ch. 678 (Liberal); *Re Hopkinson* [1949] W.N. 29 (Socialist); *Re Strakosch* [1949] Ch. 529 (appeasing racial feeling); *Re Bushnell* [1975] 1 W.L.R. 1596 (furthering socialised medicine in a socialist state).

[98] See *Baldry v Feintuck* [1972] 1 W.L.R. 552; *Webb v O'Doherty* (1991) 3 Admin. L.R. 731; *Re Koeppler's WT* [1984] Ch. 243. In *Southwood v Att.-Gen.* [2000] W.T.L.R. 1199 the Court of Appeal held that a trust to educate the public to accept that peace is best secured by demilitarisation and disarmament was political and non-charitable.

However, if a body which exists for wider charitable purposes incidentally pursues political activity so as to put pressure on the public and politicians this does not affect the charitable status of the body, e.g. the RSPCA fighting vivisection, the British Legion fighting for better pensions for former servicemen, or Guide Dogs for the Blind resisting VAT on dog food. Certain registered charities such as the Child Poverty Action Group, Oxfam and Shelter walked the tightrope so precariously that the Charity Commissioners were prompted to publish guidance on this issue, which emphasised the constraints on charities in this area. This guidance was subsequently amended to strike a more positive note, by stressing the benefits to be had from charities playing an advocacy and campaigning role.[99] The recent recognition of the promotion of human rights as a charitable purpose has also had a liberalising effect on the rules in this area,[100] which were recently reviewed in *Hanchett-Stamford v Att.-Gen.*,[101] the relevant parts of which are reproduced immediately below. **6–117**

HANCHETT-STAMFORD v ATTORNEY-GENERAL

Chancery Division [2009] Ch. 173, [2009] 2 W.L.R. 405, [2008] 4 All E.R. 323

In 1914 the Performing and Captive Animals Defence League was founded as an unincorporated association. Its purposes included bringing about a ban on performing animals. In 1949, following the decision in *National Anti-Vivisection Society v IRC*,[102] the Inland Revenue decided that the league did not have charitable status since its principal object was to change the law. Mr and Mrs Hanchett-Stamford joined the league as life members in the mid-1960s, and after her husband's death in 2006, Mrs Hanchett-Stamford was left as the sole surviving member. She decided to wind up the league and to transfer its assets to an active animal charity. Hence she sought a declaration that the work and objects of the league were charitable under the Charities Act 2006 s.2(2)(k) and an order appointing herself and her solicitor as trustees of the fund. Lewison J. refused the relief sought, holding that the league's purposes were not exclusively charitable because one of its objects was seeking a change in the law to ban performing animals. However he also held that on her husband's death the league had ceased to exist and its rules had ceased to bind Mrs Hanchett-Stamford, who was therefore entitled to its assets absolutely as its sole surviving member. His analysis of the latter point is reproduced at paras 14–76 ff. **6–118**

LEWISON J. stated the facts and continued: . . . The league has never been incorporated. It is therefore an unincorporated association. Accordingly, unless its assets are held on charitable trusts, they belong in some sense to its members for the time being. I will need to examine this generalisation more closely in due course. If, on the other hand, its assets are held on charitable trusts then none of the members of the league can have a claim to beneficial ownership of them. Nevertheless, it is convenient, for the purposes of discussion to refer to the assets as "the assets of the league". It seems to me, therefore, that the first issue I must address is: are the assets of the league held on charitable trusts? The general rule is that in order to achieve charitable status a trust, however philanthropic, must satisfy each of the following three requirements. (1) It must be of a charitable nature, within the spirit and intendment of the preamble to the Charitable Uses Act 1601 (43 Eliz. 1, c.4) as interpreted by the courts and extended by statute. (2) It must promote a public benefit of a nature recognised by the courts as a public benefit. (3) The purposes of the trust must be wholly and exclusively charitable. **6–119**

The key element of any charitable trust is that it exists for the benefit of the public. The benefit to the public may be direct or indirect. It is the indirect benefit to the public which has enabled the law to uphold **6–120**

[99] Charity Commission, *CC 9: Speaking Out—Guidance on Campaigning and Political Activities by Charities* (March 2008 version).

[100] Charity Commission, *RR 12: The Promotion of Human Rights* (January 2005 version); Charities Act 2006 s.2(2)(h). See paras 6–276 ff.; and also Charity Commission, *Decision on English PEN's Application for Registration as a Charity*, July 21, 2008

[101] [2009] Ch. 173.

[102] [1948] A.C. 31.

as charitable trusts for the prevention of cruelty to animals. The Hobbesian view of humanity that underlies this (an innate tendency to cruelty) was explained in *Re Wedgwood*:[103]

> "A gift for the benefit and protection of animals tends to promote and encourage kindness towards them, to discourage cruelty, and to ameliorate the condition of the brute creation, and thus to stimulate humane and generous sentiments in man towards the lower animals, and by these means promote feelings of humanity and morality generally, repress brutality, and thus elevate the human race."

6–121 Accordingly, a trust that had as its sole object the prevention of cruelty to performing animals would be capable of being a charitable trust. The advancement of animal welfare is now expressly recognised as a charitable purpose by section 2(2)(k) of the Charities Act 2006. I do not, however, regard this as a significant change in the law.

6–122 However, as Mr Sims points out on behalf of the Attorney-General, in principle where the purpose or one of the purposes of a trust is to change the law the courts have refused to recognise the trust as charitable. A number of reasons have been given for this approach. First, it has been said that the courts cannot evaluate whether the advocated change in the law would or would not be for the benefit of the public. In *Bowman v Secular Society Ltd* Lord Parker of Waddington said:[104]

> "It is true that a gift to an association formed for their attainment may, if the association be unincorporated, be upheld as an absolute gift to its members, or, if the association be incorporated, as an absolute gift to the corporate body; but a trust for the attainment of political objects has always been held invalid, not because it is illegal, for everyone is at liberty to advocate or promote by any lawful means a change in the law, but because the court has no means of judging whether a proposed change in the law will or will not be for the public benefit, and therefore cannot say that a gift to secure the change is a charitable gift."

6–123 However, this may be too dogmatic a view. In *National Anti-Vivisection Society v IRC*[105] the House of Lords did evaluate the competing arguments for and against the abolition of vivisection; and came to the clear conclusion that the benefits to the public in terms of scientific and medical research outweighed the harm caused by the suffering of animals that vivisection necessarily entailed. A second reason that has been given is that law cannot stultify itself by holding that it is for the public benefit that the law itself should be changed; and that each court must decide on the principle that the law is right as it stands. This was the reason put forward by both Lord Wright and Lord Simonds in the *National Anti-Vivisection Society* case. A third reason is that if the courts sanction as charitable trusts with the purpose of changing the law, they would be trespassing on the role of the legislature, whose constitutional responsibility it is to evaluate the need for such changes. This was one of the reasons given by Slade J. in *McGovern v AG*[106] and by Chadwick L.J. in *Southwood v AG*[107] This last reason seems to me to be the most persuasive. But whatever the rationale, there is no doubt that the principle remains that a trust, one of whose purposes is to change the law, cannot be charitable.

6–124 That is not to say that it is unlawful for a charity to promote or oppose changes in the law, provided that its purposes are exclusively charitable. There is a distinction between the purposes or objects of a charity and the means by which it promotes those purposes or objects. Thus the Charity Commission is able to issue guidance to charities and charity trustees about the extent to which they can engage in campaigning, including campaigns to change the law. However, that guidance still takes as its bedrock the principle that an organisation set up for the purpose of changing the law cannot be a charity.

6–125 Looking at the statement of the league's objectives there can be little doubt, in my judgment, that at least one of its significant purposes was to change the law. It is true that it asserted that the particular acts of cruelty against which it was campaigning were already illegal as a result of the Protection of Animals

---

[103] [1915] 1 Ch. 113 at 122.
[104] [1917] A.C. 406 at 442.
[105] [1948] A.C. 31.
[106] [1982] Ch. 321.
[107] [2000] W.T.L.R. 1199.

Act 1911, but plainly its founders considered that that Act was not enough and that more legislation was needed. It seems probable that the members of the league had a wider conception of cruelty than the law did. The booklet also asserted that it was impossible to train any performing animal without cruelty and it is clear, in my judgment, that the league's aim was to ban performing animals completely (hence the reference to "just compensation to the trade"). This would undoubtedly represent a change in the law just as much as banning fox-hunting or the farming of mink. In my judgment this has the consequence that at its inception the league was not a charitable organisation. Ms Maclennan, who appeared for Mrs Hanchett-Stamford, did not argue strenuously that the league was charitable at its inception. I think that there were pragmatic reasons behind her stance, but I must apply the law as I perceive it to be.

However, Ms Maclennan submits that even if the objects of the league were not charitable at its inception, they have since become charitable. She puts this argument in two ways. (i) The objects of the league have become charitable as a result of changes in the law; alternatively (ii) the objects of the league have become charitable, or its assets held on charitable trusts, as a result of the decision of Mr and Mrs Hanchett-Stamford to transfer those assets to the Born Free Foundation. **6–126**

In support of the first argument she relies on the story of the General Medical Council ("GMC"). The question of the charitable status of the GMC arose in *General Medical Council v IRC*[108] The GMC was first established by the Medical Act 1858 and incorporated by the Medical Council Act 1862. Its principal objects were to keep and publish a register of qualified medical practitioners, to exercise oversight over medical studies and examinations and to publish the British Pharmacopaeia. It also had the power to strike off practitioners in certain circumstances. Only registered practitioners were entitled to sue for their fees. The Inland Revenue decided that the GMC had not been established for exclusively charitable purposes and the GMC's appeal against that decision was dismissed both by Rowlatt J. and by the Court of Appeal. The point which decided the case was that the GMC was established principally for the benefit of the medical profession and that any benefit to the public was an incidental and secondary benefit, not least because only a registered practitioner could sue for his fees. However, in 2001 the GMC applied to the Charity Commission for registration as a charity; and this time the application succeeded. The commission summarised its decision as follows: **6–127**

> "2.2.1 There had been sufficient changes in the relevant legal framework, to the constitution and activities of the GMC and the social and economic context within which the GMC operates, taken together, for them to reconsider the charitable status of the GMC despite the prevailing legal authorities.
>
> "2.2.2 It was open to them to adopt a purposive construction to the statutory provisions constituting the GMC to ascertain the purpose for which it was established.
>
> "2.2.3 The GMC is established for the charitable purpose of the protection, promotion and maintenance of the health and safety of the community by ensuring proper standards in the practice of medicine."

The commission considered that there had been no major changes in the law, although they referred to other cases in which it had been held that the regulation of a profession could be charitable. However, the commission considered that there had been major changes to the GMC's own powers and functions with the result that the GMC was a body "significantly different to the body constituted under the Medical Act 1858 and to the body considered in the GMC case". It noted also that the introduction of the National Health Service had transformed the environment within which medical services were provided (no doubt diminishing the need for most medical practitioners to be able to sue for their fees), and also the general recognition that the regulation of professions was in the public interest. It was these cumulative changes that persuaded the commission to re-open the question of the charitable status of the GMC. **6–128**

In the present case Ms Maclennan relies on the passing of the Animal Welfare Act 2006 as amounting to the necessary change. She also points to the explicit recognition of the advancement of animal welfare as a charitable purpose by section 2(2)(k) of the Charities Act 2006. As to this last point, as I have said, the advancement of animal welfare has long been recognised as a charitable purpose, for the reasons explained in *Re Wedgwood*.[109] I do not regard this as amounting to any change in the substance of the law. **6–129**

[108] (1928) 97 L.J.K.B. 578.
[109] [1915] 1 Ch. 113.

> The Animal Welfare Act 2006 does contain provisions which create offences of causing distress to animals; but it does not go so far as to prohibit performing animals. As is clear from its statement of policies in the 1962 booklet, the league believed that it was impossible to train performing animals without cruelty. It seems to me, on such exiguous evidence as I have, that the objectives of the league have not yet been fully attained. In other words, it still appears to be one of the objects of the league to change the law. The Charities Act 2006 has not changed the fundamental principle that if one of the objects or purposes of an organisation is to change the law, it cannot be charitable.
>
> **6–130** Ms Maclennan also submitted that the public perception of animals and their welfare had changed since the late 1940s. It was plain, she said, that the social climate had changed. Even zoos had become much more akin to educational establishments rather than places where the public could simply go to satisfy its curiosity. The problem with this submission, to my mind, was that it was just a submission. There was no evidence upon which it was based and I do not consider that an alleged social transformation of that kind is one of which the court can take judicial notice. Quite apart from anything else, if the court were to attempt to weigh up the pros and cons of banning performing animals of all kinds or preventing the establishment of municipal zoos, it would be exercising the kind of value judgment which is inappropriate for the judicial process.
>
> **6–131** I cannot accept the first argument for asserting that the league became charitable. . . .

D. No Unlawful Discrimination

6–132 It is not against public policy or unlawful in a private trust to discriminate on grounds of race, religion, nationality or colour.[110] However the Race Relations Act 1976 s.34 prohibits discrimination against persons on ground of colour, race, nationality or ethnic or national origins in the case of charitable trusts, though it allows discrimination in favour of persons of a class defined by reference to race, nationality or ethnic or national origins[111]—though not by reference to colour, so that a trust for "the black community of Hackney, Haringey, Islington and Tower Hamlets" was upheld as a valid charitable trust, but only on the basis that the word "black" was deleted.[112] In exceptional circumstances the removal of any discriminatory provision unacceptable to the original trustees is possible under the *cy-près* jurisdiction.[113]

6–133 Sexually discriminating provisions in private trusts are valid. Where a charitable trust contains a provision for benefiting persons of one sex only it is valid,[114] e.g. Boy Scouts, Girl Guides, retired schoolmasters, research fellowships available for men only.[115] In the case of an educational charity, however, the trustees can apply to the Secretary of State for Education to make the trust's benefits open to both sexes. He will make the order if satisfied that to do so would conduce to the advancement of education without sex discrimination and 25 years have elapsed since creation of the trust, unless the donor (or his personal representatives) or the personal representatives of the testator have consented in writing.[116]

6–134 Discrimination against the disabled is prescribed except that charities can treat some categories of disabled more favourably than others,[117] e.g. so the Royal National Institute for the Blind can prefer

110 *Re Lysaght* [1986] Ch. 191; *Re Dominion Students' Hall Trusts* [1947] Ch. 183; *Blathwayt v Lord Cawley* [1967] A.C. 397. The Human Rights Act 1998 may affect religious conditions.

111 For discussion of "ethnic" charities, see Charity Commission, *Decision on Applications for Registration of the Ethnic-English Trust and the Ironside Community Trust*, June 28, 2007, paras 5.8–5.21.

112 *Re Harding, deceased* [2008] Ch. 235.

113 *Re Lysaght* [1966] Ch. 191; *Re Woodhams* [1981] 1 W.L.R. 493.

114 Sex Discrimination Act 1975 s.43. See, too, the Equality Act (Sexual Orientation) Regulations 2007 reg.18, which allows charities to provide benefits only to persons of a particular sexual orientation, provided that such differential treatment is justified under art.14 of the EHRC: *Catholic Care (Diocese of Leeds) v Charity Commission* [2010] EWHC 520 (Ch).

115 *Hugh-Jones v St John's College Cambridge* (1979) 123 Sol. Jo. 603.

116 Sex Discrimination Act 1975 s.78.

117 Disability Discrimination Act 1995 s.18C.

employing visually impaired persons. Similarly, the Equality Act 2006 s.58 permits charities to discriminate in favour of, but not against, groups of people defined by reference to their religious beliefs.

E. Purposes must be Exclusively Charitable

i. The Basic Rule

If, consistently with its terms, a trust may be applied exclusively for purposes which are not charitable, it is a non-charitable trust notwithstanding that, consistently with its terms, it may be applied exclusively for purposes which are charitable. Thus a trust to apply income to "registered charities or to such bodies as in the opinion of the trustees have charitable objects" is not charitable since the final clause does not state "exclusively charitable objects" and, even if it did, bodies in the opinion of the trustees having exclusively charitable objects might not be regarded by the courts as having exclusively charitable objects.[118] More obviously, the following trusts are not exclusively charitable and so are void: "for worthy causes", "for benevolent purposes", for "charitable or benevolent purposes",[119] for purposes "connected with the education and welfare of children"[120] or "for the public good".[121] **6–135**

ii. Exceptions

Notwithstanding the basic rule, a benignant construction can sometimes save a charitable trust as in *Guild v IRC*[122] where the trust deed required funds to be used for a Sports Centre in North Berwick qualifying as a valid recreational charity under the 1958 Recreational Charities Act "or some similar purpose in connection with sport", where the House of Lords held such "similar purpose" must likewise be a charitable purpose. Again, in *Armenian Patriarch of Jerusalem v Sorsino*,[123] a trust for the "education and advancement in life of Armenian children" was construed conjunctively and so for the charitable purpose of education. Note, however, that the principle which holds that ambiguous trust provisions should be construed in favour of charity[124] does not apply to the construction of company documents.[125] **6–136**

Also, if the main purpose of a corporation or trust is charitable and the only non-charitable elements in its constitution and operations are merely incidental to the effective promotion of that main purpose, then the corporation and trust are established for charitable purposes only.[126] If the non-charitable object is itself a main object, then neither the corporation nor the trust is established for charitable purposes only; but there is this difference between them: the corporation remains validly constituted, but the trust is void.[127] As Slade J. states,[128] "The distinction is between (a) those **6–137**

---

118 *Re Wootton's WT* [1968] 1 W.L.R. 681. In poverty cases the courts seem ready to restrict the opinion of trustees as to persons in needy circumstances or special need to such persons that the law recognises as within the poverty head of charity: *Re Scarisbrick* [1951] Ch. 622; *Re Cohen* [1973] 1 W.L.R. 415.

119 *Chichester Diocesan Fund v Simpson* [1944] A.C. 341; *Latimer v CIR* [2004] 1 W.L.R. 1466 at [32].

120 *Att.-Gen. of the Bahamas v Royal Trust Co* [1986] 1 W.L.R. 1001 (welfare purposes not restricted to educational welfare purposes so as to qualify as charitable).

121 *Att.-Gen. of Cayman Islands v Wahr-Hansen* [2001] 1 A.C. 75.

122 [1992] 2 A.C. 310.

123 (2002) 5 I.T.E.L.R. 125.

124 See e.g. *Hadaway v Hadaway* [1955] 1 W.L.R. 16 at 19, per Viscount Simonds.

125 *IRC v Oldham Training and Enterprise Council* [1996] S.T.C. 1218; Charity Commission, *Decision on Applications for Registration of the Ethnic-English Trust and the Ironside Community Trust*, June 28, 2007, para.5.5.

126 *Royal College of Surgeons of England v National Provincial Bank Ltd* [1952] A.C. 631; *Re Coxen* [1948] Ch. 747; *London Hospital Medical College v IRC* [1976] 1 W.L.R. 613.

127 *Chichester Diocesan Fund and Board of Finance (Incorporated) v Simpson* [1944] A.C. 341; *Oxford Group v IRC* [1949] W.N. 343; *Associated Artists Ltd v IRC* [1956] 1 W.L.R. 752.

128 *McGovern v Att.-Gen.* [1982] Ch. 321 at 341.

non-charitable activities authorised by the trust instrument which are merely incidental or subsidiary to a charitable purpose and (b) those non-charitable activities so authorised which themselves form part of the trust purpose. In the latter but not the former case the reference to non-charitable activities will deprive the trust of its charitable status."

6–138 Where a trustee is directed to apportion between charitable and non-charitable objects the trust is always good as to the charitable objects. The trust will be valid *in toto* if the non-charitable objects are certain and valid,[129] and, in the absence of apportionment by the trustee, the court will divide the fund equally between both classes of objects in accordance with the maxim that "equality is equity".[130] If the non-charitable objects are uncertain, then the trust will be good as to the charitable objects only[131] so long as they are sufficiently defined to reveal a general charitable intention.[132]

5. The Thirteen Heads of Charity

6–139 The following account is arranged in accordance with the classificatory scheme of the Charities Act 2006 s.2(2), which has been reproduced above.[133]

A. Section 2(2)(a): "The Prevention or Relief of Poverty"

6–140 Section 2(2)(a) has its origins in that part of the preamble to the Statute of Charitable Uses 1601 which speaks of "the relief of aged, impotent and poor people". At common law, these words had to be read disjunctively so that a trust was charitable if the beneficiaries were either elderly, or ill, or poor.[134] Under the scheme of the Charities Act 2006, the relief of those in need by reason of age and ill-health has been separated out from relief of the poor and appears in s.2(2)(j).

6–141 The "relief" of poverty and the "prevention" of poverty exist along a continuum of measures that can be taken for the benefit of the needy, and many charities aim to do both. However there is a difference between the two, in that prevention entails addressing the causes, while relief entails addressing the consequences of poverty, and s.2(2)(a) effected a change to the law by recognising the prevention of poverty as a stand-alone purpose. This purpose might be pursued, for example, by charities which provide money management and debt counselling advice. Many charities set up prior to the 2006 Act have aims for the relief of poverty, with no mention of the prevention of poverty. But the Charity Commission advises that it has "long accepted that charities concerned with the relief of poverty can also prevent poverty" and so it is unnecessary "for charities for the relief of poverty to extend their objects to refer specifically to the prevention of poverty", although "it is open to them to do so if that is appropriate."[135]

6–142 "Poverty" is a relative term and the expression "poor people" is not necessarily confined to the destitute poor: it includes persons who have to "go short" in the ordinary acceptation of that term, due regard being had to their station in life and so forth.[136] Thus, a trust fund for "poor and needy"

---

129 *Re Douglas* (1887) 35 Ch.D. 472.
130 *Salusbury v Denton* (1857) 3 K. & J. 529.
131 *Re Clarke* [1923] 2 Ch. 407.
132 The *cy-près* doctrine is available if required.
133 See para.6–53.
134 Age: *Re Robinson* [1951] Ch. 198; *Re Glyn's WT* [1950] 2 All E.R. 1150n.; *Re Bradbury* [1950] 2 All E.R. 1150n.; *Rowntree Memorial Trust Housing Association v Att.-Gen.* [1983] Ch. 159; impotence: *Re Elliott* (1910) 102 L.T. 528; *Re Hillier* [1944] 1 All E.R. 480; *Re Lewis* [1955] Ch. 104.
135 Charity Commission *The Prevention or Relief of Poverty for the Public Benefit* (December 2008 version) part C2.
136 *Re Segelman* [1996] Ch. 171; *Re Coulthurst* [1951] Ch. 661 at 666; *Re Young* [1953] 3 All E.R. 689: Charity Commission, *Decision to Register the AITC Foundation* (February 19, 2004).

relatives could be used to assist those who may need a helping hand from time to time in order to overcome an unforeseen crisis: the failure of a business venture, urgent repairs to a dwelling house or expenses brought on by reason of failing health. The "working classes" do not ipso facto constitute a section of the poor,[137] but in *Re Niyazi's WT*[138] a gift of residue worth about £15,000 for "the construction of or as a contribution towards the construction of a working men's hostel" in Famagusta was held charitable. The size of the gift, the grave housing shortage in Famagusta, and the term "working men's hostel" provided a sufficient connotation of poverty to make the gift charitable. The Charity Commission now advises that "For a charity carrying out its aims in England and Wales, 'people in poverty' might typically mean households living on less than 60% of median income who go short in some unacceptable way. This includes those people who, despite working, might still fall into this category and people may qualify for assistance from a poverty charity whether or not they are eligible for state benefits."[139]

Trusts for the relief of poverty (but not for the relief of elderly[140] or ill persons[141]) form an exception to the principle that because every charitable trust must be for the public benefit the beneficiaries must not be a private class defined by reference to a personal nexus with a particular person. The exception covers both the poor relations of a named individual[142] and the poor employees of a particular employer and their families.[143] However, there must be a primary intent to relieve poverty, though among a particular class of person. If the primary intent is to benefit particular persons (e.g. A, B, C and their children for their relief in needy circumstances) the trust is a private one and not charitable.[144] **6–143**

It seems that the Charity Commission would like to tighten up the rules on public benefit in this area but are constrained by legal precedent from going as far as they would like. In their most recent guidance document they state that: "Even where all the beneficiaries have to be poor, there may be circumstances in which the restrictions on who can benefit are either so limited or irrational as to outweigh the normal public character of the relief of poverty."[145] They give the example of a trust to relieve poverty among people who have attended a specific school during a specific time and were members of the school's rugby team. It is easy to understand why the Commission might baulk at trusts of this kind, but it is less easy to see why they are any different from trusts to relieve poverty among the settlor's relatives, which the Commission is bound to accept as legally valid. **6–144**

DINGLE v TURNER

House of Lords [1972] A.C. 601, [1972] 2 W.L.R. 523, [1972] 1 All E.R. 878.

VISCOUNT DILHORNE: My Lords, I agree with Lord Cross that this appeal should be dismissed and with the reasons he gives for the conclusion. **6–145**

---

137 *Re Sanders' WT* [1954] Ch. 265, ("dwellings for the working classes and their families resident in the area of Pembroke Dock or within a radius of 5 miles therefrom" held not charitable).

138 [1978] 3 All E.R. 785.

139 Charity Commission *The Prevention or Relief of Poverty for the Public Benefit* (December 2008 version) part C1.

140 *Re Dunlop* [1984] N.I. 408 (trust to found a home for old Presbyterian persons held to be for sufficient section of public to be charitable under fourth head of charity).

141 *Re Resch's WT* [1969] 1 A.C. 514.

142 *Re Scarisbrick* [1951] Ch. 662.

143 *Dingle v Turner* [1972] A.C. 601. See, too, *Cawdron v Merchant Taylors' School* [2010] P.T.S.R. 507 at [29]–[34] (trust to benefit sons of school old boys killed or disabled in the First World War).

144 *Re Scarisbrick* [1951] Ch. 662; *Re Cohen* [1973] 1 W.L.R. 415; *Re Segelman* [1995] 3 All E.R. 676 at 686–692 (26 persons in class which would increase with birth of further members).

145 Charity Commission *The Prevention or Relief of Poverty for the Public Benefit* (December 2008 version) part E3.

6–146 With Lord MacDermott, I too do not wish to extend my concurrence to what my noble and learned friend Lord Cross has said with regard to the fiscal privileges of a legal charity. Those privileges may be altered from time to time by Parliament and I doubt whether their existence should be a determining factor in deciding whether a gift or trust is charitable.

6–147 LORD MACDERMOTT: My Lords, the conclusion I have reached on the facts of this case is that the gift in question constitutes a public trust for the relief of poverty which is charitable in law. I would therefore dismiss the appeal.

6–148 I do not find it necessary to state my reasons for this conclusion in detail. In the first place, the views which I have expressed at some length in relation to an educational trust in *Oppenheim v Tobacco Securities Trust Co Ltd*[146] seem to me to apply to this appeal and to mean that it fails. And, secondly, I have had the advantage of reading the opinion prepared by my noble and learned friend, Lord Cross of Chelsea, and find myself in agreement with his conclusion for the reasons he has given. But I would prefer not to extend my concurrence to what my noble and learned friend goes on to say respecting the fiscal privileges of a legal charity. This subject may be material on the question whether what is alleged to be a charity is sufficiently altruistic in nature to qualify as such, but beyond that, and without wishing to express any final view on the matter, I doubt if these consequential privileges have much relevance to the primary question whether a given trust or purpose should be held charitable in law.

6–149 LORD HODSON: My Lords, I agree with my noble and learned friend, Lord Cross of Chelsea, that this appeal should be dismissed and with his reasons for that conclusion. With this reservation: that I share the doubts expressed by my noble and learned friends, Lord MacDermott and Viscount Dilhorne, as to the relevance of fiscal considerations in deciding whether a gift or trust is charitable.

6–150 LORD SIMON OF GLAISDALE: My Lords, I have had the advantage of reading the opinion of my noble and learned friend, Lord Cross of Chelsea, with which I agree.

6–151 LORD CROSS OF CHELSEA: My Lords, . . . Clause 8(e) was in the following terms:

> "(e) To invest the sum of ten thousand pounds in any of the investments for the time being authorised by law for the investment of trust funds in the names of three persons (hereinafter referred to as 'the Pension Fund Trustees') to be nominated for the purpose by the persons who at the time at which my Executors assent to this bequest are directors of E. Dingle & Company Limited and the Pension Fund Trustees shall hold the said sum and the investments for the time being representing the same (hereinafter referred to as 'the Pensions Fund') upon trust to apply the income thereof in paying pensions to poor employees of E. Dingle & Company Limited or of any other company to which upon any reconstruction or amalgamation the goodwill and the assets of E. Dingle & Company Limited may be transferred who are of the age of Sixty years at least or who being of the age of Forty five years at least are incapacitated from earning their living by reason of some physical or mental infirmity provided always that if at any time the Pension Fund Trustees shall for any reason be unable to apply the income of the Pension Fund in paying such pensions to such employees as aforesaid the Pension Fund Trustees shall hold the Pensions Fund and the income thereof upon trust for the aged poor in the Parish of St. Andrew, Plymouth."

Finally by clause 8(g) the testator directed his trustees to hold the ultimate residue of his estate on the trusts set out in clause 8(e).

6–152 The testator died on January 10, 1950. His widow died on October 8, 1966, having previously released her testamentary power of appointment over her husband's shares in E. Dingle & Co Ltd, which accordingly fell into the residuary estate. When these proceedings started in July 1970, the value of the fund held on the trusts declared by clause 8(e) was about £320,000 producing a gross income of about £17,800 per annum.

6–153 E. Dingle and Co Ltd was incorporated as a private company on January 20, 1935. Its capital was owned by the testator and one John Russell Baker and it carried on the business of a departmental store. At the time of the testator's death the company employed over 600 persons and there was a substantial

[146] [1951] A.C. 297.

number of ex-employees. On October 23, 1950, the company became a public company. Since the testator's death its business has expanded and when these proceedings started it had 705 full-time and 189 part-time employees and was paying pensions to 89 ex-employees.

The trustees took out an originating summons asking the court to determine whether the trust declared by clause 8(e) were valid and if so to determine various subsidiary questions of construction—as, for example, whether part-time employees or employees of subsidiary companies were eligible to receive benefits under the trust. To this summons they made defendants (1) representatives of the various classes of employees or ex-employees, (2) those who would be interested on an intestacy if the trusts failed, and (3) Her Majesty's Attorney-General. It has been common ground throughout that the trust at the end of clause 8(e) for the aged poor in the Parish of St Andrew Plymouth is dependent on the preceding trust for poor employees of the company so that although it will catch any surplus income which the trustees do not apply for the benefit of poor employees it can have no application if the preceding trust is itself void. **6–154**

The contentions of the appellant and the respondents may be stated broadly as follows. The appellant says that in the *Oppenheim* case this House decided that in principle a trust ought not to be regarded as charitable if the benefits under it are confined either to the descendants of a named individual or individuals or the employees of a given individual or company and that although the "poor relations" cases may have to be left standing as an anomalous exception to the general rule because their validity has been recognised for so long, the exception ought not to be extended to "poor employees" trusts which had not been recognised for long before their status as charitable trusts began to be called in question. The respondents, on the other hand, say, first, that the rule laid down in the *Oppenheim* case with regard to educational trusts ought not to be regarded as a rule applicable in principle to all kinds of charitable trust and, secondly, that in any case it is impossible to draw any logical distinction between "poor relations" trusts and "poor employees" trusts, and, that as the former cannot be held invalid today after having been recognised as valid for so long, the latter must be regarded as valid also. **6–155**

By a curious coincidence within a few months of the decision of this House in the *Oppenheim* case the cases on gifts to "poor relations" had to be considered by the Court of Appeal in *Re Scarisbrick*.[147] Most of the cases on this subject were decided in the eighteenth or early nineteenth centuries and are very inadequately reported but two things at least were clear. First, that it never occurred to the judges who decided them that in the field of "poverty" a trust could not be a charitable trust if the class of beneficiaries was defined by reference to descent from a common ancestor. Secondly, that the courts did not treat a gift or trust as necessarily charitable because the objects of it had to be poor in order to qualify, for in some of the cases the trust was treated as a private trust and not a charity. The problem in *Re Scarisbrick* was to determine on what basis the distinction was drawn. The Court of Appeal held that in this field the distinction between a public or charitable trust and a private trust depended on whether as a matter of construction the gift was for the relief of poverty amongst a particular description of poor people or was merely a gift to particular poor persons. The fact that the gift took the form of a perpetual trust would no doubt indicate that the intention of the donor could not have been to confer private benefits on particular people whose possible necessities he had in mind; but the fact that the capital of the gift was to be distributed at once did not necessarily show that the gift was a private trust. **6–156**

[His Lordship then reviewed the earlier cases leading up to *Gibson v South American Stores* and continued:] The facts in *Gibson v South American Stores (Gath & Chaves) Ltd*[148]—the case followed by Megarry J. in this case—were that a company had vested in trustees a fund derived solely from its profits to be applied at the discretion of the directors in granting gratuities, pensions or allowances to persons— **6–157**

> "who . . . are or shall be necessitous and deserving and who for the time being are or have been in the company's employ . . . and the wives widows husbands widowers children parents and other dependants of any person who for the time being is or would if living have been himself or herself a member of the class of beneficiaries."

[147] [1951] Ch. 622.
[148] [1950] Ch. 177.

6–158 The Court of Appeal held that this trust was a valid charitable trust but it did so without expressing a view of its own on the question of principle involved, because the case of *Re Laidlaw*[149] which was unearthed in the course of the hearing showed that the Court of Appeal had already accepted the decision in *Re Gosling*[150] as correct.

6–159 In *Oppenheim v Tobacco Securities Trust Co Ltd*[151] this House had to consider the principle laid down by the Court of Appeal in *Re Compton*.[152] There the trustees of a fund worth over £125,000 were directed to apply its income and also if they thought fit all or any part of the capital—

> "in providing for or assisting in providing for the education of children of employees or former employees of British-American Tobacco Co, Ltd . . . or any of its subsidiary or allied companies . . ."

6–160 There were over 110,000 such employees. The majority of your Lordships—namely Lord Simonds (in whose judgment Lord Oaksey concurred), Lord Normand and Lord Morton of Henryton—in holding that the trust was not a valid charitable trust gave unqualified approval to the Compton principle. They held, that is to say, that although the "poverty" cases might afford an anomalous exception to the rule, it was otherwise a general rule applicable to all charitable trusts that no class of beneficiaries can constitute a "section of the public" for the purpose of the law of charity if the distinguishing quality which links them together is relationship to a particular individual either through common descent or common employment. My noble and learned friend, Lord MacDermott, on the other hand, in his dissenting speech, while not challenging the correctness of the decisions in *Re Compton* or in the *Hobourn Aero* case[153] said that he could not regard the principle stated by Lord Greene M.R. as a criterion of general applicability and conclusiveness. He said:[154]

> ". . . I see much difficulty in dividing the qualities or attributes which may serve to bind human beings into classes into two mutually exclusive groups, the one involving individual status and purely personal, the other disregarding such status and quite impersonal. As a task this seems to me no less baffling and elusive than the problem to which it is directed, namely, the determination of what is and what is not a section of the public for the purposes of this branch of the law."

He thought that the question whether any given trust was a public or a private trust was a question of degree to be decided in the light of the facts of the particular case and that viewed in that light the trust in the *Oppenheim* case was a valid charitable trust . . .

6–161 The *Oppenheim* case was a case of an educational trust and although the majority evidently agreed with the view expressed by the Court of Appeal in the *Hobourn Aero* case,[155] that the *Compton* rule was of universal application outside the field of poverty, it would no doubt be open to this House without overruling *Oppenheim* to hold that the scope of the rule was more limited. If ever I should be called on to pronounce on this question—which does not arise in this appeal—I would as at present advised be inclined to draw a distinction between the practical merits of the *Compton* rule and the reasoning by which Lord Greene M.R. sought to justify it. That reasoning—based on the distinction between personal and impersonal relationships—has never seemed to me very satisfactory and I have always—if I may say so—felt the force of the criticism to which my noble and learned friend Lord MacDermott subjected it in his dissenting speech in the *Oppenheim* case.[156] For my part I would prefer to approach the problem on far broader lines. The phrase "a section of the public" is in truth a phrase which may mean different things to different people. In the law of charity judges have sought to elucidate its meaning by contrasting it with another

149 (January 11, 1935) unreported, the decision (and not the reasoning) only being available.
150 (1900) 48 W.R. 300.
151 [1951] A.C. 297.
152 [1945] Ch. 123.
153 [1946] Ch. 194.
154 [1951] A.C. 297 at 317.
155 [1946] Ch. 194.
156 [1951] A.C. 297. See also G. Cross, as Lord Cross then was, (1956) 72 L.Q.R. 187.

phrase "a fluctuating body of private individuals". But I get little help from the supposed contrast for as I see it one and the same aggregate of persons may well be describable both as a section of the public and as a fluctuating body of private individuals. The ratepayers in the Royal Borough of Kensington and Chelsea, for example, certainly constitute a section of the public; but would it be a misuse of language to describe them as a "fluctuating body of private individuals"? After all, every part of the public is composed of individuals and being susceptible of increase or decrease is fluctuating. So at the end of the day one is left where one started with the bare contrast between "public" and "private". No doubt some classes are more naturally describable as sections of the public than as private classes while other classes are more naturally describable as private classes than as sections of the public. The blind, for example, can naturally be described as a section of the public; but what they have in common—their blindness—does not join them together in such a way that they could be called a private class. On the other hand, the descendants of Mr Gladstone might more reasonably be described as a "private class" than as a section of the public, and in the field of common employment the same might well be said of the employees in some fairly small firm. But if one turns to large companies employing many thousands of men and women most of whom are quite unknown to one another and to the directors the answer is by no means so clear. One might say that in such a case the distinction between a section of the public and a private class is not applicable at all or even that the employees in such concerns as ICI or GEC are just as much "sections of the public" as the residents in some geographical area. In truth the question whether or not the potential beneficiaries of a trust can fairly be said to constitute a section of the public is a question of degree and cannot be by itself decisive of the question whether the trust is a charity. Much must depend on the purpose of the trust. It may well be that, on the one hand, a trust to promote some purpose, prima facie charitable, will constitute a charity even though the class of potential beneficiaries might fairly be called a private class and that, on the other hand, a trust to promote another purpose, also prima facie charitable, will not constitute a charity even though the class of potential beneficiaries might seem to some people fairly describable as a section of the public.

In answering the question whether any given trust is a charitable trust the courts—as I see it—cannot avoid having regard to the fiscal privileges accorded to charities. As counsel for the Attorney-General remarked in the course of the argument the law of charity is bedevilled by the fact that charitable trusts enjoy two quite different sorts of privilege. On the one hand, they enjoy immunity from the rules against perpetuity and uncertainty and although individual potential beneficiaries cannot sue to enforce them the public interest arising under them is protected by the Attorney-General. If this was all there would be no reason for the courts not to look favourably on the claim of any "purpose" trust to be considered as a charity if it seemed calculated to confer some real benefit on those intended to benefit by it whoever they might be and if it would fail if not held to be a charity. But that is not all. Charities automatically enjoy fiscal privileges which with the increased burden of taxation have become more and more important and in deciding that such and such a trust is a charitable trust the court is endowing it with a substantial annual subsidy at the expense of the taxpayer. Indeed, claims of trusts to rank as charities are just as often challenged by the Revenue as by those who would take the fund if the trust was invalid. It is, of course, unfortunate that the recognition of any trust as a valid charitable trust should automatically attract fiscal privileges, for the question whether a trust to further some purpose is so little likely to benefit the public that it ought to be declared invalid and the question whether it is likely to confer such great benefits on the public that it should enjoy fiscal immunity are really two quite different questions. The logical solution would be to separate them and to say—as the Radcliffe Commission proposed—that only some charities should enjoy fiscal privileges. But as things, are, validity and fiscal immunity march hand in hand and the decisions in the *Compton*[157] and *Oppenheim*[158] cases were pretty obviously influenced by the consideration that if such trusts as were there in question were held valid they would enjoy an undeserved fiscal immunity. To establish a trust for the education of the children of employees in a company in which you are interested is no doubt a meritorious act; but however numerous the employees may be the purpose which you are seeking to achieve is not a public purpose.[159] It is a company purpose and there is no reason why your fellow taxpayers should contribute to a scheme which by providing "fringe benefits" for **6–162**

[157] [1945] Ch. 123.
[158] [1951] A.C. 297.
[159] For a critical view of this approach see T.G. Watkin [1978] Conv. 277.

your employees will benefit the company by making their conditions of employment more attractive. The temptation to enlist the assistance of the law of charity in private endeavours of this sort is considerable—witness the recent case of the Metal Box scholarships—*Inland Revenue Comrs v Educational Grants Association Ltd*[160]—and the courts must do what they can to discourage such attempts. In the field of poverty the danger is not so great as in the field of education—for while people are keenly alive to the need to give their children a good education and to the expense of doing so, they are generally optimistic enough not to entertain serious fears of falling on evil days much before they fall on them. Consequently the existence of company "benevolent funds", the income of which is free of tax does not constitute a very attractive "fringe benefit". This is a practical justification—although not, of course, the historical explanation—for the special treatment accorded to poverty trusts in charity law. For the same sort of reason a trust to promote some religion among the employees of a company might perhaps safely be held to be charitable provided that it was clear that the benefits were to be purely spiritual. On the other hand, many "purpose" trusts falling under Lord Macnaghten's fourth head if confined to a class of employees would clearly be open to the same sort of objection as educational trusts. As I see it, it is on these broad lines rather than for the reasons actually given by Lord Greene M.R. that the *Compton* rule can best be justified.

6–163 My Lords, I would dismiss this appeal.

6–164 *Appeal dismissed.*

B. Section 2(2)(b): "The Advancement of Education"

6–165 This group of charitable trusts has its origins in those parts of the preamble to the Statute of Charitable Uses 1601 which speak of "the maintenance of schools of learning, free schools and scholars in universities" and "the education and preferment of orphans". It is now clear that trusts endowing fee-paying schools are charitable if the school is non-profit-making or if, though profit-making, its profits are used for school purposes only.[161] Similarly, the Incorporated Council of Law Reporting is a charity because its charges are retained for its purposes and do not enure for the benefit of its members: it provides essential material for the study of law so as to be for the advancement of education, it being immaterial that thereby lawyers are able to make money because one must not confuse the results flowing from the achievement of the purpose with the purpose itself.[162]

6–166 Education is not confined to matters formally taught in schools and universities. It includes the promotion or encouragement of the arts and graces of life: see *Re Shaw's Will Trusts*[163] ("the teaching, promotion and encouragement in Ireland of self-control, elocution, oratory, deportment, the arts of personal contact, of social intercourse, and the other arts of public, private, professional and business life"); *Royal Choral Society v IRC*[164] (choral singing in London); *Re Levien*[165] (organ music); *Re Delius*[166] (the music of the composer Delius); *Re Dupree's Deed Trusts*[167] (encouragement of chess-playing among young people in Portsmouth); and *Re South Place Ethical Society*[168] (the study and dissemination of ethical principles

160 [1967] Ch. 993.

161 *Abbey Malvern Wells Ltd v Ministry of Local Government* [1951] Ch. 728; *Customs & Excise Commissioners v Bell Concord Education Trust* [1990] 1 Q.B. 1040.

162 *Incorporated Council of Law Reporting v Att.-Gen.* [1972] Ch. 73 where two L.JJ. held the Council to fall within the educational head of charity and all three L.JJ. held it within the fourth *Pemsel* head.

163 [1952] Ch. 163.

164 [1943] 2 All E.R. 101; contrast *Associated Artists Ltd v IRC* [1956] 1 W.L.R. 752 (production of artistic dramatic works).

165 [1955] 1 W.L.R. 964.

166 [1957] Ch. 299; contrast *Re Pinion* [1965] Ch. 85 (bequest of worthless works of art to found a museum); *Sutherland's Trustees v Verschoyle* 1968 S.L.T. 43.

167 [1945] Ch. 16.

168 [1980] 1 W.L.R. 1565.

and the cultivation of a rational religious sentiment). Some of these purposes would now appear to belong under other sub-sections, most notably s.2(2)(f), which recognises as a charitable purpose "the advancement of the arts, culture, heritage or science".

The Charity Commission has upheld as charitable a Cult Information Centre (researching into and making people aware of movements concerned with the exploration of spiritual life) and Public Concern at Work (concerned with promoting business ethics and advising and protecting employees faced with ethical dilemmas at work).[169] Note, however, that the Commission will pay particular attention to the quality of instruction offered by organisations which claim to be training their users outside formal educational establishments, and will decline to register them if it considers their activities to amount to nothing more the unstructured imparting of information.[170] **6–167**

The decision of Harman J. in *Re Shaw*[171] (denying charitable status where George Bernard Shaw had bequeathed funds for pursuing inquiries into a new 40-letter alphabet) appeared to render doubtful the validity of trusts for the advancement of research, at any rate where no element of teaching was involved; but *Re Hopkins' Will Trusts* removes most of the doubts. There Wilberforce J. held that:[172] **6–168**

> "that the word 'education', as used by Harman J, must be used in a wide sense, certainly extending beyond teaching, and that the requirement is that, in order to be charitable, research must either be of educational value to the researcher or must be so directed as to lead to something which will pass into the store of educational material or so as to improve the sum of communicable knowledge in an area which education may cover . . . research of a private character, for the benefit only of the members of a society, would not normally be educational or otherwise charitable but I do not think that the research in the present case [into the works of Francis Bacon and whether he might have been the author of plays ascribed to Shakespeare] can be said to be of private character, for it is inherently inevitable and manifestly intended that the result of any discovery should be published to the world."

In *McGovern v Att.-Gen.* Slade J. summarised the principles as follows:[173] **6–169**

> "(1) A trust for research will ordinarily qualify as a charitable trust if, but only if (a) the subject matter of the proposed research is a useful subject of study; and (b) it is contemplated that knowledge acquired as a result of the research will be disseminated to others; and (c) the trust is for the benefit of the public, or a sufficiently important section of the public. (2) In the absence of a contrary context, however, the court will be readily inclined to construe a trust for research as importing subsequent dissemination of the results thereof. (3) Furthermore, if a trust for research is to constitute a valid trust for the advancement of education, it is not necessary either (a) that a teacher/pupil relationship should be in contemplation, or (b) that the persons to benefit from the knowledge to be acquired should be persons who are already in the course of receiving 'education' in the conventional sense."

The rule that trusts for research purposes are charitable only if it is contemplated that the research will be published was revisited by the Charity Commission in its guidance document on *Public Benefit and the Advancement of Education*, where it stated that:[174]

---

169 See respectively Decisions Vol.1, p.1 and Vol.2, p.5.

170 Charity Commission, *Decision on the Millennium College UK Ltd's Application for Registration as a Charity*, 27 April 2004; *Decision on Living in Radiance's Application for Registration as a Charity*, 24 August 2005.

171 [1965] Ch. 699; [1957] 1 W.L.R. 729.

172 [1965] Ch. 669 at 680–681.

173 [1982] Ch. 321 at 352.

174 (December 2008 version) para. E2.

> "This does not mean that research has to be presented in a way that is understandable by everyone. It might only be capable of being understood by people who are experts in the field. What is important is that it is published and made publicly available so that everyone who is capable of understanding it has access to it, and its benefits or usefulness are widely available to everyone."

6–170 In *IRC v McMullen*,[175] the House of Lords held that it is charitable to provide sports facilities for children and young people at school and university because physical education and development are an integral part of the education of the young. This decision is reproduced below for the court's discussion of education as a legally charitable purpose.[176] At the time when the case was decided, the promotion of sport was not a charitable object per se, but the law in this area subsequently changed as discussed below in subs.(g).[177]

6–171 The promotion of a particular type of political education[178] is not charitable; and some other forms of education may also not be for the public benefit: *Re Hummeltenberg*[179] (training of spiritualistic mediums). In *Southwood v Attorney-General*[180] the Court of Appeal held that a trust to educate the public that peace is best secured by disarmament and pacifism was not charitable because "the court cannot determine whether or not it promotes the public benefit for the public to be" so educated: "there are differing views as to how best to secure peace and avoid war . . . on the one hand it can be argued that war is best avoided by bargaining through strength; on the other hand it can be argued that peace is best secured through disarmament—if necessary, by unilateral disarmament." The court and not the settlor determines whether public benefit is present so that a testator cannot set up a charitable museum of his artistic collection if it has no artistic merit.[181] The fact that it is by means of an educational process that non-charitable purposes are to be achieved does not render such purposes charitable.[182]

6–172 A trust for the education of beneficiaries who are ascertained by reference to some personal tie (e.g. of blood or contract), such as the relations of a particular individual, the members of a particular family, the employees of a particular firm or the members of a particular trade union, lacks the necessary element of public benefit and is not charitable: *Oppenheim v Tobacco Securities Trust Co Ltd*.[183] However, this may require reconsideration in the light of *Dingle v Turner*[184] where large-scale trusts are concerned. A trust to educate the residents of a town[185] or the children of members of a particular profession[186] will be valid.

6–173 Merely creating a clearly valid charitable trust, e.g. "for the advancement of the education of children in the United Kingdom" will not confer tax advantages if the trustees run the trust as a private

---

175 [1981] A.C. 1.

176 See paras 6–177 ff.

177 See paras 6–273 ff.

178 *Bonar Law Memorial Trust v IRC* (1933) 49 T.L.R. 220; *Re Hopkinson* [1949] 1 All E.R. 346; cf. *Re Scowcroft* [1898] 2 Ch. 638 which nowadays should be regarded as of doubtful authority; and see *Re McDougall* [1957] 1 W.L.R. 81 (study of methods of government is a charitable object). For the same reason, a twist to persuade people to accept particular religious beliefs is not a charitable trust for an education purpose: Charity Commission, *Decision on the Gnostic Centre's Application for Registration as a Charity*, December 16, 2009, paras 12 to 18.

179 [1923] 1 Ch. 237. Cf. *Funnel v Stewart* [1996] 1 All E.R. 715.

180 [2000] W.T.L.R. 1199 at 1217.

181 *Re Pinion* [1965] Ch. 85.

182 *Re Koeppler's WT* [1984] Ch. 243, though reversed by the Court of Appeal [1986] Ch. 423 since the purpose was held charitable.

183 [1951] A.C. 297, reproduced below at paras 6–193 ff.

184 [1972] A.C. 601, reproduced above at paras 6–145 ff. However the majority there seemed to favour the result in *Oppenheim*, tax advantages preventing the trust being sufficiently altruistic.

185 *Re Tree* [1945] Ch. 325: a restriction to Methodists or members of the Church of England would seem valid.

186 *Hall v Derby Sanitary Authority* (1885) 16 Q.B.D. 163 approved in *Oppenheim v Tobacco Securities Trust Co* [1951] A.C. 297.

trust for certain associated persons: *IRC v Educational Grants Association*.[187] Indeed, the trustees will be acting beyond their powers and so be liable for breach of trust.

If a trust for a broad charitable class of beneficiaries gives the trustees a power, without being under any duty, to prefer a certain private class within the broader public class this does not vitiate the validity of the trust as a charitable trust.[188] However, payments to members of the private class will have unfortunate tax consequences if regarded as of such significance that they ought fairly to be considered as misuse of public funds for a private purpose. Rather than put the tax inspector on his mettle some settlors may omit the preference from the trust deed and rely on the sensible selection of beneficiaries by trustees. **6–174**

If the trust for the broad charitable class imposes a duty upon the trustees to use the whole, if possible, or an uncertain part of the funds for a specified private class then the trust cannot be a valid charitable trust.[189] If only a maximum specified part of the fund is directed to be used for the private class then while such part should not be charitable the remainder, presumably, should be severed as charitable since it can be used for exclusively charitable purposes. However, in *Re Koettgen*,[190] Upjohn J. in a brief extempore judgment held that if there was a broad primary class that was charitable the trust remained charitable despite an imperative direction imposing a duty to prefer a private class for up to a maximum of 75 per cent of the trust income. This is difficult to justify logically, but pragmatically it validates the trust, while leaving it open to the Revenue to charge tax if the trust is operated as a private trust and enabling charitable purposes to be carried out to the extent it is impossible or impracticable to benefit the preferred class. The Charity Commissioners have accepted *Re Koettgen* as good law.[191] **6–175**

Note that fee-charging schools and other educational bodies must now satisfy the Charity Commission that their activities enure to the public benefit in the ways set out in the Commission's document on *Public Benefit and Fee-Charging* (December 2008 version), parts of which have been reproduced above.[192] **6–176**

INLAND REVENUE COMMISSIONERS v MCMULLEN

House of Lords [1981] A.C. 1, [1980] 2 W.L.R. 416, [1980] 1 All E.R. 884.

LORD HAILSHAM: Four questions arose for decision below. In the first place neither the parties nor the judgments below were in agreement as to the proper construction of the trust deed itself. Clearly this is a preliminary debate which must be settled before the remaining questions are even capable of decision. In the second place the trustees contend and the Crown disputes that, on the correct construction of the deed, the trust is charitable as being for the advancement of education. Thirdly, the trustees contend and the Crown disputes that if they are wrong on the second question the trust is charitable at least because it falls within the fourth class of Lord Macnaghten's categories as enumerated in *Income Tax Special* **6–177**

---

187 [1967] Ch. 993.

188 *Re Koettgen* [1954] Ch. 252; *Caffoor v Comr of Income Tax, Colombo* [1961] A.C. 584; *IRC v Educational Grants Association* [1967] Ch. 123.

189 *Re Martin* (1977) 121 Sol. Jo. 828, *The Times*, November 17, 1977. An anomalous exception exists for the ancient English institution of educational provision for Founder's Kin in certain schools and colleges "though there seems to be virtually no direct authority as to the principle on which they rested and they should probably be regarded more as belonging to history than to doctrine": *Caffoor v Comr of Income Tax* [1961] A.C. 584 at 602.

190 [1954] Ch. 252; doubted in *IRC v Educational Grants Association* [1967] Ch. 123.

191 [1978] Annual Report, paras 86 and 89.

192 See paras 6–91 ff.

Purposes Comrs v Pemsel[193] as a trust beneficial to the community within the spirit and intendment of the preamble to the statute 43 Eliz. I, c.4.[194] Fourthly, the trustees contend and the Crown disputes that, even if not otherwise charitable, the trust is a valid charitable trust as falling within section 1 of the Recreational Charities Act 1958, that is as a trust to provide or to assist in the provision of facilities for recreation or other leisure time occupation provided in the interests of social welfare.

6–178 Since we have reached the view that the trust is a valid educational charity their Lordships have not sought to hear argument nor, therefore, to reach a conclusion on any but the first two disputed questions in the dispute. Speaking for myself, however, I do not wish my absence of decision on the third or fourth points to be interpreted as an indorsement of the majority judgments in the Court of Appeal nor as necessarily dissenting from the contrary views contained in the minority judgment of Bridge L.J. For me at least the answers to the third and fourth questions are still left entirely undecided.

6–179 I now turn to the question of construction, for which it is necessary that I reproduce the material portions of the deed . . . The objects of the Trusts are:—

> "(a) to organise or provide or assist in the organisation and provision of facilities which will enable and encourage pupils of Schools and Universities in any part of the United Kingdom to play Association Football or other games or sports and thereby to assist in ensuring that due attention is given to the physical education and development of such pupils as well as to the development and occupation of their minds and with a view to furthering this object (i) to provide or assist in the provision of Association Football or games or sports equipment of every kind for the use of such pupils as aforesaid (ii) to provide or assist in the provision of courses lectures demonstrations and coaching for pupils of Schools and Universities in any part of the United Kingdom and for teachers who organise or supervise playing and coaching of Association Football or other games or sports at such Schools and Universities as aforesaid (iii) to promote provide or assist in the promotion and provision of training colleges for the purpose of training teachers in the coaching of Association Football or other games or sports at such Schools and Universities as aforesaid (iv) to lay out manage equip and maintain or assist in the laying out management equipment and maintenance of playing fields or appropriate indoor facilities or accommodation (whether vested in the Trustees or not) to be used for the teaching and playing of Association Football or other sports or games by such pupils as aforesaid.
>
> "(b) to organise or provide or assist in the organisation or provision of facilities for physical recreation in the interests of social welfare in any part of the United Kingdom (with the object of improving the conditions of life for the boys and girls for whom the same are provided) for boys and girls who are under the age of twenty-one years and who by reason of their youth or social and economic circumstances have need of such facilities."

6–180 I pause here only to say that no question arises as to clause 3(b) above which clearly corresponds to the language of the Recreational Charities Act 1958. Controversy therefore revolves solely around clause 3(a), since it is obvious that, if this cannot be shown to be solely for charitable purposes, the whole trust ceases to be a charitable trust . . .

6–181 I agree with [the judgment of Bridge L.J.] . . . that what the deed means is that the purpose of the settlor is to promote the physical education and development of pupils at schools and universities as an addition to such part of their education as relates to their mental education by providing the facilities and assistance to games and sports in the manner set out at greater length and in greater detail in the enumerated sub-clauses of clause 3(a) of the deed . . .

6–182 On a proper analysis, therefore, I do not find clause 3(a) ambiguous. But, before I part with the question of construction, I would wish to express agreement with a contention made on behalf of the trustees and of the Attorney-General, but not agreed to on behalf of the Crown, that in construing trust deeds the intention of which is to set up a charitable trust, and in others too, where it can be claimed that there is an ambiguity, a benignant construction should be given if possible. This was the maxim of the civil law: *semper in dubiis benigniora praeferenda sunt*. There is a similar maxim in English law: *ut res magis valeat quam*

[193] [1891] A.C. 531 at 583.
[194] Charitable Uses Act 1601.

pereat. It certainly applies to charities when the question is one of uncertainty (*Weir v Crum-Brown*[195]) and, I think, also where a gift is capable of two constructions one of which would make it void and the other effectual (cf. *Bruce v Deer Presbytery*,[196] *Houston v Burns*[197] and *Bain, Public Trustee v Ross*[198]). In the present case I do not find it necessary to resort to benignancy in order to construe the clause, but, had I been in doubt, I would certainly have been prepared to do so . . .

I must now turn to the deed, construed in the manner in which I have found it necessary to construe it, to consider whether it sets up a valid charitable trust for the advancement of education. **6–183**

It is admitted, of course, that the words "charity" and "charitable" bear, for the purposes of English law and equity, meanings totally different from the senses in which they are used in ordinary educated speech, or for instance, in the Authorised Version of the Bible. But I do not share the view, implied by Stamp and Orr L.JJ. in the instant case,[199] that the words "education" and "educational" bear, or can bear, for the purposes of the law of charity, meanings different from those current in present day educated English speech. I do not believe that there is such a difference. What has to be remembered, however, is that, as Lord Wilberforce pointed out in *Re Hopkins' Will Trusts*[200] and in *Scottish Burial Reform and Cremation Society Ltd v Glasgow City Corpn*,[201] both the legal conception of charity, and within it the educated man's ideas about education are not static, but moving and changing. Both change with changes in ideas about social values. Both have evolved with the years. In particular in applying the law to contemporary circumstances it is extremely dangerous to forget that thoughts concerning the scope and width of education differed in the past greatly from those which are now generally accepted. **6–184**

In saying this I do not in the least wish to cast doubt on *Re Nottage*,[202] which was referred to in both courts below and largely relied on by the Crown here. Strictly speaking *Re Nottage* was not a case about education at all. The issue there was whether the bequest came into the fourth class of charity categorised in Lord Macnaghten's classification of 1891.[203] The mere playing of games or enjoyment of amusement or competition is not per se charitable, nor necessarily educational, though they may (or may not) have an educational or beneficial effect if diligently practised. Neither am I deciding in the present case even that a gift for physical education per se and not associated with persons of school age or just above would necessarily be a good charitable gift. That is a question which the courts may have to face at some time in the future. But in deciding what is or is not an educational purpose for the young in 1980 it is not irrelevant to point out what Parliament considered to be educational for the young in 1944 when, by the Education Act of that year in sections 7 and 53 (which are still on the statute book), Parliament attempted to lay down what was then intended to be the statutory system of education organised by the state, and the duties of the local education authorities and the Minister in establishing and maintaining the system. Those sections are so germane to the present issue that I cannot forbear to quote them both. Section 7 provides (in each of the sections the emphasis being mine): **6–185**

> "The statutory system of public education shall be organised in three progressive stages to be known as primary education, secondary education, and further education; and it shall be the duty of the local education authority for every area, so far as their powers extend, to contribute towards *the spiritual, moral, mental, and physical development of the community by securing that efficient education throughout those stages shall be available to meet the needs of the population of their area*"

and in section 53 of the same Act it is said:

> "(1) It shall be the duty of every local education authority to secure that the facilities for primary, secondary and further education provided for their area include adequate facilities for recreation *and social and*

---

195 [1908] A.C. 162 at 167.
196 (1867) L.R. 1 Sc. & Div. 96 at 97.
197 [1918] A.C. 337 at 341–342.
198 [1930] 1 Ch. 224 at 230.
199 [1979] 1 W.L.R. 130 at 135, 139.
200 [1965] Ch. 669 at 678.
201 [1968] A.C. 138 at 154.
202 [1895] 2 Ch. 649.
203 See *Income Tax Special Purposes Comrs v Pemsel* [1891] A.C. 531 at 583.

physical training, and for that purpose a local education authority, with the approval of the Secretary of State, may establish maintain and manage, or assist the establishment, maintenance, and management of *camps, holiday classes, playing fields, play centres and other places (including playgrounds, gymnasiums, and swimming baths not appropriated to any school or college), at which facilities for recreation and for such training as aforesaid are available for persons receiving primary, secondary or further education, and may organise games, expeditions and other activities for such persons, and may defray or contribute towards the expenses thereof*."

6–186 . . . I find the first instance case of *Mariette*,[204] a decision of Eve J., both stimulating and instructive. Counsel for the Crown properly reminded us that this concerned a bequest effectively tied to a particular institution. Nevertheless, I cannot forbear to quote a phrase from the judgment, always bearing in mind the danger of quoting out of context. Eve J. said:[205]

"No one of sense could be found to suggest that between those ages [10 to 19] any boy can be properly educated unless at least as much attention is given to the development of his body as is given to the development of his mind."

6–187 Apart from the limitation to the particular institution I would think that these words apply as well to the settlor's intention in the instant appeal as to the testator's in *Re Mariette*, and I regard the limitation to the pupils of schools and universities in the instant case as a sufficient association with the provision of formal education to prevent any danger of vagueness in the object of the trust or irresponsibility or capriciousness in application by the trustees. I am far from suggesting either that the concept of education or of physical education even for the young is capable of indefinite extension. On the contrary, I do not think that the courts have as yet explored the extent to which elements of organisation, instruction or the disciplined inculcation of information, instruction or skill may limit the whole concept of education. I believe that in some ways it will prove more extensive, in others more restrictive than has been thought hitherto. But it is clear at least to me that the decision in *Re Mariette*[206] is not to be read in a sense which confines its application for ever to gifts to a particular institution. It has been extended already in *Re Mellody*[207] to gifts for annual treats for schoolchildren in a particular locality (another decision of Eve J.), to playgrounds for children (*Re Chester*,[208] possibly not educational, but referred to in *Inland Revenue Comrs v Baddeley*[209]); to a children's outing (*Re Ward's Estate*[210]), to a prize for chess to boys and young men resident in the City of Portsmouth (*Re Dupree's Deed Trusts*,[211] a decision of Vaisey J.) and for the furthering of the Boy Scouts' movement by helping to purchase sites for camping, outfits, etc. (*Re Webber*,[212] another decision of Vaisey J.).

6–188 It is important to remember that in the instant appeal we are dealing with the concept of physical education and development of the young deliberately associated by the settlor with the status of pupillage in schools or universities (of which, according to the evidence, about 95 per cent are within the age-group 17 to 22). We are not dealing with adult education, physical or otherwise, as to which some considerations may be different.

6–189 I am at pains to disclaim the view that the conception of this evolving, and therefore not static, view of education is capable of infinite abuse or, even worse, proving void for uncertainty. Quite apart from the doctrine of the benignant approach to which I have already referred, and which undoubtedly comes to the assistance of settlors in danger of attack for uncertainty, I am content to adopt the approach of my predecessor Lord Loreburn L.C. in *Weir v Crum-Brown*,[213] to which attention was drawn by counsel for the

---

[204] [1915] 2 Ch. 284.
[205] [1915] 2 Ch. 284 at 288.
[206] [1915] 2 Ch. 284.
[207] [1918] 1 Ch. 228.
[208] (July 25, 1934) unreported.
[209] [1955] A.C. 572 at 596.
[210] [1937] 81 Sol. Jo. 397.
[211] [1945] Ch. 16.
[212] [1954] 1 W.L.R. 1500.
[213] [1908] A.C. 162 at 167.

Attorney-General, that if the bequest to a class of persons, is as here capable of application by the trustees, or, failing them, the court, the gift is not void for uncertainty. Lord Macnaghten also said:[214]

> "The testator has taken pains to provide competent judges. It is for the trustees to consider and determine the value of the service on which a candidate may rest his claim to participate in the testator's bounty."

Mutatis mutandis, I think this kind of reasoning should apply here. Granted that the question of application may present difficulties for the trustees, or, failing them, for the court, nevertheless it is capable of being applied, for the concept in the mind of the settlor is an object sufficiently clear, is exclusively for the advancement of education, and, in the hands of competent judges, is capable of application. **6–190**

My Lords, for these reasons I reach the conclusion that the trust is a valid charitable gift for the advancement of education, which, after all, is what it claims to be. The conclusion follows that the appeal should be allowed. **6–191**

LORD DIPLOCK and LORD SALMON merely concurred while LORD RUSSELL and LORD KEITH concurred and gave brief speeches. **6–192**

OPPENHEIM v TOBACCO SECURITIES TRUST CO LTD

House of Lords [1951] A.C. 297, [1951] 1 All E.R. 31

Investments were held by the respondents, Tobacco Securities Trust Co Ltd, on trust to apply the income in providing for "the education of children of employees or former employees of British-American Tobacco Co Ltd . . . or any of its subsidiary or allied companies without any limit of time being specified". The High Court and Court of Appeal held the trust void for perpetuity because it was not charitable on the ground that it lacked public benefit. **6–193**

LORD SIMONDS (with whom LORD NORMAND, LORD OAKSEY and LORD MORTON agreed): In the case of trusts for educational purposes the condition of the public benefit must be satisfied. The difficulty lies in determining what is sufficient to satisfy the test, and there is little to help your Lordships to solve it. **6–194**

If I may begin at the bottom of the scale, a trust established by a father for the education of his son is not a charity. The public element, as I will call it, is not supplied by the fact that from that son's education all may benefit. At the other end of the scale the establishment of a college or university is beyond doubt a charity. "Schools of learning and free schools, and scholars of universities" are the very words of the preamble to the [Charitable Uses Act 1601 (43 Eliz. I, c.4)]. So also the endowment of a college, university or school by the creation of scholarships or bursaries is a charity, and nonetheless because competition may be limited to a particular class of persons. It is on this ground, as Lord Greene M.R. pointed out in *Re Compton*,[215] that the so-called "founder's kin" cases can be rested. The difficulty arises where the trust is not for the benefit of any institution either then existing or by the terms of the trust to be brought into existence, but for the benefit of a class of persons at large. Then the question is whether that class of persons can be regarded as such a "section of the community" as to satisfy the test of public benefit. These words "section of the community" have no special sanctity, but they conveniently indicate (1) that the possible (I emphasise the word "possible") beneficiaries must not be numerically negligible, and (2) that the quality which distinguishes them from other members of the community, so that they form by themselves a section of it, must be a quality which does not depend on their relationship to a particular individual. It is for this reason that a trust for the education of members of a family or, as in *Re Compton*, of a number of families cannot be regarded as charitable. A group of persons may be numerous, but, if the nexus between them is their personal relationship to a single *propositus* or to several *propositi*, they are neither the community nor a section of the community for charitable purposes. **6–195**

I come, then, to the present case where the class of beneficiaries is numerous, but the difficulty arises in regard to their common and distinguishing quality. That quality is being children of employees of one or **6–196**

---

[214] [1908] A.C. 162 at 169.
[215] [1945] Ch. 123.

other of a group of companies. I can make no distinction between children of employees and the employees themselves. In both cases the common quality is found in employment by particular employers. The latter of the two cases, by which the Court of Appeal held itself to be bound, the *Hobourn* case, is a direct authority for saying that such a common quality does not constitute its possessors a section of the public for charitable purposes. In the former case, *Re Compton*, Lord Greene M.R. had by way of illustration placed members of a family and employees of a particular employer on the same footing, finding neither in common kinship nor in common employment the sort of nexus which is sufficient. My Lords, I am so fully in agreement with what was said by Lord Greene in both cases, and by my noble and learned friend, then Morton L.J., in the *Hobourn* case, that I am in danger of repeating without improving upon their words. It appears to me that it would be an extension [of the legal definition of charity], for which there is no justification in principle or authority, to regard common employment as a quality which constitutes those employed a section of the community. It must not, I think, be forgotten that charitable institutions enjoy rare and increasing privileges, and that the claim to come within that privileged class should be clearly established. With the single exception of *Re Rayner*,[216] which I must regard as of doubtful authority, no case has been brought to the notice of the House in which such a claim as this has been made, where there is no element of poverty in the beneficiaries, but just this and no more, that they are the children of those in a common employment.

6–197 Learned counsel for the appellant sought to fortify his case by pointing to the anomalies that would ensue from the rejection of his argument. For, he said, admittedly those who follow a profession or calling—clergymen, lawyers, colliers, tobacco-workers and so on—are a section of the public; how strange then it would be if, as in the case of railwaymen, those who follow a particular calling are all employed by one employer. Would a trust for the education of railwaymen be charitable,[217] but a trust for the education of men employed on the railways by the Transport Board not be charitable? And what of service of the Crown, whether in the civil service or the armed forces? Is there a difference between soldiers and soldiers of the King? My Lords, I am not impressed by this sort of argument and will consider on its merits if the occasion should arise, the case where the description of the occupation and the employment is in effect the same, where in a word, if you know what a man does, you know who employs him to do it. It is to me a far more cogent argument, as it was to my noble and learned friend in the *Hobourn* case, that, if a section of the public is constituted by the personal relation of employment, it is impossible to say that it is not constituted by a thousand as by 100,000 employees, and if by a thousand, then by a hundred, and, if by a hundred, then by ten. I do not mean merely that there is a difficulty in drawing the line, though that, too, is significant. I have it also in mind that, though the actual number of employees at any one moment might be small, it might increase to any extent, just as, being large, it might decrease to any extent. If the number of employees is the test of validity, must the court take into account potential increase or decrease, and, if so, as at what date? . . .

6–198 LORD MACDERMOTT (dissenting): The question is whether it is of a public nature, whether, in the words of Lord Wrenbury in *Verge v Somerville*,[218] "it is for the benefit of the community or of an appreciably important class of the community." The relevant class here is that from which those to be educated are to be selected. The appellant contends that this class is public in character; the respondent bank (as personal representative of the last surviving settlor) denies this and says that the class is no more than a group of private individuals.

6–199 Until comparatively recently the usual way of approaching an issue of this sort, at any rate where educational trusts were concerned, was, I believe, to regard the facts of each case and to treat the matter very much as one of degree. No definition of what constituted a sufficient section of the public for the purpose was applied, for none existed; and the process seems to have been one of reaching a conclusion on a general survey of the circumstances and considerations regarded as relevant rather than of making a single, conclusive test. The investigation left the course of the dividing line between what was and what was not a section of the community unexplored, and was concluded when it had gone far enough to establish to the satisfaction of the court whether or not the trust was public; and the decision as to that was, I think, very often reached by determining whether or not the trust was private.

---

216 (1920) 89 L.J. Ch. 369.
217 As to this see *Hall v Derby Sanitary Authority* (1885) 16 Q.B.D. 163.
218 [1924] A.C. 496 at 499.

6–200 If it is still permissible to conduct the present inquiry on these broad if imprecise lines, I would hold with the appellant. The numerical strength of the class is considerable on any showing. The employees concerned number over 110,000, and it may reasonably be assumed that the children, who constitute the class in question, are no fewer. The large size of the class is not, of course, decisive but in my view it cannot be left out of account when the problem is approached in this way. Then it must be observed that the propositi are not limited to those presently employed. They include former employees (not reckoned in the figure I have given) and are, therefore, a more stable category than would otherwise be the case. And, further, the employees concerned are not limited to those in the service of the "British American Tobacco Co Ltd or any of its subsidiary or allied companies"—itself a description of great width—but include the employees, in the event of the British American Tobacco Co Ltd being reconstructed or merged on amalgamation, of the reconstructed or amalgamated company or any of its subsidiary companies. No doubt the settlors here had a special interest in the welfare of the class they described, but, apart from the fact that this may serve to explain the particular form of their bounty, I do not think it material to the question in hand. What is material, as I regard the matter, is that they have chosen to benefit a class which is, in fact, substantial in point of size and importance and have done so in a manner which, to my mind, manifests an intention to advance the interests of the class described as a class rather than as a collection or succession of particular individuals . . .

6–201 The respondent bank, however, contends that the inquiry should be of quite a different character to that which I have been discussing. It advances as the sole criterion a narrower test derived from the decisions of the Court of Appeal in *Compton*,[219] and in *Hobourn*.[220] The basis and nature of this test appear from the passage in the judgment of the court in *Compton*,[221] where Lord Greene M.R., says:

> "In the case of many charitable gifts it is possible to identify the individuals who are to benefit, or who at any given moment constitute the class from which the beneficiaries are to be selected. This circumstance does not, however, deprive the gift of its public character. Thus, if there is a gift to relieve the poor inhabitants of a parish the class to benefit is readily ascertainable. But they do not enjoy the benefit, when they receive it, by virtue of their character as individuals but by virtue of their membership of the specified class. In such a case the common quality which unites the potential beneficiaries into a class is essentially an impersonal one. It is definable by reference to what each has in common with the others, and that is something into which their status as individuals does not enter. Persons claiming to belong to the class do so not because they are A.B., C.D. and E.F., but because they are poor inhabitants of the parish. If, in asserting their claim, it were necessary for them to establish the fact that they were the individuals A.B., C.D. and E.F., I cannot help thinking that on principle the gift ought not to be held to be a charitable gift, since the introduction into their qualification of a purely personal element would deprive the gift of its necessary public character. It seems to me that the same principle ought to apply when the claimants, in order to establish their status, have to assert and prove, not that they themselves are A.B., C.D., and E.F., but that they stand in some specified relationship to the individuals A.B., C.D., and E.F., such as that of children or employees. In that case, too, a purely personal element enters into and is an essential part of the qualification, which is defined by reference to something, i.e., personal relationship to individuals or an individual which is in its essence non-public."

6–202 The test thus propounded focuses upon the common quality which unites those within the class concerned and asks whether that quality is essentially impersonal or essentially personal. If the former, the class will rank as a section of the public and the trust will have the element common to and necessary for all legal charities; but, if the latter, the trust will be private and not charitable. It is suggested in the passage just quoted, and made clear beyond doubt in *Hobourn*,[222] that in the opinion of the Court of Appeal employment by a designated employer must be regarded for this purpose as a personal and not as an impersonal bond of union. In this connection and as illustrating the discriminating character of what I may

---

[219] [1945] Ch. 123.
[220] [1946] Ch. 194.
[221] [1945] Ch. 123 at 129–130.
[222] [1946] Ch. 194.

call "the *Compton*[223] test" reference should be made to that part of the judgment of the learned Master of the Rolls in *Hobourn*,[224] in which he speaks of the decision in *Hall v Derby Borough Urban Sanitary Authority*.[225] The passage runs thus:

> "That related to a trust for railway servants. It is said that if a trust for railway servants can be a good charity, so too a trust for railway servants in the employment of a particular railway company is a good charity. That is not so. The reason, I think, is that in the one case the trust is for railway servants in general and in the other case it is for employees of a particular company, a fact which limits the potential beneficiaries to a class ascertained on a purely personal basis."

6–203 My Lords, I do not quarrel with the result arrived at in the *Compton* and *Hobourn* cases, and I do not doubt that the *Compton* test may often prove of value and lead to a correct determination. But, with the great respect due to those who have formulated this test, I find myself unable to regard it as a criterion of general applicability and conclusiveness. In the first place I see much difficulty in dividing the qualities or attributes, which may serve to bind human beings into classes, into two mutually exclusive groups, the one involving individual status and purely personal, the other disregarding such status and quite impersonal. As a task this seems to me no less baffling and elusive than the problem to which it is directed, namely, the determination of what is and what is not a section of the public for the purposes of this branch of the law. After all, what is more personal than poverty or blindness or ignorance? Yet none would deny that a gift for the education of the children of the poor or blind was charitable; and I doubt if there is any less certainty about the charitable nature of a gift for, say, the education of children who satisfy a specified examining body that they need and would benefit by a course of special instruction designed to remedy their educational defects.

6–204 But can any really fundamental distinction, as respects the personal or impersonal nature of the common link, be drawn between those employed, for example, by a particular university and those whom the same university has put in a certain category as the result of individual examination and assessment? Again, if the bond between these employed by a particular railway is purely personal, why should the bond between those who are employed as railway men be so essentially different? Is a distinction to be drawn in this respect between those who are employed in a particular industry before it is nationalised and those who are employed therein after that process has been completed and one employer has taken the place of many? Are miners in the service of the National Coal Board now in one category and miners at a particular pit or of a particular district in another? Is the relationship between those in the service of the Crown to be distinguished from that obtaining between those in the service of some other employer? Or, if not, are the children of, say, soldiers or civil servants to be regarded as not constituting a sufficient section of the public to make a trust for their education charitable?

6–205 It was conceded in the course of the argument that, had the present trust been framed so as to provide for the education of the children of those engaged in the tobacco industry in a named county or town, it would have been a good charitable disposition, and that even though the class to be benefited would have been appreciably smaller and no more important than is the class here. That concession follows from what the Court of Appeal has said. But if it is sound and a personal or impersonal relationship remains the universal criterion I think it shows, no less than the queries I have just raised in indicating some of the difficulties of the problem, that the *Compton* test is a very arbitrary and artificial rule. This leads me to the second difficulty that I have regarding it. If I understand it aright it necessarily makes the quantum of public benefit a consideration of little moment; the size of the class becomes immaterial and the need of its members and the public advantage of having that need met appear alike to be irrelevant. To my mind these are considerations of some account in the sphere of educational trusts for, as already indicated, I think the educational value and scope of the work actually to be done must have a bearing on the question of public benefit.

[223] [1945] Ch. 123.
[224] [1946] Ch. 194 at 206.
[225] (1885) 16 Q.B.D. 163

Finally, it seems to me that, far from settling the state of the law on this particular subject, the *Compton* test is more likely to create confusion and doubt in the case of many trusts and institutions of a character whose legal standing as charities has never been in question. Take, for instance, a trust for the provision of university education for boys coming from a particular school. The common quality binding the members of that class seems to reside in the fact that their parents or guardians all contracted for their schooling with the same establishment or body. That the school in such a case may itself be a charitable foundation seems altogether beside the point and quite insufficient to hold the *Compton* test at bay if it is well founded in law. **6–206**

I therefore return to what I think was the process followed before the decision in *Compton's case*, and, for the reasons already given, I would hold the present trust charitable and allow the appeal. I have only to add that I recognise the imperfections and uncertainties of that process. They are as evident as the difficulties of finding something better. But I venture to doubt if it is in the power of the courts to resolve those difficulties satisfactorily as matters stand. It is a long cry to the age of Elizabeth and I think what is needed is a fresh start from a new statute. **6–207**

Appeal dismissed. **6–208**

IRC v EDUCATIONAL GRANTS ASSOCIATION LTD

Chancery Division [1967] Ch. 123, [1966] 3 W.L.R. 724, [1966] 3 All E.R. 708

The Revenue appealed from a decision of the Special Commissioners of Income Tax that the respondents were a charity entitled to exemption from income tax under section 447(1)(b) of the Income Tax Act 1952 (now section 532 of the Income Tax Act 2007). The respondents were a company limited by guarantee formed for the advancement of education. However, the promoters of the company and its management were very much connected with Metal Box Ltd. Virtually all the income came from a seven-year deed of covenant executed by Metal Box Ltd Care was taken that details of the company's objects did not leak out except to the higher ranks of Metal Box employees and their associates. Between 75 and 85 per cent of payments were for the benefit of children of Metal Box employees. The Revenue conceded that the respondents were established for charitable purposes only and so the case turned upon whether or not the payments had been applied to charitable purposes only. **6–209**

Pennycuick J. allowed the appeal holding that the absence of public benefit had the consequence that the payments had not been applied to charitable purposes only. The Court of Appeal[226] in short extempore judgments affirmed his decision but without pursuing his doubts over *Re Koettgen*. The reserved judgment of Pennycuick J. appears below as illuminating the issues more clearly than the Court of Appeal decision. **6–210**

PENNYCUICK J.: . . . I will next read the relevant part of section 447 of the Income Tax Act 1952. **6–211**

> "(1) Exemption shall be granted . . . (b) . . . from tax chargeable under Sch.D in respect of any yearly interest or other annual payment, forming part of the income of any body of persons or trust established for charitable purposes only, or which, according to the rules or regulations established by Act of Parliament, charter, decree, deed of trust or will, are applicable to charitable purposes only, and so far as the same are applied to charitable purposes only."

It will be observed that the subsection imposes two distinct requirements: (i) the income must form part of the income of a body of persons or trust established for charitable purposes only, or must, according to the rules established by the relevant instrument, be applicable to charitable purposes only; and (ii) the exemption is available only so far as the income is applied to charitable purposes only. The first requirement depends on the construction of the relevant instrument; the second requirement depends on what is in fact done with the income as it arises from time to time. I will, for convenience, consider these requirements in their application to a corporate body, since that is the case now before me. They apply equally, mutatis mutandis, in the case of a trust created by a will or settlement. **6–212**

[226] [1967] Ch. 993.

6–213 The objects of the corporation, in order that they may be exclusively charitable, must be confined to objects for the public benefit. Equally, the application of the income, if it is to be within those objects, must be for the public benefit. Conversely, the application of income otherwise than for the public benefit must be outside the objects and ultra vires. For example, under an object for the advancement of education, once that is accepted as an exclusively charitable object, the income must be applied for the advancement of education by way of public benefit. An application of income for the advancement of education by way of private benefit would be ultra vires, and nonetheless so by reason that, in the nature of things, the members of a private class are included in the public as a whole. This may perhaps explain the repetition of the words "for charitable purposes only" in the second requirement of the subsection.

6–214 Counsel for the taxpayers advanced a simple and formidable argument: viz. (i) the taxpayers are established for specified educational purposes; (ii) those purposes are admittedly charitable purposes, so the first requirement is satisfied; (iii) the income has been applied for the specified educational purposes; and (iv) therefore the income has been applied for charitable purposes, and the second requirement is satisfied. It seems to me that this argument leaves out of account the element of public benefit. It is true that it is claimed by the taxpayers and admitted by the Crown that the educational purposes specified in the taxpayers' memorandum are charitable purposes, but this by definition implies that the purposes are for the public benefit. In order that the second requirement may be satisfied, it must equally be shown that their income has been applied not merely for educational purposes as expressed in the memorandum but for those educational purposes by way of public benefit. An application of income by way of private benefit would be ultra vires. It is not open to the taxpayers first to set up a claim which can only be sustained on the basis that the purposes expressed in the memorandum are for the public benefit, and then, when it comes to the application of the income, to look only to the purposes expressed in the memorandum, leaving the element of public benefit out of account. This point may be illustrated by considering the familiar example of a case in which a fund is settled on trust for the advancement of education in general terms and the income is applied for the education of the settlor's children. Counsel for the taxpayer does not shrink from the conclusion that such an application comes within the terms of the trust and satisfies the second requirement of the subsection. I think that it does neither.

6–215 Counsel for the Crown based his argument on construction broadly on the lines which I have indicated above as being correct. He devoted much of his argument to repelling the application of the *Koettgen* case to the present one. In the *Koettgen*[227] case a testatrix bequeathed her residuary estate on trust "for the promotion and furtherance of commercial education . . .". The will provided that

> "The persons eligible as beneficiaries under the fund shall be persons of either sex who are British born subjects and who are desirous of educating themselves or obtaining tuition for a higher commercial career but whose means are insufficient or will not allow of their obtaining such education or tuition at their own expense . . .".

The testatrix further directed that in selecting the beneficiaries

> "It is my wish that the . . . trustees shall give a preference to any employees of JB & Co (London), Ltd, or any members of the families of such employees; failing a sufficient number of beneficiaries under such description then the persons eligible shall be any persons of British birth as the . . . trustees may select provided that the total income to be available for benefiting the preferred beneficiaries shall not in any one year be more than seventy-five per cent of the total available income for that year."

In the event of the failure of those trusts there was a gift over to a named charity. It was admitted that the trust was for the advancement of education, but it was contended for the charity that having regard to the direction to prefer a limited class of persons the trusts were not of a sufficiently public nature to constitute valid charitable trusts. It was held that the gift to the primary class from whom the trustees could select beneficiaries contained the necessary element of benefit to the public, and that it was when that class was ascertained that the validity of the trust had to be determined; so that the subsequent direction to

[227] [1954] Ch. 252.

prefer, as to 75 per cent of the income, a limited class did not affect the validity of the trust, which was accordingly a valid and effective charitable trust. *Oppenheim v Tobacco Securities Trust Co Ltd*,[228] was distinguished.

The other case considered by the Special Commissioners was *Caffoor (Trustees of the Abdul Gaffoor Trust) v Comr of Income Tax, Colombo*[229] in the Privy Council. In that case by the terms of a trust deed executed in Ceylon in 1942 the trust income after the death of the grantor was to be applied by the board of trustees, the appellants, in their absolute discretion for all or any of a number of purposes, which included "(2)(b) the education instruction or training in England or elsewhere abroad of deserving youths of the Islamic Faith" in any department of human activity. The recipients of the benefits were to be selected by the board "from the following classes of persons and in the following order: (i) male descendants along either the male or female line of the grantor or of any of his brothers or sisters" failing whom youths of the Islamic Faith born of Muslim parents of the Ceylon Moorish community permanently resident in Colombo or elsewhere in Ceylon. It was held that in view of what was in effect the absolute priority to the benefit of the trust income which was conferred on the grantor's own family by clause 2(b)(i) of the trust deed this was a family trust and not a trust of a public character solely for charitable purposes, and the income thereof was accordingly not entitled to the exemption claimed. In his speech, Lord Radcliffe, giving the decision of the Privy Council, made the following comments[230] on the *Koettgen* case: **6–216**

> "It was argued with plausibility for the appellants that what this trust amounted to was a trust whose general purpose was the education of deserving young people of the Islamic Faith, and that its required public character was not destroyed by the circumstances that a preference in the selection of deserving recipients was directed to be given to members of the grantor's own family. Their Lordships go with the argument so far as to say that they do not think that a trust which provides for the education of a section of the public necessarily loses its charitable status or its public character merely because members of the founder's family are mentioned explicitly as qualified to share in the educational benefits or even, possibly, are given some kind of preference in the selection. They part with the argument, however, because they do not consider that the trust which is now before them comes within the range of any such qualified exception."

Lord Radcliffe went on to say that, there, the grantor's own family had, in effect, absolute priority. Then he said of the *Koettgen* case[231]: **6–217**

> "It is not necessary for their Lordships to say whether they would have put the same construction on the will there in question as the learned judge did, or whether they regard the distinction which he made as ultimately maintainable. The decision edges very near to being inconsistent with Oppenheim's case, but it is sufficient to say that the construction of the gift which was there adopted does not tally with the construction which their Lordships are bound to place on the trust which is now before them. Here, the effect of the wording of para. 2(b)(i) is to create a primary disposition of the trust income in favour of the family of the grantor."

I am not concerned with the construction placed by Upjohn J. on the particular will before him in the *Koettgen* case. I will assume that the effect of the will was as he construed it, i.e., that it constituted a primary public class and then directed that the trustees should give preference to employees of a named company and their families, those employees being necessarily members of the whole public class. Upjohn J., held the trust to be charitable. In the *Caffoor* case, Lord Radcliffe gave a very guarded and qualified assent to that principle. The decision in *Koettgen's case* is concerned with the character of a trust on the construction of the relevant instrument, and not with the application of income. Its relevance in the latter connection is presumably that, if in the instrument creating a trust for a public class a private class **6–218**

228 [1951] A.C. 297.
229 [1961] A.C. 584.
230 [1961] A.C. 297 at 603.
231 [1961] A.C. 297 at 604.

whose members are included in the public class can be mentioned specifically and accorded a preference, then a preferential application of income for the benefit of a private class whose members are comprised in a public class is a proper execution of a trust for the public class. This is a long step, and I do not feel obliged to take it.

6–219 For myself I find considerable difficulty in the *Koettgen* decision. I should have thought that a trust for the public with preference for a private class comprised in the public might be regarded as a trust for the application of income at the discretion of the trustees between charitable and non-charitable objects. However, I am not concerned here to dispute the validity of the *Koettgen* decision. I only mention the difficulty which I feel as affording some additional reason for not applying the *Koettgen* decision by analogy in connection with the second requirement of the subsection.

6–220 I return now to the present case. The taxpayers have claimed that the purposes of the taxpayers are exclusively charitable, which imports that the purposes must be for the public benefit. The Crown have admitted that claim. I have then to consider whether the taxpayers have applied their income within their expressed objects and by way of public benefit. There is no doubt that the application has been within their expressed objects, but has it been by way of the public benefit? In order to answer this question, I must, I think, look at the individuals and institutions for whose benefit the income has been applied, and seek to discern whether these individuals and institutions possess any, and if so, what, relevant characteristics by virtue of which the income has been applied for their benefit. One may for this purpose look at the minutes of the council, circular letters and so forth. Counsel for the Crown at one time appeared to suggest that one might look at the actual intention of the members of the council. I do not think that is so.

6–221 When one makes this enquiry, one finds that between 75 per cent and 85 per cent of the income of the taxpayers has been expended on the education of children connected with Metal Box Co Ltd. The taxpayers are intimately connected with Metal Box Co Ltd, in the many respects found in the Case Stated. They derive most of their income from Metal Box Co Ltd. The council of management, as the Special Commissioners found, has followed a policy of seeking applications for grants from employees and ex-employees of Metal Box Co Ltd, though these applications are not, of course, always successful. The inference is inescapable that this part of the taxpayer's income—i.e. 75 per cent to 85 per cent—has been expended for the benefit of these children by virtue of a private characteristic: i.e., their connection with Metal Box Co Ltd Such an application is not by way of public benefit. It is on all fours with an application of 75 per cent to 85 per cent of the income of a trust fund on the education of a settlor's children. It follows, in my judgment, that, as regards the income which has been applied for the education of children of Metal Box Co Ltd's employees, the taxpayers have failed to satisfy the second requirement in the subsection, and that the claim for relief fails. No reason has been suggested why the taxpayers should not obtain relief in respect of income applied for the benefit of institutions and outside individuals; see the words "so far as" in the section.

6–222 I recognise that this conclusion involves a finding that the council of management has acted ultra vires in applying the income of the taxpayers as it has done, albeit within the expressed objects of the taxpayers' memorandum. This conclusion follows from the basis on which the taxpayers have framed their objects and based their claim. It is of course open to a comparable body to frame its objects so as to make clear that its income may be applied for private as well as public purposes, but in that case it may not obtain tax relief. It does not seem to me that such a body can have it both ways. I propose, therefore, to allow this appeal.

C. Section 2(2)(c): "The Advancement of Religion"

6–223 This category has its origin in the preamble to the 1601 Statute which speaks of "the repair of churches" but the courts soon held that the equity of the Statute extended to trusts advancing orthodox religion. With increasing religious toleration "the present position is that any religious body is entitled to charitable status so long as its tenets are not morally subversive and so long as its purposes are directed to the benefit of the public."[232]

---

[232] *Charities: A Framework for the Future* (1989) Cm. 694, para.2.20.

In rejecting the claim of an ethical society to be a charity for the advancement of religion Dillon J. said:[233] **6–224**

> "Religion is concerned with man's relations with God, and ethics are concerned with man's relations with man. The two are not the same, all are not made the same by sincere inquiry into the question: what is God? If reason leads people not to accept Christianity or any known religion, but they do believe in the excellence of qualities, such as truth, beauty and love, or believe in the platonic concept of the ideal, their beliefs may seem to them to be the equivalent of a religion, but viewed objectively they are not religion. . . . It seems to me that two of the essential attributes of religion are faith and worship: faith in a god and worship of that god. The Oxford English Dictionary gives as one of the definitions of religion: 'A particular system of faith and worship.' Then: 'Recognition on the part of man of some higher unseen power as having control of his destiny, and as being entitled to obedience, reverence and worship.' "

On this definition, however, Buddhism was not a religion since it is a "realised" rather than a "revealed" religion, and its adherents do not revere the Buddha as a "god", but instead believe that they should follow a spiritual path that he laid out which can ultimately lead to spiritual awakening. Dillon J. failed to resolve this in his judgment, but it has now been settled by the Charities Act 2006 s.2(3)(a)(ii) that for the purposes of s.2(2), religion includes "a religion which does not involve belief in a god". When the Charities Act 2006 was passing through Parliament, efforts were made by the Humanist peer Lord Wedderburn and others to include the phrase "or belief" after the word "religion" in s.2(2)(c). However these were resisted by the Government, which maintained that non-religious belief systems, such as those promoting moral and spiritual welfare, could be charitable by another route, under s.2(2)(l).[234] **6–225**

So far as theistic religions are concerned, no distinction is drawn between monotheistic and polytheistic religions. Charitable trusts have been registered for the advancement of the Church of England, Catholic,[235] Baptist,[236] Quaker,[237] Exclusive Brethren,[238] Jewish,[239] Sikh, Islamic, Hindu[240] and Spiritualist[241] religions. The Unification Church (the "Moonies")[242] has charitable status, but not the Church of Scientology. The Charity Commission[243] rejected its application for registration because although Scientologists believe in a supreme being, this belief does not find expression in conduct indicative of reverence or veneration for the supreme being: study and therapy or counselling did not amount to such worship.[244] **6–226**

---

233 *Re South Place Ethical Society* [1980] 1 W.L.R. 1565 at 1571. The society was charitable under the second and fourth heads of charity.

234 *Hansard (HL)* 28 June 2005, cols 136–152 and 12 October 2005, cols 292–298.

235 *Bradshaw v Tasker* (1834) 2 Myl. & K. 221.

236 *Re Strickland's WT* [1936] 3 All E.R. 1027.

237 *Re Manser* [1905] 1 Ch. 68.

238 *Holmes v Att.-Gen. The Times*, February 12, 1981.

239 *Neville Estates Ltd v Madden* [1962] Ch. 832 but not a trust for the settlement of Jews in Palestine: *Keren Kayemeth Le Jisroel v IRC* [1932] A.C. 650, followed in Charity Commission, *Decision on the Application for Registration of Good News for Israel* (February 5, 2004), notwithstanding the establishment of the state of Israel in the interim.

240 See (1989) Cm. 694, para.2.19, SI 1962/1421, SI 1963/2074; *Varsani v Jesani* [1999] Ch. 219.

241 Charity Commission, *Decision on the Application for Registration of the Sacred Hands Spiritual Centre* (September 5, 2003).

242 [1982] Charity Commissioners *Annual Report* paras 36–38. The Attorney-General dropped his action to deprive them of charitable status: *Hansard* February 3, 1988, p.977.

243 Decision of November 17, 1999, reproduced below at paras 6–239 ff.

244 The Church of Scientology has achieved recognition as a religious charity in other jurisdictions, e.g. Australia: *Church of the New Faith v Commissioner of Pay-roll Tax* (1983) 154 C.L.R. 120.

6–227 The Freemasons[245] and the Oxford Group[246] (as originally formed) are not religious charities, though a trust for the publication of the writings of Joanna Southcott (who claimed to be with child by the Holy Ghost and so about to give birth to a new Messiah) was held to be charitable[247] (and so void under the 1736 Mortmain and Charitable Uses Act). Indeed, a trust "for the continuance of the work of God as it has been maintained by H and myself since 1942" was held charitable[248] where the work consisted mainly in the free distribution of fundamentalist Christian tracts written by H, though the tracts were of no intrinsic merit except in confirming the beliefs of H's circle.

6–228 Trusts for adding to or repairing the fabric of a church[249] or for the upkeep of a churchyard[250] are charitable but not for the erection or upkeep of a particular tomb in a churchyard.[251] If a gift is made to an ecclesiastic in his official name and by virtue of his office then if no purposes are expressed in the gift the gift is for charitable religious purposes inherent in the office.[252] However, if the purposes are expressed in terms not confining them to exclusively charitable purposes then the charitable character of the trustee will not make the gift charitable.[253] A trust for religious purposes will be treated as for charitable religious purposes[254] but a trust for religious institutions will not be a charitable trust because some religious institutions (like a purely contemplative order of nuns) lack the necessary public benefit for a charitable trust.[255]

6–229 The courts are generally reluctant to enter into questions of the comparative worth of different religions. However, in *Gilmour v Coats*,[256] which is reproduced below, the House of Lords held that a trust for a contemplative order of nuns who did not leave their cloisters nor allow the public into them was not charitable. The benefits of their edifying example and their intercessory prayers were too vague and incapable of being proved to be of tangible benefit for the public. The court does not have to accept as proved whatever a particular religion believes. Nonetheless, in *Neville Estates Ltd v Madden* Cross J. upheld as charitable a trust for the members from time to time of the Catford Jewish Synagogue because "the court is entitled to assume that some benefit accrues to the public from the attendance at places of worship of persons who live in this world and mix with their fellow citizens".[257] Moreover, the Charity Commissioners registered as charitable the Society of the Precious Blood.[258] This was an enclosed contemplative society of Anglican Nuns but their activities included within their walls public religious services, religious and secular education of the public and the relief of suffering, sickness, poverty and distress through their counselling service.

---

245 *United Grand Lodge of Freemasons v Holborn BC* [1957] 1 W.L.R. 1080.
246 *Re Thackrach* [1939] 2 All E.R. 4; *Oxford Group v IRC* [1949] 2 All E.R. 537.
247 *Thornton v Howe* (1862) 31 Beav. 14.
248 *Re Watson* [1973] 1 W.L.R. 1472.
249 *Hoare v Osborne* (1866) L.R. 1 Eq. 585; *Re Raine* [1956] Ch. 417.
250 *Re Vaughan* (1866) 33 Ch.D. 187 at 192; *Re Douglas* [1905] 1 Ch. 279.
251 *Lloyd v Lloyd* (1852) 2 Sim. (N.S.) 225; *Re Hooper* [1932] 1 Ch. 38; see Parish Councils and Burial Authorities (Miscellaneous Provisions) Act 1970 s.1 (a burial or local authority may contract to maintain a grave or memorial for not exceeding 99 years).
252 *Re Rumball* [1956] Ch. 105.
253 *Re Simson* [1946] Ch. 299 (gift to vicar "for his work in the parish" charitable); *Farley v Westminster Bank* [1939] A.C. 430 (gift to vicar "for parish work" not charitable) applying *Dunn v Byrne* [1912] A.C. 407.
254 *MacLaughlin v Campbell* [1906] I.R. 588 to trustees "for such Roman Catholic purposes in the parish of Coleraine or elsewhere as they deem fit" void because possibility of Catholic political economic or social purposes, while there and in *Re White* [1893] 2 Ch. 41 it was accepted that a gift for "religious purposes" means impliedly "charitable religious purposes."
255 *Gilmour v Coats* [1949] A.C. 426.
256 [1949] A.C. 426.
257 [1962] Ch. 832 at 853. Clearly, the benefited class was small, and in *Dingle v Turner* [1972] A.C. 601 at 625 Lord Cross said, "A trust to promote some religion among the employees of a company might perhaps be held to be charitable, provided it was clear that the benefits were to be purely spiritual." *Re Warre's WT* [1953] 1 W.L.R. 725 (retreat house not charitable) is of dubious authority.
258 [1989] Annual Report paras 56–62; Decisions, Vol.3, p.11.

6–230 A further issue is whether or not the saying of Catholic Masses for the repose of particular souls is for the public benefit. The benefit of intercessory prayer is incapable of legal proof, but if Masses are said in public this has an edifying and improving effect on members of the public who happen to be in attendance, Masses held in private only edifying a private and not a public class of people. In both cases, however, one can argue that the money paid to the priest for saying Masses relieves the Catholic Church to that extent of its liability to provide stipends for priests and so benefits the Catholic Church and its members. In *Re Hetherington*[259] it was held that this in itself is not enough, so that the trust for Masses for the repose of particular souls was held to be charitable only by implicitly restricting it to Masses that had to be held in public. On this basis, the Charity Commissioners, in rejecting the application for registration as a charity of the Church of Scientology, held that it is the public nature of religious practice which is essential to the trust being charitable. Their decision is reproduced below.[260]

GILMOUR v COATS

House of Lords [1949] A.C. 426, [1949] 1 All E.R. 848

6–231 The income of a trust fund was to be applied to the purposes of a Carmelite convent, if those purposes were charitable. The convent was comprised of an association of strictly cloistered and purely contemplative nuns who were concerned with prayers and meditation, and who did not engage in any activities for the benefit of people outside the convent. In the view of the Roman Catholic Church, however, their prayers and meditation caused the intervention of God for the benefit of members of the public, and their life inside the convent provided an example of self-denial and concentration on religious matters which was beneficial to the public. At first instance and in the Court of Appeal it was held that the trust was not a charitable one, and the House of Lords dismissed an appeal from this conclusion.

6–232 LORD SIMONDS (with whom LORD DU PARCQ, LORD NORMAND, LORD MORTON, and LORD REID agreed): I need not go back beyond the case of *Cocks v Manners*,[261] which was decided nearly eighty years ago by Wickens V.C. In that case the testatrix left her residuary estate between a number of religious institutions, one of them being the Dominican convent at Carisbrooke, a community not differing in any material respect from the community of nuns now under consideration. The learned judge used these words,[262] which I venture to repeat, though they have already been cited in the courts below:

> "On the Act [the statute of Elizabeth] unaffected by authority I should certainly hold that the gift to the Dominican convent is neither within the letter nor the spirit of it; and no decision has been referred to which compels me to adopt a different conclusion. A voluntary association of women for the purpose of working out their own salvation by religious exercises and self-denial seems to me to have none of the requisites of a charitable institution, whether the word 'charitable' is used in its popular sense or in its legal sense. It is said, in some of the cases, that religious purposes are charitable, but that can only be true as to religious services tending directly or indirectly towards the instruction or the edification of the public; an annuity to an individual, so long as he spent his time in retirement and constant devotion, would not be charitable, nor would a gift to ten persons, so long as they lived together in retirement and performed acts of devotion, be charitable. Therefore the gift to the Dominican convent is not, in my opinion, a gift on a charitable trust."

---

259 [1990] Ch. 1 criticised by C. Rickett [1990] Conv. 34; further see *Nolan v Downes* (1917) 23 C.L.R. 546 and *Carrigan v Redwood* (1910) 30 N.Z.L.R. 244.

260 See paras 6–239 ff. For additional discussion of public benefit and religious charities see Charity Commission, *The Advancement of Religion for the Public Benefit* (December 2008 version).

261 (1871) L.R. 12 Eq. 574.

262 ibid. at 585.

6–233 Apart from what I have called the final argument, which I will deal with later, the contention of the appellant rests, not on any change in the lives of the members of such a community as this, nor, from a wider aspect, on the emergence of any new conception of the public good, but solely on the fact that for the first time certain evidence of the value of such lives to a wider public together with new arguments based on that evidence has been presented to the court. Never before, it was urged, has the benefit to be derived from intercessory prayer and from edification been brought to the attention of the court; if it had been, the decision in *Cocks v Manners* would, at least should, have been otherwise.

6–234 My Lords, I would speak with all respect and reverence of those who spend their lives in cloistered piety, and in this House of Lords spiritual and temporal, which daily commences its proceedings with intercessory prayers, how can I deny that the Divine Being may in His Wisdom think fit to answer them? But, my Lords, whether I affirm or deny, whether I believe or disbelieve, what has that to do with the proof which the court demands that a particular purpose satisfies the test of benefit to the community? Here is something which is manifestly not susceptible of proof. But, then it is said, this is a matter not of proof but of belief, for the value of intercessory prayer is a tenet of the Catholic faith, therefore, and in such a prayer there is benefit to the community. But it is just at this "therefore" that I must pause. It is, no doubt, true that the advancement of religion is, generally speaking, one of the heads of charity, but it does not follow from this that the court must accept as proved whatever a particular church believes. The faithful must embrace their faith believing where they cannot prove: the court can act only on proof. A gift to two or ten or a hundred cloistered nuns in the belief that their prayers will benefit the world at large does not from that belief alone derive validity any more than does the belief of any other donor for any other purpose. The importance of this case leads me to state my opinion in my own words but, having read again the judgment of the learned Master of the Rolls, I will add that I am in full agreement with what he says on this part of the case.

6–235 I turn to the second of the alleged elements of public benefit, edification by example, and I think that this argument can be dealt with very shortly. It is, in my opinion, sufficient to say that this is something too vague and intangible to satisfy the prescribed test. The test of public benefit has, I think, been developed in the last two centuries. Today it is beyond doubt that that element must be present. No court would be rash enough to attempt to define precisely or exhaustively what its content must be. But it would assume a burden which it could not discharge if now for the first time it admitted into the category of public benefit something so indirect, remote, imponderable and, I would add, controversial as the benefit which may be derived by others from the example of pious lives.

6–236 I must now refer to certain cases on which the appellant relied. They consist of a number of cases in the Irish courts and *Re Caus*,[263] a decision of Luxmoore J. A consideration of the Irish cases shows that it has there been decided that a bequest for the saying of masses, whether in public or in private, is a good charitable bequest: see, e.g., *Att.-Gen. v Hall*[264] and *O'Hanlon v Logue*.[265] And in *Re Caus* Luxmoore J. came to the same conclusion. I would expressly reserve my opinion on the question whether these decisions should be sustained in this House. So important a matter should not be decided except on a direct consideration of it. It is possible that, particularly in regard to the celebration of masses in public, good reason may be found for supporting a gift for such an object as both a legal and a charitable purpose. But it follows from what I have said in the earlier part of this opinion that I am unable to accept the view, which at least in the Irish cases is clearly expressed, that in intercessory prayer and edification that public benefit which is the condition of legal charity is to be found. Of the decision of Luxmoore J. in *Re Caus*, I would only say that his ratio decidendi is expressly stated to be,[266] "first, that it (i.e., a gift for the saying of masses) enables a ritual act to be performed which is recognised by a large proportion of Christian people to be the central act of their religion, and, secondly, that it assists in the endowment of priests whose duty it is to perform the ritual act." The decision, therefore, does not assist the appellant's argument in the present case and I make no further comments on it.[267]

---

263 [1934] Ch. 162.
264 [1897] 2 I.R. 426.
265 [1906] 1 I.R. 247.
266 [1934] Ch. 162 at 170.
267 See *Re Hetherington* [1990] Ch. 1 on *Re Caus*.

It remains, finally, to deal with the argument that the element of public benefit is supplied by the fact that qualification for admission to membership of the community is not limited to any group of persons but is open to any woman in the wide world who has the necessary vocation. Thus, it is said, just as the endowment of a scholarship open to public competition is a charity, so also a gift to enable any woman (or, presumably, any man) to enter a fuller religious life is a charity. To this argument, which, it must be admitted, has a speciously logical appearance, the first answer is that which I have indicated earlier in this opinion. There is no novelty in the idea that a community of nuns must, if it is to continue, from time to time obtain fresh recruits from the outside world. That is why a perpetuity is involved in a gift for the benefit of such a community, and it is not to be supposed that, to mention only three masters of this branch of the law, Wickens V.C., Lord Lindley or Lord Macnaghten failed to appreciate the point. Yet, by direct decision or by way of emphatic example, a community such as this is by them regarded as the very type of religious institution which is not charitable. I know of no consideration applicable to this case which would justify this House in unsettling a rule of law which has been established so long and by such high authority. But that is not the only, nor, indeed, the most cogent reason why I cannot accede to the appellant's argument. It is a trite saying that the law is life, not logic. But it is, I think, conspicuously true of the law of charity that it has been built up, not logically, but empirically. It would not, therefore, be surprising to find that, while in every category of legal charity some element of public benefit must be present, the court had not adopted the same measure in regard to different categories, but had accepted one standard in regard to those gifts which are alleged to be for the advancement of religion, and it may be yet another in regard to the relief of poverty. To argue by a method of syllogism or analogy from the category of education to that of religion ignores the historical process of the law. Nor would there be lack of justification for the divergence of treatment which is here assumed. For there is a legislative and political background peculiar to so-called religious trusts, which has, I think, influenced the development of the law in this matter.[268] **6–237**

Appeal dismissed. **6–238**

CHARITY COMMISSIONERS' DECISION ON APPLICATION FOR REGISTRATION OF THE CHURCH OF SCIENTOLOGY, 17 DECEMBER 1999

The Legal Test of Public Benefit under the Third Head of Charity

The Commissioners noted that it is clear (from the dicta of Lord Greene M.R. in *Coats v Gilmour*) that the burden is upon the religious organisation in question to demonstrate both its impact upon the community and that the impact is beneficial, if public benefit is to be demonstrated. **6–239**

Some clear principles emerge from the decided cases: **6–240**

> A gift for the advancement of religion must be beneficial to the public (or a sufficient section of the public)[269] and not simply for the benefit of the adherents of the particular religion themselves.[270]
>
> It is settled law that the question whether a particular gift satisfies the requirement of public benefit must be determined by the court and the opinion of the donor or testator is irrelevant.[271]
>
> The court must decide whether or not there is a benefit to the community in the light of evidence of a kind cognisable by the court.[272]

The presence or absence of the necessary element of public benefit has also been considered in a number of cases. The essential distinguishing feature seems to be whether or not the practice of the religion is essentially public. The case *In re Hetherington decd.* [1990] Ch. 1 focused on the question of public benefit **6–241**

---

[268] The Nathan Committee on Charitable Trusts rejected the suggestion of the representatives of the Roman Catholic Church that trusts for the advancement of religion should be defined to include "the advancement of religion by those means which that religion believes and teaches are means by which it does advance it": (1952) Cmnd. 8710, paras 129–130.

[269] *National Anti-Vivisection Society v IRC* [1948] A.C. 31.

[270] *Holmes v AG*, *The Times*, February 12, 1981.

[271] *Re Hummeltenberg* [1923] 1 Ch. 237 and *National Anti-Vivisection Society v IRC* (above).

[272] *Gilmour v Coats* [1949] A.C. 426.

in relation to religion. In that case the Judge summarised the principles established by the legal authorities. In concluding that a gift for the celebration of masses (assumed to be in public) was charitable he drew upon cases concerning a variety of religious practices and concluded as follows:

1. a trust for the advancement of education, the relief of poverty or the advancement of religion is charitable and assumed to be for the public benefit. The assumption can be rebutted by showing that in fact the particular trust in question cannot operate so as to confer a legally recognised benefit on the public—as in *Gilmour v Coats;*
2. the celebration of a religious rite in public does confer sufficient public benefit because of the edifying and improving effect of such celebration on the members of the public who attend; and
3. the celebration of a religious rite in private does not contain the necessary element of public benefit since any benefit of prayer or example is incapable of proof in the legal sense and any element of edification is limited to a private not public class of those present at the celebration. Following *Gilmour v Coats,*[273] *Yeap Cheah Neo v Ong Cheng Neo*[274] and *Hoare v Hoare*[275]; and
4. where there is a gift for a religious purpose which could be carried out in a way which is beneficial to the public, (i.e. by public masses) but could also be carried out in a way which would not have a sufficient element of public element (i.e. by private masses) the gift is to be construed as a gift to be carried out by methods that are charitable, all non charitable methods being excluded.

It is clear from *In re Hetherington decd*[276] and the cases cited there that it is the public nature of the religious practice which is essential to the gift being charitable.

6–242 The Commissioners concluded that the decided cases indicated that where the practice of the religion is essentially private or is limited to a private class of individuals not extending to the public generally, the element of public benefit will not be established.[277]

The Legal Test of Public Benefit under the Fourth Head

6–243 The Commissioners turned next to the legal test of public benefit under the fourth head of charity and considered the test to be that set out by Lord Wright in *National Anti-Vivisection Society v IRC.*[278] Lord Wright said that:

> "I think the whole tendency of the concept of charity in a legal sense under the fourth head is towards tangible and objective benefits, and at least, that approval by the common understanding of enlightened opinion for the time being, is necessary before an intangible benefit can be taken to constitute a sufficient benefit to the community to justify admission of the object into the fourth class."

6–244 It seemed to the Commissioners that the benefit that arises from the moral or spiritual welfare or improvement of the community is likely to be an intangible rather than a tangible one. The Commissioners considered the test in respect of an intangible benefit to mean a common consensus of opinion among people who were fair minded and free from prejudice or bias.

6–245 The Commissioners considered in particular whether the representations which it had received about Scientology generally and CoS in particular, both favourable and unfavourable amounted to such "common understanding" and concluded that they did not. The representations were not easily substantiated and in effect represented opposing ends of the spectrum of opinion about CoS or Scientology generally.

---

273 [1949] A.C. 426.
274 (1875) L.R. 6 P.C. 381.
275 (1886) 56 L.T. 147.
276 [1990] Ch. 1.
277 *In re Hetherington decd* (above); *Coats v Gilmour* [1948] Ch. 340 at 347, per Lord Evershed.
278 [1948] A.C. 31 at 49.

The Commissioners further indicated that a key factor in assessing whether the test in that case was met (i.e. whether there was a common understanding of enlightened opinion that public benefit flowed from the advancement of Scientology by CoS), was the extent to which the core practices of Scientology were readily accessible by the public generally. **6–246**

Accordingly, the Commissioners would need to consider whether there was approval by the common understanding of enlightened opinion that pursuit of Scientology doctrines and practices is beneficial to the community such that CoS may be regarded as charitable under the fourth head. **6–247**

Consideration of CoS's Arguments as to Public Benefit under the Fourth Head of Charity

The Commissioners noted CoS's arguments in this respect. One interpretation of CoS's legal arguments was to the effect that public benefit under the fourth head of charity does not have to be proved, but that it is only necessary to show that the organisation's activities may have that result. **6–248**

The Commissioners considered CoS's argument apparently based upon *Berry v St Marylebone Corporation* [1959] Ch. 406 concerning the Theosophical Society in England seeking relief from paying rates under section 8 of the Ratings and Valuation (Miscellaneous Provisions) Act 1955. The Commissioners noted that CoS appeared to rely on dicta of Romer L.J. in that case as support for the proposition that public benefit under the fourth head of charity need not be proven but should only be shown. **6–249**

The Commissioners did not accept this argument, as it was not clear to them that the case cited—*Berry v St Marylebone Corporation*—was authority for this proposition, rather it seemed to the Commissioners that it was authority for the proposition that it was necessary to show that the purpose (in that case the advancement of religion) may be likely to be advanced. This they had considered above. In any event the case related specifically to the requirements of section 8 of the Ratings and Valuation (Miscellaneous Provisions) Act 1955 and was not a discussion about charitable status such that the judge's comments were not directly applicable to charity law. **6–250**

In relation to the question of public benefit it seemed clear to the Commissioners from the dicta of Lord Wright in *National Anti-vivisection Society v IRC* that public benefit must positively be shown under the fourth head of charity. Lord Wright's comments in that case that the whole tendency of the concept of charity under the fourth head is towards tangible and objective benefits, seemed to the Commissioners to indicate quite clearly that the benefits must be identifiable and demonstrable, and that a common consensus of approval is necessary before an intangible benefit can be regarded as sufficient to satisfy the requirement of public benefit. **6–251**

Whether CoS is Established for the Public Benefit, whether under the Third or Fourth Heads of Charity

The Commissioners next sought to address the question of whether CoS had shown itself to be established for the public benefit. The Commissioners considered the considerable volume of evidence supplied by CoS in support of its arguments that CoS was established for the public benefit whether under the third or fourth heads of charity because **6–252**

> Individual churches of Scientology conduct numerous religious services freely accessible by members of the public.
>
> CoS sufficiently benefits the public through extensive charitable and public benefit programmes including anti drug campaigns, eradicating illiteracy, disaster relief and raising public morality.
>
> The Company (CoS) is limited by guarantee and its members make no profit.
>
> It is of the essence of Scientology "like most other religions" to seek to make itself available to all.
>
> Many of Mr Hubbard's teachings are already recognised as charitable and applied by existing registered charities.
>
> The Scientology movement engages in other activities which could potentially give rise to public benefit e.g. volunteer and relief programmes; rituals and practices such as "assists" (described as a form of healing); work in the field of criminal rehabilitation; observance of a moral code by individual Scientologists and promulgation of that moral code through the "Way to Happiness Foundation".

6-253 The Commissioners considered that the evidence and arguments supplied by CoS may indicate ways in which Scientology organisations, and individual Scientologists, seek to benefit the wider community. They noted that in terms of English charity law some of that work may potentially be charitable in its own right, albeit not as promoting the moral or spiritual welfare or improvement of the community nor as advancing religion.[279] However, the Commissioners noted that the evidence and argument put to them by CoS did not address the central question of whether the advancement of Scientology (whether as a religion or as a non-religious belief system) confers recognisable benefit upon the public in English charity law. CoS states that its principal activities are auditing and training and that it is through these core activities that Scientology is advanced. In the Commissioners view it therefore had to be demonstrated that the advancement of Scientology through auditing and training is beneficial to the public. The Commissioners considered that it is to the central activities of auditing and training that the question of public benefit should be addressed.

6-254 The Commissioners went on to consider whether it was demonstrated that public benefit flowed from the core practices of Scientology. The Commissioners again noted that the test of public benefit was slightly different in relation to the third and fourth heads of charity. In relation to the third head the decided cases indicated that the public or private nature of the "religious practice" of the organisation in question was central to determining the presence or absence of public benefit. In relation to the purpose of promoting the moral or spiritual welfare or improvement of the community under the fourth head of charity the legal test was that set out by Lord Wright in the *National Vivisection Society v IRC* case.

6-255 *In relation to the test of public benefit for the advancement of religion the Commissioners concluded that:*

(1) The Central "Religious" Practices of Scientology are Conducted in Private and not in Public

6-256 The "religious practices" of Scientology are auditing and training. Scientologists regard these as worship. Auditing is conducted in private on a one to one basis. It appears akin to a form of counselling and is described by Scientologists as such.[280] Training is essentially a private activity requiring the study of specialist material and access to specialist trainers. Whilst members of the public may sign up for a course of auditing and training, generally upon payment of the appropriate requested donation, these activities are not carried out "in public". Further, progression beyond introductory or initial levels of auditing and training necessitated membership of the Church.

6-257 Attendance at a session of auditing or training by members of the public generally does not appear to be a possibility. The Commissioners found it difficult therefore to see how any edifying and improving effects upon the public generally might flow from the "religious" practices of Scientology.

6-258 In relation to the fourth proposition in *In re Hetherington decd*, there was no suggestion that auditing and training could be carried out in a way that was public rather than private. It did not seem possible to construe auditing and training as religious rites which could be conducted in public rather than in private such as to render them charitable.

(2) Auditing and Training are in their Nature Private rather than Public Activities

6-259 The Commissioners considered that even if a member of the public could attend an auditing and/or training session other than as a participant but rather as an observer, these Scientology services are by their very nature directed to the particular individual receiving them. Auditing appears akin to a form of counselling and is described by Scientologists who receive it as "counselling". It is directed to the private needs of the individual receiving it. The Commissioners found it difficult to see how the public could be edified or otherwise benefited by attending and observing at such a session.

6-260 Both the above factors—that Scientology services are conducted in private, and are in their nature private being directed to the needs of the private individual in receipt of them seemed to the Commissioners to indicate that these actual activities are of a private rather than a public kind. In any event it seemed to the Commissioners that any benefit to the public that may flow from auditing and training is incapable of proof, any edification or improving effect being limited to the private individual engaging in the auditing

---

279 Much Scientology activity appeared to the Commissioners to be in the fields of education and what might broadly be termed "relief in need".

280 Video presentation "The Church of Scientology at Saint Hill—A Special presentation to the Charity Commission of England and Wales".

or training. Accordingly, the Commissioners concluded that these activities conferred no legally recognised benefit on the public.

6–261 In addition the Commissioners noted that the apparent dependence of participation in those activities upon payment of the requested donation referred to by CoS strengthened their perception that these activities were of a private rather than a public kind. Whilst CoS states that there are ways in which adherents can and do participate in auditing and training without making any form of monetary contribution, so that a lack of financial means is no bar to a member's progress in Scientology, access to auditing and training through requested donations is the norm. The Commissioners noted that the fact that a practice existed of requesting and making these payments strengthened the Commissioners in their perception that the activities were of a private rather than a public kind.

6–262 The Commissioners further noted that in its published and promotional literature, including the book "What is Scientology?", Scientology on balance presented its benefits in private rather than public terms.

6–263 In addition the Commissioners noted that a not insignificant number of individual Scientologists described the benefits of Scientology in private and personal terms this being borne out both by a number of the statements printed in Scientology's published literature and by a significant proportion of the letters of support for CoS received from individual Scientologists.

6–264 The fact that Scientology describes its benefits in private rather than public terms in its published and promotional literature, and that individual Scientologists described the benefits of Scientology to them in private and personal terms confirmed the Commissioners conclusion that CoS is not established for the public benefit.

6–265 *In relation to the test of public benefit under the fourth head of charity law for the moral or spiritual welfare or improvement of the community the Commissioners concluded that:*

The question of accessibility by the public was key to the existence of public benefit. As indicated above, the Commissioners had already concluded that the central practices of Scientology (auditing and training) were conducted in private rather than in public, and were in their nature private rather than public activities. In addition there was the practice of requesting donations in advance of receipt of those services. This led the Commissioners to conclude that the restricted access to those practices meant that any benefit flowing from Scientology as advanced by CoS is of a private rather than a public kind. In addition the description of the benefits of Scientology, both in Scientology published and promotional literature and by individual Scientologists, as already acknowledged by the Commissioners, confirmed them in this conclusion.

6–266 The Commissioners concluded that it could not be said that CoS had demonstrated that it was established for the public benefit so as to satisfy the legal test of public benefit of a charitable purpose for the advancement of religion or for the moral or spiritual welfare or improvement of the community.

D. Section 2(2)(d): "The Advancement of Health or the Saving of Lives"

6–267 The Charities Act 2006 s.2(3)(b) states that for the purposes of s.2(2)(d) "the advancement of health" includes "the prevention or relief of sickness, disease or human suffering". This encompasses measures to ease the suffering, or to assist the recovery, of people who are sick, convalescent, disabled or infirm;[281] and a person may relevantly be "sick" if he suffers from a mental disorder or an addiction.[282] The advancement of health "includes conventional methods as well as complementary, alternative or holistic methods which are concerned with healing mind, body and spirit in the alleviation of symptoms and the cure of illness."[283] However the Charity Commission also states that:[284]

---

[281] *Re Lewis* [1955] Ch. 104 (blind); *Motability* [1977] Ch. Com. Rep. paras [51]–[56] (physically disabled); *Sarah Mary Collard Fund for the Provision of Guide Dogs* [1983] Ch. Com. Rep. paras [57]–[58].

[282] *Needham v Bowers* (1888) 21 Q.B.D. 436 ("institution for the reception of insane persons"); *Cawse v Committee of the Nottingham Lunatic Hospital* [1891] 1 Q.B. 585 ("lunatic hospital").

[283] Charity Commission *Commentary on the Descriptions of Charitable Purposes in the Charities Act 2006* (August 2009) para.[25]. See too *Re Le Cren Clarke* [1996] 1 All E.R. 715 (faith healing); Charity Commission, *Decision on the Application for Registration of NSFH Charitable Trust Ltd* (15 August 2002) (spiritual healing).

[284] Charity Commission *Commentary on the Descriptions of Charitable Purposes in the Charities Act 2006* (August 2009) para.[25].

> "to be charitable there needs to be sufficient evidence of the efficacy of the method to be used. Assessing the efficacy of different therapies will depend upon what benefits are claimed for it (i.e. whether it is diagnostic, curative, therapeutic and/or palliative) and whether it is offered as a complement to conventional medicine or as an alternative. Each case is considered on its merits but the House of Lords Report on complementary and alternative medicine provides a useful guide."[285]

6–268 Section 2(2)(d) obviously takes in the provision of medical and nursing services, whether in the community,[286] or in hospitals, hospices, care homes, rest homes, etc.[287] It also includes the promotion of health by the provision of other services, items and facilities for patients,[288] the welfare of health professionals,[289] the education and training of health professionals,[290] and the organisation and regulation of their activities.[291] The pursuit of medical research also falls within the scope of s.2(2)(d),[292] as does the education of the public with regard to health and safety matters.[293] However these last few purposes also fall within s.2(2)(b), and the saving of lives by rescue services, which falls under this head,[294] also falls under s.2(2)(l).

6–269 In *Re Resch's WT*, Lord Wilberforce stated that a hospital may not be a charitable body if "the benefits it provides are not for the public, or a sufficiently large class of the public to satisfy the necessary tests of public character". However, he also considered that a private hospital which "provides only for persons of means who are capable of paying the substantial fees required as a condition of admission" does not necessarily fall foul of this rule, because "to provide, in response to public need, medical treatment otherwise inaccessible but in its nature expensive, without any profit motive, might well be charitable" albeit that "to limit admission to a nursing home to the rich would not be so."[295]

6–270 This case was distinguished by the Charity Commission in its decision to refuse registration as a charity to Odstock Private Care Ltd.[296] The applicant company was formed, by means of a loan from an NHS foundation trust, to promote the undertaking of private patient work at the trust's district hospital. It did this by entering agreements with patients and insurance companies for the provision of private care, and then contracting with the trust to provide staffed facilities to enable this work to be carried out by clinicians. The company argued that its overall aim was to provide low-cost treatment to patients, using facilities which were available to the public at large and ploughing any surpluses

---

285 *6th Report of the House of Lords Select Committee on Science and Technology, Session 1999–2000*.

286 *IRC v Peebleshire Nursing Assoc* 1927 SC 215; *Re Webster* [1912] 1 Ch. 106 (midwives).

287 *Biscoe v Jackson* (1887) 35 Ch.D. 460; *Re Weir Hospital* [1910] 2 Ch. 124; *Re Welsh Hospital (Netley) Fund* [1921] 1 Ch. 655; *Kytherian Association of Queensland v Sklavos* (1958) 101 C.L.R. 56; *Re Smith, decd* [1962] 1 W.L.R. 763; *Re Resch's WT* [1969] 1 A.C. 514.

288 *Att.-Gen. v Belgrave Hospital* [1910] 1 Ch. 73; *Re Adams* [1968] Ch. 80; Charity Commission *Annual Report for 1966* at p.32. By extension a gift to provide accommodation for relations coming to visit patients is also charitable: *Re Dean's WT* [1950] 1 All E.R. 882.

289 *Armagh County Infirmary Committee v Commissioner for Valuation for NI* [1940] N.I. 1 (house for visiting surgeon); *Re White's WT* [1951] 1 All E.R. 528 (rest home for nurses). See too *Re Pettit* [1988] 2 N.Z.L.R. 513 (relief of doctors' widows).

290 *Re Lysaght* [1966] 1 Ch. 191 (medical studentships); *London Hospital Medical College v IRC* [1976] 1 W.L.R. 613 (student union at medical school).

291 Including the promulgation and enforcement of professional standards: Charity Commission *Decision on the Application for Registration as a Charity by the General Medical Council* (2 April 2001).

292 *Taylor v Taylor* (1910) 10 C.L.R. 218; *Re Osmund* [1944] Ch. 206; *National Trust Co v Canadian Diabetes Assoc* (1993) 109 D.L.R. (4th) 232.

293 *Re Hood* [1931] 1 Ch. 240 (temperance); *McGregor v Commissioner of Stamp Duties* [1942] N.Z.L.R. 164 (obstetrics and maternal welfare); *The League of Highway Safety and Safe Drivers Ltd* [1965] Ch. Com. Rep. 27 (road safety); *The Royal Association for Disability and Rehabilitation* [1977] Ch. Com. Rep. [57] (causes of disablement and the ways in which these may be reduced or eliminated); *Auckland Medical Aid Trust v CIR* [1979] 1 NZLR 382 (human reproduction).

294 *Thomas v Howell* (1874) L.R. 18 Eq. 198 (lifeboat); *Re Wokingham Fire Brigade Trusts* [1951] Ch. 373 (fire brigade).

295 [1969] 1 A.C. 514 at 540–541.

296 September 25, 2007.

back into additional NHS facilities at the hospital. However, the Commission took the view that the scheme was not available to the public at large, but only to those who could pay the fees, and so people living in poverty would not have access to its services. As the company did not provide financial assistance to patients on low incomes, they would need to fall back on insurance, but the cost of such insurance had not been shown to be affordable to all members of the community.[297]

E. Section 2(2)(e): "The Advancement of Citizenship or Community Development"

6–271 This head takes in a broad group of charitable purposes which are directed towards support for community and social infrastructure and whose focus is on the community rather than the individual. These include the promotion of urban and rural regeneration,[298] the promotion of community capacity building,[299] and promotion of the voluntary sector.[300]

F. Section 2(2)(f): "The Advancement of the Arts, Culture, Heritage, or Science"

6–272 Charities concerned with the advancement of art and culture, such as museums[301] and art galleries,[302] must satisfy a criterion of educational or artistic merit.[303] The advancement of "heritage" takes in the preservation and conservation of historic land and buildings,[304] as well as the preservation of historical traditions by folk clubs, country dancing societies, eisteddfods, etc. The advancement of science includes scientific research projects and charities connected with learned societies and institutions, e.g. the Royal College of Surgeons[305] and the Royal Geographical Society.[306]

G. Section 2(2)(g): "The Advancement of Amateur Sport"

6–273 For many years, the promotion of sport was upheld as charitable only where it was ancillary to the pursuit of a charitable purpose: *Re Mariette*[307] (sport in a school—educational); *Re Gray*[308] (sport in an army regiment—general public benefit in promoting the efficiency of the Army); *London Hospital Medical College v IRC.*[309] (athletic, cultural and social activities of Students Union—furthering educational purposes of medical school); *IRC v McMullen*[310] (soccer and other sports in schools and universities—educational).

---

297 For further discussion of private hospitals, see D. Morris, "Fee-Paying Hospitals and Charitable Status: A New Dawn or Lost Opportunities?" (2007) 18 K.L.J. 455.

298 Charity Commission, *RR 2: Promotion of Rural and Urban Regeneration* (March 1999 version). Cf. *Re Tenant* [1996] 2 N.Z.L.R. 633 (provision of creamery).

299 Charity Commission, *RR 5: The Promotion of Community Capacity Building* (November 2000 version).

300 Charity Commission, *RR 13: Promotion of the Voluntary Sector for the Benefit of the Public* (September 2004 version). See too Charity Commission, *Decision on the Application for Registration of the Charity Bank Ltd* (April 17, 2002); Charity Commission, *Decision on the Application for Registration of Guidestar UK* (March 7, 2003); Charity Commission, *RR 14: Promoting the Efficiency and Effectiveness of Charities and the Effective Use of Charitable Resources for the Benefit of the Public* (September 2004 version).

301 *Trustees of the British Museum v White* (1826) 2 Sim. & St. 594; *Re Holburne* (1885) 53 L.T. 212.

302 *Abbott v Fraser* (1874) L.R. 6 P.C. 96.

303 Charity Commission, *RR 10: Museums and Art Galleries* (August 2002 version), paras 6–12 and Annex A.

304 *Re Verrall* [1916] 1 Ch. 100 (National Trust); *Re Cranstoun* [1932] 1 Ch. 537 (Elizabethan cottages); *Settle & Carlisle Railway Trust* [1990] Ch. Com. Rep. 23–26 (railway line). See too Charity Commission, *RR 9: Preservation and Conservation* (February 2001 version).

305 *Royal College of Surgeons of England v National Provincial Bank Ltd* [1952] A.C. 631.

306 *Beaumont v Oliviera* (1869) L.R. 4 Ch. 309.

307 [1915] 2 Ch. 284. See too *Re Geere's WT* [1954] C.L.Y. 388 (swimming pool at Marlborough College).

308 [1925] Ch. 362; but doubted in *IRC v City of Glasgow Police Athletic Assoc* [1953] A.C. 380 at 391 and 401.

309 [1976] 2 All E.R. 113. See too *Att.-Gen. v Ross* [1985] 3 All E.R. 334 (North London Polytechnic Students' Union).

310 [1981] A.C. 1, reproduced above at paras 6–177 ff.

Until recently, however, the promotion of sport as such was not a charitable object: *Re Nottage*[311] (yacht racing); *Re Clifford*[312] (angling); *Re Patten*[313] (cricket); *Re King*[314] (general sport); *Re Birchfield Harriers*[315] (competitive athletics).

6–274 In 2003, the law was changed by the Charity Commission's decision to recognise as charitable "the promotion of community participation in healthy recreation by providing facilities for playing particular sports".[316] In this context, "facilities" meant not just lands, building, and equipment, but also the organising of sporting activity such as that undertaken by community amateur sports clubs (CASCs). In practical terms, a CASC could therefore be a charity provided that: (1) the sport in question was capable of improving physical health and fitness, and (2) the club had an open membership; i.e. access to the club's facilities was genuinely available to anyone who wished to take advantage of them.[317] Some restrictions on club membership were tolerated, e.g. limited facilities and health of applicants,[318] but others were not, e.g. tests of skill for admission and membership subscriptions which are unaffordable for most of the community served by the club.[319]

6–275 In 2006 the law was changed again by the Charities Act 2006. The Government's intention was simply to codify the current position, but an amendment was agreed to the legislation during its passage through Parliament, with the result that s.2(3)(d) now provides that for the purposes of s.2(2)(g) " 'sport' means sports or games which promote health by involving physical or mental skill or exertion". Hence it can now be a charitable purpose to undertake sport and games involving mental as well as physical skill or exertion—assuming that these activities "promote health". At the time of writing, guidance is still awaited from the Charity Commission as to which sports and games it now regards as falling within the scope of the Act.

H. Section 2(2)(h): "The Advancement of Human Rights, Conflict Resolution or Reconciliation or the Promotion of Religious or Racial Harmony or Equality and Diversity"

6–276 The promotion of human rights can be accomplished in various ways including monitoring human rights abuses, obtaining redress for the victims of such abuses, and campaigning in favour of the recognition of human rights, to the extent that political activity of this kind is ancillary to the charity's main purposes.[320] The advancement of conflict resolution or reconciliation includes the resolution of international conflicts, the promotion of international co-operation,[321] and relieving the suffering and distress arising through conflict on a national and international scale. It also includes mediation and conciliation services,[322] and the promotion of restorative justice, where all the parties

311 [1885] 2 Ch. 649.
312 (1911) 106 L.T. 14.
313 [1929] 2 Ch. 276.
314 [1931] W.N. 232.
315 [1989] Ch. Com. Rep. paras 48–52.
316 Charity Commission, *RR 11: Charitable Status and Sport* (April 2003 version).
317 *RR11* at para.7.
318 *RR11* at paras 16–17.
319 *RR11* at paras 18–19.
320 See further Charity Commission, *RR 12: The Promotion of Human Rights* (January 2005 version). For discussion of political activities, see paras 6–116 ff. And for a survey of charities working in this field, see Charity Commission, *RS 16: Charities Working in the Field of Human Rights* (December 2007 version).
321 Cf. *Re Koeppler's WT* [1986] Ch. 423 (trust to fund conferences to promote co-operation in Europe charitable as for the advancement of education).
322 Mediation in Divorce (Richmond-upon-Thames); The National Family Conciliation Council [1983] Ch. Com. Rep. paras 28–34.

affected by a particular criminal offence come together to resolve collectively how to deal with its aftermath.[323]

6–277 The appeasement of racial feelings between Dutch- and English-speaking South Africans was held not to be a charitable purpose in *Re Strakosch*,[324] essentially because the court considered it to be a political purpose. Social attitudes subsequently underwent a considerable shift, however, and the enactment of the Race Relations Act 1968 indicated that Parliament considered the promotion of harmonious race relations to be for the public benefit. For this reason, the Charity Commissioners departed from *Re Strakosch* in 1983, when they stated that "promoting race relations, endeavouring to eliminate discrimination on grounds of race, and encouraging equality of opportunity" are charitable purposes.[325]

I. Section 2(2)(i): "The Advancement of Environmental Protection or Improvement"

6–278 This head includes[326] the conservation of particular species of flora and fauna, of particular geographical areas,[327] and of the environment more generally,[328] along with the promotion of sustainable development and bio-diversity and the promotion of recycling and renewable energy resources.[329] Charities for the conservation of species or of particular land must produce independent expert evidence that the species or land in question are worthy of conservation.[330]

6–279 In *Re Grove-Grady*,[331] the Court of Appeal struck down a trust to establish a sanctuary for wild birds and animals from which the public would be excluded, because the court could perceive no benefit to mankind in leaving the animals to their own devices in this way. However, ideas about environmental protection and the survival of endangered species have moved on. The Charity Commission's current approach to wildlife sanctuaries is to presume that they are not for the public benefit unless the public is given physical access to the site, but to take a flexible approach to the level of access needed, acknowledging that access "needs to be consistent with the aims of the charity so that visitors should not be allowed access at the expense of deterioration of a fragile . . . environment".[332] If an organisation can make out a case for limiting or excluding public access, it may still be able to satisfy the public benefit requirement by other means, e.g. restricting access to parts of the site, publishing books and videos about their activities, etc.[333]

J. Section 2(2)(j): "The Relief of Those in Need by Reason of Youth, Age, Ill-health, Disability, Financial Hardship or other Disadvantage"

6–280 As previously noted,[334] "the relief of aged, impotent and poor people" was specified as charitable in the Preamble to the Statute of Charitable Uses 1601, but because these words are to be construed

---

323 Charity Commission, *Decision on Application for Registration by Restorative Justice Consortium Ltd* (January 15, 2003).
324 [1949] Ch. 529.
325 [1983] Ch. Com. Rep. paras 15–20. See too *Community Security Trust* (1995) 4 Decisions of the Charity Commissioners 8. The promotion of gender equality is also a charitable purpose: *Halpin v Seear* Ch.D. 27 February 1976; *Women's Service Trust* [1977] Ch. Com. Rep. paras 34–36.
326 For a survey of charities working in this field, see Charity Commission, *Going Green: Charities and Environmental Responsibility* (December 2008 version), part 5.
327 *The Upper Teesdale Defence Fund* [1969] Ch. Comm. Rep. paras 23–24 (fund for preservation of flora and fauna of Upper Teesdale).
328 Charity Commission, *Decision on the Application for Registration of Environment Foundation* (January 24, 2003).
329 Charity Commission, *Decision on the Application for Registration of Recycling in Ottery* (April 2002).
330 Charity Commission, *RR 9: Preservation and Conservation* (February 2001 version), paras A10-A15.
331 [1929] 1 Ch. 557.
332 Charity Commission, *RR 9: Preservation and Conservation* (February 2001 version) para.A19.
333 *RR9* para.A20. Cf. *Att.-Gen. for New South Wales v Sawtell* [1978] 2 N.S.W.L.R. 200.
334 See para.6–140.

disjunctively,[335] the relief of those in need by reason of age,[336] and the relief of those in need by reason of ill-health or disability, are stand-alone charitable purposes—although they belong more obviously under s.2(2)(d). The Preamble also mentions "the education and preferment of orphans", and by analogy with this purpose, the promotion of the welfare of children generally is also a charitable purpose.[337]

K. Section 2(2)(k): "The Advancement of Animal Welfare"

6–281 Trusts for the protection or welfare of animals have been upheld as charitable provided that they benefit, or promote the moral improvement of, the community.[338] Note, however, that in *National Anti-Vivisection Society v IRC*,[339] the House of Lords held among other things that anti-vivisection is not a charitable purpose because the benefits to mankind of retaining vivisection outweighed the moral benefits of abolishing it.

L. Section 2(2)(l): "The Promotion of the Efficiency of the Armed Forces of the Crown, or of the Efficiency of the Police, Fire and Rescue Services or Ambulance Services"

6–282 This sub-section did not appear in the Charities Bill 2005, but was introduced by amendment primarily in order to safeguard the charitable status of the 15,000-odd service funds whose purposes are (broadly speaking) to further *esprit de corps* in the armed services.[340] Typically these include funds for increasing the physical fitness of members of the services through the provision of sporting facilities, equipment, and sporting competitions; funds to support messes (NCOs and Officers) and institutes (other ranks), including the provision of plate, etc.; benevolent funds for serving members, ex-serving members, widows/widowers of serving or ex-serving members, and the dependents of serving or ex-serving members who are in need; and so on.

M. Other Purposes

6–283 Section 2(2)(m) deems "any other purposes within subsection (4)" to be charitable, and s.2(4) sweeps in existing charitable purposes which do not fall under any other head (including purposes falling within the Recreational Charities Act 1958), and any new charitable purposes which are recognised in the future by analogising from existing charitable purposes. Existing purposes falling under this head include: the payment of rates and taxes;[341] the provision of public works and public

---

335 *Re Robinson* [1951] Ch. 198; *Joseph Rowntree Memorial Trust Housing Assoc Ltd v Att.-Gen.* [1983] Ch. 159.

336 *Re Dunlop* [1984] N.I. 408 (home for elderly Presbyterians); *Joseph Rowntree Memorial Trust Housing Assoc Ltd v Att.-Gen.* [1983] Ch. 159 (sheltered accommodation for the elderly). The Charities Act 2006 s.2(3)(e) specifies that "relief" of those in need under this head includes the provision of accommodation or care.

337 *D v NSPCC* [1978] A.C. 171 at 228. See too *Re Sahal's WT* [1958] 1 W.L.R. 1243 (gift of house as children's home); Charity Commission, *Decision on the Application for Registration of the Internet Content Rating Association* (September 12, 2002) (protection of children and young people from harm arising from contact with unsuitable material on the internet).

338 *Re Wedgwood* [1915] 1 Ch. 113 (promotion of humane methods of slaughtering livestock); *Re Moss* [1949] 1 All E.R. 495 (welfare of cats and kittens); *Re Green's WT* [1985] 3 All E.R. 455 (rescue, maintenance, and benefit of cruelly treated animals).

339 [1948] A.C. 31.

340 *Hansard (HL)* June 28, 2005, cols 131 ff.

341 Dating back to the Preamble which refers to the "aid or ease of any poor inhabitants concerning payment of fifteens, setting out of soldiers and other taxes." See e.g. *Nightingale v Goulburn* (1848) 2 Ph. 594.

amenities;[342] the promotion of agriculture,[343] and of industry and commerce,[344] provided that the public benefit outweighs any private benefits derived by those involved;[345] the relief of unemployment;[346] the promotion of moral or spiritual welfare;[347] the relief of refugees;[348] and the relief of victims of accidents and disasters.[349]

It also includes the provision of facilities for public recreation. Trusts of land for public use as a recreation ground have long been charitable,[350] but problems were created by the House of Lords' decision in *IRC v Baddeley*,[351] reproduced below. This concerned a trust to promote the moral, social and physical well-being of Methodists resident in West Ham and Leyton by the provision of facilities for moral, social and physical training and recreation. The court held that this was not charitable, first, because the intended beneficiaries did not comprise a sufficient section of the community, and, second, because the promotion of social well-being was not a charitable purpose. It was then feared that village halls and similar institutions which had previously been considered charitable might not be charitable after all, and so the Recreational Charities Act 1958 was enacted to remove any doubt on this point. **6–284**

The 1958 Act establishes two criteria for the validity of a recreational charity: first, the trust must be for the public benefit; and, second, the facilities must be provided in the interests of social welfare. The second criterion itself has two elements: the first is constant, namely, that the object of providing the facilities must be to improve the intended beneficiaries' conditions of life; but the second may be satisfied in alternative ways—by showing either that the beneficiaries have need of the facilities by reason of the factors enumerated in the Act, or that the facilities are available to the members or female (but not male) members of the public at large. The proper interpretation of these provisions is considered by the House of Lords in *Guild v IRC*,[352] also reproduced below. **6–285**

---

342 *Att.-Gen. v Heelis* (1824) 2 Sim. & St. 67 (town lighting, paving, drains and sewers); *Att.-Gen. v Shrewsbury Corp* (1843) 6 Beav. 220 (repair and improvement of town's bridges, towers and walls); *Scottish Burial Reform and Cremation Soc v Glasgow Corp* [1968] A.C. 138 (crematorium); *Oxford Ice-Skating Assoc Ltd* [1984] Ch. Com. Rep. paras 19–25 (ice-rink). Because the provision of amenities and services of this kind is nowadays frequently undertaken by public authorities, many trusts for their provision have been made the subject of schemes under the Charities Act 1993 s.13. See further "Charities for the Maintenance of Highways, Bridges, and Similar Works" [1968] Ch. Com. Rep. paras 66–72.

343 *IRC v Yorkshire Agricultural Soc* [1928] 1 K.B. 611.

344 *IRC v White* (1980) 55 T.C. 61 (improvement of standards of craftsmanship); *Business in the Community* [1987] Ch. Com. Rep. paras 16–19. Note that the regulation of a trade is not a charitable purpose: *Wine Standards Board of the Vintners' Company* [1978] Ch. Com. Rep. paras 95–98.

345 *IRC v Oldham Training and Enterprise Council* [1996] S.T.C. 1218.

346 *Oldham TEC* at 1234; Charity Commission, *RR 3: Charities for the Relief of Unemployment* (March 1999 version).

347 *Re South Place Ethical Society* [1980] 1 W.L.R. 1565; *Public Concern at Work* (1994) 2 Decisions of the Charity Commissioners 5 (assistance to employees faced with moral and ethical issues of whistle-blowing). But cf. Charity Commission, *Decision on the Gnostic Centre's Application for Registration as a Charity*, December 16, 2009, paras 50 to 57: furtherance of the applicant body's non-religious philosophical beliefs was not charitable because it had no demonstrable impact on the community.

348 *Re Morison* (1967) 117 N.L.J. 757.

349 *Re Hartley Colliery Accident Relief Fund* (1908) 102 L.T. 165n.; *Re North Devon and Somerset Relief Fund Trusts* [1953] 1 W.L.R. 1260. Disaster funds are entitled to charitable status only if the help is given to those in need: Charity Commission, *CC 40: Disaster Appeals* (January 2002 version).

350 *Re Hadden* [1932] 1 Ch. 133 (park); *Re Morgan* [1955] 1 W.L.R. 738 (recreation ground); *Brisbane CC v Att.-Gen. for Queensland* [1979] A.C. 411 (park); *Bath and North Eastern Somerset Council v Att.-Gen.* (2002) 5 I.T.E.L.R. 274 (recreation ground).

351 [1955] A.C. 572. See too *Londonderry Presbyterian Church House Trustees v IRC* [1946] N.I. 178; *Williams Trustees v IRC* [1947] A.C. 447.

352 [1992] 2 A.C. 310. See too Charity Commission, *RR 4: The Recreational Charities Act 1958* (August 2000 version); Charity Commission, *Decision on Application for Registration of Community Server* (September 15, 2003).

INLAND REVENUE COMMISSIONERS v BADDELEY

House of Lords [1955] A.C. 572, [1955] 2 W.L.R. 552, [1955] 1 All E.R. 525

6–286 Land was conveyed to trustees on trust to be used by certain Methodist leaders "for the promotion of the religious social and physical well-being of persons resident in . . . West Ham and Leyton . . . *by the provision of facilities for religious services and instruction* and for the social and physical training and recreation of such aforementioned persons who for the time being are in the opinion of such leaders members or likely to become members of the Methodist Church and of insufficient means otherwise to enjoy the advantages provided by these presents and by the provision of facilities for religious social and physical training and education and by promoting and encouraging all forms of such activities as are calculated to contribute to the health and well-being of such persons." A second conveyance was in the same terms but with the omission of the italicised words. The conveyances were held not to be charitable and so not exempt from stamp duty.

6–287 VISCOUNT SIMONDS: . . . This brings me to another aspect of the case, which was argued at great length and to me at least presents the most difficult problems in this branch of the law. Suppose that, contrary to the view that I have expressed that the social element prevented the trust being charitable, the trust would be a valid charitable trust, if the beneficiaries were the community at large or a section of the community defined by some geographical limits, is it the less a valid trust if it is confined to members or potential members of a particular church within a limited geographical area?

6–288 The starting point of the argument must be, that this charity (if it be a charity) falls within the fourth class in Lord Macnaghten's classification. It must therefore be a trust which is, to use the words of Sir Samuel Romilly in *Morice v Bishop of Durham*,[353] of "general public utility," and the question is what these words mean. It is, indeed, an essential feature of all "charity" in the legal sense that there must be in it some element of public benefit, whether the purpose is educational, religious or eleemosynary . . . and, as I have said elsewhere, it is possible, particularly in view of the so-called "poor relations' cases", the scope of which may one day have to be considered, that a different degree of public benefit is requisite according to the class in which the charity is said to fall. But it is said that if a charity falls within the fourth class, it must be for the benefit of the whole community or at least of all the inhabitants of a sufficient area. And it has been urged with much force that, if, as Lord Greene said in *Re Strakosch*,[354] this fourth class is represented in the preamble to the Statute of Elizabeth by the repair of bridges, etc., and possibly by the maintenance of Houses of Correction, the class of beneficiaries or potential beneficiaries cannot be further narrowed down. Some confusion has arisen from the fact that a trust of general public utility, however general and however public, cannot be of equal utility to all and may be of immediate utility to few. A sea wall, the prototype of this class in the preamble, is of remote, if any, utility to those who live in the heart of the Midlands. But there is no doubt that a trust for the maintenance of sea walls generally or along a particular stretch of coast is a good charitable trust. Nor, as it appears to me, is the validity of a trust affected by the fact that by its very nature only a limited number of people are likely to avail themselves, or are perhaps even capable of availing themselves, of its benefits. It is easy, for instance, to imagine a charity which has for its object some form of child welfare, of which the immediate beneficiaries could only be persons of tender age. Yet this would satisfy any test of general public utility. It may be said that it would satisfy the test because the indirect benefit of such a charity would extend far beyond its direct beneficiaries, and that aspect of the matter has probably not been out of sight. Indirect benefit is certainly an aspect which must have influenced the decision of the "cruelty to animal" cases. But, I doubt whether this sort of rationalisation helps to explain a branch of the law which has developed empirically and by analogy upon analogy.

6–289 It is, however, in my opinion, particularly important in cases falling within the fourth category to keep firmly in mind the necessity of the element of general public utility, and I would not relax this rule. For here is a slippery slope. In the case under appeal the intended beneficiaries are a class within a class; they are those of the inhabitants of a particular area who are members of a particular church: the area is

[353] (1805) 10 Ves. 522 at 532.
[354] [1949] Ch. 529.

comparatively large and populous and the members may be numerous. But, if this trust is charitable for them, does it cease to be charitable as the area narrows down and the numbers diminish? Suppose the area is confined to a single street and the beneficiaries to those whose creed commands few adherents: or suppose the class is one that is determined not by religious belief but by membership of a particular profession or by pursuit of a particular trade. These were considerations which influenced the House in the recent case of *Oppenheim*. That was a case of an educational trust, but I think that they have even greater weight in the case of trusts which by their normal classification depend for their validity upon general public utility.

It is pertinent, then, to ask how far your Lordships might regard yourselves bound by authority to hold the trusts now under review valid charitable trusts, if the only question in issue was the sufficiency of the public element . . . **6–290**

In [*Verge v Somerville*[355]] in which the issue was as to the validity of a gift "to the trustees of the Repatriation Fund or other similar fund for the benefit of New South Wales returned soldiers", Lord Wrenbury, delivering the judgment of the Judicial Committee, said that, to be a charity, a trust must be "for the benefit of the community or of an appreciably important class of the community. The inhabitants," he said, "of a parish or town or any particular class of such inhabitants, may, for instance, be the objects of such a gift, but private individuals, or a fluctuating body of private individuals, cannot." Here, my Lords, are two expressions: "an appreciably important class of the community" and "any particular class of such inhabitants," to which in any case it is not easy to give a precise quantitative or qualitative meaning. But I think that in consideration of them the difficulty has sometimes been increased by failing to observe the distinction, at which I hinted earlier in this opinion, between a form of relief accorded to the whole community yet by its very nature advantageous only to the few and a form of relief accorded to a selected few out of a larger number equally willing and able to take advantage of it. Of the former type repatriated New South Wales soldiers would serve as a clear example. To me it would not seem arguable that they did not form an adequate class of the community for the purpose of the particular charity that was being established. It was with this type of case that Lord Wrenbury was dealing, and his words are apt to deal with it. Somewhat different considerations arise if the form, which the purporting charity takes, is something of general utility which is nevertheless made available not to the whole public but only to a selected body of the public—an important class of the public it may be. For example, a bridge which is available for all the public may undoubtedly be a charity and it is indifferent how many people use it. But confine its use to a selected number of persons, however numerous and important: it is then clearly not a charity. It is not of general public utility: for it does not serve the public purpose which its nature qualifies it to serve. **6–291**

Bearing this distinction in mind, though I am well aware that in its application it may often be very difficult to draw the line between public and private purposes, I should in the present case conclude that a trust cannot qualify as a charity within the fourth class . . . if the beneficiaries are a class of persons not only confined to a particular area but selected from within it by reference to a particular creed. The Master of the Rolls in his judgment cites a rhetorical question asked by Mr Stamp in argument:[356] "Who has ever heard of a bridge to be crossed only by impecunious Methodists?" The *reductio ad absurdum* is sometimes a cogent form of argument, and this illustration serves to show the danger of conceding the quality of charity to a purpose which is not a public purpose. What is true of a bridge for Methodists is equally true of any other public purpose falling within the fourth class and of the adherents of any other creed. **6–292**

LORD REID [dissenting, and disagreeing with VISCOUNT SIMONDS on the "public" point]: But your Lordships are bound by a previous decision in this House, and it appears to me to be unquestionable that in *Goodman v Mayor of Saltash*[357] this House decided that there was a valid charitable trust where there was no question of poverty or disability or of education or religion, and where the beneficiaries were not by any means all the inhabitants of any particular area . . . [If] the members of a religious denomination do not constitute a section of the public (or the community) then a trust solely for the advancement of religion or of education would not be a charitable trust if limited to members of a particular church. Of course, the appellants do not contend that that is right: they could not but admit that the members of a church **6–293**

[355] [1924] A.C. 496 at 499.
[356] [1953] Ch. 504 at 519.
[357] (1882) 7 App. Cas. 633.

are a section of the community for the purpose of such trusts. But they maintain that they cease to be a section of the community when it comes to trusts within the fourth class. . . . Poverty may be in a special position but otherwise I can see no justification in principle or authority for holding that when dealing with one deed for one charitable purpose the members of the Methodist or any other church are a section of the community, but when dealing with another deed for a different charitable purpose they are only a fluctuating body of private individuals. I therefore reject this argument and on the whole matter I am of opinion that this appeal ought to be dismissed.

6–294 LORD SOMERVELL OR HARROW: I agree with the Court of Appeal in rejecting the argument that as a matter of law a trust to qualify under Lord Macnaghten's fourth class must be analogous to the repair of "bridges portes havens causwaies seabankes and highewaies", being the examples given in the preamble outside the three main categories of poverty, religion and education . . . I think, however, that a trust to be valid under this head would normally be for the public or all members of the public who needed the help or facilities which the trust was to provide. The present trust is not for the public.

6–295 I cannot accept the principle submitted by the respondents that a section of the public sufficient to support a valid trust in one category must as a matter of law be sufficient to support a trust in any other category. I think that difficulties are apt to arise if one seeks to consider the class apart from the particular nature of the charitable purpose. They are, in my opinion, interdependent. There might well be a valid trust for the promotion of religion benefiting a very small class. It would not at all follow that a recreation ground for the exclusive use of the same class would be a valid charity, though it is clear from the Mortmain and Charitable Uses Act 1888, that a recreation ground for the public is a charitable purpose.

[LORD PORTER and LORD TUCKER expressed no opinion on the "public" point.]

RECREATIONAL CHARITIES ACT 1958 SECTION 1

6–296 (1) Subject to the provisions of this Act, it shall be and be deemed always to have been charitable to provide, or assist in the provision of, facilities for recreation or other leisure-time occupation, if the facilities are provided in the interests of social welfare:

Provided that nothing in this section shall be taken to derogate from the principle that a trust or institution to be charitable must be for the public benefit.

(2) The requirement of the foregoing subsection that the facilities are provided in the interests of social welfare shall not be treated as satisfied unless—

(a) the facilities are provided with the object of improving the conditions of life for the persons for whom the facilities are primarily intended; and

(b) either—

(i) Those persons have need of such facilities as aforesaid by reason of their youth, age, infirmity or disablement, poverty or social and economic circumstances; or

(ii) The facilities are to be available to the members or female members of the public at large.

(3) Subject to the said requirement, subsection (1) of this section applies in particular to the provision of facilities at village halls, community centres and women's institutes, and to the provision and maintenance of grounds and buildings to be used for purposes of recreation or leisure-time occupation, and extends to the provision of facilities for those purposes by the organising of any activity.

[Section 2 makes special provision for trusts for miners' welfare; section 3 makes it clear that the Act does not restrict the purposes which are charitable independently of the Act.]

GUILD v IRC

House of Lords [1992] 2 A.C. 310, [1992] 2 W.L.R. 397, [1992] 2 All E.R. 10

LORD KEITH OF KINKEL (with whom LORD ROSKILL, LORD GRIFFITHS, LORD JAUNCEY and LORD LOWRY simply concurred]: My Lords, the late James Young Russell (the testator), who resided in North Berwick, died on September 11, 1982 leaving a will dated April 7, 1971 in which, after bequeathing a number of pecuniary legacies, he provided as follows: **6–297**

> "And I leave the whole, rest, residue and remainder of my said means and estate to the Town Council of North Berwick for the use in connection with the Sports Centre in North Berwick or some similar purpose in connection with sport and the receipt of the Treasurer for the time being of the Burgh of North Berwick shall be a sufficient receipt and discharge for my Executor."

In the course of his argument in relation to the first branch of the bequest counsel for the Crown accepted that it assisted in the provision of facilities for recreation or other leisure-time occupation within the meaning of sub-s. (1) of s.1 of the 1958 Act, and also that the requirement of public benefit in the proviso to the subsection was satisfied. It was further accepted that the facilities of the sports centre were available to the public at large so that the condition of sub-s. (2)(b)(ii) was satisfied. It was maintained, however, that these facilities were not provided "in the interests of social welfare" as required by sub-s. (1), because they did not meet the condition laid down in sub-s. (2)(a), namely that they should be "provided with the object of improving the conditions of life for the persons for whom the facilities are primarily intended". The reason why it was said that this condition was not met was that on a proper construction it involved that the facilities should be provided with the object of meeting a need for such facilities in people who suffered from a position of relative social disadvantage. Reliance was placed on a passage from the judgment of Walton J. in *IRC v McMullen*.[358] He said in relation to the words "social welfare" in sub-s.(1): **6–298**

> "In my view, however, these words in themselves indicate that there is some sort of deprivation, not, of course, by any means necessarily of money, which falls to be alleviated; and I think that this is made even clearer by the terms of s.1(2)(a) of the 1958 Act. The facilities must be provided with the object of improving the conditions of life for persons for whom the facilities are primarily intended. In other words, they must be to some extent and in some way deprived persons."

When the case went to the Court of Appeal[359] the majority (Stamp and Orr L.JJ.) affirmed the judgment of Walton J. on both points, but Bridge L.J. dissented. As regards the 1958 Act point he said:[360] **6–299**

> "I turn therefore to consider whether the object defined by cl.3(a) is charitable under the express terms of s.1 of the Recreational Charities Act 1958. Are the facilities for recreation contemplated in this clause to be "provided in the interests of social welfare" under s.1(1)? If this phrase stood without further statutory elaboration, I should not hesitate to decide that sporting facilities for persons undergoing any formal process of education are provided in the interests of social welfare. Save in the sense that the interests of social welfare can only be served by the meeting of some social need, I cannot accept the judge's view that the interests of social welfare can only be served in relation to some "deprived" class. The judge found this view reinforced by the requirement of s.1(2)(a) that the facilities must be provided "with the object of improving the conditions of life for the persons for whom the facilities are primarily intended". Here again I can see no reason to conclude that only the deprived can have their conditions of life improved. Hyde Park improves the conditions of life for residents in Mayfair and Belgravia as much as for those in Pimlico or the Portobello Road, and the village hall may improve the conditions of life for

[358] [1978] 1 W.L.R. 664 at 675.
[359] See [1979] 1 W.L.R. 130.
[360] [1979] 1 W.L.R. 130 at 142–143.

> the squire and his family as well as for the cottagers. The persons for whom the facilities here are primarily intended are pupils of schools and universities, as defined in the trust deed, and these facilities are in my judgment unquestionably to be provided with the object of improving their conditions of life. Accordingly the ultimate question on which the application of the statute to this trust depends, is whether the requirements of s.1(2)(b)(i) are satisfied on the ground that such pupils as a class have need of facilities for games or sports which will promote their physical education and development by reason either of their youth or of their social and economic circumstances, or both. The overwhelming majority of pupils within the definition are your persons and the tiny majority of mature students can be ignored as de minimis. There cannot surely be any doubt that young persons as part of their education do need facilities for organised games and sports both by reason of their youth and by reason of their social and economic circumstances. They cannot provide such facilities for themselves but are dependent on what is provided for them."

6–300 In the House of Lords the case was decided against the Crown upon the ground that the trust was one for the advancement of education, opinion being reserved on the point under the 1958 Act. Lord Hailsham of St Marylebone L.C. said:[361]

> ". . . I do not wish my absence of decision on the third or fourth points to be interpreted as an indorsement of the majority judgments in the Court of Appeal nor as necessarily dissenting from the contrary views contained in the minority judgment of Bridge L.J."

6–301 Counsel for the executor, for his part, relied on part of the judgment of Lord MacDermott L.C.J. in *Valuation Comr for Northern Ireland v Lurgan BC*.[362] A local authority which was the owner and occupier of an indoor swimming pool claimed exemption from rates in respect of it under s.2 of the Valuation (Ireland) Act 1854 on the ground, inter alia, that it was used exclusively for the purposes of a recreational charity under the Recreational Charities Act (Northern Ireland) 1958. A majority of the Court of Appeal held that this ground of exemption was established.

6–302 Lord MacDermott L.C.J. makes the point that s.1(2) of the 1958 Act does not exactly contain a definition but that it does state the essential elements which must be present if the requirements that the facilities should be provided in the interests of social welfare is to be met. It is difficult to envisage a case where, although these essential elements are present, yet the facilities are not provided in the interests of social welfare. Nor do I consider that the reference to social welfare in subs.(1) can properly be held to colour subs.(2)(a) to the effect that the persons for whom the facilities are primarily intended must be confined to those persons who suffer from some form of social deprivation. That this is not so seems to me to follow from the alternative conditions expressed in subs.(2)(b). If it suffices that the facilities are to be available to the members of the public at large, as sub-para.(ii) provides, it must necessarily be inferred that the persons for whom the facilities are primarily intended are not to be confined to those who have need of them by reason of one of the forms of social deprivation mentioned in sub-para.(1).

6–303 The fact is that persons in all walks of life and all kinds of social circumstances may have their conditions of life improved by the provision of recreational facilities of suitable character. The proviso requiring public benefit excludes facilities of an undesirable nature. In my opinion the view expressed by Bridge L.J. in *IRC v McMullen* is clearly correct and that of Walton J. in the same case is incorrect. Lord MacDermott L.C.J. in the *Lurgan BC* case plainly did not consider that the category of persons for whom the facilities were primarily intended was subject to any restriction. I would therefore reject the argument that the facilities are not provided in the interests of social welfare unless they are provided with the object of improving the conditions of life for persons who suffer from some form of social disadvantage. It suffices if they are provided with the object of improving the conditions of life for members of the community generally. The Lord President, whose opinion contains a description of the facilities available at the sports centre which it is unnecessary to repeat, took the view that they were so provided.[363] I respectfully agree, and indeed the contrary was not seriously maintained.

---

[361] [1981] A.C. 1 at 11.
[362] [1968] N.I. 104.
[363] See [1991] S.T.C. 281 at 288–289.

6–304 It remains to consider the point upon which the executor was unsuccessful before the First Division, namely whether or not the second branch of the bequest of residue, referring to "some similar purpose in connection with sport", is so widely expressed as to admit of the funds being applied in some manner which falls outside the requirements of s.1 of the 1958 Act. Counsel for the executor invited your Lordships, in construing this part of the bequest, to adopt the benignant approach which has regularly been favoured in the interpretation of trust deeds capable of being regarded as evincing a charitable intention. That approach is appropriate where the language used is susceptible of two constructions one of which would make it void and the other effectual.[364] It was argued for the Crown that the benignant approach was not apt in the present case, since the question was not whether the trust was valid or invalid, but whether it qualified for exemption from tax by virtue of the 1958 Act. But the importation into Scots law, for tax purposes, of the technical English law of charities involves that a Scottish judge should approach any question of construction arising out of the language used in the relevant instrument in the same manner as would an English judge who had to consider its validity as a charitable gift. The English judge would adopt the benignant approach in setting about that task, and so the Scottish judge dealing with the tax consequences should do likewise.

6–305 The matter for decision turns upon the ascertainment of the intention of the testator in using the words he did. The adjective "similar" connotes that there are points of resemblance between one thing and another. The points of resemblance here with the sports centre cannot be related only to location in North Berwick or to connection with sport. The first of these is plainly to be implied from the fact of the gift being to the town council of North Berwick and the second is expressly stated in the words under construction. So the resemblance to the sports centre which the testator had in mind must be ascertained by reference to some other characteristics possessed by it. The leading characteristics of the sports centre lie in the nature of the facilities which are provided there and the fact that those facilities are available to the public at large. These are the characteristics which enable it to satisfy s.1 of the 1958 Act. Adopting so far as necessary a benignant construction, I infer that the intention of the testator was that any other purpose to which the town council might apply the bequest or any part of it should also display those characteristics. In the result I am of opinion, the first part of the bequest having been found to be charitable within the meaning of s.1 of the 1958 Act, that the same is true of the second part, so that the funds in question qualify for exemption from capital transfer tax.

6–306 My Lords, for these reasons I would allow the appeal and set aside the determination of the commissioners.

6. The *Cy-Près* Doctrine

6–307 As discussed in Chapter 14, where a private trust is initially ineffective or subsequently fails there arises a resulting trust for the settlor or his estate if he is dead.[365] If a charitable trust is initially impracticable or impossible then again there is a resulting trust in favour of the settlor or, if he is dead, his estate (thereby normally benefiting his family[366]) unless the settlor had a general charitable intention.[367] If he had such an intention, then the trust property will be applied *cy-près* under a scheme formulated by the Charity Commission or the court, i.e. it will be applied to some other charitable purposes as nearly as possible resembling the original purposes (the term "*cy-près*" derives from the

---

364 See *IRC v McMullen* [1981] A.C. 1 at 14, per Lord Hailsham of St Marylebone L.C. and *Weir v Crum-Brown* [1908] A.C. 162 at 167, per Lord Loreburn L.C.

365 See paras 14–31 ff.

366 Disinherited family members can make a claim that the charitable bequest be reduced in their favour under the Inheritance (Provision for Family and Dependants) Act 1975.

367 *Re Rymer* [1895] 1 Ch. 19; *Re Stemson* [1970] Ch. 16. Gifts to particular Churches or to augment particular vicars' stipends may be saved under special legislation, e.g. Methodist Church Act 1976 s.15 or Endowments and Glebe Measures 1976 of the Church of England.

French expression "*aussi près que possible*"). If an effective charitable trust subsequently becomes impracticable or impossible then the trust property will be applied *cy-près* irrespective of the question of general charitable intention: the settlor or, if he is dead, his residuary legatee or next of kin are forever excluded once the property has been effectually dedicated to charity absolutely.

6–308 It is the duty of trustees to secure the effective use for charity of trust property by a *cy-près* application where appropriate,[368] although the Commission may make a scheme of its own volition if satisfied that the trustees "ought in the interests of the charity to apply for a scheme but have unreasonably refused or neglected to do so" after being approached by the Commission.[369]

6–309 Formerly, when the courts and the Commission made a scheme to change the charitable purposes for which particular property was held, they had to choose new purposes which were as close as possible to the original purposes. Under the new Charities Act 1993 s.14B,[370] however, this requirement has been relaxed: the nearness of the new purposes to the old remains, but equal weight is given to two other matters: the spirit of the gift by which the property came to the charity, and the need to ensure that, once the scheme has been made, the property is applied to purposes that are "suitable and effective in the light of current social and economic circumstances".

6–310 The case law reveals how much leeway a court has in determining whether there has been an initial failure of charitable purposes and, if so, whether there was a general charitable intention manifested by the testator or donor.

A. Whether or not There is Initial Lapse or Failure

6–311 There are three basic ways in which a testator might bequeath property: (1) for the relief of the blind in Batley; (2) for Batley Blind Home, High Street, Batley, the receipt of the treasurer for the time being to be sufficient discharge to the executors; or (3) for Batley Blind Home Ltd [a company limited by guarantee under the Companies Act 2006], High Street, Batley.

6–312 No problem arises in the first case since the purpose is not initially impracticable or impossible and purposes live for ever, although particular institutions carrying out purposes may die. If the purpose had been more specific such as building a blind home at a particular site, where there was no reasonable chance of such a blind home being erected whether because of planning permission problems or lack of cash, so that the purpose failed ab initio, then the legacy would lapse unless a general charitable intention was present to enable a *cy-près* application to be made.[371] However, if the site for the testator's project is merely incidental to his charitable intention and the preservation or use of that site is not an original purpose of the charitable gift, then an alternative site may be used without the

---

[368] Charities Act 1993 s.13(5).

[369] Charities Act 1993 s.16(6).

[370] Inserted by the Charities Act 2006 s.18.

[371] *Re Wilson* [1913] 1 Ch. 314 (to endow a school at a particular place where there was no reasonable chance of such a school being established); *Re Good's WT* [1950] 2 All E.R. 653 (funds insufficient for erection and upkeep of rest-homes); *Re Ulverston and District New Hospital Building Trusts* [1956] Ch. 622 (funds always insufficient for required purpose); *Re Mackenzie* [1962] 2 All E.R. 890 (trust to provide bursaries for education at secondary schools rendered impossible by provision of free education by state); *Re Lysaght* [1966] Ch. 191 (gift to Royal College of Surgeons on trust to provide studentships for persons not of Jewish or Catholic faith failed as the college was not prepared to act as trustees of such a trust and Buckley J., rather remarkably, held that this was the rare type of case where the identity of the trustees was vital to the trust. He further held that a paramount charitable intent was present so that a *cy-près* scheme could be directed omitting the offending religious conditions. This reveals the flexibility of *cy-près* applications which can even provide remedies in special circumstances); *Re Woodhams* [1981] 1 W.L.R. 493 (music scholarship for British boys restricted to orphans from two institutions but the trustee, the London College of Music, would not accept the trust as so restricted so Vinelott J. removed the restrictions by *cy-près* scheme).

need for a *cy-près* scheme.[372] The time for determining whether failure has occurred is the date of the inter vivos gift or, in the case of a testamentary gift, the date of the testator's death,[373] i.e. when the gift vests in interest and not when it vests in possession, e.g. after the end of a life interest. If need be, an inquiry will be directed as to "whether at the date of the death of the testator it was practicable to carry his intentions into effect or whether at the said date there was any reasonable prospect that it would be practicable to do so at some future time."[374] Where a future gift is defeasible an inquiry as to its practicability should be undertaken on the basis that the gift will not be defeated but will take effect at some future time as an interest in possession.[375] The onus of proving impracticability is on the person who is asserting it.[376]

Problems arise in the second case, where an unincorporated charitable association runs the home, if the home has ceased to exist by the testator's death. Since the association is unincorporated and charitable (not being a private members' club) the gift must necessarily be construed as a gift on trust for purposes: *Re Vernon's WT*,[377] parts of which are reproduced below. The purposes may be (a) the relief of the blind from time to time in the Batley Blind Home and nothing more, (b) the relief of the Blind in Batley, or (c) the augmentation of the endowed trust funds of the Batley Blind Home for whatever purposes such endowed trust funds might become held,[378] e.g. if amalgamated with the Bury Blind Home and the Dewsbury Deaf Home. **6–313**

In (a) where the gift is construed as a gift to a particular charitable institution just for its particular purposes then the gift lapses if the institution ceases to exist before the testator's death,[379] unless, which is most unlikely,[380] a general charitable intention can be found to justify a *cy-près* application.[381] In (b) where the gift is construed as a gift for a charitable purpose in circumstances where the existence of the particular institution carrying out the purpose is not material to the gift's validity, the gift does not lapse so long as the purpose can be carried out by other means which are to be determined by the court in cases of doubt.[382] Construction (c) ensures that so long as there are endowment funds held in trust for the named charity's purposes the gift augments such funds despite any alteration in its name or constitution or any amalgamation with other charities.[383] Thus the bequest in (c) unlike (b) could be used for the Bury Blind Home and the Dewsbury Deaf Home. However, if the constitution of the named charity does not provide for there to be a fund in existence for ever devoted to charity so that the charity is liable to dissolution under its own constitution and chooses to dissolve itself, whereupon its surplus funds on its winding up are transferred to some other charity, the gift will lapse on the basis that the charity has ceased to exist.[384] **6–314**

---

372 *Oldham BC v Att.-Gen.* [1993] Ch. 210. The council was trustee of The Clayton Playing Fields "for the benefit and enjoyment of the inhabitants of Oldham, Chatterton and Rayton" and was allowed to sell the land for supermarket development and purchase an alternative site for playing fields to benefit such inhabitants. Nothing could have been done if the purpose of the original gift was that the particular land conveyed should be used for ever as playing fields, none of the section 13 criteria for a *cy-près* application being applicable.

373 *Re Wright* [1954] Ch. 347, *Harris v Sharp* (unreported, CA March 21, 1989).

374 *Re Wright* [1954] Ch. 347; *Re White* [1955] Ch. 188; *Re Martin* (1977) 121 Sol. J. 828.

375 *Re Tacon* [1958] Ch. 447.

376 *Re Tacon* [1958] Ch. 447; *Harris v Sharp* (unreported, CA March 21, 1989).

377 [1972] Ch. 300n.

378 Cf. accretion to the funds of an unincorporated members' club: *Re Recher's WT* [1972] Ch. 526, discussed at para.5–81.

379 *Re Rymer* [1895] 1 Ch. 19, *Re Slatter's WT* [1964] Ch. 512; *Re Spence's WT* [1979] Ch. 483.

380 *Re Harwood* [1936] Ch. 285; *Re Stemson* [1970] Ch. 16 at 21.

381 As happened in *Re Finger's WT* [1972] 1 Ch. 286, on which Megarry V.C. had some reservations in *Re Spence's WT* [1978] 3 All E.R. 92.

382 *Re Watt* [1932] 2 Ch. 243; *Re Roberts* [1963] 1 W.L.R. 406; *Re Finger's W.T.* [1972] 1 Ch. 286; *Re Broadbent* [2001] W.T.L.R. 967.

383 *Re Lucas* [1948] Ch. 424 (on which see *Re Spence's WT* [1978] 3 All E.R. 92); *Re Faraker* [1912] 2 Ch. 488; *Re Bagshaw* [1954] 1 W.L.R. 238.

384 *Re Stemson's WT* [1970] Ch. 16.

6–315 In the third case where the bequest is to the Batley Blind Home Ltd, High Street, Batley, the bequest is presumed to be an out and out gift to the corporate institution beneficially as part of its general funds, unless there is something positive in the will to justify the bequest being treated as on trust for the purposes of the company's charitable objects. In the former case the gift will lapse if the company is would up before the testator dies unless, which is most unlikely, a general charitable intention can be found to justify a *cy-près* application.[385] In the latter case the trust purposes will be (a) the relief of the blind from time to time in the Batley Blind Home, High Street, Batley, as run by the Batley Blind Home Ltd, or (b) the relief of the blind from time to time in premises run by the Batley Blind Home Ltd, or (c) the relief of the blind in Batley. In (a) lapse will occur if such home ceases to exist before the testator's death, in (b) lapse will occur if the company is wound up before the testator's death, while in (c) lapse will not occur.[386]

B. *Where There is Initial Lapse or Failure*

6–316 If matters of construction cannot save the gift then the gift lapses unless the court can find a general charitable intention present. There have been many judicial statements on the meaning of the phrase. For example, in *Re Taylor*, Kay J. held that:[387]

> "If upon the whole scope and intent of the will you discover the paramount object of the testator was to benefit not a particular institution but to effect a particular form of charity independently of any special institution or mode, then, although he may have indicated the mode in which he desires that to be carried out, you are to regard the primary paramount intention chiefly, and if the particular mode for any reason fails, to use the phrase familiar to us, execute that *cy-près*, that is, carry out the general paramount intention indicated without which his intention itself cannot be effected."

6–317 Again, in *Re Lysaght*, Buckley J. held that:[388]

> "A general charitable intention . . . may be said to be a paramount intention on the part of a donor to effect some charitable purpose which the court can find a method of putting into operation, notwithstanding that it is impracticable to give effect to some direction by the donor which is not an essential part of his true intention—not, that is to say, of his paramount intention. In contrast, a particular charitable intention exists when the donor means his charitable disposition to take effect if, but only if, it can be carried into effect in a particular specified way, for example, in connection with a particular school to be established at a particular place,[389] or by establishing a home in a particular house . . .".[390]

6–318 Where the gift is to an institution described by a particular name and the institution has never existed, a general charitable intent is presumed if the name imports a charitable object;[391] but the

[385] *Re Stemson's WT* [1970] Ch. 16.
[386] *Re Meyers* [1951] Ch. 534.
[387] (1888) 58 L.T. 538 at 543.
[388] [1966] Ch. 191 at 202, approved in *Re Woodhams* [1981] 1 All E.R. 202 at 209.
[389] *Re Wilson* [1913] 1 Ch. 314.
[390] *Re Packe* [1918] 1 Ch. 437.
[391] *Re Davis* [1902] 1 Ch. 876; *Re Harwood* [1936] Ch. 285 (though Peace Societies are probably not charitable: *Re Koeppler's WT* [1984] 2 All E.R. 111 at 122, 124); but cf. *Att.-Gen. for NSW v Public Trustee* (1987) 8 N.S.W.L.R. 550.

presumption may be easily rebutted if the will also includes a residuary gift in favour of charity.[392] On the other hand, the court is assisted in discovering a general charitable intention if the gift to the non-existent institution is of a share of residue and the other residuary legatees are charities.[393]

C. Subsequent Failure

If at the testator's death the designated charity existed or it was not then impossible or impracticable to carry out the designated charitable purposes then the gifted property has become charitable property to the perpetual exclusion of the testator's residuary legatee or next of kin. Accordingly, the *cy-près* doctrine is available upon any subsequent failure: there is no need to prove any general charitable intent.[394] **6–319**

The position is the same for inter vivos gifts effectively dedicated to charity, whether the surplus funds are general assets of a charitable company that has been wound up[395] or assets held on charitable trusts by trustees for an unincorporated association that has been dissolved or for purposes that have been carried out.[396] As Jenkins L.J. remarked,[397] "Once the charity for which the fund was raised had been effectively brought into action the fund was to be regarded as permanently devoted to charity to the exclusion of any resulting trust" for the subscribers. He endorsed[398] the decision of Danckwerts J.[399] that no general charitable intention need be proved in such cases, though there are some illogical cases where the courts have gone to the lengths of excluding any resulting trust by holding that the subscribers intended to give their money out and out under a general charitable intention.[400] **6–320**

D. Cy-près under the Charities Act 1993 Section 14

In the case of initial failure of charitable purposes, s.14 permits a *cy-près* application as if a general charitable intention had been present. It is necessary to show that the donors cannot be traced or have executed written disclaimers.[401] The idea is to prevent resulting trusts arising in favour of anonymous donors contributing in the course of street collections, etc. to specific charitable appeals. However, the section seems to be superfluous, since it only applies where "any difficulty in applying **6–321**

---

392 *Re Goldschmidt* [1957] 1 W.L.R. 524.

393 *Re Knox* [1937] Ch. 109. See also *Re Satterthwaite's WT* [1966] 1 W.L.R. 277, where a misanthropic testatrix left her residuary estate in nine shares to nine named institutions, seven of which were animal charities, an anti-vivisection society (once thought charitable but now in law not charitable) and the London Animal Hospital (not ascertainable): a general charitable intent was found to infect the latter two shares of residue. In *Re Jenkin's WT* [1966] Ch. 249 residue was divided into sevenths, six for charitable institutions and one for "the British Union for the Abolition of Vivisection to do all in its power to urge and get an Act passed prohibiting atrocious unnecessary cruelty to animals": no general charitable intent was found since there was such a clearly expressed non-charitable purpose.

394 *Re Slevin* [1891] 2 Ch. 236; *Re Moon's WT* [1948] 1 All E.R. 300; *Re Wright* [1954] Ch. 347; *Re King* [1923] 1 Ch. 243; *Re Raine* [1956] Ch. 417; *Re Tacon* [1958] Ch. 447.

395 *Liverpool & District Hospital v Att.-Gen.* [1981] Ch. 193.

396 *Re Wokingham Fire Brigade Trusts* [1951] Ch. 373.

397 *Re Ulverston & District New Hospital Building Trusts* [1956] Ch. 622 at 636. To similar effect see Upjohn J. in *Re Coopers Conveyance* [1956] 1 W.L.R. 1096 and Blackburne J. in *Cawdron v Merchant Taylors' School* [2010] P.T.S.R. 507.

398 *Re Ulverston* at 637.

399 *Re Wokingham Fire Brigade Trusts* [1951] Ch. 373.

400 *Re Welsh Hospital (Netley) Fund* [1921] 1 Ch. 655; *Re North Devon & West Somerset Relief Fund Trusts* [1953] 1 W.L.R. 1260; *Re British School of Egyptian Archaeology* [1954] 1 W.L.R. 546.

401 cf. Charities Act 1993 s.14A, inserted by the Charities Act 2006 s.17, which permits *cy-près* applications where a charity has told the donors at the time of soliciting their payments that these will be applied *cy-près* if the purposes for which the money was solicited fail.

property to those purposes makes that property or the part not applicable *cy-près* available to be returned to the donors."[402] Thus, it applies only where under the general law the property is held on a resulting trust for donors. It does not apply where the property passes to the Crown as bona vacantia, as an out and out gift without any general charitable intention, nor where the property is in any event applicable *cy-près* as an out and out gift under a general charitable intention. Since 1970 it has been clear that cash put into collection boxes is by way of out and out gift[403] and so there is no scope for s.14 to apply to such cash collections.

6–322 At face value, the section purports to cover the proceeds of lotteries, competitions, entertainments or sales, but in most cases the so-called donors will have provided contractual consideration for their tickets, and so there is no question of returning their money to them by way of a resulting trust,[404] and so the section is inapplicable to such proceeds. If the money paid is ex gratia and not contractual then this will be by way of out and out gift[405] so that the section will be inapplicable. In the case of supervening failure of charitable purposes where the property has been given out and out to charity then such property is regarded as permanently devoted to charity to the exclusion of any resulting trust[406] so that s.14 can have no scope.

E. *Extension of Cy-près under the Charities Act 1993 Section 13*

6–323 The Charities Act 1993 s.13, as amended by the Charities Act 2006 s.15, was originally enacted as the Charities Act 1960 s.13. Before 1960, failure justifying *cy-près* occurred when the purposes of a trust became impossible or impracticable or there was a surplus after the purposes had been carried out. "Impracticable" came to be liberally interpreted over the years so as to include "highly undesirable",[407] but failure did not occur just because performance in another way would be more suitable or more beneficial.[408] Section 13 now extends the occasions when *cy-près* may be available but in cases of initial failure it is still necessary to show general charitable intention.[409] The section deals with difficulties over the original purposes of the trust (e.g. where £3 p.a. for clergyman and the rest to the poor when total income was £5 in 1716 and the income then rose to £800 p.a.)[410] and not over provisions as to administration of the trust (e.g. a provision for distribution of all capital for charitable purposes within 10 years of the settlor's death).[411] However, matters relating to administration of the trust may be dealt with under the court's inherent jurisdiction.[412]

6–324 Section 13 has no application of course, if there would have been no need for a scheme before s.13 of the 1960 was enacted, as appears from *Oldham BC v AG*,[413] where the council held land "upon trust

402 Charities Act 1993 s.14(7).

403 *Re West Sussex Constabulary's Benevolent Fund Trusts* [1971] Ch. 1; *Re Hillier* [1954] 1 W.L.R. 700 (out-and-out gift and general charitable intention imputed); *Re Ulverston & District New Hospital Building Fund* [1956] 1 Ch. 622 (out-and-out gift but bona vacantia since no general charitable intention imputed). In bona vacantia cases the Attorney-General normally waives the Crown's rights and has the property applied *cy-près* as emerges from *Re Ulverston* [1956] 1 Ch. 622 at 634.

404 *Re West Sussex Constabulary's Benevolent Fund Trust* [1971] Ch. 1. Previously, the courts had overlooked this and so too, naturally, did the 1960 Act.

405 See para.14–12, n.23.

406 *Re Wright* [1954] Ch. 347; *Re Ulverston* [1956] 1 Ch. 622 at 636; *Re Wokingham Fire Brigade Trusts* [1951] Ch. 373.

407 *Re Dominion Students' Hall Trust* [1947] Ch. 183 (scheme removing provision restricting Hall for Dominion students to students of European origin, i.e. white students).

408 *Re Weir Hospital* [1910] 2 Ch. 124.

409 Charities Acts 1960 and 1993 s.13(2). In *Re JW Laing Trust* [1984] 1 All E.R. 50 at 53 counsel surprisingly (and erroneously) conceded that general charitable intent was necessary for property effectively dedicated to charity in 1922.

410 *Re Lepton's Charity* [1972] Ch. 276.

411 *Re JW Laing Trust* [1984] 1 All E.R. 50.

412 *Att.-Gen. v Dedham School* (1857) 23 Beav. 350; *Re JW Laing Trust* [1984] 1 All E.R. 50.

413 [1993] Ch. 210. Before the Charities Act 1993 ss. 36–38, the Commissioners' consent was still needed to dispose of charity land.

to preserve and manage the same at all times hereafter as playing fields for the benefit and enjoyment of" local inhabitants. The council wanted to sell the land to developers and use the proceeds to buy other land with better facilities. The Court of Appeal held that this did not involve an alteration of the "original purposes" of the charitable gift so that the sale could proceed without the need for a *cy-près* scheme.

For s.13 to apply the circumstances must be fitted into one or other of the "pigeonholes" in s.13(1) (a) to (e), the largest pigeonhole being (e)(iii) "where the original purposes, in whole or in part, have, since they were laid down ceased . . . to provide a suitable and effective method of using the property available by virtue of the gift, regard being had to the appropriate considerations." Section 13(1A) then provides that "the appropriate considerations" means "(a) (on the one hand) the spirit of the gift concerned, and (b) (on the other) the social and economic circumstances prevailing at the time of the proposed alteration of the original purposes." When determining the "spirit of the gift" the court or Charity Commission must make a value judgment taking account of "the basic intention underlying the gift or the substance of the gift": it must "look beyond the original purposes as defined by the objects specified in the declaration of trust and . . . seek to identify the spirit in which the donors gave property upon trust for those purposes . . . with the assistance of the document as a whole and any relevant evidence as to the circumstances in which the gift was made."[414] **6–325**

So far as the second paragraph of s.13(1A) is concerned, the Charity Commission has written that:[415] **6–326**

> "It is clear from the Parliamentary debates on the Charities Bill that the phrase 'social and economic circumstances' is intended to be interpreted broadly, and to encompass all relevant circumstances that the trustees or the Commission might need to take into account when deciding how or whether the purposes of the charity should be altered. Other authorities have suggested that this could therefore include environmental, legal, scientific or technological considerations.
>
> "We might take into account, for example, the following:
>
> "In some cases the provision of specific articles such as food or fuel may no longer be the most practical means of relieving financial hardship or other forms of disadvantage.
>
> "Provision of care for people with disabilities is now generally based around enabling them to live in their own homes rather than housing them in institutions.
>
> "In some cases the social or economic circumstances that led to the setting up of a charity (e.g. to provide education or housing) for members of one sex only may have changed over time.
>
> "The objects of some charities may imply outdated social or moral judgements about potential beneficiaries, such as 'deserving poor' (historically, poor people who could work but didn't were officially classed as 'idle' and therefore undeserving). These may unnecessarily restrict the beneficiary class. Some objects contain language that could now be offensive or off-putting to potential beneficiaries or donors, such as 'crippled', 'handicapped', 'invalid' or 'insane'."

In *Varsani v Jesani*[416] a group of Hendon Hindus in 1967 set up a trust to promote the faith of Swaminarayan as practised in accordance with the teaching and tenets of Muktajivandasji, to provide facilities for a small united community of his followers in the Hendon area of London. After his death problems arose over his successor as divine leader of the sect so that the community divided into two **6–327**

414 *Varsani v Jesani* [1999] Ch. 219 at 238.

415 Charity Commission, *OG 2A1: Operational Guidance: Application of Property Cy-près* (March 2008 version) para.1.1. cf. *Re Hanbey* [1956] Ch. 264, where the court considered the "social utility" of the charity's objects as well as the intentions of the founder.

416 [1999] Ch. 219.

factions, each claiming that it adhered to the true faith while the other did not. The Court of Appeal held that to appropriate the property to one faction to the exclusion of the other would be contrary to the spirit in which the gift to the charitable trust was made, and that the impasse between the two factions with the majority faction excluding the minority faction meant that a *cy-près* scheme could be made under paragraph (e)(iii) to divide the trust property between the two factions.

RE VERNON'S WILL TRUSTS

Chancery Division [1972] Ch. 300n., 303

6–328 BUCKLEY J.: Every [charitable] bequest to an unincorporated charity by name without more must take effect as a gift for a charitable purpose. No individual or aggregate of individuals could claim to take such a bequest beneficially. If the gift is to be permitted to take effect at all, it must be as a bequest for a purpose, i.e., that charitable purpose which the named charity exists to serve. A bequest which is in terms made for a charitable purpose will not fail for lack of a trustee but will be carried into effect either under the sign manual or by means of a scheme. A bequest to a named unincorporated charity, however, may on its true interpretation show that the testator's intention to make the gift at all was dependent on the named charitable organisation being available at the time when the gift takes effect to serve as the instrument for applying the subject-matter of the gift to the charitable purpose for which it is by inference given. If so and the named charity ceases to exist in the lifetime of the testator, the gift fails (*Re Ovey*[417]). A bequest to a corporate body, on the other hand, takes effect simply as a gift to that body beneficially, unless there are circumstances which show that the recipient is to take the gift as a trustee. There is no need in such a case to infer a trust for any particular purpose. The objects to which the corporate body can properly apply its funds may be restricted by its constitution, but this does not necessitate inferring as a matter of construction of the testator's will a direction that the bequest is to be held in trust to be applied for those purposes: the natural construction is that the bequest is made to the corporate body as part of its general funds, that is to say, beneficially and without the imposition of any trust. That the testator's motive in making the bequest may have undoubtedly been to assist the work of the incorporated body would be insufficient to create a trust.

6–329 This dictum was applied by Goff J. in *Re Finger's WT*[418] so as to hold a gift to a dissolved unincorporated charity, the National Radium Commission, to be a purpose trust for the sort of work carried on by the Commission so as not to lapse, while a gift to a dissolved corporate charity, the National Council for Maternity and Child Welfare, he held to be for such charity absolutely beneficially, so as to lapse unless a general charitable intention could be found to justify a *cy-près* application: he found such an intention enabling the gift to pass to the National Association for Maternity and Child Welfare. Earlier he had said that:[419]

> "If the matter were *res integra* I would have thought there would be much to be said for the view that the status of the donee, whether corporate or unincorporate, can make no difference to the question whether as a matter of construction a gift is absolute or on trust for purposes. Certainly drawing such a distinction produces anomalous results."

---

417 (1885) 29 Ch.D. 560.

418 [1972] Ch. 286; and also see *Re Koeppler's WT* [1986] Ch. 423 at 434, taking the *Re Vernon's WT* [1972] Ch. 300 approach.

419 [1972] Ch. 286 at 294. See also *Montefiore Jewish Home v Howell* [1984] 2 N.S.W.L.R. 407, for treating corporate and unincorporated charities similarly.

Nevertheless, the dictum of Buckley J. was applied in *Re ARMS (Multiple Sclerosis Research) Ltd*[420] where the recipient company went into compulsory insolvent liquidation after the testator's will was made but before the testator's death, by which date the company had not been formally dissolved. Neuberger J. held that the company took the money as part of its general assets available for its creditors.

RE SPENCE'S WILL TRUSTS

Chancery Division [1979] Ch. 483, [1978] 3 W.L.R. 483, [1978] 3 All E.R. 92

MEGARRY V.C.: The testatrix, Mrs Spence, . . . made her will on December 4, 1968, and died on May 30, 1972 . . . She gave her residuary estate to her trustees on trust to sell it and to pay her funeral and testamentary expenses and debts, and then: **6–330**

> "to pay and divide the residue thereof equally between The Blind Home, Scott Street, Keighley and the Old Folks Home at Hillworth Lodge, Keighley for the benefit of the patients."

The will next provided that the receipt of the treasurer for the time being of "each of the above-mentioned institutions" should be a sufficient discharge to her trustees. Subject to the expenses of administration and to the costs of these proceedings, the net residue is now worth some £17,000 . . .

I shall first consider the gift to "The Blind Home, Scott Street, Keighley . . . for the benefit of the patients." I think it is clear that these last six words apply to the gift to the Blind Home as they apply to the gift to the Old Folks Home; and nobody contended to the contrary. The question is whether this gift carries a moiety of residue to the Keighley and District Association for the Blind and, if so, on what terms. That charity was founded in 1907 and, over the years, it has changed its name thrice. It has borne its present name for nearly 20 years and is at present governed by a trust deed dated October 25, 1963. For over 25 years it has been running a blind home at 31 Scott Street, Keighley, which provides permanent accommodation for the blind in Keighley and district. Since 1907 there have been no other premises or associations connected with the blind in Keighley. The premises in Scott Street are often called "The Blind Home"; and a memorandum of the appointment of new trustees made on June 9, 1970, refers to the meeting for that purpose held at "The Blind Home, Scott Street, Keighley." Other names are used. A board on the building calls it "The Keighley and District Home for the Blind", and a brochure in evidence calls it "Keighley Home for the Blind". It seems clear beyond a peradventure that the language of the will fits the home run by the charity at these premises. **6–331**

In those circumstances, counsel for the plaintiff felt unable to advance any argument that the gift of this moiety failed and passed as on intestacy; and in this I think he was right. That, however, does not dispose of the matter, since the charity also carries on a home for the blind at Bingley, and may of course expend some or all of its funds on this or other purposes within its objects. There is therefore the question whether the moiety should go to the charity as an accretion to its endowment, and so be capable of being employed on any of its activities, or whether it is to be confined to the particular part of the charity's activities that are carried on at The Blind Home in Scott Street, Keighley. I confess that but for the decision of the Court of Appeal in *Re Lucas*[421] I should have had little hesitation in resolving this question in the latter and narrower sense, confining the moiety to the particular Blind Home in Scott Street, Keighley. **6–332**

In *Re Lucas* the testatrix made her will on October 12, 1942, and died on December 18, 1943. The will made gifts to "the Crippled Children's Home, Lindley Moor, Huddersfield"; and it provided that the receipt of the treasurer or other officer for the time being should be a sufficient discharge. From 1916 there had been an establishment called "The Huddersfield Home for Crippled Children" at Lindley Moor, governed by the charitable trusts established by a deed dated March 29, 1915; but according to the statement of **6–333**

[420] [1997] 1 W.L.R. 877.
[421] [1948] Ch. 424.

facts in the report[422] "On October 17, 1941, this home was closed and a scheme for the future administration of its assets was made by the charity commissioners." Under that scheme the charity thereby created was to be known as "The Huddersfield Charity for Crippled Children", and the income was to be applied in sending poor crippled children to holiday or convalescent homes.

6–334 In the All England Law Reports,[423] passages in the judgments which are omitted from the Law Reports explicitly state that the scheme of the Charity Commissioners was sealed on October 17, 1941. They also show that the home had been closed not on that day but some two-and-a-half years before, on April 6, 1939, when the lease had run out. The statement of facts in the Law Reports is thus wrong in this respect. When the testatrix came to make her will on October 12, 1942, the home had been closed for some three-and-a-half years, and the charity had for almost a year had a name which, in accord with its new objects, had had the word "Home" in it replaced by "Charity". The All England Law Reports also show that the original name, "The Huddersfield Home for Crippled Children", had been given to the charity by the trust deed. The question for resolution in *Re Lucas* was thus whether the gifts to "the Crippled Children's Home, Lindley Moor, Huddersfield" took effect as gifts to "The Huddersfield Charity for Crippled Children", or whether they were gifts for the upkeep of a particular home for crippled children which had ceased to exist before the will had been made, so that they failed.

6–335 At first instance, Roxburgh J. held that the latter was the correct view: *Re Lucas*.[424] On appeal, Lord Greene M.R. delivered the reserved judgment of himself, Somervell L.J. and Jenkins J. This reversed the decision below, and held that the gifts were gifts which contributed to the endowment of the charity, and so did not fail. I have found the judgment puzzling in places. Lord Greene M.R. discussed the misdescription in the will as follows.[425]

> "As to the misdescription (i.e. 'The Crippled Children's Home' for 'the Huddersfield Home for Crippled Children') the description given by the testatrix was no more an accurate description of the particular home than it was of the charity."

Later the judgment considers the position if the testatrix "did know the correct name of the charity (i.e. 'The Huddersfield Home for Crippled Children')."

6–336 I find this puzzling. My difficulty is this. Nearly a year before the will was made, the correct name of the charity had ceased to be what the judgment says it was. The "description given by the testatrix" was "the Crippled Children's Home, Lindley Moor, Huddersfield". This, said the judgment, was "no more an accurate description of the particular home [that is, the Huddersfield Home for Crippled Children which was at Lindley Moor] than it was of the charity". Yet when the will was made the name of the charity had for nearly a year been "The Huddersfield Charity for Crippled Children", a name which did not include the word "Home". I find it difficult to see why a gift to a "Home" does not fit an entity with "Home" in its title better than it fits an entity without the word "Home" in its title, but the word "Charity", instead. If in referring to the "correct name" of the charity the judgment intends to refer to what had once been the correct name of the charity, I cannot see what it was that made the court reject the state of affairs when the will was made in favour of the past, particularly when there appears to have been no evidence about what the testatrix knew about the charity. I say what I say with all due humility, and a ready recognition that the fault may be an inability on my part to see what is plain to others; but, though humble, I remain puzzled.

6–337 The main factors in the decision of the Court of Appeal seem to have been that the words used in the will fitted the home that had been closed down no better than the charity which continued in existence, and that the will had omitted to make any specific reference to the upkeep or maintenance of the home which would indicate that the gifts were to be confined to the upkeep of the home. The gifts were accordingly gifts to the charity, and so did not fail. The question for me is whether on the case before me there ought to be a similar result, so that the moiety of residue would go to the Keighley, and District

---

[422] [1948] Ch. 424 at 425.
[423] [1947] 2 All E.R. 773 at 774; [1948] 2 All E.R. 22 at 24.
[424] [1948] Ch. 175.
[425] [1948] Ch. 424 at 428.

Association for the Blind as an addition to its endowment generally, and would not be confined to the Blind Home in Scott Street, Keighley, carried on by the association.

Counsel for the first defendant submitted that there were two substantial points of distinction between the present case and *Re Lucas*.[426] First, the words of the will fitted the Blind Home far better than they fitted the association. Indeed, although the Blind Home was from time to time described by different names, all the names used included both "Blind" and "Home": and, as I have mentioned, the appointment of new trustees in June 1970 uses the name "The Blind Home, Scott Street, Keighley", which is the precise expression used in the will. The title of the charity, "The Keighley and District Association for the Blind", is very different. True, it has the word "Blind" in common with the title used in the will. There is also the word "Keighley", though this is used adjectively and not as part of the address. But otherwise there is nothing in common. In particular, there is not the use of the word "Home" in both titles which the Court of Appeal in *Re Lucas* said was present in that case; and I think the words "Home" and "Association" are different in a real and significant sense. **6–338**

Secondly, in the case before me, there are the words "for the benefit of the patients" which follow and govern the expression "The Blind Home, Scott Street, Keighley". In *Re Lucas* there was no counterpart to this. Indeed, the absence of any reference to the upkeep or maintenance of the home in that case was, as I have indicated, one of the grounds on which the decision was based. Here, there is no reference to upkeep or maintenance as such: but I think "patients" must mean "patients of the Blind Home", and the upkeep and maintenance of the home is an obvious means of providing a benefit for the patients in it. **6–339**

In my judgment both these distinctions are valid and substantial. It therefore seems to me that the case before me is distinguishable from *Re Lucas*, so far as I have correctly understood that case. The testatrix was making provision for the benefit of the patients for the time being at a particular home, namely, the home usually known as The Blind Home at Scott Street, Keighley. She was giving the money not to augment generally the endowment of the charity which runs that home, with the consequences that the money might be used for purposes other than the benefit of the patients at that home, but was giving the money so that it would be used exclusively for the benefit of those patients. The only way in which this can conveniently be done is to give the money to the charity but to confine its use to use for the benefit of the patients for the time being at the home. That, I think, requires a scheme; but I see no need to direct that a scheme should be settled in chambers. Instead, I think that I can follow the convenient course taken by Goff J. in *Re Finger's Will Trusts*.[427] I shall therefore order by way of scheme (the Attorney-General not objecting) that the moiety be paid to the proper officer of the charity to be held on trust to apply it for the benefit of the patients for the time being of the home known as The Blind Home, Scott Street, Keighley. **6–340**

I now turn to the other moiety of residue, given by the will to "the Old Folks Home at Hillworth Lodge, Keighley for the benefit of the patients". Hillworth Lodge was built as a workhouse in 1858. Shortly before the outbreak of war in 1939 the West Riding Country Council, in whom it had become vested, closed it down: but during the war it was used to house what were generally but inelegantly called "evacuees". In 1948 it became an aged persons' home under the National Assistance Act 1948, and it continued as such until January 28, 1971, when it was finally closed down. There had been between 120 and 140 residents in it as late as 1969, but the numbers were then progressively run down, until in January 1971, just before it closed, only ten residents were left; and these were transferred to another establishment in Pudsey. The aged of the area had over the years been increasingly accommodated in purpose-designed old people's homes which provided better accommodation for the aged than could the old workhouse, despite many improvements to it. Since the building ceased to house old people it has been used as Divisional Social Services Offices. **6–341**

When the testatrix made her will in 1968 the building was accordingly still in use as an old people's home run by the local authority in accordance with their duty under the National Assistance Act 1948. As an old people's home it had no assets of its own, and residents contributed towards their maintenance in accordance with the Ministry of Social Security Act 1966 Part III. When the testatrix died on May 30, 1972, the building was no longer used as an old people's home, and was being used, or was soon to be used, as offices. The home had been run neither as nor by a charity. It formerly provided homes for those living in a **6–342**

[426] [1948] Ch. 424.
[427] [1972] 1 Ch. 286 at 300.

large area of the West Riding, and not merely Keighley; and it has not been replaced by any one home. Instead, there are many old people's homes serving the area.

6–343 Now without looking at the authorities I would have said that this was a fairly plain case of a will which made a gift for a particular purpose in fairly specific terms. The gift was for the benefit of the patients at a particular home, namely the Old Folks Home at Hillworth Lodge, Keighley. At the date of the will there were patients at that home. When the testatrix died, there was no longer any home there, but offices instead; and so there were no longer any patients there, or any possibility of them. The gift was a gift for a charitable purpose which at the date of the will was capable of accomplishment and at the date of death was not. Prima facie, therefore, the gift fails unless a general charitable intention has been manifested so that the property can be applied *cy-près*. Buttressed by authority, counsel for the plaintiff contended that the court would be slow to find a general charitable intention where the object of the gift is defined with some particularity, as it was here.

6–344 Against that, counsel for the Attorney-General advanced two main contentions. First, he said that as a matter of construction it was wrong to construe the gift as being merely for the benefit of patients who were actually at the Old Folks Home at Hillworth Lodge; admittedly, of course, there are none of these. Instead, those who were intended to benefit included all those who would have been sent to that home if it had still existed, irrespective of the type of home in which in fact they are being or will be accommodated. He emphasised that the gift was essentially a gift for old people in Keighley, and the home was merely a means of providing a benefit for them.

6–345 I do not think that this argument can be right. When the testatrix made her will there were patients at the Old Folks Home at Hillworth Lodge. The gift to that home "for the benefit of the patients" is, on this construction, to be treated as being a gift for the benefit not only of the patients who successively were for the time being at the home, but of others who never go near the home but who might or would have been sent to it in certain circumstances. The words of the will were perfectly capable of being satisfied by confining their meaning to their natural sense, namely, as relating to those who are or will in the future be patients at the home. Why is there to be forced on to those words a notional extension of uncertain effect? If at the time they were being written those words could not have their natural effect, one might indeed look round for a secondary meaning; but that is not the case.

6–346 There are further difficulties. If the notional extension is made, who are within it? As I have said, the defunct home provided for a large area of the West Riding, and not merely Keighley. How is it to be determined who can hope to benefit under the gift? Which of the occupants of the other old people's homes in such an area (the extent of which is undefined) can claim to be objects of the testatrix's bounty? Who is to decide whether any particular individual could (or would) have been sent to the defunct home had it still existed, and so would fall within the scope of the gift? I do not see how such an extension of meaning can fairly be placed on the words of the will. No doubt a scheme could cure much, but my difficulty is in seeing what on this footing, was the intention of the testatrix. For the reasons that I have given, I reject this contention.

6–347 Counsel's other contention for the Attorney-General was that the will displayed a sufficient general charitable intention for the moiety to be applied *cy-près*. In doing this he had to contend with *Re Harwood*.[428] This, and cases which apply to it, such as *Re Stemson's Will Trusts*[429] establish that it is very difficult to find a general charitable intention where the testator has selected a particular charity, taking some care to identify it, and the charity then ceases to exist before the testator's death. This contrasts with cases where the charity described in the will has never existed, when it is much easier to find a general charitable intention.

6–348 These cases have been concerned with gifts to institutions, rather than gifts for purposes. The case before me, on the other hand, is a gift for a purpose, namely, the benefit of the patients at a particular old folks home. It therefore seems to me that I ought to consider the question, of which little or nothing was said in argument, whether the principle in *Re Harwood*, or a parallel principle, has any application to such a case. In other words, is a similar distinction to be made between, on the one hand, a case in which the testator has selected a particular charitable purpose, taking some care to identify it, and before the

---

428 [1936] Ch. 285.
429 [1970] Ch. 16.

testator dies that purpose has become impracticable or impossible of accomplishment, and on the other hand a case where the charitable purpose has never been possible or practicable?

As at present advised I would answer yes to that question. I do not think that the reasoning of the *Re Harwood* line of cases is directed to any feature of institutions as distinct from purposes. Instead, I think the essence of the distinction is in the difference between particularity and generality. If a particular institution or purpose is specified, then it is that institution or purpose, and no other, that is to be the object of the benefaction. It is difficult to envisage a testator as being suffused with a general glow of broad charity when he is labouring, and labouring successfully, to identify some particular specified institution or purpose as the object of his bounty. The specific displaces the general. It is otherwise where the testator has been unable to specify any particular charitable institution or practicable purpose, and so, although his intention of charity can be seen, he has failed to provide any way of giving effect to it. There, the absence of the specific leaves the general undisturbed. It follows that in my view in the case before me, where the testatrix has clearly specified a particular charitable purpose which before her death became impossible to carry out, counsel for the Attorney-General has to face that level of great difficulty in demonstrating the existence of a general charitable intention which was indicated by *Re Harwood*. **6–349**

One way in which counsel sought to meet that difficulty was by citing *Re Finger's Will Trusts*.[430] There, Goff J. distinguished *Re Harwood* and held that the will before him displayed a general charitable intention. He did this on the footing that the circumstances of the case were "very special". The gift that failed was a gift to an incorporated charity which had ceased to exist before the testatrix died. The "very special" circumstances were, first, that apart from a life interest and two small legacies, the whole estate was devoted to charity, and that this was emphasised by the direction to hold the residue in trust for division "between the following charitable institutions and funds". Secondly, the charitable donee that had ceased was mainly, if not exclusively, a co-ordinating body, and the judge could not believe that the testatrix meant to benefit that body alone. Thirdly, there was evidence that the testatrix regarded herself as having no relatives. **6–350**

In the case before me neither of these last two circumstances applies, nor have any substitute special circumstances been suggested. As for the first, the will before me gives 17 pecuniary legacies to relations and friends, amounting in all to well over one-third of the net estate. Further, in *Re Rymer*,[431] which does not appear to have been cited, the will had prefaced the disputed gift by the words "I give the following charitable legacies to the following institutions and persons respectively". These words correspond to the direction which in *Re Finger's Will Trusts* was regarded as providing emphasis, and yet they did not suffice to avoid the conclusion of Chitty J. and the Court of Appeal that a gift to an institution which had ceased to exist before the testator's death lapsed and could not be applied *cy-près*. I am not sure that I have been able to appreciate to the full the cogency of the special circumstances that appealed to Goff J.; but however that may be I can see neither those nor any other special circumstances in the present case which would suffice to distinguish *Re Harwood*. **6–351**

The other way in which counsel for the Attorney-General sought to meet his difficulty was by relying on *Re Satterthwaite's Will Trusts*[432] and on *Re Knox*.[433] The doctrine may for brevity be described as charity by association. If the will gives the residue among a number of charities with kindred objects, but one of the apparent charities does not in fact exist, the court will be ready to find a general charitable intention and so apply the share of the non-existent charity *cy-près*. I have not been referred to any explicit statement of the underlying principle, but it seems to me that in such cases the court treats the testator as having shown the general intention of giving his residue to promote charities with that type of kindred objects, and then, when he comes to dividing the residue, as casting round for particular charities with that type of objects to name as donees. If one or more of these are non-existent, then the general intention will suffice for a *cy-près* application. It will be observed that, as stated, the doctrine depends, at least to some extent, on the detection of "kindred objects" (a phrase which comes from the judgment of Luxmoore J. in *Re Knox*[434]) in the charities to which the shares of residue are given; in this respect the charities must in some degree be ejusdem generis. **6–352**

---

[430] [1972] 1 Ch. 286.
[431] [1895] 1 Ch. 19.
[432] [1966] 1 W.L.R. 277.
[433] [1937] Ch. 109.
[434] [1937] Ch. 109 at 113.

6–353 In *Re Satterthwaite's Will Trusts*[435] the residuary gift was to nine charitable bodies which were all concerned with kindness to animals; but the gifts to two of them failed as no bodies could be found which sufficiently answered the descriptions in the will. Harman L.J. said[436] that he "felt the gravest doubts" whether a general charitable intent had been shown. However, at first instance the judge had held that in respect of one of the bodies a sufficient general charitable intention had been displayed, and as there had been no appeal as to that share, he (Harman L.J.) would reach the same conclusion in respect of the other share, which was the subject of the appeal. On the other hand, Russell L.J. had no doubt that a general charitable intention had been shown.[437] Diplock L.J. delivered a single-sentence judgment agreeing with both the other judgments. The support which this case provides for counsel for the Attorney-General accordingly seems to me to be a trifle muted.

6–354 In *Re Knox* Luxmoore J. distilled a general charitable intention out of a residuary gift in quarters to two named infirmaries, a named nursing home and Dr Barnardo's Homes. No institution existed which correctly answered the description of the nursing home, and it was held that the quarter share that had been given to it should be applied *cy-près*. I am not entirely sure what genus the judge had in mind as embracing the infirmaries and Dr Barnardo's Homes when he said that "the object of each of the other charities is a kindred object to that which is to be inferred from the name" of the nursing home: perhaps it was the provision of residential accommodation for those in need. "It will be observed that these are all cases of gifts to bodies which did not exist. In such cases, the court is ready to find a general charitable intention: see *Re Davis*.[438] The court is far less ready to find such an intention where the gift is to a body which existed at the date of the will but ceased to exist before the testator died, or, as I have already held, where the gift is for a purpose which, though possible and practicable at the date of the will, has ceased to be so before the testator's death. The case before me is, of course, a case in this latter category, so that counsel for the Attorney-General has to overcome this greater difficulty in finding a general charitable intention. Not only does counsel have this greater difficulty: he also has, I think, less material with which to meet it. He has to extract the general charitable intention for the gift which fails from only one other gift: the residue, of course, was simply divided into two. In *Re Knox* and *Re Hartley, deceased*[439] the gifts which failed were each among three other gifts, and in *Re Satterthwaite's Will Trusts* there were seven or eight other gifts. I do not say that a general charitable intention or a genus cannot be extracted from a gift of residue equally between two: but I do say that larger numbers are likely to assist in conveying to the court a sufficient conviction both of the genus and of the generality of the charitable intention.

6–355 A further point occurred to me which I think that I should mention. There are, of course, cases where there is merely a single gift, but the court is nevertheless able to see a clear general charitable intention underlying the particular mode of carrying it out that the testator has laid down. Thus in the well known case of *Biscoe v Jackson*,[440] which I read in the light of *Re Wilson*,[441] the gift was to provide a soup kitchen and cottage hospital "for the parish of Shoreditch". Despite a considerable degree of particularity about the soup kitchen and the cottage hospital that were to be provided, the court found a general charitable intention to provide a benefit for the sick and poor of the parish. In that case, of course, there would have been no real difficulty in ascertaining those who were intended to benefit. Whatever the practical difficulties, at least the concept of those who were to be included is clear enough. The only real difficulty or impossibility lay in the particular method of carrying out that intention which the testator had specified. In the present case, on the other hand, the difficulty lies not only in the particular method but also in the very nature of the general charitable intention that is said to underlie that method. For the reasons that I have already given, I find it far from clear which "patients" are intended to benefit once the touchstone of the Old Folks Home at Hillworth Lodge is removed. There is no geographical or other limitation to provide a guide. Where the difficulty or impossibility not only afflicts the method but also invades the concept of the

---

[435] [1966] 1 W.L.R. 277.
[436] [1966] 1 W.L.R. 277 at 284.
[437] [1966] 1 W.L.R. 277 at 286.
[438] [1902] 1 Ch. 876 at 884.
[439] March 15, 1978 (unreported decision of Megarry J.).
[440] (1887) 35 Ch.D. 460.
[441] [1913] 1 Ch. 314.

alleged general charitable intention, then I think that the difficulty of establishing that the will displays any general charitable intention becomes almost insuperable.

From what I have said it follows that I have been quite unable to extract from the will, construed in its context, any expression of a general charitable intention which would suffice for the moiety to be applied *cy-près*. Instead, in my judgment, the moiety was given for a specific charitable purpose which, though possible when the will was made, became impossible before the testatrix died. The gift of the moiety accordingly fails, and it passes as on intestacy. **6–356**

Questions

1. Are the following trusts charitable, and, if not, are they otherwise valid? **6–357**

   (a) To apply the income from £500,000 among such persons having the surnames Smith or Hayton, with preference so far as practicable for 50 per cent of the income to be used for the relatives of David Hayton, as my trustees may consider to merit educational assistance.
   (b) £400,000 to my trustees to invest and apply the income therefrom in educating the children of needy employees or ex-employees of London Transport for 21 years whereupon the income shall be used to provide an English Public School education for such children of European origin living in Oxford as my trustees shall determine provided that in either case no person of the Roman Catholic faith shall be so assisted.
   (c) A £10 million trust set up by ICI Plc and Barclays Bank Plc for the income to be used at the trustees' discretion in assisting towards the education of the children or grandchildren of any persons employed or formerly employed by I.C.I. or Barclays Bank or any of their subsidiary or associated companies.

2. In 2000 a public appeal for funds to establish a recreation and sports centre for the City of London Police was launched. £200,000 was donated by Hank Badman, £80,000 was obtained from street collections, £110,000 profit was made out of a pop festival in aid of the appeal and £20,000 was donated anonymously. It has now proved completely impossible in view of the size of the fund to obtain any suitable site. What should be done with the moneys? **6–358**

3. By his will dated April 1, 1999, Oscar O'Flaherty (who died three months ago) bequeathed £60,000 to his executors to use part thereof for benevolent purposes and the remainder for charitable purposes and £50,000 to the "Torquay Home for Distressed Gentlefolk for the benefit of the needy who happen to be there." The Home, an unincorporated body, closed down six months before Oscar's death, its funds and many of its inhabitants going to the Bournemouth Home for the Handicapped. Advise Oscar's executors. Would your answer differ at all if the gift had been to the Torquay Home for Distressed Gentlefolk Ltd which had gone into compulsory insolvent liquidation six months before Oscar's death although it had not been formally dissolved by his death? **6–359**

4. By his will Alan left his residuary estate to Tim and Tom "upon trust to apply the income therefrom for such of the adult residents of Greater London as my Trustees in their absolute discretion shall think fit having due regard to the need to combat the stress, squalor and expense of residing in Greater London provided that my Trustees shall have power to add as further possible beneficiaries adult residents of any other city in the United Kingdom where the stress, squalor and expense are in my Trustees' absolute discretion comparable to that of Greater London provided **6–360**

further that one day before the expiration of the period of eighty years from my death (which period I hereby specify as the perpetuity period applicable hereto) the aforesaid Trust shall determine and the capital shall be distributed equally between United Reform Churches in West Ham and Leyton to use the income therefrom to assist in the burial or cremation of members of their congregations." Alan has just died and Tim and Tom seek advice on the validity of the Trust.

PART III

VARIATION AND TERMINATION OF EXPRESS TRUSTS

7 VARIATION AND TERMINATION OF TRUSTS

1. Introduction

Obviously trusts come to an end when the trustees distribute all the trust property to the beneficiaries. Settlors can also reserve powers of revocation, appointment and amendment of the trust to themselves, or confer such powers on others, and the effect of exercising such powers may well be to vary or terminate the trust. Various legal rules can also affect the variation and termination of trusts: the rule in *Saunders v Vautier*[1] provides that the absolutely entitled sui juris beneficiaries of a trust can sometimes demand a transfer of legal title to the trust property; the courts have a limited equitable jurisdiction to vary trusts, and statutory powers of variation under the Variation of Trusts Act 1958; and the rules against perpetuities can also bring some trusts to an end once a fixed period of time has elapsed. **7–01**

2. Powers of Revocation, Appointment and Amendment

The settlor of a trust has no automatic power to revoke the trust after it has been completely constituted, but he may reserve such a power to himself,[2] although if he does so then he will be treated for tax purposes as having retained an interest in the property so that he will be liable for tax on capital gains and income generated within the settlement. A settlor may also confer a power of revocation on the trustees (or others), and it is common practice to give them such a power along with an overriding power of appointment,[3] since the latter power cannot effectively be exercised without first exercising of a power of revocation.[4] Trustees may also be given an overriding power of advancement,[5] the exercise of which may also be to vary, or even terminate, the interests under the settlement, and the same result may also follow if the trustees (e.g. of a pension trust or an insurance premiums trust deed) exercise an overriding power of amendment of the trust. However powers of the latter sort are confined to such amendments as can reasonably be considered to have been within the contemplation of the parties, and if the power is given to trustees then they must also observe their undivided duty of loyalty.[6] **7–02**

---

1 (1841) 4 Beav. 115.

2 *Schmidt v Air Products of Canada Ltd* [1994] 2 S.C.R. 611.

3 As in, e.g. *Abacus Trust Co (Isle of Man) Ltd v Barr* [2003] Ch. 409; *Stow v Stow* [2008] Ch. 461; *Howell v Lees-Millais* [2009] W.T.L.R. 1163. See too *Barclays Bank Ltd v Quistclose Investments Ltd* [1970] A.C. 567, as interpreted in *Twinsectra Ltd v Yardley* [2002] A.C. 164: where money is lent for a specific purpose, it may be held on trust for the lender, subject to a power vested in the borrower to apply the money to the agreed purpose, full or partial exercise of which will defeat the lender's beneficial interest under the trust.

4 *Re Thursby's Settlement* (1855) 6 De G.M. & G. 654 at 671; *Saunders v Evans* (1861) 8 H.L.C. 721 at 739. For capital gains tax purposes it is vital whether the power is exercised to create a resettlement (as a separate settlement occasioning a charge to tax) or a sub-settlement (on which no charge arises): *Roome v Edwards* [1982] A.C. 279; *Swires v Renton* [1991] S.T.C. 490; *West v Trennery* [2005] 1 All E.R. 827.

5 As in, e.g. *Re Hancock* [1896] 2 Ch. 173; *Pilkington v IRC* [1966] A.C. 612.

6 *Lord Napier and Ettrick v Kershaw Ltd (No.2)* [1999] 1 W.L.R. 756; *Hillsdown Holdings Plc v Pensions Ombudsman* [1997] 1 All E.R. 862.

3. The Rule in *Saunders v Vautier*

7–03 *Saunders v Vautier*,[7] reproduced below,[8] holds that if a beneficiary of full capacity has a vested, and not a contingent, interest in the trust property,[9] then he can call for a transfer of legal title from the trustees, irrespective of any material purpose that the settlor might have had in mind. As a matter of property law an absolutely entitled beneficiary can do whatever he wants with the property, and any restriction on his enjoyment is inconsistent with the absolute nature of his interest.[10] The settlor cannot oust this principle, even by express declaration.[11] Hence beneficiaries who are entitled in succession (e.g. a life tenant and remainderman) may combine to call for a transfer, provided that they are of full capacity and are collectively entitled absolutely.[12] Likewise, if all the beneficiaries of a discretionary trust are of full capacity and are entitled absolutely to the property between them, then they too may call for a transfer, provided that they act together.[13] Indeed, the rule in *Saunders v Vautier* applies even where there are nothing more than powers of appointment with a gift over in default of appointment.[14]

7–04 *Stephenson v Barclays Bank*,[15] reproduced below,[16] further establishes that if several beneficiaries are together absolutely entitled as co-owners of the trust property, then the rule applies to each of them separately, provided that each beneficiary's share can be severed from the trust fund without harm to the remainder.[17] The rule also applies to severable parts of, or interests in, the trust fund. So, for example, if income is payable during a certain period to such of A, B and C as the trustees shall select, with separate trusts affecting the capital, then A, B and C can jointly demand that the income be paid as they direct.[18]

7–05 Note, however, that the rule does not apply where a beneficiary has only a contingent interest: i.e. where his entitlement under the trust does not arise until the happening of a specified event, such as the beneficiary attaining 25 years of age.[19] Nor does it apply where there is a fluctuating body of beneficiaries from time to time within a class,[20] even where the likelihood of another beneficiary being

---

7 (1841) 4 Beav. 115, affirmed (1841) 1 Cr. & Ph. 240. The principle articulated in the case was not new; previous decisions to the same effect included: *Lord Pawlet's case* (1685) 2 Vent. 366; *Love v L'Estrange* (1727) 5 Bro. P.C. 59; *Barnes v Rowley* (1797) 3 Ves. Jun. 305; *Barton v Briscoe* (1822) Jac. 603; *Dawson v Hearn* (1831) 1 Russ. & My. 606.

8 At paras 7–09 ff.

9 For the principles of construction which determine whether a beneficiary has a vested or contingent interest, see *Harrison v Tucker* [2003] W.T.L.R. 883.

10 *Weatherall v Thornburgh* (1878) 5 Ch.D. 261 at 270, per Cotton L.J.

11 *Stokes v Cheek* (1860) 28 Beav. 620.

12 *Barton v Briscoe* (1822) Jac. 603; *Haynes v Haynes* (1866) 35 L.J. Ch. 303; *Re Millner* (1872) L.R. 14 Eq. 245; *Anson v Potter* (1879) 13 Ch.D. 141; *Re Bowes* [1896] 1 Ch. 507; *Re White* [1901] 1 Ch. 570.

13 *Re Nelson* [1928] Ch. 920n.; *Re Smith* [1928] Ch. 915; *Sir Moses Montefiore Jewish Home v Howell & Co (No.7) Pty Ltd* [1984] 2 N.S.W.L.R. 406 at 410.

14 *Schmidt v Rosewood Trust* [2003] 2 A.C. 709 at [41].

15 [1975] 1 W.L.R. 882. See too *Pearson v Lane* (1809) 17 Ves. 101; *Re Marshall* [1914] 1 Ch. 192; *Re Sandeman's WT* [1937] 1 All E.R. 368; *Crowe v Appleby* [1975] 1 W.L.R. 1539 at 1543.

16 At paras 7–12 ff.

17 For cases concerning shareholdings in a private company where this was an issue, see e.g. *Re Weiner's WT* [1956] 1 W.L.R. 579; *Lloyds Bank Plc v Duker* [1987] 1 W.L.R. 1324.

18 *Re Smith* [1928] Ch. 915; *Re AEG Unit Trust* [1957] Ch. 415 at 422.

19 *Re Couturier* [1907] 1 Ch. 470 at 473, where Joyce J. points out the distinction between giving a person an interest *contingent* on his reaching a specified age, and giving him a *vested* interest and postponing the enjoyment of it to a specified age. See too *Gosling v Gosling* (1859) John 265; *Re Lord Nunburnholme* [1912] 1 Ch. 489. If a contingent interest is given, but the specified event does not occur, then either the trust deed will specify that someone else then becomes entitled to the trust property, as in e.g. *Re Bellville's ST* [1964] Ch. 163, or it will go to the settlor or his estate on a resulting trust.

20 *Re Levy* [1960] Ch. 346 at 363; *Re Westphal* [1972] N.Z.L.R. 792 at 794–795.

born before the fund is exhausted is remote.[21] Nor does it apply where other persons have an interest in the accumulations of income which the beneficiaries would like to stop.[22]

Where trusts arise out of contractual relationships it is possible for the parties who are beneficiaries to contract out of their *Saunders v Vautier* rights. So, for example, unit-holders in a unit trust cannot terminate the trust and claim the trust property while the trust is operating as a going concern and before it is wound up as agreed pursuant to the trust deed. Also the rule does not apply if the trust property consists of a non-assignable contract under which there are outstanding obligations to be performed by the trustee.[23] **7–06**

The rule in *Saunders v Vautier* does not give beneficiaries the right to control the trustee in the exercise of any discretion conferred upon him by statute or the trust instrument.[24] However, if property is held on trust for beneficiaries all of whom are ascertained and of full capacity then the beneficiaries, acting collectively, may force the trustees to retire in favour of new trustees whom they have nominated.[25] **7–07**

As Paul Matthews has observed,[26] the rule in *Saunders v Vautier* is connected with the further rule of English law that prohibits restraints on the inalienability of trust interests.[27] Interestingly, neither rule forms part of the law of many American states, which have tended instead to follow the Massachusetts case of *Claflin v Claflin*,[28] in holding either that the rule in *Saunders v Vautier* does not apply at all, or else that, if there remains some material purpose of the settlor still to be carried out, then the rule cannot be applied to bring the trust to an end, even though that is what all the beneficiaries want.[29] The fact that so many American states can manage satisfactorily without the rule in *Saunders v Vautier* suggests that it is not "fundamental to the trust concept, any more than the rule against rendering trust interests inalienable is . . . because a trust can still create property interests, belonging to beneficiaries and good against third parties even if . . . the beneficiaries cannot on their own alienate their interests or terminate the trust prematurely."[30] **7–08**

SAUNDERS v VAUTIER

Master of the Rolls (1841) 4 Beav. 115; Cr. & Ph. 240; 10 L.J.Ch. 354

A testator bequeathed his stock on trust to accumulate the dividends until V should attain the age of twenty-five, and then to transfer the principal, together with the accumulated dividends, to V. V, having attained twenty-one, claimed to have the fund transferred to him. It was contended for him that he had "a vested interest, and that as the accumulation and postponement of payment was for his benefit alone, he might waive it and call for an immediate transfer of the fund." **7–09**

---

[21] *Thorpe v HMRC* [2009] S.T.C. 2107 at [14]–[15].

[22] *Berry v Geen* [1938] A.C. 575.

[23] *Don King Productions Inc v Warren* [2000] Ch. 291 at 321, citing *Re Brockbank* [1948] Ch. 206.

[24] *Re Brockbank* [1948] Ch. 206; *Re George Whichelow Ltd* [1954] 1 W.L.R. 5; *Holding and Management Ltd v Property Holdings Plc* [1990] 1 All E.R. 938 at 948.

[25] Trusts of Land and Appointment of Trustees Act 1996, ss. 19 and 20 (assuming that no-one else has the power to nominate new trustees). For further discussion see para.8–11.

[26] P. Matthews, "The Comparative Importance of the Rule in *Saunders v Vautier*" (2006) 122 L.Q.R. 266.

[27] For which see *Brandon v Robinson* (1811) 18 Ves. 429; *Green v Spicer* (1830) Russ. & My. 395; *Re Dugdale* (1888) 38 Ch.D. 176 at 182.

[28] 20 N.E. 454 (1889).

[29] The wider socio-economic implications of this are also explored in J. Getzler, "Transplantation and Mutation in Anglo-American Trust Law" (2009) 10 Theoretical Inquiries in Law 355.

[30] Matthews, above, p.294.

7–10 LORD LANGDALE M.R.: I think that principle has been repeatedly acted upon; and where a legacy is directed to accumulate for a certain period, or where the payment is postponed the legatee, if he has an absolute indefeasible interest in the legacy, is not bound to wait until the expiration of that period, but may require payment the moment he is competent to give a valid discharge.

7–11 On a question raised, with reference to a previous order for maintenance, as to whether there was a vested interest in V before he attained twenty-five, the petition stood over, with liberty to apply to the Lord Chancellor. Held, by the Lord Chancellor, the fund was intended wholly for the benefit of V, although the enjoyment of it was postponed: it vested immediately, and he could now claim the transfer.

STEPHENSON v BARCLAYS BANK TRUST CO LTD

Chancery Division [1975] 1 W.L.R. 88; [1975] 1 All E.R. 625

7–12 WALTON J.: I think it may be desirable to state what I conceive to be certain elementary principles. (1) In a case where the persons who between them hold the entirety of the beneficial interests in any particular trust fund are all sui juris and acting together ("the beneficial interest holders"), they are entitled to direct the trustees how the trust fund may be dealt with. (2) This does not mean, however, that they can at one and the same time override the pre-existing trusts and keep them in existence. Thus, in *Re Brockbank*[31] itself the beneficial interest holders were entitled to override the pre-existing trusts by, for example, directing the trustees to transfer the trust fund to X and Y, whether X and Y were the trustees of some other trust or not, but they were not entitled to direct the existing trustees to appoint their own nominee as a new trustee of the existing trust. By so doing they would be pursuing inconsistent rights. (3) Nor, I think, are the beneficial interest holders entitled to direct the trustees as to the particular investment they should make of the trust fund. I think this follows for the same reasons as the above. Moreover, it appears to me that once the beneficial interest holders have determined to end the trust they are not entitled, unless by agreement, to the further services of the trustees. Those trustees can of course be compelled to hand over the entire trust assets to any person or persons selected by the beneficiaries against a proper discharge, but they cannot be compelled, unless they are in fact willing to comply with the directions, to do anything else with the trust fund which they are not in fact willing to do. (4) Of course, the rights of the beneficial interest holders are always subject to the right of the trustees to be fully protected against such matters as duty, taxes, costs or other outgoings; for example, the rent under a lease which the trustees have properly accepted as part of the trust property.

7–13 So much for the rights of the beneficial interest holders collectively. When the situation is that a single person who is sui juris has an absolutely vested beneficial interest in a share of the trust fund, his rights are not, I think, quite as extensive as those of the beneficial interest holders as a body. In general, he is entitled to have transferred to him (subject, of course, always to the same rights of the trustees as I have already mentioned above) an aliquot share of each and every asset of the trust fund which presents no difficulty so far as division is concerned. This will apply to such items as cash, money at the bank or an unsecured loan, stock exchange securities and the like. However, as regards land, certainly, in all cases, as regards shares in a private company in very special circumstances (see *Re Weiner's Will Trusts*[32]) and possibly (although the logic of the addition in facts escapes me[33]) mortgage debts (see *Re Marshall*[34] per Cozens-Hardy M.R.) the situation is not so simple, and even a person with a vested interest in possession in an aliquot share of the trust fund may have to wait until the land is sold, and so forth, before being able to call on the trustees as of right to account to him for his share of the assets.

---

[31] [1948] Ch. 206.
[32] [1956] 1 W.L.R. 579.
[33] In *Crowe v Appleby* [1975] 1 W.L.R. 1539 at 1543, Goff J. endorsed Walton J.'s views and pointed out that "the logic of the addition of mortgages is that they include not only the debt but the estate and powers of the mortgagee."
[34] [1914] 1 Ch. 192 at 199.

4. Judicial Variation of Trusts

A. *Equitable Jurisdiction*

The rule in *Saunders v Vautier* applies only where all the trust beneficiaries are of full capacity so that they can use their rights under the rule to demand a transfer of legal title. Where they are not of full capacity, the decision of the House of Lords in *Chapman v Chapman*[35] in 1954 made it clear that the court did not possess plenary powers to alter a trust on the ground that alteration would be advantageous to infant or unborn beneficiaries. However, there were some limited exceptions to this principle. Some of these related to acts done by the trustees in regard to the trust property in the administration of the trust, while others went beyond this and conferred a limited power to remould the beneficial interests when this was to the advantage of the beneficiaries. **7–14**

i. Trustees' Administrative Acts

Salvage. This group of cases involved the alienation of infants' property and established the proposition that the court could sanction a mortgage or sale of part of an infant's beneficial interest for the benefit of the part retained in cases of absolute necessity.[36] **7–15**

Emergency. This exception can be regarded as an extension of the salvage cases. The salvage cases required proof of absolute necessity. The principle of the emergency cases was somewhat wider and enabled the court to sanction departure from the terms of a trust where an emergency had arisen which the settlor had not foreseen and which required to be dealt with by the conferment of extraordinary powers on the trustees.[37] **7–16**

Trustee Act 1925 s.57. Section 57 rested the court's jurisdiction on expediency—a basis which, it is conceived, is wider than that of salvage or emergency. The section provides that: **7–17**

> "Where in the management or administration of any property vested in trustees, any sale, lease, mortgage, surrender, release or other disposition or any purchase, investment, acquisition, expenditure, or other transaction is in the opinion of the court expedient, but the same cannot be effected by reason of the absence of any power for that purpose vested in the trustees by the trust instrument, if any, or by law, the court may by order confer upon the trustees, either generally or in any particular instance, the necessary power for the purpose, in such terms, and subject to such provisions and conditions, if any, as the court may think fit and may direct in what manner any money authorised to be expended, and the costs of any transaction, are to be paid or borne as between capital and income."

The object of the section is to enable the court to authorise specific dealings with the trust property which it might not have been able to do on the basis of salvage or emergency, but it was no part of the legislative aim to disturb the rule that the court will not rewrite a trust,[38] and so the section does not empower the court to vary the beneficial interests under a settlement.[39] **7–18**

---

[35] [1954] A.C. 429. Legislation was later enacted to undo the bad effects of this decision, in the shape of the Variation of Trusts Act 1958, and the variation of trust sought by the applicants in *Chapman* was subsequently granted under the statute: *Re Chapman's ST (No.2)* [1959] 1 W.L.R. 372.

[36] *Re Jackson* (1882) 21 Ch.D. 786; *Conway v Fenton* (1888) 40 Ch.D. 512; cf. *Re De Teissier* [1893] 1 Ch. 153; *Re Montagu* [1897] 2 Ch. 8.

[37] *Re New* [1901] 2 Ch. 534; *Re Tollemache* [1903] 1 Ch. 457; *Saipem SpA v Rafidain Bank* [1994] C.L.C. 253.

[38] *Re Downshire* [1953] Ch. 218.

[39] *Sutton v England* [2010] W.T.L.R. 335 at [27]–[43], per Mann J., following *Re Freeston's Charity* [1978] 1 W.L.R. 741.

7–19 Section 57 is an overriding section, the provisions of which are read into every settlement.[40] The powers of the court are limited only by expediency, though the proposed transaction must be for the benefit not of one beneficiary but of the whole trust.[41] The power has been used to authorise the sale of chattels settled on trusts which prevent sale,[42] the sale of land where a consent requisite to sale has been refused,[43] the partitioning of land where there was no power to partition,[44] the blending of two charitable funds into one,[45] the investment of funds in assets of any kind as if the trustees were beneficial owners subject to obtaining professional investment advice,[46] and the making of distributions out of an "exempt approved" pension fund in the form of taxable payments.[47]

ii. Remoulding of the Beneficial Interests

7–20 *Maintenance.*[48] Where a settlor made a provision for a family but postponed the enjoyment, either for a particular purpose or generally for the increase of the estate, it was assumed that he did not intend that the children should be left unprovided for, or in a state of such moderate means that they could not be educated properly for the position which he intended them to have, and the court accordingly broke in upon the accumulation and provided maintenance for the children. The exercise of this jurisdiction resulted in an alteration of beneficial interests since income was applied in maintaining beneficiaries notwithstanding the fact that the settlor had directed that it should be accumulated or applied in reduction of incumbrances. The jurisdiction was not confined to cases of emergency or necessity.[49]

7–21 *Compromise.* It has long been clear that where the rights of the beneficiaries under a trust are the subject of doubt or dispute, the court has jurisdiction on behalf of all interested parties, whether adult, infant or unborn, to sanction a compromise by substituting certainty for doubt.[50] The issue in *Re Downshire, Re Blackwell* and *Re Chapman* before the Court of Appeal,[51] and in the last-named case[52] before the House of Lords, was whether the court had jurisdiction to do the same with regard to rights which were admittedly not in dispute. Their Lordships emphatically rejected the view that the courts had so ample a jurisdiction.

7–22 *The Settled Land Act 1925 s.64.* Section 64(1) provides that any transaction affecting or concerning the settled land, or any part thereof, or any other land (not being a transaction otherwise authorised by the Act, or by the settlement) which in the opinion of the court would be for the benefit of the settled land, or any part thereof, or the persons interested under the settlement, may, under an order of the court, be effected by a tenant for life, if it is one which could have been validly effected by an absolute owner. "Transaction" is defined by subs.(2) to include "any sale, extinguishment of manorial incidents, exchange, assurance, grant, lease, surrender, reconveyance, release, reservation or other

---

40 *Re Mair* [1935] Ch. 218.
41 *Re Craven's Estate (No.2)* [1937] Ch. 431.
42 *Re Hope's WT* [1929] 2 Ch. 136.
43 *Re Beale's ST* [1932] 2 Ch. 15.
44 *Re Thomas* [1930] 1 Ch. 194. A power to partition is now given by the Trusts of Land and Appointment of Trustees Act 1996 s.13, on which see *Rodway v Landy* [2001] Ch. 703.
45 *Re Harvey* [1941] 3 All E.R. 284.
46 *Anker-Petersen v Anker-Petersen* [2000] W.T.L.R. 581.
47 *NBPF Pension Trustees Ltd v Warnock-Smith* [2008] 2 All E.R. (Comm) 740.
48 *Erratt v Barlow* (1807) 14 Ves. Jun. 202; *Greenwell v Greenwell* (1800) 5 Ves. Jun. 194; *Havelock v Havelock* (1880) 17 Ch.D. 807; *Re Collins* (1886) 32 Ch.D. 229; *Re Walker* [1901] 1 Ch. 879.
49 *Haley v Bannister* (1820) 4 Madd. 275.
50 *Brooke v Mostyn* (1864) 2 De G. J. & S. 415; *Re Barbour's Settlement* [1974] 1 All E.R. 1188.
51 [1953] Ch. 218.
52 [1954] A.C. 429.

disposition, any purchase or other acquisition, any covenant, contract, or option, and any application of capital money . . . and any compromise or other dealing or arrangement".

"Transaction" is a word of very wide import, and enables beneficial interests to be altered even without the consent of beneficiaries of full age and capacity. Section 64 has been held wide enough to enable trustees to transfer part of their trust property to another settlement of which they were trustees even though benefiting some other persons,[53] and to enable the 11th Duke of Marlborough to convey the Blenheim estate to trustees of a new settlement giving his troublesome son a protected life interest instead of a fee tail, such interest being under a trust for sale and not under an SLA trust so that the son had no power as tenant for life.[54] **7–23**

Trustee Act 1925 s.53. Section 53 provides that where an infant is beneficially entitled to any property the court may with a view to the application of the capital or income thereof for the maintenance, education or benefit of the infant make an order appointing a person to convey such property upon such terms as the court may think fit. The effect of this section may be summarised as follows. Where (a) an infant is beneficially entitled to any interest in property, whether real or personal; (b) the interest itself is not under the settlement applicable for his maintenance, education or benefit, nor is it producing any income which is so applicable; and (c) a proposal is made that the court should authorise a "conveyance"[55] of the infant's interest with a view to the application of the capital or income, arising out of such conveyance, for the maintenance, education or benefit of the infant; then the court has jurisdiction to sanction the proposal upon such terms as it thinks fit. Thus the sale of an infant's contingent reversionary interest to the life-tenant in order to minimise liability to estate duty was made with a view to, and was, an application of the proceeds of sale for the infant's benefit, where they amounted to more than he would have been likely to receive if no sale had taken place, and they were to be settled upon[56] and not paid outright to him.[57] **7–24**

B. *The Variation of Trusts Act 1958*

The decision in *Chapman v Chapman*[58] was criticised by the Law Reform Committee, whose report[59] led to the enactment of the Variation of Trusts Act 1958. Essentially, the Act enables the court on behalf of persons who cannot themselves give their approval (e.g. because unborn, unascertainable or minors) to approve arrangements varying or revoking beneficial and administrative provisions under trusts so long as such arrangements are for the benefit of the individual persons in question. Exceptionally, in the case of persons with contingent discretionary interests under protective trusts, where the interest of the protected beneficiary has not failed or determined, the court can give an approval on behalf of (and against the will of) ascertained adults and no benefit to them is required.[60] **7–25**

The Act has been useful for saving tax by exporting trusts and by partitioning the trust fund between the life tenant (who might have a protected interest) and the remaindermen (who might be minors, unborn or unascertained). However, where no alteration of beneficial interests is sought, and it is merely sought to expand the trustees' administrative powers, it is simpler and cheaper to invoke **7–26**

---

[53] *Raikes v Lygon* [1988] 1 W.L.R. 28.

[54] *Hambro v Duke of Marlborough* [1994] Ch. 158.

[55] Including a mortgage: *Re Gower's Settlement* [1934] Ch. 365; *Re Bristol's Settled Estates* [1965] 1 W.L.R. 469.

[56] *Re Meux* [1958] Ch. 154.

[57] *Re Heyworth's Contingent Reversionary Interest* [1956] Ch. 364.

[58] [1954] A.C. 429.

[59] (1957) Cmnd. 310.

[60] Variation of Trusts Act 1958 s.1(1)(d) and proviso. Here the settlor's intentions have much significance: *Re Steed's WT* [1960] Ch. 407; *Goulding v James* [1997] 2 All E.R. 239 at 250. For general discussion of protective trusts, see paras 1–145 ff.

the Trustee Act 1925 s.57, which also obviates the need to obtain the consent of every adult beneficiary.[61] To illustrate the approach taken by the courts towards the exercise of their jurisdiction under the 1958 Act, *Wyndham v Egremont*[62] is reproduced below.[63] The following points should also be noted.

i. Variation Cannot be Resettlement

7–27 It is often said that the Act does not extend beyond a variation to a completely new resettlement.[64] However, in *Re Ball's Settlement* Megarry J. stated:[65]

> "If an arrangement changes the whole substratum of the trust, then it may well be that it cannot be regarded merely as varying that trust. But if, an arrangement, whilst leaving the substratum, effectuates the purpose of the trust by other means, it may still be possible to regard that arrangement as merely varying the original trusts, even though the means employed are wholly different and even though the form is completely changed . . . in essence the court is merely contributing on behalf of infants and unborn and unascertained persons the binding assets which they, unlike an adult beneficiary, cannot give. So far as is proper, the power of the court to give that consent should be assimilated to the wide powers which the ascertained adults have."

In the case a settlement conferred a life interest on the settlor (subject to a power of appointment in favour of his sons and grandchildren) and the capital was in default of appointment to be divided between the two sons of the settlor or their issue *per stirpes* if either son predeceased the settlor. The approved arrangement revoked the beneficial and administrative provisions of the settlement and replaced them with new provisions whereby each half of the trust fund was held on trust for one of the sons for life and, subject thereto, for such of that son's children equally as were born before a certain date. This jurisdictional limit is thus unlikely in practice to cause much difficulty.

ii. Benefit

7–28 "Benefit" may be financial, moral or social[66] or the facilitation of the administration of the settlement.[67] Unfortunately, the reported cases all too often show, as one commentator puts it,[68] "that benefit and the measure of it is simply what the court says it is." An extreme case is *Re Remnant's WT*[69] where the children of two sisters, Dawn and Merrial, had contingent interests under a testamentary trust which contained a forfeiture provision in respect of any child who practised Roman Catholicism or was married to a Catholic at the time of vesting, with an accruer provision in favour of the children of the other sister. Dawn's children were Protestant while Merrial's children were Catholic. In the interests of family harmony an application was made inter alia for deletion of the forfeiture provision. Pennycuick J. acceded to the application in the interests of family harmony and freedom of marital

---

[61] *Anker-Petersen v Anker-Petersen* [2000] W.T.L.R. 581.
[62] [2009] W.T.L.R. 1473.
[63] At paras 7–38 ff.
[64] *Re T's Settlement Trusts* [1964] Ch. 158 at 162; *Re Holt's Settlement* [1969] 1 Ch. 100 at 117; *Wyndham v Egremont* [2009] W.T.L.R. 1473 at [21].
[65] [1968] 1 W.L.R. 899 at 905.
[66] *Re Towler's ST* [1964] Ch. 158; *Re Holt's Settlement* [1969] 1 Ch. 100; *Re Weston's Settlement* [1969] 1 Ch. 224; *Re Remnant's ST* [1970] 1 Ch. 560; but cf. *Re Tinker's Settlement* [1960] 1 W.L.R. 1011.
[67] *Re University of London Charitable Trusts* [1964] Ch. 282; *Re Seale's Marriage Settlement* [1961] Ch. 574.
[68] R.B.M. Cotterell (1971) 34 M.L.R. 96, p.98.
[69] [1970] 1 Ch. 560.

choice, though defeating the testator's clear intentions and though financially disadvantageous to Dawn's children who otherwise had a good chance of gaining under the accruer clause. *Re Tinker's Settlement*[70] was not cited where Russell J. had refused approval to inserting a provision (omitted in error) which would have taken away a sister's children's chance of obtaining property under an accruer clause on the brother's death under 30. Further, Pennycuick J. did not consider whether the Protestant children, when adult, would in all probability be happy to forgo a larger share in the trust fund resulting from their cousins' Catholicism, this being the test taken by Cross J. in *Re CL*[71] to distinguish *Re Tinker* from *Re CL*, where he approved a mental patient giving up certain life interests in favour of her adopted daughters with interests in remainder. Perhaps one may artificially reconcile *Re Remnant's WT* with *Re Tinker's Settlement* on the basis that in the former both sides of the family could benefit in theory while in the latter only one side of the family could benefit.[72]

So long as the arrangement is for the benefit of the incapable or unborn beneficiaries it does not matter that it is contrary to the settlor's wishes,[73] the operation of the rule in *Saunders v Vautier* entitling the beneficiaries collectively to deal with their property as they want and the court's approval operating as the collective consent of the unborn or incapable beneficiaries. Exceptionally, in the case of protective trust cases under s.1(1)(d) of the 1958 Act, where it is immaterial that there is no benefit for the class of contingent beneficiaries, the settlor's purpose to protect the protected life tenant from improvident dealings is a significant consideration.[74] **7–29**

The court may sanction a proposed arrangement which involves an element of risk to infant or unborn beneficiaries if the risk is one which an adult might well be prepared to take.[75] It will not sanction an arrangement involving an appointment made under a special power considered to be a fraud on the power. Thus, if a life tenant exercises a power to appoint capital to his two minor children to the exclusion of any of his future children, with the ulterior intent of receiving a larger share of the capital than otherwise would be possible this can be invalidated.[76] **7–30**

The court may be willing to approve an arrangement varying the trusts of a settlement with a view to mitigating potential tax burdens,[77] but it is likely to be unwilling to approve an arrangement which has adverse tax consequences for those on whose behalf it is concerned to give its approval, unless those consequences are more than outweighed by other benefits.[78] **7–31**

In *Re Cohen's WT*,[79] Danckwerts J. said that the court could take a risk on behalf of an infant if it was a risk an adult would be prepared to take. In a later case of the same name, however,[80] Stamp J. stressed that (i) the court had to be satisfied that there was a benefit in the case of each individual infant and not merely of the whole class to which the infant belonged; and (ii) while the court need not be satisfied that each individual infant is bound to be better off than he would otherwise have been, it must be sure that he is making a bargain which is a reasonable one which an adult would be **7–32**

---

[70] [1960] 1 W.L.R. 1011.
[71] [1969] 1 Ch. 587.
[72] P.J. Clarke [1987] Conv. 69. And cf. *S v T* [2006] W.T.L.R. 1461 (following intestate death of applicant's unmarried father, variation made to statutory trusts arising under Administration of Estates Act 1925, to give him lump sum in exchange for surrendering the remainder of the trust fund to his paternal grandmother, all of which he would otherwise lose following his adoption).
[73] *Goulding v James* [1997] 2 All E.R. 239.
[74] *Goulding* at 249–251, based on *Re Steed's WT* [1960] Ch. 407.
[75] *Re Cohen's WT* [1959] 1 W.L.R. 865; *Re Holt's Settlement* [1969] 1 Ch. 100; *Re Robinson's ST* [1976] 1 W.L.R. 806.
[76] *Re Brook's Settlement* [1968] 1 W.L.R. 1661; and cf. *Re Wallace's Settlements* [1963] 1 W.L.R. 711.
[77] *Ridgewell v Ridgewell* [2008] S.T.C. 1883.
[78] *Wyndham v Egremont* [2009] W.T.L.R. 1473 at [25].
[79] [1959] 1 W.L.R. 865 at 868; criticised at (1960) 76 L.Q.R. 22 (R. E. M.).
[80] *Re Cohen's WT* [1965] 1 W.L.R. 1229.

prepared to make. It seems, further, that the court may take a broad reasonable view but not a galloping gambling view.[81]

iii. Parties to the Application

7–33 Application is by claim form (under Pt 8 of the Civil Procedure Rules) supported by affidavits to which a draft scheme of arrangement will be exhibited. The proper claimants are the adult beneficiaries and not the trustees.[82] The trustees are supposed to be "watch-dogs" concerned with the interests of those who may possibly be adversely affected by the arrangement proposed. The defendant should be the trustees, the settlor, any beneficiary not a claimant, and any person who may become entitled to an interest under the trusts as being at a future date or on the happening of a future event a person of any specified description or a member of any specified class (e.g. next-of-kin of S, still alive) who would be of that description or of that class if the said date had fallen or the said event had happened (e.g. S's death) at the date of the application to the court, being the date of issue of the claim form.[83] No other persons who might eventually fulfil that description or be members of that class (e.g. distant relatives who might be next-of-kin if the nearer relatives conveniently died) need be made parties, nor need possible objects of a power of appointment which has not actually been exercised in their favour, or persons whose only interest is under discretionary trusts in a protective trust where the interest of the protected beneficiary has not failed or determined. However, a person who has an actual interest conferred directly on him by a settlement, however remote or contingent, has been held not to be a person who may become entitled to an interest so the court cannot approve on his behalf.[84]

iv. The Effect of Approval by the Court

7–34 The variation takes effect as soon as the order of the court is made without any further instrument,[85] and the order may be liable to stamp duty.[86] A fundamental question is whether it is the order of the court or the arrangement which that order approves which has the effect of varying the trusts. The former view was taken in *Re Hambleden's WT*.[87] The latter view is supported by dicta of Lords Reid and Wilberforce in *Re Holmden's Settlement*.[88]

7–35 In *Re Holt's Settlement*,[89] decided before *Re Holmden's Settlement* was reported, Megarry J. rejected the view taken in *Re Hambleden's WT*, canvassed the difficulties arising from such rejection and accepted counsel's submission that,[90] "when the adults by their counsel assented to the arrangement and the court on behalf of the infants by order approved the arrangement then there was an arrangement which varied the trusts." The variation is thus effected by the consent of all parties on *Saunders v Vautier*[91] principles, the court supplying the consents of the unborn, the unascertained and infants. This was endorsed in *Goulding v James* by Mummery L.J., who said that:[92]

---

[81] *Re Robinson's ST* [1976] 1 W.L.R. 806.
[82] *Re Druce's ST* [1962] 1 W.L.R. 363. Trustees should only act as claimants where they are satisfied that the proposed arrangement is beneficial and that no beneficiary is willing to make the application.
[83] *Knocker v Youle* [1986] 1 W.L.R. 934 at 938.
[84] *Knocker v Youle* [1986] 1 W.L.R. 934.
[85] *Re Holmden's Settlement* [1968] A.C. 685; *Re Holt's Settlement* [1969] 1 Ch. 100.
[86] Practice Note [1966] 1 W.L.R. 345; *Re Holt's*, above; *Thorn v IRC* [1976] 1 W.L.R. 915, though N.B. ad valorem duty on gifts was abolished by the Finance Act 1985 s.82.
[87] [1960] 1 W.L.R. 82.
[88] [1968] A.C. 685 at 701, 702, 710 and 713.
[89] [1969] 1 Ch. 100.
[90] [1969] 1 Ch. 100 at 115.
[91] See paras 7–03 ff.
[92] [1997] 2 All E.R. 239 at 247.

"The court is merely contributing on behalf of infants and unborn and unascertained persons the binding assents to the arrangements which they, unlike an adult beneficiary, cannot give. The 1958 Act has thus been viewed by the courts as a statutory extension of the consent principle embodied in the rule in *Saunders v Vautier*. The principle recognises the rights of beneficiaries who are sui juris and together absolutely entitled to the trust property, to exercise their proprietary rights to overbear and defeat the intention of a testator or settlor."

Adult beneficiaries who give their own consents to the variation would seem to be pro tanto disposing of their subsisting equitable interests so that signed writing is required by s.53(1)(c) of the Law of Property Act 1925. However, in *Re Holt's Settlement*[93] Megarry J. held that the court's power under the 1958 Act was to approve arrangements that actually did vary the trusts effectively so the court's order approving the arrangement makes it effective irrespective of whether there is any signed writing provided by the consenting adults. The 1958 Act by implication ousted s.53(1)(c). Furthermore, where the arrangement consisted of a specifically enforceable contract the beneficial interests would have passed under a constructive trust to the purchasers, such a trust being effective under s.53(2) without signed writing. **7–36**

VARIATION OF TRUSTS ACT 1958 SECTION 1

(1) Where property, whether real or personal, is held on trusts arising, whether before or after the passing of this Act, under any will, settlement or other disposition, the court may if it thinks fit by order approve on behalf of— **7–37**

(a) any person having, directly or indirectly, an interest, whether vested or contingent, under the trusts who by reason of infancy or other incapacity is incapable of assenting,[94] or
(b) any person (whether ascertained or not) who may become entitled, directly or indirectly, to an interest under the trusts as being at a future date or on the happening of a future event a person of any specified description[95] or a member of any specified class of persons, so however that this paragraph shall not include any person who would be of that description, or a member of that class, as the case may be, if the said date had fallen or the said event had happened at the date of the application to the court,[96] or
(c) any person unborn, or
(d) any person[97] in respect of any discretionary interest of his under protective trusts where the interest of the principal beneficiary has not failed or determined,

any arrangement (by whomsoever proposed,[98] and whether or not there is any other person beneficially interested who is capable of assenting thereto) varying or revoking all or any of the trusts,

---

93 [1969] 1 Ch. at 115–116.

94 Objects of a discretionary trust are treated as included: *Re Clitheroe's ST* [1959] 3 All E.R. 784; but not objects of a power of appointment: *Knocker v Youle* [1986] 1 W.L.R. 934.

95 Unascertained future spouses are included: *Re Steed's WT* [1960] Ch. 407.

96 This refers inter alia to the potential next-of-kin of a living person, who must make up their own minds whether or not to give their consent: *Re Suffert's Settlement* [1961] Ch. 1. The relevant date is the date of issue of the claim form: *Knocker v Youle* [1986] 1 W.L.R. 934 at 938.

97 Including an unascertained or unborn person: *Re Turner's WT* [1960] Ch. 122. This approval may be given without the need to show "benefit".

98 The arrangement need not be in the nature of a contract between the parties: *Re Steed's WT* [1959] Ch. 354; but must not amount to a completely new settlement: *Re T's ST* [1964] Ch. 158; *Re Ball's ST* [1968] 1 W.L.R. 899; and it must be practical and businesslike: *Re Van Jenisen's WT* [1964] 1 W.L.R. 449.

or enlarging[99] the powers of the trustees of managing or administering any of the property subject to the trusts:

Providing that except[100] by virtue of paragraph (d) of this subsection the court shall not approve an arrangement on behalf of any person unless the carrying out thereof would be for the benefit[101] of that person.

(2) In the foregoing subsection "protective trusts" means the trusts specified in paragraphs (i) and (ii) of subsection (1) of section thirty-three of the Trustee Act 1925 or any like trusts, "the principal beneficiary" has the same meaning as in the said subsection (1) and "discretionary interest" means an interest arising under the trust specified in paragraph (ii) of the said subsection (1) or any like trust.[102]

(3) The jurisdiction conferred by subsection (1) of this section shall be exercisable by the High Court, except that the question whether the carrying out of any arrangement would be for the benefit of a person falling within paragraph (a) of the said subsection (1) who lacks capacity (within the meaning of the Mental Capacity Act 2005) to give his assent is to be determined by the Court of Protection. . . .

(5) Nothing in the foregoing provisions of this section shall apply to trusts affecting property settled by Act of Parliament.

(6) Nothing in this section shall be taken to limit the powers conferred by section sixty-four of the Settled Land Act 1925, section fifty-seven of the Trustee Act 1925, or the powers of the Court of Protection.

WYNDHAM v EGREMONT

Chancery Division [2009] W.T.L.R. 1473

7–38 BLACKBURNE J.: In this matter I have approved in exercise of the jurisdiction conferred by section 1(1) of the Variation of Trusts Act 1958 ("the 1958 Act") an arrangement varying the trusts of a fund referred to as "George's Fund" comprised in settlement known as Lord Egremont's 1969 Settlement ("the 1969 Settlement") which was created by a deed dated 28 February 1969 and deeds supplemental thereto. I did so at the conclusion of counsels' submissions on 24 July 2009 and indicated that, in view of the matters raised in the course of argument, I would set out briefly in writing my reasons for giving that approval. This I now do.

7–39 The claimant, George Ronan Valentine Wyndham ("George"), after whom the fund in question is named . . . is the only son of John Max Henry Scawen Wyndham, Second Baron Egremont ("Lord Egremont"). George attained his 26th birthday on 31 July 2009. He is unmarried.

7–40 George's Fund, which I shall refer to simply as "the Fund", consists of investments, cash, life policies, land in Cumbria and a great deal of agricultural and other land—indeed the major part of the Wyndham family estate—at Petworth in West Sussex. It is worth many millions. Petworth House was made over to the National Trust by Lord Egremont's great-uncle in 1947. Petworth—the house and estate—has been the family seat since it came into the ownership of the Wyndham family in the 18th century and, traced through the female line, has been in the ownership of Lord Egremont's ancestors for many generations

---

99 e.g. conferring wider investment powers: *Re Coates's Trusts* [1959] 1 W.L.R. 375; *Re Byng's WT* [1959] 1 W.L.R. 375; *Re Allen's ST* [1960] 1 W.L.R. 6; *Re Royal Naval and Royal Marine Children's Homes, Portsmouth* [1959] 1 W.L.R. 755.

100 Even in the excepted case the court must exercise its discretion judicially: *Re Burney's Settlement* [1961] 1 W.L.R. 545; *Re Baker's ST* [1964] 1 W.L.R. 336.

101 The court will not approve an arrangement which is a fraud on a power (*Re Robertson's WT* [1960] 1 W.L.R. 1050) or is contrary to public policy (*Re Michelham's WT* [1964] Ch. 550). Nor will the court use the Act as a justification for rectifying a settlement on the basis of mistake (*Re Tinker's Settlement* [1960] 1 W.L.R. 1011) or for making an order which can be made without the aid of the Act (*Re Pettifor's WT* [1966] Ch. 257 where the female beneficiary was 70 years old and so well past child-bearing age).

102 For "like" trusts, see *Re Wallace's Settlement* [1968] 1 W.L.R. 711 at 716.

before that. It is where Lord Egremont and his family still live. It is this fact among others that has led to some of the terms of the arrangement which I was asked to approve. . . .

I do not need to trace the various instruments by which the trusts had been established upon which the Fund had come to be held by the time of the hearing before me to approve the arrangement varying them ("the pre-arrangement trusts"). It is sufficient to note that they start with the 1969 Settlement (itself the result of the exercise of a power of appointment contained in an earlier instrument) and end with a deed dated 18 July 2008 ("the 2008 Deed"). Those trusts were as follows: **7–41**

- (i) the Fund was held in trust for George during his lifetime;
- (ii) if George should be living on the Vesting Day the Fund would thereupon vest in him absolutely;
- (iii) the Trustees had power at any time or times before the Vesting Day to transfer the Fund to George absolutely or to apply the same for his benefit in such manner as they with his consent should think fit;
- (iv) subject as aforesaid the Fund was held upon such trusts for the benefit of George's children and remoter issue as he by deed or deeds revocable or irrevocable executed before the Vesting Day should appoint or if he should die before then as he by will or codicil should appoint;
- (v) subject to and in default of appointment the Fund was held on trust for George's eldest or only son living on the Vesting Day or if his eldest or only son should have died before the Vesting Day then on trust for such son's eldest or only son living on the Vesting Day;
- (vi) if the foregoing trusts should fail or determine the Fund was to devolve on George or his personal representatives.

Paragraph (vi) of the above summary—the ultimate trust—needs more explanation. As a result of various appointments, the Fund became absolutely vested in George on his 18th birthday but on to that absolute interest various trusts had been engrafted which, in the events that have happened, were those summarised at paragraph (i) to (v) above by the time of my approval of the arrangement. The ultimate trust takes effect therefore under the rule in *Hancock v Watson*.[103] **7–42**

For the purpose of the pre-arrangement trusts the expression "Vesting Day" had been redefined by the 2008 Deed to be the day on which should expire the period of 20 years from the death of the last survivor of the issue, whether children or more remote, of His late Majesty King George V living on 20 May 1940. (The choice of Royal Lives by reference to that date derived from the terms of the 1969 Settlement which itself derived from the exercise of a power of appointment contained in an earlier instrument.) **7–43**

Under the pre-arrangement trusts the only living beneficiary is George. He is entitled to: an immediate life interest, and an absolute interest in capital if he is living on the Vesting Day (as defined by the 2008 Deed); the right in the meantime to be considered for a capital advance; and the ultimate trust if he should die before the Vesting Day leaving no son or grandson living on the Vesting Day. Given the ages of the remaining Royal Lives in being under the definition of "the Vesting Day" contained in the 2008 Deed, the youngest of whom (HRH Princess Alexandra) is presently 72, those trusts will inevitably come to an end in the not too distant future and, since George is only 26, in all likelihood in George's lifetime. **7–44**

The arrangement varying the trusts of the Fund is designed to achieve two aims: (1) to ensure, in accordance with George's wishes, that the ancestral estates at Petworth continue to be attached to the two baronies and thus to devolve for as long as possible down the senior male line and (2) to defer, by an extension of the applicable trust period, the very considerable tax charges which under current legislation—absent the arrangement—will arise on the termination of the pre-arrangement trusts and which could only be met by the sale of a significant part of the ancestral lands as the major constituent of the Fund. **7–45**

---

[103] [1902] A.C. 14.

7–46 With those objectives in mind the arrangement has involved the following modifications to the pre-arrangement trusts:

(i) the redefinition of "the Vesting Day" as the day on which expires the period of 21 years after the death of the last survivor of the issue of His late Majesty King George V and the issue of George's great-grandfather, the Fifth Baron Leconfield, living on the date of the order approving the arrangement (in the event 24 July 2009);

(ii) the deletion of the contingent capital trust in favour of George (being the trust summarised at (ii) of paragraph 5 above);

(iii) the substitution for the default trust in favour of George's son or grandson of a default trust of the Fund (and also of the income thereof in the meantime) in favour of that one of George's male issue in the male line who shall be living on the Vesting Day and then hold the baronies of Egremont and Leconfield;

(iv) the addition of a default power of appointment of the Fund and the income thereof among the male issue in the male line of the Fifth Baron Leconfield (other than the present Lord Egremont) exercisable by the trustees with George's consent during his lifetime and otherwise at their discretion; and

(v) the addition of a default trust of the Fund (and also of the income thereof in the meantime) in favour of that one of the Fifth Baron Leconfield's male issue in the male line (other than the present Lord Egremont) who shall be living on Vesting Day and shall then hold the baronies of Egremont and Leconfield or the barony of Leconfield.

The ultimate trust is, as before, for George and his personal representatives under the trusts of the 1969 Settlement and supplemental deeds.

7–47 The proposed variation, if it is to be approved by the court under section 1(1), must be for the benefit of the only other class of beneficiaries potentially entitled under the pre-arrangement trusts, namely George's future eldest or only son living on the Vesting Day and, if he should have died by then, the eldest or only son living on the Vesting Day of George's eldest or only son. This very restricted class, which is currently unborn, is represented by the defendants who are the trustees of the Fund in their capacity as trustees of the 1969 Settlement. They have appeared before me by Mr Hedley Marten.

7–48 Mr Marten has submitted, and I agree, that the variation to the pre-arrangement trusts brings two very clear benefits to the unborns. The first is the elimination of the likelihood, given George's young age and the relative imminence of the current Vesting Day, that George will be alive on the Vesting Day and thus take all, leaving nothing for the unborns. Since George is one of the measuring lives for the purpose of the new trust period under the trusts as varied, he can no longer take under the proposed contingent trust of capital. The deferment of the absolute vesting of capital by a significant period of time means, it is true, that the prospect of George's son or grandson taking an absolute interest in capital if George were to die before the present Vesting Date is correspondingly deferred and may possibly be eliminated altogether if that son or grandson should not survive to the new Vesting Day. But, in the meantime, following George's death, such son or grandson will be entitled to the intermediate income earned by the Fund.

7–49 The second benefit is that the Vesting Day will under existing legislation give rise to a deemed disposal of the Fund and thus trigger a substantial charge to capital gains tax. Present estimates are that the liability will exceed £3 million. The postponement of the Vesting Day under the proposed arrangement to the expiry of the period of 21 years from the death of the last survivor of the legitimate issue, whether children or more remote, living on 24 July 2009 (when I approved the arrangement) of His late Majesty King George V and the Fifth Baron Leconfield is intended to effect a postponement of the charge to tax by a very significant period. Mr Marten submitted, and I agree, that the deferment of that charge is a clear and substantial benefit to the unborns. Mr Marten accepted, as I have mentioned, that the postponement of the Vesting Day reduces or eliminates the chances of a future son or grandson of George taking absolutely, but submitted that it was nevertheless realistic to assume that such persons would wish to take steps to avoid the severe tax consequences of such absolute vesting. I agree. In the meantime, such son or grandson has the income of the Fund following George's death.

The addition of a new clause extending the default trusts (under the pre-arrangement trusts they are limited to the two named unborns) to male issue of all degrees in the male line of George does not either advantage or disadvantage those unborns since it merely adds trusts behind the existing trusts in their favour. The same, Mr Marten submitted, applies to the new trusts to be added in favour of the male issue in the male line of the Fifth Baron Leconfield. Although these additions are not specifically for the benefit of the unborns, the trustees consider it appropriate to support them in view of the historic connection between the Wyndham family and Petworth. **7–50**

I do not see that the addition of these trusts causes any difficulty. The fact that these additional provisions are not specifically for the benefit of the unborns does not matter provided that I am satisfied, as I was, that overall the unborns are benefited by the arrangement. **7–51**

Subject only to the following three points, which were elaborated at some length in the skeleton arguments and other papers before me and to which Mr Barlow referred in some detail, I was satisfied therefore that the arrangement was one which I could properly approve under section 1(1) of the 1958 Act. **7–52**

The first concerns the propriety of inserting a new perpetuity date into the trusts of the Fund. As to this, it is well established that an arrangement under section 1(1) enables the court to approve a variation which includes a new perpetuity period applicable to the settlement in question. In *Re Holt's Settlement*[104] Megarry J. approved an arrangement which substituted in place of a common law period a new statutory period of eighty years and also added a new twenty-one year accumulation period, both of which were made possible by the Perpetuities and Accumulations Act 1964 ("the 1964 Act") and neither of which was available under the settlement that was being varied, since it took effect prior to the commencement of the 1964 Act on 15 July 1964. Megarry J. observed that:[105] **7–53**

> "Any variation owes its authority not to anything in the initial settlement but to the statute [i.e. the 1958 Act] and the consent of the adults coming, as it were, ab extra. This certainly seems to be so in any case not within the Act where a variation or resettlement is made under the doctrine of *Saunders v Vautier* by all the adults joining together; and I cannot see any real difference in principle in a case where the court exercises its jurisdiction on behalf of the infants under the Act of 1958 . . ."

Megarry J. then went on to consider whether it was permissible to insert a new perpetuity period into the settlement by reference to the statutory period made available by section 1(1) of the 1964 Act. This turned on whether a variation approved by the court in exercise of the jurisdiction conferred by section 1(1) of the 1968 Act constituted an "instrument" within the meaning of section 15(5) of the 1964 Act. Megarry J, held that it did and therefore that it was open to the court to approve the arrangement in that case.

A few days after the judgment in *Re Holt's Settlement* was delivered, the House of Lords gave judgment in *IRC v Holmden*.[106] In that case, a settlement provided that during the life of the settlor's widow the income should be held upon discretionary trusts for a class of beneficiaries consisting of the widow, her children and their issue. On 12 January 1960 the court approved (under section 1(1) of the 1958 Act) an arrangement whereby the discretionary trusts should last during the widow's life or twenty-one years, whichever was the longer. The widow who was already aged 84 at the time of the court's order approving the arrangement died less than three years later and the question was whether estate duty was payable on the widow's death. If there had been no arrangement, the funds would have passed on her death so that duty would have been payable under section 1 of the Finance Act 1894. It was contended for the Revenue that under the arrangement the interest in income "has been disposed of or has determined" so that duty was chargeable under section 43 of the Finance Act 1940. In evaluating this contention, the House of Lords considered the effect of an arrangement approved by the court under the 1958 Act. Lord Reid pointed out[107] that the court did not itself amend or vary the trusts; the beneficiaries were bound because they had consented, the court supplying the consent for the infant and unascertained beneficiaries. It followed, in his view, that the arrangement brought to an end the original provisions and substituted for **7–54**

[104] [1969] 1 Ch. 100.
[105] At 120.
[106] [1968] A.C. 685.
[107] At 701.

them new provisions arranged by the beneficiaries. To like effect was Lord Guest.[108] Lord Wilberforce reached a similar conclusion:[109]

> "If all the beneficiaries under the settlement had been sui juris, they could, in my opinion, have joined together with the trustees and declared different trusts which would supersede those originally contained in the settlement. Those new trusts would operate *proprio vigore*, by virtue of a self-contained instrument—namely, the deed of arrangement or variation. The original settlement would have lost any force or relevance. The effect of an order made under the Variation of Trusts Act, 1958, is to make good by act of the court any want of capacity to enter into a binding arrangement of any beneficiary not capable of binding himself and of any beneficiary unborn: the nature and effect of any arrangement so sanctioned is the same as that I have described."

7–55 . . . Here, there is no wish to insert a new perpetuity period by reference to section 1(1) of the 1964 Act but to introduce what is, in effect, a new common law period by reference to stated lives in being measured as at the date of approval of the arrangement, plus twenty-one years. In my judgment, there is ample power to do so just as there is, in appropriate cases, to insert a new perpetuity period by reference to the statutory period made available by the 1964 Act.

7–56 Necessarily implicit in the fact that the court's power under section 1(1) of the 1958 Act to approve an arrangement operates as a statutory extension of the consent principle embodied in the rule in *Saunders v Vautier*[110] is that merely because that is the basis for the jurisdiction does not mean that every exercise of the jurisdiction gives rise to a resettlement. Section 1(1) of the 1958 Act authorises the court to approve an arrangement varying (or revoking) all or any of the trusts of a will, settlement or other disposition. It does not authorise the court to approve a resettlement.[111] This leads to the second of the matters raised in argument before me which was whether by seeking to introduce a term extending the trust period, and doing so for potentially so lengthy a period, when coupled with the other amendments and insertions, it might be said that the arrangement was not by way of a variation of the trusts of the Fund at all but, in truth, was to be regarded as a resettlement of the Fund.

7–57 There is no bright-line test for determining whether it is the one or the other. In *Re Balls Settlement Trusts* Megarry J stated that:[112]

> "If an arrangement, while leaving the substratum effectuates the purpose of the original trusts by other means, it may still be possible to regard that arrangement as merely varying the original trusts, even though the means employed are wholly different and even though the form is completely changed."

That does rather beg what is meant by "the substratum" of the trust and "the purpose of the original trust" and how one is to distinguish these elements.

7–58 Useful guidance for determining whether what is proposed is a variation rather than a resettlement, indeed the analogy is very close, is to be found in *Roome v Edwards*.[113] The case was concerned with a claim for capital gains tax. It was material to that claim to decide whether the exercise of a power of appointment contained in a settlement gave rise to a settlement separate from the main settlement. Lord Wilberforce (with whose speech three of the other four Law Lords agreed: Lord Roskill delivered a separate speech) said this, speaking generally on the topic:[114]

> "There are a number of obvious indicia which may help to show whether a settlement, or a settlement separate from another settlement, exists. One might expect to find separate and defined property;

[108] At 710–711.
[109] At 713.
[110] See *Goulding v James* [1997] 2 All E.R. 239.
[111] See *Re T's Settlement Trusts* [1964] Ch. 158 at 162.
[112] [1968] 1 W.L.R. 899 at 905.
[113] [1982] A.C. 279.
[114] At 292–293.

separate trusts; and separate trustees. One might also expect to find a separate disposition bringing the separate settlement into existence. These indicia may be helpful, but they are not decisive. For example, a single disposition, e.g., a will with a single set of trustees, may create what are clearly separate settlements, relating to different properties, in favour of different beneficiaries, and conversely separate trusts may arise in what is clearly a single settlement, e.g. when the settled property is divided into shares. There are so many possible combinations of fact that even where these indicia or some of them are present, the answer may be doubtful, and may depend upon an appreciation of them as a whole.

"Since 'settlement' and 'trusts' are legal terms, which are also used by business men or laymen in a business or practical sense, I think that the question whether a particular set of facts amounts to a settlement should be approached by asking what a person, with knowledge of the legal context of the word under established doctrine and applying this knowledge in a practical and common-sense manner to the facts under examination, would conclude. To take two fairly typical cases. Many settlements contain powers to appoint a part or a proportion of the trust property to beneficiaries: some may also confer power to appoint separate trustees of the property so appointed, or such power may be conferred by law.[115] It is established doctrine that the trusts declared by a document exercising a special power of appointment are to be read into the original settlement.[116] If such a power is exercised, whether or not separate trustees are appointed, I do not think that it would be natural for such a person as I have presupposed to say that a separate settlement had been created: still less so if it were found that provisions of the original settlement continued to apply to the appointed fund, or that the appointed fund were liable, in certain events, to fall back into the rest of the settled property. On the other hand, there may be a power to appoint and appropriate a part or portion of the trust property to beneficiaries and to settle it for their benefit. If such a power is exercised, the natural conclusion might be that a separate settlement was created, all the more so if a complete new set of trusts were declared as to the appropriated property, and if it could be said that the trusts of the original settlement ceased to apply to it. There can be many variations on these cases each of which will have to be judged on its facts."

With that guidance in mind I have no doubt that the alterations to the pre-arrangement trusts contained in the arrangement which I have approved constitute a variation of those trusts and not a resettlement. The trustees remain the same, the subsisting trusts remain largely unaltered and the administrative provisions affecting them are wholly unchanged. The only significant changes are (1) to the trusts in the remainder, although the ultimate trust in favour of George and his personal representatives remains the same, and (2) the introduction of the new and extended perpetuity period. **7–59**

That leads to the last and related question which is whether the arrangement will have adverse tax consequences. Just as the court may be willing to approve an arrangement varying the trusts of a settlement with a view to mitigating potential tax burdens, it is likely to be unwilling to approve an arrangement which has adverse tax consequences for those on whose behalf it is concerned to give its approval unless those consequences are more than outweighed by other benefits. The concern here is whether, on the ground that they give rise to a resettlement, the variations to the trust, principally the extension of the trust period, might be said to give rise to a "deemed disposal" under section 71(1) of the Taxation of Capital Gains Act 1992 or might lead to adverse consequences for inheritance tax or Stamp Duty Land Tax purposes. I propose to take this very shortly because, in my view, the approach of Lord Wilberforce in *Roome v Edwards* (cited earlier) is in point. I do not consider, for the reasons already summarised, that the arrangement does give rise to a resettlement. This view cannot of course bind HM Revenue and Customs who, I should note, were approached with a view to commenting on a joint opinion of counsel to the effect that the variations of the pre-arrangement trusts effected by the arrangement would not give rise to adverse tax consequences but who declined—as I understand it in accordance with a change of practice in such matters—to be joined to the proceedings or to comment one way or the other on counsels' opinion or otherwise to make any representations. **7–60**

[115] See Trustee Act 1925 s.37.

[116] See *Muir (or Williams) v Muir* [1943] A.C. 468.

C. *The Matrimonial Causes Act 1973*

7-61 Under the Matrimonial Causes Act 1973 ss. 21(2)(c) and 24(1)(c), the court has very extensive powers to make an order varying any "ante-nuptial or post-nuptial"[117] settlement made on the parties to the marriage for the benefit of the parties and/or the children of the marriage, so long as it is for the benefit of some of them. An order extinguishing or reducing the interest of either of the spouses may even be made under s.24(1)(d). The trustees should be made parties and may be replaced, while the terms of the settlement may be completely rewritten.[118]

5. The Rules against Perpetuities

7-62 The law holds that private (i.e. non-charitable) trusts may not continue indefinitely.[119] Reference is often made to a trust offending the rule against perpetuities without it being made clear whether the trust infringes the rule against remoteness of vesting, directed at persons' interests vesting at too remote a time, or infringes the rule against inalienability, directed at immediately effective interests which can go on for too long, so tying up the use of the income of trust property for too long. The two rules are mutually exclusive, the former applying to "people" trusts and the latter to "purpose" trusts. The Perpetuities and Accumulations Act 2009, which has now superseded the 1964 legislation in this area, helps to validate people trusts, but does not affect the rule against inalienability that can invalidate private purpose trusts.

A. *The Rule against Remoteness of Vesting*

i. The Common Law Rule

7-63 Where capital is set on one side to be kept intact ("endowment" capital) with only the income thereof being used, this cannot last indefinitely. A settlor cannot be allowed to rule the living from his grave for thousands of years nor to compel capital to be used for ever as "safe" trust capital instead of absolutely owned capital available for risky entrepreneurial ventures. Thus, where a settlor created successive interests a future interest (contingent on birth or whatever) was, under the common law rule, void unless at the creation of the trust it was absolutely certain that the contingency would be satisfied—and so the interest would become "vested in interest"—within the perpetuity period.

7-64 The perpetuity period cannot exceed 21 years from the death of some expressly or impliedly relevant life in being at the creation of the trust. A settlor can expressly stipulate that his beneficiaries are only those described by him who take a vested interest before the expiry of 21 years from the death of the last survivor of all the descendants of King George VI living at the date of the settlement (a "royal lives" clause). If T died, leaving his estate on trust for his widow, W, for life, remainder to S, his only child, for life, remainder to such of his grandchildren who attained 21 years of age, all the trusts are valid. W has a life interest "vested in possession" (a present right of present enjoyment), S has a life interest "vested in interest" (a present right to future enjoyment), while grand-children under 21 have contingent interests (a contingent right to future enjoyment), which must become vested in interest within 21 years of

---

[117] *Brooks v Brooks* [1996] A.C. 375; but pension schemes that amount to nuptial settlements are now outside the MCA 1973 because pension-splitting is now possible under the Welfare Reform and Pensions Act 1999.

[118] *E v E (Financial Provision)* [1990] 2 F.L.R. 233; *T v Y (Joinder of Third Parties)* [1996] 2 F.L.R. 357.

[119] For discussion of the reasons for this and an overview of the legal position prior to the enactment of the perpetuities and Accumulations Act 2009, see Law Commission, *The Rules Against Perpetuities and Excessive Accumulations* (Law Com. No.251, 1998), reviewed in Gallanis (2000) 59 C.L.J. 284.

the deaths of S and his spouse, even though in the case of class gifts a member's interest does not vest in interest (for perpetuity purposes) until the size of the share is fixed when the last class member is ascertained. The grandchildren's parents' lives are impliedly causally relevant in restricting the period within which the contingent interests inevitably must, if at all, become vested interests.

ii. The Statutory "Wait and See" Rule

If, by any stretch of the imagination, a contingent interest might possibly not become vested in interest within the perpetuity period, it was void. To mitigate this harshness the Perpetuities and Accumulations Act 1964 radically reformed the rule against remoteness. Where a contingent future interest would have been void at common law, the statute provided that one should instead "wait and see" what actually happened in a statutory perpetuity period.[120] The interest was valid until it became clear that it must vest in interest (if at all) outside the period prescribed by statute, which replaced causally relevant common law lives by a list of statutory lives in being[121] and, as an alternative, expressly allowed a specified period of years not exceeding 80 to be chosen as the perpetuity period.[122] Common practice was to use the 80-year period because one then knew in advance exactly when the trust would terminate. **7–65**

In 1998 the Law Commission published a consultation paper proposing reform of the rules against perpetuities and accumulations,[123] and recommending among other things that the range of permitted perpetuity periods should be replaced by a single period of 125 years. Legislation to this effect has now been enacted in the form of the Perpetuities and Accumulations Act 2009 s.5. The "wait and see" rule is preserved by s.7, and applies in all cases where, at the outset, it is possible that an interest will not vest within the perpetuity period. Hence the relevant provision will be treated as entirely valid unless and until it becomes clear that the interest cannot vest, or the relevant power will not be exercised, or fully exercised, within the perpetuity period. **7–66**

Section 8 further provides that, where it is or becomes clear that the inclusion of future or potential members of a class of beneficiaries would cause the interest to be void for remoteness, those members are automatically excluded from the class unless the effect of so doing would be to exhaust the class. Sections 9 and 10 remove some inconvenient consequences that would otherwise flow from the "wait and see" rule. Section 9 validates any interest, that would otherwise be valid, that follows or is dependent on a disposition which is void for remoteness, and enables such an interest to be accelerated. Section 10 substantially re-enacts ss.3 and 12 of the 1964 Act, and provides that, where the gift over expectant on a determinable interest is void for remoteness, the determinable interest becomes absolute. Section 11 defines differing kinds of special powers of appointment, which are among the dispositions to which the "wait and see" rule applies. **7–67**

iii. *Re Denley*-Type Locus Standi Purpose Trusts

As discussed in Chapter 5,[124] *Re Denley*[125] upheld a trust of land to be maintained and used as a recreation or sports ground for the benefit of employees from time to time of a particular company, while in *Wicks v Firth*[126] the House of Lords assumed that there can be a valid trust to award scholarships to assist in the education of children of employees of a company from time to time. Both trusts were **7–68**

---

120 Perpetuities and Accumulations Act 1964 s.3(1), (2), (3).
121 Section 3(5).
122 Section 1.
123 Law Commission, *The Rules Against Perpetuities and Excessive Accumulations* (Law Com. 251, 1998).
124 See para.5–15.
125 [1969] 1 Ch. 373.
126 [1983] A.C. 214.

limited expressly to a valid perpetuity period, but what would have happened if such trusts were left open-ended to last indefinitely?

7–69 It seems likely that for perpetuity purposes such a trust would have been regarded as analogous to a discretionary trust before the 1964 Act.[127] Thus, because the powers of the trustees to benefit the beneficiaries were not bound to have been exhaustively exercised within the common law perpetuity period the trusts would have been void. Under the statutory "wait and see" rule, however, the trusts are valid to the extent that the trustees exercise their fiduciary powers within the statutory perpetuity period. At the end of the period the property will then be held on resulting trust for the settlor. An alternative approach would be to say that *Re Denley*-type purpose trusts should be treated like other permitted non-charitable purpose trusts[128] and so be subject not to the rule against remoteness but to the rule against inalienability.[129] This would make them void unless at the outset it is certain that by the end of the perpetuity period the trust fund will be wholly alienable by some absolute owners.[130] However, in light of the modern judicial tendency to facilitate, rather than frustrate, the intentions of settlors and testators, it seems likely that the courts will not invoke the harsh rule against inalienability that applies to purpose trusts but will regard *Re Denley*-type purpose trusts as trusts for those persons with locus standi to sue.[131]

B. The Rule against Inalienability (or Perpetual Purpose Trusts)

7–70 The common law rule against remoteness ensured that endowment trusts for persons were void unless one could be absolutely sure from the outset that by the end of the perpetuity period the beneficiaries would have obtained vested interests enabling them to deal with the trust fund as they wished. Under the rule in *Saunders v Vautier*[132] if trustees hold property on trust for A absolutely or for B for life, remainder to C absolutely, then (assuming that each is sui juris) A or B and C, as the case may be, can direct the trustees how to deal with the property, e.g. vest it in A absolutely or divide it absolutely between B and C in the shares agreed by B and C. Persons like B must obtain vested interests before the end of the perpetuity period but there is no requirement that their interests must terminate within the perpetuity period so that someone must become absolutely entitled to the relevant property in such period.[133] Thus, if at the end of the period B has a life interest the trust continues till C acquires the property on B's death.

7–71 The rule against inalienability makes the few permitted[134] non-charitable endowment purpose trusts void unless from the outset it is certain that persons will become absolutely entitled beneficiaries by the end of the perpetuity period,[135] i.e. 21 years from the death of the last survivor of any causally relevant lives in being.[136] Such a rule was necessary because purposes unlike individuals can last forever and because a rule against remoteness of vesting is inappropriate when interests cannot vest in purposes as opposed to persons. Thus, testamentary trusts to erect and then maintain a sepulchral monument, or to say private masses for the testator, are void unless restricted to a specified perpetuity period, which will be 21 years unless, say, a royal lives clause is used.

---

127 See *Re Grant's WT* [1979] 3 All E.R. 359 at 368.
128 See paras 5–12 ff.
129 *Re Northern Developments (Holdings) Ltd* (October 6, 1978, unreported) at (1991) 107 L.Q.R. 608 at 611.
130 See next sub-heading.
131 See Vinelott J. in *Re Grant's WT* [1979] 3 All E.R. 359 at 368; P.J. Millett QC (now Lord Millett) (1985) 101 L.Q.R. 268 at 281–282.
132 (1841) 4 Beav. 115.
133 *Re Chardon* [1928] Ch. 464; Re Gage [1898] 1 Ch. 506; *Wainwright v Miller* [1897] 2 Ch. 255.
134 See paras 5–12 ff.
135 *Leahy v Att.-Gen. for New South Wales* [1959] A.C. 457; *Cocks v Manners* (1871) L.R. 12 Eq. 574.
136 *Re Astor's ST* [1952] Ch. 534; *Re Khoo Cheng Teow* [1932] Straits Settlement Reports 226. The statutory period of 125 years introduced by the 2009 Act applies only to the rule against remoteness: see s.18 which provides that "This Act does not affect the rule of law which limits the duration of noncharitable purpose trusts."

Whatever happen from time to time to be the particular trust assets comprised in the trust fund will be alienable under the Settled Land Act 1925, or the Law of Property Act 1925, or the Trustee Act 2000. However, if trust income has to be used for a particular purpose then the trust fund producing that income must be kept intact for as long as the income is required for that purpose. The inalienability of the trust income inevitably leads to the inalienability of the trust fund. The rule against inalienability is concerned to ensure that the length of time for which trustees must retain the trust fund (in whatever assets it is from time to time invested) does not exceed the perpetuity period. **7–72**

If the trustees do not have to keep the capital intact and use only the income thereof but can spend trust money on the trust purposes without the need to consider whether or not the money represents capital or income and whether the purpose is a "capital" or "income" type of purpose, then the rule against inalienability has no application.[137] Usually, the settlor will make it clear if the trustees are to hold his property on trust only to use the income within a specified perpetuity period for particular purposes and at the end of the period to distribute the capital to beneficiaries. Exceptionally, he may make it clear that his property is to be used without distinction between capital and income until fully consumed. **7–73**

C. *The Rule against Excessive Accumulations*

Fearful of the implications for the English economy if mega-wealthy men like Peter Thellusson could by will[138] have the income of their estate accumulated for the full perpetuity period of royal lives plus 21 years—and more fearful for the finances of themselves and their children—English MPs passed the Accumulations Act 1800 (the "Thellusson Act") to restrict the period for which income could be accumulated. Subsequent legislation in the area meant that until recently, where it was sought to give trustees a power to accumulate, it was crucial to restrict the accumulation to one of the six periods allowed by ss. 164–166 of the Law of Property Act 1925 and s.13 of the 1964 Act.[139] However, the rule against excessive accumulation has now been abolished for most purposes by the Perpetuities and Accumulations Act 2009 s.13, which repeals the relevant sections of the 1925 and 1964 statutes. The effect of this should be to provide settlors and testators with considerable freedom to accumulate income within settlements, although the rule against perpetuities effectively limits the life of a trust and so provides an upper limit on any accumulation. **7–74**

PERPETUITIES AND ACCUMULATIONS ACT 2009

1. Application of the Rule

(1) The rule against perpetuities applies (and applies only) as provided by this section. **7–75**

(2) If an instrument limits property in trust so as to create successive estates or interests the rule applies to each of the estates or interests.

---

137 *Re Lipinski's WT* [1976] Ch. 235 at 245; *Re Drummond* [1914] 2 Ch. 90 at 98; *Re Prevost* [1930] 2 Ch. 383 at 388; *Re Price* [1943] Ch. 422 at 428, 430; *Re Macaulay's Estate* [1943] Ch. 435 at 436. In *Leahy v Att.-Gen. for New South Wales* [1959] A.C. 457 at 483. Viscount Simonds doubted whether a society's liberty to spend the capital and income of a gift as it saw fit saved a gift on trust to the society unless its members are treated as the immediate beneficiaries capable of disposing of the gifted property. This is too restrictive a view of the beneficiary principle: there can be *Re Denley*-type purpose trusts benefiting individuals within a fluctuating class who have no right to make the trust property their own but do have a right to ensure that the property is used for their benefit.

138 *Thellusson v Woodford* (1799) 4 Ves. 227, for a full account of which, see P. Polden, *Peter Thellusson's Will of 1797 and Its Consequences on Chancery Law* (2002).

139 Unless s.31 of the Trustee Act 1925 allowed accumulations during a beneficiary's minority.

(3) If an instrument limits property in trust so as to create an estate or interest which is subject to a condition precedent and which is not one of successive estates or interests, the rule applies to the estate or interest.

(4) If an instrument limits property in trust so as to create an estate or interest subject to a condition subsequent the rule applies to—

(a) any right of re-entry exercisable if the condition is broken, or
(b) any equivalent right exercisable in the case of property other than land if the condition is broken.

(5) If an instrument which is a will limits personal property so as to create successive interests under the doctrine of executory bequests, the rule applies to each of the interests.

(6) If an instrument creates a power of appointment the rule applies to the power. . . .

(8) This section has effect subject to the exceptions made by section 2 and to any exceptions made under section 3.

2. Exceptions to Rule's Application

7–76 (1) This section contains exceptions to the application of the rule against perpetuities.

(2) The rule does not apply to an estate or interest created so as to vest in a charity on the occurrence of an event if immediately before the occurrence an estate or interest in the property concerned is vested in another charity.

(3) The rule does not apply to a right exercisable by a charity on the occurrence of an event if immediately before the occurrence an estate or interest in the property concerned is vested in another charity.

(4) The rule does not apply to an interest or right arising under a relevant pension scheme.

(5) The exception in subsection (4) does not apply if the interest or right arises under—

(a) an instrument nominating benefits under the scheme, or
(b) an instrument made in the exercise of a power of advancement arising under the scheme. . . .

5. Perpetuity Period

7–77 (1) The perpetuity period is 125 years (and no other period).

(2) Subsection (1) applies whether or not the instrument referred to in section 1(2) to (6) specifies a perpetuity period; and a specification of a perpetuity period in that instrument is ineffective.

6. Start of perpetuity period

7–78 (1) The perpetuity period starts when the instrument referred to in section 1(2) to (6) takes effect; but this is subject to subsections (2) and (3).

(2) If section 1(2), (3) or (4) applies and the instrument is made in the exercise of a special power of appointment the perpetuity period starts when the instrument creating the power takes effect; but this is subject to subsection (3).

(3) If section 1(2), (3) or (4) applies and—

(a) the instrument nominates benefits under a relevant pension scheme, or
(b) the instrument is made in the exercise of a power of advancement arising under a relevant pension scheme,

the perpetuity period starts when the member concerned became a member of the scheme.

(4) The member concerned is the member in respect of whose interest in the scheme the instrument is made.

7. Wait and See Rule

(1) Subsection (2) applies if (apart from this section and section 8) an estate or interest would be void on the ground that it might not become vested until too remote a time. 7–79

(2) In such a case—

(a) until such time (if any) as it becomes established that the vesting must occur (if at all) after the end of the perpetuity period the estate or interest must be treated as if it were not subject to the rule against perpetuities, and

(b) if it becomes so established, that does not affect the validity of anything previously done (whether by way of advancement, application of intermediate income or otherwise) in relation to the estate or interest.

(3) Subsection (4) applies if (apart from this section) any of the following would be void on the ground that it might be exercised at too remote a time—

(a) a right of re-entry exercisable if a condition subsequent is broken;

(b) an equivalent right exercisable in the case of property other than land if a condition subsequent is broken;

(c) a special power of appointment.

(4) In such a case—

(a) the right or power must be treated as regards any exercise of it within the perpetuity period as if it were not subject to the rule against perpetuities, and

(b) the right or power must be treated as void for remoteness only if and so far as it is not fully exercised within the perpetuity period.

(5) Subsection (6) applies if (apart from this section) a general power of appointment would be void on the ground that it might not become exercisable until too remote a time.

(6) Until such time (if any) as it becomes established that the power will not be exercisable within the perpetuity period, it must be treated as if it were not subject to the rule against perpetuities.

8. Exclusion of Class Members to Avoid Remoteness

(1) This section applies if— 7–80

(a) it is apparent at the time an instrument takes effect or becomes apparent at a later time that (apart from this section) the inclusion of certain persons as members of a class would cause an estate or interest to be treated as void for remoteness, and

(b) those persons are potential members of the class or unborn persons who at birth would become members or potential members of the class.

(2) From the time it is or becomes so apparent those persons must be treated for all the purposes of the instrument as excluded from the class unless their exclusion would exhaust the class.

(3) If this section applies in relation to an estate or interest to which section 7 applies, this section does not affect the validity of anything previously done (whether by way of advancement, application of intermediate income or otherwise) in relation to the estate or interest.

(4) For the purposes of this section—

(a) a person is a member of a class if in that person's case all the conditions identifying a member of the class are satisfied, and

(b) a person is a potential member of a class if in that person's case some only of those conditions are satisfied but there is a possibility that the remainder will in time be satisfied. . . .

9. Saving and Acceleration of Expectant Interests

7–81 (1) An estate or interest is not void for remoteness by reason only that it is ulterior to and dependent on an estate or interest which is so void.

(2) The vesting of an estate or interest is not prevented from being accelerated on the failure of a prior estate or interest by reason only that the failure arises because of remoteness.

10. Determinable Interests Becoming Absolute

7–82 (1) If an estate arising under a right of reverter on the determination of a determinable fee simple is void for remoteness the determinable fee simple becomes absolute.

(2) If an interest arising under a resulting trust on the determination of a determinable interest is void for remoteness the determinable interest becomes absolute.

11. Powers of Appointment

7–83 (1) Subsection (2) applies to a power of appointment exercisable otherwise than by will (whether or not it is also exercisable by will).

(2) For the purposes of the rule against perpetuities the power is a special power unless—

(a) the instrument creating it expresses it to be exercisable by one person only, and
(b) at all times during its currency when that person is of full age and capacity it could be exercised by that person so as immediately to transfer to that person the whole of the interest governed by the power without the consent of any other person or compliance with any other condition (ignoring a formal condition relating only to the mode of exercise of the power).

(3) Subsection (4) applies to a power of appointment exercisable by will (whether or not it is also exercisable otherwise than by will).

(4) For the purposes of the rule against perpetuities the power is a special power unless—

(a) the instrument creating it expresses it to be exercisable by one person only, and
(b) that person could exercise it so as to transfer to that person's personal representatives the whole of the estate or interest to which it relates.

(5) Subsection (6) applies to a power of appointment exercisable by will or otherwise.

(6) If for the purposes of the rule against perpetuities the power would be a special power under one but not both of subsections (2) and (4), for the purposes of the rule it is a special power.

Questions

1. "Where there is a trust for A, B and C absolutely, A, B and C are in a strong position." **Discuss**.
2. "It has been said that the courts have no jurisdiction under the Variation of Trusts Act 1958 to approve a resettlement, but in reality they have approved arrangements which amount to resettlements in all but name." **Discuss**.
3. Brian leaves his cricket field and pavilion to trustees to hold on trust solely for the present and future members of Slogworthy Cricket Club. Consider in the light of the Perpetuities and Accumulations Act 2009. Would the position be different if such property had been left on trust to further the playing of cricket by persons resident in Slogworthy?
4. What would happen if the facts in *Re Denley* resulted from a 2010 conveyance which omitted to restrict the trusts to any specified perpetuity period?

PART IV

RIGHTS AND DUTIES OF EXPRESS TRUSTEES

8 APPOINTMENT, RETIREMENT, REMOVAL AND PAYMENT OF TRUSTEES

1. Introduction

8–01 It is vital to ensure that the appointment, retirement and removal of trustees are correctly carried out. If they are not, then various problems may ensue: the old trustees will remain liable to account to the beneficiaries as trustees, while the new "trustees" will become liable to account as trustees *de son tort*;[1] also the new "trustees" may not be the legal owners of the trust property, with potentially significant consequences for the validity of their purported dispositions of trust property, and for the tax treatment of the settlement.[2]

8–02 Reflecting the principle that a trustee may not occupy a position where his personal interest and the beneficiaries' interests might conflict,[3] trustees may not generally receive payment for their services. However, there are some exceptions to this rule, and trustees are also entitled to be indemnified for costs which they incur in the course of carrying out the trust affairs.

2. Appointment of Trustees

8–03 When a settlor creates a trust in his lifetime, he will usually appoint the first trustees of the trust, e.g. by declaring himself trustee, or by including a clause in the trust instrument appointing himself and/or others as the trustees. Once the trust has come into existence, however, the settlor has no right to appoint new trustees unless he reserves a power of appointment to himself in the trust instrument. Alternatively he may give such a power to another person.[4] In either case the power to appoint new trustees will be a fiduciary power and so it cannot be exercised by the donee of the power to appoint himself as this would create a conflict between his personal interest and the interests of the beneficiaries.[5] In the case of a testamentary trust, the settlor obviously can do no more than appoint the first trustees, but again he may give a power to appoint new trustees to another person.

8–04 If no power to appoint new trustees is conferred by the trust instrument, either generally or in some specific situation, then they may be appointed either under the statutory powers contained in the Trustee Act 1925 s.36 or Trusts of Land and Appointment of Trustees Act 1996 s.19, or by the court.

8–05 Note that a person appointed trustee may disclaim the office, for "a man cannot have an estate put into him in spite of his teeth". The disclaimer of a trust by a person appointed trustee must be a

[1] See paras 12–06 ff.
[2] e.g. *Jasmine Trustees Ltd v Wells & Hind (a firm)* [2008] Ch. 194.
[3] See paras 9–14 ff.
[4] e.g. *Re Walker and Hughes* (1883) 24 Ch.D. 698; *Re Sheppard's ST* [1888] W.N. 234.
[5] *Re Skeats Settlement* (1889) L.R. 42 Ch.D. 522.

disclaimer of the whole trust; it cannot be partial.[6] Ideally it ought to be in writing (or by deed), but it may also be oral,[7] by conduct,[8] by mere inactivity (it seems),[9] or signified on behalf of the person appointed trustee by counsel at the Bar.[10] If a person is appointed both executor and trustee and he proves the will, he thereby accepts the trust. But if he renounces probate, he does not thereby necessarily disclaim the trust.[11]

8–06 Note, too, that trusts do not fail for want of trustees. If a testator creates a trust in his will, but fails to appoint trustees or appoints trustees who refuse or are unable to act or have ceased to exist, then the trust does not fail[12] (unless its operation was conditional upon a specific trustee undertaking the trust[13]). Nor does it fail if the intended trustees disclaim ownership of shares or land secretly transferred into their names by a settlor. The property or the beneficial interest therein remains in the settlor or the personal representatives of the testator to be held upon the trusts of the settlement or the will as the case may be.[14]

8–07 On the death of a sole or sole surviving trustee the trust property vests in his personal representatives subject to the trusts and by the Trustee Act 1925 s.18(2), they are capable of exercising or performing any power or trust which the deceased trustee could have exercised or performed. They are not bound to accept the position and duties of trustees and may exercise their power of appointing new trustees under s.36 with a right to payment of the costs thereof from the trust moneys.[15] If need be the court may appoint new trustees under s.41[16] or itself execute the trust.[17]

8–08 What happens if a deceased trustee's powers devolve upon his personal representative who then dies himself, without having appointed new trustees? If he accepted the trustee role under s.18(2) then he should himself be treated as a trustee for his powers to devolve under s.18(2) to his own personal representative.[18] If he was an executor of the deceased trustee and appointed an executor under his own will, then his executor would be executor by representation of the trustee[19] and so have the s.18(2) powers in any event.

A. Statutory Powers of Appointment

8–09 The Trustee Act 1925 s.36 gives a power to appoint new trustees to the following persons in the following order: (i) the person(s) nominated in the trust instrument (s.36(1)(a)); (ii) if there is no such person, or no such person able or willing to act, the surviving and continuing trustees (s.36(1)(b)); or (iii) if there is no surviving or continuing trustee, the personal representatives of the last or only surviving trustee (s.36(1)(b)).

---

6 *Re Lord and Fullerton* [1896] 1 Ch. 228.
7 *Bingham v Clanmorris* (1828) 2 Moll. 253; doubted by Wood V.C. in *Re Ellison* (1856) 2 Jur. 62.
8 *Stacey v Elph* (1883) 1 My. & K. 195; *Re Birchall* (1889) 40 Ch.D. 436.
9 *Re Clout and Frewer* [1924] 2 Ch. 230.
10 *Landbroke v Bleaden* (1852) 16 Jur. (O.S.) 630; *Foster v Dawber* (1860) 8 W.R. 646.
11 *Mucklow v Fuller* (1821) Jac. 198; *Ward v Butler* (1824) 2 Moll. 533; *Dix v Burford* (1854) 19 Beav. 409 at 412, per Romilly M.R.
12 *Re Willis* [1921] 1 Ch. 44; *Re Armitage* [1972] Ch. 438; *Re Morrison* (1967) 111 S.J. 758.
13 *Re Lysaght* [1966] 1 Ch. 191.
14 *Mallot v Wilson* [1903] 2 Ch. 494, accepted as good law by the Court of Appeal in *Harris v Sharp* [2003] W.T.L.R. 1541. P. Matthews [1981] Conv. 141 contends that disclaimer of an inter vivos transfer to a trustee should make the transfer void and the trust fail; but one may treat the transferor as constructive trustee by *Re Rose* [1952] Ch. 499 principles, for which see paras 2–87 ff. See also *Standing v Bowring* (1885) 31 Ch.D. 282 at 288; *Tett v Phoenix* [1984] B.C.L.C. 599; and on the unilateral and bilateral nature of gifts see J. Hill (2001) 117 L.Q.R. 127.
15 *Re Benett* [1906] 1 Ch. 216.
16 *Jones v Jones* (1874) 31 L.T. 538.
17 *McPhail v Doulton* [1971] A.C. 424 at 457.
18 P.W. Smith, "The Chains of Trusteeship" (1977) 41 Conv. 423.
19 Administration of Estates Act 1925 s.7.

Where the power to appoint new trustees vests in the current trustees, it is a fiduciary power[20] and when exercising it they must pay due regard to the interests of the trust and of the conflicting interests of the beneficiaries. Their function is a paternalistic one requiring them to protect the beneficiaries from themselves.[21] Thus, before 1996 even if the beneficiaries were all of full capacity and between them absolutely entitled, they still could not compel the trustees under s.36 to appoint their nominee: the trustees were entitled to exercise their independent judgment.[22] All that the beneficiaries could do was put an end to the existing settlement under the rule in *Saunders v Vautier*[23] and then create a new settlement of which, as settlors, they were be able to appoint new trustees—but this had fiscal disadvantages. **8–10**

However, the position was changed by the enactment of the Trusts of Land and Appointment of Trustees Act 1996 s.19 of which provides that if all the beneficiaries are ascertained and of full age and capacity then they have a right to require the trustees to retire and to direct the trustees to appoint specified persons to be new trustees, such right not existing where a person nominated in the trust instrument (not the current trustees) has the power to appoint new trustees.[24] **8–11**

The provision in the Trustee Act 1925 s.36(1) which enables a trustee who remains out of the United Kingdom for more than 12 months to be replaced does not make persons resident abroad ineligible to be appointed as trustees, as held by Pennycuick V.C. in *Re Whitehead's WT*.[25] However, while accepting that the appointment of non-resident trustees had been a proper valid one in the case before him, he went on to say that in the absence of special circumstances (e.g. the beneficiaries having taken up permanent residence in a foreign country where the newly-appointed trustees reside) the appointment of non-residents was improper (though neither void nor illegal) so that the court would be likely to interfere at the instance of the beneficiaries.[26] **8–12**

This approach is now out of date where the trustees are exercising their discretion to appoint foreign trustees and are merely seeking the declaratory authorisation of the court for their own protection. In *Richard v Mackay*[27] Millett J. stated: **8–13**

> "The appropriateness is for the trustees to decide, and different minds may have different views on what is appropriate in particular circumstances. Certainly, in the conditions of today when one can have an international family with international interests and where they are as likely to make their home in one country as in another and as likely to choose one jurisdiction as another for the investment of their capital, I doubt that the language of Sir John Pennycuick is really in tune with the times. In my judgment, where the trustees retain their discretion, as they do in the present case, the court should need to be satisfied only that the proposed transaction is not so inappropriate that no reasonable trustee could entertain it."

Thus, the trustees (in case United Kingdom exchange control was reintroduced) could properly transfer part of the trust fund to the trustees of a trust to be established in Bermuda with Bermudan **8–14**

---

[20] Indeed, even if the power of appointing new trustees is reserved to the settlor while alive it will be presumed to be a fiduciary power: *IRC v Schroder* [1983] S.T.C. 480; *Re Osiris Trustees Ltd* [2000] W.T.L.R. 933. The settlor needs to act in altruistic good faith.

[21] *Head v Gould* [1898] 2 Ch. 250.

[22] *Re Brockbank* [1948] Ch. 206.

[23] (1841) 4 Beav. 115. See paras 7–06 ff.

[24] Section 19(1)(a). Section 19 is inapplicable to a pre-Act trust if the settlor subsequently executes a deed stating it is to be inapplicable: s.21(6).

[25] [1971] 1 W.L.R. 833.

[26] It thus seems that the appointment is voidable by the beneficiaries, and that: the Revenue will have no locus standi to object unless the appointment was void as part of a criminal conspiracy to defraud the Revenue.

[27] (1997) 11 Tru. L. I. 22, noted by R. Bramwell QC in (1990) 1 O.T.P.R. 1, and followed in *Re Beatty's WT (No.2)* (1997) 11 Trust L.I. (3) 77.

resident trustees, Bermuda having a stable English system of law and very experienced corporate trustees, even though the beneficiaries had no connection with Bermuda. Although the proposal was not to appoint new trustees of an existing trust nothing turns on the distinction, as recognised in *Re Whitehead's WT*.[28]

8–15 However, Millett J. contrasted cases where the court is asked to exercise a discretion of its own (e.g. under the Variation of Trusts Act 1958[29] or the Trustee Act 1925 s.41[30]) with cases where the trustees are exercising their own discretion. In the former situation the applicants have to make out a positive case for the court's exercise of its discretion "and the court is unlikely to assist them where the scheme is nothing more than a device to avoid tax and has no other advantages of any kind."

8–16 Tax-saving is, of course, a proper consideration for trustees[31] and where it is clear that the proposed transaction is not so inappropriate that no reasonable trustee could entertain it the appointment of foreign trustees can now proceed without seeking any confirmation from the court.

8–17 Under the Trustee Act 1925 s.37(1)(c) "a trustee shall not be discharged from his trust unless there will be either a trust corporation or at least two persons to act as trustees to perform the trust." This subsection was amended (with prospective effect only) in 1996, having previously specified that at least two "individuals" must have been appointed if resigning trustees were to be discharged, the word "individuals" meaning natural persons only, so that resigning trustees were not discharged following the appointment as the new trustees, e.g. of a human being and a company that was not a trust corporation.[32] This trap was eliminated in 1996 by the replacement of the word "individuals" with the word "persons". Note, however, that "trust corporation" still cannot cover a company that is not incorporated in a Member State of the European Union,[33] and that if a sole corporate trustee is appointed then the purportedly replaced trustees remain as trustees if the new corporate trustee does not rank as a "trust corporation."[34]

8–18 However, it seems that s.37(1)(c) is subject to express contrary intention so that the trust instrument can expressly authorise the discharge of trustees from the trusts by replacing them with the appointment as sole trustee of a corporation ranking as a trust corporation by the law of the State of its incorporation, except for trust property consisting of land in England and Wales.[35] After all, a valid receipt for the proceeds of sale of such land can only be given by a trust corporation or two persons acting as trustees.[36]

TRUSTEE ACT 1925 SECTIONS 36–37[37]

8–19 36.—(1) Where a trustee,[38] either original or substituted, and whether appointed by a court or otherwise, is dead, or remains out of the United Kingdom for more than twelve months,[39] or desires to be

[28] [1971] 1 W.L.R. 833 at 838.
[29] See paras 7–25 ff.
[30] See para. 8–25.
[31] [1971] 1 W.L.R. 833 at 839.
[32] *Jasmine Trustees Ltd v Wells & Hind (a firm)* [2008] Ch. 194 at [22]–[32]. For trust corporations, see para.8–36.
[33] See Trustee Act 1925 s.68(18).
[34] e.g. *Adam & Co International Trustees Ltd v Theodore Goddard* (2000) 2 I.T.E.L.R. 634, [2000] W.T.L.R. 349. See too para 1–161.
[35] Trustee Act 1925 ss. 69(2), 71(3); *London Regional Transport Pension Fund Trust Co v Hatt* [1993] P. L.R. 227 at 260, accepted in *Adam & Co*, above.
[36] Trustee Act 1925 s.14(2), (3); Law of Property Act 1925 s.27(2).
[37] This section reproduces, with amendments and additions, the Trustee Act 1893 s.10(1), (3) and (4). *Wolstenholme & Cherry's Conveyancing Statutes* (13th edn), by J.T. Farrand, Vol.4, provides a most useful commentary on all sections of the Trustee Act.
[38] "Trustee" is used as to exclude personal representatives. Accordingly, no power is conferred to appoint executors. By the Administration of Estates Act 1925 s.7, an executor of a sole or last surviving executor of a testator is the executor by representation of that testator.
[39] It does not follow that there is an absolute bar to the appointment of non-resident trustees: *Re Whitehead's WT* [1971] 1 W.L.R. 833 discussed by R. Bramwell QC in (1990) 1 O.T.P.R. 1. Further see *Richard v Mackay* (1997) 11 Tru. L.I. 22.

discharged from all or any of the trusts or powers reposed in or conferred on him, or refuses or is unfit to act therein, or is incapable of acting therein, or is an infant, then, subject to the restrictions imposed by this Act on the number of trustees[40]—

(a) the person or persons nominated for the purpose of appointing new trustees by the instrument, if any, creating the trust;[41] or
(b) if there is no such person, or no such person able and willing to act, then the surviving or continuing[42] trustees or trustee for the time being, or the personal representatives of the last surviving or continuing trustee[43]:

may, by writing,[44] appoint one or more other persons (whether or not being the persons exercising the power) to be a trustee or trustees in the place of[45] the trustee so deceased, remaining out of the United Kingdom, desiring to be discharged, refusing, or being unfit or being incapable, or being an infant, as aforesaid.

(2) Where a trustee has been removed under a power contained in the instrument creating the trust, a new trustee or new trustees may be appointed in the place of the trustee who is removed, as if he were dead, or, in the case of a corporation, as if the corporation desired to be discharged from the trust, and the provisions of this section shall apply accordingly, but subject to the restrictions imposed by this Act on the number of trustees.

(3) Where a corporation being a trustee is or has been dissolved, either before or or after the commencement of this Act, then, for the purposes of this section and of any enactment replaced thereby, the corporation shall be deemed to be and to have been from the date of the dissolution incapable of acting in the trusts or powers reposed in or conferred on the corporation.

(4) The power of appointment given by subsection (1) of this section or any similar previous enactment to the personal representatives of a last surviving or continuing trustee shall be and shall be deemed always to have been exercisable by the executors for the time being (whether original or by representation) of such surviving or continuing trustee who have proved the will of their testator or by the administrators for the time being of such trustee without the concurrence of any executor who has renounced or has not proved.

---

[40] Maximum of four trustees except for charities: Trustee Act 1925 s.34 and see s.36(5).

[41] See *Re Wheeler* [1896] 1 Ch. 315: a decision on s.10(1) of the Trustee Act of 1893, which is re-enacted by s.36(1) of the Act of 1925. In that case the settlor, instead of nominating X the person to appoint new trustees generally—as in *Re Walker and Hughes* (1883) 24 Ch.D. 698—nominated X to appoint new trustees in certain specified events. One of the trustees became bankrupt and absconded, whereupon he became "unfit" to act, but not "incapable" of acting. The events specified by the settlor included the event of a trustee becoming "incapable", but not that of a trustee becoming "unfit". The question was whether the proper person to nominate a new trustee was X, as being "the person or persons nominated for the purpose of appointing new trustees by the instrument, if any, creating the trust"—s.36(1)(a)—or whether the proper person was the surviving or continuing trustees or trustee under s.36(1)(b). Kekewich J. held that if a power of appointment contained in the instrument of trust is a limited one, and the event which has actually happened is not one of the events contemplated by that power, then the nominee is not "the person or persons nominated for the purpose of appointing new trustees by the instrument, if any, creating the trust." Hence the proper person to appoint a new trustee in *Re Wheeler* was to be found in s.36(1)(b). *Re Wheeler* was followed, with reluctance, by Neville J. in *Re Sichel* [1916] 1 Ch. 358. The Act of 1925 does not seem to alter the position.

[42] A continuing trustee is one who is to continue to act after completion of the intended appointment: *Re Coates to Parsons* (1886) 34 Ch.D. 370.

[43] Persons appointed executors and trustees of wills of land must formally assent in favour of themselves qua trustees so as to take advantage of s.40: *Re King's WT* [1964] Ch. 542. An executor who has not proved his testator's will can exercise the power but the trustee appointed in such circumstances can only prove his title by reference to a proper grant of representation so that such a grant is, in practice, vital: *Re Crowhurst Park* [1974] 1 W.L.R. 583. If a will creates trusts but the trustees predecease the testator then s.36 is inapplicable: *Nicholson v Field* [1893] 2 Ch. 511.

[44] For the desirability of making the appointment by deed, see s.40 of the Trustee Act 1925.

[45] See *Adam Co International Trustee Ltd v Theodore Goddard* [2000] W.T.L.R. 349 at 355.

(5) But a sole or last surviving executor intending to renounce, or all the executors where they all intend to renounce, shall have and shall be deemed always to have had power, at any time before renouncing probate, to exercise the power of appointment given by this section, or by any similar previous enactment, if willing to act for the purpose and without thereby accepting the office of executor.

(6) Where, in the case of any trust, there are not more than three trustees[46]

(a) the person or persons nominated for the purpose of appointing new trustees by the instrument, if any creating the trust; or

(b) if there is no such person, or no such person able and willing to act, then the trustee or trustees for the time being;

may, by writing, appoint another person or other persons[47] to be an additional trustee or additional trustees, but it shall not be obligatory to appoint any additional trustee, unless the instrument, if any, creating the trust, or any statutory enactment provides to the contrary, nor shall the number of trustees be increased beyond four by virtue of any such appointment.

[(6)A to (6)D deal with the position of an attorney for a trustee making an appointment on behalf of the trustee: added by Trustee Delegation Act 1999, s.8].

(7) Every new trustee appointed under this section as well before as after all the trust property becomes by law, or by assurance, or otherwise, vested in him, shall have the same powers, authorities, and discretions, and may in all respects act as if he had been originally appointed a trustee by the instrument, if any, creating the trust.

(8) The provisions of this section relating to a trustee who is dead include the case of a person nominated trustee in a will but dying before the testator, and those relative to a continuing trustee include a refusing or retiring trustee, if willing to act in the execution of the provisions of this section.[48]

(9) Where a trustee lacks capacity to exercise his functions as trustee and is also entitled in possession to some beneficial interest in the trust property, no appointment of a new trustee in his place shall be made by virtue of paragraph (b) of subsection (1) of this section unless leave to make the appointment has been given by the Court of Protection.[49]

8–20 37.—(1) On the appointment of a trustee for the whole or any part of trust property—

(a) the number of trustees may, subject to the restrictions imposed by this Act on the number of trustees, be increased; and

(b) a separate set of trustees, not exceeding four, may be appointed for any part of the trust property held on trusts distinct from those relating to any other part or parts of the trust property, notwithstanding that no new trustees or trustee are or is to be appointed for other parts of the trust property, and any existing trustee may be appointed or remain one of such separate set

---

46 This broad provision was inserted by the Trusts of Land and Appointment of Trustees Act 1996 Sch.3 para.3(11).

47 An appointor cannot appoint himself additional trustee: *Re Power's ST* [1951] Ch. 1074.

48 In *Re Stoneham's ST* [1953] Ch. 59, X and Y were the trustees of a settlement. Y remained out of the United Kingdom for a period longer than 12 months. X executed a deed retiring from the trust and appointing C and D to be trustees in place of himself and Y. Y challenged the validity of the new appointments on the ground that he was entitled to participate in making them. Danckwerts J. rejected his contention, first because he had been validly removed from the trust owing to his continuous absence from the United Kingdom for more than 12 months, even though the removal might have been against his will, and second because he was not a "continuing trustee" within the meaning of s.36(8) of the Act of 1925. He was not a "refusing or retiring" trustee but a trustee who had been compulsorily removed from the trust and so his concurrence in the new appointments could be dispensed with: *Re Coates to Parsons* (1886) 34 Ch.D. 370 explained.

49 As amended by the Mental Capacity Act 2005.

of trustees, or, if only one trustee was originally appointed, then, save as hereinafter provided, one separate trustee may be so appointed; and

(c) it shall not be obligatory, save as hereinafter provided, to appoint more than one new trustee where only one trustee was originally appointed, or to fill up the original number of trustees where more than two trustees were originally appointed, but, except where only one trustee was originally appointed, and a sole trustee when appointed will be able to give valid receipts for all capital money, a trustee shall not be discharged from his trust unless there will be either a trust corporation or at least two persons to act as trustees to perform the trust; and

(d) any assurance or thing requisite for vesting the trust property, or any part thereof, in a sole trustee, or jointly in the persons who are the trustees, shall be executed or done.

(2) Nothing in this Act shall authorise the appointment of a sole trustee, not being a trust corporation where the trustee, when appointed, would not be able to give valid receipts for all capital money arising under the trust.

TRUSTS OF LAND AND APPOINTMENT OF TRUSTEES ACT 1996 SECTIONS 19–21

19.—(1) This section applies in the case of a trust where— **8–21**

(a) there is no person nominated for the purpose of appointing new trustees by the instrument, if any, creating the trust, and

(b) the beneficiaries under the trust are of full age and capacity and (taken together) are absolutely entitled to the property subject to the trust.

(2) The beneficiaries may give a direction or directions of either or both of the following descriptions—

(a) a written direction to a trustee or trustees to retire from the trust, and

(b) a written direction to the trustees or trustee for the time being (or, if there are none, to the personal representative of the last person who was a trustee) to appoint by writing to be a trustee or trustees the person or persons specified in the direction.

(3) Where—

(a) a trustee has been given a direction under subsection (2)(a),

(b) reasonable arrangements have been made for the protection of any rights of his in connection with the trust,

(c) after he has retired there will be either a trust corporation or at least two persons to act as trustees to perform the trust, and

(d) either another person is to be appointed to be a new trustee on his retirement (whether in compliance with a direction under subsection (2)(b) or otherwise) or the continuing trustees by deed consent to his retirement,

he shall make a deed declaring his retirement and shall be deemed to have retired and be discharged from the trust.

(4) Where a trustee retires under subsection (3) he and the continuing trustees (together with any new trustee) shall (subject to any arrangements for the protection of his rights) do anything necessary to vest the trust property in the continuing trustees (or the continuing and new trustees).

(5) This section has effect subject to the restrictions imposed by the Trustee Act 1925 on the number of trustees.

20.—(1) This section applies where— **8–22**

(a) a trustee lacks capacity (within the meaning of the Mental Capacity Act 2005) to exercise his functions as trustee,

(b) there is no person who is both entitled and willing and able to appoint a trustee in place of him under section 36(1) of the Trustee Act 1925, and
(c) the beneficiaries under the trust are of full age and capacity and (taken together) are absolutely entitled to the property subject to the trust.

(2) The beneficiaries may give to—

(a) deputy appointed for the trustee by the Court of Protection,
(b) an attorney acting for him under the authority of an enduring power of attorney or lasting power of attorney registered under the Mental Capacity Act 2005, or
(c) a person authorised for the purpose by the Court of Protection under Part VII of the Mental Health Act 1983

a written direction to appoint by writing the person or persons specified in the direction to be a trustee or trustees in place of the incapable trustee.

8–23 21.—(1) For the purposes of s.19 or 20 a direction is given by beneficiaries if—

(a) a single direction is jointly given by all of them, or
(b) (subject to subsection (2)) a direction is given by each of them (whether solely or jointly with one or more, but not all, of the others),

and none of them by writing withdraws the direction given by him before it has been complied with.

(2) Where more than one direction is given each must specify for appointment or retirement the same person or persons.

(3) Subsection (7) of section 36 of the Trustee Act 1925 (powers of trustees appointed under that section) applies to a trustee appointed under section 19 or 20 as if he were appointed under that section.

(4) A direction under section 19 or 20 must not specify a person or persons for appointment if the appointment of that person or those persons would be in contravention of section 35(1) of the Trustee Act 1925 or section 24(1) of the Law of Property Act 1925 (requirements as to identity of trustees).

(5) Sections 19 or 20 do not apply in relation to a trust created by a disposition in so far as provision that they do not apply is made by the disposition.

(6) Sections 19 and 20 do not apply in relation to a trust created before the commencement of this Act by a disposition in so far as provision to the effect that they do not apply is made by a deed executed—

(a) in a case in which the trust was created by one person and he is of full capacity, by that person, or
(b) in a case in which the trust was created by more than one person, by such of the persons who created the trust as are alive and of full capacity.

(7) A deed executed for the purpose of subsection (6) is irrevocable.

(8) Where a deed is executed for the purposes of subsection (6)—

(a) it does not affect anything done before its execution to comply with a direction under section 19 or 20, but
(b) a direction under section 19 or 20 which has been given but not complied with before its execution shall cease to have effect.

B. Appointment of Trustees by the Court

The court has power to appoint new trustees under the Trustee Act 1925 s.41,[50] but an application should not be made to the court if the power of appointing new trustees contained in s.36(1) of the Act can be exercised.[51] The principles which guide the court in making an appointment are set out in *Re Tempest*,[52] which is reproduced below. If non-resident trustees are to be appointed the beneficiaries must usually[53] have a real and substantial connection with the country where the proposed trustees are resident. **8–24**

TRUSTEE ACT 1925 SECTION 41

(1) The court, may, whenever it is expedient to appoint a new trustee or new trustees, and it is found inexpedient, difficult or impracticable so to do without the assistance of the court, make an order appointing a new trustee or trustees either in substitution for or in addition to any existing trustee or trustees, or although there is no existing trustee. **8–25**

In particular and without prejudice to the generality of the foregoing provision, the court may make an order appointing a new trustee in substitution for a trustee who is lacks capacity to exercise his functions as trustee, or is a bankrupt, or is a corporation which is in liquidation or has been dissolved.

RE TEMPEST

Court of Appeal in Chancery (1866) L.R. 1 Ch. 485; 35 L.J.Ch. 632; 14 L.T. 688; 12 Jur.(n.s.) 539; 14 W.R. 850

TURNER L.J. (with whom KNIGHT-BRUCE L.J. agreed): In making such appointments the court acts upon and exercises its discretion; and this, no doubt, is generally true; but the discretion which the court has and exercises in making such appointments is not, as I conceive, a mere arbitrary discretion, but a discretion in the exercise of which the court is, and ought to be, guided by some general rules and principles, and, in my opinion, the difficulty which the court has to encounter in these cases lies not so much in ascertaining the rules and principles by which it ought to be guided, as in applying those rules and principles to the varying circumstances of each particular case. The following rules and principles may, I think, safely be laid down as applying to all cases of appointments by the court of new trustees. **8–26**

First, the court will have regard to the wishes of the persons by whom the trust has been created, if expressed in the instrument creating the trust, or clearly to be collected from it.[54] I think this rule may be safely laid down, because if the author of the trust has in terms declared that a particular person, or a person filling a particular character, should not be a trustee of the instrument, there cannot, as I apprehend, be the least doubt that the court would not appoint to the office a person whose appointment was so **8–27**

---

[50] Under the section a trustee may be displaced against his will: *Re Henderson* [1940] Ch. 764. The section authorises removal of trustees by replacement but not otherwise: *Re Harrison's ST* [1965] 3 All E.R. 795 at 799.

[51] *Re Gibbon's Trusts* (1882) 30 W.R. 287; 45 L.T. 756. Otherwise, if it is uncertain whether the power under s.36(1) of the Act is exercisable: *Re May's Will Trusts* [1941] Ch. 109.

[52] (1866) L.R. 1 Ch. 485.

[53] In *Re Chamberlain* (1976) 126 N.L.J. 1034 (reported in article by J. B. Morcom) the court approved Guernsey trustees where the beneficiaries were domiciled and resident some in France some in Indonesia.

[54] See also *Re Badger* [1915] W.N. 166; 84 L.J. Ch. 567: the court will not appoint an additional trustee against the wishes of a sole trustee appointed by the settlor, in the absence of allegations against his honesty, even at the unanimous request of the beneficiaries of full capacity (not between them absolutely entitled to the whole beneficial interest so as to be able to invoke the Trusts of Land and Appointment of Trustees Act 1996 s.19), except where land is trust property since a valid receipt cannot be given by less than two trustees or a trust corporation: Law of Property Act 1925 s.27(2).

prohibited, and I do not think that upon a question of this description any distribution can be drawn between express declarations and demonstrated intention. The analogy of the course which the court pursued in the appointment of guardians affords, I think, some support to this rule. The court in those cases attends to the wishes of the parents, however informally they may be expressed.

8–28 Another rule which may, I think, safely be laid down is this—that the court will not appoint a person to be trustee with a view to the interest of some of the persons interested under the trust, in opposition either to the wishes of the testator or to the interests of others of the cestuis que trust. I think so for this reason, that it is of the essence of the duty of every trustee to hold an even hand between the parties interested under the trust. Every trustee is in duty bound to look to the interests of all, and not of any particular member or class of members of his cestuis que trust.

8–29 A third rule which, I think, may safely be laid down is that the court in appointing a trustee will have regard to the question whether his appointment will promote or impede the execution of the trust, for the very purpose of the appointment is that the trust may be better carried into execution . . .[55]

8–30 There cannot, I think, be any doubt that the court ought not to appoint a trustee whose appointment will impede the due execution of the trust; but, on the other hand, if the continuing or surviving trustee refuses to act with a trustee who may be proposed to be appointed . . . I think it would be going too far to say that the court ought, on that ground alone, to refuse to appoint the proposed trustee; for this would, as suggested in the argument, be to give the continuing or surviving trustee a veto upon the appointment of the new trustee. In such a case, I think it must be the duty of the court to inquire and ascertain whether the objection of the surviving or continuing trustee is well founded or not, and to act or refuse to act upon it accordingly. . . .[56]

C. *Protection of a Purchaser of Land of which New Trustees have been Appointed*

TRUSTEE ACT 1925 SECTION 38

8–31 (1) A statement, contained in any instrument coming into operation after the commencement of this Act by which a new trustee is appointed for any purpose connected with land, to the effect that a trustee has remained out of the United Kingdom for more than twelve months or refuses or is unfit to act, or is incapable of acting, or that he is not entitled to a beneficial interest in the trust property in possession, shall, in favour of a purchaser of a legal estate, be conclusive evidence of the matter stated.

(2) In favour of such purchaser any appointment of a new trustee depending on that statement, and any vesting declaration, express or implied, consequent on the appointment, shall be valid.

Where an appointment is invalid the general rule is that the old trustee remains trustee with the powers and liabilities of a trustee[57] though the invalidly appointed new trustee will become liable as trustee *de son tort* if he intermeddles with the property.[58]

---

[55] A person will thus not be appointed if so to do would place him in a position in which his interest and duty would be likely to conflict: *Re Parsons* [1940] Ch. 973.

[56] The court may postpone an order for appointment of new trustees in order to protect the interests of the existing trustees, e.g. *Re Pauling ST (No.2)* [1963] Ch. 576.

[57] *Adam & Co International Trustees Ltd v Theodore Goddard* (2000) 2 I.T.E.L.R. 634, [2000] W.T.L.R. 389.

[58] *Pearce v Pearce* (1856) 22 Beav. 248.

D. Vesting of Trust Property in New or Continuing Trustees

The Trustee Act 1925 s.40 automatically vests trust property in new and/or continuing trustees as joint tenants without the need for any formal conveyance or assignment. The section is widely drafted to cover choses in action as well interests in land or chattels.[59] **8–32**

TRUSTEE ACT 1925 SECTION 40

(1) Where by a deed a new trustee is appointed to perform any trust, then— **8–33**

(a) if the deed contains a declaration by the appointor to the effect that any estate or interest in any land subject to the trust, or in any chattel so subject, or the right to recover or receive any debt or other thing in action so subject, shall vest in the persons who by virtue of the deed become or are the trustees for performing the trust, the deed shall operate,[60] without any conveyance or assignment, to vest in those persons as joint tenants and for the purposes of the trust the estate interest or right to which the declaration relates; and

(b) if the deed is made after the commencement of this Act and does not contain such a declaration, the deed shall, subject to any express provision to the contrary therein contained, operate as if it had contained such a declaration by the appointor extending to all the estates interests and rights with respect to which a declaration could have been made.

(2) Where by a deed a retiring trustee is discharged under the statutory power without a new trustee being appointed, then—

(a) if the deed contains such a declaration as aforesaid by the retiring and continuing trustees, and by the other person, if any, empowered to appoint trustees, the deed shall, without any conveyance or assignment, operate to vest in the continuing trustees alone, as joint tenants, and for the purposes of the trust, the estate, interest, or right to which the declaration relates; and

(b) if the deed is made after the commencement of this Act and does not contain such a declaration, the deed shall, subject to any express provision to the contrary therein contained, operate as if it had contained such a declaration by such persons as aforesaid extending to all the estates, interests and rights with respect to which a declaration could have been made.

(3) An express vesting declaration, whether made before or after the commencement of this Act, shall, notwithstanding that the estate, interest or right to be vested is not expressly referred to, and provided that the other statutory requirements were or are complied with, operate and be deemed always to have operated (but without prejudice to any express provision to the contrary contained in the deed of appointment on discharge) to vest in the persons respectively referred to in subsections (1) and (2) of this section, as the case may require, such estates, interests and rights as are capable of being and ought to be vested in those persons.

(4) This section does not extend—

(a) to land conveyed by way of mortgage for securing money subject to the trust, except land conveyed on trust for securing debentures or debenture stock;

(b) to land held under a lease which contains any covenant, condition or agreement against assignment or disposing of the land without licence or consent, unless, prior to the execution of the deed containing expressly or impliedly the vesting declaration, the requisite licence or

[59] As noted in *Gregson v HAE Trustees Ltd* [2009] 1 All E.R. (Comm) 457 at [48].

[60] Even when the estate, interest or right is not vested in the person making the appointment. cf. Law of Property Act 1925 s.9; but not as in *Re King's WT* [1964] Ch. 542, where the legal estate is held by the appointor in his capacity as personal representative, not having executed an assent in his favour as trustee. Entry on the register is needed for registered land. The practice is for the current registered proprietor(s) to execute a transfer to the new trustees as new registered proprietors: this saves the Registrar from having to check on the validity of the deed of appointment and then altering the register.

consent has been obtained, or unless, by virtue of any statute or rule of law, the vesting declaration, express or implied, would not operate as a breach of covenant or give rise to a forfeiture;

(c) to any share, stock, annuity or property which is only transferable in books kept by a company or other body, or in manner directed by or under an Act of Parliament.

In this subsection "lease" includes an underlease and an agreement for a lease or underlease.

(5) For purposes of registration of the deed in any registry, the person or persons making the declaration expressly or impliedly, shall be deemed the conveying party or parties, and the conveyance shall be deemed to be made by him or them under a power conferred by this Act. . . .

E. Special Types of Trustee

8–34 Although most trustees are appointed by the settlors of express trusts, and are charged with active duties to hold and manage the trust property for the benefit of the beneficiaries, some special types of trustee are appointed in different circumstances and/or owe a different range of duties.

i. Custodian Trustees[61]

8–35 Custodian trustees are distinct from the usual managing trustees. They hold the trust property and the trust documents of title (e.g. title deeds, share certificates) and all sums payable to or out of the income or capital of the trust property are paid to or by them except that dividends and other income derived from the trust property may be paid to such other persons as they direct, e.g. the managing trustees or a beneficiary.[62] The day-to-day running of the trust is left to the managing trustees whose instructions must be obeyed by the custodian trustee unless aware that they involve a breach of trust.[63] The following may be appointed custodian trustees: the Public Trustee, the Official Custodian for Charities and trust corporations.[64] A trustee cannot be custodian trustee and managing trustee of the same trust.[65]

ii. Trust Corporations

8–36 A trust corporation can act alone where otherwise two trustees would be required, e.g. receipt of capital moneys on a sale of land. The following are trust corporations:[66] the Public Trustee, the Treasury Solicitor, the Official Solicitor, certain charitable corporations and corporations either appointed by the court in any particular case or entitled to act as custodian trustees under the Public Trustee Act 1906. Corporations so entitled include those constituted under United Kingdom law or the law of an

---

[61] Generally see S.G. Maurice (1960) 24 Conv. (N.S.) 196; P. Pearce (1972) 36 Conv. (N.S.) 260–261; Keeton's *Modern Developments in the Law of Trusts*, Ch.3; P. Matthews, "All About Bare Trusts: Part 1" [2005] P.C.B. 266, pp. 266–269.

[62] Public Trustee Act 1906 s.4(2).

[63] Public Trustee Act 1906 s.4(2). Exceptionally, in the case of an authorised unit trust, the trustee, which must be a corporate EU trustee independent of the manager of the unit trust, has to take reasonable care to ensure that the manager acts within its powers, keeps adequate records and manages the scheme in accordance with the Financial Service Authority's Regulations for Collective Investment Schemes.

[64] Public Trustee Rules 1912 r.30, as substituted by the Public Trustee (Custodian Trustees) Rules 1975, SI 1975/1189 and amended by SI 1976/836, SI 1981/358, SI 1984/109, SI 1985/132; SI 1987/1891.

[65] *Forster v Williams Deacon's Bank Ltd* [1935] Ch. 359; *Arning v James* [1936] Ch. 58.

[66] Law of Property Act 1925 s.205(1)(xxviii); Trustee Act 1925 s.68(18); Law of Property (Amendment) Act 1925 s.3 (including trustees in bankruptcy).

EU state and having a place of business in the United Kingdom and empowered to undertake trust business, which are either incorporated by special Act or Royal Charter or else registered United Kingdom or other European Union state companies with an issued capital of at least £250,000 (or its foreign equivalent) of which at least £100,000 (or its equivalent) has been paid up in cash.

iii. The Public Trustee[67] in the Official Solicitor's Office

The Public Trustee was established in 1906 as a corporation sole available to deal with the difficulty persons might have in finding someone willing to act as trustee especially of low value trusts. However, it cannot accept charitable trusts, insolvent estates or, normally, trusts involving the carrying on of a business. It can act as personal representative, ordinary managing trustee, custodian trustee or judicial trustee. Since April 1, 2001 the Official Solicitor is also the Public Trustee. **8–37**

iv. Judicial Trustees

The Judicial Trustees Act 1896 established judicial trustees in order "to provide a middle course in cases where the administration of the estate by the ordinary trustees had broken down and it was not desired to put the estate to the expense of a full administration" by the court.[68] Judicial trustees can only be appointed by the court upon a claim in existing proceedings or an original Pt 8 claim. Trouble-shooting accountants are often appointed to sort out the muddled situation. The judicial trustee is an officer of the court so that he can at any time obtain the court's directions as to the way in which he should act without the necessity of a formal application by summons though he has as much authority as ordinary trustees to act on his own initiative, and, for example, compromise claims.[69] **8–38**

v. Can there be a "Controlling Trustee"?

The basic position is that all trustees are equal and must act unanimously, trusteeship being a joint office par excellence, so that one trustee cannot be "controlling trustee" whom the other trustees can safely leave on his or her own to deal with all trust matters.[70] However, as where two trustees are needed to give a good receipt for capital moneys derived from land, the trust instrument can effectively provide for T2 always to do whatever T1 decides without being liable in any way for any breach of trust unless T2 was aware that he was assisting T1 to commit a breach of trust.[71] Similarly, there is no reason why a trust instrument might not effectively provide for T1 to have a casting vote if T1 and T2 cannot agree on a trust matter.[72] **8–39**

67 The Hutton Committee of Enquiry into the Public Trustee Office (1972) Cmnd. 4913 recommended that it be wound up and merged with the Official Solicitor's Department but the government did not take any action on the Committee's recommendations. By the Public Trustee and Administration of Funds Act 1986 the Public Trustee was given the powers of a judge of the Court of Protection concerned with mental patients' property and affairs, but since April 1, 2001 the mental health functions were taken from the Public Trustee by the Public Guardian's Office, now see Mental Capacity Act 2005 ss. 57–60.

68 *Re Ridsdell* [1947] Ch. 597 at 605, per Jenkins J. See *Judicial Trustee Rules 1983 and Practice Note* [2003] 3 All E.R. 974.

69 *Re Ridsdell* [1947] Ch. 597.

70 It is a breach of trust to leave matters to a co-trustee: all co-trustees must positively involve themselves with all trust matters; see paras 9–09 and 11–02.

71 *Re Arnott* [1899] I.R. 201.

72 After all, the settlor can provide for trustees to act by majority decisions, but if only an even number of trustees subsists then the chairman of the trustees is to have a casting vote where the trustees are equally divided.

3. Retirement of Trustees

8–40 Where a trustee retires and a new trustee is appointed to fill the vacancy,[73] the retirement and new appointment are effected under s.36(1) of the Trustee Act 1925. Where all the beneficiaries require retirement under s.19 of the 1996 Act, the retiring trustee must execute a deed discharging himself under s.19(3). Where a new trustee is not appointed to fill the vacancy, the retirement is effected under s.39.

8–41 Independently of statute, a trustee may also retire under a power of retirement contained in the trust instrument,[74] or by the consent of all the beneficiaries, the latter being of full capacity,[75] or by authority of the court, to which the trustee has a right to apply to be discharged from the trust (although costs will depend on whether he has reasonable grounds for desiring to be discharged).[76]

8–42 Normally, retirement will be effected by the one deed executed by the retiring trustee and the remaining trustees—*and* any person (an "appointor") empowered to appoint new trustees. If, by mistake, with the oral consent of his co-trustees, T simply retires by executing a deed retiring from the trust, then it seems that matters can be regularised by a subsequent deed executed by the remaining trustees and the appointor, if any.[77] What happens if T2 and T3, blissfully unaware that T1 has remained a trustee despite T1 having executed a deed retiring from the trust, subsequently execute a deed in which they can only achieve what they intend to achieve by executing the deed if they alone are the trustees? At the date of this subsequent deed T1 is treated as effectively discharged by this deed with the consent of T2 and T3 who alone become the proper trustees, so that they achieve what they intended to achieve.[78]

TRUSTEE ACT 1925 SECTION 39[79]

8–43 (1) Where a trustee is desirous of being discharged from the trust, and after his discharge there will be either a trust corporation or at least two individuals to act as trustees to perform the trust, then, if such trustee as aforesaid by deed declares that he is desirous of being discharged from the trust, and if his co-trustees and such other person, if any, as is empowered to appoint trustees, by deed consent to the discharge of the trustee, and to the vesting in the co-trustees alone of the trust property, the trustee desirous of being discharged shall be deemed to have retired from the trust, and shall, by the deed, be discharged therefrom under this Act, without any new trustee being appointed in his place.

(2) Any assurance or thing requisite for vesting the trust property in the continuing trustees alone shall be executed or done.

4. Removal of Trustees

8–44 If the conditions in s.36(1) for replacing a trustee with another person cannot be satisfied for the removal of such trustee, then removal will require an express power in the trust instrument or an

---

[73] If no one else can be found the Public Trustee will usually be willing to act.
[74] *Camoys v Best* (1854) 19 Beav. 414.
[75] *Wilkinson v Parry* (1828) 4 Russ. 472 at 476.
[76] *Gardiner v Dounes* (1856) 22 Beav. 395; *Barker v Peile* (1865) 2 Dr. & Sm. 340; *Re Chetwynd* [1902] 1 Ch. 692.
[77] *Re Epona Trustees Ltd and Pentera Trustees Ltd* [2009] W.T.L.R. 87 (Jersey Royal Ct).
[78] *Re Epona*, applying *Davis v Richards and Wallington Industries* [1990] 1 W.L.R. 1511 and *Re Morgan* [1857] 7 Ir. Ch. R. 18.
[79] Section 39, like s.37(1)(c), is subject to contrary intention e.g. if the trust instrument authorises retirement if a non European Union trust corporation remains a trustee: *Adam & Co International Trustee Ltd v Theodore Goddard* (2000) 2 I.T.E.L.R. 634, [2000] W.T.L.R. 349.

application to the court. The trust instrument may confer a power of removal,[80] though if it is conferred on a majority of the trustees and they are not unanimous then a meeting will need to be held.[81] It needs to be borne in mind that the benefit of property passing from the old trustees to the new trustees under s.40 only applies if a new trustee is appointed in place of the old trustee and not if the old trustee is simply removed.

The court has a jurisdiction, independent of statute, to remove trustees, as illustrated by *Letterstedt v Broers*,[82] which appears immediately below. This case also makes it clear that while dishonest misconduct will certainly lead the court to remove a trustee, want of proper capacity to execute the duties of trustee will also suffice.[83] Under s.41, the court may also remove a trustee on appointing a new trustee.[84] On appointment of a new trustee under s.36 the appointors may remove a trustee. If hostility between trustees prevents them from acting unanimously (as they must do unless the trust instrument authorises otherwise) then one or all should be removed and replaced.[85] **8–45**

In an emergency, trustees may be removed on an ex parte interim application and a receiver appointed of the trust assets until appointment of new trustees at an inter partes hearing.[86] **8–46**

The Occupational Pensions Regulatory Authority has power under the Pensions Act 1995 ss. 4 to 9 to suspend or remove trustees and appoint new trustees in the case of pension trust schemes, while the Charity Commission has similar powers under the Charities Act 1993 s.18.[87] **8–47**

LETTERSTEDT v BROERS

Privy Council (1884) 9 App. Cas. 371; 51 L.T. 169

The Board of Executors of Cape Town were the sole surviving executors and trustees of a will under which the appellant was a beneficiary. The appellant alleged misconduct in the administration of the trust, and claimed that the Board were unfit to be entrusted with the management of the estate and should be removed in favour of a new appointment. The Supreme Court of the Cape of Good Hope had refused the application to remove the Board. The beneficiary appealed successfully. **8–48**

LORD BLACKBURN: . . . the whole case has been argued here, and, as far as their Lordships can perceive, in the court below, as depending on the principles which should guide an English court of equity when called upon to remove old trustees and substitute new ones. It is not disputed that there is a jurisdiction "in cases requiring such a remedy", as is said in Story's *Equity Jurisprudence*, s.1287, but there is very little to be found to guide us in saying what are the cases requiring such a remedy; so little that their Lordships are compelled to have recourse to general principles **8–49**

---

80 A power of removal, e.g. vested in a protector, will be presumed a fiduciary power not to be exercised for the personal benefit of the power-holder but for the beneficiaries as a whole or perhaps even for the benefit of the settlor (although the trust instrument should spell this out): *Von Knierem v Bermuda Trust Co* (1994) Butts, O.C.M. Vol.1 at 116; *Re Osiris* [2000] W.T.L.R. 933.

81 *Att.-Gen. v Scott* (1750) 1 Ves. Sen. 413.

82 (1884) 9 App. Cas. 371.

83 See too *Thomas and Agnes Carvel Foundation v Carvel* [2008] Ch. 395 at [51]; *Jones v Firkin-Flood* [2008] EWHC 2417 (Ch) at [283] ff.

84 If there is a dispute as to fact then instead of taking out a summons under s.41 a writ should be issued for administration or execution of the trusts invoking the inherent jurisdiction to remove trustees: *Re Henderson* [1940] Ch. 764.

85 *Re Consiglis' Trusts (No.1)* (1973) 36 D.L.R. (3d) 658. On the exercise of the court's jurisdiction see *Monty v Delmo* [1996] 1 V.R. 65 and *Titterton v Oates* [2001] W.T.L.R. 319.

86 *Clarke v Heathfield* (1985) 82 Law Soc. Gaz. 599; [1985] I.C.R. 203.

87 Considered in *Weth v Att.-Gen. (No.2)* [1999] 1 W.L.R. 686; *Seray-Wurie v Charity Commission* [2008] EWHC 1091 (CL).

8–50 Story says, section 1289: "But in cases of positive misconduct, courts of equity have no difficulty in interposing to remove trustees who have abused their trust; it is not indeed every mistake or neglect of duty, or inaccuracy of conduct of trustees, which will induce courts of equity to adopt such a course. But the acts or omissions must be such as to endanger the trust property or to show a want of honesty, or a want of proper capacity to execute the duties, or a want of reasonable fidelity."

8–51 It seems to their Lordships that the jurisdiction which a court of equity has no difficulty in exercising under the circumstances indicated by Story is merely ancillary to its principal duty, to see that the trusts are properly executed. This duty is constantly being performed by the substitution of new trustees in the place of original trustees for a variety of reasons in non-contentious cases. And therefore, though it should appear that the charges of misconduct were either not made out, or were greatly exaggerated, so that the trustee was justified in resisting them, and the court might consider that in awarding costs, yet if satisfied that the continuance of the trustee would prevent the trusts being properly executed, the trustee might be removed. It must always be borne in mind that trustees exist for the benefit of those to whom the creator of the trust has given the trust estate.

8–52 The reason why there is so little to be found in the books on this subject is probably that suggested by Mr Davey in his argument. As soon as all questions of character are as far settled as the nature of the case admits, if it appears clear that the continuance of the trustee would be detrimental to the execution of the trusts, even if for no other reason than that human infirmity would prevent those beneficially interested, or those who act for them, from working in harmony with the trustee, and if there is no reason to the contrary from the intentions of the framer of the trust to give this trustee a benefit or otherwise, the trustee is always advised by his own counsel to resign, and does so. If, without any reasonable ground, he refused to do so, it seems to their Lordships that the court might think it proper to remove him; but cases involving the necessity of deciding this, if they ever arise, do so without getting reported. It is to be lamented that the case was not considered in this light by the parties in the court below, for, as far as their Lordships can see, the Board would have little or no profit from continuing to be trustees, and as such coming into continual conflict with the appellant and her legal advisers, and would probably have been glad to resign, and get out of an onerous and disagreeable position. But the case was not so treated.

8–53 In exercising so delicate a jurisdiction as that of removing trustees, their Lords do not venture to lay down any general rule beyond the very broad principle above enunciated, that their main guide must be the welfare of the beneficiaries. Probably it is not possible to lay down any more definite rule in a matter so essentially dependent on details often of great nicety. . . .

8–54 It is quite true that friction or hostility between trustees and the immediate possessor of the trust estate is not of itself a reason for the removal of the trustees. But where the hostility is grounded on the mode in which the trust has been administered, where it has been caused wholly or partially by substantial overcharges against the trust estate, it is certainly not to be disregarded.

8–55 Looking, therefore, at the whole circumstances of this very peculiar case, the complete change of position, the unfortunate hostility that has arisen, and the difficult and delicate duties that may yet have to be performed, their Lordships can come to no other conclusion than that it is necessary, for the welfare of the beneficiaries, that the Board should no longer be trustees.

8–56 Probably if it had been put in this way below they would have consented. But for the benefit of the trust they should cease to be trustees, whether they consent or not . . .

5. Remuneration of Trustees

8–57 The basic rule is that trustees must administer the trust gratuitously for otherwise "the trust estate might be loaded and made of little value."[88] There is an obvious conflict between their self-interest and their duty, but the position has been much liberalised and modernised by the Trustee Act 2000. The cases in which the trustee is entitled to payment for his services are as follows.

[88] *Robinson v Pett* (1734) 3 P. Wms. 249 at 251.

8–58 First, in a suitable case the court has an inherent jurisdiction to authorise a trustee to receive remuneration prospectively or retrospectively and it may also increase the remuneration authorised by the trust deed. To do so the court must be satisfied that the trustee's services have been or will be of exceptional benefit to the estate.[89] On occasion the power to award remuneration has been exercised even in favour of a trustee who has been ordered to disgorge unauthorised profits,[90] but it is hard to predict when such awards will be made, following Lord Goff's statement in *Guinness Plc v Saunders*, that the exercise of the courts' jurisdiction should be restricted to cases where an award would not have the effect of encouraging fiduciaries to put themselves in a position of conflict.[91] The court, when appointing a corporation (other than the Public Trustee) to act, also has a statutory jurisdiction[92] under s.42 of the Trustee Act 1925 to authorise it to charge for its services.

8–59 Second, if the settlement authorises the trustee to charge for his services then he is entitled to be paid, but charging clauses used to be construed strictly with the onus on the trustee to show that the charge which he proposes to make is covered by the terms of the settlement. Thus, where a solicitor-trustee was authorised to make "professional charges," and even where the words "for his time and trouble" were added, he was not allowed to charge for time and trouble expended other than in his position as solicitor.[93] But where a will authorised the solicitor-trustee to make "the usual professional or other proper and reasonable charges for all business done and time expended in relation to the trusts of the will, whether such business is usually within the business of a solicitor or not", the solicitor was permitted to charge for business not strictly of a professional nature transacted by him in relation to the trust,[94] though, apparently, not for work altogether outside his professional vocation that a layman could do.[95]

8–60 However, in a radical fashion s.28(2) of the Trustee Act 2000 now treats a trustee entitled under the trust instrument to charge for services provided by him as entitled to receive payment "in respect of services even if they are services which are capable of being provided by a lay trustee", so long as the trustee is "a trust corporation or is acting in a professional capacity"—and the services were provided after January 2001.[96] A trustee acts in a professional capacity[97] "if he acts in the course of a profession or business which consists of or includes the provision of services in connection with (a) the management or administration of trusts generally or a particular kind of trust, or (b) any particular aspect of the management or administration of trusts generally or a particular kind of trust." A person acts as a "lay trustee" if he does not act in a professional capacity and is not a trust corporation.[98]

8–61 Third, by s.29 of the Trustee Act 2000 (unless provision as to entitlement to remuneration has been made by the trust instrument or by primary or subordinate legislation[99]—and unless the trust is a

---

[89] *Marshall v Holloway* (1820) 2 Swans. 432; *Docker v Somes* (1834) 2 My. & K. 655; *Re Freeman* (1887) 37 Ch.D. 148; *Re Macadam* [1946] Ch. 73; *Re Masters* [1953] 1 W.L.R. 51; *Re Duke of Norfolk's ST* [1982] Ch. 61; *Foster v Spencer* [1996] 2 All E.R. 672.

[90] *Boardman v Phipps* [1967] 2 A.C. 46 at 102 and 112; *O'Sullivan v Management Agency and Music Ltd* [1985] Q.B. 42; *Badfinger Music Ltd v Evans* [2001] W.T.L.R. 1. And see para.15–82.

[91] *Guinness Plc v Saunders* [1990] 2 A.C. 663 at 701, followed in e.g. *Quarter Master UK Ltd (in liq) v Pyke* [2005] 1 B.C.L.C. 245 at [76]–[77], though cf. *Nottingham University v Fishel* [2000] I.C.R. 1462 at 1499–1500. See too *Imageview Management Ltd v Jack* [2009] Bus. L.R. 1034 at [54]–[60].

[92] The Public Trustee has a statutory right to charge under the Public Trustee Act 1906 s.9, as have custodian trustees acting as custodian trustees *only* under the Public Trustee Act 1906 s.4: *Forster v Williams Deacon's Bank* [1935] Ch. 359. Judicial trustees may charge under the Judicial Trustees Act 1896 s.1.

[93] *Re Chapple* (1884) 27 Ch.D. 584; *Re Orwell's WT* [1982] 1 W.L.R. 1337.

[94] *Re Ames* (1883) 25 Ch.D. 72.

[95] *Clarkson v Robinson* [1900] 2 Ch. 722.

[96] Trustee Act 2000 s.31(1).

[97] Trustee Act 2000 s.28(5).

[98] Trustee Act 2000 s.28(6).

[99] Trustee Act 2000 s.29(5).

charitable trust[100]) a trustee which is a trust corporation is entitled to "reasonable remuneration",[101] while a trustee who acts in a "professional capacity" (as defined in the last paragraph) and is not a sole trustee, is also entitled to reasonable remuneration if each other trustee has agreed in writing that he may be remunerated for the services he provides to the trust,[102] including services capable of being provided by a lay trustee.[103] The power for a trustee to agree that another trustee be remunerated for her services is a power to be exercised in the interests of the beneficiaries as a whole and not for the personal benefit of the trustee to be remunerated or of the person exercising the power,[104] hoping perhaps for a reciprocal agreement for him to be remunerated. However, because it is the legislation that has placed a trustee in an invidious position where there is a sensible possibility of a conflict between self-interest and fiduciary duty, the exercise of the power to agree remuneration of a trustee is not impeachable by reason only that a conflict situation has arisen.[105] Where T1 and T2 are to be trustees it is better not to rely on s.29 but on an express remuneration clause: in the absence of the latter, T1 and T2 agreeing to each other being remunerated would be vulnerable to attack by disaffected beneficiaries so that to protect themselves T1 and T2 would want to obtain the prior consent of adult beneficiaries[106] or the authorisation of the court.[107]

8–62 Fourth, the rules governing payment of charity trustees have been relaxed by the Charities Act 2006 ss.36–37, inserting new ss.73A–73C of the Charities Act 1993.[108] It remains the case that charity trustees can be paid for their services as trustees only in restricted circumstances, but under the new sections they can now be paid for providing other services in the absence of an express power to pay them, provided that certain conditions are met, namely: (a) that the number of trustees receiving payment must be in a minority; (b) the amount paid must be reasonable and set out in a written agreement between the trustee and the charity; and (c) the governing document must not contain any specific provision forbidding this type of payment. The payment of charity trustees is a contentious issue because charities are told simultaneously that voluntarism is a fundamental feature of their activities and that they must undertake these activities in a professional manner.

8–63 Fifth, if the beneficiaries are all of full capacity and between them absolutely entitled to the trust estate, they may authorise the trustee to be paid. If the beneficiaries then sue the trustee for breach of trust in paying trust moneys to himself the trustee has their authorisation as a defence unless undue influence was exercised by him.

8–64 Sixth, the general rule of gratuitous service was particularly severe in the case of solicitor-trustees. Thus in *Christophers v White*,[109] it was held that a solicitor-trustee's firm was not entitled to charge for professional services rendered to the trust by a partner in the firm even though the partner was not one of the trustees.[110] But where a solicitor-trustee employed his partner, as distinct from his firm, under an express agreement that the partner should be individually entitled to charges, these were allowed on the ground that where such an agreement is carried out there is no infringement of the

100 Trustee Act 2000 s.29(1)(b) and (2)(b).
101 As defined in s.29(3).
102 Trustee Act 2000 s.29(2).
103 Trustee Act 2000 s.29(4).
104 Law Commission, *Report on Trustees' Powers and Duties* (Law Com. No.260, 1999) para.7.10 and Explanatory Note to Trustees Act 2000, para.103.
105 *Edge v Pensions Ombudsman* [1998] Ch. 512.
106 A trustee can invoke the Trustee Act 1925 s.62, to claim an indemnity from a beneficiary who consented to a breach of trust, so inhibiting action by a descendant of such a beneficiary.
107 *Lewin on Trusts* (17th edn) para.20–149D.
108 For general discussion, see Charity Commission, *CC11: Trustee Expenses and Payments* (June 2008 version).
109 (1847) 10 Beav. 523.
110 See also *Re Gates* [1933] Ch. 913 and *Re Hill* [1934] Ch. 623.

rule that a trustee may not make his office a source of remuneration.[111] Moreover, the severity of the rule was relaxed by the case of *Cradock v Piper*,[112] in which a solicitor-trustee acted as solicitor for himself and his co-trustees in legal proceedings relating to the trust, and was held to be entitled to his usual charges. The rule is that unlike a sole trustee acting as solicitor to the trust, a solicitor-trustee acting in legal proceedings[113] for a body of trustees, of whom he himself is one, is entitled to his usual charges if the fact of his appearing for himself and his co-trustees jointly has not increased the costs which would have been incurred if he had appeared for those co-trustees only.

Seventh, where the trust property is situate abroad and the law of the foreign country permits payment, the trustee is entitled to keep any remuneration which he has received. Thus in *Re Northcote*,[114] a testator who left assets both in this country and in the USA died domiciled in England, and the principal forum of administration was therefore English. The executors took out an English grant, and on doing so they were put on terms by the Revenue, the English effects being insufficient to pay the English duty, to undertake themselves personally to obtain a grant in New York in respect of the American assets. In due course they obtained such a grant, and got in the assets. Under the law of New York they were entitled to commission for so doing, and Harman J. held that they were under no duty to account for it to the beneficiaries. **8–65**

TRUSTEE ACT 2000 SECTIONS 28–33

28.—(1) Except to the extent (if any) to which the trust instrument makes inconsistent provision, subsections (2) to (4) apply to a trustee if— **8–66**

(a) there is a provision in the trust instrument entitling him to receive payment out of trust funds in respect of services provided by him to or on behalf of the trust, and
(b) the trustee is a trust corporation or is acting in a professional capacity.

(2) The trustee is to be treated as entitled under the trust instrument to receive payment in respect of services even if they are services which are capable of being provided by a lay trustee.

(3) Subsection (2) applies to a trustee of a charitable trust who is not a trust corporation only—

(a) if he is not a sole trustee, and
(b) to the extent that a majority of the other trustees have agreed that it should apply to him.

(4) Any payments to which the trustee is entitled in respect of services are to be treated as remuneration for services (and not as a gift) for the purposes of—

(a) section 15 of the Wills Act 1837 (gifts to an attesting witness to be void), and
(b) section 34(3) of the Administration of Estates Act 1925 (order in which estate to be paid out).

(5) For the purposes of this Part, a trustee acts in a professional capacity if he acts in the course of a profession or business which consists of or includes the provision of services in connection with—

(a) the management or administration of trusts generally or a particular kind of trust, or
(b) any particular aspect of the management or administration of trusts generally or a particular kind of trust,

---

111 *Cluck v Carlon* (1861) 30 L.J. Ch. 639.
112 (1850) 1 Mac. & G. 664.
113 Legal proceedings need not necessarily be hostile litigation but may be friendly proceedings in chambers: *Re Corsellis* (1887) 34 Ch.D. 675. It must be work in connection with a writ or an originating summons rather than general advisory work relating to legal proceedings.
114 [1949] 1 All E.R. 442; see also *Chambers v Goldwin* (1802) 9 Ves. 271.

and the services he provides to or on behalf of the trust fall within that description.

(6) For the purposes of this Part, a person acts as a lay trustee if he—

(a) is not a trust corporation, and
(b) does not act in a professional capacity.

8–67 29.—(1) Subject to subsection (5), a trustee who—

(a) is a trust corporation, but
(b) is not a trustee of a charitable trust,

is entitled to receive reasonable remuneration out of the trust funds for any services that the trust corporation provides to or on behalf of the trust.

(2) Subject to subsection (5), a trustee who—

(a) acts in a professional capacity, but
(b) is not a trust corporation, a trustee of a charitable trust or a sole trustee,

is entitled to receive reasonable remuneration out of the trust funds for any services that he provides to or on behalf of the trust if each other trustee has agreed in writing that he may be remunerated for the services.

(3) "Reasonable remuneration" means, in relation to the provision of services by a trustee, such remuneration as is reasonable in the circumstances for the provision of those services to or on behalf of that trust by that trustee and for the purposes of subsection (1) includes, in relation to the provision of services by a trustee who is an authorised institution under the Banking Act 1987 and provides the services in that capacity, the institution's reasonable charges for the provision of such services.

(4) A trustee is entitled to remuneration under this section even if the services in question are capable of being provided by a lay trustee.

(5) A trustee is not entitled to remuneration under this section if any provision about his entitlement to remuneration has been made—

(a) by the trust instrument, or
(b) by any enactment or any provision of subordinate legislation.

(6) This section applies to a trustee who has been authorised under a power conferred by Part IV or the trust instrument—

(a) to exercise functions as an agent of the trustees, or
(b) to act as a nominee or custodian,

as it applies to any other trustee.

8–68 30.—(1) The Secretary of State may by regulations make provision for the remuneration of trustees of charitable trusts who are trust corporations or act in a professional capacity.

(2) The power under subsection (1) includes power to make provision for the remuneration of a trustee who has been authorised under a power conferred by Part IV or any other enactment or any provision of subordinate legislation, or by the trust instrument—

(a) to exercise functions as an agent of the trustees, or
(b) to act as a nominee or custodian.

8–69 31.—(1) A trustee—

(a) is entitled to be reimbursed from the trust funds, or
(b) may pay out of the trust funds,

expenses properly incurred by him when acting on behalf of the trust.

(2) This section applies to a trustee who has been authorised under a power conferred by Part IV or any other enactment or any provision of subordinate legislation, or by the trust instrument—

(a) to exercise functions as an agent of the trustees, or
(b) to act as a nominee or custodian,

as it applies to any other trustee.

32.—(1) This section applies if, under a power conferred by Part IV or any other enactment or any provision of subordinate legislation, or by the trust instrument, a person other than a trustee has been— **8–70**

(a) authorised to exercise functions as an agent of the trustees, or
(b) appointed to act as a nominee or custodian.

(2) The trustees may remunerate the agent, nominee or custodian out of the trust funds for services if—

(a) he is engaged on terms entitling him to be remunerated for those services, and
(b) the amount does not exceed such remuneration as is reasonable in the circumstances for the provision of those services by him to or on behalf of that trust.

(3) The trustees may reimburse the agent, nominee or custodian out of the trust funds for any expenses properly incurred by him in exercising functions as an agent, nominee or custodian.

33.—(1) Subject to subsection (2), sections 28, 29, 31 and 32 apply in relation to services provided to or on behalf of, or (as the case may be) expenses incurred on or after their commencement on behalf of, trusts whenever created. **8–71**

(2) Nothing in section 28 or 29 is to be treated as affecting the operation of—

(a) section 15 of the Wills Act 1837, or
(b) section 34(3) of the Administration of Estates Act 1925,

in relation to any death occurring before the commencement of section 28 or (as the case may be) section 29.

6. Indemnity of Trustees[115]

A. Indemnity Out of, and Lien Over, the Trust Estate

Few individuals would become trustees unless they could recoup themselves for the liabilities which they incur while managing the trust affairs,[116] and by the Trustee Act 2000 s.31(1): "A trustee (a) is entitled to be reimbursed from the trust funds, or (b) may pay out of the trust funds, expenses properly incurred by him when acting on behalf of the trust." What then, if he employs an agent or nominee or custodian, who incurs expenses and charges for remuneration? By s.32(3): "The trustees may reimburse the agent, nominee or custodian out of the trust funds for any expenses properly incurred by him in exercising functions as an agent, nominee or custodian." However, by s.32(2) the trustees can only "remunerate the agent, nominee or custodian out of the trust funds for services" if "the amount **8–72**

[115] See generally A.W. Scott, "Liabilities Incurred in the Administration of Trusts" (1915) 28 H.L.R. 725; Stone. "A Theory of Liability of Trust Estates for the Contracts and Torts of the Trustee" (1922) 22 Col. L.R. 527; A. J. Hawkins, "The Personal Liability of Charity Trustees" (1979) 95 L.Q.R. 99; D. J. Hayton, "Trading Trusts", Chapter in J. Glasson (ed.), *International Trust Laws*.

[116] *Worrall v Harford* (1802) 8 Ves. Jun. 4 at 8; *Re Exhall Coal Co Ltd* (1866) 35 Beav 449 at 453.

does not exceed such remuneration as is reasonable in the circumstances for the provision of those services by him to or on behalf of that trust."

8–73 These provisions reflect the established position that trustees only have power to pay "proper costs incident to the execution of the trust".[117] As Lord Selborne L.C. stated in *Stott v Milne*,[118] "The right of trustees to indemnity against all costs and expenses properly incurred by them in the execution of the trust is a first charge on all the trust properly, both income and corpus. The trustees, therefore, had a right to retain the costs out of the income until provision could be made for raising them out of the corpus."

8–74 However, no indemnity can be claimed by a trustee in respect of a liability improperly incurred,[119] e.g. because of lack of power under the trust instrument; or because of lack of due authorisation under internal requirements;[120] or because the transaction entails a breach of duty by the trustee, e.g. to diversify investments, to supervise agents, or to invest with the statutory duty of care. Moreover, a trustee cannot reimburse himself out of the trust fund if he is indebted to the trust by reason of some unconnected breach of trust, since his right to reimbursement depends ultimately on the state of accounts between him and the beneficiaries and it is limited to the balance, if any, in his favour.[121] Finally, no right of indemnity exists to the extent that this has been excluded in the trust instrument, as may happen where the trustee has a liberal right to remuneration under a charging clause intended to cover expenses.[122]

8–75 The trustee can protect himself against the problems created by his lack of power or authority by taking the advice of lawyers or even the guidance of the court but this takes time and money. He can also protect himself against allegations that, in breach of his equitable duties, he involved himself as claimant or defendant in an action involving the trust and a third party, so that he should personally pay his own costs and the costs of the other (winning) side in the action. To do this, he seeks in private a *Beddoe's* order[123] from the court which will entitle him to be reimbursed costs out of the trust fund no matter the result of the litigation, so long as full and frank disclosure was made to the court. However, where the claim seeks to undermine the trust wholly or partly (e.g. claims by the settlor's creditors or trustee in bankruptcy[124] or an adverse proprietary tracing claim) the trustee may be required to be neutral and only have a right of indemnity for the costs of acting neutrally,[125] unless no other person is appropriate to represent the interests of beneficiaries who are unborn or otherwise unascertained.[126]

---

117 *Holding and Management Ltd v Property Holding and Investment Trust Plc* [1998] 1 W.L.R. 1313 at 1324, per Nicholls L.J. See too *Re Grimthorpe* [1958] Ch. 615 at 623.

118 (1884) 25 Ch.D. 710 at 715.

119 Exceptionally, if the trustee acted in good faith and the transaction benefited the trust fund he should have a right of indemnity to the extent of the benefit to prevent unjust enrichment of the beneficiaries: *Vyse v Foster* (1872) 8 Ch. App. 309 at 336–337; *Conway v Fenton* (1888) 11 Ch.D. 512 at 518—or the trust deed might expressly permit indemnity even beyond the extent of the benefit to the whole expense.

120 e.g. for trustee unanimity, or for the beneficiaries' consent, or for a meeting to be duly held before any decision is taken.

121 *Ex parte Edmonds* (1862) 4 De G.F. & J. 488 at 498; *Re Johnson* (1880) 15 Ch.D. 548; *Re British Power Traction & Lighting Co Ltd* [1910] 2 Ch. 470.

122 *Ex parte Chippendale, Re German Mining Co* (1854) 4 De G.M. & G 19 at 52; *McLean v Burns Philip Trustee Co Pty. Ltd* [1985] 2 N.S.W.L.R. 623 (the right to indemnity excluded in unit trusts so as not to affect the marketability of units).

123 *Re Beddoe* [1893] 1 Ch. 547: this is in a separate action and the judge who hears it will not hear the main action. For details see *Lewin on Trusts* (17th edn) paras 21–106 to 21–119.

124 Insolvency Act 1986 ss.339–342 and 423–425.

125 *Alsop Wilkinson v Neary* [1996] 1 W.L.R. 1220.

126 *Re Hall* [1994–95] Cayman I.L.R. 456, *Lloyds Bank v Bylevan Corp SA* [1994–95] C.I.L.R. 519.

The right of indemnity of a trustee is bolstered by an equitable proprietary right in the nature of a non-possessory lien,[127] which enables the trustee to retain assets against actual, contingent or possible liabilities[128] or to seek a sale of the assets[129] if in the ownership of a successor trustee. The equitable lien will continue to bind successor trustees,[130] but it will not bind beneficiaries to whom the assets are distributed unless expressly preserved by the distributing trustee(s), the recipient beneficiary normally receiving the assets (whether expressly or by necessary implication) discharged from the interests of other beneficiaries and from the prior equitable interests of trustees.[131] **8–76**

Trustees should reimburse themselves as soon as possible because they are not entitled to interest on the money they paid out to meet expenses.[132] This rule probably derives from the practical consideration that it would be inconvenient if interest were to accrue on each item of a trustee's expenditure on a piecemeal basis, but it can cause hardship and injustice to trustees where costs have mounted up over an extended period.[133] It seems, though, that the courts have a discretion to award interest in hard cases.[134] **8–77**

B. Indemnity by the Beneficiary Personally

A trustee's right of indemnity in respect of expenses properly incurred—e.g. in respect of costs, a call on shares, solicitor's, stockbroker's or auctioneer's charges—is a right of indemnity against the trust estate, not against the beneficiary. Hence, the trustees of an ordinary club are entitled to be indemnified out of the club property, not by the club members,[135] unless, as is often the case, the club rules allow this. But a trustee's indemnity extends beyond the trust estate to the beneficiary personally where the trustee accepted the trust at the request of the settlor who is also a beneficiary so as to raise an implied contract of indemnity[136] and also where the beneficiary is a sole beneficiary sui juris and entitled absolutely,[137] or where there are several beneficiaries who are sui juris and between them collectively entitled absolutely.[138] This can prove very useful where a trustee for such beneficiaries properly borrows money to carry out authorised trading or investing and the borrowings exceed the **8–78**

---

127 *Jennings v Mather* [1901] 1 K.B. 108 at 113–114, [1902] 1 K.B. 1 at 6 and 9; *Stott v Milne* (1884) 25 Ch.D. 710 at 715; *Commissioner of Stamp Duties v ISPT* (1999) 2 I.T.E.L.R. 1 at 18; *Octavo Investments Pty Ltd v Knight* (1979) 114 C.L.R. 360; *Dimos v Dikeatos Nominees Ltd* (1997) 149 A.L.R. 113.

128 *X v A* [2000] 1 All E.R. 490.

129 *Re Pumfrey* (1882) 22 Ch.D. 255 at 262.

130 *Dimos v Dikeatos Nominees Ltd* (1997) 149 A.L.R. 113.

131 Australian cases (like *Dimos* and *Chief Commissioner of Stamp Duties v Buckle* (1998) 72 A.L.J.R. 242) treat the trustee's right not as an "encumbrance" but as a proprietary right equivalent to (but ranking ahead of) the equitable interests of beneficiaries.

132 *Gordon v Trail* (1820) 8 Price 416; *Foster v Spencer* [1996] 2 All E.R. 672 at 678.

133 *Foster v Spencer* [1996] 2 All E.R. 672 at 678.

134 *Re German Mining Co* (1853) 4 De G. M. & G. 19 at 36 and 43; *Murray's Executors' Case* (1854) 5 De G. M. & G. 746 at 753.

135 *Wise v Perpetual Trustee Co* [1903] A.C. 139, establishing a presumption that the members of an unincorporated association do not intend to pledge their personal credit for any larger sum than the amount of their membership dues. For critical comment, see T.C. Williams (1903) 19 L.Q.R. 386; R.W. Rideout, "Limited Liability of Unincorporated Associations" (1996) 49 C.L.P. 187, pp. 198–204; R. Flannigan, "Contractual Responsibility in Non-Profit Associations" (1998) 18 O.J.L.S. 631, pp. 641–644.

136 *Ex parte Chippendale* (1854) 4 De G.M. & G. 19 at 54; *Jervis v Wolferstan* (1874) L.R. 18 Eq. 18, as explained by Lord Blackburn in *Fraser v Murdoch* (1881) 6 App. Cas. 855 at 872; *Matthews v Ruggles-Brise* [1911] 1 Ch. 194. In that case it was also held that where a beneficiary is personally liable to indemnify his trustee, an assignment by him of his beneficial interest does not affect that liability as it stood at the date of the assignment.

137 *Hardoon v Belilios* [1901] A.C. 118.

138 *Buchan v Ayre* [1915] 2 Ch. 474 at 477; *Re Reid* (1971) 17 D.L.R. (3d) 199; *Balkin v Peck* (1997) 43 N.S.W.L.R. 766 (English executor recovered from Australian beneficiaries when he overlooked the tax payable on proceeds remitted to Australia).

assets when things go dreadfully wrong as occurred in *JW Broomhead (Vic) Pty Ltd (in liq.) v JW Broomhead Pty Ltd*[139] where McGarvie J. held "where there are several beneficiaries entitled to separate benefits, a beneficiary who gets a proportion of the benefit should bear that proportion of its burdens unless he can show why the trustee should bear the proportion of them himself." He further held that where a beneficiary is insolvent the loss in respect of his proportion falls on the trustee and not the other beneficiaries. He also accepted that "a request from a beneficiary to the trustee to assume the office of trustee or to incur liabilities obviously justifies the imposition of a personal liability to indemnify on the beneficiary and this should be so even if the beneficiary has only a limited interest."

8–79 The beneficiary's obligation to indemnify the trustee does not depend on the beneficiary having requested the trustee to incur the liability, but arises out of the principle that "the cestui que trust who gets all the benefit of the property should bear its burden"[140]—although consistently with this the beneficiary can escape his liability by disclaiming his interest in the trust property.[141] It also follows that a beneficiary who takes an interest by assignment from the original beneficiary is bound to indemnify the trustee,[142] although in this case the original beneficiary also remains liable to indemnify.[143] Note that the trustee's right to be indemnified by the beneficiaries is separate from his right to be indemnified out of the trust assets, and it is no answer to a trustee's claim to be indemnified by the beneficiaries personally that he should have recouped himself out of the trust property when he had a chance to do so.[144]

C. *Subrogation of Third Parties and the Trustees' Indemnity Rights*[145]

8–80 In carrying out the trusts or powers a trustee is personally liable to the extent of his whole fortune or patrimony for debts, contracts, torts or taxes arising in respect of his acts or omissions as trustee. After all, the trust property is not an entity that can be regarded as a person to be made liable. Having transferred his property, usually by way of gift, to the trustees the settlor has disappeared from the picture. The trustees are not agents for the beneficiaries nor are they in a partnership with them so there is no legal connection between the beneficiaries and any creditors. Thus, the trustees are personally liable and remain so even after retiring as trustees: hence the need for an indemnity from the new trustees or reliance upon their equitable lien.

8–81 As a matter of contract law a trustee and a third party may agree that the trustee may limit or exclude his personal liability and that the trustee shall pay the debt out of the trust property under his statutory right of indemnity.[146] The onus lies on the trustee to displace the strong presumption of personal liability so that contracting descriptively "as trustee" is not sufficient,[147] but contracting "as

---

[139] [1985] V.R. 891 at 936–939.

[140] *Hardoon v Belilos* [1901] AC 118 at 125, per Lord Lindley. See too *Balkin v Peck* (1997) 43 NSWLR 706 at 711–712, per Mason P.

[141] *Hardoon* at 125.

[142] *Hardoon* at 125.

[143] *Matthews v Ruggles-Brise* [1911] 1 Ch. 194 at 203.

[144] *Balkin v Peck* (1997) 43 N.S.W.L.R. 706 at 714, per Mason P.

[145] In 1999, the Trust Law Committee, an English law reform body based at King's College London, published a report recommending various statutory reforms of the law in this area: Trust Law Committee *Rights of Creditors against Trustees and Trust Funds* (June 1999): *www.kcl.ac.uk/content/1/c6/01/11/90/TLCCredRightsReport140499_1.pdf*. For general discussion, see too C. Mitchell and S. Watterson, *Subrogation: Law and Practice* (2007) Ch.12.

[146] *Muir v City of Glasgow Bank* (1879) 4 App. Cas. 337 at 355. It is possible for the trustee, if authorised, to go further and charge the trust property with payment of the debt: such an intention to create a charge is not likely to be inferred merely from an agreement that the creditor is to look to the trust property and not to the trustee for payment: cf. *Swiss Bank Corp v Lloyds Bank* [1980] 2 All E.R. 419 at 426; aff'd [1981] 2 All E.R. 449.

[147] *Watling v Lewis* [1911] 1 Ch. 414 at 424; *Marston Thompson & Evershed Plc v Benn* [2007] W.T.L.R. 315.

trustee and not otherwise" will suffice since the phrase would be meaningless if not excluding personal liability.[148]

8–82 Where a trustee does not pay a creditor out of his own moneys or out of trust moneys available under his statutory right of indemnity the creditor may have a claim by way of subrogation to the trustee's right of indemnity.[149] The problem is that the creditor's right is derivative: he stands in the shoes of the trustee and has no better right than the trustee.[150] Thus, for the creditor to be paid out of the trust assets he will need to show that the right of indemnity was not excluded by the trust instrument,[151] that the debt was properly incurred in the authorised carrying on of the trust, and that the state of accounts between the trustee and the beneficiaries (taking into account any losses caused by any breach of trust on the trustee's part) is such that there is some balance in the trustee's favour to which the right of indemnity may attach. However, where there are two or more trustees and one of them does not have a clear account (e.g. because of an outstanding claim against him for a breach of trust) the creditor can rely on the right to indemnity enjoyed by the other trustee.[152]

8–83 In addition to his proprietary right of indemnity, a trustee in some limited circumstances (already discussed above) may have a personal right of indemnity against a beneficiary personally. The right of subrogation in respect of the proprietary right of a trustee to an indemnity from the trust property arose out of the Court of Chancery's practice in administration of trust estates in an administration action. There was no similar practice for allowing a right of subrogation in respect of a trustee's right of indemnity against a beneficiary personally but, in principle, there should be such a right of subrogation.

8–84 A person contracting with a trustee is in a particularly invidious position due to her derivative right being worthless if the trustee happens to be or become indebted to the trust fund for some unconnected breach of trust or if the trustee happens to be in breach of some equitable duty of care in negotiating the contract. In the absence of a power to create a fixed charge over specific assets or to create an equitable interest in the fluctuating trust fund in the nature of a floating charge, what can be done to protect the creditor's interests?

8–85 To deal with the unconnected indebtedness problem it seems possible to negotiate as part of the price of the contract a necessarily incidental, but express, term that the trustee is in no way personally liable upon the contract, but the creditor shall have a personal non-proprietary direct independent right of recourse to the trust fund, so that it is immaterial whether or not the trustee's right of indemnity has been extinguished by indebtedness to the trust fund. It would be better, however, if statute were to provide that the indebtedness of a trustee to the trust at the time a contractual creditor (or a victim of a tort) seeks an indemnity out of the trust fund should not be a reason for refusing such an indemnity to such creditor (or victim).

8–86 Dealing with a trustee who may be in breach of his equitable duty of care is fraught with danger. If the creditor believes he is getting too good a bargain perhaps he should disclose this to help ensure that the trustee satisfies the equitable duty—but this would seem to place intending contractors with

148 *Re Robinson's Settlement* [1912] 1 Ch. 717 at 729; *Muir v City of Glasgow Bank* (1879) 4 App. Cas. 337 at 362.

149 *Re Johnson* (1880) 15 Ch.D. 548 at 552; *Re Blundell* (1889) 44 Ch.D. 1 at 11; *Vacuum Oil Pty Ltd v Wiltshire* (1945) 72 C.L.R. 319 at 325 and 336; *Re Raybould* [1900] 1 Ch. 199.

150 *Ex parte Edmonds* (1862) 4 De G.F. & J. 488 at 498; *Re Johnson* (1880) 15 Ch.D. 548; *Re British Power Traction & Lighting Co Ltd* [1910] 2 Ch. 470.

151 Unlike the Trustee Act 1925 s.69(2) which expressly allowed s.30(2) to be subject to contrary intent, no provision in Trustee Act 2000 allows this in respect of s.31 (the successor to s.30(2) of the 1925 Act), but it is considered that no court would permit a trustee to exploit s.31 if its generous remuneration was premised upon no recovery of expenses. A court could hold s.31 inapplicable on the basis the trustee was acting not "on behalf of the trust" but on behalf of itself in order to earn its generous remuneration or could hold the benefit of the remuneration was only available as burdened by the obligation not to claim expenses.

152 *Re Frith* [1902] 1 Ch. 342 at 346.

trustees under a fiduciary obligation which seems inappropriate and impractical in the commercial context. Perhaps, the House of Lords or even the Court of Appeal might restrict "properly incurred" to mean incurred by virtue of authority in the trust instrument and complying with any internal procedures so that it would be immaterial[153] that there had been a breach of equitable duties of care in investing or in supervising agents. It would be better if statute were to provide that a trustee's breach of equitable duties should not prevent a creditor having a right of indemnity out of the trust fund unless dishonestly implicated in such breach. Furthermore, where a trustee's conduct made him a tortfeasor and such conduct amounted to a breach of his equitable duties (e.g. of care) this should not prevent the victim from having a right of indemnity out of the trust fund. In *Re Raybould*,[154] reproduced immediately below, it was fortunate for the claimant that the subsidence damage was caused by the proper management of the colliery by the trustee. In *Re Christian Brothers of Ireland in Canada*[155] the Brothers operated schools where some of the teachers unlawfully sexually abused pupils, and it was held that all the property of the charity was available to satisfy pupils' claims.

RE RAYBOULD

Chancery Division [1900] 1 Ch. 199, 69 L.J. Ch. 249

8–87 The surviving trustee and executor of a deceased's estate properly worked one of the testator's collieries. Earthworks caused a subsidence damaging the buildings and machinery of the adjoining owners, Roberts & Cooper. They obtained a judgment against the trustee for damage and costs. In the present proceedings they sought an order that this amount and cost be paid out of the testator's estate.

8–88 BYRNE J.: The first question I have to consider is whether the same principle ought to be applied to the case of a trustee claiming a right to indemnity for liability for damages for a tort, as is applied to the simpler case of claims made against a trustee by ordinary business creditors, where they have been allowed the benefit of his right to indemnity, by proving directly against the assets: the kind of case of which *Dowse v Gorton*[156] is a recent illustration. It has been argued that there is no authority to justify me in holding that, where damages have been recovered against a trustee in respect of a tort, the person so recovering can avail himself of the trustee's right to indemnity, and so go direct against the trust estate; but the authority of *Bennett v Wyndham*[157] goes to show that if a trustee in the course of the ordinary management of his testator's estate, either by himself or his agent, does some act whereby some third person is injured, and that third person recovers damages against the trustee in an action for tort, the trustee, if he has acted with due diligence and reasonably, is entitled to be indemnified out of his testator's estate. When once a trustee is entitled to be this indemnified out of his trust estate, I cannot myself see why the person who has recovered judgment against the trustee should not have the benefit of this right to indemnify and go direct against the trust estate or the assets, as the case may be, just as an ordinary creditor of a business carried on by a trustee or executor has been allowed to do, instead of having to go through the double process of suing the trustee, recovering the damages from him and leaving the trustee to recoup himself out of the trust estate. I have the parties interested in defending the trust estate before me, and I have also the trustee, and he claims indemnity, and, assuming that a proper case for indemnifying him is made out by the evidence, I think his claim should be allowed.

---

[153] Assuming the problem of indebtedness to the trust fund for such breach of trust was overcome.
[154] [1900] 1 Ch. 199.
[155] (2000) 184 D.L.R. (4th) 445, noted D.R. Wingfield (2003) 119 L.Q.R. 44, and discussed in M.H. Ogilvie, "Vicarious Liability and Charitable Immunity in Canadian Sexual Torts Law" (2004) 4 O.U.C.L.J. 167.
[156] [1891] A.C. 190.
[157] (1862) D.F. & J. 259.

> The next question I have to decide is whether this trustee has worked the colliery in such a way as to be entitled to be indemnified. Having considered all the evidence, I am not prepared to say that the injury done to the applicants' land was occasioned by reckless or improper working, or otherwise than by the ordinary and reasonable management of the colliery; and I therefore come to the conclusion that the trustee is entitled to be indemnified out of the assets against the damages and costs which he has been ordered to pay to Messrs Roberts & Cooper. It follows, therefore, for the reasons already given, that Messrs Roberts & Cooper are entitled to stand in the trustee's place for the purpose of obtaining this indemnity direct from this testator's estate. The result, therefore, is that this summons succeeds . . . **8–89**

Questions

1. Given that the absolutely entitled beneficiaries of a trust can use their *Saunders v Vautier* rights to wind up the trust if they are unhappy with their trustees, what is the practical significance of their rights to force the trustees to retire and appoint new ones under the Trusts of Land and Appointment of Trustees Act 1996? **8–90**

2. If trustees seek to retire how can this be achieved? **8–91**

3. What happens when (a) one of two trustees dies, and then (b) the survivor dies? **8–92**

4. How does trust property become vested in new trustees? **8–93**

5. Can the courts ever award an equitable allowance for services to a defaulting fiduciary, given Lord Goff's statement in *Guinness Plc v Saunders* that such awards should not be made if they will encourage fiduciaries to put themselves in a position of conflict? **8–94**

6. Michael and Naomi are the trustees of a large family trust, who run the trust affairs out of an office which they rent from Larry. Michael and Naomi commit various negligent and fraudulent breaches of trust and then become bankrupt. **8–95**

   Advise Larry, who wishes to know whether he can recover rent arrears out of the trust fund, or from the beneficiaries.

9 DUTIES OF TRUSTEES

1. Introduction

9–01 A trustee has two roles to perform: a distributive role, concerned with distributing income and capital to appropriate beneficiaries, and an administrative or managerial role, concerned with safeguarding and developing the value of the trust fund. When performing both of these roles, the trustee owes prescriptive equitable duties of skill and care and proscriptive duties of keeping within the terms of the trust and of exhibiting undivided loyalty and good faith towards the beneficiaries.[1]

A. The Distributive Role

9–02 When performing his distributive role the trustee must ensure that trust property is distributed only to those who are entitled to benefit under the terms of the trust.[2] He must exercise any discretionary power in a responsible fashion for the purposes intended by the settlor, and he must not exercise any such power capriciously or in a way that is contrary to any sensible expectation of the settlor.[3] In a disinterested and impartial fashion, he must take account of all relevant factors and ignore all irrelevant factors, so that it cannot be said that he would have made a different decision if he had taken all relevant factors into account and ignored all irrelevant factors.[4] This rule is reminiscent of the *Wednesbury* test[5] for unreasonableness in public law.[6]

B. The Managerial Role

9–03 When administering and managing the trust property the trustee, again, is bound by the terms of the trust deed, and he may not, for example, exceed his powers of sale and purchase, either by selling trust assets which he is bound to retain, or by buying assets for investment purposes that lie outside the range of permissible investments. The beneficiaries can obtain an injunction to restrain him from acting in an unauthorised way,[7] or, if it is too late and his unauthorised actions turn out badly, they

---

1 *Bristol & West BS v Mothew* [1998] Ch. 1 at 18.

2 Equity does not allow the trustee's accounts to show that he transferred property to a third party who was not entitled to receive it under the trust instrument; if he submits accounts which record such an unauthorised transaction then the accounts will be "falsified" by deleting the record of the disbursement so that they show that the property remains part of the trust fund; the trustee must then make this true by replacing the property either by acquiring substitute property or by paying in its current monetary value. For discussion see paras 11–09 ff.

3 *Re Hay's ST* [1982] 1 W.L.R. 202 at 209; *Re Beatty's WT* [1990] 3 All E.R. 844 at 846; *McPhail v Doulton* [1971] A.C. 424 at 449, *Re Manisty's Settlement* [1994] Ch. 17 at 26.

4 *Re Hastings-Bass* [1975] Ch. 25 41; *Mettoy Pensions Trustees Ltd v Evans* [1991] 2 All E.R. 513 at 553; *Abacus Trustees Ltd v Barr* [2000] Ch. 409; *Sieff v Fox* [2005] 1 W.L.R. 811; *St Mary and St Michael Parish Advisory Co Ltd v Westminster Roman Catholic Diocese Trustee* [2006] W.T.L.R. 881 at [122].

5 Named for *Associated Provincial Picture Houses Ltd v Wednesbury Corporation* [1948] 1 KB 223.

6 As noted in *Sieff v Fox* [2005] 1 W.L.R. 811 at [76], per Lloyd L.J., following *Harris v Lord Shuttleworth* [1994] I.C.R. 51 and *Edge v Pensions Ombudsman* [1998] Ch. 512, affirmed [2000] Ch. 602 at 627.

7 As in e.g. *Fox v Fox* (1870) L.R. 11 Eq. 142; *Buttle v Saunders* [1950] 2 All E.R. 193.

can require him to reconstitute the trust fund. On the other hand, if his unauthorised actions turn out well, for example because he buys an unauthorised investment that increases in value, they can ratify his actions and treat them as a duly authorised exercise of his powers.[8]

When performing his managerial role, the trustee is generally required to display "no higher degree of diligence than a man of ordinary prudence would exercise in the management of his own private affairs".[9] In the investment sphere, however, his duty is "not to take such care only as a prudent man would take if he had only himself to consider; the duty rather is to take such care as an ordinary prudent man would take if he were minded to make an investment for the benefit of other people for whom he felt morally bound to provide".[10] Note, though, that with the advent of professional paid trustees and trust companies it has become established that a higher degree of care is expected of them, so that they are judged according to the standards of care which they profess.[11] In 2000 this equitable duty of care was replaced by a statutory duty of care covering most, though not all, activities of trustees. **9–04**

Section 1 of the Trustee Act 2000 lays down "the duty of care" applicable to trustee activities relating to investments, using agents, nominees and custodians, compounding liabilities, insuring, valuing, and auditing. When carrying on such activities, a trustee: **9–05**

"must exercise such care and skill as is reasonable in the circumstances, having regard in particular—

(a) to any special knowledge or experience that he has or holds himself out as having, and
(b) if he acts as a trustee in the course of a business or profession, to any special knowledge or experience that it is reasonable to expect of a person acting in the course of that kind of business or profession."

Note that (a) involves a subjective element relating to any extra knowledge or experience of the trustee personally, while (b) objectively relates to persons engaged in the trustee's business or profession generally. In (b) there is a distinction between a trustee who carries on trust business in the course of practising generally as a solicitor or accountant, and a trustee who specialises in trust work in the course of the specific business of being a trustee: the latter will normally be governed by a higher standard. Note, too, that the statutory duty of care laid down in section 1 may be excluded by an express term of the trust instrument.[12] **9–06**

If a trustee performs his managerial and administrative functions with an appropriate degree of skill and care then he will not be liable for loss which occurs as a result of his actions (also assuming that these are authorised). So, for example, he will not be liable for resulting losses if he takes a reasonable decision to buy investments which then depreciate in value following a drop in the securities market. Nor will he be liable for profits that he would have made if he had been more dynamic and skilful, e.g. in more actively selling and buying shares. When determining whether trustees have breached their duties of skill and care in making decisions (e.g. on selling or buying particular investments) the court will treat them in the same way as other professionals, who would only be "liable for **9–07**

---

[8] Which explains the remark famously attributed to Selwyn L.J. by Sir Nathaniel Lindley M.R. in the course of argument in *Perrins v Bellamy* [1899] 1 Ch. 797 at 798: "My old master, the late Selwyn L.J., used to say 'The main duty of a trustee is to commit judicious breaches of trust.' "

[9] *Learoyd v Whiteley* (1887) 12 A.C. 727 at 733, per Lord Watson.

[10] *Re Whiteley* (1886) 33 Ch.D. 347, 355, per Lindley L.J., endorsed in *Cowan v Scargill* [1985] Ch. 270 at 289; *Nestlé v National Westminster Bank Plc* [1994] 1 All E.R. 118, at 126 and 140.

[11] *Bartlett v Barclays Bank Trust Co* [1980] 1 All E.R. 139 at 152. See too Lord Nicholls, "Trustees and Their Broader Community: Where Duty, Morality and Ethics Converge" (1995) 9 Tru. L.I. 71 at p.73.

[12] Trustee Act 2000 Sch 1 para.7. For general discussion of exemption clauses, see paras 9–215 ff.

damage caused by their advice, acts or omissions in the course of their professional work which no member of the profession who was reasonably well-informed and competent would have given or done or omitted to do".[13]

C. *Protection by Court Applications*

9–08 If any doubts arise, then the trustee should apply to the Chancery Division for directions to guide and protect him. As a last resort a trustee who is found to have breached a duty may ask the court to excuse him under the Trustee Act 1925 s.61. This section empowers the court to excuse a trustee from part or all of his liability for breach of trust if he has acted "honestly and reasonably, and ought fairly to be excused for the breach of trust and for omitting to obtain the directions of the court in the matter in which he committed such breach". A paid trustee is much less likely to be excused than an unpaid trustee.[14]

D. *Co-trustees*

9–09 Where there is more than one trustee, as is usually the case, each trustee is personally responsible for the acts performed in the administration of the trust and so should personally consider each act that needs to be done: if things turn out badly, it is no defence that one was a "sleeping trustee" blindly relying on one's co-trustees.[15] It is not possible for the trustees collectively to delegate their duties to another person, except where this is authorised under the trust instrument or by the Trustee Act 2000, which gives them broad powers to delegate their managerial, but not their distributive, functions.[16] The trustees must act unanimously except where the settlement or the court otherwise directs, or in the case of charitable trusts or pension trusts, where the trustees may act by a majority.[17] So, for example, if there is a trust to sell land with a power to postpone sale, then the power to postpone is only effective so long as all the trustees wish to postpone sale: once one wishes the trust to sell the sale must be carried out, all the trustees being under a duty to sell unless the power to postpone sale is exercised unanimously.[18] Conversely, if there is a trust is to hold land with power to sell it,[19] then sale requires the agreement of all the trustees or an application to the court.[20]

---

13 *Saif Ali v Sydney Mitchell & Co* [1980] A.C. 198 at 218, per Lord Diplock, applied in *Wight v Olswang (No.2)* [2000] W.T.L.R. 783, and on appeal [2001] W.L.T.R. 291. See too *Bristol & West BS v Mothew* [1998] Ch. 1 at 17–18.

14 *Re Rosenthal* [1972] 1 W.L.R. 1273; *Re Pauling's ST* [1964] Ch. 303 at 338 and 339; *National Trustee Co of Australasia v General Finance Co* [1905] A.C. 373. See paras 11–105 to 11–106 for further discussion.

15 *Munch v Cockerell* (1840) 5 Myl. & Cr. 178; *Bahin v Hughes* (1886) 31 Ch.D. 390; *Re Turner* [1897] 1 Ch. 536; *Head v Gould* [1898] 2 Ch. 250. There is no automatic vicarious liability for a co-trustee's breaches of trust, but a trustee will be liable for his own breach of trust if he fails to act jointly with the others and take reasonable steps to monitor their conduct: see e.g. *Re Lucking's WT* [1968] 1 W.L.R. 866.

16 Trustee Act 2000 Pt IV. An individual trustee may delegate his own functions, including distributive functions, under the Trustee Delegation Act 1999. For further discussion see paras 9–211 ff.

17 *Luke v South Kensington Hotel Ltd* (1879) 11 Ch.D. 121; *Re Whiteley* [1910] 1 Ch. 600 at 608 (charitable trusts); Pensions Act 1995 s.32 (pension trusts); *Re Butlin's ST* [1976] Ch. 251 (rectification to allow majority decisions). If decision by majority is allowed then it is not enough that a majority sign a paper recording the decision: the trustees must meet (*Att.-Gen. v Scott* (1750) 1 Ves. Sen. 413).

18 *Re Mayo* [1943] Ch. 302. However, the letter of the trust will not be enforced if so to do would defeat the spirit of the trust: *Jones v Challenger* [1961] 1 Q.B. 176.

19 This is normal for co-ownership under Trusts of Land and Appointment of Trustees Act 1996.

20 Trusts of Land and Appointment of Trustees Act 1996 ss.14, 15.

E. New Trustees

When accepting office as a trustee a person should ascertain the terms of the trust and check that he has been properly appointed. He should inspect all trust documents and ensure that all trust property is properly invested and is in the joint names of himself and his co-trustees,[21] or in the name of a duly authorised nominee or custodian.[22] It is often best to have title deeds or share certificates deposited at a bank in the joint names of the trustees, but in the absence of special circumstances the court will not order one trustee who has possession of the documents to do this.[23] A person who is appointed as a new trustee of an existing trust must investigate any suspicious circumstances which suggest that a breach of trust may have occurred prior to his appointment, so that action can be taken to recoup the trust fund if necessary.[24] **9–10**

2. Compliance with the Terms of the Trust and the General Law

A trustee owes a duty to hold the trust property in an authorised form for the beneficiaries (or for the charitable purposes) identified by the settlor, and to account for his dealings with the property to the beneficiaries (or to the Attorney-General or Charity Commission). To enable the trustee to carry out his managerial and distributive roles, he is typically given powers—to buy and sell trust property, to accumulate income, to distribute income and capital, and so on—but he may not exercise these powers in a way that would be inconsistent with the terms of the trust, most obviously by distributing property to anyone who is not a beneficiary (or applying charitable funds to some unauthorised purpose[25]). Additional limits may also be placed on the trustee's powers by the settlor or by the general law: for example, he may be unable to sell particular trust assets, or to buy particular types of property for investment purposes. **9–11**

When describing these limits on a trustee's powers, it can be said that he owes a proscriptive duty to comply with the terms of the trust and the general law. However, this is not a duty breach of which leads to an award of compensation in the same way that breach of a primary duty to perform a contract triggers an obligation to pay compensatory damages. Hence it may be more illuminating to say that the rules constraining the exercise of trustees' powers disable them from carrying out transactions that are not authorised by the trust instrument or by the general law. **9–12**

The reason why this matters becomes clear when one considers the claims which beneficiaries can bring, and the remedies to which they are entitled, in cases where the trustee purports to dispose of trust property in an unauthorised transaction. For example, he may purport to take trust property for himself or to transfer it to a third party, neither of them being beneficiaries; or to sell trust assets where he lacks the requisite power of sale; or to use trust money to buy a new asset where he lacks the requisite power of investment. In such cases, the courts do not ask whether the trustee has committed a breach of duty, and then calculate the extent of the trustee's liability by asking which of the **9–13**

---

[21] *Hallows v Lloyd* (1888) 39 Ch.D. 686 at 691; *Harvey v Olliver* (1887) 57 L.T. 239; *Tiger v Barclays Bank* [1952] W.N. 38; *Lewis v Nobbs* (1878) 8 Ch.D. 591. For those classes of property not vesting in the new trustee under Trustee Act 1925 s.40, the ordinary modes of transferring the property will have to be used.

[22] Trustee Act 2000 ss.16–23.

[23] *Re Sisson's Settlements* [1903] 1 Ch. 262. Bearer securities have to be deposited with a custodian unless otherwise authorised by the trust instrument: Trustee Act 2000 s.18.

[24] *Re Strahan* (1856) 8 De G. M. & G. 291; *Re Forest of Dean Coal Co* (1878) 10 Ch.D. 250.

[25] cf. Charity Commission, *CC 12: Managing Financial Difficulties and Insolvency in Charities* (Septermber 2004 version), para.34: "It is a breach of trust to use restricted funds for purposes other than those for which they were given"; *The Prevention or Relief of Poverty for the Public Benefit* (December 2008 version), para.G1: "a breach of trust can arise where trustees act outside their duties or powers, including using their charity's property and other resources for something that falls outside the charity's aims".

beneficiaries' losses have been caused by this breach. Instead they treat his unauthorised disposal of trust property as a nullity and order him to perform his continuing duty to hold the trust property in an authorised form, either by returning misapplied assets *in specie*, or by handing over replacement property, or by paying the current monetary value of the property. The mechanics of this, and the ways in which the beneficiaries' remedy differs from an award of damages at common law, are discussed in Chapter 11.

3. Conflicts of Interest

9–14 To maintain confidence in the trust institution by ensuring that the trustee consistently prioritises the beneficiaries' interests over his own interests, Equity holds that a trustee may not place himself in a position where his personal interest and the beneficiaries' interests could possibly conflict.[26]

A. A Disabling Rule

9–15 This rule, like the rule which holds that trustees may not enter unauthorised transactions, has traditionally been understood as a "disabling rule".[27] Historically, the Chancery courts did not hold that trustees owed a positive duty to avoid conflicts of interest, breach of which led to the imposition of a loss- or gain-based liability. Rather, they held that trustees were disabled from entering transactions which entailed an actual or potential conflict of interest.[28] Where a trustee purported to enter such a transaction with the beneficiaries, it followed that the transaction was voidable at the beneficiaries' option. But the Chancery courts did not think of the fiduciary duty of good faith and loyalty as a prescriptive duty, breach of which could lead to the award of a compensatory remedy.[29] Moreover, where the trustee made a profit for himself out of the trust property or his office as trustee, he was disabled from asserting that this profit belonged to him, and was treated instead as though he had intended all along to acquire the profit for the beneficiaries, who were therefore entitled to an order that he should account to them for the profit, or to an order the profit was held on a constructive trust for them.[30]

9–16 In recent years, there has been a significant shift in judicial thinking about the nature of fiduciary duties, particularly in other Commonwealth jurisdictions, as a result of which compensatory claims for breach of fiduciary duty have come to be seen as a conceptually viable possibility.[31] The courts have

---

[26] *Parker v McKenna* (1874) L.R. 10 Ch. App. 96 at 124–125; *Bray v Ford* [1896] A.C. 44 at 51; *Boardman v Phipps* [1967] 2 A.C. 46; *Murad v Al-Saraj* [2005] W.T.L.R. 1573.

[27] See e.g. T. Lewin, *A Practical Treatise on the Law of Trusts and Trustees* (1837), p.376; J. Hill, *A Practical Treatise on the Law Relating to Trustees* (1845), pp. 554–561; E. Vintner, *The History and Law of Fiduciary Relationship and Resulting Trust* 3rd ed (1955), Ch.1.

[28] *Tito v Waddell (No.2)* [1977] Ch. 106 at 248, per Megarry V.C.: "what equity does is to subject trustees to particular disabilities in cases falling within the self-dealing and fair-dealing rules." See too *Re Bloye's WT* (1849) 1 Mac. & G. 488 at 495, per Lord Cottenham L.C.; *McPherson v Watt* (1877) 3 App. Cas. 254 at 266, per Lord O'Hagan.

[29] L. Sealy, "Some Principles of Fiduciary Obligation" [1963] C.L.J. 119, esp. at pp. 124 and 135–137; "Fiduciary Obligations: Forty Years On" (1995) 9 J.C.L. 37 at pp. 51–52; and "Directors' Duties Revisited" (2001) 22 Co. Law. 79 at pp. 80–81. For a contrary (but in our view less plausible) reading of the C19 authorities, see M. Conaglen, "Equitable Compensation for Breach of the Fiduciary Dealing Rules" (2003) 119 L.Q.R. 246.

[30] *Regal (Hastings) Ltd v Gulliver* [1967] 2 A.C. 134 at 159, per Lord Porter: "Directors, no doubt, are not trustees, but they occupy a fiduciary position towards the company whose board they form. Their liability in this respect does not depend upon breach of duty but upon the proposition that a director must not make a profit out of property acquired by reason of his relationship to the company of which he is a director." See too *Fawcett v Whitehouse* (1829) 1 Russ. & M. 132 at 149; *Re Canadian Oil Works Corp* (1875) L.R. 10 Ch. App. 593 at 601; *Furs Ltd v Tomkies* (1936) 54 C.L.R. 583 at 592; *Scott v Scott* (1963) 109 C.L.R. 649; *Guinness Plc v Saunders* (1987) 3 B.C.C. 271 at 287.

[31] e.g. *Warman International Ltd v Dwyer* (1995) 182 C.L.R. 544 at 559; *Breen v Williams* (1996) 186 C.L.R. 71 at 113; *Swindle v Harrison* [1997] 4 All E.R. 705; *Aequitas v AEFC* (2001) 19 A.C.L.C. 1,006 at [428] and [442]; *Re MDA Investment Management Ltd* [2005] B.C.C. 783 at [70]; *Stevens v Premium Real Estate Ltd* [2009] 2 N.Z.L.R. 284. And note *Nocton v Lord Ashburton* [1914] A.C. 465.

also begun to characterise a trustee's liability to account for unauthorised profits as a wrong-based remedy for breach of his duty "not to promote his personal interest by making or pursuing a gain in circumstances in which there is a conflict or a real or substantial possibility of a conflict between his personal interests and those of the persons whom he is bound to protect."[32] We share Lord Millett's view that this represents a departure from Equity's traditional approach, which was to insist that the trustee "must be taken to have received the money for and on behalf of [the beneficiary] and accordingly must account to him for it":[33] i.e. Equity did not traditionally say that the trustee had wrongfully committed a breach of duty, for the profits of which he had to account; rather, it said that the trustee was disabled from doing anything other than the right thing by holding unauthorised profits for the beneficiaries.

The rules governing unauthorised fiduciary profits, and the constructive trusts that can be imposed on them, are discussed further in Chapter 15,[34] and the rules governing the payment of trustees for the performance of their duties are considered in Chapter 8.[35] In the rest of this section we shall discuss the situation where trustees purchase trust property. **9–17**

B. *Purchase of Trust Property by Trustees*

A trustee who is the sole legal owner of trust property cannot sell or lease the property to himself,[36] but often there is more than one trustee, in which case rights might be transferred from the trustees collectively to an individual trustee for his own benefit. A trustee might also buy his beneficiary's equitable interest, so that the legal and equitable titles become merged and he becomes the absolute beneficial owner of the property. In cases of this kind, the trustee must beware of the "fair dealing" and "self-dealing rules", defined by Megarry V.C. in *Tito v Waddell (No.2)* as follows:[37] **9–18**

> "The self-dealing rule is . . . that if a trustee sells the trust property to himself, the sale is voidable by any beneficiary *ex debito justitiae*, however fair the transaction. The fair-dealing rule is . . . that if a trustee purchases the beneficial interest of any of his beneficiaries, the transaction is not voidable *ex debito justitiae*, but can be set aside by the beneficiary unless the trustee can show that he has taken no advantage of his position and has made full disclosure to the beneficiary, and that the transaction is fair and honest."

Megarry V.C. thought that these are "two rules: the consequences are different, and the property and the transactions which invoke the rules are different."[38] However, the better view is that the rules are not separate, but applications of the same principle to differing sets of facts, namely the principle that "no one who has a duty to perform shall place himself in a situation to have his interests conflicting with that duty."[39] The rules are often thought to be distinct because the substantive **9–19**

---

[32] *Hospital Products Ltd v United States Surgical Corp* (1984) 156 C.L.R. 41 at 103, per Mason J. For a case which equivocates between the old and new approaches, see *Gwembe Valley Development Co Ltd v Koshy (No.3)* [2002] 1 B.C.L.C. 478, esp. at [103]–[108].

[33] Lord Millett, "Book Review" (2002) 2 O.U.C.L.J. 291, at p.295. See too Lord Millett, "Proprietary Restitution" in S. Degeling and J. Edelman (eds), *Equity in Commercial Law* (2005).

[34] See para.15–71.

[35] See paras 8–57 ff.

[36] *Rye v Rye* [1962] A.C. 496; *Ingram v IRC* [2000] 1 A.C. 293, as affected by the Law of Property Act 1925 s.72. Further see B.H. McPherson, "Self-dealing Trustees" in A.J. Oakley (ed.), *Trends in Contemporary Trust Law* (1996).

[37] [1977] Ch. 106 at 241.

[38] *Tito* at 241.

[39] *Broughton v Broughton* (1855) 5 De G.M. & G. 160 at 164, quoted in *Movitex Ltd v Bulfield* [1988] B.C.LC 104 at 117.

fairness of the impugned transaction is relevant to the validity of transactions caught by the "fair dealing rule", but irrelevant to the validity of transactions caught by the "self-dealing rule". However, this difference is more apparent than real, because the relevance of the fairness of the transaction in "fair dealing" cases is simply that it provides evidence as to whether the trustee has made full disclosure of all the material facts to the beneficiaries with whom he has dealt, and whose consent he needs before he can act in a way that might cause a conflict between their interests and his own.[40]

9–20 The prohibition against purchase by a trustee applies whether or not he himself fixes the price. In *Wright v Morgan*,[41] a testator left land on trust for sale with power to postpone sale for seven years and provided that it should be offered at a price to be fixed by valuers to one of his sons, X, who was one of the trustees. X assigned his right (which was treated as an option and not a right of pre-emption) to his brother, Y, who was also one of the trustees, but who was not authorised to purchase the land by the terms of the will. Y arranged for the sale to himself, retired from his office as trustee, and purchased the land at a price fixed by the valuers. If X had assigned his right to a stranger, Z, then Z could properly have purchased the land (assuming that the right was assignable and not personal to X). Nevertheless, it was held that the sale could be set aside. A potential conflict of interest existed because Y, as a trustee, was one of those responsible for determining when the land was first to be offered for sale (and prices could fluctuate over the years), and for determining the terms of payment, e.g. cash or instalments with interest payable. Of course, if X had exercised his right and had the land conveyed to him, then a subsequent conveyance to Y would have been unimpeachable.

9–21 The prohibition against purchase by the trustee is applicable where the sale is conducted at an auction held by the trustee himself,[42] since the trustee is in a position to discourage bidders. Furthermore, where the sale is conducted, not by the trustee, but a third party, as, for example, where a trustee holds trust property subject to a mortgage and the mortgagee sells under his power of sale, the trustee may not buy the property, since he might otherwise prefer his personal interest to his duty,[43] and this is so whether or not he could have prevented the sale.[44] The rule is a strong one and is not circumvented by the device of the trustee selling to a third party to hold on trust for him.[45] But if there is no prior agreement and the sale is in all respects bona fide, then there is no objection to the trustee subsequently buying the trust property from the person to whom he sold it,[46] although if he contracts to sell the property to X, a stranger, and before the conveyance is made he purchases the benefit of the contract from X, then the contract can be set aside.[47] Moreover, if the trustee has retired from the trust with the intention of purchasing the property then the sale can be avoided,[48] but it is otherwise if at the date of his retirement he had no idea of making the purchase, unless the circumstances show that when he made the purchase he used information acquired by him while a trustee.[49]

---

[40] M. Conaglen, "A Re-Appraisal of the Fiduciary Self-Dealing and Fair Dealing Rules" [2006] C.L.J. 366.
[41] [1926] A.C. 788.
[42] *Whelpdale v Cookson* (1747) 1 Ves. Sen. 9; *Campbell v Walker* (1800) 5 Ves. 678 at 682.
[43] *Newgate Stud Co v Penfold* [2008] 1 B.C.L.C. 46 at [222]. See too A. W. Scott, "The Trustee's Duty of Loyalty" (1936) 49 Harvard Law Review 521 at 529–530.
[44] *Griffith v Owen* [1907] 1 Ch. 195, where it was held that the tenant for life of an equity of redemption could not purchase the property for himself from the mortgagee selling under his power of sale.
[45] *Michoud v Girod* (1846) 4 How. 503 (US).
[46] *Re Postlethwaite* (1888) 37 W.R. 200.
[47] *Williams v Scott* [1900] A.C. 499.
[48] *Wright v Morgan* [1926] A.C. 788.
[49] *Re Boles and British Land Co's Contract* [1902] 1 Ch. 244. A trustee who has disclaimed is not caught by the rule: *Stacey v Elph* (1833) 1 Myl. & K. 195; cf. *Clark v Clark* (1884) 9 App. Cas. 733 at 737.

The rule is sufficiently strong and elastic to prevent a trustee from selling the trust property to a company of which he is the principal shareholder,[50] managing director or other principal officer,[51] or to a partnership of which he is a member.[52] Of course, the rule also applies to corporate trustees, so that a trust corporation cannot in the absence of authorisation by the trust instrument or consent of the beneficiaries or approval of the court sell the trust property either to itself or to its subsidiaries.[53] However, sale of property to a trustee's spouse is not absolutely prohibited by the self-dealing rule; rather, by virtue of the fair dealing rule, the trustee must discharge the burden of showing that the transaction is in the best interests of the beneficiaries.[54] **9–22**

Where a sale takes place in breach of the rules outlined above, the beneficiaries have a number of remedies open to them. They may claim any profit made by the trustee on a resale of the property. If the property has not been resold then they can insist on a reconveyance, or alternatively they can demand that it be offered for sale again. If on this occasion a higher price is bid than the price which the trustee paid, then it will be sold at that price. If not, then the trustee may at the option of the beneficiaries be allowed to retain the property, and in the nature of things the beneficiaries will confer this doubtful favour upon him where the property has fallen in value since he purchased it.[55] The right which the beneficiaries have to avoid the sale is an equitable one, and as such is liable to be lost through laches, but for laches to apply the beneficiaries must have full knowledge of the facts and must acquiesce in the situation for an unreasonably long period.[56] Further, the right to have the sale set aside may be lost if the court in the exercise of its inherent jurisdiction sets the seal of its approval on the transaction, and it seems that not only may the court authorise a sale which is about to take place, but in a suitable case it may ratify one which has already occurred.[57] **9–23**

This all presupposes that the sale has taken place without the consent of the beneficiaries. However, where they are of full capacity they may authorise the sale, which will then stand, provided that the trustee made a full disclosure,[58] and did not induce the sale by taking advantage of his relation to the beneficiaries or by other improper conduct, as evidenced by the fact that the transaction was apparently fair and reasonable.[59] The onus of proof is on the trustee to show affirmatively that these conditions existed, but there is no objection to the consent of the beneficiaries being obtained after the sale to the trustees.[60] Sales will also stand if they are expressly or impliedly authorised by the trust instrument,[61] if they are authorised by the court, and if they are made pursuant to a contract or option[62] arising before the trusteeship arose. **9–24**

---

[50] *Silkstone & Haigh Moor Coal Co v Edey* [1900] 1 Ch. 167; *Farrars v Farrars Ltd* (1888) 40 Ch.D. 395. A mortgagee can exercise his power of sale in favour of a company in which he is interested only if he shows he acted in good faith and took all reasonable steps to obtain the best price reasonably obtainable: *Tse Kwong Lam v Wong Chit Sen* [1983] 1 W.L.R. 1349; cf. *Bank of Scotland v Neath Port Talbot CBC* [2008] B.C.C. 376.

[51] *Re Thompson's Settlement* [1986] Ch. 99 at 114–115; cf. *Eberhardt v Christiana Window Glass Co* (1911) 9 Del. Ch. 284 (US).

[52] *Colgate's Executor v Colgate* (1873) 23 N.J. Eq. 372 (US).

[53] *Purchase v Atlantic Safe Deposit and Trust Co* (1913) 81 N.J. Eq. 334 (U.S.).

[54] *Newgate Stud Co v Penfold* [2008] 1 B.C.L.C. 46 at [233] ff., following *Burrell v Burrell's Trustees* 1915 S.C. 33. See too *Ferraby v Hobson* (1847) 2 Ph. 255 at 261; *Re Douglas* [1928] 29 S.R. (N.S.W.) 48; *Re King's WT* (1959) 173 E.G. 627; *Tito v Waddell (No.2)* [1977] Ch. 106 at 240.

[55] For further details, see *Holder v Holder* [1966] 2 All E.R. 116 at 130, per Cross J.

[56] For discussion, see para.11–135.

[57] *Farmer v Dean* (1863) 32 Beav. 327; *Campbell v Walker* (1800) 5 Ves. 678.

[58] *Newgate Stud Co v Penfold* [2008] 1 B.C.L.C. 46 at [227].

[59] *Gibson v Jeyes* (1801) 6 Ves. 266; *Coles v Trecothick* (1804) 9 Ves. 234; *Morse v Royal* (1806) 12 Ves. 355; cf. *Fox v Mackreth* (1788) 2 Bro. C.C. 400. These factors can make it difficult for the trustee to find a purchaser when he himself wishes to sell, as a purchaser will be bound by a beneficiary's equity to set aside the transaction if he has actual or constructive notice.

[60] T.B. Ruoff, "Purchases in Breach of Trust: A Suggested Cure" (1954) 18 Conv. (N.S.) 528.

[61] *Sargeant v National Westminster Bank* (1990) 61 P. & C.R. 518; *Edge v Pensions Ombudsman* [1998] Ch. 512, affirmed [2000] Ch. 602; *Breakspear v Ackland* [2009] Ch. 32.

[62] *Re Mulholland's WT* [1949] 1 All E.R. 460.

4. Notification of Beneficiaries and Provision of Trust Information

A. Notification of Beneficiaries

9–25 In *Armitage v Nurse*, Millett L.J. (as he then was) stated that:[63]

> "there is an irreducible core of obligations owed by the trustees to the beneficiaries and enforceable by them which is fundamental to the concept of a trust. If the beneficiaries have no rights enforceable against the trustees there are no trusts."

If a trust is purportedly created for a beneficiary who can never actually exercise his rights against the trustee because he does not know that he is a beneficiary, then it cannot meaningfully be said that he has any enforceable rights, and so it cannot be said that there is a trust at all. Hence, to give substance to the beneficiary's core right to performance of the trust, a sui juris beneficiary has the right to be told that he is a beneficiary, and the trustee owes a concomitant duty to notify him of this fact.[64] However, the trustee's duty of notification is only a duty to take reasonable steps in all the circumstances, and if the objects of a power consist of more than one category of person, e.g. for issue, relatives and employees of the settlor, then the court is likely to consider that by necessary implication the settlor only intended that the trustee should inform the first group, as the primary objects of his bounty.[65]

9–26 In *Schmidt v Rosewood Trust Ltd*,[66] parts of which are reproduced below,[67] Lord Walker stressed that no bright-line distinction should be made between beneficiaries under discretionary trusts and objects of discretionary powers of appointment for the purposes of the rules on disclosure of trust information. By extension his comments must also apply to notification. The nub of the matter is the strength of the claimant's claim to benefit, depending upon whether he is intended to receive significant bounty from the settlor via his trustees, a question of fact and of degree in all the circumstances, including the contents of any letter of wishes (discussed further below).[68]

9–27 Suppose, for example, that a settlor declares a discretionary trust for his descendants, his other relatives known to his trustees, and employees and ex-employees of X Co Ltd (which he founded). In this case, the latter two classes are likely to be treated as peripheral with the result that they do not have as extensive rights as the former two classes. Similarly, if there was also a power of appointment vested in the trustees in favour of English charities benefiting children or of any charity in Vanuatu, such charities' interests should also be considered peripheral. Conversely, however, suppose that there is a discretionary trust to accumulate income for the trust period and then distribute the capital between such English charities as the trustees then see fit in their discretion, but with a power, instead, to appoint income or capital from time to time to the descendants of the settlor and their spouses or cohabitants. In this case, the descendant-objects are likely to be the primary focus of the

---

63 [1998] Ch. 241 at 253. See too D.J. Hayton, "The Irreducible Core Content of Trusteeship" in A.J. Oakley (ed.) *Trends in Contemporary Trust Law* (1996).

64 *Brittlebank v Goodwin* (1868) L.R.5 Eq. 541 at 550; *Hawkesley v May* [1956] 1 Q.B. 304; *Foreman v Kingston* [2005] W.T.L.R. 823 at [85]. The beneficiary also has the right to be told the name and address of the trustee to whom a request can be made for a discretionary distribution: *Re Murphy's ST* [1999] 1 W.L.R. 282, where the judge treated the claimant as a primary object of a power of appointment in a discretionary trust. In the case of a testamentary trust or the statutory intestacy trust, the executor is under no duty to disclose the gift to the specified beneficiaries (*Re Lewis* [1904] Ch. 656) until the estate has been fully administered and the net trust fund ascertained in which the beneficiaries for the first time acquire an equitable proprietary interest (that is different from the equitable chose in action to have the estate duly administered: see para.1–122).

65 *Re Manisty's Settlements* [1974] Ch. 17 at 25.

66 [2003] 2 A.C. 709 at [66].

67 At paras 9–37 ff.

68 See D.J. Hayton, "Beneficiaries' and Objects' Rights to Information" (2003) 10 Jo. Int. Trust & Corp. P. 139.

settlor's bounty with the charities only having a peripheral interest in the capital, if any, left at the end of the period.

B. Provision of Trust Accounts

A beneficiary has the right, exercisable at reasonable intervals, to inspect accounts prepared by the trustees explaining the current whereabouts of the trust property and the history of their dealings with it.[69] The trustees owe a correlative duty to keep proper accounts and to produce these on demand, along with supporting oral or documentary information.[70] Trustees "who indefensibly fail to produce accounts may be ordered to pay not only the costs of proceedings to obtain the accounts but also the costs of taking the account which is ordered".[71] Note that "every beneficiary is entitled to see the trust accounts, whether his interest is in possession or not".[72] Thus, any beneficiary with a future interest,[73] including (so far as practicable) a person who is merely the likely object of a discretionary trust or power which may never actually be exercised in his favour,[74] has the means to discover a breach of trust which he may then take action to redress.[75] **9–28**

C. Other Trust Documents

In *Re Londonderry's Settlement*,[76] the Court of Appeal drew a distinction between trust accounts and other "trust documents" which could be inspected by a beneficiary, and material which did not count as "trust documents", and which was therefore not available for inspection, for example correspondence between the trustees themselves, or between the trustees and beneficiaries, and the agenda for trustees' meetings. Moreover, while "trust documents" included minutes of trustees' meetings and other documents of the trustees disclosing their deliberations on the exercise of their discretions or their reasons for any particular exercise of their discretions or "the material upon which such reasons were or might have been based", these were exempt from the beneficiaries' right to inspect trust documents. Otherwise, the right of trustees not to be obliged to give reasons for the exercise of their discretionary distributive functions would be undermined.[77] This still enabled beneficiaries to see a factual aide-memoire on the state of the fund, past distributions and future possibilities, and legal advice as to the law relating to the manner in which trustees were entitled to exercise their discre- **9–29**

---

[69] He can take copies of these accounts at his own expense or pay the trustee for copies provided by the trustee for an agreed sum representing the cost to the trustee: *Kemp v Burn* (1863) 4 Giff. 348; *Re Watson* (1904) 49 Sol. Jo. 54.

[70] *White v Lady Lincoln* (1803) 8 Ves. Jun. 363; *Pearse v Green* (1819) 1 Jac. & W. 135 at 140; *Eglin v Sanderson* (1862) 3 Giff. 434 at 440; *Re Cowin* (1886) 33 Ch.D. 179; *Re Rabaiotti's 1989 Settlement* [2000] W.T.L.R. 953; *Schmidt v Rosewood Trust Ltd* [2003] 2 A.C. 709.

[71] *Mason v Coleman* [2007] EWHC 3149 (Ch) at [93]. See too *Kemp v Burn* (1863) 4 Giff 348; *Jefferys v Marshall* (1870) 23 L.T. 548; *Re Skinner* [1904] 1 Ch. 289; *Re Den Haag Trust* (1997/98) 1 O.F.L.R. 495.

[72] *Armitage v Nurse* [1998] Ch. 241 at 261, per Millett L.J. Unless there is a possibility of income being accumulated and added to capital it seems that a capital beneficiary is, however, not entitled to see the income accounts disposing of income to income beneficiaries: *Nestlé v National Westminster Bank* [2000] W.T.L.R. 795 at 822; but he must be entitled to check that the investment policy keeps an equitable balance between income and capital beneficiaries: see paras 9–140 ff.

[73] Including contingent interests: *Re Tillott* [1892] 1 Ch. 86; *Att.-Gen. of Ontario v Stavro* (1995) 119 D.L.R. (4th) 750.

[74] *Chaine-Nickson v Bank of Ireland* [1976] I.R. 393; *Spellson v George* (1987) 11 N.S.W.L.R. 300 at 315–316; *Hartigan Nominees Pty Ltd v Rydge* (1992) 29 N.S.W.L.R. 405; *Re Rabbaiotti's 1989 Settlement* [2000] W.T.L.R. 953; *Schmidt v Rosewood Trust Ltd* [2003] 2 A.C. 709.

[75] Although time does not begin to run against him until he obtains a present interest in the trust property because "he should not be compelled to litigate (at considerable personal expense) in respect of an injury to an interest which he may never live to enjoy": *Armitage* at 261.

[76] [1965] Ch. 818.

[77] *Re Beloved Wilkes' Charity* (1851) 3 Mac. & G. 440; *Wilson v Law Debenture Trust Corp* [1995] 2 All E.R. 337.

tions; but there was no right to see legal advice obtained by a trustee (which should be at his own expense) for his own protection when aware of likely proceedings against him[78] or to any evidence on a *Beddoe's* application by trustees for directions whether to take proceedings against a beneficiary.[79]

9–30 Following the Privy Council's decision in *Schmidt v Rosewood Trust Ltd*,[80] however, it now seems futile to try to distinguish "trust documents" from other documents that a beneficiary or an object of a power seeks to inspect. When acting in its inherent equitable jurisdiction to supervise, and if appropriate to intervene in, the administration of trusts, the court can order the trustee to give the claimant access to all documents and information relating to the trusteeship functions that the court thinks it appropriate for the beneficiary to see. Once the claimant has satisfied the court that he has more than a theoretical possibility of benefiting, not having a remote or peripheral or likely defeasible interest, then the court will order disclosure, unless there are issues as to personal[81] or commercial[82] confidentiality, in which case the court must balance the competing interests of different beneficiaries, the trustees themselves, and third parties.[83] It may be that some documents will be disclosed in redacted form or with parts obliterated, while safeguards may be imposed (whether by undertakings to the court or arrangements for inspection only by the claimant's professional advisers or otherwise) to limit the use which may be made of documents or information disclosed under the order of the court.[84] In particular, discretionary beneficiaries and objects are not entitled to the reasons for the exercise by trustees of their discretion but must respect the autonomy of the trustees in exercising their discretionary distributive functions.[85]

D. Letters of Wishes

9–31 Difficult issues arise where a settlor provides the trustees with a letter of wishes that he intends to guide them when they exercise their discretionary powers (e.g. to appoint property to the beneficiaries of a discretionary trust). Such letters have special significance after the settlor's death, because while alive the settlor should in any event be consulted by the trustees before a significant exercise of their discretionary distributive functions.[86] Such letters are brought into existence for the purposes of the operation of the trust, and they must be handed on from a retiring trustee to the new trustee, some regard needing to be had to them before a discretionary decision is taken on any matter to which they refer, even if the trustees exercising their independent discretion then decide to ignore a particular wish.[87] Thus, a letter of wishes is a trust document that is legally significant, although not so significant as the trust deed itself unless, exceptionally, the settlor intends the letter to be legally binding so as to override the trust deed to the extent necessary to give effect to what was laid down in the letter.[88]

---

[78] *Talbot v Marshfield* (1865) 2 Dr. & Sm. 549; *Bacon v Bacon* (1876) 3 4 L.T. 349.
[79] *Re Eaton* [1964] 1 W.L.R. 1269; *Midland Bank Trust Co Ltd v Green* [1980] Ch. 590 at 604–609.
[80] [2003] 2 A.C. 709.
[81] e.g. as to a beneficiary's needs as a drug addict or an HIV positive person.
[82] e.g. where a rival businessman or litigant against the trustees purchases an equitable interest under a trust to discover more about trust matters: *Rouse v 100F Australia Trustees Ltd* [2002] W.T.L.R. 111 at 128–129.
[83] *Schmidt* at [67].
[84] *Schmidt* at [54].
[85] *Re Londonderry's Settlement* [1965] Ch. 918; *Foreman v Kingston* [2005] W.T.L.R. 823 at [99]. Quaere whether the beneficiaries of pension trusts may earn more extensive rights?
[86] *Abacus Trust Co v Barr* [2003] Ch. 409 at [23]–[25].
[87] *Bank of Nova Scotia Trust Co (Bahamas) Ltd v Ricart de Barletta* 1 Butterworths Offshore Cases & Materials 5, discussed by H. Thompson in (1994) 3 Jo. Int. T. & Corp. P. 35. Further see D.J. Hayton (1999) 32 Vanderbilt Jo. of Transnat. Law 555, at pp. 573–576.
[88] *Chase Manhattan Equities Ltd v Goodman* [1991] B.C.L.C. 897 at 923.

Nevertheless, in *Breakspear v Ackland*,[89] reproduced below,[90] Briggs J. held that letters of wishes are generally subject to the *Londonderry* principle that the exercise by trustees of their dispositive discretionary powers should be regarded, from start to finish, as an essentially confidential process. A document brought into existence for the sole or predominant purpose of being used in such a process is itself properly to be regarded as confidential, so that the trustees ordinarily need not disclose it to beneficiaries merely because they ask to see it, unless, in the trustees' view, disclosure is in the interests of the sound administration of the trust, and the exercise of their discretions. **9–32**

Upon reaching the latter stage, however, one wonders why the beneficiaries should not have a right to see the letter of wishes where it concerns a matter of which they complain involving the sound administration of the trust and the proper exercise of the trustees' discretions. After all, the trustees' discretions can only be exercised in a responsible manner for the purposes for which they were conferred upon the trustees,[91] as indicated by the settlor in his legally significant letter of wishes. How can a beneficiary make the trustees account to him for the exercise of their discretions unless he knows the purposes for which these discretions were conferred? In trying to establish a prima facie case the beneficiary is fighting the trustee in circumstances where the beneficiary is blind-folded and has one arm tied behind his back. **9–33**

Consider the case of a discretionary trust for A, B, C, D, E and F where the trustees are directed not to inform D, E and F that they are beneficiaries, and so are not to show them the trust deed, and that the settlor's letter of wishes is expressly confidential to the trustees and A, B and C. Should the court not hold that not only are D, E and F entitled to be told they are beneficiaries, and to see the trust deed, but that they are also entitled to see the letter of wishes? The first two restrictions, amounting to keeping the trust deed confidential, are repugnant to, or inconsistent with, the trust concept which requires the beneficiaries having an irreducible core of rights against the trustees.[92] Is not a confidentiality restriction in a letter of wishes similarly repugnant to the trust concept because, if it prevents a beneficiary from knowing what is the purpose behind a particular discretionary power, then he cannot possibly allege the trustee is not responsibly exercising the power for the purpose for which it was conferred on the trustee by the settlor? **9–34**

What if the letter of wishes was expressed to be confidential between the settlor and the trustee so as not to be disclosed to A, B, C, D, E or F? Is the position the equivalent of the trust deed being expressed to be similarly confidential, which would clearly be ignored as repugnant to the trust concept unless one accepted it as forming the basis of a claim that the trust was a sham? Such argument has a logical attraction which may yet appeal to a court taking account of its broad inherent jurisdiction expounded in *Schmidt v Rosewood Trust Ltd*.[93] To avoid problems, the letter of wishes should provide for it to be disclosed to, say, two responsible members of the class of beneficiaries or if, as yet, there are no ascertained beneficiaries of full capacity to, say, two members of a class of objects of the power who have a right to make the trustees account; or, if there are none yet ascertained of full capacity, then to a person designated as a protector until there is an ascertained person of full capacity with a right to make the trustees account. However, it would be open to a court to require the letter to be made generally available to beneficiaries or objects subject to deletion of any personal or commercial confidential information. **9–35**

---

[89] [2009] Ch 32. See too *Re Rabbaiotti's 1989 Settlement* [2000] W.T.L.R. 953; *Hartigan Nominees Pty Ltd v Rydge* (1992) 29 N.S.W.L.R 405.
[90] At paras 9–43 ff.
[91] *Re Hay's ST* [1982] 1 W.L.R. 202 at 209; *Re Beatty's WT* [1990] 3 All E.R. 844 at 846; *McPhail v Doulton* [1971] A.C. 424 at 449.
[92] *Armitage v Nurse* [1998] Ch. 241 at 253.
[93] [2003] 2 A.C. 709.

E. Beneficiaries' Rights to Disclosure in Course of Civil Litigation

9–36 So far, we have been concerned with the rights of a beneficiary or object of a fiduciary power, to whom the trustee must account for the trusteeships to obtain disclosure of trust documents and supporting information under the law of trusts. Quite separately, under the Civil Procedure Rules governing civil litigation,[94] if a beneficiary can make out a properly particularised claim (so that it cannot be struck down as a mere "fishing expedition" to see if material can be found to support a claim) then this triggers standard disclosure of documents that can advance or hinder either party's case. Subsequent applications can also be made in relation to specific disclosure of documents not disclosed pursuant to standard disclosure. Previously, a similar procedure was known as "discovery", and the order in *Re Londonderry's Settlement* was expressly made "without prejudice to any right of the defendant to discovery in separate proceedings against the plaintiffs." As Robert Walker J. has pointed out:[95]

> "If a decision taken by trustees is directly attacked in legal proceedings, the trustees may be compelled either legally (through discovery or subpoena) or practically (in order to avoid adverse inferences being drawn) to disclose the substance of the reasons for their decision".

SCHMIDT v ROSEWOOD TRUST LIMITED

Privy Council [2003] 2 A.C. 709; [2003] 2 W.L.R. 1442; [2003] 3 All E.R. 76

9–37 The petitioner sought disclosure of documents relating to two settlements of which his late father was a settlor. He was himself a possible object of a power of appointment vested in the trustees, and the administrator of his father's estate, his father also having been a possible object of a power of appointment vested in the trustees. The trustees resisted disclosure, arguing that trust documents only need to be disclosed to trust beneficiaries by virtue of the beneficiaries' proprietary interests in the documents, with the result that they need not be disclosed to the objects of powers of appointment. This proprietary analysis of disclosure rights was rejected by the Privy Council.

LORD WALKER (speaking for the court, which consisted of LORD NICHOLLS, LORD HOPE, LORD HUTTON, LORD HOFFMANN and LORD WALKER):

Disclosure to Discretionary Beneficiaries: A Proprietary Basis?

9–38 Much of the debate before the Board addressed the question whether a beneficiary's right or claim to disclosure of trust documents should be regarded as a proprietary right. Mr Brownbill argued that it should be classified in that way, and from that starting point he argued that no object of a mere power could have any right or claim to disclosure, because he had no proprietary interest in the trust property . . .

9–39 Their Lordships consider that the more principled and correct approach is to regard the right to seek disclosure of trust documents as one aspect of the court's inherent jurisdiction to supervise, and if necessary to intervene in, the administration of trusts. The right to seek the court's intervention does not depend on entitlement to a fixed and transmissible beneficial interest. The object of a discretion (including a mere power) may also be entitled to protection from a court of equity, although the circumstances in which he may seek protection, and the nature of the protection he may expect to obtain, will depend on the court's

[94] CPR Pt 31 and the related Practice Direction. It is also possible to obtain pre-action disclosure of specific documents discoverable under standard disclosure post-action: see CPR r.31.16 and *Black v Sumitomo Corp* [2002] 1 W.L.R. 156 (if desirable to save costs or dispose fairly of the proceedings or assist the dispute to be resolved without proceedings).

[95] *Scott v National Trust* [1998] 2 All E.R. 705 at 719, and to similar effect Buxton L.J. in *Taylor v Midland Bank Trust Co* (2000) 2 I.T.E.L.R. 439 at 459–461.

discretion.[96] Mr Brownbill's submission to the contrary effect tends to prove too much, since he would regard the object of a discretionary trust as having a proprietary interest even though it is not transmissible (except in the special case of collective action taken unanimously by all the members of a closed class).

9–40 Their Lordships are therefore in general agreement with the approach adopted in the judgments of Kirby P. and Sheller J.A. in the Court of Appeal of New South Wales in *Hartigan Nominees Pty Ltd v Rydge*.[97] . . . It will be observed that Kirby P. said that for an applicant to have a proprietary right might be sufficient, but was not necessary. In the Board's view it is neither sufficient nor necessary. Since *In re Cowin*[98] well over a century ago the court has made clear that there may be circumstances (especially of confidentiality) in which even a vested and transmissible beneficial interest is not a sufficient basis for requiring disclosure of trust documents; and *In re Londonderry's Settlement*[99] and more recent cases have begun to work out in some detail the way in which the court should exercise its discretion in such cases. There are three such areas in which the court may have to form a discretionary judgment: whether a discretionary object (or some other beneficiary with only a remote or wholly defeasible interest) should be granted relief at all; what classes of documents should be disclosed, either completely or in a redacted form; and what safeguards should be imposed (whether by undertakings to the court, arrangements for professional inspection, or otherwise) to limit the use which may be made of documents or information disclosed under the order of the court. . . .

Conclusion

9–41 Their Lordships have already indicated their view that a beneficiary's right to seek disclosure of trust documents, although sometimes not inappropriately described as a proprietary right, is best approached as one aspect of the court's inherent jurisdiction to supervise (and where appropriate intervene in) the administration of trusts. There is therefore in their Lordships' view no reason to draw any bright dividing-line either between transmissible and non-transmissible (that is, discretionary) interests, or between the rights of an object of a discretionary trust and those of the object of a mere power (of a fiduciary character). The differences in this context between trusts and powers are (as Lord Wilberforce demonstrated in *McPhail v Doulton*[100]) a good deal less significant than the similarities. The tide of Commonwealth authority, although not entirely uniform, appears to be flowing in that direction.

9–42 However the recent cases also confirm (as had been stated as long ago as *In re Cowin* in 1886) that no beneficiary (and least of all a discretionary object) has any entitlement as of right to disclosure of anything which can plausibly be described as a trust document. Especially when there are issues as to personal or commercial confidentiality, the court may have to balance the competing interests of different beneficiaries, the trustees themselves, and third parties. Disclosure may have to be limited and safeguards may have to be put in place. Evaluation of the claims of a beneficiary (and especially of a discretionary object) may be an important part of the balancing exercise which the court has to perform on the materials placed before it. In many cases the court may have no difficulty in concluding that an applicant with no more than a theoretical possibility of benefit ought not to be granted any relief.

BREAKSPEAR v ACKLAND

Chancery Division [2009] Ch. 32, [2008] 3 W.L.R. 698, [2008] 2 All E.R. (Comm) 62

9–43 The settlor of a family discretionary trust gave a non-binding "wish letter" to the trustees in which he requested that they take stated matters into account when exercising their dispositive powers. Three of the beneficiaries (who were the settlor's children) asked the trustees to disclose the contents of the letter in

[96] See Lord Wilberforce in *Gartside v IRC* [1968] A.C. 553 at 617–618, and in *McPhail v Doulton* [1971] A.C. 424 at 456–457; Templeman J. in *Re Manisty's Settlement* [1974] Ch. 17 at 27–28; and Warner J. in *Mettoy Pension Trustees Ltd v Evans* [1990] 1 W.L.R. 1587 at 1617–1618.
[97] (1992) 29 N.S.W.L.R. 405.
[98] (1886) 33 Ch.D. 179.
[99] [1965] Ch. 918.
[100] [1971] A.C. 424.

order to evaluate their future expectations under the trust, but the trustees refused on the ground that the wish letter was confidential and its disclosure would cause family discord. The beneficiaries successfully brought an action for disclosure of the letter. The passages of Briggs J.'s judgment reproduced here concern the general principles governing disclosure of letters of wishes.

9–44 BRIGGS J.: The essential characteristic of a wish letter . . . is that it is a mechanism for the communication by a settlor to trustees of the settlement of non-binding requests by him to take stated matters into account when exercising their discretionary powers. Typically, wish letters are concerned with the exercise of dispositive discretions, but they may include wishes in relation to the exercise of powers of investment, or of other purely administrative powers. . . . The large increase in the use of wish letters has gone hand in hand with the rise in the popularity of discretionary trusts, in preference to the more detailed fixed interest trust. The combination of a broad discretionary trust accompanied by a wish letter may be said to have two particular advantages. The first, an advantage which it enjoys over the old-fashioned fixed interest trust, is that it preserves flexibility for the trustees in responding to changes in the beneficiaries' circumstances which are not or cannot be foreseen by the settlor. The second advantage, which stems from the placing of the trusts affecting the property and the settlor's non-binding wishes into separate documents, is that the settlor may make use of a confidential wish letter as the medium for the written expression of facts, beliefs, expectations, concerns and (occasionally) prejudices about the beneficiaries which it would or might be hurtful, impolitic or simply undesirable for him to include in a document which the beneficiaries had a right to inspect. That advantage may be summarised in the word confidentiality, so long as it is appreciated that the word has both a subjective and an objective connotation. Confidentiality may serve a purely selfish desire of the settlor to keep his wishes, beliefs and the communication of certain facts secret from the family. Objectively speaking, that secrecy may in many cases be thoroughly beneficial, since it may tend to preserve family harmony and mutual respect, while enabling trustees to be briefed as to matters relevant to the exercise of their discretionary powers, rather than kept in ignorance of them.

9–45 . . . Since few would argue that clearly and rationally expressed wishes and relevant information included by settlors in wish letters could be treated by trustees as wholly irrelevant to the exercise of their discretionary powers, it is inescapable that their content will potentially be relevant, both to beneficiaries in monitoring the performance by trustees of their fiduciary obligations, and to the court in enforcing that performance where necessary and appropriate. Furthermore, the contents of a relevant wish letter may make all the difference to a beneficiary in understanding, in the context of an otherwise broadly drafted discretionary trust, what are or may be his or her expectations of benefit from the assets of a family settlement. While such expectations may on occasion be damaging, in particular to young beneficiaries, a broad knowledge of their prospects may be of significant advantage to them in planning both their own lives, and the education and maintenance of their children and other dependants. It is incidentally for this latter purpose that the claimants say that they have made their claim to disclosure.

9–46 There is therefore an inevitable tension between on the one hand the advantages of confidentiality, and on the other hand, the advantages of disclosure, in relation to wish letters. It is precisely this tension which has generated the controversy evident in the Australian, New Zealand and Channel Islands authorities. It is tempting to say that the infinitely variable weight to be given to those competing considerations in any particular case is best resolved by the exercise of discretion by the judge resorted to for the resolution of the impasse, rather than by the laying down of rules or even guidelines. But in my judgment this superficially attractive solution has real disadvantages. The first is that unless the principles are generally understood, settlors are likely to treat the uncertainty as to the general confidentiality of wish letters as a disincentive to their beneficial use. The second is that the uncertainty is likely to lead to more rather than less applications to court to resolve questions of disclosure, and will therefore be a recipe for litigation. In the context of the likely asset base of even wealthy families, the attendant cost should be avoided if at all possible. . . .

9–47 [Briggs J. reviewed a series of cases,[101] then drew the following conclusions]: The first question is whether it is either permissible or appropriate in the light of *O'Rourke v Darbishire* and the *Londonderry*

[101] *Re Beloved Wilkes's Charity* (1851) 3 Mac. & G. 440; *O'Rourke v Darbishire* [1920] A.C. 581; *Re Londonderry's Settlement* [1965] Ch. 918; *Hartigan Nominees Pty Ltd v Rydge* (1992) 29 N.S.W.L.R. 405; *Wilson v Law Debenture Trust Corp Plc* [1995] 2 All E.R. 337; *Re Rabaiotti's Settlements* [2000] W.T.L.R. 953; *Schmidt v Rosewood Trust Ltd* [2003] 2 A.C. 709; *Foreman v Kingstone* [2005] W.T.L.R. 823; *Countess Bathurst v Kleinwort Benson (Channel Islands) Trustees Ltd* [2007] W.T.L.R. 959.

case for me to decide at first instance that the basis upon which trustees and the court should approach a request for disclosure of a wish letter (or of any other document in the possession of trustees in their capacity as such) is one calling for the exercise of discretion rather than the adjudication upon a proprietary right. In my judgment it is both permissible and appropriate to answer that question in the affirmative. My review of the authorities demonstrates that there is now virtual unanimity in the relevant common law jurisdictions to that effect. Furthermore, as I have sought to demonstrate, even the Court of Appeal in the *Londonderry* case itself found the proprietary analysis to be both inconclusive and unsatisfactory, by comparison with the recognition of a clear, principled basis for refusing disclosure even in cases where there appeared to be a prima facie proprietary right to disclosure.

On that basis, the second question is whether the *Londonderry* principle remains good law, at least in England. In my opinion, it is still good law and, in any event, law by which a first instance judge remains bound, unless and until released by some higher judicial or parliamentary authority. **9–48**

At the heart of the *Londonderry* principle is the unanimous conclusion (most clearly expressed by Danckwerts L.J.) that it is in the interests of beneficiaries of family discretionary trusts, and advantageous to the due administration of such trusts, that the exercise by trustees of their dispositive discretionary powers be regarded, from start to finish, as an essentially confidential process. It is in the interests of the beneficiaries because it enables the trustees to make discreet but thorough inquiries as to their competing claims for consideration for benefit without fear or risk that those inquiries will come to the beneficiaries' knowledge. They may include, for example, inquiries as to the existence of some life-threatening illness of which it is appropriate that the beneficiary in question be kept ignorant. Such confidentiality serves the due administration of family trusts both because it tends to reduce the scope for litigation about the rationality of the exercise by trustees of their discretions, and because it is likely to encourage suitable trustees to accept office, undeterred by a perception that their discretionary deliberations will be subjected to scrutiny by disappointed or hostile beneficiaries, and to potentially expensive litigation in the courts. **9–49**

I recognise the force of the contrary proposition, best enunciated by the editors of *Underhill & Hayton*,[102] that the conferral of a general confidentiality upon the exercise by trustees of their discretionary powers may in particular cases reduce the practical extent to which they can be held to account. Trustees undoubtedly are accountable for the exercise of those powers, but it seems to me quite wrong to suppose that the courts have been mindless of the existence of that core principle of accountability, during the period of more than 150 years when the law has been that it is better for confidentiality to be afforded. While Kirby P. and those who sympathise with his views may be right in recognising that, in society generally, the principle of fiduciary accountability has gained ground in recent years, it seems to me that this is better described as a process whereby the strict principles whereby a trustee has always been accountable have spread to other areas of society, where the concept of fiduciary obligations by those who hold property or exercise power or authority on behalf of others, or over their affairs, has come to be more generally recognised. **9–50**

Nor can I see any persuasive basis for thinking that the reasoning which led the English courts to think it appropriate in the interests of beneficiaries, and in the administration of trusts, to confer confidentiality on the exercise by family trustees of their discretionary dispositive powers has ceased to hold good. It is not obvious that the potentially disastrous consequences of a resort to civil litigation about the administration of family trust property, in terms of the expenditure of time and cost, are much less of a potential evil than they were in the 19th century. Nor is there any less need today than there always has been to avoid deterring suitable family trustees from accepting an arduous unpaid office. Of course there is a risk that the conferral of such confidentiality may enable unworthy trustees to use it as a shield for the concealment of their culpable inadequacies, but this risk cannot have been ignored in the 19th century, and now that it is recognised that the general principle of confidentiality is subject to being overridden as a matter of discretion by the court, it may fairly be supposed that the risk has if anything become more rather than less manageable. **9–51**

My reason for concluding that, regardless of my own opinion, I am bound to continue to treat the *Londonderry* principle as still being good law is simply because it formed part of the ratio of that decision, it has never been overruled, and because, if anything, it received a general endorsement rather than criticism in *Schmidt v Rosewood Trust Ltd*.[103] **9–52**

---

[102] *Underhill & Hayton's Law of Trusts and Trustees*, 17th edn (2007), para.60.5.

[103] [2003] 2 A.C. 709.

9–53 I turn therefore to the question whether, and if so in what way, the *Londonderry* principle applies to wish letters. In that context I am content to limit myself to wish letters arising in the context of family discretionary trusts, rather than employee trusts, pension trusts or other business trusts, leaving for another occasion the manner in which the *Londonderry* principle is applicable to them. The defining characteristic of a wish letter is that it contains material which the settlor desires that the trustees should take into account when exercising their (usually dispositive) discretionary powers. It is therefore brought into existence for the sole purpose of serving and facilitating an inherently confidential process. It seems to me axiomatic that a document brought into existence for the sole or predominant purpose of being used in furtherance of an inherently confidential process is itself properly to be regarded as confidential, to substantially the same extent and effect as the process which it is intended to serve. . . .

9–54 While in a sense a wish letter is the companion of the trust deed, it by no means follows that it therefore needs or ought to be afforded similar treatment in the hands of the trustees. The trust deed is a document which confers and identifies the trustees' powers. There is in principle nothing confidential about the existence and precise boundaries of those powers. By contrast, the wish letter, operating exclusively within those boundaries and purely in furtherance of the trustees' confidential exercise of discretionary powers, may properly be afforded a status of confidentiality which the trust deed itself entirely lacks. . . .

9–55 I shall briefly summarise what I consider to be [the practical effect of these principles] in relation to family discretionary trusts, separately in relation to each of the three stages in which the issue may typically arise. First, trustees should in general regard a wish letter (that is a document from the settlor the sole or predominant purpose of which is or appears to be to assist them in the exercise of their discretionary powers) as invested with a confidentiality designed to be maintained, relaxed, or if necessary abandoned, as they judge best serves the interests of the beneficiaries and the due administration of the trust. This discretion to maintain, relax or abandon confidence arises regardless of a request for disclosure by a beneficiary, and persists regardless of the incapacity, death or change of heart on the part of the settlor.

9–56 Where a beneficiary makes a request for disclosure, that in my judgment merely triggers an occasion upon which the trustees need to exercise (or reconsider the exercise of) that discretion, giving such weight to the making of and reasons for that request as they think fit. Having made their decision the trustees are not obliged to give reasons for it, any more than in relation to any other exercise of their discretionary powers. In a difficult case the trustees may, as always, seek the directions of the court on the question whether to disclose but, bearing in mind the inevitable cost associated with doing so, the trustees will need to think twice before concluding that the difficulty of the question justifies the expenditure. It is by no means a matter for criticism (of the type levelled against the trustees in this case) that trustees do not either give reasons or apply to the court for directions, if minded not to accede to a beneficiary's request for disclosure.

9–57 If application is made to the court by trustees for directions whether to disclose a wish letter, then it is a fundamental principle that full disclosure must be made to the court. It will almost always be necessary to include the wish letter itself in that disclosure to the court. Furthermore the court is unlikely to determine the question of disclosure without joinder of at least the requesting beneficiary, and the court would have to give anxious consideration to the question whether, and if so to what extent, to restrict disclosure of the relevant materials to that beneficiary or his legal advisers, for the purposes of enabling submissions to be made on his behalf, in the same way as occurs in the context of *In re Beddoe* applications,[104] where the opposite party to the proposed or threatened litigation is a beneficiary of the trust.

9–58 At the second stage (i.e. determination of the disclosure issue by the court in proceedings brought solely for that purpose), the matter may be presented, at least in theory, in four different ways. In its simplest form the trustees may seek to surrender their discretion to the court, in which case (if it permits the surrender, which it is not obliged to do) the court is exercising its own discretion afresh, rather than reviewing any negative exercise of discretion by the trustees. Alternatively, the trustees may, without surrendering their discretion, invite the court in effect to bless their refusal. Thirdly the case may be brought by the disappointed beneficiary by way of a challenge to the trustees' negative exercise of their discretion to disclose. Finally, the beneficiary may seek simply to invoke an original discretion in the court, as part of its jurisdiction in the administration of trusts.

[104] [1893] 1 Ch. 547.

9–59 The second and third of those types of application involve a review of the trustees' negative exercise of their discretion to disclose. If the trustees themselves apply, then it is in practice inevitable that they will have to disclose their reasons. If the disappointed beneficiary applies, then it seems to me that the *Londonderry* principle will entitle the trustees, if they choose to do so, to decline to give reasons, and to defend the challenge upon the basis that, if it be the case, the disappointed beneficiary has disclosed no grounds for impugning either the fairness or the honesty of their decision, their reasoning being off-limits for that purpose.

9–60 Finally, if the disappointed beneficiary seeks to invoke the court's administrative jurisdiction, then it will be incumbent upon him to demonstrate, by reference to whatever facts may be available to him, that an occasion has arisen which calls for the interference of the court. A mere refusal to disclose a wish letter, unaccompanied by reasons or evidence of *mala fides* or unfairness, would not ordinarily justify such intervention. Of course, if the trustees volunteer reasons for their refusal, the court may investigate those reasons, and call for such factual material or further explanation from the trustees as may be thought fit.

9–61 The third stage (where disclosure is sought from the court to facilitate the determination of an issue to which the wish letter is alleged to be relevant) gives rise to different considerations, governed by the law and practice as to disclosure in civil proceedings. For those purposes, the relevance of the foregoing detailed analysis of the status of a wish letter is that identified by Danckwerts L.J. in the *Londonderry* case,[105] namely that if the document in question does no more than illuminate the trustees' reasons for the making of a discretionary decision, it may be simply irrelevant, unless the trustees by a partial disclosure of their reasons have put into play the issue as to their rationality. . . .

5. Reduction of the Trust Property into Possession

9–62 It has already been noted that upon accepting trusteeship a new trustee should ensure that all trust property is put into the joint names of himself and his co-trustees or into the name of a duly authorised nominee.[106] However he also needs to be aware of the following statutory powers.

TRUSTEE ACT 1925 SECTION 15

Power to Compound Liabilities

9–63 A personal representative or two or more trustees acting together, subject to the restrictions[107] imposed in regard to receipts by a sole trustee not being a trust corporation, a sole acting trustee where by the instrument, if any, creating the trust, or by statute, a sole trustee is authorised to execute the trusts and powers reposed in him, may, if and as he or they think fit—

(a) accept any property, real or personal, before the time at which it is made transferable or payable; or

(b) sever and apportion any blended trust funds or property; or

(c) pay or allow any debt or claim on any evidence that he or they think sufficient; or

(d) accept any composition or any security, real or personal, for any debt or for any property, real or personal, claimed; or

(e) allow any time of payment of any debt; or

(f) compromise, compound, abandon, submit to arbitration, or otherwise settle any debt, account, claim or thing whatever relating to the testator's or intestate's estate or to the trust[108];

---

[105] [1965] Ch. 918 at 936.
[106] See para.9–10.
[107] See the Law of Property Act 1925 s.27; Trustee Act 1925 s.14.
[108] See *Re Strafford (Earl of)* [1980] Ch. 28 for a useful examination of the scope of this.

and for any of those purposes may enter into, give, execute, and do such agreements, instruments of composition or arrangement, releases, and other things as to him or them seem expedient, without being responsible for any loss occasioned by any act or thing so done by him or them if he has or they have discharged the duty of care set out in section 1(1) of the Trustee Act 2000.[109]

9–64 This section replaces, with amendments and additions, the Trustee Act 1893 s.21, which itself replaced the Conveyancing Act 1881 s.37. In *Re Brogden*[110] the Court of Appeal held that trustees must demand payment of funds due to the trust, and take legal proceedings, if necessary, to enforce payment if the demand is not complied with within a reasonable time, unless they reasonably believe that such action would be fruitless. In this case the breach of trust occurred before the Conveyancing Act 1881 came into force. Where trustees of a pension trust are desirous of ensuring that a s.15 compromise of their claim against the employer to add funds to the trust will be a proper exercise of their powers they can obtain confirmation from the court.[111]

TRUSTEE ACT 1925 SECTION 22

Reversionary Interests, Valuations and Audit

9–65 (1) Where trust property includes any share or interest in property not vested in the trustees, or the proceeds of the sale of any such property, or any other thing in action, the trustees on the same falling into possession, or becoming payable or transferable may—

(a) agree or ascertain the amount or value thereof or any part thereof in such manner as they may think fit;

(b) accept in or towards satisfaction thereof, at the market or current value, or upon any valuation or estimate of value which they may think fit, any authorised investments;

(c) allow any deductions for duties, costs, charges and expenses which they may think proper or reasonable;

(d) execute any release in respect of the premises so as effectually to discharge all accountable parties from all liability in respect of any matter coming within the scope of such release;

without being responsible in any such case for any loss occasioned by any act or thing so done by them if they have discharged the duty of care set out in section 1(1) of the Trustee Act 2000.[112]

(2) The trustees shall not be under any obligation and shall not be chargeable with any breach of trust by reason of any omission—

(a) to place any distringas notice or apply for any stop or other like order upon any securities or other property out of or on which such share or interest or other thing in action as aforesaid is derived, payable or charged; or

(b) to take any proceedings on account of any act, default, or neglect on the part of the persons in whom such securities or other property or any of them or any part thereof are for the time being, or had at any time been, vested;

---

109 Before February 1, 2001 trustees only needed to have acted "in good faith".

110 (1888) 38 Ch.D. 546.

111 *Bradstock Group Pension Scheme Trustees Ltd v Bradstock Group Plc* [2003] W.T.L.R. 1281.

112 Before February 1, 2001 trustees only needed to have acted "in good faith".

unless and until required in writing so to do by some person, or the guardian of some person, beneficially interested under the trust, and unless also due provision is made to their satisfaction for payment of the costs of any proceedings required to be taken.

Provided that nothing in this subsection shall relieve the trustees of the obligation to get in and obtain payment or transfer of such share or interest or other thing in action on the same falling into possession.

(3) Trustees may, for the purpose of giving effect to the trust, or any of the provisions of the instrument, if any, creating the trust or of any statute, from time to time (by duly qualified agents) ascertain and fix the value of any trust property in such manner as they think proper, and any valuation so made shall be binding upon all persons interested under the trust if the trustees have discharged the duty of care set out in section 1(1) of the Trustee Act 2000.

(4) Trustees may, in their absolute discretion, from time to time, but not more than once in every three years unless the nature of the trust or any special dealings with the trust property make a more frequent exercise of the right reasonable, cause the accounts of the trust property to be examined or audited by an independent accountant, and shall, for that purpose, produce such vouchers and give such information to him as he may require; and the costs of such examination or audit, including the fee of the auditor, shall be paid out of the capital or income of the trust property, or partly in one way and partly in the other, as the trustees, in their absolute discretion, think fit, but, in default of any direction by the trustees to the contrary in any special case, costs attributable to capital shall be borne by capital and those attributable to income by income.

6. Investment of the Trust Property

The trustees must invest and manage the trust fund so that there is adequate income and capital available when they exercise their distributive function. They must familiarise themselves with their powers of investment so that they know which investments are within or outside their powers. When deciding whether to sell or purchase investments within the authorised range of investments, they must also comply with further duties: in this section we consider their duty of care and their duty to obtain the best financial return for all the beneficiaries, and in the next section we discuss their duty to act even-handedly between different classes of beneficiaries. **9–66**

A. The Range of Authorised Investments

Trustees are under a fundamental duty to invest the trust funds in investments authorised expressly or impliedly by the trust instrument, or by the court,[113] or in default by the Trustee Act 2000. A properly drafted trust instrument will contain very extensive powers of investment so that there is no need to apply to the court for wider powers, or otherwise to rely upon the Trustee Act 2000 which applies to pre-existing trusts (from February 1, 2001) as well as new trusts. If a testator by specific gift leaves certain investments (e.g. my apartments in Tenerife) to trustees for A for life, then B absolutely, this impliedly authorises the trustees to retain such investments but not to purchase any more.[114] If personal representatives appropriate property to trustees under the Administration of Estates Act 1925 s.41, then the property is thereafter treated as an authorised investment for purposes of retention but not for purchasing more of the same. **9–67**

113 The court's powers are in the Trustee Act 1925 s.57, and the Variation of Trusts Act 1958.

114 *Re Pugh* [1887] W.N. 143; *Re Whitfield* (1920) 125 L.T. 61.

9–68 If an express investment power is void for uncertainty[115] (e.g. "to invest in blue chip shares and such other investments as my trustees know I would approve of") then the trustees are relegated to the powers under the 2000 Act unless they obtain wider powers from the court.

B. Duties when Investing

i. To Act Like a Prudent Person Conducting Another's Affairs

9–69 Trustees must exhibit the statutory duty of care laid down by the Trustee Act 2000 s.1,[116] which is reproduced above.[117] When exercising his powers of investment, a trustee must act like a prudent person investing for other people, reviewing the portfolio of investments regularly,[118] and if lacking investment knowledge seeking professional advice and considering such advice before acting upon it.[119] A prudent person might reasonably select some speculative investments for himself that he should avoid if investing for the benefit of another person who depends on the trust fund as a safe basis for securing her future. Thus, the 2000 Act has not affected the following risk averse approach summarised by Lord Nicholls:[120]

> "It is not enough that a trustee should act honestly. Promotion of the trust purpose requires a trustee to be prudent and exercise the degree of care he would in conducting his own affairs but mindful, when making investment decisions, that he is dealing with another's property. The classic formulation of this standard of conduct was enunciated by Lindley L.J. in *Re Whiteley*.[121] The duty of a trustee is not to take such care only as a prudent man would take if he had only himself to consider; the duty is rather to take such care as an ordinary prudent man would take if he were minded to make an investment for the benefit of other people for whom he felt morally bound to provide. . . . This 'ordinary prudent person conducting another's affairs' is the equitable counterpart of the reasonable man who is so ubiquitous in the common law. . . . A comment is needed here on the ordinary prudent person. His standards are the minimum standards expected of trustees. If the trustee is a person professing particular expertise in the management of trusts, and he has been appointed for that reason, his conduct will be judged by the standards he professes. A professional person, a trust corporation, held out as an expert, will be expected to display the degree of skill and care and diligence such an expert would have."

9–70 Lord Nicholls went on to endorse the view of Hoffmann J. (as he then was) who had stated that:[122]

> "Modern trustees acting within their investment powers are entitled to be judged by the standards of current portfolio theory, which emphasises the risk level of the entire portfolio rather than the risk attaching to each investment taken in isolation."

---

115 *Re Kolb's WT* [1962] Ch. 531.
116 The duty may be excluded or modified by the trust deed: Trustee Act 2000 Sch.1 para.7.
117 At para 9–05.
118 *Nestlé v National Westminster Bank Plc* [1994] 1 All E.R. 118.
119 *Cowan v Scargill* [1985] Ch. 279; *Jones v AMP Perpetual Trustee Co NZ Ltd* [1994] 1 N.Z.L.R. 690. Pension trustees are required to seek advice by the Pensions Act 1995 s.36, for breach of which duty the defendant trustees were held liable in *Adams v Bridge* [2009] Pens. L.R. 153.
120 Lord Nicholls, "Trustees and Their Broader Community: Where Duty, Morality and Ethics Converge" (1995) 9 Tru. L.I. 71 at 73.
121 (1886) 33 Ch.D. 347 at 355.
122 *Nestlé v National Westminster Bank Plc* (1988) [2000] W.T.L.R. 795 at 802. See, too, *British Museum Trustees v Att.-Gen.* [1984] 1 W.L.R. 418 AT 425, per Megarry V.C.; *Dominica Social Security Board v Nature Island Investment Co Ltd* [2008] UKPC 19 at [30], per Lord Walker.

In Lord Nicholls' view:[123]

> "Investment policy is aimed at producing a portfolio of investments which is balanced overall and suited to the needs of the particular trust. Different investments are accompanied by different degrees of risk, which are reflected in the expected rate of return. A large fund with a widely diversified portfolio of securities might justifiably include modest holdings of high risk securities which would be imprudent and out of place in a smaller fund. In such a case it would be inappropriate to isolate one particular investment out of a vast portfolio and enquire whether that can be justified as a trust investment. Such a 'line by line' approach is misplaced. The inquiry, rather, should be to look at a particular investment and enquire whether that is justified as a holding in the context of the overall portfolio. Traditional warnings against the need for trustees to avoid speculative or hazardous investments are not to be read as inhibiting trustees from maintaining portfolios of investments which contain a prudent and sensible mixture of low risk and higher risk securities. They are not to be so read, because they were not directed at a portfolio which is a balanced exercise in risk management."

This requires portfolio securities having a low co-variance with each other, where a positive co-variance means the values of two assets are likely to move in the same direction, and a low co-variance means the values are likely to move in opposite directions. Having dissimilar investments is not sufficient: real estate and government bonds are different, but when interest rates increase both types of investment suffer and vice versa. The proportions of different types of asset within the portfolio are crucial for achieving the purposes of the fund, the most basic proportion being that between equity and debt, viz. between stocks and shares and fixed interest securities, e.g. 60 per cent to 40 per cent or vice versa. **9–71**

Sections 4 and 5 of the Trustee Act 2000 now expressly impose such duties upon trustees as follows. **9–72**

TRUSTEE ACT 2000 SECTION 4

(1) In exercising any power of investment, whether arising under this Part or otherwise, a trustee must have regard to the standard investment criteria. **9–73**

(2) A trustee must from time to time review the investments of the trust and consider whether, having regard to the standard investment criteria, they should be varied.

(3) The standard investment criteria, in relation to a trust, are—

(a) the suitability to the trust of investments of the same kind as any particular investment proposed to be made or retained and of that particular investment as an investment of that kind, and

(b) the need for diversification of investments of the trust, in so far as is appropriate to the circumstances of the trust.[124]

[123] (1995) 9 Tru. L.I. 71 at 74. On modern portfolio theory, see J. Langbein, "The Uniform Prudent Investor Act and the Future of Trust Investing" (1996) 81 Iowa L.R. 641; I.N. Legair, "Modern Portfolio Theory: A Primer" (2000) 14 Tru L.I. 75.

[124] The trustees might legitimately decide against diversification if instructed by the settlor to retain particular assets within the trust fund: *Gregson v HAE Trustees Ltd* [2009] 1 All E.R. (Comm.) 457 at [70]–[92],

TRUSTEE ACT 2000 SECTION 5

9–74 (1) Before exercising any power of investment, whether arising under this Part or otherwise, a trustee must (unless the exception applies) obtain and consider proper advice about the way in which, having regard to the standard investment criteria, the power should be exercised.

(2) When reviewing the investments of the trust, a trustee must (unless the exception applies) obtain and consider proper advice about whether, having regard to the standard investment criteria, the investments should be varied.

(3) The exception is that a trustee need not obtain such advice if he reasonably concludes that in all the circumstances it is unnecessary or inappropriate to do so.

(4) Proper advice is the advice of a person who is reasonably believed by the trustee to be qualified to give it by his ability in and practical experience of financial and other matters relating to the proposed investment.

9–75 It will be seen that proper advice is not needed if the trustee reasonably concludes that in all the circumstances it is unnecessary or inappropriate (e.g. the investment seems a safe one and a small one or the trustee is an experienced knowledgeable investor), while it would seem that proper advice could be that of a co-trustee or an employee who is reasonably believed by the trustee to be qualified to give it. It will be advisable to have the advice in writing and also to record in writing when advice is considered unnecessary or inappropriate.

9–76 Often trustees will delegate their asset management functions[125] to a land agent or a discretionary portfolio manager and have investments held by a nominee or custodian.[126] There must be a written agreement as to the terms of asset management delegation coupled with a policy statement, while there is a duty to keep the delegation arrangements and the policy statement under regular review.[127]

9–77 In practice, claims for breach of the duty of care are most likely to succeed where a trustee has recklessly or negligently purchased a wholly inappropriate investment. Exceptionally, it may be possible to make out a case that the trustee who has systematically pursued a wrong-headed investment strategy, or who has done nothing to review and consider changes to the portfolio over a long period, should be liable to compensate the beneficiaries for the lost gains that would have been made if the trustee had acted reasonably.[128] However, as Hoffmann J. said,[129] "In reviewing the conduct of trustees over a period of more than 60 years, one must be careful not to endow the prudent trustee with prophetic vision or expect him to have ignored the received wisdom of his time", e.g. as to the balance between gilt-edged securities and company shares. Where trustees invest in authorised investments it is difficult to make them liable for negligent breach of their equitable and statutory duties of care, as it must be proved that their conduct was a course which no properly informed prudent trustee could have followed. This is the ratio of *Nestlé v National Westminster Bank Plc*.[130]

---

125 Trustee Act 2000 ss.11, 12, 13, 14, 15.
126 Trustee Act 2000 ss.16, 17, 19, 20. Pension trustees are governed by the Pensions Acts 1995 and 2004.
127 See para.9–206.
128 *Nestlé v National Westminster Bank Plc* [1993] 1 W.L.R. 1260 at 1268 and 1280.
129 *Nestlé v National Westminster Bank Plc* (1988) [2000] W.T.L.R. 795 at 802.
130 [1993] 1 W.L.R. 1260.

NESTLÉ v NATIONAL WESTMINSTER BANK PLC

Court of Appeal [1993] 1 W.L.R. 1260, [1994] 1 All E.R. 118

STAUGHTON L.J. (with whom DILLON and LEGGATT L.JJ. agreed): When Mr William Nestlé died in 1922, 9–78
the value of his trust fund (after payment of debts, legacies and estate duty) was about £50,000. In November 1986, when the plaintiff, his granddaughter Miss Georgina Nestlé, became absolutely entitled after the death of the last life tenant, it was worth £269,203. That, it might be thought, was a substantial improvement. But during the same period the cost of living had multiplied by a factor of 20, so that it would have required £1m to provide equivalent wealth: see the BZW equity-gilt study of 1988. The same source shows that an equity price index rose by 5203 per cent in that period. An equivalent appreciation in the value of the trust fund would have left it worth £2.6m in 1986. It is true that a small portion of the fund was advanced to life tenants, that some capital was used to supplement income for an annuity, and that there were no doubt transaction costs; against that, a sum of about £5,000 was added to the fund in 1959 when Mr Nestlé's house and contents were sold. Nevertheless, it is apparent that the investments retained or made by the trustees fell woefully short of maintaining the real value of the fund, let alone matching the average increase in price of ordinary shares.

Of course it is not a breach of trust to invest the trust fund in such a manner that its real value is not 9–79
maintained. At times that will be impossible, and at others it will require extraordinary skill or luck. The highest that even the plaintiff puts her claim is that, if the equity portion in the fund as it stood in 1922 (74 per cent) had been invested so as to achieve no more than the index, the fund as a whole would have been worth over £1.8m in 1986 . . .

In the experts' reports and during the course of the trial it appeared that there were four main strands 9–80
to the plaintiff's case. (1) The trustees misunderstood the investment clause in the will. (2) The trustees failed to conduct a regular and periodic review of the investments. (3) Throughout the trust period, but in particular in the later stages when there were life tenants domiciled abroad, they retained or bought too high a proportion of fixed interest securities and too few ordinary shares. (4) To the extent that the trustees did invest in ordinary shares, they concentrated too heavily on shares in banking and insurance companies, to the exclusion of other sectors.

Misunderstanding, and Failure to Review

In my judgment the first two charges were proved. It was admitted that at times the trustees misunder- 9–81
stood the investment clause; but the evidence showed that they continually misunderstood it, and there is nothing to show that they ever understood it correctly. To a novice in these matters it seems that they might deserve to be forgiven, since only among much other detail are to be found the words "stocks shares bonds debentures or securities of any railway or other company." But there is authority which shows plainly that the word "company" in such a clause is not limited by its context. Trustees are not allowed to make mistakes in law; they should take legal advice, and if they are still left in doubt they can apply to the court for a ruling. Either course would have revealed their mistake in this case.

I also consider that, for a substantial period, the trustees failed to conduct regular periodic reviews 9–82
of the investments. From 1922 to 1959 there was only one change of an investment, other than changes which were forced on the trustees by rights issues or because a security reached its redemption date . . .

However, the misunderstanding of the investment clause and the failure to conduct periodic reviews do 9–83
not by themselves, whether separately or together, afford the plaintiff a remedy. They were symptoms of incompetence or idleness—not on the part of National Westminster Bank but of their predecessors; they were not, without more, breaches of trust. The plaintiff must show that, through one or other or both of those causes, the trustees made decisions which they should not have made or failed to make decisions which they should have made. If that were proved, and if at first sight loss resulted, it would be appropriate to order an inquiry as to the loss suffered by the trust fund.

It may be difficult to discharge that burden, and particularly to show that decisions were not taken when 9–84
they should have been. But that does not absolve a plaintiff from discharging it, and I cannot find that it was discharged in this case . . .

The Balance of the Fund between Equities and Gilts

9–85 That brings me to what I regard as the substance of the case, the failure to invest a higher proportion of the trust fund in ordinary shares. Here one must take care to avoid two errors. First, the trustees' performance must not be judged with hindsight: after the event even a fool is wise, as a poet said nearly 3,000 years ago. Secondly (unless this is the same point), one must bear in mind that investment philosophy was very different in the early years of this trust from what it became later. Inflation was non-existent, overall, from 1921 to 1938. It occurred in modest degree during the war years, and became a more persistent phenomenon from 1947 onwards. Equities were regarded as risky during the 1920s and 1930s, and yielded a higher return then gilt-edged securities. It was only in 1959 that the so-called reverse yield gap occurred.

9–86 During the period from 1922 until the death of Mrs Barbara Nestlé in 1960, the proportion of ordinary shares in the trust fund as a whole varied between 46 and 82 per cent. Until 1951 it never rose above 57 per cent; there was then quite a sharp rise until 1960, not caused by any change in investment policy but presumably by a general rise in the value of ordinary shares (183 per cent, according to the index, between 1950 and 1960).

9–87 In my judgment the trustees are not shown to have failed in their duties at any time up to 1959 in this respect. I cannot say that, in the light of investment conditions then prevailing, they were in breach of trust by not holding a higher proportion of ordinary shares. In addition, they were charged with the duty of providing an annuity of £1,500 after tax for the widow of Mr William Nestlé, and of setting aside a fund for that purpose. The plaintiff's expert witnesses were themselves disinclined to criticise the balance of the fund, as between fixed interest and ordinary shares, in that period.

9–88 After 1959 the situation had changed. Mrs Barbara Nestlé died in October 1960, and the trustees were relieved of the task of providing for her annuity. The cult of the equity had begun by then, if not some years before. From that date I would accept the evidence of the plaintiff's experts that, all other things being equal, there should be at least 50 per cent of the fund in ordinary shares.

9–89 The trustees' experts countered that on two grounds. First, they pointed to evidence that pension funds and life assurance companies continued to invest less than half their funds in equities, and a substantial proportion in gilt-edged securities. Counsel for the plaintiff provided us with a calculation which was said to disprove this in the case of pension funds. But it had not been made in the court below or put to witnesses, and was incomplete for this purpose . . .

9–90 There is in my opinion a better answer to this comparison. Life assurance companies and pension funds have as their primary duty an obligation to pay at some future date a sum that is fixed in monetary terms. No doubt they offer profits, or an increase on the promised pension; and it may be that even in 1959 there was competition between companies by reference to their past records of success. But I am convinced that they could be expected to follow a policy of considerable caution in order to ensure that, come what may, their minimum obligations in monetary terms were fulfilled. I do not regard them as a reliable guide to what would have been done by private investors, or should have been done by trustees of a private family trust.

9–91 The second point is this, Professor Briston, who gave evidence for the plaintiff, made a calculation on the basis that the part of the trust fund which was invested in ordinary shares initially remained in ordinary shares throughout. His calculation shows that, if one takes the 74 per cent proportion of equities when Mr William Nestlé died, the fund as a whole would have grown to £1.8m in 1986. Alternatively, the portfolio had a proportion of 54 per cent in equities after the setting up of the annuity fund and some restructuring between 1922 and 1924; if that part of the fund had remained in ordinary shares, the value of the fund as a whole would in 1986 have been £1.36m.

9–92 I have already expressed the view that, in the light of investment conditions then prevailing, the trustees are not to be criticised over the balance of the fund between fixed interest and equities in the period from 1922 to 1959. It follows that I do not accept the evidence of Professor Briston that they ought to have acted differently in that period. Neither did he persist in it when cross-examined . . .

9–93 In my judgment they should, in the investment climate prevailing from 1960 onwards, have followed Professor Briston's policy, subject only to one important consideration—the overseas domicile of life tenants. If all the beneficiaries had been subject to United Kingdom tax, they should have regarded the 76.8 per cent of the fund that was in ordinary shares in 1959 (or even the 82.6 per cent in 1960) as devoted to equity investment, and only the balance as available for fixed interest securities. No doubt there were times during the period from 1960 to 1986 when it would not have been a breach of trust, and may even have been wise, to depart temporarily from that policy. But in the main I am convinced that it is the policy which they should have followed. With hindsight, one can see that the BZW Equity Index rose from 789.9 to 6353.2 in that period; the gilt index fell from 74.6 to 48.4. But my conclusion is based on the evidence of Professor Briston and Mr Harris, not on hindsight.

That, however, assumes that all the beneficiaries were subject to United Kingdom tax, which they were not. George Nestlé lived in Tanganyika from 1933 to 1963, when he moved to Malta and lived there until he died in 1972. Elsie, his widow, continued to live there until 1980, when she returned to England. She died in 1982. John Nestlé went to live in Cyprus in 1969, and died there in 1986. The fiscal effects of residence/ordinary residence/domicile overseas were, as I understand it, twofold: first, the life tenant would not be liable for United Kingdom income tax on investments outside the United Kingdom, or (more significantly) on the income from gilt-edged securities which were tax exempt; secondly, neither estate duty nor capital transfer tax would be payable on the death of a life tenant in respect of such securities. **9–94**

The obligation of a trustee is to administer the trust fund impartially, or fairly (I can see no significant difference), having regard to the different interests of beneficiaries. Wilberforce J. said in *Re Pauling's Settlement Trusts (No.2)*:[131] **9–95**

> "The new trustees would be under the normal duty of preserving an equitable balance, and if at any time it was shown they were inclining one way or the other, it would not be a difficult matter to bring them to account."

At times it will not be easy to decide what is an equitable balance. A life tenant may be anxious to receive the highest possible income, whilst the remainderman will wish the real value of the trust fund to be preserved. If the life tenant is living in penury and the remainderman already has ample wealth, common sense suggests that a trustee should be able to take that into account, not necessarily by seeking the highest possible income at the expense of capital but by inclining in that direction. However, before adopting that course a trustee should, I think, require some verification of the facts. In this case the trustees did not, so far as I am aware, have any reliable information as to the relative wealth of the life tenants and the plaintiff. They did send an official to interview Mr John Nestlé in Cyprus on one occasion; but the information which they obtained was conflicting and (as it turned out) incomplete. **9–96**

Similarly I would not regard it as a breach of trust for the trustees to pay some regard to the relationship between Mr George Nestlé and the plaintiff. He was merely her uncle, and she would have received nothing from his share of the fund if he had fathered a child who survived him. The trustees would be entitled, in my view, to incline towards income during his life tenancy and that of his widow, on that ground. Again common sense suggests to me that such a course might be appropriate, and I do not think that it would be a breach of the duty to act fairly, or impartially. **9–97**

The dominant consideration for the trustees, however, was that George's fund from 1960, and John's from 1969, would not be subject to United Kingdom income tax in so far as it was invested in exempt gilts. That was a factor which the trustees were entitled—and I would say bound—to take into account. A beneficiary who has been left a life interest in a trust fund has an arguable case for saying that he should not be compelled to bear tax on the income if he is not lawfully obliged to do so. **9–98**

It was no more than a factor for the trustees to bear in mind, and would rarely justify more than a modest degree of preference for income paid gross over capital growth. **9–99**

A trustee should also bear in mind, as these trustees did, that estate duty or capital transfer tax is likely to be reduced in such a case if part of the fund is invested in tax-exempt gilts. That may provide a compensating benefit for the remainderman. Of course it is by no means certain that the benefit will materialise; the life tenant may return to this country, as happened in the case of Mrs Elsie Nestlé. It has been said that nothing in this world is certain except death and taxes. But even the tax benefit was imponderable, since it could not be forecast what rate of tax would be applicable on the death of a life tenant. **9–100**

131 [1963] Ch. 576 at 586.

9–101 It is said that the trustees should have anticipated that Elsie would return to the United Kingdom, or at least have made inquiries as to her intentions. I can see some force in the second part of that argument. It would have been prudent to ask her to let them know if she planned to come back to this country. But this was never put to the bank's witnesses. And I cannot find that any loss to the trust fund resulted from failure to request information from Elsie. From time to time during her life tenancy there were indications that she might return, but it was only at a late stage that this attained any degree of probability; and I doubt whether even then it would have been right for the trustees to switch investments, thus reducing her income and foregoing any prospect of a saving in capital transfer tax.

9–102 I do not consider it necessary to examine separately the balance of the two different funds from 1961 to 1986. From the point of view of the plaintiff, what mattered was the balance of the fund as a whole. The proportion in ordinary shares varied between 59.55 per cent and 35.9 per cent. On occasion the lower figure may be attributable not to a change in investments but to a fall in the value of equities, for example in 1974 when there was a catastrophic fall. But there can be no doubt that there were other occasions when money was switched from ordinary shares to gilt-edged securities.

9–103 The policy of the trustees during this period was to achieve a 50/50 split between equities and fixed-interest. This was not to be an initial division of the kind favoured by Professor Briston, which would have resulted in a much higher proportion of equities by 1986; it was to be a division that was rebalanced from time to time, as envisaged by Professor Brealey. Whilst I much prefer Professor Briston's method in general for trust funds during this period, I consider that the circumstances of this trust and in particular the overseas life tenants, justified the policy which the trustees adopted. They did not fail to act fairly or impartially by adopting it.

9–104 But it is said that the trustees failed to implement their own policy: the proportion of ordinary shares fell on one occasion to 35.9 per cent, and in six years it was below 40 per cent. In my judgment the trustees were not obliged to rebalance the fund annually, still less at more frequent intervals. It would have been questionable to switch immediately into equities when they fell through the floor in 1974, merely because the ordinary shares then held were only 36.37 per cent of the fund. There was evidence that it is not a wise policy for trustees to be changing investments continually; and whilst I would not regard that as a justification for sheer inertia, I accept that an ordinary fund manager who has no special expertise should not busy himself with constant changes. The equity content started as 59.55 per cent in 1961 and ended as 51.31 per cent in 1986. Over those 26 years the average, according to my arithmetic, was 44.56 per cent. I would not regard that as revealing a serious departure from the trustees' policy, or a failure to act fairly and impartially. But I should add that, if I had found a breach of trust in this respect I would have been reluctant to accept that compensation should be measured by the difference between the actual performance of the fund and the very least that a prudent trustee might have achieved. There is said to be 19th century authority to that effect; but I would be inclined to prefer a comparison with what a prudent trustee was likely to have achieved—in other words, the average performance of ordinary shares during the period.

Diversification

9–105 The complaint here is that there was undue emphasis on the shares of banks and insurance companies during the period from 1922 to 1960. Indeed the equities in the annuity fund when it was set up in 1922 were entirely of that description.

9–106 However, there was evidence from the experts on both sides that bank and insurance shares were regarded as safest in the earlier period of this trust, "a low risk portfolio". I am inclined to agree with Professor Briston that there should have been diversification in the 1950s, rather than from 1960 onwards. But I cannot accept that failure to diversify in that decade was a course which no prudent trustee would have followed . . .

9–107 I would dismiss the appeal. . . . It is not shown that there was loss arising from a breach of trust for which the trustees ought to compensate the trust fund . . .

ii. To Do the Best they can Financially for the Beneficiaries as a Whole

9–108 If trustees have agreed to sell land so as to be morally bound but not yet legally bound by a contract, they are under a duty to gazump (i.e. negotiate with someone putting in a serious higher offer) so as to obtain a higher price for the beneficiaries, even if as honourable men they would prefer to implement the bargain to which they felt in honour bound. This is the ratio of *Buttle v Saunders*.[132] If trustees have strong opinions against alcohol or smoking or the arms trade, then if such investments would be likely to be more beneficial financially than other proposed investments they must purchase those investments even though they find them disagreeable. This is the ratio of *Cowan v Scargill*,[133] reproduced below. However, if trustees obtain professional advice that particular investments other than in companies engaging in such activities are equally satisfactory for the portfolio from a financial point of view then, of course, they can proceed to purchase those other investments. Thus, Lord Nicholls has concluded that:[134]

> "In practice in these cases where trustees or [beneficiaries] have strong views about particular investments on non-financial grounds it should be possible for trustees to exercise their investment powers in a manner avoiding embarrassment to all concerned without upsetting the balance of the portfolio. . . . The range of investment is so extensive that there is scope for trustees to give effect to moral considerations without thereby prejudicing beneficiaries' financial interests."

A settlor, of course, can always restrict the trustees' powers of investment by excluding certain types of investments and can always reduce the duties owed by the trustees, e.g. by permitting or directing the trustees to invest only in companies whose products or policies are ecologically more beneficial than those of other competing companies in the opinion of the trustees and by exempting the trustees from any liability so long as they acted in good faith.[135] **9–109**

In the case of charitable trusts, the trustees must consider whether a particular investment is consistent with its charitable purposes so that, for example, it would not be proper for a trust concerned to rehabilitate alcoholics and prevent alcoholism to invest in companies manufacturing and distributing alcoholic drinks or for a trust for the Society of Friends to invest in shares in companies engaged in the armaments industry.[136] According to the Charity Commission:[137] **9–110**

> "Some trustees may . . . wish to adopt an ethical investment policy, even though it does or may detract from the objective of obtaining the best direct financial return. The circumstances in which they may do this are . . . [where they] adopt an ethical investment policy which will involve:
>
> - Avoiding investments in a particular business that would for practical reasons conflict with the aims of the charity; for example, a charity with objects for the protection of the environment and wildlife may decide not to invest in businesses which pollute what the charity is trying to protect.
> - Avoiding investments that might hamper a charity's work, either by making potential beneficiaries unwilling to be helped because of the source of the charity's money, or by alienating supporters. This requires trustees to strike a balance between the likely cost of lost support, if the charity were to hold the investments, and any risk of financial under-performance if those investments are excluded from its portfolio."

---

132 [1950] 2 All E.R. 193.

133 [1985] Ch. 270.

134 Lord Nicholls, "Trustees and Their Broader Community: Where Duty, Morality and Ethics Converge" (1995) 9 Tru. L.I. 71 at 75.

135 On exemption clauses see paras 9–215 ff.

136 *Martin v Edinburgh DC* [1989] Pensions L.R. 9; *Harries v Church Commissioners* [1992] 1 W.L.R. 1241.

137 Charity Commission, *CC 14: Investment of Charitable Funds: Basic Principles* (December 2004 version), paras 34 and 35.

COWAN v SCARGILL

Chancery Division [1985] Ch. 270, [1984] 3 W.L.R. 501, [1984] 2 All E.R. 750

9–111 Under a mineworkers' pension scheme set up by the National Coal Board, a committee of management was formed of ten trustees (five appointed by the board and five by the National Union of Mineworkers) to control and administer funds provided by members' contributions to the scheme and by contributions by the board of approximately the same amount. The funds totalled some £3,000 million, with some £200 million available for investment each year, and the committee had wide powers of investment which they used with the assistance of an advisory panel of experts. An investment plan was submitted by a sub-committee for approval but the five union trustees on the committee of management objected to investments in oil, investments overseas, and the acquisition of land overseas. The board trustees sought the court's directions as to whether the union trustees were in breach of their fiduciary duties in holding up the adoption of the 1982 plan. Megarry V.C. held that they were, because their objections could not be justified on broad economic grounds and were only remotely in the interests of beneficiaries, for whom there would be no advantage in excluding investments overseas or investments in competition with the coal industry.

9–112 MEGARRY V.C.: I turn to the law. The starting point is the duty of trustees to exercise their powers in the best interests of the present and future beneficiaries of the trust, holding the scales impartially between different classes of beneficiaries. This duty of the trustees towards their beneficiaries is paramount. They must, of course, obey the law; but subject to that, they must put the interests of their beneficiaries first. When the purpose of the trust is to provide financial benefits for the beneficiaries, as is usually the case, the best interests of the beneficiaries are normally their best financial interests. In the case of a power of investment, as in the present case, the power must be exercised so as to yield the best return for the beneficiaries, judged in relation to the risks of the investments in question; and the prospects for the yield of income and capital appreciation both have to be considered in judging the return from the investment.

9–113 The legal memorandum that the union obtained from their solicitors is generally in accord with these views. In considering the possibility of investment for "socially beneficial reasons which may result in lower returns to the fund", the memorandum states that "the trustees' only concern is to ensure that the return is the maximum possible consistent with security"; and then it refers to the need for diversification. However, it continues by saying that:

> "Trustees cannot be criticised for failing to make a particular investment for social or political reasons, such as in South African stock for example, but may be held liable for investing in assets which yield a poor return or for disinvesting in stock at inappropriate times for non-financial criteria."

9–114 This last sentence must be considered in the light of subsequent passages in the memorandum which indicate that the sale of South African securities by trustees might be justified on the ground of doubts about political stability in South Africa and the long-term financial soundness of its economy, whereas trustees could not properly support motions at a company meeting dealing with pay levels in South Africa, work accidents, pollution control, employment conditions for minorities, military contracting and consumer protection. The assertion that trustees could not be criticised for failing to make a particular investment for social or political reasons is one that I would not accept in its full width. If the investment in fact made is equally beneficial to the beneficiaries, then criticism would be difficult to sustain in practice, whatever the position in theory. But if the investment in fact made is less beneficial, then both in theory and in practice the trustees would normally be open to criticism.

9–115 This leads me to the second point, which is a corollary of the first. In considering what investments to make trustees must put on one side their own personal interests and views. Trustees may have strongly held social or political views. They may be firmly opposed to any investment in South Africa or other countries, or they may object to any form of investment in companies concerned with alcohol, tobacco, armaments or many other things. In the conduct of their own affairs, of course, they are free to abstain from making any such investments. Yet under a trust, if investments of this type would be more beneficial to the beneficiaries than other investments, the trustees must not refrain from making the investments by reasons of the views that they hold.

Trustees may even have to act dishonourably (though not illegally) if the interests of their beneficiaries require it. Thus where trustees for sale had struck a bargain for the sale of trust property but had not bound themselves by a legally enforceable contract, they were held to be under a duty to consider and explore a better offer that they received, and not to carry through the bargain to which they felt in honour bound.[138] In other words, the duty of trustees to their beneficiaries may include a duty to "gazump", however honourable the trustees. As Wynn-Parry J. said trustees "have an overriding duty to obtain the best price which they can for their beneficiaries".[139] . . . **9–116**

Powers must be exercised fairly and honestly for the purposes for which they are given and not so as to accomplish any ulterior purpose, whether for the benefit of the trustees or otherwise.[140] **9–117**

Third, by way of a caveat I should say that I am not asserting that the benefit of the beneficiaries which a trustee must make his paramount concern inevitably and solely means their financial benefit, even if the only object of the trust is to provide financial benefits. Thus if the only actual or potential beneficiaries of a trust are all adults with very strict views on moral and social matters, condemning all forms of alcohol, tobacco and popular entertainment, as well as armaments, I can well understand that it might not be for the "benefit" of such beneficiaries to know that they are obtaining rather larger financial returns under the trust by reason of investments in those activities than they would have received if the trustees had invested the trust funds in other investments. The beneficiaries might well consider that it was far better to receive less than to receive more money from what they consider to be evil and tainted sources. "Benefit" is a word with a very wide meaning, and there are circumstances in which arrangements which work to the financial disadvantage of a beneficiary may yet be for his benefit.[141] But I would emphasise that such cases are likely to be very rare, and in any case I think that under a trust for the provision of financial benefits the burden would rest, and rest heavy, on him who asserts that it is for the benefit of the beneficiaries as a whole to receive less by reason of the exclusion of some of the possibly more profitable forms of investment. Plainly the present case is not one of this rare type of case. Subject to such matters, under a trust for the provision of financial benefits, the paramount duty of the trustees is to provide the greatest financial benefits for the present and future beneficiaries. **9–118**

Fourth, the standard required of a trustee in exercising his powers of investment is that he must "take such care as an ordinary prudent man would take if he were minded to make an investment for the benefit of other people for whom he felt morally bound to provide".[142] That duty includes the duty to seek advice on matters which the trustee does not understand, such as the making of investments, and on receiving that advice to act with the same degree of prudence. This requirement is not discharged merely by showing that the trustee has acted in good faith and with sincerity. Honesty and sincerity are not the same as prudence and reasonableness. Some of the most sincere people are the most unreasonable; and Mr Scargill told me that he had met quite a few of them. Accordingly, although a trustee who takes advice on investments is not bound to accept and act on that advice, he is not entitled to reject it merely because he sincerely disagrees with it, unless in addition to being sincere he is acting as an ordinary prudent man would act. **9–119**

Fifth, trustees have a duty to consider the need for diversification of investments. By section 6(1) of the Trustee Investments Act 1961: **9–120**

> "In the exercise of his powers of investment a trustee shall have regard—(a) to the need for diversification of investments of the trust, in so far as is appropriate to the circumstances of the trust; (b) to the suitability to the trust of investments of the description of investment proposed and of the investment proposed as an investment of that description."

The degree of diversification that is practicable and desirable for a large fund may plainly be impracticable or undesirable (or both) in the case of a small fund.

---

138 *Buttle v Saunders* [1950] 2 All E.R. 193.

139 *Buttle* at 195.

140 See *Duke of Portland v Topham* (1864) 11 H.L. Cas. 32, a case on a power of appointment that must apply a fortiori to a power given to trustees as such.

141 See, for example, *Re Towler's Settlement Trusts* [1964] Ch. 158; *Re CL* [1969] 1 Ch. 587.

142 See *Re Whiteley* (1886) 33 Ch.D. 347 at 355, per Lindley L.J. and see also at 350, 358; *Learoyd v Whiteley* (1887) 12 App. Cas. 727.

9–121 In the case before me, it is not in issue that there ought to be diversification of the investments held by the fund. The contention of the defendants, put very shortly, is that there can be a sufficient degree of diversification without any investment overseas or in oil, and that in any case there is no need to increase the level of overseas investments beyond the existing level. Other pension funds got on well enough without overseas investments, it was said, and in particular the NUM's own scheme had, in 1982, produced better results than the scheme here in question . . .

9–122 I shall not pursue this matter. Even if other funds in one particular year, or in many years, had done better than the scheme which is before me, that does not begin to show that it is beneficial to this scheme to be shorn of the ability to invest overseas. . . .

9–123 Sixth, there is the question whether the principles that I have been stating apply, with or without modification, to trusts of pension funds. Counsel for the plaintiffs asserted that they applied without modification, and that it made no difference that some of the funds came from the members of the pension scheme, or that the funds were often of a very substantial size. Mr Scargill did not in terms assert the contrary. He merely said that this was one of the questions to be decided, and that pension funds may be subject to different rules. I was somewhat unsuccessful in my attempts to find out from him why this was so, and what the differences were. What it came down to, I think, was that the rules for trusts had been laid down for private and family trusts and wills a long time ago; that pension funds were very large and affected large numbers of people; that in the present case the well-being of all within the coal industry was affected; . . .

9–124 I can see no reason for holding that different principles apply to pension fund trusts from those which apply to other trusts. Of course, there are many provisions in pension schemes which are not to be found in private trusts, and to these the general law of trusts will be subordinated. But subject to that, I think that the trusts of pension funds are subject to the same rules as other trusts. The large size of pension funds emphasises the need for diversification, rather than lessening it, and the fact that much of the fund has been contributed by members of the scheme seems to me to make it even more important that the trustees should exercise their powers in the best interests of the beneficiaries. In a private trust, most, if not all, of the beneficiaries are the recipients of the bounty of the settlor, whereas under the trusts of a pension fund many (though not all) of the beneficiaries are those who, as members, contributed to the funds so that in due time they would receive pensions. It is thus all the more important that the interests of the beneficiaries should be paramount, so that they may receive the benefits which in part they have paid for. I can see no justification for holding that the benefits to them should run the risk of being lessened because the trustees were pursuing an investment policy intended to assist the industry that the pensioners have left, or their union . . .

9–125 I reach the unhesitating conclusion that the trusts of pension funds are in general governed by the ordinary law of trusts, subject to any contrary provision in the rules or other provisions which govern the trust. In particular, the trustees of a pension fund are subject to the overriding duty to do the best that they can for the beneficiaries, the duty that in the United States is known as "the duty of undivided loyalty to the beneficiaries".[143]

9–126 In considering that duty, it must be remembered that very many of the beneficiaries will not in any way be directly affected by the prosperity of the mining industry or the union. Miners who have retired, and the widows and children of deceased miners, will continue to receive their benefits from the fund even if the mining industry shrinks: for the scheme is fully funded, and the fund does not depend on further contributions to it being made. I cannot regard any policy designed to ensure the general prosperity of coal mining as being a policy which is directed to obtaining the best possible results for the beneficiaries, most of whom are no longer engaged in the industry, and some of whom never were. The connection is far too remote and insubstantial. Further, the assets of even so large a pension fund as this are nowhere near the size at which there could be expected to be any perceptible impact from the adoption of the policies for which Mr Scargill contends . . .

[143] See *Blankenship v Boyle* 329 F.Supp.1089 at 1095.

C. *The Trustee Act 2000 Default Powers*

In the absence of wider express powers in the trust instrument and subject to any restriction or exclusion in such instrument or in primary or subordinate legislation, the Trustee Act 2000 (after repealing most of the Trustee Investments Act 1961) confers on trustees of old or new trusts[144] first, a "general power of investment", extending to loans secured on land (whether by way of legal or equitable mortgage or charge) but not to acquiring land, and second, a power to acquire legal estates in freehold or leasehold land in the UK as an investment or for occupation by a beneficiary or for any other reason. **9–127**

By s.3(1) "a trustee may make any kind of investment that he could make if he were absolutely entitled to the assets of the trust", but by subs.(3) "the general power of investment does not permit a trustee to make investments in land other than in loans secured on land". Investments can thus properly be made in assets anywhere in the world, including loans secured on foreign land, so long, of course, as the various equitable and statutory duties of care are observed. An "investment" was originally considered to be an asset acquired for the sake of the income it was expected to yield[145] but, nowadays, with the emphasis on "total return",[146] taking account of income yield and capital appreciation in accordance with modern portfolio theory, an investment is considered to cover an asset acquired for the sake of either or both an income yield or a likely capital profit.[147] It follows, for example, that the purchase of depreciating chattels for a villa owned by the trustees or of a depreciating vehicle for use by a beneficiary or of a lottery ticket fall outside the general power of investment, so that the beneficiary will need to have trust income or capital properly distributed to him or her and then use it to purchase the chattels or vehicle or lottery ticket for himself or herself. **9–128**

By s.8(1) "a trustee may acquire freehold or leasehold land in the United Kingdom (a) as an investment, (b) for occupation by a beneficiary, or (c) for any other reason." In England and Wales "freehold or leasehold land"[148] means a legal estate in land and, particularly in purchasing leases, the trustees will need to ensure that they observe their equitable and statutory duties of care. Then, by s.8(3), "for the purpose of exercising his functions as a trustee, a trustee who acquires land under this section has all the powers of an absolute owner in relation to the land." For trustees who have acquired land other than under s.8(3), e.g. because the settlor settled land[149] on the trustees, the Trusts of Land and Appointment of Trustees Act 1996 s.6(3) provides, "The trustees of land have power to acquire land under the power conferred by section 8 of the Trustee Act 2000." Under s.8(3) it seems that the use of the present tense enables trustees to acquire the land with the assistance of a mortgage thereon and, to that extent, "gear up" the value of the trust fund. Otherwise, gearing up by money borrowed on the security of existing assets to acquire new assets needs express authorisation.[150] **9–129**

---

144 Trustee Act 2000 ss.7(1) and 10(2).

145 *Re Wragg* [1919] 2 Ch. 58 at 64 and 65; *Re Power's WT* [1947] Ch. 576; *Tootal Broadhurst Lee Co Ltd v I.R.C.* [1949] 1 All E.R. 261 at 265.

146 *Cowan v Scargill* [1985] Ch. 270 at 287; *Harries v Church Commissioners* [1992] 1 W.L.R. 1241 at 1246; *JW v Morgan Trust Co of the Bahamas Ltd* (2000) 4 I.T.E.L.R. 541. See, too, para.9–142.

147 In *Cook v Medway Housing Soc* [1997] S.T.C. 90 at 98, "investment" was said to amount to the "laying out of moneys in anticipation of a profitable capital or income return". See too *Weston v IRC* [2001] W.T.L.R. 1217 at [18].

148 Trustee Act 2000 s.8(2). Interests in foreign land may be acquired by acquiring shares in a company that owns foreign land.

149 But land that is within the Settled Land Act 1925 is governed exclusively by such Act: Trustee Act 2000 s.10(1).

150 *Re Suenson-Taylor's ST* [1974] 1 W.L.R. 1280.

D. *Express Investment Clauses*

9–130 Express investment clauses are found in virtually all trusts (other than those arising on a person's death intestate or those arising without the assistance of legal advice), although clauses in trust instruments more than 40 or 50 years old will usually be much more limited than modern clauses drafted in the light of the variety of financial products now on offer. Powers (to acquire investments in a safe list of authorised investments) in default of express powers of investment were conferred by the Trustee Act 1925 and then the Trustee Investments Act 1961, but such powers soon became increasingly out-dated and ineffective in safeguarding and developing the value of the trust fund.

9–131 Draftsmen have developed their own sophisticated investment clauses and will continue to use them (rather than rely on the default powers in the Trustee Act 2000) so as to confer the broadest possible powers on the trustees, who, however broad their powers, have their opportunities much narrowed by the equitable and statutory duties of care imposed upon them (except to the extent expressly modified or excluded by the trust instrument). To confer the broadest possible powers, draftsmen will often employ clauses like "to apply or invest in the purchase or acquisition of assets or investments of whatsoever nature and wherever situated, and whether or not yielding income or being appreciating or depreciating assets, and including the acquisition of derivatives but only for the purpose of limiting risks and not for the purpose of speculation." However, if most exceptionally, speculation is desired, the draftsman can insert "or speculate" after "or invest" and omit the limitation on the acquisition of derivatives, while providing that in exercising such flexible powers the trustees "are under a duty to speculate with the trust fund as would an absolute beneficial owner who could afford to lose an amount equivalent to the value of the trust fund without it affecting his standard of living in any way whatever" and "are not to be liable for any conduct unless acting dishonestly".[151] The draftsman can also confer an express power to "gear up" the trust fund by borrowing on the security of existing trust property in order to acquire further property for the trust[152] and an express power to lend merely on the security of a personal promise of the borrower to repay,[153] when a high interest rate will of course be payable because a personal promise provides no security at all in the event of non-payment. Ethical investment clauses that give a large discretion to trustees can also be included, e.g. "to select only those investments which the trustees in their absolute discretion consider to be ethically acceptable".

9–132 At one stage the courts took a narrow restrictive approach to the interpretation of investment clauses as extending the default powers as little as possible, but for the last 50 years the courts[154] have been interpreting investment clauses[155] according to the natural and proper meaning of the words used in their context so as to empower investment in a fairly-construed wide range of investments. However, the courts have been strict in refusing to treat the conferment of a power for a trustee to invest in his absolute discretion in all respects as if he were the absolute beneficial owner of the trust fund as exempting such a trustee from the need to exhibit the appropriate duties of care.[156]

---

151 Such exemption clauses are valid if known of and approved by the settlor: *Armitage v Nurse* [1998] Ch. 241; *Bogg v Raper* (1998) 1 I.T.E.L.R. 267. See paras 9–215 ff.
152 Otherwise not permitted: *Re Suenson-Taylor's ST* [1974] 1 W.L.R. 1280.
153 Otherwise not permitted: *Khoo Tek Keong v Ch'ng Joo Tuan Neoh* [1934] A.C. 529.
154 *Re Harari's ST* [1949] 1 All E.R. 430; *Re Peczenik's Settlement* [1964] 1 W.L.R. 270; *Re Douglas' WT* [1959] 1 W.L.R. 744.
155 In *R v Clowes (No.2)* [1994] 2 All E.R. 316 at 327–330 the CA held that a clause "to place any uninvested funds with any body on such terms and conditions as you see fit" was not an investment clause to be treated liberally: it merely allowed money to be placed temporarily pending investment.
156 *Re Maberly* (1886) 33 Ch.D. 455 at 458; *Bartlett v Barclays Bank Trust Co Ltd* [1980] Ch. 515 at 536.

7. Capital and Income: The Trustee's Duty of Impartiality

A. Introduction

9–133 There are several reasons why it is often essential for trustees to distinguish between capital and income when they manage the trust property. First, this distinction is crucial for taxation purposes. Second, where investments are held on trust for interests in succession (e.g. "A for life, remainder to B"), investment returns will be allocated to the life tenant or the remainderman according to whether they are classified as income or capital receipts. This consideration is likely to affect the investment strategy adopted by the trustees, given their duty to maintain a fair balance between the needs of differing classes of beneficiaries when investing the trust funds. Third, where property forms part of the permanent endowment of a charitable trust, a receipt classified as capital will usually form part of that endowment and will not normally be available to be spent for charitable purposes. This consideration is also likely to affect the trustee's investment strategy. Fourth, the distinction between capital and income can affect the allocation of trustee expenses to different parts of the trust fund. Fifth, while trust law does not give trustees any general flexibility in classifying the returns from investments, it has developed certain equitable rules of apportionment which require the sharing of certain returns and outgoings between capital and income, and in some cases impose a duty to sell certain trust property. These matters will all be discussed here in turn. It should be noted at the outset that they were all recently reviewed by the Law Commission, which published a report in 2009 on *Capital and Income in Trusts: Classification and Entitlement.*[157]

A. Classification of Receipts

9–134 Broadly speaking, property which can be categorised as the "tree" is capital, and the "fruit" which it produces is categorised as income, e.g. rents, interest payments, dividends from shares. However, receipts by trustees from companies raise special problems.

9–135 Except for the purposes of taxation, no distinction is made between a company's trading profits (being the excess of trading receipts over the costs of trading) and a company's capital profits (arising from selling an asset in excess of its balance sheet value). Both sorts are available for distribution to shareholders, but the company's capital itself can only be distributed to shareholders[158] on liquidation of the company or under an authorised reduction of share capital (or a payment out of a special share premium account[159]) or a bonus issue of stock or shares which capitalises company profits. What is paid out by the company as capital goes to benefit remaindermen: what is paid out as dividend goes to the life tenant.

9–136 Distributions of capital profits can cause great unfairness. For example, in *Re Sechiari*,[160] a trust fund included shares in Thomas Tilling & Co Ltd. The company was nationalised, and was obliged to sell its road transport interests to the British Transport Commission in return for BTC stock. It decided to distribute £5 of BTC stock for each £1 of stock held by its shareholders. This led to a 75 per cent drop in the value of its shares. The life tenant was held to be entitled to the distribution as income, thus receiving much more than was fair in view of the drastic diminution in value of the capital for the remaindermen.

---

157 Law Com. No.315, 2009.
158 *Hill v Permanent Trustee Company of New South Wales Ltd* [1930] A.C. 720.
159 Tantamount to an authorised reduction of capital: *Re Duff's Settlements* [1951] Ch. 923.
160 [1950] 1 All E.R. 417 based on the rule in *Bouch v Sproule* (1885) 12 App. Cas. 385.

9–137 This case was distinguished in *Sinclair v Lee*,[161] where ICI Plc had hived off its bioscience activities to its subsidiary Zeneca Ltd and then transferred the shares in Zeneca Ltd to Zeneca Group Plc, the shares in which were then distributed to ICI shareholders. This indirect, as opposed to direct, demerger halved the value of the ICI shares. Nicholls V.C. boldly, but artificially, distinguished this from the direct demerger cases like the Thomas Tilling case, so that the Zeneca Group Plc shares were held to be capital for the benefit of the remaindermen, thereby preventing the life tenant from obtaining an unfair windfall and preserving the value of capital for the remaindermen.

9–138 In the case of ordinary scrip dividends, where a company declares a dividend but affords shareholders the option to take the dividend either as cash or as bonus shares, the receipt is income even if the shares are taken instead of cash: the company's intention is to pay a dividend and not to capitalise its profits. In the case of enhanced scrip dividends the bonus shares are issued at a price below market value in circumstances where the company has a third party lined-up ready to pay the market price for the shares. Shareholders are thus better off if taking and then selling the bonus shares, so the company's intention prima facie seems to be to capitalise the profits. However, so long as the trustee's decisions on what the trustee believed to be the company's intention were consistent, the Revenue[162] was prepared to accept the trustee's decision that the bonus shares and their proceeds were wholly capital or wholly income or, indeed, capital subject to a lien in favour of the life tenant for the amount of the cash dividend[163] (such lien being satisfied out of the proceeds of sale of the bonus shares).

9–139 In its 2009 Report, the Law Commission considered that the legal rules for the classification of corporate receipts are problematic and unpopular, and can cause significant difficulties in trust administration. In particular, it thought that the artificial distinction between direct and indirect demergers created by the decision in *Sinclair v Lee* is confusing and unprincipled. Hence it recommended that shares distributed in a tax-exempt demerger should be classified as capital for trust law purposes, so that shares would be classified as capital whether they were received as a result of direct and indirect demergers. It also recommended that when such a distribution is made, trustees should have a power to make a payment of capital to beneficiaries interested in income where otherwise there would be prejudice to those beneficiaries. The Law Commission would have liked to have gone further, to recommend that all corporate receipts should be classified by reference to a new set of rules based on the form of receipts, and to recommend additionally that settlors should be allowed to opt into a regime under which trustees would have the power to allocate trust receipts between income and capital. However, it was dissuaded from making this recommendation by HMRC, which advised that this would produce highly adverse tax consequences for interest in possession trusts.[164]

---

161 [1993] Ch. 497.

162 Statement of Practice 4/94 in the days when companies had to pay advance corporation tax on cash dividends, something they wished to avoid.

163 As permitted in *Re Malam* [1894] 3 Ch. 578.

164 HMRC considered that the proposed power of allocation would enable the trustees to make a decision as to the entitlement of the income beneficiary under an interest in possession trust, with the result that the trust income would then be regarded as accumulated or discretionary income for income tax purposes and the trust fund would be regarded as falling within the relevant property regime for IHT purposes. For discussion of the current tax treatment of trusts see paras 1–85 ff.

B. Investment Policy

9–140 As Hoffmann J. stated in *Nestlé v National Westminster Bank Plc*,[165] a "trustee must act fairly in making investment decisions which may have different consequences for differing classes of beneficiaries." Where there is a life tenant the distinction between capital and income is crucial, since the trustees have a discretion to choose whether to buy income-producing investments or capital-growth investments, and opting for an investment policy which lays too much stress on one objective or the other would unfairly favour the life tenant over the remainderman or vice versa.[166] The point can be illustrated by reference to a New Zealand case, *Re Mulligan*.[167] The settlor's widow was both a trustee and a life tenant, and she browbeat her co-trustees (a firm of solicitors who should have known better) into joining her in an investment strategy that was designed to maximise income, to the detriment of the remainderman. After her death the remainderman successfully sued her co-trustees for breach of trust, and they were held liable to make up the decline in capital value suffered by the trust fund.

9–141 Again, suppose that trustees use their power under the Trustee Act 2000 s.8, to purchase or retain a short lease of premises leased out so that the life-tenant can receive all rents during the last 10 or 12 years of the authorised lease, leaving nothing for the remainderman. In such a case, depending on what other assets form part of the trust fund, the trustees might be in breach of their overriding duty to keep an even hand between the beneficiaries, and they may also be in breach of their duty to invest prudently.[168] They would probably be in breach of this duty for purchasing such a lease in the first place,[169] and it would also be imprudent to retain it until it expires or for any longer period than reasonably necessary to sell the depreciating leases.[170] It would also seem that the remainderman could specifically invoke ss.14 and 15 of the Trusts of Land and Appointment of Trustees Act 1996 for the court to compel the trustees to sell or he could take advantage of his inherent right to call for conversion if the land was held on trust for sale.[171]

9–142 Where there is a power to appoint capital to the life tenant, the trustees will have the flexibility to invest a greater part than otherwise would be possible in assets yielding little or no income but where much capital growth is expected, so that they can then sell some of the assets and appoint the proceeds (capital) to the life tenant to make up for the income lost by investing in fewer assets yielding a good income. This would entail taking a "total return" approach to the trust investments, according to which income yield and capital growth are viewed as the combined investment objective for the fund. On this approach, if £1 million of trust assets appreciate to be worth £1,100,000 at the end of the year and yield income of £40,000, then the total return of £140,000 less an amount for inflation

---

165 (1988) [2000] W.T.L.R. 795 at 803. In an exceptional case it may even be necessary for the trustees to balance fairly the interests of beneficiaries belonging to the same class, e.g. several beneficiaries who are entitled to fixed shares of the capital. So where a trust fund included 999 shares in a private company, the trustees could reject the claim of a beneficiary entitled to 46/80 of a trust fund to have 574 of the shares, since such a majority shareholding is worth much more than 46/80 of the proceeds of sale of the 999 shares. In such a case the only fair course is to sell all the shares and divide the proceeds pro rata: *Lloyds Bank Plc v Duker* [1987] 1 W.L.R. 1324.

166 In the case of charitable trusts which have a permanent endowment, which must be kept intact as capital, a balance also needs to be kept between capital and income.

167 [1998] 1 N.Z.L.R. 481.

168 For which see paras 9–69 ff.

169 e.g. *Re Maberly* (1886) 33 Ch.D. 455 (should not invest as directed in Irish land but in statutorily authorised investments).

170 e.g. *Beauclerk v Ashburnham* (1845) 8 Beav. 322; 14 L.J.Ch. 241 where trustees were authorised and required by and with the consent and direction in writing of the life-tenant to invest in leaseholds. Obviously, the trustees could not object to investment in leaseholds as such, but they had a discretion whether or not to agree to a particular investment proposed "because it must be agreed at once that it would not be fit for them to lay out the trust moneys in a low, bad and deteriorating situation", per Lord Langdale M.R. at 8 Beav. 328.

171 *Thornton v Ellis* (1852) 15 Beav. 193; *Wightwick v Lord* (1857) 6 H.L.C. 217; and cf. *Page v West* [2010] EWHC 504 (Ch).

could be spent without the trust fund being any worse off than it was at the outset. To make allowance for annual ups and downs of the stock market it may be advisable to have a policy, if the terms of the trust allow it, to pay out the equivalent of 5 per cent of the value of the fund at the end of the year including the income produced that year. This can be done for well-drafted discretionary trusts or even well-drafted fixed interest trusts where the trustees have power to appoint capital to any beneficiary.

9–143 Unfortunately, however, trustees' scope for pursuing a "total return" investment policy is restricted by the rules that classify trust receipts as income or capital. The effect of these rules is to prevent trustees from distributing "capital receipts" to life tenants as income, with the result that they may be forced to invest more of the trust fund in income-yielding investments than would produce the best total return, in order to discharge their duty to maintain a balance between life tenant and remainderman. In its 2009 Report, the Law Commission regarded this as unsatisfactory, and would have liked to recommend that settlors should be allowed to opt into a regime under which trustees would have the power to allocate trust receipts between income and capital. As previously noted, however, it decided against making this recommendation because of the tax consequences of giving such a power to the trustees of interest in possession trusts.

9–144 Finally, note that the Charities Act 1993 ss.75, 75A, and 75B, inserted by the Charities Act 2006 s.43, now provide that even funds that form part of a charity's permanent endowment can be spent in some circumstances. The trustees of small charities can spend all or part of the capital of the permanent endowment if they consider that the purposes applicable to it could be carried out more effectively in doing so, and so can the trustees of large charities with the consent of the Charity Commission. In its 2009 Report the Law Commission has recommended there should be a general statutory power to enable all charities to resolve that the endowment fund, or some portion of it, should be freed from restrictions with respect to expenditure of capital in order that they might operate total return investment in accordance with regulations made by the Charity Commission without seeking special authorisation.[172]

C. *Expenses*

9–145 In the absence of express provision in the trust instrument, it is a matter for the general law to determine whether an expense incurred by a trust (such as accountancy fees or the cost of repairing buildings) is chargeable to income or to capital. The answer to this question can have significant tax implications, because an expense that is properly chargeable to income reduces the income tax payable.

9–146 The leading authority is *Carver v Duncan*,[173] which concerned the proper classification of various expenses, including insurance premiums and investment advisers' fees, for the purposes of the statutory precursor to the Income Tax Act 2007 s.484.[174] The House of Lords held that these expenses had been incurred for the benefit of the whole estate and were therefore properly chargeable to capital. Lord Templeman stated that:[175]

> "Trustees are entitled to be indemnified out of the capital and income of their trust fund against all obligations incurred by the trustees in the due performance of their duties and the due exercise of their powers. The trustees must then debit each item of expenditure either against income or

172 Law Com. No.315, para.8.80.

173 [1985] A.C. 1082.

174 Finance Act 1973 s.16, subsequently the Income and Corporation Taxes Act 1988 s.686.

175 *Carver* at 1120.

against capital. The general rule is that income must bear all ordinary outgoings of a recurrent nature, such as rates and taxes, and interest on charges and encumbrances. Capital must bear all costs, charges and expenses incurred for the benefit of the whole estate."

These principles were revisited by the Court of Appeal in *HMRC v Trustees of the Peter Clay Discretionary Trust*,[176] parts of which are reproduced immediately below. One issue was whether the executive trustees' fees should be treated as a trust expense for tax purposes—a question to which Lindsay J. gave a positive answer at first instance, from which no appeal was made. The case also concerned the question whether a range of expenses incurred by the trustees should be debited against capital or income: investment management fees, bank charges, custodian charges, accountancy and administration fees, and trustees' remuneration. The Court of Appeal held that only those expenses which relate wholly and exclusively to income can be attributed to income: an expense which relates both to income and to capital must be charged wholly to capital. However, where trustees can show that part of a single fee relates to work done for income alone, then the trustees can apportion the expense, detaching the income element and charging it to income. That is the case whether or not the invoice is itemised; apportionment is possible provided an evidence-based estimate can be made. **9–147**

COMMISSIONERS FOR HM REVENUE & CUSTOMS v TRUSTEES OF THE PETER CLAY DISCRETIONARY TRUST

Court of Appeal [2009] Ch. 296; [2009] 2 W.L.R. 1353; [2009] 2 All E.R. 683

SIR JOHN CHADWICK (with whom ARDEN and LLOYD L.JJ. agreed): In their grounds of appeal, annexed to the appellants' notice, the trustees do not seek to challenge the principle that capital must bear all costs charges and expenses incurred for the benefit of the whole estate. But it is said on their behalf that the judge was in error in failing to recognise that trustees' fees and remuneration are in part incurred not for the benefit of capital but for the distinct benefit of income "in so far as it is necessary to get in, account for (and make tax returns of) income as such, and distribute or determine how to deal with the income (depending on the terms of the trust)", that these are concerns of trustees which do not in any way impinge on capital, and that accordingly part of the burden of such fees and remuneration (not being incurred for the benefit of the whole estate) is not covered by the *Carver v Duncan*[177] principle and should be charged to income. Further, it is said that all costs of dealing with any income should be charged to that income; and that that the costs of capitalising income (like costs incurred in distributing income) are themselves costs of dealing with the income in question and should be charged to that income. **9–148**

The Benefit of the Whole Estate

As I have said it is common ground that expenses incurred "for the benefit of the whole estate" are chargeable to capital. But there is, I think, no true consensus between the parties as to the meaning of the expression "for the benefit of the whole estate". It is necessary, therefore, to examine the judgments of this court in [*Re Bennett*][178] and the speeches in the House of Lords in *Carver v Duncan* in order to understand the sense in which that expression is used. . . . **9–149**

[After reviewing these two cases, Sir John Chadwick concluded that:] . . . it is, I think, beyond argument that an expense is incurred "for the benefit of the whole estate" in the present context when the purpose or object for which that expense is incurred is to confer benefit both on the income beneficiaries and on those entitled to capital on the determination of the income trusts. The expression "expenses incurred for **9–150**

176 [2009] Ch. 296.
177 [1985] A.C. 1082.
178 [1896] 1 Ch. 778.

the benefit of the whole estate" must be understood in that sense. It is common ground—and, if it were not, this court would be bound by the authority of *Carver v Duncan* so to hold—that expenses which are of that nature are to be charged against capital. . . .

The Fee of the Executive Trustee

9–151 At the time the appellants' notice was filed—and the grounds of appeal settled in the terms to which I have referred—the trustees and their advisers were entitled to think that it was the Revenue's contention that no part or parts of the trustees' fees were properly chargeable to income. But it was made clear, in the skeleton argument filed on behalf of the Revenue in this Court, that the Revenue no longer maintained that contention. The Revenue's position in this Court is set out in paragraph 5 of that skeleton argument:

> "5. Regarding the fee of the executive trustee, HMRC have hitherto contended that no part of the fee is properly chargeable to income. However, as explained below, in the light of the facts found by the Special Commissioners, HMRC now accept that the Special Commissioners correctly held that a proportion of the fee is properly chargeable to income."

9–152 The basis upon which the Revenue accepts that apportionment of the executive trustee's fee and remuneration is permissible is explained at paragraphs 12 to 14 of the skeleton argument. After referring (at paragraph 11) to the proposition (endorsed by the judge at paragraph [36] of his judgment) that "an expense which is incurred for the benefit of both the income and capital beneficiaries must be regarded as incurred for the benefit of the whole estate" the Revenue went on to say this:

> "12. However, HMRC do not contend that the rule is all or nothing, precluding the apportionment of a single expense. But apportionment is not based upon the general principle of achieving fairness between beneficiaries. Instead it is based upon the ability to demonstrate that part of the expense relates to the trustee's duties to the income beneficiaries alone. That is, if it can be shown that an identified or identifiable part of an expense is for work carried out for the benefit of the income beneficiaries alone, then that part is properly chargeable to income."

For the reasons which I have set out in the previous section of this judgment, I regard that as a correct statement of the general law. It leads to the conclusion stated in the following paragraphs of the Revenue's skeleton argument:

> "13. The fee of the executive trustee in the present case is an example of a single expense which can be apportioned. The Special Commissioners found (decision, para.4(2) and (3)) that the fee was calculated on a time basis and that one-half of the time which the trustee spent on the Trust was spent on the income of the Trust alone. From this they held (decision, para.19(3)) that the fee could be attributed in part to income in exactly the same way as if a bank trustee had charged separate income and capital fees.
>
> "14. In the light of the Special Commissioners' finding of fact, HMRC now accept that they cannot challenge this decision as erroneous in law. Therefore HMRC no longer contend that no part of the executive trustee's fee is properly chargeable to income."

9–153 It seems to me, if I may say so, that a challenge to the Special Commissioners' decision that a proportion of the fee paid to the executive trustee is properly chargeable to income was incapable of being sustained once the Revenue had accepted (as it did before the judge) that a proportion of the trustees' expenses under head (v)—professional fees for accountancy and administration—were properly so chargeable. To put the point shortly: if professional fees incurred by the trustees for accountancy services can properly be apportioned (on a time basis) between fees attributable to dealing with the income of the trust fund and fees attributable to dealing with the capital of the fund, then it is impossible to see why the fees charged by the executive trustee for time spent in applying his professional judgment to the matters in relation to which those accountancy services are required should not also be capable of a proper apportionment.

9–154 It follows that the appeal must be allowed, at least to the extent of varying the order of 15 November 2007 so as to permit apportionment of the executive trustee's fee and (as I have already mentioned) to permit apportionment of bank charges, custodian fees and professional fees for accountancy and administration. The only expenses now in dispute (as the Revenue accepts, at paragraph 6 of its skeleton in this Court) are the fee paid to the non-executive trustees and the fees of the investment managers.

The Fee Paid to the Non-Executive Trustees

As I have said, the Special Commissioners held that it would not be appropriate to attribute to income any part of the fixed fee paid to the non-executive trustees. They drew a distinction between that fee—which, as they said, did not vary according to the amount of work attributed to income—and the fee paid to the executive trustee—which did vary according to the amount of work attributed to income. On the basis of that distinction they concluded that the fee paid to the non-executive trustees should properly be treated as an expense incurred for the benefit of the whole estate; and so should be charged to capital in accordance with their understanding of the *Carver v Duncan* principle. The judge did not find it necessary to address, separately, the fixed fee paid to the non-executive trustees: he had held that none of the fees paid to trustees (whether executive or non-executive) could properly be apportioned to income. **9–155**

The trustees submit that if apportionment is permissible in respect of the time-based fee paid to the executive trustee then there is no reason to deny apportionment in respect of the fixed fee paid to the non-executive trustees. The argument is summarised at paragraph 20 of counsel's supplementary skeleton argument in this court: **9–156**

> "20. . . . if the remuneration of any trustee must be supposed to take account of the work involved for income as well as for capital and if there is work of any substance involved in getting in and dealing with income (as plainly here was so) it cannot be right to differentiate between the fees payable to the different trustees. Each trustee has to deal with trust business some of which will be for the benefit of the trust as a whole and some of which will be for the purpose solely of making sure that income (the 'annual harvest') is properly accounted for and properly dealt with—the latter element is an income element as clearly as is the commission payable to an estate agent in getting in the rent from a tenanted building. So apportionment is appropriate for all trustees."

On this issue the Revenue adopts the reasoning of the Special Commissioners. It is said that, in contrast to the position in respect of the executive trustee (where the Revenue now accept that apportionment is permitted), "the fixed fee of the non-executive trustees in the present case is an example of a single expense which cannot be apportioned". The reason is said to be that "this fee, being fixed, did not vary according to the amount of work carried out for the benefit of income".

To assert that the fixed fee paid to the non-executive trustees did not vary according to the amount of work attributed to income—or "according to the amount of work carried out for the benefit of income"—is, if I may say so, a statement of the obvious. The nature of a fixed fee is that it does not vary with the amount of work actually done to earn it: whether that work be attributable solely to income, solely to capital or to both income and capital. But the fact that the fee is fixed does not of itself prevent the fee from being apportioned into two or more parts. The amount of each part is ascertained by applying the appropriate proportion to the whole. So, if it could be established (say, by the keeping of time records) that the non-executive trustees spent one half of their time addressing matters which were exclusively for the benefit of the income beneficiaries, there would be no difficulty in principle in making an attribution of one half of the fixed fee to income. The hurdle which faces the trustees' claim to charge a part of the fixed fee against income does not arise because the fee is fixed: it arises because, in the absence of time records, it will be difficult for the trustees to establish whether any (and, if any, what proportion) of the time of the non-executive trustees was spent addressing matters which were exclusively for the benefit of income. **9–157**

The Special Commissioners made no finding as to the proportion of the time spent by the non-executive trustees in addressing matters which were exclusively for the benefit of the income beneficiaries. As I have said, they took the view (at paragraph 19(3) of their decision) that the fact that the fee paid to the non-executive trustees was fixed in amount was sufficient, of itself, to preclude apportionment. For the reasons just set out, I am satisfied that they were incorrect in that view. It is, I think, self-evident that—in the administration of discretionary trusts of income—the trustees may be expected to spend part of their time in addressing matters which are exclusively for the benefit of the income beneficiaries. By way of example, if the circumstances of individual beneficiaries are such as to require the trustees (in a proper exercise of their discretion) to make a distribution of income, they may be expected to spend time **9–158** considering to whom and in what amounts such distribution should be made. As it seems to me, the Special Commissioners needed to make a finding whether, in the present case, the non-executive trustees did devote part of their time addressing such matters; and, if so, what proportion of their time was devoted to that task. It is, I think, no answer to say that, in the absence of time records, determination of that proportion will, necessarily, be imprecise: a realistic estimate can be made.

The Fees of Investment Advisers

9–159 The trustees accept—as they must, in the light of the decision in *Carver v Duncan*—that advice as to the investment of capital or of income already accumulated should be charged to the relevant fund: their claim to charge the expense of obtaining investment advice is limited to "that element of investment advice required for the purpose of determining whether and if so how the current year's income should be capitalised". It is said on their behalf (at paragraph 21 of counsel's supplementary skeleton argument) that:

> "The argument is that if income is accumulated (as it was on a large scale in this case) then the process of capitalisation involves investment and the cost of dealing with that process is as much the cost of dealing with income as is any other cost involved in the process of taking current income through to its eventual destination, whether it goes into the hands of a recipient beneficiary or goes in a capitalised form in the hands of a trustee required to keep it as such. Expense incurred before income has completed this process, and needed for the purpose of dealing with that income, must be an income expense because it is part of the expense of getting in and dealing with the annual harvest of the trust, not part of the cost of looking after the source of that harvest".

9–160 The Special Commissioners took the view that once the trustees had resolved to accumulate the income, the monies to be accumulated ought properly to be regarded as capital; so that the expenses incurred in connection with the investment of those monies could not be said to be chargeable to income. They accepted that the position might be otherwise if the trustees were temporarily investing income while deciding whether to accumulate it. The judge took a similar view.[179] As he put it: "the advice [in respect of income which was to be accumulated] amounted to advice as to how best to make the income into capital, advice which, surely, redounded for the benefit of the estate as a whole". The Revenue support that analysis.

9–161 In my view the Special Commissioners' analysis is correct. The first question is whether the expenses incurred in connection with the investment of income were incurred before or after the trustees had made the decision to accumulate that income. If the expenses were incurred after the trustees had made the decision to accumulate, they cannot, as it seems to me, be said to be expenses incurred exclusively for the benefit of the income beneficiaries. They must be charged against the capital of the accumulated funds. If the expenses were incurred before the trustees had made the decision to accumulate—and can be properly be characterised as expenses incurred for the purpose of temporarily investing income while deciding whether or not to distribute that income to the income beneficiaries—then (at least to the extent that the income was, in the event, distributed and not accumulated) the expenses could be said to have been incurred exclusively for the benefit of the income beneficiaries. But that is not said to be the present case.

D. *The Apportionment Rules*

9–162 The rules of apportionment are all logical developments of the rules classifying trust property as capital and income, and of the duty to balance the interests of beneficiaries interested in capital and income. However they were formulated a long time ago, in circumstances much less likely to arise today, they are prescriptive, they are unclear in places, and they generally require complex calculations relating to disproportionately small sums of money. They are invariably excluded by well-drafted

[179] At para.[38] of his judgment.

trust instruments and where they are not excluded they are often ignored or cause considerable inconvenience. For all these reasons the Law Commission recommended in its 2009 Report that the apportionment rules should not apply to any future trusts, subject to contrary provision in the trust instrument.[180] However, since this recommendation has not yet been acted upon, a brief account of the rules will be given here.

Where a testator's residuary estate is left on trust for A for life, remainder to B absolutely, debts, expenses, and legacies have to be paid out of residue in the course of the year traditionally allowed to the executor to wind up distribution of the deceased's estate. These payments are treated under the rule in *Allhusen v Whittell*[181] as coming partly from income and partly from capital. One must ascertain that sum which together with interest for the year would amount to the total expended on debts, expenses and legacies: such sum is borne by B as out of capital, while the excess of the total expenditure over that sum is borne by A. The rate of interest is based on the ratio subsisting between the actual net income after tax for the year and the gross capital value of the estate.[182] **9–163**

Once the net residue has been ascertained there are problems if A is receiving too high an income from unauthorised investments of a wasting or hazardous nature or if A is receiving too little income because some assets are non-income-producing (e.g. an equitable reversionary interest under another trust where the income is going to the prior life tenant). Under the rule in *Howe v Earl of Dartmouth*[183] the unauthorised[184] investments must be sold and the life tenant only receives an income of 4 per cent[185] of the value of the property, excess income having to be invested in authorised securities. Under the rule in *Re Earl of Chesterfield's Trusts*[186] once a capital value has materialised for the non-income-producing asset, whether by selling it or waiting until the death of the life tenant in the case of a reversionary interest, then the capital is apportioned between income and capital. One must ascertain that sum which, invested at 4 per cent from the date of the testator's death and accumulating at compound interest with yearly rests, would, with the accumulations, have produced the amount of capital to be apportioned: that ascertained sum is treated as capital and the excess as income. **9–164**

A need for an apportionment also arises if a trustee lends money on a security that turns out to be insufficient to repay principal and arrears of interest. Where this was an authorised investment the sum realised from the security is apportioned between life tenant and remainderman by reference to the ratio of the arrears of interest to the amount of outstanding principal.[187] Where the investment was unauthorised, then the proceeds of realisation of the investment plus any income from such investment must be apportioned between the life tenant and remainderman in the proportion which the income which the life tenant ought to have received had the unauthorised investment not been made bears to the value of the sum wrongly invested, but the life tenant must bring into hotchpot all the income actually received during the currency of the unauthorised investment.[188] **9–165**

---

180 Law Com. No.315, 2009.
181 (1867) 4 Eq. 295. See too *Re Wills* [1915] 1 Ch. 769.
182 *Re Oldham* [1927] W.N. 113.
183 (1802) 7 Ves. Jr. 137.
184 After the Trustee Act 2000, unless there is a contrary intention in the testator's will, the executor and trustee will be treated as being authorised to invest in any kind of investment other than land outside the UK. However, it may well be that an investment may be regarded as an unauthorised one from the date of the testator's death if after complying with the core duty to obtain and consider proper advice the executor decides it is not proper to retain the investment.
185 The percentage figure is supposed to represent a fair current rate: *Re Fawcett* [1940] Ch. 402, *Re Parry* [1947] Ch. 23; *Re Berry* [1962] Ch. 97.
186 (1883) 24 Ch.D. 643.
187 *Re Atkinson* [1904] 2 Ch. 160.
188 *Re Bird* [1901] 1 Ch. 916.

9–166 In the case of a purchase or sale of shares "*cum*" (with) or "*ex*" (without) dividend the trustees may prefer capital or income beneficiaries as the case may be. However, no apportionment is made unless a really glaring injustice would otherwise be caused.[189]

9–167 Finally, the Apportionment Act 1870 s.2 requires payments in the nature of income to be treated as accruing from day to day and be apportioned accordingly, which creates difficulties for a testator's life tenant (when payments received after death are apportioned to the pre-death period) as well as for classes of beneficiaries benefiting under s.31 of the Trustee Act 1925 as made clear in *Re Joel's WT*.[190]

8. Distribution of the Trust Property

9–168 Trustees typically have powers to appoint trust property to the beneficiaries, to apply the trust income to the maintenance of minor beneficiaries, and to advance capital for the benefit of beneficiaries. We will consider the duties owed by trustees when exercising each of these powers in turn.

A. Powers of Appointment

9–169 Trustees may not appoint trust property to anyone who is not a beneficiary. In *Eaves v Hickson*,[191] trustees were induced by a forgery to pay trust funds to persons not entitled, and Romilly M.R. held that, as between trustee and beneficiary, the loss fell on the former.[192] Note, however, that the Trustee Act 1925 s.61 is now available as a defence to a trustee who honestly and reasonably makes a wrongful payment through circumstances similar to those in *Eaves v Hickson*, or through an erroneous construction of the trust instrument.[193]

9–170 Before paying trust funds to an alleged assignee from a beneficiary a trustee must investigate the assignee's title. If he relies merely on the alleged assignee's statement, he is not acting reasonably. If the assignee happens also to be solicitor to the trust the trustee will still be liable[194] unless excused under s.61.[195] But although the trustee must investigate the assignee's title, he cannot require actual delivery up to him of the assignee's document of title.[196]

9–171 If a trustee, through inadvertence or a mistake of construction or of fact, has overpaid one beneficiary at the expense of another, and the court is administering the estate, then the court will adjust accounts out of future payments.[197] If the estate is not being administered by the court, an adjustment can be made with the court's assistance; and might presumably be made without any application to the court. If the underpaid beneficiary can identify the fund erroneously paid, he has, in addition, the remedy of tracing it into the hands of the overpaid beneficiary or an assignee (except a bona fide purchaser) and asserting a proprietary claim, or a personal claim in

---

189 *Bulkeley v Stephens* [1896] 2 Ch. 241; and *Hitch v Ruegg* [1986] T.L. & P. 62 disapproving *Re Winterstoke's WT* [1938] Ch. 158.
190 [1967] Ch. 14.
191 (1861) 30 Beav. 136. However, only if the forger or the wrong recipients could not compensate the beneficiary.
192 See also *Ashby v Blackwell* (1765) 2 Eden 299 at 302; *Sutton v Wilders* (1871) L.R. 12 Eq. 373, *Boulton v Beard* (1853) 3 De G.M. & G. 608; *Sporle v Barnaby* (1864) 10 Jur. 1142.
193 *Re Smith* (1902) 71 L.J. Ch. 411; *National Trustees Company of Australasia v General Finance Co of Australasia* [1905] A.C. 381; *Re Allsop* [1914] 1 Ch. 1. For discussion of s.61, see paras 11–105 ff.
194 *Davis v Hutchings* [1907] 1 Ch. 356.
195 *Re Allsop* [1914] 1 Ch. 1. It is possible protection may be available under Trustee Act 2000 ss. 11 and 23.
196 *Re Palmer* [1907] 1 Ch. 486; see *Warter v Anderson* (1853) 11 Hare 301.
197 *Dibbs v Goren* (1849) 11 Beav. 483; *Re Musgrave* [1916] 2 Ch. 417. Not until *Kleinwort Benson Ltd v Lincoln CC* [1999] 2 A.C. 349 did the common law allow recovery for mistakes of law as well as fact.

knowing receipt if he can prove that the recipient had the requisite degree of knowledge.[198] If he is a beneficiary under a will he will also have a personal action against a recipient under *Ministry of Health v Simpson* principles, according to which the recipient's knowledge is irrelevant and he is strictly liable to repay the value of the assets received.[199]

If a trustee-beneficiary underpays himself, however, then, according to *Re Horne*,[200] he suffers by his mistake, although it may be that, nowadays, he should be allowed to recoup himself out of trust property in his hands.[201] **9–172**

In 1982 the Law Reform Committee made the following recommendation:[202] **9–173**

> "where it appears that the cost of taking out a summons is out of all proportion to the amount at stake, trustees should be empowered to take the advice of counsel (in the case of trusts having adult beneficiaries only) or Chancery Queens Counsel or conveyancing counsel of the court (where there are infant beneficiaries) and to distribute on the basis of that advice if no adult beneficiary starts proceedings within three months of being sent a copy of the relevant opinion."

As a half-way measure the Administration of Justice Act 1985 s.48 gives the court power (without an oral hearing) to authorise action to be taken concerning the construction of a will or trust in reliance on a written opinion of a person with a ten year High Court qualification within the Courts and Legal Services Act 1990 s.71.

B. Powers of Maintenance

Under the Trustee Act 1925 s.31, trustees have a power to apply trust income to the maintenance of minor beneficiaries. This power is of fundamental importance in the administration of trusts for the assistance it may provide to minors, for the taxation repercussions flowing from the way in which it can convert what are vested interests under the terms of the trust into contingent interests and also flowing from a beneficiary's entitlement to income at 18 years of age,[203] and for the apportionment problems it creates where there is a class of beneficiaries. **9–174**

The trustees must be aware of these points and they must consciously exercise their discretion whether to exercise the power. In *Wilson v Turner*[204] they automatically paid over the income to the minor's father without any request from him and without any attempt to ascertain whether any income was required for the minor's maintenance: the father was ordered to repay the income. Trustees should particularly review the situation a month or two before the minor attains 18 years since the statutory power to apply income and its accumulations over the years expires on his 18th birthday. **9–175**

Under the statutory power, so long as income is legally available,[205] there is a duty to accumulate the income for the period of the beneficiary's minority, so far as it is not used under a power to apply it for the maintenance, education or benefit of the beneficiary. During this period accumulations may be used as if they were current income despite having accrued to the capital.[206] Once the beneficiary **9–176**

---

198 See paras 12–09 ff. and 13–96 ff.
199 [1951] A.C. 251.
200 [1905] 1 Ch. 76.
201 See *Re Reading* [1916] W.N. 262.
202 Law Reform Committee, *Powers and Duties of Trustees* (Cmnd. 8733, 1982), para.5.4.
203 See para.1–91.
204 (1883) 22 Ch.D. 521.
205 A trust instrument may oust s.31 expressly or by necessary implication and s.31 only applies in the case of a contingent interest if the interest carries the intermediate income.
206 Section 31(2).

attains 18, however, the trustees must pay the income from the capital (including the accumulations which become part of the capital) to the beneficiary even if the beneficiary's interest is still contingent under the trust terms, e.g. to B if he attains 25 years.[207]

9–177 Section 31(2) may convert what appear to be indefeasible vested interests into defeasible or contingent interests, since accumulations of income will not pass to a beneficiary with a vested interest in income under the terms of the trust unless he satisfies a contingency within s.31(2)(i), or unless he is entitled not just to income but also to the capital to which the accumulations automatically accrue, as where personalty is settled on a minor not for life but absolutely (s.31(2)(ii)). The contingencies within s.31(2)(i) are (a) attaining the age of 18 or marrying thereunder when having a vested interest in income during his infancy, and (b) attaining the age of 18 or marrying thereunder when thereupon becoming entitled to the capital from which the income arose in fee simple absolute or determinable[208] (realty) or absolutely and indefeasibly[209] (personalty) or for an entailed interest (realty and personalty). Thus, if B is an unmarried minor and under a trust an apparently indefeasible vested interest is conferred on him (e.g. to B for life), then in substance B's interest in income is defeasible or contingent[210] since he has no right to income as it arises (the trustees being under a duty to accumulate it in so far as not exercising their power to use it if they see fit for B's maintenance, education or benefit), and he has no right to accumulated income unless he attains 18 or marries thereunder.

9–178 Section 31 may be ousted wholly or partly by a contrary intention expressed directly or indirectly in the trust instrument. Its provisions will be inapplicable if on a fair reading of the instrument in question one can say that such application would be inconsistent with the purport of the instrument.[211]

TRUSTEE ACT 1925 SECTION 31

Power to Apply Income for Maintenance and to Accumulate Surplus Income during a Minority

9–179 (1) Where any property is held by trustees in trust for any person for any interest whatsoever, whether vested or contingent, then, subject to any prior interests[212] or charges affecting that property—

(i) during the infancy of any such person, if his interest so long continues, the trustees may, at their sole discretion, pay to his parent or guardian, if any, or otherwise apply for or towards his maintenance, education, or benefit, the whole or such part, if any, of the income of that property as may, in all the circumstances, be reasonable, whether or not there is—(a) any other fund applicable to the same purpose; or (b) any person bound by law to provide for his maintenance or education; and

---

207 This gives the beneficiary an interest in possession which has had much significance for IHT purposes in the past, but note the changes to the IHT regime made in 2006, discussed at paras 1–95 ff.

208 *Re Sharp's ST* [1973] Ch. 331 treats this as a determinable fee in the strict sense distinct from a fee simple on condition though the Settled Land Act 1925 s.117(1)(iv) (not cited) treats "determinable fee" as meaning a fee determinable whether by limitation or condition. Consider Trustee Act 1925 s.68(1)(xviii).

209 The interest will not be absolute if defeasible by an overriding power or a condition: *Re Sharp's ST*, above.

210 *Stanley v IRC* [1944] K.B. 255; *Re Delamere's ST* [1984] 1 W.L.R. 813.

211 *IRC v Bernstein* [1961] Ch. 399 at 412; *Re Delamere's ST* [1984] 1 All E.R. 584 at 588. See too *Price v Williams-Wynn* [2006] W.T.L.R. 1633, where trustees executed a deed with the intention of creating an immediate interest in possession, but failed to exclude s.31 with the result that their purpose was frustrated; the deed was rectified to exclude the section.

212 If there is a prior direction to set apart and accumulate income, the trustees have no power to apply intermediate income for maintenance under this section: *Re Reade-Revell* [1930] 1 Ch. 52, but the court may do so under its inherent jurisdiction: *Re Walker* [1901] 1 Ch. 879.

(ii) if such person on attaining the age of [eighteen][213] years has not a vested[214] interest in such income, the trustees shall[215] thenceforth pay the income of that property and of any accretion thereto under subsection (2) of this section to him, until he either attains a vested interest therein or dies, or until failure of his interest:

Provided that, in deciding whether the whole or any part of the income of the property is during a minority to be paid or applied for the purposes aforesaid, the trustees shall have regard to the age of the infant and his requirements and generally to the circumstances of the case, and in particular to what other income, if any, is applicable for the same purposes; and where trustees have notice that the income of more than one fund is applicable for those purposes, then, so far as practicable, unless the entire income of the funds is paid or applied as aforesaid or the court otherwise directs, a proportionate part only of the income of each fund shall be so paid or applied.

(2) During the infancy of any such person, if his interest so long continues, the trustees shall accumulate all the residue of that income by investing it, and any profits from so investing it from time to time in authorised investments, and shall hold those accumulations as follows:

(i) If any such person—(a) attains the age of eighteen years, or marries under that age, and his interest in such income during his infancy or until his marriage is a vested interest; or (b) on attaining the age of eighteen years or on marriage under that age becomes entitled to the property from which such income arose in fee simple, absolute or determinable, or absolutely,[216] for an entailed interest; the trustees shall hold the accumulations in trust for such person absolutely, but without prejudice to any provision with respect thereto contained in any settlement by him made under any statutory powers during his infancy, and so that the receipt of such person after marriage, and though still an infant, shall be a good discharge; and

(ii) In any other case the trustees shall,[217] notwithstanding that such person had a vested interest in such income, hold the accumulations as an accretion to the capital of the property from which such accumulations arose,[218] and as one fund with such capital for all purposes, and so that, if such property is settled land, such accumulations shall be held upon the same trusts as if the same were capital money arising therefrom; but the trustees may, at any time during the infancy of such person if his interest so long continues, apply those accumulations, or any part thereof, as if they were income arising in the then current year.

(3) This section applies in the case of a contingent interest only if the limitation or trust carries the intermediate income[219] of the property, but it applies to a future or contingent legacy by the

---

213 For interests under any instruments made before January 1, 1970, 21 years remain the relevant age: Sch.III para.5(1). In such a case money may be paid direct to the beneficiary once he attains 18 instead of to his parent or guardian, Sch.III para.5(2). For appointments made after 1969 under a pre-1970 settlement the relevant age is 18: *Re Delamere's ST* [1984] 1 All E.R. 584 at 588; *Begg-McBrearty v Stilwell* [1996] 1 W.L.R. 951.

214 The section does not apply if the person has a vested interest, even if it is liable to be divested: *Re McGeorge* [1963] Ch. 544.

215 The word "shall" prima facie imports a "duty" as distinct from a "power". In this context, however, it imports a "power" which can be overriden by the expression of a contrary intention: see the Trustee Act 1925 s.69(2); *Re Turner's WT* [1937] Ch. 15. Provisions made by the settlor or testator if inconsistent with the statutory power amount to contrary intention, e.g. a direction to accumulate: *Re Erskine's ST* [1971] 1 W.L.R. 162; *Re Henderson's Trusts* [1969] 1 W.L.R. 651 at 659. But if there is no contrary intention the trustees are under a duty to pay the income to the beneficiary on his attaining the age of 18: *Re Jones' WT* [1947] Ch. 48. Even though the beneficiary may not be entitled to the capital till attaining 30 years of age the fact that he is entitled to the income will give him an interest in possession for inheritance tax purposes.

216 This applies exclusively to personalty and requires the interest in personalty to be indefeasible so that there is an odd distinction between realty and personalty: *Re Sharp's ST* [1973] Ch. 331.

217 This may be excluded if its application would be inconsistent with the purport of the instrument in question, e.g. where an appointment of income to six minors "in equal shares absolutely" reveals in context an intention that each was to take an indefeasible share even if dying before attaining 18: *Re Delamere's ST* [1984] 1 All E.R. 584.

218 Thus accumulation subject to an overriding power of appointment form an accretion to the respective shares of the beneficiaries subject to the overriding power: *Re Sharp's ST* [1973] Ch. 331, following *Re Joel's WT* [1967] Ch. 14.

219 As to this, see the Law of Property Act 1925 s.175.

parent of, or a person standing in loco parentis to, the legatee, if and for such period as, under the general law, the legacy carries interest for the maintenance of the legatee, and in any such case as last aforesaid the rate of interest shall (if the income available is sufficient, and subject to any rules of court to the contrary[220]) be five pounds per centum per annum.

(4) This section applies to a vested annuity in like manner as if the annuity were the income of property held by trustees in trust to pay the income thereof to the annuitant for the same period for which the annuity is payable, save that in any case accumulations made during the infancy of the annuitant shall be held in trust for the annuitant or his personal representatives absolutely.

(5) This section does not apply where the instrument, if any, under which the interest arises came into operation before the commencement of this Act.[221]

LAW OF PROPERTY ACT 1925 SECTION 175

Contingent and Future Testamentary Gifts Carry Intermediate Income

9–180 (1) A contingent or future specific devise or bequest of property, whether real or personal, and a contingent residuary devise of freehold land, and a specific or residuary devise of freehold land to trustees upon trust for persons whose interests are contingent or executory shall, subject to the statutory provisions relating to accumulations, carry the intermediate income of that property from the death of the testator, except so far as such income, or part thereof, may be otherwise expressly disposed of.

(2) This section applies only to wills coming into operation after the commencement of this Act.

9–181 In the case of an infant with a vested interest the Trustee Act 1925 s.31 requires income to be accumulated except so far as it is applied for the maintenance of the infant unless the income is disposed of in favour of someone else or directed only to be accumulated.[222] But if the infant's interest is contingent, then by s.31(3) income is not required to be dealt with in this way, unless the limitation or trust carries the intermediate income. The rules in regard to this are as follows (subject to any contrary intention):

- A contingent gift by will of residuary personalty carries with it all the income which it produces after the testator's death.[223] If the income is accumulated until the contingency occurs, then any applicable rules limiting the period of accumulation, must be complied with.[224] On the other hand, a residuary bequest, whether vested or contingent, which is expressly deferred to a future date does not carry intermediate income.[225]

---

220 4 per cent is now prescribed pursuant to CPR Practice Direction 40.15.

221 The section applies to an appointment made after 1925 under a power created before 1926: *Re Dickinson's Settlements* [1939] Ch. 27.

222 *Re Turner's WT* [1937] Ch. 15; *Re Ransome* [1957] Ch. 348; *Re Reade-Revell* [1930] 1 Ch. 52; *Re Stapleton* [1946] 1 All E.R. 323.

223 *Re Adams* [1893] 1 Ch. 329 at 334.

224 *Countess of Bective v Hodgson* (1864) 10 H.L.C. 656. But note that the Law of Property Act 1925 ss.164–166 and the Perpetuities and Accumulations Act 1964 s.13 have now been abolished for most purposes by the Perpetuities and Accumulations Act 2009 s.13.

225 *Re Oliver* [1947] 2 All E.R. 162 at 166; *Re Gillett's WT* [1950] Ch. 102; *Re Geering* [1964] Ch. 136.

- A contingent residuary devise of freehold land and a residuary devise of freehold land to trustees upon trust for persons, whose interests are contingent, carry the intermediate income which they produce.[226]
- A contingent or future specific bequest of personalty carries the intermediate income,[227] and so does a contingent or future specific devise of realty.[228]
- An inter vivos contingent interest will be of specific property and will carry the intermediate income (unless the income is disposed of in favour of someone else or directed to be accumulated).
- Where a testator directs that a general or pecuniary contingent legacy (e.g. "a thousand ICI Plc shares" or "£15,000") be set apart from the rest of his estate for the benefit of the minor contingent legatee this will carry the intermediate income produced by such separate fund.[229]

Section 31(3) further makes s.31 apply to a future or contingent legacy by a parent or person in loco parentis so far as under the general law the legacy carries interest for the maintenance of the legatee. Where a future or contingent legacy has not been directed to be set apart so as itself to produce intermediate income, it will be paid in due course at the appropriate time out of the residuary estate, and usually the legatee just receives the legacy without being allowed any interest for the period before the legacy became payable.[230] Exceptionally, a legacy carries 4 per cent interest[231] payable from the testator's death out of the residuary estate income if the testator was the parent or in loco parentis to the minor legatee, the legacy was direct to the minor and not to trustees for him,[232] no other fund was set aside for the maintenance of the minor,[233] and, if the legacy was contingent, the contingency related to the legatee's minority and so was not the attaining of an age greater than the age of majority.[234] In this exceptional case the provisions of s.31 apply. **9–182**

There is a further exceptional case where a contingent legacy carries 6 per cent interest before it becomes payable: where the testator's will reveals an intention that the legacy should carry interest from the testator's death for the maintenance of the minor.[235] Here the testator need not be the parent of or in loco parentis to the minor and the contingency may be the attainment of an age exceeding majority.[236] It would seem that this was overlooked so that, strictly, s.31 is inapplicable, so that there must be used for the maintenance of the legatee interest at 4 per cent rather than the higher actual income produced if, on winding up the testator's estate, the executors for convenience sake set aside the capital to which the legatee will be entitled on attaining, say, 25 years of age. It will be troublesome that the balance of income over the sum representing 4 per cent interest will fall into **9–183**

---

226 Law of Property Act 1925 s.175.
227 Law of Property Act 1925 s.175.
228 *Re McGeorge* [1963] Ch. 544.
229 *Re Medlock* (1886) 55 L.J. Ch. 738; Re Woodin [1895] 2 Ch. 309; Re Couturier [1907] 1 Ch. 470. Income will be carried from the end of the executor's year unless intended to provide for the maintenance of a minor legatee as from the testator's death.
230 *Re Raine* [1929] 1 Ch. 716.
231 Trustee Act 1925 s.31(3); CPR Practice Direction 40.15.
232 *Re Pollock* [1943] Ch. 338.
233 *Re West* [1913] 2 Ch. 345.
234 *Re Abrahams* [1911] 1 Ch. 108.
235 *Re Churchill* [1909] 2 Ch. 431 (intention implied from a power to apply the whole or any part of the contingent legacy for the advancement or otherwise for the benefit of the legatee at any time before attaining 21 years of age, which clearly authorised payments for the minor's maintenance), *Re Selby Walker* [1949] 2 All E.R. 178.
236 *Re Jones* [1932] 1 Ch. 108 (beware the incorrect headnote).

residue. However, it would probably strain s.31(3) too much to construe "contingent interest" which "carries the intermediate income" to include contingent legacies to the extent they indirectly (via interest payable out of the residuary estate income) carry intermediate income so as to cover this further exceptional case, especially when the latter half of the subsection deals with legacies which carry interest for maintenance.

C. *Powers of Advancement*

9–184 Under the Trustee Act 1925 s.32, trustees have the power to advance trust capital for the benefit of beneficiaries. When exercising this power they must be careful for a mistake will mean that both capital and income disappear, probably for good. Danckwerts J. has said that " 'benefit' is the widest possible word one could have and it must include payment direct to the beneficiary but that does not absolve the trustees from making up their minds whether the payment in the particular manner which they contemplate is for the benefit of the beneficiary";[237] and Viscount Radcliffe has said that benefit "means any use of money which will improve the material situation of the beneficiary".[238] In *Re Hampden*[239] a transfer to trustees for the benefit of the beneficiary's children was held to have been authorised by an express power to benefit the beneficiary. In *Re Clore's ST*[240] making a donation to a charity at a wealthy beneficiary's request to discharge what he felt to be a moral obligation was held to be an advancement for his benefit, but in *X v A*[241] it was held that the existence of a beneficiary's moral obligation to make charitable gifts was an objective question that did not merely turn on the beneficiary's personal opinion.

9–185 *Re Pauling's ST*[242] provides a sorry, salutary story for compulsory reading before trustees exercise their power of advancement. It is a fascinating case but too long to set out in any detail. Essentially, the father of the beneficiaries was so charming and forceful that the trustees frittered away much of the capital in ways that enabled the wife's overdraft to be paid off, a house to be bought for the father and his wife absolutely and an overly high standard of living to be maintained for the family. The lessons to be drawn are that requests for advancements from young adults unemancipated from the undue influence of their parents must be treated with caution and the moneys requested applied by the trustees themselves for a particular purpose if previous experience indicates that otherwise the purported purpose is unlikely to be effected.

9–186 Reviewing *Pauling's* case in the New Zealand Supreme Court in *Kain v Hutton*, Tipping J. said that:[243]

> "in spite of the width of the concept of benefit, [the case] shows that it is insufficient simply to make an advancement on the basis that any receipt of money or other property ahead of the date of vesting in possession must be of benefit to the recipient. The concept of benefit is wide but not wholly unrestricted.
>
> For example, proposed advancements close to the date of vesting in possession should be viewed cautiously. Trustees must make sure that there really is a good reason to advance the date. Similarly, advancements when the trustees are or should be aware that the beneficiary may be

---

237 *Re Moxon's WT* [1958] 1 W.L.R. 165. For "benefit" under an express clause see *Re Buckinghamshire's ST, The Times*, March 29, 1977.

238 *Pilkington v IRC* [1964] A.C. 612 at 635.

239 [2001] W.T.L.R. 195; *Re Esteem Settlement* [2001] W.T.L.R. 641.

240 [1966] 1 W.L.R. 955.

241 [2006] 1 W.L.R. 741.

242 [1964] Ch. 303.

243 [2008] 3 N.Z.L.R. 589 at [56]–[59] (footnotes omitted).

> going to use the money or other property unwisely should also be viewed with caution, unless the advancement is by means of a protective trust.
>
> Need, as such, is not the touchstone but if there is a total absence of material or moral need the interests of those who take in default should be preferred to those of the proposed advancee. The position, in short, is that trustees may exercise their discretionary power to make an advancement only if they have formed the considered view that there is good reason to do so and it truly will be of benefit to the advanced beneficiary to exercise the power in the manner contemplated. . . .
>
> In this respect powers of advancement are different from powers of appointment. A person exercising a power of appointment is exercising a discretionary power to select who should take from a group of potential beneficiaries. That is a materially different task from that required of someone exercising a power of advancement. There, the essential question is whether a distribution should be made ahead of the time at which the beneficiary would otherwise receive possession of property in which they already have an interest."

An advancement may be by way of settlement that benefits someone other than the beneficiary so long as the beneficiary receives significant benefit,[244] e.g. receiving a life interest in the advanced moneys, remainder to his widow for life, remainder to his children equally. To deal with a dictum of Upjohn J.[245] and cases narrowly construing powers of appointment in outdated fashion the power of advancement has often been expressly extended to permit delegation of duties and discretions to make clear that a re-settlement may be by way of discretionary trusts or by way of protective trusts which may end up after forfeiture as discretionary trusts. However, the modern consensus, supported by Viscount Radcliffe in *Pilkington v IRC*,[246] is that no question of delegation of the trustees' functions arises where they transfer property to be held on new trusts which may contain discretionary trusts and powers, because the new trustees are not exercising delegated functions but are exercising new original functions of their own as a result of the outright advancement. **9–187**

It is necessary to ensure that the rule against remoteness is not infringed, for the perpetuity period relevant to the exercise of the power of advancement runs from the date of the settlement and not from the date of the exercise of the power.[247] If part of the exercise of the power of advancement is void for remoteness and the resultant effect of the intended advancement is such that it could not reasonably be regarded as being beneficial to the beneficiary intended to be advanced, then the advancement fails for it cannot be authorised as within the powers of the trustees under s.32: otherwise the part of the advancement not void for remoteness will stand as within the trustees' powers,[248] e.g. C's life interest stands where the advancement is to trustees for C for life with remainders to his issue where the remainders are void for remoteness. The fact that in such a case no effective beneficial trusts of capital are created does not mean that there has been no payment or application of capital as required by s.32: the transfer of capital to the trustees of the settlement for C for life is an application of capital within s.32.[249] **9–188**

---

244 *Pilkington v IRC* [1964] A.C. 612; *Re Hampden* [2001] W.T.L.R. 195.
245 *Re Wills' Trusts* [1959] Ch. 1 at 13.
246 [1964] A.C. 612 at 639.
247 *Pilkington v IRC* [1964] A.C. 612. For the purposes of the Perpetuities and Accumulations Act 2009 the exercise of a power of advancement is treated as the exercise of a special power.
248 *Re Abraham's WT* [1969] 1 Ch. 463 as cut down by the interpretation of the CA in *Re Hastings-Bass* [1975] Ch. 25 explored in *Mettoy Pension Trustees v Evans* [1990] 1 W.L.R. 1587.
249 *Re Hastings-Bass* [1975] Ch. 25.

TRUSTEE ACT 1925 SECTION 32

9–189 (1) Trustees may[250] at any time or times pay or apply any capital money[251] subject to a trust, for the advancement or benefit, in such manner as they may, in their absolute discretion, think fit, of any person entitled to the capital[252] of the trust property or of any share thereof, whether absolutely or contingently on his attaining any specified age or on the occurrence of any other event, or subject to a gift over on his death under any specified age or on the occurrence of any other event, and whether in possession or in remainder or reversion, and such payment or application may be made notwithstanding that the interest of such person is liable to be defeated by the exercise of a power of appointment or revocation, or to be diminished by the increase of the class to which he belongs:

Provided that—

(a) the money so paid or applied for the advancement or benefit of any person shall not exceed altogether in amount one-half[253] of the presumptive or vested share or interest of that person in the trust property; and

(b) if that person is or becomes absolutely and indefeasibly entitled to a share in the trust property the money so paid or applied shall be brought into account as part of such share; and

(c) no such payment or application shall be made so as to prejudice any person entitled to any prior life or other interest,[254] whether vested or contingent, in the money paid or applied unless such person is in existence and of full age and consents in writing to such payment or application.[255]

(2) This section applies only where the trust property consists of money or securities or of property held upon trust for sale calling in and conversion, and such money or securities, or the proceeds of such sale calling in and conversion are not by statute or in equity considered as land, or applicable as capital money for the purposes of the Settled Land Act 1925.

(3) This section does not apply to trusts constituted or created before the commencement of this Act.

---

250 The section confers a power; it does not impose a duty: hence it cannot be utilised if the settlement contains a contrary intention: see *IRC v Bernstein* [1961] Ch. 399; *Re Henderson's Trusts* [1969] 1 W.L.R. 651; *Re Evans' Settlement* [1967] 1 W.L.R. 1294. While a duty to accumulate is necessarily inconsistent with the power of maintenance it is not necessarily inconsistent with the power of advancement: *IRC v Bernstein* [1961] Ch. 399. Section 32 is not excluded by the accumulation trust in s.31 nor by express accumulation and maintenance trusts in similar form to s.31.

251 Assets can be transferred *in specie: Re Collard's WT* [1961] Ch. 293. When brought into account on final distribution of the trust property they will be taken into account as of their cash value when originally received: *Re Gollin's Declaration of Trust* [1969] 1 W.L.R. 1858.

252 The section does not apply where the beneficiary is given only an interest in income: *Re Winch's Settlement* [1917] 1 Ch. 633.

253 If A and B are the two beneficiaries contingently equally entitled to a trust fund of £200,000 and B receives the maximum advancement of £50,000 does this mean that the power can no longer be exercised in his favour or, if the fund remaining appreciates to £250,000, can B maintain that the fund is now notionally worth £250,000 plus his advanced £50,000 so that an advancement of half of half of £300,000, i.e., £75,000, may be made to him so that he may receive a further £25,000 on top of the £50,000 he has already received? Consider s.32(1) proviso (b), and also *Re Marquess of Abergavenny's Estate Act Trusts* [1981] 1 W.L.R. 843 (trustees had express power to advance to the life tenant "any part or parts not exceeding in all one half in value of the settled fund". Goulding J. held an advance of half the value of the settled fund exhausted the exercise of the power so that it ceased to be exercisable in the future even though the retained assets had later increased in value).

254 A beneficiary under a discretionary trust is not entitled to such a prior interest as to render his consent requisite: *Re Beckett's Settlement* [1940] Ch. 279 but where income is held on the protective trusts in Trustee Act 1925 s.33, and there has been no forfeiture the "principal beneficiary" has a prior interest within para.(c) his consent not incurring a forfeiture: *Re Harris' Settlement* (1940) 162 L.T. 358; *Re Rees' WT* [1954] Ch. 202. Further see *IRC v Bernstein* [1961] Ch. 399. Often the power to advance is extended to the whole, rather than half, of the prospective share but the life tenant's consent remains requisite: *Henley v Wardell, The Times*, January 29, 1988. In the case of a small trust fund for a minor the half may be extended to the whole under the Variation of Trusts Act 1958: *D v O* [2004] 3 All E.R. 780.

255 The remainderman's power to withhold consent to a proposed exercise by trustees of their powers under s.32 is a personal rather than a fiduciary power: *C v C* [2009] W.T.L.R. 1419 at [15].

9. Delegation of Duties and Powers

A. Introduction

The law's attitude towards the delegation of trustee duties has shifted over time. The classical rule of equity was *delegatus non potest delegare* ("a delegate is not able to delegate"), reflected in Langdale M.R.'s comment in *Turner v Corney*[256] that "trustees who take on themselves the management of property for the benefit of others have no right to shift their duty on other persons; and if they employ an agent, they remain subject to the responsibility towards their cestuis que trust, for whom they have undertaken the duty". In other words, trustees owed a continuing duty to account for the trust property to the beneficiaries that could not be discharged by transferring the property into the hands of an agent. If trustees did this, and the agent dealt with the property to good effect, then the beneficiaries could ratify the trustees' acts; but if the agent absconded with the property or negligently lost it, then the beneficiaries could hold the trustees liable to account for its value because the transfer to the agent was an unauthorised transaction that would be struck out on a taking of accounts—i.e. the accounts would be "falsified" to show that the transfer had never taken place, leaving the trustees with an ongoing duty hold the property for the beneficiaries that they would have to perform substitutively by paying its market value into the trust fund.[257] **9–190**

By the 1880s, however, the courts had become concerned that this rule operated too harshly against trustees who needed to be able to delegate their investment functions to professionals with expertise in investing in an increasingly sophisticated financial marketplace. Hence in *Speight v Gaunt*[258] the Court of Appeal, affirmed by the House of Lords, held that trustees had an implied authority to delegate their managerial responsibilities to an agent if, in the circumstances, delegation was either reasonably necessary or in the ordinary course of affairs. If these conditions were satisfied then the trustee would owe no continuing duty to account for property transferred to the agent. However, the trustee still had to be prudent in his selection and supervision, and he could not employ an agent to do an act outside the scope of the agent's business.[259] Thus the trustee could still be made liable for loss arising through the agent's default if he failed to exercise reasonable care in selecting and supervising the agent.[260] Moreover, the trustees would not be relieved from such liability by an express or statutory provision[261] authorising a wide use of agents in ministerial matters and exempting a trustee from liability for loss caused by the acts or defaults of an agent unless the loss occurred through the trustee's "wilful default".[262] **9–191**

The Trustee Act 1925 radically enlarged trustees' collective powers to delegate implementation of their decisions to an agent because s.23(1) enabled them to delegate whether or not there was any reasonable need for this, and lazy trustees could therefore delegate matters they could have seen to personally. However, they could not delegate the exercise of their own discretion to decide what should be done except, as before, in the case of managing overseas property (although under s.23(2) **9–192**

---

256 (1841) 5 Beav. 515 at 517.

257 *Att.-Gen. v Scott* (1749) 1 Ves. Sen. 413 at 417; *Clough v Bond* (1838) 3 My. & Cr. 440 at 496–497; *Rowland v Witherden* (1851) 3 Mac. & G. 568. Falsification of accounts and substitutive performance claims are discussed in Chapter 11.

258 (1883) 22 Ch.D. 727, affirmed (1883) 9 App. Cas. 1; discussed in C Stebbings, *The Private Trustee in Victorian England* (2001) Ch.5, esp. 151–155.

259 *Fry v Tapson* (1884) 28 Ch.D. 268.

260 *Matthews v Brise* (1845) 10 Jur. (O.S.) 105.

261 *Underwood v Stevens* (1816) 1 Mer. 712; Trustee Act 1925 s.30(1). The position is now governed by the Trustee Act 2000 s.23.

262 *Re Brier* (1884) 26 Ch.D. 238 at 243, per Lord Selborne L.C. Also see *Re Chapman* [1896] 2 Ch. 763 at 776, per Lindley L.J.: "Wilful default which includes want of ordinary prudence on the part of the trustees must be proved." In *Speight v Gaunt* (1883) 9 App. Cas. 1 at 13–15 and 22–23, the HL treated wilful default as including want of ordinary prudence.

they could now do this whether or not there was any reasonable necessity for it). Following the enactment of the 1925 legislation, it was uncertain whether trustees still owed a duty to select and supervise agents with the care of the prudent business person. Traditionalists considered that they did, and would be liable if they were personally guilty of wilful default in the traditional equitable sense which covered deliberate, reckless and negligent conduct.[263] Modernists believed in a literal, rather than a history-based, interpretation of s.23(1) so that in cases where use of agents was permissible trustees should not be personally "responsible for the default of any such agent if employed in good faith", although there could be personal liability for trustees guilty of wilful default in the common law sense of deliberate or reckless conduct.[264] In *Armitage v Nurse*,[265] the Court of Appeal, without full consideration of the arguments favouring the traditional approach, accepted the modernists' interpretation.[266]

B. Collective Delegation under the Trustee Act 2000

9–193 The Trustee Act 2000 ss.11 to 27 confer the following powers on trustees collectively, subject to the following duties, and subject also to any restriction or exclusion imposed by the trust instrument or by any other legislation.[267]

i. Agents

TRUSTEE ACT 2000 SECTION 11

9–194 (1) Subject to the provisions of this Part, the trustees of a trust may authorise any person to exercise any or all of their delegable functions as their agent.

(2) In the case of a trust other than a charitable trust, the trustees' delegable functions consist of any function other than—

(a) any function relating to whether or in what way any assets of the trust should be distributed,
(b) any power to decide whether any fees or other payment due to be made out of the trust funds should be made out of income or capital,
(c) any power to appoint a person to be a trustee of the trust, or
(d) any power conferred by any other enactment or the trust instrument which permits the trustees to delegate any of their functions or to appoint a person to act as a nominee or custodian.

(3) In the case of a charitable trust, the trustees' delegable functions are—

(a) any function consisting of carrying out a decision that the trustees have taken;
(b) any function relating to the investment of assets subject to the trust (including, in the case of land held as an investment, managing the land and creating or disposing of an interest in the land);
(c) any function relating to the raising of funds for the trust otherwise than by means of profits of a trade which is an integral part of carrying out the trust's charitable purpose;
(d) any other function prescribed by an order made by the Secretary of State.

---

[263] G.H. Jones, "Delegation by Trustees: A Reappraisal" (1959) 22 M.L.R. 381; J.H. Stannard, "Wilful Default" [1979] Conv. 345.
[264] *Re Vickery* [1931] 1 Ch. 572.
[265] [1998] Ch. 241.
[266] See paras 9–216 ff. for further discussion.
[267] Trustee Act 2000 s.26.

(4) For the purposes of subsection (3)(c) a trade is an integral part of carrying out a trust's charitable purpose if the profits are applied solely to the purposes of the trust and either—

(a) the trade is exercised in the course of the actual carrying out of a primary purpose of the trust, or

(b) the work in connection with the trade is mainly carried out by beneficiaries of the trust.

It will be seen that s.11 is concerned with trustees' management or administrative functions, and not their discretionary distributive functions. It extends to a sole trustee,[268] but not to trustees of authorised unit trusts,[269] nor to enable pension trustees to delegate investment functions.[270] **9–195**

TRUSTEE ACT 2000 SECTION 12

(1) Subject to subsection (2), the persons whom the trustees may under section 11 authorise to exercise functions as their agent include one or more of their number. **9–196**

(2) The trustees may not authorise two (or more) persons to exercise the same function unless they are to exercise the function jointly.

(3) The trustees may not under section 11 authorise a beneficiary to exercise any function as their agent (even if the beneficiary is also a trustee).

(4) The trustees may under section 11 authorise a person to exercise any function as their agent even though he is also appointed to act as their nominee or custodian (whether under section 16, 17 or 18 or any other power).

It is important that the trustees can employ one of themselves for particular tasks so long as he is not a beneficiary, there then being conflict of interest possibilities with a beneficiary-agent being vulnerable to the charge of preferring his or her own interests to those of other beneficiaries. Exceptionally under s.9(1) of the Trusts of Land and Appointment of Trustees Act 1996, "The trustees of land may, by power of attorney, delegate to any beneficiary or beneficiaries of full age and beneficially entitled to an interest in possession in land subject to the trust any of their functions as trustees which relate to the land." This power of attorney may be for any period or indefinite,[271] must be given by all the trustees jointly, may be revoked by any one or more of them and will be revoked by the appointment of a new trustee.[272] Such power can be exercised to enable a life tenant to decide upon sale or lease of the land but cannot enable the life tenant to receive or give receipts for capital money,[273] two trustees being required for this purpose[274] (considering the practical danger of permitting an income beneficiary to receive capital moneys). Beneficiaries exercising delegated functions are in the same **9–197**

[268] Trustee Act 2000 s.25.
[269] Trustee Act 2000 s.37.
[270] On which see the Pensions Act 1995 ss.34 to 36.
[271] Trusts of Land and Appointment of Trustees Act 1996 (TOLATA) s.9(5).
[272] TOLATA s.9(3).
[273] TOLATA s.9(7).
[274] Law of Property Act 1925 s.27; Trustee Act 1925 s.14.

position as trustees (with the same duties and liabilities) but are not regarded "as trustees for any other purposes (including the purposes of any enactment permitting the delegation of functions by trustees or imposing requirements relating to the payment of capital money)."[275]

9–198 As to be expected if an agent is employed under s.11 to carry out a function (like investment) then he is subject to the same duties and restrictions attached to the function (like having regard to the standard investment criteria) as if the trustees themselves were exercising the function.[276]

TRUSTEE ACT 2000 SECTION 15

9–199 (1) The trustees may not authorise a person to exercise any of their asset management functions as their agent except by an agreement which is in or evidenced in writing.

(2) The trustees may not authorise a person to exercise any of their asset management functions as their agent unless—

(a) they have prepared a statement that gives guidance as to how the functions should be exercised ("a policy statement"), and
(b) the agreement under which the agent is to act includes a term to the effect that he will secure compliance with—

(i) the policy statement, or
(ii) if the policy statement is revised or replaced under section 22, the revised or replacement policy statement.

(3) The trustees must formulate any guidance given in the policy statement with a view to ensuring that the functions will be exercised in the best interests of the trust.

(4) The policy statement must be in or evidenced in writing.

(5) The asset management functions of trustees are their functions relating to—

(a) the investment of assets subject to the trust,
(b) the acquisition of property which is to be subject to the trust, and
(c) managing property which is subject to the trust and disposing of, or creating or disposing of an interest in, such property.

9–200 Clearly, this authorises the common useful, if not necessary, practice of employing a discretionary portfolio manager, but it extends to employing an estate agent to sell a trust property at the best price. It is noteworthy that the section applies to all asset management delegations, whether under the Act or otherwise (e.g. under the terms of the trust instrument).

TRUSTEE ACT 2000 SECTION 14

9–201 (1) Subject to subsection (2) and sections 15(2) and 29 to 32, the trustees may authorise a person to exercise functions as their agent on such terms as to remuneration and other matters as they may determine.

---

275 TOLATA s.9(7).

276 Trustee Act 2000 s.13.

(2) The Trustees may not authorise a person to exercise functions as their agent on any of the terms mentioned in subsection (3) unless it is reasonably necessary for them to do so.

(3) The terms are—

(a) a term permitting the agent to appoint a substitute;
(b) a term restricting the liability of the agent or his substitute to the trustees or any beneficiary;
(c) a term permitting the agent to act in circumstances capable of giving rise to a conflict of interest.

9–202 It will be seen that an objective test of what is "reasonably necessary" in all the circumstances applies to use of s.14 to authorise the potentially detrimental terms specified in s.4(3). An express power may liberally permit trustees to authorise any terms if the trustees subjectively bona fide believe such terms to be reasonably necessary in the best interests of the beneficiaries. It is doubtful whether a term ousting the liability of an agent (e.g. by excluding some otherwise applicable duty) is covered as "a term restricting the liability of" an agent[277] although, in any event, it may be difficult to justify any such ouster as "reasonably necessary".

9–203 In engaging a discretionary portfolio manager it may well be reasonably necessary to permit it to appoint a substitute for a foreign portfolio of shares, to permit it to exclude liability for negligence, to permit it as a market-maker in shares in a particular company to sell such shares to the trustees and to permit it to place business with a subsidiary or associated company entitled to charge for its services. At the time of the engagement it will be good practice for the trustees to record the factors making them consider that particular terms were reasonably necessary.

TRUSTEE ACT 2000 SECTION 32

9–204 (1) This section applies if, under a power conferred by Part IV or any other enactment or any provision of subordinate legislation, or by the trust instrument, a person other than a trustee has been—

(a) authorised to exercise functions as an agent of the trustees, or
(b) appointed to act as a nominee or custodian.

(2) The trustees may remunerate the agent, nominee or custodian out of trust funds for services if—

(a) he is engaged on terms entitling him to be remunerated for those services, and
(b) the amount does not exceed such remuneration as is reasonable in the circumstances for the provision of those services by him to or on behalf of that trust.

(3) The trustees may reimburse the agent, nominee or custodian out of the trust funds for any expenses properly incurred by him in exercising functions as an agent, nominee or custodian.

9–205 If a trustee has been appointed agent, nominee or custodian, then he can claim properly incurred expenses out of the trust fund, but entitlement to remuneration for his services will be based on a clause in the trust instrument or, otherwise, the Trustee Act 2000 s.29.

[277] Ouster of one particular duty, however, may be said to reduce or restrict the overall possible liability of the agent.

9-206 Trustees are under the statutory duty of care[278] when selecting the person who is to act, when determining any terms on which that person is to act, and, if that person is to exercise asset management functions, when preparing a policy statement under s.15, such duty applying whether the appointment is made under the Trustee Act 2000 or otherwise[279] (e.g. under the terms of the trust instrument, except, of course, to the extent the statutory duty is modified or excluded in the trust instrument[280]).

9-207 Under the Trustee Act 2000 s.22, while the agent continues to act for the trustees (a) they must keep under review the arrangements under which the agent acts and how those arrangements are being put into effect, (b) if circumstances make it appropriate to do so, they must consider whether there is a need to exercise any power of intervention that they have (e.g. a power to revoke the appointment or to give directions to the agent) and (c) if they consider that there is a need to exercise such a power, they must do so. The position is the same[281] where trustees of land delegate their functions under s.9 of the Trusts of Land and Appointment of Trustees Act 1996. In the case of an agent authorised to exercise asset management functions, the trustees' duties include a duty to consider whether there is any need to revise or replace the s.15 policy statement, a duty to revise or replace it if they consider that there is such a need, and a duty to assess whether the current policy statement is being complied with.[282] The revision or replacement must be in, or evidenced in, writing and must be formulated with a view to ensuring that the delegated functions will be exercised in the best interests of the trust beneficiaries as a whole.[283] The statutory duty of care applies to the exercise of these supervisory duties under s.22 of the Trustee Act 2000[284] and s.9A (3) of the Trusts of Land and Appointment of Trustees Act 1966,[285] but delegations made under s.9 before February 2001 remain subject to the old law, including the prospectively repealed s.9(8).[286]

9-208 In deciding whether or not to exercise their powers of delegation under the Trustee Act 2000 the trustees can suit themselves and do not need to prove it was reasonably necessary to exercise the power or that exercise of the power was in the best interests of the trust beneficiaries. However, the statutory duty of care applies to trustees of land in deciding whether or not to delegate any of their extensive functions under s.9 of the Trusts of Land and Appointment of Trustees Act 1996 to a beneficiary with an interest in possession[287]—because the extensive powers conferred upon such a beneficiary can be exercised with little constraint and much impact.

ii. Nominees and Custodians

9-209 The need for speedy settlement of share dealings within three days, the introduction of dematerialised holding and transfer of shares via the London Stock Exchange CREST system, and the use of computerised clearing systems in other financial markets make it vital that trustees are given broad powers to use nominees and custodians. These broad powers are contained in ss.16, 17 and 18 of the Trustee Act 2000.

---

[278] Trustee Act 2000 s.1; see para.9-05.
[279] Trustee Act 2000 Sch.1 para.3, and s.21(3).
[280] Trustee Act 2000 Sch.1 para.7.
[281] TOLATA s.9A(2)-(5).
[282] Trustee Act 2000 s.23(2).
[283] Trustee Act 2000 s.15.
[284] Trustee Act 2000 Sch.1 para.3(1)(e).
[285] TOLATA s.9A(5).
[286] TOLATA s.9A(7).
[287] TOLATA s.9A(1).

Trustees are under the statutory duty of care when selecting the nominee or custodian and determining its terms of engagement, whether under the Trustee Act 2000 or otherwise[288] (e.g. under the trust instrument, unless it provides otherwise). They also need to keep under review the arrangements under which the nominee or custodian acts and how those arrangements are being put into effect, considering whether any power of intervention needs to be exercised and then exercising it if called for.[289] The statutory duty of care applies to this reviewing duty[290] but not to deciding whether or not to exercise the powers to utilise the services of custodians or nominees. **9–210**

C. *Delegation by Individual Trustees*

Section 25 of the Trustee Act 1925 for the first time allowed an individual trustee to delegate all or any of his discretionary functions, whether distributive functions or administrative functions, if he would be absent from the UK for more than a month. The Powers of Attorney Act 1971 then amended s.25 of the 1925 Act so that the facility was generally available to a trustee (whether or not absent abroad for a period) but the period for delegation was confined to 12 months, although another power of attorney could then forthwith be created for another 12 months and so on, if appropriate. The Trustee Delegation Act 1999 slightly further amended s.25 and repealed s.3(3) of the Enduring Powers of Attorney Act 1985. This subsection had been a last-minute amendment to the 1985 Act, to reverse a particular recent case involving co-owners of land[291] but it accidentally had the vastly greater effect of enabling a trustee by an enduring power of attorney to delegate all his trusteeships to another person for an unlimited period. The 1999 Act further made special provision[292] for co-owners of land so that a trustee who also has a beneficial interest in trust land (or the proceeds thereof) can simply grant an ordinary power of attorney under the Powers of Attorney Act 1971 to his co-owner, enabling such co-owner to make a valid overreaching sale of the land. The amended s.25 of the Trustee Act 1925 is reproduced immediately below. **9–211**

TRUSTEE ACT 1925 SECTION 25

(1) Notwithstanding any rule of law or equity to the contrary, a trustee may, by power of attorney, delegate the execution or exercise of all or any of the trusts, powers and discretions vested in him as trustee either alone or jointly with any other person or persons. **9–212**

(2) A delegation under this section—

(a) commences as provided by the instrument creating the power or, if the instrument makes no provision as to the commencement of the delegation, with the date of the execution of the instrument by the donor; and

(b) continues for a period of twelve months or any shorter period provided by the instrument creating the power.

(3) The persons who may be donees of a power of attorney under this section include a trust corporation.

---

[288] Trustee Act 2000 s.21(3) and Sch.1 para.3.

[289] Trustee Act 2000 s.22.

[290] Trustee Act 2000 Sch.1 para.3.

[291] *Walia v Michael Naughton Ltd* [1985] 1 W.L.R. 1115; Hansard (HL) Vol.465, June 24, 1985, cols 548–549.

[292] Trustee Delegation Act 1999 ss.1, 2, 3.

(4) Before or within seven days after giving a power of attorney under this section the donor shall give written notice of it (specifying the date on which the power comes into operation and its duration, the donee of the power, the reason why the power is given and, where some only are delegated, the trusts, powers and discretions delegated) to—

(a) each person (other than himself), if any, who under any instrument creating the trust has power (whether alone or jointly) to appoint a new trustee; and

(b) each of the other trustees, if any; but failure to comply with this subsection shall not, in favour of a person dealing with the donee of the power, invalidate any act done or instrument executed by the donee.

(5) A power of attorney given under this section by a single donor—

(a) in the form set out in subsection (6) of this section; or

(b) in a form to the like effect but expressed to be made under this subsection, shall operate to delegate to the person identified in the form as the single donee of the power the execution and exercise of all the trusts, powers and discretions vested in the donor as trustee (either alone or jointly with any other person or persons) under the single trust so identified.

(6) The form referred to in subsection (5) of this section is as follows—"THIS GENERAL TRUSTEE POWER OF ATTORNEY is made on [date] by [name of one donor] of [address of donor] as trustee of [name or details of one trust]. I appoint [name of one donee] of [address of donee] to be my attorney [if desired, the date on which the delegation commences or the period for which it continues (or both)] in accordance with section 25 (5) of the Trustee Act 1925. [To be executed as a deed]".

(7) The donor of a power of attorney given under this section shall be liable for the acts or defaults of the donee in the same manner as if they were the acts or defaults of the donor.

(8) For the purpose of executing or exercising the trusts or powers delegated to him, the donee may exercise any of the powers conferred on the donor as trustee by statute or by the instrument creating the trust, including power, for the purpose of the transfer of any inscribed stock, himself to delegate to an attorney power to transfer, but not including the power of delegation conferred by this section.

9–213 This amended s.25 applies to powers of attorney created from March 1 2000 onwards. The duration of the delegation cannot exceed 12 months reckoned from the specified date or, in default, from the date of execution of the power.[293] It is now possible to delegate to a sole co-trustee[294] but, unless this be a trust corporation, such sole attorney-co-trustee can give no valid overreaching receipt for capital moneys arising from a disposition of land.[295] Sub-delegation by the attorney is still prohibited.[296] A statutory short form of power of attorney is available for use but, if used, a separate one has to be used for each trust fund to which the delegation is to apply.[297] However, there is nothing to stop a partner in a firm of solicitors who is trustee of ten trusts from executing one power of attorney delegating to a fellow partner the trusteeship powers of all ten trusts while enjoying six months sabbatical leave.

9–214 Delegation under s.25 is intended as a temporary measure, the donor of the power being aut omatically liable for the acts and defaults of the donee as if the donor's[298] and also having to give

---

293 Trustee Act 1925 s.25(2).
294 Trustee Act 1925 s.25(3).
295 Trustee Delegation Act 1999 s.7.
296 Trustee Act 1925 s.25(8).
297 Trustee Act 1925 s.25(5)–(6).
298 Trustee Act 1925 s.25(7).

written notification to the person, if any, having power to appoint new trustees and to the donor's co-trustees,[299] who have the same power in default of any such person.[300] They might then consider it more appropriate to replace the donor as trustee. If not, the delegation lasts till the expiry of the 12 months (or lesser specified period) unless the donor earlier dies or becomes mentally incompetent, except that if the power was executed as an enduring power of attorney then mental incapacity will not vitiate the delegation.[301]

10. Exemption Clauses

9–215 It should first be noted that the jurisdiction of the court as to pure matters of law cannot be ousted by provisions in the trust instrument giving the trustees power to determine all questions arising in the execution of the trusts under the instrument.[302] However, the decision of trustees or of a third party can be binding and conclusive on matters of fact, assuming that the specified factual circumstances are conceptually certain,[303] while the decision of someone with expert knowledge in the relevant factual area can even conclusively determine an incidental question of construction.[304]

9–216 If trustees can prove that the settlor knew of, and approved, a clause in the trust instrument exempting the trustees from liability for a breach of trust upon a fair non-restrictive construction of the clause,[305] then they will escape liability for the breach unless it was a dishonest breach of trust. This was held by the Court of Appeal in *Armitage v Nurse*,[306] reproduced below,[307] in giving effect to a clause protecting the trustee from liability "unless such loss or damage shall be caused by his own actual fraud". "Fraud" was held simply to mean dishonesty which "connotes at the minimum an intention on the part of the trustee to pursue a particular course of action, either knowing that it is contrary to the interests of the beneficiaries or being recklessly indifferent whether it is contrary to their interests or not".[308] Whether a trustee has acted dishonestly is tested by the court against objective standards of honest conduct and it is irrelevant whether the trustee genuinely believes that his conduct is honest—i.e. there is no need to show that he has been "self-consciously dishonest".[309]

9–217 Thus, it is permissible for an exemption clause to exempt a trustee from liability for loss arising from negligence of whatever kind, in contrast to Scots law, which follows other civil law systems in distinguishing gross negligence and ordinary negligence, and which does not permit exemption clauses that protect trustees from liability for gross negligence.[310] Similarly, the Trusts (Jersey) Law 1984 art.30(10) provides that "nothing in the terms of a trust shall relieve, release or exonerate a trustee from liability for breach of trust arising from the trustee's own fraud, willful misconduct or gross

---

[299] Trustee Act 1925 s.25(4).
[300] Trustee Act 1925 s.36.
[301] Trustee Delegation Act 1999 ss.6 and 9.
[302] *Re Wynn* [1952] Ch. 271.
[303] *Re Coxen* [1948] Ch. 747; *Re Jones* [1953] Ch. 125; *Re Wright's WT* [1981] Law.S. Gaz 841.
[304] *The Glazier* (1996) 1 Ll. Rep.370; *Re Tuck's ST* [1978] Ch. 49; *Dundee General Hospitals Board v Walker* [1952] 1 All E.R. 896.
[305] *Walker v Stones* [2001] Q.B. 902 at 935 and 941. See too *Bonham v Blake Lapthorn Linell (a firm)* [2007] W.T.L.R. 189 at [177], per Kitchin J., stressing that "anything which is not clearly within [an exemption clause] should be treated as falling outside it", but adding that "trustees accept office on the terms of a document for which they are not responsible, and are entitled to have the document construed according to the natural meaning of the words used." *Bonham* is discussed further at para.11–71.
[306] [1998] Ch. 241.
[307] At paras 9–223 ff.
[308] *Armitage* at 251.
[309] *Barnes v Tomlinson* [2007] W.T.L.R. 377 at [78].
[310] *Seton v Dawson* (1841) 4 D 310, 316–317; *Knox v Mackinnon* (1888) 13 App. Cas. 753 at 765; *Clarke v Clarke's Trustees* 1925 S.C. 693; *Lutea Trustees Ltd v Orbis Trustees* [1998] S.L.T. 471.

negligence"; and the Trusts (Guernsey) Law 1989 art.34(7) provides that "nothing in the terms of a trust shall relieve a trustee of liability for a breach of trust arising from his own fraud or wilful misconduct or gross negligence". In its 2006 Report on exemption clauses, the Law Commission considered introducing a similar measure into English law, but rejected this on the basis that English law does not clearly distinguish between gross and ordinary negligence.[311]

9–218 Further uncertainty exists where trustees consciously act beyond their powers (e.g. making an investment which they know to be unauthorised), thereby deliberately committing a breach of trust, but do so in good faith and in the honest belief that they are acting in the best interests of the beneficiaries as a whole. Lord Nicholls[312] considered this to be fraudulent because the trustees are taking a risk to the prejudice of another person's rights, which they know to be a risk which they have no right to take. In *Armitage*, however, Millett L.J.[313] (as he then was) considered that this would not be fraudulent, perhaps assuming that if the trustees honestly think there is a risk which they ought to take, then they can justifiably believe they have a right to take it—although he accepted that[314] "a trustee who relied on the presence of an exemption clause to justify what he proposed to do would thereby lose its protection: he would be acting recklessly in the proper sense of the term." Trustees will be well-advised to accept Lord Nicholls' view and not to commit a deliberate breach of trust in the belief it will be profitable or, if not, will be covered by a wide exemption clause. They should not proceed except with extended powers conferred by the court[315] or, perhaps, if they have sufficient beneficiaries of full capacity to provide them with an indemnity backed with some security.

9–219 A trustee who is a solicitor and who inserts a clause into the settlor's trust instrument to exempt himself from liability for breaches of trust unless fraudulent, will also be well-advised if he tells the settlor to seek independent legal advice. After all, such a solicitor-prospective trustee is in a fiduciary relationship with the settlor, so that one would expect that he would be disabled from relying on such a broad clause unless independent legal advice was suggested.[316] Somewhat surprisingly, however, the Court of Appeal held in *Bogg v Raper*[317] that the solicitor as prospective executor and trustee, who drafted the testamentary trusts, did not have to prove that he had advised the testator to take independent legal advice, so long as it was proved the testator had known and approved the will—which must always be the case where probate of the will has been granted. Millett L.J. stated:

> "The fundamental fallacy in the [plaintiffs'] argument is that clause 12 does not confer a benefit on the persons responsible for advising the testator on the contents of the will. In the first place, it does not discriminate between the persons who advised the testator in connection with his will and other persons who become executors or trustees and who have had no part in the preparation of his will. In the second place, it does not confer a benefit on the executors and trustees but defines the extent of the potential liabilities. Unlike a trustee charging clause, it does not enable the executors and trustees to profit from their position, but it protects them from loss thereby. The inclusion of the clause does not, therefore, conflict with the rule that, in the absence of clear words, a trustee may not profit form his trust."

---

311 Law Commission, *Trustee Exemption Clauses* (Law Com. No.301, 2006).
312 *Royal Brunei Airlines v Tan* [1995] 2 A.C. 378 at 390.
313 *Armitage v Nurse* [1998] Ch. 241 at 252.
314 *Armitage* at 254.
315 Under the Trustee Act 1925 s.57.
316 *Rutanen v Ballard* 424 Mass. 723 at 733 (1997); *Baskerville v Thurgood* [1992] Sask. LR. 214.
317 (1998/99) 1 I.T.E.L.R. 267 at 285.

In its 2003 Consultation Paper on *Trustee Exemption Clauses*,[318] the Law Commission suggested that some legislative reform was required in this area, and proposed drawing a distinction between lay and professional trustees, suggesting that lay trustees should generally continue to be able to rely on trustee exemption clauses,[319] but that professional trustees should be unable to rely on an exemption clause where their conduct has been so unreasonable, irresponsible or incompetent that in fairness to the beneficiaries their conduct should not be excused.[320] However, in its 2006 Report on the subject, the Law Commission seems to have succumbed to special pleading by professional trustees, weakly concluding that reform would be undesirable because it could lead to increased costs, delays in trust administration, a greater tendency towards defensive trusteeship, and a general loss of flexibility in the operation of trusts.[321] Instead it tamely suggested that a rule of practice should be recognised and enforced by regulatory and professional bodies along the following lines: "Any paid trustee who causes a settlor to include a clause in a trust instrument which has the effect of excluding or limiting liability for negligence must before the creation of the trust take such steps as are reasonable to ensure that the settlor is aware of the meaning and effect of the clause."[322] **9–220**

So far, it has been the basic type of exemption clause that has been considered, namely a clause exempting from liability for a breach of duty. However, a clause may alternatively oust any duty in the first place so that there can then be no breach of duty. In *Hayim v Citibank SA*,[323] for example, Citibank was appointed executor of the testator's American will on terms that the executor "shall have no responsibility or duty with respect to" a Hong Kong house until the deaths of the testator's very elderly brother and sister who resided in the house. This house was given by a Hong Kong will to another executor on trust for Citibank as executor of the American will. Citibank declined to take steps to have the house sold for the benefit of the beneficiaries under the American will who wanted the house to be sold and the siblings to be evicted from it. Substantial losses flowed from the delayed sale of the house. The Privy Council held the clause was "understandable and explicable". To avoid death duties (payable if the siblings had interests in possession in the house) and to avoid placing them at the mercy of the beneficiaries, the clause enabled Citibank to permit the siblings to remain living in the house without Citibank owing any duties to the beneficiaries (other than to account to them if Citibank used the house for its own purposes). **9–221**

It is also not uncommon to see clauses that oust the trustee's duty to diversify investments, e.g. where 90 per cent of the value of the trust fund is in the controlling shareholding of a company transferred by the settlor to the trustees. The statutory duty of care when investing can also be excluded. Thus, a big lottery winner might settle £2 million on trustees to speculate with it for 21 years as if they were the absolute beneficial owners of it and could afford to lose all of it without it affecting their standard of living in any way. Of course, all the duties of trustees cannot be ousted or the trustees would either be nominee-resulting trustees for the settlor or themselves be absolute beneficial owners. The trustees must be left under a duty to perform the trust honestly and in good faith for the benefit of beneficiaries having a correlative right to make the trustees account for performance of their duty.[324] **9–222**

---

318 LCCP No.171, 2003.
319 LCCP No.171, para.4.39.
320 LCCP No.171, para.4.78.
321 Law Com. No.301, para.5.99.
322 Law Com. No.301, para.6.65.
323 [1987] A.C. 730.
324 *Armitage v Nurse* [1998] Ch. 241 at 253.

ARMITAGE v NURSE

Court of Appeal [1998] Ch. 241, [1997] 3 W.L.R. 1048, [1997] 2 All E.R. 705

9–223 Under clause 15 of the settlement, "No Trustee shall be liable for any loss or damage which may happen . . . from any cause whatsoever unless such loss or damage shall be caused by his own actual fraud." As a matter of construction, the court first held "clause 15 exempts the trustee from liability for loss or damage to the trust property no matter how indolent, imprudent, lacking in diligence, negligent or wilful he may have been, so long as he has not acted dishonestly."

MILLETT L.J. (with whom HIRST and HUTCHISON agreed):

The Permitted Scope of Trustee Exemption Clauses

9–224 It is submitted on behalf of Paula that a trustee exemption clause which purports to exclude all liability except for actual fraud is void, either for repugnancy or as contrary to public policy. . . . What is pleaded is, at the very lowest, culpable and probably gross negligence. So the question reduces itself to this: can a trustee exemption clause validly exclude liability for gross negligence?

9–225 It is a bold submission that a clause taken from one standard precedent book and to the same effect as a clause found in another, included in a settlement drawn by Chancery counsel acting for an infant settlor and approved by the court on her behalf, should be so repugnant to the trusts or contrary to public policy that it is liable to be set aside at her suit. But the submission has been made and we must consider it. In my judgment it is without foundation.

9–226 There can be no question of the clause being repugnant to the trust. In *Wilkins v Hogg*[325] Lord Westbury L.C. challenged counsel to cite a case where an indemnity clause protecting the trustee from his ordinary duty had been held so repugnant as to be rejected. Counsel was unable to do so. No such case has occurred in England or Scotland since.

9–227 I accept the submission made on behalf of Paula that there is an irreducible core of obligations owed by the trustees to the beneficiaries and enforceable by them which is fundamental to the concept of a trust. If the beneficiaries have no rights enforceable against the trustees there are no trusts. But I do not accept the further submission that these core obligations include the duties of skill and care, prudence and diligence. The duty of the trustees to perform the trusts honestly and in good faith for the benefit of the beneficiaries is the minimum necessary to give substance to the trusts, but in my opinion it is sufficient. As Mr Hill pertinently pointed out in his able argument, a trustee who relied on the presence of a trustee exemption clause to justify what he proposed to do would thereby lose its protection: he would be acting recklessly in the proper sense of the term.

9–228 It is, of course, far too late to suggest that the exclusion in a contract of liability for ordinary negligence or want of care is contrary to public policy. What is true of a contract must be equally true of a settlement. It would be very surprising if our law drew the line between liability for ordinary negligence and liability for gross negligence. In this respect English law differs from civil law systems, for it has always drawn a sharp distinction between negligence, however gross, on the one hand and fraud, bad faith and wilful misconduct on the other. The doctrine of the common law is that: "Gross negligence may be evidence of *mala fides*, but is not the same thing."[326] But while we regard the difference between fraud on the one hand and mere negligence, however gross, on the other as a difference in kind, we regard the difference between negligence and gross negligence as merely one of degree. English lawyers have always had a healthy disrespect for the latter distinction. In *Hinton v Dibbin*,[327] Lord Denman C.J. doubted whether any intelligible distinction exists; while in *Grill v General Iron Screw Collier Co*[328] Willes J. famously observed that gross negligence is ordinary negligence with a vituperative epithet. But civilian systems draw the line in a different place. The doctrine is *culpa lata dolo aequiparetur*; and although the maxim itself is not Roman the

[325] (1861) 31 L.J. Ch. 41 at 42.
[326] See *Goodman v Harvey* (1836) 4 A & E 870 at 876, per Lord Denman C.J.
[327] (1842) 2 Q.B. 646.
[328] (1866) 35 L.J.C.P. 321 at 330.

principle is classical. There is no room for the maxim in the common law; it is not mentioned in *Broom Selection of Legal Maxims Classified and Illustrated*.[329]

9–229 The submission that it is contrary to public policy to exclude the liability of a trustee for gross negligence is not supported by any English or Scottish authority. The cases relied on are the English cases of *Wilkins v Hogg*[330] and *Pass v Dundas*;[331] and the Scottish cases of *Knox v Mackinnon*[332] and *Rae v Meek*,[333] *Wyman or Ferguson (Pauper) v Paterson*[334] and *Clarke v Clarke's Trustees*.[335] These cases, together with two other Scottish cases, *Seton v Dawson*[336] and *Carruthers v Carruthers*,[337] and cases from the Commonwealth and America, were reviewed by the Jersey Court of Appeal in *Midland Bank Trustee (Jersey) Ltd v Federated Pension Services Ltd*[338] in a masterly judgment delivered by Sir Godfray Le Quesne QC.

9–230 I agree with the conclusion of the Jersey Court of Appeal that all these cases are concerned with the true construction of the particular clauses under consideration or of similar clauses in standard form in the nineteenth century. None of them deals with the much wider form of clause which has become common in the present century, and none of them is authority for the proposition that it is contrary to public policy to exclude liability for gross negligence by an appropriate clause clearly worded to have that effect.

9–231 At the same time, it must be acknowledged that the view is widely held that these clauses have gone too far, and that trustees who charge for their services and who, as professional men, would not dream of excluding liability for ordinary professional negligence, should not be able to rely on a trustee exemption clause excluding liability for gross negligence. Jersey introduced a law in 1989 which denies effect to a trustee exemption clause which purports to absolve a trustee from liability for his own "fraud, wilful misconduct or gross negligence". . . . If clauses such as cl.15 of the settlement are to be denied effect, then in my opinion this should be done by Parliament.

Questions

9–232
1. In September 2009 Tim died, bequeathing £800,000 to his executor and trustee, Eric, on trust for his widow for life, remainder to his children Alan, Brian and Charles equally. Their children were then aged 30, 25 and 15 years respectively. The will contained various administrative provisions including wide powers of investment, and also a clause exempting the trustee from liability for any breach of trust that is not dishonest.

   Although Eric was himself an experienced investor, upon winding up Tim's estate in March 2003 he gave the £800,000 for investment to Whizz Kid & Co, which specialises in discretionary portfolio management for clients and for itself. Eric signed the Company's current customer agreement in 2003. Its terms enable the Company inter alia to sell its own shares to the trust at a price no higher than that generally available at the time and to purchase for itself the trust's shares at a price no lower than that generally available at the time and provide that the Company shall not be liable for any loss arising from its negligence. The Company reports back to Eric every six months and follows his written policy statement concerning income and capital growth.

---

329 10th edn, 1939.
330 (1861) 31 L.J. Ch. 41.
331 (1880) 43 L.T. 665.
332 (1888) 13 App. Cas. 753.
333 (1889) 14 App. Cas. 558.
334 [1900] A.C. 271.
335 1925 S.C. 693.
336 (1841) 4 D. 310.
337 [1896] A.C. 659.
338 [1995] Jersey L.R. 352.

The investments are now only worth £400,000. At the end of 2003 the Company sold £30,000 of its own ABC Plc shares to the trust and these shares are now only worth £5,000. In 2003 the Company bought from the trust for £20,000 XYZ Plc shares now worth £80,000. About £200,000 of the loss is due to the negligence of Jason, an employee of the Company, who is addicted to cocaine. Eric's son knew about Jason's addiction and had told Eric about it.

Advise Tim's widow, who has heard that Whizz Kid & Co is having financial problems and would also like to have the trust property sold up and its proceeds divided between her and her children.

9–233 2. A domineering, secretive, prospective settlor seeks your advice on how much he can keep in the dark persons interested under a very flexible discretionary trust and whether he can sensibly insert a provision, "No breach of trust action may be brought where the trustees have received written permission from the settlor in the relevant matter unless the action is brought within one month of the grant of such permission."

9–234 3. The Mega Trust Co Ltd would like you to draft some provisions for its standard forms of trust instrument. In particular, it would like provisions which

(a) exclude as much trustee liability for breach of trust as possible;
(b) permit the trustee to continue to act even where it has a conflict of interest, whether in its own right or as trustee of another trust;
(c) make clear that the trustee has no duty to supervise the activities of any company in which it owns shares (even a majority shareholding) or to seek representation on the board of directors.

Advise the Company how far (if at all) it is possible in English law to achieve these objectives.

10 CONTROL OF TRUSTEE POWERS

1. Introduction

10–01 Trustees are frequently vested with discretionary powers, which may be distributive (e.g. powers of appointment) or managerial (e.g. powers of investment). This chapter considers some of the ways in which the courts control the exercise of such powers. As we shall see, the rules governing the control of powers vested in the trustees of family trusts differ from the rules affecting pension fund trustees, and so these are treated separately.

10–02 Under a family discretionary trust the trustees have a duty to exercise their discretion by distributing income (or, ultimately, capital) in some sort of amounts to some of the beneficiaries (unless, under a power to accumulate, they have decided to accumulate income). If the trustees neglect or refuse or are unable (till the outcome of a case) to discharge their duty, then the court will let them remedy this[1] or will positively have the settlor's intentions carried out, "by appointing new trustees or by authorising or directing representative persons of the classes of beneficiaries to prepare a scheme for distribution, or even, should the proper basis for distribution appear, by itself directing the trustees so to distribute."[2]

10–03 In the case of distributive powers of appointment, advancement or maintenance, the trustees have a duty to consider from time to time whether or not to exercise the power but they need not exercise the power.[3] Thus, if a power to distribute income to X instead of to trust beneficiaries is not exercised within a reasonable period (in default of an expressly specified period), then the power lapses in respect of that income so that the income devolves on the trust beneficiaries entitled in default of a valid exercise of the power.[4]

10–04 If a trustee's attitude is that he is not going to bother about using any powers to benefit a beneficiary, B, as B does not deserve any consideration (e.g. because B married against his wishes), then the court will intervene to remove the trustee or direct a payment that no trustee could refuse to make unless being spiteful or malicious. This is the ratio of *Klug v Klug*,[5] where legacy duty had to be paid by a beneficiary in four equal instalments but the beneficiary's income was insufficient to pay these instalments. Neville J. said:[6]

---

1 *Re Locker's ST* [1978] 1 All E.R. 216.
2 *McPhail v Doulton* [1971] A.C. 424 at 451, per Lord Wilberforce.
3 *Re Hay's ST* [1981] 3 All E.R. 786 at 792–793.
4 *Re Allen-Meyrick's WT* [1966] 1 W.L.R. 499.
5 [1918] 2 Ch. 67. See too Re *Lofthouse* (1885) 29 Ch.D. 921 (where trustees had refused to pay maintenance to a beneficiary under a discretionary power and Bacon V.C. ordered £400 p.a. to be paid; on appeal his order was discharged without more ado since the trustees were agreeable to pay £250 pa). There was an interventionist attitude in some 19th-century cases concerning powers to benefit a beneficiary, especially if the beneficiary was a ward of court: *Re Hodges* (1878) 7 Ch.D. 754; *Re Roper's Trusts* (1879) 11 Ch.D. 271.
6 *Klug* at 71.

> "When the summons was previously before me, I decided that the trustees could in the exercise of their discretion under the powers of advancement, if they thought fit, advance out of capital a sum sufficient to pay this legacy duty. The public trustee thinks that their discretion should be so exercised, but his co-trustee, the mother, declines to join him in so doing, not because she has considered whether or not it would be for her daughter's welfare, that the advance should be made, but because her daughter has married without her consent, and her letters show, in my opinion, that she has not exercised her discretion at all. . . . In such circumstances, it is the duty of the court to interfere and to direct a sum to be raised out of capital sufficient to pay off . . . the legacy duty."

It seems that no other course of action could be taken by the trustees (unless they acted in a way that no rational adequately informed body of trustees could act) so the court should direct such course.

10–05 Exceptionally in the pensions fund context the courts[7] have also been prepared positively to exercise fiduciary powers to augment pensions of beneficiaries where there is no one who can exercise the power, the employer-trustee being a company in liquidation and the liquidator being in the irreconcilable position of acting for the creditors interested in a non-exercise of the power to benefit the ordinary beneficiary-members of the pension scheme, while acting as trustee required to look after such members' interests. The court[8] acts in the manner in which a reasonable trustee could be expected to act in the light of all the material circumstances so as to do what is just and equitable.

10–06 One accepts this in the pensions context where the member-beneficiaries have earned their entitlements as deferred pay and as settlors have some justified expectations that powers to augment their entitlement out of surpluses will be seriously considered for exercising in certain circumstances. In the private family trust context, however, where the trustees are in a position to exercise their powers in favour of persons who are not beneficiaries at all but only objects of a power of appointment, and the trustees choose not to exercise them, stating that they have fairly considered exercising their powers but have chosen not to, then one might expect that should be the end of the matter.

10–07 However, in *Schmidt v Rosewood Trust Ltd*[9] Lord Walker asserted the court's inherent jurisdiction to supervise, and if necessary to intervene in, the administration of trusts, whether dealing with the rights of beneficiaries under discretionary trusts or the rights of objects of fiduciary powers of appointment. Thus, in an extreme case where, in the light of the settlor's letters of wishes, the trustees are not exercising their fiduciary powers of appointment in the manner intended by the settlor, the trustees can be replaced by more amenable trustees or even a particular exercise of the power could be directed by the court if it would be perverse to any sensible expectation of the settlor to exercise—or no rational trustee could possibly exercise—the power other than in the directed fashion.[10]

2. Family Trusts

10–08 Various legal rules affect the exercise of discretionary powers by trustees.[11] First, there are mandatory rules of law governing the *creation* of powers in the first place, e.g. rules against perpetuity which

---

[7] *Mettoy Pension Trustees Ltd v Evans* [1990] 1 W.L.R. 1587; *Bridge Trustees Ltd v Noel Penny (Turbines) Ltd* [2008] Pens. L.R. 345; *Scully v Coley* [2009] UKPC 29 at [29].

[8] *Thrells Ltd v Lomas* [1993] 1 W.L.R. 456. Now, under Pensions Act 1995 s.25(2) an independent person as trustee exists to exercise the power.

[9] [2003] 2 A.C. 709 at [51].

[10] cf. *Klug v Klug* [1918] 2 Ch. 67.

[11] P. Matthews, "The Doctrine of Fraud on a Power, Part 1" [2007] P.C.B. 131; R.C. Nolan, "Controlling Fiduciary Power" (2009) 68 C.L.J. 293.

prevent certain powers being created at all,[12] and rules on certainty of objects which invalidate powers of appointment if the class of objects is conceptually uncertain.[13] Second, there are rules determining the *extent* of powers, e.g. rules of construction which enable the court to determine a power's scope, the rules which hold that a power of appointment must be exercised in favour of a person who is within the class of objects, and within the limits laid down by the power itself,[14] and the doctrine of fraud on a power, which holds that a purported exercise of a power is a nullity if the trustee acts for an improper purpose. Third, there are rules which go to the trustee's *exercise* of a power, under which the court may review the trustee's decision-making and set a transaction to one side if they find that this is flawed, for example by invoking the rule in *Re Hastings-Bass*,[15] which holds that trustees must consider relevant matters and exclude irrelevant matters from consideration when exercising powers. In this section we will look at the doctrine of fraud on a power and the rule in *Re Hastings-Bass*.

A. Fraud on a Power[16]

In *Vatcher v Paull* Lord Parker said that:[17] **10–09**

> "The term [fraud] in connection with frauds on a power does not necessarily denote any conduct on the part of the appointor amounting to fraud in the common law meaning of the term or any conduct which could properly be termed dishonest or immoral. It merely means that the power has been exercised for a purpose, or with an intention, beyond the scope of or not justified by the instrument creating the power."

Thus a trustee may commit a fraud on a power even though he acts in good faith, for example because he purports to exercise a power to achieve a purpose that is impermissible on its face, e.g. by appointing property to a person who is not a beneficiary.[18] He may also commit a fraud on a power if he purports to exercise a power in a way that produces a permissible outcome on its face, but with the bad faith intention of achieving a larger purpose that is impermissible. For example, it might well constitute a fraud on a power for trustees to appoint property to a beneficiary who has previously agreed to apply the property for the benefit of a person who is not an object, as in *Wong v Burt*,[19] which is reproduced below.[20] As Lord Parker noted in *Vatcher*,[21] it would also constitute a fraud on a power for a father to exercise a power of appointment in favour of his child, although such an appointment is basically valid,[22] if he does so when the child is ill with the intention of taking the child's estate for himself on the child's death—and in such a case, the appointment will constitute a fraud on the power even if the child subsequently recovers.[23]

---

12 *Re De Sommery* [1912] 2 Ch. 622 at 630.
13 *Re Gulbenkian's ST* [1970] A.C. 508. For discussion, see para.4–105.
14 *Re Keele Estates (No.2) Ltd* [1952] Ch. 603; *Re Brinkley's WT* [1968] Ch. 407.
15 [1975] Ch. 25.
16 See P. Matthews, "The Doctrine of Fraud on a Power, Parts 1 and 2" [2007] P.C.B. 131 and 191.
17 [1915] A.C. 372 at 378. See too *Duke of Portland v Topham* (1864) 11 H.L. Cas. 32 at 54.
18 *Kain v Hutton* [2008] 3 N.Z.L.R. 589 at [18].
19 [2005] 1 N.Z.L.R. 91. See too *Lane v Page* (1755) Amb. 233; *Re Turner's Settled Estates* (1884) 28 Ch.D. 205; *Re Greaves* [1954] Ch. 434. But cf. *Netherton v Netherton* [2000] W.T.L.R. 1171, followed in *Re X Trust* (2003) 5 I.T.E.L.R. 119; *Kain v Hutton* [2008] 3 N.Z.L.R. 589.
20 At paras 10–13 ff.
21 *Vatcher* at 379–380.
22 See too *Henty v Wrey* (1882) 21 Ch.D. 232.
23 See too *Lord Hinchbrooke v Seymour* (1789) 1 Bro. C.C. 395.

10–10 To determine what the proper purpose of a power is, reference must be made to the settlor's (objectively understood) expectations,[24] although trustees must beware of slavishly following a settlor's directions and exercising no independent judgment of their own as this could lead to a finding that the purported trust is a sham.[25]

10–11 If a personal power is released so as to benefit the person entitled in default of the exercise of such power so that he can then benefit the person who has released the power, this is outside the fraud on a power doctrine, the person who released the power not being in a conflict of interest situation and the default beneficiary being the owner of the property (subject to divestment by exercise of the power) and capable of dealing with it as he or she likes.[26] However, if the donee of a personal power of appointment positively exercises it, then like the donee of a fiduciary power, he is subject to the fraud on a power doctrine, since it would constitute a wrong against those entitled in default of appointment for the donee to exercise the power for an improper purpose.[27]

10–12 As Lloyd L.J. noted in *Sieff v Fox*:[28]

> "If the exercise of a power is vitiated by the doctrine of fraud on a power, the result appears to be that the exercise is declared void: see *Topham v Duke of Portland*,[29] and the form of order made in that case,[30] and see also *Cloutte v Storey*.[31] This may be because the appointment is treated as having been, in effect, to a non-object, and plainly a direct appointment to such a person would be void. On the other hand, if, as Warner J held in the *Mettoy* case,[32] the principle could result in part of a document being set aside but not the rest, the process would come close to rectification, and it would be difficult to say that a part of it was altogether void."

WONG v BURT

New Zealand Court of Appeal [2005] 1 N.Z.L.R. 91

10–13 HAMMOND J.: The essential facts relating to this issue can be shortly stated.

10–14 Clause 5 of William Wong's will, in summary, provided as follows:

- The residuary estate was to be held in trust with the net annual income payable to Estelle Wong until her death.
- After the death of Estelle Wong, the net annual income was to be payable in equal shares to those of Phillipa and Wong Liu Sheung who were still alive. It is of singular importance to this case that there was no substitutionary provision in favour of grandchildren, if one of those daughters predeceased Estelle; in that event, all the income was to be paid to the other surviving daughter.

---

[24] *Re Manisty's Settlement* [1974] Ch. 17 at 26; *Re Hay's S.T.* [1982] 1 W.L.R. 202 at 209; *Re Beatty's WT* [1990] 1 W.L.R. 1503 at 1506.
[25] See paras 4–28 ff.
[26] *Re Somes* [1896] 1 Ch. 250. Similarly revocation of a revocable appointment made under a personal special power of appointment, even coupled with a release of the power, falls outside the fraud on a power doctrine unless the revocation is solely for the purpose of making a new appointment which is a fraud on the power: *Re Greaves* [1954] Ch. 434.
[27] *Mettoy Pension Trustees Ltd v Evans* [1990] 1 W.L.R. 1587 at 1613–1614, citing *Re Mills* [1930] 1 Ch. 654 and *Re Greaves* [1954] Ch. 434. See too *Hillsdown Holdings Plc v Pensions Ombudsman* [1997] 1 All E.R. 862.
[28] [2005] 1 W.L.R. 3811 at [78].
[29] (1869) L.R. 5 Ch. App. 40.
[30] Printed in *Seton's Judgments and Orders*, 7th edn, vol.2 (1912), p.1672.
[31] [1911] 1 Ch. 18.
[32] *Mettoy Pension Trustees Ltd v Evans* [1990] 1 W.L.R. 1587.

- After the death of the last surviving child, the estate is to be distributed among the children, or grandchildren, or great grandchildren of Phillipa. The exclusion of Wong Liu Sheung's children appears to have been quite deliberate, as a result of a family falling out.

Clause 6 of the will conferred upon the trustees a discretion to pay to Estelle, out of the capital of the estate: **10–15**

"... such sum or sums as they in their absolute discretion may think fit if they shall consider it necessary, desirable or expedient so to do by reason of the state of my wife's health or her desire to travel or to acquire a home or by reason of a fall in the purchasing power of money or for any other reasons whatsoever whether similar or dissimilar to the foregoing."

When Phillipa Wong died in 1995 Mrs Estelle Wong became concerned as to the position of Mei-Ling and Matthew. She viewed the inability of these two children to take their mother's share of the estate income, in the event of their mother's death, as inappropriate, and unfair. **10–16**

To overcome this disability, in 1996 the trustees distributed $250,000 of the capital of the William Wong estate to Estelle. Estelle then lent this sum of $250,000 to the Phillipa Estelle Wong Trust (PEW Trust). The beneficiaries of PEW are Mei-Ling and Matthew. **10–17**

In effecting this payment of $250,000, the trustees relied on their powers under clause 6 of the will. The debt was then periodically forgiven over a period of years, and by this will. **10–18**

The Claim in the High Court

Wong Liu Sheung bought proceedings in the High Court claiming that, in so proceeding, the trustees: **10–19**

- had acted ultra vires the terms of the trust;
- breached their duty to exercise their discretion for a proper purpose; and
- breached their duty to act impartially and even handedly towards all classes of beneficiaries.

The Judgment in the High Court

Ronald Young J. dismissed this claim, in its entirety, in a judgment delivered on 6 May 2003. . . . **10–20**

The Grounds of Appeal

Ms Peters argued that the exercise of the discretion by the trustees in the impugned respect was for an improper purpose. This submission rested essentially on two propositions. First, that the sole purpose of the exercise of the discretion was to "remedy" a perceived inequality that had arisen under clause 5 of the will (the appellants really say as a device to circumvent the plain meaning of clause 5). Second, that the distribution made was to benefit a person who was not an object of the clause 6 discretion (i.e. not Estelle). **10–21**

As to remedies, Ms Peters submitted that the $250,000 can be traced to the PEW Trust, and as such, the trustees of that trust hold the funds as constructive trustees for the William Wong estate. **10–22**

Alternatively, the appellants submit that the trustees are personally liable. The essential issue both under clause 13 of the will (the exoneration provision) and s.73 is whether the trustees acted dishonestly. The appellants submit that the trustees' actions, particularly when they were specifically warned that the will prohibited the course of conduct proposed, amounted (at least) to "recklessness". . . . **10–23**

The Law

The notion of a fraud on a power itself rests on the fundamental juristic principle that any form of authority may only be exercised for the purposes conferred, and in accordance with its terms. This principle is one of general application. **10–24**

The particular expression, a "fraud on a power", applies to both a power and a discretion. The word "fraud" here denotes an improper motive, in the sense that a power given for one purpose is improperly used for another purpose. **10–25**

Over the years a number of attempts have been made to categorise the circumstances in which a fraud on a power will arise. For instance, Hanbury and Martin, *Modern Equity*[33] divides the cases into three **10–26**

[33] 16th edn, 2001, p.188.

categories. The first arises where the appointment is made as a result of a prior agreement or bargain with the appointee as to what he or she will do with the proceeds. Secondly, there are those cases where the power is exercised improperly so as to benefit the appointor. The third category are those cases in which an appointment is drafted so that the intent appears to benefit objects of the power, but the real intent is to benefit non-objects.

10–27 These distinctions are useful for analytic and descriptive purposes, but it is necessary to recall that the sine qua non which makes the exercise of a discretion or power "improper" is the improper intention of the person exercising it. The central principle is that if the power is exercised with the intention of benefiting some non-object of the discretionary power, whether that person is the person exercising it, or anybody else for that matter, the exercise is void. If, on the other hand, there is no such improper intention, even although the exercise does in fact benefit a non-object, it is valid.[34]

10–28 In the case of a discretionary power to be exercised in favour of one of its objects, but in the "hope" that the recipient will benefit a non-object, the validity of such an exercise will depend upon whether the recipient had legal and moral freedom of action.[35]

10–29 The case law in this area is difficult, not so much for the underlying principles, which seem plain enough, but in their application to often quite complex estates, or interrelated transactions. Assume, for instance, a case in which a discretionary power is exercisable in favour of an adult male (X) who states that, if it is in fact exercised in his favour, he will give part of the relevant fund to his parents, Y and Z, who are not objects of the discretionary power. If the true intention of the appointment is to benefit the parents, the exercise is invalid. If that is not the case, but X is under some distinct pressure to benefit Y and Z, the exercise would also be invalid.[36] On the other hand, if X has genuine freedom of action and wishes to give Y and Z a benefit, then it appears that the exercise of the power would be good.[37]

10–30 As to the effect of a finding of a fraud on a power, it has long been held that where a power is successfully impugned, its exercise is totally invalid,[38] unless the improper element in the appointment can be severed from the remainder of that appointment.[39]

This Case

10–31 It is necessary at this point to add some further facts. On the evidence, Mrs Estelle Wong was devastated by the death from cancer of her daughter Phillipa, in August of 1995. Phillipa was then only 43 years old, and Matthew and Mei-Ling were teenagers. Estelle was very close to Phillipa. Although Phillipa's family were in Australia, Estelle spoke regularly to Phillipa, and she would frequently go to Australia to visit her daughter.

10–32 On one occasion, after she had returned from Australia, Estelle expressed concern to Mr Burt (who is now a retired chartered accountant and had a long association with the Wong family) "about the effect of Bill Wong's will". Estelle suddenly came to appreciate that, under the will, Phillipa's share of the income would not pass to her children.

10–33 It was in those circumstances that advice was sought from Chapman Tripp on this issue. It seems that it was Mr Burt who calculated various figures, and "concluded that $250,000 would partly redress the situation and should be loaned to the PEW Trust, and successively forgiven". As Mr Burt put it, "the purpose of the loan and forgiveness programme was to restore the expected benefit that Mei-Ling and Matthew would have received on their mother's death had they been entitled under Bill's will to her life interest in the PW Estate Trust. . . .

10–34 In their opinion (which was disclosed to the Court) Chapman Tripp advised that clause 5 must be read in "its plain words". The solicitors said, "In other words there is no statutory remedy to allow Phillipa's two children to receive the income that she would have received". The solicitors then detailed three options which, as they saw it, were "available to remedy this matter". One was to resort to the discretionary power available to the trustees under clause 6 of the will, which "[Estelle] could then invest in [her] own name".

---

[34] See *Vatcher v Paull* [1915] A.C. 372 at 378, per Lord Parker.
[35] *Birley v Birley* (1858) 25 Beav. 299.
[36] *Re Dick* [1953] Ch. 343.
[37] *Re Marsden's Trusts* (1859) 4 Drew. 594; and see Parker and Mellows, *The Modern Law of Trusts* (8th edn, Oakley), p.222.
[38] *Re Cohen* [1911] 1 Ch. 37.
[39] *Topham v Duke of Portland* (1858) 1 De G.J. & S. 517.

Estelle could then amend her will to provide for that sum to be left equally to Mei-Ling and Matthew. Secondly, the capital sum received from the estate could be loaned to the PEW Trust and then, on Estelle's death, the assets of that trust automatically vest in Mei-Ling and Matthew. A third option was identified as being an interest-free loan from the husband's estate, but repayable on Janice's death.

Although some disadvantages in each of these alternatives were identified, it was at no point suggested by the solicitors that the potential difficulties relating to a fraud on a power might have to be addressed in relation to the first option. **10–35**

The evidence in the case in this respect is well documented and quite clear. In summary, on Phillipa's premature death, Mrs Estelle Wong became concerned that there was no gift-over provision as to income for Phillipa's children. A member of Chapman Tripp recorded in a file note: "this is of great concern to Mrs Wong and although she accepts that her late husband may never have anticipated their daughter predeceasing Mrs Wong she is adamant that it would have been his intention for Phillipa's share of the income to pass to her children". Thus it was that a scheme was settled by Mrs Wong, with the trustees, and after taking legal advice, which had the overt and pre-determined idea that the trustees would utilise clause 6 of the will to avoid the effect of clause 5 of the will, in the circumstances which had arisen. This exercise was not undertaken as a distinct, or separate advance to Mrs Wong or in the "hope" that Estelle Wong would benefit a non-object. The exercise was already constrained by a pre-considered course of action which also avoided Mrs Estelle Wong having to resort to any assets under her control or direction to assist her grandchildren. **10–36**

In our view, this deliberate, and pre-conceived, device amounted to a fraud on the power. If Mrs Estelle Wong had simply been advanced the money out of the estate and had then exercised genuine freedom of action to benefit the children (as for instance by setting up a trust for them), that would not have been unlawful. But what was knowingly erected was a deliberate scheme to subvert the terms of the will. What was overlooked was that the property was vested in those entitled in default of the exercise of the power, subject to its being divested by a proper exercise of the power in clause 6, and the steps in fact taken gave rise to a fraud on those entitled in default. **10–37**

Held: to the extent that the $250,000 could not be recovered by tracing into the PEW Trust, the trustees were personally accountable and were not protected by an exemption clause which provided that they should "not liable for any loss not attributable to dishonesty". **10–38**

C. *The Rule in Re Hastings-Bass*

The Court of Appeal's decision in *Re Hastings-Bass*[40] has now obtained the status of a "rule" or "principle". The case concerned a statutory advancement that was made out of an old settlement into a new settlement with intent to avoid estate duty at 75 per cent. It transpired that the advancement of capital out to trustees for B for life, with remainders over to his family, was void for perpetuity as to these remainders. The Revenue argued that an advancement of capital only for B's life did not fully dispose of the capital, so that this fell outside the scope of the Trustee Act 1925 s.32 so as to be void, or was not "for the benefit of B" when the remainders failed so that it was outside s.32 and void.[41] The Court of Appeal held[42] that where the trustee "acts in good faith" the court should not interfere with his action: **10–39**

> "notwithstanding that it does not have the full effect which he intended, unless (1) what he has achieved is unauthorised by the power conferred on him or (2) it is clear that he would not have acted as he did (a) had he not taken into account considerations which he should not have taken

[40] [1975] Ch. 25.
[41] As in *Re Abrahams WT* [1969] 1 Ch. 463.
[42] [1975] Ch. 25 at 41.

> into account or (b) had he not failed to take into account considerations which he ought to have taken into account".

10–40 The trustee's action in advancing capital only to B for life was not void because it was authorised under s.32 and the overlooking of the voidness of the remainders after B's lifetime, so that there was a resulting trust of the capital to the old settlement, did not prevent the advancement of capital to B for his life being for his benefit and so valid when this achieved the substantial tax-saving intended by the trustee. B would still have received his life-interest if the trustee had appreciated the need to restrict the remainders to the perpetuity period provided for in the old settlement.

10–41 In *Sieff v Fox*, parts of which are reproduced below,[43] Lloyd L.J. restated the *Hastings-Bass* principle in a positive form, as follows:[44]

> "Where trustees act under a discretion given to them by the terms of the trust, in circumstances in which they are free to decide whether or not to exercise that discretion,[45] but the effect of the exercise is different from that which they intended,[46] the court will interfere with their action if it is clear that they would not have acted as they did had they not failed to take into account considerations which they ought to have taken into account, or taken into account considerations which they ought not to have taken into account."

He also said that the courts should "take a reasonable and not over-exigent view of what it is that the trustees ought to have taken into account" and "adopt a critical approach to contentions that the trustees would have acted differently if they had realised the true position."[47]

10–42 Applying the rule, Lloyd L.J. set aside an appointment of property by trustees to the Duke of Bedford, who had subsequently assigned the property to the trustees of a second settlement. The purpose of these transactions was to prevent the risk of a significant charge to inheritance tax arising in the event of the Duke's death while he was entitled to an interest in possession under the first settlement. However, he and the trustees of the first settlement had failed to appreciate that the appointment would trigger a £1 million capital gains tax liability which would not have arisen if the appointment had been differently drafted. On the facts the trustees would not have made the appointment if they had been aware of this.

10–43 The trustees had acted on legal advice, and their solicitors (and their insurers) must have been relieved when Lloyd L.J. made his declaration, for an expensive negligence suit would surely have followed if he had dismissed the claim. On the other hand, the decision cannot have pleased HMRC. Yet it is a curiosity of *Sieff*, and of other recent cases where the rule has been invoked,[48] that HMRC

---

[43] At paras 10–47 ff.

[44] [2005] 1 W.L.R. 3811 at [119].

[45] As noted by Sir Andrew Park in *Smithson v Hamilton* [2009] I.C.R. 1 at [53], this is "the commonest situation where the principle may arise, but (as Lloyd L.J. explains at other points in his judgment) it can also apply where the trust imposes an obligation on the trustee to act but the precise way in which he acts is left for him to determine." Hence the rule covers the exercise of distributive powers by discretionary trustees although they are not free to decide whether or not to exercise their discretion in favour of beneficiaries: they must exercise it, although they have leeway to decide who gets how much.

[46] In *Smithson* at [53] Sir Andrew Park also glossed this part of Lloyd L.J.'s formulation, stressing that "it is certainly not the case that the *Hastings-Bass* principle only applies where an action taken by trustees fails to achieve the direct legal effect which they intended. Indeed, at least in cases involving private trusts the usual situation is that the action which the trustees take achieves exactly the legal effect intended, but has unwelcome consequences, usually tax consequences, which the trustees failed to foresee."

[47] *Sieff* at [82].

[48] e.g. *Green v Cobham* [2000] W.T.L.R. 1101; *Abacus Trust Co (Isle of Man) Ltd v NSPCC* [2001] S.T.C. 1344; *Burrell v Burrell* [2005] S.T.C. 569.

declined an invitation to be joined as a party to the proceedings. The result has been that significant cases have been decided in the past few years without the benefit of counter-argument from a party with a real financial interest in opposing the application, a fact which has led to judicial expressions of concern, lest the principle develop into an easy way for trustees and their professional advisers to escape responsibility for the consequences of their negligent behaviour—to the potential detriment of third parties, and with potentially disruptive effects for the administration of trust affairs.[49] HMRC have now said that in the light of their "increasing concern (which is shared by many commentators) that the principle as currently formulated is too wide in its scope, [they will] . . . give active consideration to participating in future cases where large amounts of tax are at stake and/or where it is felt that [they] could make a useful contribution to the elucidation and development of the principle."[50]

The scope and effect of the rule are discussed in the passages from *Sieff* that are reproduced below. **10–44** The following points should also be noted. First, it may be that the rule applies only to powers that are exercisable in respect of trust property in favour of beneficiaries or objects of powers of appointment, as opposed to administrative or management powers. Thus, the power to appoint new trustees and transfer legal title to the trust property to them has been held to fall outside the scope of the rule,[51] as has the power to enter a contract with a third party or agree to a variation or cancellation of such a contract.[52] The discretion to decide that a beneficiary or object should receive a payment out of the trust fund is an equitable discretion conferred by the trust instrument and exercisable according to trust law, and the right which the beneficiary or object has to call for a transfer of legal title to the relevant assets depends on the proper exercise of the trustee's discretion. In contrast, the exercise of legal contractual or dispositive powers of management in favour of third parties is a function of the trustee's own common law legal capacity to contract, or to dispose of owned property. A contract or a transfer of property made by a trustee will be legally valid even if unauthorised and made in breach of trust law.[53]

Second, the question arises whether the rule in *Re Hastings-Bass* should be aligned with the equitable rules governing the rescission of deeds executed by mistake. **10–45** Millett J. stated in *Gibbon v Mitchell* that a deed will not be set aside unless the mistake was "as to the effect of the transaction itself and not merely as to its consequences or the advantage to be gained by entering into it".[54] He seems to have transposed this distinction from cases on the doctrine of rectification,[55] but it is probably unworkable in the rescission context, and it is out of line with Lindley L.J.'s wider statement in *Ogilvie v Littleboy* that "a donor can only obtain back property which he has given away by showing that he was under some mistake of so serious a character as to render it unjust on the part of the donee to retain the property given to him".[56] More recent cases have applied a causative mistake test without regard to the *Gibbon* effects/consequences decision.[57] These authorities suggest that a causative mistake as to the fiscal consequences of a transaction should suffice to entitle an appointor to ask for rescission, which would be consistent with the findings made in *Sieff* and other cases that such a

---

[49] e.g. *Breadner v Granville-Grossman* [2001] Ch. 523 at [61] and [95]; *Sieff* at [81]. See too Sir Robert Walker, "The Limits of the Principle in *Re Hastings-Bass*" (2002) 13 K.C.L.J. 173, p.183.

[50] HMRC, *Tax Bulletin No.83* (2006). See too *Gresh v RBC Trust Co (Guernsey) Ltd*, Royal Court of Guernsey, May 29, 2009, where HMRC unsuccessfully applied to be joined to a set of *Re Hastings-Bass* proceedings; this decision is currently under appeal.

[51] *Re Duxbury's ST* [1995] 1 W.L.R. 425 at 428.

[52] *Donaldson v Smith* [2007] W.T.L.R. 421 at [54]–[55].

[53] *Rolled Steel Products (Holdings) Ltd v British Steel Corp* [1986] Ch. 246 at 303.

[54] [1990] 1 W.L.R. 1304 at 1309.

[55] For which see paras 17–277 ff. Millett J.'s distinction was cited with approval by the CA in a rectification case: *Allnutt v Wilding* [2007] W.T.L.R. 941.

[56] (1897) 13 T.L.R. 399, endorsed on appeal (1899) 15 T.L.R. 294.

[57] *Re Griffiths, deceased* [2009] Ch. 162; *Fender v National Westminster Bank Plc* [2008] 3 E.G.L.R. 80; *P v Atlas Trust Co (Jersey) Ltd* [2009] W.T.L.R. 873; *Bhatt v Bhatt* [2009] S.T.C. 1540; but cf. *Pitt v Holt* [2010] EWHC 45 (Ch) at [49] ff.

mistake can also bring the rule in *Re Hastings-Bass* into play.[58] This also suggests that Lloyd L.J. was right to reject Lightman J.'s finding in *Abacus Trust Co (Isle of Man) Ltd v Barr*[59] that the rule applies only where it was a breach of the trustee's duties that led him to ignore a relevant consideration or to act upon an irrelevant consideration. As noted by Brian Green, this finding was also desirable from a policy perspective, because:[60]

> "if relief [were] to be conditional on a finding of want of proper care and diligence on the part of the trustee, the whole nature of the proceedings [would] change from one of technical failure . . . to one involving a finding of trustee negligence. The proceedings [would] become ones that trustees [would be] less likely to bring, and ones which if brought [might] well have to be actively defended. The scope, scale, and cost of such proceedings [would be] liable to change accordingly."

10–46 Finally, the question arises whether the application of the rule in *Re Hastings-Bass* leads to the trustee's impeached exercise of a discretionary equitable power being declared void ab initio, or merely voidable, suggesting that it cannot be set aside if too great a time has elapsed or if third party rights have intervened, and suggesting, too, that HMRC have no standing to intervene in an application under the rule. Those who are concerned that the rule is too broad (including HMRC) would like the Court of Appeal to resolve this question by holding that it merely renders transactions voidable, but against this it can be argued that the rule holds that a trustee is only authorised to exercise his distributive powers if he is adequately informed of all relevant considerations, and that if he is not so informed then his exercise of such a power amounts to a fraud on the power and is accordingly void. The latter view was recently taken by Norris J. in *Futter v Futter* [61] but he reached his decision without the benefit of detailed argument, and it is currently under appeal.

SIEFF v FOX

Chancery Division [2005] 1 W.L.R. 3811; [2005] 3 All E.R. 693

LLOYD L.J. (sitting as a High Court judge) stated the facts and continued:

The Hastings-Bass Principle

10–47 . . . So far as acts by trustees in the exercise of a discretionary power are concerned, traditionally the courts are reluctant to interfere. It has been said that, when a power has been exercised in good faith and within its terms, the court will not interfere: see *Gisborne v Gisborne*.[62] This judicial reticence is further emphasised by the well established entitlement of trustees not to give reasons for their exercise of discretionary distributive powers. That has not been a feature of the recent cases from the *Hastings-Bass* case[63] onwards, as the trustees have been open with the court and the beneficiaries about the circumstances of the appointment or other relevant act. Nevertheless, if the trustees do not vouchsafe their reasons it is the more difficult for a beneficiary to challenge the exercise of their discretions unless a defect is apparent from the documents. In *Tempest v Lord Camoys*[64] the court would not override the refusal of one of two trustees to agree with a course of action proposed by the other involving the purchase of particular land

---

[58] See too *Abacus Trust Co (Isle of Man) Ltd v NSPCC* [2001] S.T.C. 1344 at [16].
[59] [2003] Ch. 409.
[60] B. Green QC, "The Law Relating to Trustees' Mistakes—Where Are We Now?" (2003) 17 Tru L.I. 114, pp. 120–121.
[61] [2010] EWHC 449 (Ch) at [31]–[35]. See too P. Matthews, "The Doctrine of Fraud on a Power" [2007] P.C.B. 131, pp. 138–139.
[62] (1877) 2 App. Cas. 300.
[63] [1975] Ch. 25.
[64] (1882) 21 Ch.D. 571.

and the raising of some of the purchase money on mortgage. Conversely, in *Klug v Klug*[65] the refusal of one of two trustees (the mother of the relevant beneficiary) to agree to an advance to a beneficiary to provide funds for the payment of legacy duty, which the other trustee, the Public Trustee, considered would be a proper exercise of a power, was overridden where it appeared that the mother's refusal to agree was due to the daughter having married without her consent. The mother's refusal to exercise the power in her daughter's favour was disregarded because of her irrelevant motivation.

There are several different categories of case where an exercise by trustees of a discretionary power may be held to be invalid. **10–48**

(i) There may be a formal or procedural defect, such as the failure to use the stipulated form of document, for example a document under hand instead of a deed, or to obtain a necessary prior consent. (In some such cases, and for the benefit of some interested persons, equity may relieve against such a formal or procedural defect.)

(ii) The power may have been exercised in a way which it does not authorise, for example with an unauthorised delegation, or by the inclusion of beneficiaries who are not objects of the power.

(iii) The exercise may infringe some rule of the general law, such as the rule against perpetuities.

(iv) The trustees may have exercised the power for an improper purpose, in cases known as fraud on the power. *Cloutte v Storey*,[66] among the cases cited to me, is an example of this, where the power was exercised in favour of one of the objects, but under a private arrangement whereby he passed the benefit back to his parents, who had made the appointment. Another example, in a different context, was *Hillsdown Holdings Plc v Pensions Ombudsman*.[67] I take it that references, for example in *Gisborne v Gisborne* (and in the *Hastings-Bass* case itself), to good faith are to be understood in this context, so that an exercise which is not in good faith is, or at any rate includes, a case where the exercise is a fraud on the power.

(v) The trustees may have been unaware that they had any discretion to exercise: see *Turner v Turner*,[68] an extreme and highly unusual case on the facts, which has been described as equitable non est factum.

(vi) To these categories, of which the first four are clear and well established, the rule or principle in the *Hastings-Bass* case is said to add a further class of case, namely where the trustees have failed to have regard to some relevant consideration which they ought to have taken into account.

[Lloyd L.J. discussed *Re Baron Vestey's Settlement*,[69] *Re Pilkington's WT*,[70] *Re Abrahams' WT*,[71] and *Re Hastings-Bass*[72] before turning to more recent authorities]: A positive formulation [of the principle in *Re Hastings-Bass*] was first put forward by Warner J. in *Mettoy Pension Trustees Ltd v Evans*.[73] That case concerned the exercise by pension trustees of a power to amend the rules applying to the pension scheme. In most respects no issue arose as to the terms of the amended rules, but the amendments did change the position as regards the allocation of any surplus in a winding up, which had been at the disposition of the trustees, but which, after the amendments, was to be decided on by the company. The evidence was that the trustees were unaware of this particular point in the new rules. The judge held that the discretion conferred on the company was fiduciary. Nevertheless, the representatives of employees and pensioners **10–49**

---

[65] [1918] 2 Ch. 67.
[66] [1911] 1 Ch. 18.
[67] [1997] 1 All E.R. 862.
[68] [1984] Ch. 100.
[69] [1951] Ch. 209.
[70] [1959] Ch. 699.
[71] [1969] 1 Ch. 463.
[72] [1975] Ch. 25.
[73] [1990] 1 W.L.R. 1587.

argued that the power of amendment had not been validly exercised to the extent of the change in the power over any surplus, and relied on *Re Hastings-Bass* as authority for this. At the outset of the passage in his judgment in which he deals with the submissions on this point, Warner J. set out the proposition as the positive converse of what the Court of Appeal had said in the *Hastings-Bass* case itself:[74]

> "where a trustee acts under a discretion given to him by the terms of the trust, the court will interfere with his action if it is clear that he would not have acted as he did had he not failed to take into account considerations which he ought to have taken into account."

10–50 He then considered the submissions made to him, as to whether there was any such rule, and if so what it amounted to. He held that such a rule did exist, and was not limited to cases of invalidity for, so to speak, external reasons (such as the rule against perpetuities), and that it could invalidate part only of a disposition in an appropriate case. He then said:[75]

> "I have come to the conclusion that there is a principle which may be labelled 'the rule in *Hastings-Bass*'. I do not think that the application of that principle is confined, as Mr Nugee suggested, to cases where an exercise by trustees of a discretion vested in them is partially ineffective because of some rule of law or because of some limit on their discretion which they overlooked. If, as I believe, the reason for the application of the principle is the failure of the trustees to take into account considerations that they ought to have taken into account, it cannot matter whether that failure is due to their having overlooked (or to their legal advisers having overlooked) some relevant rule of law or limit on their discretion, or is due to some other cause.
>
> "For the principle to apply, however, it is not enough that it should be shown that the trustees did not have a proper understanding of the effect of their act. It must also be clear that, had they had a proper understanding of it, they would not have acted as they did."

10–51 Applying these principles to the facts, the judge said that three questions arose. (1) What were the trustees under a duty to consider? (2) Did they fail to consider it? (3) If so, what would they have done if they had considered it? Having reviewed the evidence, and in the light of his finding that the company's power over surplus was fiduciary, he held that the new rules were not in any respect invalidated under the rule in *Re Hastings-Bass*. . . .

10–52 Warner J. delivered that judgment in December 1989. In July 1990 he gave judgment in another case in which the *Hastings-Bass* case, and what he had said about it in the *Mettoy* case, were relied on: *Stannard v Fisons Pension Trust Ltd*.[76] That case concerned the amount to be transferred from one pension scheme to another upon the sale by Fisons of part of its business to a third party. The purchaser (in effect) claimed that the amount which had been paid was inadequate. One of the arguments in favour of not ordering an additional payment was based on the *Hastings-Bass* principle, to the extent of submitting that unless that principle were satisfied, the trustees' decision as to the amount to be transferred should not be disturbed. The judge distinguished the *Hastings-Bass* case and the *Mettoy* case on a number of grounds. In particular, in the *Stannard* case[77] he pointed out that those cases had concerned the voluntary exercise by trustees of a discretion, whereas in the *Stannard* case the trustees were under an obligation to exercise their discretion at a particular time and after fulfilling a given condition, and he had found that they had not complied with that obligation, so that the question was how their failure to perform that obligation should be remedied.

10–53 The *Stannard* case was appealed unsuccessfully to the Court of Appeal.[78] Dillon L.J., with whom Ralph Gibson L.J. agreed, decided the case on the basis of legal principles set out in another Court of Appeal

[74] At 1621.
[75] At 1624.
[76] [1990] 1 Pens. L.R. 179.
[77] At [183].
[78] [1991] Pens. L.R. 225.

case: *Kerr v British Leyland (Staff) Trustees Ltd.*[79] He held that the trustees' decision was vitiated by the fact that they were not, at the relevant moment, properly informed as to the value of the fund and the implications of its value in relation to future contributions, and that if they had been properly informed as to those matters it might materially have affected their decision. He also said that he had no difficulty reconciling the judgment in the *Kerr* case with that in the *Hastings-Bass* case but he did not elaborate on that point. Staughton L.J. agreed in the result but for somewhat different reasons, and did not find it necessary to refer to either the *Kerr* case or the *Hastings-Bass* case.

Mr Herbert submitted to me that the *Kerr* case and the *Stannard* case are in a different and distinct line of authority from the *Hastings-Bass* case, because they are concerned with circumstances in which the trustees are under an obligation to act, whereas the *Hastings-Bass* case concerned a voluntary exercise of a discretion, as did the *Mettoy* case. . . . He submitted, on this basis, that the proposition that the matter overlooked "might" have led the trustees to act differently cannot properly be transferred from the *Kerr* case line of cases to the *Hastings-Bass* principle, both because of this distinction and because it is inconsistent with the Court of Appeal's judgment in the *Hastings-Bass* case itself. **10–54**

The issue in the *Kerr* case was whether a member of a pension scheme was entitled to an incapacity payment or, more exactly, whether the trustees' decision that he was not so entitled was valid and effective. The judge had held that the decision made by the trustees was based on inadequate and misleading information as to Mr Kerr's state of health, due to failures of communication and misunderstandings. The Court of Appeal agreed that this vitiated the decision. Fox L.J. said:[80] **10–55**

> "If the board had appreciated that aspect of the case I think that it might materially have affected their decision and that they might well have concluded that the proper course was to defer a decision until more was known about the effect which the remedial steps were having upon Mr Kerr."

The Court of Appeal allowed the appeal, but only because the judge had considered that the court could itself decide that Mr Kerr was entitled to the incapacity payment. The Court of Appeal upheld his order that the decision taken was of no effect, and directed the trustee board to reconsider the claim. **10–56**

The *Kerr* case is thus a rather different kind of case, where the trustees are the arbiters of a beneficiary's entitlement to a particular benefit under the rules of the pension scheme, and that entitlement is derived not from pure bounty, as would be the case in a family trust, but from the contract of employment. In those circumstances, and given the inadequate information provided to the trustees on which to take their decision, it seems to me logical that a relatively low threshold of relevance ("might") should have been adopted by the court as the test of whether the deficiency of information entitles the beneficiary to have his case, in effect, reconsidered. *Mihlenstedt v Barclays Bank International Ltd*[81] was a similar case, though there the decision lay with the employer, not the trustees, and the claim failed on the facts. *Harris v Lord Shuttleworth*[82] was also a similar type of case. **10–57**

Likewise in the *Stannard* case the trustees were under an obligation to act, by appropriating an amount to be applied for the benefit of the transferring employees, though they had to decide, after consulting the actuary, what amount should be appropriated, as being the amount which they decided to be just and equitable. Although on its facts the *Stannard* case is a different kind of case from the *Kerr* case, it seems to me that the analogy is fair. Both were pension cases, so that the rights of the members or beneficiaries arose in the context of the contract of employment. Both were cases in which the trustees were under a duty to act, though with some freedom as to how they proceeded. It is true that even outside this type of case, if trustees have a discretionary power, they are under obligations in relation to it, including to consider from time to time whether to exercise it, and if they do decide to exercise it they are under duties in respect of that process, but it seems to me that there is a real distinction between such a case (which *Re Abrahams' WT, Re Hastings-Bass* and the present case are) and cases such as the *Kerr* case and the **10–58**

[79] [2001] W.T.L.R. 1071.
[80] At 1079.
[81] [1989] I.R.L.R. 522.
[82] [1994] I.C.R. 991.

Stannard case where the trustees are under a duty to act, not merely a duty to consider from time to time whether to act. I consider, therefore, that Mr Herbert's submissions in this respect are well founded.

10–59 Since the decisions in the *Mettoy* case and the *Stannard* case, the *Hastings-Bass* principle has been applied in a number of cases, especially in the last five years, in which the principle has been stated in different terms. Some disquiet has been expressed both judicially[83] and extra-judicially[84] as to the ease with which the principle may allow the court to set aside what appear to be valid exercises of a trustee's discretion. . . .

10–60 [Lloyd L.J. reviewed *Green v Cobham*,[85] *Breadner v Granville-Grossman*,[86] *AMP (UK) Plc v Barker*,[87] *Abacus Trust Co (Isle of Man) Ltd v NSPCC*,[88] and *Hearn v Younger*,[89] then continued:] Next in time came a family trust case, in which the *Hastings-Bass* principle was the basis of the judge's decision: *Abacus Trust Co (Isle of Man) v Barr*.[90] In this case, a settlor had created a trust in the Isle of Man under which he had a life interest subject to an overriding power of appointment. He expressed the wish that the trustees should exercise that power in respect of 40 per cent of the trust property to create discretionary trusts for the benefit of his two sons, to the exclusion of any benefit for himself and his wife. By some mistake or misunderstanding, the trustees thought that his wish was that the trusts should be created in respect of 60 per cent of the fund. They acted accordingly in April 1992. The error was soon discovered but the settlor, without legal advice, decided at that time not to do anything about it. Again in 1994 he thought about it but did not take legal advice and took no further steps. In 2001 the trustees received legal advice that the appointment was open to challenge, and the settlor decided that the point should be tested in proceedings.

10–61 Lightman J. had cited to him all the cases that I have mentioned, and Sir Robert Walker's article mentioned above. He held that the principle did apply to the exercise of the power of appointment, but that it rendered the appointment voidable, not void. He left over for further argument the question whether it should be avoided. One of the striking consequences, if he had held the appointment void, would have been that any sums distributed pursuant to the discretionary trusts in favour of the sons since the appointment would have been repayable (subject to possible defences of change of position) even though the grounds for challenging the appointment had been known since August 1992, and decisions had been taken in 1992 and 1994 not to do anything about it. It is understandable that the judge should have been attracted by an argument which gave the court a degree of control over whether, and perhaps if so on what basis or terms, the appointment should be set aside. He took it that none of that would be possible if the appointment were void.[91]

10–62 The judge said that the principle had only been changed significantly in one respect in the course of the sequence of judicial decisions, namely by the use of the "might" test in the *Stannard* case, but that it was unnecessary to consider which test was correct, since on the facts of the case the "would" test would be satisfied. He rejected the submission that the mistake must have been as to something fundamental, in favour of the conventional test, that the unconsidered relevant consideration would (or might) have affected the trustees' decision.

10–63 He did hold that it is relevant to consider how the mistake arose. The settlor's contention was that the fact of a mistake was enough, regardless of how it came to be made. The judge held that the principle is based on the proposition that the trustees have acted in breach of duty by failing to take into account a relevant consideration, or taking into account an irrelevant consideration. Accordingly, if they have acted without any breach of duty, having identified the relevant considerations and used all proper care and diligence in obtaining the relevant information and advice relating to those considerations, the decision

---

83 By Park J. in *Breadner v Granville-Grossman* [2001] Ch. 523 at [61].
84 See Sir Robert Walker "The Limits of the Principle in *Re Hastings-Bass*" [2002] P.C.B. 226, and see also Underhill and Hayton, *Law of Trusts and Trustees*, 16th edn (2003), pp.694–699.
85 [2002] S.T.C. 820.
86 [2001] Ch. 523.
87 [2001] Pens. L.R. 77.
88 [2001] S.T.C. 1344.
89 [2002] W.T.L.R. 1317.
90 [2003] Ch. 409.
91 At [23].

cannot be impugned merely because, without any fault on the part of the trustees (or of any person acting on behalf of the trustees), some information relied on turns out to be inaccurate.

His decision that the defective appointment was voidable rather than void is consistent with this last point; he said that it accorded with ordinary principles of equity that a decision challenged on grounds of breach of fiduciary duty is voidable, not void. **10–64**

The next, and most recent, case in which the *Hastings-Bass* principle has been considered is *Burrell v Burrell*,[92] again a family trust case, and one where the mistake was as to the fiscal consequences of the appointment. Trustees held property on trusts under which a young man had an interest in possession but they had an overriding power of appointment exercisable on or after his 19th birthday. They were asked to consider exercising it before the declaration of a dividend by a company some of whose shares were comprised in the trust property, which was expected to happen three days after the birthday. They exercised the power by appointing the shares in the company on discretionary trusts. The shares were of a nature such as to qualify for business property relief for inheritance tax. However, a condition of the application of that relief was overlooked, namely that the transferor (in this case, the person entitled to the interest in possession) had to have held the shares for at least two years before the transfer, whereas he had only held them for one year. Accordingly, the appointment gave rise to a substantial charge to inheritance tax. **10–65**

The trustees brought the proceedings to have the appointment set aside. They said, and Mann J. accepted, that they had executed the appointment under a mistaken belief as to its tax consequences, and that if they had known what those consequences would be they would not have executed it. All parties before the court supported the application. As in the present case the Inland Revenue had declined the invitation to take part in the proceedings. Most, if not all, of the cases which I have mentioned were cited to the judge. He held that the trustees ought to have borne the fiscal consequences of the appointment in mind, that they did not give full and proper consideration to those consequences, and that if they had done so they would not have acted as they did. Because of Lightman J.'s decision in *Abacus Trust Co (Isle of Man) v Barr* the judge considered whether the trustees or their advisers or agents were in breach of duty, and held that both the trustees and their solicitors were. Accordingly he held that the deed should be set aside, it being unnecessary for him to decide between "would" and "might", and between void and voidable. **10–66**

It is apparent from this survey that the cases have come a long way from the propositions discussed in the *Vestey* case and *Re Abrahams' WT*. In those cases the criterion was said to be whether the partial invalidity imposed externally by the rule against perpetuities, as explained in the *Pilkington* case, or by the non-application of section 31 in the *Vestey* case, rendered the effect of the trustees' act substantially or essentially different from that which was intended. The *Hastings-Bass* case was the same kind of case. I have already suggested a reframing of the *Mettoy* version of the *Hastings-Bass* statement of principle. The question whether the difference in effect has to be substantial in order for the principle to apply comes into the test as part of the process of answering the question whether, if the trustees had been aware of the true position, they would not have acted as they did. **10–67**

One element introduced in the *Hastings-Bass* formulation is whether the trustees took into account matters which they ought not to have done, or failed to take into account matters which they ought to have. This is reminiscent of public law and the *Wednesbury* test,[93] though that case does not seem to have been cited in the *Hastings-Bass* case itself. That is now established as a relevant test in relation to the exercise of a discretion by trustees, as a result of *Edge v Pensions Ombudsman*.[94] In that case the Court of Appeal, affirming the decision of Sir Richard Scott V.C.,[95] and following earlier decisions of the Court of Appeal including *Harris v Lord Shuttleworth*, held that trustees to whom the exercise of a discretionary power is entrusted were under a duty to exercise that power (if they chose to exercise it) only for the purpose for which it is given, giving proper consideration to the matters which are relevant and excluding from consideration matters which are irrelevant.[96] The introduction into trust law of what might seem to be a public law concept has been criticised, at any rate in relation to private family trusts as distinct from pension **10–68**

---

[92] [2005] S.T.C. 569.
[93] See *Associated Provincial Picture Houses Ltd v Wednesbury Corp* [1948] 1 K.B. 223
[94] [2000] Ch. 602.
[95] [1998] Ch. 512.
[96] [2000] Ch. 602 at 627.

funds,[97] but it seems to me that this formulation respects the traditional view, that it is for the trustees to exercise the power, and to decide whether or not to do so (unless they have an obligation to do so, as in the *Kerr* or the *Stannard* type cases), and is at the same time consistent with the cases about fraud on the power or other examples of caprice or bad faith, such as *Cloutte v Storey*[98] or *Klug v Klug*.[99] In those cases the defaulting trustee was motivated by irrelevant considerations in deciding whether or not to exercise the power, and if so how: the advantage of a non-object in cases such as the *Cloutte* case (or *Hillsdown Holdings Plc v Pensions Ombudsman*[100]) or an irrelevant consideration in relation to an object in the *Klug* case.

10–69 It seems to me that, for the purposes of a case where the trustees are not under a duty to act, the relevant test is still that stated in the *Hastings-Bass* case, namely whether, if they had not misunderstood the effect that their actual exercise of the discretionary power would have, they would have acted differently. In my judgment that is correct both on authority, starting with the *Hastings-Bass* case itself, and on principle. Only in a case where the beneficiary is entitled to require the trustees to act, such as the *Kerr* case or the *Stannard* case, should it suffice to vitiate the trustees' decision to show that they might have acted differently. The word "might" has been used, as matter of decision, only in those two cases. In two cases it has been said (not as a matter of decision) that the "might" test applies to a voluntary exercise of a power: *AMP (UK) Plc v Barker* and *Hearn v Younger*. I respectfully disagree with those observations, having had the benefit of what may have been fuller, and were no doubt different, submissions on the point. If an act by trustees is set aside, where the trustees have acted under an obligation, then the beneficiaries can require the trustees to start again, on the correct basis. It seems to me that the lower test of "might" is appropriate in such cases. If the trustees' act was voluntary, so that they cannot be compelled to act again if the act is set aside, the more demanding test of "would" is justified in order to decide whether the trustees' act can be set aside. (The *Vestey* case was a case where the trustees were under a duty to act, but the test applied there was expressed in different and more general terms.)

10–70 Another unresolved question on the cases is whether, if the trustees' exercise is vitiated on this principle, the result is that the trustees' act is void or voidable. Lightman J. in *Abacus Trust Co (Isle of Man) v Barr* held that it was voidable, and adjourned the question whether it should be avoided. In *Re Abrahams' WT* Cross J. held that the defective appointment in that case was void. Since it was the Inland Revenue that sought this result, it was only on the basis of it being void that the submission could have been accepted. That body would not have standing to seek to have a voidable act set aside. If the exercise of a power is vitiated by the doctrine of fraud on a power, the result appears to be that the exercise is declared void: see *Topham v Duke of Portland*,[101] and the form of order made in that case,[102] and see also *Cloutte v Storey*.[103] This may be because the appointment is treated as having been, in effect, to a non-object, and plainly a direct appointment to such a person would be void. On the other hand, if, as Warner J. held in the *Mettoy* case, the principle could result in part of a document being set aside but not the rest, the process would come close to rectification, and it would be difficult to say that a part of it was altogether void. He did not have to consider that aspect, since on the facts he held that no part was to be set aside.

10–71 Lightman J. held that the exercise was voidable, rather than void, because its being set aside resulted from a breach of the trustees' duty. Some acts of trustees which are set aside for breach of duty are voidable; they will not be set aside if no one with the right to do so applies for that remedy, and such an application may be defeated on discretionary and equitable grounds which would not be available if the disposition was void, such as affirmation or laches. It is also fair to say (as Lightman J. clearly bore in mind, and as Park J. mentioned in *Breadner v Granville-Grossman*) that if the consequence of the doctrine is that the exercise is void, this might have dramatic and potentially unfair disruptive consequences for the trustees and the beneficiaries. To hold that the defect makes the appointment voidable, rather than void, is therefore attractive.

---

97 See Underhill and Hayton, *Law of Trusts and Trustees* 16th edn (2003), p.696.
98 [1911] 1 Ch. 18.
99 [1918] 2 Ch. 67.
100 [1997] 1 All E.R. 862.
101 (1869) L.R. 5 Ch. App. 40.
102 Printed in *Seton's Judgments and Orders*, 7th edn, vol.2 (1912), p.1672.
103 [1911] 1 Ch. 18.

Nevertheless it seems to be questionable whether the application of the doctrine should be regarded as depending on a breach of duty, and whether its consequences should be aligned with those of a breach of trust. It seems to me that it would have been hard to say that the trustees who made the advancement which was held to be completely ineffective in *Re Abrahams' WT* acted in breach of their duty. What was wrong with their act was the application of the rule against perpetuities in a way quite different from that which seems to have been regarded as normal and legitimate at the time, and which was held valid by Danckwerts J. at first instance in the *Pilkington* case.[104] **10–72**

Taking together, first, the fact that only if the exercise was void could the Inland Revenue have succeeded in having the advancement set aside in *Re Abrahams' WT* (and, at first instance, in the *Hastings-Bass* case itself) and, secondly, the difficulty of showing that in either of those cases there was any breach of the trustees' duty, it seems to me that Lightman J.'s conclusion that the appointment was voidable is open to doubt, as also is his introduction of a factor, not previously mentioned in the cases, that the trustees or their advisers or agents must have been at fault in some way for the principle to apply. I respectfully agree with him that the application of the principle is of potentially worrying breadth if it cannot be confined or controlled by reference to equitable principles, and that it would be more satisfactory if substantial delay in raising the point, with knowledge of the problem (as in the case before him), could be treated as relevant to the grant or withholding of relief. Mr Taube submitted that, because the remedy lay in equity, and the grant of a declaration is discretionary, matters affecting the conscience of the parties, including laches or acquiescence, could be taken into account by the court in deciding what, if any, relief to grant, even if, on the true analysis, an appointment which is vitiated by the *Hastings-Bass* principle is void, not merely voidable. **10–73**

I do not need to decide between "void" and "voidable" in order to decide this case: all counsel agreed that nothing turned on that distinction in this instance. It seems to me, however, that on authority, the main ways at present open to the court to control the application of the principle are: (a) to insist on a stringent application of the tests as they have been laid down, (b) to take a reasonable and not over-exigent view of what it is that the trustees ought to have taken into account, and (c) to adopt a critical approach to contentions that the trustees would have acted differently if they had realised the true position, perhaps especially so in cases (unlike the present) where it is in the interests of all who are before the court that the appointment should be set aside. As Park J. said in *Breadner v Granville-Grossman*: "It cannot be right that whenever trustees do something which they later regret and think that they ought not to have done, they can say that they never did it in the first place."[105] **10–74**

The position would also be more flexible if equitable considerations can be taken into account in deciding whether or not to grant any and if so what relief. The court's task might be easier in some cases if the Inland Revenue did not always decline the invitation to take part in cases of this kind, but there are no doubt policy reasons of one kind or another for that attitude, of which the court is not aware. **10–75**

Mr Herbert submits that it is not enough to bring the principle into play that the trustees be mistaken as to the fiscal effects of the transaction, and that the mistake must be as to the substantive legal effect of the appointment or other act, as *Re Abrahams' WT*, the *Hastings-Bass* case and the *Mettoy* case, or as to a matter of fact, such as the true nature of the settlor's wishes in *Abacus Trust Co (Isle of Man) v Barr*. He submits that this follows from the formulation of the rule by reference to the effect of the exercise being different from that which the trustees intended. He says that the "effect" in this context excludes consequential matters such as tax liabilities. He relies for this on an analogy with *Gibbon v Mitchell*[106] and other cases about mistake by an individual donor. **10–76**

He submits that, in cases concerning the setting aside of dispositions by individuals for mistake, fiscal consequences have never been held to be a sufficient or relevant reason. I will deal with those cases later in this judgment, but it seems to me that there are at least two significant differences. First, trustees are dealing with assets which are not their own, and in relation to which they owe duties to beneficiaries, whereas individual beneficial owners owe no legal duty to anyone else as to how they deal with their **10–77**

104 [1959] Ch. 699.
105 [2001] Ch. 523 at [61].
106 [1990] 1 W.L.R. 1304.

own assets. Secondly, the fiscal treatment of trust property is much more complex than that applying to disposals by individuals. I do not accept that, even if fiscal consequences are irrelevant as regards cases of mistakes by individual donors, that is a sufficient reason for regarding them as irrelevant to the application of the *Hastings-Bass* principle.

10–78 Mr Herbert's submission has to be seen in context with the question what are the considerations which trustees ought to take into account. It seems to me that, for this submission to be right, logically he would have to submit that an accurate appreciation of fiscal consequences is not among them. This would be a very difficult proposition to advance, at any rate in relation to a private trust: pension trusts or charitable trusts may be different in this respect, being largely tax exempt. . . . In the circumstances of a substantial private trust . . . the fact is that trustees do have regard to the fiscal treatment of the trust property, as it is or would be according to whether they do nothing, or act in one or another of various ways that may be open to them, and they are right to do so. It does not follow that they need to know every detail of the tax consequences of acting as they propose, or, by comparison, of not taking that action, or taking other action that may be open to them. Being unaware of some subtle, and perhaps unforeseeable, detail of the tax consequences may not result in their decision being held to be vitiated by the *Hastings-Bass* principle. There might be scope for argument as to whether the provisions of UK capital gains tax law about the treatment of several settlements, with different trustees, as one composite settlement, and about the treatment of professional trustees as resident or non-resident, held to be relevant in *Green v Cobham*, might have been regarded as too subtle and arcane for the British Virgin Islands based trustees of the will trust to have been obliged to take them into account. Park J. clearly considered that the "abstruse and recondite" technical defect of the 1976 appointment in *Breadner v Granville-Grossman* was not a point which could bring the principle into play. If the discrepancy between the intended and actual fiscal consequences were the result of a later court decision by which the position was held to be otherwise than had previously been supposed, it would be very surprising if that change could have the effect of invalidating acts by trustees done on the basis of the previous understanding of the position. But I have no doubt that fiscal consequences may be relevant considerations which the trustees ought to take into account, and that a material difference between the intended and actual fiscal consequences of the act may be sufficient to bring the principle into play. . . .

3. Pension Trusts

A. Introduction

10–79 Occupational pension schemes are of two types, defined benefit (or final salary) schemes and defined contribution (or money-purchase) schemes. Usually, both employer and employee pay contributions to trustees. In the case of defined benefit schemes the contributions are used by the trustees for themselves to build up a large trust fund that is security[107] for payment to scheme members of their pensions and for payment of death-in-service benefits and pensions to surviving spouses, partners, cohabitants or dependants: the company is at risk as liable to make up any shortfall in the scheme. In the case of defined contribution schemes, the contributions are used by the trustees for regular investment on behalf of each contributing employee with an assurance company which invests in a range of shares or unit trusts, so that, on retirement or death-in-service, funds will be available to purchase an annuity and provide a limited lump sum as well; no question of any shortfall arises for the company to meet. However, employees do less well under these schemes than under defined benefit schemes, not least because their contributions are smaller than under defined benefit schemes.

[107] *Wrightson Ltd v Fletcher Challenge Nominees Ltd* [2001] Pens. L.R. 207 at [28]. This does not mean that any surplus belongs to the employer which is liable to make up any deficit, because scheme members have expectations of enhanced benefits: the terms of the scheme and the exercise of powers of amendment thereof are crucial, coupled with Pensions Act 1995 s.37 as substituted by Pensions Act 2004 s.25. Further see *National Grid Plc v Mayes* [1999] Pens. L.R. 37.

The employee's contract of employment leads to him becoming a member of the pension scheme upon its terms and conditions, so that his rights arise under the scheme.[108] Each employee is settlor of a separate settlement within the head trust established originally by the employer.[109] The employee is normally contractually obliged to contribute to the pension fund via deduction from his wages or salary while the employer is also contractually obliged to contribute. These bilateral contributions, which arise from the employee's unilateral work, are the source of the benefits to which the employee is entitled as a scheme member. The employee is thus directly and indirectly the settlor of the amount of money needed as security for his entitlements to benefits. It is thus the employee's expectations as settlor that the trustees must focus upon when exercising their discretions. **10–80**

Moreover, over many years the employee has earned his rights under the pension scheme as deferred remuneration. He expects his trustees to give serious and special consideration to any claims he may have to take early retirement or to any partial or total disability benefits and to any claims of his cohabitants or dependants in respect of benefits arising from his death. These matters will often be crucial to living standards. Furthermore, the discretion afforded to the trustees will often be much more limited than in the case of ordinary family discretionary trusts because the pension trustees' discretionary fiduciary obligation is restricted to deciding whether a person is entitled to a payment on establishment of certain factual requirements.[110] **10–81**

In the case of a family discretionary trust the expectation of the settlor is for his trustees to have autonomous leeway over the trust period to make the sorts of gifts in their discretion as he would have made if still alive and absolute beneficial owner of the property.[111] Beneficiaries and objects of discretionary powers are not intended to have much scope at all to complain that they have received less than others, except in blatant circumstances where the trustees' integrity can be challenged, e.g. in reaching a decision perverse to any sensible expectation of the settlor or a decision that no rational body of trustees could reach. **10–82**

Moreover, in such family trusts a holder of a personal, as opposed to a fiduciary, power can exercise it spitefully and capriciously,[112] but if an employer holds a personal power in a pensions trust structure it must not exercise the power in a manner likely seriously to damage the relationship of confidence between employee and employer.[113] **10–83**

B. No Need for a Fair Hearing but Reasons Need be Disclosed for Pension Trusts

In the context of traditional family trusts there is clearly no need for a fair hearing even if there may be said to be two sides involved with a particular issue; e.g. the objects of a power of appointment and the beneficiaries entitled in default of exercise of such power.[114] Where the trustees know what the settlor wanted, then it is permitted for them to do what he wanted without giving much consideration to the interests of other persons capable of benefiting under the trust.[115] Such persons may think this is rough on them, so all they are getting is "rough justice", but if this is what the settlor intended, then **10–84**

---

108 *Imperial Group Pension Trust Ltd v Imperial Tobacco Ltd* [1991] 1 W.L.R. 589.
109 *Air Jamaica Ltd v Charlton* [1999] 1 W.L.R. 1399 at 1408.
110 *Telstra Super Pty Ltd v Flegeltaub* [2000] 2 V.R. 276 at [25].
111 *Re Wills Trust Deeds* [1964] Ch. 219 at 228–229; *Sayseng v Kellogg Superannuation Pty Ltd* [2003] NSWSC 945 at [59].
112 *Re Wright* [1920] 1 Ch. 108 at 118.
113 *Imperial Group Pension Trust Ltd v Imperial Tobacco Ltd* [1991] 1 W.L.R. 589; *National Grid Plc v Laws* [1997] Pens. L.R. 157 at 177. Further see D.J. Hayton, "Pension Trusts and Traditional Trusts: Drastically Different Species of Trusts" [2005] Conv. 229.
114 *Scott v National Trust* [1998] 2 All E.R. 705 at 718; *R v Charity Commissioners, ex parte Baldwin* [2001] W.T.L.R. 137 at 148–149; *Re B* [1987] 2 All E.R. 475 at 478; *Yates v Air Canada* (2004) 5 E.T.R. (3d) 281.
115 *Karger v Paul* [1984] V.R. 161; *Breadner v Granville-Grossman* [2001] Ch. 523; *Re Esteem Settlement* [2004] W.T.L.R. 1.

so be it. If a settlor could have lived for 130 years and then would likely have done with his own property what his trustees did with the trust property under the terms of his trust created when he was 60 years old, then the trustees' conduct cannot be impugned unless their integrity can be challenged.

10–85 However, the pension trust context is very different. As Santow J.A. said in the New South Wales Court of Appeal in *Hannover Life Re of Australasia Ltd v Sayseng*:[116]

> "whereas a superannuation trust may once have been perceived as having a function as an exercise of bounty on the part of the employer, this [does] not accord with modern day realities of the employment relationship in which employees contribute their own funds and bargain for employer contributions which serve the economic function of being part of the reward for employment services. . . . Hence there is a strong shared expectation that benefits will actually be available as contemplated by the parties to that bilateral relationship."

This is so whether a scheme member has a specific individual interest in an early retirement pension or a permanent disability payment, or a more general class interest in the amount of pension fund to be transferred to the new employer taking over the business in which the class members work or in the amount of augmented benefits for the class if there is a fund surplus available for such augmentation, or whether a third party claims a pension as a cohabitant or a lump sum as designee of a member's indicative power of designation of death-in-service benefits.

10–86 The interest at stake of a scheme member or third party is so important to him as relating to his expected standard of living that the Pensions Ombudsman has held that it is "injustice in consequence of maladministration" to fail to give reasons to a claimant for rejecting his claim because he cannot understand or appeal to the Pensions Ombudsman against a decision for which no reasons are given.[117] Acceptable standards of administration require provision of a reasoned decision together with copies of documents relied upon in the decision[118] (with appropriate deletions of any confidential information concerning others). This reflects the common law approach to decisions of administrative bodies where cases where reasons are not required are becoming exceptions to a general rule.[119]

10–87 When someone capable of benefiting under a trust goes to court to seek significant information withheld by the trustee, the Privy Council in *Schmidt v Rosewood Trust Ltd*,[120] in a seminal advice provided by Lord Walker extolling the broad flexible power of the "court's inherent jurisdiction to supervise (and where appropriate intervene in) the administration of trusts", has emphasised the need to look at the strength of such person's claim. A claim can hardly be much stronger than that of an employee who claims his health circumstances justify an early retirement with a pension and payment of a hefty lump sum for permanent disablement, even though the trustee in its discretion needs to hold the opinion that such is justified by the employee's health circumstances.

10–88 The claimant will produce as much medical evidence as he can to support his claim and, if the trustees' delegate to deal with these matters then requires it, the delegate will seek further evidence from the claimant's doctors or independent doctors and perhaps from an inquiry agent; he should

---

116 (2005) 13 A.N.Z. Ins. Cas. 90–123 at [32]. This consideration may also affect the court's approach to construing the terms of a pension scheme: *British Airways Pension Trustees v British Airways Plc* [2002] Pens. L.R. 247 at [26] ff., followed in *Re IMG Pension Plan* at [2010] Pens. L.R. 23 at [110] ff.

117 *Allen v TKM Group Pension Trust Ltd* [2002] Pens. L.R. 333; *Manship v IMI Pensions Trust Ltd* November 26, 2002; *Annual Report* 2001–2002, p.7.

118 Very relevant for internal appeals: consider Pensions Act 1995 s.50, as substituted by Pensions Act 2004 s.273.

119 *Stefan v General Medical Council* [1999] 1 W.L.R. 1293; *R. v Higher Education Funding Council, ex parte Institute of Dental Surgery* [1994] 1 W.L.R. 241.

120 [2003] 2 A.C. 709 at [66].

then afford the claimant the opportunity to deal with matters then arising that are adverse to the claim so that all relevant considerations are present in the adjudicatory framework. No formal oral hearing with rights of reply is needed: all that is needed is that the trustee has in place procedures[121] to ensure that it is adequately informed of relevant considerations[122] so that a real and genuine determination of the claim is made.[123] It is up to the trustees sensibly to decide how it goes about being adequately informed of relevant considerations.

10–89 What then if the trustees determine to reject the claim stating "We have properly taken account of all relevant considerations and ignored all irrelevant considerations but in our opinion your claim fails" or "We have taken account of the original material supplied by you, of further material obtained by us and of your response (with supporting materials) to queries raised by us, but in our opinion your claim fails"? The trustees refuse to do anything more.

10–90 In 1994 Rattee J. in *Wilson v Law Debenture Trust Corp Plc*[124] upheld the entitlement of pension trustees to refuse to provide any reasoning for their decisions, just as under *Re Londonderry's Settlement*[125] trustees of a family trust are entitled to refuse to provide any reasons, despite the key differences already detailed above. This led Lord Walker (when Robert Walker J.) to criticise the judge's view in a scholarly paper,[126] where he cited Lord Browne-Wilkinson's dictum in *Target Holdings Ltd v Redferns* that "It is important . . . to distinguish between the basic principles of trust law and those specialist rules developed in relation to traditional trusts and the rationale of which has no application to trusts of quite a different kind."[127] In *Schmidt v Rosewood Trust Ltd* Lord Walker subsequently stressed that the likelihood of the court exercising its broad inherent jurisdiction to supervise and, if appropriate, intervene in trust affairs will increase with the strength of the claimant's interest. Surely the strength of the interest of a pension scheme member whose claim has been rejected to be able to know the reasons and to see any supporting documents (subject to any deletions of confidential material) is such that he should now be entitled to obtain such reasons and supporting documents from the trustee.

10–91 After all, the claimant has the core right to an early retirement pension and a lump sum if the relevant factual circumstances are established in the fiduciary opinion of the trustee and he has the vital ancillary right to strike down the trustee's opinion if it might have been different but for ignoring a relevant consideration or taking account of an irrelevant consideration.[128] Surely these rights are not meaningful and without substance unless the claimant can ascertain whether or not he has such rights[129] by ascertaining the reasoning of the trustee. We must not forget that the claimant was led to become an employee and to continue in employment as settlor of the contributions giving rise to his rights as deferred remuneration on the basis that he did have meaningful and substantial rights.

---

[121] *Stannard v Fisons Pension Trust Ltd* [1991] Pens. L.R. 225 at [65]; *Hearn v Younger* [2002] W.T.L.R. 1317 at [91]; *Tonkin v Western Mining Corp* [1998] 10 A.N.Z. Ins. Cas. 61–397. Now see Pensions Act 2004 s.273 substituting new Pensions Act 1995 s.50.

[122] *Edge v Pensions Ombudsman* [2002] Ch. 602.

[123] *Maciejewski v Telstra Super Pty Ltd* (1998) 44 N.S.W.L.R. 601; *Knudsen v Kara Kar Holdings Pty Ltd* [2000] NSWSC 715 at [55]; *Telstra Super Pty Ltd v Flegeltaub* [2000] 2 V.R. 276 at [29]–[30]; *Dundee General Hospitals Board v Walker* [1952] 1 All E.R. 896 at 905.

[124] [1995] 2 All E.R. 337.

[125] [1965] Ch. 918.

[126] "Some Trust Principles in the Pensions Context" in A. J. Oakley (ed.), *Trends in Contemporary Trust Law* (1996), p.131.

[127] [1996] A.C. 421 at 435.

[128] See paras 10–93 to 10–94.

[129] See, e.g. *Re Murphy's Settlements* [1999] 1 W.L.R. 282; *Scally v Southern Health and Social Services Board* [1992] 1 A.C. 294 at 306–307. Beneficiaries need a meaningful right to make the trustee account for its actions: *Foreman v Kingston* [2004] 1 N.Z.L.R. 841.

10–92 Thus, in the field of pension trusts, while there is no need for a fair hearing as such, there is a need for an adequately informed reasoned decision after procedures enabling the trustee to be adequately informed to come to a fair conclusion. In the field of traditional family trusts there just needs to be an adequately informed decision, often requiring the trustees to do very little to be adequately informed where the settlor's wishes as to whom he wants benefited are clear.

C. Decisions that "Would" or "Might" have been Different if Trustee Adequately Informed

10–93 The rule in *Re Hastings-Bass*[130] has already been discussed.[131] It applies to pension trusts as well as family trusts, but with a variation confirmed by Lloyd L.J. in *Sieff v Fox*. There he was faced with a split in the authorities going to the question whether it must be shown that the trustees "would" or "might" have acted differently before the rule applies. In most of the cases, starting with *Re Hastings-Bass* itself, the view has been taken that an application will succeed only if it can be shown that the trustees would have acted differently. But the less stringent requirement that the trustees might have acted differentlyh was applied by the Court of Appeal in *Kerr v British Leyland (Staff) Trustees Ltd*,[132] followed by the Court of Appeal in *Stannard v Fisons Ltd*.[133] Lloyd L.J. resolved this inconsistency by distinguishing *Kerr* and *Stannard* from the main run of cases, as authorities concerned with pension trusts under which the "rights of the . . . beneficiaries arose in the context of the contract of employment" rather than from the settlor's pure bounty, and where the trustees were "under a duty to act, not merely a duty to consider from time to time whether to act". In such cases, it seemed logical to Lloyd L.J. "that a relatively low threshold of relevance ('might') should have been adopted by the court as the test", and he contrasted the case where trustees have exercised a power voluntarily: here "the more demanding test of 'would' is justified in order to decide whether the trustees' act can be set aside".[134]

10–94 This was a neat and principled way of reconciling the cases, trailed in *Kerr* and *Stannard* themselves: in the former case, for example, Fox L.J. stressed that it was the duty of the trustees "to give properly informed consideration" to an application by the member of an occupational pension scheme who had "purchased [his] rights", when determining whether he met the conditions for payment of an ill-health early retirement pension.[135] Where beneficiaries are challenging a decision made by pension trustees to reject their claim, it seems proper that they can compel trustees to reconsider a decision made on incomplete evidence (so that relevant facts are missing) if the decision might be different once the evidence is complete. Beneficiaries may be regarded as having earned a legitimate reasonable expectation of this in the light of becoming settlor-beneficiaries by virtue of entering into a contract of employment with the company. In contrast, "would" makes perfect sense in the family trust context where the patriarchal settlor would not wish his discretionary beneficiaries to be able to whine from time to time that the trustees "might" have done this, that or the other, and so put the trustees to the trouble and expense of proving that they would not have made a different decision.

---

130 [1975] Ch. 25.
131 See paras 10–39 ff.
132 Decided in 1986, and reported at [2001] W.T.L.R. 1071.
133 [1992] I.R.L.R. 27.
134 *Sieff* at [56], [55], and [77].
135 *Kerr* at 1079.

D. Negative and Positive Judicial Interference with Trustees' Decisions

Where a beneficiary's claim to particular benefits under a pension scheme is wrongly rejected, then since nothing has happened it is easy to declare the rejection ineffective (or void), so that the matter must be reconsidered in proper fashion. However, where the trustees' wrongful decision has achieved positive ends, then the court should investigate matters carefully and, if favouring restricting or undoing the trustees' decision, the court should consider whether there is some discretionary factor against this, e.g. delay or change of position. In one area, the court should also be prepared to make a positive decision itself, rather than just negate the trustees' decision and leave it to the trustees properly to reconsider the matter and come up with a proper decision within the large leeway afforded to trustees. English[136] and Canadian[137] administrative law on abuse of discretionary powers is beginning to indicate that where all other decisions would be irrational ones that no sensible adequately informed decision-maker could make, then the matter should not be referred back for reconsideration: the court itself should make the only rational decision and implement it. **10–95**

Support for this in the trusts context can be found in *Mettoy Pension Trustees Ltd v Evans*[138] where Warner J. in 1989 concluded that discretionary powers of trustees will be enforced by the court appointing new trustees or, should the proper basis for distribution appear, by itself directing the trustees so to distribute trust property, in the same way that Lord Wilberforce in *McPhail v Doulton*[139] had said that discretionary trusts could be enforced by the courts "in the manner best calculated to give effect to the settlor's intentions". In 2003 Warner J.'s views were endorsed in Lord Walker's advice in *Schmidt v Rosewood Trust Ltd*,[140] and in 2008, in *Bridge Trustees Ltd v Noel Penny (Turbines) Ltd*,[141] Judge Purle QC held that where the donee of a fiduciary power "is bound to exercise the power, but declines to do so, the court may intervene, under its inherent jurisdiction to execute a trust, to exercise the power or cause it to be exercised in whatever way and by whatever means it thinks fit". The judge disposed of the case by appointing a new trustee to exercise the power, but he also considered that:[142] **10–96**

> "The most obvious way in which the court will intervene is by directing the donee as to how the power should be exercised. As the power in this case is imperative, and the defendant is bound to exercise the power in some way, the court's intervention does not depend on any surrender of discretion by the defendant. The court would be intervening to ensure that the trust is executed in accordance with its terms."

In 2009, this was also taken to be the correct approach by Lord Collins in *Scully v Coley*, who said that if an employer-trustee does not exercise a fiduciary power whether or not to approve a scheme to allocate a surplus, "the court will do so".[143]

---

136 *R. (Bibi) v Newham LBC* [2002] 1 W.L.R. 237; *R. v North and East Devon HA* [2001] Q.B. 213.

137 *Mount Sinai Hospital v Quebec* [2001] 2 S.C.R. 281 at [67]–[68].

138 [1990] 1 W.L.R. 1587 at 1617–1618, noting the advancement ordered by the court in *Klug v Klug* [1918] 2 Ch. 67. In the circumstances the court itself exercised the power so that the employer received one third and the beneficiaries two thirds of the available fund. The case was followed in *Thrells v Lomas* [1993] 2 All E.R. 546 before the Pensions Act 1995 s.25(2) avoids the need for court intervention where the liquidator is conflicted out of exercising the company's power, his power being vested in an independent person as trustee.

139 [1971] A.C. 424 at 457.

140 [2003] 2 A.C. 709 at [42] and [51].

141 [2008] Pens. L.R. 345 at [25].

142 *Bridge Trustees* at [26].

143 [2009] UKPC 29 at [29]. On the facts the trustee did not refuse to exercise such a power.

10–97 Where the beneficiary's claim is an all or nothing one as in most pension claims, but not as in claims to have a discretionary family trust distribution within a broad value range, it is easier for the court to find that the only rational possibility is to accept the claim in the light of the evidence produced by the claimant and the trustees to justify their conflicting attitudes, so that the court can substitute the only rational decision for the flawed decision of the trustees.[144] If further evidence is required, then the court can quash the trustees' rejection of the claim, direct the trustees as to the nature of the further evidence needed and direct the trustees to exercise their discretion afresh in the light of such further evidence and of the guidance in the court's judgment.[145]

10–98 Where a claim relates to the claimant having become totally and permanently disabled "in the opinion of the trustee" in circumstances where the trustee has effected a policy of insurance to cover only beneficiaries who become so disabled, it will almost invariably be irrational for the trustee not to pay the proceeds of the policy to the claimant if the insurer in its opinion has considered the claimant to be so disabled. The claimant's difficulties thus lie with persuading the insurer that he has become totally and permanently disabled.

10–99 The grounds upon which "the opinion of the insurer" can be challenged are generally similar to the grounds on which the opinion of the trustee can be challenged but the consequences of a successful challenge are more radical. As stated by Bryson J. in *Sayseng v Kellogg Superannuation Pty Ltd*:[146]

> "The court regards the reference to the insurer's opinion as means adopted by the parties for ascertainment of the facts to which the opinion relates: contractual entitlement depends on the facts, not primarily on the opinion which is the means of ascertaining them, and if the insurer has actually failed to form the opinion, or has constructively failed by acting on some wrong basis, the court proceeds to determine the facts."

If the incidental machinery to give effect to a contract breaks down then the court gives effect to the contract.[147] Thus, the decision of the court can take the place of the insurer's opinion[148] (e.g. as to whether the claimant is totally and permanently disabled or whether the deceased's death was self-inflicted) if the court decides that the insurer's opinion is to be disregarded as in breach of its contractual and fiduciary duties. If the court then decides that the insurable event has occurred, it can direct the insurer to pay the requisite amount to the trustee, whose only rational course is to pay it to the beneficiary, or the court can simply order payment directly to the beneficiary.

10–100 In the traditional trust context, rights of beneficiaries are to be determined solely by means of the machinery of the trustee exercising its discretion, so that if such an exercise has to be disregarded as in breach of the trustee's fiduciary duties, then the exercise of the discretion has to be referred back to those same trustees or, in an extreme case, to new trustees after removal of the old trustees.[149]

---

144 *Minehan v AGL Employees Superannuation Pty Ltd* (1998) 134 A.C.T.R. 1 at [66]–[69], following *Dillon v Burns Philp Finance Ltd* (NSW Sup Ct, July 20, 1988); *Dunstone v Irving* [2000] VSC 488 at [131]–[134].

145 As in administrative law cases: *R. (Bibi) v Newham LBC* [2002] 1 W.L.R. 237.

146 [2003] NSWSC 945 at [77]; affirmed sub nom. *Hannover Life Re of Australasia Ltd v Sayseng* (2005) 13 A.N.Z. Ins. Cas. 90–123.

147 e.g. *Beaufort Developments (NI) Ltd v Gilbert-Ash (NI) Ltd* [1999] 1 A.C. 266 at 288–289, 291–292.

148 *McArthur v Mercantile Mutual Life Insurance Co Ltd* [2002] Qd. R. 197; *Sayseng v Kellogg Superannuation Pty Ltd* [2003] NSWSC 945 at [82]–[85], [94]–[97]; *Butcher v Port* [1985] 1 N.Z.L.R. 491 at 496–497; the defendant cannot take advantage of his own wrongdoing: *Edward v Aberayron Mutual Ship Assurance Society* (1876) 1 Q.B.D. 563.

149 *Edge v Pensions Ombudsman* [1998] Ch. 512 at 534 endorsed [2000] Ch. 602 at 627, 630 (a pensions case involving a discretionary power of amendment to take account of an actuarial surplus, not a power relating to a factual issue); *Kerr v British Leyland (Staff) Trustees Ltd* (1986) [2001] W.T.L.R. 1071 at 1080 (assumed traditional rules applied to pension trustees so the court could not substitute its view for that of the trustees).

However, in the pensions trust context why should the courts, in the light of the broad discretion to intervene emphasised by the Privy Council in *Schmidt*,[150] not treat the discretion of the trustee in certain areas involving complex consideration as the sole machinery for determining the rights of beneficiaries but in other areas merely to be the incidental machinery for giving effect to beneficiaries' rights on establishment of particular facts? If the incidental machinery does not duly operate, then the court intervenes to determine whether or not particular facts have been established. In the pensions trust context there is not the rationale that there is in family trusts for the all-pervasive centrality of the trustees' discretion as the sole machinery for determining the rights of beneficiaries. **10–101**

Thus, where the opinion of the trustee as to the establishment of certain facts is required before payment out of benefits, e.g. as to a permanent disability or whether death was self-inflicted or whether a person was a dependant or cohabitant of the beneficiary at his death, the court should be able to decide the matter itself if the opinion of the trustee is a nullity for breach of its fiduciary obligations.[151] The court should decide the matter itself if it has enough material to reach a decision. If it does not have enough material, then it should afford the claimant and the trustees the opportunity to obtain further evidence for the trustees then to act in accordance with the court's earlier guidance. Failure so to act will then lead to the court resolving the matter. **10–102**

However, in other areas where there is plenty of scope for discretion (e.g. as to distributing death-in-service benefits where trustees have a discretion after taking account of person(s) designated by the beneficiary in his lifetime, but circumstances may have changed significantly since the making of such indicative designation, or as to augmenting the benefits of different classes of beneficiary) if the discretionary decision is fatally flawed, then the court should refer the exercise of the discretion back to the trustees (or replacement trustees if more appropriate). **10–103**

E. Legislative Intervention

The facilitative simple nature of trust law permits the creation of a ring-fenced fund protected against the insolvency of its trustee-owner, but otherwise stacked with provisions favouring the employer at the expense of the employee-beneficiaries. In a laisser-faire era the employer, influenced by the trade union, was hopefully left to be trusted to look after the pension fund for employees in benevolent altruistic fashion, whether as itself trustee or having its directors as trustees. The only statutory intervention needed was to exempt these long-running trust funds from the rule against remoteness,[152] while much on-going fiscal regulation has prevented exploitation of favourable tax provisions in Finance Acts, with caps placed upon the amount of contributions and of the amount ultimately available for a senior employee's pension. **10–104**

In defined benefit schemes if the contributions of employees and employer prove inadequate to provide the promised pension benefits then the onus lies on the employer to make up the deficit. For a substantial period this caused no worries due to a rising stock market for investments and due to a good job market causing many employees to leave their jobs before reaching retirement age. Also dividends from shares were tax-free for pension funds until the Government in 1998 removed this valuable benefit worth £5 billion p.a. **10–105**

However, it was appreciated that there was a need for a Pensions Ombudsman to provide cheap speedy relief for scheme members where there was maladministration.[153] This involves "bias, neglect, **10–106**

---

150 [2003] 2 A.C. 709.

151 See *Minehan v AGL Employees Superannuation Pty Ltd* (1998) 134 A.C.T.R. 1 at [66]–[69].

152 Now Pension Schemes Act 1993 s.163, originally Superannuation and other Funds (Validation) Act 1927.

153 Post created in Social Security Act 1990, but currently governed by Pensions Scheme Act 1993 as amended by Pensions Act 1995 and 2004.

inattention, delay, incompetence, ineptitude, perversity, turpitude, arbitariness and so on".[154] For such he can direct apologies be made, order the holding of another meeting, award compensation for financial loss or even for distress,[155] order specific performance as by making someone a scheme member from a particular date. However, where the maladministration amounts to a breach of trust the range of his remedies is limited to those available to the High Court,[156] though this is not too restrictive if that range is fairly wide in the light of *Schmidt v Rosewood Trust Ltd* and other matters discussed above.

10–107 A crisis then arose in respect of significant pension funds the property of which was misappropriated by the well-known, swashbuckling Robert Maxwell before his mysterious death by drowning. The Government set up a Committee under (now Sir) Roy Goode which reported[157] that trust law was a good basis for pension funds but only if the freedom to minimise the obligations of the trustees was drastically restricted and if actuarially supervised minimum funding requirements were imposed. The Pensions Act 1995 was thus enacted, also setting up an Occupational Pensions Regulatory Authority ("OPRA"). Thereafter, the Government removed the tax-free perquisite for dividends received by pension trusts and there was a poor three-year performance of the stock markets. Accounting standards also tightened, so that companies found that notional actuarial surpluses had become deficits which the companies needed to provide for out of their own resources—and which affected the price of the shares. Many companies closed their defined benefit schemes and switched to direct contribution schemes. Indeed, some companies went into liquidation and wound up their pension funds in circumstances where there was a large deficit. Employees, who thought they would be well-provided for, found there was very little for them, throwing them back on a very basic State pension.

10–108 These matters led to the Pensions Act 2004. This replaces OPRA with the Pensions Regulator, inheriting OPRA's powers but with extra powers[158] for a more proactive role, much assisted by obligations[159] upon persons involved with pension schemes to report breaches of the legislation to the Regulator, so he can protect members' benefits, promote good administration of pension schemes, and take steps to reduce the likelihood of claims against the new Pension Protection Fund.

10–109 The Regulator's most significant determinations have to be made on his behalf by a Determinations Tribunal.[160] An appeal lies to the Pension Regulator Tribunal[161] from which appeal on a point of law may be made, with leave, to the Court of Appeal.

10–110 The 2004 Act also establishes a Pension Protection Fund ("PPF") to provide compensation for members of defined benefit schemes if the sponsoring employer is insolvent and the scheme underfunded.[162] A £15 per head flat-rate levy in respect of the members of such pension schemes is made on the trustees thereof, though 80 per cent of the money raised is due to come from a risk-based levy according to different risk ratings of different pension trusts. The Board of the PPF may be required to review its decision and a PPF Ombudsman may then deal with matters.[163]

---

154 *Hillsdown Holdings Plc v Pensions Ombudsman* [1997] 1 All E.R. 862 at 884.

155 *Wild v Smith* [1996] O.P.L.R. 129.

156 *Wakelin v Read* [2000] Pens. L.R. 319; *Arjo Wiggins Ltd v Ralph* [2010] Pens. L.R. 11 at [13]. But the Pensions Ombudsman can order that a claimant should be made a member of a scheme retrospective to a particular date subject to paying contributions rather than order damages even if in the High Court damages would have to be ordered if the claimant did not seek specific performance: *Henderson v Stephenson Harwood* [2005] Pens. L.R. 209.

157 See "Pension Law Reform", 1993 Cm. 2342, and the case for trust law in D.J. Hayton, "Trust Law and Occupational Pension Schemes" [1993] Conv. 283; also see note of R. Nobles on Pensions Act 1995 in (1996) 59 M.L.R. 241.

158 Pensions Act 2004 ss.13 to 32.

159 ibid. ss.70–71.

160 ibid. ss.9–10.

161 ibid. ss.102–105.

162 ibid. ss.107–119.

163 ibid. ss.209–217.

The Act provides for at least one third of trustees (or of directors of a corporate trustee) in every scheme to be nominated and selected by the members,[164] while the trustees (or directors of a corporate trustee) are required to be conversant with relevant scheme documentation and have appropriate knowledge and understanding of pensions and trust law and of the principles underpinning investment of assets and funding of liabilities.[165] The Regulator has to issue a Code of Practice to provide practical guidance on these matters.[166] **10–111**

The old Minimum Funding Requirement with its "one size fits all" approach is replaced with new scheme funding requirements which are flexible enough to take into account scheme-specific factors when determining the most appropriate funding strategy and to allow for a longer-term view of investments and for correcting funding deficiencies.[167] The trustees and the employer must in the light of actuarial valuations (at least once every three years) agree a strategy, with the Pensions Regulator having powers of last resort to help resolve differences.[168] The Regulator also has to issue a Code of Practice for trustees on scheme funding.[169] **10–112**

There is a morass of cumbersome protective legislation to be found in the Pension Schemes Act 1993, the Pensions Act 1995 (181 sections and 7 Schedules), the Welfare Reform and Pensions Act 1999, and the Pensions Act 2004 (325 sections and 13 schedules). It is beyond the scope of this book to deal with pension trusts any further, other than to note that the power to amend the trust deed so as to affect subsisting rights is closely circumscribed.[170] **10–113**

PENSIONS ACT 1995 SECTIONS 32–34

32.—(1) Decisions of the trustees of a trust scheme may, unless the scheme provides otherwise, be taken by agreement of a majority of the trustees. **10–114**

(2) Where decisions of the trustees of a trust scheme may be taken by agreement of a majority of the trustees—

(a) the trustees may, unless the scheme provides otherwise, by a determination under this subsection require not less than the number of trustees specified in the determination to be present when any decision is so taken, and

(b) notice of any occasions at which decisions may be so taken must, unless the occasion falls within a prescribed class or description, be given to each trustee to whom it is reasonably practicable to give such notice.

(3) Notice under subsection (2)(b) must be given in a prescribed manner and not later than the beginning of a prescribed period.

33.—(1) Liability for breach of an obligation under any rule of law to take care or exercise skill in the performance of any investment functions, where the function is exercisable— **10–115**

(a) by a trustee of a trust scheme, or

(b) by a person to whom the function has been delegated under section 34,

164 ibid. ss.241–243.
165 ibid. ss.247–248.
166 ibid. s.90.
167 ibid. ss.221–233.
168 ibid. s.231.
169 ibid. s.90.
170 ibid. s.262 substituting an extended Pensions Act 1995 s.67.

cannot be excluded or restricted by any instrument or agreement.

(2) In this section, references to excluding or restricting liability include—

(a) making the liability or its enforcement subject to restrictive or onerous conditions,
(b) excluding or restricting any right or remedy in respect of the liability, or subjecting a person to any prejudice in consequence of his pursuing any such right or remedy, or
(c) excluding or restricting rules of evidence or procedure.

(3) This section does not apply—

(a) to a scheme falling within any prescribed class or description, or
(b) to any prescribed description of exclusion or restriction.

10–116 34.—(1) The trustees of a trust scheme have, subject to section 36(1) and to any restriction imposed by the scheme, the same power to make an investment of any kind as if they were absolutely entitled to the assets of the scheme.

(2) Any discretion of the trustees of a trust scheme to make any decision about investments—

(a) may be delegated by or on behalf of the trustees to a fund manager to whom subsection (3) applies to be exercised in accordance with section 36, but
(b) may not otherwise be delegated except under section 25 of the Trustee Act 1925 (delegation of trusts during absence abroad) or subsection (5) below.

(3) This subsection applies to a fund manager who, in relation to the decisions in question, falls, or is treated as falling, within any of paragraphs (a) to (c) of section 191(2) of the Financial Services Act 1986 (occupational pension schemes: exemptions where decisions taken by authorised and other persons).

(4) The trustees are not responsible for the act or default of any fund manager in the exercise of any discretion delegated to him under subsection (2)(a) if they have taken all such steps as are reasonable to satisfy themselves or the person who made the delegation on their behalf has taken all such steps as are reasonable to satisfy himself—

(a) that the fund manager has the appropriate knowledge and experience for managing the investments of the scheme, and
(b) that he is carrying out his work competently and complying with section 36.

(5) Subject to any restriction imposed by a trust scheme—

(a) the trustees may authorise two or more of their number to exercise on their behalf any discretion to make any decision about investments, and
(b) any such discretion may, where giving effect to the decision would not constitute carrying on investment business in the United Kingdom (within the meaning of the Financial Services Act 1986), be delegated by or on behalf of the trustees to a fund manager to whom subsection (3) does not apply to be exercised in accordance with section 36;

but in either case the trustees are liable for any acts or defaults in the exercise of the discretion if they would be so liable if they were the acts or defaults of the trustees as a whole.

(6) Section 33 does not prevent the exclusion or restriction of any liability of the trustees of a trust scheme for the acts or defaults of a fund manager in the exercise of a discretion delegated to him under subsection (5)(b) where the trustees have taken all such steps as are reasonable to satisfy themselves, or the person who made the delegation on their behalf has taken all such steps as are reasonable to satisfy himself—

(a) that the fund manager has the appropriate knowledge and experience for managing the investments of the scheme, and
(b) that he is carrying out his work competently and complying with section 36;

and subsection (2) of section 33 applies for the purposes of this subsection as it applies for the purposes of that section.

(7) The provisions of this section override any restriction inconsistent with the provisions imposed by any rule of law or by or under any enactment, other than an enactment contained in, or made under, this Part or the Pension Schemes Act 1993.

PENSIONS ACT 2004 SECTIONS 244 AND 247–249

244. Investment Principles

For section 35 of the Pensions Act 1995 (investment principles) substitute— 10–117

35 *Investment principles*

(1) The trustees of a trust scheme must secure—

(a) that a statement of investment principles is prepared and maintained for the scheme, and
(b) that the statement is reviewed at such intervals, and on such occasions, as may be prescribed and, if necessary, revised.

(2) In this section "statement of investment principles", in relation to a trust scheme, means a written statement of the investment principles governing decisions about investments for the purposes of the scheme.

(3) Before preparing or revising a statement of investment principles, the trustees of a trust scheme must comply with any prescribed requirements.

(4) A statement of investment principles must be in the prescribed form and cover, amongst other things, the prescribed matters.

(5) Neither a trust scheme nor a statement of investment principles may impose restrictions (however expressed) on any power to make investments by reference to the consent of the employer.

(6) If in the case of a trust scheme—

(a) a statement of investment principles has not been prepared, is not being maintained or has not been reviewed or revised, as required by this section, or
(b) the trustees have not complied with the obligation imposed on them by subsection (3),

section 10 applies to any trustee who has failed to take all reasonable steps to secure compliance.

(7) Regulations may provide that this section is not to apply to any scheme which is of a prescribed description.

247. Requirement for Knowledge and Understanding: Individual Trustees

(1) This section applies to every individual who is a trustee of an occupational pension scheme. 10–118

(2) In this section, "relevant scheme", in relation to an individual, means any occupational pension scheme of which he is a trustee.

(3) An individual to whom this section applies must, in relation to each relevant scheme, be conversant with—

(a) the trust deed and rules of the scheme,
(b) any statement of investment principles for the time being maintained under section 35 of the Pensions Act 1995 (c.26),

(c) in the case of a relevant scheme to which Part 3 (scheme funding) applies, the statement of funding principles most recently prepared or revised under section 223, and

(d) any other document recording policy for the time being adopted by the trustees relating to the administration of the scheme generally.

(4) An individual to whom this section applies must have knowledge and understanding of—

(a) the law relating to pensions and trusts,
(b) the principles relating to—

(i) the funding of occupational pension schemes, and
(ii) investment of the assets of such schemes, and

(c) such other matters as may be prescribed.

(5) The degree of knowledge and understanding required by subsection (4) is that appropriate for the purposes of enabling the individual properly to exercise his functions as trustee of any relevant scheme.

248. Requirement for Knowledge and Understanding: Corporate Trustees

10–119 (1) This section applies to any company which is a trustee of an occupational pension scheme.

(2) In this section, "relevant scheme", in relation to a company, means any occupational pension scheme of which it is a trustee.

(3) A company to which this section applies must, in relation to each relevant scheme, secure that each individual who exercises any function which the company has as trustee of the scheme is conversant with each of the documents mentioned in subsection (4) so far as it is relevant to the exercise of the function.

(4) Those documents are—

(a) the trust deed and rules of the scheme,
(b) any statement of investment principles for the time being maintained under section 35 of the Pensions Act 1995,
(c) in the case of a relevant scheme to which Part 3 (scheme funding) applies, the statement of funding principles most recently prepared or revised under section 223, and
(d) any other document recording policy for the time being adopted by the trustees relating to the administration of the scheme generally.

(5) A company to which this section applies must secure that any individual who exercises any function which the company has as trustee of any relevant scheme has knowledge and understanding of—

(a) the law relating to pensions and trusts,
(b) the principles relating to—

(i) the funding of occupational pension schemes, and
(ii) investment of the assets of such schemes, and

(c) such other matters as may be prescribed.

(6) The degree of knowledge and understanding required by subsection (5) is that appropriate for the purposes of enabling the individual properly to exercise the function in question.

(7) References in this section to the exercise by an individual of any function of a company are to anything done by the individual on behalf of the company which constitutes the exercise of the function by the company.

(8) In this section "company" means a company within the meaning given by section 735(1) of the Companies Act 1985 (c. 6) or a company which may be wound up under Part 5 of the Insolvency Act 1986 (c. 45) (unregistered companies).

249. Requirement for Knowledge and Understanding: Supplementary

(1) For the purposes of sections 247 and 248, a person's functions as trustee of a relevant scheme are any functions which he has by virtue of being such a trustee and include, in particular— 10–120

(a) any functions which he has as one of the trustees authorised under section 34(5)(a) of the Pensions Act 1995 (c.26) (delegation of investment discretions) in the case of the scheme, and
(b) any functions which he otherwise has as a member of a committee of the trustees of the scheme.

(2) Regulations may provide for any provision in section 247 or 248—

(a) not to apply, or
(b) to apply with modifications,

to a trustee in prescribed circumstances.

(3) Nothing in either of those sections affects any rule of law requiring a trustee to have knowledge of, or expertise in, any matter. . . .

Questions

1. "So long as trustees consciously exercise their distributive discretions there is precious little a beneficiary can do to impeach such exercise, while objects of a power are even worse off: everyone is at the mercy of the trustees." **Discuss**. **10–121**

2. "The scope and limits of the rule in *Re Hastings-Bass* are uncertain, but there are good reasons for thinking that it lets trustees (and beneficiaries) escape the bad consequences of the trustees' negligent decision-making too easily." **Discuss**. **10–122**

3. "Pension fund beneficiaries must have stronger rights than beneficiaries under discretionary family trusts, particularly if entitled to benefits in the event of the occurrence of a particular factual situation.". **Discuss**. **10–123**

PART V

BREACH OF TRUST

11 PERSONAL COMPENSATORY LIABILITY OF TRUSTEES FOR BREACH OF TRUST

1. Remedies for Breach of Trust

A. What is a Breach of Trust?

11-01 Any act or neglect on the part of a trustee which is contrary to the duties imposed upon him, and which is not excused by law,[1] or by the terms of the trust instrument,[2] is a breach of trust. Thus, as Millett L.J. observed in *Armitage v Nurse*:[3]

> "A breach of trust may be deliberate or inadvertent; it may consist of an actual misappropriation or misapplication of the trust property or merely of an investment or other dealing which is outside the trustees' powers; it may consist of a failure to carry out a positive obligation of the trustees or merely of a want of skill and care on their part in the management of the trust property; it may be injurious to the interests of the beneficiaries or be actually to their benefit."

11-02 Trustees are liable only for their own breaches of duty. Note, though, that, it constitutes a breach of duty for a trustee to leave the trust affairs in the hands of a co-trustee to be dealt with as he sees fit,[4] or to leave trust property in his sole control,[5] or to stand by with knowledge that he is committing a breach of duty,[6] or to take no steps to obtain redress on becoming aware that he has committed a

---

[1] Note the Trustee Act 1925 s.61, discussed at paras 11–105 ff.

[2] Where a trust instrument contains a clause qualifying the extent of the trustee's duties, or otherwise exempting him from liability unless guilty of dishonesty, the court should construe the clause restrictively, against the trustee, but should bear in mind that the clause was inserted by the settlor, rather than the trustee himself, so that a strict *contra proferentem* approach would be unjustified: *Midland Bank Trustee (Jersey) Ltd v Federated Pension Services Ltd* [1996] P.L.R. 179 at 192; *Bogg v Raper* (1999) 1 I.T.E.L.R. 267 at 281. See too *Wight v Olswang (No.1)* (1999) 1 I.T.E.L.R. 783; *Wight v Olswang (No.2)* (2000) 2 I.T.E.L.R. 689.

[3] [1998] Ch. 241 at 250, adding that breaches of trust can be committed fraudulently or in good faith. Various rules turn upon this distinction, e.g. the rules governing exemption clauses (paras 9–215 ff.), limitation periods (paras 11–135 ff.), and the release of a trustee's bankruptcy debts by discharge (Insolvency Act 1986 s.281(3), considered in *Woodland-Ferrari v UCL Group Retirement Benefits Scheme* [2003] Ch. 115; but not the rules concerning the removal of trustees (paras 8–44 ff.) as held in *Letterstedt v Broers* (1884) 9 App. Cas. 371, followed in *Jones v Firkin-Flood* [2008] EWHC 2417 (Ch) (trustees may be removed whether or not they acted in bad faith).

[4] *Wynne v Tempest* (1897) 13 T.L.R. 360; *Re Lucking's WT* [1968] 1 W.L.R. 866. This assumes that there has been no proper delegation, e.g. under the Trustee Act 2000 ss. 11 and 12. Exceptionally a settlor may provide that a trustee must act as his co-trustee directs, in which case he will not be liable unless he dishonestly assists his co-trustee to commit a breach of trust: *Re Arnott* [1899] I.R. 201.

[5] *Lewis v Nobbs* (1878) 8 Ch.D. 591. This assumes that the co-trustee is not an authorised nominee or custodian under the Trustee Act 2000 s.19.

[6] *Booth v Booth* (1838) 1 Beav. 125; *Gough v Smith* [1872] W.N. 18.

breach of trust,[7] or to retire from being a trustee with the object of facilitating a breach of trust which the remaining, or new, trustees then commit.[8] Trustees who cause the same damage to their beneficiaries by their respective breaches of duty are jointly and severally liable: i.e. the beneficiaries can require two or more of them jointly, or one of them individually, to discharge their common liability.[9] If a trustee is obliged to pay more than his fair share of a common liability for breach of trust, then he can recover a contribution from the others, or even require them to reimburse him in full.[10]

B. Compensatory Remedies

11–03 Various remedies are available for breach of trust, but the focus of this chapter is on personal compensatory remedies: i.e. orders that a trustee should pay a sum of money in order to compensate the beneficiaries for loss. Two types of compensatory award can be made against trustees: an order that they should pay a money substitute for performance of their primary obligation to hold the trust assets for the beneficiaries and deliver them in specie when called upon to do so; and an order that they should pay money to redress harm which the beneficiaries have sustained through the trustees' breach of duty. Both types of award have traditionally been mediated through proceedings for an account of the trust property, but they are different in nature, essentially because the second type of claim depends on the assertion that the trustees have committed a breach of trust, while the first type of claim does not. Both types of claim are sometimes described as "restitutionary",[11] but this usage is best avoided, both to avoid confusing the two types of claim with one another, and to avoid confusing both of them with liability in unjust enrichment when it is clear that in this context the word "restitution" is used to mean "compensation".[12]

11–04 Where trustees misapply trust property, the beneficiaries may be able to follow and/or trace the assets or their identifiable proceeds into the hands of the recipients, and they may then be entitled to assert a proprietary claim to the assets or their traceable proceeds.[13] If they prefer to do so, then the beneficiaries are free to assert such a proprietary claim, rather than pursuing the trustees with a view to fixing them with a personal compensatory liability.[14]

C. Other Remedies

11–05 Other remedies for breach of trust can also be awarded, depending on the circumstances of the case. Trustees must account for gains made contrary to their fiduciary duty to subordinate their personal interests to those of the beneficiaries.[15] Transactions between trustees and third parties entered in

---

7 *Wilkins v Hogg* (1861) 8 Jur. 25 at 26.

8 *Head v Gould* [1898] 2 Ch. 250; *Kingdom v Castleman* (1877) 36 L.T. 141.

9 *Charitable Corp v Sutton* (1742) 2 Atk 400 at 406; *Walker v Symonds* (1818) 3 Swan 1 at 75; *Ashurst v Mason* (1875) L.R. 20 Eq. 225 at 233; *Re Duckwari Plc* [1999] Ch. 253 at 262.

10 See paras 11–148 ff.

11 In substitutive performance claims it is often said that the trustee must effect "restitution" or "restoration" of the trust assets for which he has failed to account, or their money equivalent: e.g. *Re Dawson* [1966] 2 N.S.W.R. 211 at 216; *Bartlett v Barclays Bank Trust Co Ltd (No.2)* [1980] Ch. 515 at 543; *Target Holdings Ltd v Redferns* [1996] A.C. 421 at 433. But in reparation claims, too, it is sometimes said that the trustee's liability is "restitutionary": e.g. *Hodgkinson v Simms* [1994] 3 S.C.R. 377 at 440; *Re Mulligan* [1998] 1 N.Z.L.R. 481 at 507; *Swindle v Harrison* [1997] 4 All E.R. 705 at 733.

12 *Bartlett v Barclays Bank Trust Co Ltd (No.2)* [1980] Ch. 515 at 545, per Brightman L.J. See too S.B. Elliott, "Restitutionary Compensatory Damages for Breach of Fiduciary Duty?" [1998] R.L.R. 135.

13 See Chapter 12.

14 Denning J., "The Recovery of Money" (1949) 65 L.Q.R. 37, 44; *Hagan v Waterhouse* (1994) 34 N.S.W.L.R. 308 at 369–370; *Foskett v McKeown* [2001] 1 A.C. 102 at 130; *Wong v Burt* (2004) 7 I.T.E.L.R. 263 at [59].

15 See paras 9–14 to 9–17 and 15–79 ff.

breach of trust can be set aside at the beneficiaries' suit, although not if the third party is a bona fide purchaser for value without notice of the trust.[16] Declarations can be made, setting out the nature and extent of a beneficiary's interest,[17] or a trustee's duty.[18] Prohibitory injunctions can be issued, restraining trustees from committing a breach of trust.[19] Trustees can be removed and new trustees appointed.[20] Judicial trustees and, exceptionally, receivers of trust property[21] can also be appointed, where this is necessary to preserve the trust assets and no other remedy, e.g. the appointment of new trustees, is feasible.

Can an award of exemplary damages be made in a case of outrageous misconduct by a trustee? **11–06**
In *Re Brogden*,[22] North J. said that "the court will not punish a trustee pecuniarily for his breach of trust except so far as loss has resulted therefrom to the trust estate", and historically no English court has ever awarded exemplary damages against a defaulting trustee.[23] Until recently, it was thought that the English courts had no power to award exemplary damages in respect of equitable wrongdoing because there was no case pre-dating 1964 where this had been done.[24] However, they may wish to reconsider the position, now that the cause of action test for the award of exemplary damages has been discredited in *Kuddus v Chief Constable of Leicestershire*.[25] Elsewhere, the appellate courts of Canada and New Zealand have held that an award of exemplary damages can be made in relation to a breach of fiduciary duty.[26] In Australia, the leading case is now the New South Wales Court of Appeal's decision in *Harris v Digital Pulse Pty Ltd*,[27] where Heydon J.A. vehemently opposed the award of exemplary damages for equitable wrongdoing, but Mason P. strongly favoured their award in suitable cases. The third judge, Spigelman C.J., thought it unnecessary and undesirable to decide the case on the basis that a punitive monetary award can never be awarded in equity, because remedial flexibility is a characteristic of equity jurisprudence. In our view, the courts should be able to award exemplary damages in cases of outrageous misconduct by trustees and other fiduciaries.

---

[16] *Peffer v Rigg* [1977] 1 W.L.R. 285.

[17] The courts have an unfettered discretion to make binding declarations under CPR rule 40.20, but they will not normally entertain theoretical questions with no practical application: *Padden v Arbuthnot Pensions and Investments Ltd* [2004] EWCA Civ 582 at [24] and [31]. The proper form of a declaration of equitable interest under rule 40.20 is discussed in *Powell v Wilshire* [2005] 1 Q.B. 117 at [39]–[45]. The Trusts of Land and Appointment of Trustees Act 1996 s.14(2)(b) enables a person with an interest in property that is subject to a trust of land to obtain an order declaring the nature or extent of his interest, as in, e.g. *Oxley v Hiscock* [2004] 2 F.L.R. 669.

[18] *Cowan v Scargill* [1985] Ch. 270.

[19] *Fox v Fox* (1870) L.R. 11 Eq. 142 (improper distribution of assets); *Dance v Goldingham* (1873) L.R. 8 Ch. App. 902; *Buttle v Saunders* [1950] 2 All E.R. 193 (sale of assets at an undervalue).

[20] See Chapter 8.

[21] *Att.-Gen. v Schonfield* [1980] 1 W.L.R. 1182; *Clarke v Heathfield* [1985] I.C.R. 203; *Derby & Co Ltd v Weldon (Nos 3 and 4)* [1990] Ch. 65 (freezing injunction); *Younghams v Candoora No.19 Pty Ltd* (2000) 3 I.T.E.L.R. 154; *ASIC v Takaran Pty. Ltd (No.2)* (2002) 43 A.C.S.R. 334.

[22] (1886) 38 Ch.D. 546 at 557. See too *Att.-Gen. v Alford* (1855) 4 De G.M. & G. 843; *Vyse v Foster* (1872) L.R. 3 Ch. App. 309 at 333, affirmed (1874) L.R. 7 H.L. 318.

[23] The Pensions Act 1995 s.10 permits penalty fines for maladministration of occupational pension schemes, but to date no such fine has been imposed in a reported case.

[24] *AB v South West Water Services Ltd* [1993] Q.B. 507. See too Law Commission, *Aggravated, Exemplary, and Restitutionary Damages* (Law Com. No.247, 1997) paras [5.54]–[5.56], recommending legislation to give the courts a power to award exemplary damages in relation to breaches of equitable duty. This recommendation has not been acted upon by Parliament.

[25] [2002] 2 A.C. 122.

[26] Canada: *Norberg v Wynrib* [1992] 2 S.C.R. 226; *KM v HM* [1992] 3 S.C.R. 6; *Whiten v Pilot Insurance Co* [2002] 1 S.C.R. 595; *Chudy v Merchant Law Group* (2008) 300 D.L.R. (4th) 56. New Zealand: *Aquaculture Corp v New Zealand Green Mussel Co Ltd* [1990] 3 N.Z.L.R 299; *Cook v Evatt (No.2)* [1992] 1 N.Z.L.R. 676.

[27] (2003) 56 N.S.W.L.R. 298.

D. *Standing to Sue*

11–07 Proceedings to have a breach of trust redressed "may be taken by a beneficiary against a trustee or a former trustee or the estate of a former trustee".[28] This includes the beneficiary of a discretionary trust, who can obtain an injunction to compel the proper administration of the trust even though his interest is nothing more than a mere expectancy.[29] Proceedings to redress a breach of trust can also be taken by a trustee against a co-trustee or former trustee,[30] without joining the beneficiaries,[31] and it is no answer to the claim that the trustee himself participated in the breach.[32]

2. Compensation Claims against Trustees

11–08 Equity recognises two different types of compensation claim against trustees, which will be termed substitutive performance claims and reparation claims.[33] Substitutive performance claims are claims for a money payment as a substitute for performance of the trustees' core obligation to hold and deliver trust assets on demand. Claims of this sort are apposite when trust property has been misapplied, and the amount claimed is the objective value of the property which the trustees should have been able to produce when asked to do so. Reparation claims are claims for a money payment to make good the damage caused by a breach of trust, and the amount claimed is measured by reference to the loss sustained by the beneficiaries. Claims of this sort are often brought where trustees have carelessly mismanaged trust property, but they lie more generally wherever a fiduciary has harmed his principal by committing a breach of duty. Both types of claim have traditionally been mediated through proceedings for an account, as we shall discuss.[34]

A. *Substitutive Performance Claims*

11–09 "The duty of a trustee is properly to preserve the trust fund, to pay the income and the corpus to those who are entitled to them respectively, and to give all his cestuis que trust on demand information with respect to the mode in which the trust fund has been dealt with, and where it is."[35] The beneficiaries have corresponding rights to obtain trust accounts and to insist that the trust assets are maintained or disbursed solely in accordance with the trust instrument.[36] The beneficiaries can obtain a court

---

[28] *Young v Murphy* [1996] 1 V.R. 279 at 281. See too *Re Cross* (1881) 20 Ch.D. 109; *Space Investments Ltd v Canadian Imperial Bank of Commerce Trust Co (Bahamas) Ltd* [1986] 1 W.L.R. 1072 at 1074.

[29] *Gartside v IRC* [1968] A.C. 553 at 617. See too *Spellson v George* (1987) 11 N.S.W.L.R. 300 at 316, considered in *Schmidt v Rosewood Trust Ltd* [2003] 2 A.C. 709 at [59]–[60]; *Armitage v Nurse* [1998] Ch. 241 at 261; *Johns v Johns* [2004] 3 N.Z.L.R. 202 at [34]. The objects of a fiduciary power of appointment are similarly entitled.

[30] *Young v Murphy* [1996] 1 V.R. 279 at 281.

[31] *Young* at 283. See too *Greenwood v Wakeford* (1839) 1 Beav 576; *Re Cross* (1881) 20 Ch.D. 109; *Williams v Barton* [1927] 2 Ch. 9; *Montrose Investment Ltd v Orion Nominees Ltd* [2004] W.T.L.R. 133 at [24]. If a trustee pursues proceedings against a co-trustee to judgment, the beneficiaries are generally bound by the outcome of the proceedings and forbidden to bring subsequent proceedings in their own right against the same defendant in respect of the same breach of trust: *Norton v Levy* (1883) 48 L.T. 703 at 704; *Re De Leeuw* [1922] 2 Ch. 540 at 550–551.

[32] *Young* at 283. See too *Baynard v Woolley* (1855) 20 Beav. 583 at 585; *Butler v Butler* (1877) 7 Ch.D. 116 at 120–121.

[33] Using terminology suggested by Steven Elliott in his Oxford PhD thesis: *Compensation Claims against Trustees* (2002), parts of which have been published as: S.B. Elliott, "Restitutionary Compensatory Damages for Breach of Fiduciary Duty?" [1998] R.L.R. 135; S.B. Elliott, "Fiduciary Liability for Client Mortgage Frauds" (1999) 13 Tru. L.I. 74; S.B. Elliott, "Remoteness Criteria in Equity" (2002) 65 M.L.R. 588; S.B. Elliott and C. Mitchell, "Remedies for Dishonest Assistance" (2004) 67 M.L.R. 16, esp. at pp.23–34; S.B. Elliott and J. Edelman, "Money Remedies against Trustees" (2004) 18 Tru. L.I. 116.

[34] See paras 11–66 ff.

[35] *Low v Bouverie* [1891] 3 Ch. 82 at 99, per Lindley L.J.

[36] *Target Holdings Ltd v Redferns* [1996] A.C. 421 at 434. These rights and duties arise immediately that the trustee receives trust assets in a fiduciary capacity: *Att.-Gen. v Cocke* [1988] Ch. 414 at 420.

order commanding the trustees to perform their duties,[37] and to obtain such an order they need not assert that the trustees have done anything wrong. Their claim resembles a claim for specific performance of the primary obligations owed under a contract,[38] rather than a claim for damages for breach of contract or tort.[39]

If a trustee cannot perform his core obligation to account for and deliver a trust asset *in specie*, for example because he has misapplied it, then the court can order him instead to pay money as a substitute for performance of his duty. In this situation, the trustee has committed a breach of trust, but there is no need for the beneficiaries to plead or prove this breach of trust in order to obtain their remedy.[40] The reason is that their claim is still a claim for performance of the trustee's primary obligation to deliver the asset, but with the difference that it is a claim for substitute performance of this obligation by the payment of a money sum. It is not a claim for money to compensate the beneficiaries for any harm which they may have suffered as a consequence of the trustee's failure to perform his obligation *in specie*. The amount payable is accordingly measured by the objective value of the property which the trustee should have delivered: it "looks not so much to the loss suffered as to what is required to restore the trust fund".[41] The amount is calculated by requiring the trustee to produce accounts which omit no relevant incomings and record only authorised outgoings, by inspecting these to determine what property makes up the trust fund, and then, if the trustee cannot produce this property *in specie*, by ordering him to pay over a money substitute—either directly to the beneficiaries, or more usually, into the trust fund so that the trust can remain on foot. Thus, as Kekewich J. held in *Head v Gould*:[42] **11–10**

> "As against a trustee who, on the accounts being taken, is shewn to have improperly applied part of the trust estate, the right of a cestui que trust is to have those accounts set straight—that is, to compel the trustee to pay such a sum as will make them balance."

Because their claim is not founded on an assertion that the trustee has committed a breach of duty, the beneficiaries need not prove that the trustee's actions or omissions have caused them a loss,[43] nor **11–11**

---

[37] *Re Locker's ST* [1977] 1 W.L.R. 1323 (trustees ordered to exercise obligatory discretionary power of appointment). The courts can also make a vesting order directing trustees to transfer trust assets to an absolutely entitled beneficiary: Trustee Act 1925 ss.44(vi) and 51(1)(d); *Re Knox's Trusts* [1895] 2 Ch. 483; cf. *Quinton v Proctor* [1998] 4 V.R. 469; *Davis v Williams* [2003] NSWCA 371 at [41]. Where one or more beneficiaries are absolutely beneficially entitled to land held on a trust of land, so that they have rights to replace the trustees under the Trusts of Land and Appointment of Trustees Act 1996 s.19, the English courts should also be willing to vest the land directly in the beneficiaries, preferring the approach in *Re Godfrey's Trusts* (1883) 23 Ch.D. 205 to that in *Re Holland* (1881) 16 Ch.D. 672 and *Re Carrie* (1878) 10 Ch.D. 93.

[38] A claim for specific performance may succeed even though it is issued before the date when contractual performance is required, so that by definition no breach of contract can yet have occurred: *Hasham v Zenab* [1960] A.C. 316, noted R.E. Megarry (1960) 76 L.Q.R. 200.

[39] Compare the statement in *Ex p. Adamson* (1878) 8 Ch. App. 807 at 819, that Chancery suits for breach of trust were always for "an equitable debt or liability in the nature of a debt", with the comment in *Jervis v Harris* [1996] Ch. 195 at 202–203, that "The plaintiff who claims payment of a debt need not prove anything beyond the occurrence of the event or condition on the occurrence of which the debt becomes due. He need prove no loss; the rules as to remoteness of damage and mitigation of loss are irrelevant."

[40] *Bacon v Clarke* (1837) 2 My. & Cr. 294; Re Stevens [1898] 1 Ch. 162; *Ahmed Angullia bin Hadjee Mohamed Salleh Angullia v Estate and Trust Agencies (1927) Ltd* [1938] A.C. 624 at 637.

[41] *New Cap Reinsurance Corp Ltd v General Cologne Re Australia Ltd* (2004) 7 I.T.E.L.R. 295 at [55], per Young C.J. in Eq. See too *Re Anglo-French Co-operative Soc* (1882) 21 Ch.D. 492 at 506; *Re Windsor Steam Coal Co (1901) Ltd* [1929] 1 Ch. 151 at 166–167; *Knight v Haynes Duffell, Kentish & Co (a firm)* [2003] EWCA Civ 223 at [36]–[39]; *Re Lehman Brothers International (Europe) (in admin.) (No.2)* [2009] EWHC 2141 (Ch) at [53], per Blackburne J.: a beneficiary's remedy for breach of trust is "principally directed to securing performance of the trust, rather than to the recovery of compensation or damages".

[42] [1898] 2 Ch. 250 at 266. See too *Wiglesworth v Wiglesworth* (1852) 16 Beav. 269 at 272; *Chaplin v Young* (1864) 33 Beav. 330 at 343.

[43] *Cocker v Quayle* (1830) 1 Russ. & M. 353; *Salway v Salway* (1831) 2 Russ. & M. 215; *Youyang Pty Ltd v Minter Ellison Morris Fletcher* (2003) 212 C.L.R. 484 at [63] and [69].

do the concepts of remoteness[44] and contributory negligence[45] have any bearing on their claim. Moreover, no deduction will be made for tax which would have been payable by the trustees on the relevant property but for their default,[46] and the beneficiaries' tax liabilities do not enter the picture because they arise when capital or income is distributed out of the fund, and not when the trustee pays the value of the relevant asset back into the trust fund. The amount due from the trustee to make the accounts balance may be the value of misapplied (or wrongfully retained) trust income,[47] or of a misapplied capital sum plus interest.[48] Where some other property than money has been misapplied, he may be liable to pay the market value of the property at the date of misapplication plus interest,[49] or, if this is a higher sum, the market value of the property at the date of judgment,[50] along with the amount of any income that would otherwise have been generated by the property between the date of misapplication and the date of judgment.[51]

11–12 When deciding whether a trustee's payments are justified and should therefore be allowed to stand on the taking of the account, the court will generally disallow unauthorised disbursements, with the result that unauthorised purchases are treated as having been made with the trustee's own money.[52] However, there are exceptional cases where unauthorised disbursements are allowed, and the trustee exonerated from performance of his duty to hold the relevant property for the beneficiaries. One such case is where the beneficiaries elect to adopt the trustee's actions and ask the court to treat these as though they had been authorised all along. Beneficiaries would wish to do this where the trustee has bought an unauthorised investment which has increased in value,[53] or where the trustee has wrongfully sold trust property whose current market value is lower than the value of the sale proceeds plus interest.[54]

11–13 Sometimes the courts also relieve a trustee from the performance of his duty where they consider that this would be inequitable. For example, in *Jones v Lewis*, Lord Hardwicke L.C. held that:[55]

> "if a trustee is robbed, that robbery properly proved shall be a discharge, provided he keeps [the trust property] so as he would keep his own."

---

[44] *Clough v Bond* (1838) 3 My. & Cr. 490; *Magnus v Queensland National Bank* (1888) 37 Ch.D. 466; *Re Dawson* [1966] 2 N.S.W.R. 211 at 214; *Re Duckwari Plc (No.2)* [1999] Ch. 268 at 272; *McCann v Switzerland Insurance Australia Ltd* (2000) 203 C.L.R. 579 at 621–622.

[45] *Alexander v Perpetual Trustees (WA) Ltd* (2004) 216 C.L.R. 109 at [44] and esp. [104]: contributory negligence is inapt because "the basic principle that a fiduciary's liability to a beneficiary for breach of trust is one of restoration."

[46] *Bartlett v Barclays Bank Trust Co Ltd (No.2)* [1980] Ch. 515 at 543; *Re Bell's Indenture* [1980] 1 W.L.R. 1217; *John v James* [1986] S.T.C. 352 at 361.

[47] *Sharma v Farlam Ltd* [2009] EWHC 1622 (Ch) at [401] ff.

[48] *Docker v Somes* (1834) 2 My. & K. 655; *Burdick v Garrick* (1870) 5 Ch. App. 233; *Re Davis* [1902] 2 Ch. 314; *Gordon v Gonda* [1955] 1 W.L.R. 885; *Kemp v Sims* [2009] Pens. L.R. 83.

[49] *Shepherd v Mouls* (1845) 4 Hare 500 at 504.

[50] *Re Massingberd's Settlement* (1890) 63 L.T. 296; *Re Bell's Indenture* [1980] 1 W.L.R. 1217.

[51] *Kellaway v Johnson* (1842) 5 Beav. 319 at 324; *Hewett v Foster* (1843) 6 Beav. 259; *Dixon v Dixon* (1878) 9 Ch.D. 587.

[52] *Jackson v Dickinson* [1903] 1 Ch. 947, esp. at 951–952 (where the consequences of this rule are fully explored).

[53] *Re Patten* (1883) 52 L.J. Ch. 787; *Re Jenkins* [1903] 2 Ch. 362; *Wright v Morgan* [1926] A.C. 788 (PC) 799. If the beneficiaries choose to adopt the investment, they cannot *also* demand that the trustees pay in the difference between the current value of the investment and the (higher) current value of an authorised asset that was sold to make the purchase: *Thornton v Stokill* (1855) 1 Jur. 751, which should be preferred on this point to *Re Lake* [1903] 1 K.B. 439.

[54] *Harrison v Harrison* (1740) 2 Atk. 121; *Bostock v Blakeney* (1794) 2 Bro. C.C. 653 at 656; *Pocock v Reddington* (1801) 5 Ves. Jun. 794 at 800.

[55] (1750) 2 Ves. Sen. 240 at 241. See too *Morley v Morley* (1678) 2 Chan. Cas. 2; *Jobson v Palmer* [1893] 1 Ch. 71. And cf. *ex parte Belchier* (1754) Amb. 218 at 219 (trustee not answerable for property lost on banker's bankruptcy); *Job v Job* (1875) 6 Ch.D. 562 at 563–564 (similar rule for executors).

It is tempting, but wrong, to conclude from the fact that trustees need not account for stolen trust property which they kept with reasonable care that the courts will never require trustees to reach into their own pockets unless they have committed a breach of duty. Various cases have already been cited for the rule that substitutive performance claims do not depend on the assertion that the trustee has committed a breach of duty. Another is *Eaves v Hickson*,[56] where Romilly M.R. declined to relieve a trustee who made unauthorised distributions on presentation of a forged document. No finding was made that the trustee had failed to examine this document carefully, and although counsel cited *Jones* and other robbery cases,[57] his Lordship concluded that the trustee was still "bound to pay the trust fund to the right person".[58]

It follows that much can turn on the question whether a trustee's acts are unauthorised (in which case liability to perform his primary duties will subsist unless he is relieved) or authorised (in which case no liability will ensue unless he commits a breach of duty such as a breach of his duty of care). This has sometimes led the courts to reclassify as authorised types of trustee action that were previously held to be unauthorised, with a view to moderating the law's severity. For example, in *Speight v Gaunt*[59] the Court of Appeal and House of Lords changed the law when they held that the delegation of a trustee's investment duties to a broker was not an unauthorised action, although it was an action that had to be done carefully. **11–14**

To give some examples of substitutive performance claims, let it be supposed that a trustee T makes an unauthorised distribution of £x to A, who is now bankrupt; that T makes an unauthorised investment of £y in a villa in South Africa, which has now halved in value; and that T makes an unauthorised transfer of assets worth £z to an agent, B, who has now absconded with the money. Because T had no power under the trust to distribute the £x to A or to spend the £y on the villa, he will be treated as though he carried out these transactions with his own money, and he will be required to pay £x and £y back into the trust fund,[60] with compound interest at 1% above the clearing banks' base rate.[61] So far as the assets worth £z are concerned, T will now have to pay their replacement value back into the trust fund, even if this has risen to £2z in the interim,[62] and it makes no difference whether the assets were lost through an innocent accident or through B's negligence or dishonesty: see *Clough v Bond*[63] and *Caffrey v Derby*,[64] which are discussed in the extract from *Re Dawson*[65] that is reproduced below.[66] **11–15**

In *Target Holdings Ltd v Redferns*,[67] parts of which are also reproduced below,[68] the claimant company agreed to lend money to a borrower to purchase property. Repayment of the loan was to be secured by a charge on the property. The money was placed with the defendant solicitors on trust for payment to the borrower's order, once a duly executed charge over the property and supporting **11–16**

---

[56] (1861) 30 Beav 136. See also *Ashby v Blackwell* (1765) 2 Eden 299; *Bostock v Flyer* (1865) L.R. 1 Eq. 26; *Sutton v Wilders* (1871) L.R. 12 Eq. 373.
[57] *Eaves* at 139.
[58] *Eaves* at 141.
[59] (1883) 22 Ch.D. 727, affirmed (1883) 9 App. Cas. 1; discussed in C. Stebbings, *The Private Trustee in Victorian England* (2001) ch.5, esp. at pp.151–155. See para.9–191.
[60] *Knott v Cottee* (1852) 19 Beav. 77; *Re Duckwari Plc (No.2)* [1999] Ch. 268 at 272; *Wong v Burt* (2004) 7 I.T.E.L.R. 263 at [59].
[61] *Wallersteiner v Moir (No.2)* [1975] Q.B. 373 at 397.
[62] *Shepherd v Mouls* (1845) 24 Hare 500 at 504; *Re Massingberd* (1890) 63 L.T. 296.
[63] (1838) 3 My. & Cr. 490 at 496–497, per Lord Cottenham L.C., endorsed in *Target Holdings Ltd v Redferns* [1996] 1 A.C. 421 at 434, per Lord Browne-Wilkinson.
[64] (1801) 6 Ves. 488.
[65] [1966] 2 N.S.W.R. 211.
[66] At paras 11–20 ff.
[67] [1996] 1 A.C. 421.
[68] At paras 11–22 ff.

documents of title were delivered. The solicitors paid the money over to the borrower's order without first obtaining the charge or other documents, although these were later delivered. The borrower defaulted on the loan and it then transpired that the property had been fraudulently overvalued, so that the claimant was left substantially out of pocket after it had exercised its power of sale. The Court of Appeal held that the solicitors had committed a breach of trust by releasing the money before receiving the documents, and that at this moment there had been "an immediate loss placing the trustee under an immediate duty to restore the moneys to the trust fund".[69] They concluded that the solicitors were liable for the full amount of the money, but to prevent double recovery they required the claimant to give credit for the amount realised by the sale of the property.

11–17 The House of Lords agreed that there had been a breach of trust, but disagreed that the clock should be stopped at the date of breach for the purpose of quantifying the solicitors' liability. Their Lordships held that the relevant date was the date of judgment, i.e. after the transaction had been completed, and that the solicitors would therefore be liable only if the claimant could prove that its loss would not have occurred but for the early payment of the money without taking any security. Hence the case was sent back to the High Court for determination of this point.

11–18 Unfortunately, Lord Browne-Wilkinson's leading speech is hard to follow.[70] He clearly thought that the claimant should have to prove a causal link between its loss and the solicitor's breach of duty. Yet, as Lord Millett later observed (extra-judicially),[71] the claim was for substitutive performance of the solicitor's duty to hold and disburse the trust money in accordance with the terms of the trust, and so the question whether the claimant had suffered a loss as a result of the solicitor's breach of duty was beside the point. In Lord Millett's view, the case should therefore have been decided on the different basis that the solicitor's payment without taking the documents was a breach of trust, but that where a trustee has misapplied trust assets, his "obligation to restore the trust property is not an obligation to restore it in the very same form in which he disbursed it, but an obligation to restore it in any form authorised by the trust".[72] Hence, when the solicitor acquired the title deeds and delivered them to the claimant, it performed its obligation to restore the trust property, not in specie, but in the form of an authorised substitute. Hence the solicitor should not have been liable for anything.

11–19 This rationalisation of the case leaves intact Lord Browne-Wilkinson's finding that the quantum of the liability owed by a trustee who misapplies trust property is not determined at the date of breach, even though he comes under an immediate liability to restore the property.[73] However, this does not mean that the court can look at events occurring after the breach to see whether the beneficiaries would ultimately have suffered the same loss anyway.[74] Instead, its significance lies in the fact that the court can look to see whether the trustee has rectified matters in an authorised fashion since the date of breach. Also, if the trustee has not done this, the value of his obligation to hand over the property will vary according to its current market value, or, where the property is money, according to the amount of (compound) interest accrued on the money between the date of breach and the date of judgment.

---

[69] [1994] 1 W.L.R. 1089 at 1103, per Peter Gibson L.J.

[70] Essentially he failed to distinguish substitutive performance claims and reparation claims. The source of this confusion was the Supreme Court of Canada's incoherent decision in *Canson Enterprises Ltd v Boughton & Co* [1991] 3 S.C.R. 534, as explained in J. Edelman and S.B. Elliott, "Money Remedies against Trustees" (2004) 18 Tru L.I. 116, at pp. 122–125.

[71] Sir P. Millett, "Equity's Place in the Law of Commerce" (1998) 114 L.Q.R. 214, at pp. 225–227. See too Lord Millett, "Proprietary Restitution" in S. Degeling and J. Edelman (eds), *Equity in Commercial Law* (2005).

[72] Millett (L.Q.R.) at p.227.

[73] See too *Youyang Pty Ltd v Minter Ellison Morris Fletcher* (2003) 212 C.L.R. 484 at [35].

[74] *Cocker v Quayle* (1830) 1 Russ. & M. 535.

RE DAWSON

New South Wales Supreme Court [1966] 2 N.S.W.R. 211 (endorsed by Brightman L.J. in *Bartlett v Barclays Bank Trust Co Ltd (No.2)* [1980] Ch. 515 at 543)

STREET J.: The obligation of a defaulting trustee is essentially one of effecting a restitution to the estate. **11–20**
The obligation is of a personal character and its extent is not to be limited by common law principles governing remoteness of damage. In *Caffrey v Darby*,[75] trustees were charged with neglect in failing to recover possession of part of the trust assets. The assets were lost and it was argued by the trustees that the loss was not attributable to their neglect. The Master of the Rolls, in stating his reasons, asked "will they be relieved from that by the circumstance that the loss has ultimately happened by something that is not a direct and immediate consequence of their negligence?" His answer to this question was that, even supposing that "they could not look to the possibility" of the actual event which occasioned the loss, "yet, if they have already been guilty of negligence they must be responsible for any loss in any way to that property; for whatever may be the immediate cause the property would not have been in a situation to sustain that loss if it had not been for their negligence. If they had taken possession of the property it would not have been in his possession. If the loss had happened by fire, lightning, or any other accident, that would not be an excuse for them, if guilty of previous negligence. That was their fault." *Caffrey v Darby* is consistent with the proposition that if a breach has been committed then the trustee is liable to place the trust estate in the same position as it would have been in if no breach had been committed. Considerations of causation, foreseeability and remoteness do not readily enter into the matter. To the same effect is the case of *Clough v Bond*.[76] It was argued before Lord Cottenham L.C. that "the principle of the court is to charge persons in the situation of trustees as parties to the breach of trust, wherever they have acted irregularly, and the irregularity, however well intended, has in the result enabled their co-trustees to commit a breach of trust, or has been, however remotely, the origin of the loss." . . . The principles embodied in this approach do not appear to involve any inquiry as to whether the loss was caused by or flowed from the breach. Rather the inquiry in each instance would appear to be whether the loss would have happened if there had been no breach.

. . . The cases to which I have referred demonstrate that the obligation to make restitution, which courts of **11–21**
equity have from very early times imposed on defaulting trustees and other fiduciaries, is of a more absolute nature than the common-law obligation to pay damages for tort or breach of contract. . . . Moreover the distinction between common law damages and relief against a defaulting trustee is strikingly demonstrated by reference to the actual form of relief granted in equity in respect of breaches of trust. The form of relief is couched in terms appropriate to require the defaulting trustee to restore to the estate the assets of which he deprived it. Increases in market values between the date of breach and the date of recoupment are for the trustee's account: the effect of such increases would, at common law, be excluded from the computation of damages but in equity a defaulting trustee must make good the loss by restoring to the estate the assets of which he deprived it notwithstanding that market values may have increased in the meantime. The obligation to restore to the estate the assets of which he deprived it necessarily connotes that, where a monetary compensation is to be paid in lieu of restoring assets, that compensation is to be assessed by reference to the value of the assets at the date of restoration and not at the date of deprivation. In this sense the obligation is a continuing one and ordinarily, if the assets are for some reason not restored in specie, it will fall for quantification at the date when recoupment is to be effected, and not before.

TARGET HOLDINGS LTD v REDFERNS (A FIRM)

House of Lords [1996] 1 A.C. 421, [1995] 3 W.L.R. 352, [1995] 3 All E.R. 785

The claimant mortgagee alleged that it had been the victim of a mortgage fraud as part of which the insol- **11–22**
vent second defendant had overvalued the mortgaged property at £2 million. The first defendant, a firm

[75] (1801) 6 Ves. 488.
[76] (1838) 3 My. & Cr. 490.

of solicitors, had acted not just for the claimant but also for the mortgagor, Crowngate Ltd, and also for two other companies, Kohli Ltd and Panther Ltd. The owner of the property, Mirage Ltd, had agreed to sell to Crowngate for £775,000, but Crowngate had arranged matters so that Mirage would sell to Panther for £775,000, which would then sell the property on to Kohli for £1,250,000, which would then sell to Crowngate for £2 million. The claimant knew nothing of these arrangements, the point of which was to create a false impression of the property's value. The claimant paid £1,525,000 to the defendant solicitors to be held on a bare trust to pay the money to Crowngate's order only when the property was transferred to Crowngate and charges over it were executed in the claimant's favour. In breach of trust the money was paid over a month before the charges were executed. Crowngate became insolvent and the claimant sold the property for only £500,000. The claimant sued the defendant solicitors for breach of their duty of care as the claimant's solicitor in failing to alert the claimant to the suspicious circumstances, and also for breach of trust in paying the money away without authority. The claimant sought summary judgment for breach of trust; Warner J. granted leave to defend, conditional upon payment into court of £1 million. The Court of Appeal granted summary judgment.

11–23 LORD BROWNE-WILKINSON (with whom LORD KEITH, LORD ACKNER, LORD JAUNCEY and LORD LLOYD agreed): Peter Gibson L.J., with whom Hirst L.J. agreed, held that the basic liability of a trustee in breach of trust is not to pay damages but to restore to the trust fund that which has been lost to it or to pay compensation to the beneficiary for what he has lost. He held that, in assessing the compensation payable to the beneficiary, causation is not irrelevant but common law rules of causation, as such, do not apply: the beneficiary is to be put back in the position he would have been in but for the breach of trust. He held that in cases where the breach of trust does not involve paying away trust money to a stranger (e.g. making an unauthorised investment), the answer to the question whether any loss has been thereby caused and the quantification of such loss will depend upon events subsequent to the commission of the breach of trust. But he held that in cases such as the present where the trustee has paid away trust moneys to a stranger, there is an immediate loss to the trust fund and the causal connection between the breach and the loss is obvious: the trustee comes under an immediate duty to restore the moneys to the trust fund. He held that the remedies of equity are sufficiently flexible to require Target (as it has always accepted) to give credit for the moneys received on the subsequent realisation of its security. But otherwise Redferns' liability was to pay to Target the whole of the moneys wrongly paid away . . .

11–24 Before considering the technical issues of law which arise, it is appropriate to look at the case more generally. Target alleges, and it is probably the case, that it was defrauded by third parties (Mr Kohli and Mr Musafir and possibly their associates) to advance money on the security of the property. If there had been no breach by Redferns of their instructions and the transaction had gone through, Target would have suffered a loss . . . [which] would have been wholly caused by the fraud of the third parties. The breach of trust committed by Redferns left Target in exactly the same position as it would have been if there had been no such breach: Target advanced the same amount of money, obtained the same security and received the same amount on the realisation of that security. In any ordinary use of words, the breach of trust by Redferns cannot be said to have caused the actual loss ultimately suffered by Target unless it can be shown that, but for the breach of trust, the transaction would not have gone through, e.g. if Panther could not have obtained a conveyance from Mirage otherwise than by paying the purchase money to Mirage out of the moneys paid out, in breach of trust, by Redferns to Panther on 29 June. If that fact can be demonstrated, it can be said that Redferns' breach of trust was a cause of Target's loss: if the transaction had not gone through, Target would not have advanced the money at all and therefore Target would not have suffered any loss. But the Court of Appeal decided,[77] and it is common ground before your Lordships, that there is a triable issue as to whether, had it not been for the breach of trust, the transaction would have gone through. Therefore the decision of the Court of Appeal in this case can only be maintained on the basis that, even if there is no causal link between the breach of trust and the actual loss eventually suffered by Target (i.e. the sum advanced less the sum recovered) the trustee in breach is liable to bear (at least in part) the loss suffered by Target. . . .

11–25 At common law there are two principles fundamental to the award of damages. First, that the defendant's wrongful act must cause the damage complained of. Second, that the plaintiff is to be put "in the

[77] See [1994] 1 W.L.R. 1089 at 1100 and 1104, per Ralph Gibson and Peter Gibson L.JJ.

same position as he would have been in if he had not sustained the wrong for which he is now getting his compensation or reparation".[78] Although, as will appear, in many ways equity approaches liability for making good a breach of trust from a different starting point, in my judgment those two principles are applicable as much in equity as at common law. Under both systems liability is fault based: the defendant is only liable for the consequences of the legal wrong he has done to the plaintiff and to make good the damage caused by such wrong. He is not responsible for damage not caused by his wrong or to pay by way of compensation more than the loss suffered from such wrong. The detailed rules of equity as to causation and the quantification of loss differ, at least ostensibly, from those applicable at common law. But the principles underlying both systems are the same. On the assumptions that had to be made in the present case until the factual issues are resolved (i.e. that the transaction would have gone through even if there had been no breach of trust), the result reached by the Court of Appeal does not accord with those principles. Redferns as trustees have been held liable to compensate Target for a loss caused otherwise than by the breach of trust. I approach the consideration of the relevant rules of equity with a strong predisposition against such a conclusion.

The considerations urged before your Lordships, although presented as a single argument leading to the conclusion that the views of the majority in the Court of Appeal are correct, on analysis comprise two separate lines of reasoning, viz.: **11–26**

(A) an argument developed by Mr Patten QC (but not reflected in the reasons of the Court of Appeal) that Target is now (i.e. at the date of judgment) entitled to have the "trust fund" restored by an order that Redferns reconstitute the trust fund by paying back into client account the moneys paid away in breach of trust. Once the trust fund is so reconstituted, Redferns as bare trustee for Target will have no answer to a claim by Target for the payment over of the moneys in the reconstituted "trust fund". Therefore, Mr Patten says, it is proper now to order payment direct to Target of the whole sum improperly paid away, less the sum which Target has received on the sale of property; and

(B) the argument accepted by the majority of the Court of Appeal that, because immediately after the moneys were paid away by Redferns in breach of trust there was an immediate right to have the "trust fund" reconstituted, there was then an immediate loss to the trust fund for which loss Redferns are now liable to compensate Target direct.

The critical distinction between the two arguments is that argument (A) depends upon Target being entitled now to an order for restitution to the trust fund whereas argument (B) quantifies the compensation payable to Target as beneficiary by reference to a right to restitution to the trust fund at an earlier date and is not dependent upon Target having any right to have the client account reconstituted now. **11–27**

Before dealing with these two lines of argument, it is desirable to say something about the approach to the principles under discussion. The argument both before the Court of Appeal and your Lordships concentrated on the equitable rules establishing the extent and quantification of the compensation payable by a trustee who is in breach of trust. In my judgment this approach is liable to lead to the wrong conclusions in the present case because it ignores an earlier and crucial question, viz. is the trustee who has committed a breach under any liability at all to the beneficiary complaining of the breach? There can be cases where, although there is an undoubted breach of trust, the trustee is under no liability at all to a beneficiary. For example, if a trustee commits a breach of trust with the acquiescence of one beneficiary, that beneficiary has no right to complain and an action for breach of trust brought by him would fail completely. Again there may be cases where the breach gives rise to no right to compensation. Say, as often occurs, a trustee commits a judicious breach of trust by investing in an unauthorised investment which proves to be very profitable to the trust. A carping beneficiary could insist that the unauthorised investment be sold and the proceeds invested in authorised investments: but the trustee would be under no liability to pay compensation either to the trust fund or to the beneficiary because the breach has caused no loss to the trust fund. Therefore, in each case the first question is to ask what are the rights of the beneficiary: only if some relevant right has been infringed so as to give rise to a loss is it necessary to consider the extent of the trustee's liability to compensate for such loss. **11–28**

[78] See *Livingstone v Rawyards Coal Co* (1880) 5 App. Cas. 25 at 39, per Lord Blackburn.

11–29 The basic right of a beneficiary is to have the trust duly administered in accordance with the provisions of the trust instrument, if any, and the general law. Thus, in relation to a traditional trust where the fund is held in trust for a number of beneficiaries having different, usually successive, equitable interests (e.g. A for life with remainder to B), the right of each beneficiary is to have the whole fund vested in the trustees so as to be available to satisfy his equitable interest when, and if, it falls into possession. Accordingly, in the case of a breach of such a trust involving the wrongful paying away of trust assets, the liability of the trustee is to restore to the trust fund, often called "the trust estate", what ought to have been there.

11–30 The equitable rules of compensation for breach of trust have been largely developed in relation to such traditional trusts, where the only way in which all the beneficiaries' rights can be protected is to restore to the trust fund what ought to be there. In such a case the basic rule is that a trustee in breach of trust must restore or pay to the trust estate either the assets which have been lost to the estate by reason of the breach or compensation for such loss. Courts of Equity did not award damages but, acting in personam, ordered the defaulting trustee to restore the trust estate.[79] If specific restitution of the trust property is not possible, then the liability of the trustee is to pay sufficient compensation to the trust estate to put it back to what it would have been had the breach not been committed.[80] Even if the immediate cause of the loss is the dishonesty or failure of a third party, the trustee is liable to make good that loss to the trust estate if, but for the breach, such loss would not have occurred.[81] Thus the common law rules of remoteness of damage and causation do not apply. However, there does have to be some causal connection between the breach of trust and the loss to the trust estate for which compensation is recoverable, viz. the fact that the loss would not have occurred but for the breach.[82]

11–31 Hitherto I have been considering the rights of beneficiaries under traditional trusts where the trusts are still subsisting and therefore the right of each beneficiary, and his only right, is to have the trust fund reconstituted as it should be. But what if at the time of the action claiming compensation for breach of trust those trusts have come to an end? Take as an example again the trust for A for life with remainder to B. During A's lifetime B's only right is to have the trust duly administered and, in the event of a breach, to have the trust fund restored. After A's death, B becomes absolutely entitled. He of course has the right to have the trust assets retained by the trustees until they have fully accounted for them to him. But if the trustees commit a breach of trust, there is no reason for compensating the breach of trust by way of an order for restitution and compensation to the trust fund as opposed to the beneficiary himself. The beneficiary's right is no longer simply to have the trust duly administered: he is, in equity, the sole owner of the trust estate. Nor, for the same reason, is restitution to the trust fund necessary to protect other beneficiaries. Therefore, although I do not wholly rule out the possibility that even in those circumstances an order to reconstitute the fund may be appropriate, in the ordinary case where a beneficiary becomes absolutely entitled to the trust fund the court orders, not restitution to the trust estate, but the payment of compensation directly to the beneficiary. The measure of such compensation is the same, i.e. the difference between what the beneficiary has in fact received and the amount he would have received but for the breach of trust. . . .

Argument (A)

11–32 As I have said, the critical step in this argument is that Target is now entitled to an order for reconstitution of the trust fund by the repayment into client account of the moneys wrongly paid away, so that Target can now demand immediate repayment of the whole of such moneys without regard to the real loss it has suffered by reason of the breach.

11–33 Even if the equitable rules developed in relation to traditional trusts were directly applicable to such a case as this, as I have sought to show, a beneficiary becoming absolutely entitled to a trust fund has no automatic right to have the fund reconstituted in all circumstances. Thus, even applying the strict rules so developed in relation to traditional trusts, it seems to me very doubtful whether Target is now entitled to

[79] See *Nocton v Lord Ashburton* [1914] A.C. 932 at 952, per Viscount Haldane L.C.

[80] See *Caffrey v Darby* (1801) 6 Ves. 488 and *Clough v Bond* (1838) 3 My. & Cr. 490.

[81] See Underhill and Hayton, *Law of Trusts and Trustees* 14th edn (1987), pp. 734–736, *Re Dawson (decd)* [1966] 2 N.S.W.R. 211 and *Bartlett v Barclays Bank Trust Co Ltd (No.2)* [1980] 2 Ch. 515.

[82] See also *Re Miller's Deed Trusts* (1978) 75 L.S. Gaz. 454 and *Nestlé v National Westminster Bank Plc* [1993] 1 W.L.R. 1260.

have the trust fund reconstituted. But in my judgment it is in any event wrong to lift wholesale the detailed rules developed in the context of traditional trusts and then seek to apply them to trusts of quite a different kind. In the modern world the trust has become a valuable device in commercial and financial dealings. The fundamental principles of equity apply as much to such trusts as they do to the traditional trusts in relation to which those principles were originally formulated. But in my judgment it is important, if the trust is not to be rendered commercially useless, to distinguish between the basic principles of trust law and those specialist rules developed in relation to traditional trusts which are applicable only to such trusts and the rationale of which has no application to trusts of quite a different kind.

This case is concerned with a trust which has at all times been a bare trust. Bare trusts arise in a number of different contexts: e.g. by the ultimate vesting of the property under a traditional trust, nominee shareholdings, and, as in the present case, as but one incident of a wider commercial transaction involving agency. In the case of moneys paid to a solicitor by a client as part of a conveyancing transaction, the purpose of that transaction is to achieve the commercial objective of the client, be it the acquisition of property or the lending of money on security. The depositing of money with the solicitor is but one aspect of the arrangements between the parties, such arrangements being for the most part contractual. Thus, the circumstances under which the solicitor can part with money from client account are regulated by the instructions given by the client: they are not part of the trusts on which the property is held. I do not intend to cast any doubt on the fact that moneys held by solicitors on client account are trust moneys or that the basic equitable principles apply to any breach of such trust by solicitors. But the basic equitable principle applicable to breach of trust is that the beneficiary is entitled to be compensated for any loss he would not have suffered but for the breach. I have no doubt that, until the underlying commercial transaction has been completed, the solicitor can be required to restore to client account moneys wrongly paid away. But to import into such trust an obligation to restore the trust fund once the transaction has been completed would be entirely artificial. The obligation to reconstitute the trust fund applicable in the case of traditional trusts reflects the fact that no one beneficiary is entitled to the trust property and the need to compensate all beneficiaries for the breach. That rationale has no application to a case such as the present. To impose such an obligation in order to enable the beneficiary solely entitled (i.e. the client) to recover from the solicitor more than the client has in fact lost flies in the face of common sense and is in direct conflict with the basic principles of equitable compensation. In my judgment, once a conveyancing transaction has been completed the client has no right to have the solicitor's client account reconstituted as a "trust fund". **11–34**

Argument (B)

. . . The key point in the reasoning of the Court of Appeal is that where moneys are paid away to a stranger in breach of trust, an immediate loss is suffered by the trust estate: as a result, subsequent events reducing that loss are irrelevant. They drew a distinction between the case in which the breach of trust consisted of some failure in the administration of the trust and the case where a trustee has actually paid away trust moneys to a stranger. There is no doubt that in the former case, one waits to see what loss is in fact suffered by reason of the breach, i.e. the restitution or compensation payable is assessed at the date of trial, not of breach. However, the Court of Appeal considered that where the breach consisted of paying away the trust moneys to a stranger it made no sense to wait: it seemed to Peter Gibson L.J. obvious that in such a case "there is an immediate loss, placing the trustee under an immediate duty to restore the moneys to the trust fund".[83] The majority of the Court of Appeal therefore considered that subsequent events which diminished the loss in fact suffered were irrelevant, save for imposing on the compensated beneficiary an obligation to give credit for any benefit he subsequently received. In effect, in the view of the Court of Appeal one "stops the clock" at the date the moneys are paid away: events which occur between the date of breach and the date of trial are irrelevant in assessing the loss suffered by reason of the breach. **11–35**

A trustee who wrongly pays away trust money, like a trustee who makes an unauthorised investment, commits a breach of trust and comes under an immediate duty to remedy such breach. If immediate proceedings are brought, the court will make an immediate order requiring restoration to the trust fund of the assets wrongly distributed or, in the case of an unauthorised investment, will order the sale of the unauthorised investment and the payment of compensation for any loss suffered. But the fact that there is an **11–36**

[83] [1994] 1 W.L.R. 1089 at 1103.

accrued cause of action as soon as the breach is committed does not in my judgment mean that the quantum of the compensation payable is ultimately fixed as at the date when the breach occurred. The quantum is fixed at the date of judgment, at which date, according to the circumstances then pertaining, the compensation is assessed at the figure then necessary to put the trust estate or the beneficiary back into the position it would have been in had there been no breach. I can see no justification for "stopping the clock" immediately in some cases but not in others: to do so may, as in this case, lead to compensating the trust estate or the beneficiary for a loss which, on the facts known at trial, it has never suffered.

11–37 Moreover, in my judgment the distinction is not consistent with the decision in *Re Dawson (decd)*.[84] In that case a testator had established separate executors for his New Zealand and his Australian estates. In 1939 the New Zealand estate was under the administration of attorneys for, among others, PSD. PSD arranged that New Zealand £4,700 should be withdrawn from the New Zealand estate and paid away to a stranger, X, who in turn was supposed to lend the moneys to an Australian company in which PSD was interested. X absconded with the money. In that case, therefore, the trust money had been paid away to a stranger. Street J. had to decide whether the liability of PSD to compensate the estate was to be satisfied by paying sufficient Australian pounds to buy New Zealand £4,700 at the rate of exchange at the date of breach (when there was parity between the two currencies) or at the date of judgment (when the Australian pound had depreciated against the New Zealand pound). He held that the rate of exchange was to be taken as at the date of judgment. Although, contrary to the present case, this decision favoured the beneficiaries at the expense of the defaulting trustee, the principle is of general application whether operating to the benefit or the detriment of the beneficiaries. The equitable compensation for breach of trust has to be assessed as at the date of judgment and not at an earlier date.

11–38 In *Canson Enterprises Ltd v Boughton & Co*[85] the plaintiffs had bought some property in a transaction in which they were advised by the defendant, a solicitor. To the knowledge of the solicitor, but not of the plaintiffs, there was an improper profit being made by the vendors. If the plaintiffs had known that fact, they would not have completed the purchase. The defendant solicitor was in breach of his fiduciary duties to the plaintiffs. After completion the plaintiffs built a warehouse on the property, which due to the negligence of engineers and builders, was defective. The question was whether the defendant solicitor was liable to compensate the plaintiffs for the defective building, the plaintiffs contending that "but for" the defendant's breach of fiduciary duty they would not have bought the property and therefore would not have built the warehouse. Although the Supreme Court of Canada were unanimous in dismissing the claim, they reached their conclusions by two differing routes. The majority considered that damages for breach of fiduciary duty fell to be measured by analogy with common law rules of remoteness, whereas the minority considered that the equitable principles of compensation applied. Your Lordships are not required to choose between those two views. But the judgment of McLachlin J. (expressing the minority view) contains an illuminating exposition of the rules applicable to equitable compensation for breach of trust. Although the whole judgment deserves study, I extract the following statements:

11–39 "While foreseeability of loss does not enter into the calculation of compensation for breach of fiduciary duty, liability is not unlimited. Just as restitution in specie is limited to the property under the trustee's control, so equitable compensation must be limited to loss flowing from the trustee's acts in relation to the interest he undertook to protect. Thus, Davidson states 'It is imperative to ascertain the loss *resulting from breach of the relevant equitable duty*'.[86] . . .

"A related question which must be addressed is the time of assessment of the loss. In this area tort and contract law are of little help. . . . The basis of compensation at equity, by contrast, is the restoration of the actual value of the thing lost through the breach. The foreseeable value of the items is not in issue. As a result, the losses are to be assessed as at the time of trial, *using the full benefit of hindsight*[87] . . .

[84] [1966] 2 N.S.W.R. 211.
[85] [1991] 3 S.C.R. 534.
[86] I. Davidson, "The Equitable Remedy of Compensation" (1982) 3 Melb. U.L.R. 349, 354 (McLachlin J.'s emphasis).
[87] McLachlin J.'s emphasis.

"In summary, compensation is an equitable monetary remedy which is available when the equitable remedies of restitution and account are not appropriate. By analogy with restitution, it attempts to restore to the plaintiff what has been lost as a result of the breach, i.e. the plaintiff's lost opportunity. The plaintiff's actual loss as a consequence of the breach is to be assessed with the full benefit of hindsight. Foreseeability is not a concern in assessing compensation, but it is essential that the losses made good are only those which, *on a common sense view of causation*, were caused by the breach."[88]

In my view this is good law. Equitable compensation for breach of trust is designed to achieve exactly what the word compensation suggests: to make good a loss in fact suffered by the beneficiaries and which, using hindsight and common sense, can be seen to have been caused by the breach. . . . **11–40**

Mr Patten for Target relied on *Nant-y-glo and Blaina Ironworks Co v Grave*[89] as showing that a trustee can be held liable to recoup to the trust fund the value of shares at the highest value between the date of breach and the date of judgment. In my view that case has no relevance. The claim there was not for breach of trust but for account of profits made by a fiduciary (a company director) from shares which he had improperly received in breach of his duty. The amount recoverable in an action claiming an account of profits is dependent upon the profit made by the fiduciary, not the loss suffered by the beneficiary. **11–41**

Mr Patten also relied on *Jaffray v Marshall*,[90] where the principles applicable in an action for an account of profits were, to my mind wrongly, applied to a claim for compensation for breach of trust. In my judgment that case was wrongly decided not only because the wrong principle was applied but also because the judge awarded compensation by assessing the quantum on an assumption (viz. that the house in question would have been sold at a particular date) when he found as a fact that such sale would not have taken place even if there had been no breach of trust. **11–42**

For these reasons I reach the conclusion that, on the facts which must currently be assumed, Target has not demonstrated that it is entitled to any compensation for breach of trust. Assuming that moneys would have been forthcoming from some other source to complete the purchase from Mirage if the moneys had not been wrongly provided by Redferns in breach of trust, Target obtained exactly what it would have obtained had no breach occurred, i.e. a valid security for the sum advanced. Therefore, on the assumption made, Target has suffered no compensatable loss. Redferns are entitled to leave to defend the breach of trust claim. **11–43**

However, I find it very difficult to make that assumption of fact. There must be a high probability that, at trial, it will emerge that the use of Target's money to pay for the purchase from Mirage and the other intermediate transactions was a vital feature of the transaction. The circumstances of the present case are clouded by suspicion, which suspicion is not dissipated by Mr Bundy's untruthful letter dated 30 June informing Target that the purchase of the property and the charges to Target had been completed. If the moneys made available by Redferns' breach of trust were essential to enable the transaction to go through, but for Redferns' breach of trust Target would not have advanced any money. In that case the loss suffered by Target by reason of the breach of trust will be the total sum advanced to Crowngate less the proceeds of the security. It is not surprising that Mr Sumption QC was rather muted in his submission that Redferns should have had unconditional leave to defend and that the order for payment into court of £1m. should be set aside. In my judgment such an order was fully justified. **11–44**

I would therefore allow the appeal, set aside the order of the Court of Appeal and restore the order of Warner J. **11–45**

B. Reparation Claims

Reparation claims are claims that trustees should make good the harm which the beneficiaries have suffered as a consequence of the trustees' breach of duty. They depend on the assertion that the trustees have committed a wrong,[91] and the award made is calculated by reference to the loss **11–46**

[88] Lord Browne-Wilkinson's emphasis.
[89] (1878) 12 Ch.D. 738.
[90] [1993] 1 W.L.R. 1285.
[91] *Partington v Reynolds* (1858) 4 Drew 253 at 255–256; *Dowse v Gorton* [1891] A.C. 190 at 202; *Re Stevens* [1898] 1 Ch. 162 at 170.

suffered by the beneficiaries,[92] including the loss of a chance to avoid a detriment or make a gain.[93] The beneficiaries must prove that their loss has been factually caused by the trustees' breach of duty, using a "but-for" causation test in all cases, regardless of whether the breach was innocent, negligent or fraudulent.[94] Canadian authorities also indicate that their claims are subject to the principle of novus actus interveniens,[95] and that where the beneficiaries have become aware that their trustees are not to be trusted, losses flowing from clearly unreasonable behaviour by the beneficiaries thereafter will be judged to have been caused by this behaviour and not by the breach.[96]

11–47 A reparation claim might be brought, for example, where a trustee fails to exhibit the requisite degree of care in negligently making an authorised investment which subsequently declines in value,[97] or again, where he has failed to do something, e.g. to collect the rents payable on the trust property,[98] or to diversify investments,[99] or to sell particular assets,[100] or to monitor the activities of a 99 per cent owned company, as in *Bartlett v Barclays Bank Trust Co Ltd (No.2)*,[101] which is reproduced below.[102] In cases of this sort, it must be shown that the loss could not have occurred, but for the trustee's failure to do what no reasonable trustee (viz. a properly informed trustee exhibiting the due standard of care) could have failed to do. Proving this can be difficult,[103] but it seems that a claim would lie where trustees take a positive decision to take specific action, e.g. to sell particular shares as soon as practicable, and then fail to implement their decision without any conscious reason. Another way of analysing this situation, however, would be to draw an analogy with the case where a trust instrument requires a particular original investment to be sold as soon as practicable. If the trustees fail to perform this duty, then a substitutive performance claim will lie against them for the amount that would have been realised if they had sold investment within a reasonable time.[104]

11–48 In the *Bartlett* case, Brightman L.J. thought that where trustees are ordered to pay money to make good the harm caused to the beneficiaries by the trustees' negligence, the award is "not readily distinguishable from damages except with the aid of a powerful legal microscope."[105] This comment was later echoed by Millett L.J. in *Bristol & West BS v Mothew*, who held that:[106]

---

92 *Elder's Trustee and Executor Co Ltd v Higgins* (1963) 113 C.L.R. 426 at 453; *Fales v Canada Permanent Trust Co* [1977] 2 S.C.R. 302 at 320.

93 *Sanders v Parry* [1967] 1 W.L.R. 753 at 767; *Nestlé v National Westminster Bank Plc* [1993] 1 W.L.R. 1260 at 1269; *Colour Control Centre Pty Ltd v Ty* N.S.W. Sup. Ct. (Eq. Div.) July 24, 1995; *Bank of New Zealand v New Zealand Guardian Trust Co Ltd* [1999] 1 N.Z.L.R. 664 at 685–686.

94 *Target Holdings Ltd v Redferns* [1996] A.C. 421 at 436; *Collins v Brebner* [2000] Lloyds Rep. P.N. 587; *Hulbert v Avens* [2003] EWHC 76 (Ch) at [56]; *Gwembe Valley Development Co Ltd v Koshy (No.3)* [2004] 1 B.C.L.C. 131 at [147]. But cf. *Bairstow v Queen's Moat Houses Plc* [2001] 2 B.C.L.C. 531 at [53]–[54]. On the question whether reparation claims are subject to a remoteness cap, see S.B. Elliott, "Remoteness Criteria in Equity" (2002) 65 M.L.R. 588; and also *Olszanecki v Hillocks* [2004] W.T.L.R. 975.

95 *Hodgkinson v Simms* [1994] 3 S.C.R. 377 at 443; *Waxman v Waxman* (2004) 7 I.T.E.L.R. 162 at [663].

96 *Canson Enterprises Ltd v Boughton & Co* [1991] 3 S.C.R. 534 at 554, endorsed in *Corporaçion del Cobre de Chile v Sogemin Metals Ltd* [1997] 1 W.L.R. 1396 at 1403–1404. See too *Lipkin Gorman v Karpnale Ltd* [1992] 4 All E.R. 331 at 361.

97 In these circumstances no question can arise of the beneficiaries choosing whether to adopt or reject the transaction: the investment forms part of the trust estate, but the trustee may be personally liable to pay compensation for the loss caused by his negligence: *Re Salmon* (1888) 42 Ch.D. 351 at 369 and 371.

98 *M'Donnel v White* (1865) 9 HLC 570 at 584.

99 *Nestlé v National Westminster Bank* [1993] 1 W.L.R. 1265 at 1281; *Re Mulligan* [1998] 1 N.Z.L.R. 181.

100 *Wight v Olswang (No.2)* [2000] W.T.L.R. 783, reversed [2001] W.T.L.R. 291; *Re Ambrazevicius Estate* (2002) 164 Man. R. (2d) 5.

101 [1980] Ch. 515.

102 At paras 11–52 ff.

103 Consider *Nestlé v National Westminster Bank* [1993] 1 W.L.R. 1265 discussed at para.9–77.

104 *Fry v Fry* (1859) 27 Beav. 144; *Fales v Canada Permanent Trust Co* (1976) 70 D.L.R. (3d) 257 at 274.

105 [1980] Ch. 515 at 545.

106 [1998] Ch. 1 at 18, adopting *Permanent BS v Wheeler* (1994) 11 W.A.R. 187 at 237. See too *Bank of New Zealand v New Zealand Guardian Trust Co Ltd* [1999] 1 N.Z.L.R. 664 at 687; *Hilton v Barker Booth & Eastwood (a firm)* [2005] 1 W.L.R. 1597 at [29]; *Langlands v SG Hambros Trust Co (Jersey) Ltd* [2007] EWHC 627 (Ch) at [25].

> "Equitable compensation for breach of the duty of skill and care [owed by a fiduciary] resembles common law damages in that it is awarded by way of compensation to the plaintiff for his loss. There is no reason in principle why the common law rules of causation, remoteness of damage and measure of damages should not be applied by analogy in such a case. It should not be confused with equitable compensation for breach of fiduciary duty, which may be awarded in lieu of rescission or specific restitution."

It is a controversial question whether trustees and other fiduciaries who harm their principals by their negligent acts or omissions should be treated in the same way as tortfeasors at common law, or whether the fact that they are fiduciaries justifies treating them more stringently. When considering this question it is important to distinguish clearly between substitutive performance claims and reparation claims, and to bear in mind that either type of claim might lie on some sets of facts, e.g. where trustees make an unauthorised negligent investment. As Millet L.J. stresses in the passage quoted above, analogies with tort claims are simply inapt if a substitutive performance claim is brought, but we may legitimately ask whether a reparation claim should be governed by rules of causation, remoteness and contributory negligence which are identical with, or more claimant-friendly than, the rules which apply to tort claims for compensatory damages. **11–49**

The authorities are divided on this point. Proponents of the stringent view emphasise that a fiduciary and his principal are not "independent and equal actors, concerned primarily with their own self-interest" but parties in a special relationship under which one "pledges itself to act in the best interest of the other", so that "when breach occurs, the balance favours the person wronged".[107] Proponents of the opposite view deny that there is a valid reason to treat a trustee or other fiduciary differently from anyone else who injures another person by his negligence, and that "regardless of the doctrinal underpinning, plaintiffs should not be able to recover higher damage awards merely because their claim is characterised as a breach of fiduciary duty, as opposed to breach of contract or tort."[108] **11–50**

This debate is often conducted in all-or-nothing terms, but in our view the best way forward is for the courts to acknowledge that it can be appropriate to treat different kinds of fiduciary in different ways.[109] For example, there is an important difference between traditional family trusts and modern commercial trusts for absolutely entitled beneficiaries where the parties are on a more equal footing and the management role of the trustee is extensive and complex. In the latter case at least, the justification is much weaker for imposing a more stringent liability for negligent conduct than the trustee would incur at common law. **11–51**

---

107 *Canson Enterprises Ltd v Boughton & Co* [1991] 3 S.C.R. 534 at 543, per McLachlin J., quoted with approval in *Youyang Pty Ltd v Minter Ellison Morris Fletcher* (2003) 212 C.L.R. 484 at [40]. See too *Norberg v Wynrib* [1992] 2 S.C.R. 226 at 272, quoted with approval in *Pilmer v Duke Group Ltd (in liq.)* (2001) 207 C.L.R. 165 at [71]; *Maguire v Makaronis* (1997) 188 C.L.R. 449 at 473. The argument that equity should exert prophylactic pressure on fiduciaries by stringent treatment of their breaches of skill and care as well as their breaches of fiduciary duty has been made by Joshua Getzler in three articles: "Equitable Compensation and the Regulation of Fiduciary Relationships" in P. Birks and F.D. Rose (eds), *Restitution and Equity: Resulting Trusts and Equitable Compensation* (2000); "Duty of Care" in P. Birks and A. Pretto (eds), *Breach of Trust* (2002); "Am I My Beneficiary's Keeper? Fusion and Loss-Based Fiduciary Remedies" in S. Degeling and J. Edelman (eds), *Equity in Commercial Law* (2005).

108 *Martin v Goldfarb* (1998) 41 O.R. (3d) 161 at 173, per Finlayson J.A. See too *Day v Mead* [1987] 2 N.Z.L.R. 443 at 451; *Canson Enterprises Ltd v Boughton & Co* [1991] 3 S.C.R. 534 at 585–589, per La Forest J.; *Waxman v Waxman* (2004) 7 I.T.E.L.R. 162 at [660]–[662]; J. Edelman and S. B. Elliott, "Money Remedies against Trustees" (2004) 18 Tru L.I. 116 at pp. 119–122; A.S. Burrows, *Remedies for Torts and Breach of Contract* 3rd edn (2004), at pp. 600–606.

109 See further C.E.F. Rickett, "Compensating for Loss in Equity: Choosing the Right Horse for Each Course" in P. Birks and F.D. Rose (eds), *Restitution and Equity, Vol.1* (2000); D.J. Hayton "Unique Rules for the Unique Institution, the Trust" in S. Degeling and J. Edelman (eds), *Equity in Commercial Law* (2005).

BARTLETT v BARCLAYS BANK TRUST CO LTD

Chancery Division [1980] Ch. 515; [1980] 1 All E.R. 139

11–52 The claimant sued the trustees for failing to exercise proper supervision over the management of the family company, "BTL", which they controlled through possession of a 99.8 per cent shareholding. Subsequently BTL became a wholly-owned subsidiary of another company, "BTH", which the trustees also controlled through a 99.8 per cent shareholding. The trustees' failure to supervise BTL and then BTH led to the company losing over £1/2 million in a disastrous property speculation.

11–53 BRIGHTMAN J.: The situation may be summed up as follows. BTH made a large loss as a result of the involvement of itself and BTL in the Old Bailey project. This loss reduced the value of the BTH shares and thereby caused a loss to the trust fund of the 1920 settlement. The bank, had it acted in time, could be reason of its shareholding have stopped the board of BTL embarking on the Old Bailey project; and, had it acted in time, could have stopped the board of BTL and later the board of BTH (it is unnecessary to differentiate) from continuing with the project; and could, had it acted in time, have required BTH to sell its interest in Far to Stock Conversion on the no-loss or small-loss terms which (as I find) were available for the asking. This would not have necessitated the draconian course of threatening to remove, or actually removing, the board in favour of compliant directors. The members of the board were reasonable persons, and would (as I find) have followed any reasonable policy desired by the bank had the bank's wishes been indicated to the board. The loss to the trust fund could have been avoided (as I find) without difficulty or disruption had the bank been prepared to lead, in a broad sense, rather than to follow.

11–54 What, then, was the duty of the bank and did the bank fail in its duty? It does not follow that because a trustee could have prevented a loss it is therefore liable for the loss. The questions which I must ask myself are: (i) what was the duty of the bank as the holder of 99.8 per cent of the shares in BTL and BTH? (2) Was the bank in breach of duty in any and if so what respect? (3) If so, did that breach of duty cause the loss which was suffered by the trust estate? (4) If so, to what extent is the bank liable to make good that loss? In approaching these questions, I bear in mind that the attack on the bank is based, not on wrongful acts, but on wrongful omissions, that is to say, non-feasance not misfeasance.

11–55 The cases establish that it is the duty of a trustee to conduct the business of the trust with the same care as an ordinary prudent man of business would extend towards his own affairs.[110] In applying this principle, Lindley L.J. added in *Re Whiteley*:[111]

> ". . . care must be taken not to lose sight of the fact that the business of the trustee, and the business which the ordinary prudent man is supposed to be conducting for himself, is the business of investing money for the benefit of persons who are to enjoy it at some future time, and not for the sole benefit of the person entitled to the present income. The duty of a trustee is not to take such care only as a prudent man would take if he had only himself to consider; the duty rather is to take such care as an ordinary prudent man would take if he were minded to make an investment for the benefit of other people for whom he felt morally bound to provide. The is the kind of business the ordinary prudent man is supposed to be engaged in; and unless this is borne in mind the standard of a trustee's duty will be fixed too low; lower than it has ever yet been fixed, and lower certainly than the House of Lords or this Court endeavoured to fix it in [*Re Speight*]."

11–56 . . . If the trust had existed without the incorporation of BTL, so that the bank held the freehold and leasehold properties and other assets of BTL directly on the trusts of the settlement, it would in my opinion have been a clear breach of trust for the bank to have hazarded trust money in the Old Bailey development project in partnership with Stock Conversion. The Old Bailey project was a gamble, because it involved buying into the site at prices in excess of the investment values of the properties, with no certainty

110 See *Re Speight* (1883) 22 Ch.D. 727 at 739, per Jessel M.R., and 762, per Bowen L.J.; affirmed on appeal (1883) 9 App. Cas. 1., and see Lord Blackburn at 19.

111 (1886) 33 Ch.D. 347 at 355.

or probability, with no more than a chance, that planning permission could be obtained for a financially viable redevelopment, that the numerous proprietors would agree to sell out or join in the scheme, that finance would be available on acceptable terms, and that the development would be completed, or at least become a marketable asset, before the time came to start winding up the trust. However one looks at it, the project was a hazardous speculation on which no trustee could properly have ventured without explicit authority in the trust instrument. I therefore hold that the entire expenditure in the Old Bailey project would have been incurred in breach of trust, had the money been spent by the bank itself. The fact that it was a risk acceptable to the board of a wealthy company like Stock Conversion has little relevance.

I turn to the question, what was the duty of the bank as the holder of shares in BTL and BTH? I will first answer this question without regard to the position of the bank as a specialist trustee, to which I will advert later. The bank, as trustee, was bound to act in relation to the shares and to the controlling position which they conferred, in the same manner as a prudent man of business. The prudent man of business will act in such manner as is necessary to safeguard his investment. He will do this in two ways. If facts come to his knowledge which tell him that the company's affairs are not being conducted as they should be, or which put him on enquiry, he will take appropriate action. Appropriate action will no doubt consist in the first instance of enquiry of and consultation with the directors, and in the last but most unlikely resort, the convening of a general meeting to replace one or more directors. What the prudent man of business will not do is to content himself with the receipt of such information on the affairs of the company as a shareholder ordinarily receives at annual general meetings. Since he has the power to do so, he will go further and see that he has sufficient information to enable him to make a responsible decision from time to time either to let matters proceed as they are proceeding, or to intervene if he is dissatisfied. This topic was considered by Cross J. in *Re Lucking's Will Trusts*.[112] In that case nearly 70 per cent of the shares in the company were held by two trustees, L and B, as part of the estate of the deceased; about 29 per cent belonged to L in his own right, and 1 per cent belonged to L's wife. The directors in 1954 were Mr and Mrs L and D, who was the manager of the business. In 1956 B was appointed trustee to act jointly with L. The company was engaged in the manufacture and sale of shoe accessories. It had a small factory employing about 20 people, and one or two travellers. It also had an agency in France. D wrongfully drew some £15,000 from the company's bank account in excess of his remuneration, and later became bankrupt. The money was lost. Cross J. said this:[113] 11–57

> "The conduct of the defendant trustees is, I think, to be judged by the standard applied in *Re Speight*, namely, that a trustee is only bound to conduct the business of the trust in such a way as an ordinary prudent man would conduct a business of his own. Now, what steps, if any, does a reasonably prudent man who finds himself a majority shareholder in a private company take with regard to the management of the company's affairs? He does not, I think, content himself with such information as to the management of the company's affairs as he is entitled to as shareholder, but ensures that he is represented on the board. He may be prepared to run the business himself as managing director or, at least, to become a non-executive director while having the business managed by someone else. Alternatively, he may find someone who will act as his nominee on the board and report to him from time to time as to the company's affairs. In the same way, as it seems to me, trustees holding a controlling interest ought to ensure so far as they can that they have such information as to the progress of the company's affairs as directors would have. If they sit back and allow the company to be run by the minority shareholder and receive no more information than shareholders are entitled to, they do so at their risk if things go wrong."

I do not understand Cross J. to have been saying that in every case where trustees have a controlling interest in a company it is their duty to ensure that one of their number is a director or that they have a nominee on the board who will report from time to time on the affairs of the company. He was merely outlining convenient methods by which a prudent man of business (as also a trustee) with a controlling interest in a private company, can place himself in a position to make an informed decision whether any action is appropriate to be taken for the protection of his asset. Other methods may be equally satisfactory and 11–58

[112] [1968] 1 W.L.R. 866.
[113] [1968] 1 W.L.R. 866 at 874–875.

convenient, depending on the circumstances of the individual case. Alternatives which spring to mind are the receipt of the copies of the agenda and minutes of board meetings if regularly held, the receipt of monthly management accounts in the case of a trading concern, or quarterly reports. Every case will depend on its own facts. The possibilities are endless. It would be useless, indeed misleading, to seek to lay down a general rule. The purpose to be achieved is not that of monitoring every move of the directors, but of making it reasonably probable, so far as circumstances permit, that the trustee or (as in *Re Lucking's Will Trusts*) one of them will receive an adequate flow of information in time to enable the trustees to make use of their controlling interest should this be necessary for the protection of their trust asset, namely the shareholding. The obtaining of information is not an end in itself, but merely a means of enabling the trustees to safeguard the interest of their beneficiaries.

11–59 . . . So far, I have applied the test of the ordinary prudent man of business. Although I am not aware that the point has previously been considered, except briefly in *Re Waterman's Will Trusts*,[114] I am of opinion that a higher duty of care is plainly due from someone like a trust corporation which carries on a specialised business of trust management. A trust corporation holds itself out in its advertising literature as being above ordinary mortals. With a specialist staff of trained trust officers and managers, with ready access to financial information and professional advice, dealing with and solving trust problems day after day, the trust corporation holds itself out, and rightly, as capable of providing an expertise which it would be unrealistic to expect and unjust to demand from the ordinary prudent man or woman who accepts, probably unpaid and sometimes reluctantly from a sense of family duty, the burdens of a trusteeship. Just as, under the law of contract, a professional person possessed of a particular skill is liable for breach of contract if he neglects to use the skill and experience which he professes, so I think that a professional corporate trustee is liable for breach of trust if loss is caused to the trust fund because it neglects to exercise the special care and skill which it professes to have. The advertising literature of the bank was not in evidence (other than the scale of fees) but counsel for the bank did not dispute that trust corporations, including the bank, hold themselves out as possessing a superior ability for the conduct of trust business, and in any event I would take judicial notice of that fact. Having expressed my view of the higher duty required from a trust corporation, I should add that the bank's counsel did not dispute the proposition.

11–60 In my judgment the bank wrongfully and in breach of trust neglected to ensure that it received an adequate flow of information concerning the intentions and activities of the boards of BTL and BTH. It was not proper for the bank to confine itself to the receipt of the annual balance sheet and profit and loss account, detailed annual financial statements and the chairman's report and statement, and to attendance at the annual general meetings and the luncheons that followed, which were the limits of the bank's regular sources of information. Had the bank been in receipt of more frequent information it would have been able to step in and stop, and ought to have stopped, Mr Roberts and the board embarking on the Old Bailey project. That project was imprudent and hazardous and wholly unsuitable for a trust whether undertaken by the bank direct or through the medium of its wholly owned company. Even without the regular flow of information which the bank ought to have had, it knew enough to put it on enquiry. There were enough obvious points at which the bank should have intervened and asked questions. Assuming, as I do, that the questions would have been answered truthfully, the bank would have discovered the gamble on which Mr Roberts and his board were about to embark in relation to the Old Bailey site, and it could have, and should have, stopped the initial move towards disaster, and later on arrested further progress towards disaster. . . .

11–61 I hold that the bank failed in its duty whether it is judged by the standard of the prudent man of business or of the skilled trust corporation. The bank's breach of duty caused the loss which was suffered by the trust estate. If the bank had intervened as it could and should have, that loss would not have been incurred. By "loss", I mean the depreciation which took place in the market value of the BTL and BTH shares, by comparison with the value which the shares would have commanded if the loss on the Old Bailey project had not been incurred, and reduction of dividends through loss of income. The bank is liable for the loss so suffered by the trust estate, except to the extent that I shall heareafter indicate. . . .

11–62 The bank also relies on clause 18 of the settlement. Clause 18 entitled the bank to:

[114] [1968] 1 W.L.R. 866.

> "act in relation to [BTL] or any other company and the shares securities and properties thereof in such way as it shall think best calculated to benefit the trust premises and as if it was the absolute owner of such shares securities and property."

In my judgment this a clause which confers on the bank power to engage in a transaction which might otherwise be outside the scope of its authority; it is not an indemnity protecting the bank against liability for a transaction which is a breach of trust because it is one that a prudent man of business would have eschewed. . . .

11–63 Section 61 of the Trustee Act 1925 is pleaded. There is no doubt that the bank acted honestly. I do not think it acted reasonably. Nor do I think it would be fair to excuse the bank at the expense of the beneficiaries.

11–64 There remains this defence, which I take from paragraph 26 of the amended pleading:

> "In about 1963 the Old Company purchased a site at Woodbridge Road, Guildford, pursuant to the policy pleaded in paragraph 19 hereof, for the sum of £79,000, and re-sold the same for £350,000 to MEPC Ltd in 1973. The net profit resulting from such sale was £271,000. If, which is denied, the Defendant is liable for breach of trust, whether as alleged in the amended Statement of Claim or otherwise, the Defendant claims credit for such sum of £271,000 or other sum found to be gained in taking any accounts or inquiries."

11–65 The general rule as stated in all the textbooks, with some reservations, is that where a trustee is liable in respect of distinct breaches of trust, one of which has resulted in a loss and the other in a gain, he is not entitled to set off the gain against the loss, unless they arise in the same transaction. . . . The relevant cases are, however, not altogether easy to reconcile. All are centenarians and none is quite like the present. The Guildford development stemmed from exactly the same policy and (to a lesser degree because it proceeded less far) exemplified the same folly as the Old Bailey project. Part of the profit was in fact used to finance the Old Bailey disaster. By sheer luck the gamble paid off handsomely, on capital account. I think it would be unjust to deprive the bank of this element of salvage in the course of assessing the cost of the shipwreck. My order will therefore reflect the bank's right to an appropriate set-off. . . .

C. *Accountability*

11–66 At the core of an express trust is the trustees' duty to produce accounts that are available for the beneficiaries to examine. The beneficiaries are entitled to the production of these accounts without any court order, but they can also obtain an order for an account as a means of enforcing their rights to performance of the trustees' primary duties and reparation for losses flowing from the trustees' breaches of duty.[115] Lewison J. explained this process in *Ultraframe (UK) Ltd v Fielding*:[116]

> "The taking of an account is the means by which a beneficiary requires a trustee to justify his stewardship of trust property. The trustee must show what he has done with that property. If the beneficiary is dissatisfied with the way that a trustee has dealt with trust assets, he may surcharge or falsify the account. He surcharges the account when he alleges that the trustee has not obtained for the benefit of the trust all that he might have done, if he had exercised due care and diligence. If the allegation is proved, then the account is taken as if the trustee had received, for the benefit of

---

115 "Trustees who indefensibly fail to produce accounts may be ordered to pay not only the costs of proceedings to obtain the accounts but also the costs of taking the account which is ordered": *Mason v Coleman* [2007] EWHC 3149 (Ch) at [93]. See too *Kemp v Burn* (1863) 4 Giff. 348; *Jefferys v Marshall* (1870) 23 L.T. 548.

116 [2007] W.T.L.R. 835 at [1513].

the trust, what he would have received if he had exercised due care and diligence. The beneficiary falsifies the account when he alleges that the trustee has applied trust property in a way that he should not have done (e.g. by making an unauthorised investment). If the allegation is proved, then the account will be taken as if the expenditure had not been made; and as if the unauthorised investment had not formed part of the assets of the trust. Of course, if the unauthorised investment has appreciated in value, the beneficiary may choose not to falsify the account: in which case the asset will remain a trust asset and the expenditure on it will be allowed in taking the account."

11–67 Before the Judicature Acts, beneficiaries could only make hostile claims against their trustees by bringing an administration suit. This was a suit for the judicial execution of the trust, asking the court to assume responsibility for the trust's performance. Beneficiaries can still bring full execution proceedings, but they can now also bring narrower proceedings for discrete relief by asking the court for an order that the trustees should present an account of their dealings for judicial scrutiny, adding the common form plea for administration of the trust estate "if and so far as necessary".[117]

11–68 As explained in *Glazier v Australian Men's Health (No.2)*,[118] parts of which are reproduced below,[119] there are three types of accounting order which a court might make. An order for an account in common form is the most common, as the name suggests. The trustees are directed to submit a set of accounts which identify the original trust property, what the trustees have received, what they have disbursed for costs and expenses,[120] what they have distributed to the beneficiaries, and what they have left in hand. These accounts can then be challenged by the beneficiaries, but the fact that a court has ordered trustees to present accounts in this form need not imply that they have done anything wrong, as orders for common accounts can be made simply in order to clarify matters.[121] In contrast, an order for an account on the basis of wilful default is entirely grounded on the trustees' misconduct,[122] and requires them to account not only for what they have received but also for what they would have received if they had not committed a breach of duty.[123] The term "wilful default" is a misleading one in this context since it encompasses all breaches of duty, running from inadvertent non-compliance with the terms of the trust through to deliberate fraud.[124] Finally, an order for an account of profits requires the trustees to account for specific gains.

11–69 An account of profits will be ordered in connection with a claim that the trustees should be required to hand over improper gains, and an account on the basis of wilful default will be ordered in connection with a reparation claim. An account in common form can be ordered where the beneficiaries make a claim for substitutive performance; however, it can also be used where they seek reparation. In all cases, the onus lies on the trustees to prove and justify their records, and evidential presumptions are made against them if they fail to do so.[125] In the event that a court decides, following its scrutiny of the

---

117 *Iliffe v Trafford* [2002] W.T.L.R. 507 at [8].
118 [2001] NSWSC 6. Austin J.'s decision was overturned on appeal, but nothing was said by the NSWCA that contradicted his structural analysis of accounting in equity: *Meehan v Glazier Holdings Pty Ltd* (2002) 54 N.S.W.L.R. 146.
119 At paras 11–73 ff.
120 Note the Trustee Act 2000 s.31, discussed at paras 8–72 ff., which empowers trustees to take properly incurred expenses out of the trust funds. For discussion of the question whether trustees can recover an indemnity for expenses incurred in the course of unauthorised conduct, see *Fitzwood Pty Ltd v Unique Goal Pty Ltd (in liq.)* (2001) 188 A.L.R. 566.
121 *Partington v Reynolds* (1858) 4 Drew 253 at 256.
122 *Partington* at 256.
123 *Re Tebbs* [1976] 1 W.L.R. 924; *Bartlett v Barclays Bank Co Ltd* [1980] Ch. 15; *Coulthard v Disco Mix Club Ltd* [1999] 2 All E.R. 457 at 481; *Armitage v Nurse* [1998] Ch. 241 at 252; *Iliffe v Trafford* [2002] W.T.L.R. 507 at [9].
124 *Walker v Symonds* (1818) 3 Swans 1 at 69; *Re Chapman* [1896] 2 Ch. 763 at 776 and 779–780. See too J.H. Stannard "Wilful Default" [1979] Conv. 345, esp. 348.
125 *Campbell v Hogg* [1930] 3 DLR 673 (P.C.); *Maintemp Heating & Air Conditioning Inc v Monat Developments Inc* (2002) 59 O.R. (3d) 270 at [40]–[44]; *Sinclair v Sinclair* [2009] EWHC 926 (Ch) at [39]–[41].

trustees' accounts, that they owe the beneficiaries a personal liability of some kind, then different forms of order can be made against them, according to the nature of the trust. Where the trust is absolute and there is no need to reconstitute the fund, the court can simply order them to transfer trust assets or pay money directly to the beneficiaries.[126] Where the trust is still on foot, the trustees will be ordered to reconstitute the fund in a proper state, or where they have been replaced by new trustees, to transfer assets or pay money to the new trustees, to be held by them under the terms of the trust.[127]

The various types of claim which can be brought against trustees are mediated through proceedings for an account in different ways. In the case of a substitutive performance claim where the trustees have made an unauthorised distribution, the court will not permit the trustees to enter the distribution into the accounts as an outgoing as it will not allow them to say that they acted in breach of duty.[128] Instead, they will be treated as though they have spent their own money and kept the trust assets in hand. The accounts will be "falsified" to delete the unauthorised outgoing, and the trustees will be required to produce the relevant trust property in specie or pay a money substitute out of their own pockets.[129] **11–70**

In *Bonham v Blake Lapthorn Linell (a firm)*[130] an exemption clause provided that trustees would incur no liability for loss unless it was caused by their wilful and individual fraud or wrongdoing. However the beneficiaries sought to avoid the operation of this clause with the following argument. Where a trustee makes an unauthorised payment out of trust funds, the beneficiaries' remedy is to falsify the accounts—i.e. to insist on accounts which do not show the disbursement, and to require the trustee to make up any deficiency out of his own pocket. This being so, a clause exempting liability for "loss" would not apply in such a case, because the law does not recognise unauthorised payments on the taking of accounts, and so it cannot be said that a "loss" has ever taken place. Kitchin J. rejected this, stating that:[131] **11–71**

> "just because the account cannot be drawn so as to reflect the loss caused by the trustee's default it does not follow that the trust has not sustained a loss. The drawing of the account is the formal process by means of which the extent of the liability to reconstitute the trust is identified. It enables the parties to compare the accounts as drawn with the actual state of the trust. Following the drawing of the account, there remains an obligation to restore the deficiency, and I believe that deficiency is a loss."

Reparation claims are brought into the conceptual scheme of the accounts in a rather different way. The loss claimed by the beneficiaries is translated into an accounting item by "surcharging" the trustees with the amount of the loss as if the trustees had already received this amount for the beneficiaries. They must then pay an equivalent amount into the trust funds out of their pockets in order to balance the accounts.[132] Essentially the same procedure is followed in the case of a claim for unauthorised profits: the trustees are treated as though they had received this sum for the benefit of the beneficiaries, and the accounts are surcharged accordingly. As a sanction to underpin and emphasise the trustee's duty of loyalty in cases where trustees have improperly received particular assets, e.g. shares, **11–72**

---

126 *Target Holdings Ltd v Redferns* [1996] A.C. 421 at 435; *Roxborough v Rothmans of Pall Mall Australia Ltd* (2002) 185 A.L.R. 335 at 353.

127 *Partridge v Equity Trustees Executors and Agency Co Ltd* (1947) 75 C.L.R. 149; *Hillsdown Plc v Pensions Ombudsman* [1997] 1 All E.R. 862 at 897; *Chellaram v Chellaram (No.2)* [2002] 3 All E.R. 17 at [159]; *Patel v London Borough of Brent* [2004] W.T.L.R. 577 esp. at [32].

128 *Re Smith* [1896] 1 Ch. 71 at 77; *Re Biss, deceased* [1903] 2 Ch. 40.

129 *Knott v Cottee* (1852) 16 Beav. 77 at 79–80; *Re Bennion* (1889) 60 L.T. 859; *Re Salmon* (1889) 42 Ch.D. 351 at 357.

130 [2007] W.T.L.R. 189.

131 *Bonham* at [180].

132 *Meehan v Glazier Holdings Pty. Ltd* (2002) 54 N.S.W.L.R. 146 at 149–150; *Re Ambrazevicius Estate* (2002) 164 Man. R. (2d) 5.

in breach of duty, they will be liable to account to the beneficiaries for the highest market value of the assets between the date of breach and the date of judgment. The justification for this rule is that the trustees owe a continuing duty throughout this period to realise the assets for the beneficiaries at the most opportune moment.[133] Where trustees divert business contracts to themselves in breach of fiduciary duty, they must account for all the profits which are properly attributable to the breach, but need not account for profits which they make through their legitimate business activities.[134]

GLAZIER v AUSTRALIAN MEN'S HEALTH (NO.2)

New South Wales Supreme Court [2000] NSWSC 6 (reversed in *Meehan v Glazier Holdings Pty Ltd* (2002) 54 N.S.W.L.R. 146, without casting doubt on the following summary of legal principles)

AUSTIN J.:

Accounting for Administration in Common Form or for Wilful Default, and Accounting for Profit or Replenishing Loss

11–73 In equity an order for the taking of accounts may be made in a wide variety of circumstances. In the present context it is important to distinguish between two kinds of orders. One kind (which I shall call an order for an account of administration) is made where the overall administration of a business enterprise or fund or other property is to be established or accounted for. Another kind (which I shall call an order for an account of profits) is made to provide a remedy for specific equitable wrongdoing.

Order for Account of Administration

11–74 An order for an account of administration is made for the taking of accounts of money received and disbursed by the person who is responsible for the administration of a business enterprise or fund or other property, and for payment of any amount found to be due by that person upon the taking of the accounts. For example, the court routinely orders the taking of accounts of the administration of an estate by an executor, or upon the dissolution of a partnership, or of the administration of property by a mortgagee in possession, or of a trust fund such as a solicitor's trust account. In such a case the making of the order need not imply any wrongdoing by the defendant.

Order for an Account of Administration in Common Form

11–75 The usual form of order, referred to as an order in common form or for common accounts, requires the defendant to account only for what he or she has actually received, and his or her disbursement and distribution of it. The defendant prepares accounts and it is open to the other parties to surcharge or falsify items in those accounts. A surcharge is the showing of an omission for which credit ought to have been given, while a falsification is the showing of a charge which has been wrongly inserted, the falsifying party alleging that money shown in the account as paid was either not paid or improperly paid[135] . . .

Order for an Account of Administration on Basis of Wilful Default

11–76 Sometimes the court orders that accounts be taken on the basis of wilful default (or in the earlier cases, wilful neglect or default). The order is "entirely grounded on misconduct", the defendant being required to account not only for what he or she has received, but also for what he or she might have received had it not been for the default.[136] To obtain an order for the taking of accounts in common form against an executor, for example, the plaintiff need only show that the defendant is the executor, and need not show

---

133 *Nant-y-glo and Blaina Ironworks Co v Grave* (1878) 12 Ch.D. 738, accepted in *Target Holdings Ltd v Redferns* [1996] A.C. 421 at 440; *Re Caerphilly Colliery Co* (1877) L.R. 5 Ch.D. 336 at 341, endorsed in *Att.-Gen. for Hong Kong v Reid* [1994] 1 A.C. 324 at 335.

134 *CMS Dolphin Ltd v Simonet* [2001] 2 B.C.L.C. 704 at [97]. The timing of the account is helpfully discussed in *Crown Dilmun v Sutton* [2004] 1 B.C.L.C. 468 at [205]–[214].

135 G.P. Stuckey and C.D. Parker (eds) *Parker's Practice in Equity (New South Wales)* 2nd edn (1949), p.269.

136 *Partington v Reynolds* (1858) 4 Drew 253 at 255–256.

anything about the defendant's dealings with the estate; whereas to obtain an order on the basis of wilful default the plaintiff must allege and prove "that there is some part of the deceased's personal estate which ought to have been and might have been received by the defendant, and which he has omitted to receive by his own wilful neglect or default".[137]

It appears that in the present context, the concept of "wilful default" is confined to cases where there has been "a loss of assets received, or assets which might have been received".[138] In that case the failure of executors to cause the proceeds of an insurance policy to be paid to the policy's mortgagee for nearly seven years, during which time interest accrued to the mortgagee, was held not to amount to wilful default for the purposes of an application for an accounting on that basis. However, the concept is evidently not confined to cases of conscious wrongdoing.[139] Obviously the concept here is not necessarily the same as the concept of "wilful default" used in other parts of the law.[140] **11–77**

As will be seen the court may make an order that general accounts be taken on the footing of wilful default if at least one instance of wilful default has been proved. However the court has a discretion whether to make such an order. The test is this: "is the past conduct of the trustees such as to give rise to a reasonable prima facie inference that other breaches of trust not yet known to the plaintiff or the court have occurred?"[141] **11–78**

An order for accounts based on wilful default has the effect of casting a much more substantial burden of proof on the accounting party than applies in the case of common accounts. On a falsification, the onus is on the accounting party to justify the account, unless the account is a settled account. . . .[142] An accounting on the footing of wilful default leads to an order requiring the defendant to replenish funds wrongfully depleted by him or her and in that sense to make restitution for the benefit of the plaintiff. **11–79**

Order for Account of Profits for Specific Equitable Wrongdoing

An order for an account of profits is made where specific wrongdoing such as breach of trust or fiduciary duty has been found or is suspected. It is usually ancillary to the grant of an injunction.[143] An order for an account of profits typically requires the wrongdoer to account to the plaintiff for profits made in consequence of the wrongdoing, although the court has a discretion to fashion the order to suit the circumstances of the case, and (for example) will not order the defendant to account for the entire profits of a business established in breach of fiduciary duty, where it would be inequitable to do so.[144] The accounting relates to specified gains rather than the general administration of a fund. Since the order is premised upon a finding of specific wrongdoing, the distinction between an order in common form and an order on the basis of wilful default is irrelevant. **11–80**

Comparison of Order for Account of Profits with Orders for Account of Administration in Common Form and on Basis of Wilful Default

The contrast between an order for an account of profits and an order for an account of administration in common form is obvious. The former provides a remedy for specific wrongdoing, while the latter "supposes no misconduct".[145] The difference between an order for an account of profits and an order for an account of administration on the basis of wilful default is much less sharp. This is especially so when one bears in mind that an order on the footing of wilful default can be limited to an account of part only of the administration, and even to that part of the administration in respect of which wilful default has been proved (as in *Re Tebbs*). **11–81**

---

137 *Partington* at 256.

138 *Re Stevens* [1898] 1 Ch. 162 at 171.

139 *Bartlett v Barclays Trust Co Ltd* [1980] 1 Ch. 515 at 546.

140 See, e.g. *Wilkinson v Feldworth Financial Services Pty Ltd* (1998) 29 A.C.S.R. 642 at 696–700.

141 *Re Tebbs* [1976] 1 All E.R. 858 at 863; see also *Russell v Russell* (1891) 17 V.L.R. 729.

142 *Parker*, p.269; *Daniell's Practice of the High Court of Chancery* (5th edn, 1871), 1120ff. and 575ff.; *Seton's Forms of Judgment and Orders* (6th edn, 1901), Vol.II, 1356ff. and 1382ff.; and note the forms of falsification and surcharge in Miller and Horsell's *Equity Forms and Precedents* (1934), 195–196; and as to settled accounts, see *Pit v Cholmondeley* (1754) 2 Ves. 565.

143 *Colbeam Palmer Ltd v Stock Affiliates Pty Ltd* (1968) 122 C.L.R. 25 at 34.

144 *Warman International Ltd v Dwyer* (1995) 182 C.L.R. 544.

145 *Partington v Reynolds* at 256.

Confusion has arisen because in both cases, it is necessary to establish at least one instance of wrongdoing, and yet in one case the order is directed only to the specific wrongdoing that has been proved, while in the other case proof of an instance of wrongdoing leads to a process which "assumes the probability that other improper transactions may have occurred"[146] throughout the administration or some specified part of it.

11–82 There is another source of confusion between cases where it is appropriate to order the taking of accounts on the basis of wilful default, and cases where relief is sought because of a specific breach of trust or duty. In action for breach of trust or duty, an order for an account of profits is one of the many equitable remedies available if the plaintiff makes out an appropriate case. Another remedy is an order that the defendant replenish the fund that he or she has wrongfully depleted (in an administration action, this may take the form of an order charging the executor with the asset). Confusion can arise because an order of that kind is similar in effect to, though more specific than, an order for the taking of accounts on the basis of wilful default, since the latter order includes a provision requiring that the defendant replenish the fund by the amount certified to be due when accounts have been taken.

Active and Passive Misconduct

11–83 In a case where an account of administration on the basis of wilful default is appropriate, emphasis is placed on whether the defendant has failed to discharge his or her duty, rather than whether the plaintiff has established active conduct in breach of duty. This could lead one to infer that the difference between accounting on the basis of wilful default and accounting for profit is that in the first case the wrongdoing is passive whereas in the second case there is active wrongdoing. In my view that would be an oversimplification.

11–84 [His Lordship then considered *Re Wrightson*,[147] *Bartlett v Barclays Bank Trust Co (No.2)*,[148] and *Gava v Grljusich*,[149] and continued:] In my view the distinction drawn in these cases is not the mere distinction between active and passive conduct. The circumstances that give rise to a breach of trust will commonly involve active and passive elements. For example, in *Re Tebbs* the wrongdoing was active conduct, involving the sale of land at an undervalue, but it was regarded as wilful default by Slade J. and his characterisation of it was accepted by Kennedy J. in *Gava v Grljusich*.[150] In *Bartlett v Barclays Trust Co Ltd* the wrongdoing was found to be wilful default, although it involved the "active" conduct of allowing directors to occupy residential premises at an undervalue as well as the "passive" default of not intervening to prevent the unauthorised investment. In *Re Symons*,[151] the plaintiffs' complaints related to conduct with active and passive elements but the case was treated as one of wilful default. Similarly, in the present case there is evidence that the trustee failed to keep proper accounting records. That involved omission to make accurate and complete entries recording the receipt and disbursement of trust money (passive breaches), and preparation and maintenance of accounting records that were not in proper form for a trust (active conduct). More importantly, it is hard to see why in principle there should be such a dramatic difference in consequences between cases where the breach is active and cases where it is passive. The true distinction identified by the quoted passages is the distinction between an order for administration, made in cases where the defendant is required to administer a fund for the benefit of others over time, and fails to do so properly (and is therefore guilty of "passive" breaches by not doing what he or she ought to have done), and an order for an account of profits or replenishment of a fund, made in cases where the complaint is about specific instances of wrongdoing ("active" breaches, although they may be as much non-feasance as misfeasance) . . .

[146] *Re Tebbs* at 864.
[147] [1908] 1 Ch. 789.
[148] [1980] Ch. 539.
[149] [1999] WASC 13.
[150] [1999] WASC 13 at [31].
[151] (1882) 21 Ch.D. 757.

D. *Examples*

i. Making Unauthorised Investments and Negligently Investing

Where trustees make an unauthorised investment they are liable for the amount of the money improperly invested, but they are entitled to claim a credit for the sale proceeds of the property when it is sold, as held in *Knott v Cottee*,[152] which is reproduced immediately below. However, "what the prudent man should do at any time depends on the economic and financial conditions of that time—not on what judges of the past, however eminent, have held to be the prudent course in the conditions if 50 or 100 years before" as Dillon L.J. has indicated.[153] Thus, he and his brethren further indicated[154] that if a negligent investment policy (one that no prudent trustee could have pursued) causes loss, the trustee can be required to make good to the trust fair compensation for the capital growth there would have been if a proper investment policy had been followed, i.e. compensation for loss of profit taking account, it seems, of the average performance of authorised investments during the period. It would seem to follow that if trustees invest in unauthorised investments (as contrasted with negligent investment in authorised investments) they could be similarly accountable for the profit that would have been made if they had properly invested in authorised investments. **11–85**

In *Re Mulligan*,[155] in order to favour the life tenant, the trustees did not diversify by investing in equities. It was held that they should have diversified in 1972 to the extent of 40 per cent of the capital and such 40 per cent holdings in equities would have appreciated at 75 per cent of an appropriate index of equities. The 25 per cent discount took account of dealing costs and the fact that the fund was not large enough for the trustees to be expected to rival the index. Nowadays investment can be in "tracker funds" which track and reflect the index, so obviating the need for such a discount. **11–86**

KNOTT v COTTEE

Master of the Rolls (1852) 16 Beav. 77; 16 Jur. (O.S.) 752

A testator who died in January 1844 directed his executor-trustees to invest in "the public or Government stocks or funds of Great Britain, or upon real security in England and Wales." In 1845 and 1846, the defendant executor-trustee invested part of the estate in Exchequer bills, which in 1846 were ordered into court, and in the same year sold at a loss. By a decree made in 1848, the court declared that the investment in Exchequer bills was improper. If, however, the investment had been retained, its realisation at the time of the decree of 1848 would have resulted in a profit. The judge held that "the executor ought to be charged with the amount improperly invested, and credited with the produce of the Exchequer bills in 1846." **11–87**

ROMILLY M.R.: Here is an executor who had a direct and positive trust to perform, which was, to invest the money upon government stocks or funds, or upon real securities, and accumulate at compound interest all the balances after maintaining the children. He has made certain investments, which the court has declared to be improper. The case must either be treated as if these investments had not been made, or had been made for his own benefit out of his own moneys, and that he had at the same time retained moneys of the testator in his hands. I think, therefore, that there must be a reference back, to ascertain what balances the executor retained from time to time, it being clear that he has retained some balances. . . . **11–88**

As to the mode of charging the executor in respect of the Exchequer bills, I treat the laying out in Exchequer bills in this way: The persons interested were entitled to earmark them, as being bought with **11–89**

[152] (1852) 16 Beav. 77.
[153] *Nestlé v National Westminster Bank Plc* [1994] 1 All E.R. 118 at 126.
[154] *Nestlé* at 126–127 (criticising *Robinson v Robinson* (1851) 1 De. G.M. & G. 247).
[155] [1998] 1 N.Z.L.R. 481.

the testator's assets, in the same manner as if the executor had bought a house with the trust funds; and though they do not recognise the investment, they had a right to make it available for what was due; and though part of the property of the executor, it was specifically applicable to the payment. When the Exchequer bills were sold and produced £3,955, the court must consider the produce as a sum of money refunded by the executor to the testator's estate on that day; and on taking the account, the master must give credit for this amount as on the day on which the Exchequer bills were sold. . . .

ii. Improper Retention of Unauthorised Investments

11–90 Where trustees retain an unauthorised investment which depreciates in value,[156] they are liable for the difference between the price obtainable on sale at the proper time and the proceeds of sale of the unauthorised investment when eventually sold.

FRY v FRY

Master of the Rolls (1859) 27 Beav. 144, 28 L.J.Ch. 591, 34 L.T. (O.S.) 51, 5 Jur. 1047

11–91 A testator who died in March 1834, after devising his residuary real estate to two trustees on trust to pay the rents (except those of the Langford Inn) to his wife during her widowhood, with remainder over, and bequeathing his residuary personal estate upon trust for conversion for his wife during her widowhood, with remainder over, directed the trustees: "And as for and concerning all that messuage or dwelling-house called Langford Inn . . . upon trust, as soon as convenient after my decease, to sell and dispose of the same, either by auction or private sale, and for the most money that could be reasonably obtained for the same." In April 1836 the trustees advertised the Langford Inn for sale for £1,000. They refused an offer of £900, made in 1837. One of the trustees died in 1842. A railway opened in 1843 caused the property to depreciate in value through the diversion of traffic. The property was again advertised for sale in 1845, but no offer was received. The other trustee died in 1856. Langford Inn was still unsold and could not be sold except at a low price.

11–92 Held, by ROMILLY M.R., that the trustees had committed a breach of trust by reason of their negligence in not selling the property for so many years, that the property must be sold, and that the estates of the trustees were "liable to make good the deficiency between the amount which should be produced by the sale of the inn and the sum of £900, in case the purchase-money thereof should not amount to that sum."[157]

11–93 It was held by the Court of Appeal in *Re Chapman*[158] and in *Rawsthorne v Rowley*,[159] that a trustee is not liable for a loss arising through the retention of an authorised investment unless he was guilty of wilful default,[160] which requires proof of want of ordinary prudence on the part of the trustee.[161] The position is now governed by the Trustee Act 2000 ss. 1, 4, and 5. The trustees must from time to time

---

156 Where the investment increases in value the beneficiaries can adopt its purchase and the gain will then belong to the trust: *Piety v Stace* (1799) 4 Ves. 620 at 622–623.

157 See also *Grayburn v Clarkson* (1868) 3 Ch. App. 605; *Dunning v Gainsborough* (1885) 54 L.J. Ch. 891. Where the proper time during which the unauthorised investments, e.g. shares, should have been sold is a period during which fluctuations occur in the value of the shares one may take half the sum of the lowest and highest prices at which the shares might have been sold in the period commencing when the shares could first have been sold to advantage and ending at the date by which they should reasonably have been sold: *Fales v Canada Permanent Trust Co* (1976) 70 D.L.R. (3d) 257 at 274.

158 [1896] 2 Ch. 763.

159 [1909] 1 Ch. 409n.

160 See also *Baud v Fardell* (1855) 4 W.R. 40; *Henderson v Hunter* (1843) 1 L.T. (O.S.) 359 at 385; *Robinson v Murdoch* (1881) 45 L.T. 417; *Re Oddy* (1910) 104 L.T. 128 at 131; *Re Godwin* (1918) 87 L.J. Ch. 645.

161 *Re Chapman* [1896] 2 Ch. 763 at 776, per Lindley L.J.

obtain and consider proper advice on whether retention of the investment is satisfactory having regard to the need for diversification and the suitability of the investments. In deciding what to do the statutory duty of care needs to be observed (except to the extent excluded).

iii. Improper Realisation of Proper Investments

It is clearly a breach of trust if trustees sell an authorised investment for the purpose of investing in an **11–94** unauthorised investment or for the purpose of paying the proceeds to the life-tenant in breach of trust. In such cases the trustees are liable to replace the authorised investment or the proceeds of sale of the authorised investment, whichever is the greater burden.[162] Replacement of the authorised investment will be at its value at the date it is actually replaced or at the date of the court judgment if not earlier replaced or, exceptionally, at the date the authorised investment would, in any event, have been sold.[163]

PHILLIPSON v GATTY

Vice-Chancellor (1848) 6 Hare 26, affirmed (1850) 7 Hare 516

The trustees of a sum of consols, who had power to convert and reinvest in the public funds or upon real **11–95** security, realised part of the stock and invested it in an unauthorised investment.

WIGRAM V.C.: . . . Then comes another material question—are the trustees to replace the stock, or the **11–96** money produced by the sale? Mr Wood argued that they were liable to make good the money only, distinguishing the sale, which he said was lawful, from the investment, which I have decided to have been a breach of trust. My opinion is, that the trustees must replace the stock. There was no authority to sell, except with a view to the reinvestment; and here the sale was made with a view to the investment I have condemned. It was all one transaction, and the sale and investment must stand or fall together. . . .

Held, therefore, that the trustees must replace the stock improperly realised. Affirmed on appeal.[164] **11–97**

iv. Non-Investment of Trust Funds

A trustee ought not to leave trust moneys uninvested for an unreasonable length of time. If he unnec- **11–98** essarily retains trust moneys which he ought to have invested, he is chargeable with interest.[165] While an investment is being sought, however, a trustee has statutory powers to pay trust moneys into an interest-bearing account.[166] If a trustee, having been directed to invest in a specific investment, makes no investment at all, and the price of the specified investment rises, he may be required to purchase so much of that investment as would have been obtained by a purchase at the proper time.[167] This applies equally where he is directed to invest in a specific investment and he makes some investment other than the one specified.[168] But if he is directed to invest in a specified range of investments, and

---

162 Thus, if an authorised investment is sold for £10,000, then invested in an unauthorised investment sold for £8,000 and when matters are discovered the authorised investment can be repurchased for £7,000, the trustees must top up the £8,000 to £10,000, the true figure that should be in the accounts (after falsifying them) as retained for the beneficiaries: *Shepherd v Mouls* (1845) 4 Hare 500 at 504; *Watts v Girdlestone* (1843) 6 Beav. 188.

163 *Re Bell's Indenture* [1980] 3 All E.R. 425 at 437–439, pointing out that in *Re Massingberd* (1890) 63 L.T. 296 the reference to the date of the writ for ascertaining the value of the property sold in breach of trust was per incuriam and should be the date of the judgment.

164 Followed in *Re Massingberd* (1890) 63 L.T. 296.

165 *Re Jones* (1883) 49 L.T. 91. For lost capital appreciation see *Midland Bank Trustee Ltd v Federated Pension Services* [1995] Jersey L.R. 352.

166 Trustee Act 2000 ss. 3 and 16–24.

167 *Byrchall v Bradford* (1822) 6 Madd. 235.

168 *Pride v Fooks* (1840) 2 Beav. 430 at 432.

he makes no investment at all, it has been held that he is chargeable only with the trust fund itself, and not with the amount of one or other of the investments which might have been purchased.[169] The reason was stated by Wigram V.C in *Shepherd v Mouls* as follows:[170]

> "The discretion given to the trustees to select an investment among several securities makes it impossible to ascertain the amount of the loss (if any) which has arisen to the trust from the omission to invest, except, perhaps, in the possible case (which has not occurred here) of a particular security having been offered to the trustees, in conformity with the terms of the trust."

Nowadays, however, in view of *Nestlé v National Westminster Bank*[171] as discussed above,[172] the trustees would be charged with the loss of profit that would have been made taking account of the average performance of the investments within the specified range.

v. Trust Funds in Trade

11–99 If a trustee in breach of trust lends funds to a third party who knows they are trust funds but not that the loan is a breach of trust and employs the trust funds in trade, the beneficiaries cannot claim from the third party a share of the profits. For example, a trustee in breach of trust lends £1,000 of trust moneys to X, who employs the fund in his trade. The agreement between the trustee and X provides that X is to pay interest at the rate of 15 per cent. By employing this fund of £1,000 in his trade, X makes a profit during the first year of £300. The beneficiaries cannot claim from X a share of that profit; all that they can require is that he replace, with interest, the fund which he borrowed. What is the position if X knew, not merely that the funds were trust funds, but also that the loan was itself a breach of trust? In this latter case, it would seem that X is a constructive trustee, that he may not "traffic in his trust", and must therefore account for his profit.[173] Of course, if the instrument of trust authorises a loan of trust funds to a third party, and such a loan is made, the beneficiaries have no right to claim profits.[174]

11–100 On the other hand, if it is the trustee himself who in breach of trust employs trust funds in his own trade, the beneficiaries may, instead of taking interest, require him to account for the profit. Thus, if in breach of trust he employs £1,000 of trust moneys in his own trade and thereby makes a profit during the first year of £200, the beneficiaries (on calling upon him to replace the fund of £1,000), may, instead of taking interest on that sum, claim the profit of £200.[175]

11–101 Even if the trust funds so employed by the trustee in his own trade were mixed up with his private moneys, so that the fund used by him was a mixed one, the beneficiaries may still claim a proportionate share of the profits.[176] But it is either the one or the other, either interest or profit. They cannot, even if they find it advantageous to do so, claim interest for part of the time and profit for the other part.[177]

---

169 *Shepherd v Mouls* (1845) 4 Hare 500; *Robinson v Robinson* (1851) 1 De G.M. & G. 247.

170 *Shepherd* at 504.

171 [1994] 1 All E.R. 118.

172 See para.11–85.

173 *Stroud v Gwyer* (1860) 25 Beav. 130; *Vyse v Foster* (1872) 8 Ch. App. 309 at 334; *Belmont Finance Co Ltd v Williams Furniture Ltd* [1979] Ch. 250; *Beach Petroleum NL v Johnson* (1993) 43 F.C.R. 1; *Robins v Incentive Dynamics Pty Ltd (in liq.)* (2003) 45 A.C.S.R. 244.

174 *Parker v Bloxam* (1855) 20 Beav. 295 at 302–304; *Evans v London Co-operative Society Ltd, The Times*, July 6, 1976.

175 *Jones v Foxall* (1852) 15 Beav. 388; *Williams v Powell* (1852) 15 Beav. 461; *Townsend v Townsend* (1859) 1 Giff. 201; *Re Davis* [1902] 2 Ch. 314.

176 *Docker v Somes* (1834) 2 My. & K. 655; *Edinburgh TC v Lord Advocate* (1879) 4 App. Cas. 823. Indeed, if the trust funds were the sine qua non of the purchase of a valuable asset later sold at a profit it is arguable that the trust should take the whole profit for to allow the trustee a proportion for himself would be to allow him to profit from his position.

177 *Heathcote v Hume* (1819) 1 Jac. & W. 122; *Vyse v Foster* (1872) 8 Ch. App. 309 at 334; *Tang Man Sit v Capacious Investments Ltd* [1996] A.C. 514.

3. Impounding the Trustee's Beneficial Interest and the Rule in *Re Dacre*[178]

If a beneficiary is also trustee, but is in default to the estate in his character of trustee, he is not entitled to receive any further part of his beneficial interest until his default is made good. His beneficial interest may also be applied in satisfaction of his liability. Take X who is a trustee, for himself for life, remainder to Y. X commits a breach of trust, and has not yet satisfied his liability. Until he does so, he cannot receive any further part of his beneficial interest, and that interest may be applied in satisfaction of his liability. The rule holds good where X's beneficial interest is derivative as well as where it is original. For example, X holds on trust for several beneficiaries, of which he is not himself one. He is in default to the estate in his character of trustee. One of the beneficiaries dies, and then X becomes entitled to that beneficiary's share as intestate successor or as legatee or devisee. X is now derivatively a beneficiary, and the rule applies as stated above. **11–102**

What is the position of an assignee from the trustee-beneficiary X? The assignee is in the same position as his assignor, i.e. he takes subject to the equity available against the trustee-beneficiary.[179] He takes subject to that equity even if the trustee-beneficiary's default to the estate was subsequent to the assignment.[180] **11–103**

It can, in fact, be most unsafe to take an assignment of the beneficial interest of a trustee-beneficiary, especially if that interest is reversionary. But it was held in *Re Towndrow*[181] that the rule does not apply to a case in which the trustee-beneficiary's liability relates to one trust (of a specific legacy) and his beneficial interest is derived from another trust (of the residuary estate), even though he is trustee of both trusts and both trusts are created by the same will. The rule in *Re Dacre* therefore applies only where the default relates to, and the beneficial interest is derived from, the same trust. **11–104**

4. Defences

A. Power of the Court to Relieve Trustees from Personal Liability

Section 61 of the Trustee Act 1925 states that:[182] **11–105**

> "If it appears to the court that a trustee, whether appointed by the court or otherwise, is or may be[183] personally liable for any breach of trust, whether the transaction alleged to be a breach of trust occurred before or after the commencement of this Act, but has acted honestly and reasonably, and ought fairly to be excused for the breach of trust and for omitting to obtain the directions of the court in the matter in which he committed such a breach, then the court may relieve him either wholly or partly from personal liability for the same."

---

178 [1916] 1 Ch. 344. See too *Jacubs v Rylance* (1874) L.R. 17 Eq. 341; *Re Brown* (1886) 32 Ch.D. 597; *Selangor United Rubber Estates Ltd v Cradock (No.4)* [1969] 1 W.L.R. 1773 at 1776–1779.

179 *Irby v Irby (No.3)* (1858) 25 Beav. 632.

180 *Doering v Doering* (1889) 42 Ch.D. 203; *Re Knapman* (1881) 18 Ch.D. 300 at 307.

181 [1911] 1 Ch. 662.

182 Re-enacting the Judicial Trustees Act 1896 s.3. See L. Sheridan, "Excusable Breaches of Trust" (1955) 19 Conv. (N.S.) 420; Lord Maugham, "Excusable Breaches of Trust" (1898) 14 L.Q.R. 159; C. Stebbings, *The Private Trustee in Victorian England* (2002), Ch.6; J. Lowry and R. Edwards, "Excuses" in P. Birks and A. Pretto (eds) *Breach of Trust* (2002).

183 This does not authorise relief in respect of future anticipated breaches of trust: it relates to an existing situation where the trustee may or may not be liable for breach of trust: *Re Rosenthal* [1972] 1 W.L.R. 1273.

This enables the court to excuse not just breaches of trust in the management of trust property but also payments to the wrong persons.[184] The question of fairness should be considered separately from whether the trustee acted honestly and reasonably: is it fair for the trustee to be excused when the inevitable result is to deny compensation to the beneficiaries? The burden is on the trustee[185] to satisfy the threefold obligation[186] of proving he acted honestly, reasonably and ought fairly to be excused. An appellate court will be reluctant to interfere with the lower court's exercise of discretion.[187]

11–106 The courts are reluctant to grant relief to a paid trustee but may do so in special circumstances.[188] The taking of legal advice will be a significant consideration if such advice is followed but a breach of trust occurs because the advice was erroneous: the standing of the legal adviser and the value of the property affected by the advice will be relevant considerations.[189] If the adviser were a negligent solicitor then the trustee should sue the solicitor to recover the loss for the trust and it seems hardly likely that the court would excuse the trustee if he failed to sue.[190] One must distinguish between trustees obtaining advice on behalf of the trust beneficiaries and trustees obtaining advice for their own personal protection and benefit. In the former case any cause of action arising from negligent advice will be a trust asset so that, if not barred by the limitation period, the beneficiaries could sue for themselves on joining the trustees as co-defendants with the adviser if the trustees refused to sue; in the latter case the beneficiaries generally have no rights against the adviser, being able only to sue the trustees for any breach of trust.[191]

B. An Instigating or Consenting Beneficiary Cannot Sue the Trustee and May Be Liable to Indemnify the Trustee

11–107 A beneficiary[192] who is of full capacity,[193] and who knowingly concurs in a breach of trust,[194] cannot afterwards complain of it against the trustees,[195] unless they knew or ought to have known that the beneficiary's concurrence was the result of undue influence.[196] The position was summarised by Wilberforce J. in a passage in *Re Pauling's ST*:[197]

> "The court has to consider all the circumstances in which the concurrence of the cestui que trust was given with a view to seeing whether it is fair and equitable that, having given his concurrence, he should afterwards turn round and sue the trustees: that, subject to this, it is not necessary that he should know

---

184 *Re Alsop* [1914] 1 Ch. 1; *Ward-Smith v Jebb* (1964) 108 Sol. Jo. 919; *Re Wightwick* [1950] 1 Ch. 260; *Re Evans* [1999] 2 All E.R. 777.

185 *Re Stuart* [1897] 2 Ch. 583; *Re Turner* [1897] 1 Ch. 536.

186 *Marsden v Regan* [1954] 1 W.L.R. 423 at 434–435, per Evershed M.R. See too *Mitchell v Halliwell* [2005] EWHC 937 (Ch) at [49] (no relief for honest trustee who unreasonably failed to ensure that beneficiaries took independent advice).

187 *Marsden v Regan* [1954] 1 W.L.R. 423.

188 *National Trustees Co of Australasia v General Finance Co* [1905] A.C. 373; *Re Windsor Steam Coal Co* [1929] 1 Ch. 151; *Hawkesley v May* [1956] 1 Q.B. 304; *Re Pauling's ST* [1964] Ch. 303 (partial relief); *Re Rosenthal* [1972] 1 W.L.R. 1273.

189 *National Trustees Co of Australasia*, above; *Re Allsop* [1914] 1 Ch. 1 at 13; *Marsden v Regan* [1954] 1 All E.R. 475 at 482; *Wong v Burt* (2004) 7 I.T.E.L.R. 263 at [49]–[58]; *Re Equilift Ltd* [2010] B.P.I.R. 116 at [15].

190 *National Trustees Co of Australasia*, above.

191 *Wills v Cooke* (1979) 76 L.S.G. 706; *Parker-Tweedale v Dunbar Bank Plc* [1990] 2 All E.R. 577 at 583. But for exceptions to this rule, see *Hayim v Citibank NA* [1987] A.C 730 at 747–748; *Bradstock Trustee Services Ltd v Nabarro Nathanson* [1995] 1 W.L.R. 1405; *HR v JAPT* [1997] P.L.R. 99.

192 In charitable trusts only the Attorney-General can consent or acquiesce in a breach of trust: *Re Freeston's Charity* [1978] 1 All E.R. 481 at 490, though the Court of Appeal found it unnecessary to say anything on this point: [1979] 1 All E.R. 51 at 63.

193 *Wilkinson v Parry* (1828) 4 Russ. 272 at 276; *Montford v Cadogan* (1816) 19 Ves. 635. He may not fraudulently misrepresent his age to obtain money and then claim the money again on majority: *Overton v Banister* (1844) Hare 503.

194 *Phipps v Boardman* [1964] 2 All E.R. 187 at 204–205, 207; the point was not appealed.

195 *Fletcher v Collis* [1905] 2 Ch. 24. If he instigates or requests the breach then a fortiori he cannot sue.

196 *Re Pauling's ST* [1964] Ch. 303 at 338. Trustees must take special care in the case of young adults living with their parents.

197 [1962] 1 W.L.R. 86 at 108; approved by the Court of Appeal in *Holder v Holder* [1968] Ch. 353 at 369.

that what he is concurring in is a breach of trust, provided that he fully understands what he is concurring in, and that it is not necessary that he should himself have directly benefited by the breach of trust."

So if a beneficiary consents to an act which the trustees know to be unauthorised although they refrain from telling him this, then he may still sue them. The trustees must put the beneficiaries fully in the picture and must not withhold crucial information.[198] If, however, they themselves do not appreciate that what they propose is a breach of trust and the beneficiary fully understands and agrees with the proposal then he cannot sue them if things turn out badly. *Fletcher v Collis*,[199] reproduced below, establishes that these principles apply whether the beneficiary's consent or acquiescence[200] is before or after the breach of trust, and they prevent him from suing for breach of trust, whether or not he benefited from consenting to such breach.

Where the beneficiary instigated, requested or consented to a breach of trust which the trustees then committed and another beneficiary called upon the trustee to make good the breach of trust, the court has always had jurisdiction to order the trustee to be indemnified out of the interest of the beneficiary who, being of full capacity, either instigated, requested or concurred in the breach. A motive of personal benefit on the part of the beneficiary was sufficient to invoke the jurisdiction in cases of instigation[201] or request;[202] but personal benefit actually derived by the beneficiary was necessary in cases of concurrence.[203] In order to succeed in claiming an indemnity, the trustee had to show that the beneficiary knew the facts which constituted the breach of trust although it was not necessary to show that the beneficiary knew that these facts amounted in law to a breach of trust: *Re Somerset*,[204] reproduced below.[205] **11–108**

Section 62 of the Trustee Act 1925[206] enlarges the jurisdiction as follows: "Where a trustee commits a breach of trust at the instigation or request or with the consent in writing[207] of a beneficiary, the court may if it thinks fit make such order as to the court seems just for impounding all or any part of the interest of the beneficiary in the trust estate by way of indemnity to the trustee[208] or persons claiming through him." However, the factors of motive and actual benefit are likely to continue to influence the court in exercising its discretion. **11–109**

The section provides for impounding the interest of the "beneficiary in the trust estate". In *Ricketts v Ricketts*[209] there was a marriage settlement for a mother for her life, remainder to her son. The son, on his marriage, assigned his reversionary interest under that settlement to the trustees of his own marriage settlement, under which latter settlement he was a beneficiary for life. Notice of the assignment was given to the trustees of the first settlement. By that assignment the son divested himself of **11–110**

---

198 *Phipps v Boardman* [1964] 2 All E.R. 187 at 204–205; *Mitchell v Halliwell* [2005] EWHC 937 (Ch) esp. at [41]–[52].

199 [1905] 2 Ch. 24.

200 Mere delay (subject to Limitation Act 1980) is not enough; there must be conduct and circumstances making it inequitable to assert a claim e.g. having knowledge of entitlement to sue but doing nothing, so that the trustee does things that would otherwise not have been done: *De Busche v Alt* (1877) 8 Ch.D. 286, 314; *Nelson v Rye* [1996] 1 W.L.R. 1378.

201 *Trafford v Boehm* (1746) 3 Atk. 440 at 442; *Raby v Ridehalgh* (1855) 7 De G.M. & G. 104.

202 *M'Gachen v Dew* (1851) 15 Beav. 84; *Hanchett v Briscoe* (1856) 22 Beav. 496.

203 *Cocker v Quayle* (1830) 1 Russ. & M. 535 at 538; *Booth v Booth* (1838) 1 Beav. 125 at 130; *Blyth v Fladgate* [1891] 1 Ch. 337 at 363. It makes no difference that the concurring beneficiary became a beneficiary after the date of his concurrence; *Evans v Benyon* (1887) 37 Ch.D. 329 at 344. These factors of motive and actual benefit may still influence the exercise of discretion of the court determining whether all or any part of the beneficial interest should be impounded: *Bolton v Curre* [1895] 1 Ch. 544 at 549; *Re Somerset* [1894] Ch. 231 at 275.

204 [1894] 1 Ch. 231. See also *Rehden v Wesley* (1861) 29 Beav. 213 at 215.

205 At paras 000ff.

206 Replacing the Trustee Act 1893 s.45, itself replacing the Trustee Act 1888 s.6.

207 The requirement of writing only refers to consent and not instigation or request: *Re Somerset* [1894] 1 Ch. 231.

208 An order for indemnity can be made in favour of a former trustee: *Re Pauling's ST (No.2)* [1963] Ch. 576. It would be absurd if the trustee who, ex hypothesi, is in breach of trust had to remain trustee in order to have an impounding order for an indemnity.

209 (1891) 64 L.T. 263.

his character of beneficiary under the first settlement, and substituted in his place the trustees of the second settlement. Afterwards the son instigated the trustees of the first settlement to commit a breach of trust in his favour by applying trust capital in discharging his debts, and when those trustees proceeded against him under the section for an indemnity, they discovered that he was not a beneficiary against whom they could proceed. Their beneficiary was now to be found in the trustees of the second settlement, who were trustees for the son who instigated the breach of trust to pay off his debts. He was not a "beneficiary in the trust estate".

RE SOMERSET

Court of Appeal [1894] 1 Ch. 231

11–111 Kekewich J. held that a £34,612 mortgage was a proper investment except in so far as the trustees had advanced too much, so that they were liable for a breach of trust in respect only of the amount excessively advanced: Trustee Act 1888 s.5. He considered that the largest sum which in the circumstances the trustees could properly have advanced was £26,000. He further held that the trustees were entitled to have the plaintiff's life interest impounded by way of indemnity under the Trustee Act 1888 s.6; as to which the plaintiff appealed.

11–112 LINDLEY L.J. (with whom A. L. SMITH and DAVEY L.JJ. agreed): The second question is whether, in order to indemnify the trustees, the court ought to impound the income of the trust funds during the life of the appellant. This question turns on the construction of section 6,[210] and on the conduct of the parties.

11–113 Did the trustees commit the breach of trust for which they have been made liable at the instigation or request, or with the consent in writing, of the appellant? The section is intended to protect trustees, and ought to be construed so as to carry out that intention. But the section ought not, in my opinion, to be construed as if the word "investment" had been inserted instead of "breach of trust". An enactment to that effect would produce great injustice in many cases. In order to bring a case within this section the cestui que trust must instigate, or request or consent in writing to some act or omission which is itself a breach of trust and not to some act or omission which only becomes a breach of trust by reason of want of care on the part of the trustees. If a cestui que trust instigates, requests or consents in writing to an investment not in terms authorised by the power of investment, he clearly falls within the section; and in such a case his ignorance or forgetfulness of the terms of power would not, I think, protect him—at all events, not unless he could give some good reason why it should, e.g., that it was caused by the trustee. But if all that a cestui que trust does is to instigate, request or consent in writing to an investment which is authorised by the terms of the power, the case is, I think, very different. He has a right to expect that the trustees will act with proper care in making the investment, and if they do not they cannot throw the consquences on him unless they can show that he instigated, requested or consented in writing to their non-performance of their duty in this respect. This is, in my opinion, the true construction of this section.

11–114 As regards the necessity for a writing, I agree with the decision of Mr Justice Kekewich in *Griffith v Hughes*,[211] that an instigation or request need not be in writing, and that the words "in writing" apply only to the consent.

11–115 I pass now to the facts. It is, in my opinion, perfectly clear that the appellant instigated, requested and consented in writing to the investment by the trustees of the trust money on a mortgage of Lord Hill's estate. This, indeed, was not disputed. But the evidence does not, that I can see, go further than this. He certainly never instigated, requested or consented in writing to an investment on the property without inquiry; still less, if upon inquiry the rents payable in respect of the lands mortgaged were found to be less than the interest payable on the mortgage.

11–116 Whether the appellant knew the rental is a very important question. Mr Justice Kekewich has found that he did. But the evidence does not, in my opinion, warrant this inference . . . .

[210] The Trustee Act 1888 s.6 is now the Trustee Act 1925 s.62.
[211] [1892] 3 Ch. 105.

The solicitors obtained the valuation for and on behalf of the trustees; they obtained the second opinion of the valuers for the benefit of the borrower, and for the protection of the trustees. In obtaining the valuation and opinion the solicitors were not acting for or on behalf of the appellant; and considering that they never disclosed the valuation or opinion to the appellant, and never informed him of their effect, he cannot, in my opinion, be held to have known them. It is important to observe that the statute does not make a cestui que trust responsible for a breach of trust simply because he had actual or constructive notice of it; he must have instigated or requested it, or have consented to it in writing. Even if the knowledge of his solicitors could be imputed to him for some purposes, it is not true in fact that the appellant did by himself or his agent instigate, request or consent in writing to a breach of trust.[212] Even if the appellant had constructive notice through his solicitors of the valuation, the court, in exercising the power conferred on it by the statute, would, in my opinion, be acting unjustly, and not justly, if, under the circumstances of this case, it held the appellant liable to indemnify the trustees. The court would be treating the appellant as having done more than he did, and I can see no justification for such a course. It must be borne in mind that the plaintiff was not seeking to benefit himself at the expense of the remaindermen as in *Raby v Ridehalgh*.[213] He was seeking a better security for the trust money for the benefit of everyone interested in it. . . . **11–117**

Held, therefore, by the Court of Appeal that the defendants were not entitled to have the plaintiff's life interest impounded by way of indemnity.[214] **11–118**

FLETCHER v COLLIS

Court of Appeal [1905] 2 Ch. 24

Securities were settled on trust for the husband for life, remainder to the wife for life, remainder to children. At the request of the wife and with the (written) consent of the husband, the trustee in 1885 sold off the whole of the trust fund and handed the proceeds to the wife, who spent them. In June 1891 the husband was adjudicated bankrupt. In August 1891 the present action was commenced by the remaindermen against the trustee to make him replace the loss, but proceedings were stayed on an undertaking by the trustee, on the security of (inter alia) certain policies on his life, to make good the trust fund. By means of payments by the trustee and of the policies which fell in on his death in 1902, the whole of the trust fund was replaced, together with interest from August 1891. **11–119**

The personal representative of the deceased trustee then took out a summons for a declaration that she was entitled, during the life of the husband, to the income of the trust fund replaced by the deceased trustee. It was argued for her that a beneficiary who concurs in a breach of trust cannot afterwards complain of it against his trustee. The capital had in fact been replaced by the trustee at the instance of the remaindermen, but since the husband himself had by virtue of his concurrence no claim against the trustee, the income of the capital so replaced should (during the life of the husband) go to her as personal representative of the trustee who replaced it. **11–120**

For the husband's trustee in bankruptcy, who resisted the claim of the personal representative, it was contended that the authorities showed that mere concurrence by a beneficiary does not preclude him from complaining against his trustee: it must be shown that the beneficiary also derived a personal benefit from the breach of trust, which was not the case here. **11–121**

---

212 On this point, A.L. Smith L.J. observed (at 270): "In my opinion, upon the true reading of this section, a trustee, in order to obtain the benefit conferred thereby, must establish that the beneficiary knew the facts which rendered what he was instigating, requesting or consenting to in writing a breach of trust." Davey L.J. observed (at 274): ". . . in order to bring the case within the section the beneficiary must have requested the trustee to depart from and go outside the terms of his trust. It is not, of course, necessary that the beneficiary should know the investment to be in law a breach of trust."

213 (1855) 7 De G.M. & G. 104.

214 In accordance with this case is *Mara v Browne* [1892] 2 Ch. 69 at 92–93, where North J. held that the trustee was not entitled to impound the interest of the beneficiary because the beneficiary, though she had consented in writing, had not consented to those acts which constituted the breach of trust. On appeal [1896] 1 Ch. 199 the point did not arise. The life tenant's interest was impounded in *Jaffray v Marshall* [1993] 1 W.L.R. 1285.

11–122 ROMER L.J. (with whom VAUGHAN WILLIAMS and STIRLING L.JJ. agreed): There was one proposition of law urged by the counsel on behalf of the respondents before us to which I accede. It is this: If a beneficiary claiming under a trust does not instigate or request a breach of trust, is not the active moving party towards it, but merely consents to it, and he obtains no personal benefit from it, then his interest in the trust estate would not be impoundable in order to indemnify the trustee liable to make good loss occasioned by the breach. I think this is what was meant and referred to by Chitty J. in his judgment in *Sawyer v Sawyer*,[215] where he says: "It strikes me as a novelty in law, and a proposition not founded on principle, to say that the person who merely consents is bound to do more than what he says he consents to do. It does not mean that he makes himself personally liable, nor does he render any property liable to make it good." But that proposition of law must be taken to be subject to the following right of the trustee as between himself and the beneficiaries. In the case I have before referred to in respect to the general proposition, the beneficiary who knowingly consented to the breach could not, if of full contracting age and capacity, and in the absence of special circumstances, afterwards be heard to say that the conduct of the trustee in committing the breach of trust was, as against him the particular beneficiary, improper, so as to make the trustee liable to the beneficiary for any damage suffered in respect of that beneficiary's interest in the trust estate by reason of the loss occasioned by the breach, and of course if satisfactorily proved the consent of the beneficiary to the breach need not be in writing.

11–123 I will illustrate what I have said by a concrete case, not only to make my meaning perfectly plain, but also because the illustration will have a bearing upon the case now before us. Take a simple case of a trust under a settlement, say, of £3,000, for a tenant for life, and after the death of the tenant for life for certain remaindermen. Suppose the trustee commits a breach of trust and sells out £1,000, and pays it over to some third person, so that the cestui que trust does not benefit by it himself, and suppose that the tenant for life, being of full age and sui juris, knows of that act of the trustee and consents to it. What would be the position of the trustee in reference to that breach of trust if he were made liable at the instance of the remaindermen for the loss accruing to the trust estate by the breach of trust, assuming the £1,000 to have been lost? The remaindermen would have the right of saying, so far as their interest in remainder is concerned, the capital must be made good by the trustee; but the tenant for life who consented could not himself have brought an action against the trustee to make him liable for the loss of income suffered by the tenant for life by reason of the breach of trust as to the £1,000. On the other hand, the trustee would not have had a right, as against the cestui que trust, the tenant for life, to have impounded the tenant for life's interest on the remaining £2,000 of the trust fund in order to indemnify himself. Now suppose the remaindermen having brought an action to make good the breach of trust against the trustee, and the tenant for life is a co-plaintiff, a defence is put in by the trustee raising his right as against the tenant for life seeking relief in respect of the loss of income, but admitting the right of the remaindermen: what would the court in such a case do if the question between the tenant for life and the trustee had to be tried out, and the tenant for life was found to have consented knowingly to the breach of trust? To my mind the right thing for the court to do would have been clear. It might order the £1,000 to be paid into court by the trustee; but, pending the life of the tenant for life, it might also order the income to be paid to the trustee, because the income of the £1,000 would have been out of the pocket of the trustee just as much as the corpus from which it proceeded, and not to have given that relief to the trustee would have been to ignore his right, and to have acceded to the claim of the tenant for life in the action by him that I have indicated. Now suppose that the tenant for life is not a plaintiff, but co-defendant with the trustee, so that the question cannot be tried out at the trial as between the tenant for life and the trustee: what might the court do, if so advised, in that case? It might order the £1,000 to be paid into court by the trustee, and it might reserve the question of the right as between the tenant for life and the trustee to the income to be determined at some later period. It will be found that that illustration is pertinent to the case that is now before us. In such a case when the question as to income arose the trustee would be able to say: "The remaindermen are clearly not entitled to the income on the trust fund I have replaced, if the tenant for life is not entitled to it as against me. I replaced it; it is my money, and I am entitled to it"; and, therefore, when the question came to be tried out ultimately as between the tenant for life and the trustee, if that income was still under the control of the court, the court would again have the right to say to the trustee who replaced the corpus: "The income is yours in the absence of the right of the beneficiary, the tenant for life, to claim as against you to make you liable for that income."

[215] (1885) 28 Ch.D. 595 at 598.

Now that right of a trustee which I have been dealing with, the right to resist the claim by the beneficiary to make good as against him the income, has clearly not been affected either by section 6 of the Trustee Act of 1888, or by section 45 of the Trustee Act of 1893. As I pointed out in *Bolton v Curre*,[216] those sections were intended to and did extend the powers of the court for the benefit of the trustee. They clearly extended the powers of court so far as concerns the case of a married woman restrained from anticipation; but they also extended them in another respect by giving power to the court to impound any part of the interest in the trust property of any beneficiary who consented to a breach of trust, provided that consent was in writing. But clearly there was nothing in those sections which was intended to, and nothing in my opinion which operated so as to, deprive the trustee of the right I previously indicated, namely, the right of saying as against a beneficiary who has consented to a breach of trust that the beneficiary cannot make him, the trustee, personally liable to recoup, to the beneficiary who consented, the loss accruing to that beneficiary by the breach of trust committed with his consent. The beneficiary, if he consented to the breach of trust, could not be heard to make that a ground of complaint or a ground of action as against the trustee. . . . **11–124**

Is not this matter that we have to deal with on this appeal in substance one where a beneficiary who has consented to a breach of trust is now for his own benefit calling upon the trustee to make good the loss accruing to the beneficiary by reason of the breach? I think it is **11–125**

Held, therefore, by the Court of Appeal that the personal representative of the deceased trustee was entitled, during the life of the husband tenant for life, to the income of the fund replaced by the trustee. **11–126**

HOLDER v HOLDER

Court of Appeal [1968] Ch. 353, [1968] 2 W.L.R. 237, [1968] 1 All E.R. 665

The plaintiff was seeking to set aside a sale made to the third defendant by the first two defendant trustees when the third defendant was technically a trustee. HARMAN L.J. (with whom DANCKWERTS and SACHS L.JJ. agreed on this point) dealt as follows with the defence of the plaintiff's consent or acquiescence. **11–127**

There arises a further defence, namely, that of acquiescence, and this requires some further recital of the facts. **11–128**

Completion of the sale was due for Michaelmas, 1961, but by that time the third defendant was not in a position to find the purchase money. The proving executors served a notice to complete in October, 1961, and, the validity of this notice being questioned, served a further notice in December. In February 1962 the plaintiff's solicitor pressed the defendants to forfeit the third defendant's deposit and this was a right given by the contract of sale and is an affirmation of it. Further, in May, 1962, the plaintiff issued a writ for a common decree of administration against the proving executors, seeking thus to press them to complete the contract and wind up the estate. The contract was in fact completed in June, 1962, and in the same month £2,000 on account was paid to and accepted by the plaintiff as his share and he thereupon took no further steps with his action. In order to complete, the third defendant borrowed £21,000 from the Agricultural Mortgage Corporation with interest at 7 1/2 per cent. He also borrowed £3,000 from his mother with interest at 6 1/2 per cent, and a like sum from his sister at a similar rate of interest. In November 1962 the third defendant demanded possession of Glebe Farm house from the plaintiff, who at that time changed his solicitors, and it was suggested by the new solicitors in February 1963 that the third defendant was disqualified from bidding at the auction. This was the first time any such suggestion had been made by anyone. The writ was not issued till a year later. **11–129**

I have found this question a difficult one. The plaintiff knew all the relevant facts but he did not realise nor was he advised till 1963 that the legal result might be that he could object to his brother's purchase because he continued to be a personal representative. There is no doubt strong authority for the proposition that a man is not bound by acquiescences until he knows his legal rights. In *Cockerell v Cholmeley*[217] Sir John Leach M.R. said this: **11–130**

[216] [1895] 1 Ch. 544 at 549.
[217] (1830) 1 Russ. & M. 418 at 425.

"It has been argued that the defendant, being aware of the facts of the case in the lifetime of Sir Henry Englefield has, by his silence, and by being a party to the application to Parliament, confirmed the title of the plaintiffs. In equity it is considered, as good sense requires it should be, that no man can be held by any act of his to confirm a title, unless he was fully aware at the time, not only of the fact upon which the effect of title depends, but of the consequence in point of law; and there is no proof that the defendant, at the time of the acts referred to, was aware of the law on the subject . . .".

11–131 There, however, the judge was asked to set aside a legal right. In *Wilmott v Barber*[218] Fry J. said this:

"A man is not to be deprived of his legal rights unless he has acted in such a way as would make it fraudulent for him to set up those rights. What, then, are the elements or requisites necessary to constitute fraud of that description? In the first place the plaintiff must have made a mistake as to his legal rights. Secondly, the plaintiff must have expended some money or must have done some act (not necessarily upon the defendant's land) on the faith of his mistaken belief. Thirdly, the defendant, the possessor of the legal right, must know of the existence of his own right which is inconsistent with the right claimed by the plaintiff. If he does not know of it he is in the same position as the plaintiff, and the doctrine of acquiescence is founded upon conduct with a knowledge of your legal rights."

On the other hand, in *Stafford v Stafford*[219] Knight Bruce L.J. said this:

"Generally, when the facts are known from which a right arises, the right is presumed to be known . . .".

11–132 Like the judge, I should desire to follow the conclusion of Wilberforce J. who reviewed the authorities in *Re Pauling's Settlement Trusts;*[220] and this passage was mentioned without dissent in the same case in the Court of Appeal:[221]

"The result of these authorities appears to me to be that the court has to consider all the circumstances in which the concurrence of the cestui que trust was given with a view to seeing whether it is fair and equitable that, having given his concurrence, he should afterwards turn round and sue the trustees: that, subject to this, it is not necessary that he should know that what he is concurring in is a breach of trust, provided that he fully understands what he is concurring in, and that it is not necessary that he should himself have directly benefited by the breach of trust."

There is, therefore, no hard and fast rule that ignorance of a legal right is a bar, but the whole of the circumstances must be looked at to see whether it is just that the complaining beneficiary should succeed against the trustee.[222]

11–133 On the whole I am of the opinion that in the circumstances of this case it would not be right to allow the plaintiff to assert his right (assuming he had one) because with full knowledge of the facts he affirmed the sale. He has had £2,000 as a result. He has caused the third defendant to embark on liabilities which he cannot recoup. There can in fact be no restitutio in integrum which is a necessary element in rescission.

11–134 The plaintiff is asserting an equitable and not a legal remedy. He has by his conduct disentitled himself to it. It is extremely doubtful whether the order if worked out would benefit anyone, I think we should not assent to it, on general equitable principles.

---

[218] (1880) 15 Ch.D. 96 at 105.
[219] (1857) 1 De G. & J. 193 at 202.
[220] [1961] 3 All E.R. 713 at 730.
[221] [1964] Ch. 303.
[222] Endorsed in *Re Freeston's Charity* [1979] 1 All E.R. 51 at 62. The third proposition of Fry J. in *Wilmott v Barber* (1880) 15 Ch.D. 96 at 105 has also been rejected in *Taylor Fashions Ltd v Liverpool Victoria Trustees Co Ltd* [1981] 1 All E.R. 897 at 915–918 and *Habib Bank Ltd v Habib Bank AG Zurich* [1981] 2 All E.R. 650 at 666, 668.

C. *Limitation*

i. Equitable Rules

11–135 The Limitation Act 1980 s.36 provides that "nothing in the Act shall affect any equitable jurisdiction to refuse relief on the ground of acquiescence or otherwise." This section therefore preserves the equitable doctrine of "laches". "Laches" is an old Law French term that means "neglect" or "slackfulness", and, in essence, the doctrine bars equitable claims where there has been a substantial lapse of time coupled with the existence of circumstances which make it inequitable to enforce the claim. In the words of Lord Selborne L.C., the doctrine is available:[223]

> "where it would be practically unjust to give a remedy, either because the party has, by his conduct, done that which might fairly be regarded as equivalent to a waiver of it, or where by his conduct and neglect he has, though perhaps not waiving that remedy, yet put the other party in a situation in which it would not be reasonable to place him if the remedy were afterwards asserted."

11–136 According to Lord Walker in *Fisher v Brooker,* detrimental reliance by the defendant is "usually an essential ingredient", but this is not an "immutable requirement".[224]

The field of operation of the doctrine has been narrowed by statute.[225] Nowadays, it is the statutory six-year period which operates against a beneficiary in respect of a claim against the trustee for a breach of trust[226] and not the equitable doctrine of "laches". But there are cases outside the Act (e.g. claims against trustees who have fraudulently concealed their breaches of trust from the beneficiaries[227]) and cases under the Act[228] in which the liability of the trustee is subject to no statutory period of limitation at all (e.g. a claim against trustees for property or proceeds thereof retained by them). In such a case the right of the beneficiary will only be barred by an unreasonably long period of delay amounting to laches.[229]

11–137 The ability of equity to act by analogy to the statute is expressly recognised and preserved, for s.36(1) of the 1980 Act provides that the six-year period which it lays down is not to apply to "any claim for specific performance of a contract or for an injunction or for other equitable relief" save in so far as

---

223 *Lindsay Petroleum Co v Hurd* (1874) L.R. 5 P.C. 221 at 239–240. See also *Weld v Petre* [1929] 1 Ch. 33 at 51–52; *Holder v Holder* [1968] Ch. 353; *Nelson v Rye* [1986] 2 All E.R. 186 at 200–205, although incorrect on other points: *Paragon Finance Plc v Thakerar & Co* [1999] 1 All E.R. 400 at 415–416; *Companhia de Seguros Imperio v Heath Ltd* [2001] 1 W.L.R. 112; *J.J. Harrison (Properties) Ltd v Harrison* [2002] 1 B.C.L.C. 162.

224 [2009] 1 W.L.R. 1764 at [64]. See too *Patel v Shah* [2005] W.T.L.R. 359 at [32], endorsing *Frawley v Neill* [2000] C.P. Rep. 20: the modern approach is to determine "whether it would be unconscionable in all the circumstances for a party to be permitted to assert his beneficial right."

225 Trustee Act 1888 s.8; Limitation Act 1939 replaced by Limitation Act 1980. The history of the limitation statutes and their impact on equity's limitation rules is discussed in W. Swadling, "Limitation" in P. Birks and A. Pretto (eds), *Breach of Trust* (2002).

226 See Limitation Act 1939 s.19(2), replaced by Limitation Act 1980 s.21(3); *Re Pauling's ST* [1964] Ch. 303.

227 Limitation Act 1980 s.32(1)(b). In *Tito v Waddell (No.2)* [1977] Ch. 106 at 248–251, Megarry J. held that breaches of the self-dealing rule would also be outside the Act, but the CA declined to follow him on this point in *Gwembe Valley Development Co Ltd v Koshy (No.3)* [2004] 1 B.C.L.C. 131, holding at [108] that it would be anomalous and unnecessarily complicated to apply different limitation periods to claims for breach of fiduciary duty and claims against trustees who purchase trust property.

228 Limitation Act 1980 s.21(1).

229 *McDonnell v White* (1865) 11 H.L.C. 271; *Sleeman v Wilson* (1871) L.R. 13 Eq. 36; *Tito v Waddell (No.2)* [1977] Ch. 106 at 248–250; *Re Loftus, deceased* [2007] 1 W.L.R. 591 at [33]–[41].

a court of equity may apply it by analogy.[230] But the analogous application of s.36(1) is limited to claims for which no express provision is to be found elsewhere in the statute.[231]

11–138 Thus it was held in *Re Diplock*[232] that even if the claims in equity were analogous to the common law action for money had and received (which they were not), they were also "actions in respect of a claim to the personal estate of a deceased person" for which under s.20 of the 1939 Act (now s.22 of the 1980 Act) the relevant period of limitation was one of 12 years from the date when the right to receive the share or interest accrued; accordingly, there was no scope for applying any other period by way of analogy or otherwise.

11–139 The equitable rule that time would not run against the plaintiff in cases of fraud and mistake is adopted by s.32(1) of the 1980 Act (replacing and amending s.26 of the 1939 Act) which provides that:[233]

> "Where in the case of any action for which a period of limitation is prescribed by this Act, either:
>
> (a) the action is based upon the fraud of the defendant or his agent or of any person through whom he claims or his agent, or
> (b) any fact relevant to the plaintiff's right of action has been deliberately concealed from him by any such person as aforesaid, or
> (c) the action is for relief from the consequences of mistake,
>
> the period of limitation shall not begin to run until the plaintiff has discovered the fraud concealment or mistake, as the case may be, or could with reasonable diligence have discovered it.

Subsection (3) goes on to protect purchasers taking under transactions without notice of the fraud having been committed or the concealment or mistake having been made, as the case may be. "Deliberate commission of a breach of duty in circumstances in which it is unlikely to be discovered for some time amounts to deliberate concealment of the facts involved in that breach of duty."[234] The House of Lords[235] has held that where after a cause of action has arisen there was a deliberate concealment of facts relevant to the claimant's cause of action time does not begin to run until the concealment was or should have been discovered. In a separate case, the House of Lords has also

---

230 On this and actions for an account, see *Tito v Waddell (No.2)* [1977] Ch. 106 at 250–252 discussing Limitation Act 1939 s.2(7) replaced by Limitation Act 1980 s.36(1).

231 A case like *Re Robinson* [1911] 1 Ch. 502 would be decided today in accordance with the provisions of s.21(3) of the Limitation Act 1980 and not by the use of any analogy to the statute. But note that in *Gwembe Valley Development Co. Ltd v Koshy (No.3)* [2004] 1 B.C.L.C. 131 the CA resolved a limitation point in relation to a claim against a company director both on the basis that he was a constructive trustee and so a trustee within s.21 and on the basis that the rules governing claims by beneficiaries for recovery of trust property should apply by way of analogy under s.36.

232 [1948] Ch. 465 at 502–516; when the case reached the House of Lords, sub nom. *Ministry of Health v Simpson* [1951] A.C. 251, their Lordships approved the views of the Court of Appeal on the applicability of s.20 of the Limitation Act 1939 (now s.22 of the 1980 Act) and it therefore became unnecessary to express an opinion on the applicability of s.26 thereof (now s.32 of the 1980 Act). It seems that s.22 of the 1980 Act applies even after the personal representatives have become trustees, but it does not apply to claims against the personal representative of an intestate in respect of real estate which remains unsold or, as to claims in respect of personal estate, at a time when he is not in a position to distribute assets in his hands because the costs, funeral and testamentary and administration expenses, debts and other liabilities properly payable have not been paid and any pecuniary legacies provided for: *Re Loftus, deceased* [2007] 1 W.L.R. 591.

233 *Nocton v Lord Ashburton* [1914] A.C. 932 at 936, 958; *Kitchen v RAF Association* [1958] 1 W.L.R. 563 (solicitor's negligence); *Baker v Medway Supplies* [1958] 1 W.L.R. 1216 (fraudulent conversion of money); *Bartlett v Barclays Bank Trust Co* [1980] 1 All E.R. 139 at 154; *Peco Arts Inc v Hazlitt Gallery Ltd* [1983] 3 All E.R. 193 (reasonable diligence in discovering drawing not an original).

234 Limitation Act 1980 s.32(2); *King v Victor Parsons & Co* [1973] 1 W.L.R. 29 at 33, per Lord Denning M.R. This reflects the old case law on (b) when it was known as fraudulent concealment in Limitation Act 1939 s.26.

235 *Sheldon v RH Outhwaite (Underwriting Agencies) Ltd* [1996] A.C. 102. The meaning of deliberate concealment in subs.32(1)(b) and 32(2) is also reviewed in *Williams v Fanshaw Porter Hazelhurst* [2004] P.N.L.R. 544 and *Newgate Stud Co v Penfold* [2008] 1 B.C.L.C. 46.

held that a defendant does not deliberately commit a breach of duty unless he intends to commit the act which constitutes the breach of duty and realises that the act involves a breach of duty.[236]

It has been held in several cases[237] that para.(c) applies only to cases where a mistake has been made and has had certain consequences and the claimant is seeking to be relieved from those consequences, e.g. actions to recover money paid under a mistake; to rescind or rectify contracts on the ground of mistake; to reopen accounts settled in consequence of mistakes. It applies, in fact, only where mistake is an essential ingredient of the cause of action, and it does not help a claimant to ascertain the amount still due to him after the ordinary period of limitation has expired. The anomalous result is that a person who has by mistake paid too much can take advantage of the section, but the person who has by mistake received too little cannot avail himself of it.[238] **11–140**

ii. Statutory Rules Affording Little Protection to Trustees

LIMITATION ACT 1980 SECTION 21

(1) No period of limitation prescribed by this Act shall apply to an action by a beneficiary under a trust, being an action: **11–141**

(a) in respect of any fraud or fraudulent breach of trust to which the trustee was a party or privy; or
(b) to recover from the trustee trust property or the proceeds thereof in the possession of the trustee, or previously received by the trustee and converted to his use.

(2) Where a trustee who is also a beneficiary under the trust receives or retains trust property or its proceeds as his share on a distribution of trust property under the trust, his liability in any action brought by virtue of subsection (1)(b) above to recover that property or its proceeds after the expiration of the period of limitation prescribed by this Act for bringing an action to recover trust property shall be limited to the excess over his proper share.

This subsection only applies if the trustee acted honestly and reasonably in making the distribution.

(3) Subject to the preceding provisions of this section an action by a beneficiary to recover trust property or in respect of any breach of trust, not being an action for which a period of limitation is prescribed by any other provision of this Act,[239] shall not be brought after the expiration of six years from the date on which the right of action accrued. For the purposes of this subsection the right of action shall not be treated as having accrued to any beneficiary entitled to a future interest in the trust property until the interest fell into possession.

(4) No beneficiary as against whom there would be a good defence under this Act shall derive any greater or other benefit from a judgment or order obtained by any other beneficiary than he could have obtained if he had brought the action and this Act had been pleaded in defence.

---

[236] *Cave v Robinson Jarvis and Rolf* [2003] 1 A.C. 384.

[237] *Phillips-Higgins v Harper* [1954] 1 Q.B. 411; *Malkin v Birmingham CC* (C.A., January 12, 2000) at [23]; *Europcar UK Ltd v HMRC* [2008] S.T.C. 2751 at [63]–[64]; *Test Claimants in the FII Group Litigation v HMRC* [2010] EWCA Civ 103 at [230] ff., followed in *FJ Chalke Ltd v HMRC* [2010] EWCA Civ 313 at [42]–[44]. Compare the contrary obiter views of Lord Walker and Lord Hoffmann in *Deutsche Morgan Grenfell Group Plc v IRC* [2007] 1 A.C. 558 at [22] and [147].

[238] As in *Phillips-Higgins*.

[239] Where personal representatives have become trustees upon completing administration of an estate the relationship between s.21(3) and s.22 is unclear. It would seem that the breadth of s.22 (formerly s.20 of the 1939 Act) makes the 12-year period applicable: *Re Diplock* [1948] Ch. 465 at 511–513; *Ministry of Health v Simpson* [1951] A.C. 251 at 276–277.

11–142 The word "trustee" is defined for the purposes of s.21 by reference to s.68(17) of the Trustee Act 1925. This definition excludes persons owing the duties incident to an estate conveyed by way of mortgage,[240] but includes constructive trustees and personal representatives. It has been held to include the directors of a company,[241] but not trustees in bankruptcy[242] nor apparently the liquidators of companies in voluntary liquidation.[243] The section is limited to actions by beneficiaries in respect of trust property. It is thought, however, that a newly-appointed trustee would have the same rights as the beneficiaries themselves against the surviving trustees.[244] A claim by the Attorney-General against trustees of a charitable trust (which has no beneficiary) is outside the section.[245]

11–143 Perpetual liability is confined under this section as under the 1888 Act for express trustees to cases of (a) fraudulent[246] breaches of trust and (b) of retention or conversion of the trust property. It appears from *Thorne v Heard*[247] that the negligence of a trustee, resulting in his solicitor embezzling the trust funds, was insufficient to render the trustee "party or privy" to the fraud. On the face of it, it appears that there could be perpetual liability for an innocent recipient of trust property from a fraudulent trustee,[248] although it would be fairer for there only to be such liability if the recipient were privy to the fraud.

11–144 The section speaks of property "previously received by the trustee and converted to his use". In *Re Howlett*[249] it was contended that this referred to an actual receipt of property, but Danckwerts J. held that it included a notional receipt, and so he was able to charge a trustee who had occupied trust property for some 20 years with an occupation rent. To fall foul of s.21(1)(b) a trustee's retention or conversion must be some wrongful application in his own favour.[250] Exceptionally, though, he has some protection under s.21(2) so that if he had distributed one-third of the trust property to himself, honestly and reasonably believing that only three beneficiaries existed, he will be liable to a fourth beneficiary turning up after six years not for a quarter share but only for the one-twelfth difference between the one-third share he took and the one-quarter share which was truly his.

11–145 Section 21(3) of the Act prescribes a six-year period of limitation for breach of trust cases not falling within s.21(1) or (2) or within any other provision of the Act. Thus, if a trustee can show that an innocent or negligent breach of trust led him to part with the trust property, then the six-year period is the appropriate one to limit his liability. The six-year period is also appropriate if the trust funds were dissipated by a co-trustee,[251] and it also applies to claims against knowing recipients of misdirected trust property and dishonest assistants in a breach of trust, which are discussed further in Chapter 12.[252]

---

240 But a prior mortgagee of land exercising his power of sale is a trustee of the surplus for subsequent mortgagees after meeting his own claims. See *Thorne v Heard* [1894] 1 Ch. 599; the Law of Property Act 1925 s.105.

241 *Re Lands Allotments Co* [1894] 1 Ch. 616 at 631, 638, 643 and *Whitwam v Watkin* (1898) 78 L.T. 188.

242 *Re Cornish* [1896] 1 Q.B. 99.

243 *Re Windsor Steam Coal Co* (1901) Ltd [1928] Ch. 609; affirmed on a different ground [1929] 1 Ch. 151.

244 See *Re Bowden* (1890) 45 Ch.D. 444, a case decided under the 1888 Act which was not limited to actions by beneficiaries.

245 *Att.-Gen. v Cocke* [1988] Ch. 414.

246 See *North American Land Co v Watkins* [1904] 1 Ch. 242; [1904] 2 Ch. 233; *Vane v Vane* (1872) L.R. 8 Ch. 383; *Armitage v Nurse* [1998] Ch. 241 at 260.

247 [1895] A.C. 495.

248 *GL Baker Ltd v Medway Building and Supplies Ltd* [1958] 1 W.L.R. 1216 at 1221–1222.

249 [1949] Ch. 767.

250 *Re Gurney* [1893] 1 Ch. 590; *Re Page* [1893] 1 Ch. 304; *Re Fountaine* [1909] 2 Ch. 382.

251 *Re Tufnell* (1902) 18 T.L.R. 705; *Re Fountaine* [1909] 2 Ch. 382.

252 Knowing recipients: *Taylor v Davies* [1920] A.C. 636, esp. at 653; *Clarkson v Davies* [1923] A.C. 100 at 110–111; *Paragon Finance Plc v DB Thakerar & Co* [1999] 1 All E.R. 400 at 408–414. Dishonest assistants: *Dubai Aluminium Co Ltd v Salaam* [2003] 2 A.C. 366 at [141]; *Cattley v Pollard* [2007] Ch. 353, which should be preferred to *Statek Corp v Alford* [2008] W.T.L.R. 1089 for the reasons discussed in C. Mitchell, "Dishonest Assistance, Knowing Receipt, and the Law of Limitation" [2008] Conv. 226. See too Lord Hoffmann's comments in the Hong Kong Final Court of Appeal in *Peconic Industrial Development Ltd v Lau Kwok Fai* [2009] W.T.L.R. 999 at [18]ff.

The last sentence of s.21(3) protects reversionary interests by enacting that time shall not run against a beneficiary until his interest has fallen into possession.[253] Even before that date a remainderman can sue for breach of trust. In such a case if the prior beneficiary is himself barred the trustees must nevertheless replace the fund at the suit of the remainderman, but during the continuance of the prior beneficiary's interest they will be entitled to the income of the property: for a judgment recovered by one beneficiary is not to improve the position of one who is already barred.[254] **11–146**

Where a beneficiary is merely interested under a discretionary trust until obtaining a life interest in possession on attaining 25 years, the Court of Appeal has held[255] that time does not run until the beneficiary obtains the interest in possession on his 25th birthday. It matters not that at 18 a beneficiary, whether her interest is in possession or not, is entitled to see trust accounts, etc. so as to be able to discover a breach of trust. The rationale for s.23(1) "is not that a beneficiary with a future interest has not the means of discovery, but that the beneficiary should not be compelled to litigate (at considerable personal expense) in respect of an injury to an interest which he may never live to enjoy. Similar reasoning would apply to exclude a person who is merely the object of a discretionary trust or power which may never be exercised in his favour."[256] This might seem to suggest that the liability of trustees of a discretionary trust is open-ended, except for those objects who received a distribution (thereby acquiring an absolute interest in possession before the relevant breach of trust and so have six years in which to act). However, in *Johns v Johns*[257] the New Zealand Court of Appeal reviewed Millett L.J.'s words, and concluded that a discretionary beneficiary would fit the rationale identified by his Lordship only if he had a further interest in the trust fund capable of falling into possession at a future date. Otherwise he "would not fit the clear requirement of a future interest in the trust property".[258] **11–147**

5. Liability of Trustees between Themselves

Contribution claims between trustees formerly lay in equity: they now lie under the Civil Liability (Contribution) Act 1978 between trustees who are liable "in respect of the same damage".[259] Because trustees in this position are jointly and severally liable to the beneficiaries,[260] one trustee may find himself obliged to pay more than his fair share of their common liability to restore the trust fund or otherwise compensate the beneficiaries for loss. In this case, he can recover a contribution of between 1 and 100 per cent of his payment from one or more of the others,[261] depending on the court's assessment of the shares in which their common liability should be borne. **11–148**

It seems likely that when apportioning liability between trustees the courts will continue to draw on the principles which were developed in the Chancery jurisdiction prior to the enactment of the 1978 Act. Thus, they will start with the presumption that co-trustees should share equal responsibility towards the beneficiaries,[262] and they will then look to see whether there are any reasons for **11–149**

---

[253] Consent by a life-tenant to an advance in favour of a remainderman does not amount to a release of the life interest so as to convert the remainderman's interest into an interest in possession: *Re Pauling's ST* [1964] Ch. 303.

[254] *Re Somerset* [1894] 1 Ch. 231; s.19(3) of the Limitation Act 1939 and s.21(4) of the 1980 Act; *Mara v Browne* [1895] 2 Ch. 69 reversed on another point [1896] 1 Ch. 199.

[255] *Armitage v Nurse* [1998] Ch. 241.

[256] *Armitage* at 261, per Millett L.J.

[257] [2004] 3 N.Z.L.R. 202.

[258] *Johns* at [40].

[259] Civil Liability (Contribution) Act 1978 ss.1 and 6. Hence a trustee cannot recover a contribution from a co-trustee who is liable only respect of some other damage, or who is not liable to the beneficiaries at all: cf. *Alexander v Perpetual Trustee (WA) Ltd* (2004) 216 C.L.R. 109.

[260] See para.11–02.

[261] Complete reimbursement is expressly allowed for by s.2(2) of the 1978 Act.

[262] *Lingard v Bromley* (1812) 1 V. & B. 114: *Jesse v Bennett* (1856) 6 De G. M. & G. 609; *Robinson v Harkin* [1896] 2 Ch. 415 at 426; *Gilchrist v Dean* [1960] V.R. 266 at 270–271.

departing from this rule. A trustee who has wrongfully misapplied trust funds to his own exclusive use,[263] or who has exclusively benefited as a beneficiary from the breach of trust,[264] must reimburse the others in full in the event that they are ordered to restore the trust fund. So too must a trustee who has acted fraudulently if the others have acted in good faith.[265]

11–150 The courts' general tendency in the cases pre-dating the 1978 Act was to reject the argument that a trustee who played an active part in the management of trust affairs should be liable for a greater share of trust losses than a passive trustee who did nothing and so failed to prevent the losses from occurring.[266] However, this tough line was moderated to the extent that lay trustees were permitted to shift the burden of paying for trust losses on to professional trustees, upon whose expertise the lay trustees had reasonably relied.[267] It may be that the modern proliferation of trust companies will invest this line of authority with increasing significance.[268] But compare a New Zealand case, *Re Mulligan*,[269] where a lay trustee (and life tenant) insisted on her solicitor co-trustee pursuing an investment policy that was designed to maximise the trust income, and no steps were taken to protect the trust capital by investing in shares. After her death, the remaindermen successfully sued the lay trustee's estate and the solicitor trustee, but neither trustee was entitled to an indemnity from the other because neither had acted reasonably, and the lay trustee would have benefited more from the income from share dividends than the investments actually made.

11–151 Contribution claims also lie between wrongdoing trustees and third parties who have incurred liability for knowing receipt of misdirected trust property and dishonest assistants in a breach of trust.[270] The same general principles of apportionment apply to these claims as to claims between trustees. Hence unequal apportionments should be made where one party has acted in good faith and another in bad faith, and where one party has made a gain and another has not. For example, in *Dubai Aluminium Co Ltd v Salaam*,[271] the House of Lords agreed with Rix J.'s finding at first instance that two fraudsters who had received all the money extracted from the a company by a wrongdoing fiduciary should reimburse the other defendants who had compensated the company for its loss, because "it cannot be just and equitable to require one party to contribute in a way which would leave another party in possession of his spoils."[272] Similar findings were made by the High Court of Australia in *Burke v LFOT Pty Ltd*,[273] and by the Court of Appeal in *Niru Battery Manufacturing Co v Milestone Trading Ltd (No.2)*, where Clarke L.J. held that the principle applies both where the recipient still has the money at the time of the contribution proceedings, and where he pays it away other than in good faith.[274] In *Charter Plc v City Index Ltd*,[275] Morritt C. was led by this dictum to conclude that there was no prospect of the claimant recovering a contribution and therefore struck out the claim. On appeal,

---

263 *Lincoln v Wright* (1841) 4 Beav. 427; *Thompson v Finch* (1856) 22 Beav. 316 at 327; *Bahin v Hughes* (1886) 31 Ch.D. 390 at 395; *Wynne v Tempest* [1897] 1 Ch. 110; *Goodwin v Duggan* (1996) 41 N.S.W.L.R. 158 at 166.

264 *Chillingworth v Chambers* [1896] 1 Ch. 685.

265 *Baynard v Woolley* (1855) 20 Beav. 583 at 585–586; *Elwes v Barnard* (1865) 13 L.T. 426; *Bellemore v Watson* (1885) 1 T.L.R. 241 at 242; *Re Smith* [1896] 1 Ch. 71.

266 *Lingard v Bromley* (1812) 1 V. & B.114 at 117; *Wilson v Moore* (1833) 1 My. & K. 126 at 147; *Bahin v Hughes* (1886) 31 Ch.D. 390 at 396; *Bacon v Camphausen* (1888) 55 L.T. 851 at 852.

267 *Lockhart v Reilly* (1856) 25 L.J. Ch. 697, affirmed (1857) 27 L.J. Ch. 54: *Thompson v Finch* (1856) 22 Beav. 316; *Wilson v Thomson* (1875) L.R. 20 Eq. 459: *Re Partington* (1887) 57 L.T. 654; *Re Turner* [1897] 1 Ch. 536; *Re Linsley* [1904] 2 Ch. 785; and cf. *Linsley v Kirstiuk* (1986) 28 D.L.R. (4th) 495.

268 Cf. *Fales v Canada Permanent Trust Co* [1977] 2 S.C.R. 302; *Blair v Canada Trust Co* (1986) 32 D.L.R. (4th) 515.

269 [1998] 1 N.Z.L.R. 181.

270 For general discussion of third party liability for breach of trust, see Chapter 12.

271 [2003] 2 A.C. 366 at [50]–[54] and [162]–[164], followed in *Pulvers (a firm) v Chan* [2008] P.N.L.R. 9 at [401].

272 [1999] 1 Lloyd's Rep. 415 at 475, following Ferris J.'s observations to the same effect in *K v P* [1993] Ch. 140 at 149.

273 (2002) 209 C.L.R. 282.

274 [2004] 2 All E.R. (Comm.) 289 at [50].

275 [2007] 1 W.L.R. 26 at [33]–[53].

Carnwath L.J. disagreed because he thought that a party who receives money for his own benefit and then pays it away should be in a "similar position" to a party who never receives anything.[276] However, this is only true if the party has acted in good faith. If he has not (and in *City Index* the claimant had not), then it would surely be inequitable to let him recover a portion of his bad faith expenditure from the defendant.

BAHIN v HUGHES

Court of Appeal (1886) 31 Ch. D. 390, 55 L.J. Ch. 472, 54 L.T. 188, 34 W.R. 311, 2 T.L.R. 276

A testator, Robert Hughes, bequeathed a legacy of £2,000 to his three daughters—Eliza Hughes, Mrs Burden and Mrs Edwards—on trust to invest in specified securities and in real securities in England and Wales. Eliza Hughes, who was the active trustee, and Mr Burden invested the fund on the (unauthorised) security of leasehold properties, an investment discovered by Mr Burden. Mrs Edwards had been informed of the proposal, but her concurrence was not obtained. The security proving insufficient, the tenant for life and remaindermen brought this action against Eliza Hughes, Mr Edwards (whose wife had died) and Mr and Mrs Burden, claiming that the defendants were liable to make good the trust fund.[277] Edwards served a third-party notice on Eliza Hughes claiming to be indemnified by her, on the ground that she had assumed the role of sole trustee, that the investment had been made at her instigation, and that she had represented to Mrs Edwards that the mortgage was a proper and sufficient security. **11–152**

Held, by Kay J., that the defendants were jointly and severally liable to replace the £2,000, and that the defendant Edwards had no right of indemnity against Eliza Hughes. Edwards appealed. **11–153**

COTTON L.J. (with whom BOWEN and FRY L.JJ. agreed): . . . On going into the authorities, there are very few cases in which one trustee, who has been guilty with a co-trustee of breach of trust and held answerable, has successfully sought indemnity as against his co-trustee. In *Lockhart v Reilly*[278] it appears from the report of the case in the Law Journal that the trustee by whom the loss was sustained had been not only trustee, but had been and was a solicitor, and acting as solicitor for his self and his co-trustee, and it was on his advice that Lockhart had relied in making the investment which gave rise to the action of the cestui que trust. The Lord Chancellor (Lord Cranworth) refers to the fact that he was a solicitor, and makes the remark: "The whole thing was trusted to him. He was the solicitor, and, independently of the consideration that one cannot help seeing it was done with a view of favouring his own family, yet if that had not been so, the co-trustee leaves it with the solicitor-trustee, by whose negligence (I use no harsher word) all this evil, in a great degree, has arisen." Therefore the Lord Chancellor, in giving his decision, relies upon the fact of the trustee being a solicitor. In *Thompson v Finch*[279] a right was conceded to prove against the estate of the deceased trustee for the full loss sustained; but it appears that in this case also he was a solicitor, and that he really took this money to himself, for he mixed it with his own money, and invested it on a mortgage; and therefore it was held that the trustee was entitled to indemnity from the estate of the co-trustee, who was a solicitor. This was affirmed in the Court of Appeal; and the Court of Appeal took so strong a view of the conduct of the solicitor that both of the judges concurred in thinking that he ought to be called on to show cause why he should not be struck off the rolls. Of course, where one trustee has got the money into his own hands, and made use of it, he will be liable to his co-trustee to give him an indemnity. Now I think it wrong to lay down any limitation of the circumstances under which one trustee would be held liable to the other for indemnity, both having been held liable to the cestui que trust; but so far as cases have gone at present, relief has only been granted against a trustee who has himself got the benefit of the breach of trust, or between whom and his co-trustees there has existed a relation which will justify the court in treating him solely liable for the breach of trust. . . . **11–154**

---

[276] [2008] Ch. 313 at [59].

[277] Prior to s.18 of the Married Women's Property Act of 1882 (which did not apply to the present case) a married woman could not act as trustee without the participation of her husband (Mr Edwards); he was necessarily a trustee through her trusteeship, and was responsible for her breaches of trust.

[278] (1856) 25 L.J. Ch. 697 at 702.

[279] (1856) 25 L.J. Ch. 681.

11–155 Miss Hughes was the active trustee and Mr Edwards did nothing, and in my opinion it would be laying down a wrong rule that where one trustee acts honestly, though erroneously, the other trustee is to be held entitled to indemnity who by doing nothing neglects his duty more than the acting trustee. That Miss Hughes made an improper investment is true, but she acted honestly, and intended to do the best she could, and believed that the property was sufficient security for the money, although she made no inquiries about their being leasehold houses. In my opinion the money was lost just as much by the default of Mr Edwards as by the innocent though erroneous action of his co-trustee, Miss Hughes. All the trustees were in the wrong, and every one is equally liable to indemnify the beneficiaries.

11–156 Appeal dismissed.

HEAD v GOULD

Chancery Division [1898] 2 Ch. 250, 67 L.J. Ch. 480, 78 L.T. 739

11–157 Miss Head and Mr Gould were appointed new trustees of certain marriage settlements (the beneficial interests being the same under both settlements), and thenceforth Gould acted as solicitor to the trusts. Miss Head was one of the remaindermen under these settlements, the tenant for life being her mother. The new trustees sold a house forming part of the trust, and in breach of trust handed the proceeds of sale to the tenant for life. Part of the trust property consisted also of certain policies on the life of Mrs Head, policies which Mrs Head had mortgaged to the trust by way of security for advances of trust capital which the former trustees had made to her at her urgent request for the purpose of assisting the family. These policies were (in breach of trust) surrendered by the new trustees with the concurrence of Mrs Head.

11–158 Miss Head claimed to be indemnified by her co-trustee, Gould, under circumstances which appear from the judgment:

11–159 KEKEWICH J.: . . . It will be convenient here at once to deal with the claim made by Miss Head against her co-trustee, Gould. By her third party notice she seeks to be indemnified by him against loss by reason of the breaches of trust, on the ground that the loss and misapplication (if any) of the trust funds, or any part thereof, were occasioned entirely by his acts or defaults, and that he assumed to act as solicitor to the trust estate and as the sole trustee thereof, and exercised control of the administration of the trust funds, and that whatever was done by herself in connection with the trust was at his instigation and in reliance upon his advice.

11–160 This is a serious charge, and if it had been proved would have entitled her to the relief claimed according to well-known and well-recognised principles. . . . There is before me no evidence bringing the case within those principles, or showing that the charge which is correctly formulated on them is consistent with the facts. My conclusion from such evidence as there is before the court is distinctly adverse to the claim. I know that, before the appointment of herself and Gould as trustees, Miss Head was an active party to the importunities of her mother which induced the former trustees to commit a breach of trust for their benefit, and that she looked to the change of trustees as a means of, in some way or other, obtaining further advances. I know, further, that she was well acquainted with the position of the trust, and that it was all-important to maintain the policies and to appropriate the rents of the house to that purpose. She now affects to ignore all that has been done since her appointment, and professes not to remember having executed the several instruments which must have been executed by her for the sale of the house and the surrender of the policies, or the receipt of moneys arising therefrom. With regret, and under a painful sense of duty, I am bound to say that I do not credit her testimony. True it is that the defendant, Gould, is a solicitor, and that he was appointed a trustee for that very reason. True no doubt, also, that the legal business was managed by him, and I do not propose to absolve him from any responsibility attaching to him on that ground; but I do not myself think that Byrne J. or any other judge ever intended to hold that a man is bound to indemnify his co-trustee against loss merely because he was a solicitor, when that co-trustee was an active participator in the breach of trust complained of, and is not proved to have participated merely in consequence of the advice and control of the solicitor. . . .

11–161 Held, therefore, that the trustee, Miss Head, had no claim of indemnity against her co-trustee.

Questions

1. "It is misleading to speak of breach of trust as if it were the equitable counterpart of breach of contract at common law. . . . It is tempting, but wrong, to assume that a trustee is . . . under a primary obligation to perform the trust and a secondary obligation to pay equitable compensation if he does not. . . . The primary remedy of the beneficiary . . . is to have the account taken, to surcharge and falsify the account, and to require the trustee to restore to the trust estate any deficiency which may appear when the account is taken." (Lord Millett, writing in the *Law Quarterly Review* in 1998.) Discuss. **11–162**

2. What should the measure of liability be in the following alternative circumstances where, in breach of trust, Samantha Smith and Roger Robinson, trustees of a family trust: **11–163**

   (a) transfer the £2 million portfolio of investments and cash to a discretionary portfolio manager and either (i) two months later before any of the investments have been replaced there is a stock-market collapse, so that the portfolio is worth only £1.5 million or (ii) four years later, after the original investments have all been replaced, there is a stock-market collapse, so that the portfolio is worth only £1.5 million, having been worth £2.5 million earlier;

   (b) transfer investments worth £200,000 to their children Amanda Smith and Jack Robinson in consideration of their marriage and either (i) two months later before any of the investments have been sold there is a stock-market collapse, so that the investments are worth only £150,000 or (ii) four years later, after the investments have been sold and used to purchase a £250,000 house (now worth £300,000) there is a stock-market collapse, so that if the investments had been retained they would have depreciated from £250,000 to £150,000.

12 PERSONAL COMPENSATORY LIABILITY OF THIRD PARTIES INVOLVED IN A BREACH OF TRUST

1. Introduction

A. Overview

12–01 Third parties involved in a breach of trust can become personally liable to the beneficiaries in various ways. First, a person who is neither a trustee, nor authorised by the trustees, but who takes it upon himself to deal with trust property that has come into his hands as though he were a trustee, is personally liable to account to the beneficiaries for the property, as a trustee *de son tort*.

12–02 Second, a person who acts unconscionably by receiving misdirected trust property for his own benefit with knowledge that it has been paid to him in breach of trust, or by receiving such property innocently but later acquiring knowledge of the breach and then dealing with it for his own benefit, is personally liable to account to the beneficiaries for the property. It is a controversial question whether such defendants also owe a concurrent, strict, personal liability in unjust enrichment to repay the value of the property received. If such a liability arises, then an innocent recipient of misdirected trust funds who does not know of their improper provenance at the time of receipt, and who never acquires such knowledge before disposing of them, is also personally liable to repay the value of the property received, unless he can rely on the defence of change of position.

12–03 Third, a person who dishonestly assists in a breach of trust is fixed with a duplicative liability which mirrors the liability of the wrongdoing trustees, with the result that he is personally liable to restore the trust fund, or to compensate the beneficiaries for loss, to the same extent as the trustees. It is a controversial question whether he is also personally liable to pay the beneficiaries the amount of any profits made by the trustees. But is it clear that he is personally liable to account to the beneficiaries for any profits that he makes for himself through his wrongdoing.

B. Personal Liability to Account as a Constructive Trustee

12–04 Trustees *de son tort*, knowing recipients, and dishonest assistants are all commonly said to owe a personal liability to account to the beneficiaries as constructive trustees. Confusingly, however, the courts do not always mean the same thing when they use this expression. In the case of a trustee *de son tort*, they mean that when the defendant acquires trust property and deals with it as though he were an express trustee, then he is personally liable to account for it in the same way as an express trustee of the property would be liable to account for it to the beneficiaries.[1] Similarly, when a knowing recipient acquires trust property he is liable to account for it to the beneficiaries as though he were an express trustee of the property for them, although he is not.[2] Consistently with this, the remedies awarded against trustees *de son tort* and knowing recipients who fail to deal with the trust property in accordance with the beneficiaries' rights are essentially the same as those which are awarded against express trustees who fail to act in accordance with the terms of the trust: claims are made through the same proceedings for an account, and liability is quantified by reference to the same principles, as those which are described in the discussion of express trustee liability in Chapter 11.

In the case of dishonest assistants, the expression means something different. A dishonest assistant can be personally liable whether or not he has received trust property which might be impressed with a constructive trust for the beneficiaries.[3] Hence when the courts say that he is personally liable to account to the beneficiaries as a constructive trustee, they cannot mean that he is himself a trustee of property for which he must account to them: "there is no real trust and usually no chance of a proprietary remedy" against him.[4] Instead, the courts mean that he can be treated, by a legal fiction, as though he were one of the trustees in whose breach of trust he has participated, so as to fix him with the same personal liabilities as are owed by that trustee: his liability derives from and duplicates the liability of that trustee.[5] Another way of putting this is to say that dishonest assistants can incur a civil secondary liability, analogous to the criminal secondary liability of those who procure, aid or abet a crime.[6] This has important consequences for the remedies which can be awarded against dishonest assistants, since it means that these remedies may simply duplicate the remedies awarded against the trustees whose breaches of duty have been assisted. Note, however, that dishonest assistants can also incur a direct primary liability in their own right, to disgorge profits which they have made for themselves through their equitable wrongdoing, whether or not the trustees have shared in these profits, and whether or not they correspond to a loss to the trust estate. **12–05**

2. Trusteeship *De Son Tort*

In *Mara v Browne*, A.L. Smith L.J. held that:[7] **12–06**

> "If one, not being a trustee and not having authority from a trustee, takes upon himself to intermeddle with trust matters or to do acts characteristic of the office of trustee he may thereby make himself what is called in law a trustee of his own wrong, i.e. a trustee *de son tort*, or as it is also termed, a constructive trustee."

---

[1] e.g. *Jasmine Trustees Ltd v Wells & Hind (a firm)* [2008] Ch. 194 at [42].

[2] e.g. *Jesse v Bennett* (1856) 6 De G. M. & G. 609 at 612; *Morgan v Stephens* (1861) 3 Giff. 226 at 237; *Rolfe v Gregory* (1865) 4 De G. J. & S. 576 at 578; *John v Dodwell & Co Ltd* [1918] A.C. 563 at 569.

[3] *Royal Brunei Airlines Sdn Bhd v Tan* [1995] 2 A.C. 378 at 382; *Houghton v Fayers* [2000] Lloyd's Rep. Bank. 145 at 149.

[4] *Coulthard v Disco Mix Club Ltd* [2000] 1 W.L.R. 707 at 731.

[5] *US Surgical Corp v Hospital Products International Pty Ltd* (1982) 2 N.S.W.L.R. 766 at 817 (not considered on appeal); *Arab Monetary Fund v Hashim* Q.B.D. 29 July 1994, per Chadwick J.; *Royal Brunei Airlines Sdn Bhd v Tan* [1995] 2 A.C. 378 at 385; *Australian Securities Commission v AS Nominees Ltd* (1995) 62 F.C.R. 504 at 523; *Equiticorp Industries Ltd v R. (No.47)* [1998] 2 N.Z.L.R. 481 at 658; *Bankgesellschaft Berlin AG v Makris* Q.B.D. (Comm. Ct.) 22 January 1999, per Cresswell J.; *Grupo Torras SA v Al-Sabah (No.5)* [2001] Lloyd's Rep. Bank. 36 at 61–62.

[6] *Ultraframe (UK) Ltd v Fielding* [2007] W.T.L.R. 835 at [1506], per Lewison J.: "liability as a dishonest assistant, as the law has developed, is a secondary liability akin to the criminal liability of one who aids and abets the commission of a criminal offence."

[7] [1896] 1 Ch. 199 at 209. See too *Blyth v Fladgate* [1891] 1 Ch. 337; *Lyell v Kennedy* (1899) 14 App. Cas. 437; *Taylor v Davies* [1920] A.C. 636 at 651; *Selangor United Rubber Ltd v Cradock (No.3)* [1968] 1 W.L.R. 1555 at 1579; *Carl Zeiss Stiftung v Herbert Smith (No.2)* [1969] 2 Ch. 276 at 289. In *Dubai Aluminium Co Ltd v Salaam* [2003] 2 A.C. 366 at [138], Lord Millett preferred the term "de facto trustee" to the term "trustee *de son tort*".

12–07 A trustee *de son tort* does not purport to act for himself, but for the beneficiaries,[8] and there is no need to show that he has acted dishonestly in order to fix him with liability: he may have been honest and well intentioned, a busybody of excessive probity.[9] His conduct is equated to a declaration of himself as a trustee,[10] and he is expected to familiarise himself with the extent of his duties on taking office, and thereafter he may be liable for a breach of these duties, as though he were an express trustee.[11] However, this does not mean that he has the same powers that he would have if he were an express trustee, and he cannot validly exercise dispositive discretions conferred on the trustees by the trust instrument.[12]

12–08 In the event that trust property comes into the hands of a trustee *de son tort* he will hold it on constructive trust for the beneficiaries, to whom he will owe a duty to account for his stewardship of the property. Thus in *Blyth v Fladgate*,[13] where a sole trustee had solicitors invest trust funds in Exchequer Bills and, after his death and before appointment of any new trustees, the bills were sold by the solicitors and the proceeds invested in a loan on mortgage, the solicitors were liable for the loss arising when the security proved insufficient.

3. Knowing Receipt

A. Ingredients of Liability

12–09 In *El Ajou v Dollar Land Holdings Plc*,[14] Hoffmann L.J. stated that for the purposes of a claim for knowing receipt:

> "the plaintiff must show, first, a disposal of his assets in breach of fiduciary duty; secondly, the beneficial receipt by the defendant of assets which are traceable as representing the assets of the plaintiff; and thirdly, knowledge on the part of the defendant that the assets he received are traceable to a breach of fiduciary duty."

12–10 Several points arise out of this statement. First, liability for knowing receipt is not confined to cases concerning misapplied trust property: it may also be incurred where a defendant receives misdirected assets which were controlled by a person, such as a company director, who owed fiduciary duties to a principal in respect of his handling of the property.[15] Second, there is no need to show that the trustee or fiduciary misapplied the relevant property with a dishonest state of mind.[16] Third, receipt of trust property includes receipt of the traceable proceeds of trust property, as identified in accordance with the relevant tracing rules.[17] Fourth, the defendant must receive legal title to the property; if he does not, then he may be strictly liable to repay the amount of the property at common law, but no question can

---

[8] *Nolan v Nolan* [2004] VSCA 109 at [29].

[9] *Lyell v Kennedy* (1889) 14 App. Cas. 437 at 459; *Mara v Browne* [1896] 1 Ch. 199 at 209; *Life Association of Scotland v Siddal* (1861) 3 De G. F. & J. 58; *Baden, Delvaux v Société Générale pour Favoriser le Développement du Commerce et de l'Industrie en France SA* [1993] 1 W.L.R. 509 at 577; *Dubai Aluminium Co Ltd v Salaam* [2003] 2 A.C. 366 at [138]

[10] *Life Association of Scotland v Siddal* (1861) 3 De G. F. & J. 58 at 72.

[11] *Pearce v Pearce* (1856) 22 Beav. 248 at 252.

[12] *Jasmine Trustees Ltd v Wells & Hind (a firm)* [2008] Ch. 194 at [52]–[57].

[13] [1891] 1 Ch. 337. See too *Goddard v DFC New Zealand Ltd* [1991] 3 N.Z.L.R. 580.

[14] [1994] 2 All E.R. 685 at 700.

[15] *Russell v Wakefield Waterworks Co* (1875) L.R. 20 Eq. 474 at 479; *Belmont Finance Corp Ltd v Williams Furniture Ltd (No.2)* [1980] 1 All E.R. 393; *Agip (Africa) Ltd v Jackson* [1991] Ch. 547; *CMS Dolphin Ltd v Simonet* [2001] 2 B.C.L.C. 704.

[16] *Polly Peck International Plc v Nadir (No.2)* [1992] 4 All E.R. 769 at 777; *El Ajou v Dollar Land Holdings Plc* [1994] 2 All E.R. 685 at 700.

[17] *Agip (Africa) Ltd v Jackson* [1990] Ch. 265 at 289–292; *El Ajou v Dollar Land Holdings Plc* [1994] 2 All E.R. 685 at 700; *Boscawen v Bajwa* [1996] 1 W.L.R. 328 at 334; *Foskett v McKeown* [2001] 1 A.C. 102 at 128; *Trustor AB v Smallbone (No.2)* [2001] 1 W.L.R. 1177 at 1184. For the rules of tracing, see paras 13–16ff.

arise of his holding the property on constructive trust for the claimant.[18] Fifth, the defendant must have received the property beneficially for himself: he will not be liable if he receives property ministerially, i.e. in his capacity as agent for a third party to whom he owes an immediate duty to account for the property, and who is himself immediately liable to the beneficiaries on the defendant's receipt.[19] Sixth, the defendant must not be in a position to raise the defence of bona fide purchase for value of the legal estate without notice of the beneficiaries' interest.[20] Seventh, knowing receipt claims are usually brought where the recipient no longer has the property, since in cases where he still has it, the beneficiaries will generally seek an order that the property be reconveyed.[21] But there is no rule forbidding them to claim a money remedy in knowing receipt in the latter class of case,[22] unless the property is registered land and the transfer is made for valuable consideration, in which case the Land Registration Act 2002 s.29, which avoids the beneficiaries' equitable interests in the property, should also immunise the recipient from personal liability in knowing receipt.[23]

B. Requirement of Knowledge

Until 2000, the starting point for the courts when investigating the degree of knowledge possessed by a defendant in an action for knowing receipt was *Baden, Delvaux v Société Générale pour Favoriser le Développement du Commerce et de l'Industrie en France SA*.[24] This case concerned liability for assisting in a breach of trust, but Peter Gibson J. adopted a five-fold classification of knowledge there that was later used in knowing receipt cases as well. He distinguished between: (i) actual knowledge; (ii) wilfully shutting one's eyes to the obvious; (iii) wilfully and recklessly failing to make such inquiries as an honest and reasonable man would make; (iv) knowledge of circumstances which would indicate the facts to an honest and reasonable man; and (v) knowledge of circumstances which would put an honest and reasonable man on inquiry.[25] **12–11**

There was no clear alignment between actual knowledge, *Baden, Delvaux* categories (i)–(iii), and dishonesty, on the one hand, and between constructive knowledge, *Baden, Delvaux* categories (iv)–(v), and negligence, on the other. Hence it is difficult to translate decisions that were expressed in the language of the *Baden, Delvaux* classification into the language of dishonesty and negligence. Nevertheless, the weight of authority indicated that dishonesty of the sort typically displayed by defendants falling into categories (i)–(iii) was sufficient, but not necessary, for liability,[26] and these cases were **12–12**

---

18 *Criterion Properties Plc v Stratford* [2004] 1 W.L.R. 1846; cf. *Trustee of the Property of FC Jones & Sons (a firm) v Jones* [1997] Ch. 159. Trustees generally have the power to transfer legal title to trust property even where they act in breach of trust: *Rolled Steel Products (Holdings) Ltd v British Steel Corp* [1986] Ch. 246 at 303.

19 *Barnes v Addy* (1874) 9 Ch. App. 244 at 254–255; *Agip (Africa) Ltd v Jackson* [1990] Ch. 265 at 291–292; *Twinsectra Ltd v Yardley* [2002] 2 A.C. 164 at 194; *Evans v European Bank Ltd* (2004) 7 I.T.E.L.R. 19 at [164]–[176]. In these circumstances, the defendant may still be liable for dishonest assistance, depending on his state of mind, as in, e.g. *British North American Elevator Co v Bank British North American* [1919] A.C. 658; *Papamichael v National Westminster Bank Plc* [2003] 1 Lloyd's Rep. 341.

20 *Re Diplock* [1948] Ch. 465 at 535 and 544; *Carl Zeiss Stiftung v Herbert Smith & Co (a firm) (No.2)* [1969] 2 Ch. 276 at 289; *Cowan de Groot Properties Ltd v Eagle Trust Plc* [1991] B.C.L.C. 1045 at 1110.

21 *Ultraframe (UK) Ltd v Fielding* [2007] W.T.L.R. 835 at [1486].

22 *Ultraframe* at [1577].

23 M. Conaglen and A. Goymour, "Knowing Receipt and Registered Land" in C. Mitchell (ed.), *Constructive and Resulting Trusts* (2010).

24 [1993] 1 W.L.R. 509 (the case was decided in 1983).

25 *Baden, Delvaux* at 575–587.

26 *Selangor United Rubber Estates Ltd v Cradock (No.3)* [1968] 1 W.L.R. 1555; *Belmont Finance Corp v Williams Furniture Ltd (No.2)* [1980] 1 All E.R. 399 at 405; *International Sales and Agencies Ltd v Marcus* [1982] 3 All E.R. 551 at 558; *Baden, Delvaux v Société Générale pour Favoriser le Développement du Commerce et de l'Industrie en France SA* [1993] 1 W.L.R. 509 at 582; *Houghton v Fayers* [2000] 1 B.C.L.C. 511.

probably inconsistent with others which held that carelessness of the kind typically exhibited by defendants falling into categories (iv)–(v) was not enough.[27]

12–13 In 1995, in *Royal Brunei Airlines Sdn Bhd v Tan*,[28] the Privy Council held that liability for assisting in a breach of trust should no longer be decided with reference to the *Baden, Delvaux* classification, which had become over-theorised and obscure.[29] Then, in 2000, in *BCCI (Overseas) Ltd v Akindele*,[30] the Court of Appeal said the same thing with respect to knowing receipt. Nourse L.J. held that dishonesty will suffice, but is not required, to make a defendant liable where he has received and dealt with misapplied trust property for his own benefit,[31] and that as a general rule a defendant will be liable whenever his "state of knowledge [is] . . . such as to make it unconscionable for him to retain the benefit of the receipt."[32] It may be doubted whether unconscionability is a sufficiently certain concept to bring clarity and predictability to the law in this area,[33] and indeed, it was expressly rejected by Lord Nicholls in *Royal Brunei* as the test for assistance liability for precisely this reason.[34] Nevertheless, there is much to be said for abandoning the over-subtle distinctions of *Baden, Delvaux*, and in practice the courts do not seem to have much trouble with applying Nourse L.J.'s test. A sceptic might say that this is unsurprising since the test makes liability turn on the exercise of a judicial discretion. Be that as it may, *Akindele* has been reaffirmed by the Court of Appeal on several occasions,[35] although there has been no move to relabel this head of liability "unconscionable receipt", as might have been anticipated given the rebranding of "knowing assistance" as "dishonest assistance" which followed the *Royal Brunei* case.[36]

C. Remedies

12–14 A knowing recipient's core duty as constructive trustee of the property he receives, and generally his only duty of practical significance, is to restore the property immediately.[37] In this respect his position differs from that of express trustees, who have continuing duties to hold the trust property for the beneficiaries. However, if a knowing recipient breaches his core restorative duty by dealing with the property for himself, or indeed by applying it in any other way that is inconsistent with the beneficiaries' rights, then the mechanisms by which they can hold him liable to account are essentially the same as those by which they can hold an express trustee liable to account for unauthorised expenditure, as discussed in Chapter 11.[38] By analogy with the express trustee cases, the knowing recipient can be ordered to restore the property *in specie* if it is still in his hands. By the same analogy, if he has disposed of the property then

---

27 *Re Montagu's ST* [1987] Ch. 264; *Lipkin Gorman v Karpnale Ltd* [1987] 1 W.L.R. 987 at 1005; *Barclays Bank Plc v Quincecare Ltd* [1992] 4 All E.R. 363 at 375; *Eagle Trust Plc v SBC Securities Ltd* [1992] 4 All E.R. 488 at 509; *Cowan de Groot Properties Ltd v Eagle Trust Plc* [1991] B.C.L.C. 1045 at 1110; *Polly Peck International Plc v Nadir (No.2)* [1992] 4 All E.R. 769 at 777; *Jonathan v Tilley* (1988) 12 Tru. L.I. 36.

28 [1995] 2 A.C. 378.

29 See para.12–71.

30 [2001] Ch. 437.

31 *BCCI* at 448.

32 *BCCI* at 455.

33 Consider the different readings of *BCCI* in *Papamichael v National Westminster Bank Plc* [2003] 1 Lloyd's Rep. 341 at [246]–[247] and *Criterion Properties Plc v Stratford UK Properties LLC* [2003] 1 W.L.R. 2108 at [20]–[39], not reviewed on appeal [2004] 1 W.L.R. 1846.

34 [1995] 2 A.C. 378 at 392.

35 *Criterion Properties Plc v Stratford UK Properties LLC* [2003] 1 W.L.R. 2108 at [20]–[39], not reviewed on appeal [2004] 1 W.L.R. 1846; *Charter Plc v City Index Ltd* [2008] Ch. 313; *Uzinterimpex JSC v Standard Bank Plc* [2008] Bus. L.R. 1762.

36 cf. S.B. Thomas "Goodbye Knowing Receipt. Hello Unconscientious Receipt" (2001) 21 OJLS 239.

37 cf. *Re Holmes* [2005] 1 W.L.R. 857 at [22]; *Darkingjung Pty Ltd v Darkingjung Local Aboriginal Land Council* [2006] NSWSC 1217 at [47].

38 See paras 11–08 ff.

he must show that this disposal was authorised, or else the account will be falsified, and an order for substitutive performance made, requiring him to pay the current monetary value of the property, or where the property was money, the capital sum plus interest.[39]

Beneficiaries do not have to allege a breach of duty against an express trustee before they can obtain an order of either kind, and for the same reasons they do not have to allege a breach of duty against the knowing recipient. Once they have established that he knowingly received the trust property and was therefore placed under a primary restorative duty, they need not show that he breached this duty by failing to return the property, as they are entitled without more to an order for specific or substitutive performance of his primary duty. For example, in *Green v Weatherill*[40] a daughter received money from her father, to be held on trust for him, and she transferred part of the money to her sister, who knew that this transfer was in breach of trust. The sister was ordered to pay the relevant sum into court, although there was no allegation in the pleadings that she had committed any breach of her duty as constructive trustee to return the money. **12–15**

Note, too, that in many cases the measure of a knowing recipient's liability is different from the measure of other liabilities that he might owe on a different footing. Suppose, for example, that a knowing recipient receives and then disposes of trust property that subsequently increases in value. If the recipient owed a concurrent liability in unjust enrichment, a possibility considered in the next section, then the measure of his liability would be the value of the property at the time of receipt. But if he were chargeable with the property as a knowing recipient, then he would be liable as constructive trustee to account to the beneficiaries for its current monetary value.[41] A vivid example is an American case, *Re Rothko*,[42] where executors of the renowned painter, Mark Rothko, improperly transferred a large number of his paintings to third parties, who subsequently disposed of them. The value of Rothko's works then appreciated hugely, and in proceedings by the beneficiaries of his estate, the New York Court of Appeals held that the third parties were liable to pay the current market value of the paintings. **12–16**

In some circumstances, a knowing recipient might also be concurrently liable for dishonest assistance, and again the remedies available against him under these two heads might be different according to the circumstances. Suppose, for example, that a trustee misappropriates shares, converts them to cash, and gives the cash to a defendant, who knows that the transfer is a breach of trust. The value of the shares subsequently doubles. If the defendant's liability were for dishonest assistance, then he would be liable for the current value of the shares, because his liability would replicate the liability of the trustee to pay a money substitute for the shares which he can no longer produce when called upon to do so.[43] In contrast, if the defendant's liability were as a knowing recipient, then the trustee's liability would not be attributed to him. His liability would instead be a primary liability for the substitutive performance of his own custodial duties, which only arose in respect of the property which he received. Thus his liability would be for the value of the cash, plus interest. **12–17**

---

[39] For further discussion see C. Mitchell and S. Watterson, "Remedies for Knowing Receipt" in C. Mitchell (ed.), *Constructive and Resulting Trusts* (2010). And cf. R. Nolan, "Equitable Property" (2006) L.Q.R. 232, pp. 239–240, who cites various old cases for the proposition that unless they give consideration even the innocent recipients of misdirected trust property are "liable to the trust in the same manner as the trustees themselves were": e.g. *Pye v Gorge* (1710) 1 P. Wms. 128 at 128; *Mansell v Mansell* (1732) P. Wms. 678 at 681. We agree that recipients can owe duties akin to those owed by express trustees, but we consider that Nolan places insufficient emphasis on the fact that in all of these cases the defendant still had the property when proceedings were brought, by which time he must have known of the breach of trust even if he had previously been unaware of it.

[40] [1929] 2 Ch 213 at 222–223.

[41] For this reason the High Court of Australia was incorrect to say in *Farah Constructions Pty Ltd v Say-Dee Pty Ltd* (2007) 230 C.L.R. 89 at [134] that "recognising [strict liability in unjust enrichment as] a new and additional avenue of relief . . . is an avenue which tends to render [liability for knowing receipt] otiose."

[42] 43 N.Y. 2d 305; 372 N.E. 2d 291 (1977).

[43] See para.12–81.

D. Liability in Unjust Enrichment for Misdirected Trust Funds?

12–18 Some scholars have argued that recipients of misdirected trust property should owe a strict liability in unjust enrichment for the value of the property received.[44] This argument has been accepted by some eminent judges in obiter dicta and extra-judicial writings,[45] but in *BCCI (Overseas) Ltd v Akindele*,[46] Nourse L.J. considered that a decision of the House of Lords would be needed to recognise such a claim in English law.[47] Presumably he thought that recognising a strict liability claim would be inconsistent with all the knowing receipt cases since *Barnes v Addy*,[48] which require proof of fault. However these cases only make fault a prerequisite for (compensatory) liability to account as a constructive trustee, and they say nothing about (restitutionary) liability in unjust enrichment to repay the value of the benefit received.

12–19 Three strands of authority could be drawn upon by a claimant arguing for the introduction of such a claim. First, it was held by the House of Lords in *Ministry of Health v Simpson*[49] that the recipients of funds improperly distributed in the administration of a deceased person's estate are strictly liable to repay the persons properly entitled to the estate, and it could be argued that there is no compelling reason why this situation should be treated differently from the situation where a defendant receives misdirected trust assets. Second, it was held by the House of Lords in *Lipkin Gorman v Karpnale Ltd*[50] that a common law action for money had and received would lie where a claimant's property was wrongfully taken from him by a third party and transferred without his knowledge to the defendant, and again it could be argued that there is no compelling reason why this situation should be treated differently from the situation where a defendant receives misdirected trust assets. Third, it has been held that where trust assets are misappropriated by a trustee and used to pay off a security charged on property belonging to an innocent third party, the beneficiaries are entitled to be subrogated to the extinguished rights which were formerly possessed by the charge-holder, and to be treated, by a legal fiction, as though these rights were not extinguished, but were instead assigned to the beneficiaries in order that they might enforce them against the innocent third party.[51] The English courts have held that subrogation is a remedy awarded to reverse unjust enrichment,[52] and if beneficiaries are entitled to acquire proprietary rights against innocent third parties via subrogation on the ground of unjust enrichment, then a fortiori they should also be entitled to a direct personal claim in unjust enrichment against innocent third parties who have been enriched at the beneficiaries' expense.

---

[44] e.g. P. Birks, "Receipt" in P. Birks and A. Pretto (eds) *Breach of Trust* (2002) 213; A. Burrows, *The Law of Restitution* 2nd edn (2004) 202–206; R. Chambers and J. Penner, "Ignorance" in S. Degeling and J. Edelman (eds), *Restitution in Commercial Law* (2008) (identifying "want of authority" rather than "ignorance" as the reason for restitution). An argument against the recognition of a claim in unjust enrichment is offered by L.D. Smith, "Unjust Enrichment, Property, and the Structure of Trusts" (2000) 116 L.Q.R. 412.

[45] Lord Nicholls, "Knowing Receipt: The Need for a New Landmark", in W.R. Cornish et al. (eds) *Restitution: Past, Present and Future* (1998); Lord Walker, "Dishonesty and Unconscionable Conduct in Commercial Life—Some Reflections on Accessory Liability and Knowing Receipt" (2005) 27 Sydney L.R. 187 at 202; Lord Millett, "Proprietary Restitution" in S. Degeling and J. Edelman *Equity in Commercial Law* (2005) at 311. See too *Twinsectra Ltd v Yardley* [2002] 2 A.C. 164 at 194 and *Dubai Aluminium Co Ltd v Salaam* [2003] 2 A.C. 366 at [87].

[46] [2001] Ch. 437 at 456.

[47] An opportunity for the House of Lords to decide whether such a claim lies in English law seemed to have arisen in 2009 when the CA's decision in *Charter Plc v City Index Ltd* [2008] Ch. 313 was appealed. However the parties' dispute was settled before the appeal was heard.

[48] (1874) L.R. 9 Ch. App. 244

[49] [1951] A.C. 251.

[50] [1991] 2 A.C. 548.

[51] *McCullough v Marsden* (1919) 45 D.L.R. 645 at 646–647; *Primlake Ltd (in liq.) v Matthews Assocs* [2007] 1 B.C.L.C. 666 at [340].

[52] *Banque Financière de la Cité v Parc (Battersea) Ltd* [1999] A.C. 221 at 228 and 234, followed in *Niru Battery Manufacturing Co v Milestone Trading Ltd (No.2)* [2004] 2 All E.R. (Comm.) 289, at [27]–[28]; *Filby v Mortgage Express (No.2) Ltd* [2004] EWCA Civ 759 at [62].

E. Other Jurisdictions

12–20 The question whether the recipients of misdirected trust funds owe a liability in unjust enrichment has been addressed by the courts of several other jurisdictions. In *Farah Constructions Pty Ltd v Say-Dee Pty Ltd*,[53] the High Court of Australia held that they do not, essentially because the court denied that unjust enrichment is an independent source of rights and obligations in Australian law, a view that was out of line with many previous High Court decisions which hold that it is[54]. In *Gold v Rosenberg*[55] and *Citadel General Assurance Co v Lloyds Bank Canada*,[56] the Supreme Court of Canada held that the "essence" of a knowing receipt claim is that the defendant has been unjustly enriched at the claimant's expense. Unfortunately the court's analysis conflates liability to account for trust property and liability in unjust enrichment to repay the value of property received, with the result that the important remedial differences between these two types of liability were obscured.[57] In *Re Esteem Settlement*,[58] the Royal Court of Jersey held that liability for knowing receipt is not itself a liability in unjust enrichment, but that all recipients of misdirected trust property owe a strict liability in unjust enrichment, whether or not they know of the breach of trust, so that a knowing recipient owes concurrent liabilities in knowing receipt and unjust enrichment. If the English courts decide to recognise a claim in unjust enrichment against the recipients of misdirected trust funds, then it is submitted that the Jersey rather than the Canadian model would be preferable.

F. Change of Position Defence

12–21 If the English courts do hold that a claim in unjust enrichment lies against the recipients of misapplied trust property, then it seems likely that recipients who are sued on this basis will often attempt to raise a change of position defence. It therefore seems apposite to give a brief account here of the circumstances in which this defence is available. Note that change of position is not a defence to claims in knowing receipt, first, because it is only a defence to claims in unjust enrichment, which knowing receipt claims are not; and, second, because the unconscionability of the defendant's behaviour would automatically debar him from relying on the defence, which is only available to those who have acted in good faith.

12–22 In practice, the defence of change of position is most often relied on by defendants who have incurred extraordinary expenditure in reliance on their receipt of the benefit: i.e. they have been led to spend their money on something which they would not have bought if they had not received the benefit.[59] However, the defence is available to a wider class of defendants than this, and there is no need to show that the change in a defendant's position came about because he consciously chose to spend the money, although there must be a causal link, at least on a "but-for" basis, between the receipt of the benefit and the change in the defendant's position.[60] Thus, a defendant who is paid £5,000 in banknotes and then immediately loses them when his wallet is stolen can raise the defence although it cannot be said that he changed his position in reliance on his receipt. A defendant who changes his position in anticipation of a benefit which is subsequently paid to him can also raise the defence.[61] However

---

[53] (2007) 230 C.L.R. 89 at [148]–[158].
[54] e.g. *Pavey & Matthews Pty Ltd v Paul* (1987) 162 C.L.R. 221 at 227 and 256–257; *David Securities Pty Ltd v Commonwealth Bank of Australia* (1992) 175 C.L.R. 353 at 379 and 392; *ANZ Banking Group v Westpac Banking Corp* (1998) 164 C.L.R. 662 at 673.
[55] [1997] 3 SCR 767.
[56] [1997] 3 SCR 805.
[57] For these differences, see para.12–16.
[58] 2002 JLR 53 at [148]–[161].
[59] As in e.g. *Philip Collins Ltd v Davis* [2000] 3 All ER 808 at 827–830.
[60] *Scottish Equitable Plc v Derby* [2001] 3 All E.R. 818 at 827; *Rose v AIB Group (UK) Plc* [2003] 2 B.C.L.C. 374 at [49]; *Cressman v Coys of Kensington (Sales) Ltd* [2004] 1 W.L.R. 2775 at [49].
[61] *Dextra Bank & Trust Co Ltd v Bank of Jamaica* [2002] 1 All E.R. (Comm.) 193.

a defendant who changes his position by purchasing an asset which remains in his possession at the time of the claim cannot rely on the defence to the extent that he remains enriched by his possession of the asset.[62]

12–23 In *Lipkin Gorman v Karpnale Ltd*,[63] Lord Goff held that the defence is not available to those who act in bad faith nor to wrongdoers. This good faith requirement clearly excludes defendants who have been self-consciously dishonest, but it can also exclude those who have failed "to act in a commercially acceptable way" and those who have engaged in "sharp practice of a kind that falls short of outright dishonesty".[64] On the other hand, "mere negligence on the part of the recipient is not sufficient to deprive him of the defence of change of position".[65]

BANK OF CREDIT AND COMMERCE INTERNATIONAL (OVERSEAS) LTD v AKINDELE

Court of Appeal [2001] Ch. 437, [2000] 3 W.L.R. 1423, [2000] 4 All E.R. 221

12–24 The defendant, Chief Akindele, entered a contract with two companies, ICIC (Overseas) Ltd and BCCI (Overseas) Ltd, for the purchase of shares in their holding company, BCCI Holdings (Luxembourg) SA. The contract provided that the defendant would pay US$10 million to BCCI (Overseas) Ltd in exchange for 250,000 shares in the holding company, and on terms that after two years BCCI (Overseas) Ltd would arrange for their sale at a price that would give the defendant a 15 per cent annual return on his investment. The defendant paid the money, and by a further agreement, the shares were later sold and the defendant was paid US$16.679 million. Following the insolvent liquidation of ICIC (Overseas) Ltd and BCCI (Overseas) Ltd, it emerged that these arrangements had been procured as part of a fraudulent scheme by officers of the BCCI group, acting in breach of their fiduciary duty to their employers, the point of which had been to give the false impression that certain dummy loans had been performing normally. The liquidators of the two companies claimed that the defendant was liable to account to them for US$6.679m as a constructive trustee on the basis that he had knowingly assisted the breaches of fiduciary duty or had received the US$16.679 million with knowledge of these breaches. At first instance Carnwath J. dismissed the action on the ground that dishonesty by the defendant was the essential foundation of the claimants' case whether under the head of knowing assistance or of knowing receipt and that this had not been established by the claimants. The liquidators appealed.

NOURSE L.J. (with whom WARD L.J. and SEDLEY L.J. agreed) stated the facts and then continued:

The Claimants' Case in this Court

12–25 The judge[66] identified the two main issues arising on the pleadings as being, first, was the defendant liable for dishonestly assisting or participating in breaches of trust by Mr Naqvi, Mr Hafeez and Mr Kazmi (knowing assistance) and, secondly, was the defendant liable for receiving the divestiture payment with knowledge of the breaches of trust (knowing receipt). In this court the claimants' case has been maintained under both heads. In regard to knowing assistance, while accepting the judge's findings of primary fact, Mr Sheldon submitted that he was wrong not to infer from them that the defendant had acted dishonestly. I cannot accept that submission. Having seen and heard the defendant give evidence and found him to be a credible witness on most points, and after a conscientious consideration of the evidence as a whole, the

---

62 *Lipkin Gorman v Karpnale Ltd* [1991] 2 A.C. 548 at 560.

63 *Lipkin Gorman* at 580; *Credit Suisse (Monaco) SA v Attar* [2004] EWHC 374 (Comm) at [98].

64 *Niru Battery Manufacturing Co v Milestone Trading Ltd (No.1)* [2002] 2 All E.R. (Comm.) 705 at [125], per Moore-Bick J., affirmed [2004] 1 Lloyd's Rep. 344.

65 *Niru* at [125], per Moore-Bick J., relying on *Dextra Bank & Trust Co Ltd v Bank of Jamaica* [2002] 1 All E.R. (Comm.) 193, where at [42]–[45] the Privy Council declined to hold that the relative fault of the claimant and the defendant can affect the availability of the defence.

66 [1999] B.C.C. 669 at 675–676.

judge was entitled to find that he had acted honestly. It cannot be said either that there was no evidence to support that finding or that it was against the weight of the evidence as a whole. The defendant not having acted dishonestly, the case in knowing assistance is bound to fail. If the claim is to succeed at all, it can only be in knowing receipt.

Knowing Receipt

The essential requirements of knowing receipt were stated by Hoffmann L.J. in *El Ajou v Dollar Land Holdings Plc*:[67] **12–26**

> "For this purpose the plaintiff must show, first, a disposal of his assets in breach of fiduciary duty; secondly, the beneficial receipt by the defendant of assets which are traceable as representing the assets of the plaintiff; and thirdly, knowledge on the part of the defendant that the assets he received are traceable to a breach of fiduciary duty."

In the present case the first two requirements were satisfied in relation to the defendant's receipt of the US$16.679m paid to him pursuant to the divestiture agreement. But the satisfaction of the third requirement, knowledge on the part of the defendant that the sum received by him was traceable to a breach or breaches of fiduciary duty by Mr Naqvi, Mr Hafeez and Mr Kazmi, is problematical. **12–27**

So far as the law is concerned, the comprehensive arguments of Mr Sheldon and Mr Moss have demonstrated that there are two questions which, though closely related, are distinct: first, what, in this context, is meant by knowledge; second, is it necessary for the recipient to act dishonestly? Because the answer to it is the simpler, the convenient course is to deal with the second of those questions first. **12–28**

Knowing Receipt—Dishonesty

As appears from the penultimate sentence of his judgment, Carnwath J. proceeded on an assumption that dishonesty in one form or another was the essential foundation of the claimants' case, whether in knowing assistance or knowing receipt. That was no doubt caused by the acceptance before him (though not at any higher level) by Mr Sheldon, recorded at p.677f, that the thrust of the recent authorities at first instance was that the recipient's state of knowledge must fall into one of the first three categories listed by Peter Gibson J. in *Baden, Delvaux v Société Générale pour Favoriser le Développement du Commerce et de l'Industrie en France SA*,[68] on which basis, said Mr Justice Carnwath, it was doubtful whether the test differed materially in practice from that for knowing assistance. However, the assumption on which the judge proceeded, derived as I believe from an omission to distinguish between the questions of knowledge and dishonesty, was incorrect in law. While a knowing recipient will often be found to have acted dishonestly, it has never been a prerequisite of the liability that he should. **12–29**

An authoritative decision on this question, the complexity of whose subject transactions has sometimes caused it to be overlooked in this particular context, is *Belmont Finance Corporation v Williams Furniture Ltd (No.2)*,[69] where the plaintiff ("Belmont") was the wholly-owned subsidiary of the second defendant ("City"), which in turn was the wholly-owned subsidiary of the first defendant ("Williams"). The chairman of all three companies and the sole effective force in the management of their affairs was Mr John James. Reduced to its essentials, what had happened there was that the shareholders of a fourth company ("Maximum") had agreed to sell its shares to Belmont for £500,000 and to buy the share capital of Belmont from City for £489,000, a transaction which, as carried out, constituted a contravention of section 54 of the Companies Act 1948 (prohibition of provision of financial assistance by a company for the purchase of its own shares) and was thus a misapplication of Belmont's funds. **12–30**

Belmont having subsequently become insolvent, its receiver obtained an independent valuation of the shares in Maximum as at the date of the transaction which suggested that, instead of being worth £500,000, they were only worth some £60,000. The receiver brought an action in Belmont's name principally against Williams, City and the shareholders of Maximum, claiming that they were liable to Belmont, **12–31**

[67] [1994] 2 All E.R. 685 at 700.
[68] [1993] 1 W.L.R. 509 at 575–576.
[69] [1980] 1 All E.R. 393.

first, for damages for conspiracy and, secondly, as constructive trustees on the grounds of both knowing assistance and knowing receipt. At the trial, Foster J. found that Mr James genuinely believed that to buy the capital of Maximum for £500,000 was a good commercial proposition for Belmont. He held that there had been no contravention of section 54 and dismissed the action.

12–32 On Belmont's successful appeal to this court Buckley L.J. is recorded[70] as having pointed out that Mr James had genuinely believed that the transaction was a good commercial proposition for Belmont without having any good grounds for that belief. He continued:

> "After careful consideration I do not feel that we should be justified in disturbing the judge's finding that Mr James genuinely believed that the agreement was a good commercial proposition for Belmont. It was a belief which, on his view of the commercial aspects of the case, Mr James could have sincerely held."

12–33 Having observed that Mr James, as a director of both Williams and City knew perfectly well what the objects of the transaction were, that other officers of City had the same knowledge and that their knowledge must be "imputed" to the respective companies,[71] and having referred[72] to the judgment of Lord Selborne L.C. in *Barnes v Addy*,[73] Buckley L.J. dealt with the claim in constructive trust:[74]

> "In the present case, the payment of the £500,000 by Belmont to [the shareholders of Maximum], being an unlawful contravention of section 54, was a misapplication of Belmont's money and was in breach of the duties of the directors of Belmont. £489,000 of the £500,000 so misapplied found their way into the hands of City with City's knowledge of the whole circumstances of the transaction. It must follow, in my opinion, that City is accountable to Belmont as a constructive trustee of the £489,000 under the first of Lord Selborne L.C.'s two heads. There remains the question whether City is chargeable as a constructive trustee under Lord Selborne's second head on the ground that Belmont's directors were guilty of dishonesty in buying the shares of Maximum and that City with knowledge of the facts assisted them in that dishonest design. As I understand Lord Selborne L.C.'s second head, a stranger to a trust notwithstanding that he may not have received any of the trust fund which has been misapplied will be treated as accountable as a constructive trustee if he has knowingly participated in a dishonest design on the part of the trustee to misapply the fund; he must himself have been in some way a party to the dishonesty of the trustees. It follows from what I have already held that the directors of Belmont were guilty of misfeasance but not that they acted dishonestly."

12–34 Goff L.J. also held that City was liable in knowing receipt.[75] Waller L.J. did not add anything of his own on the question of constructive trust. Accordingly, though the claim in knowing assistance failed because the directors of Belmont did not act dishonestly, the claim in knowing receipt succeeded. I will return to that decision when dealing with the question of knowledge.

12–35 *Belmont Finance Corporation v Williams Furniture Ltd (No.2)* is clear authority for the proposition that dishonesty is not a necessary ingredient of liability in knowing receipt. There have been other, more recent, judicial pronouncements to the same effect. Thus in *Polly Peck International Plc v Nadir (No.2)*,[76] Scott L.J. said that liability in a knowing receipt case did not require that the misapplication of the trust funds should be fraudulent. While in theory it is possible for a misapplication not to be fraudulent and the recipient to be dishonest, in practice such a combination must be rare. Similarly, in *Agip (Africa) Ltd v Jackson*,[77] Millett J. said that in knowing receipt it was immaterial whether the breach of trust was fraudulent or not. The point was made most clearly by Vinelott J. in *Eagle Trust Plc v SBC Securities Ltd*:[78]

---

70 At 403.
71 At 404.
72 At 405.
73 (1874) L.R. 9 Ch. App. 244 at 251.
74 At 405.
75 At 410–412.
76 [1992] 4 All E.R. 769 at 777.
77 [1990] Ch. 265 at 292.
78 [1993] 1 W.L.R. 484 at 497.

> "What the decision in *Belmont (No. 2)* shows is that in a 'knowing receipt' case it is only necessary to show that the defendant knew that the moneys paid to him were trust moneys and of circumstances which made the payment a misapplication of them. Unlike a 'knowing assistance' case it is not necessary, and never has been necessary, to show that the defendant was in any sense a participator in a fraud."

Knowing Receipt—The Authorities on Knowledge

With the proliferation in the last 20 years or so of cases in which the misapplied assets of companies have come into the hands of third parties, there has been a sustained judicial and extra-judicial debate as to the knowledge on the part of the recipient which is required in order to found liability in knowing receipt. Expressed in its simplest terms, the question is whether the recipient must have actual knowledge (or the equivalent) that the assets received are traceable to a breach of trust or whether constructive knowledge is enough. The instinctive approach of most equity judges, especially in this court, has been to assume that constructive knowledge is enough. But there is now a series of decisions of eminent first instance judges who, after considering the question in greater depth, have come to the contrary conclusion, at all events when commercial transactions are in point. In the Commonwealth, on the other hand, the preponderance of authority has been in favour of the view that constructive knowledge is enough. 12–36

In *Karak Rubber Co Ltd v Burden*,[79] Brightman J. referred to a person: 12–37

> "who is a constructive trustee because (though not nominated as a trustee) he has received trust property with actual or constructive notice that it is trust property transferred in breach of trust . . .".

In *Belmont (No.2)*,[80] Buckley L.J. referred to the principle, established by the decision of this court in *Re Lands Allotment Co*,[81] that the directors of a company are treated as if they were actual trustees of the assets of the company which are in their hands or under their control. He continued: 12–38

> "So, if the directors of a company in breach of their fiduciary duties misapply the funds of their company so that they come into the hands of some stranger to the trust who receives them with knowledge (actual or constructive) of the breach, he cannot conscientiously retain those funds against the company unless he has some better equity. He becomes a constructive trustee for the company of the misapplied funds."

Goff L.J. said that what Belmont had to show, among other things, was that City received all or part of the £500,000 "knowing or in circumstances in which it ought to know, that it was a breach of trust".[82] He answered that question, saying:[83] 12–39

> "In my judgment the answer to that question must plainly be Yes for they are fixed with all the knowledge that Mr James had. Now, he had actual knowledge of all the facts which made the agreement illegal and his belief that the agreement was a good commercial proposition for Belmont can be no more a defence to City's liability as constructive trustees than in conspiracy. Apart from this, clearly, in my judgment, Mr James knew or ought to have known all the facts that I have rehearsed, showing that there was in any event a misfeasance apart from illegality."

Similarly, in *Rolled Steel Products (Holdings) Ltd v British Steel Corporation*,[84] Browne-Wilkinson L.J. said: 12–40

> "A third party who has notice—actual or constructive—that a transaction, although intra vires the company, was entered into in excess or abuse of the powers of the company cannot enforce such

[79] [1972] 1 W.L.R. 602 at 632.
[80] At 405.
[81] [1894] 1 Ch. 616.
[82] At 410.
[83] At 412.
[84] [1986] Ch. 246 at 306.

transaction against the company and will be accountable as constructive trustee for any money or property of the company received by [him]."

12–41 In *Agip (Africa) Ltd v Jackson*,[85] Millett J., in reference to a person who receives for his own benefit trust property transferred to him in breach of trust, said:

"He is liable as a constructive trustee if he received it with notice, actual or constructive, that it was trust property and that the transfer to him was a breach of trust. . .".

12–42 In *Houghton v Fayers*,[86] I myself said that it was enough for the claimant company to establish that the second defendant "knew or ought to have known that the money had been paid to him in breach of [the first defendant's] fiduciary duty to [the claimant]".

12–43 Collectively, those observations might be thought to provide strong support for the view that constructive knowledge is enough. But it must at once be said that in each of the three cases in this court (including, despite some apparent uncertainty in the judgment of Goff L.J.,[87] *Belmont (No.2)*) actual knowledge was found and, further, that the decisions in *Karak* and *Agip* were based on knowing assistance, not knowing receipt. Thus in none of the five cases was it necessary for the question to be examined in any depth and there appears to be no case in which such an examination has been conducted in this court. The groundwork has been done in other cases at first instance. I will refer to those of them in which the question has been considered in depth.

12–44 The seminal judgment, characteristically penetrative in its treatment of authority and, in the best sense, argumentative, is that of Megarry V.C. in *Re Montagu's Settlement Trusts*.[88] It was he who first plumbed the distinction between notice and knowledge. It was he who, building on a passage in the judgment of this court in *Re Diplock*,[89] first emphasised the fundamental difference between the questions which arise in respect of the doctrine of purchaser without notice on the one hand and the doctrine of constructive trusts on the other. Reading from his earlier judgment in the same case, he said:[90]

"The former is concerned with the question whether a person takes property subject to or free from some equity. The latter is concerned with whether or not a person is to have imposed upon him the personal burdens and obligations of trusteeship. I do not see why one of the touchstones for determining the burdens on property should be the same as that for deciding whether to impose a personal obligation on a [person]. The cold calculus of constructive and imputed notice does not seem to me to be an appropriate instrument for deciding whether a [person's] conscience is sufficiently affected for it to be right to bind him by the obligations of a constructive trustee."

12–45 He added that there is more to being made a trustee than merely taking property subject to an equity.

12–46 The practical importance of that distinction had been explained by the Vice-Chancellor in his earlier judgment. The question in that case was whether the widow and executrix of the will of the 10th Duke of Manchester was liable to account to the 11th Duke in respect of certain settled chattels or the proceeds of sale thereof. Having found that the 10th Duke had had no knowledge that the chattels received by him were still subject to any trust and that he believed that they had been lawfully and properly released to him by the trustees, Megarry V.C. continued:[91]

"If liability as a constructive trustee depended on his knowledge, then he was not liable as a constructive trustee, and his estate is not liable for any chattels that have been disposed of, as distinct from any traceable proceeds of them. Even if he was not a constructive trustee and was a mere volunteer, his

---

[85] At 291.
[86] [2000] 1 B.C.L.C. 511 at 516.
[87] At 412.
[88] [1987] Ch. 264.
[89] [1948] Ch. 465 at 478–479.
[90] At 278.
[91] At 272.

> estate is liable to yield up any chattels that remain, or the traceable proceeds of any that have gone. . . . But unless he was a constructive trustee, there appears to be no liability if the chattels have gone and there are no traceable proceeds."

Megarry V.C. summarised his conclusions in eight subparagraphs.[92] I read the first three: **12–47**

> "(1) The equitable doctrine of tracing and the imposition of a constructive trust by reason of the knowing receipt of trust property are governed by different rules and must be kept distinct. Tracing is primarily a means of determining the rights of property, whereas the imposition of a constructive trust creates personal obligations that go beyond mere property rights. (2) In considering whether a constructive trust has arisen in a case of the knowing receipt of trust property, the basic question is whether the conscience of the recipient is sufficiently affected to justify the imposition of such a trust. (3) Whether a constructive trust arises in such a case primarily depends on the knowledge of the recipient, and not on notice to him; and for clarity it is desirable to use the word 'knowledge' and avoid the word 'notice' in such cases."

The effect of the Vice-Chancellor's decision, broadly stated, was that, in order to establish liability in knowing receipt, the recipient must have actual knowledge (or the equivalent) that the assets received are traceable to a breach of trust and that constructive knowledge is not enough. **12–48**

In *Eagle Trust Plc v SBC Securities Ltd*,[93] Vinelott J. did not think it would be right to found a decision that the statement of claim in that case disclosed no cause of action solely on the authority of *Re Montagu's Settlement Trusts*. However, on the ground that he (unlike Megarry V.C.) was dealing with a commercial transaction, he arrived at the same conclusion and held that in such a transaction constructive knowledge is not enough. He cited[94] a well known passage in the judgment of Lindley L.J. in *Manchester Trust v Furness*,[95] the latter part of which reads thus: **12–49**

> "In dealing with estates in land title is everything, and it can be leisurely investigated; in commercial transactions possession is everything, and there is no time to investigate title; and if we were to extend the doctrine of constructive notice to commercial transactions we should be doing infinite mischief and paralyzing the trade of the country."

The decision of Vinelott J. was followed by Knox J. in *Cowan de Groot Properties Ltd v Eagle Trust Plc*[96] (another case of a commercial transaction) and the decisions of both of them by Arden J. at the trial of the action in *Eagle Trust Plc v SBC Securities Ltd*.[97] **12–50**

We were also referred to three decisions in New Zealand and one in Canada. In each of *Westpac Banking Corp v Savin*,[98] *Equiticorp Industries Group Ltd v Hawkins*,[99] and *Lankshear v ANZ Banking Group (New Zealand) Ltd*,[100] the preferred view was that constructive knowledge was enough, although in the last-named case the point went by concession. All of them were cases of commercial transactions. In *Westpac Banking Corp v Savin*, a decision of the Court of Appeal, Richardson J., having expressed a provisional preference for the view that constructive knowledge was enough, said:[101] **12–51**

> "Clearly Courts would not readily import a duty to enquire in the case of commercial transactions where they must be conscious of the seriously inhibiting effects of a wide application of the doctrine. Nevertheless there must be cases where there is no justification on the known facts for allowing a commercial man

---

92 At 285.
93 At 503.
94 At 504.
95 [1895] 2 Q.B. 539 at 545.
96 [1992] 4 All E.R. 700.
97 See [1996] 1 B.C.L.C. 121.
98 [1985] 2 N.Z.L.R. 41.
99 [1991] 3 N.Z.L.R. 700.
100 [1993] 1 N.Z.L.R. 481.
101 At 53.

who has received funds paid to him in breach of trust to plead the shelter of the exigencies of commercial life."

12–52 In *Citadel General Assurance Co v Lloyds Bank Canada*,[102] another case of a commercial transaction, the Supreme Court of Canada held, as a matter of decision, that constructive knowledge was enough.

The *Baden* Case

12–53 It will have been observed that up to this stage I have made no more than a passing reference to the five-fold categorisation of knowledge accepted by Peter Gibson J. in the *Baden* case:[103] (i) actual knowledge; (ii) wilfully shutting one's eyes to the obvious; (iii) wilfully and recklessly failing to make such enquiries as an honest and reasonable man would make; (iv) knowledge of circumstances which would indicate the facts to an honest and reasonable man; (v) knowledge of circumstances which will put an honest and reasonable man on inquiry. Reference to the categorisation has been made in most of the knowing receipt cases to which I have referred from *Re Montagu's Settlement Trusts* onwards. In many of them it has been influential in the decision. In general, the first three categories have been taken to constitute actual knowledge (or its equivalent) and the last two constructive knowledge.

12–54 Two important points must be made about the *Baden* categorisation. First, it appears to have been propounded by counsel for the plaintiffs, accepted by counsel for the defendant and then put to the judge on an agreed basis. Secondly, though both counsel accepted that all five categories of knowledge were relevant and neither sought to submit that there was any distinction for that purpose between knowing receipt and knowing assistance (a view with which the judge expressed his agreement[104]), the claim in constructive trust was based squarely on knowing assistance and not on knowing receipt.[105] In the circumstances, whatever may have been agreed between counsel, it is natural to assume that the categorisation was not formulated with knowing receipt primarily in mind. This, I think, may be confirmed by the references to "an honest and reasonable man" in categories (iv) and (v). Moreover, in *Agip* Millett J. warned against over refinement or a too ready assumption that categories (iv) and (v) are necessarily cases of constructive knowledge only.[106]

Knowing Receipt—The Recipient's State of Knowledge

12–55 In *Royal Brunei Airlines Sdn Bhd v Tan*,[107] which is now the leading authority on knowing assistance, Lord Nicholls of Birkenhead, in delivering the judgment of the Privy Council, said that "knowingly" was better avoided as a defining ingredient of the liability, and that in that context the *Baden* categorisation was best forgotten.[108] Although my own view is that the categorisation is often helpful in identifying different states of knowledge which may or may not result in a finding of dishonesty for the purposes of knowing assistance, I have grave doubts about its utility in cases of knowing receipt. Quite apart from its origins in a context of knowing assistance and the reservations of Millett and Knox JJ., any categorisation is of little value unless the purpose it is to serve is adequately defined, whether it be fivefold, as in *Baden*, or twofold, as in the classical division between actual and constructive knowledge, a division which has itself become blurred in recent authorities.

12–56 What then, in the context of knowing receipt, is the purpose to be served by a categorisation of knowledge? It can only be to enable the court to determine whether, in the words of Buckley L.J. in *Belmont (No.2)*, the recipient can "conscientiously retain [the] funds against the company" or, in the words of Megarry V.C. in *Re Montagu's Settlement Trusts*, "[the recipient's] conscience is sufficiently affected for it to be right to bind him by the obligations of a constructive trustee". But if that is the purpose, there is no need for categorisation. All that is necessary is that the recipient's state of knowledge should be such as to make it unconscionable for him to retain the benefit of the receipt.

---

[102] (1997) 152 D.L.R. (4th) 411.
[103] [1993] 1 W.L.R. 509, 575–576.
[104] At 582.
[105] See 572.
[106] [1990] Ch. 265 at 293, reservations which were shared by Knox J. in *Cowan de Groot* [1992] 4 All E.R. 700 at 761.
[107] [1995] 2 A.C. 378.
[108] At 392.

12–57 For these reasons I have come to the view that, just as there is now a single test of dishonesty for knowing assistance, so ought there to be a single test of knowledge for knowing receipt. The recipient's state of knowledge must be such as to make it unconscionable for him to retain the benefit of the receipt. A test in that form, though it cannot, any more than any other, avoid difficulties of application, ought to avoid those of definition and allocation to which the previous categorisations have led. Moreover, it should better enable the courts to give common-sense decisions in the commercial context in which claims in knowing receipt are now frequently made, paying equal regard to the wisdom of Lindley L.J. on the one hand and of Richardson J. on the other.

Knowing Receipt—A Footnote

12–58 We were referred in argument to "Knowing Receipt: The Need for a New Landmark", an essay by Lord Nicholls;[109] a work of insight and scholarship taking forward the writings of academic authors, in particular those of Professors Birks, Burrows and Gareth Jones. It is impossible to do justice to such a work within the compass of a judgment such as this. Most pertinent for present purposes is the suggestion made by Lord Nicholls,[110] in reference to the decision of the House of Lords in *Lipkin Gorman v Karpnale Ltd*:[111]

> "In this respect equity should now follow the law. Restitutionary liability, applicable regardless of fault but subject to a defence of change of position, would be a better-tailored response to the underlying mischief of misapplied property than personal liability which is exclusively fault-based. Personal liability would flow from having received the property of another, from having been unjustly enriched at the expense of another. It would be triggered by the mere fact of receipt, thus recognising the endurance of property rights. But fairness would be ensured by the need to identify a gain, and by making change of position available as a default in suitable cases when, for instance, the recipient had changed his position in reliance on the receipt."

12–59 Lord Nicholls goes on to examine the *Re Diplock*[112] principle, suggesting that it could be reshaped by being extended to all trusts but in a form modified to take proper account of the decision in *Lipkin Gorman v Karpnale Ltd*.[113]

12–60 No argument before us was based on the suggestions made in Lord Nicholls' essay. Indeed, at this level of decision, it would have been a fruitless exercise. We must continue to do our best with the accepted formulation of the liability in knowing receipt, seeking to simplify and improve it where we may. While in general it may be possible to sympathise with a tendency to subsume a further part of our law of restitution under the principles of unjust enrichment, I beg leave to doubt whether strict liability coupled with a change of position defence would be preferable to fault-based liability in many commercial transactions, for example where, as here, the receipt is of a company's funds which have been misapplied by its directors. Without having heard argument it is unwise to be dogmatic, but in such a case it would appear to be commercially unworkable and contrary to the spirit of the rule in *Royal British Bank v Turquand*[114] that, simply on proof of an internal misapplication of the company's funds, the burden should shift to the recipient to defend the receipt either by a change of position or perhaps in some other way. Moreover, if the circumstances of the receipt are such as to make it unconscionable for the recipient to retain the benefit of it, there is an obvious difficulty in saying that it is equitable for a change of position to afford him a defence.

Knowing Receipt—The Facts of the Present Case

12–61 I return to the facts of the present case, in order to determine whether the defendant is liable in knowing receipt to repay (together with interest) US$6.679m of the sum received by him pursuant to the divestiture agreement, being the excess over the US$10m he paid to ICIC Overseas pursuant to the 1985 agreement. (By a decision whose forensic good sense dispensed with an analysis of its juristic foundation the claimants

---

109 In Cornish, Nolan, O'Sullivan and Virgo (eds) *Restitution Past, Present and Future* (1998).

110 At p.238.

111 [1991] 2 A.C. 548.

112 [1948] Ch. 465.

113 At p.241.

114 (1856) 6 E. & B. 327.

abandoned a claim for the full US$16.679m.) The answer to that question depends on whether the judge's findings, though made in the course of an inquiry as to the defendant's honesty, are equally supportive of a conclusion that his state of knowledge was not such as to make it unconscionable for him to retain the benefit of the receipt.

12–62 I start with the defendant's state of knowledge at the date of the 1985 agreement. As to that, the judge found that there was no evidence that anyone outside BCCI had reason to doubt the integrity of its management at that time. More specifically, it is clear that the judge was of the view that the defendant had no knowledge of the underlying frauds within the BCCI group either in general or in relation to the 1985 agreement. He found that the defendant saw it simply as an arm's-length business transaction. Moreover, he was not prepared to draw the conclusion that the high rate of interest and the artificial nature of the agreement were sufficient to put an honest person in the defendant's position on notice that some fraud or breach of trust was being perpetrated. He said that the defendant would have had no reason to question the form of the transaction.

12–63 Those findings, expressed in language equally appropriate to an inquiry as to constructive notice, appear to me to be consistent only with the view that the defendant's state of knowledge at the date of the 1985 agreement was not such as to make it unconscionable for him to enter into it. However, that point, though of great importance, is not in itself decisive. We have also to consider the defendant's state of knowledge at the date of the divestiture agreement, by which time, as the judge said, he did have suspicions as to the conduct of BCCI's affairs.

12–64 In order to understand the judge's reference, it is necessary to go back to what he said:[115]

> "Towards the end of 1988 the defendant decided to end his relationship with BCCI, and in particular to terminate the share agreement. A number of factors led to this decision. In late 1987 there had been rumours in the Nigerian press of irregularities involving BCCI. He had received warnings from senior business figures in Nigeria. One was Dr Onaolapo Soleye, a former Nigerian Minister of Finance, who has provided a witness statement. He says that he informed the defendant of 'unorthodox and irregular banking practices around the world', and warned him of the effect a scandal relating to BCCI could have on his business image and that of BCCI Nigeria. The defendant also became aware later in 1988 that various BCCI officials had been arrested by US Customs in Tampa in connection with money laundering offences. He considered selling his shares in BCCI Nigeria, but was dissuaded from doing so by Dr Soleye and others, because of the tribal imbalance it would create within the bank. At this time the defendant was seeking to realise £20m of his own money, and to raise a further £40m, to finance a property investment venture in the UK. The major banks involved including NM Rothschild in London and BNP, objected to him raising part of the finance from BCCI."

12–65 So in late 1987, more than two years after the 1985 agreement was entered into, there were press rumours of irregularities involving BCCI and warnings to the defendant from senior business figures in Nigeria of unorthodox and irregular banking practices around the world. Later in 1988 the defendant became aware that various BCCI officials had been arrested in connection with money laundering offences. He also knew that the major banks involved in financing his property investment venture in the United Kingdom objected to his raising part of the finance from BCCI.

12–66 There having been no evidence that the defendant was aware of the internal arrangements within BCCI which led to the payment to him of the US$16.679m pursuant to the divestiture agreement, did the additional knowledge which he acquired between July 1985 and December 1988 make it unconscionable for him to retain the benefit of the receipt? In my judgment it did not. The additional knowledge went to the general reputation of the BCCI group from late 1987 onwards. It was not a sufficient reason for questioning the propriety of a particular transaction entered into more than two years earlier, at a time when no one outside BCCI had reason to doubt the integrity of its management and in a form which the defendant had no reason to question. The judge said that the defendant was entitled to take steps to protect his own interest, and that there was nothing dishonest in his seeking to enforce the 1985 agreement. Nor was there anything unconscionable in his seeking to do so. Equally, had I thought that that was still the appropriate

[115] At p.675.

test, I would have held that the defendant did not have actual or constructive knowledge that his receipt of the US$6.79m was traceable to a breach or breaches of fiduciary duty by Messrs Naqvi, Hafeez and Kazmi.

Conclusion

For these reasons, though by a different route in relation to knowing receipt, I have come to the conclusion that Mr Justice Carnwath's decision to dismiss the action was correct. I would affirm it and dismiss the claimants' appeal. **12–67**

4. Dishonest Assistance

A. The Primary Breach

Claims for dishonest assistance clearly lie against defendants who assist in misapplications of property by trustees, whether express, constructive, or resulting,[116] and other fiduciaries, e.g. company directors.[117] Most probably claims also lie against defendants who assist in breaches of fiduciary duty that do not entail the misapplication of property.[118] **12–68**

There was originally no requirement that a defendant should have assisted in a dishonest breach of duty.[119] Then, in an unreserved judgment not discussing the earlier cases, Lord Selborne L.C. held that assistants in a breach of trust could not be liable unless "they assist with knowledge in a dishonest and fraudulent design on the part of the trustees".[120] In his speech for the Privy Council in *Royal Brunei Airlines Sdn Bhd v Tan*, Lord Nicholls declined to apply this rule, holding that the claimant did not need to show that the breach of trust assisted by the defendant had been a dishonest breach.[121] This finding was affirmed by the House of Lords in *Twinsectra Ltd v Yardley*.[122] **12–69**

B. The Defendant's State of Mind

Turning to the defendant's own state of mind, the cases on this point had got into a sorry state prior to *Royal Brunei*. In the *Baden, Delvaux* case,[123] Peter Gibson J. had held that a defendant might be liable for assisting in a breach of trust even if his behaviour fell short of dishonesty,[124] and he had accepted that any of the five types of knowledge he identified there would serve to render a defendant liable as an assistant in a breach of trust.[125] Subsequently a consensus emerged that, contrary **12–70**

---

116 For the latter, see: *Bank Tejerat v Hong Kong and Shanghai Banking Corp (CI) Ltd* [1995] 1 Lloyd's Rep. 239; *Heinl v Jyske Bank (Gibraltar) Ltd* [1999] Lloyd's Rep. Bank. 511.

117 *Selangor United Rubber Estates Ltd v Cradock (No.3)* [1968] 1 W.L.R. 1555; *Belmont Finance Corp Ltd v Williams Furniture Ltd (No.2)* [1980] 1 All E.R. 393; *Heinl v Jyske Bank (Gibraltar) Ltd* [1999] Lloyd's Rep. Bank. 511.

118 *JD Wetherspoon Plc v Van den Berg & Co Ltd* [2009] EWHC 639 (Ch) at [518]. See too *Goose v Wilson Sandford (a firm)* [2000] EWCA Civ 73; *Waxman v Waxman* (2004) 7 I.T.E.L.R. 162 at [546]. But contrast *Cowan de Groot Properties Ltd v Eagle Trust Plc* [1991] B.C.L.C. 1045 at 1103; *Satnam Investments Ltd v Dunlop Heywood & Co Ltd* [1999] 1 B.C.L.C. 385 at 404; *Petrotrade Inc v Smith* [2000] 1 Lloyd's Rep. 486 at 491–492.

119 *Fyler v Fyler* (1841) 3 Beav. 550; *Att.-Gen v Corporation of Leicester* (1844) 7 Beav. 176.

120 *Barnes v Addy* (1874) L.R. 9 Ch. App. 244 at 252, confirmed in *Belmont Finance Corp v Williams* [1979] Ch. 250 at 257.

121 [1995] 2 A.C. 378 at 385.

122 [2002] 2 A.C. 164 at 171 and 195.

123 [1993] 1 W.L.R. 509 (the case was decided in 1983).

124 *Baden, Delvaux* at 577. For Peter Gibson J.'s five-fold classification, see para.12–11.

125 *Baden, Delvaux* at 575–587.

to Peter Gibson J.'s view, a defendant must have been dishonest to incur liability,[126] but a line of cases pre-dating *Baden, Delvaux*, and holding that a defendant can be liable if he has honestly but negligently failed to investigate the circumstances of an impugned transaction, was never overruled.[127] The body of law founded on the *Baden, Delvaux* classification also suffered from the more general problem that it was over-theorized: as Lord Nicholls put it in *Royal Brunei*, the courts were led into "tortuous convolutions" in their efforts to investigate the "sort" of knowledge possessed by defendants, "when the truth is that 'knowingly' is inapt as a criterion when applied to the gradually darkening spectrum where the differences are of degree and not kind."[128]

12–71 In *Royal Brunei*, Lord Nicholls therefore decided to start afresh. He held that knowledge is best avoided as a defining ingredient of liability, and that the *Baden, Delvaux* scale is best forgotten in this context.[129] He rejected the idea that unconscionability should be the touchstone for liability, unless it is made clear "what, *in this context*, unconscionable *means*",[130] and he held that to fix a defendant with liability, it must be shown that he acted dishonestly. He emphasised that the test for dishonesty in this context is not purely subjective, in the sense that individuals are not "free to set their own standards of honesty in particular circumstances",[131] and must be judged by reference to the standards of right-thinking members of society. So, as the courts have put it in subsequent cases, there is no "Robin Hood" defence to an action for dishonest assistance.[132]

12–72 Did Lord Nicholls mean to lay down a test of self-conscious dishonesty analogous to the test laid down in criminal law by Lord Lane C.J. in *R. v Ghosh*[133]; i.e. must a defendant have done something that right-thinking people would regard as dishonest, and also have been aware that they would view his actions in this light? There are strong pointers in Lord Nicholls' speech that he did not mean to say this, particularly his statement that:[134]

> "Whatever may be the position in some criminal or other contexts (see, for instance, *R. v Ghosh*), in the context of the accessory liability principle acting dishonestly, or with a lack of probity, which is synonymous, means simply not acting as an honest person would in the circumstances. This is an objective standard."

12–73 Notwithstanding this, however, a majority of the House of Lords subsequently held in *Twinsectra Ltd v Yardley* that self-conscious dishonesty was required. Lord Hutton stated that "dishonesty requires knowledge by the defendant that what he was doing would be regarded as dishonest by honest people".[135] Likewise, Lord Hoffmann held that there must be "a dishonest state of mind, that is to say, consciousness that one is transgressing ordinary standards of honest behaviour."[136] Applying this test to the facts of the case, the majority concluded that a solicitor who had enabled a client to commit a

---

126 e.g. *Agip (Africa) Ltd v Jackson* [1990] 1 Ch. 265 at 292–293, on appeal: [1991] Ch. 547 at 569; *Lipkin Gorman v Karpnale Ltd* [1989] 1 W.L.R. 1340 at 1354–1355.

127 *Selangor United Rubber Estates Ltd v Cradock (No.3)* [1968] 1 W.L.R. 1555; *Karak Rubber Co Ltd v Burden (No.2)* [1972] 1 W.L.R. 602; *Rowlandson v National Westminister Bank Ltd* [1978] 1 W.L.R. 798.

128 [1995] 2 A.C. 378 at 391.

129 *Royal Brunei* at 392.

130 *Royal Brunei* at 392 (his emphasis).

131 *Royal Brunei* at 389

132 *Grupo Torras SA v Al-Sabah (No.5)* [2001] Lloyd's Rep. Bank. 36 at 60; *Walker v Stones* [2001] Q.B. 902 at 939; *Twinsectra Ltd v Yardley* [2002] 2 A.C. 164 at 172. Cf. *Consul Developments Pty Ltd v DPC Estates Pty Ltd* (1975) 132 C.L.R. 373 at 398.

133 [1982] Q.B. 1053.

134 [1995] 2 A.C. 378 at 389.

135 [2002] 2 A.C. 164 at [36].

136 *Twinsectra* at [20].

breach of trust by releasing trust money to the client absolutely had not acted dishonestly, although he was aware from the terms of an undertaking given by another solicitor that the client had been meant to take the money as trustee and not as absolute owner.

The majority speeches in *Twinsectra* depended on a very strained reading of Lord Nicholls' words in *Royal Brunei*. However the point was then revisited by the Privy Council, in *Barlow Clowes International Ltd v Eurotrust International Ltd*.[137] There a fraudster laundered several million pounds stolen from the claimant company through bank accounts held in the names of various Isle of Man companies administered by Eurotrust, another company in the Isle of Man which provided offshore financial services. One of the Eurotrust directors was found by the trial judge to have strongly suspected that the money passing through his hands had been stolen, but to have consciously decided not to make inquiries lest he discover the truth. The judge also held that he might have seen nothing wrong with this behaviour, because he had had an "exaggerated notion of dutiful service to clients, which produced a warped moral approach that it was not improper to treat carrying out clients' instructions as being all important."[138] **12–74**

On appeal from the finding that the director was liable for dishonest assistance, counsel argued that on these facts he could not have been relevantly dishonest because he had not been aware that his actions were dishonest by ordinary standards, as required by *Twinsectra*. Lord Hoffmann rejected this. Conceding that there had been "an element of ambiguity" in Lord Hutton's remarks in *Twinsectra*, he held that neither he nor Lord Hutton had meant to say there that a defendant must have considered what normally acceptable standards of honest conduct might be: they had merely meant to say that a defendant must have known about those aspects of the relevant transaction which made his participation transgress those standards.[139] Applying this test to the facts of *Eurotrust*, the defendant was liable. **12–75**

In subsequent cases, the courts have taken Lord Hoffmann at his word and followed *Eurotrust* rather than *Twinsectra*, although the former is a decision of the Privy Council and the latter a decision of the House of Lords.[140] Hence it may now be said that the mental element for dishonest assistance is not self-conscious dishonesty of the kind described by Lord Lane C.J. in *Ghosh* but objective dishonesty of the kind described by Lord Nicholls in *Royal Brunei* and Lord Hoffmann in *Eurotrust*. **12–76**

C. *Dishonesty and Knowledge*

Although he held that knowledge is not the defining ingredient of accessory liability in *Royal Brunei*, Lord Nicholls acknowledged that the honesty of a defendant's conduct can only be assessed in the light of what he knew when he acted. Obviously, the facts which a defendant must have known before he can be said to have acted dishonestly vary from case to case, but it seems that at the very least the defendant must have known "that the person he is assisting is not entitled to do what he is doing."[141] He need not have known all the details of the primary wrongdoer's whole design, though, according to Lewison J. in *Ultraframe (UK) Ltd v Fielding*, although by analogy with criminal accessory liability, he must have known in broad terms what the design was, and his liability should not extend to unforeseen and uncontemplated actions by the primary wrongdoer which lay outside the scope of the joint enterprise in which he participated.[142] **12–77**

---

137 [2006] 1 W.L.R. 1476.
138 [2004] W.T.L.R. 1365 at [133].
139 [2006] 1 W.L.R. 1476 at [15]–[16].
140 e.g. *Abouh-Rahmah v Abacha* [2007] Bus. L.R. 220 at [43]; *Statek Corp v Alford* [2008] W.T.L.R. 1089 at [98]. But cf. *Starglade Properties Ltd v Nash* [2010] EWHC 99 (ch) at [51].
141 *Ultraframe (UK) Ltd v Fielding* [2007] W.T.L.R. 835 at [1504], per Lewison J.
142 *Ultraframe* at [1506].

12–78 Is a defendant relevantly dishonest if he thinks that he is participating in some wrongful transaction other than the breach of trust in which he has actually participated? The cases are divided on this point,[143] but in principle, defendants should not be allowed to make the disreputable argument that they did not think they were helping to steal from the claimant because they thought they were helping to steal from someone else. As Fox L.J. held in *Agip (Africa) Ltd v Jackson*,[144] "persons who [need] to demonstrate that they [have] acted honestly [cannot] shelter behind transactions or objects which [are] themselves disreputable."

D. Causation

12–79 Generally speaking, the law of civil wrongs, like the criminal law, is "moulded on the philosophy of autonomy",[145] with the result that it does not generally regard loss flowing from the actions of a primary wrongdoer as having been caused by the actions of a participant who has induced or assisted in the commission of the wrong.[146] However, liability for dishonest assistance is an exception to this general rule: a defendant is liable for loss flowing from the primary wrong even where there is no direct causal link between his actions and the loss. Thus, in *Grupo Torras SA v Al-Sabah (No.5)* Mance L.J. held that:[147]

> "The starting point . . . is that the requirement of dishonest assistance relates not to any loss or damage which may be suffered, but to the breach of trust or fiduciary duty. The relevant enquiry is . . . what loss or damage resulted from the breach of trust or fiduciary duty which has been dishonestly assisted."

This was affirmed on appeal,[148] and then reaffirmed by a differently constituted Court of Appeal, in *Casio Computer Ltd v Sayo*, where Tuckey L.J. stated that:[149]

> "*Grupo Torras* . . . establishes that in a claim for dishonest assistance it is not necessary to show a precise causal link between the assistance and the loss . . . [and that loss] caused by the breach of fiduciary duty is recoverable from the accessory."

12–80 Of course, where a defendant's actions have made no difference at all to the implementation of a breach of trust or fiduciary duty, "there is no causative effect and therefore no assistance . . . [so that] the requirements of conscience [do not] require any remedy."[150] Hence a claimant must at least show that the defendant's actions have made the fiduciary's breach of duty easier than it would otherwise have been. But the causation requirement for dishonest assistance is no stronger than this, and it is no answer to a claim, for example, that the claimant's loss would have occurred anyway, because the wrongdoing fiduciary would have committed the breach even if the defendant had not assisted him.

---

143 Yes: *Agip (Africa) Ltd v Jackson* [1990] 1 Ch. 265 at 295, affirmed [1991] Ch. 547 at 569; *Ultraframe (UK) Ltd v Fielding* [2007] W.T.L.R. 835 at [1500]. No: *Brink's Ltd v Abu-Saleh* [1999] C.L.C. 133; *Grupo Torras SA v Al-Sabah (No.5)* [1999] C.L.C. 1469 at 1665–1666, affirmed [2001] Lloyd's Rep Bank 36 at 59.

144 [1991] Ch 547 at 569.

145 G. Williams, "Complicity, Purpose and the Draft Code" [1990] Crim. L.R. 4, 6.

146 H.L.A. Hart and A.M. Honoré, *Causation in the Law*, 2nd edn (1985), p.385.

147 [1999] C.L.C. 1469 at 1667.

148 [2001] Lloyd's Rep Bank 36 at 61.

149 [2001] I.L.Pr. 43 at [16].

150 *Brown v Bennett* [1999] 1 B.C.L.C. 649 at 659, per Morritt L.J.

Thus a defendant can be liable for actions or omissions which precede the breach,[151] although he cannot be liable if his actions or omissions only occurred after the breach was fully implemented.[152] However, where the breach has entailed the misapplication of funds, the courts are likely to hold that it was not fully implemented until the funds were hidden away where the beneficiaries could not find them, with the consequence that those who assist in money-laundering activities after trust funds have been removed from a trust account can be fixed with liability for dishonest assistance.[153]

E. Remedies

Different remedies can be awarded against dishonest assistants in different situations.[154] If the wrong-doing trustee incurs a liability to pay money as a form of substitutive performance of his obligation to account for trust property,[155] then the dishonest assistant will be jointly and severally liable for the same amount, as in these circumstances the law will fix him with a civil secondary liability which derives from and duplicates the liability of the trustee.[156] Similarly, the dishonest assistant can also be ordered to pay the same measure of compensation as the trustee would have had to pay if the principal had sued him for reparation.[157] And again, there are a series of Canadian cases,[158] and several English decisions,[159] which hold that where the trustee has incurred a liability to disgorge unauthorised profits,[160] the dishonest assistant will be jointly and severally liable for the same amount—although in *Ultraframe (UK) Ltd v Fielding*,[161] Lewison J. declined to make a finding to this effect because he thought it would amount to a punitive measure. Finally, however, where a dishonest assistant makes profits for himself by his wrongdoing, he will be primarily liable to disgorge these profits.[162] **12–81**

---

151 R.P. Austin, "Constructive Trusts" in P.D. Finn (ed.), *Essays in Equity* (1985), pp.196, 236–237, discussing *Adams v Bank of New South Wales* [1984] 1 N.S.W.L.R. 285. See too *Aequitas Ltd v Sparad No.100 Ltd* (2001) 19 A.C.L.C. 1006.

152 *Brown v Bennett* [1998] 2 B.C.L.C. 97 at 105.

153 *Heinl v Jyske Bank (Gibraltar) Ltd* [1999] Lloyd's Rep. Bank. 511 at 523, approving *Agip (Africa) Ltd v Jackson* [1990] Ch. 265 at 293. See too *Casio Computer Co Ltd v Sayo* [2001] I.L.Pr. 43 at [22].

154 For further discussion, see S.B. Elliott and C. Mitchell, "Remedies for Dishonest Assistance" (2004) 67 M.L.R. 16; P. Ridge, "Justifying the Remedies for Dishonest Assistance" (2008) 124 L.Q.R. 445; M.S. Clapton, "Gain-Based Remedies for Knowing Assistance: Ensuring Assistants Do Not Profit From Their Wrongs" (2008) 45 Alberta L.R. 989; C. Mitchell and S. Watterson, "Remedies for Knowing Receipt" in C. Mitchell (ed.) *Constructive and Resulting Trusts* (2010) at pp.150–154.

155 See paras 11–09 ff, above.

156 See e.g. *Macdonald v Hauer* (1976) 72 D.L.R. (3d) 110 at 129; *Re Bell's Indenture* [1980] 1 W.L.R. 1217 at 1231–1233; *Commercial Union Life Assurance Co of Canada v John Ingle Insurance Group Inc* (2002) 22 C.C.L.I. 221, affirmed (2002) 217 D.L.R. (4th) 178; *NCR Australia Pty Ltd v Credit Connection Pty Ltd (in liq.)* [2004] NSWSC 1 at [150].

157 See paras 11–46 ff. Awards of this sort were made against dishonest assistants in, e.g. *Colour Control Centre Pty Ltd v Ty* N.S.W. Sup. Ct. (Eq. Div.) 24 July 1995; *Equiticorp Industries Group Ltd v R. (No.47)* [1998] 2 N.Z.L.R. 481 at 658; *Fyffes Group Ltd v Templeman* [2000] 2 Lloyd's Rep. 643.

158 Running from *Canada Safeway Ltd v Thompson* [1951] 3 D.L.R. 295 through to *Glenko Enterprises Ltd v Keller* [2001] 1 W.W.R. 229 at 257–258.

159 *Ostrich Farming Corp Ltd v Wallstreet LLC* Ch.D., Lawtel Report 8 October 1998; *Comax Secure Business Services Ltd v Wilson* Q.B.D. 21 June 2001; *CMS Dolphin Ltd v Simonet* [2001] 2 B.C.L.C. 704, followed in *Quarter Master UK Ltd v Pyke* [2005] 1 B.C.L.C. 245.

160 See paras 15–79 ff.

161 [2007] W.T.L.R. 835 at [1589]–[1601].

162 *Consul Development Pty Ltd v DPC Estates Pty Ltd* (1972) 132 C.L.R. 373 at 397, followed in *US Surgical Corp v Hospital Products International Pty Ltd* (1982) 2 N.S.W.L.R. 766 at 817, and quoted with approval in *Fyffes Group Ltd v Templeman* [2000] 2 Lloyd's Rep. 643 at 672. See too *Crown Dilmun v Sutton* [2004] 1 B.C.L.C. 468 at [204]; *Ultraframe (UK) Ltd v Fielding* [2007] W.T.L.R. 835 at [1595]. In *Nanus Asia Co Inc v Standard Chartered Bank* [1990] 1 H.K.L.R. 396 at 417–419, the judge went one step further and held that a dishonest assistant's profits were held on constructive trust; but in *Sinclair Investment Holdings SA v Versailles Trade Finance Ltd (in admin. rec.)* [2007] 2 All E.R. (Comm.) 993, a dishonest assistant was held only to owe a personal liability to disgorge profits.

ROYAL BRUNEI AIRLINES v TAN

Privy Council [1995] 2 A.C. 378, [1995] 3 W.L.R. 64, [1995] 3 All E.R. 97

The judgment of their Lordships was delivered by LORD NICHOLLS OF BIRKENHEAD:

12–82 The proper role of equity in commercial transactions is a topical question. Increasingly plaintiffs have recourse to equity for an effective remedy when the person in default, typically a company, is insolvent. Plaintiffs seek to obtain relief from others who were involved in the transaction, such as directors of the company, or its bankers, or its legal or other advisers. They seek to fasten fiduciary obligations directly onto the company's officers or agents or advisers, or to have them held personally liable for assisting the company in breaches of trust or fiduciary obligations.

12–83 This is such a case. An insolvent travel agent company owed money to an airline. The airline seeks a remedy against the travel agent's principal director and shareholder. Its claim is based on the much-quoted dictum of Lord Selborne L.C., sitting in the Court of Appeal in Chancery, in *Barnes v Addy*:[163]

> "[The responsibility of a trustee] may no doubt be extended in equity to others who are not properly trustees, if they are found . . . actually participating in any fraudulent conduct of the trustee to the injury of the cestui que trust. But . . . strangers are not to be made constructive trustees merely because they act as the agents of trustees in transactions within their legal powers, transactions, perhaps of which a court of equity may disapprove, unless those agents receive and become chargeable with some part of the trust property, or unless they assist with knowledge in a dishonest and fraudulent design on the part of the trustees."

12–84 In the conventional shorthand, the first of these two circumstances in which third parties (non-trustees) may become liable to account in equity is "knowing receipt", as distinct from the second, where liability arises from "knowing assistance". Stated even more shortly, the first limb of Lord Selborne L.C.'s formulation is concerned with the liability of a person as a recipient of trust property or its traceable proceeds. The second limb is concerned with what, for want of a better compendious description, can be called the liability of an accessory to a trustee's breach of trust. Liability as an accessory is not dependent upon receipt of trust property. It arises even though no trust property has reached the hands of the accessory. It is a form of secondary liability in the sense that it only arises where there has been a breach of trust. In the present case the plaintiff airline relies on the accessory limb. The particular point in issue arises from the expression "a dishonest and fraudulent design on the part of the trustees . . .".

12–85 In short, the issue on this appeal is whether the breach of trust which is a prerequisite to accessory liability must itself be a dishonest and fraudulent breach of trust by the trustee.

The Honest Trustee and the Dishonest Third Party

12–86 It must be noted at once that there is a difficulty with the approach adopted on this point in the *Belmont* case.[164] Take the simple example of an honest trustee and a dishonest third party. Take a case where a dishonest solicitor persuades a trustee to apply trust property in a way the trustee honestly believes is permissible but which the solicitor knows full well is a clear breach of trust. The solicitor deliberately conceals this from the trustee. In consequence, the beneficiaries suffer a substantial loss. It cannot be right that in such a case the accessory liability principle would be inapplicable because of the innocence of the trustee. In ordinary parlance, the beneficiaries have been defrauded by the solicitor. If there is to be an accessory liability principle at all, whereby in appropriate circumstances beneficiaries may have direct recourse against a third party, the principle must surely be applicable in such a case, just as much as in a case where both the trustee and the third party have been dishonest. Indeed, if anything, the case for liability of the dishonest third party seems stronger where the trustee is innocent, because in such a case the third party alone was dishonest and that was the cause of the subsequent misapplication of the trust property.

12–87 The position would be the same if, instead of procuring the breach, the third party dishonestly assisted in the breach. Change the facts slightly. A trustee is proposing to make a payment out of the trust fund to

[163] (1874) L.R. 9 Ch. App. 244 at 251–252.
[164] [1979] Ch. 250.

a particular person. He honestly believes he is authorised to do so by the terms of the trust deed. He asks a solicitor to carry through the transaction. The solicitor well knows that the proposed payment would be a plain breach of trust. He also well knows that the trustee mistakenly believes otherwise. Dishonestly he leaves the trustee under his misapprehension and prepares the necessary documentation. Again, if the accessory principle is not to be artificially constricted, it ought to be applicable in such a case.

These examples suggest that what matters is the state of mind of the third party sought to be made liable, not the state of mind of the trustee. The trustee will be liable in any event for the breach of trust, even if he acted innocently, unless excused by an exemption clause in the trust instrument or relieved by the court. But his state of mind is essentially irrelevant to the question whether the third party should be made liable to the beneficiaries for the breach of trust. If the liability of the third party is fault-based, what matters is the nature of his fault, not that of the trustee. In this regard dishonesty on the part of the third party would seem to be a sufficient basis for his liability, irrespective of the state of mind of the trustee who is in breach of trust. It is difficult to see why, if the third party dishonestly assisted in a breach, there should be a further prerequisite to his liability, namely that the trustee also must have been acting dishonestly. The alternative view would mean that a dishonest third party is liable if the trustee is dishonest, but if the trustee did not act dishonestly that of itself would excuse a dishonest third party from liability. That would make no sense. **12–88**

Earlier Authority

The view that the accessory liability principle cannot be restricted to fraudulent breaches of trust is not to be approached with suspicion as a latter-day novelty. Before the accessory principle donned its *Barnes v Addy* strait-jacket, judges seem not to have regarded the principle as confined in this way. In *Fyler v Fyler*,[165] Lord Langdale M.R. expressed the view that, if trustees invested in an unauthorised investment, solicitors who knowingly procured that to be done for their own benefit "ought to be considered as partakers in the breach of trust" even though the trustees intended in good faith that the investment would be beneficial to the life tenant and not prejudicial to the beneficiaries with interests in capital. The same judge, in *Attorney-General v Corporation of Leicester*,[166] stated: **12–89**

> "it cannot be disputed that, if the agent of a trustee, whether a corporate body or not, knowing that a breach of trust is being committed, interferes and assists in that breach of trust, he is personally answerable, although he may be employed as the agent of the person who directs him to commit that breach of trust."

In *Eaves v Hickson*[167] trustees, acting in good faith, paid over the fund to William Knibb's adult children on the strength of a forged marriage certificate produced to them by William Knibb. Sir John Romilly M.R. held that William Knibb was liable to replace the fund, to the extent that it was not recovered from his children, and to do so in priority to the liability of the trustees. Far from this being a case of fraud by the trustees, Sir John Romilly M.R.[168] described it as a very hard case on the trustees, who were deceived by a forgery which would have deceived anyone who was not looking out for forgery or fraud.

This point did not arise in *Barnes v Addy*. There the new sole trustee was engaged in a dishonest and fraudulent design. He intended to misapply the trust fund as soon as it reached his hands. The two solicitors were held not liable because there was no evidence that either of them had any knowledge or suspicion of this. **12–90**

What has gone wrong? Their Lordships venture to think that the reason is that, ever since the *Selangor* case[169] highlighted the potential uses of equitable remedies in connection with misapplied company funds, there has been a tendency to cite and interpret and apply Lord Selborne L.C.'s formulation in *Barnes v Addy* as though it were a statute. This has particularly been so with the accessory limb of Lord Selborne L.C.'s apothegm. This approach has been inimical to analysis of the underlying concept. Working within **12–91**

[165] (1841) 3 Beav. 550 at 568.
[166] (1844) 7 Beav. 176 at 179.
[167] (1861) 30 Beav. 136.
[168] At 141.
[169] [1968] 1 W.L.R. 1555.

this constraint, the courts have found themselves wrestling with the interpretation of the individual ingredients, especially "knowingly" but also "dishonest and fraudulent design on the part of the trustees", without examining the underlying reason why a third party who has received no trust property is being made liable at all. . . .

12–92 To resolve this issue it is necessary to take an overall look at the accessory liability principle. A conclusion cannot be reached on the nature of the breach of trust which may trigger accessory liability without at the same time considering the other ingredients including, in particular, the state of mind of the third party. It is not necessary, however, to look even more widely and consider the essential ingredients of recipient liability. The issue on this appeal concerns only the accessory liability principle. Different considerations apply to the two heads of liability. Recipient liability is restitution-based; accessory liability is not. . . .

Fault-Based Liability

12–93 Given, then, that in some circumstances a third party may be liable directly to a beneficiary, but given also that the liability is not so strict that there would be liability even when the third party was wholly unaware of the existence of the trust, the next step is to seek to identify the touchstone of liability. By common accord dishonesty fulfils this role. Whether, in addition, negligence will suffice is an issue on which there has been a well-known difference of judicial opinion. The *Selangor* decision in 1968 was the first modern decision on this point. Ungoed-Thomas J. held that the touchstone was whether the third party had knowledge of circumstances which would indicate to "an honest, reasonable man" that the breach in question was being committed or would put him on inquiry.[170] Brightman J. reached the same conclusion in *Karak Rubber Co Ltd v Burden (No.2)*.[171] So did Peter Gibson J. in 1983 in *Baden v Société Générale pour Favoriser le Développement du Commerce et de l'Industrie en France SA*.[172] In that case the judge accepted a five-point scale of knowledge which had been formulated by counsel.

12–94 Meanwhile doubts had been expressed about this test by Buckley and Goff L.JJ. in the *Belmont* case.[173] Similar doubts were expressed in Australia by Jacobs P. in *DPC Estates Pty Ltd v Grey and Consul Development Pty Ltd*.[174] When that decision reached the High Court of Australia, the doubts were echoed by Barwick C.J., Gibbs and Stephen JJ.[175]

12–95 Since then the tide in England has flowed strongly in favour of the test being one of dishonesty: see, for instance, Sir Robert Megarry V.C. in *Re Montagu's Settlement Trusts*[176] and Millett J. in *Agip (Africa) Ltd v Jackson*.[177] In *Eagle Trust Plc v SBC Securities Ltd*,[178] Vinelott J. stated that it could be taken as settled law that want of probity was a prerequisite to liability. This received the imprimatur of the Court of Appeal in *Polly Peck International Plc v Nadir (No.2)*.[179] . . .

Dishonesty

12–96 Before considering this issue further it will be helpful to define the terms being used by looking more closely at what dishonesty means in this context. Whatever may be the position in some criminal or other contexts (see, for instance, *R. v Ghosh*[180]), in the context of the accessory liability principle acting dishonestly, or with a lack of probity, which is synonymous, means simply not acting as an honest person would in the circumstances. This is an objective standard. At first sight this may seem surprising. Honesty has a connotation of subjectivity as distinct from the objectivity of negligence. Honesty, indeed, does have a strong subjective element in that it is a description of a type of conduct assessed in the light of what a person actually knew at the time, as distinct a from what a reasonable person would have known or appreciated. Further, honesty and its counterpart dishonesty are mostly concerned with advertent conduct, not

170 [1968] 1 W.L.R. 1555 at 1590.
171 [1972] 1 W.L.R. 602.
172 [1993] 1 W.L.R. 509.
173 [1979] Ch. 250 at 267 at 275.
174 [1974] 1 N.S.W.L.R. 443 at 459.
175 See *Consul Development Pty Ltd v DP Estates Pty Ltd* (1975) 132 C.L.R. 373 at 376, 398, 412.
176 [1987] Ch. 264 at 285.
177 [1990] Ch. 265 at 293.
178 [1993] 1 W.L.R. 484 at 495.
179 [1992] 4 All E.R. 769 at 777, per Scott L.J.
180 [1982] Q.B. 1053.

inadvertent conduct. Carelessness is not dishonesty. Thus for the most part dishonesty is to be equated with conscious impropriety. However, these subjective characteristics of honesty do not mean that individuals are free to set their own standards of honesty in particular circumstances. The standard of what constitutes honest conduct is not subjective. Honesty is not an optional scale, with higher or lower values according to the moral standards of each individual. If a person knowingly appropriates another's property, he will not escape a finding of dishonesty simply because he sees nothing wrong in such behaviour.

In most situations there is little difficulty in identifying how an honest person would behave. Honest people do not intentionally deceive others to their detriment. Honest people do not knowingly take others' property. Unless there is a very good and compelling reason, an honest person does not participate in a transaction if he knows it involves a misapplication of trust assets to the detriment of the beneficiaries. Nor does an honest person in such a case deliberately close his eyes and ears, or deliberately not ask questions, lest he learn something he would rather not know, and then proceed regardless. However, in the situations now under consideration the position is not always so straightforward. This can best be illustrated by considering one particular area: the taking of risks. **12–97**

Taking Risks

All investment involves risk. Imprudence is not dishonesty, although imprudence may be carried recklessly to lengths which call into question the honesty of the person making the decision. This is especially so if the transaction serves another purpose in which that person has an interest of his own. **12–98**

This type of risk is to be sharply distinguished from the case where a trustee, with or without the benefit of advice, is aware that a particular investment or application of trust property is outside his powers, but nevertheless he decides to proceed in the belief or hope that this will be beneficial to the beneficiaries or, at least, not prejudicial to them. He takes a risk that a clearly unauthorised transaction will not cause loss. A risk of this nature is for the account of those who take it. If the risk materialises and causes loss, those who knowingly took the risk will be accountable accordingly. This is the type of risk being addressed by Peter Gibson J. in the *Baden* case,[181] when he accepted that fraud includes taking "a risk to the prejudice of another's rights, which risk is known to be one which there is no right to take." **12–99**

This situation, in turn, is to be distinguished from the case where there is genuine doubt about whether a transaction is authorised or not. This may be because the trust instrument is worded obscurely, or because there are competing claims, as in *Carl Zeiss Stiftung v Herbert Smith & Co (No.2)*,[182] or for other reasons. The difficulty here is that frequently the situation is neither clearly white nor clearly black. The dividing edge between what is within the trustee's powers and what is not is often not clear-cut. Instead there is a gradually darkening spectrum which can be described with labels such as clearly authorised, probably authorised, possibly authorised, wholly unclear, probably unauthorised and, finally, clearly unauthorised. **12–100**

The difficulty here is that the differences are of degree rather than of kind. So far as the trustee himself is concerned the legal analysis is straightforward. Honesty or lack of honesty is not the test for his liability. He is obliged to comply with the terms of the trust. His liability is strict. If he departs from the trust terms he is liable unless excused by a provision in the trust instrument or relieved by the court. The analysis of the position of the accessory, such as the solicitor who carries through the transaction for him, does not lead to such a simple, clear-cut answer in every case. He is required to act honestly; but what is required of an honest person in these circumstances? An honest person knows there is doubt. What does honesty require him to do? **12–101**

The only answer to these questions lies in keeping in mind that honesty is an objective standard. The individual is expected to attain the standard which would be observed by an honest person placed in those circumstances. It is impossible to be more specific. Knox J. captured the flavour of this, in a case with a commercial setting, when he referred to a person who is "guilty of commercially unacceptable conduct in the particular context involved".[183] Acting in reckless disregard of others' rights or possible rights can be a tell-tale sign of dishonesty. An honest person would have regard to the circumstances known to him, including the nature and importance of the proposed transaction, the nature and importance of his role, the ordinary course of business, the degree of doubt, the practicability of the trustee or the third party **12–102**

181 [1993] 1 W.L.R. 509 at 574.
182 [1969] 2 Ch. 276.
183 *Cowan de Groot Properties Ltd v Eagle Trust Plc* [1992] 4 All E.R. 700 at 761.

proceeding otherwise and the seriousness of the adverse consequences to the beneficiaries. The circumstances will dictate which one or more of the possible courses should be taken by an honest person. He might, for instance, flatly decline to become involved. He might ask further questions. He might seek advice, or insist on further advice being obtained. He might advise the trustee of the risks but then proceed with his role in the transaction. He might do many things. Ultimately, in most cases, an honest person should have little difficulty in knowing whether a proposed transaction, or his participation in it, would offend the normally accepted standards of honest conduct.

12–103 Likewise, when called upon to decide whether a person was acting honestly, a court will look at all the circumstances known to the third party at the time. The court will also have regard to personal attributes of the third party, such as his experience and intelligence, and the reason why he acted as he did.

12–104 Before leaving cases where there is real doubt, one further point should be noted. To inquire, in such cases, whether a person dishonestly assisted in what is later held to be a breach of trust is to ask a meaningful question, which is capable of being given a meaningful answer. This is not always so if the question is posed in terms of "knowingly" assisted. Framing the question in the latter form all too often leads one into tortuous convolutions about the "sort" of knowledge required, when the truth is that "knowingly" is inapt as a criterion when applied to the gradually darkening spectrum where the differences are of degree and not kind.

Negligence

12–105 It is against this background that the question of negligence is to be addressed. This question, it should be remembered, is directed at whether an honest third party who receives no trust property should be liable if he procures or assists in a breach of trust of which he would have become aware had he exercised reasonable diligence. Should he be liable to the beneficiaries for the loss they suffer from the breach of trust?

12–106 The majority of persons falling into this category will be the hosts of people who act for trustees in various ways: as advisers, consultants, bankers and agents of many kinds. This category also includes officers and employees of companies in respect of the application of company funds. All these people will be accountable to the trustees for their conduct. For the most part they will owe to the trustees a duty to exercise reasonable skill and care. When that is so, the rights flowing from that duty form part of the trust property. As such they can be enforced by the beneficiaries in a suitable case if the trustees are unable or unwilling to do so. That being so, it is difficult to identify a compelling reason why, in addition to the duty of skill and care vis-à-vis the trustees which the third parties have accepted, or which the law has imposed upon them, third parties should also owe a duty of care directly to the beneficiaries. They have undertaken work for the trustees. They must carry out that work properly. If they fail to do so, they will be liable to make good the loss suffered by the trustees in consequence. This will include, where appropriate, the loss suffered by the trustees, being exposed to claims for breach of trust.

12–107 Outside this category of persons who owe duties of skill and care to the trustees, there are others who will deal with trustees. If they have not accepted, and the law has not imposed upon them, any such duties in favour of the trustees, it is difficult to discern a good reason why they should nevertheless owe such duties to the beneficiaries.

12–108 There remains to be considered the position where third parties are acting for, or dealing with, dishonest trustees. In such cases the trustees would have no claims against the third party. The trustees would suffer no loss by reason of the third party's failure to discover what was going on. The question is whether in this type of situation the third party owes a duty of care to the beneficiaries to, in effect, check that a trustee is not misbehaving. The third party must act honestly. The question is whether that is enough.

12–109 In agreement with the preponderant view, their Lordships consider that dishonesty is an essential ingredient here. There may be cases where, in the light of the particular facts, a third party will owe a duty of care to the beneficiaries. As a general proposition, however, beneficiaries cannot reasonably expect that all the world dealing with their trustees should owe them a duty to take care lest the trustees are behaving dishonestly. . . .

The Accessory Liability Principle

12–110 Drawing the threads together, their Lordships' overall conclusion is that dishonesty is a necessary ingredient of accessory liability. It is also a sufficient ingredient. A liability in equity to make good resulting loss attaches to a person who dishonestly procures or assists in a breach of trust or fiduciary obligation. It is not necessary that, in addition, the trustee or fiduciary was acting dishonestly, although this will usually be so where the third party who is assisting him is acting dishonestly. "Knowingly" is better avoided as a defining ingredient of the principle and in the context of this principle the *Baden* scale of knowledge is best forgotten.

Conclusion

From this statement of the principle it follows that this appeal succeeds. The money paid to BLT on the sale of tickets for the airline was held by BLT upon trust for the airline. This trust, on its face, conferred no power on BLT to use the money in the conduct of its business. The trust gave no authority to BLT to relieve its cash flow problems by utilising for this purpose the rolling 30-day credit afforded by the airline. Thus BLT committed a breach of trust by using the money instead of simply deducting its commission and holding the money intact until it paid the airline. The defendant accepted that he knowingly assisted in that breach of trust. In other words, he caused or permitted his company to apply the money in a way he knew was not authorised by the trust of which the company was trustee. Set out in these bald terms, the defendant's conduct was dishonest. By the same token, and for good measure, BLT also acted dishonestly. The defendant was the company, and his state of mind is to be imputed to the company. 12–111

The Court of Appeal held that it was not established that BLT was guilty of fraud or dishonesty in relation to the amounts it held for the airline. Their Lordships understand that by this the Court of Appeal meant that it was not established that the defendant intended to defraud the airline. The defendant hoped, maybe expected, to be able to pay the airline, but the money was lost in the ordinary course of a poorly-run business with heavy overhead expenses. These facts are beside the point. The defendant had no right to employ the money in the business at all. That was the breach of trust. The company's inability to pay the airline was the consequence of that breach of trust. 12–112

BARLOW CLOWES INTERNATIONAL LTD (IN LIQ.) v EUROTRUST INTERNATIONAL LTD

Privy Council [2006] 1 W.L.R. 1476, [2006] 1 All E.R. 333

The judgment of their Lordships was delivered by LORD HOFFMANN:

In the mid-1980s Mr Peter Clowes, through a Gibraltar company called Barlow Clowes International Ltd ("Barlow Clowes"), operated a fraudulent off-shore investment scheme purporting to offer high returns from the skilled investment of funds in UK gilt-edged securities. He attracted about £140 million, mainly from small UK investors. Most of the money was dissipated in the personal business ventures and extravagant living of Mr Clowes and his associates. In 1988 the scheme collapsed and Mr Clowes was afterwards convicted and sent to prison. 12–113

Some of the investors' funds were paid away during 1987 through bank accounts maintained by companies administered from the Isle of Man by a company providing off-shore financial services which was then called International Trust Corporation (Isle of Man) Ltd ("ITC"). The principal directors were Mr Peter Henwood and Mr Andrew Sebastian. In proceedings in the Common Law Division of the High Court of the Isle of Man, Barlow Clowes (now in liquidation) claimed that Mr Henwood, Mr Sebastian and, through them, ITC, dishonestly assisted Mr Clowes and one of his principal associates, Mr Cramer, to misappropriate the investors' funds. 12–114

After a trial lasting 31 days, during which Mr Henwood and Mr Sebastian gave evidence and were cross-examined at length, the Acting Deemster (Hazel Williamson QC) found that Mr Henwood was liable for dishonestly assisting in the misappropriation of three sums: £577,429 paid away on 8 June 1987, £6 million paid away on 7 July 1987 and £205,329 paid away on 12 November 1987. She found Mr Sebastian similarly liable for the same sums and an additional £1,799,603.32 paid away on 22 June 1987 and ITC liable, through Mr Henwood and Mr Sebastian, for all four payments. She dismissed a limitation defence. 12–115

All three defendants appealed to the Staff of Government Division of the High Court. Mr Sebastian and ITC appealed solely on the limitation point and their appeals were dismissed. Mr Henwood's appeal against the finding that he had given dishonest assistance was allowed on the ground that it was not supported by the evidence. Against that decision Barlow Clowes appeals to Her Majesty in Council. Mr Sebastian and ITC have taken no further part in the proceedings. 12–116

The circumstances in which Mr Henwood and ITC came to be involved in the affairs of Barlow Clowes are set out with exemplary clarity in the judgment of the Acting Deemster and only the briefest summary is 12–117 necessary here. ITC provided off-shore financial services. In particular, it formed and administered off-shore companies, provided off-shore directors who would act upon the instructions of beneficiaries, opened bank accounts and moved money, sometimes through its own client account. In 1985 it was introduced to Mr Guy Cramer, a young businessman who was an associate of Mr Clowes but who had ventures of his own, probably funded with Barlow Clowes investors' money. He instructed ITC to form and administer a number of off-shore companies.

12–118 Between May 1986 and February 1987 ITC dealt with a series of payments from Barlow Clowes to off-shore companies which they administered on behalf of Mr Cramer. The Acting Deemster considered 10 such transactions, mostly in amounts of between £100,000 and £250,000, but with one payment of £1,137,500, from Barlow Clowes to companies under Mr Cramer's personal control. There was no apparent commercial purpose for these transactions, still less any reason for their being routed through the ITC client account or from one off-shore Cramer company to another. Counsel for Barlow Clowes invited the judge to find that even at that stage Mr Henwood and Mr Sebastian must have entertained strong suspicion that the money had been misappropriated and that the services of ITC were being used to conceal its origins. The judge found that Mr Sebastian probably did have suspicions but refused to find that Mr Henwood did so. ITC had a good deal of other business besides that of Mr Cramer. Mr Henwood, she said, was not of a naturally curious disposition concerning matters which did not affect him personally and might not have applied his mind to what was happening.

12–119 All this changed in the spring of 1987 when Mr Cramer and Mr Clowes decided to merge their interests by a "reverse take-over" by Barlow Clowes of a listed company called James Ferguson Holdings Plc ("JFH") controlled by Mr Cramer. ITC began to provide off-shore services for the combined entity and became much more involved in its affairs. On 2 April 1987 Mr Henwood went to Gibraltar and met Mr Clowes. Later that month, Mr Henwood went to the Bahamas with Mr Cramer and they discussed the possibility of absorbing Mr Henwood's ITC business into the JFH group, providing financial services from the Barlow Clowes offices in Geneva. Mr Henwood saw the possibility of becoming virtually a partner of Mr Clowes and Mr Cramer and began to take a lively interest in their business. On 5 June 1987 Mr Henwood went with Mr Clowes and Mr Cramer to Geneva to plan the development of the Barlow Clowes business, including the integration of ITC Mr Henwood learned a great deal about the nature of the Barlow Clowes business and the source of its liquid funds.

12–120 It was during this summer of 1987 that the two impugned transactions, referred to by the judge as transactions 11 and 15, took place. The first part of transaction 11 was the payment on 3 March 1987 of £1,886,415 from Barlow Clowes through ITC's client account to a Cramer company called Ryeman Ltd. The money was required to enable Ryeman to put itself forward as a sub-underwriter of a rights offer by JFH which formed part of the reverse takeover by which the Barlow Clowes companies were injected into JFH. The money was not required for sub-underwriting and remained in the Ryeman account until 8 June 1987 when Mr Henwood authorised the payment of £577,429 for Mr Cramer's personal business. The judge found that by that time Mr Henwood knew enough about the origins of the money to have suspected misappropriation and that he acted dishonestly in assisting in its disposal.

12–121 The first part of transaction 15 was the payment on 22 June 1987 by Barlow Clowes to Ryeman of £7 million in connection with a proposed bid for a brewery company which was being made by Mr Clowes and Mr Cramer. On 7 July 1987 Mr Henwood and Mr Sebastian authorised the transfer of £6 million of this money to Mr Cramer's personal account. Here again, the judge held that Mr Henwood was acting dishonestly. In November 1987 Mr Henwood and Mr Sebastian authorised the payment of £205,329 of the remaining transaction 15 money to a company controlled by Mr Clowes. The judge found this also to be dishonest assistance.

12–122 The judge stated the law in terms largely derived from the advice of the Board given by Lord Nicholls of Birkenhead in *Royal Brunei Airlines Sdn Bhd v Tan*.[184] In summary, she said that liability for dishonest assistance requires a dishonest state of mind on the part of the person who assists in a breach of trust. Such a state of mind may consist in knowledge that the transaction is one in which he cannot honestly participate (for example, a misappropriation of other people's money), or it may consist in suspicion combined with a conscious decision not to make inquiries which might result in knowledge.[185] Although a dishonest state

[184] [1995] 2 A.C. 378.
[185] See *Manifest Shipping Co Ltd v Uni-Polaris Insurance Co Ltd* [2003] 1 A.C. 469.

of mind is a subjective mental state, the standard by which the law determines whether it is dishonest is objective. If by ordinary standards a defendant's mental state would be characterised as dishonest, it is irrelevant that the defendant judges by different standards. The Court of Appeal held this to be a correct state of the law and their Lordships agree.

The judge found that during and after June 1987 Mr Henwood strongly suspected that the funds passing through his hands were monies which Barlow Clowes had received from members of the public who thought that they were subscribing to a scheme of investment in gilt-edged securities. If those suspicions were correct, no honest person could have assisted Mr Clowes and Mr Cramer to dispose of the funds for their personal use. But Mr Henwood consciously decided not to make inquiries because he preferred in his own interest not to run the risk of discovering the truth. **12–123**

Their Lordships consider that by ordinary standards such a state of mind is dishonest. The judge found that Mr Henwood may well have lived by different standards and seen nothing wrong in what he was doing. He had an: **12–124**

> "exaggerated notion of dutiful service to clients, which produced a warped moral approach that it was not improper to treat carrying out clients' instructions as being all important. Mr Henwood may well have thought this to be an honest attitude, but, if so, he was wrong."

Lord Neill of Bladen QC, who appeared for Mr Henwood, submitted to their Lordships that such a state of mind was not dishonest unless Mr Henwood was aware that it would by ordinary standards be regarded as dishonest. Only in such a case could he be said to be consciously dishonest. But the judge made no finding about Mr Henwood's opinions about normal standards of honesty. The only finding was that by normal standards he had been dishonest but that his own standard was different. **12–125**

In submitting that an inquiry into the defendant's views about standards of honesty is required, Lord Neill relied upon a statement by Lord Hutton in *Twinsectra Ltd v Yardley*,[186] with which the majority of their Lordships agreed: **12–126**

> "There is, in my opinion, a further consideration which supports the view that for liability as an accessory to arise the defendant must himself appreciate that what he was doing was dishonest by the standards of honest and reasonable men. A finding by a judge that a defendant has been dishonest is a grave finding, and it is particularly grave against a professional man, such as a solicitor. Notwithstanding that the issue arises in equity law and not in a criminal context, I think that it would be less than just for the law to permit a finding that a defendant had been 'dishonest' in assisting in a breach of trust where he knew of the facts which created the trust and its breach but had not been aware that what he was doing would be regarded by honest men as being dishonest. . . . I consider that the courts should continue to apply that test and that your Lordships should state that dishonesty requires knowledge by the defendant that what he was doing would be regarded as dishonest by honest people, although he should not escape a finding of dishonesty because he sets his own standards of honesty and does not regard as dishonest what he knows would offend the normally accepted standards of honest conduct."

Their Lordships accept that there is an element of ambiguity in these remarks which may have encouraged a belief, expressed in some academic writing, that *Twinsectra* had departed from the law as previously understood and invited inquiry not merely into the defendant's mental state about the nature of the transaction in which he was participating but also into his views about generally acceptable standards of honesty. But they do not consider that this is what Lord Hutton meant. The reference to "what he knows would offend normally accepted standards of honest conduct" meant only that his knowledge of the transaction had to be such as to render his participation contrary to normally acceptable standards of honest conduct. It did not require that he should have had reflections about what those normally acceptable standards were. **12–127**

Similarly in the speech of Lord Hoffmann, the statement[187] that a dishonest state of mind meant "consciousness that one is transgressing ordinary standards of honest behaviour" was in their Lordships' view intended to **12–128**

[186] [2002] 2 A.C. 164 at [35]–[36].
[187] At [20].

require consciousness of those elements of the transaction which make participation transgress ordinary standards of honest behaviour. It did not also to require him to have thought about what those standards were.

12–129 On the facts of *Twinsectra*, neither the judge who acquitted Mr Leach of dishonesty nor the House undertook any inquiry into the views of the defendant solicitor Mr Leach about ordinary standards of honest behaviour. He had received on behalf of his client a payment from another solicitor whom he knew had given an undertaking to pay it to Mr Leach's client only for a particular use. But the other solicitor had paid the money to Mr Leach without requiring any undertaking. The judge found that he was not dishonest because he honestly believed that the undertaking did not, so to speak, run with the money and that, as between him and his client, he held it for his client unconditionally. He was therefore bound to pay it upon his client's instructions without restriction on its use. The majority in the House of Lords considered that a solicitor who held this view of the law, even though he knew all the facts, was not by normal standards dishonest.

12–130 Their Lordships therefore reject Lord Neill's submission that the judge failed to apply the principles of liability for dishonest assistance which had been laid down in *Twinsectra*. In their opinion they were no different from the principles stated in *Royal Brunei Airlines v Tan* which were correctly summarised by the judge.

12–131 Their Lordships now address the grounds upon which the Staff of Government Division allowed Mr Henwood's appeal. Having set out the Acting Deemster's findings at some length, they said that she could have held Mr Henwood liable unless she could find that he had

> "solid grounds for suspicion, which he consciously ignored, that the disposals in which Mr Henwood participated involved dealings with misappropriated funds."

12–132 Their Lordships think that, on the facts of the case, this was an accurate way of putting the matter. The question for the Staff of Government Division was whether there was evidence upon which the Acting Deemster could have made such a finding.

12–133 The court referred to the judge's findings that Mr Henwood had been made fully aware of the nature of Barlow Clowes' business by his visits to Gibraltar and Geneva, that he knew that over £1 million had been "propelled" through an off-shore shell company controlled by Mr Cramer in three tranches between 5 and 14 May 1987 and that in consequence of the talks about merging ITC into the Clowes/Cramer group, Mr Henwood had begun to wonder where all Mr Cramer's money came from. She concluded that:

> "it did come home to Mr Henwood during this period that there must be some real possibility that the monies which Mr Cramer was putting through ITC, emanating as he knew from Barlow Clowes, could well be gilt investors' money."

12–134 Another matter which the judge took into account was Mr Henwood's knowledge of previous dishonesty by Mr Cramer. No sooner had he become a client of ITC in 1985 than he enlisted their support (which was willingly given) in a fraudulent scheme to pretend that a company he controlled had entered into leases at substantial rents with independent tenants. The charade even included Mr Cramer (through ITC) placing advertisements in the *Financial Times* and answering them himself in the guise of a different company. The sub-underwriting agreement which led to the transaction 11 payment of £1,886,415 to Ryeman had also involved a pretence, which Mr Henwood knew to have been dishonest, that Ryeman was independent of Mr Cramer and Barlow Clowes.

12–135 Finally, the judge had regard to the lies which Mr Henwood told in evidence. In flat contradiction to what he had said on previous occasions, he denied that he had had any knowledge of the Barlow Clowes business or the money-laundering transactions which passed through ITC and the companies it was administering. With conspicuous fairness the judge noted that people sometimes tell lies for reasons other than a belief that they are necessary to conceal guilt: compare *R. (on the application of Ruth) v Lucas*.[188] She said of Mr Henwood's denial that he knew about the nature of the Barlow Clowes business:

> "This is quite obviously a lie, and it is so desperate a lie, that I ask myself why he should resort to it. It *could* be that when he learned about the nature of Barlow Clowes' business he was not prompted to be

188 [1981] Q.B. 720.

> suspicious, and he is now lying out of fear that this would not be believed—or it could be that he did become suspicious and he is lying in such an extreme way because he does not think that merely denying that he drew suspicious conclusions is a credible position. This could only be because he himself would not think it potentially credible. Given that there is some evidence that Mr Henwood was, indeed, beginning to question the source of Mr Cramer's supposed wealth, I find that the latter is the more likely explanation. I think Mr Henwood lied about actually gaining knowledge of Barlow Clowes' business at this time precisely because such knowledge caused him to ask himself questions which he now realises are damning."

The Staff of Government Division dealt with this mass of evidence by saying: **12–136**

> "The evidential basis for [the finding of suspicions which were consciously ignored] therefore wholly stems from the Acting Deemster's legitimate disbelief of much of Mr Henwood's oral testimony coupled with the inferences she draws from it. These are that he knew the money came from members of the Barlow Clowes group and because he knew the money came from this source and the general nature of the group's business he must, as a matter of objective assessment, also have appreciated that the disposals were of money which had been misappropriated in breach of trust."

This is, with all respect, a travesty of the judge's findings. Her findings did not stem wholly from her disbelief of Mr Henwood's evidence. The appellate court had itself recounted the other matters upon which the judge relied and which have been summarised above. She did not say that "as a matter of objective assessment" Mr Henwood must have appreciated that the disposals were of misappropriated money. She said that as matter of Mr Henwood's subjective state of mind, he suspected this to have been the case. **12–137**

The court went on to say that the judge's reasoning displayed the dangers of "drawing inferences from inferences", a process which they had earlier said was "notoriously productive of injustice". Their Lordships have some difficulty in understanding what this means. Mr Henwood's various subjective states of mind—whether or not he suspected misappropriation and whether he consciously decided not to ask questions about the transactions in which he was assisting—were facts. Since there is no window into another mind, the only way to form a view on these matters is to draw inferences from what Mr Henwood knew, said and did, both then and later, including what he said in evidence. That is what the judge did and it is hard to see what other method could have been adopted. The Acting Deemster, who had seen Mr Henwood giving evidence for six days, was in a far better position than the Staff of Government Division to arrive at the right answer. **12–138**

The appellate court then went on to say that because Mr Henwood knew the general nature of the businesses of the members of the Barlow Clowes group, it was not a necessary inference that he would have concluded that the disposals were of moneys held in trust. That was because there was no evidence that Mr Henwood: **12–139**

> "knew anything about, for example, the actual conduct of the businesses of members of the Barlow Clowes group, the contractual arrangements made with investors, the mechanisms for management of funds under the group's control, the investment and distribution policies and the precise involvement of Mr Cramer in the group's affairs."

[28] Their Lordships consider that this passage displays two errors of law. First, it was not necessary (as the Staff of Government Division had themselves said earlier in the judgment) that Mr Henwood should have concluded that the disposals were of moneys held in trust. It was sufficient that he should have entertained a clear suspicion that this was the case. Secondly, it is quite unreal to suppose that Mr Henwood needed to know all the details to which the court referred before he had grounds to suspect that Mr Clowes and Mr Cramer were misappropriating their investors' money. The money in Barlow Clowes was either held on trust for the investors or else belonged to the company and was subject to fiduciary duties on the part of the directors. In either case, Mr Clowes and Mr Cramer could not have been entitled to make free with it as they pleased. In *Brinks Ltd v Abu-Saleh*[189] Rimer J. expressed the opinion that a person cannot be **12–140**

[189] [1996] C.L.C. 133 at 151.

liable for dishonest assistance in a breach of trust unless he knows of the existence of the trust or at least the facts giving rise to the trust. But their Lordships do not agree. Someone can know, and can certainly suspect, that he is assisting in a misappropriation of money without knowing that the money is held on trust or what a trust means.[190] And it was not necessary to know the "precise involvement" of Mr Cramer in the group's affairs in order to suspect that neither he nor anyone else had the right to use Barlow Clowes money for speculative investments of their own.

12–141 Their Lordships accordingly consider that there was abundant evidence on which the judge was entitled to make the findings of fact which she did about the disposal of £577,429 of the transaction 11 money on 8 June 1987. The Staff of Government Division should not have set them aside.

12–142 By the time of the later transactions, Mr Henwood had even more reason to be suspicious. In particular, he had been told on 2 July 1987 by two employees in the Geneva office that Mr Clowes and Mr Cramer were misappropriating clients' money. Mr Clowes had subsequently persuaded the employees to say that they had been misunderstood, but Mr Henwood knew he had understood them perfectly well. The Staff of Government nevertheless found that even in these circumstances, the judge was not entitled to find that he must have entertained suspicions which he chose not to investigate. They said that he might have thought his suspicions would somehow be disabused or that he might have relied upon the word of Mr Clowes that all was well.

12–143 The difficulty about this reasoning is that Mr Henwood never said in evidence that he thought his suspicions might be disabused or that he had made inquiries of Mr Clowes and been given a reassuring answer. Mr Henwood's evidence, which the judge found to be untruthful, was that he knew nothing and had no reason to suspect anything. A state of mind in which suspicion had been allayed was entirely the invention of the Staff of Government Division. There was no evidence that Mr Henwood had tried to seek any explanation whatever and their Lordships consider that the judge was fully justified in concluding that this was the result of a deliberate and dishonest decision.

12–144 Their Lordships will therefore humbly advise Her Majesty that the appeal should be allowed and the decision of the Acting Deemster restored. Mr Henwood must pay the appellants' costs in the Staff of Government Division and before their Lordships' Board.

Questions

12–145 1. What do the courts mean when they say that trustees *de son tort*, knowing recipients and dishonest assistants variously owe a "personal liability to account" to the beneficiaries, and how does this affect the measure of compensation that each may have to pay following a breach of trust?

12–146 2. In *Barnes v Addy* (1874) L.R. 9 Ch. App. 244 at 252, Lord Selborne L.C. thought that "if persons dealing honestly as agents are at liberty to rely on the legal power of the trustees, [and] are not to have the character of trustees constructively thrust upon them, then the transactions of mankind can safely be carried through; and I apprehend those who create trusts do expressly intend, in the absence of fraud and dishonesty, to exonerate such agents of all classes from the responsibilities which are expressly incumbent by reason of the fiduciary relation upon the trustees." In light of these comments do you think that fault should be a prerequisite for third party liability for breach of trust; and if so, what degree of fault?

12–147 3. "The majority of the House of Lords in *Twinsectra* clearly misinterpreted Lord Nicholls' discussion of the fault requirement for accessory liability in *Royal Brunei*. In *Eurotrust* Lord Hoffmann could not admit this if he wanted to get things back on the right track while sitting in the Privy Council." **Discuss.**

[190] See *Twinsectra Ltd v Yardley* [2002] 2 A.C. 164, at [19], per Lord Hoffmann, and [135], per Lord Millett.

4. A stockbroker is directed by trustees to sell an authorised investment and to apply the proceeds to the purchase of an unauthorised investment. He knowingly does so because he bona fide believes this to be in the beneficiaries' best financial interests. Most surprisingly the unauthorised investment halves in value within a year. Can the beneficiaries sue the stockbroker if the trustees are now insolvent; and if so, what might be the measure of his liability? **12–148**

5. An accountant agrees to falsify his client's records, and certify them as accurate, in what he believes to be a conspiracy to evade the payment of VAT. In fact his client has misappropriated trust funds and the beneficiaries now wish to know whether they can sue the accountant. Would it make any difference if the client would have stolen the money anyway? **12–149**

13 PROPRIETARY CLAIMS FOLLOWING A BREACH OF TRUST

1. Introduction

13–01 Various proprietary claims can lie where trustees make an unauthorised investment, or misappropriate trust property for themselves, or misdirect trust property to third parties. The beneficiaries[1] may be entitled to assert a continuing equitable proprietary interest in misdirected trust property; to assert a new equitable proprietary interest in the traceable proceeds of trust property; to acquire an equitable lien over property in a defendant's hands; or to acquire a charge over a defendant's property via subrogation.

A. The Key Features of Proprietary Claims

13–02 These claims differ in that the first and second are claims to ownership of property, while the third and fourth are claims to security over property belonging to a defendant. However, all four claims bring the advantage of priority in a defendant's insolvency. If a defendant has never owned an asset free from a claimant's equitable ownership interest, then this interest will be unaffected by his insolvency because the asset can never have formed part of his estate. If the claimant has a charge over a defendant's property, then this will give him priority over the defendant's unsecured creditors, and possibly over his other secured creditors as well, depending on the relevant priority rules.

13–03 If a claimant has an ownership right in an asset which appreciates in value, then the increase will accrue to the claimant. If a claimant has a charge over a defendant's property to secure the repayment of a particular sum, and the property depreciates in value, then the claimant can still enforce the whole amount of his charge against the property, and if necessary recover any outstanding difference via a personal action.[2]

13–04 Pending the hearing of a proprietary claim a claimant is entitled almost as of right to an interim injunction preserving the claimed assets until the outcome of the trial.[3]

---

[1] In the case of misdirected funds, claims can also be made by the trustees: *Montrose Investment Ltd v Orion Nominees Ltd* (2004) 7 I.T.E.L.R. 255 at [24]–[25]; *Pulvers (a firm) v Chan* [2008] P.N.L.R. 9 at [380].

[2] *Serious Fraud Office v Lexi Holdings Plc (in administration)* [2009] Q.B. 376 at [40]: an equitable lien is "a cumulative remedy in aid of an equitable in personam claim, not an alternative remedy".

[3] If part of his proprietary claim is weak the court has discretion to grant the requested injunction only over part of the claimed assets: *Polly Peck International Plc v Nadir (No.2)* [1992] 4 All E.R. 769.

B. Following, Tracing and Claiming

13–05 If a trustee takes trust property for himself and retains the property in its original form, then it will often be a simple matter for the beneficiaries to identify the property which forms the subject-matter of their proprietary claim. However, matters may be less straightforward than this. If a trustee transfers a trust asset to a third party, then the beneficiaries must follow the asset from the trustee's hands into the third party's hands as a necessary evidential preliminary to asserting a proprietary claim against the asset: i.e. they must first prove that the asset held by the third party was formerly held for them by the trustee. Again, if a trustee or a third party recipient exchanges a trust asset for a new asset, then the beneficiaries must trace the value inherent in the trust asset into the value inherent in the new asset before they can assert a proprietary claim to the new asset.[4]

13–06 In *Foskett v McKeown* Lord Millett explained the relationship between the rules of following, tracing and claiming in these terms:[5]

> "[Following and tracing] are both exercises in locating assets which are or may be taken to represent an asset belonging to the plaintiffs and to which they assert ownership. The processes of following and tracing are, however, distinct. Following is the process of following the same asset as it moves from hand to hand. Tracing is the process of identifying a new asset as the substitute for the old. Where one asset is exchanged for another, a claimant can elect whether to follow the original asset into the hands of the new owner or to trace its value into the new asset in the hands of the same owner. . . . Tracing is also distinct from claiming. It identifies the traceable proceeds of the claimant's property. It enables the claimant to substitute the traceable proceeds for the original asset as the subject matter of his claim. But it does not affect or establish his claim. That will depend on a number of factors including the nature of his interest in the original asset . . . [and] his claim may also be exposed to potential defences as a result of intervening transactions."

13–07 Thus, "the rules of following and tracing . . . [are] evidential in nature", and they are distinct from "rules which determine substantive rights": "the former are concerned with identifying property in other hands or in another form; the latter with the rights that a claimant can assert against the property in its present form".[6] Consistently with this, the discussion in this chapter is divided into two sections, the first dealing with the rules of following and tracing, and the second with the rules that govern proprietary claims following a breach of trust.

C. Common Law and Equitable Tracing Rules

13–08 For many years it was thought that there were different tracing rules in equity and at common law, and that the equitable rules are more favourable to claimants than the common law rules, most significantly because claimants at common law could not trace through mixtures of money in bank

[4] Different rules apply to "clean substitutions" and "mixed substitutions", the former occurring where the new asset is acquired solely with trust property, the latter occurring where the new asset is acquired with a mixture of trust property and the defendant's own property: *Foskett v McKeown* [2001] 1 A.C. 102 at 130.

[5] *Foskett v McKeown* [2001] 1 A.C. 102 at 127–128.

[6] *Glencore International AG v Metro Trading International Ltd* [2001] 1 Lloyd's Rep. 284 at [180], per Moore-Bick J. See too *Boscawen v Bajwa* [1996] 1 W.L.R. 328 at 334; *Waxman v Waxman* (2004) 7 I.T.E.L.R. 162 at [582].

accounts, something which equity allows.[7] It was also thought that a claimant had to show that his property was held on trust or subject to some other fiduciary relationship before he could take advantage of the equitable tracing rules with a view to tracing through mixtures in bank accounts.[8]

13–09 As Professor Lionel Smith has explained, these findings were always suspect as a matter of authority.[9] They were inconsistent with a long line of subrogation cases in which claimants were not required to establish a fiduciary relationship before invoking the equitable tracing rules to show that their money was used to discharge securities to which they sought to be subrogated.[10] They were also inconsistent with *Marsh v Keating*,[11] where the House of Lords advised by 12 common law judges was willing to accept that the common law could trace through a mixed bank account. Finally, Viscount Haldane L.C.'s finding in *Sinclair v Brougham*[12] that there can be no tracing at common law where money has been lent and placed in a bank account was founded on a misunderstanding of Thesiger L.J.'s statement in *Re Hallett's Estate*[13] that a claimant who makes an unsecured loan cannot generally make a proprietary claim against the borrower's assets to secure repayment of the loan.

13–10 These objections to the traditional view are now of subsidiary importance, however, following *Foskett v McKeown*, where Lord Steyn[14] and Lord Millett[15] both considered that there is now only one set of tracing rules in English law, applicable to common law and equitable claimants alike. Their comments on this point were obiter, but it seems likely that they will be followed in future cases.[16] Developing the law in this way would certainly be desirable in principle. In the past, the courts have been apt to discover fiduciary relationships between the parties to litigation, not because their relationship has been of the sort that would normally attract the imposition of fiduciary duties, but because the courts have wished to let the claimant take advantage of the "equitable" tracing rules. So, for example, it has been held that a thief owes a fiduciary duty to his victim, with the result that the victim can invoke the "equitable" rules in order to trace through the thief's sale of the stolen property and mixing of the proceeds in a bank account.[17] Instrumental findings of this sort debase the currency of the fiduciary concept.

---

7 *Sinclair v Brougham* [1914] A.C. 398 at 419–420; *Banque Belge pour l'Étranger v Hambrouck* [1921] 1 K.B. 321 at 328 and 330; *Re Diplock* [1948] Ch. 465 at 518; *Agip (Africa) Ltd v Jackson* [1991] Ch. 547 at 566. The point was conceded in *Lipkin Gorman v Karpnale Ltd* [1991] 2 A.C. 548. See too *Taylor v Plumer* (1815) 3 M. & S. 562, which has often been said to stand for the proposition that tracing through mixtures in bank accounts is not possible at common law, but which in fact lays down a rule about claiming; moreover, the case was ultimately decided on equitable principles, as confirmed in *Trustee of FC Jones & Son (a firm) v Jones* [1997] Ch. 159 at 169.

8 *Sinclair v Brougham* [1914] A.C. 398 at 421; *Re Diplock* [1948] Ch. 465 at 536–537; *Agip (Africa) Ltd v Jackson* [1991] Ch. 547 at 566.

9 L.D. Smith, *The Law of Tracing* (1997), 123–130 and 168–174.

10 e.g. *Marlow v Pitfeild* (1719) 1 P. Wms. 558; *Baroness Wenlock v River Dee Co* (1887) 19 Q.B.D. 15; *Orakpo v Manson Investments Ltd* [1978] A.C. 95.

11 (1834) 2 Cl. & Fin. 250; discussed in J. Edelman, "*Marsh v Keating*" in C. Mitchell and P. Mitchell (eds), *Landmark Cases in the Law of Restitution* (2006).

12 [1914] A.C. 398 at 419–421.

13 (1880) 13 Ch.D. 696 at 723–724.

14 [2001] 1 A.C. 102. at 113.

15 *Foskett* at 128–129.

16 cf. *BMP Global Distribution Inc v Bank of Nova Scotia* (2009) 304 D.L.R. (4th) 292 at [79]–[85] where the Supreme Court of Canada cites *Foskett* in the course of denying that tracing through mixtures in bank accounts is impossible at common law. But compare *Bracken Partners Ltd v Gutteridge* [2003] 2 B.C.L.C. 83 at [31] (not considered on appeal [2004] 1 B.C.L.C. 377) with *Shalson v Russo* [2005] Ch. 281 at [103]–[104] and *London Allied Holdings Ltd v Lee* [2007] EWHC 2061 (Ch) at [256].

17 *Black v Freedman* (1910) 12 C.L.R. 105 at 110, endorsed by Lord Templeman in *Lipkin Gorman v Karpnale Ltd* [1991] 2 A.C. 548 at 565–566; *Bishopsgate Investment Management Ltd v Maxwell* [1993] 1 Ch. at 70; *Westdeutsche Landesbank Girozentrale v Islington LBC* [1996] A.C. 669 at 716.

2. Following and Tracing

A. *Following*

In many cases, following a misdirected trust asset into the hands of a third party recipient presents no great evidential difficulty. However, problems can arise when the recipient mixes the asset with other assets in such a way that they lose their discrete identity.[18] Different rules are used to resolve these problems, depending on whether the asset has been incorporated into a fungible mixture, i.e. a mixture composed of mutually interchangeable units, each of which can readily be separated from the others without causing any damage.[19] **13–11**

i. Fungible Mixtures

Suppose that trust assets are mixed with other assets in such a way that no one can tell who has contributed what to the mixture, but it remains possible to divide the mixture into identical parts: suppose, for example, that trust crude oil is mixed with other crude oil,[20] or trust shares with other shares.[21] Where the whole mixture is still intact, the beneficiaries' contribution must still be somewhere in the mixture even though it has lost its discrete identity, and so the rule in this case is that the beneficiaries can identify any proportionate part of the mixture as their property.[22] **13–12**

However, if part of the mixture is consumed or transferred to a third party, then the evidential problem becomes more acute. In this case no one can know whether the beneficiaries' contribution subsists in the remainder. Two rules are used to resolve this problem. In the absence of wrongdoing, the remainder is apportioned rateably between contributors to the mixture: e.g. if 20,000 barrels of trust oil are mixed with 100,000 barrels of oil belonging to others, and 30,000 barrels are consumed, then one-sixth of the 90,000 barrels remaining (i.e. 15,000 barrels) are deemed to be trust oil.[23] However, where the mixing is done wrongfully, as in the case where a trustee fails to segregate trust assets from his own assets, a different rule applies, namely that evidential uncertainty created by wrongdoing is resolved against the wrongdoer.[24] This does not mean that the wrongdoer is debarred from following his own contribution into the mixture, but it does mean that losses from the mixture are deemed to have come out of his portion first.[25] So, for example, if a trustee mixes 100 tons of trust gravel with 100 tons of his own gravel, and 80 tons of gravel are then stolen out of the mixture, the trustee can **13–13**

[18] See generally P. Birks, "Mixtures of Goods" in N. Palmer and E. McKendrick (eds), *Interests in Goods*, 2nd edn (1993); P. Matthews, "The Limits of Common Law Tracing" in P. Birks (ed.), *Laundering and Tracing* (1995), pp. 42–46; L.D. Smith, *The Law of Tracing* (1997), ch.2; R.J.W. Hickey, "Dazed and Confused: Accidental Mixtures of Goods and the Theory of Acquisition of Title" (2003) 66 M.L.R. 368.

[19] *Rysaffe Trustee Co (CI) Ltd v IRC* [2002] S.T.C. 872 at [32]; *Glencore International AG v Alpina Insurance Co Ltd (No.2)* [2004] 1 All E.R. (Comm.) 858 at [16]. See too J. Austin, *Lectures on Jurisprudence* 4th edn (1879) p.807; R. Goode, "Are Intangible Assets Fungible?" in P. Birks and A. Pretto (eds), *Themes in Comparative Law* (2002).

[20] *Indian Oil Corp. v Greenstone Shipping SA* [1988] Q.B. 345; *Glencore International AG v Metro Trading International Ltd* [2001] 1 Lloyd's Rep. 284.

[21] *Brady v Stapleton* (1952) 88 C.L.R. 322.

[22] *Lupton v White* (1808) 15 Ves. Jun. 432 at 441; *Indian Oil Corp v Greenstone Shipping SA* [1988] Q.B. 345 at 369–371; *Foskett v McKeown* [2001] 1 A.C. 102 at 143; *Glencore International AG v Metro Trading International Ltd* [2001] 1 Lloyd's Rep. 284 at [185].

[23] *Spence v Union Marine Insurance Co* (1868) L.R. 3 C.P. 427.

[24] This is a rule of general application in the law of evidence: *Armory v Delamirie* (1722) 1 Str. 505; *Infabrics Ltd v Jaytex Ltd* [1985] F.S.R. 75.

[25] *Harris v Truman* (1881) 7 Q.B.D. 340 at 358, affirmed (1882) 9 Q.B.D. 264; *Indian Oil Corp v Greenstone Shipping SA* [1988] Q.B. 345 at 370–371; *Foskett v McKeown* [2001] 1 A.C. 102 at 132; *Glencore International AG v Metro Trading International Ltd* [2001] 1 Lloyd's Rep. 284 at [159] and [182].

identify 20 tons of the remaining gravel as his own, but he must allow the beneficiaries to identify the remainder as theirs.

ii. Non-Fungible Mixtures

13–14 The process of following an asset inevitably comes to an end if the asset is destroyed. The law provides that it also comes to an end because the asset is deemed to have been destroyed, in three situations:

- where the asset is physically attached to another, "dominant", asset so that it would cause serious damage, or be disproportionately expensive, to separate the two: here the asset is said to "accede" to the dominant asset;[26]
- where the asset is physically attached to land in such a way that it would cause serious damage, or be disproportionately expensive, to separate the two: here the asset is said to become a "fixture" on the land;[27] and
- where the asset is combined with other items to create a wholly new product, under the doctrine of "specification".[28]

13–15 At least in the case of specification, however, these rules are modified where the mixing is performed by a wrongdoer. Here, despite the creation of the new thing, the owner of the assets which are wrongfully used to create the new asset can follow his property into the new asset. So, in *Jones v De Marchant*,[29] a husband wrongfully took 18 beaver skins belonging to his wife and used them, together with four skins of his own, to have a fur coat made up which he gave to his mistress. The wife was allowed to recover the coat, a result which can only be explained on the basis that she was permitted to follow her property into the new asset.

B. Tracing

13–16 The rules on tracing resemble the rules on following, insofar as they provide that gains and losses to a mixture must be shared rateably between innocent contributors to the mixture. They also provide that evidential uncertainty created by wrongdoing must be resolved against the wrongdoer.

i. Where a Trustee Mixes Trust Money with his Own Money

13–17 Suppose that a trustee mixes £25,000 of his own money with £25,000 of trust money in such a way that the funds lose their separate identities. Suppose that he takes £20,000 out of the mixture and loses it, and then takes a further £20,000 out of the mixture and uses it to buy a painting which triples

---

[26] *Hendy Lennox (Industrial Engines) Ltd v Grahame Puttick Ltd* [1984] 1 W.L.R. 485; *McKeown v Cavalier Yachts Pty Ltd* (1988) 13 N.S.W.L.R. 303 at 311. Which of two assets accedes to the other depends on which is the "dominant" entity, a point which is decided rather impressionistically by reference to overall physical significance rather than monetary value. The doctrine of "accession" derives from the Roman doctrine of *accessio*.

[27] *Hobson v Gorringe* [1897] 1 Ch 182; *Reynolds v Asby & Son* [1904] A.C. 406; *Melluish (Inspector of Taxes) v BMI (No.3) Ltd* [1996] A.C. 454; *Elitestone Ltd v Morris* [1997] 1 W.L.R. 687; *Chelsea Yacht & Boat Co Ltd v Pope* [2000] 1 W.L.R. 1941. See too H.N. Bennett, "Attachment of Chattels to Land" in N. Palmer and E. McKendrick (eds), *Interests in Goods*, 2nd edn (1993).

[28] *International Banking Corp v Ferguson, Shaw & Sons* 1910 S.C. 182; *Borden (UK) Ltd v Scottish Timber Products Ltd* [1981] Ch. 25. The doctrine derives from the Roman doctrine of *specificatio*.

[29] (1916) 28 D.L.R. 561, endorsed in *Foskett v McKeown* [2001] 1 A.C. 102 at 132–133. See too *Spence v Union Marine Insurance Co Ltd* (1868) L.R. 3 C.P. 427 at 437–438; *Sandeman & Sons v Tyzack and Branfoot Steamship Co Ltd* [1923] A.C. 680 at 694–695. An attempt to extend the principle to mixtures of ideas leading to the creation of a patentable product failed in *IDA Ltd v University of Southampton* [2006] R.P.C. 21 at [40]–[42].

in value. It is impossible to say whose money was lost, whose money bought the painting, and whose money is left. Because the trustee is a wrongdoer, Equity resolves the evidential problem against him,[30] by allowing the beneficiaries to "cherry-pick" from two rules in order to reach the best result for themselves.[31] The rule in *Re Hallett's Estate*[32] provides that the trustee may not say that the beneficiaries' money was lost, and that the beneficiaries may say that the trustee lost his own money. The rule in *Re Oatway*[33] provides that the trustee may not say that he used his own money to buy the painting, and that the beneficiaries may say that their money was used for this purpose. This produces the result that the beneficiaries can trace their money into the painting and £5,000 of the remaining cash, the balance being attributable to the trustee. Note that the rule in *Clayton's case*, considered below, does not apply in this situation.[34]

The rules in *Re Hallett's Estate* and *Re Oatway* are designed to resolve evidential uncertainty. Hence they have no bite in a situation that is not evidentially uncertain. Suppose that a trustee mixes £50,000 of his own money and £50,000 of trust money and places the mixture in an empty bank account. Suppose that he withdraws £80,000, loses it, and then adds another £30,000 of his own money, so that there is now £50,000 in the account. Here, the beneficiaries cannot invoke the rule in *Re Hallett's Estate* to identify more than £20,000 in the account as their property because it is not evidentially uncertain that at least £30,000 of the remaining funds came from the trustee's own resources.[35] This rule, established in *James Roscoe (Bolton) Ltd v Winder*,[36] is known as "the lowest intermediate balance rule": "absent any payment in of money with the intention of making good earlier depredations, tracing cannot occur through a mixed account for any larger sum than is the lowest balance in the account between the time the beneficiary's money goes in, and the time the remedy is sought."[37] **13–18**

ii. Where a Trustee Mixes Trust Funds Together

If trust funds are mixed together and the beneficiaries are equally innocent victims of the trustee's wrongdoing, then the beneficiaries will generally have equally strong claims to a rateable share of gains, and equally weak claims to avoid taking a rateable share of losses, to the mixed fund.[38] Hence, gains and losses are generally shared between the beneficiaries pro rata.[39] **13–19**

---

[30] *Gray v Haig* (1855) 20 Beav. 214 at 226.

[31] *Shalson v Russo* [2005] Ch. 281 at [144], per Rimer J., which is to be preferred on this point to *Turner v Jacob* [2008] W.T.L.R. 307 at [100]–[102], per Patten J.

[32] (1880) 13 Ch.D. 696, esp. at 727, per Jessel M.R.: "where a man does an act which may be rightfully performed . . . he is not allowed to say against the person entitled to the property or the right that he has done it wrongfully." See too *Halley v Law Society* [2002] EWHC 139 (Ch) at [160].

[33] [1903] 2 Ch. 356, esp. at 360, per Joyce J.: the trustee "cannot maintain that the investment which remains represents his money alone and what has been spent and can no longer be traced or recovered was money belonging to the trust." See too *Grey v Haig* (1855) 20 Beav. 214 at 226.

[34] *Re Hallett's Estate* (1880) 13 Ch.D. 696 at 728.

[35] cf. *Law Society of Upper Canada v Toronto-Dominion Bank* (1999) 169 D.L.R. (4th) 353, where the Ontario CA failed to grasp this point, as noted by L.D. Smith (2000) 33 Can. Bus. L.J. 75.

[36] [1915] 1 Ch. 62, endorsed in *Re Goldcorp Exchange Ltd* [1995] 1 A.C. 74 at 107–108, also in *Bishopsgate Investment Management Ltd v Homan* [1995] Ch. 211 at 219 and 220.

[37] *Re French Caledonia Travel Service Pty. Ltd* (2003) 59 N.S.W.L.R. 361 at [175], per Campbell J. For application of the principle where goods are successively withdrawn and deposited in a mixed bulk, see *Glencore International AG v Metro Trading International Ltd* [2001] 1 Lloyd's Rep. 284 at [201]–[202], revisited in *Glencore International AG v Alpina Insurance Co Ltd (No.2)* [2004] 1 All E.R. (Comm.) 858 at [14]–[20]. For a case falling within the scope of Campbell J.'s proviso, see *Westdeutsche Landesbank Girozentrale v Islington LBC* [1994] 4 All E.R. 890 at 939 (not considered on appeal).

[38] But it seems that if a trustee mixes two trust funds in one account and then purports to withdraw a sum for the beneficiary of one trust but actually uses it for his own purposes then that sum should be allocated to that particular trust: *Re Stillman and Wilson* (1950) 15 A.B.C. 68; *Re Registered Securities Ltd* [1991] 1 N.Z.L.R. 545. Quaere whether these cases can be reconciled with the principal that a wrong doing trustee's intentions are generally irrelevant (see para.13–29)?

[39] *Edinburgh Corp v Lord Advocate* (1879) 4 App. Cas. 823; *Re Diplock* [1948] Ch 465 at 533, 534 and 539.

13–20 Until recently, there was thought to be an exception to this principle, deriving from *Clayton's case*.[40] This concerned a dispute centring on the appropriation of payments as between a bank and its customer, but it came to be seen as authority for the rule that if a trustee places money belonging to two different sets of beneficiaries into the same unbroken running account,[41] any withdrawals that he makes from the account are deemed to be made in the same order as the payments in, on a "first in, first out" basis.[42] Thus, for example, if he puts £10,000 from Trust A into a current bank account, and then puts in £10,000 from Trust B, and then withdraws £10,000 and loses it (or uses it to buy an asset which triples in value), then the loss (or gain) will be attributed solely to the beneficiaries of Trust A.

13–21 As between the beneficiaries of Trust A and Trust B this is an arbitrary and unfair result, and for this reason the "first in, first out" rule has been discarded in many Commonwealth jurisdictions, in favour of a pro rata approach.[43] In *Barlow Clowes International Ltd v Vaughan*,[44] the Court of Appeal reaffirmed the general application of *Clayton's case* in English law, except where its application would be impracticable or would result in injustice between the parties. However, more recent English cases suggest that the rule will not often be applied, for the courts are now swift to find that the rule is an impracticable or unjust method of resolving disputes between the victims of shared misfortune, particularly in cases of large-scale fraud.[45]

13–22 *Barlow Clowes* concerned the liquidation of an investment company whose fraudulent managers had stolen most of the company's assets, leaving thousands of investors out of pocket. The question arose as to how the surviving assets should be distributed between the investors. The court held that the rule in *Clayton's case* should not be used to resolve this question because the investors had all intended that their money should be pooled in a single fund for investment purposes, so that it would conform with their original intentions if they all shared rateably in what remained in the pool. However, Woolf and Leggatt L.JJ.[46] also indicated that a "rolling charge" solution might be fairer than rateable sharing so that claimants should share losses and gains to the fund in proportion to their interest in the fund immediately prior to each withdrawal.

13–23 This would work as follows. Suppose that a trustee pays £2,000 from Trust A and then £4,000 from Trust B into an empty current bank account. He then withdraws £3,000 and loses it. He then pays in £3,000 from Trust C before withdrawing another £3,000 to buy shares whose value increases tenfold. He then withdraws the remaining £3,000 and loses it. Applying the "rolling charge" rule, the first loss must be borne by A and B in the ratio 1:2, and C need not bear this loss at all. Immediately after the

---

40 (1816) 1 Mer. 529. For the history of the case see L.D. Smith, *The Law of Tracing* (1997), pp. 183–194; *Re French Caledonia Travel Service Pty Ltd* (2003) 59 N.S.W.L.R. 361 at [20]–[172].

41 e.g. a current bank account, a solicitor's trust account or a moneylender's account. The rule does not apply where there are distinct and separate debts: *The Mecca* [1897] A.C. 286; *Re Sherry* (1884) 25 Ch.D. 692 at 702. Nor does the rule apply to entries on the same day: it is the end-of-day balance which counts: *The Mecca* at 291.

42 *Pennell v Deffell* (1853) 4 De G.M. & G. 372; *Hancock v Smith* (1889) 41 Ch.D. 456 at 461; *Re Stenning* [1895] 2 Ch. 433; *Re Diplock* [1948] Ch. 465 at 553–554.

43 *Re Ontario Securities Commission* (1985) 30 D.L.R. (4th) 1, affirmed (1998) 52 D.L.R. (4th) 767; *Re Registered Securities Commission* [1991] 1 N.Z.L.R. 545; *Keefe v Law Society of New South Wales* (1998) 44 N.S.W.L.R. 451; *ASIC v Enterprise Solutions 2000 Pty Ltd* [2001] QSC 82; *Re Esteem Settlement* 2002 J.L.R. 53; *Re French Caledonia Travel Service Pty Ltd* (2003) 59 N.S.W.L.R. 361; *Re International Investment Unit Trust* [2005] 1 N.Z.L.R. 270.

44 [1992] 4 All E.R. 22.

45 *El Ajou v Dollar Land Holdings Plc (No.2)* [1995] 2 All E.R. 213 at 222; *Russell-Cooke Trust Co v Prentis* [2003] 2 All E.R. 478 at 495; *Commerzbank Aktiengesellschaft v IMB Morgan Plc* [2005] Lloyd's Rep. 298 at [43]–[49]; *Re Ahmed & Co* (2006) 8 I.T.E.L.R. 779 at [131]–[138]. Note too that in *El Ajou (No.2)*, at 223–224, Robert Walker J. held that where A and B's money is mixed in an account and *Clayton's case* deems A's money (and not B's) to have been paid to D, B can still trace into the money received by D and claim against him if A makes no claim and is unlikely to do so. This finding was followed in *Campden Hill Ltd v Chakrani* [2005] EWHC 911 (Ch) at [76]–[77].

46 *Barlow Clowes* at 35 and 44.

first withdrawal the remaining £3,000 would be attributed to A and B in the ratio 1:2, and after the next deposit, the £6,000 in the account would be attributable to A, B, and C in the ratio 1:2:3. Hence, the shares should be attributed to them in the same proportion, leaving A with shares worth £5,000, B with shares worth £10,000 and C with shares worth £15,000. In contrast, the pro rata rule would attribute all gains and losses in proportion to the total contributions made by each Trust, giving a ratio of 2:4:3, and leaving A with shares worth £6,667, B with shares worth £13,333, and C with shares worth £10,000. The "first in, first out" rule, meanwhile, would produce the result that all of A's money is lost, that £1,000 of B's money is lost, that all the shares belong to B, and that all of C's money is lost.

In *Shalson v Russo*,[47] Rimer J. suggested that the rolling charge rule should always be used to resolve cases of this kind, because the pro rata rule ignores evidence of what has actually happened to the claimants' money: thus, in the example, we know that no part of Trust C's £3,000 can have gone into the trustee's first withdrawal, suggesting that Trust C should not have to share this loss with Trust A and Trust B. Rimer J.'s position can certainly be supported by reference to *Roscoe v Winder*,[48] but in a case involving thousands of investors and hundreds of thousands of deposits and withdrawals, the expense and practical difficulties of calculation using the rolling charge rule may be prohibitive, leaving the claimants with a choice between the rough justice of the pro rata rule, and the even rougher justice of "first in, first out". **13–24**

iii. Where Recipients of Trust Money Mix it with their Own Money

Where a trustee misdirects trust funds to a bona fide purchaser for value without notice of the trust interest the beneficiaries may be able to follow the property into his hands and trace its inherent value through his subsequent mixtures and substitutions, but it will be pointless for them to do this as he will have a defence to any proprietary claim that they might bring.[49] However, where a trustee misdirects trust property to a recipient who is not a bona fide purchaser, the beneficiaries may well wish to follow the property into the recipient's hands and then trace its inherent value through subsequent mixtures and substitutions into the value inherent in some new asset. **13–25**

The tracing rules that apply in this case will vary according to whether the recipient has acted in good faith. If he is a bona fide volunteer, then the rules governing the situation will be the same as those which govern the case where money belonging to the innocent beneficiaries of separate trust funds is mixed together by the trustee[50]: gains and losses will be shared rateably, possibly subject to the rule in *Clayton's case*[51] if the court sees fit to apply it.[52] If the recipient takes the property with knowledge of the breach of trust, however, then he cannot innocently mix the property with his own property. He will owe the beneficiaries a duty as constructive trustee to account to them for the trust property. Hence if he mixes it with his own property he will be counted as a wrongdoer,[53] and the case will be governed by **13–26**

---

[47] [2005] Ch. 281 at [150].

[48] [1915] 1 Ch. 62, discussed in para.13–18, above.

[49] *Miller v Race* (1758) 1 Burr. 542; *Pilcher v Rawlins* (1872) L.R. 7 Ch. App. 259; *Taylor v Blakelock* (1886) 32 Ch.D. 560; *Re Diplock* [1948] Ch. 465 at 539; *Foskett v McKeown* [2001] 1 A.C. 102 at 130. See too D. Fox, "Bona Fide Purchase and the Currency of Money" (1996) 55 C.L.J. 547.

[50] *Re Diplock* [1948] Ch. 465 at 524 and 539.

[51] *Re Diplock* [1948] Ch. 465 at 554.

[52] See paras 13–20 to 13–24. If the recipient pays the trust money into an interest-bearing account designated as a trust account as soon as he learns of the trust claim, this will be regarded as effectively unmixing the fund so that the trust claim will then relate only to the money in the designated account: *Re Diplock* [1948] Ch. 465 at 551–552, dealing with the claim against the National Institute for the Deaf, reversed on an amended statement of the facts: ibid. at 559.

[53] *Boscawen v Bajwa* [1996] 1 W.L.R. 328 at 336–338; *Banton v CIBC Trust Corp* (2001) 197 D.L.R. (4th) 212.

the same rules as those which govern the case where an express trustee wrongfully mixes trust funds with his own money: evidential uncertainties will be resolved against the trustee.[54]

iv. Payment of Debts

13–27 Like the process of following property from hand to hand, the process of tracing the value inherent in property through mixtures and substitutions must come to an end if the asset in which the value resides is dissipated or destroyed. So, if a trustee (or third party recipient) uses trust funds to buy a meal which he consumes, or a house which burns down, then his purchases leave no traceable residue (assuming that the house is uninsured): nothing is left in his hands to which the beneficiaries might assert a proprietary claim. As the Court of Appeal stated in *Re Diplock*:[55]

> "The equitable remedies [available to beneficiaries making proprietary claims] presuppose the continued existence of the [trust] money either as a separate fund or as part of a mixed fund or as latent in property acquired by means of such a fund. If such continued existence is not established equity is . . . helpless."

13–28 The rule that the tracing process comes to an end when the value being traced is dissipated generally applies in the case where a defendant uses trust money to pay off a debt, for example, by paying the money into an overdrawn bank account, as in *Bishopsgate Investment Management Ltd v Homan*,[56] which is reproduced below. However, there are two exceptions to this principle. First, if the debt was secured by a charge over the defendant's property then Equity can treat the debt and the charge, by a legal fiction, as though they were not extinguished by the payment, thereby enabling the beneficiaries to trace the value inherent in their money into the value inherent in the creditor's fictionally subsisting chose in action against the defendant.[57] Second, if a defendant borrows money and uses it to buy an asset, and subsequently uses trust money to repay his creditor, then the beneficiaries can trace "backwards" through the loan transaction into the asset and identify the value inherent in the asset as the proceeds of the value inherent in the trust money.[58]

v. The Role of Intention

13–29 Backwards tracing was an issue in *Foskett v McKeown* in the Court of Appeal, where Scott V.C. expressed the view that beneficiaries should be allowed to trace "backwards" through the payment of a debt with trust money into an asset purchased with the borrowed money only if they could prove that it was the trustee's intention at the time of borrowing the money to repay the lender with

---

[54] See paras 13–17 and 13–18.

[55] [1948] Ch. 465 at 521.

[56] [1995] Ch. 211 see too *Northern Counties of England Fire Insurance Co v Whipp* (1884) 26 Ch.D. 482 at 495–496; *Thomson v Clydesdale Bank Ltd* [1893] A.C. 282. And note that where a defendant has several accounts with the same bank, the asset into which a deposit can be traced is the net balance due from the bank on *all* the accounts, and not only the account against which the deposit is credited: *Cooper v PRG Powerhouse Ltd* [2008] 2 All E.R, (Comm.) 964 at [32].

[57] *Boscawen v Bajwa* [1996] 1 W.L.R. 328 at 340, rejecting *Re Diplock* [1948] Ch. 465 at 549–550; *Primlake Ltd (in liq.) v Matthews Assocs* [2007] 1 B.C.L.C. 666 at [340]. As discussed at para.13–107, the point of this is that the beneficiaries can acquire the fictionally subsisting security via subrogation and enforce it for their own benefit.

[58] L.D. Smith, "Tracing into the Payment of a Debt" [1995] C.L.J. 290, esp. 292–295, expanded in L.D. Smith, *The Law of Tracing* (1997), pp.146–152. This analysis has the support of Dillon L.J. in *Bishopsgate Investment Management Ltd v Homan* [1995] Ch. 211 at 216–217 (but was disapproved by Leggatt L.J. at 221 and 222). It was also adopted by Hobhouse J. in *Westdeutsche Landesbank Girozentrale v Islington LBC* [1994] 4 All E.R. 890 at 939–940 (approved by CA without comment); by Scott V.C. in *Foskett v McKeown* [1998] Ch. 265 at 283–284 (not considered on appeal to HL); by Rimer J. in *Shalson v Russo* [2005] Ch. 281 at [144] (obiter); and (in effect) by David Richards QC, sitting as a deputy High Court judge in *Law Society v Haider* [2003] EWHC 2486 (Ch) at [40]–[41].

trust money.[59] No doubt he was concerned that beneficiaries might otherwise be able to "backwards trace" into every asset bought by a trustee with money withdrawn from an overdrawn account into which the trustee later pays trust money. However, the tracing rules are not generally concerned with a defendant's intentions, but with establishing transactional links between assets in order to identify the current whereabouts of the value which was formerly in the claimant's property.[60] As Ungoed-Thomas J. stated in *Re Tilley's Will Trusts*[61]:

> "if, having regard to all the circumstances of the case objectively considered, it appears that the trustee has in fact, whatever his intention, laid out trust moneys in or towards a purchase, then the beneficiaries are entitled to the property purchased and any profits which it produces to the extent to which it has been paid for out of the trust money."

The law's focus on transactional links may seem to produce some unpalatable results. Suppose that a trustee misdirects £5 of trust money to an innocent donee X who uses it to buy a winning lottery ticket that pays out £1 million. X can prove that he could have used his own resources to buy the ticket, and that he would have done so if he had known the improper provenance of the trust money. Nonetheless, the beneficiaries can say that the £1 million are the traceable proceeds of the trust money. Again, suppose that a trustee steals £5,000 of trust money and uses it to pay his rent, and then uses another £5,000 of his own to buy a diamond. The beneficiaries cannot trace into the ring even if they can prove that the trustee could not have afforded to pay the rent and buy the jewel out of his own resources. In our view, however, the answer to problems of the former sort does not lie in reformulating the tracing rules by requiring beneficiaries to prove causal rather than transactional links between misapplied trust property and substitute assets,[62] but in revisiting the rules of claiming the fruits of misdirected trust property.[63] So far as the problems of the latter sort are concerned, we are not convinced that the beneficiaries should have anything more than a personal claim against the trustee, a view which is borne out by the courts' treatment of Lord Templeman's "swollen assets theory" in *Space Investments Ltd v Canadian Imperial Bank of Commerce Trust Co.*[64] **13–30**

vi. The Swollen Assets Theory

Space Investments concerned a bank trustee that was empowered by the trust instrument to lend trust money to itself. The bank lawfully exercised this power, and then went into liquidation. The beneficiaries were unable to trace their money into any particular surviving asset and so the Privy Council held that their claims ranked as unsecured debts. In obiter dicta, however, Lord Templeman contrasted the situation with the case where a trustee unlawfully dissipates trust money and the beneficiaries cannot trace their money into a particular surviving asset. Here, in his Lordship's view, "equity allows the beneficiaries to trace the trust money to all the assets of the bank and to recover the trust money by the exercise of an equitable charge over all the assets of the bank."[65] **13–31**

---

59 [1998] Ch. 265 at 283–284.

60 Similarly, the rules of following are concerned with identifying the current whereabouts of particular assets, and with deeming them to be in particular locations when no-one can say where they have actually gone. See further L.D. Smith, *The Law of Tracing* (1997) pp. 69–70, 82–85 and 136–139.

61 [1967] Ch. 1179 at 1193.

62 As urged in D.A. Oesterle, "Deficiencies of the Restitutionary Right to Trace" (1983) 68 Cornell L.R. 172; C. Rotherham, "The Metaphysics of Tracing: Substituted Title and Property Rhetoric" [1996] Osgoode Hall L.J. 321; S. Evans, "Rethinking Tracing and the Law of Restitution" (1999) 115 L.Q.R. 469.

63 See further paras 13–96 ff.

64 [1986] 3 All E.R. 75.

65 *Space Investments* at 76–77, overlooking *Re Hallett & Co* [1894] 2 Q.B. 237 at 245.

13–32 In support of this conclusion he cited Jessel M.R.'s comment in *Re Hallett's Estate*,[66] that "if a man mixes trust funds with his own, the whole will be treated as trust property". However, this was to misread Jessel M.R.'s judgment, which was concerned with the case where a trustee mixes £X of trust money with £Y of his own money in a particular account and then dissipates part of the mixture. Jessel M.R. said nothing to support Lord Templeman's assertion that in such a case the whole of the trustee's assets constitutes one colossal fund which should be regarded as having been mixed with the trust money, so that if the money in the account is dissipated the beneficiaries can switch their attention to some other asset in the trustee's hands.

13–33 Moreover, Lord Templeman's analysis is inconsistent with the *Roscoe v Winder* principle discussed earlier,[67] that presumptions are made against wrongdoing trustees only where there is evidential uncertainty. In a case where it is certain that a trustee has dissipated trust money out of a particular bank account, this principle prevents the beneficiaries from arguing that some other asset in the trustee's hands should be deemed to represent the traceable proceeds of their property. Essentially for this reason, Lord Templeman's dicta were repudiated by the Court of Appeal in *Serious Fraud Office v Lexi Holdings Plc (in administration)*, Keene L.J. stating that:[68]

> "For [an] equitable charge to attach [to assets in the trustee's hands] it must attach to assets in existence which derive from the misappropriated trust funds. There must be a nexus. Were it otherwise the principles of following and tracing could become otiose. On the contrary, tracing in this area is a vital process: just because it is by that process that the necessary nexus is established and the proprietary remedy, be it by way of constructive trust or equitable charge, made effectual."

13–34 The *Lexi Holdings* case was followed in *Re Lehman Bros (International) Europe (in admin.)*,[69] where Briggs J. held that the claimants could not rely on the *Space Investments* dicta, and could only identify the traceable proceeds of their money in line with orthodox tracing principles. He also rejected the suggestion that these principles:[70]

> "are old-fashioned, unduly restrictive and therefore inappropriate for the protection of investors in the modern world. On the contrary, they represent the fruits of equity judges' and lawyers' endeavours over very many years to find and refine techniques of identifying and recovering trust property, in circumstances where the common law has failed to assist. The purpose of the process has been to help beneficiaries rather than to hinder them, and the techniques are only constrained by the unavoidable requirement to identify property to which it is appropriate to attach a proprietary claim. It is true that their use as an evidential tool can frequently be prohibitively slow and expensive, but this is usually the consequence of the evidential obstacles caused by the trustee's misappropriation of the property in the first place, not by any inherent or obviously curable defect in the tracing principles themselves."

---

[66] (1880) 13 Ch.D. 696 at 719.

[67] See para.13–18.

[68] [2009] Q.B. 376 at [49]–[50]. Lord Templeman's dicta had previously been restrictively distinguished in *Re Goldcorp Exchange Ltd* [1995] 1 A.C. 74 and *Bishopsgate Investment Management Ltd v Homan* [1995] Ch. 211; and on the same theme, note Lewison J.'s comments in *Ultraframe (UK) Ltd v Fielding* [2007] W.T.L.R. 835 at [1470]–[1475] and Lord Neuberger's judgment (in the CA) in *Re BA Peters Plc (in admin)* [2009] B.P.I.R. 248.

[69] [2009] EWHC 3228 (Ch) at [190] ff.

[70] *Lehman Bros* at [198].

BISHOPSGATE INVESTMENT MANAGEMENT LTD v HOMAN

Court of Appeal [1995] Ch. 211, [1994] 3 W.L.R. 1270, [1995] 1 All E.R. 347

DILLON L.J.: This is an appeal, by leave of the judge, by Bishopsgate Investment Management Ltd ("BIM") against an order of Vinelott J. made on 21 December 1993. BIM, which is now in liquidation, is the trustee of certain of the assets of various pension schemes for employees of companies with which the late Robert Maxwell was associated. 13–35

The respondents to the appeal, Mr Homan and three colleagues who are partners in Price Waterhouse & Co, are the court-appointed administrators of Maxwell Communication Corporation Plc ("MCC"). The judge's order was made on an application by the administrators under the Insolvency Act 1986 for directions. MCC, which was known at an earlier stage as the British Printing Corporation Ltd, was a publicly quoted company and the most prominent of a large number of companies, for which it was the holding company. There is a second group of companies, which have been referred to as the Maxwell private sector companies; essentially they were companies the share capitals of which were beneficially owned, directly or indirectly, by Robert Maxwell and members of his family or trusts established by him. 13–36

On the unexpected death of Robert Maxwell on 5 November 1991 it was discovered that very large amounts of pension fund moneys of BIM had been improperly paid, during his lifetime, directly or indirectly into various bank accounts of the private sector companies and of MCC with National Westminster Bank. At the time of each wrongful payment of BIM's pension fund moneys into MCC's accounts those accounts were overdrawn, or later became overdrawn. It was also found that MCC was hopelessly insolvent. . . . 13–37

The administrators, who have realised a substantial amount of MCC's assets although the administration is far from complete, wanted to make an interim distribution among the creditors of MCC. But the liquidators claimed that BIM was entitled to an equitable charge, in priority to all other unsecured creditors of MCC, on all the assets of MCC for the full amount of the pension moneys of BIM wrongly paid to MCC. Accordingly the administrators applied to the Companies Court for directions. 13–38

Vinelott J. approached the application on the basis that if the claims of BIM were plainly not maintainable in law the court ought to make a declaration to that effect, in order that an interim distribution could be made without regard to unfounded claims. But, if it was possible that on a further investigation of the facts there might be a claim, valid in law, by BIM to an equitable charge on a particular asset, the proceeds of that asset ought not to be distributed until the particular facts had been investigated. 13–39

The judge declared by his order that the administrators were entitled to deal with specified notices of claim as if they do not give rise to any proprietary claims, and he declared also that BIM was not entitled to any equitable charge over the assets of MCC in respect of proprietary claims notified to the administrators to the extent that such assets were acquired before any moneys or assets misappropriated from BIM were paid or transferred to or so as to be under the control of MCC and were not acquired in anticipation of or otherwise in connection with the misappropriation of such assets or moneys. In essence the judge held that BIM could only claim an equitable charge on any assets of MCC in accordance with the recognised principles of equitable tracing and these principles do not permit tracing through an overdrawn bank account—whether an account which was already overdrawn at the time the relevant moneys were paid into it or an account which was then in credit, but subsequently became overdrawn by subsequent drawings. 13–40

The judge reserved, however, the position if it were shown that there was a connection between a particular misappropriation of BIM's moneys and the acquisition by MCC of a particular asset. The judge gave as an instance of such a case what he called "backward tracing"—where an asset was acquired by MCC with moneys borrowed from an overdrawn or loan account and there was an inference that when the borrowing was incurred it was the intention that it should be repaid by misappropriations of BIM's moneys. Another possibility was that moneys misappropriated from BIM were paid into an overdrawn account of MCC in order to reduce the overdraft and so make finance available within the overdraft limits for MCC to purchase some particular asset. 13–41

By a respondent's notice by way of cross-appeal, the administrators ask us to overrule these reservations of the judge, and hold that even if the possible facts which the judge envisages were clearly proved that could not in law give BIM any equitable charge on the particular asset acquired. For my part I would not interfere at all with this aspect of the judge's exercise of his discretion. In my judgment, if the connection he 13–42 postulates between the particular misappropriation of BIM's money and the acquisition by MCC of a particular asset is sufficiently clearly proved, it is at least arguable, depending on the facts, that there ought to be an equitable charge in favour of BIM on the asset in question of MCC.

13–43 But the main claims of BIM are put much more widely as claims to an equitable charge on all the assets of MCC. These claims are not founded on proving any particular intention of Robert Maxwell or others in charge of MCC but on general principles which it is said that the court ought to apply. They are founded primarily on certain observations of Lord Templeman in giving the judgment of the Privy Council in *Space Investments Ltd v Canadian Imperial Bank of Commerce Trust Co (Bahamas) Ltd*.[71] In particular, in that case Lord Templeman said:[72]

> "In these circumstances it is impossible for the beneficiaries interested in trust money misappropriated from their trust to trace their money to any particular asset belonging to the trustee bank. But equity allows the beneficiaries, or a new trustee appointed in place of an insolvent bank trustee . . . to trace the trust money to all the assets of the bank and to recover the trust money by the exercise of an equitable charge over all the assets of the bank. . . . [That] equitable charge secures for the beneficiaries and the trust priority over the claims of the customers . . . and . . . all other unsecured creditors."

13–44 What Lord Templeman there said was strictly obiter, in that on the facts the Privy Council held that the bank trustee was authorised by the trust instruments to deposit trust money with itself as banker and so there had been no misappropriation. The beneficiaries or their new trustee therefore could merely prove with the other general creditors of the insolvent bank trustee for a dividend in respect of the moneys so deposited.

13–45 Vinelott J. rejected the submissions of BIM founded on the *Space Investments* case. He considered that Lord Templeman could not have intended to effect such a fundamental change to the well-understood limitations to equitable tracing; Lord Templeman was only considering the position of an insolvent bank which had been taking deposits and lending money.

13–46 In the notice of appeal to this court, BIM's first ground of appeal relies on the *Space Investments* case and it is said that the judge erred in his interpretation of what Lord Templeman had said. There is a second, and alternative, ground of appeal to which I will refer later. . . .

13–47 As I read the judgment of the Privy Council in *Re Goldcorp Exchange Ltd*[73] delivered by Lord Mustill, it makes it clear that Lord Templeman's observations in the *Space Investments* case were not concerned at all with the situation we have in the present case where trust moneys have been paid into an overdrawn bank account, or an account which has become overdrawn. Lord Mustill said in the clearest terms:[74]

> "Their Lordships should, however, say that they find it difficult to understand how the judgment of the Board in *Space Investments Ltd v Canadian Imperial Bank of Commerce Trust Co (Bahamas) Ltd* on which the claimants leaned heavily in argument, would enable them to overcome the difficulty that the moneys said to be impressed with the trust were paid into an overdrawn account and thereupon ceased to exist.[75] The observations of the Board in the *Space Investments* case were concerned with a mixed, not a non-existent, fund."

13–48 Thus the wide interpretation of those observations put forward by Cooke P. [in the New Zealand Court of Appeal in *Re Goldcorp Exchange Ltd*[76]], which is the basis of the first ground of appeal in the present case, is rejected. Instead the decision of the Court of Appeal in *Re Diplock* is endorsed. There it was said:[77]

[71] [1968] 1 W.L.R. 1072.
[72] ibid. at 1074.
[73] [1995] 1 A.C. 74.
[74] ibid. at 104.
[75] See, e.g. *Re Diplock* [1948] Ch. 465.
[76] *Liggett v Kensington* [1993] 1 N.Z.L.R. 257 at 274.
[77] [1948] Ch. 465 at 521.

"The equitable remedies presuppose the continued existence of the money either as a separate fund or as part of a mixed fund or as latent in property acquired by means of such a fund. If, on the facts of any individual case, such continued existence is not established, equity is as helpless as the common law itself."

Also endorsed, in my judgment, in the decision of the Board delivered by Lord Mustill is the long-standing first instance decision in *James Roscoe (Bolton) Ltd v Winder*,[78] which Mr Heslop for BIM, in his submissions in March, invited us to overrule. That was a decision that, in tracing trust moneys into the bank account of a trustee in accordance with *Re Hallett's Estate*,[79] tracing was only possible to such an amount of the balance ultimately standing to the credit of the trustee as did not exceed the lowest balance of the account during the intervening period. Thus as is said in the headnote to the report: **13–49**

"Payments into a general account cannot, without proof of express intention, be appropriated to the replacement of trust money which has been improperly mixed with that account and drawn out."

That reflects the statement by Sargant J. in the *James Roscoe* case[80];

"it is impossible to attribute to him"—i.e. the account holder—"that by the mere payment into the account of further moneys, which to a large extent he subsequently used for purposes of his own, he intended to clothe those moneys with a trust in favour of the plaintiffs."

Mr Heslop, for BIM, referred, however, to later passages in the opinion of Lord Mustill. First Lord Mustill stated that the law relating to the creation and tracing of equitable proprietary interests is still in a state of development.[81] He referred to two recent decisions[82] on facts not particularly relevant to the present case as instances where equitable proprietary interests have been recognised in circumstances which might previously have been regarded merely as circumstances for common law relief. . . . **13–50**

Mr Heslop submitted that the beneficiaries under the pension schemes of which BIM is trustee are in a different position from the other creditors, who are mainly banks, of BIM. He did not, of course, adopt the simple populist approach that pensioners, like widows and orphans, are "goodies" while banks, like usurers, are "baddies" and so the court should use its powers to ensure that the goodies are paid in full ahead of the baddies. But he did say that the beneficiaries under the pension schemes never undertook the risk that their pension funds would be misappropriated and paid into the overdrawn bank account of an insolvent company, whereas all the banks which lent money to MCC took their chance, as a commercial risk, on MCC's solvency. **13–51**

Mr Heslop therefore relied on the second ground in the notice of appeal, whereby BIM claims (as it has been explained to us) to be entitled to an equitable charge as security for its claims against MCC (i) over any moneys standing to the credit at the time of the appointment of the administrators of MCC of any banking account maintained by MCC into which any moneys of BIM or the proceeds of any assets of BIM misappropriated from it were paid and (ii) over any assets acquired out of any such bank account, whether or not in credit as at the date such assets were acquired. **13–52**

So far as (i) is concerned, the point is that the National Westminster Bank account into which the misappropriated BIM trust moneys were paid happened to be in credit when the administrators were appointed. BIM therefore claims a lien on that credit balance in the National Westminster Bank account for the amount of the misappropriated trust moneys. It is difficult to suppose, however, in the circumstances of Robert Maxwell's last days—and I know no evidence—that Robert Maxwell intended to make good the misappropriation of the BIM pension moneys by the cryptic expedient of arranging to put MCC's **13–53**

[78] [1915] 1 Ch. 62.
[79] (1880) 13 Ch.D. 696.
[80] [1915] 1 Ch. 62 at 69.
[81] [1995] 1 A.C. 74 at 109.
[82] *Att.-Gen. for Hong Kong v Reid* [1994] A.C. 324 and *Lord Napier and Ettrick v Hunter* [1993] A.C. 713.

account with National Westminster Bank into credit—but without repaying the credit balance this created to BIM. But in the absence of clear evidence of intention to make good the depredations on BIM it is not possible to assume that the credit balance has been clothed with a trust in favour of BIM and its beneficiaries.[83]

13–54 As to (ii), this seems to be going back to the original wide interpretation of what Lord Templeman said in the *Space Investments* case and applying it to an overdrawn account because the misappropriated moneys that went into the account were trust moneys and thus different from other moneys that may have gone into that account. But the moneys in the *Space Investments* case were also trust moneys, and so, if argument (ii) is valid in the present case, it would also have been valid, as a matter of law, in the *Space Investments* case. But that was rejected in *Re Goldcorp Exchange Ltd* because equitable tracing, though devised for the protection of trust moneys misapplied, cannot be pursued through an overdrawn and therefore non-existent fund. Acceptance of argument (ii) would, in my judgment, require the rejection of *Re Diplock*, which is binding on us, and of Lord Mustill's explanation of Lord Templeman's statement in the *Space Investments* case in *Re Goldcorp Exchange Ltd*.

13–55 It is not open to us to say that because the moneys were trust moneys the fact that they were paid into an overdrawn account or have otherwise been dissipated presents no difficulty to raising an equitable charge on assets of MCC for their amount in favour of BIM. The difficulty Lord Mustill referred to is not displaced. Accordingly I would reject both grounds of appeal, and dismiss both the appeal and the cross-appeal.

13–56 On consideration, I do not regard it as appropriate to give any further directions to the judge.

13–57 LEGGATT L.J.: . . . There can be no equitable remedy against an asset acquired before misappropriation of money takes place, since *ex hypothesi* it cannot be followed into something which existed and so had been acquired before the money was received and therefore without its aid.

13–58 The concept of a "composite transaction" is in my judgment fallacious. What is envisaged is (a) the purchase of an asset by means of an overdraft, that is, a loan from a bank, and (b) the discharge of the loan by means of misappropriated trust money. The judge thought that the money could be regarded as having been used to acquire the asset. His conclusion was that "It is sufficient to say that proof that trust moneys were paid into an overdrawn account of the defaulting trustee may not always be sufficient to bar a claim to an equitable charge".

13–59 I see the force of Mr Kosmin's submission that, if an asset were used as security for an overdraft which was then discharged by means of misappropriated money, the beneficiary might obtain priority by subrogation. But there can ordinarily be no tracing into an asset which is already in the hands of the defaulting trustee when the misappropriation occurs.

13–60 In *Liggett v Kensington*[84] Cooke P. applied the principle which he derived from the *Space Investments* case that those who do not take a risk of insolvency are entitled to an equitable charge over all the assets of the trustee, giving them priority over those who are to be regarded as having taken such a risk. That decision is authority for no wider proposition than that, where a bank trustee wrongly deposits money with itself, the trustee can trace into all the bank's credit balances.

13–61 Consistently with Mr Kosmin's submissions on this appeal, Lord Mustill, delivering the judgment of the Board in *Re Goldcorp Exchange Ltd*,[85] stated that their Lordships found it difficult to understand how it would enable the claimants in that case to "overcome the difficulty that the moneys said to be impressed with the trust were paid into an overdrawn account and thereupon ceased to exist." Lord Mustill emphasised that the observations of the Board were concerned with a mixed, not a non-existent, fund. He also cited with approval *James Roscoe (Bolton) Ltd v Winder* as conventionally exemplifying the principles of tracing.

13–62 I therefore consider that the judge came to the right conclusion, though I do not accept that it is possible to trace through an overdrawn bank account or to trace misappropriated money into an asset bought before the money was received by the purchaser. I agree that the appeal should be dismissed.

[83] See *James Roscoe (Bolton) Ltd v Winder* [1915] 1 Ch. 62.
[84] [1993] 1 N.Z.L.R. 257.
[85] [1995] 1 A.C. 74 at 104.

HENRY L.J.: I agree with both judgments. 13–63

Appeal dismissed with costs. 13–64

FOSKETT v MCKEOWN

House of Lords [2001] 1 A.C. 102, [2000] 2 W.L.R. 1299, [2000] 3 All E.R. 97

The claimant purchasers paid money to Murphy on trust for themselves, intending that the money should be used to buy land for investment purposes in Portugal. Murphy had previously bought a life insurance policy on his own life, on trust for his children (who would receive 90 per cent of the policy proceeds in the event of his death) and his mother (who would receive 10 per cent). Murphy paid the first two annual premiums with his own money; the source of the money which he used to pay the third premium was disputed; and in breach of trust he used the claimants' money to pay the fourth and fifth premiums. Murphy then committed suicide and the insurer paid £1 million to the surviving trustees of the policy settlement. The claimants sued the trustees, arguing that at least 40 per cent of the insurance proceeds was held on constructive trust for them because at least 40 per cent of the insurance premiums had been paid with trust money misappropriated by Murphy. A majority of the House of Lords allowed the claim, and refused to restrict the claimants to a lien over the proceeds for the amount of money paid towards the premiums. 13–65

LORD MILLETT (with whom LORD BROWNE-WILKINSON and LORD HOFFMANN agreed, and with whom LORD STEYN and LORD HOPE disagreed on the question of remedy): My Lords, this is a textbook example of tracing through mixed substitutions. At the beginning of the story the purchasers were beneficially entitled under an express trust to a sum standing in the name of Mr Murphy in a bank account. From there the money moved into and out of various bank accounts where in breach of trust it was inextricably mixed by Mr Murphy with his own money. After each transaction was completed the purchasers' money formed an indistinguishable part of the balance standing to Mr Murphy's credit in his bank account. The amount of that balance represented a debt due from the bank to Mr Murphy, that is to say a chose in action. At the penultimate stage the purchasers' money was represented by an indistinguishable part of a different chose in action, viz. the debt prospectively and contingently due from an insurance company to its policyholders, being the trustees of a settlement made by Mr Murphy for the benefit of his children. At the present and final stage it forms an indistinguishable part of the balance standing to the credit of the respondent trustees in their bank account. 13–66

Tracing and Following

The process of ascertaining what happened to the purchasers' money involves both tracing and following. These are both exercises in locating assets which are or may be taken to represent an asset belonging to the purchasers and to which they assert ownership. The processes of following and tracing are, however, distinct. Following is the process of following the same asset as it moves from hand to hand. Tracing is the process of identifying a new asset as the substitute for the old. Where one asset is exchanged for another, a claimant can elect whether to follow the original asset into the hands of the new owner or to trace its value into the new asset in the hands of the same owner. In practice his choice is often dictated by the circumstances. In the present case the purchasers do not seek to follow the money any further once it reached the bank or insurance company, since its identity was lost in the hands of the recipient (which in any case obtained an unassailable title as a bona fide purchaser for value without notice of the purchasers' beneficial interest). Instead the purchasers have chosen at each stage to trace the money into its proceeds, viz. the debt presently due from the bank to the account holder or the debt prospectively and contingently due from the insurance company to the policy holders. 13–67

Having completed this exercise, the purchasers claim a continuing beneficial interest in the insurance money. Since this represents the product of Mr Murphy's own money as well as theirs, which Mr Murphy mingled indistinguishably in a single chose in action, they claim a beneficial interest in a proportionate part of the money only. The transmission of a claimant's property rights from one asset to its traceable proceeds is part of our law of property, not of the law of unjust enrichment. There is no "unjust factor" to justify restitution (unless "want of title" be one, which makes the point). The claimant succeeds if at all by virtue of his own title, not to reverse unjust enrichment. Property rights are determined by fixed rules and 13–68 settled principles. They are not discretionary. They do not depend upon ideas of what is "fair, just and reasonable". Such concepts, which in reality mask decisions of legal policy, have no place in the law of property.

13–69 A beneficiary of a trust is entitled to a continuing beneficial interest not merely in the trust property but in its traceable proceeds also, and his interest binds every one who takes the property or its traceable proceeds except a bona fide purchaser for value without notice. In the present case the purchasers' beneficial interest plainly bound Mr Murphy, a trustee who wrongfully mixed the trust money with his own and whose every dealing with the money (including the payment of the premiums) was in breach of trust. It similarly binds his successors, the trustees of the children's settlement, who claim no beneficial interest of their own, and Mr Murphy's children, who are volunteers. They gave no value for what they received and derive their interest from Mr Murphy by way of gift.

Tracing

13–70 We speak of money at the bank, and of money passing into and out of a bank account. But of course the account holder has no money at the bank. Money paid into a bank account belongs legally and beneficially to the bank and not to the account holder. The bank gives value for it, and it is accordingly not usually possible to make the money itself the subject of an adverse claim. Instead a claimant normally sues the account holder rather than the bank and lays claim to the proceeds of the money in his hands. These consist of the debt or part of the debt due to him from the bank. We speak of tracing money into and out of the account, but there is no money in the account. There is merely a single debt of an amount equal to the final balance standing to the credit of the account holder. No money passes from paying bank to receiving bank or through the clearing system (where the money flows may be in the opposite direction). There is simply a series of debits and credits which are causally and transactionally linked. We also speak of tracing one asset into another, but this too is inaccurate. The original asset still exists in the hands of the new owner, or it may have become untraceable. The claimant claims the new asset because it was acquired in whole or in part with the original asset. What he traces, therefore, is not the physical asset itself but the value inherent in it.

13–71 Tracing is thus neither a claim nor a remedy. It is merely the process by which a claimant demonstrates what has happened to his property, identifies its proceeds and the persons who have handled or received them, and justifies his claim that the proceeds can properly be regarded as representing his property. Tracing is also distinct from claiming. It identifies the traceable proceeds of the claimant's property. It enables the claimant to substitute the traceable proceeds for the original asset as the subject matter of his claim. But it does not affect or establish his claim. That will depend on a number of factors including the nature of his interest in the original asset. He will normally be able to maintain the same claim to the substituted asset as he could have maintained to the original asset. If he held only a security interest in the original asset, he cannot claim more than a security interest in its proceeds. But his claim may also be exposed to potential defences as a result of intervening transactions. Even if the purchasers could demonstrate what the bank had done with their money, for example, and could thus identify its traceable proceeds in the hands of the bank, any claim by them to assert ownership of those proceeds would be defeated by the bona fide purchaser defence. The successful completion of a tracing exercise may be preliminary to a personal claim[86] or a proprietary one, to the enforcement of a legal right,[87] or an equitable one.

13–72 Given its nature, there is nothing inherently legal or equitable about the tracing exercise. There is thus no sense in maintaining different rules for tracing at law and in equity. One set of tracing rules is enough. The existence of two has never formed part of the law in the United States.[88] There is certainly no logical justification for allowing any distinction between them to produce capricious results in cases of mixed substitutions by insisting on the existence of a fiduciary relationship as a precondition for applying equity's tracing rules. The existence of such a relationship may be relevant to the nature of the claim which the plaintiff can maintain, whether personal or proprietary, but that is a different matter. I agree with the passages which my noble and learned friend Lord Steyn has cited from Professor Birks' essay "The Necessity

[86] As in *El Ajou v Dollar Land Holdings Plc* [1993] 3 All E.R. 717.
[87] As in *Trustees of the Property of FC Jones & Sons (a firm) v Jones* [1997] Ch. 159.
[88] See Scott, *The Law of Trusts* (4th edn, 1989), 605–609.

of a Unitary Law of Tracing",[89] and with Dr Lionel Smith's exposition in his comprehensive monograph *The Law of Tracing*.[90]

This is not, however, the occasion to explore these matters further, for the present is a straightforward case of a trustee who wrongfully misappropriated trust money, mixed it with his own, and used it to pay for an asset for the benefit of his children. Even on the traditional approach, the equitable tracing rules are available to the purchasers. There are only two complicating factors. The first is that the wrongdoer used their money to pay premiums on an equity linked policy of life assurance on his own life. The nature of the policy should make no difference in principle, though it may complicate the accounting. The second is that he had previously settled the policy for the benefit of his children. This should also make no difference. The claimant's rights cannot depend on whether the wrongdoer gave the policy to his children during his lifetime or left the proceeds to them by his will; or if during his lifetime whether he did so before or after he had recourse to the claimant's money to pay the premiums. The order of events does not affect the fact that the children are not contributors but volunteers who have received the gift of an asset paid for in part with misappropriated trust moneys. **13–73**

The Cause of Action

As I have already pointed out, the purchasers seek to vindicate their property rights, not to reverse unjust enrichment. The correct classification of the purchasers' cause of action may appear to be academic, but it has important consequences. The two causes of action have different requirements and may attract different defences. **13–74**

A plaintiff who brings an action in unjust enrichment must show that the defendant has been enriched at the plaintiff's expense, for he cannot have been unjustly enriched if he has not been enriched at all. But the plaintiff is not concerned to show that the defendant is in receipt of property belonging beneficially to the plaintiff or its traceable proceeds. The fact that the beneficial ownership of the property has passed to the defendant provides no defence; indeed, it is usually the very fact which founds the claim. Conversely, a plaintiff who brings an action like the present must show that the defendant is in receipt of property which belongs beneficially to him or its traceable proceeds, but he need not show that the defendant has been enriched by its receipt. He may, for example, have paid full value for the property, but he is still required to disgorge it if he received it with notice of the plaintiff's interest. **13–75**

Furthermore, a claim in unjust enrichment is subject to a change of position defence, which usually operates by reducing or extinguishing the element of enrichment. An action like the present is subject to the bona fide purchaser for value defence, which operates to clear the defendant's title. **13–76**

The Tracing Rules

The insurance policy in the present case is a very sophisticated financial instrument. Tracing into the rights conferred by such an instrument raises a number of important issues. It is therefore desirable to set out the basic principles before turning to deal with the particular problems to which policies of life assurance give rise. **13–77**

The simplest case is where a trustee wrongfully misappropriates trust property and uses it exclusively to acquire other property for his own benefit. In such a case the beneficiary is entitled at his option either to assert his beneficial ownership of the proceeds or to bring a personal claim against the trustee for breach of trust and enforce an equitable lien or charge on the proceeds to secure restoration of the trust fund. He will normally exercise the option in the way most advantageous to himself. If the traceable proceeds have increased in value and are worth more than the original asset, he will assert his beneficial ownership and obtain the profit for himself. There is nothing unfair in this. The trustee cannot be permitted to keep any profit resulting from his misappropriation for himself, and his donees cannot obtain a better title than their donor. If the traceable proceeds are worth less than the original asset, it does not usually matter how the beneficiary exercises his option. He will take the whole of the proceeds on either basis. This is why it is not possible to identify the basis on which the claim succeeded in some of the cases. **13–78**

---

[89] In R. Cranston (ed.), *Making Commercial Law: Essays in Honour of Roy Goode* (1997).

[90] L.D. Smith *The Law of Tracing* (1997). See particularly pp.120–130, 277–279 and 342–347.

13–79 Both remedies are proprietary and depend on successfully tracing the trust property into its proceeds. A beneficiary's claim against a trustee for breach of trust is a personal claim. It does not entitle him to priority over the trustee's general creditors unless he can trace the trust property into its product and establish a proprietary interest in the proceeds. If the beneficiary is unable to trace the trust property into its proceeds, he still has a personal claim against the trustee, but his claim will be unsecured. The beneficiary's proprietary claims to the trust property or its traceable proceeds can be maintained against the wrongdoer and anyone who derives title from him except a bona fide purchaser for value without notice of the breach of trust. The same rules apply even where there have been numerous successive transactions, so long as the tracing exercise is successful and no bona fide purchaser for value without notice has intervened.

13–80 A more complicated case is where there is a mixed substitution. This occurs where the trust money represents only part of the cost of acquiring the new asset. As James Barr Ames pointed out in "Following Misappropriated Property into its Product",[91] consistency requires that, if a trustee buys property partly with his own money and partly with trust money, the beneficiary should have the option of taking a proportionate part of the new property or a lien upon it, as may be most for his advantage. In principle it should not matter (and it has never previously been suggested that it does) whether the trustee mixes the trust money with his own and buys the new asset with the mixed fund or makes separate payments of the purchase price (whether simultaneously or sequentially) out of the different funds. In every case the value formerly inherent in the trust property has become located within the value inherent in the new asset.

13–81 The rule, and its rationale, were stated by Samuel Williston in "The Right to Follow Trust Property when Confused with Other Property"[92]:

> "If the trust fund is traceable as having furnished in part the money with which a certain investment was made, and the proportion it formed of the whole money so invested is known or ascertainable, the cestui que trust should be allowed to regard the acts of the trustee as done for his benefit, in the same way that he would be allowed to if all the money so invested had been his; that is, he should be entitled in equity to an undivided share of the property which the trust money contributed to purchase—such a proportion of the whole as the trust money bore to the whole money invested. The reason in one case as in the other is that the trustee cannot be allowed to make a profit from the use of the trust money, and if the property which he wrongfully purchased were held subject only to a lien for the amount invested, any appreciation in value would go to the trustee."

If this correctly states the underlying basis of the rule (as I believe it does), then it is impossible to distinguish between the case where mixing precedes the investment and the case where it arises on and in consequence of the investment. It is also impossible to distinguish between the case where the investment is retained by the trustee and the case where it is given away to a gratuitous donee. The donee cannot obtain a better title than his donor, and a donor who is a trustee cannot be allowed to profit from his trust.

13–82 In *Re Hallett's Estate*,[93] Jessel M.R. acknowledged that where an asset was acquired exclusively with trust money, the beneficiary could either assert equitable ownership of the asset or enforce a lien or charge over it to recover the trust money. But he appeared to suggest that in the case of a mixed substitution the beneficiary is confined to a lien. Any authority that this dictum might otherwise have is weakened by the fact that Jessel M.R. gave no reason for the existence of any such rule, and none is readily apparent. The dictum was plainly obiter, for the fund was deficient and the plaintiff was only claiming a lien. It has usually been cited only to be explained away.[94] It was rejected by the High Court of Australia in *Scott v Scott*.[95] It has not been adopted in the United States.[96] In *Primeau v Granfield* Learned Hand J. expressed himself in forthright terms: "On principle there can be no excuse for such a rule."[97]

91 (1906) 19 Harvard L.R. 511.
92 (1888) 2 Harvard L.R. 28, 29.
93 (1880) 13 Ch.D. 696 at 709.
94 See e.g. *Re Tilley's Will Trusts* [1967] Ch. 1179 at 1186, per Ungoed-Thomas J.; A. Burrows, *The Law of Restitution* (1993), p.368.
95 (1963) 109 C.L.R. 649 at 661–662, cited by Morritt L.J. below: [1998] Ch. 265 at 300–301.
96 See the American Law Institute, *Restatement of the Law, Trusts 2d* (1959) at p.202(h).
97 (1911) 184 F. 480 at 482.

13–83 In my view the time has come to state unequivocally that English law has no such rule. It conflicts with the rule that a trustee must not benefit from his trust. I agree with Burrows that the beneficiary's right to elect to have a proportionate share of a mixed substitution necessarily follows once one accepts, as English law does, (i) that a claimant can trace in equity into a mixed fund and (ii) that he can trace unmixed money into its proceeds and assert ownership of the proceeds.

13–84 Accordingly, I would state the basic rule as follows. Where a trustee wrongfully uses trust money to provide part of the cost of acquiring an asset, the beneficiary is entitled at his option either to claim a proportionate share of the asset or to enforce a lien upon it to secure his personal claim against the trustee for the amount of the misapplied money. It does not matter whether the trustee mixed the trust money with his own in a single fund before using it to acquire the asset, or made separate payments (whether simultaneously or sequentially) out of the differently owned funds to acquire a single asset.

13–85 Two observations are necessary at this point. First, there is a mixed substitution (with the results already described) whenever the claimant's property has contributed in part only towards the acquisition of the new asset. It is not necessary for the claimant to show in addition that his property has contributed to any increase in the value of the new asset. This is because, as I have already pointed out, this branch of the law is concerned with vindicating rights of property and not with reversing unjust enrichment. Secondly, the beneficiary's right to claim a lien is available only against a wrongdoer and those deriving title under him otherwise than for value. It is not available against competing contributors who are innocent of any wrongdoing. The tracing rules are not the result of any presumption or principle peculiar to equity. They correspond to the common law rules for following into physical mixtures (though the consequences may not be identical). Common to both is the principle that the interests of the wrongdoer who was responsible for the mixing and those who derive title under him otherwise than for value are subordinated to those of innocent contributors. As against the wrongdoer and his successors, the beneficiary is entitled to locate his contribution in any part of the mixture and to subordinate their claims to share in the mixture until his own contribution has been satisfied. This has the effect of giving the beneficiary a lien for his contribution if the mixture is deficient.

13–86 Innocent contributors, however, must be treated equally inter se. Where the beneficiary's claim is in competition with the claims of other innocent contributors, there is no basis upon which any of the claims can be subordinated to any of the others. Where the fund is deficient, the beneficiary is not entitled to enforce a lien for his contributions; all must share rateably in the fund.

13–87 The primary rule in regard to a mixed fund, therefore, is that gains and losses are borne by the contributors rateably. The beneficiary's right to elect instead to enforce a lien to obtain repayment is an exception to the primary rule, exercisable where the fund is deficient and the claim is made against the wrongdoer and those claiming through him. It is not necessary to consider whether there are any circumstances in which the beneficiary is confined to a lien in cases where the fund is more than sufficient to repay the contributions of all parties. It is sufficient to say that he is not so confined in a case like the present. It is not enough that those defending the claim are innocent of any wrongdoing if they are not themselves contributors but, like the trustees and Mr Murphy's children in the present case, are volunteers who derive title under the wrongdoer otherwise than for value. On ordinary principles such persons are in no better position than the wrongdoer, and are liable to suffer the same subordination of their interests to those of the claimant as the wrongdoer would have been. They certainly cannot do better than the claimant by confining him to a lien and keeping any profit for themselves.

13–88 Similar principles apply to following into physical mixtures.[98] There are relatively few cases which deal with the position of the innocent recipient from the wrongdoer, but *Jones v De Marchant*[99] may be cited as an example. A husband wrongfully took 18 beaver skins belonging to his wife and used them, together with four skins of his own, to have a fur coat made up which he then gave to his mistress. Unsurprisingly the wife was held entitled to recover the coat. The mistress knew nothing of the true ownership of the skins, but her innocence was held to be immaterial. She was a gratuitous donee and could stand in no better

98 See *Lupton v White* (1808) 15 Ves. Jun. 432; and *Sandeman & Sons v Tyzack and Branfoot Steamship Co Ltd* [1913] A.C. 680 at 695, where Lord Moulton said: "If the mixing has arisen from the fault of 'B', 'A' can claim the goods."

99 (1916) 28 D.L.R. 561.

position than the husband. The coat was a new asset manufactured from the skins and not merely the product of intermingling them. The problem could not be solved by a sale of the coat in order to reduce the disputed property to a divisible fund, since (as we shall see) the realisation of an asset does not affect its ownership. It would hardly have been appropriate to require the two ladies to share the coat between them. Accordingly it was an all or nothing case in which the ownership of the coat must be assigned to one or other of the parties. The determinative factor was that the mixing was the act of the wrongdoer through whom the mistress acquired the coat otherwise than for value.

13–89 The rule in equity is to the same effect, as Page Wood V.C. observed in *Frith v Cartland*:[100]

> ". . . if a man mixes trust funds with his own, the whole will be treated as the trust property, except so far as he may be able to distinguish what is his own."

This does not, in my opinion, exclude a pro rata division where this is appropriate, as in the case of money and other fungibles like grain, oil or wine. But it is to be observed that a pro rata division is the best that the wrongdoer and his donees can hope for. If a pro rata division is excluded, the beneficiary takes the whole; there is no question of confining him to a lien. *Jones v De Marchant* is a useful illustration of the principles shared by the common law and equity alike that an innocent recipient who receives misappropriated property by way of gift obtains no better title than his donor, and that if a proportionate sharing is inappropriate the wrongdoer and those who derive title under him take nothing.

Insurance Policies

13–90 In the case of an ordinary whole-life policy the insurance company undertakes to pay a stated sum on the death of the assured in return for fixed annual premiums payable throughout his life. Such a policy is an entire contract, not a contract for a year with a right of renewal. It is not a series of single premium policies for one year term assurance. It is not like an indemnity policy where each premium buys cover for a year after which the policyholder must renew or the cover expires. The fact that the policy will lapse if the premiums are not paid makes no difference. The amounts of the annual premiums and of the sum assured are fixed in advance at the outset and assume the payment of annual premiums throughout the term of the policy. The relationship between them is based on the life expectancy of the assured and the rates of interest available on long term government securities at the inception of the policy.

13–91 In the present case the benefits specified in the policy are expressed to be payable "in consideration of the payment of the first Premium already made and of the further Premiums payable". The premiums are stated to be "£10220.00 payable at annual intervals from 06 Nov 1986 throughout the lifetime of the life assured". It is beyond argument that the death benefit of £1m paid on Mr Murphy's death was paid in consideration for all the premiums which had been paid before that date, including those paid with the purchasers' money, and not just some of them. Part of that sum, therefore, represented the traceable proceeds of the purchasers' money.

13–92 It is, however, of critical importance in the present case to appreciate that the purchasers do not trace the premiums directly into the insurance money. They trace them first into the policy and thence into the proceeds of the policy. It is essential not to elide the two steps. In this context, of course, the word "policy" does not mean the contract of insurance. You do not trace the payment of a premium into the insurance contract any more than you trace a payment into a bank account into the banking contract. The word "policy" is here used to describe the bundle of rights to which the policyholder is entitled in return for the premiums. These rights, which may be very complex, together constitute a chose in action, viz. the right to payment of a debt payable on a future event and contingent upon the continued payment of further premiums until the happening of the event. That chose in action represents the traceable proceeds of the premiums; its current value fluctuates from time to time. When the policy matures, the insurance money represents the traceable proceeds of the policy and hence indirectly of the premiums.

13–93 It follows that, if a claimant can show that premiums were paid with his money, he can claim a proportionate share of the policy. His interest arises by reason of and immediately upon the payment of the premiums, and the extent of his share is ascertainable at once. He does not have to wait until the policy

[100] (1865) 2 H. & M. 417 at 420.

matures in order to claim his property. His share in the policy and its proceeds may increase or decrease as further premiums are paid; but it is not affected by the realisation of the policy. His share remains the same whether the policy is sold or surrendered or held until maturity; these are merely different methods of realising the policy. They may affect the amount of the proceeds received on realisation but they cannot affect the extent of his share in the proceeds. In principle the purchasers are entitled to the insurance money which was paid on Mr Murphy's death in the same shares and proportions as they were entitled in the policy immediately before his death.

Since the manner in which an asset is realised does not affect its ownership, and since it cannot matter whether the claimant discovers what has happened before or after it is realised, the question of ownership can be answered by ascertaining the shares in which it is owned immediately before it is realised. Where A misappropriates B's money and uses it to buy a winning ticket in the lottery, B is entitled to the winnings. Since A is a wrongdoer, it is irrelevant that he could have used his own money if in fact he used B's. This may seem to give B an undeserved windfall, but the result is not unjust. Had B discovered the fraud before the draw, he could have decided whether to keep the ticket or demand his money back. He alone has the right to decide whether to gamble with his own money. If A keeps him in ignorance until after the draw, he suffers the consequence. He cannot deprive B of his right to choose what to do with his own money; but he can give him an informed choice. **13–94**

The application of these principles ought not to depend on the nature of the chose in action. They should apply to a policy of life assurance as they apply to a bank account or a lottery ticket **13–95**

3. Claiming

In this section we describe the different proprietary claims that can be made against trust property or its traceable proceeds, assuming that all necessary following and tracing processes have been successfully completed. We then consider possible sources of the beneficiaries' proprietary rights. **13–96**

A. Proprietary Claims

i. Where a Trustee Misappropriates Trust Property for Himself

If a trustee misappropriates trust assets for himself and retains them in their original form, then the beneficiaries can demand that he reconstitute the trust estate, where necessary by conveying legal title to the assets to new trustees who have been appointed in the meantime.[101] If a trustee misappropriates trust property and uses it exclusively to acquire other property for his own benefit (a "clean substitution"), then the beneficiaries can elect either to claim the new property in specie, or to enforce an equitable lien over the new property to secure their personal claim against the trustee to restore the trust fund.[102] If a trustee misappropriates trust property and mixes it with his own property before buying a new asset out of the mixture (a "mixed substitution"), then again the beneficiaries can elect either to claim a proportionate ownership interest in the new asset, or to enforce an equitable lien over the property to secure their personal claim against the trustee.[103] **13–97**

---

[101] See para.11–69. Before the Judicature Acts it would have been necessary for the beneficiaries to bring full execution proceedings, although these would usually have been aborted once relief had been granted in respect of the particular misapplication: see e.g. *Re Medland* (1889) 41 Ch.D. 476 at 482. Today there is almost never a call for full judicial execution of a trust, but the same principles are applied, the overriding object being to enforce the performance of the trust according to its terms.

[102] *Re Hallett's Estate* (1880) 13 Ch.D. 696 at 709; *Foskett v McKeown* [1998] Ch. 265 at 277; [2001] 1 A.C. 102 at 130.

[103] *Scott v Scott* (1962) 109 C.L.R. 649; *Re Tilley's WT* [1967] Ch. 1178 (where the point was conceded); *British Columbia Teachers' Credit Union v Betterley* (1975) 61 D.L.R. (3d) 755; *Foskett v McKeown* [1998] Ch. 265 at 277; [2001] 1 A.C. 102 at 130–131.

13–98 If a trustee misappropriates money from two different trust sources and uses it to buy a new asset, then[104]:

> "neither set of beneficiaries can claim a first charge over the asset to recover its money. The equities as between the two sets of beneficiaries will be equal. Neither will be entitled to priority as against the other. It follows that they must share proportionately in the asset, bearing pro rata any shortfall and enjoying pro rata any increase in value."

13–99 If beneficiaries assert an ownership interest in property which generates income, then they can claim the income as well: so, for example, if they trace into a house which has been let for rent, then they can claim the rental income as well as the house.[105] If a trustee uses trust funds to buy a house in the trustee's name, with the help of a mortgage loan that the trustee personally covenants to repay, the courts do not treat the trustee as having personally contributed the mortgage money when calculating the quantum of the beneficiaries' claim. So, for example, if the trustee uses £25,000 of trust money to buy a house with the help of a £75,000 purchase loan secured by a mortgage on the property, and the house increases in value, then the beneficiaries can claim the whole house, subject to a counter-claim for any mortgage payments actually made by the trustee: but for the £25,000 of trust funds the trustee would not have been able to provide the necessary security for the mortgage loan and so the fruits of the transaction should go to the beneficiaries.[106]

13–100 An equitable lien is "essentially a positive right to obtain . . . an order for sale of the subject property or for actual payment from the subject fund" and it "may, in general, be enforced in the same way as any other equitable charge, namely, by sale in pursuance of court order or, where the lien is over a fund, by an order for payment thereout."[107] Since an ownership interest in property will "rise or fall in value with the property"[108] it will be to the beneficiaries' advantage to elect for an equitable lien in cases where the property has decreased in value, and pursue a personal claim against the defendant for the difference. An equitable lien can also be a potent remedy in a case where the beneficiaries can trace into a number of different assets and funds. Suppose that a trustee has several bank accounts and mixes £100,000 of trust money with his own money in his No.1 account, then transfers money from the No.1 account to his No.2 and No.3 accounts, and then buys a painting with money from the No.1 account, a car with money from the No.2 account, and a flat with money from the No.3 account. In this case, "as against the wrongdoer and his successors in title, the beneficiary is entitled to locate his contribution in any part of the mixture [i.e. in any part of the value remaining in the three accounts, the painting, the car, and the flat] and to subordinate their claims to share in the mixture till his own contribution has been satisfied."[109]

13–101 If the trustee reinstates the trust by returning the trust property then the beneficiaries will have no claim against him. However, if a trustee uses trust money to buy assets which increase in value it is not enough for him to repay the value of the trust money originally taken: he must account to the beneficiaries for the increase in value as well.[110]

---

104 *Foskett v McKeown* [1998] Ch. 265 at 278, per Scott V.C. See too Lord Millett's comments on appeal: [2001] 1 A.C. 102 at 132.
105 *Banton v CIBC Corp* (1999) 182 D.L.R. (4th) 486 at 504–505; *Greenwood v Lee* [2003] O.P.L.R. 1.
106 *Paul Davies Pty Ltd v Davies* [1983] N.S.W.L.R. 440; *Re Marriage of Wagstaff* (1990) 99 F.L.R. 390.
107 *Hewett v Court* (1983) 149 C.L.R. 638 at 664, per Deane J.
108 *Australian Postal Corp v Lutak* (1991) 21 N.S.W.L.R. 584 at 590, per Bryson J.
109 *Foskett v McKeown* [2001] 1 A.C. 102 at 132, per Lord Millett. See too *El Ajou v Dollar Land Holdings Plc* [1993] 3 All E.R. 713 at 735–736; on appeal: [1994] 2 All E.R. 685 at 701; *Re Goldcorp Exchange Ltd* [1994] 2 All E.R. 806 at 831.
110 *Scott v Scott* (1962) 109 C.L.R. 649; *Re Hughes* [1970] I.R. 237.

13–102 If a trustee has honestly done work or spent money improving an asset claimed by the beneficiaries then he may be entitled to an allowance at the court's discretion.[111]

ii. Where Trust Property is Misdirected to a Third Party

13–103 Where trust property is misdirected to a third party recipient, then again, the beneficiaries can assert an ownership right in the property or its traceable proceeds unless the recipient is a bona fide purchaser for value without notice of the beneficiaries' equitable interest.[112] Even if he has acted in good faith, the recipient must "yield up any [trust property that remains], or the traceable proceeds of any that [has been exchanged for a new asset]".[113] This proprietary liability is not dependent on proof of fault and it must be distinguished from the personal liability which the recipient may additionally incur for knowing receipt if he has acted with the requisite degree of fault.[114] If the recipient has mixed trust property with his own, then the beneficiaries can claim the traceable residue of their property,[115] the identity of the residue being determined by rules which vary according to whether the recipient has acted in good faith, as discussed above.[116]

13–104 As previously noted,[117] the rules of tracing permit beneficiaries to trace into assets bought by an innocent recipient even though he can prove that he could have bought the asset with his own money, and that he would have done so, had he known that the money which he actually used to buy the asset belonged to the beneficiaries. In the event that the asset increases in value, then it follows from the foregoing discussion that the beneficiaries can capture the whole of the increase by asserting an ownership claim to the asset. In a case where the defendant is a wrongdoing trustee, or a donee from a wrongdoing trustee, as in *Foskett v McKeown*, above, this outcome may not offend us, but where he has acted in good faith, it is "an affront to our notions of justice" that he should be liable in this way, as Lord Millett has observed.[118] Suppose that an innocent recipient uses £5 of misapplied trust funds to buy a lottery ticket which pays out £5 million where he could and would have used his own £5 for the purpose, had he known of the trust money's tainted source. In our view, the most to which the beneficiaries should be entitled in this situation is an equitable lien over the winnings to secure repayment of the £5.[119]

iii. Where a Trustee Makes an Unauthorised Investment

13–105 When an express trust is declared, "the trust fund" is generally defined in the trust deed in terms such as "property transferred to the trustees to hold on the terms of this settlement and all the property from time to time representing the same", but the latter clause can simply be regarded as spelling out what is inevitably involved in the settlor creating a trust. The reason is that the trustees will be given

---

111 *Re Berkeley Applegate (Investment Consultants) Ltd* [1988] 3 All E.R. 71 at 83; *Badfinger Music Ltd v Evans* [2001] W.T.L.R. 1.
112 *Foskett v McKeown* [2001] 1 A.C. 102 at 127 and 130.
113 *Re Montagu's ST* [1987] Ch. 264 at 272, per Megarry V.C.
114 *Agip (Africa) Ltd v Jackson* [1990] 1 Ch. 265 at 290; *Allan v Rea Brothers Trustees Ltd* [2002] P.L.R. 169 at [55]; *Waxman v Waxman* (2004) 7 I.T.E.L.R. 162 at [583]; *NABB Brothers Ltd v Lloyds Bank International (Guernsey) Ltd* [2005] I.L.Pr. 37 at [72]. Also *Clark v Cutland* [2004] 1 W.L.R. 783 (innocent D can hold property on constructive trust for C even though C concedes that D not personally liable to account for lost money). Personal liability for knowing receipt is discussed at paras 12–09 ff.
115 *Re Diplock* [1948] Ch. 465 at 524 and 539.
116 See para.13–26.
117 See para.13–30.
118 "Proprietary Restitution" in S. Degeling and J. Edelman (eds), *Equity in Commercial Law* (2005).
119 An outcome which is supported by *Re Tilley's WT* [1967] Ch. 1179, as discussed in D.J. Hayton, "Equity's Identification Rules" in P. Birks (ed.) *Laundering and Tracing* (1995) pp. 10–12.

powers of disposition, sale and investment, and for these to be effective, the trustees must be able to transfer their legal title to trust assets clear of the beneficiaries' equitable interest. Hence the doctrine of overreaching provides that whenever the trustees exercise a power to sell or dispose of trust assets in an authorised fashion, the recipient takes clear legal title, and in the case of sale, the trust will instantly attach instead to the proceeds of sale.[120] Again, if the trustees use trust money to buy a new asset in a valid exercise of their powers of investment, then the same thing happens: the beneficiaries' equitable interest in the money is overreached, the vendor gets clear legal title to the money, and the trust attaches to the new asset.

13–106 Now consider the case where trustees act in an unauthorised way when they sell trust assets or use trust money to buy new assets. In *Wright v Morgan*, Viscount Dunedin held that where[121]:

> "a trustee has made an improper investment, the law is well settled. The *cestuis que trustent* as a whole have a right, if they choose, to adopt the investment and to hold it as trust property. But if there is not unanimity then it is not trust property, but the trustee who has made it must keep the investment himself. He is debtor to the trust for the money which has been applied in its purchase."

These rules would be worked out in proceedings for an account either by affirming the purchase in a case where the beneficiaries all consent to that outcome, or else, in a case where they do not, by falsifying the account to delete the unauthorised expenditure from the record and requiring the trustees to reconstitute the trust fund by paying over the amount of the outgoing from their own pockets.[122] In a case where the trustee uses trust money to make an unauthorised investment which triples in value, and the beneficiaries cannot all consent to take the investment because some are minors or unborn, can the trustee keep it for himself and repay the amount of the purchase money plus interest? Presumably he cannot. In this case, the adult beneficiaries could apply (at the trustee's expense) to the court under the Trustee Act 1925 s.57 for an order authorising the purchase; alternatively, they could move to replace the trustee, and the new trustee could then demand the investment on the beneficiaries' behalf.[123]

iv. Where Trust Funds are Used to Pay Off a Mortgage

13–107 Suppose that a trustee misappropriates trust money and uses it to pay off a debt secured by a mortgage on his house, or suppose that a trustee misdirects trust money to a third party who does the same thing. Here, the courts can allow the beneficiaries, by means of a legal fiction, to trace their money into the discharged mortgage,[124] and to be treated as though they had acquired the mortgage as security for the repayment of their money.[125] This remedy is termed "subrogation", which literally means "substitution": the beneficiaries are treated, by a fiction, as though they were substitutes for the original mortgagee.[126]

---

120 *State Bank of India v Sood* [1997] Ch. 276. See too C. Harpum, "Overreaching, Trustees' Powers, and the Reform of the 1925 Property Legislation" [1990] C.L.J. 277; D. Fox, "Overreaching" in P. Birks and A. Pretto (eds) *Breach of Trust* (2002); R.C. Nolan "Property in a Fund" (2004) 120 L.Q.R. 108, pp. 111–117; R.C. Nolan, "Understanding the Limits of Equitable Property" (2006) 1 Journal of Equity 18, pp.24–28.

121 [1926] A.C. 788 at 798, citing *Parker v McKenna* (1874) L.R. 10 Ch. 96. See too *Re Patten* (1883) 52 L.J. (Ch.) 787; *Power v Banks* [1901] 2 Ch. 487 at 496; *Re Jenkins and HE Randall and Co's Contract* [1903] 2 Ch. 362.

122 *Re Biss, deceased* [1903] 2 Ch. 40. For discussion of the accounting process, see paras 11-66 ff.

123 *Young v Murphy* [1996] 1 V.R. 279.

124 See para.13–28.

125 *McCullough v Marsden* (1919) 45 D.L.R. 645; *Primlake Ltd (in liq.) v Matthews Assocs* [2007] 1 B.C.L.C. 666 at [340].

126 Because subrogation entails a fictional process of revival and transfer of the mortgagee's extinguished rights, the courts have a discretion to decide how many of the mortgagee's advantages should accrue to a claimant: *Banque Financière de la Cité v Parc (Battersea) Ltd* [1999] 1 A.C. 221; *Cheltenham & Gloucester Plc v Appleyard* [2004] EWCA Civ 291 at [32]–[44]; *Kali Ltd v Chawla* [2008] B.P.I.R. 415.

Boscawen v Bajwa,[127] parts of which are reproduced below,[128] was arguably a case of this kind. The claimant building society lent money to a borrower for the sole purpose of buying a house, and the borrower's solicitors paid the money over to the vendor prematurely, before the sale documents were properly completed. The vendor used the money to discharge a mortgage over the property, and then the sale fell through. The Court of Appeal allowed the claimant to acquire the mortgage via subrogation, and although it was not pleaded in this way, the case can be explained on the basis that the claimant's money was subject to a *Quistclose* trust[129] that was breached when the money was transferred to the vendor before the sale documents were completed.[130] **13–108**

B. Sources of Proprietary Rights

It is easier to describe the different types of proprietary claim which the beneficiaries can bring following a breach of trust than it is to explain why the beneficiaries are entitled to bring such claims. In *Foskett v McKeown*,[131] the majority of the House of Lords held that the beneficiaries are given a proprietary claim to the whole or part of a traced asset in order to vindicate their proprietary rights in the trust fund. The following discussion considers what this means. **13–109**

i. Rights in Traceable Substitutes

We must first distinguish proprietary claims to trust assets in their original form from proprietary claims to the traceable proceeds of trust assets. Suppose that a trustee misappropriates a trust painting for himself, or misdirects it to a recipient who is not a bona fide purchaser for value without notice. In this case, nothing happens to interrupt the beneficiaries' continuing equitable ownership of the painting, and they can enforce their continuing rights by obtaining a declaration of ownership and an order for reconveyance if necessary. **13–110**

Now contrast the case where a trustee uses trust assets to buy an unauthorised investment for the beneficiaries, or a new asset for himself, or where a trustee misdirects trust property to a third party who uses it to buy a new asset. Here, assuming that the beneficiaries can trace and follow as necessary into the new asset, they can assert a proprietary claim to the new asset. But, strictly speaking, their proprietary right to the new asset cannot be the same right as their proprietary right to the original trust property. The reason is that a property right is a right to a specific thing which cannot be detached from the thing to which it relates and reattached to some new thing.[132] For example, an ownership right in land relates to the land, and so it cannot be the same right as the right to the sale proceeds of the land, even if one right is exchanged for the other. **13–111**

In *Foskett*, their Lordships ignored this, focussing their attention on the beneficiaries' interests as interests in the trust fund established by the settlor. Lord Browne-Wilkinson held that[133]: **13–112**

---

[127] [1996] 1 W.L.R. 328.

[128] At paras 13–120 ff.

[129] See paras 5–33 ff.

[130] cf. *Hillel v Christoforides* (1991) 63 P. & C.R. 301 at 307; *Chohan v Saggar* [1992] B.C.C. 750 at 756; *Filby v Mortgage Express (No.2) Ltd* [2004] EWCA Civ 759 at [19].

[131] [2001] 1 A.C. 102.

[132] P. Birks, "Tracing, Property, and Unjust Enrichment" (2002) 54 C.L.P. 231, 244–245; R. Chambers, "Tracing and Unjust Enrichment" in J. W. Neyers et al. (eds), *Understanding Unjust Enrichment* (2004), pp. 273–274. See too A. Burrows, "Proprietary Restitution: Unmasking Unjust Enrichment" (2001) 117 L.Q.R. 412.

[133] [2001] 1 A.C. 102 at 110. Cf. *Taylor v Plumer* (1815) 3 M. & S. 562 at 575.

> "The only trusts at issue are the express trusts of the purchasers' trust deed. Under those express trusts the purchasers were entitled to equitable proprietary interests in the original moneys [which they paid over to the trustee]. Like any other equitable proprietary interest, those equitable proprietary interests under the purchasers' trust deed which originally existed in the moneys paid to [the trustee] now exist in any other property which, in law, now represents the original trust assets. . . . If, as a result of tracing, it can be said that certain of the policy moneys are what now represent part of the assets subject to the trusts of the purchasers trust deed, then as a matter of English property law the purchasers have an absolute interest in such moneys."

Similarly, Lord Millett held that the beneficiaries have "a continuing beneficial interest not merely in the trust property but in its traceable proceeds also",[134] and he has since written extra-judicially that "'the fiction of persistence' is not a fiction [because the] beneficiaries' interests in the new investment are exactly the same as their interest in the old."[135] However, this cannot be true: the new asset is not the old asset, and prior to the acquisition of the new asset with trust funds, no one owed any obligation to the beneficiaries in respect of the new asset. It follows that the beneficiaries' right in the new asset after it has been acquired must be a new right whose existence calls for explanation.

ii. Sources of Rights in Traceable Substitutes

13–113 To the extent that they recognised this, the majority of the House of Lords in *Foskett* explained the beneficiaries' new right in the traceable proceeds of trust property as a right which arose in order to "vindicate their property rights" in the original trust property.[136] However, it should be stressed that the mere fact of the beneficiaries' ownership of the original trust property is not enough in itself to explain their acquisition of a new proprietary right in a traceable substitute.[137] In Professor Birks' terms, it is not an "event" to which the new right can respond.[138] For this event, one must look instead to the substitution by means of which the new asset was acquired with the trust property.

13–114 Take the case where a trustee uses trust funds to purchase an authorised investment.[139] Here, by virtue of an agreement between the settlor and the trustee, the trustee holds the original trust property, subsequently added property, and property substituted for such property, as a trust fund for the beneficiaries. When the trustee buys an authorised investment with trust funds, the beneficiaries' interest in the funds is overreached, and they acquire a new interest in the new investment, by a process which the beneficiaries cannot subsequently dispute. In our view, the source of the beneficiaries' new rights in this case is the settlor's intention, agreed to by the trustee, to give the beneficiaries' proprietary rights in the original trust assets and the proceeds thereof, mediated through the trustee's authorised

---

134 *Foskett* at 127.

135 Lord Millett, "Proprietary Restitution" in S. Degeling and J. Edelman (eds), *Equity in Commercial Law* (2005) pp.315–316, adding that "wrongfully substituted assets are [not] held on a constructive trust . . . [but] continue to be held on the same trusts throughout. If the claimant was the beneficiary under an express trust, the substituted assets are held on the same express trusts." In his essay in the same volume, "Old and New in the Law of Tracing", Professor Charles Rickett says essentially the same thing when he writes at pp.135–138 and 140–144 that equitable property rights possess the attribute of "transmissibility", arguing that if this were not so then every time a trustee effects an authorised substitution of trust property for a new asset, the new asset would be held on a new trust, and the disposal of the original asset would have to comply with the formality rules which govern the disposition of subsisting equitable interests.

136 [2001] 1 A.C. 102 at 129, per Lord Millett. See too Lord Browne-Wilkinson's comments at 110 and Lord Hoffmann's comments at 115.

137 As suggested in R. Grantham and C. Rickett, "Property Rights: A Legally Significant Event" [2003] C.L.J. 417; Lord Millett, 'Proprietary Restitution' in S. Degeling and J. Edelman (eds), *Equity in Commercial Law* (2005); G. Virgo *The Principles of the Law of Restitution* 2nd edn (2006) pp. 570–574.

138 See, e.g. P. Birks, "Tracing, Property, and Unjust Enrichment" (2002) 54 C.L.P. 231, p.245.

139 See para.13–105.

exercise of his powers of sale and investment to acquire new assets for the beneficiaries, to be held by him on the same terms as those on which he held the original trust assets.[140]

The same analysis can also be used to explain the case where the trustees purport to acquire new assets for the beneficiaries, but act beyond the scope of their powers. As noted above,[141] the beneficiaries can retrospectively adopt the unauthorised investment, which looks like an ad hoc variation of the trust, retrospectively giving the beneficiaries rights whose source, again, is the settlor's intention, agreed to by the trustee, to create such rights in their favour. **13–115**

The case where a trustee misappropriates trust funds and uses them to acquire new assets for himself resembles the case where a trustee makes an unauthorised profit from his position. As argued in Chapter 9, the constructive trust imposed on the trustee's gain in the latter situation responds to the fact that a trustee binds himself by agreement at the moment when he assumes office to hold all the profits of his office for the beneficiaries as and when he receives them.[142] A fortiori, one can also say that a trustee binds himself to hold whatever traceable proceeds of trust funds come into his hands for the beneficiaries, and that the beneficiaries' proprietary right to these therefore responds to the trustee's intention that the beneficiaries should have them. Obviously it is tempting to say of this situation that the trustee does not intend the beneficiaries to acquire the new assets, but intends to take them for himself. However, it is not the trustee's current intention, but his original intention at the time of taking office, to which the beneficiaries' proprietary right responds. Equity will not allow the trustee to go back on his word, and will, in effect, specifically enforce his promise to act for the beneficiaries. **13–116**

Finally, we come to the case where the traceable proceeds of misdirected trust assets are in the hands of third party recipients. Here, the recipients have not previously agreed to hold the new assets for the beneficiaries, and the beneficiaries' right to them should therefore be explained either on the basis that the recipient commits a wrong (analogous to conversion at common law) when he interferes with the beneficiaries' rights in the original trust property, or else that he is unjustly enriched at the beneficiaries' expense when trust assets are used to acquire new assets for the benefit of the recipient.[143] **13–117**

In *Foskett*, Lord Millett denied that beneficiaries can claim the traceable proceeds of trust property in the hands of third parties on the ground of unjust enrichment.[144] However, his Lordship's reasons for saying this do not stand up to scrutiny. They depend on the premise that the law of property and the law of unjust enrichment cannot both be in issue in a single claim. This premise entails a categorical error, since property and unjust enrichment are not categories that can be opposed: the first is a type of right, and the second a source of rights.[145] Moreover, his Lordship purports to analyse claims to traceable proceeds in the hands of third parties in the same way that he analyses claims to traceable proceeds in the hands of trustees. Yet the two types of claim are different, since the trustees have previously agreed to hold the proceeds for the beneficiaries while the third parties have not. **13–118**

iii. Does it Matter?

There are practical reasons why all this matters, as noted by Lord Millett in *Foskett*.[146] Most significantly, it seems from his Lordship's comments there that the defence of change of position is not **13–119**

---

140 See too R. Chambers, "Tracing and Unjust Enrichment" in J. W. Neyers et al. (eds), *Understanding Unjust Enrichment* (2004) pp. 263, 267.

141 See para.13–106.

142 See para.9–15.

143 P. Birks, "Property and Unjust Enrichment: Categorical Truths" [1997] N.Z.L.Rev. 623, 661; A. Burrows, *The Law of Restitution* 2nd ed (2002), pp.64–66 and 208–209.

144 [2001] 1 A.C. 102 at 127.

145 P. Birks, *Unjust Enrichment* 2nd ed (2005), pp.32–38.

146 [2001] 1 A.C. 102 at 129.

available to a third party recipient of trust funds unless the beneficiaries' claim is founded on unjust enrichment.[147] Extra-judicially, however, he has suggested that even where this is not the basis of the claim, such a third party should have an equitable allowance for work done improving any trust asset that he has received.[148]

BOSCAWEN v BAJWA

Court of Appeal [1996] 1 W.L.R. 328, [1995] 4 All E.R. 769

13–120 Dave & Co, solicitors for the prospective purchaser of Bajwa's house, acted also for the Abbey National Building Society, which transferred £140,000 to Dave & Co to be used only to complete the purchase and until then to be held for the Abbey National. In breach of trust Dave paid £137,405 to Bajwa's solicitors to hold to Dave's order until completion and then sent them Dave's cheque for £2,595 which "bounced" just after Bajwa's solicitors had precipitately paid £140,000 to Bajwa's mortgagee, the Halifax Building Society, to discharge its mortgage on Bajwa's house. The sale fell through. The claimant, a judgment creditor of Bajwa, obtained a charging order absolute over the house, which was sold and the £105,311 net proceeds of sale were paid into court. It was held that the Abbey National was entitled to all of these proceeds. It had priority over the claimant because its moneys could be traced into the payment to the Halifax and it was entitled to be subrogated to the Halifax's charge: i.e. Bajwa's freehold was already subject to a charge in equity by way of subrogation in favour of the Abbey National when the plaintiff obtained his interest under the charging order.

MILLETT L.J. (with whom WAITE and STUART-SMITH L.JJ. agreed):

Tracing and Subrogation

13–121 The submission that the deputy judge illegitimately conflated two different causes of action, the equitable tracing claim and the claim to a right of subrogation, betrays a confusion of thought which arises from the admittedly misleading terminology which is traditionally used in the context of equitable claims for restitution. Equity lawyers habitually use the expressions "the tracing claim" and "the tracing remedy" to describe the proprietary claim and the proprietary remedy which equity makes available to the beneficial owner who seeks to recover his property in specie from those into whose hands it has come. Tracing properly so-called, however, is neither a claim nor a remedy but a process. Moreover, it is not confined to the case where the plaintiff seeks a proprietary remedy; it is equally necessary where he seeks a personal remedy against the knowing recipient or knowing assistant. It is the process by which the plaintiff traces what has happened to his property, identifies the persons who have handled or received it, and justifies his claim that the money which they handled or received. Unless he can prove this, he cannot (in the traditional language of equity) raise an equity against the defendant or (in the modern language of restitution) show that the defendant's unjust enrichment was at his expense.

13–122 In such a case, the defendant will either challenge the plaintiff's claim that the property in question represents his property (i.e. he will challenge the validity of the tracing exercise), or he will raise a priority dispute (e.g. by claiming to be a bona fide purchaser without notice). If all else fails, he will raise the defence of innocent change of position. This was not a defence which was recognised in England before 1991, but it was widely accepted throughout the common law world. In *Lipkin Gorman (a firm) v Karpnale Ltd*[149] the House of Lords acknowledged it to be part of English law also. The introduction of this defence not only provides the court with a means of doing justice in future, but allows a re-examination of many decisions of the past in which the absence of the defence may have led judges to distort basic principles in order to avoid injustice to the defendant.

---

[147] For general discussion of the change of position defence, see paras 12–21 ff.; and for discussion of the question whether the defence should be available in response to proprietary claims, see P. Birks, "Change of Position and Surviving Enrichment" in W. Swadling (ed.), *The Limits of Restitutionary Claims: A Comparative Analysis* (1997), 36 at pp.42 ff.

[148] "Proprietary Restitution" in S. Degeling and J. Edelman (eds), *Equity in Commercial Law* (2005).

[149] [1991] 2 A.C. 548.

If the plaintiff succeeds in tracing his property, whether in its original or in some changed form, into the hands of the defendant and overcomes any defences which are put forward on the defendant's behalf, he is entitled to a remedy. The remedy will be fashioned to the circumstances. The plaintiff will generally be entitled to a personal remedy; if he seeks a proprietary remedy he must usually prove that the property to which he lays claim is still in the ownership of the defendant. If he succeeds in doing this, the court will treat the defendant as holding the property on a constructive trust for the plaintiff and will order the defendant to transfer it in specie to the plaintiff. But this is only one of the proprietary remedies which is available to a court of equity. If the plaintiff's money has been applied by the defendant, for example, not in the acquisition of a landed property but in its improvement, then the court may treat the land as charged with the payment to the plaintiff of a sum representing the amount by which the value of the defendant's land has been enhanced by the use of the plaintiff's money. And if the plaintiff's money has been used to discharge a mortgage on the defendant's land, then the court may achieve a similar result by treating the land as subject to a charge by way of subrogation in favour of the plaintiff. **13–123**

Subrogation, therefore, is a remedy, not a cause of action.[150] It is available in a wide variety of different factual situations in which it is required in order to reverse the defendant's unjust enrichment. Equity lawyers speak of a right of subrogation, or of an equity of subrogation, but this merely reflects the fact that it is not a remedy which the court has a general discretion to impose whenever it thinks it just to do so. The equity arises from the conduct of the parties on well-settled principles and in defined circumstances which make it unconscionable for the defendant to deny the proprietary interest claimed by the plaintiff. A constructive trust arises in the same way. Once the equity is established the court satisfies it by declaring that the property in question is subject to a charge by way of subrogation in the one case or a constructive trust in the other. **13–124**

Accordingly, there was nothing illegitimate in the deputy judge's invocation of the two doctrines of tracing and subrogation in the same case. They arose at different stages of the proceedings. Tracing was the process by which the Abbey National sought to establish that its money was applied in the discharge of the Halifax's charge; subrogation was the remedy which it sought in order to deprive Mr Bajwa (through whom the appellants claim) of the unjust enrichment which he would thereby otherwise obtain at the Abbey National's expense. **13–125**

Tracing

It is still a prerequisite of the right to trace in equity that there must be a fiduciary relationship which calls the equitable jurisdiction into being.[151] That requirement is satisfied in the present case by the fact that from the first moment of its receipt by Dave in its general client account the £140,000 was trust money held in trust for the Abbey National. The appellants do not dispute that the Abbey National can successfully trace £137,405 of its money into Hill Lawson's client account. But they do dispute the judge's finding that it can trace the sum further into the payment to the Halifax. **13–126**

The £137,405 was paid into Hill Lawson's general client account at the bank because it was only intended to be kept for a short time. Funds which were held for clients for any length of time were held in separate designated accounts. Hill Lawson's ledger cards showed Mr Bajwa as the relevant client. According to Mr Duckney, Hill Lawson also held other funds for Mr Bajwa which were the result of an inheritance which he had received. These were the source from which Hill Lawson made good the shortfall of £2,595 which arose when Dave's cheque was dishonoured. The amount of these other funds is unknown, though it was certainly nothing like £140,000. The evidence does not show whether they were held in Hill Lawson's general client account or whether they were held in a separate designated account. If they were held in the general client account, the £137,405 received from Dave was (quite properly) mixed not only with moneys belonging to other clients but also with money belonging to Mr Bajwa. Hill Lawson can be presumed not to have committed a breach of trust by resorting to moneys belonging to other clients, but they were perfectly entitled to use Mr Bajwa's own money to discharge the Halifax's charge on his **13–127**

[150] See Goff and Jones *Law of Restitution* (4th edn, 1993) at 589 ff; *Orakpo v Manson Investments Ltd* [1978] A.C. 95 at 104 per Lord Diplock; and *Re TH Knitwear (Wholesale) Ltd* [1988] Ch. 275 at 284 per Slade L.J.

[151] See *Agip (Africa) Ltd v Jackson* [1991] Ch. 547 at 566, per Fox L.J. (N.B. Lord Millett subsequently changed his mind about this in *Foskett v McKeown* [2001] 1 A.C. 102 at 128–129.)

property. Whether they did so or not cannot be determined in the absence of any evidence of the amount involved. Accordingly, it is submitted, the Abbey National has failed to establish how much of its money was applied in the discharge of the Halifax's charge and how much of the money which was applied for this purpose was Mr Bajwa's own money.

13–128 The Abbey National answers this submission in two ways. First, it submits that Hill Lawson's ledger cards show that Hill Lawson appropriated the £137,405 which it had received from Dave towards the payment of the sum of £140,000 to the Halifax, and resorted to Mr Bajwa's other funds only when Dave's cheque for the balance was dishonoured. The ledger cards were, of course, made up after the event, though long before any litigation ensued, so they are not primary evidence of actual appropriation; but they are reliable evidence of the appropriation which Hill Lawson believed that they had made.

13–129 I accept this submission. It is not necessary to apply artificial tracing rules where there has been an actual appropriation. A trustee will not be allowed to defeat the claim of his beneficiary by saying that he has resorted to trust money when he could have made use of own; but if the beneficiary asserts that the trustee has made use of the trust money there is no reason why he should not be allowed to prove it.

13–130 The second way in which the Abbey National answers the appellants' submission is by reliance on equity's ability to follow money through a bank account where it has been mixed with other moneys by treating the money in the account as charged with the repayment of his money. As against a wrongdoer the claimant is not obliged to appropriate debits to credits in order to ascertain where his money has gone. Equity's power to charge a mixed fund with the repayment of trust moneys enables the claimant to follow the money, not because it is his, but because it is derived from a fund which is treated as if it were subject to a charge in his favour.[152]

13–131 The appellants accept this, but submit that for this purpose Mr Bajwa was not a wrongdoer. He was, as I have said, not guilty of any impropriety or want of probity. He relied on his solicitors, and they acted unwisely, perhaps negligently, and certainly precipitately, but not dishonestly. Mr Bajwa, it is submitted, was an innocent volunteer who mixed trust money with his own. As such, he was not bound to give priority to the Abbey National, but could claim parity with it. Accordingly, Mr Bajwa and the Abbey National must be treated as having contributed pari passu to the discharge of the Halifax's charge; and in the absence of the necessary evidence the amounts which were provided by Mr Bajwa and the Abbey National respectively cannot be ascertained. (In fact, on this footing the Abbey National would be entitled to succeed to the extent of one-half of its claim, but that is by the way.)

13–132 For this proposition the appellants rely on a passage in *Re Diplock's Estate*,[153] as follows:

> "Where an innocent volunteer (as distinct from a purchaser for value without notice) mixes 'money' of his own with 'money' which in equity belongs to another person, or is found in possession of such a mixture, although that other person cannot claim a charge on the mass superior to the claim of the volunteer, he is entitled, nevertheless, to a charge ranking pari passu with the claim of the volunteer. . . . But this burden on the conscience of the volunteer is not such as to compel him to treat the claim of the equitable owner as paramount. That would be to treat the volunteer as strictly as if he himself stood in a fiduciary relationship to the equitable owner which *ex hypothesi* he does not. The volunteer is under no greater duty of conscience to recognise the interest of the equitable owner than that which, lies on a person having an equitable interest in one of two trust funds of 'money' which have become mixed towards the equitable owner of the other. Such a person is not in conscience bound to give precedence to the equitable owner of the other of the two funds."

13–133 This would be highly relevant if the distinction which the court was there making was between the honest and the dishonest recipient. But it was not. The distinction was between the innocent recipient who had no reason to suspect that the money was not his own to dispose of as he pleased, and the recipient who knew or ought to have known that the money belonged to another. In *Re Diplock's Estate* the defendants were the recipients of grants made to them by the personal representatives of a deceased testator in

152 See *Re Hallett's Estate* (1880) 13 Ch.D. 696; *Re Oatway* [1903] 2 Ch. 356; and *El Ajou v Dollar Land Holdings Plc* [1993] 3 All E.R. 717.

153 [1948] Ch. 465 at 524.

accordance with the terms of the residuary gift in his will. The gift was afterwards held by the House of Lords to be ineffective, with the result that the testator's residue passed on intestacy. The next of kin then brought proceedings to recover the moneys paid away. The defendants found themselves in an unenviable position. Not only had they received the money honestly and in good faith, but they had had no reason to think that it was not theirs. There was no question of their having consciously mixed money which belonged to another with their own.

But the present case is very different. Neither Mr Bajwa nor his solicitors acted dishonestly, but nor were they innocent volunteers. Hill Lawson knew that the money was trust money held to Dave's order pending completion and that it would become available for use on behalf of their client only on completion. They were manifestly fiduciaries. Mr Bajwa, who was plainly intending to redeem the Halifax's mortgage out of the proceeds of sale of the property, must be taken to have known that any money which his solicitors might receive from the purchasers or their mortgagees would represent the balance of the proceeds of sale due on completion and that, since he had made no arrangement with the purchasers to be advanced any part of that amount before completion, it would be available to him only on completion. He cannot possibly have thought that he could keep both the property and the proceeds of sale. Had he thought about the matter at all, he would have realised that the money was not his to mix with his own and dispose of as he saw fit. The only reason that he and his solicitors can be acquitted of dishonesty is that he relied on his solicitors and they acted in the mistaken belief that, save for the tidying up of some loose ends, they were on the point of completing. **13–134**

It follows that Mr Bajwa cannot avail himself of the more favourable tracing rules which are available to the innocent volunteer who unconsciously mixes trust money with his own. **13–135**

Subrogation

The appellants submit that the mere fact that the claimant's money is used to discharge someone else's debt does not entitle him to be subrogated to the creditor whose debt is paid. There must be "something more".[154] From this the appellants derive the proposition that in order to be subrogated to the creditor's security the claimant must prove (i) that the claimant intended that his money should be used to discharge the security in question (that being the "something more" required by Oliver J.) and (ii) that he intended to obtain the benefit of the security by subrogation. **13–136**

I cannot accept that formulation as a rule of general application regardless of the circumstances in which the remedy of subrogation is sought. The cases relied on were all cases where the claimant intended to make an unsecured loan to a borrower who used the money to discharge a secured debt. In such a case the claimant is not entitled to be subrogated to the creditor's security since this would put him in a better position than he had bargained for. **13–137**

The mere fact that the payer of the money intended to make an unsecured loan will not preclude his claim to be subrogated to the personal rights of the creditor whose debt is discharged if the contractual liability of the original borrower proves to be unenforceable.[155] . . . **13–138**

In cases such as *Butler v Rice*[156] and *Ghana Commercial Bank v Chandiram*,[157] where the claimant paid the creditor direct and intended to discharge his security, the court took the claimant's intention to have been to keep the original security alive for his own benefit save in so far as it was replaced by an effective security in favour of himself. In the present case the Abbey National did not intend to discharge the Halifax's charge in the events which happened, that is to say in the event that completion did not proceed. But it did not intend its money to be used at all in that event. If *Butler v Rice* and similar cases are relied upon to support the proposition that there can be no subrogation unless the claimant intended to keep the original security alive for its own benefit save in so far as it was replaced by a new and effective security, with the result that the remedy is not available where the claimant had no direct dealings with the creditor and did not intend his money to be used at all, then I respectfully dissent from that proposition. I prefer the **13–139**

---

[154] *Paul v Speirway Ltd (in liq.)* [1976] Ch. 220 at 230 per Oliver J.; and see *Orakpo v Manson Investments Ltd* [1978] A.C. 95 at 105.

[155] See e.g. *Re Wrexham, Mold & Connah's Quay Railway Co* [1899] 1 Ch. 440 (where the borrowing was ultra vires) and *B Liggett (Liverpool) Ltd v Barclays Bank Ltd* [1928] 1 K.B. 48 (where the borrowing was unauthorised).

[156] [1910] 2 Ch. 277.

[157] [1960] A.C. 732.

view of Slade L.J. in *Re TH Knitwear (Wholesale) Ltd*[158] that in some situations the doctrine of subrogation is capable of applying even though it is impossible to infer a mutual intention to this effect on the part of the creditor and the person claiming to be subrogated to the creditor's security. In the present case the payment was made by Hill Lawson, and it is their intention which matters. As fiduciaries, they could not be heard to say that they had paid out their principal's money otherwise than for the benefit of their principal. Accordingly, their intention must be taken to have been to keep the Halifax's charge alive for the benefit of the Abbey National pending completion. In my judgment this is sufficient to bring the doctrine of subrogation into play.

13–140 The application of the doctrine in the present case does not create the problem which confronted Oliver J. in *Paul v Speirway*. The Abbey National did not intend to be an unsecured creditor of anyone. It intended to retain the beneficial interest in its money unless and until that interest was replaced by a first legal mortgage on the property. The factual context in which the claim to subrogation arises is a novel one which does not appear to have arisen before, but the justice of its claim cannot be denied. The Abbey National's beneficial interest in the money can no longer be restored to it. If it is subrogated to the Halifax's charge its position will not be improved nor will Mr Bajwa's position be adversely affected. Both parties will be restored as nearly as may be to the positions which they were respectively intended to occupy.

13–141 The appellants place much reliance on a passage in *Re Diplock*,[159] where the court was dealing with the claim against the Leaf Homeopathic Hospital. The hospital received a grant for the specific purpose of enabling it to pay off a secured bank loan. The passage in question reads:

> "Here, too, we think that the effect of the payment to the bank was to extinguish the debt and the charge held by the bank ceased to exist. The case cannot, we think, be regarded as one of subrogation, and if the appellants were entitled to a charge it would have to be a new charge created by the court. The position in this respect does not appear to us to be affected by the fact that the payment off of this debt was one of the objects for which the grant was made. The effect of the payment off was that the charity, which had previously held the equity of redemption, became owners of unincumbered property. That unencumbered property derived from a combination of two things, the equity of redemption contributed by the charity and the effect of the Diplock money in getting rid of the incumbrance. If equity is now to create a charge (we say 'create' because there is no survival of the original charge) in favour of the judicial trustee, it will be placing him in a position to insist upon a sale of what was contributed by the charity. The case, as it appears to us, is in effect analogous to the cases where Diplock money is expended on improvements to charity land. The money was in this case used to remove a blot on the title; to give the judicial trustee a charge in respect of the money so used would, we think, be equally unjust to the charity who, as a result of such a charge, would have to submit to a sale of the interest in the property which it brought in. We may point out that if the relief claimed were to be accepted as a correct application of the equitable principle, insoluble problems might arise in a case where in the meanwhile fresh charges on the property had been created or money been expended upon it."

13–142 The passage is not without its difficulties and is in need of reappraisal in the light of the significant developments in the law of restitution which have taken place in the last 50 years. The second sentence is puzzling. The discharge of the creditor's security at law is certainly not a bar to subrogation in equity; it is rather a precondition. But the court was probably doing no more than equating the remedy to the creation of a new charge for the purpose of considering whether this was justified.

13–143 It is also unclear what conclusion was thought to follow from the observation that the unencumbered property derived from two sources, the equity of redemption contributed by the charity and the money belonging to the next of kin which was used to redeem the mortgage. If the money had been used to buy the property without any contribution from the charity, the next of kin would have sought a declaration that they were solely and beneficially entitled to the property under a constructive trust. Their claim

[158] [1988] Ch. 275 at 286.
[159] [1948] Ch. 465, 549–550.

to be subrogated to the security which had been discharged with their money reflected the respective contributions which they and the charity had made, and did not encroach upon the charity's equity of redemption at all.

Nor is it clear to me why insoluble problems would arise in a case where there had been fresh charges created on the property in the meantime. The next of kin would obtain a charge by subrogation with the same priority as the charge which had been redeemed except that it would not enjoy the paramountcy of the legal estate. A subsequent incumbrancer who obtained a legal estate for value without notice of the interest of the next of kin would take free from it. . . . **13–144**

Taken as a whole, however, the passage cited is an explanation of the reasons why, in the particular circumstances of that case, it was considered unjust to grant the remedy of subrogation. The hospital had changed its position to its detriment. It had in all innocence used the money to redeem a mortgage held by the bank, which, no doubt, was willing to allow its advance to remain outstanding indefinitely so long as it was well secured and the interest was paid punctually. The next of kin were seeking to be subrogated to the bank's security in order to enforce it and enable a proper distribution of the estate to be made. This would have been unjust to the hospital. It may be doubted whether in its anxiety to avoid injustice to the hospital the court may not have done an even greater injustice to the next of kin, who were denied even the interest on their money. Justice did not require the withholding of any remedy, but only that the charge by subrogation should not be enforceable until the hospital had had a reasonable opportunity to obtain a fresh advance on suitable terms from a willing lender, perhaps from the bank which had held the original security. **13–145**

Today, considerations of this kind would be regarded as relevant to a change of position defence rather than as going to liability. . . . **13–146**

Questions

1. Is the following approach sensible for a claimant beneficiary where his trustee has misdirected trust funds? **13–147**

   (a) Go for a proprietary claim to trust assets or their traceable proceeds, if possible.
   (b) Go for personal liability: (i) of the trustees for breach of trust; (ii) of any third party who has dishonestly assisted in a breach of trust and is therefore personally liable to the same extent as the trustee or fiduciary whose breach he has assisted; (iii) of any third party who has beneficially received the trust property but has disposed of it after his conscience was affected that he had improperly received the property; or (iv) of any third party who has beneficially received the trust property and who has disposed of it, on the basis that his knowledge or ignorance of its improper provenance is irrelevant because he is strictly liable to repay the value received in unjust enrichment unless he can establish a change of position defence.

2. Theo is the sole trustee of a trust for Baz. In September 2007, Theo enters a contract to buy a vintage car under which he pays the car dealer £40,000 and promises to pay him the £20,000 balance of the purchase price in one year's time. In September 2008, Theo decides not to make this payment out of his personal resources and instead transfers £20,000 to the car dealer's bank account from the Baz Trust Account, which he maintains at Caring Bank Plc. The car has now doubled in value. At the same time Theo transfers another £5,000 out of the trust account into his personal account with the bank, bringing the balance in that account from £5,000 up to £10,000. He then takes £5,000 out of his current account and uses it to buy shares which have now doubled in value. Finally he transfers another £5,000 out of the trust account into his **13–148**

girlfriend Gigi's personal account. Innocently believing the money to be a legitimate birthday gift, Gigi spends it all. Theo makes all three transfers from the trust account with the help of the bank manager Roxy, whom he tells untruthfully that the purpose of the transfers is to evade tax. Roxy is happy to assist him as she believes that paying tax is morally wrong because the Government spends some of it on nuclear weapons. Advise Baz.

PART VI

TRUSTS IMPOSED BY LAW

14 RESULTING TRUSTS

1. Introduction

A. Resulting and Constructive Trusts

14–01 As explained in Chapter 1, trusts are either express trusts or trusts imposed by law, and if we lay statutory trusts to one side, then there are only two types of trust imposed by law: resulting trusts and constructive trusts.[1] Resulting trusts, examined in this chapter, are imposed where one party transfers legal title to property to another, and receives nothing in exchange; in these circumstances a trust is imposed on the property for the transferor unless the transferee can prove that he intended to make a gift. The word "resulting" derives from the Latin *resalire*, meaning "to jump back", and describes the movement of beneficial ownership of the property back to the transferor from the transferee. Constructive trusts, discussed in the following chapter, are imposed where the law holds it appropriate to deem a defendant to have conferred the same rights on a claimant as he would have acquired, had the defendant validly declared an express trust in his favour.

14–02 On these definitions of "resulting" and "constructive", the circumstances in which these two types of trust might be imposed can sometimes overlap, but although resulting trusts might conceivably be viewed as a particular type of constructive trust, the converse is not true, since constructive trusts are often imposed that are not "resulting" in pattern. Hence the best view seems to be that these trusts are not simply interchangeable, and that there are differences between them that we can only understand if we investigate the underlying reasons why they are imposed.[2]

14–03 So far as resulting trusts are concerned, there are two main schools of thought: on one view, they respond to the transferor's actual or presumed intention that the transferee should hold the property on trust for him; on another view, they respond to the transferee's unjust enrichment at the transferor's expense. These two schools of thought are discussed further below.[3]

14–04 Constructive trusts, in contrast, are imposed in a wider range of situations, and more explanations have been advanced for their imposition, e.g. to perfect the defendant's intention to transfer beneficial ownership to the claimant; to compensate the claimant for the loss that he detrimentally incurs in reliance on the defendant's assurances; to strip the defendant of the profits of his wrongdoing; or to reverse the defendant's unjust enrichment at the claimant's expense. These explanations are all reviewed in the next chapter.[4]

B. Personal and Proprietary Rights

14–05 There is a significant difference between a beneficiary's proprietary rights under a resulting or constructive trust, and his personal rights against the trustee. In *Westdeutsche Landesbank Girozentrale v*

[1] See paras 1–135 ff.
[2] See the authorities cited at para.1–139, n.179.
[3] See paras 14–162 ff.
[4] See paras 15–137 ff.

Islington LBC,[5] Lord Browne-Wilkinson thought that it would be inappropriate to fix a resulting or constructive trustee with personal liability to account to the beneficiaries for the trust property, unless his conscience were affected with knowledge of the circumstances which led to the creation of the beneficiary's equitable proprietary interest. Situations can certainly be imagined in which it would be harsh to hold a resulting or constructive trustee liable to make good losses out of the trust funds when he does not know that the beneficiary has an equitable interest in the property: where the trustee is an infant, for example.[6] However, it need not follow from this, as Lord Browne-Wilkinson also held, that a resulting or constructive trust should not arise at all unless and until the trustee's conscience is affected by knowledge of the relevant circumstances.[7]

14–06 Less drastic strategies than denying the existence of the trust altogether are open to a court that wishes to avoid fixing a resulting or constructive trustee with personal liability for spending the trust assets in good faith: for example, placing the trustee under no greater duty than "an obligation to restore the property on demand, if still in possession of it" at the time when the trustee becomes aware of the trust's existence.[8] Various authorities contradict the view that trusts cannot be imposed by law unless and until the trustee's conscience is affected,[9] and in Robert Chambers' words:[10]

> "delaying the creation of the trust until the trustees have sufficient notice to affect their consciences may have a drastic effect on a number of important matters which depend on the timing of the creation of the resulting [or constructive] trust, such as entitlement to income, liability for taxation, risk and insurance, commencement of limitation periods, transfer and transmission of property interests, and priority of competing claims."

14–07 In principle, therefore, the best view is that a resulting or constructive trust can arise whatever the state of the trustee's conscience, and that when it arises the beneficiary immediately acquires an equitable proprietary interest in the trust assets[11] along with a concomitant right to see an account of the trustee's dealings with the property from the moment of receipt. However, this need not mean that the trustee will be personally liable for disposing of the trust assets before his conscience is affected by knowledge of the circumstances which led to the imposition of the trust.[12] Until the trustee acquires such knowledge, and for as long as the trust property remains in his hands, the beneficiary

---

5 [1996] A.C. 669 at 705–706.

6 As in *Re Vinogradoff* [1935] W.N. 68.

7 [1996] A.C. 669 at 706–707, recognising that an equitable proprietary interest can burden a defendant's legal estate before his conscience is affected, but refusing to use the term "trust" to describe this interest.

8 J. Hackney, *Understanding Equity & Trusts* (1987), p.167. Other possible strategies are explored in R. Chambers, *Resulting Trusts* (1997), pp.209–212.

9 *Birch v Blagrave* (1755) Amb. 264; *Childers v Childers* (1857) 1 De G. & J. 482; *Re Vinogradoff* [1935] W.N. 68; *Re Diplock* [1948] Ch. 465; *Re Muller* [1953] N.Z.L.R. 879.

10 R. Chambers, *Resulting Trusts* (1997), p.206.

11 Cf. *Hardoon v Belilios* [1901] A.C. 118 at 123, per Lord Lindley: a trust exists when "the legal title [is] in the plaintiff and the equitable title in the defendant."

12 *R. v Chester and North Wales Legal Aid Area Office, ex parte Floods of Queensferry Ltd* [1998] 1 W.L.R. 1496 at 1500, per Millett L.J.; *Allan v Rea Brothers Trustees Ltd* [2002] P.L.R. 169 at [55], per Robert Walker L.J.; *Clark v Cutland* [2004] 1 W.L.R. 783; *Nabb Brothers Ltd v Lloyds Bank International (Guernsey) Ltd* [2005] EWHC 405 (Ch) at [69]; *Ultraframe (UK) Ltd v Fielding* [2007] W.T.L.R. 835 at [1518]. See too R. Chambers, *Resulting Trusts* (1997), pp. 200–209; W.J. Swadling, "Property and Conscience" (1998) 14 Tru L.I. 228; Lord Millett, "Restitution and Constructive Trusts" (1998) 114 L.Q.R. 399, pp.403–406. For associated discussion of the personal liability to account as a constructive trustee that is owed by knowing recipients see paras 12–14 ff.

simply has a power[13] to fix him with a duty to reconvey the property by bringing the existence of the trust to his attention.[14] Moreover, even after the beneficiary exercises this power, the trustee's duty to reconvey the property is generally the limit of his obligations, and the beneficiary does not enjoy the same personal rights against him as those which are generally enjoyed by the beneficiaries of an express trust.[15]

C. *Exemption from Formality Rules Applying to Express Trusts*

14–08 Neither resulting nor constructive trusts are subject to the Law of Property Act 1925 s.53(1), a fact which takes on particular significance in cases where spouses or unmarried cohabitees have both contributed towards the purchase or upkeep of a shared home without any writing being used to set out the respective size of each party's equitable interest in the property.[16]

2. Classifying Resulting Trusts

14–09 Lord Millett has written extra-judicially that: "Resulting trusts arise in three situations: voluntary payment or transfer; purchase in the name of another; and incomplete disposal of the beneficial interest. The first two have been described as 'apparent gifts'; the last as 'failing trusts'."[17] We shall adopt this classification for the purpose of expounding the cases in Sections 3 and 4. First, though, we must explain what lawyers mean when they speak of "automatic" and "presumed resulting trusts", and we must examine the role of presumptions and intention in this area of the law.

14–10 In *Re Vandervell's Trusts (No.2)*,[18] the relevant parts of which are reproduced below, Megarry J. held that there are two types of resulting trusts: "automatic resulting trusts" and "presumed resulting trusts". In his Lordship's view, the former arise "automatically" when some or all of the beneficial interest in property held on an express trust has not been exhausted. On Megarry J.'s view, for example, an "automatic resulting trust" would arise if X transferred property to Y on trust for Z, for the period of Z's life, remainder to Z's children, and Z then died without issue. In this situation, X would

---

13 As noted in B. McFarlane, *The Structure of Property Law* (2008) pp.306–307 and 309–310, the exercise of this power by the beneficiary is not the *only* way in which a trustee may come under a duty because his conscience becomes affected by knowledge: this may also happen e.g. if the trustee's knowledge derives from a third party or arises when he checks his records.

14 *Allied Carpets Group Plc v Nethercott* Q.B.D. January 28, 2000, Colman J.; *Re Holmes* [2005] 1 All E.R. 490 at [22], per Burnton J. Hence the beneficiary can obtain an order against the trustee akin to the orders for conveyance made in *Dillwyn v Llewelyn* (1862) 4 De G. F. & J. 517 at 523, per Lord Westbury L.C., and more recently in *Riches v Hogben* [1985] 2 Qd. R. 292 at 302, per McPherson J. The trustee may also be obliged to get in the trust estate where this is necessary: *Evans v European Bank Ltd* (2004) 7 I.T.E.L.R. 19 at [116], per Spigelman C.J.; *Bracken Partners Ltd v Gutteridge* [2004] 1 B.C.L.C. 373.

15 *Lonrho Plc v Fayed (No. 2)* [1992] 1 W.L.R. 1 at 12, per Millett J. See too R.H. Maudsley, "Constructive Trusts" (1977) 28 N.I.L.R. 123, p.124; R. Chambers, *Resulting Trusts* (1997), pp. 194–200; L.D. Smith, "Constructive Fiduciaries?" in P. Birks (ed.), *Privacy and Loyalty* (1997), pp.263–267; Lord Millett, "Restitution and Constructive Trusts" (1998) 114 L.Q.R. 399, pp.404–405. Clearly the trustee need not undertake the administrative and managerial duties with which express trustees are commonly charged, as discussed in Chapter 9. Quaere, though, whether the trustee owes a duty to avoid conflicts of interest once he becomes aware of the trust's existence? On one view such a duty can only be imposed on those fiduciaries who have assumed office voluntarily: A. Scott, "The Fiduciary Principle" (1949) 37 Cal. L.R. 539, p.540; *Hospital Products Ltd v United States Surgical Corp* (1984) 156 C.L.R. 41 at 96–97. But cf. C. Mitchell and S. Watterson, "Remedies for Knowing Receipt" in C. Mitchell (ed.), *Constructive and Resulting Trusts* (2010) pp.142–144. And on the question whether a resulting or constructive trustee enjoys the same right of indemnity as an express trustee, see *Nolan v Collie* (2003) 7 V.R. 287 at [32]–[34]; *Re Loftus, deceased* [2005] 1 W.L.R. 1890 at [202], not considered on appeal [2007] 1 W.L.R. 591.

16 See paras 15–13 ff.

17 Lord Millett, "Pension Schemes and the Law of Trusts" (2000) 14 Tru L.I. 66, p.73.

18 [1974] Ch. 269 at 288 ff., glossing *Vandervell v IRC*. [1967] 2 A.C. 291 at 312 ff., per Lord Upjohn.

have failed to dispose of the whole beneficial interest in the trust property, and since it cannot have been his intention for the remainder interest to go to Y, or to the Crown as bona vacantia, a resulting trust "automatically" returns it to X.

14–11 In contrast, Megarry J. thought that a "presumed resulting trust" would arise in cases where X buys property in Y's name, or transfers property to Y, and Y gives X no consideration for the property. In these situations, X may have made his intentions clear, but if he does not, then equity presumes what they must have been. It is inherently more likely in these cases than in the first case that X intended to give Y the property. Nonetheless equity views the transaction with a cynical eye and raises a presumption in X's favour, failure to rebut which by Y will lead to the imposition of a resulting trust in X's favour. In Megarry J.'s view, the relevant presumption in cases of this sort is that X intends Y to be trustee for him, a point to which we shall return below.

14–12 There is certainly something to be said for the view that these two classes of case are different, since in the first X clearly intends Y to be a trustee but fails to make it clear where the whole of the equitable ownership should go, while in the second it may not be clear that X intends Y to be a trustee at all.[19] Nevertheless, Megarry J.'s analysis was doubted by Lord Browne-Wilkinson in *Westdeutsche Landesbank Girozentrale v Islington LBC*,[20] parts of which are also reproduced below. His Lordship considered that there is no real difference between the two classes of case which Megarry J. identified.[21] In the first case, as in the second, X transfers legal title to property to Y and gets nothing in return for it. In the first case, as in the second, the imposition of a resulting trust leads to the creation of a new equitable property right for X, and as a new right, as Professor Chambers has written, "it cannot be explained as the inertia of a pre-existing beneficial interest".[22] In the first case, as in the second, a resulting trust will not arise if Y can prove that X meant to benefit him. So, in the example given above, Y could keep the remainder interest for himself if he could show that X meant him to do so in the event that Z died childless.[23] This all suggests that there are not two types of resulting trust, but only one, imposed by law when property is transferred gratuitously and the transferee cannot establish that the transferor meant him to take the beneficial interest for himself.

---

[19] A point well made in J. Mee, "'Automatic' Resulting Trusts: Retention, Restitution, or Reposing Trust?" in C. Mitchell (ed.) *Constructive and Resulting Trusts* (2010).

[20] [1996] A.C. 669.

[21] See too Lord Browne-Wilkinson, "Constructive Trusts and Unjust Enrichment" (1996) 10 Tru. L.I. 98, pp.99–100; Lord Millett, "Restitution and Constructive Trusts" (1998) 114 L.Q.R. 399, p.402 n.17; Lord Millett, "Pension Schemes and the Law of Trusts" (2000) 14 Tru L.I. 66, p.73.

[22] R. Chambers, "Resulting Trusts in Canada" (2000) 38 Alberta L.R. 379, p.389.

[23] A resulting trust would also be precluded in this case if X intended to abandon the property, as it would then go to the Crown as bona vacantia. The courts are generally reluctant to find that settlors mean to abandon their property: *Davis v Richards & Wallington Ltd* [1990] 1 W.L.R. 1511 at 1540–1542, per Scott J., following *Jones v Williams*, Ch.D., 15 March 1988, Knox J. But for a rare case where the court so found, see *Environment Agency v Hilldridge Ltd* [2004] 2 B.C.L.C. 358, and note too that in the case of street collections, where thousands of individual donors contribute money towards a purpose which is then accomplished leaving a surplus, the courts are likely to find a general intention to part utterly with contributed money so as to exclude any resulting trust in their favour. In such cases, the money will pass to the Crown, as in e.g. *Re West Sussex Constabulary's Fund Trusts* [1971] Ch. 1, unless accruing to the funds of an unincorporated association for which the collections were made, as in e.g. *Re Bucks Constabulary Fund Friendly Society (No.2)* [1979] 1 W.L.R. 936. cf. Lord Millett, "Pension Schemes and the Law of Trusts" (2000) 14 Tru L.I. 66, p.74, professing the unorthodox view that if no resulting trust arises on the failure of an express trust, then the trustees should become the beneficial owners of the trust assets, so that these would become bona vacantia only if the trustees disclaimed their interest.

RE VANDERVELL'S TRUSTS (NO.2)

Chancery Division [1974] Ch. 269; [1973] 3 W.L.R. 744; [1974] 1 All E.R. 47

MEGARRY J.: It seems to me that the relevant points on resulting trusts may be put in a series of propositions . . . as follows. 14–13

(1) If a transaction fails to make any effective disposition of any interest it does nothing. This is so at law and in equity, and has nothing to do with resulting trusts. 14–14

(2) Normally the mere existence of some unexpressed intention in the breast of the owner of the property does nothing: there must at least be some expression of that intention before it can effect any result. To yearn is not to transfer. 14–15

(3) Before any doctrine of resulting trust can come into play, there must at least be some effective transaction which transfers or creates some interest in property. 14–16

(4) Where A effectually transfers to B (or creates in his favour) any interest in any property, whether legal or equitable, a resulting trust for A may arise in two distinct classes of case. For simplicity, I shall confine my statement to cases in which the transfer or creation is made without B providing any valuable consideration, and where no presumption of advancement can arise; and I shall state the position for transfers without specific mention of the creation of new interests. 14–17

(a) The first class of case is where the transfer to B is not made on any trust. If, of course, it appears from the transfer that B is intended to hold on certain trusts, that will be decisive, and the case is not within this category; and similarly if it appears that B is intended to take beneficially. But in other cases there is a rebuttable presumption that B holds on a resulting trust for A. The question is not one of the automatic consequences of a dispositive failure by A, but one of presumption: the property has been carried to B, and from the absence of consideration and any presumption of advancement B is presumed not only to hold the entire interest on trust, but also to hold the beneficial interest for A absolutely. The presumption thus establishes both that A is to take on trust and also what that trust is. Such resulting trusts may be called "presumed resulting trusts".

(b) The second class of case is where the transfer to B is made on trusts which leave some or all of the beneficial interest undisposed of. Here B automatically holds on a resulting trust for A to the extent that the beneficial interest has not been carried to him or others. The resulting trust here does not depend on any intentions or presumptions, but is the automatic consequence of A's failure to dispose of what is vested in him. Since *ex hypothesi* the transfer is on trust, the resulting trust does not establish the trust but merely carries back to A the beneficial interest that has not been disposed of. Such resulting trusts may be called "automatic resulting trusts".

(5) Where trustees hold property in trust for A, and it is they who, at A's direction, make the transfer to B, similar principles apply, even though on the face of the transaction the transferor appears to be the trustees and not A. If the transfer to B is on trust, B will hold any beneficial interest that has not been effectually disposed of on an automatic resulting trust for the true transferor, A. If the transfer to B is not on trust, there will be a rebuttable presumption that B holds on a resulting trust for A. 14–18

WESTDEUTSCHE LANDESBANK GIROZENTRALE v ISLINGTON LBC

House of Lords [1996] A.C. 669; [1996] 2 W.L.R. 802; [1996] 2 All E.R. 961

See para.14–165 below for the facts of the case. 14–19

LORD BROWNE-WILKINSON: Under existing law a resulting trust arises in two sets of circumstances: 14–20

> (A) Where A makes a voluntary payment to B or pays (wholly or in part) for the purchase of property which is vested either in B alone or in the joint names of A and B, there is a presumption that A did not intend to make a gift to B: the money or property is held on trust for A (if he is the sole provider of the money) or in the case of a joint purchase by A and B in shares proportionate to their contributions. It is important to stress that this is only a presumption, which presumption is easily rebutted either by the counter-presumption of advancement or by direct evidence of A's intention to make an outright transfer.[24]
>
> (B) Where A transfers property to B on express trusts, but the trusts declared do not exhaust the whole beneficial interest.[25]
>
> 14–21 Both types of resulting trust are traditionally regarded as examples of trusts giving effect to the common intention of the parties. A resulting trust is not imposed by law against the intentions of the trustee (as is a constructive trust) but gives effect to his presumed intention. Megarry J. in *Re Vandervell's Trusts (No.2)* suggests that a resulting trust of type (B) does not depend on intention but operates automatically. I am not convinced that this is right. If the settlor has expressly, or by necessary implication, abandoned any beneficial interest in the trust property, there is in my view no resulting trust: the undisposed-of equitable interest vests in the Crown as bona vacantia.[26]

14–22 On the traditional view of the law espoused by Megarry J. in *Re Vandervell's Trusts (No.2)* and by Lord Browne-Wilkinson in the *Westdeutsche* case, resulting trusts arise where property is transferred gratuitously, and the transferor X's intentions are unclear, because he is presumed to intend that the transferee Y should hold the property on trust for him.[27] However, this analysis suffers from a significant drawback: it cannot account for cases where resulting trusts have been imposed, but it is clear that X had no intention that Y should be his trustee, or even that the one thing X intended was precisely that Y should not be his trustee. In such cases, Y should have been able to rebut a presumption that he was to hold the property on trust, and yet a resulting trust was still imposed. For example, in *Vandervell v IRC*,[28] as we have seen,[29] Vandervell thought that he had disposed of his property completely, and did not want the remainder of the property to result to him, as this rendered him liable to tax that he had sought to avoid; in *Re Vinogradoff*,[30] the transferor could not have intended the transferee to be trustee for her because the transferee was her seven-year-old grand-daughter; and in *El Ajou v Dollar Land Holdings Plc*,[31] the transferor had no such intention because it was unaware of the fact that the property had been taken from it in the first place.

14–23 This problem can be solved by recognising that resulting trusts are not imposed in response to X's (actual or presumed) intention to create a trust, but in response to the fact that X (actually or presumably) did not intend to make a gift to Y.[32] This analysis makes sense of all the cases, including those listed above: it is clear, for example, that although Vandervell did not wish the share option to result

---

24 *Underhill & Hayton*, pp.317 ff.; *Vandervell v IRC* [1967] 2 A.C. 291 at 312 ff.; *Re Vandervell's Trusts (No.2)* [1974] Ch. 269 at pp.288ff.
25 ibid. and *Barclays Bank Ltd v Quistclose Investments Ltd* [1970] A.C. 567.
26 *Re West Sussex Constabulary's Widows, Children and Benevolent (1930) Fund Trusts* [1971] Ch. 1.
27 W.J. Swadling, "A New Role for Resulting Trusts?" (1996) 16 L.S. 110, p. 115; W.J. Swadling, "Explaining Resulting Trusts" (2008) 124 L.Q.R. 72, pp.79–85.
28 [1967] 2 A.C. 291.
29 Above at paras 3–100 to 3–101.
30 [1935] W.N. 68.
31 [1993] 3 All E.R. 717.
32 R. Chambers, *Resulting Trusts* (1997), pp.19–27; P. Birks, *Unjust Enrichment* (2003), pp.136–137.

to him, he did not wish to make an outright gift of it to the trustee company, either, as Lord Millett pointed out in *Air Jamaica Ltd v Charlton*.[33] Hence, as Lord Phillips M.R. held in *Lavelle v Lavelle*, the best view of the law is that:[34]

> "where one person, A, transfers the legal title of a property he owns or purchases to another, B, without receipt of any consideration, the effect will depend on his intention. . . . Normally there will be evidence of the intention with which a transfer is made. Where there is not, the law applies presumptions. Where there is no close relationship between A and B, there will be a presumption that A does not intend to part with the beneficial interest in the property . . . [If B fails to rebut this presumption, then he will] take the legal title under a resulting trust for A."[35]

There are also cases where X transfers property to Y and he does actually intend that Y should hold the property on trust for X. If all relevant formalities are complied with, then the arrangement will simply take effect as an express trust. If they are not, then the express trust intended by X will be unenforceable, and if X is to receive an equitable beneficial interest then it must be under a resulting trust, as in *Hodgson v Marks*,[36] reproduced below. However, even cases of this sort can be explained on the basis that evidence of X's intention to create a trust for himself demonstrates that he had no intention to benefit Y. **14–24**

Resulting trusts respond only to a transferor's lack of intention to benefit a transferee. Lord Browne-Wilkinson thought that "a resulting trust arises in order to give effect to the intention of the parties":[37] i.e. he saw them as responding to the intentions of both the transferor and the transferee. In this, however, his Lordship confused resulting trusts with common intention constructive trusts,[38] and his view is inconsistent with cases where resulting trusts were imposed on property held by transferees who had no intention of becoming trustees, for example because they were legally incapable of forming any intention at all.[39] Hence, the better view is that the only person whose intentions are relevant is the transferor.[40] **14–25**

A presumption in the transferor's favour will only be made in cases where there is no evidence that he intended to create a trust, or to make a gift, or to make a loan of the property to the transferee.[41] In cases where the court has heard sufficient evidence to determine the transferor's intention on the facts, there is no need for any presumption to be made.[42] **14–26**

---

[33] [1999] 1 W.L.R. 1399 at 1412. See too *Twinsectra Ltd v Yardley* [2000] W.T.L.R. 527 at 562, per Potter L.J.; [2002] 2 A.C. 164 at [91], per Lord Millett.

[34] [2004] 2 F.C.R. 418 at [13]–[14].

[35] Where there is a close relationship between A and B, such as father and child, a countervailing presumption of advancement will be raised: see paras 14–102 ff.

[36] [1971] Ch. 892.

[37] "Constructive Trusts and Unjust Enrichment" (1996) 10 Tru L.I. 98, 99, echoed in *Tinsley v Milligan* [1994] 1 A.C. 340 at 371; *Westdeutsche Landesbank Girozentrale v Islington LBC* [1996] A.C. 669 at 708.

[38] For which see paras 15–13 ff. It seems likely that his Lordship was misled by Lord Diplock's unfortunately expressed speech in *Gissing v Gissing* [1971] A.C. 886 at 904–905 and 922. Certainly a misreading of this speech led the Canadian courts to use unorthodox "common intention resulting trusts" to resolve shared homes cases (e.g. *Rathwell v Rathwell* [1978] 2 S.C.R. 436), an approach which has now given way to the application of statutes and constructive trust reasoning: *Oosterhoff on Trusts* 6th edn (2004), pp.554–560.

[39] e.g. *Lench v Lench* (1805) 10 Ves. Jun. 511; *Childers v Childers* (1857) 1 De G. & J. 482; *Re Vinogradoff* [1935] W.N. 68.

[40] R. Chambers, *Resulting Trusts* (1997), pp. 35–37; J. Mee, *The Property Rights of Cohabitees* (1999), pp. 39–43. This is not to deny that a transferee's intentions can be relevant as circumstantial evidence of the transferor's intentions, as in, e.g. *Ali v Khan* (2002) 5 I.T.E.L.R. 232 at [28], per Morritt V.C.

[41] *Air Jamaica Ltd v Charlton* [1999] 1 W.L.R. 1399 at 1412, per Lord Millett; *Twinsectra Ltd v Yardley* [2000] W.T.L.R. 527 at 562, per Potter L.J.; *Lavelle v Lavelle* [2004] 2 F.C.R. 418 at [13], per Lord Phillips M.R.

[42] *Stockholm Finance Ltd v Garden Holdings Inc* Ch.D. October 26, 1995, per Robert Walker J.; *United Overseas Bank Ltd v Iwuanyanwu* Ch.D. 5 March 2001 at [33]; *Ali v Khan* (2002) 5 I.T.E.L.R. 232 at [30], per Morritt V.C.; *Popely v Ayton Ltd* [2004] EWHC 843 (Ch) at [7].

HODGSON v MARKS

Court of Appeal [1971] Ch. 892; [1971] 2 W.L.R. 1263; [1971] 2 All E.R. 684

14–27 Mrs Hodgson was an elderly widow who transferred legal title to her house to her lodger, Mr Evans, to stop her nephew from turning him out of the house. Mr Evans sold the house to Mr Marks, who granted a registered mortgage over the house to a building society to secure a purchase loan. Mr Marks and Mrs Hodgson knew nothing of one another at this time. When she found out what had happened, she sued Mr Marks and the building society, and asked for the house to be reconveyed to her free of the mortgage. At first instance the judge held that Mrs Hodgson had not intended to make a gift to Mr Evans, but that she had intended that he should hold the house on an express trust for her. This trust was prima facie unenforceable for non-compliance with the LPA 1925 s.53(1)(b), but relying on *Rochefoucauld v Boustead*,[43] the judge held that the statute should not be used to prevent her from giving evidence of fraud, with the result that she should be permitted to prove the oral trust. However, the judge dismissed Mrs Hodgson's claim because he considered that she had no overriding interest under the LRA 1925 s.70(1)(g) as a person "in actual occupation of the land". On appeal, the Court of Appeal held that she did have an overriding interest binding on Mr Marks and the building society.

14–28 RUSSELL L.J. (with whom BUCKLEY and CAIRNS L.JJ. agreed, decided that Mrs Hodgson had relevantly been in "actual occupation" of the house during the relevant period, and then proceeded:) I turn next to the question whether s.53(1) of the Law of Property Act 1925 prevents the assertion by the plaintiff of her entitlement in equity to the house. Let me first assume that, contrary to the view expressed by the judge, the first defendant is not debarred from relying on the section, and the express oral arrangement or declaration of trust between the plaintiff and Mr Evans found by the judge was not effective as such. Nevertheless, the evidence is clear that the transfer was not intended to operate as a gift and, in those circumstances, I do not see why there was not a resulting trust of the beneficial interest to the plaintiff, which would not, of course, be affected by s.53(1). It was argued that a resulting trust is based on implied intention, and that where there is an express trust for the transferor intended and declared—albeit ineffectively—there is no room for such an implication. I do not accept that. If an attempted express trust fails, that seems to me just the occasion for implication of a resulting trust, whether the failure be due to uncertainty, or perpetuity, or lack of form. It would be a strange outcome if the plaintiff were to lose her beneficial interest because her evidence had not been confined to negativing a gift but had additionally moved into a field forbidden by s.53(1) for lack of writing. I remark in this connection that we are not concerned with the debatable question whether on a voluntary transfer of land by A to stranger B there is a presumption of a resulting trust. The accepted evidence is that this was not intended as a gift, notwithstanding the reference to love and affection in the transfer, and s.53(1) does not exclude that evidence. . . .

14–29 On the above footing it matters not whether the first defendant was or was not debarred from relying on s.53(1) by the principle that the section is not to be used as an instrument for fraud. The first defendant was in fact ignorant of her interest and it is forcefully argued that there is nothing fraudulent in his taking advantage of the section. I do not propose to canvass the general point further, more particularly in the light of the nature of the subject-matter with which we are dealing—an overriding interest. Quite plainly Mr Evans could not have placed any reliance on s.53, for that would have been to use the section as an instrument of fraud. Accordingly, at the moment before registration of the first defendant as registered proprietor there was in existence an overriding interest in the plaintiff, and by force of the statute the registration could only take effect subject thereto.

[43] [1897] 1 Ch. 196.

Questions

Did the trust which arose in Mrs Hodgson's favour respond to her intention to create a trust for herself,[44] or to her lack of intention to give the house to Mr. Evans? If the former, then did it not subvert the underlying purpose of the formality rules contained in s.53 to give her enforceable rights against Mr Marks and the building society? Would a resulting trust have arisen in Mrs Hodgson's favour if she had transferred the house to Mr Evans on an unenforceable oral trust for the benefit of a third party? **14–30**

3. Failing Trusts

A. Where Resulting Trusts Arise

Resulting trusts arise in favour of the settlor where he has transferred property to trustees[45] on express trusts which fail, whether for failure of marriage consideration, uncertainty, lapse, disclaimer, perpetuity, illegality, non-compliance with requisite statutory formalities, or for any other reason.[46] They also arise if settlors fail to dispose exhaustively of the whole beneficial interest under their express trusts.[47] Where express trusts of funds subscribed by many settlors do not exhaust the funds there is a resulting trust in favour of the settlors rateably in proportion to the amounts subscribed by them.[48] In the case of charitable trusts that fail the funds will usually be applied cy-près as has been seen in Chapter 6. **14–31**

Whether or not the settlor has failed to dispose effectively of the entire beneficial interest is often a difficult matter. In *Re Abbott*[49] a fund had been subscribed for the maintenance and support of two deaf and mute women and Stirling J. held, not as a matter of construction of the documents by which the subscriptions had been sought, but as an inference from all the facts, that the surplus left after both women had died was held on a resulting trust for the subscribers. In *Re Andrew's Trust*[50] a fund was subscribed solely for the education of the children of a deceased clergyman and not for the exclusive use of one child or for equal division among them but as necessary, and after the formal education of the children had been completed Kekewich J. held that the children were entitled to the balance equally. He construed "education" in the broadest sense as an ongoing process that did not come to an end with the conclusion of formal education, and he treated the reference to education as expressing merely the motive of the gift. Thus, he held that:[51] **14–32**

---

[44] As argued in W.J. Swadling, "A Hard Look at *Hodgson v Marks*", in P. Birks and F.D. Rose (eds), *Restitution and Equity* (2000).

[45] If a settlor declares himself trustee of a trust which fails, he will become absolute beneficial owner of the property once more. A resulting trust is not needed to accomplish this, and in fact would be impossible, as a person cannot be a trustee solely for his own benefit: *Westdeutsche Landesbank Girozentrale v Islington LBC* [1996] A.C. 669 at 703, per Lord Browne-Wilkinson.

[46] *Hodgson v Marks* [1971] Ch. 892 at 933, per Russell L.J.; *Re Ames's Settlement* [1946] Ch. 217 though see now ss.16 and 24 of the Matrimonial Causes Act 1973. If the settlor were a testator then the property would result to his estate: if the property were specifically devised or bequeathed it would fall into residue; if the property were comprised in the residuary gift then it would pass to the next-of-kin under the intestacy rules set out in the Administration of Estates Act 1925 as amended. On the impact of illegality, see paras 14–110 ff.

[47] *Re West* [1900] 1 Ch. 84; *Re Gillingham Bus Disaster Fund* [1958] Ch. 300.

[48] See too *Re British Red Cross Balkan Fund* [1914] 2 Ch. 419 (where in the absence of the Att.-Gen. a resulting trust was erroneously admitted); *Re Welsh Hospital Fund* [1921] 1 Ch. 655 at 662; *Re Hobourn Aero Components Ltd's Air Raid Disaster Fund* [1946] Ch. 194; *Air Jamaica Ltd v Charlton* [1999] 1 W.L.R. 1399 (for which, see paras 14–39 ff.).

[49] [1900] 2 Ch. 326.

[50] [1905] 2 Ch. 48.

[51] ibid. at 52–53, citing Page-Wood V.C. in *Re Sanderson's Trust* (1857) 3 K. & J. 497 at 503.

"If a gross sum be given, or if the whole income of property be given, and a special purpose be assigned for the gift this court [rebuttably] regards the gift as absolute and the purpose merely as the motive of the gift, and therefore holds that the gift takes effect as to the whole sum or the whole income as the case may be."

14–33 This was applied by the Court of Appeal in *Re Osoba*[52] holding that a bequest to the testator's widow upon trust "for her maintenance and for the training of my daughter Abiola up to university grade and for the maintenance of my aged mother" was a trust for the three women absolutely as joint tenants so that nothing resulted to the testator's estate after Abiola finished her university education, the widow and the mother having died by then, so that Abiola was absolutely entitled as the surviving joint tenant.

14–34 Following *Barclays Bank Ltd v Quistclose Investments Ltd*,[53] it was thought that a resulting trust conforming to the pattern described here would also arise following the failure of a purpose trust to apply money lent for a specific purpose. However, the *Quistclose* case and subsequent authorities were reinterpreted in *Twinsectra Ltd v Yardley*[54] in such a way as to render this analysis otiose, Lord Millett holding that money lent for a specific purpose can be subject to an immediate express trust for the lender, subject to a power to apply the money to the purpose. These cases are discussed in Chapter 5.[55]

B. *Where Resulting Trusts do not Arise*

14–35 There is no resulting trust for the settlor or his estate on the failure of an express trust if the trustee is expressly intended to take the property beneficially for himself subject to a charge for some purpose. Thus, in *Re Foord*[56] where a testator left his estate to his sister "absolutely . . . on trust" to pay his widow an annuity and the estate exceeded the annuity the sister was held beneficially entitled to the balance. Likewise, there is no resulting trust where the rule in *Hancock v Watson*[57] applies. This rule states that "if you find an absolute gift to a legatee in the first instance, and trusts are engrafted or imposed on that absolute interest which fail, either from lapse or invalidity or any other reason, then the absolute gift takes effect so far as the trusts have failed to the exclusion of the residuary legatee or next-of-kin as the case may be."[58] The rule is equally applicable to inter vivos settlements.[59]

14–36 There is no resulting trust if the doctrine of acceleration applies to prevent there being a temporary failure to exhaust the beneficial interest under a trust.[60] Thus, if T by will leaves property to A for life and after A's death to B absolutely, and A disclaims his interest, B's interest is accelerated so as to take effect immediately, thereby ousting any possible resulting trust of the income until A's death. For the doctrine to apply the remainderman must have a vested interest and there must be no contrary intention manifested in the trust document.[61]

---

[52] [1979] 2 All E.R. 393.
[53] [1970] A.C. 567. See too *Re ETVR* [1987] B.C.L.C. 646.
[54] [2002] A.C. 164.
[55] See paras 5–33 to 5–34.
[56] [1922] 2 Ch. 519. See too *Cook v Hutchinson* (1836) 1 Keen 42. But contrast the resulting trust in *Re West* [1900] 1 Ch. 84.
[57] [1902] A.C. 14. See too *Lassence v Tierney* (1849) 1 Mac. & G. 551.
[58] *Hancock* at 22 (Lord Davey).
[59] *Att.-Gen. v Lloyd's Bank* [1935] A.C. 382; *Re Burton's ST* [1955] Ch. 348; *Watson v Holland* [1985] 1 All E.R. 290.
[60] *Re Flower's ST* [1957] 1 W.L.R. 401.
[61] *Re Scott* [1975] 2 All E.R. 1033.

There is usually no resulting trust where a party has transferred property under a contract (save for the rare cases in which a *Quistclose*-style arrangement has been agreed by the parties[62]). Thus, in the case of a society formed to raise funds by subscriptions from its members for the purpose of providing for their widows, which had surplus funds after the death of the last widow, there could be no resulting trust for the deceased members' estates: each member had parted absolutely with his money in return for contractual benefits for his widow.[63] Similarly, no resulting trust can arise where donors part absolutely with their money for tickets contractually entitling them to participate in raffles, sweepstakes, beetle drives, whist drives, discos, or to watch live entertainment, and the purposes for which such money has been raised fail to exhaust the profits arising after deducting expenses.[64] **14–37**

Davis v Richard & Wallington Ltd[65] concerned a surplus within a pension scheme. The funds of the scheme were held on trust but the trust deed was silent as to the destination of any surplus, and there was no way to amend the deed to deal with the surplus.[66] Scott J. held that the surplus derived primarily from over-funding arising from the contributions of the employer (which was obliged to make up any deficiencies if the employees' contributions proved inadequate), and that the portion of the surplus which derived from the employer's contributions should result to the employer. However, as regards the surplus derived from the employees' contributions he held that this should pass to the Crown as bona vacantia because the circumstances of the case pointed "firmly and clearly to the conclusion that a resulting trust in favour of the employees should be excluded". Why? Because equity should not impute to the employees an intention that would lead to an unworkable result, the value of benefits being different for each employee.[67] Nor should equity impose a resulting trust if this would lead to employees receiving more than the legislature intended when stipulating the statutory limits under exempt approved schemes. However, these reasons for refusing to impose a resulting trust for the employees were regarded as unconvincing by Lord Millett in *Air Jamaica Ltd v Charlton*.[68] **14–38**

AIR JAMAICA LTD v CHARLTON

Privy Council [1999] 1 W.L.R. 1399

Air Jamaica Ltd was privatised and its employee pensions plan was discontinued, leaving a surplus of $400 million. The pensions plan was established by a trust deed, one clause of which (clause 13.3) provided that "any balance of the Fund shall be applied to provide additional benefits for Members and after their death for their widows or their designated beneficiaries in such equitable and non-discriminatory manner as the Trustees may determine". The surplus would have been distributed in line with this clause if it had been valid, but the Privy Council advised that it was void for perpetuity. Clause 4 of the trust deed stated: "No moneys which at any time have been contributed by the Company under the terms hereof shall in any circumstances be repayable to the Company". The company purported to amend the trust deed, by removing clause 4 and replacing clause 13.3 with a clause providing that the surplus would be held on trust for the company. The Privy Council advised that clause 4 invalidated these amendments, but that it did not prevent a resulting trust from arising in the company's favour in respect of the surplus funds. **14–39**

---

62 See para.5–33.
63 *Cunnack v Edwards* [1896] 2 Ch. 679.
64 *Re West Sussex Constabulary's Benevolent Fund Trusts* [1971] Ch. 1.
65 [1990] 1 W.L.R. 1511.
66 See now Pensions Act 1985 ss.68, 69.
67 But if the proportionate return under a resulting trust were effectively impossible to calculate and administer, why not have a per capita distribution to cut the Gordian knot, in line with Goff J.'s recommendation in *Re West Sussex Constabulary's Fund Trusts* [1970] 1 All E.R. 544 at 548?
68 [1999] 1 W.L.R. 1399.

14–40 LORD MILLETT (speaking for the court, which also consisted of LORD STEYN, LORD HOPE, SIR CHRISTOPHER SLADE and SIR ANDREW LEGGATT): Prima facie the surplus is held on a resulting trust for those who provided it. This sometimes creates a problem of some perplexity. In the present case, however, it does not. Contributions were payable by the members with matching contributions by the company. In the absence of any evidence that this is not what happened in practice, the surplus must be treated as provided as to one half by the company and as to one half by the members.

14–41 The Attorney General contended that neither the company nor the members can take any part in the surplus, which has reverted to the Crown as bona vacantia. He argued that cl.4 of the trust deed precludes any claim by the company, while the members cannot claim any part of the surplus because they have received all that they are entitled to. There is authority for both propositions. Their Lordships consider that they can be supported neither in principle nor as a matter of construction.

14–42 In *Re ABC Television Ltd Pension Scheme*[69] Foster J. held that a clause similar to cl.4 of the present trust deed "negatives the possibility of implying a resulting trust". This is wrong in principle. Like a constructive trust, a resulting trust arises by operation of law, though unlike a constructive trust it gives effect to intention. But it arises whether or not the transferor intended to retain a beneficial interest—he almost always does not—since it responds to the absence of any intention on his part to pass a beneficial interest to the recipient. It may arise even where the transferor positively wished to part with the beneficial interest, as in *Vandervell v IRC*.[70] In that case the retention of a beneficial interest by the transferor destroyed the effectiveness of a tax avoidance scheme which the transferor was seeking to implement. The House of Lords affirmed the principle that a resulting trust is not defeated by evidence that the transferor intended to part with the beneficial interest if he has not in fact succeeded in doing so. As Plowman J. had said in the same case at first instance:[71]

> "As I see it, a man does not cease to own property simply by saying 'I don't want it'. If he tries to give it away the question must always be, has he succeeded in doing so or not?"

Lord Upjohn expressly approved this.[72]

14–43 Consequently their Lordships think that clauses of this kind in a pension scheme should generally be construed as forbidding the repayment of contributions under the terms of the scheme, and not as a pre-emptive but misguided attempt to rebut a resulting trust which would arise dehors the scheme. The purpose of such clauses is to preclude any amendment that would allow repayment to the company. Their Lordships thus construe cl.4 of the trust deed as invalidating the 1994 amendments, but not as preventing the company from retaining a beneficial interest by way of a resulting trust in so much of the surplus as is attributable to its contributions.

14–44 The members' contributions stand on a similar footing. In *Davis v Richards & Wallington Industries Ltd*[73] Scott J. held that the fact that a party has received all that he bargained for is not necessarily a decisive argument against a resulting trust, but that in the circumstances of the case before him a resulting trust in favour of the employees was excluded. The circumstances that impressed him were twofold. He considered that it was impossible to arrive at a workable scheme for apportioning the employees' surplus among the different classes of employees and he declined[74] to "impute to them an intention that would lead to an unworkable result". He also considered that he was precluded by statute from "imputing to the employees an intention" that they should receive by means of a resulting trust sums in excess of the maximum permitted by the relevant tax legislation.

14–45 These formulations also adopt the approach to intention that their Lordships have already considered to be erroneous. Their Lordships would observe that, even in the ordinary case of an actuarial surplus, it is not obvious that, when employees are promised certain benefits under a scheme to which they have

[69] May 22, 1973, unreported.
[70] [1967] 1 All E.R. 1.
[71] [1966] Ch. 261 at 275.
[72] [1967] 1 All E.R. 1 at 9.
[73] [1991] 2 All E.R. 563.
[74] At 1544.

> contributed more than was necessary to fund them, they should not expect to obtain a return of their excess contributions. In the present case, however, the surplus does not arise from over-funding but from the failure of some of the trusts. It is impossible to say that the members "have received all that they bargained for". One of the benefits they bargained for was that the trustees should be obliged to pay them additional benefits in the event of the scheme's discontinuance. It was the invalidity of this trust that gave rise to the surplus. Their Lordships consider that it would be more accurate to say that the members claim such part of the surplus as is attributable to their contributions because they have not received all that they bargained for.
>
> Pension schemes in Jamaica, as in England, need the approval of the Inland Revenue if they are to secure the fiscal advantages that are made available. The tax legislation in both countries places a limit on the amount which can be paid to the individual employee. Allowing the employees to enjoy any part of the surplus by way of resulting trust would probably exceed those limits. This fact is not, however, in their Lordships' view a proper ground on which to reject the operation of a resulting trust in favour of the employees. The Inland Revenue had an opportunity to examine the pension plan and to withhold approval on the ground that some of its provisions were void for perpetuity. They failed to do so. There is no call to distort principle in order to meet their requirements. The resulting trust arises by operation of the general law, dehors the pension scheme and the scope of the relevant tax legislation. **14–46**
>
> Scott J. was impressed by the difficulty of arriving at a workable scheme for apportioning the surplus funds among the members and the executors of deceased members. This was because he thought it necessary to value the benefits that each member had received in order to ascertain his share in the surplus. On the separate settlement with mutual insurance analysis which their Lordships have adopted in the present case, however, no such process is required. The members' share of the surplus should be divided pro rata among the members and the estates of deceased members in proportion to the contributions made by each member without regard to the benefits each has received and irrespective of the dates on which the contributions were made. **14–47**

C. *Dissolution of Unincorporated Associations*

When an unincorporated association is dissolved it is necessary to ascertain whether its property falls to be distributed on a resulting trust to persons providing such property or on a contractual basis to the members of the association or as bona vacantia to the Crown. **14–48**

The rules of an unincorporated association usually vest the assets of the association in trustees on trust for the members. However, this trust bears no relation to the members' claims to the surplus assets when the association is dissolved. So far as these are concerned, the old view[75] that they arise under resulting trusts has been totally discredited. It is now well established that the interests and rights of persons who are members of any type of unincorporated association are governed exclusively by contract.[76] Hence, if the rules of the association by which the members are contractually bound *inter se* provide for a particular method of distribution when the association is dissolved, this method will be used,[77] subject to the rights of third parties to share in the surplus assets. **14–49**

---

[75] *Re Printers and Transferrers Amalgamated Trades Protection Society* [1899] 2 Ch. 184; *Re Lead Co's Workmen's Fund Society* [1904] 2 Ch. 196.

[76] *Tierney v Tough* [1914] 1 I.R. 142; *Re St. Andrew's Allotment Association* [1969] 1 W.L.R. 229; *Re William Denby Ltd's Sick Fund* [1971] 1 W.L.R. 973; *Re West Sussex Constabulary's Benevolent Fund Trusts* [1971] Ch. 1; *Re Sick & Funeral Society of St John's Sunday School* [1973] Ch. 51 (per capita basis but child members only to have a half share); *Re GKN Nuts and Bolts Ltd Sports and Social Club* [1982] 1 W.L.R. 774; *Re Bucks Constabulary Fund Friendly Society (No.2)* [1979] 1 All E.R. 623; *Boyle v Collins* [2004] 2 B.C.L.C. 471 at [26]–[27], per Lewison J., considering *Abbatt v Treasury Solicitor* [1969] 1 W.L.R. 561.

[77] Otherwise, distribution will be on the basis of equality.

14–50 Third party rights to share in the fund will arise either by the duly authorised procedure in the association's constitution for creating contracts or express trusts, or by declarations of trust made by a donor at the time of transferring property to the association. However, to avoid invalidating a donor's declaration of trust for infringing the beneficiary principle or perpetuity rules, the courts tend to interpret such gifts not as declarations of trust, but as out-and-out gifts to the members as an accretion to the funds which are the subject-matter of the contract by which the members are all bound *inter se*, with the result that such gifts will fall to be dealt with in just the same way as the funds which the members themselves have subscribed to the association's funds.[78]

14–51 The present position is set out in *Re Bucks Constabulary Fund Friendly Society (No.2)*,[79] reproduced below. This decision should be preferred to *Re West Sussex Constabulary's Benevolent Fund*,[80] parts of which are also reproduced here, because it pays proper attention to the primacy of the members' contracts in determining beneficial entitlements to the assets of the association, as stipulated in *Re Recher's WT*.[81] Finally, however, we also reproduce part of Lewison J.'s recent judgment in *Hanchett-Stamford v Att.-Gen.*,[82] where he considers the situation where an association becomes moribund because all the members but one have died, and refuses to follow Walton J.'s *dictum* in *Re Bucks (No.2)*, that in such a case the assets should be treated as bona vacantia and pass to the Crown.

RE WEST SUSSEX CONSTABULARY'S WIDOWS, CHILDREN AND BENEVOLENT (1930) FUND TRUSTS

Chancery Division [1971] Ch. 1; [1970] 2 W.L.R. 848; [1970] 1 All E.R. 544

14–52 In 1930 members of the West Sussex Constabulary established a fund to provide for their widows and orphans. In 1968 the West Sussex Constabulary was amalgamated with other forces, and the question arose how the assets of the fund should be dealt with. These came from (1) contributions of past and present members; (2) entertainments, raffles, sweepstakes; (3) collecting boxes; (4) donations and legacies. Goff J. held that (4) were held on resulting trusts for the donors while (1), (2), and (3) were bona vacantia. These holdings are now of doubtful value in view of *Re Bucks (No.2)*, but the following dicta are still good law.

14–53 GOFF J.: I must now turn to the moneys raised from outside sources. Counsel for the Treasury Solicitor made an overriding general submission that there cannot be a resulting trust of any of the outside moneys because in the circumstances it is impossible to identify the trust property; no doubt something could be achieved by complicated accounting, but this, he submitted, would not be identification but notional reconstruction. I cannot accept that argument. In my judgment, in a case like the present, equity will cut the Gordian knot by simply dividing the ultimate surplus in proportion to the sources from which it has arisen. . . . There may be cases of tolerable simplicity where the court will be more refined, but in general, where a fund has been raised from mixed sources, interest has been earned over the years and income—and possibly capital—expenditure has been made indiscriminately out of the fund as an entirety, and then the venture comes to an end prematurely or otherwise, the court will not find itself baffled but will cut the Gordian knot as I have said.

14–54 Then counsel divided the outside moneys into three categories, first, the proceeds of entertainments, raffles and sweepstakes; secondly, the proceeds of collecting-boxes; and, thirdly, donations, including legacies if any, and he took particular objections to each.

---

[78] *Re Recher's WT* [1972] Ch. 526; *Re Lipinski's WT* [1976] Ch. 235.
[79] [1979] 1 All E.R. 623.
[80] [1971] Ch. 1.
[81] [1972] Ch. 526 at 538–539.
[82] [2009] Ch. 173.

I agree that there cannot be any resulting trust with respect to the first category. I am not certain whether Harman J. in *Re Gillingham Bus Disaster Fund*[83] meant to decide otherwise. In stating the facts he referred to "street collections and so forth".[84] In the further argument[85] there is mention of whist drives and concerts but the judge himself did not speak of anything other than gifts. If, however, he did, I must respectfully decline to follow his judgment in that regard, for whatever may be the true position with regard to collecting-boxes, it appears to me to be impossible to apply the doctrine of resulting trust to the proceeds of entertainments and sweepstakes and such-like money-raising operations for two reasons: first, the relationship is one of contract and not of trust, the purchaser of a ticket may have the motive of aiding the cause or he may not; he may purchase a ticket merely because he wishes to attend the particular entertainment or to try for the prize, but whichever it be, he pays his money as the price of what is offered and what he receives; secondly, there is in such cases no direct contribution to the fund at all; it is only the profit, if any, which is ultimately received and there may even be none. **14–55**

In any event, the first category cannot be any more susceptible to the doctrine than the second to which I now turn. Here one starts with the well-known dictum of P.O. Lawrence J. in *Re Welsh Hospital (Netley) Fund* where he said[86]: **14–56**

> "So far as regards the contributors to entertainments, street collections etc., I have no hesitation in holding that they must be taken to have parted with their money out-and-out. It is inconceivable that any person paying for a concert ticket or placing a coin in a collecting-box presented to him in the street should have intended that any part of the money so contributed should be returned to him when the immediate object for which the concert was given or the collection made had come to an end. To draw such an inference would be absurd on the face of it."

This was adopted by Upjohn J., in *Re Hillier's Trusts*[87] where the point was actually decided.

. . . In *Re Ulverston and District New Hospital Building Trusts*[88] Jenkins L.J. threw out a suggestion that there might be a distinction in the case of a person who could prove that he put a specified sum in a collecting-box, and, in the *Gillingham* case[89] Harman J. after noting this, decided that there was a resulting trust with respect to the proceeds of collections. He said:[90] **14–57**

> "In my judgment the Crown has failed to show that this case should not follow the ordinary rule merely because there was a number of donors who, I will assume, are unascertainable. I see no reason myself to suppose that the small giver who is anonymous has any wider intention than the large giver who can be named. They all give for the one object. If they can be found by enquiry the resulting trust can be executed in their favour. If they cannot I do not see how the money could then, with all respect to Jenkins L.J., change its destination and become bona vacantia. It will be merely money held upon a trust for which no beneficiary can be found. Such cases are common and where it is known that there are beneficiaries the fact that they cannot be ascertained does not entitle the Crown to come in and claim. The trustees must pay the money into court like any other trustee who cannot find his beneficiary. I conclude, therefore, that there must be an enquiry for the subscribers to this fund."

. . . [For] for my part I cannot reconcile the decision of Upjohn J. in *Re Hillier's Trusts* with that of Harman J. in the *Gillingham* case. As I see it, therefore, I have to choose between them. On the one hand it may be said that Harman J. had the advantage, which Upjohn J. had not, of considering the suggestion made by **14–58**

[83] [1958] Ch. 300.
[84] ibid. at 304.
[85] ibid. at 309.
[86] [1921] 1 Ch. 655 at 660.
[87] [1954] 1 W.L.R. 9.
[88] [1956] Ch. 622 at 633.
[89] [1958] Ch. 300.
[90] ibid. at 314.

Jenkins L.J. On the other hand that suggestion with all respect, seems to me somewhat fanciful and unreal. I agree that all who put their money into collecting-boxes should be taken to have the same intention, but why should they not all be regarded as intending to part with their money out and out absolutely in all circumstances? I observe that P.O. Lawrence J. in *Re Welsh Hospital*[91] used very strong words. He said any other view was inconceivable and absurd on the face of it. That commends itself to my humble judgment, and I therefore prefer and follow the judgment of Upjohn J. in *Re Hillier's Trusts*.

RE BUCKS CONSTABULARY FUND FRIENDLY SOCIETY (NO.2)

Chancery Division [1979] 1 W.L.R. 936; [1979] 1 All E.R. 623

14–59 The Bucks Constabulary Fund Friendly Society was established to provide for the relief of widows and orphans of deceased members of the Bucks Constabulary. It was an unincorporated association registered under the Friendly Societies Act 1896 but it had no rules providing for the distribution of its assets in the event of it being wound up. When it was wound up the question arose whether the surplus assets were bona vacantia passing to the Crown or whether they should be distributed among the members equally per capita or on some other basis.

14–60 WALTON J.: There are basically two claimants to the fund, the Solicitor for the Affairs of Her Majesty's Treasury, who claims the assets as ownerless property, bona vacantia, and the members of the friendly society at the date of its dissolution on 14th October 1969.

14–61 Before considering the relevant legislation . . . and the decided cases, it is I think desirable to view the question of the property of unincorporated associations in the round. If a number of persons associate together, for whatever purpose, if that purpose is one which involves the acquisition of cash or property of any magnitude, then, for practical purposes, some one or more persons have to act in the capacity of treasurers or holders of the property. In any sophisticated association there will accordingly be one or more trustees in whom the property which is acquired by the association will be vested. These trustees will of course not hold such property on their own behalf. Usually there will be a committee of some description which will run the affairs of the association; though of course in a small association the committee may well comprise all the members; and the normal course of events will be that the trustee, if there is a formal trustee, will declare that he holds the property of the association in his hands on trust to deal with it as directed by the committee. If the trust deed is a shade more sophisticated it may add that the trustee holds the assets on trust for the members in accordance with the rules of the association. Now in all such cases it appears to me quite clear that, unless under the rules governing the association the property thereof has been wholly devoted to charity, or unless and to the extent to which the other trusts have validly been declared of such property, the persons, and the only persons, interested therein are the members. Save by way of a valid declaration or trust in their favour, there is no scope for any other person acquiring any rights in the property of the association, although of course it may well be that third parties may obtain contractual or proprietary rights, such as a mortgage, over those assets as the result of a valid contract with the trustees or members of the committee as representing the association.

14–62 I can see no reason for thinking that this analysis is any different whether the purpose for which the members of the association associate are a social club, a sporting club, to establish a widows' and orphans' fund, to obtain a separate Parliament for Cornwall, or to further the advance of alchemy. It matters not. All the assets of the association are held in trust for its members (of course subject to the contractual claims of anybody having a valid contract with the association) save and expect to the extent to which valid trusts have otherwise been declared of its property. I would adopt the analysis made by Brightman J. in *Re Recher's Will Trusts*.[92] . . .

14–63 All this doubtless seems quite elementary, but it appears to me to have been lost sight of to some extent in some of the decisions which I shall hereafter have to consider in detail in relation to the destination on dissolution of the funds of unincorporated associations.

---

[91] [1921] Ch. 655 at 661.
[92] [1972] Ch. 526 at 538–539.

Now in the present case I am dealing with a society which was registered under the Friendly Societies Act 1896. This does not have any effect at all on the unincorporated nature of the society, or (as I have in substance already indicated) on the way in which its property is held. But the latter point is in fact made very explicit by the provisions of s.49(1) of the 1896 Act which reads as follows: **14–64**

> "All property belonging to a registered society, whether acquired before or after the society is registered, shall vest in the trustees for the time being of the society, for the use and benefit of the society and the members thereof, and of all persons claiming through the members according to the rules of the society."

There can be doubt, therefore, that in the present case the whole of the property of the society is vested in the trustees for the use and benefit of the society and the members thereof and of all persons claiming through the members according to the rules of the society. I do not think I need go through the rules in detail. They are precisely what one would expect in the case of an association whose main purpose in life was to enable members to make provision for widows and orphans. Members paid a contribution in exchange for which in the event of their deaths their widows and children would receive various benefits. There is a minimal benefit for which provision is made in the case of a member suffering very severe illness indeed, but, as counsel for the Treasury Solicitor was able to demonstrate from an analysis of the accounts, virtually the entire expenditure of the association was, as indeed one would expect, on the provision of widows' and orphans' benefits. But, of course, there is no trust whatsoever declared in their favour. I am not called on, I think, to decide whether they are, within the meaning of s.49(1), persons claiming through the members according to the rules of the society, or whether they are simply the beneficiaries of stipulations by the members for the benefit of third parties. All parties are agreed that accrued rights of such persons must be given full effect. There is indeed no rule which says what is to happen to surplus assets of the society on a dissolution. But in view of s.49(1) there is no need. The assets must continue to be held, the society having been dissolved, and the widows and orphans being out of the way, simply for the use and benefit of the members of the society, albeit they will all now be former members. **14–65**

This indeed appears so obvious that in a work of great authority on all matters connected with friendly societies, Baden Fuller, the learned author says this:[93] **14–66**

> "If the rules provide for the termination of the society they usually also provide for the distribution of the funds in that event, but if on the termination of a society no provision has been made by the rules for the distribution of its funds, such funds are divisible among the existing members at the time of the termination or dissolution in proportion to the amount contributed by each member for entrance fees and subscriptions, but irrespective of fines or payments made to members in accordance with the rules."

In my judgment this accurately represents the law, at any rate so far as the beneficiaries of the trust on dissolution are concerned, although not necessarily so far as the quantum of their respective interests is concerned; a matter which still remains to be argued. The effective point is that the claims of the Treasury Solicitor to the funds as bona vacantia are unsustainable in the present case. I say "in the present case" because there are undoubtedly cases where the assets of an unincorporated association do become bona vacantia. To quote Baden Fuller again:[94] **14–67**

> "A society may sometimes become defunct or moribund by its members either all dying or becoming so reduced in numbers that it is impossible either to continue the society or to dissolve it by instrument; in such cases the surplus funds, after all existing claims (if any) under the rules have been satisfied or provided for, are not divisible among the surviving members . . . or the last survivor . . . or the representative of the last survivor . . . nor is there any resulting trust in favour of the personal representatives of the members of the society . . . not even in favour of honorary members in respect of donations by them . . . but a society which, though moribund, had at a testator's death one member and three

[93] *The Law of Friendly Societies* (4th edn, 1926), p.186.
[94] ibid., pp.186–187.

annuitant beneficiaries, was held to be existing so as to prevent the lapse of a legacy bequeathed to it by the testator. . . . In these circumstances two cases seem to occur: if the purposes of the society are charitable, the surplus will be applicable cy-près . . . but if the society is not a charity, the surplus belongs to the Crown as bona vacantia."

14–68 Before I turn to a consideration of the authorities, it is I think pertinent to observe that all unincorporated societies rest in contract to this extent, that there is an implied contract between all of the members inter se governed by the rules of the society. In default of any rule to the contrary, and it will seldom if ever be that there is such a rule, when a member ceases to be a member of the association he ipso facto ceases to have any interest in its funds. Once again, so far as friendly societies are concerned, this is made very clear by s.49(1), that it is the members, the present members, who, alone, have any right in the assets. As membership always ceases on death, past members or the estates of deceased members therefore have no interest in the assets. Further, unless expressly so provided by the rules, unincorporated societies are not really tontine societies, intended to provide benefits for the longest liver of the members. Therefore, although it is difficult to say in any given case precisely when a society becomes moribund, it is quite clear that if a society is reduced to a single member neither he, still less his personal representatives on his behalf, can say he is or was the society and therefore entitled solely to its fund. It may be that it will be sufficient for the society's continued existence if there are two members, but if there is only one the society as such must cease to exist. There is no association, since one can hardly associate with oneself or enjoy one's own society. And so indeed the assets have become ownerless.

14–69 [The judge referred to various cases and went on:] Finally . . . there comes a case which gives me great concern, *Re West Sussex Constabulary's Widows, Children and Benevolent (1930) Fund Trusts*.[95] The case is indeed easily distinguishable from the present case in that what was there under consideration was a simple unincorporated association and not a friendly society, so that the provisions of s.49(1) of the 1869 Act do not apply. Otherwise the facts in that case present remarkable parallels to the facts in the present case. Goff J. decided that the surplus funds had become bona vacantia. . . .

14–70 It will be observed that the first reason given by the judge for his decision is that he could not accept the principle of the members' clubs as applicable. This is a very interesting reason, because it is flatly contrary to the successful argument of Mr Ingle Joyce who appeared for the Attorney-General in the case Goff J. purported to follow, *Cunnack v Edwards*. His argument was as follows:[96]

"This society was nothing more than a club, in which the members had no transmissible interest: *Re St James' Club*.[97] Whatever the members, or even the surviving member, might have done while alive, when they died their interest in the assets of the club died with them";

and in the Court of Appeal[98] he used the arguments he had used below. If all that Goff J. meant was that the purposes of the fund before him were totally different from those of a members' club then of course one must agree, but if he meant to imply that there was some totally different principle of law applicable one must ask why that should be. His second reason is that in all the cases where the surviving members had taken, the organisation existed for the benefit of the members for the time being exclusively. This may be so, so far as actual decisions go, but what is the principle? Why are the members not in control, complete control, save as to any existing contractual rights, of the assets belonging to their organisation? One could understand the position being different if valid trusts had been declared of the assets in favour of third parties, for example charities, but that this was emphatically not the case was demonstrated by the fact that Goff J. recognised that the members could have altered the rules prior to dissolution and put the assets into their own pockets. If there was no obstacle to their doing this, it shows in my judgment quite clearly that the money was theirs all the time. Finally he purports to follow *Cunnack v Edwards* and it will be seen from the analysis which I have already made of that case that it was extremely special in its facts,

95 [1971] Ch. 1.
96 [1895] 1 Ch. 489 at 494.
97 (1852) 2 De G. M. & G. 383 at 387.
98 [1896] 2 Ch. 679.

resting on a curious provision of the 1829 Act which is no longer applicable. As I have already indicated, in the light of s.49(1) of the 1896 Act the case before Goff J.[99] is readily distinguishable, but I regret that, quite apart from that, I am wholly unable to square it with the relevant principles of law applicable.

14–71 The conclusion therefore is that, as on dissolution there were members of the society here in question in existence, its assets are held on trust for such members to the total exclusion of any claim on behalf of the Crown. The remaining question under this head which falls now to be argued is, of course, whether they are simply held per capita, or, as suggested in some of the cases, in proportion to the contributions made by each. . . .

14–72 I think that there is no doubt that, as a result of modern cases springing basically from the decision of O'Connor M.R. in *Tierney v Tough*,[100] judicial opinion has been hardening and is now firmly set along the lines that the interests and rights of persons who are members of any type of unincorporated association are governed exclusively by contract, that is to say the rights between themselves and their rights to any surplus assets. I say that to make it perfectly clear that I have not overlooked the fact that the assets of the society are usually vested in trustees on trust for the members. But that is quite a separate and distinct trust bearing no relation to the claims of the members *inter se* on the surplus funds so held on trust for their benefit.

14–73 That being the case, prima facie there can be no doubt at all but that the distribution is on the basis of equality, because, as between a number of people contractually interested in a fund, there is no other method of distribution if no other method is provided by the terms of the contract, and it is not for one moment suggested here that there is any other method of distribution provided by the contract. We are, of course, dealing here with a friendly society, but that really makes no difference to the principle. The Friendly Societies Acts do not incorporate the friendly society in any way and the only effect that it has is, as I pointed out in my previous judgment in this case, that there is a section which makes it crystal clear in the Friendly Societies Act 1896 that the assets are indeed held on trust for the members.

14–74 Now the fact that the prima facie rule is a matter of equality has been recently laid down, not of course for the first time, in two cases to which I need to no more than refer, *Re St Andrew's Allotment Association's Trusts*,[101] a decision of the late Ungoed-Thomas J., and *Re Sick and Funeral Society of St John's Sunday School, Golcar*,[102] a decision of Megarry J. Neither of those cases was, however, the case of a friendly society, and there are a number of previous decisions in connection with friendly societies, and, indeed *Tierney v Tough* itself is such a case, where the basis of distribution according to the subscriptions paid by the persons among whom the fund is to be distributed has been applied, and it has been suggested that perhaps those decisions are to be explained along the lines that a friendly society, or similar society, is thinking more of benefits to members, and that, thinking naturally of benefits to members, you think, on the other side of the coin, of subscriptions paid by members. But in my judgment that is not a satisfactory distinction of any description, because one is now dealing with what happens at the end of the life of the association; there are surplus funds, funds which have not been required to carry out the purposes of the association, and it does not seem to me it is a suitable method of distribution to say that one then looks to see what the purposes of the society were while the society was a going concern.

14–75 An ingenious argument has been put up by counsel for the third and fifth defendants, who are *ad idem* on this particular point, which runs very simply as follows: the members of the society are entitled in equity to the surplus funds which are distributable among them, therefore they are to be distributed among them according to equitable principles and those principles should, like all equitable principles, be moulded to fit the circumstances of the case, and in one case it would therefore be equitable to distribute in equal shares, in another case it might be equitable to distribute in proportion to the subscriptions that they have paid, and I suppose that in another case it might be equitable to distribute according to the length of their respective feet, following a very well known equitable precedent. Well, I completely deny the basic premise. The members are not entitled in equity to the fund: they are entitled at law. It is a matter, so far as the members are concerned, of pure contract, and, being a matter of pure contract, it is, in my judgment, as

---

99 [1971 Ch. 1.
100 [1914] I.R. 142.
101 [1969] 1 W.L.R. 229.
102 [1973] Ch. 51.

far as distribution is concerned, completely divorced from all questions of equitable doctrines. It is a matter of simple entitlement, and that entitlement, in my judgment, at this time of day must be, and can only be, in equal shares.

HANCHETT-STAMFORD v ATTORNEY-GENERAL

Chancery Division [2009] Ch. 173, [2009] 2 W.L.R. 405, [2008] 4 All E.R. 323

14–76 The facts are summarised at para.6–118.

14–77 LEWISON J. (after reviewing *Re Bucks (No.2)* continued): . . . There is, I think, no difficulty in accepting Walton J.'s ultimate conclusion. Nor is there any difficulty in accepting that the member's rights are contractual rather than equitable. Nor is there any difficulty in accepting that on a member's death he ceases to have any interest in the assets of the unincorporated association. Accretion on death is inherent in the beneficial interest in any asset being held by joint tenants in equity; and is no doubt reinforced by contractual restrictions such as the rules of an association. It, therefore, follows that the estate of a deceased member can have no claim to the assets. In *Neville Estates Ltd v Madden*[103] Cross J. applied the same principle to cessation of membership through resignation. This must be a facet of the contractual relations between members. Walton J. also said that if there is only one member of an unincorporated association, it must cease to exist. That, too, must I think be right both for the reasons that Walton J gave; and also because if the members' rights are based in contract, a contract must cease to bind once there is no other party who can enforce it.

14–78 However, what I find more difficult to accept is that a member who has a beneficial interest in an asset, albeit subject to contractual restrictions, can have that beneficial interest divested from him on the death of another member. It leads to the conclusion that if there are two members of an association which has assets of, say £2m, they can by agreement divide those assets between them and pocket £1m each, but if one of them dies before they have divided the assets, the whole pot goes to the Crown as bona vacantia. Since Walton J. was not dealing with a case in which there was only one surviving member, his observations were obiter. Nor did he explain his reasoning on this question beyond the extract from his judgment that I have quoted.

14–79 I must, I think, look a little more carefully at the authorities that are said to have this effect. In *Cunnack v Edwards*[104] a society was established to raise a fund, by the subscriptions, fines and forfeitures of its members, to provide annuities for the widows of its deceased members. There was also a category of honorary members. In 1848 Mr Edwards became an ordinary member and remained a member until his death in 1878, when he died a widower. He was the last surviving ordinary member. It appeared that all the other members had predeceased him, except Sir Vyvyan, an honorary member, and it was believed the only honorary member of the society. On joining the society he had signed a declaration that his object in joining the society was not that any widow of his should claim any benefit from it (to which he relinquished his right), but merely for the encouragement of the society. Sir Vyvyan died in 1879. The last annuitant had also died. Thus at the date when the matter came before the court there were no surviving members of the society and all the widows' pensions had been paid. The question was: what was to happen to the surplus funds. The two original claimants were the personal representatives of Mr Edwards and the Crown. The personal representatives of Sir Vyvyan made no claim. The Crown argued that the surplus was either held on charitable trusts and ought to be applied cy-près; or that the surplus was bona vacantia. Chitty J. held that the fund was not a charitable fund, and stood over the question of bona vacantia, giving leave to add as a party a representative of deceased members of the society generally. The argument for the Crown was:[105]

> "This society was nothing more than a club, in which the members had no transmissible interest . . . Whatever the members, or *even the surviving member*, might have done while alive, when they died their interest in the assets of the club died with them. The earlier deceased members have had all the benefit

[103] [1962] Ch. 832.
[104] [1895] 1 Ch. 489 and (on appeal) [1896] 2 Ch. 679.
[105] [1895] 1 Ch. 489 at 494–495. (Emphasis added by Lewison J.).

> they bargained for when they joined—their widows have received their annuities. When Edwards was alive he and Sir R. Vyvyan might have dissolved the society in the statutory way and voted themselves the funds; but they did not do so. As a fact, Sir R. Vyvyan was the surviving member, and his representatives disclaim all beneficial interest; still he had just as much right to this fund as Edwards."

Thus the argument for the Crown turned on the fact that at the date of the proceedings there were no surviving members, but it did not exclude the possibility that if there had been a surviving member that surviving member could have claimed the assets. Chitty J. dealt with the claim of the personal representatives of Mr Edwards as follows:[106] **14-80**

> "The claim of the representative of the last surviving member may be disposed of in a few words. The society was not a tontine society, and there is no ground for saying that the fund belonged in equity to the last survivor. There is nothing in the rules, or in any principle of equity, applicable to the case on which this claim can be rested. It was said that the last surviving member might have held a meeting under section 26 of the statute of George IV, and voted the funds to himself. To this proposition, extravagant as it is, it is sufficient answer to say that the last survivor never attempted to do anything of the kind."

In the result Chitty J. held that the surplus was held on a resulting trust for its contributors. The case then went to the Court of Appeal. On appeal Mr Edwards's personal representatives abandoned his claim and the contest was between the deceased members generally on the one hand, and the Crown on the other. Counsel for the Crown repeated the same arguments that he had advanced before Chitty J., which included the passage I have emphasised. The Court of Appeal held that when each subscriber paid money to the society his entire beneficial interest in the money was exhausted. Lord Halsbury said:[107] **14-81**

> "There never was and there never could be any interest remaining in the contributor other than the right that his wife, if she survived him, should become entitled to a widow's portion thus provided. This was the final and exhaustive destination of all the sums contributed to the common fund. Under these circumstances, I am at a loss to see what room there is for the contention that there is any resulting trust."

A.L. Smith L.J. said:[108] **14-82**

> "As the member paid his money to the society, so he divested himself of all interest in this money for ever, with this one reservation, that if the member left a widow she was to be provided for during her widowhood. Except as to this he abandoned and gave up the money for ever."

Accordingly, the case turned on the circumstances in which the money was paid to the society. Thus the entirety of the bargain was that the money was to be used to pay widows' pensions, and not to return any part of the money to the contributor. On the facts, there were no surviving members of the association when the case came to court, so that the question before me did not arise; and the successful argument for the Crown admitted of the possibility that a single surviving member could during his lifetime claim the assets of the friendly society. In addition, as Walton J. pointed out in *Re Bucks Constabulary (No.2)*, the case concerned a friendly society and the legislation then in force required the rules to state all the uses applicable to the assets of the society, and they stated none in favour of members. I do not consider that this case is authority for the proposition that the sole surviving member of an unincorporated association, while still alive, cannot lay claim to its assets. Moreover although it was no doubt true, as Chitty J. held and as Walton J. emphasised, that the society was not a tontine society in the sense that it was not its intention to provide benefits for the ultimate survivor, any case in which property is held on a joint tenancy in equity produces a tontine effect, even if that is not its purpose. **14-83**

---

106 At 496.
107 [1896] 2 Ch 679 at 681.
108 At 683.

14–84 [He reviewed *Tierney v Tough*[109] and *Abbatt v Treasury Solicitor*,[110] then continued:] The thread that runs through all these cases is that the property of an unincorporated association is the property of its members, but that they are contractually precluded from severing their share except in accordance with the rules of the association; and that, on its dissolution, those who are members at the time are entitled to the assets free from any such contractual restrictions. It is true that this is not a joint tenancy according to the classical model; but since any collective ownership of property must be a species of joint tenancy or tenancy in common, this kind of collective ownership must, in my judgment, be a subspecies of joint tenancy, albeit taking effect subject to any contractual restrictions applicable as between members. In some cases (such as *Cunnack v Edwards*) those contractual restrictions may be such as to exclude any possibility of a future claim. In others they may not. The cases are united in saying that on a dissolution the members of a dissolved association have a beneficial interest in its assets, and Lord Denning M.R. goes as far as to say that it is a "beneficial equitable joint tenancy". I cannot see why the legal principle should be any different if the reason for the dissolution is the permanent cessation of the association's activities or the fall in its membership to below two. The same principle ought also to hold if the contractual restrictions are abrogated or varied by agreement of the members. I do not find in the authorities considered by Walton J. anything that binds me to hold that where there is one identifiable and living member of an unincorporated association that has ceased to exist, the assets formerly held by or for that association pass to the Crown as bona vacantia. In addition, article 1 of the First Protocol of the European Convention for the Protection of Human Rights and Fundamental Freedoms guarantees the peaceful enjoyment of possessions. It says: "No one shall be deprived of his possessions except in the public interest and subject to the conditions provided for by law . . .".

14–85 On the face of it for one of two members of an unincorporated association to be deprived of his share in the assets of the association by reason of the death of the other of them, and without any compensation, appears to be a breach of this article. It is also difficult to see what public interest is served by the appropriation by the state of that member's share in the association's assets. This, in my judgment, provides another reason why the conclusion that a sole surviving member of an unincorporated association, while still alive, cannot claim its assets is unacceptable.

14–86 I therefore respectfully decline to follow Walton J.'s obiter dictum that a sole surviving member of an unincorporated association cannot claim the assets of the association, and that they vest in the Crown as bona vacantia. I might add that the Attorney General suggested in argument, without arguing in favour of one outcome, that there were three possible outcomes: first, that the last surviving member is entitled to the assets; secondly, that the assets are held jointly between the last surviving member and the estate of the member whose death caused the dissolution; thirdly, that the assets were ownerless or bona vacantia. For the reasons I have given, I conclude the first outcome is correct and I reject the second and third.

4. Apparent Gifts

A. Where Resulting Trusts Arise

i. Purchase in the Name of Another

14–87 If X buys property (real or personal) and tells the vendor to convey the property to Y, then Y must rebut the presumption that X did not mean him to take the property beneficially for himself.[111] The most obvious way for Y to do this is to prove that X intended to make him a gift.[112] Another way is for Y to prove that X intended to lend Y the purchase money, as in this case X must have intended Y to have beneficial

109 [1914] 1 I.R. 142.
110 [1969] 1 W.L.R. 561.
111 *Dyer v Dyer* (1788) 2 Cox 92; *Vandervell v IRC* [1967] 2 A.C. 291.
112 As in e.g. *Loosemore v McDonnell* [2007] EWCA Civ 1531.

ownership of the property, and to owe him a personal obligation to repay the amount of the loan. Thus, if X provides £25,000 of the £100,000 purchase price of a house in Y's name, and provides the money as purchaser, then he will be entitled to a quarter share of the house unless he intends to make Y a gift of the money, the onus being on Y to prove this.[113] But if X provides the £25,000 as a lender to Y, then he will only be entitled as Y's creditor to the repayment of the £25,000 and any agreed interest. In general, therefore, we may say that loan agreements are inconsistent with resulting trusts,[114] although in some exceptional cases where X lends Y money for a specified purpose, the parties may arrange matters so that Y holds the money on trust for X, but has a power to apply the money to the specified purpose, the exercise of which will defeat X's equitable proprietary interest in the money.[115]

ii. Purchase in the Joint Names of Oneself and Another

If X purchases property (real or personal) and tells the vendor to convey the property into the joint names of himself and Y, then Y must prove that X meant to give him a share of the property, or else X and Y will together hold the property on resulting trust for X.[116] **14–88**

iii. Joint Purchase

Suppose that X and Y jointly purchase property (real or personal) in the name of Y alone. They both contribute towards the purchase money, but the conveyance is taken in Y's name alone. Unless Y proves that X intended a gift, he will hold the property on resulting trust for X and Y in shares proportionate to their contributions.[117] **14–89**

If X and Y purchase a yearly tenancy for £3,000 each in Y's name then Y will hold it on resulting trust in equal shares unless he can show that X meant a gift. However, if no capital sum is paid and Y alone takes on the tenancy, having arranged for X to share the rent and gas and electricity bills, and X does so, then X cannot claim a half share under a resulting trust in the tenancy, or indeed of the freehold in the event that Y purchases this on favourable terms (even if X reimburses Y half the price of the freehold).[118] Payments of a capital nature, as opposed to income, are required before a resulting trust can arise. Thus, if X and Y buy a shared home in Y's name for £100,000, and X pays £50,000 directly, and Y provides £50,000 borrowed from a lender which takes a mortgage over the property to secure repayment of the loan, Y cannot claim a greater share than half under a resulting trust. It makes no difference whether the amounts actually paid by Y to the mortgage lender amount to more or less than £50,000. **14–90**

What if X and Y jointly purchase property (real or personal) as legal joint tenants? Again, in the absence of evidence that they intended otherwise, the parties will hold the property on resulting trust for themselves in the proportions in which they contributed.[119] If X dies, then Y will take legal title to the whole by survivorship, but will be treated as a tenant in common in equity, and will hold X's share of the purchase or mortgage money on resulting trust for X's estate.[120] **14–91**

---

113 *Seldon v Davidson* [1968] 1 W.L.R. 1083; *Dewar v Dewar* [1975] 1 W.L.R. 1532.

114 *Aveling v Knipe* (1815) 19 Ves. Jun. 441; *Re Sharpe* [1980] 1 All E.R. 198 at 201; *Winkworth v Edward Baron Development Co Ltd* [1987] 1 All E.R. 114 at 118, per Lord Templeman.

115 As in *Twinsectra Ltd v Yardley* [2002] A.C. 164. See para.5–33.

116 *Benger v Drew* (1721) P. Wms. 781; *Rider v Rider* (1805) 10 Ves. 360.

117 *The Venture* [1908] P. 218; *Bull v Bull* [1955] 1 Q.B. 234.

118 *Savage v Dunningham* [1974] Ch. 181.

119 *Calverley v Green* (1984) 155 C.L.R. 242; *Springette v Defoe* [1992] 2 F.L.R. 388 at 392, per Dillon L.J., followed in *R. (on the application of Kelly) v Hammersmith & Fulham LBC* [2004] EWHC 435 (Admin) at [19], per Richards J. But cf. *Stack v Dowden* [2007] 2 A.C. 432, discussed below at paras 14–92 ff., where Baroness Hale indicated that such cases should henceforth be resolved using constructive trust principles.

120 *Re Jackson* (1887) 34 Ch.D. 732; *Cobb v Cobb* [1955] 2 All E.R. 696. See too Law of Property Act 1925 s.111 enabling the survivor to give a good receipt.

iv. Joint Purchase of Shared Homes

14–92 Until recently, it was clear that these principles would also apply in cases where X and Y buy a shared family home together but foolishly do not make an express written declaration of trust as to their shares.[121] Again, in the absence of clear evidence as to their intentions, it would be presumed that neither intended to make a gift or loan of his or her contribution to the purchase price. Unless this presumption was rebutted, the property would be held on resulting trust for the pair of them, the amount of their equitable interests corresponding to the contributions which they had made to the purchase.[122] So, for example, in the case of a house costing £100,000, if X paid £40,000 and Y paid £60,000, then X would be equitably entitled to 40 per cent and Y to 60 per cent, and the position was the same if X did not actually pay £40,000 but obtained a £40,000 discount off the market price, as a sitting tenant of the house.[123]

14–93 Following the House of Lords' decision in *Stack v Dowden*,[124] however, it has become rather uncertain when the courts should refer to resulting trust principles when allocating equitable interests in shared family homes. In *Stack* Baroness Hale held that the courts should generally avoid using resulting trust reasoning as a means of establishing equitable interests in shared homes,[125] because it is too focused on one type of contribution to the parties' relationship, viz. financial contributions, to the exclusion of other types, e.g. home-making, child-care, etc., with the result that it delivers outcomes that are unfair and discriminatory against women who support their partners by staying at home while their partners go out to work. Speaking for the Privy Council in *Abbott v Abbott*, Baroness Hale reiterated this point, stating that "It is now clear that the constructive trust is generally the more appropriate tool of analysis in most matrimonial cases."[126]

14–94 In *Stack*, however, Lord Neuberger considered that resulting trusts should not be completely abandoned in this context, as he believed that they might still have a role to play,[127] and in *Laskar v Laskar*,[128] a case in which he subsequently sat as a judge of the Court of Appeal, Lord Neuberger specifically rejected the argument that the only way to establish an equitable interest in a family home is by way of a constructive trust. In *Laskar* a mother and daughter bought a house together as an investment, without intending to live in it. The court used a traditional resulting trust analysis under which the parties' shares were allocated in proportion to their contributions to the purchase price, and Lord Neuberger said that "it would not be right to apply the reasoning in *Stack v Dowden* to such a case as this, where the parties primarily purchased the property as an investment for rental income and capital appreciation, even where their relationship is a familial one."[129] It seems, therefore, that there are still some family home cases in which resulting trust reasoning should be used to determine the parties' equitable interests.

---

121 An express written declaration of trust signed by the parties is conclusive in the absence of fraud or mistake (*Goodman v Gallant* [1986] Fam. 106) or undue influence (*Humphreys v Humphreys* [2005] 1 F.C.R. 712).

122 *Pettit v Pettit* [1970] A.C. 777 at 814. Quaere whether acquisition costs, e.g. legal fees and stamp duty, are part of the purchase price? *Huntingford v Hobbs* [1993] 1 F.L.R. 736 suggests that they are, but in *Curley v Parkes* [2004] EWCA Civ 1515 at [22], Peter Gibson L.J. held otherwise. At [23] he also held that removal costs do not form part of the purchase price either.

123 *Abbey National BS v Cann* (1989) 59 P. & C.R 381; *Springette v Defoe* [1992] 2 F.L.R. 388; *Mckenzie v Mckenzie* [2003] EWHC 601 (Ch) at [81]; *R (on the application of Kelly) v Hammersmith & Fulham LBC* [2004] EWHC 435 (Admin). See too *Laskar v Laskar* [2008] 1 W.L.R. 2695 at [22]–[26].

124 [2007] 2 A.C. 432.

125 *Stack* at [60], with the agreement of Lord Hoffmann at [1], Lord Hope at [3], and Lord Walker at [31]. See too *Fowler v Barron* [2008] 2 F.L.R. 831 at [30] and [52].

126 [2008] 1 F.L.R. 1451 at [4].

127 *Stack* at [110] ff.

128 [2008] 1 W.L.R. 2695.

129 *Laskar* at [17].

It follows that at least in a *Laskar*-type "investment" case, the pre-*Stack* case-law will continue to govern the allocation of equitable interests in family homes where the property has been purchased with the help of a mortgage loan—e.g. where X and Y buy a house together, X provides £40,000, and the £60,000 balance is provided by way of mortgage. In such a case, the mortgage will have to be granted by the new legal owners of the house who will thereby be directly liable to the mortgagee for the amount of the mortgage loan. Where the legal title is taken in the names of X and Y this means that X and Y will be jointly and severally liable to the mortgagee, with a right of indemnity against each other for half the money unless they have agreed otherwise between themselves. Thus, if X and Y undertake liability for a £60,000 mortgage on their £100,000 house they will prima facie be regarded as thereby providing £30,000 of the purchase price each.[130] However, if X provides £40,000 of the purchase price in cash and agrees with Y that Y will be solely responsible for repaying the mortgage lender, who has supplied the balance of £60,000, then Y will be regarded as providing £60,000 of the purchase price.[131] **14–95**

"Under a resulting trust, the existence of the trust is established once and for all at the date on which the property is acquired."[132] Because the shares of X and Y under a resulting trust crystallise at the date of acquisition, neither can subsequently claim a larger share under the resulting trust on the basis that he has paid for improvements to the property or paid a higher proportion of the mortgage instalments than the parties agreed at the time of acquisition.[133] This holds true even if the parties fall out and one subsequently makes all the mortgage payments, although on sale of the property, equitable accounting principles can require deductions to be made against the other party's share of the sale proceeds.[134] **14–96**

v. Transfer from One to Another

We now turn to cases where X gratuitously transfers property into Y's name. In the cases we have considered so far, the transaction was a purchase; here it is a transfer. Property already stands in the name of X, who gratuitously transfers it into the name of Y. Here, again, there is a presumption that X does not intend to make a gift to Y, which Y must rebut if he does not wish to hold the property on resulting trust for X. **14–97**

This presumption will be raised whenever the property gratuitously transferred by X to Y is personal property (e.g. cash, shares, etc.).[135] Exceptionally, however, no presumption will be raised if the property is land. Under the Law of Property Act 1925 s.60(3): "In a voluntary conveyance a resulting trust for the grantor shall not be implied merely by reason that the property is not expressed to be **14–98**

---

130 *Harwood v Harwood* [1991] 2 F.L.R. 274 at 292; *Springette v Defoe* (1992) 65 P. & C.R. 1; *Ammala v Savimaa* (1993) 17 Fam.L.R. 529 (Fed. Ct of Australia).

131 *Huntingford v Hobbs* [1993] 1 F.L.R. 736; *Ivin v Blake* (1994) 67 P. & C.R. 265; *Carlton v Goodman* [2002] 2 F.L.R. 259 at [22] and [38]–[42]; *McKenzie v McKenzie* [2003] EWHC 601 (Ch) at [80]–[81]; *Trowbridge v Trowbridge* [2003] 2 F.L.R. 231.

132 Lord Browne-Wilkinson, "Constructive Trusts and Unjust Enrichment" (1996) 10 Tru L.I. 98, p.100. See too *Pettitt v Pettitt* [1970] A.C. 777 at 800 and 816; *Gissing v Gissing* [1971] A.C. 886 at 900; *Calverley v Green* (1984) 155 C.L.R. 242 at 257; *Sekhon v Alissa* [1989] 2 F.L.R. 94 at 100; *Huntingford v Hobbs* [1993] 1 F.L.R. 736; *Carlton v Goodman* [2002] 2 F.L.R. 259; *Curley v Parkes* [2004] EWCA Civ 1515 at [14] and [15]; *Barrett v Barrett* [2008] 2 P. & C.R. 17 at [6].

133 The position is different in Ireland where an "extended resulting trust" analysis is used to give contributors a resulting trust interest calculated by reference to their contributions both to the purchase price and to ongoing mortgage payments: J. Mee, *The Property Rights of Cohabitees* (1999), Ch.3.

134 *Bernard v Jacobs* [1982] Ch. 391; *Re Gorman* [1990] 1 W.L.R. 616; *Huntingford v Hobbs* [1993] 1 F.L.R. 736; *Re Pavlou* [1993] 1 W.L.R. 1046; *Ryan v Dries* (2002) 4 I.T.E.L.R. 829; *Re Byford* [2004] 1 F.L.R. 56; *Stack v Dowden* [2007] 2 A.C. 432 at [117], per Lord Neuberger.

135 *Fowkes v Pascoe* (1875) 10 Ch. App. 343 at 348; *Hepworth v Hepworth* (1870) L.R. 11 Eq. 10; *Standing v Bowring* (1885) 16 Ch.D. 282; *Re Vinogradoff* [1935] W.N. 68; *Vandervell v IRC* [1967] 2 A.C. 291 at 312–313; *Re Vandervell's Trusts (No.2)* [1974] Ch. 269; *Tinsley v Milligan* [1994] 1 A.C. 340 at 371.

conveyed for the use or benefit of the grantee." In *Lohia v Lohia*,[136] it was held that this means what it says: if X conveys land to Y and receives nothing in return, there will be no presumption in X's favour that Y must rebut if he wishes to keep the property for himself. It follows that the sub-section creates inconsistencies between the rules for real and personal property, and also between the rules for purchase of property in another's name and transferring property into another's name.

14–99 Arguably, however, these inconsistencies are justified.[137] There are many reasons why X might buy property in Y's name without intending to make a gift to Y that do not obtain in the case of a transfer of property from X to Y: e.g. overlooking the need to protect X's position in the course of a complex transaction involving vendors and mortgagees.[138] Moreover, formality rules apply to conveyances of land which do not apply to transfers of personal property, increasing the likelihood that a transferor has thought carefully about whether he really wants to hand his property over to another person, and so reducing the need for a backstop rule that he should be presumed not to have intended this.

vi. Transfer into Joint Names of Oneself and Another

14–100 Suppose that property stands in the name of X, but instead of transferring it into the sole name of Y, as in v. above, he gratuitously transfers it into the joint names of himself and Y. Again there will be a presumption that X does not intend to make a gift to Y of his share,[139] unless the property in question is land in which case there will be no such presumption, by dint of the Law of Property Act 1925 s.60(3). An example is *Young v Sealey*,[140] where X opened a joint bank account with Y, but during her life X retained complete control of the account, and Y neither paid anything into, nor drew anything out of the account. On X's death Y took the legal title by survivorship. Did he hold it on resulting trust for X's estate? Romer J. held not. A presumption arose in favour of the estate, but Y was able to rebut this with evidence of X's intentions.

14–101 What if X and Y open a joint bank account, and X provides in his will that Y should receive whatever is left in the account, X having had control of the account during his lifetime, and Y having had no sole drawing rights until X's death? Does the provision in X's will amount to a testamentary disposition? Following the lead of the High Court of Australia,[141] English courts of first instance[142] have held that no testamentary disposition is involved, there being "an immediate gift [at the time of opening the joint account] of a fluctuating asset consisting of the chose in action for the time being constituting the balance in the bank account."[143] Likewise, the Irish Supreme Court held in *Lynch v Burke*[144] that there was no testamentary disposition on similar facts, either because there was a gift subject to the contingency of surviving the donor, or because the donee had been given contractual rights under documents signed by the donee and enforceable against the bank and the donor's executor.

---

136 [2001] W.T.L.R. 101, affirmed on a different point [2001] EWCA Civ 1691, and cited with approval in *Ali v Khan* (2002) 5 I.T.E.L.R. 232 at [24], per Morritt V.C.

137 R. Chambers (2001) 15 Tru. L.I. 26, p. 29.

138 cf. *Brown v Brown* (1993) 31 N.S.W.L.R. 582.

139 *Re Vinogradoff* [1935] W.N. 68.

140 [1949] Ch. 278. See too *Re Reid* (1921) 50 Ont. L.R. 595; *Russell v Scott* (1936) 55 C.L.R. 440; *Aroso v Coutts & Co* [2002] 1 All E.R. (Comm) 241.

141 *Russell v Scott* (1936) 56 C.L.R. 440.

142 *Young v Sealey* [1943] Ch. 278; *Re Figgis* [1969] 1 Ch. 123.

143 *Re Figgis* [1969] 1 Ch. 123 at 149, per Megarry J.

144 [1995] 2 I.R. 159.

B. *Where Resulting Trusts do not Arise*

i. Presumption of Advancement[145]

14–102 As we have said, where X gratuitously transfers property to Y, and there is no clear evidence of X's intentions, Equity generally presumes that X did not intend Y to take the property beneficially for himself. Exceptionally, however, Equity makes the opposite presumption when X and Y are in a special relationship such as that which exists between a father and his child. Here, a presumption of advancement is made: it is presumed that X intends Y to take the property beneficially for himself because fathers generally wish to advance their children in life by helping them financially. Note that the presumption here is not that X intends to maintain Y, in discharge of his (common law) duty to maintain his infant children, but rather that he intends to establish Y as an independent economic actor.[146]

14–103 The presumption of advancement is made where X is the father of Y, or stands in loco parentis to Y,[147] or is the husband of Y, or the fiancé of Y.[148] It does not arise where X is merely cohabiting with Y,[149] nor where X is the wife of Y.[150] The English cases are divided on the question whether the presumption arises as between a mother and her children,[151] but authorities from elsewhere in the Commonwealth say that it does.[152]

14–104 These distinctions derive from cases which date back several hundred years, and some have ceased to reflect contemporary socio-economic reality and ideas of gender equality. Specifically, there is no longer a good reason to think that fathers but not mothers have the financial wherewithal to advance their children in life, nor to think that husbands but not wives have the means to benefit their spouses. In the latter case, it seems most likely that the courts will redress the present inequality of treatment by doing away with presumptions of advancement between spouses altogether, since the strength of the presumption between husband and wife is now said to be very weak.[153] Moreover, the gender bias inherent in the rules affecting spouses probably contravenes art.5 of the Seventh Protocol to the European Convention of Human Rights, which asserts the equality of spousal rights and responsibilities.[154]

14–105 Of the former case, it has been said that although the question whether the presumption arises between mother and child is uncertain, this is "of little practical importance, since very slight intention is sufficient to establish advancement, there being very little additional motive required beyond

---

145 Shortly before this book went to press, Lord Lester of Herne Hill moved an amendment to the Equality Bill 2008–09 to 2009–10, to abolish the presumption of advancement, and this was accepted by the Government: *Hansard* (HL) February 9, 2010, cols 707 ff. If the legislation is enacted in its newly amended form, then parts of the discussion in this section will become otiose.

146 J. Glister, "The Presumption of Advancement" in C. Mitchell (ed.), *Constructive and Resulting Trusts* (2010), pp.310–312.

147 *Hepworth v Hepworth* (1870) L.R. 11 Eq. 10; *Shephard v Cartwright* [1955] A.C. 431; *Re Cameron The Times* April 2, 1999; *Lavelle v Lavelle* [2004] 2 F.C.R. 418 at [14]. For a presumption of advancement to arise on the basis that a transferor is in loco parentis to a transferee, it must be shown that he assumed the duty of a father to make provision for a child: *Bennett v Bennett* [876] l0 Ch.D. 414 at 477, followed in *Sansom v Gardner* [2009] EWHC 3369 (QB) (where this was not established on the facts).

148 *Tinker v Tinker* [1970] P. 136; *Silver v Silver* [1958] 1 W.L.R. 259; *Moate v Moate* [1948] 2 All E.R. 486 (intended husband: marriage afterwards solemnised); Law Reform (Miscellaneous Provisions) Act 1970 s.2(1); *Mossop v Mossop* [1988] 2 All E.R. 202.

149 *Rider v Kidder* (1805) 10 Ves. Jun. 360; *Napier v Public Trustee* (1980) 32 A.L.R. 153 at 158; *Calverley v Green* (1984) 56 A.L.R. 483; *Lowson v Coombes* [1999] 1 F.L.R. 799.

150 *Re Curtis* (1885) 52 L.T. 244; *Mercier v Mercier* [1903] 2 Ch. 98; *Abrahams v Trustee of Property of Abrahams* [2000] W.T.L.R. 593.

151 Yes, at least where she is a widowed mother: *Garrett v Wilkinson* (1848) 2 De G. & Sm. 244 at 246; *Sayre v Hughes* (1886) L.R. 5 Eq. 376; *Re Grimes* [1937] I.R. 470. No: *Re De Visme* (1863) 2 De G.J. & S. 17; *Bennet v Bennet* (1879) 10 Ch.D. 474; *Sekhon v Alissa* [1989] 2 F.L.R. 94.

152 *Re Brownlie* [1990] 3 N.Z.L.R. 243; *Brown v Brown* (1993) 31 N.S.W.L.R. 582 at 591; *Re Dreger Estate* (1994) 97 Manitoba R. (2d) 39; *Nelson v Nelson* (1995) 184 C.L.R. 538; *Pecore v Pecore* [2007] 1 S.C.R. 795 at [32]–[33].

153 *Pettitt v Pettitt* [1970] A.C. 777 at 793; *McGrath v Wallis* [1995] 2 F.L.R. 114 at 155; *Ali v Khan* (2002) 5 I.T.E.L.R. 232 at [30].

154 Written Answer, *Hansard* (HL) April 21, 1998, vol.588, col.197.

the mother/child relationship to induce a mother to make a gift to her child."[155] It should be borne in mind, however, that the existence of the presumption can still be crucial, and that much can still turn "upon the precise family relationship" between the parties, "so that, for example, distinctions between a wife or partner, a child or brother become central", when the courts are asked to determine "the enforceability of a transaction between two parties implicated in illegal purpose".[156]

14–106 In *Pecore v Pecore*[157] and *Madsen Estate v Saylor*,[158] the Supreme Court of Canada considered that the presumption of advancement should no longer apply to transfers by parents to their adult children, reasoning that:[159]

> "it is common nowadays for ageing parents to transfer their assets into joint accounts with their adult children in order to have that child assist them in managing their financial affairs. There should therefore be a rebuttable presumption that the adult child is holding the property in trust for the ageing parent to facilitate the free and efficient management of that parent's affairs."

ii. Rebutting the Presumptions

14–107 In some cases, the presumption that a transferor does not intend a gift, and also the opposite presumption that a transferor intends a gift where he is in a special relationship with the transferee, can be rebutted by comparatively slight evidence,[160] but speaking generally, the strength of the evidence required to rebut either presumption will vary with the strength of the presumption, which in turn will depend on the facts and circumstances giving rise to it.[161] To give some examples:

> "if a young woman in her first job, not very well paid, were to raise as much as she could on mortgage in order to buy a flat, what would we make of the fact that her well-to-do uncle, a man on affable terms with her, provided a minor part of the purchase price? The most obvious explanation is not that he wanted a part of the speculation. It is more credible that it was meant to be a loan or, perhaps, a gift."[162]

On the other hand, if an unmarried couple both contribute to the purchase of a shared home, and only one appears on the legal title, there is only "a fairly strong presumption" that the other does not intend to make a gift of her contribution because "modern couples usually have the property conveyed into their joint names and, if they do not, one may wonder why."[163] If a father conveys property into his child's name, but retains the title deeds and simultaneously declares that the transaction is not a gift, then that is sufficient to rebut the presumption of advancement,[164] although the retention

---

155 *Crown Prosecution Service v Malik* [2003] EWHC 660 (Admin) at [27], per Richards J.
156 *Collier v Collier* (2002) 6 I.T.E.L.R. 270, at [97], per Mance L.J.
157 [2007] 1 S.C.R. 795.
158 [2007] 1 S.C.R. 838.
159 *Pecore* at [36], per Rothstein J. But cf. *McDonnell v Loosemore* [2007] EWCA Civ 1531 at [33], per Toulson L.J.: "It is not unusual for a person of advancing years and in poor health to decide to pass on his capital assets to his family immediately, trusting that they will behave honourably towards him by not letting him become homeless and destitute . . . that is sufficient to rebut a presumption of a resulting trust".
160 *Pettitt v Pettitt* [1970] A.C. 777 at 813, 824; *Falconer v Falconer* [1970] 1 W.L.R. 1333; *McGrath v Wallis* [1995] 2 F.L.R. 114.
161 *Vajpeyi v Yusaf* [2004] W.T.L.R. 989 at [71], per Peter Prescott QC (sitting as a deputy High Court judge), following *Fowkes v Pascoe* (1875) L.R. 10 Ch. 343 at 352–353, per Mellish L.J.
162 *Vajpeyi* at [77].
163 *Vajpeyi* at [76].
164 *Warren v Gurney* [1944] 2 All E.R. 472.

of title deeds without such a declaration may be insufficient.[165] If land is purchased in the name of a company which is formed for the purpose and controlled by the provider of the funds, then it would be "perverse" to think that he does not wish the company to take the property beneficially for itself, since his likely intention is to use the company to deal with the property.[166]

Before the First World War, it was held that acquiescence by a child, in whose name a purchase had been made, in the receipt by his father during his life of the rents or other income from the property does not rebut the presumption of advancement,[167] at any rate where the child has not already been fully advanced to set him up in life.[168] The reason given was that if the child were an infant then it would be natural that the father should receive the profits, while if the child were an adult, then it would be an act of good manners on his part not to dispute their reception by his father. In the 2010s, however, it seems less likely that the court would regard good manners as an explanation of the child's conduct sufficient to justify his retention of the property. **14–108**

In *Shephard v Cartwright*[169] Viscount Simonds held that evidence of acts subsequent to the transfer, though not admissible in favour of the party doing the acts, is admissible against him. However, this rule was abandoned in *Lavelle v Lavelle*,[170] in favour of the "less rigid" approach taken in *Pettitt v Pettitt*.[171] According to Lord Phillips M.R.:[172] **14–109**

> "Equity searches for the subjective intention of the transferor. It . . . is not satisfactory to apply rigid rules of law to the evidence that is admissible to rebut the presumption of advancement. Plainly, self-serving statements or conduct of a transferor, who may long after the transaction be regretting earlier generosity, carry little or no weight. But words or conduct more proximate to the transaction itself should be given the significance that they naturally bear as part of the overall picture. Where the transferee is an adult, the words or conduct of the transferor will carry more weight if the transferee is aware of them and makes no protest or challenge to them."

These comments bear out the view that there should be no absolute bar against the admissibility of a transferor's subsequent acts or declarations, given the modern trend of civil litigation, to place all relevant evidence before the court and let the court decide on the weight to be attached to it.[173]

iii. Illegality

When considering the evidence that may be offered to rebut the presumptions one must also bear in mind the maxims "he who comes to equity must come with clean hands", "*ex turpi causa non oritur actio*" ("no legal action arises out of bad conduct"), and "*in pari delicto potior est conditio defendetis* (or *possidentis*)" ("when both parties are in the wrong the defendant (or the possessor of property) is **14–110**

165 *Scawin v Scawin* (1841) 1 Y. & C.C.C. 65.
166 *Arab Monetary Fund v Hashim* Ch.D. June 15, 1994, per Chadwick J., followed in *Trade Credit Finance (No.1) Ltd v Bilgin* [2004] EWHC 2732 (Comm). Cf. *United Overseas Bank Ltd v Iwuanyanwu* Ch.D. 5 March 2001, aff'd [2001] EWCA Civ 616.
167 *Commissioner of Stamp Duties v Byrnes* [1911] A.C. 386; cf. Wickens V.C. in *Stock v McAvoy* (1872) L.R. 15 Eq. 55 at 59; *Northern Canadian Trust Co v Smith* [1947] 3 D.L.R. 135; *Re Gooch* (1890) 62 L.T. 384.
168 *Grey v Grey* (1677) 2 Swans. 594; and see *Hepworth v Hepworth* (1870) L.R. 11 Eq. 10.
169 [1955] A.C. 431.
170 [2004] 2 F.C.R. 418. See too *Pecore v Pecore* [2007] 1 S.C.R. 795 at [56]–[59]. *Shephard* was followed by the P.C. in *Antoni v Antoni* [2007] W.T.L.R. 1335 at [20], but Lord Scott does not seem to have had the benefit of Lord Phillips' comments in *Lavelle*.
171 [1970] A.C. 777.
172 [2004] 2 F.C.R. 418 at [19].
173 E. Fung, "The Scope of the Rule in *Shephard v Cartwright*" (2006) 122 L.Q.R. 651.

in the stronger position"). These maxims may come into play when a person gratuitously transfers legal title to property to another person as part of an illegal scheme, e.g. to defraud the Revenue, to defeat his creditors or to defeat his wife's claims on divorce. In cases of this sort, the law may simply hold that the transfer is ineffective, a possibility that is considered in iv. below.[174] First, though, we will discuss the situation where the transfer of legal title is valid, but the transferor subsequently wishes to claim that the property is held on a resulting trust for him.

14–111 Where the presumption of advancement applies (e.g. where X transfers property to his wife W or son S) the onus is on the transferor X to produce evidence rebutting the presumption. If he honestly transfers the property to defeat his creditors then this could not lawfully be achieved without the beneficial ownership passing with the legal title, and so the presumption of advancement is strengthened that this was what he intended to accomplish, as held in *Tinker v Tinker*.[175] If he dishonestly transfers the legal title to W or S to cloak the truth from his creditors, with a view to recovering the property for himself afterwards, then he cannot usually rely on evidence of his illegal purpose to rebut the presumption of advancement.[176] However, *Tribe v Tribe*, which is reproduced below,[177] establishes that he can rely on such evidence if the creditors were not actually deceived (e.g. because matters were resolved without the need to resort to the relevant property): he can recover his property so long as the illegal purpose has not been "wholly or partly carried into effect".[178] In effect, therefore, the law provides him with a safety net if he transfers property as part of an illegal plan which later becomes unnecessary. Is this satisfactory?

14–112 According to the majority of the House of Lords in *Tinsley v Milligan*,[179] which is also reproduced below,[180] matters are different where a presumption is made that a transferor X does not intend to make a gift (e.g. where X transfers property to his brother B). Here, X need not rely on evidence of his own illegal purpose. He simply needs to show that he transferred the property to B and received nothing in return for it. B must then prove that a gift was intended, or a resulting trust for X will be imposed, and B will be unable to do this where he has received property transferred to him by X for the purpose of deceiving some third party. Hence, once the coast is clear and the third party has been defrauded, X can recover the property, an iniquitous result which Millett L.J. wished to avoid in *Tribe*,[181] but which the House of Lords' decision in *Tinsley v Milligan* clearly mandates.[182]

---

174 See paras 14–149 ff, discussing the Insolvency Act 1986 ss.339–342 and 423–425; the Matrimonial Causes Act 1973 s.37; and the Inheritance (Provisions for Family and Dependents) Act 1975 s.10.

175 [1970] P. 136; but note Insolvency Act 1986 ss.339–342, 423–425.

176 *Gascoigne v Gascoigne* [1918] 1 K.B. 223 (where there were existing creditors and where tax was paid on the basis that the bungalow belonged to the wife); *Re Emery's Investment Trusts* [1959] Ch. 410 (where it seems that American withholding tax was evaded).

177 At paras 14–134 ff.

178 [1996] Ch. 107 at 134, per Millett L.J. See too *Symes v Hughes* (1875) L.R. 9 Eq. 475; *Petherpermal Chetty v Muniandi Servai* (1908) 24 T.L.R. 462; *Perpetual Executors Association of Australia Ltd v Wright* (1917) 23 C.L.R. 185; *Martin v Martin* (1959) 110 C.L.R. 297; *Chettiar v Chettiar* [1962] A.C. 294 at 302; *Sekhon v Alissa* [1989] 2 F.L.R. 94; *Collier v Collier* (2002) 6 I.T.E.L.R. 270, esp. [103]–[107]. And for a case where the party wishing to invoke the doctrine had gone too far down the road, see *Q v Q* [2009] 1 F.L.R. 935 at [126]–[130].

179 [1994] 1 A.C. 340.

180 At paras 14–116 ff.

181 [1996] Ch. 107 at 129: "The transferor's own conduct would be inconsistent with the retention of any beneficial interest in the property" because "the only way in which a man can protect his property from his creditors is by divesting himself of all beneficial interest in it." Yet Milligan's conduct in defrauding the DHSS on the basis that she had no beneficial interest was inconsistent with her having any beneficial interest, and the Lords' majority gave no sign that Tinsley could exploit this fact against her.

182 [1994] 1 A.C. 340 at 376, per Lord Browne-Wilkinson, endorsing *Gorog v Kiss* (1977) 78 D.L.R. (3d) 690.

As pointed out by the High Court of Australia,[183] the English Court of Appeal,[184] and the English Law Commission,[185] it is highly unsatisfactory to make a transferor's ability to recover property transferred for an illegal purpose turn on the essentially irrelevant question of whether or not he and the transferee are in a special relationship giving rise to a presumption of advancement. Matters are worsened by the fact that there is uncertainty as to which presumption applies to transfers from wife to husband and mother to child. Thus, the minority of the House of Lords in *Tinsley v Milligan* preferred the harsh but certain approach that "a court of equity will not assist a claimant who does not come to equity with clean hands", producing the result that the transferred property is left in the hands of the defendant.[186] All their Lordships rejected the flexible rule relied upon by the Court of Appeal,[187] which made the transferor's ability to recover the property turn upon the extent to which the public conscience would be affronted by recognising rights arising out of illegal transactions. **14–113**

In principle, however, matters would be greatly improved if the law were amended in line with the Law Commission's recommendation, published in 1999, that there should be a structured statutory discretion to decide the effects of illegality on resulting trusts. Factors to be taken into account would be "(a) the seriousness of the illegality; (b) the knowledge and intent of the illegal trust beneficiary; (c) whether invalidity would tend to deter the illegality; (d) whether invalidity would further the purpose of the rule which renders the trust 'illegal'; and (e) whether invalidity would be a proportionate response to the claimant's participation in the illegality."[188] No legislation was enacted in response to this recommendation, and in 2010, the Law Commission published another report[189] in which it noted that the courts have begun to develop a structured discretion to deal with illegality cases at common law,[190] and concluded that there is no need for general legislation in this area. However, it still considered that more targeted legislation is needed to abolish the *Tinsley* reliance principle and give the courts a discretion to determine the effect of illegality on trusts. **14–114**

Finally, it should be noted that if illegality prevents a transferor from recovering under a resulting trust then his personal representative is in no better position.[191] Should public policy allow his trustee in bankruptcy to be in a better position?[192] **14–115**

TINSLEY v MILLIGAN

House of Lords [1994] 1 A.C. 340; [1993] 3 W.L.R. 126; [1993] 3 All E.R. 65

Stella Tinsley and Kathleen Milligan jointly purchased a house which they registered only in Tinsley's name to enable Milligan (with the knowledge and assent of Tinsley) to make false social security benefit claims for the benefit of both of them cohabiting as lovers. Their relationship ended after four years, when Tinsley moved out. She claimed possession of the house as legal owner, and Milligan counterclaimed for an order for sale and a declaration that the house was held by Tinsley on trust for the two of them in equal **14–116**

183 *Nelson v Nelson* (1995) 184 C.L.R. 538.
184 *Tribe v Tribe* [1996] Ch. 107 at 118; *Silverwood v Silverwood* (1997) 74 P. & C.R. 453 at 458–459; *Lowson v Coombes* [1999] Ch. 373 at 385; *Collier v Collier* (2002) 6 I.T.E.L.R. 270, at [105]–[106]. See too *Q v Q* [2009] 1 F.L.R. 935 at [138].
185 Law Commission, *Illegal Transactions: The Effect of Illegality on Contracts and Trusts* (Law Com. No.154, 1999), paras 3.19–3.24.
186 "Let the estate lie where it falls": *Muckleton v Brown* (1801) 6 Ves. Jun. 52 at 69.
187 [1992] Ch. 310.
188 Law Commission, *Illegal Transactions: The Effect of Illegality on Contracts and Trusts* (Law Com. No. 154, 1999), para.8.63.
189 *The Illegality Defence* (Law Com. No.320, 2010).
190 *Stone & Rolls Ltd (in liq.) v Moore Stephens (a firm)* [2009] 1 A.C. 1391; *Gray v Thames Trains Ltd* [2009] 1 A.C. 1339.
191 *Ayerst v Jenkins* (1873) L.R. 16 Eq. 275 at 281, per Lord Selborne L.C. The contrary view of Lord Eldon in *Mackleston v Brown* (1801) 6 Ves. Jun. 52 at 68 seems unsound.
192 cf. *Ayerst v Jenkins* (1873) 16 Eq. 275 at 283; *Trautwein v Richardson* [1946] Argus L.R. 129 at 134, per Dixon J.; *Caddy v McInnes* (1995) 131 A.L.R. 277.

shares. Milligan confessed her fraud to the Department of Social Security, with whom she made her peace, and thereafter was paid benefit on a lawful basis. Tinsley was prosecuted, convicted, and fined, and had to make some repayment to the Department.

14–117 LORD BROWNE-WILKINSON (with whom LORD JAUNCEY and LORD LOWRY agreed, but with whom LORD KEITH and LORD GOFF disagreed): My Lords, I agree with the speech of my noble and learned friend, Lord Goff of Chieveley, that the consequences of being a party to an illegal transaction cannot depend, as the majority in the Court of Appeal held, on such an imponderable factor as the extent to which the public conscience would be affronted by recognising rights created by illegal transactions. However, I have the misfortune to disagree with him as to the correct principle to be applied in a case where equitable property rights are acquired as a result of an illegal transaction.

14–118 Neither at law nor in equity will the court enforce an illegal contract which has been partially, but not fully, performed. However, it does not follow that all acts done under a partially performed contract are of no effect. In particular it is now clearly established that at law (as opposed to in equity), property in goods or land can pass under, or pursuant to, such a contract. If so, the rights of the owner of the legal title thereby acquired will be enforced, provided that the plaintiff can establish such title without pleading or leading evidence of the illegality. It is said that the property lies where it falls, even though legal title to the property was acquired as a result of the property passing under the illegal contract itself. I will first consider the modern authorities laying down the circumstances under which a legal proprietary interest acquired under an illegal transaction will be enforced by the courts. I will then consider whether the courts adopt a different attitude to equitable proprietary interests so acquired. . . .

14–119 From these authorities the following propositions emerge: (1) property in chattels and land can pass under a contract which is illegal and therefore would have been unenforceable as a contract; (2) a plaintiff can at law enforce property rights so acquired provided that he does not need to rely on the illegal contract for any purpose other than providing the basis of his claim to a property right; (3) it is irrelevant that the illegality of the underlying agreement was either pleaded or emerged in evidence: if the plaintiff has acquired legal title under the illegal contract that is enough.

14–120 I have stressed the common law rules as to the impact of illegality on the acquisition and enforcement of property rights because it is the appellant's contention that different principles apply in equity. In particular it is said that equity will not aid Miss Milligan to assert, establish or enforce an equitable, as opposed to a legal, proprietary interest since she was a party to the fraud on the DSS. The house was put in the name of Miss Tinsley alone (instead of joint names) to facilitate the fraud. Therefore, it is said, Miss Milligan does not come to equity with clean hands: consequently, equity will not aid her.

14–121 Most authorities to which we were referred deal with enforcing proprietary rights under a trust: I will deal with them in due course. But before turning to them, I must point out that if Miss Tinsley's argument is correct, the results would be far reaching and, I suggest, very surprising. There are many proprietary rights, apart from trusts, which are only enforceable in equity. For example, an agreement for a lease under which the tenant has entered is normally said to be as good as a lease, since under such an agreement equity treats the lease as having been granted and the "lessee" as having a proprietary interest enforceable against the whole world except the bona fide purchaser for value without notice. . . .

14–122 In my judgment to draw such distinctions between property rights enforceable at law and those which require the intervention of equity would be surprising. More than 100 years has elapsed since the administration of law and equity became fused. The reality of the matter is that, in 1993, English law has one single law of property made up of legal and equitable interests. Although for historical reasons legal estates and equitable estates have differing incidents, the person owning either type of estate has a right of property, a right in rem not merely a right in personam. If the law is that a party is entitled to enforce a property right acquired under an illegal transaction, in my judgment the same rule ought to apply to any property right so acquired, whether such right is legal or equitable.

14–123 In the present case, Miss Milligan claims under a resulting or implied trust. The court below have found, and it is not now disputed, that apart from the question of illegality Miss Milligan would have been entitled in equity to a half share in the house in accordance with the principles exemplified in *Gissing v Gissing*;[193]

[193] [1971] A.C. 886.

Grant v Edwards;[194] and *Lloyds Bank Plc v Rosset*.[195] The creation of such an equitable interest does not depend upon a contractual obligation but on a common intention acted upon by the parties to their detriment. It is a development of the old law of resulting trust under which, where two parties have provided the purchase money to buy a property which is conveyed into the name of one of them alone, the latter is presumed to hold the property on a resulting trust for both parties in shares proportionate to their contributions to the purchase price. In arguments, no distinction was drawn between strict resulting trusts and a *Gissing v Gissing* type of trust.

14–124 A presumption of resulting trust also arises in equity when A transfers personalty or money to B.[196] Before 1925, there was also a presumption of resulting trust when land was voluntarily transferred by A to B: it is arguable, however, that the position has been altered by the 1925 property legislation.[197] The presumption of a resulting trust is, in my view, crucial in considering the authorities. On that presumption (and on the contrary presumption of advancement) hinges the answer to the crucial question "does a plaintiff claiming under a resulting trust have to rely on the underlying illegality?" Where the presumption of resulting trust applies, the plaintiff does not have to rely on the illegality. If he proves that the property is vested in the defendant alone but that the plaintiff provided part of the purchase money, or voluntarily transferred the property to the defendant, the plaintiff establishes his claim under a resulting trust unless either the contrary presumption of advancement displaces the presumption of resulting trust or the defendant leads evidence to rebut the presumption of resulting trust. Therefore, in cases where the presumption of advancement does not apply, a plaintiff can establish his equitable interest in the property without relying in any way on the underlying illegal transaction. In this case Miss Milligan as defendant simply pleaded the common intention that the property should belong to both of them and that she contributed to the purchase price: she claimed that in consequence the property belonged to them equally. To the same effect was her evidence in chief. Therefore Miss Milligan was not forced to rely on the illegality to prove her equitable interest. Only in the reply and the course of Miss Milligan's cross-examination did such illegality emerge: it was Miss Tinsley who had to rely on that illegality.

14–125 Although the presumption of advancement does not directly arise for consideration in this case, it is important when considering the decided cases to understand its operation. On a transfer from a man to his wife, children or others to whom he stands in loco parentis, equity presumes an intention to make a gift. Therefore in such a case, unlike the case where the presumption of resulting trust applies, in order to establish any claim the plaintiff has himself to lead evidence sufficient to rebut the presumption of gift and in so doing will normally have to plead, and give evidence of, the underlying illegal purpose.

14–126 Against this background, I turn to consider the authorities dealing with the position in equity where A transferred property to B for an illegal purpose. The earlier authorities, primarily Lord Eldon, support the appellant's proposition that equity will not aid a plaintiff who has transferred property to another for an illegal purpose. . . .

14–127 [His Lordship reviewed various authorities, and then continued:] During the 19th century, there was originally a difference of view as to whether a transaction entered into for an illegal purpose would be enforced at law or in equity if the party had repented of his illegal purpose before it had been put into operation, i.e. the doctrine of *locus poenitentiae*. It was eventually recognised both at law and in equity that if the plaintiff had repented before the illegal purpose was carried through, he could recover his property.[198] The principle of *locus poenitentiae* is in my judgment irreconcilable with any rule that where property is transferred for an illegal purpose no equitable proprietary right exists. The equitable right, if any, must arise at the time at which the property was voluntarily transferred to the third party or purchased in the name of the third party. The existence of the equitable interest cannot depend upon events occurring after that date. Therefore if, under the principle of *locus poenitentiae*, the courts recognise that an equitable interest did arise out of the underlying transaction, the same must be true where the illegal purpose was

---

194 [1986] Ch. 638.
195 [1991] 1 A.C. 107.
196 See *Snell's Equity*, 29th edn (1990), pp.183–184; *Standing v Bowring* (1885) 31 Ch.D. 282 at 287, per Cotton L.J.; and *Dewar v Dewar* [1975] 1 W.L.R. 1532 at 1537.
197 See *Snell's Equity*, p.182.
198 See *Taylor v Bowers* (1876) 1 Q.B.D. 291; *Symes v Hughes* (1870) L.R. 9 Eq. 475.

carried through. The carrying out of the illegal purpose cannot, by itself, destroy the pre-existing equitable interest. The doctrine of *locus poenitentiae* therefore demonstrates that the effect of illegality is not to prevent a proprietary interest in equity from arising or to produce a forfeiture of such right: the effect is to render the equitable interest unenforceable in certain circumstances. The effect of illegality is not substantive but procedural. The question therefore is, "In what circumstances will equity refuse to enforce equitable rights which undoubtedly exist."

14–128 It is against this background that one has to assess the more recent law. Although in the cases decided during the last 100 years there are frequent references to Lord Eldon's wide principle, with one exception . . . none of the English decisions are decided by simply applying that principle. They are all cases where the unsuccessful party was held to be precluded from leading evidence of an illegal situation in order to rebut the presumption of advancement. Lord Eldon's rule would have provided a complete answer whether the transfer was made to a wife or child (where the presumption of advancement would apply) or to a stranger. Yet with one exception none of the cases in this century has been decided on that simple basis.

14–129 The majority of cases have been those in which the presumption of advancement applied: in those authorities the rule has been stated as being that a plaintiff cannot rely on evidence of his own illegality to rebut the presumption applicable in such cases that the plaintiff intended to make a gift of the property to the transferee. Thus in *Gascoigne v Gascoigne*;[199] *McEvoy v Belfast Banking Co Ltd*;[200] *Re Emery's Investments Trusts*;[201] *Chettiar v Chettiar*;[202] and *Tinker v Tinker*,[203] the crucial point was said to be the inability of the plaintiff to lead evidence rebutting the presumption of advancement. In each case the plaintiff was claiming to recover property voluntarily transferred to, or purchased in the name of, a wife or child, for an illegal purpose. Although reference was made to Lord Eldon's principle, none of those cases was decided on the simple ground (if it were good law) that equity would not in any circumstances enforce a resulting trust in such circumstances. On the contrary in each case the rule was stated to be that the plaintiff could not recover because he had to rely on the illegality to rebut the presumption of advancement.

14–130 In my judgment, the explanation for this departure from Lord Eldon's absolute rule is that the fusion of law and equity has led the courts to adopt a single rule (applicable both at law and in equity) as to the circumstances in which the court will enforce property interests acquired in pursuance of an illegal transaction, viz., the *Bowmakers* rule.[204] A party to an illegality can recover by virtue of a legal or equitable property interest if, but only if, he can establish his title without relying on his own illegality. In cases where the presumption of advancement applies, the plaintiff is faced with the presumption of gift and therefore cannot claim under a resulting trust unless and until he has rebutted that presumption of gift: for those purposes the plaintiff does have to rely on the underlying illegality and therefore fails.

14–131 The position is well illustrated by two decisions in the Privy Council [viz. *Singh v Ali*[205] and *Chettiar v Chettiar*[206]]. . . . In my judgment these two cases show that the Privy Council was applying exactly the same principle in both cases although in one case the plaintiff's claim rested on a legal title and in the other on an equitable title. The claim based on the equitable title did not fail simply because the plaintiff was a party to the illegal transaction; it only failed because the plaintiff was bound to disclose and rely upon his own illegal purpose in order to rebut the presumption of advancement. The Privy Council was plainly treating the principle applicable both at law and in equity as being that a man can recover property provided that he is not forced to rely on his own illegality.

14–132 I therefore reach the conclusion that, although there is no case overruling the wide principle stated by Lord Eldon, as the law has developed the equitable principle has become elided into the common law rule.

---

199 [1918] 1 K.B. 223.
200 [1934] N.I. 67.
201 [1959] Ch. 410.
202 [1962] A.C. 294.
203 [1970] P. 136 at 141, 142.
204 [1945] K.B. 65.
205 [1960] A.C. 167.
206 [1962] A.C. 294.

In my judgment the time has come to decide clearly that the rule is the same whether a plaintiff founds himself on a legal or equitable title: he is entitled to recover if he is not forced to plead or rely on the illegality, even if it emerges that the title on which he relied was acquired in the course of carrying through an illegal transaction.

As applied in the present case, that principle would operate as follows. Miss Milligan established a resulting trust by showing that she had contributed to the purchase price of the house and that there was common understanding between her and Miss Tinsley that they owned the house equally. She had no need to allege or prove why the house was conveyed into the name of Miss Tinsley alone, since that fact was irrelevant to her claim: it was enough to show that the house was in fact vested in Miss Tinsley alone. The illegality only emerged at all because Miss Tinsley sought to raise it. Having proved these facts, Miss Milligan had raised a presumption of resulting trust. There was no evidence to rebut that presumption. Therefore Miss Milligan should succeed. This is exactly the process of reasoning adopted by the Ontario Court of Appeal in *Gorog v Kiss*[207] which in my judgment was rightly decided. **14–133**

TRIBE v TRIBE

Court of Appeal [1996] Ch. 107; [1995] 3 W.L.R. 913; [1995] 4 All E.R. 237

Fearful of dilapidations claims against him as the tenant of two properties, the claimant transferred 459 out of 500 shares in the family company that operated out of the properties to one of his four children. The transfer was purportedly made in exchange for a payment of £78,030, but this payment was never made, nor was it ever intended that it should be. The presumption of advancement was allowed to be rebutted by the claimant's evidence that the purpose of the transfer was to deceive his creditors by creating the appearance that he no longer owned the shares. This illegal purpose had never been carried into effect because, without disclosing the transfer, the claimant surrendered one lease for value and purchased the reversion on the other lease. **14–134**

MILLETT L.J. (with whom NOURSE and OTTON L.JJ. agreed, reviewed a line of authorities culminating with *Tinsley v Milligan*, and then continued): Prior to *Tinsley v Milligan* no transferor had ever succeeded in recovering his property by enforcing a resulting trust where he had transferred the property for an illegal purpose and that purpose had been carried out. In *Re Great Berlin Steamboat Co*[208] the transferor failed to recover for this very reason; in other cases where the transferor has succeeded he did so only because the illegal purpose had not been carried out. **14–135**

In *Tinsley v Milligan* the parties, who both contributed to the purchase of a house, arranged for the conveyance to be taken in the name of the appellant alone but on the understanding that it was to belong to them jointly. The purpose of this arrangement was to enable the respondent to perpetrate frauds on the Department of Social Security, and over a number of years the respondent, with the connivance of the appellant, made false claims for benefit. Despite this the respondent was allowed to recover. **14–136**

In his dissenting speech Lord Goff refused to draw any distinction between cases where the presumption of advancement applied and cases in which the plaintiff could rely on a resulting trust. From the authorities he derived a single principle: that if one party puts property in the name of another for a fraudulent or illegal purpose neither law nor equity will allow him to recover the property. Even if he can establish a resulting trust in his favour he cannot enforce it. Given Lord Goff's opinion that there was but one principle in play, it was natural for him to describe the doctrine of the *locus poenitentiae* as an exception to that principle. Since the respondent could not bring herself within the exception, he would have allowed the appeal. **14–137**

This was not, however, the view of the majority. Lord Browne-Wilkinson expressly held that the rule was the same whether the plaintiff founded himself on a legal or an equitable title: he was entitled to succeed if he was not forced to rely on his own illegality, even if it emerged that the title on which he relied was acquired in the course of carrying through an illegal transaction. The respondent had established a resulting trust by showing that she had contributed to the purchase price and that there was a common understanding between her and the appellant that they should own the house equally. She had no need to **14–138**

[207] (1977) 78 D.L.R. (3d) 690.
[208] (1884) 26 Ch.D. 616.

allege or prove why she had allowed the house to be conveyed into the sole name of the appellant, since that fact was irrelevant to her claim.

14–139 The necessary consequence of this is that where he can rely on a resulting trust the transferor will normally be able to recover his property if the illegal purpose has not been carried out. In *Tinsley v Milligan* she recovered even though the illegal purpose had been carried out. It does not, however, follow that the transferor will invariably succeed in such circumstances, so that the presence or absence of a *locus poenitentiae* is irrelevant where the transfer gives rise to a resulting trust. A resulting trust, like the presumption of advancement, rests on a presumption which is rebuttable by evidence.[209] The transferor does not need to allege or prove the purpose for which property was transferred into the name of the transferee; in equity he can rely on the presumption that no gift was intended. But the transferee cannot be prevented from rebutting the presumption by leading evidence of the transferor's subsequent conduct to show that it was inconsistent with any intention to retain a beneficial interest. Suppose, for example, that a man transfers property to his nephew in order to conceal it from his creditors, and suppose that he afterwards settles with his creditors on the footing that he has no interest in the property. Is it seriously suggested that he can recover the property? I think not. The transferor's own conduct would be inconsistent with the retention of any beneficial interest in the property. I can see no reason why the nephew should not give evidence of the transferor's dealings with his creditors to rebut the presumption of a resulting trust and show that a gift was intended. He would not be relying on any illegal arrangement but implicitly denying it. The transferor would have to give positive evidence of his intention to retain a beneficial interest and dishonestly conceal it from his creditors, evidence which he would not be allowed to give once the illegal purpose had been carried out.

14–140 This analysis is not, in my view, inconsistent with a passage in Lord Browne-Wilkinson's speech where he said:[210]

> "The equitable right, if any, must arise at the time at which the property was voluntarily transferred to the third party or purchased in the name of the third party. The existence of the equitable interest cannot depend upon events occurring after that date. Therefore if, under the principle of *locus poenitentiae*, the courts recognise that an equitable interest did arise out of the underlying transaction, the same must be true where the illegal purpose was carried through. The carrying out of the illegal purpose cannot, by itself, destroy the pre-existing equitable interest."

14–141 But it does not follow that subsequent conduct is necessarily irrelevant. Where the existence of an equitable interest depends upon a rebuttable presumption or inference of the transferor's intention, evidence may be given of his subsequent conduct in order to rebut the presumption or inference which would otherwise be drawn.

14–142 *Tinsley v Milligan* is, in my opinion, not authority for the proposition that a party who transfers property for an illegal purpose in circumstances which give rise to a resulting trust can invariably enforce the trust and recover the property even though the illegal purpose has been carried into effect. I do not accept the suggestion that cases such as *Re Great Berlin Steamboat Co* have been impliedly overruled or that the dicta in the many cases, including *Taylor v Bowers*[211] and *Singh v Ali*,[212] indicating that the result would have been otherwise if the illegal purpose had or had not been carried out, must be taken to have been overruled.

14–143 The question in the present case is the converse: whether the transferor can rebut the presumption of advancement by giving evidence of his illegal purpose so long as the illegal purpose has not been carried into effect. . . .

14–144 There is no modern case in which restitution has been denied in circumstances comparable to those of the present case where the illegal purpose has not been carried out. In *Tinsley v Milligan* Lord Browne-Wilkinson expressly recognised the availability of the doctrine of the *locus poenitentiae* in a restitutionary

209 See *Standing v Bowring* (1885) 31 Ch.D. 282 at 287.
210 [1994] 1 A.C. 340 at 374.
211 (1876) 1 Q.B.D. 291.
212 [1960] A.C. 167.

context, and cited *Taylor v Bowers* as well as *Symes v Hughes*[213] without disapproval. In my opinion the weight of the authorities supports the view that a person who seeks to recover property transferred by him for an illegal purpose can lead evidence of his dishonest intention whenever it is necessary for him to do so provided that he has withdrawn from the transaction before the illegal purpose has been carried out. It is not necessary if he can rely on an express or resulting trust in his favour; but it is necessary (i) if he brings an action at law and (ii) if he brings proceedings in equity and needs to rebut the presumption of advancement. The availability of the *locus poenitentiae* is well documented in the former case. I would not willingly adopt a rule which differentiated between the rule of the common law and that of equity in a restitutionary context. . . .

At heart the question for decision in the present case is one of legal policy. The primary rule which precludes the court from lending its assistance to a man who founds his cause of action on an illegal or immoral act often leads to a denial of justice. The justification for this is that the rule is not a principle of justice but a principle of policy.[214] The doctrine of the *locus poenitentiae* is an exception which operates to mitigate the harshness of the primary rule. It enables the court to do justice between the parties even though, in order to do so, it must allow a plaintiff to give evidence of his own dishonest intent. But he must have withdrawn from the transaction while his dishonesty still lay in intention only. The law draws the line once the intention has been wholly or partly carried into effect. . . . **14–145**

In my opinion the following propositions represent the present state of the law. **14–146**

(1) Title to property passes both at law and in equity even if the transfer is made for an illegal purpose. The fact that title has passed to the transferee does not preclude the transferor from bringing an action for restitution.

(2) The transferor's action will fail if it would be illegal for him to retain any interest in the property.

(3) Subject to (2) the transferor can recover the property if he can do so without relying on the illegal purpose. This will normally be the case where the property was transferred without consideration in circumstances where the transferor can rely on an express declaration of trust or a resulting trust in his favour.

(4) It will almost invariably be so where the illegal purpose has not been carried out. It may be otherwise where the illegal purpose has been carried out and the transferee can rely on the transferor's conduct as inconsistent with his retention of a beneficial interest.

(5) The transferor can lead evidence of the illegal purpose whenever it is necessary for him to do so provided that he has withdrawn from the transaction before the illegal purpose has been wholly or partly carried into effect. It will be necessary for him to do so (i) if he brings an action at law or (ii) if he brings proceedings in equity and needs to rebut the presumption of advancement.

(6) The only way in which a man can protect his property from his creditors is by divesting himself of all beneficial interest in it. Evidence that he transferred the property in order to protect it from his creditors, therefore, does nothing by itself to rebut the presumption of advancement; it reinforces it. To rebut the presumption it is necessary to show that he intended to retain a beneficial interest and conceal it from his creditors.

(7) The court should not conclude that this was his intention without compelling circumstantial evidence to this effect. The identity of the transferee and the circumstances in which the transfer was made would be highly relevant. It is unlikely that the court would reach such a conclusion where the transfer was made in the absence of an imminent and perceived threat from known creditors.

. . . It is impossible to reconcile all the authorities on the circumstances in which a party to an illegal contract is permitted to withdraw from it. At one time he was allowed to withdraw so long as the contract had not been completely performed but later it was held that recovery was barred once it had been partly **14–147**

[213] (1870) L.R. 9 Eq. 475.

[214] See the much-quoted statement of Lord Mansfield C.J. in *Holman v Johnson* (1775) 1 Cowp. 341 at 343.

> performed.[215] It is clear that he must withdraw voluntarily, and that it is not sufficient that he is forced to do so because his plan has been discovered. In *Bigos v Bousted*[216] this was (perhaps dubiously) extended to prevent withdrawal where the scheme has been frustrated by the refusal of the other party to carry out his part.
>
> 14–148 . . . I would hold that genuine repentance is not required. Justice is not a reward for merit; restitution should not be confined to the penitent. I would also hold that voluntary withdrawal from an illegal transaction when it has ceased to be needed is sufficient. It is true that this is not necessary to encourage withdrawal, but a rule to the opposite effect could lead to bizarre results. Suppose, for example, that in *Bigos v Bousted* exchange control had been abolished before the foreign currency was made available: it is absurd to suppose that the plaintiff should have been denied restitution.

iv. Attempts by a Transferor to Deprive his Creditors

14–149 The foregoing discussion of the effect of illegality on resulting trust principles is premised on the assumption that the transfer of legal title between the parties is valid. Note, however, that some statutes invalidate transfers of legal title if they are undertaken with a view to defeating creditors.[217]

14–150 For example, the Insolvency Act 1986 ss.339–342 and 423–425 catch many dispositions in favour of third parties. Sections 339 and 341 only apply if the settlor is adjudged bankrupt (and apply only in favour of the trustee in bankruptcy) and only if the transfer was not undertaken more than five years before the bankruptcy, but no purposive intent to defraud creditors is required: merely entering into a transaction at an undervalue suffices.[218] Valuation of the transaction (e.g. assignment of a life policy) to see if there was an undervalue can take account of subsequent events (e.g. where the assignment was made one week after the assignor learned of the policy-holder's imminent death which followed two months later).[219]

14–151 The basic period is within two years of presentation of the bankruptcy petition but is extended to five years if the transferor was insolvent, as defined in s.341(3), at the time of the transfer or became so as a result of the transfer. It is rebuttably presumed that such insolvency existed if the transfer benefited "associates", including relatives of the bankrupt or spouse, as defined in s.435.

14–152 Section 423 operates independently of any bankruptcy of the transferor and covers all transfers which are made "for the purpose (a) of putting assets beyond the reach of a person who is making, or may at some time make, a claim against him, or (b) of otherwise prejudicing the interests of such a person in relation to the claim which he is making or may make." This purpose needs to be a substantial purpose (e.g. a co-equal purpose) but not a dominant purpose,[220] and in the words of Sales J.:[221]

---

[215] See *Kearley v Thompson* (1890) 24 Q.B.D. 742.

[216] [1951] 1 All E.R. 92.

[217] These statutory sections may also catch transfers into settlements, as in e.g. *Re Butterworth* (1882) 19 Ch.D. 588; *Midland Bank Plc v Wyatt* [1995] 1 F.L.R. 696; *Hill v Spread Trustee Co Ltd* [2007] 1 W.L.R. 2404.

[218] *Agricultural Mortgage Corp v Woodward* [1996] 1 F.L.R. 226.

[219] *Reid v Ramlort Ltd* [2003] 1 B.C.L.C. 499.

[220] *IRC v Hashmi* [2002] W.T.L.R. 1027. There is no limitation period for a claim under s.423 but if an action is brought 20 or 30 years after the relevant transaction it could be attacked under the right to a fair hearing in art.6 of the Human Rights Convention.

[221] *4Eng Ltd v Harper* [2010] 1 B.C.L.C. 176 at [9].

> "A claim under s.423 is a claim for some appropriate form of restorative remedy, to restore property to the transferor for the benefit of creditors, who may then seek to execute against that property in respect of obligations owed by the transferor to them. In an appropriate case, an order might be made to require the transferee to pay sums or transfer property direct to the creditors, if the position in relation to execution is clear and any further costs associated with execution ought to be avoided. But often the appropriate order will be for the transferee to pay sums or transfer property back to the transferor, leaving the distribution of those sums or property as between the creditors of the transferor to be governed by the general law. This may be particularly important if the transferor is bankrupt or in liquidation (or about to become bankrupt or go into liquidation) and has a range of creditors not all of whom are before the court on the application made under s.423."

Section 423 clearly extends to "present" creditors (with existing enforceable claims) and "subsequent" creditors (identifiable persons who have claims that may reasonably be anticipated to mature into existing enforceable claims). Moreover a victim within s.423(5) need not be a person who the debtor has in mind, either specifically or as a member of a class, for the purpose of satisfying the purpose requirement of s.423(3).[222] The burden of proving the transferor's purpose is on the applicant while the burden of proving exemption under s.425(2) is on the transferee who seeks exemption.[223] Proving the settlor's purpose is a question of fact and the surrounding circumstances may be capable of establishing a rebuttable presumption that the requisite purpose was present, e.g. where the settlor settles virtually all his assets, or settles so much of his assets that his liabilities then exceed what he has left, or makes the settlement secretly and hastily.[224] **14–153**

Under s.37 of the Matrimonial Causes Act 1973 the Family Division has jurisdiction to set aside dispositions made with the intention of defeating a spouse's claim to financial relief.[225] Under s.37(5) such an intention is presumed for a disposition made within three years of the application to the court if it actually has the effect of defeating such claim. **14–154**

Under the Inheritance (Provision for Family and Dependants) Act 1975 the court has power to make various orders in relation to dispositions effected by a deceased, other than for full valuable consideration, and made with the intention of defeating applications for financial provision.[226] Section 10 applies to dispositions made less than six years before the deceased's death but not including appointments made in exercise of a special power of appointment. **14–155**

INSOLVENCY ACT 1986 SECTIONS 339, 341–342, AND 423–425

339. Transactions at an Undervalue

(1) Subject as follows in this section and sections 341 and 342, where an individual is adjudged bankrupt and he has at a relevant time (defined in section 341) entered into a transaction with any person at an undervalue, the trustee of the bankrupt's estate may apply to the court for an order under this section. **14–156**

---

[222] *Hill v Spread Trustee Co Ltd* [2007] 1 W.L.R. 2404.

[223] *Random House UK Ltd v Allason* [2008] EWHC 2854 (Ch).

[224] *Re Wise* (1886) 17 Q.B.D. 290; *Freeman v Pope* (1870) 5 Ch. App.538; *Re Sinclair* (1884) 26 Ch.D. 319; *Lloyds Bank Ltd v Marcan* [1974] 1 W.L.R. 370; *Agricultural Mortgage Corp v Woodward* [1995] 1 B.C.L.C. 1.

[225] e.g. *Kemmis v Kemmis* [1988] 1 W.L.R. 1307; *Sherry v Sherry* [1991] 1 F.L.R. 307; but a notice to quit given to a landlord by a joint tenant of a periodic tenancy is not a disposition of any property, such notice merely signifying the tenant was not willing to consent to the continuation of the tenancy beyond the date when if would otherwise expire: *Newlon Housing Trust v Alsulaimen* [1999] 1 A.C. 813.

[226] e.g. *Re Dawkins* [1986] 2 F.L.R. 360.

(2) The court shall, on such an application, make such order as it thinks fit for restoring the position to what it would have been if that individual had not entered into that transaction.

(3) For the purposes of this section and sections 341 and 342, an individual enters into a transaction with a person at an undervalue if—

(a) he makes a gift to that person or he otherwise enters into a transaction with that person on terms that provide for him to receive no consideration,
(b) he enters into a transaction with that person in consideration of marriage, or
(c) he enters into a transaction with that person for a consideration the value of which, in money or money's worth, is significantly less than the value, in money or money's worth, of the consideration provided by the individual.

341. "Relevant Time" under Sections 339, 340

14–157 (1) Subject as follows, the time at which an individual enters into a transaction at an undervalue . . . is a relevant time if the transaction is entered into or the preference given—

(a) in the case of a transaction at an undervalue at a time in the period of 5 years ending with the day of the presentation of the bankruptcy petition on which the individual is adjudged bankrupt . . .

(2) Where an individual enters into a transaction at an undervalue . . . at a time mentioned in paragraph (a) . . . of subsection (1) (not being, in the case of a transaction at an undervalue, a time less than 2 years before the end of the period mentioned in paragraph (a)), that time is not a relevant time for the purposes of section 339 . . . unless the individual—

(a) is insolvent at that time, or
(b) becomes insolvent in consequence of the transaction . . . but the requirements of this subsection are presumed to be satisfied, unless the contrary is shown, in relation to any transaction at an undervalue which is entered into by an individual with a person who is an associate of his (otherwise than by reason only of being his employee).

(3) For the purposes of subsection (2), an individual is insolvent if—

(a) he is unable to pay his debts as they fall due, or
(b) the value of his assets is less than the amount of his liabilities, taking into account his contingent and prospective liabilities.

342. Orders under Sections 339, 340

14–158 . . . (2) An order under section 339 or 340 may affect the property of, or impose any obligation on, any person whether or not he is the person with whom the individual in question entered into the transaction . . . but such an order—

(a) shall not prejudice any interest in property which was acquired from a person other than that individual and was acquired in good faith and for value or prejudice any interest deriving from such an interest, and
(b) shall not require a person who received a benefit from the transaction . . . in good faith and for value to pay a sum to the trustee of the bankrupt's estate, except where he was a party to the transaction . . .

(2A)[227] Where a person has acquired an interest in property from a person other than the individual in question, or has received a benefit from the transaction . . . and at the time of that acquisition or receipt—

[227] These provisions came into force on July 26, 1994 by virtue of Insolvency (No.2) Act 1994 s.6 to remove the previous difficulties for purchasers of property that had been given away in the previous five years and who could be adversely affected merely because they had notice of such a transaction at an undervalue. A purchaser will now be protected if his conveyancing searches do not reveal any bankruptcy proceedings being brought against the donor.

(a) he had notice of the relevant surrounding circumstances and of the relevant proceedings, or
(b) he was an associate of, or was connected with, either the individual in question or the person with whom that individual entered into that transaction . . .

then, unless the contrary is shown, it shall be presumed for the purposes of para.(a) or para.(b) of subsection (2) that the interest was acquired or the benefit was received otherwise than in good faith.

(4) For the purposes of subsection (2A)(a), the relevant surrounding circumstances are

(a) the fact that the individual in question entered into the transaction at an undervalue; or
(b) . . .

(5) For the purposes of subsection (2A)(a), a person has notice of the relevant proceedings if he has notice—

(a) of the fact that the petition on which the individual in question is adjudicated bankrupt has been presented; or
(b) of the fact that the individual in question has been adjudged bankrupt.

423. Transactions Defrauding Creditors

(1) This section relates to transactions entered into at an undervalue; and a person[228] enters into such a transaction with another person if— **14–159**

(a) he makes a gift to the other person or he otherwise enters into a transaction with the other on terms that provide for him to receive no consideration;
(b) he enters into a transaction with the other in consideration of marriage; or
(c) he enters into a transaction with the other for a consideration the value of which, in money or money's worth, is significantly less than the value, in money or money's worth, of the consideration provided by himself.

(2) Where a person has entered into such a transaction, the court may, if satisfied under the next subsection, make such order as it thinks fit[229] for—

(a) restoring the position to what it would have been if the transaction had not been entered into, and
(b) protecting the interests of persons who are victims of the transaction.

(3) In the case of a person entering into such a transaction, an order shall only be made if the court is satisfied that it was entered into by him for the purpose—

(a) of putting assets beyond the reach of a person who is making, or may at some time make, a claim against him, or
(b) of otherwise prejudicing the interests of such a person in relation to the claim which he is making or may make. . . .

(5) In relation to a transaction at an undervalue, references here and below to a victim of the transaction are to a person who is, or is capable of being, prejudiced by it; and in the following two sections the person entering into the transaction is referred to as "the debtor."

424. Those who May Apply for an Order under Section 423

(1) An application for an order under section 423 shall not be made in relation to a transaction except— **14–160**

---

228 The section has extraterritorial effect: *Re Paramount Airways* [1993] Ch. 223. See also Enterprise Act 2002 s.254, and note that by s.262 thereof a trustee in bankruptcy cannot bring an action under ss.339, 340 or 423 without the consent of the creditors' committee or of the court.

229 Section 425(1) sets out specific orders "without prejudice to the generality of s.423."

(a) in a case where the debtor has been adjudged bankrupt or is a body corporate which is being wound up or in relation to which an administration order is in force, by the official receiver, by the trustee of the bankrupt's estate or the liquidator or administrator of the body corporate or (with the leave of the court) by a victim of the transaction . . . .

(c) in any other case, by a victim of the transaction.

(2) An application made under any of the paragraphs of subsection (1) is to be treated as made on behalf of every victim of the transaction.

425. Provision which May be Made by Order under Section 423

14–161 . . . (2) An order under section 423 may affect the property of, or impose any obligation on, any person whether or not he is the person with whom the debtor entered into the transaction; but such an order—

(a) shall not prejudice any interest in property which was acquired from a person other than the debtor and was acquired in good faith, for value and without notice[230] of the relevant circumstances, or prejudice any interest deriving from such an interest, and

(b) shall not require a person who received a benefit from the transaction in good faith, for value and without notice of the relevant circumstances to pay any sum unless he was a party to the transaction.

(3) For the purposes of this section the relevant circumstances in relation to a transaction are the circumstances by virtue of which an order under section 423 may be made in respect of the transaction.

5. Why Are Resulting Trusts Imposed?

14–162 There are two main schools of thought. On one view, resulting trusts are imposed in order to give effect to the transferor's intention to create a trust for himself;[231] on another view, they are imposed in order to reverse the transferee's unjust enrichment at the transferor's expense.[232] Claims in unjust enrichment arise under English law when a defendant is enriched at the expense of a claimant in circumstances which make his enrichment unjust,[233] the question whether his enrichment is relevantly unjust being governed by "the binding authority of previous decisions", so that the courts do not have "a discretionary power to order repayment whenever it seems in the circumstance of the particular case just and

---

230 Notice will include constructive notice: *Lloyds Bank Ltd v Marcan* [1973] 1 W.L.R. 339 at 345.

231 C.E.F. Rickett, "The Classification of Trusts" (1999) 18 N.Z Law Rev. 305; C.E.F. Rickett and R. Grantham, "Resulting Trusts: A Rather Limited Doctrine" in P. Birks and F.D. Rose (eds), *Restitution and Equity* (2000). Swadling distinguishes "presumed resulting trusts" which he takes to respond to the transferor's intention, from "automatic resulting trusts", which he now regards as inexplicable: W.J. Swadling, "A New Role for Resulting Trusts?" (1996) 16 L.S. 110; "Explaining Resulting Trusts" (2008) 124 L.Q.R. 72. Mee argues that "automatic resulting trusts" respond to the transferor's intention to create a trust for *somebody*, the law specifying that the beneficiary should be the transferor himself when the transferor fails to identify anyone else: J. Mee, " 'Automatic' Resulting Trusts: Retention, Restitution, or Reposing Trust?" in C. Mitchell (ed.) *Constructive and Resulting Trusts* (2010); cf. F.W. Maitland *Equity* (1936) p.77: "I have made A a trustee for somebody, and a trustee he must be—if for no one else then for me or my representatives".

232 P. Birks, "Restitution and Resulting Trusts" in S. Goldstein (ed.), *Equity and Contemporary Legal Developments* (1992) 361; R. Chambers, *Resulting Trusts* (1997); R. Chambers, "Resulting Trusts in Canada" (2000) 38 Alberta L.R. 378, reprinted (2002) 16 Tru. L.I. 104 and 138; R. Chambers, "Resulting Trusts" in A. Burrows and Lord Rodger (eds), *Mapping the Law: Essays in Memory of Peter Birks* (2006).

233 *Banque Financière de la Cité v Parc (Battersea) Ltd* [1999] 1 A.C. 221 at 227 and 234; *Kleinwort Benson Ltd v Lincoln CC* [1999] 2 A.C. 349 at 373 and 407–408; *Cressman v Coys of Kensington (Sales) Ltd* [2004] 1 W.L.R. 2775 at [22]; *Niru Battery Manufacturing Co v Milestone Trading Ltd (No.2)* [2004] 1 All E.R. (Comm.) 289 at [28] and [41]; *Sempra Metals Ltd v IRC* [2008] 1 A.C. 561 at [23].

equitable to do so".[234] In *Westdeutsche Landesbank Girozentrale v Islington LBC*,[235] parts of which are reproduced below, Lord Browne-Wilkinson rejected the argument that resulting trusts respond to unjust enrichment, and favoured the view that they respond to the transferor's intention to create a trust;[236] in *Air Jamaica Ltd v Charlton*[237] and *Twinsectra Ltd v Yardley*[238] Lord Millett took the opposite view.

14–163 Viewed from the perspective of principle, the main objection to the theory that resulting trusts respond to the transferor's intention to create a trust for himself is that it cannot explain cases where resulting trusts have been imposed despite clear evidence that the transferor never thought about it, or else formed a clear intention that he did not want to acquire a new equitable beneficial interest in the property, as in *Vandervell v IRC*,[239] for example. Nor can it explain why an unwritten intention to create a trust of land takes effect as a resulting trust when it does not take effect as an express trust because of non-compliance with the LPA 1925 s.53(1)(c); an example is *Hodgson v Marks*.[240]

14–164 The main objection to the theory that resulting trusts respond to unjust enrichment is that it proves too much. Pushed to its logical limits, it suggests that a resulting trust should arise whenever a claimant transfers property to a defendant, and his intention to benefit the defendant is vitiated by mistake or undue influence, or is conditional on the happening of a future event which subsequently fails to materialise. In principle, however, it seems very doubtful that claimants in these various situations should all be given proprietary rights and thus priority over the defendant's unsecured creditors, rather than a personal restitutionary remedy or a right to rescind the transfer.[241] It certainly might seem most surprising that a claimant who pays money to a defendant under a standard unsecured loan agreement should be given a proprietary remedy when the defendant defaults, although Professor Chambers would argue that even here we should distinguish between cases where the basis for the claimant's payment fails at some time after receipt of the benefit, and cases where it fails immediately, so that there is no moment at which the defendant has held the relevant asset free of any claim.[242] If that is right, then it suggests that *Sinclair v Brougham*,[243] overruled by the House of Lords in *Westdeutsche*, may have been correctly decided after all, depending on whether the ultra vires depositors' claim to recover their money on the ground of failure of consideration was founded on the assertion that the building society had failed to repay their money, or on the assertion that their contracts with the building society had been void from the beginning.[244]

---

234 *Kleinwort Benson Ltd v Birmingham CC* [1996] 4 All E.R. 733 at 737. See too *Sempra Metals Ltd v IRC* [2008] 1 A.C. 561 at [46]. For an excellent introductory account of the circumstances which render a defendant's enrichment unjust, see A. Burrows *The Law of Restitution* 2nd edn (2002), Chs 3–13.

235 [1996] A.C. 669.

236 See paras 14–165 ff.

237 [1999] 1 W.L.R. 1399.

238 [2000] A.C. 164.

239 [1967] 2 A.C. 29. As noted by J. Penner, "Resulting Trusts and Unjust Enrichment: Three Controversies" in C. Mitchell (ed.), *Constructive and Resulting Trusts* (2010), a number of shared homes cases are also like this, because resulting trusts were imposed although the court held on the facts that the legal owner had had no intention to create a trust in his cohabitant's favour: *Springette v Defoe* [1992] 2 F.C.R. 561 at 567–567; *Midland Bank Plc v Cooke* [1995] 4 All E.R. 562 at 568–570; *Oxley v Hiscock* [2004] 2 F.L.R. 669 at 676. (These cases pre-date *Stack v Dowden* [2007] 2 A.C. 432, where it was said that resulting trust reasoning should no longer generally be used in this context: see para.14–93.)

240 [1971] Ch. 892.

241 Lord Millett, "Restitution and Constructive Trusts" (1998) 114 L.Q.R. 399, p.416; Lord Millett, "The Law of Restitution: Taking Stock" (1999) 14 Amicus Curiae 1, pp. 7–8.

242 R. Chambers, *Resulting Trusts* (1997), pp. 110 and 155–170. See too P. Birks, *Unjust Enrichment* (2003), pp.162–178; P. Birks, "Retrieving Tied Money" in W. Swadling (ed.), *The Quistclose Trust: Critical Essays* (2004), pp.130–138.

243 [1914] A.C. 398.

244 Another example of immediate failure of basis is arguably provided by *Nesté Oy v Lloyds Bank Plc* [1983] 2 Lloyd's Rep.658, where to the knowledge of the payee no performance at all could have taken place under the contract for which the payment formed the consideration. See too *Re Ames' Settlement* [1946] Ch. 217; *Criterion Properties Plc v Stratford* [2004] 1 W.L.R. 1846 at [4]; *Re Farepak Food & Gifts Ltd* [2007] 2 B.C.L.C. 1, further proceedings [2009] EWHC 2580 (Ch).

WESTDEUTSCHE LANDESBANK GIROZENTRALE v ISLINGTON LBC

House of Lords [1996] A.C. 669; [1996] 2 W.L.R. 802; [1996] 2 All E.R. 961

14–165 The appellant bank sued the respondent council to recover £1,145,525 paid under an interest rate swap agreement that was void because beyond the powers of the council. The Court of Appeal upheld the judge's decision that the bank was entitled to recover the money on the ground that the council had been unjustly enriched at the bank's expense, with compound interest. The council appealed against the award of compound interest, arguing that the court could only have had jurisdiction to make such an interest award if the money had been held on trust for the bank, and arguing too that no trust had arisen in the bank's favour. The House of Lords unanimously held that although the bank had a personal claim to recover the money in a common law action for money had and received, it had no proprietary equitable claim; by a 3:2 majority, it followed that only simple interest was payable (Lords Goff and Woolf dissenting on the basis that compound interest should be awarded by way of an equitable remedy in aid of the common law, so that the bank could have restitution of the user value of its money[245]).

14–166 LORD BROWNE-WILKINSON (with whom LORD SLYNN and LORD LLOYD agreed, but with whom LORD GOFF and LORD WOOLF disagreed, reviewed the courts' jurisdiction to make awards of compound interest, and then continued):

Was there a Trust? The Argument for the Bank in Outline

14–167 The bank submitted that, since the contract was void, title did not pass at the date of payment either at law or in equity. The legal title of the bank was extinguished as soon as the money was paid into the mixed account, whereupon the legal title became vested in the local authority. But, it was argued, this did not affect the equitable interest, which remained vested in the bank (the retention of title point). It was submitted that whenever the legal interest in property is vested in one person and the equitable interest in another, the owner of the legal interest holds it on trust for the owner of the equitable title: "the separation of the legal from the equitable interest necessarily imports a trust." For this latter proposition (the separation of title point) the bank, of course, relies on *Sinclair v Brougham*[246] and *Chase Manhattan Bank NA v Israel-British Bank (London) Ltd.*[247]

14–168 The generality of these submissions was narrowed by submitting that the trust which arose in this case was a resulting trust "not of an active character" (see *Sinclair v Brougham*,[248] per Viscount Haldane L.C.). This submission was reinforced, after completion of the oral argument, by sending to your Lordships Professor Peter Birks' paper "Restitution and Resulting Trusts".[249] Unfortunately your Lordships have not had the advantage of any submissions from the local authority on this paper, but an article by William Swadling "A New Role for Resulting Trusts?"[250] puts forward counter-arguments which I have found persuasive. . . .

The Breadth of the Submission

14–169 Although the actual question in issue on the appeal is a narrow one, on the arguments presented it is necessary to consider fundamental principles of trust law. Does the recipient of money under a contract subsequently found to be void for mistake or as being ultra vires hold the moneys received on trust even where he had no knowledge at any relevant time that the contract was void? If he does hold on trust, such trust must arise at the date of receipt or, at the latest, at the date the legal title of the payer is extinguished by mixing moneys in a bank account: in the present case it does not matter at which of those dates the legal title was extinguished. If there is a trust two consequences follow: (a) the recipient will be personally

[245] See now *Sempra Metals Ltd v IRC* [2008] A.C. 561, which holds that claims in unjust enrichment do lie to recover the user value of money as compound interest.
[246] [1914] A.C. 398.
[247] [1981] Ch. 105.
[248] [1914] A.C. 398 at 421.
[249] Published in S. Goldstein (ed.), *Equity and Contemporary Legal Developments* (1992).
[250] (1996) 16 L.S. 110.

liable, regardless of fault, for any subsequent payment away of the moneys to third parties even though, at the date of such payment, the "trustee" was still ignorant of the existence of any trust;[251] (b) as from the date of the establishment of the trust (i.e. receipt or mixing of the moneys by the "trustee") the original payer will have an equitable proprietary interest in the moneys so long as they are traceable into whomsoever's hands they come other than a purchaser for value of the legal interest without notice. Therefore, although in the present case the only question directly in issue is the personal liability of the local authority as a trustee, it is not possible to hold the local authority liable without imposing a trust which, in other cases, will create property rights affecting third parties because moneys received under a void contract are "trust property".

The Practical Consequences of the Bank's Argument

Before considering the legal merits of the submission, it is important to appreciate the practical consequences which ensue if the bank's arguments are correct. Those who suggest that a resulting trust should arise in these circumstances accept that the creation of an equitable proprietary interest under the trust can have unfortunate, and adverse, effects if the original recipient of the moneys becomes insolvent: the moneys, if traceable in the hands of the recipient, are trust moneys and not available for the creditors of the recipient. However, the creation of an equitable proprietary interest in moneys received under a void contract is capable of having adverse effects quite apart from insolvency. The proprietary interest under the unknown trust will, quite apart from insolvency, be enforceable against any recipient of the property other than the purchaser for value of a legal interest without notice. **14–170**

Take the following example. T (the transferor) has entered into a commercial contract with R1 (the first recipient). Both parties believe the contract to be valid but it is in fact void. Pursuant to that contract: (i) T pays £1m to R1 who pays it into a mixed bank account; (ii) T transfers 100 shares in X company to R1, who is registered as a shareholder. Thereafter R1 deals with the money and shares as follows: (iii) R1 pays £50,000 out of the mixed account to R2 otherwise than for value; R2 then becomes insolvent, having trade creditors who have paid for goods not delivered at the time of the insolvency. (iv) R1 charges the shares in X company to R3 by way of equitable security for a loan from R3. **14–171**

If the bank's arguments are correct, R1 holds the £1m on trust for T once the money has become mixed in R1's bank account. Similarly R1 becomes the legal owner of the shares in X company as from the date of his registration as a shareholder but holds such shares on a resulting trust for T. T therefore has an equitable proprietary interest in the moneys in the mixed account and in the shares. **14–172**

T's equitable interest will enjoy absolute priority as against the creditors in the insolvency of R2 (who was not a purchaser for value) provided that the £50,000 can be traced in the assets of R2 at the date of its insolvency. Moreover, if the separation of title argument is correct, since the equitable interest is in T and the legal interest is vested in R2, R2 also holds as trustee for T. In tracing the £50,000 in the bank account of R2, R2 as trustee will be treated as having drawn out "his own" moneys first, thereby benefiting T at the expense of the secured and unsecured creditors of R2. Therefore in practice one may well reach the position where the moneys in the bank account of R2 in reality reflect the price paid by creditors for goods not delivered by R2: yet, under the tracing rules, those moneys are to be treated as belonging in equity to T. **14–173**

So far as the shares in the X company are concerned, T can trace his equitable interest into the shares and will take in priority to R3, whose equitable charge to secure his loan even though granted for value will pro tanto be defeated. **14–174**

All this will have occurred when no one was aware, or could have been aware, of the supposed trust because no one knew that the contract was void. **14–175**

I can see no moral or legal justification for giving such priority to the right of T to obtain restitution over third parties who have themselves not been enriched, in any real sense, at T's expense and indeed have had no dealings with T. T paid over his money and transferred the shares under a supposed valid contract. If the contract had been valid, he would have had purely personal rights against R1. Why should he be better off because the contract is void? **14–176**

[251] A. Burrows, "Swaps and the Friction between Common Law and Equity" [1995] R.L.R. 15.

14–177 My Lords, wise judges have often warned against the wholesale importation into commercial law of equitable principles inconsistent with the certainty and speed which are essential requirements for the orderly conduct of business affairs.[252] If the bank's arguments are correct, a businessman who has entered into transactions relating to or dependent upon property rights could find that assets which apparently belong to one person in fact belong to another; that there are "off balance sheet" liabilities of which he cannot be aware; that these property rights and liabilities arise from circumstances unknown not only to himself but also to anyone else who has been involved in the transactions. A new area of unmanageable risk will be introduced into commercial dealings. If the due application of equitable principles forced a conclusion leading to these results, your Lordships would be presented with a formidable task in reconciling legal principle with commercial common sense. But in my judgment no such conflict occurs. The resulting trust for which the bank contends is inconsistent not only with the law as it stands but with any principled development of it.

The Relevant Principles of Trust Law

14–178 (i) Equity operates on the conscience of the owner of the legal interest. In the case of a trust, the conscience of the legal owner requires him to carry out the purposes for which the property was vested in him (express or implied trust) or which the law imposes on him by reason of his unconscionable conduct (constructive trust).

14–179 (ii) Since the equitable jurisdiction to enforce trusts depends upon the conscience of the holder of the legal interest being affected, he cannot be a trustee of the property if and so long as he is ignorant of the facts alleged to affect his conscience, i.e. until he is aware that he is intended to hold the property for the benefit of others in the case of an express or implied trust, or, in the case of a constructive trust, of the factors which are alleged to affect his conscience.

14–180 (iii) TIn order to establish a trust there must be identifiable trust property. The only apparent exception to this rule is a constructive trust imposed on a person who dishonestly assists in a breach of trust who may come under fiduciary duties even if he does not receive identifiable trust property.[253]

14–181 (iv) Once a trust is established, as from the date of its establishment the beneficiary has, in equity, a proprietary interest in the trust property, which proprietary interest will be enforceable in equity against any subsequent holder of the property (whether the original property or substituted property into which it can be traced) other than a purchaser for value of the legal interest without notice.

14–182 These propositions are fundamental to the law of trusts and I would have thought uncontroversial. However, proposition (ii) may call for some expansion. There are cases where property has been put into the name of X without X's knowledge but in circumstances where no gift to X was intended. It has been held that such property is recoverable under a resulting trust.[254] These cases are explicable on the ground that, by the time action was brought, X or his successors in title have become aware of the facts which gave rise to a resulting trust; his conscience was affected as from the time of such discovery and thereafter he held on a resulting trust under which the property was recovered from him. There is, so far as I am aware, no authority which decides that X was a trustee, and therefore accountable for his deeds, at any time before he was aware of the circumstances which gave rise to a resulting trust.

[252] *Barnes v Addy* (1874) L.R. 9 Ch. App. 244 at 251 at 255, and *Scandinavian Trading Tanker Co AB v Flota Petrolera Ecuatoriana* [1983] 2 A.C. 694 at 703–704.

[253] [Editor's note: Lord Browne-Wilkinson refers here to the personal liability of a dishonest assistant to account in equity "as a constructive trustee"; dishonest assistants often do not handle misapplied trust property, and in such cases therefore cannot hold it on constructive trust for anyone as Lord Millett makes clear in *Dubai Aluminium Co Ltd v Salaam* [2003] 2 A.C. 366 at [141]–[142]. See para.12–05.]

[254] *Birch v Blagrave* (1755) Amb. 264; *Childers v Childers* (1857) 1 De G. & J. 482; *Re Vinogradoff* [1935] W.N. 68; *Re Muller* [1953] N.Z.L.R. 879.

Those basic principles are inconsistent with the case being advanced by the bank. The latest time at which there was any possibility of identifying the "trust property" was the date on which the moneys in the mixed bank account of the local authority ceased to be traceable when the local authority's account went into overdraft in June 1987. At that date, the local authority had no knowledge of the invalidity of the contract but regarded the moneys as its own to spend as it thought fit. There was therefore never a time at which both (a) there was defined trust property and (b) the conscience of the local authority in relation to such defined trust property was affected. The basic requirements of a trust were never satisfied. . . . **14–183**

The Retention of Title Point

It is said that, since the bank only intended to part with its beneficial ownership of the moneys in performance of a valid contract, neither the legal nor the equitable title passed to the local authority at the date of payment. The legal title vested in the local authority by operation of law when the moneys became mixed in the bank account but, it is said, the bank "retained" its equitable title. **14–184**

I think this argument is fallacious. A person solely entitled to the full beneficial ownership of money or property, both at law and in equity, does not enjoy an equitable interest in that property. The legal title carries with it all rights. Unless and until there is a separation of the legal and equitable estates, there is no separate equitable title. Therefore to talk about the bank "retaining" its equitable interest is meaningless. The only question is whether the circumstances under which the money was paid were such as, in equity, to impose a trust on the local authority. If so, an equitable interest arose for the first time under that trust. **14–185**

This proposition is supported by *Re Cook,*[255] *Vandervell v IRC,*[256] per Lord Upjohn and Lord Donovan, *Commissioner of Stamp Duties v Livingston,*[257] and *Underhill and Hayton's Law of Trusts and Trustees.*[258] **14–186**

The Separation of Title Point

The bank's submission, at its widest, is that if the legal title is in A but the equitable interest in B, A holds as trustee for B. **14–187**

Again I think this argument is fallacious. There are many cases where B enjoys rights which, in equity, are enforceable against the legal owner, A, without A being a trustee, for example an equitable right to redeem a mortgage, equitable easements, restrictive covenants, the right to rectification and an insurer's right by subrogation to receive damages subsequently recovered by the assured.[259] Even in cases where the whole beneficial interest is vested in B and the bare legal interest is in A, A is not necessarily a trustee, for example where title to land is acquired by estoppel as against the legal owner; a mortgagee who has fully discharged his indebtedness enforces his right to recover the mortgaged property in a redemption action, not an action for breach of trust. **14–188**

The bank contended that where, under a pre-existing trust, B is entitled to an equitable interest in trust property, if the trust property comes into the hands of a third party, X (not being a purchaser for value of the legal interest without notice), B is entitled to enforce his equitable interest against the property in the hands of X because X is a trustee for B. In my view the third party, X, is not necessarily a trustee for B: B's equitable right is enforceable against the property in just the same way as any other specifically enforceable equitable right can be enforced against a third party. Even if the third party, X, is not aware that what he has received is trust property B is entitled to assert his title in that property. If X has the necessary degree of knowledge, X may himself become a constructive trustee for B on the basis of knowing receipt. But unless he has the requisite degree of knowledge he is not personally liable to account as trustee: *Re Diplock*[260] and *Re Montagu's ST.*[261] Therefore, innocent receipt of property by X subject to an existing equitable interest does not by itself make X a trustee despite the severance of the legal and equitable titles. *Underhill and Hayton Law of Trusts and Trustees,*[262] while accepting that X is under no personal **14–189**

[255] [1948] Ch. 212.
[256] [1967] 2 A.C. 291 at 311 and 317.
[257] [1965] A.C. 694 at 712.
[258] 15th edn, 1995, p.866.
[259] *Lord Napier and Ettrick v Hunter* [1993] A.C. 713.
[260] [1948] Ch. 465 at 478.
[261] [1987] Ch. 264.
[262] 15th edn, pp.369–370.

liability to account unless and until be becomes aware of B's rights, does describe X as being a constructive trustee. This may only be a question of semantics: on either footing, in the present case the local authority could not have become accountable for profits until it knew that the contract was void.

Resulting Trust

14–190 This is not a case where the bank had any equitable interest which predated receipt by the local authority of the upfront payment. Therefore, in order to show that the local authority became a trustee, the bank must demonstrate circumstances which raised a trust for the first time either at the date on which the local authority received the money or at the date on which payment into the mixed account was made. Counsel for the bank specifically disavowed any claim based on a constructive trust. This was plainly right because the local authority had no relevant knowledge sufficient to raise a constructive trust at any time before the moneys, upon the bank account going into overdraft, became untraceable. Once there ceased to be an identifiable trust fund, the local authority could not become a trustee: *Re Goldcorp Exchange Ltd.*[263] Therefore, as the argument for the bank recognised, the only possible trust which could be established was a resulting trust arising from the circumstances in which the local authority received the upfront payment.

14–191 [His Lordship explained the circumstances under which resulting trusts arise, as set out at paras 14–19 to 14–21, and continued:] Applying these conventional principles of resulting trust to the present case, the bank's claim must fail. There was no transfer of money to the local authority on express trusts: therefore a resulting trust of type (B) above could not arise. As to type (A) above, any presumption of resulting trust is rebutted since it is demonstrated that the bank paid, and the local authority received, the upfront payment with the intention that the moneys so paid should become the absolute property of the local authority. It is true that the parties were under a misapprehension that the payment was made in pursuance of a valid contract. But that does not alter the actual intentions of the parties at the date the payment was made or the moneys were mixed in the bank account. As the article by William Swadling demonstrates,[264] the presumption of resulting trust is rebutted by evidence of any intention inconsistent with such a trust, not only by evidence of an intention to make a gift.

14–192 Professor Birks,[265] while accepting that the principles I have stated represent "a very conservative form" of definition of a resulting trust, argues from restitutionary principles that the definition should be extended so as to cover a perceived gap in the law of "subtractive unjust enrichment"[266] so as to give a plaintiff a proprietary remedy when he has transferred value under a mistake or under a contract the consideration for which wholly fails. He suggests that a resulting trust should arise wherever the money is paid under a mistake (because such mistake vitiates the actual intention) or when money is paid on a condition which is not subsequently satisfied.

14–193 As one would expect, the argument is tightly reasoned but I am not persuaded. The search for a perceived need to strengthen the remedies of a plaintiff claiming in restitution involves, to my mind, a distortion of trust principles. First, the argument elides rights in property (which is the only proper subject matter of a trust) into rights in "the value transferred".[267] A trust can only arise where there is defined trust property: it is therefore not consistent with trust principles to say that a person is a trustee of property which cannot be defined. Second, Professor Birks' approach appears to assume (e.g. in the case of a transfer of value made under a contract the consideration for which subsequently fails) that the recipient will be deemed to have been a trustee from the date of his original receipt of money, i.e. the trust arises at a time when the "trustee" does not, and cannot, know that there is going to be a total failure of consideration. This result is incompatible with the basic premise on which all trust law is built, viz. that the conscience of the trustee is affected. Unless and until the trustee is aware of the factors which give rise to the supposed trust, there is nothing which can affect his conscience. Thus neither in the case of a subsequent failure of consideration nor in the case of a payment under a contract subsequently found to be void for mistake or failure of condition will there be circumstances, at the date of receipt, which can impinge on the

---

263 [1995] 1 A.C. 74.
264 "A New Role for Resulting Trusts?" (1996) 16 L.S. 110, 133.
265 "Restitution and Resulting Trusts" in S. Goldstein (ed.), *Equity and Contemporary Legal Developments* (1992), p.360.
266 ibid. at p.368.
267 ibid. at p.361.

conscience of the recipient, thereby making him a trustee. Thirdly, Professor Birks has to impose on his wider view an arbitrary and admittedly unprincipled modification so as to ensure that a resulting trust does not arise when there has only been a failure to perform a contract, as opposed to total failure of consideration.[268] Such arbitrary exclusion is designed to preserve the rights of creditors in the insolvency of the recipient. The fact that it is necessary to exclude artificially one type of case which would logically fall within the wider concept casts doubt on the validity of the concept.

If adopted, Professor Birks' wider concepts would give rise to all the practical consequences and injustices to which I have referred. I do not think it right to make an unprincipled alteration to the law of property (i.e. the law of trusts) so as to produce in the law of unjust enrichment the injustices to third parties which I have mentioned and the consequential commercial uncertainty which any extension of proprietary interests in personal property is bound to produce. **14–194**

The Authorities

Three cases were principally relied upon in direct support of the proposition that a resulting trust arises where a payment is made under a void contract. **14–195**

(A) *Sinclair v Brougham*[269]

The case concerned the distribution of the assets of the Birkbeck Permanent Benefit Building Society, an unincorporated body which was insolvent. The society had for many years been carrying on business as a bank which, it was held, was ultra vires its objects. The bank had accepted deposits in the course of its ultra vires banking business and it was held that the debts owed to such depositors were themselves void as being ultra vires. In addition to the banking depositors, there were ordinary trade creditors. The society had two classes of members, the A shareholders who were entitled to repayment of their investment on maturity and the B shareholders whose shares were permanent. By agreement, the claims of the ordinary trade creditors and of the A shareholders had been settled. Therefore the only claimants to the assets of the society before the court were the ultra vires depositors and the B shareholders, the latter of which could take no greater interest than the society itself. **14–196**

The issues for decision arose on a summons taken out by the liquidator for directions as to how he should distribute the assets in the liquidation. In the judgments, it is not always clear whether this House was laying down general propositions of law or merely giving directions as to the proper mode in which the assets in that liquidation should be distributed. The depositors claimed, first, in quasi-contract for money had and received. They claimed secondly, as the result of an argument suggested for the first time in the course of argument in the House of Lords,[270] to trace their deposits into the assets of the society. **14–197**

Money Had and Received

The House of Lords was unanimous in rejecting the claim by the ultra vires depositors to recover in quasi-contract on the basis of moneys had and received. In their view, the claim in quasi-contract was based on an implied contract. To imply a contract to repay would be to imply a contract to exactly the same effect as the express ultra vires contract of loan. Any such implied contract would itself be void as being ultra vires. **14–198**

Subsequent developments in the law of restitution demonstrate that this reasoning is no longer sound. The common law restitutionary claim is based not on implied contract but on unjust enrichment: in the circumstances the law imposes an obligation to repay rather than implying an entirely fictitious agreement to repay.[271] In my judgment, your Lordships should now unequivocally and finally reject the concept that the claim for moneys had and received is based on an implied contract. I would overrule *Sinclair v Brougham* on this point. **14–199**

It follows that in *Sinclair v Brougham* the depositors should have had a personal claim to recover the moneys at law based on a total failure of consideration. The failure of consideration was not partial: the depositors had paid over their money in consideration of a promise to repay. That promise was ultra vires and void; **14–200**

---

[268] ibid. at pp. 356–359 and 362.
[269] [1914] A.C. 398.
[270] ibid. at 404.
[271] *Fibrosa Spolka Akcyjna v Fairbairn Lawson Combe Barbour Ltd* [1943] A.C. 32 at 63–64, per Lord Wright; *Pavey & Matthews Pty Ltd v Paul* (1987) 69 A.L.R. 577 at 579, 583, 603; *Lipkin Gorman (a firm) v Karpnale Ltd* [1991] 2 A.C. 548 at 578; *Woolwich Building Society v IRC (No.2)* [1993] A.C. 70.

therefore the consideration for the payment of the money wholly failed. So in the present swaps case (though the point is not one under appeal) I think the Court of Appeal were right to hold that the swap moneys were paid on a consideration that wholly failed. The essence of the swap agreement is that, over the whole term of the agreement, each party thinks he will come out best: the consideration for one party making a payment is an obligation on the other party to make counter-payments over the whole term of the agreement.

14–201 If in *Sinclair v Brougham* the depositors had been held entitled to recover at law, their personal claim would have ranked pari passu with other ordinary unsecured creditors, in priority to the members of the society who could take nothing in the liquidation until all creditors had been paid.

The Claim in Rem

14–202 The House of Lords held that, the ordinary trade creditors having been paid in full by agreement, the assets remaining were to be divided between the ultra vires depositors and the members of the society pro rata according to their respective payments to the society. . . .

14–203 As has been pointed out frequently over the 80 years since it was decided, *Sinclair v Brougham* is a bewildering authority: no single ratio decidendi can be detected; all the reasoning is open to serious objection; it was only intended to deal with cases where there were no trade creditors in competition and the reasoning is incapable of application where there are such creditors. In my view the decision as to rights in rem in *Sinclair v Brougham* should also be overruled. Although the case is one where property rights are involved, such overruling should not in practice disturb long-settled titles. However, your Lordships should not be taken to be casting any doubt on the principles of tracing as established in *Re Diplock*.

14–204 If *Sinclair v Brougham*, in both its aspects, is overruled the law can be established in accordance with principle and commercial common sense: a claimant for restitution of moneys paid under an ultra vires, and therefore void, contract has a personal action at law to recover the moneys paid as on a total failure of consideration; he will not have an equitable proprietary claim which gives him either rights against third parties or priority in an insolvency; nor will he have a personal claim in equity, since the recipient is not a trustee.

(B) *Chase Manhattan Bank NA v Israel-British Bank (London) Ltd*[272]

14–205 In that case Chase Manhattan, a New York bank, had by mistake paid the same sum twice to the credit of the defendant, a London bank. Shortly thereafter, the defendant bank went into insolvent liquidation. The question was whether Chase Manhattan had a claim in rem against the assets of the defendant bank to recover the second payment.

14–206 Goulding J. was asked to assume that the moneys paid under a mistake were capable of being traced in the assets of the recipient bank: he was only concerned with the question whether there was a proprietary base on which the tracing remedy could be founded.[273] He held that, where money was paid under a mistake, the receipt of such money without more constituted the recipient a trustee: he said that the payer "retains an equitable property in it and the conscience of [the recipient] is subjected to a fiduciary duty to respect his proprietary right".[274]

14–207 It will be apparent from what I have already said that I cannot agree with this reasoning. First, it is based on a concept of retaining an equitable property in money where, prior to the payment to the recipient bank, there was no existing equitable interest. Further, I cannot understand how the recipient's "conscience" can be affected at a time when he is not aware of any mistake. Finally, the judge found that the law of England and that of New York were in substance the same. I find this a surprising conclusion since the New York law of constructive trusts has for a long time been influenced by the concept of a remedial constructive trust, whereas hitherto English law has for the most part only recognised an institutional constructive trust.[275] In the present context, that distinction is of fundamental importance. Under an institutional constructive trust, the trust arises by operation of law as from the date of the circumstances which give rise to it: the function of the court is merely to declare that such trust has arisen in the past. The consequences that flow from such trust having arisen (including the possibly unfair consequences to third parties who in the interim have received the trust property) are also determined by rules of law, not under a discretion. A remedial constructive trust, as I understand it, is different. It is a judicial remedy giving rise to an enforceable equitable

[272] [1981] Ch. 105.
[273] ibid. at 116.
[274] ibid. at 119.
[275] *Metall und Rohstoff AG v Donaldson Lufkin & Jenrette Inc* [1990] 1 Q.B. 391 at 478–480.

obligation: the extent to which it operates retrospectively to the prejudice of third parties lies in the discretion of the court. Thus for the law of New York to hold that there is a remedial constructive trust where a payment has been made under a void contract gives rise to different consequences from holding that an institutional constructive trust arises in English law.

However, although I do not accept the reasoning of Goulding J., *Chase Manhattan* may well have been rightly decided. The defendant bank knew of the mistake made by the paying bank within two days of the receipt of the moneys.[276] The judge treated this fact as irrelevant,[277] but in my judgment it may well provide a proper foundation for the decision. Although the mere receipt of the moneys, in ignorance of the mistake, gives rise to no trust, the retention of the moneys after the recipient bank learned of the mistake may well have given rise to a constructive trust.[278] **14–208**

[His Lordship considered *Re Ames' Settlement*,[279] and then continued:] **14–209**

The Stolen Bag of Coins

The argument for a resulting trust was said to be supported by the case of a thief who steals a bag of coins. **14–210** At law those coins remain traceable only so long as they are kept separate: as soon as they are mixed with other coins or paid into a mixed bank account they cease to be traceable at law. Can it really be the case, it is asked, that in such circumstances the thief cannot be required to disgorge the property which, in equity, represents the stolen coins? Moneys can only be traced in equity if there has been at some stage a breach of fiduciary duty, i.e. if either before the theft there was an equitable proprietary interest (e.g. the coins were stolen trust moneys) or such interest arises under a resulting trust at the time of the theft or the mixing of the moneys. Therefore, it is said, a resulting trust must arise either at the time of the theft or when the moneys are subsequently mixed. Unless this is the law, there will be no right to recover the assets representing the stolen moneys once the moneys have become mixed.

I agree that the stolen moneys are traceable in equity. But the proprietary interest which equity is **14–211** enforcing in such circumstances arises under a constructive, not a resulting, trust. Although it is difficult to find clear authority for the proposition, when property is obtained by fraud equity imposes a constructive trust on the fraudulent recipient: the property is recoverable and traceable in equity. Thus, an infant who has obtained property by fraud is bound in equity to restore it.[280]

Restitution and Equitable Rights

Those concerned with developing the law of restitution are anxious to ensure that, in certain circumstances, **14–212** the plaintiff should have the right to recover property which he has unjustly lost. For that purpose they have sought to develop the law of resulting trusts so as to give the plaintiff a proprietary interest. For the reasons that I have given in my view such development is not based on sound principle and in the name of unjust enrichment is capable of producing most unjust results. The law of resulting trusts would confer on the plaintiff a right to recover property from, or at the expense of, those who have not been unjustly enriched at his expense at all, for example the lender whose debt is secured by a floating charge and all other third parties who have purchased an equitable interest only, albeit in all innocence and for value.

Although the resulting trust is an unsuitable basis for developing proprietary restitutionary remedies, **14–213** the remedial constructive trust, if introduced into English law, may provide a more satisfactory road forward. The court by way of remedy might impose a constructive trust on a defendant who knowingly retains property of which the plaintiff has been unjustly deprived. Since the remedy can be tailored to the circumstances of the particular case, innocent third parties would not be prejudiced and restitutionary defences, such as change of position, are capable of being given effect. However, whether English law should follow the United States and Canada by adopting the remedial constructive trust will have to be decided in some future case when the point is directly in issue.

---

276 [1981] Ch. 105 at 115.
277 ibid. at 114.
278 *Snell's Equity* (29th edn, 1991), p.193, Pettit *Equity and the Law of Trusts* (7th edn, 1993) p.168; *Metall und Rohstoff AG v Donaldson Lufkin & Jenrette Inc* [1990] 1 Q.B. 391 at 473–474.
279 [1946] Ch. 217.
280 *Stocks v Wilson* [1913] 2 K.B. 235 at 244; *R Leslie Ltd v Sheill* [1914] 3 K.B. 607. Moneys stolen from a bank account can be traced in equity: *Bankers Trust Co v Shapira* [1980] 1 W.L.R. 1274 at 1282. See also *McCormick v Grogan* (1869) L.R. 4 H.L. 82 at 97.

Questions

14–214 1. "A resulting trust is a default mechanism to locate the beneficial ownership of property and not a proprietary remedy for unjust enrichment." **Discuss.**

14–215 2. The members of the Ravers Anonymous Club, an unincorporated association whose purposes are not charitable have dissolved the association one week after having received £10,000 from Sir Lancelot Hellfire for the purposes of the Club, and one month after having received £1,000 from various raffles and sweepstakes, along with £150 from collections taken at a public meeting held to publicise the Club. In accordance with the Club rules the members received ten days' written notice of the meeting called to dissolve the association. **What should happen to the above sums?**

14–216 3. Six years before her death Miss Spry opened a current account with Barclays Bank in the joint names of herself and her nephew, Neal Smug. Both of them called on the manager when they came to open the joint account. Miss Spry told the manager that as she was getting frail her nephew would look after her banking affairs for her. She also said that if she died before her nephew then he could keep any credit balance in the account on her death. It was arranged that the bank would honour cheques drawn on the account either by Miss Spry or by Neal. Although Miss Spry kept the cheque book in her desk, all the cheques were signed by Neal. As envisaged by the parties, only Miss Spry paid money into the account. At her death a credit balance of £2,000 remained. **Who is entitled to this money if Miss Spry left her estate to the RSPCA in her will?**

14–217 4. Fearing that his wife might divorce him at some time, and that a new business venture might prove financially damaging, Harold transferred legal title to his cottage to Simon, who agreed that when matters had resolved themselves so that it was safe to do so he would reconvey the cottage to Harold. The conveyance purported to be for £200,000, but in fact, as agreed, Simon paid nothing. **Advise Harold who now seeks to recover the cottage. Does it matter (a) if Simon is Harold's brother or his son, or (b) if only six months have elapsed and Harold's wife is still living with him and he is sufficiently secure financially to pay his debts as they fall due?**

14–218 5. "The courts should be given a statutory discretion to determine the effects of illegality in resulting trust cases." **Discuss.**

14–219 6. Sharp transferred various assets to trustees to be held on trust for Sharp himself for life or until he should become bankrupt or his property should otherwise become available to his creditors. On any such event occurring the trustees were directed to pay the income to Sharp's wife for her life. Subject to those trusts the trustees were to hold on trust for Sharp's children absolutely in equal shares. Four years after making the settlement Sharp was adjudicated bankrupt when he had a wife and two adult children. **Advise Sharp's trustee in bankruptcy as to the position if he wishes (1) to sell or (2) to retain Sharp's interest under the settlement.**

15 CONSTRUCTIVE TRUSTS

1. Introduction

When a constructive trust is imposed on property in a defendant's hands, the beneficiaries acquire the same proprietary rights in the trust assets as they would under an express trust. The property forms no part of the defendant's estate and his creditors have no claim against it in the event of his insolvency. If the property increases in value, then the increase belongs to the beneficiaries. If the defendant uses the property to acquire new property, then the beneficiaries can trace into this new property and claim it for themselves, and if he transfers the property to any third party other than a bona fide purchaser for value without notice of the beneficiaries' equitable interest, then they can follow the property into the third party's hands and claim it for themselves.[1] Until trial the beneficiaries can preserve the position by obtaining (virtually[2] as of right) an interim injunction restraining dealings with "their" property. Moreover, if a constructive trust is imposed on property and the defendant's conscience is affected with knowledge of the circumstances which led to the imposition of the trust, then he will be personally liable to account to the beneficiaries for his dealings with the property in his capacity as trustee of the constructive trust.[3] **15–01**

Under English law, constructive trusts arise as a result of legal rules which state that they arise in certain circumstances. These rules do not give the courts a discretion to impose constructive trusts, or to refuse to do so, according to their assessment of the equities of a case: the courts' role is purely declaratory. In contrast, some other Commonwealth jurisdictions, e.g. Canada[4] and Australia,[5] distinguish "substantive" or "institutional" constructive trusts from "remedial" constructive trusts. Different judges and legal scholars use these terms to mean different things,[6] but most use them to distinguish constructive trusts which arise through the inflexible operation of legal rules from constructive trusts which arise following the exercise of a judicial discretion, either retrospectively or prospectively from **15–02**

---

1 See Chapter. 13.

2 *Polly Peck International Plc v Nadir (No.2)* [1992] 4 All E.R. 769 at 784 (claim too speculative).

3 See paras 12–09 ff. Note that the courts also use the language of personal liability to account as a constructive trustee when describing the liability of dishonest assistants in a breach of trust, in which case they mean something different. This is discussed at paras 12–04 ff.

4 *Sorochan v Sorochan* [1986] 2 S.C.R. 38; *Lac Minerals Ltd v International Corona Resources Ltd* [1989] 2 S.C.R. 574; *Soulos v Korkontzilas* [1997] 2 S.C.R. 217.

5 *Muschinski v Dodds* (1985) 160 C.L.R. 583; *Re Stevenson Nominees Pty Ltd* (1987) 76 A.L.R. 485; *Bathurst CC v PWC Properties Pty Ltd* (1998) 195 C.L.R. 566; *Giumelli v Giumelli* (1999) 196 C.L.R. 101. But cf. *Parsons v McBain* (2001) 109 F.C.R. 120; *Parianos v Melluish* (2003) 30 Fed. L.R. 524.

6 G. Elias, *Explaining Constructive Trusts* (1990), pp.159–163; C. Rotherham, *Proprietary Remedies in Context* (2002), pp.7–32. Some judges have used the term "remedial constructive trust" to refer to the personal liability of strangers who dishonestly participate in a breach of trust (see n.3 above): e.g. *Clarke v Marlborough Fine Art (London) Ltd* [2002] 1 W.L.R. 1731 at [66]; *Kilcarne Holdings Ltd v Targetfollow (Birmingham) Ltd* [2005] 2 P. & C.R. 8 at [261]. This usage seems to have been prompted by *Paragon Finance Plc v DB Thakerar & Co (a firm)* [1999] 1 All E.R. 400 at 408–409, where Millett L.J. distinguished constructive trusts of property from the personal liability of dishonest participants in a breach of trust. However it is best avoided, lest this personal liability become confused with the "discretionary proprietary remedy" to which Millett L.J. also refers at 414.

the date of the court order.[7] It is controversial whether the courts should have a discretion to vary property rights in this way,[8] but whatever the rights and wrongs of this question, viewed from the standpoint of principle, English law does not currently recognise "remedial" constructive trusts of this kind.[9]

15–03 Constructive trusts have been imposed in a wide variety of circumstances. This makes it hard to understand why they are imposed, and how (if at all) they differ from resulting trusts. At the end of the chapter we shall consider some of the answers which have been offered to these questions. First, though, we shall examine various situations in which constructive trusts have been imposed. We have discussed several of these already, elsewhere in the book, namely (a) cases concerning incomplete transfers and the rule in *Re Rose*;[10] (b) cases concerning secret and half-secret trusts;[11] and (c) cases concerning mutual wills.[12] In this chapter we shall look at some further situations, under these headings: (d) specifically enforceable contracts of sale; (e) assignments for value of future property; (f) purchasers' undertakings; (g) the rule in *Pallant v Morgan*; (h) shared homes; (i) unauthorised fiduciary gains; (j) proceeds of breach of confidence; (k) proceeds of crime; and (l) vitiated transfers.

2. Specifically Enforceable Contracts of Sale

15–04 If two parties enter a specifically enforceable contract to sell land or other property, then the vendor will hold the property on constructive trust for the vendor until the contract is completed by conveyance of the property.[13] However, as Mason J. observed in *Chang v Registrar of Titles*:[14]

> "there has been controversy as to the time when the trust relationship arises and as to the character of that relationship. Lord Eldon considered that a trust arose on execution of the contract.[15] Plumer M.R. thought that until it is known whether the agreement will be performed the vendor 'is not even in the situation of constructive trustee; he is only a constructive trustee *sub modo*, and providing nothing happens to prevent it. It may turn out that the title is not good, or the purchaser may be unable to pay.'[16] Lord Hatherley said that the vendor becomes a trustee for the purchaser when

---

7 e.g. *Fortex Group Ltd v Macintosh* [1998] 3 N.Z.L.R. 171 at 172–173, endorsed in *Regal Casting Ltd v Lightbody* [2009] 2 N.Z.L.R. 433 at [162]–[163].

8 P. Loughlan, "No Right to the Remedy? An Analysis of Judicial Discretion in the Imposition of Equitable Remedies" (1989) 17 Melbourne L.R. 132; P.D. Finn, "Equitable Doctrine and Discretion in Remedies" in W. Cornish et al. (eds), *Restitution: Past, Present and Future* (1998) 251; D. Wright, *The Remedial Constructive Trust* (1998), reviewed by P. Birks (1999) 115 L.Q.R. 681; P. Birks, "Rights, Wrongs, and Remedies" (2000) 20 O.J.L.S. 1; S. Evans, "Defending Discretionary Remedialism" (2001) 23 Sydney L.R. 463; D.W.M. Waters, "Liability and Remedy: An Adjustable Relationship" (2001) 64 Sask. L.R. 426; D.M. Jensen, "The Rights and Wrongs of Discretionary Remedialism" [2003] S.J.L.S. 178; S. Gardner, *Introduction to the Law of Trusts* 2nd edn (2003), pp. 124–126; T. Etherton, "Constructive Trusts: A New Model for Equity and Unjust Enrichment" [2008] C.L.J. 265. See too Etherton J.'s comments in *London Allied Holdings Ltd v Lee* [2007] EWHC 2061 (Ch) at [273]–[274].

9 *Re Goldcorp Exchange Ltd* [1995] 1 A.C. 74 at 104; *Westdeutsche Landesbank Girozentrale v Islington LBC* [1996] A.C. 669 at 714–716; *Re Polly Peck International Ltd (No.2)* [1998] 3 All E.R. 812 at 827 and 831, followed in *OJSC Oil Co Yugraneft v Abramovich* [2008] EWHC 2613 (Comm) at [378]; *Sinclair Investment Holdings SA v Versailles Trade Finance Ltd (in admin. rec'ship)* [2006] 1 B.C.L.C. 60 at [37] and [42]; *Turner v Jacob* [2008] W.T.L.R. 307 at [85]. But cf. *Thorner v Major* [2009] 1 W.L.R. 776 at [20]–[21].

10 Named for *Re Rose* [1952] Ch. 499. See too *Mascall v Mascall* (1984) 49 P. & C.R. 119; *Corin v Patton* (1990) 169 C.L.R. 450; *Pennington v Waine* [2002] 1 W.L.R. 2075. For discussion, see paras 2–87 ff.

11 e.g. *Ottaway v Norman* [1972] Ch. 698; *Blackwell v Blackwell* [1929] A.C. 318. For discussion, see paras 3–120 ff.

12 e.g. *Re Walters, deceased* [2009] Ch. 212. For discussion, see paras 3–168 ff.

13 *Holroyd v Marshall* (1862) 10 H.L.C. 191 at 209; *Dougan v Ley* (1946) 71 C.L.R. 142; *Oughtred v IRC* [1960] A.C. 206; *Neville v Wilson* [1997] Ch. 44.

14 (1976) 137 C.L.R. 177 at 184. See too *Martin Commercial Fueling Inc v Virtanen* (1997) 144 D.L.R. (4th) 290, esp. at [8]–[10].

15 *Paine v Meller* (1801) 6 Ves. Jun. 349; *Broome v Monck* [1803–1813] All E.R. Rep. 631 (1805).

16 *Wall v Bright* (1820) 1 Jac. & W 494.

the contract is completed, as by payment of the purchase money.[17] Jessel M.R. held that a trust *sub modo* arises on the execution of the contract but that the constructive trust comes into existence when title is made out by the vendor or is accepted by the purchaser."[18]

In *Jerome v Kelly*, Lord Walker reviewed these authorities and concluded that:[19]

> "[it would] be wrong to treat an uncompleted contract for the sale of land as equivalent to an immediate, irrevocable declaration of trust (or assignment of beneficial interest) in the land. Neither the seller nor the buyer has unqualified beneficial ownership. Beneficial ownership of the land is in a sense split between the seller and buyer on the provisional assumptions that specific performance is available and that the contract will in due course be completed, if necessary by the court ordering specific performance. In the meantime, the seller is entitled to enjoyment of the land or its rental income. The provisional assumptions may be falsified by events, such as rescission of the contract (either under a contractual term or on breach). If the contract proceeds to completion the equitable interest can be viewed as passing to the buyer in stages, as title is made and accepted and the purchase price is paid in full."

Consistently with this, a vendor who enters a specifically enforceable contract to sell property must **15–05** "use reasonable care to preserve the property in a reasonable state of preservation, and, so far as may be, as it was when the contract was made", or "take reasonable care that the property is not deteriorated in the interval before completion".[20] This rule may be exploited by a purchaser upon whom a vendor has served a notice to complete[21] making time of the essence of the contract: the purchaser can claim that the notice was invalid because the vendor was not ready, able and willing to complete the contract owing to breach of his equitable duty of preservation.[22] However, if the contract goes off then the vendor cannot be liable to the purchaser for failing to preserve the property.[23]

The vendor also has the right to protect his own interest prior to completion.[24] He can keep the **15–06** rents and profits until the date fixed for completion,[25] and retain possession of the property until the contract is completed by payment of the purchase price.[26] If he parts with possession to the purchaser before actual completion, or even conveys the land, then he may fall back on his equitable lien over the property to ensure that he is paid.[27] If the vendor in breach of the constructive trust sells the property to a third party, then the purchaser can trace the value in the property into the value in the

---

17 *Shaw v Foster* (1872) L.R. 5 H.L. 321.

18 *Lysaght v Edwards* (1876) 2 Ch.D. 499, accepted in *Rayner v Preston* (1881) 18 Ch.D. 1.

19 [2004] 1 W.L.R. 1409 at [32]. See too *Englewood Properties Ltd v Patel* [2005] 1 W.L.R. 1961 at [40] ff.; *Underwood v HMRC* [2009] S.T.C. 239 at [38].

20 *Clarke v Ramuz* [1891] 2 Q.B. 456 at 460 and 468; *Davron Estates Ltd v Turnshire* (1983) 133 N.L.J. 937. At law, however, risk passes to the purchaser after exchange of contracts in so far as concerns anything not caused by a breach of the vendor's duties: *Rayner v Preston* (1881) 18 Ch.D. The effect of this decision is to require both the vendor and the purchaser to insure the property, a wasteful outcome that is rightly criticised in M. Thompson, "Must the Purchaser Buy a Charred Ruin?" (1984) 48 Conv. 43, 50–52. Note though, that the parties may provide otherwise by contract: Standard Conditions of Sale, Condition 5.1 (subject to contrary agreement).

21 Standard Conditions of Sale, Condition 6.6.

22 Purchasers have taken this point where squatters have managed to break into the property which forms the subject-matter of the contract: so far the cases seem to have been settled without the need to spend days in court arguing whether or not the vendor's precautions were reasonable.

23 *Plews v Samuel* [1904] 1 Ch. 464; *Ridoul v Fowler* [1904] 1 Ch. 658, [1904] 2 Ch. 93.

24 *Shaw v Foster* (1872) L.R. 5 H.L. 321 at 328; *Re Watford Corporation's Contract* [1943] Ch. 82 at 85.

25 *Cuddon v Tite* (1858) 1 Giff. 395.

26 *Gedge v Montrose* (1858) 26 Beav. 45; *Phillips v Silvester* (1872) L.R. 8 Ch. 173.

27 *Nives v Nives* (1880) 15 Ch.D. 649; *Re Birmingham* [1959] Ch. 523; *London & Cheshire Insurance Co Ltd v Laplagrene* [1971] Ch. 499.

sale proceeds received by the vendor, and assert a proprietary claim to these proceeds, subject to accounting to the vendor for the price agreed between the two of them.[28] This will be useful if the contractual claim against the vendor for damages is not worthwhile, e.g. if the vendor is bankrupt or has generated a surplus through his dealings with the third party.[29] Note, too, that a vendor of shares in an unquoted company can use his votes to protect his lien for the price, but he cannot use them for any purpose that might damage the purchaser.[30]

3. Assignments for Value of Future Property

15–07 As Swinfen Eady L.J. stated in *Re Lind*:[31]

> "An assignment for value of future property actually binds the property itself directly it is acquired—automatically on the happening of the event, and without any future act on the part of the assignor—and does not merely rest in, and amount to, a right in contract, giving rise to an action. The assignor, having received the consideration, becomes in equity on the happening of the event, trustee for the assignee of the property devolving upon or acquired by him, and which he had previously sold and been paid for."

15–08 Here a constructive trust arises as a result of the maxim "Equity regards as done that which ought to be done".[32] If A makes a settlement in consideration of marriage under which he covenants to pay to trustees T1 and T2 any money inherited from X, then such money will be held on a constructive trust for T1 and T2 at the moment when A receives it.[33] Similarly, if F, for a consideration received from G, contracts to hold on trust for G any future receipts arising in respect of payments for specified future sales or services, then such payments are immediately subject to the trust when F receives them.[34] In the latter case, it is crucial that G has actually paid the consideration to F.

4. Purchasers' Undertakings

15–09 A contractual licence to occupy a house or flat is not an interest in land, and binds the contracting parties alone.[35] However, a purchaser P may undertake to a vendor V that he will take the property positively subject to the rights of a contractual licensee C. After completion of the purchase, C might be able to take advantage of a term for his benefit in V and P's contract under the Contracts (Rights of Third Parties) Act 1999. But if he cannot, then P might try to evict C by claiming that C only has contractual personal rights against V. In *Ashburn Anstalt v Arnold*,[36] the Court of Appeal held that Equity would prevent this by imposing a constructive trust on the property, compelling P to recognise C's rights under the contractual licence. However, as this case also reveals, if V conveys or contracts to convey the property defensively subject to whatever rights C may happen to have, so as to satisfy V's obligation to disclose all possible incumbrances and to protect him against any possible claim by

---

[28] *Bunny Industries Ltd v FSW Enterprises Pty Ltd* [1982] Qd. R. 712.
[29] *Lake v Bayliss* [1974] 1 W.L.R. 1073.
[30] *Michaels v Harley House (Marylebone) Ltd* [2000] Ch. 104.
[31] [1915] 2 Ch. 354 at 360.
[32] *Palette Shoes Pty Ltd v Krohn* (1937) 58 C.L.R. 1 at 16; *Associated Alloys Pty Ltd v ACN 001 452 106 Pty Ltd* (2000) 202 C.L.R. 588.
[33] *Pullan v Koe* [1913] 1 Ch. 9; *Re Gillott's Settlement* [1934] Ch. 97 at 158–159.
[34] *Barclays Bank Plc v Willowbank International Ltd* [1987] B.C.L.C. 717; *Associated Alloys*, above.
[35] *Ashburn Anstalt v Arnold* [1989] Ch. 1.
[36] *Ashburn Anstalt*, above.

P, then P is not bound by C's rights which are merely personal and not proprietary. In other words, it is essential that P must have agreed to confer a new right on C: he must have "undertaken a new obligation, not otherwise existing, to give effect to the relevant incumbrance or prior interest. If, but only if, he has undertaken such a new obligation will a constructive trust be imposed".[37] This new right may give C the same rights against P as he would have enjoyed against V, had V never sold the land. But it may also protect C even if C had no right against V, e.g. because he failed to register his interest,[38] and equally if C's valid right against V was destroyed by the transfer to P.[39]

The "constructive trust" used by the courts to protect C's interests in cases of this sort is probably not a trust at all. The courts find P's conscience to be personally affected by an obligation to give effect to C's interest, and therefore treat him constructively as though he were a trustee, to the limited extent that is necessary to place him under a personal obligation to C.[40] This does not mean that C acquires an equitable interest in the land, for otherwise his contractual licence would be a valid equitable interest binding the land, as would an unregistered void estate contract. **15–10**

5. The Rule in *Pallant v Morgan*

"If A and B agree that A will acquire some specific property for the joint benefit of A and B on terms yet to be agreed and B in reliance on A's agreement is thereby induced to refrain from attempting to acquire the property equity ought not to permit A when he acquires the property to insist on retaining the whole benefit for himself to the exclusion of B".[41] The source of this rule is *Pallant v Morgan*,[42] where the parties both wished to buy a piece of land that was to be sold at auction. They agreed that the claimant would refrain from bidding in order to keep the price down, and that the defendant would divide the land between them after he had bought it. After the defendant bought the land, they failed to agree on the details of division and so the defendant kept it all for himself. Harman J. held that the agreement was too uncertain to be specifically enforceable, but that the defendant should nonetheless hold the land on trust for himself and the claimant jointly because his bid had been made on the basis of an agreement for division and it would be "tantamount to sanctioning fraud" to allow him to retain all the land for himself.[43] **15–11**

This decision was given a wide interpretation in *Banner Homes Group Plc v Luff Developments Ltd (No.2)*,[44] where Chadwick L.J. noted that the *Pallant v Morgan* equity is often triggered in cases where the claimant has suffered detriment, but held that a constructive trust can also be imposed where the claimant has suffered no detriment, but the defendant has gained an advantage by acting on the parties' arrangement. This may be the aspect of his Lordship's decision that was considered "quite difficult" by an Australian judge, Bryson J., in *Seyffer v Adamson*,[45] adding that "what is altogether necessary, however, is that there be some agreement, arrangement or shared understanding about the way in which some interest in land will be acquired or dealt with". Consistently with this, **15–12**

---

[37] *Lloyd v Dugdale* [2002] 2 P. & C.R. 13 at [52], per Sir Christopher Slade.

[38] *Lyus v Prowsa Developments Ltd* [1982] 1 W.L.R. 1044; *Bahr v Nicolay (No.2)* (1988) 62 A.L.J.R. 268 at 288–289; *I.D.C. Group Ltd v Clark* [1992] 1 E.G.L.R. 187 at 190.

[39] *Melbury Road Properties 1995 Ltd v Kreidi* [1999] 3 E.G.L.R. 10; *Lloyd v Dugdale* [2002] 2 P. & C.R. 13.

[40] *Baybut v Eccle Riggs Country Park Ltd* (Ch.D., 2 November 2006) at [60].

[41] *Holiday Inns of America Inc v Broadhead* Ch.D., 19 December 1969, per Megarry J., quoted in *Banner Homes Group Plc v Luff Developments Ltd (No.2)* [2000] Ch. 372 at 391.

[42] [1953] 1 Ch. 43.

[43] *Pallant* at 48.

[44] [2000] Ch. 372 at 396–399, followed in *Cox v Jones* [2004] 2 F.L.R. 1010 at [46]. In both cases, the claimant suffered detriment on the facts.

[45] [2001] NSWSC 1132.

Mummery L.J. held in *London & Regional Investments Ltd v TBI Plc*[46] that a constructive trust can be imposed even though the parties have failed to enter a binding contract, but that no trust will be imposed if the parties have positively agreed not to be bound unless and until formal contracts have been exchanged: where the parties expressly negative an intention to create legal relations, equity should follow the law in declining to place them under enforceable obligations.

6. Shared Homes

A. Background

15–13 In recent decades a growing number of disputes have come before the courts where two parties have lived together in a marital or quasi-marital relationship, and legal ownership of their shared home does not reflect the contributions, financial or otherwise, that each made to the continuance of their ongoing relationship, and/or to the purchase and/or to the upkeep of the property. If the parties' relationship has come to an end, or if the property has been charged to a lender that now seeks to enforce its security, the question can then arise whether the value inherent in the property should be allocated in line with legal ownership, or whether equity should reallocate this value between the parties? To resolve this question, the courts must decide some complex and politically charged questions: what kinds of contribution, made in the context of what kinds of relationship, and born of what kinds of expectation, should engender an equitable interest at variance with the parties' legal rights?[47]

15–14 Most of the cases in this area concern a man and a woman in a heterosexual relationship, legal title to whose shared home is vested in the man alone. Hence the parties will be referred to here as M and W, although this usage is inapt when applied to situations where the woman is the legal owner, and situations concerning couples in a homosexual relationship. If M and W are married and a property dispute arises between them on their decision to divorce, then this will be resolved under divorce legislation[48] that does not apply in cases where the parties are unmarried, where equitable principles may come into play.[49] However, if a dispute arises between W and a bank which has taken a charge over the property from M, then W can invoke equitable principles against the bank whether or not she and M are married.

15–15 If M makes a written declaration of trust of the property in W's favour which complies with the LPA 1925 s.53(1)(b), or else the parties enter a written contract under which W takes a share of the property, and which complies with the Law of Property (Miscellaneous Provisions) Act 1989 s.2, then W will be entitled to a share of the property under the trust or contract. If this has not been done—and very often it will not have been done, no matter how desirable it might have been for the parties to arrange things more carefully[50]—then W will have to rely on alleging an equitable right under a common intention constructive trust, or else bring a proprietary estoppel claim.

---

[46] [2002] EWCA Civ 355 at [47]–[48]. See too *Thames Cruises Ltd v George Wheeler Launches Ltd* [2003] EWHC 3093 (Ch); *Kilcarne Holdings Ltd v Targetfollow (Birmingham) Ltd* [2005] 2 P. & C.R. 105; *Kinane v Mackie-Conteh* [2005] W.T.L.R. 345; *Cobbe v Yeoman's Row Management Ltd* [2008] 1 W.L.R. 1752 at [30]–[37]; *Benedetti v Sawiris* [2009] EWHC 1330 (Ch) at [504] ff.; *Clarke v Corless* [2009] EWHC 1636 (Ch) at [21]–[24].

[47] Various perspectives on these questions are offered by: L. Flynn and A. Lawson, "Gender, Sexuality and the Doctrine of Detrimental Reliance" (1995) 3 Feminist Legal Studies 105; A. Bottomley, "Women and Trust(s): Portraying the Family in the Gallery of the Law", in S. Bright and J. Dewar (eds), *Land Law: Themes and Perspectives* (1998); J. Mee, *The Property Rights of Cohabitees* (1998), ch.1; J. Miles, "Property Law v Family Law: Resolving the Problems of Family Property" (2003) 23 J.L.S. 624.

[48] For disputes between spouses the Matrimonial Causes Act 1973 s.24 affords the courts plenty of discretion to take into account the wife's home-making and child-raising activities. Substantial contributions to improvements to M's property can enable M's spouse or fiancée to obtain a beneficial interest under the Matrimonial Property and Proceedings Act 1970 s.37.

[49] But see now the Civil Partnership Act 2004 ss. 65–68.

[50] For an empirical study reporting high levels of ignorance and misapprehension about the rights generated by "common law marriage" (over 50% of those surveyed), see G. Douglas, J. Pearce and H. Woodward, "Cohabitation and Conveyancing Practice: Problems and Solutions" [2008] Conv. 365.

If W directly contributed to the purchase of the property, or undertook with M to contribute a proportion of the purchase price (e.g. using money lent on mortgage), then one might have thought that M should hold the legal title on resulting trust for M and W in proportion to their respective contributions or undertakings.[51] In this situation, however, resulting trust reasoning would give W no more than the share which she paid for (or undertook to pay for) at the outset. This was viewed as unsatisfactory (because it gave W too little) in cases such as *Midland Bank Plc v Cooke*,[52] where the courts accordingly held that if W could establish an interest under a resulting trust, then she could always use this as a "springboard" into establishing that she also had a (larger) interest under a common intention constructive trust. Since then, Baroness Hale has gone still further, in *Stack v Dowden*,[53] holding that the courts should avoid using resulting trust reasoning altogether when establishing equitable interests in shared homes, because it discriminates against women by focusing too narrowly on one type of contribution to the parties' relationship, viz. financial contributions, to the exclusion of other types, e.g. home-making, child-care, etc. Hence the courts will now ignore resulting trust reasoning in most cases and will instead turn immediately to the common intention constructive trust when deciding whether W has an equitable interest.[54] **15–16**

Legal title to shared homes is not invariably vested in M alone: sometimes it is vested in M and W as joint legal owners, in which case the courts should take the following approach, according to Baroness Hale in *Stack v Dowden*:[55] **15–17**

> "Just as the starting point where there is sole legal ownership is sole beneficial ownership, the starting point where there is joint legal ownership is joint beneficial ownership. The onus is upon the person seeking to show that the beneficial ownership is different from the legal ownership. So in sole ownership cases it is upon the non-owner to show that [she] has any interest at all. In joint ownership cases, it is upon the joint owner who claims to have other than a joint beneficial interest."

The essence of the common intention constructive trust is unconscionability. If M is the sole legal owner but W makes a contribution to the accrual of wealth inherent in the property, in reliance on a common understanding between the parties that they would share the beneficial ownership, then a constructive trust will be imposed on the basis that it would be unconscionable for M to keep the whole of the property for himself. Likewise, if the parties are joint legal owners, but W contributes more than M to the repayment of a mortgage loan, household expenses, etc. and does so in reliance on a common understanding that she should have a larger share of the property than M, then again a constructive trust will be imposed on the basis that it would be unconscionable for M to take half of the beneficial ownership. In the following discussion we will first look at the requirement that there must have been a common intention to share ownership, and then discuss the requirement that W must have detrimentally relied on this common intention. **15–18**

---

[51] See paras 14–87 to 14–96.
[52] [1995] 2 F.L.R. 915.
[53] [2007] 2 A.C. 432 at [60]. See too *Abbott v Abbott* [2008] 1 F.L.R. 1451 at [4]; *Fowler v Barron* [2008] 2 F.L.R. 831 at [30] and [52].
[54] But cf. *Laskar v Laskar* [2008] 1 W.L.R. 2695: resulting trust reasoning is still relevant where the parties have bought the property for investment purposes only.
[55] *Stack* at [56].

B. Common Intention

15–19 The common intention constructive trust requires a bilateral understanding between the parties that W should obtain a share of the property. As Lord Diplock stated in *Gissing v Gissing*:[56]

> "the relevant intention of each party is the intention which was reasonably understood by the other party to be manifested by that party's words or conduct notwithstanding that he did not consciously formulate that intention in his own mind or even acted with some different intention which he did not communicate to the other party."

15–20 It is not enough for the parties to have shared an intention to share the use of the property: W must show that they commonly intended to share the ownership of the property. Thus, in *Lloyd's Bank Plc v Rosset*, reproduced below,[57] Lord Bridge considered that:[58]

> "The question [is whether the parties have] entered an agreement, made an arrangement, reached an understanding or formed a common intention that the beneficial interest in the property would be jointly owned. . . . Spouses living in amity will not normally think it necessary to formulate or define their respective interests in property in any precise way. The expectation of parties to every happy marriage is that they will share the practical benefits of occupying the matrimonial home whoever owns it. But this is something quite distinct from sharing the beneficial interest in the property asset which the matrimonial home represents."

15–21 It was formerly the case that the parties must also have shared an understanding that W would acquire an interest in the property in exchange for some quid pro quo.[59] However, in *Lloyd's Bank Plc v Rosset*, Nicholls L.J. held that there is:[60]

> "no reason in principle why, if the parties' common intention is that the wife should have a beneficial interest in the property, and if thereafter to the knowledge of the husband she acts to her detriment in reliance on that common intention, the wife should not be able to assert an equitable interest against the husband just as much as she could in a case where the common intention was that, by acting in a certain way, she would acquire a beneficial interest. In each case the question is whether, having regard to what has occurred, it would be inequitable to permit the party in whom the legal estate is vested to deny the existence of the beneficial interest which they both intended should exist."

On appeal, Lord Bridge implicitly accepted this, stating that once there is a finding that there was an express common intention for the property to be shared beneficially:[61]

> "It will only be necessary for the partner asserting a claim to a beneficial interest against the partner entitled to the legal estate to show that he or she has acted to his or her detriment or significantly altered his or her position in reliance on the agreement in order to give rise to a constructive trust or proprietary estoppel."

---

56 [1971] A.C. 886 at 906.
57 At paras 15–40 ff.
58 [1991] 1 A.C. 107 at 127–128.
59 *Gissing v Gissing* [1971] A.C. 887 at 905, per Lord Diplock; *Austin v Keele* (1987) 61 A.L.J.R. 605 at 610, per Lord Oliver.
60 [1989] Ch. 350 at 381.
61 [1991] 1 A.C. 107 at 132.

A distinction must be made between cases based on evidence capable of establishing an express agreement between the parties and cases where there is no such evidence, but where there is evidence of conduct from which the court can infer the existence of an agreement. For a court to hold that the parties formed an express common intention, evidence of discussions is required, "however imperfectly remembered and however imprecise their terms may have been".[62] Excuses may suffice for this purpose, so that if M gives W an excuse as to why legal title to the property should be vested in his name alone, this may be interpreted as evidence that they commonly intended the beneficial ownership to be shared, as otherwise there would have been no need for an excuse.[63] A claimant must provide in her statement of claim as much particularity as possible of discussions between the parties, with the result that "the tenderest exchanges of a common law courtship may assume an unforeseen significance many years later when they are brought under equity's microscope and subjected to an analysis under which many thousands of pounds of value may be liable to turn on fine questions as to whether the relevant words were spoken in earnest or in dalliance and with or without representational intent."[64] It does not suffice that each party happened separately to form the same intention, because an express common intention means one that is communicated between the parties: it is the external manifestation of intention by one party to the other that is crucial, regardless of uncommunicated private intentions.[65] **15–22**

As Lord Bridge stated in *Lloyd's Bank Plc v Rosset*,[66] if there is no evidence of express discussions between the parties, however reasonable it might have been for the parties to discuss the matter and reach an arrangement on beneficial ownership, then the courts will be thrown back "on the conduct of the parties both as to the basis from which to infer a common intention to share the property beneficially and as the conduct relied on to give rise to a constructive trust." In this situation, Lord Bridge thought that "direct contributions to the purchase price by the partner who is not the legal owner, whether initially or by payment of mortgage instalments, will readily justify the inference necessary to the creation of a constructive trust", but he also stated that "it is at least extremely doubtful that anything less will do." **15–23**

In the case, M and W decided to buy and renovate a semi-derelict farmhouse, which they purchased for £57,000. The purchase money was provided by the trustees of a family trust who insisted that the property be bought in M's name alone. Without W's knowledge, M mortgaged the property to Lloyds Bank to secure a £15,000 loan with interest. W spent some time supervising the builders doing renovatory works, did some preparatory cleaning work, and did some skilful painting and decorating herself. The House of Lords held that such conduct was insufficient to justify any inference that there was a common intention for her to acquire a beneficial interest in the farmhouse capable of binding the mortgagee. The value of her work in relation to a farmhouse worth about £72,000 was trifling. It followed that she had no equitable beneficial interest in the property, and so the bank as mortgagee could evict her as well as M in order to be able to sell the property with vacant possession. **15–24**

Rosset clearly established that domestic contributions to the welfare of the household could not justify the court in drawing the inference that the parties must have shared an intention that W would obtain a share in the house. On the court's view, it would have been "unnatural", and would therefore have required an express agreement, for W to have done such things in the belief that she would **15–25**

---

[62] *Lloyd's Bank Plc v Rosset* [1991] 1 A.C. 107 at 132, per Lord Bridge.

[63] *Eves v Eves* [1975] 1 W.L.R. 1338; *Grant v Edwards* [1986] Ch. 638. cf. *Williamson v Sheikh* [2008] EWCA Civ 990 (declaration of express trust drafted but not executed because M told W that she could trust him to do the right thing if they separated).

[64] *Hammond v Mitchell* [1991] 1 W.L.R. 1127 at 1139, per Waite J.

[65] *Springette v Defoe* (1992) 24 H.L.R. 552; *Mollo v Mollo* [2000] W.T.L.R. 227 at 242–243; *Lightfoot v Lightfoot-Brown* [2005] 2 P. & C.R. 22.

[66] [1991] A.C. 107 at 132–133.

thereby acquire a beneficial interest in the home, since such actions were readily explicable on the basis that W was motivated by love for M and their children and by the desire to live in a pleasant and happy environment.[67] Before the court would infer the existence of a common intention from W's behaviour, something more was required and only two things would suffice: direct contributions to the purchase money paid for the property at the outset or direct contributions to the payment of mortgage instalments afterwards.

15–26 There were good reasons for thinking that indirect contributions to the payment of mortgage instalments should also have been enough, particularly the suggestion in Lord Diplock's speech in *Gissing v Gissing* that a court could draw the necessary inference of common intention where:[68]

> "the wife's efforts or her earnings made it possible for the husband to raise the initial loan or the mortgage or [where] the relieving of the husband from the expense of buying clothing for [the wife] and for their son was undertaken in order to enable him the better to meet the mortgage instalments or to repay the loan."

However, the question whether indirect mortgage repayments should also suffice has now been overtaken by the House of Lords' decision in *Stack v Dowden*,[69] which is reproduced below.[70] In *Stack* Baroness Hale held that the law has moved on since *Rosset*, in response to changing social and economic conditions, and that "the search is to ascertain the parties' shared intentions, actual, inferred or imputed, with respect to the property in the light of their whole course of conduct in relation to it."[71] She also stressed that:[72]

> "Many more factors than financial contributions may be relevant to divining the parties' true intentions. These include: any advice or discussions at the time of the transfer which cast light upon their intentions then . . . the purpose for which the home was acquired; the nature of the parties' relationship; whether they had children for whom they both had responsibility to provide a home; how the purchase was financed, both initially and subsequently; how the parties arranged their finances, whether separately or together or a bit of both; how they discharged the outgoings on the property and their other household expenses. . . . The parties' individual characters and personalities may also be a factor in deciding where their true intentions lay."

15–27 These comments were made in the context of a case where M and W were joint legal owners of the property, so that the question before the court was not whether the parties had a common intention to share beneficial ownership of their house (they obviously did since they had decided to share legal ownership), but whether they had a common intention that the size of their respective shares should be something other than half and half. Nevertheless it seems that the House of Lords meant to hold that in cases where legal title is vested in M only, the courts should take a similar "holistic" approach to the question whether the parties had a common intention to share beneficial ownership. This seems to be the only explanation of Baroness Hale's and Lord Walker's statements in *Stack* that the

---

[67] e.g. *Coombes v Smith* [1986] 1 W.L.R. 808.
[68] [1971] A.C. 886 at 910–11. See too *Burns v Burns* [1984] Ch. 317 at 328–329 and 344; *Le Foe v Le Foe* [2001] 2 F.L.R. 970 at [50].
[69] [2007] 2 A.C. 432.
[70] At paras 15–49 ff.
[71] *Stack* at [50].
[72] *Stack* at [69].

law has moved on since *Rosset*, which were echoed by Baroness Hale in the Privy Council in *Abbott v Abbott*.[73]

In *Stack*, Baroness Hale also stressed that "the search is still for the result which reflects what the parties must, in the light of their conduct, be taken to have intended", and that it is impermissible for the court "to abandon that search in favour of the result which the court itself considers fair."[74] This seems to be consistent with Lord Diplock's statement in *Gissing v Gissing*[75] that it is not open to the court to "impute" a "common intention" to the parties, as the most that it can do is to "infer" a common intention from the evidence of their words and actions. However, Baroness Hale also said that "the search is to ascertain the parties' shared intentions, actual, inferred or imputed",[76] triggering an objection from Lord Neuberger, who said in his dissenting speech that "imputation involves concluding what the parties would have intended, whereas inference involves concluding what they did intend", and held that "to impute an intention would not only be wrong in principle and a departure from [two previous House of Lords decisions[77]] . . . but it also would involve a judge in an exercise which was difficult, subjective and uncertain."[78] **15–28**

As observed by Nicholas Strauss QC, sitting as a deputy judge in *Jones v Kernott*,[79] it follows that there is "a doubt which arises from [Baroness Hale's speech] . . . as to whether, and if so how far, it is open to the court to consider what is 'fair'." He resolved this doubt by interpreting her to mean "that the court should not override the intention of the parties, in so far as that appears from what they have said or from their conduct, in favour of what the court itself considers to be fair", but that "to the extent that the intention of the parties cannot be inferred, the court is free . . . to impute a common intention to the parties."[80] It seems likely that in most cases there will be ample evidence of the parties' words and conduct from which the court can form a view of their intentions one way or the other.[81] However, it can be foreseen that cases will arise where imputation will be needed, for example, those like *Midland Bank Plc v Cooke*,[82] where the parties explicitly state in evidence that they never turned their minds to beneficial ownership of the property. **15–29**

C. Detrimental Reliance

To the extent that the court can now impute a common intention to the parties, detrimental reliance would seem to have fallen by the wayside, since there can be no point in the court investigating whether W has relied to her detriment on a fictional common intention that the court has invented. However, assuming that the *Jones v Kernott* rationalisation of *Stack* is correct, there will still be many **15–30**

[73] [2008] 1 F.L.R. 1451 at [4]–[6]. See too *Fowler v Barron* [2008] 2 F.L.R. 831 at [56]. In *Abbott* at [4] Baroness Hale acknowledged the difference between a common intention that W should have a share and a common intention respecting the size of W's share, but even so the distinction is unfortunately blurred in her speeches. Nevertheless it seems likely that the courts will prefer to take a "holistic" approach towards establishing the first type of common intention, rather than the over-restrictive approach taken in *Rosset*: S. Gardner, "Family Property Today" (2008) 124 L.Q.R. 422, pp.426–427. See too N. Piska, "Constructive Trusts and Constructing Intention" in M. Dixon (ed.), *Modern Studies in Property Lrty Law, Vol.5* (2009).

[74] *Stack* at [61].

[75] [1971] A.C. 886 at 904, accepting that he had been wrong to hold otherwise in his minority speech in *Pettitt v Pettitt* [1970] A.C. 777 at 822–825.

[76] *Stack* at [60].

[77] i.e. *Pettitt* and *Gissing*.

[78] *Stack* at [126]–[127].

[79] [2010] 1 F.L.R. 38 at [4].

[80] *Jones* at [30]–[31].

[81] For a recent case where the judge concluded on the evidence that the parties had no common intention to share ownership, and that W chose to give up her job for other reasons, see *Walsh v Singh* [2010] 1 F.C.R. 177.

[82] [1995] 2 F.L.R. 915.

cases in which the courts can discover a "real" common intention between the parties, e.g. from evidence of discussions in which M and W have agreed to share beneficial ownership, and in such cases it will remain a pertinent question whether W has acted to her detriment in reliance on the parties' agreement in such a way that it would be unconscionable for M to deny her beneficial interest in the property.[83]

15–31 The case law pre-dating *Stack* suggests that to establish detriment, W need not show that her conduct was related to M's acquisition of the property:[84] it should be enough for W to have made direct or indirect financial contributions to the acquisition of the property or payment of mortgage instalments,[85] and other types of conduct by W can also suffice, as can be seen from *Eves v Eves*,[86] for example, where the conduct relied on by W was painting the house, breaking up a patio with a sledge-hammer, disposing of the rubble, and building a new garden shed. In *Hyett v Stanley*,[87] Sir Martin Nourse reaffirmed his own finding in *Grant v Edwards*,[88] that W's conduct "must have been conduct on which [she] could not reasonably have been expected to embark unless she was to have an interest in the house". However, this is difficult to reconcile with Browne-Wilkinson V.C.'s finding in the latter case that examples of detrimental reliance might include "setting up house together" and "having a baby",[89] and with his further finding that by "analogy" with the rules on proprietary estoppel, the burden of proof should lie on M to show that W's conduct was attributable to mutual love and affection rather than reliance on the parties' common intention.[90]

D. Size of F's Interest

15–32 Where there is evidence of express discussions leading to a finding of common intention, it seems that the court should continue to start by asking whether the parties have expressly agreed what the size of W's share should be.[91] For as Peter Gibson L.J. observed in *Clough v Killey*:[92]

> "it is only common sense that where the parties form a common intention as to the specific shares they are to take, those shares prima facie are the shares to which the court will give effect."

Even in this case, however, the court may vary the size of W's entitlement in order to give her a "fair share" if subsequent dealings suggest that this would be appropriate, and in cases where no express agreement about the size of her share has been reached, the court must review the whole course of the parties' dealings, as Baroness Hale held in *Stack v Dowden*.[93]

---

[83] cf. *Grant v Edwards* [1986] 1 Ch. 638 at 656; *Lloyds Bank Plc v Rosset* [1991] 1 A.C. 107 at 132.

[84] *Gissing v Gissing* [1971] A.C. 886 at 805; *Grant v Edwards* [1986] Ch. 638 at 647 and 652; *Lloyds Bank Plc v Rosset* [1991] 1 A.C. 107 at 132.

[85] *Halifax BS v Brown* [1996] 1 F.L.R. 103 at 109; *Grant v Edwards* [1986] 1 Ch. 638 at 650.

[86] [1975] 1 W.L.R. 1338. See too *Lalani v Crump Holdings Ltd* Ch.D. June 18, 2004, at [47]: the acts alleged to give rise to detriment need not be "dealings with the property by way of contributions or by way of improvements [and other] conduct, contributions or sacrifices may suffice".

[87] [2004] 1 F.L.R. 394 at [19]. On the facts, W had acted to her detriment by rendering herself jointly and severally liable for M's debts, the repayment of which was secured by way of mortgage on their shared home.

[88] [1986] 1 Ch. 638 at 648.

[89] *Grant* at 657.

[90] *Grant* at 657. On the relationship between common intention constructive trusts and the doctrine of proprietary estoppel, see paras 15–34 ff.

[91] *Gissing v Gissing* [1971] A.C. 886 at 908; *Grant v Edwards* [1986] Ch. 638 at 655; *Chan Pui Chun v Leung Kam Ho* [2003] 1 F.L.R. 23 at [40] and [99].

[92] (1996) 72 P. & C.R. D22.

[93] [2007] 2 A.C. at [61], reviewing *Oxley v Hiscock* [2004] 2 F.L.R. 669.

15–33 Where the parties have agreed that W should receive a particular share—say, half—in exchange for a quid pro quo, the courts have assumed that this will then be the size of her share if the quid pro quo is provided.[94] However, no court appears to have considered what should happen if W provides some but not all of the quid pro quo. Moreover in cases where the parties agree that W should receive a particular share, in exchange for which she need provide no quid pro quo at all, the further question arises whether the amount which W receives under a constructive trust should be tailored to reflect the amount of detriment which she has suffered? Should a small amount of detriment win W the same size of interest as a large amount of detriment, assuming that both are sufficient to make it unconscionable for M to deny that she should get anything at all? One approach to these questions might be that suggested by Browne-Wilkinson V.C. in *Grant v Edwards*,[95] viz. for the court to act only to the extent necessary to prevent M from acting unconscionably. Thus, in some cases, instead of the promised half share, W might only obtain a quarter share, or indeed might not be entitled to an interest under a constructive trust at all, and might instead be given some other remedy by application of the doctrine of proprietary estoppel, e.g. a charge on the property to secure a sum representing the amount of her financial contributions, or a licence to live in the property until this amount is repaid.[96] It may be, however, that after *Stack v Dowden* the courts will not wish to investigate the terms of any "deal" between the parties too closely, given that the whole of the parties' relationship is grist to the court's mill and given, too, that the intentions of the parties as regards their interests in the property may change, or be taken as having changed, over time.[97]

E. Relationship with Proprietary Estoppel

15–34 An account of the doctrine of proprietary estoppel has been given in Chapter 2.[98] It has often been said that common intention constructive trust principles and proprietary estoppel principles cover much the same ground where family homes are concerned, and it has been suggested that the two bodies of law are underpinned by the same concern to prevent M from unconscionably denying W's entitlement to a remedy where W has detrimentally relied on M'ss assurances.[99] Following *Stack*, however, these two bodies of law now seem to be diverging rather than converging.

15–35 One reason is that the circumstances in which a common intention constructive trust may be imposed now seem to be wider than those in which the doctrine of proprietary estoppel is engaged, given that the court may now impute a fictional common intention to share ownership, and impose a trust to give effect to this "intention", where there have been no assurances and no reliance.

15–36 A second reason is that the remedies available in a proprietary estoppel case are more numerous, and are often weaker, than the award of an equitable interest under a constructive trust, and according to Lord Walker in *Stack v Dowden* they are awarded on a different basis:[100]

---

94 *Gissing* at 905 and 908; *Midland Bank Ltd v Dobson* [1986] 1 F.L.R. 171; *Allen v Snyder* [1977] 2 N.S.W.L.R. 685; *Grant v Edwards* [1986] Ch. 638 at 657; *Savill v Goodall* [1993] 1 F.L.R. 755.

95 [1986] Ch. 638 at 657.

96 *Re Sharpe* [1980] 1 All E.R. 198 at 202; *Maharaj v Chand* [1986] A.C. 898; *Lim Teng Huan v Ang Jwee Chan* [1992] 1 W.L.R. 113; *Burrows v Sharp* [1989] 23 H.L.R. 82; cf. *Tanner v Tanner* [1975] 1 W.L.R. 1346.

97 As stressed in *Stack* at [62] and [138]. See too *Jones v Kernott* [2010] 1 F.L.R. 38 at [27].

98 See paras 2–78 ff.

99 e.g. *Grant v Edwards* [1986] Ch. 638 at 656; *Austin v Keele* (1987) A.L.J.R. 605; *Lloyds Bank v Rosset* [1991] A.C. 107; *Stokes v Anderson* [1991] 1 F.L.R. 391; *Birmingham Midshires v Sabherwal* (1999) 80 P. & C.R. 256 at 263; *Yaxley v Gotts* [2000] Ch. 162 at 176; *Banner Homes v Luff Developments Ltd* [2000] 2 All E.R. 117 at 126; *Oxley v Hiscock* [2004] 2 F.L.R. 669 at [66].

100 *Stack* at [37] applied in *Powell v Benney* [2007] EWCA Civ 1283 at [24].

> "Proprietary estoppel typically consists of asserting an equitable claim against the conscience of the 'true owner'. The claim is a 'mere equity'. It is to be satisfied by the 'minimum award necessary to do justice', which may sometimes lead to no more than a monetary award. A 'common intention' constructive trust, by contrast, is identifying the true beneficial owner or owners, and the size of their beneficial interests."

The "minimum equity to do justice" to W and to prevent M's unconscionable assertion of his strict legal rights depends upon the conduct and relationship of the parties from the date of M's original conduct up until the date when the court makes its decree, and the likely outcome of W's claim may fluctuate during this period.[101] In a proprietary estoppel case, the court is apparently tailoring the remedy to fit the wrong and is not upholding already-existing rights of a proprietary nature.[102] Hence W cannot insist on having the expected interest, as she is a supplicant for the court's discretionary assistance and the court may decide that something less is appropriate.

15–37 In *Thorner v Major*,[103] Lord Scott thought that cases where the claimant relies on a promise that he will be left property on the owner's death can be resolved using constructive trust reasoning, but cannot be resolved using proprietary estoppel reasoning, because circumstances might make it inequitable for the estoppel to be satisfied. However, none of the other members of the court agreed with this, and as Lord Neuberger later observed extrajudicially, it was to get things exactly the wrong way round, by "overestimat[ing] the flexibility of the constructive trust concept, and . . . fail[ing] to appreciate the flexibility of the remedies available in proprietary estoppel."[104]

15–38 A third, related, reason why the two bodies of law now seem to be diverging after a period of convergence concerns the retrospectivity of the courts' orders and their effect on third parties. Previously it was accepted that where M expressed an intention to confer an ownership share on W, but failed to comply with the LPA 1925 s.53(1)(b), the imposition of a constructive trust in W's favour could vindicate the express oral trust by giving her the interest that she would have had if M's express trust had been declared in signed writing.[105] W's interest was therefore assumed to be retrospective,[106] but the date of the oral declaration could not be the date when her interest arose because the trust was then unenforceable.[107] If there was no detrimental reliance by W before M mortgaged the home to X then just as M was not subject to an enforceable trust at that time, so neither was X, who derived title from M. The priority of X over W crystallised at this stage so as not to be affected if W subsequently acted to her detriment or subsequently persuaded M to sign a memorandum evidencing the trust within the Law of Property Act 1925 s.53(1)(b). However, where X acquired a mortgage after W acted detrimentally and W subsequently alleged that she had an interest that bound X, the courts assumed without argument that any interest established in due course by W would indeed bind X.[108]

15–39 Historically, the doctrine of proprietary estoppel was similarly understood to have retrospective effect,[109] but it was later argued that a proprietary estoppel was different,[110] because it gave rise not to

---

[101] *Crabb v Arun DC* [1976] Ch. 179; *Williams v Staite* [1979] Ch. 291; *Dodsworth v Dodsworth* (1973) 228 E.G. 1115; *Griffiths v Williams* (1977) 248 E.G. 947; *Sledmore v Dalby* (1996) 72 P. & C.R. 196.

[102] cf. S. Bright and B. MacFarlane "Personal Liability in Proprietary Estoppel" [2005] Conv. 14.

[103] [2009] 1 W.L.R. 776.

[104] Lord Neuberger, "The Stuffing of Minerva's Owl? Taxonomy and Taxidermy in Equity" (2009) 68 C.L.J. 537, p.549. A sceptical view of Lord Scott's approach is also taken in *Cook v Thomas* [2010] EWCA Civ 227 at [105], per Lloyd L.J.

[105] *Allen v Snyder* [1977] 2 N.S.W.L.R. 685, per Glass J.A.

[106] *Midland Bank v Dobson* [1986] 1 F.L.R. 171; *Lloyds Bank v Rosset* [1989] Ch. 350.

[107] *Gissing v Gissing* [1971] A.C. 887; *Midland Bank v Dobson* [1986] 1 F.L.R. 171. See too paras 3–54 ff.

[108] See e.g. *Midland Bank Plc v Cooke* [1995] 2 F.L.R. 915.

[109] *Plimmer v Mayor of Wellington* (1884) 9 App. Cas. 699; *Re Sharpe* [1980] 1 W.L.R. 219 at 225.

[110] See e.g. P. Ferguson "Constructive Trusts—A Note of Caution" (1993) 109 L.Q.R. 114, p.121.

a beneficial interest, but to a "mere equity", a right to seek an equitable remedy from the court, that could not bind third parties until after the court declared that the claimant had a proprietary interest.[111] Judges and academic writers were divided on this issue, some arguing that court orders in proprietary estoppel cases could generate interests with retrospective effect that were capable of binding third parties, and others that they could not.[112] The Law Commission therefore sought to resolve the issue, at least for registered land, in its Report and draft bill which later became the Land Registration Act 2002 s.116 of which provides that:

> "It is hereby declared for the avoidance of doubt that, in relation to registered land, each of the following—
>
> (a) an equity by estoppel, and
> (b) a mere equity,
>
> has effect from the time the equity arises as an interest capable of binding successors in title (subject to the rules about the effect of dispositions on priority)."

The enactment of s.116 therefore seemed to bring the law of proprietary estoppel and the law of common intention constructive trusts closer together, but *Stack* now seems to be pushing them apart again, because it seems that detrimental reliance is unnecessary in the case of "imputed" common intention constructive trusts.[113] It remains to be seen whether the courts conclude from this that such trusts can be imposed with prospective effect only.[114]

LLOYDS BANK PLC v ROSSET

House of Lords [1991] 1 A.C. 107; [1990] 2 W.L.R. 867; [1990] 1 All E.R. 1111

LORD BRIDGE (with whom LORD GRIFFITHS, LORD ACKNER, LORD OLIVER and LORD JAUNCEY concurred) cited the judge's findings on Mrs Rosset's cleaning, painting and decorating, and then continued: It is clear from these passages in the judgment that the judge based his inference of a common intention that Mrs Rosset should have a beneficial interest in the property under a constructive trust essentially on what Mrs Rosset did in and about assisting in the renovation of the property between the beginning of November 1982 and the date of completion on 17 December 1982. Yet by itself this activity, it seems to me, could not possibly justify any such inference. It was common ground that Mrs Rosset was extremely anxious that the new matrimonial home should be ready for occupation before Christmas if possible. In these circumstances, it would seem the most natural thing in the world for any wife, in the absence of her husband abroad, to spend all the time she could spare and to employ any skills she might have, such as the ability to decorate a room, in doing all she could to accelerate progress of the work quite irrespective of any expectation she might have of enjoying a beneficial interest in the property. The judge's view that some of this work was work "on which she could not reasonably have been expected to embark unless she was to have an interest in the house" seems to me, with respect, quite untenable. **15–40**

On any view the monetary value of Mrs Rosset's work expressed as a contribution to a property acquired at a cost exceeding £70,000 must have been so trifling as to be almost de minimis. I should myself have **15–41**

---

111 K. Gray and S.F. Gray *Elements of Land Law* 4th edn (2005) para.10.212.

112 See sources cited in B. McFarlane "Proprietary Estoppel and Third Parties after the Land Registration Act 2002" (2003) 62 C.L.J. 661, p.662 nn. 4 and 5.

113 See paras 15–28 to 15–30.

114 As suggested in T. Etherton, "Constructive Trusts: A New Model for Equity and Unjust Enrichment" (2008) 67 C.L.J. 265, p.283. For an excellent historical survey of the relationship between proprietary estoppel and common intention constructive trusts, see P. Matthews, "The Words Which Are Not There: A Partial History of the Constructive Trust" in C. Mitchell (ed.), *Constructive and Resulting Trusts* (2010) pp.24–60.

had considerable doubt whether Mrs Rosset's contribution to the work of renovation was sufficient to support a claim to a constructive trust in the absence of writing to satisfy the requirements of s.53 of the Law of Property Act 1925 even if her husband's intention to make a gift to her of half or any other share in the equity of the property had been clearly established or if he had clearly represented to her that that was what he intended. But here the conversations with her husband on which Mrs Rosset relied, all of which took place before November 1982, were incapable of lending support to the conclusion of a constructive trust in the light of the judge's finding that by that date there had been no decision that she was to have any interest in the property. The finding that the discussions "did not exclude the possibility" that she should have an interest does not seem to me to add anything of significance.

15–42 These considerations lead me to the conclusion that the judge's finding that Mr Rosset held the property as constructive trustee for himself and his wife cannot be supported and it is on this short ground that I would allow the appeal. In the course of the argument your Lordships had the benefit of elaborate submissions as to the test to be applied to determine the circumstances in which the sole legal proprietor of a dwelling house can properly be held to have become a constructive trustee of a share in the beneficial interest in the house for the benefit of the partner with whom he or she has cohabited in the house as their shared home. Having in this case reached a conclusion on the facts which, although at variance with the views of the courts below, does not seem to depend on any nice legal distinction and with which, I understand, all your Lordships agree, I cannot help doubting whether it would contribute anything to the illumination of the law if I were to attempt an elaborate and exhaustive analysis of the relevant law to add to the many already to be found in the authorities to which our attention was directed in the course of the argument. I do, however, draw attention to one critical distinction which any judge required to resolve a dispute between former partners as to the beneficial interest in the home they formerly shared should always have in the forefront of his mind.

15–43 The first and fundamental question which must always be resolved is whether, independently of any inference to be drawn from the conduct of the parties in the course of sharing the house as their home and managing their joint affairs, there has at any time prior to acquisition, or exceptionally at some later date, been any agreement, arrangement or understanding reached between them that the property is to be shared beneficially. The finding of an agreement or arrangement to share in this sense can only, I think, be based on evidence of express discussions between the partners, however imperfectly remembered and however imprecise their terms may have been. Once a finding to this effect is made it will only be necessary for the partner asserting a claim to a beneficial interest against the partner entitled to the legal estate to show that he or she has acted to his or her detriment or significantly altered his or her position in reliance on the agreement in order to give rise to a constructive trust or proprietary estoppel.

15–44 In sharp contrast with this situation is the very different one where there is no evidence to support a finding of an agreement or arrangement to share, however reasonable it might have been for the parties to reach such an arrangement if they had applied their minds to the question, and where the court must rely entirely on the conduct of the parties both as the basis from which to infer a common intention to share the property beneficially and as the conduct relied on to give rise to a constructive trust. In this situation direct contributions to the purchase price by the partner who is not the legal owner, whether initially or by payment of mortgage instalments, will readily justify the inference necessary to the creation of a constructive trust. But, as I read the authorities, it is at least extremely doubtful whether anything less will do.

15–45 The leading cases in your Lordships' House are *Pettitt v Pettitt*[115] and *Gissing v Gissing*.[116] Both demonstrate situations in the second category to which I have referred and their Lordships discuss at great length the difficulties to which these situations give rise. The effect of these two decisions is very helpfully analysed in the judgment of Lord MacDermott L.C.J. in *McFarlane v McFarlane*.[117]

15–46 Outstanding examples on the other hand of cases giving rise to situations in the first category are *Eves v Eves*[118] and *Grant v Edwards*.[119] In both these cases, where the parties who had cohabited were unmarried, the female partner had been clearly led by the male partner to believe, when they set up home together, that the property would belong to them jointly. In *Eves v Eves* the male partner had told the

115 [1970] A.C. 777.
116 [1971] A.C. 886.
117 [1972] N.I. 59.
118 [1975] 1 W.L.R. 1338.
119 [1986] Ch. 638.

female partner that the only reason why the property was to be acquired in his name alone was because she was under 21 and that, but for her age, he would have had the house put into their joint names. He admitted in evidence that this was simply an "excuse". Similarly, in *Grant v Edwards* the female partner was told by the male partner that the only reason for not acquiring the property in joint names was because she was involved in divorce proceedings and that, if the property were acquired jointly, this might operate to her prejudice in those proceedings. As Nourse L.J. put it:[120]

> "Just as in *Eves v Eves*, these facts appear to me to raise a clear inference that there was an understanding between the plaintiff and the defendant, or a common intention, that the plaintiff was to have some sort of proprietary interest in the house; otherwise no excuse for not putting her name onto the title would have been needed."

The subsequent conduct of the female partner in each of these cases, which the court rightly held sufficient to give rise to a constructive trust or proprietary estoppel supporting her claim to an interest in the property, fell far short of such conduct as would by itself have supported the claim in the absence of an express representation by the male partner that she was to have such an interest. It is significant to note that the share to which the female partners in *Eves v Eves* and *Grant v Edwards* were held entitled were one-quarter and one-half respectively. In no sense could these shares have been regarded as proportionate to what the judge in the instant case described as a "qualifying contribution" in terms of the indirect contributions to the acquisition or enhancement of the value of the houses made by the female partners. **15–47**

I cannot help thinking that the judge in the instant case would not have fallen into error if he had kept clearly in mind the distinction between the effect of evidence on the one hand which was capable of establishing an express agreement or an express representation that Mrs Rosset was to have an interest in the property and evidence on the other hand of conduct alone as a basis for an inference of the necessary common intention. **15–48**

STACK v DOWDEN

House of Lords [2007] 2 A.C. 432, [2007] 2 W.L.R. 831, [2007] 2 All E.R. 929

The parties began a relationship in 1975 and in 1983 the defendant bought a house in her sole name in which the parties lived together and had four children. The defendant earned more money than the claimant, and made all the payments due under the mortgage and paid the household bills. The parties improved the house and in 1993 it was sold for three times the amount that the defendant had paid for it. The parties then bought another property, which was conveyed into their joint names. Over 65 per cent of the purchase price was paid out of funds from a building society account held in the defendant's sole name, which included the proceeds of sale of the previous house. The balance was provided by a loan secured by a mortgage in the parties' joint names and two endowment policies, one in their joint names and one in the defendant's sole name. The claimant paid the mortgage interest and the premiums due under the endowment policy in their joint names and the defendant paid the premiums due under the endowment policy in her sole name. The parties kept separate bank accounts and made separate savings and investment. The mortgage loan was paid off by a series of lump sum payments of which the defendant provided just under 60 per cent of the capital. The parties separated in 2002 and the claimant left the property while the defendant remained there with the children. The claimant successfully applied to the judge for an order for sale of the property and an equal division of the proceeds. The Court of Appeal allowed the defendant's appeal and ordered that the net proceeds of sale be divided 65 per cent to 35 per cent in the defendant's favour, a decision that was upheld by the House of Lords. The majority of the court agreed with Baroness Hale, who used constructive trust reasoning to arrive at the result; in his dissenting speech Lord Neuberger largely agreed with the result but preferred to use resulting trust reasoning. **15–49**

[120] [1986] Ch. 638 at 649.

15–50 BARONESS HALE (with whom LORD HOFFMANN, LORD HOPE and LORD WALKER agreed): My Lords, the issue before us is the effect of a conveyance into the joint names of a cohabiting couple, but without an explicit declaration of their respective beneficial interests, of a dwelling house which was to become their home. This is, so far as I am aware, the first time that this issue has come before the House, whether the couple be married or, as in this case, unmarried. The principles of law are the same, whether or not the couple are married, although the inferences to be drawn from their conduct may be different.[121]

15–51 **How Does this Problem Come About?**

It may be that, in practice, this is a temporary and transitional problem. It has come about because of developments over the last few decades which would not have been foreseen when the applicable principles and presumptions were first devised. The first development is, of course, the huge expansion in home ownership which has taken place since the Second World War and was given a further boost by the "right to buy" legislation of the 1980s. Coupled with this has been continuing house price inflation, albeit with occasional interruptions such as occurred at the end of the 1980s. This has meant that it is almost always more advantageous for someone who has contributed to the acquisition of the home to claim a share in its ownership rather than the return of the money contributed, even with interest.

15–52 Another development has been the recognition in the courts that, to put it at its lowest, the interpretation to be put on the behaviour of people living together in an intimate relationship may be different from the interpretation to be put upon similar behaviour between commercial men. To put it at its highest, an outcome which might seem just in a purely commercial transaction may appear highly unjust in a transaction between husband and wife or cohabitant and cohabitant. . . . There was a period during which it was thought that the problem might be solved by resort to the power contained in section 17 of the Married Women's Property Act 1882, in disputes between husband and wife as to the title to or possession of property, to make such order "as it thinks fit". The high-water mark of this approach was *Hine v Hine*,[122] in which Lord Denning M.R. held that this discretion "transcends all rights, legal or equitable". That section 17 conferred any discretion to interfere with established titles was firmly rejected by this House in *Pettitt v Pettitt*.[123] Nevertheless, the opinions in that case and in *Gissing v Gissing*[124] contain vivid illustrations of how difficult it is to apply simple assumptions to the complicated, interdependent and often-changing arrangements made between married couples. As Lord Reid famously put it in *Gissing v Gissing*,[125] "It cannot surely depend on who signs which cheques".

15–53 As between married couples, the problem has been addressed (if not solved) by the comprehensive redistributive powers in the Matrimonial Causes Act 1973, if the couple divorce, and in the Inheritance (Provision for Family and Dependants) Act 1975, if one of them dies. The question of who owns what takes second place to the statutory criteria and the approach to those criteria established in cases such as *White v White*.[126] The 1975 Act also gives some more limited help to the survivor of an unmarried cohabiting couple. (Neither, of course, is of any assistance in third party challenges, for example from other relatives.)

15–54 Inter vivos disputes between unmarried cohabiting couples are still governed by the ordinary law. These disputes have become increasingly visible in recent years as more and more couples live together without marrying. The full picture has recently been painted by the Law Commission in *Cohabitation: The Financial Consequences of Relationship Breakdown—A Consultation Paper*.[127] For example, the 2001 Census recorded over 10m married couples in England and Wales, with over 7.5m dependent children; but it also recorded over 2m cohabiting couples, with over 1.25m children dependent upon them. This was a 67 per cent increase in cohabitation over the previous ten years and a doubling of the numbers of such households with dependent children. The Government Actuaries Department predicts that the proportion of couples cohabiting will continue to grow, from the present one in six of all couples to one in four by 2031.

---

121 *Bernard v Josephs* [1982] Ch. 391 at 402, per Griffiths L.J.
122 [1962] 1 W.L.R. 1124 at 1127–1128.
123 [1970] A.C. 777.
124 [1971] A.C. 886.
125 At 987.
126 [2001] 1 A.C. 596.
127 LCCP No.179 (2006) Pt 2 of the Act, and its overview paper, paras 2.3–2.11.

Cohabitation comes in many different shapes and sizes. People embarking on their first serious relationship more commonly cohabit than marry. Many of these relationships may be quite short-lived and childless. But most people these days cohabit before marriage—in 2003, 78.7 per cent of spouses gave identical addresses before marriage, and the figures are even higher for second marriages. So many couples are cohabiting with a view to marriage at some later date—as long ago as 1998 the British Household Panel Survey found that 75 per cent of current cohabitants expected to marry, although only a third had firm plans.[128] Cohabitation is much more likely to end in separation than is marriage, and cohabitations which end in separation tend to last for a shorter time than marriages which end in divorce. But increasing numbers of couples cohabit for long periods without marrying and their reasons for doing so vary from conscious rejection of marriage as a legal institution to regarding themselves "as good as married" anyway.[129] There is evidence of a wide-spread myth of the "common law marriage" in which unmarried couples acquire the same rights as married after a period of cohabitation.[130] There is also evidence that "the legal implications of marriage are a long way down the list of most couples' considerations when deciding whether to marry".[131] **15–55**

The history of attempts at law reform is another illustration of the complexity of the problem. Under item 1 of its *Eighth Programme of Law Reform* (2001),[132] the Law Commission set out to review "the law as it relates to the property rights of those who share a home" (the Commission had in fact been working on the problem for some time). This therefore covered "a broad range of people, including friends and relatives who share a home as well as unmarried couples and married couples (other than on the breakdown of the marriage)". It commented that "It is widely accepted that the present law is unduly complex, arbitrary and uncertain in its application. It is ill-suited to determining the property rights of those who, because of the informal nature of their relationship, may not have considered their respective entitlements." In 2002, however, the commission published *Sharing Homes, A Discussion Paper*.[133] Unlike most Law Commission publications, this did not contain even provisional, let alone final, proposals for reform. Its principal conclusion was that:[134] **15–56**

> "It is quite simply not possible to devise a statutory scheme for the ascertainment and quantification of beneficial interests in the shared home which can operate fairly and evenly across the diversity of domestic circumstances which are now to be encountered."

While this conclusion is not surprising, its importance for us is that the evolution of the law of property to take account of changing social and economic circumstances will have to come from the courts rather than Parliament.

Just as the starting point where there is sole legal ownership is sole beneficial ownership, the starting point where there is joint legal ownership is joint beneficial ownership. The onus is upon the person seeking to show that the beneficial ownership is different from the legal ownership. So in sole ownership cases it is upon the non-owner to show that he has any interest at all. In joint ownership cases, it is upon the joint owner who claims to have other than a joint beneficial interest. . . . **15–57**

The issue as it has been framed before us is whether a conveyance into joint names indicates only that each party is intended to have some beneficial interest but says nothing about the nature and extent of that beneficial interest, or whether a conveyance into joint names establishes a prima facie case of joint and equal beneficial interests until the contrary is shown . . . at least in the domestic consumer context, a conveyance into joint names indicates both legal and beneficial joint tenancy, unless and until the contrary is proved. **15–58**

---

[128] John Ermisch, *Personal Relationships and Marriage Expectations* (2000) Working Papers of the Institute of Social and Economic Research: Paper 2000–27.

[129] LCCP No.179, Pt 2, para.2.45.

[130] Anne Barlow et al., "Just a Piece of Paper? Marriage and Cohabitation", in Alison Park et al. (eds), *British Social Attitudes: Public Policy, Social Ties. The 18th Report* (2001), pp.29–57.

[131] LCCP No.179, Pt 5, para.5.10.

[132] Law Com. No.274.

[133] Law Com. No.278.

[134] Para.1.31.

15–59 The question is, how, if at all, is the contrary to be proved? Is the starting point the presumption of resulting trust, under which shares are held in proportion to the parties' financial contributions to the acquisition of the property, unless the contributor or contributors can be shown to have had a contrary intention? Or is it that the contrary can be proved by looking at all the relevant circumstances in order to discern the parties' common intention?

15–60 The presumption of resulting trust is not a rule of law. According to Lord Diplock in *Pettitt v Pettitt*,[135] the equitable presumptions of intention are "no more than a consensus of judicial opinion disclosed by reported cases as to the most likely inference of fact to be drawn in the absence of any evidence to the contrary". Equity, being concerned with commercial realities, presumed against gifts and other windfalls (such as survivorship). But even equity was prepared to presume a gift where the recipient was the provider's wife or child. These days, the importance to be attached to who paid for what in a domestic context may be very different from its importance in other contexts or long ago. As Kevin Gray and Susan Francis Gray, in *Elements of Land Law*, point out:[136]

> "In recent decades a new pragmatism has become apparent in the law of trusts. English courts have eventually conceded that the classical theory of resulting trusts, with its fixation on intentions presumed to have been formulated contemporaneously with the acquisition of title, has substantially broken down. . . . Simultaneously the balance of emphasis in the law of trusts has transferred from crude factors of money contribution (which are pre-eminent in the resulting trust) towards more subtle factors of intentional bargain (which are the foundational premise of the constructive trust). . . . But the undoubted consequence is that the doctrine of resulting trust has conceded much of its field of application to the constructive trust, which is nowadays fast becoming the primary phenomenon in the area of implied trusts."

There is no need for me to rehearse all the developments in the case law since *Pettitt v Pettitt* and *Gissing v Gissing*, discussed over more than 70 pages . . . by Chadwick L.J. in *Oxley v Hiscock*,[137] and most importantly by my noble and learned friend, Lord Walker of Gestingthorpe, in his opinion, which make good that proposition. The law has indeed moved on in response to changing social and economic conditions. The search is to ascertain the parties' shared intentions, actual, inferred or imputed, with respect to the property in the light of their whole course of conduct in relation to it.

15–61 *Oxley v Hiscock* was, of course, a different case from this. The property had been conveyed into the sole name of one of the cohabitants. The claimant had first to surmount the hurdle of showing that she had any beneficial interest at all, before showing exactly what that interest was. The first could readily be inferred from the fact that each party had made some kind of financial contribution towards the purchase. As to the second, Chadwick L.J. said:[138]

> "in many such cases, the answer will be provided by evidence of what they said and did at the time of the acquisition. But, in a case where there is no evidence of any discussion between them as to the amount of the share which each was to have—and even in a case where the evidence is that there was no discussion on that point—the question still requires an answer. It must now be accepted that (at least in this court and below) the answer is that *each is entitled to that share which the court considers fair having regard to the whole course of dealing between them in relation to the property*. And in that context, 'the whole course of dealing between them in relation to the property' includes the arrangements which they make from time to time in order to meet the outgoings (for example, mortgage contributions, council tax and utilities, repairs, insurance and housekeeping) which have to be met if they are to live in the property as their home."

[135] [1970] A.C. 777 at 823.
[136] 4th edn (2005), p.864, para.10.21.
[137] [2005] Fam. 211.
[138] At [69]. (Emphasis supplied by Baroness Hale.)

Oxley v Hiscock has been hailed by Gray and Gray as "an important breakthrough".[139] The passage quoted is very similar to the view of the Law Commission in *Sharing Homes, A Discussion Paper*, on the quantification of beneficial entitlement:[140]

> "If the question really is one of the parties' 'common intention', we believe that there is much to be said for adopting what has been called a 'holistic approach' to quantification, undertaking a survey of the whole course of dealing between the parties and taking account of all conduct which throws light on the question what shares were intended."

That may be the preferable way of expressing what is essentially the same thought, for two reasons. First, it emphasises that the search is still for the result which reflects what the parties must, in the light of their conduct, be taken to have intended. Second, therefore, it does not enable the court to abandon that search in favour of the result which the court itself considers fair. For the court to impose its own view of what is fair upon the situation in which the parties find themselves would be to return to the days before *Pettitt v Pettitt* without even the fig leaf of section 17 of the 1882 Act.

Furthermore, although the parties' intentions may change over the course of time, producing what my noble and learned friend, Lord Hoffmann, referred to in the course of argument as an "ambulatory" constructive trust, at any one time their interests must be the same for all purposes. They cannot at one and the same time intend, for example, a joint tenancy with survivorship should one of them die while they are still together, a tenancy in common in equal shares should they separate on amicable terms after the children have grown up, and a tenancy in common in unequal shares should they separate on acrimonious terms while the children are still with them. **15–62**

We are not in this case concerned with the first hurdle. There is undoubtedly an argument for saying, as did the Law Commission in *Sharing Homes, A Discussion Paper*,[141] that the observations, which were strictly obiter dicta, of Lord Bridge of Harwich in *Lloyds Bank Plc v Rosset*[142] have set that hurdle rather too high in certain respects. But that does not concern us now. It is common ground that a conveyance into joint names is sufficient, at least in the vast majority of cases, to surmount the first hurdle. The question is whether, that hurdle surmounted, the approach to quantification should be the same. **15–63**

The majority of cases reported since *Pettitt v Pettitt* and *Gissing v Gissing* have concerned homes conveyed into the name of one party only and it is in that context that the more flexible approach to quantification identified by Chadwick L.J. in *Oxley v Hiscock* has emerged.[143] **15–64**

Curiously, it is in the context of homes conveyed into joint names but without an express declaration of trust that the courts have sometimes reverted to the strict application of the principles of the resulting trust.[144] However, Chadwick L.J. commented in *Oxley v Hiscock*:[145] **15–65**

> "47. It is, I think, important to an understanding of the reasoning in the judgments in *Springette v Defoe* that each member of this court seems to have thought that when Lord Bridge referred, in *Lloyds Bank Plc v Rosset*,[146] to the need to base a 'finding of an agreement or arrangement to share in this sense' on 'evidence of express discussions between the partners' he was addressing the secondary, or consequential, question—'what was the common intention of the parties as to the extent of their respective beneficial interests'—rather than the primary, or threshold, question—'was there a common intention that each should have a beneficial interest in the property?' . . .

---

139 *Elements of Land Law*, 4th edn, p.931, para.10.138.

140 At para.4.27.

141 At para.4.23.

142 [1991] 1 A.C. 107.

143 See, in particular, *Grant v Edwards* [1986] Ch. 638, described by Chadwick L.J. as "an important turning point" and referred to with "obvious approval" in *Lloyds Bank Plc v Rosset* [1991] 1 A.C. 107; *Stokes v Anderson* [1991] 1 F.L.R. 391; *Midland Bank Plc v Cooke* [1995] 2 F.L.R. 915; and *Drake v Whipp* [1996] 1 F.L.R. 826.

144 See *Walker v Hall* [1984] F.L.R. 126 and two cases decided by the same court on the same day, *Springette v Defoe* [1992] 2 F.L.R. 388 and *Huntingford v Hobbs* [1993] 1 F.L.R. 736 ; but cf. *Crossley v Crossley* [2006] 2 F.L.R. 813.

145 [2005] Fam. 211 at 235.

146 [1991] 1 A.C. 107 at 132.

> "48. For the reasons which I have sought to explain, I think that the better view is that, in the passage in *Rosset's case*, to which both Dillon L.J. and Steyn L.J. referred in *Springette v Defoe*[147] Lord Bridge was addressing only the primary question—'was there a common intention that each should have a beneficial interest in the property?' He was not addressing the secondary question—'what was the common intention of the parties as to the extent of their respective beneficial interests?' As this court had pointed out in *Grant v Edwards* and *Stokes v Anderson*, the court may well have to supply the answer to that secondary question by inference from their subsequent conduct. . . ."

In the case before us, he observed:[148]

> ". . . I have not altered my view that, properly understood, the authorities before (and after) *Springette v Defoe* do not support the proposition that, absent discussion between the parties as to the extent of their respective beneficial interests at the time of purchase, it must follow that the presumption of resulting trust is not displaced and the property is necessarily held in beneficial shares proportionate to the respective contributions to the purchase price."

With these passages I entirely agree. The approach to quantification in cases where the home is conveyed into joint names should certainly be no stricter than the approach to quantification in cases where it has been conveyed into the name of one only. To the extent that *Walker v Hall, Springette v Defoe*, and *Huntingford v Hobbs* hold otherwise, they should not be followed.

15–66 However, Chadwick L.J. went on to say that:[149]

> "there is no reason in principle why the approach to the second question—'what is the extent of the parties' respective beneficial interests in the property?'—should be different, in a case where the property is registered in the joint names of cohabitees, from what it would be if the property were registered in the sole name of one of them; although the fact that it has been registered in joint names is, plainly, to be taken into account when having regard 'to the whole course of dealing between them in relation to the property'."

But the questions in a joint names case are not simply "what is the extent of the parties' beneficial interests?" but "did the parties intend their beneficial interests to be different from their legal interests?" and "if they did, in what way and to what extent?" There are differences between sole and joint names cases when trying to divine the common intentions or understanding between the parties. I know of no case in which a sole legal owner (there being no declaration of trust) has been held to hold the property on a beneficial joint tenancy. But a court may well hold that joint legal owners (there being no declaration of trust) are also beneficial joint tenants. Another difference is that it will almost always have been a conscious decision to put the house into joint names. Even if the parties have not executed the transfer, they will usually, if not invariably, have executed the contract which precedes it. Committing oneself to spend large sums of money on a place to live is not normally done by accident or without giving it a moment's thought.

15–67 This is not to say that the parties invariably have a full understanding of the legal effects of their choice: there is recent empirical evidence from a small scale qualitative study to confirm that they do not.[150] But that is so whether or not there is an express declaration of trust and no-one thinks that such a declaration can be overturned, except in cases of fraud or mistake. Nor do they always have a completely free choice in the matter. Mortgagees used to insist upon the home being put in the name of the person whom they assumed would be the main breadwinner. Nowadays, they tend to think that it is in their best interests that the home be jointly owned and both parties assume joint and several liability for the mortgage. (It is, of course, a matter of indifference to the mortgagees where the beneficial interests lie.) Here again, this factor does not invalidate the parties' choice if there is an express declaration of trust, nor should it automatically count against it where there is none.

[147] See [1992] 2 F.L.R. 388 at 393 and 395, agreed with by Sir Christopher Slade at 397.

[148] At [24].

[149] At [26].

[150] See Gillian Douglas, Julia Pearce and Hilary Woodward, "Dealing with Property Issues on Cohabitation Breakdown" [2007] Fam. Law. 36.

15–68 The burden will therefore be on the person seeking to show that the parties did intend their beneficial interests to be different from their legal interests, and in what way. This is not a task to be lightly embarked upon. In family disputes, strong feelings are aroused when couples split up. These often lead the parties, honestly but mistakenly, to reinterpret the past in self-exculpatory or vengeful terms. They also lead people to spend far more on the legal battle than is warranted by the sums actually at stake. A full examination of the facts is likely to involve disproportionate costs. In joint names cases it is also unlikely to lead to a different result unless the facts are very unusual. Nor may disputes be confined to the parties themselves. People with an interest in the deceased's estate may well wish to assert that he had a beneficial tenancy in common. It cannot be the case that all the hundreds of thousands, if not millions, of transfers into joint names using the old forms are vulnerable to challenge in the courts simply because it is likely that the owners contributed unequally to their purchase.

15–69 In law, "context is everything" and the domestic context is very different from the commercial world. Each case will turn on its own facts. Many more factors than financial contributions may be relevant to divining the parties' true intentions. These include: any advice or discussions at the time of the transfer which cast light upon their intentions then; the reasons why the home was acquired in their joint names; the reasons why (if it be the case) the survivor was authorised to give a receipt for the capital moneys; the purpose for which the home was acquired; the nature of the parties' relationship; whether they had children for whom they both had responsibility to provide a home; how the purchase was financed, both initially and subsequently; how the parties arranged their finances, whether separately or together or a bit of both; how they discharged the outgoings on the property and their other household expenses. When a couple are joint owners of the home and jointly liable for the mortgage, the inferences to be drawn from who pays for what may be very different from the inferences to be drawn when only one is owner of the home. The arithmetical calculation of how much was paid by each is also likely to be less important. It will be easier to draw the inference that they intended that each should contribute as much to the household as they reasonably could and that they would share the eventual benefit or burden equally. The parties' individual characters and personalities may also be a factor in deciding where their true intentions lay. In the cohabitation context, mercenary considerations may be more to the fore than they would be in marriage, but it should not be assumed that they always take pride of place over natural love and affection. At the end of the day, having taken all this into account, cases in which the joint legal owners are to be taken to have intended that their beneficial interests should be different from their legal interests will be very unusual.

15–70 This is not, of course, an exhaustive list. There may also be reason to conclude that, whatever the parties' intentions at the outset, these have now changed. An example might be where one party has financed (or constructed himself) an extension or substantial improvement to the property, so that what they have now is significantly different from what they had then. . . .

7. Unauthorised Fiduciary Gains

15–71 As previously noted in Chapter 9,[151] a trustee may not place himself in a position where his personal interest and the beneficiaries' interests may conflict, and this principle underpins the rule that a trustee must account to his beneficiaries for any unauthorised profits that he makes from his trusteeship, and indeed that a constructive trust will be imposed on these profits or their traceable proceeds. Reasoning by way of analogy from the relationship between trustees and beneficiaries, the courts have generalised this rule and have also applied it to other relationships where one party (the "fiduciary") voluntarily assumes power over, and responsibility for, the financial and/or legal affairs of another (the "principal").

A. *Who is a Fiduciary?*

15–72 The relationship of trustee and beneficiary is the original fiduciary relationship and provides the guidelines for determining when other persons are in a fiduciary relationship to each other by virtue of the

[151] See paras 9–14 ff.

position and power of one in respect of the other and the latter's reasonably induced expectation that the former will act exclusively in the interests of the latter or of their joint interest.[152] Trustees are persons who are under a duty to act exclusively in the interests of the trust beneficiaries, who are vulnerable, if the trustees seek to abuse their position, because the trustees have rights and powers that are capable of being exercised so as detrimentally to affect the beneficiaries. Thus, if such aspects are present in other relationships these are treated as fiduciary relationships as a matter of law, e.g. personal representatives and beneficiaries of deceased's estate,[153] solicitor and client,[154] principal and agent[155] (including a self-appointed agent[156]), partner and partner,[157] promoter and company,[158] director and company,[159] underwriter and Lloyd's names,[160] employee and employer while the employment relationship subsists.[161]

15–73 Once a fiduciary relationship has been established it is necessary to ascertain the scope and ambit of the fiduciary's duties of fidelity and loyalty, which will be affected by the terms of any contract between the parties.[162] Then one can examine whether the fiduciary has placed himself in a position where his personal interest may possibly conflict with those duties. If so, then he is accountable for all profits made from acting within the scope and ambit of his fiduciary duties.[163] Note that he cannot escape liability to account for profits obtained in breach of fiduciary duty by resigning his post and then taking an opportunity for himself that came to him in his capacity as fiduciary.[164]

15–74 Separate from fiduciary relationships arising as a matter of law from status[165] are fact-based fiduciaries who become subject to fiduciary duties because of a particular factual situation where the imposition of such duties is considered appropriate in the interests of justice because of the claimant's particular vulnerability to being taken advantage of by the defendant upon whose loyalty he is reasonably relying, e.g. in the case of a financier using confidential information imparted by A

---

152 Generally see P.D. Finn, "The Fiduciary Principle" in T.G. Youdan (ed.), *Equity, Trusts and Fiduciary Relationships* (1989); P.D. Finn, "Fiduciary Law and the Modern Commercial World" in E. McKendrick (ed.), *Commercial Aspects of Trusts and Fiduciary Obligations*; P. Birks (ed.), *Privacy and Loyalty* (1997) Chapters 8, 10 and 11; P. Birks, "The Content of Fiduciary Obligation" (2002) 16 Tru. L.I. 34; L. Smith, "The Motive, Not the Deed" in J. Getzler (ed.), *Rationalizing Property, Equity and Trusts* (2003); S. Worthington, *Equity* (2003), pp.117–131; M Conaglen, "The Nature and Function of Fiduciary Loyalty" (2005) 121 L.Q.R. 452.

153 *Re Diplock* [1948] Ch. 465.

154 *Nocton v Lord Ashburton* [1914] A.C. 932; *McMaster v Byrne* [1952] 1 All E.R. 1362; *Clark Boyce v Mouat* [1994] 1 A.C. 428; *Hilton v Barker Booth & Eastwood (a firm)* [2005] 1 W.L.R. 567.

155 *Lowther v Lowther* (1806) 13 Ves. 95 at 103; *Parker v McKenna* (1874) 10 Ch. App. 96 at 124–125; *Boston Deep Sea Fishing Co v Ansell* (1888) 39 Ch.D. 389; *Att.-Gen. of Hong Kong v Reid* [1994] 1 A.C. 324 on how *Lister v Stubbs* (1890) 45 Ch.D. 1 should have been decided; *Fyffes Group Ltd v Templeman* [2000] 2 Lloyd's Rep. 643; *Imageview Management Ltd v Jack* [2009] Bus. L.R. 34.

156 *English v Dedham Vale Properties Ltd* [1978] 1 W.L.R. 93.

157 *Bentley v Craven* (1853) 18 Beav. 75; *Thompson's Trustee v Heaton* [1974] 1 All E.R. 1239; *John Taylors (a firm) v Masons* [2005] W.T.L.R. 1519

158 *Lydney Iron Ore Co v Bird* (1886) 33 Ch.D. 85 at 94; *Gluckstein v Barnes* [1900] A.C. 240.

159 *Furs Ltd v Tomkies* (1936) 54 C.L.R. 583; *Regal (Hastings) Ltd v Gulliver* [1967] 2 A.C. 134; *Ke Allied Business & Financial Consultants Ltd* [2009] 2 B.C.L.C. 666.

160 *Sphere Drake Insurance Ltd v Euro International Underwriting Ltd* [2003] Lloyd's Rep. I.R. 525 at [40]–[47].

161 *Att.-Gen. v Blake* [1998] Ch. 439; *Nottingham University v Fishel* [2000] I.C.R. 1462; *Neary v Dean of Westminster* [1999] I.R.L.R. 288.

162 *Kelly v Cooper* [1993] A.C. 205.

163 *Phipps v Boardman* [1967] 2 A.C. 46 at 128–129; *Warman International Ltd v Dwyer* (1995) 69 A.L.J.R. 362.

164 *Industrial Development Consultants Ltd v Cooley* [1972] 1 W.L.R. 443; *Canadian Aero Services Ltd v O'Malley* (1973) 40 D.L.R. (3d) 371; *Abbey Glen Pty Co v Stumborg* (1978) 85 D.L.R. (3d) 35; *CMS Dolphin Ltd v Simonet* [2001] 2 B.C.L.C. 704. Contrast *Queensland Mines Ltd v Hudson* (1978) 18 A.L.R. 1; *Island Export Finance Ltd v Umunna* [1986] B.C.L.C. 460; *Framlington Group Plc v Anderson* [1995] 1 B.C.L.C. 475; *Foster Bryant Surveying Ltd v Bryant* [2007] Bus. L.R. 1565.

165 *Hodgkinson v Simms* (1994) 117 D.L.R. (4th) 161 at 176, 215; P.D. Finn, in T.G. Youdan (ed.) *Equity, Trusts and Fiduciary Relationships*, pp. 33–44; Law Commission, *Fiduciary Duties and Regulatory Rules* (Law Com. No.124), para.2.4.3.

(when seeking a loan) to help B conclude a deal to the exclusion of A and to the profit of B and the financier,[166] or of the parties to a joint venture where they were entitled to expect that the other would act in their joint interest to the exclusion of his own several interest.[167]

The distinction between fact-based fiduciaries and status-based fiduciaries is illuminated by contrasting the position of financial advisers and of discretionary portfolio managers. It seems that the latter should be regarded automatically as fiduciaries with their unilateral powers to invest and disinvest as they see fit.[168] In the case of the former it is a question of fact whether or not the parties' relationship was such as to give rise to a fiduciary duty on the part of the adviser: the circumstances can cover the whole spectrum from total reliance upon the adviser to total independence of the adviser.[169] **15–75**

B. Scope of Fiduciary Duties

The scope of a defendant's fiduciary obligations depends upon the nature and scope of his relationship with the claimant.[170] He is not to be made liable in respect of profits derived by him outside the scope of the claimant's business nor to be obliged to prefer the claimant's interests to his own outside such scope. "A person may be in a fiduciary position *quoad* a part of his activities and not *quoad* other parts."[171] Thus, a partner is not accountable to his partners for profits made from a business outside the scope of the partnership business.[172] A director is a fiduciary in relation to his company[173] but not to any shareholder[174] (unless exceptionally the shareholder had turned to the director so as to place special reliance on the director[175]), while the director's obligations, particularly in respect of business opportunities, depend upon the actual and prospective line(s) of business of the company.[176] **15–76**

While a solicitor is a status-based fiduciary, his negligence in carrying out his duties does not amount to a breach of fiduciary duty.[177] Such a breach requires breach of the fiduciary's obligation of loyalty, e.g. acting for a client in a matter that the solicitor has a personal interest without fully disclosing this or acting for both sides in a transaction without disclosing this to one of them.[178] While an agent is a status-based fiduciary, if the principal allows the agent to mix moneys paid in respect of **15–77**

---

166 *United Pan Europe Communications NV v Deutsche Bank AG* [2000] 2 B.C.L.C. 461.

167 *Lac Minerals Ltd v International Corona Resources Ltd* (1989) 61 D.L.R. (4th) 14; *Hospital Products Ltd v US Surgical Corp* (1984) 156 C.L.R. 41; *Noranda Australia Ltd v Lachlan Resources* (1988) 14 N.W.S.L.R. 1; *John v James* [1991] F.S.R. 397 at 433; *Elliott v Wheeldon* [1993] B.C.L.C. 53 at 57; *Murad v Al-Saraj* [2005] W.T.L.R. 1573.

168 *Glennie v McDougall* [1935] S.C.R. 357 at 276; *Hewson v Stock Exchange* [1968] 2 N.S.W.L.R. 245.

169 *Woods v Martin's Bank* [1959] 1 Q.B. 55; *Daly v Sydney Stock Exchange* (1986) 160 C.L.R. 371; *Hodgkinson v Simms* (1994) 117 D.L.R. (4th) 161; *JP Morgan Bank v Springwell Navigation Corp* [2008] EWHC 1186 (Comm).

170 "To say that a man is a fiduciary only begins analysis: it gives direction to further enquiry. To whom is he a fiduciary? What obligations does he owe as a fiduciary? In what respect has he failed to discharge these obligations? And what are the consequences of his deviation from duty?" per Frankfurter J. in *SEC v Chenery Corp* 318 U.S. 80 at 85–86 (1943), endorsed by Lord Mustill in *Re Goldcorp Exchange Ltd* [1995] A.C. 74 at 98.

171 *New Zealand Netherlands Society Oranje Inc v Kuys* [1973] 2 All E.R. 1222 at 1225; *Vercoe v Rutland Fund Management Ltd* [2010] EWHC 424 (Ch) at [348]–[350].

172 *Aas v Benham* [1891] 2 Ch. 244.

173 *Regal Hastings Ltd v Gulliver* [1967] 2 A.C. 134n; *Industrial Development Consultants v Cooley* [1972] 1 W.L.R. 443.

174 *Percival v Wright* [1902] 2 Ch. 421; *North-West Transportation Co Ltd v Beatty* (1887) 12 App. Cas. 589.

175 *Coleman v Myers* [1977] 2 N.Z.L.R. 225; *Brunninghausen v Glaranics* (1999) 46 N.S.W.L.R. 538; *Peskin v Anderson* [2001] 1 B.C.L.C. 372 at [27]–[37].

176 *Queensland Mines Ltd v Hudson* (1978) 52 A.L.J.R. 394; *Canadian Aero Services Ltd v O'Malley* (1973) 40 D.L.R. (3rd) 371, *CMS Dolphin Ltd v Simonet* [2001] 2 B.C.L.C. 704; *Bhullar v Bhullar* [2003] 2 B.C.L.C. 241.

177 *Bristol & West BS v Mothew* [1998] Ch. 1, CA. As Lord Mustill said in *Re Goldcorp Exchange Ltd* [1995] A.C. 74 at 98, "The essence of a fiduciary relationship is that it creates obligations of a different character from those deriving under the contract itself".

178 *Clark Boyce v Mouat* [1994] 1 A.C. 428; *Farrington v Row McBride & Partners* [1985] 1 N.Z.L.R. 83; *Witten-Hannah v Davis* [1995] 2 N.Z.L.R. 141.

sums due to the principal with the agent's own money and account monthly to the principal for the moneys owed to the principal, the agent is only personally liable in debt to the principal.[179] However, if the agent had agreed to hold all money received on the principal's behalf from the principal's debtors separate from his own money for the principal's exclusive benefit, the principal would have an equitable proprietary interest in the money held by the agent as fiduciary.[180]

15–78 Where the fiduciary relationship arises from a contract or a partnership or trust deed or other instrument then the terms of the instrument are relevant for qualifying the scope of the fiduciary's obligations.[181] However, a fiduciary relationship can arise in the course of negotiating the terms of a contract or trust,[182] in which case abuse of such relationship or the exercise of undue influence can prevent the fiduciary relying on a clause exempting him from negligence or breach of fiduciary duties.[183]

C. Unauthorised Profits

15–79 Trustees and other fiduciaries owe a personal liability to account for unauthorised profits made in the course of their engagement and, if necessary, a constructive trust will be imposed to capture these profits for the beneficiaries or principal. These rules ultimately derive from Lord King L.C.'s decision in *Keech v Sandford*,[184] which is reproduced below.[185] They take in the case where a trustee makes unauthorised gains through the misuse of trust property, whether by using trust funds to acquire a new asset,[186] or by other means.[187] They also take in many other situations where a fiduciary makes unauthorised gains by reason of his office: for example, where he is paid unauthorised remuneration for his services,[188] takes a bribe to act against his principal's best interests,[189] or misappropriates a profit-making opportunity which comes to him in his fiduciary capacity.[190] The rule is strictly applied. It makes no difference that the fiduciary has acted in good faith, that his actions have caused the principal no loss, nor even that they have left him better off.[191] The courts have traditionally given two reasons for this strict approach: first, that fiduciaries must be given "an incentive . . . to resist the temptation to misconduct themselves";[192] and second, that a principal would often face insuperable

---

179 *Henry v Hammond* [1953] 2 K.B. 515; *Commissioners of Customs & Excise v Richmond Theatre* [1995] S.T.C. 257; *R. v Clowes (No.2)* [1994] 2 All E.R. 316.

180 *Lord Napier and Ettrick v Hunter* [1993] A.C. 713 at 744; *Re Fleet Disposal Services Ltd* [1995] 1 B.C.L.C. 345.

181 *Kelly v Cooper* [1993] A.C. 205; *New Zealand Netherlands Society Oranje Inc v Kuys* [1973] 2 All E.R. 1222; *Hilton v Barker Booth and Eastwood (a firm)* [2005] 1 W.L.R. 567 at [30].

182 *Swain v Law Society* [1981] 3 All E.R. 797 at 817.

183 *Tate v Williamson* (1866) 2 Ch. App.55 at 61; *Baskerville v Thurgood* (1992) 100 Sask. L.R. 214.

184 (1726) Sel. Cas. T. King 61. The history of the case is discussed in J. Getzler, "Rumford Market and the Genesis of Fiduciary Obligations", in A. Burrows and Lord Rodger (eds), *Mapping the Law: Essays in Honour of Peter Birks* (2006).

185 At paras 15–93 ff.

186 *Foskett v McKeown* [2001] 1 A.C. 102 at 127.

187 e.g. *Aberdeen Town Council v Aberdeen University* (1877) 2 App. Cas. 544 (Crown grant of salmon fishings made to trustees as owners of trust land); *Brown v IRC* [1965] A.C. 244 (interest earned on money in solicitors' client account); *Wells v Wells* (1967) 204 E.G. 687 (trust property let to trustee for less than market rent).

188 Fiduciaries must act gratuitously unless payment is authorised: *Robinson v Pett* (1734) 3 P. Wms 249; *Barrett v Hartley* (1866) L.R. 2 Eq. 789. Where shares are held on trust and the trustee uses his voting rights to obtain a remunerated appointment as a director of the company, he must account for his remuneration to the beneficiaries: *Re Francis* (1905) 74 L.J. Ch. 198; *Re Gee* [1948] Ch. 284.

189 *Att.-Gen. for Hong Kong v Reid* [1994] 1 A.C. 324.

190 *Phipps v Boardman* [1967] 2 A.C. 46; *Bhullar v Bhullar* [2003] 2 B.C.L.C. 241.

191 *Regal (Hastings) Ltd v Gulliver* [1967] 2 A.C. 134 at 144–5; *Warman International Ltd v Dwyer* (1995) 182 C.L.R. 544 at 558.

192 *Murad v Al-Saraj* [2005] W.T.L.R. 1573 at [74], per Arden L.J. The reports contain many similar dicta, e.g. *Docker v Somes* (1834) 2 My. & K. 655 at 665; *Bray v Ford* [1896] A.C. 44 at 51; *Guinness Plc v Saunders* [1990] 2 A.C. 663 at 701; *Lindsley v Woodfull* [2004] 2 B.C.L.C. 131 at [30].

evidential difficulties, were he required to prove that his fiduciary had acted in bad faith and had failed to do everything he could have done.[193]

15–80 It can be questioned whether deterrence is a convincing rationale for the firm treatment meted out to fiduciaries in this class of case. In Lionel Smith's view,[194] deterrence reasoning comprises an undesirable incursion of public law into the private law sphere: it disrupts the internal rationality of private law because it looks outside the relationship between the claimant and defendant, and the conduct giving rise to the litigation. More pragmatically, he has also observed that "a rule that only takes away the defendant's gain is not much of a deterrent" by comparison with a penalty[195]—which the English courts have always declined to impose on defaulting fiduciaries.[196] Taking a different tack, John Langbein has pointed to the harmful *over-deterrent* effect of a rule which can strip fiduciaries of unauthorised gains made through transactions which are prudently entered in their principals' best interests.[197] The rule has bad effects for principals because it deters fiduciaries from seeking out and developing opportunities in a way that would benefit the principals as well as the fiduciaries. By stifling entrepreneurship it is also bad for the economy as a whole.[198]

15–81 Langbein has also questioned the continued validity of the second, evidence-based rationale, observing that the strict rules governing fiduciary liability were developed 200 years ago when shortcomings in the fact-finding processes of the Chancery courts set a premium on rules that avoided fact-finding. The fusion of the Chancery and common law courts, and successive reforms of civil procedure, have left the courts far better equipped in this respect, and at the same time:[199]

> "improvements in the standards, practices and technology of trust recordkeeping, as well as enhanced duties of disclosure . . . have largely defused the old concern that a trustee operating under a potential conflict could easily conceal wrongdoing."

15–82 Obviously the courts are not blind to such concerns, and they have sometimes sought to moderate the law's harshness by making allowances to honest fiduciaries who have contributed time, skill and effort towards making the gains for which they are liable to account.[200] However, the courts have baulked at developing this line of authority to the point of apportioning profits between the

---

193 This was a frequent refrain of Lord Eldon's: e.g. *ex parte Lacey* (1802) 6 Ves. Jun. 625 at 627; *ex parte James* (1803) 8 Ves. Jun. 337 at 345. Lord Wright expressed similar concerns in *Regal (Hastings) Ltd v Gulliver* [1967] 2 A.C. 134 at 154.

194 L. Smith, "The Motive, Not the Deed", in J. Getzler (ed.), *Rationalizing Property, Equity and Trusts* (2003) 53, pp.60–61.

195 Smith, p.60. But cf. R. Cooter and B.J. Freedman, "The Fiduciary Relationship: Its Economic Character and Legal Consequences" (1991) 66 N.Y.U. Law Review 1045, pp.1048–1056, arguing that the rules requiring disgorgement of fiduciary gains have a greater deterrent effect than Smith admits because they require disgorgement even in cases where the fiduciary has not acted disloyally.

196 e.g. *Re Brogden* (1886) 38 Ch.D. 546 at 557. Saying that a rule has a weak deterrent effect is obviously not the same thing as saying that it has *no* deterrent effect: M. Conaglen, "The Nature and Function of Fiduciary Loyalty" (2005) 121 L.Q.R. 452, p.464.

197 J.H. Langbein, "Questioning the Trust Law Duty of Loyalty: Sole Interest or Best Interest?" (2005) 114 Yale L.J. 929. See too J.H. Langbein, "Mandatory Rules in the Law of Trusts" (2004) 98 Northwestern University Law Review 1105. But compare M.B. Leslie, "In Defense of the No Further Inquiry Rule: A Response to Professor John Langbein" (2005) 47 William and Mary Law Review 541.

198 J. Lowry and R. Edmunds, "The No Conflict–No Profit Rules and the Corporate Fiduciary: Challenging the Orthodoxy of Absolutism" [2000] J.B.L. 122, arguing (at p.123) that the answer is "to draw upon the US model and to assimilate the corporate opportunities doctrine". This is doubted in D. Kershaw, "Lost in Translation: Corporate Opportunities in Comparative Perspective" (2005) 25 O.J.L.S. 603.

199 Langbein (2005), above, p.932.

200 As in e.g. *Phipps v Boardman* [1967] 2 A.C. 46 at 102 and 112; *O'Sullivan v Management Agency and Music Ltd* [1985] Q.B. 42; *Badfinger Music Ltd v Evans* [2001] W.T.L.R. 1.

parties,[201] and in England they have become less willing even to make a quantum meruit award following Lord Goff's statement in *Guinness Plc v Saunders*, that the exercise of the courts' jurisdiction should be restricted to cases where an award would not have the effect of encouraging fiduciaries to put themselves in a position of conflict.[202] In *Murad v Al-Saraj* the Court of Appeal suggested in obiter dicta that the time may have come for the English courts to "revisit the operation of the inflexible rule of equity in harsh circumstances",[203] and to take a more nuanced approach where the fiduciary has acted in good faith, but this suggestion has not yet been taken up.

15–83 The fiduciary "must account . . . for any benefit or gain which has been obtained or received in circumstances where a conflict or significant possibility of conflict existed between his fiduciary duty and his personal interest in the pursuit or possible receipt of such a benefit or gain."[204] He also "must account . . . for any benefit or gain which was obtained or received by use or by reason of his fiduciary position or of opportunity or knowledge resulting from it" where he is "actually misusing his position for his personal advantage" rather than for the advantage of his principal(s). However, if information is acquired by a fiduciary in the course of his duties and it is not classified as confidential information he is free to use the information for the benefit of himself or of another trust of which he is trustee if there is no reasonably foreseeable possibility of his needing to use that information for his original principal(s).[205] Where information acquired by a fiduciary or his "tippee" (to whom he passes the information) is confidential so that its disclosure could be prevented by a court injunction then, although such information has insufficient "property" nature for the law of theft, it may have sufficient "property" nature for profits made by use of such information to be held on constructive trust,[206] though since then abuse of position (in addition to exploitation of fiduciary property) has been held sufficient to justify the imposition of a constructive trust on property obtained as a result of such abuse.[207]

15–84 Before a defaulting fiduciary must account for a gain in his hands, the principal must establish a causal link between the gain and the breach of fiduciary duty committed by the defendant.[208] Otherwise, a principal who proved a breach of duty would be entitled to recover *every* gain made by the fiduciary and "no fiduciary is liable for all the profits he ever made from any source".[209] The test used

201 *Warman International Ltd v Dwyer* (1995) 182 C.L.R. 544 at 562. The courts' reluctance to do this stands in marked contrast to cases such as *Foskett v McKeown* [2001] 1 A.C. 102 where assets are bought with a mixture of beneficiaries' money and the trustee's own money and the capital profits on resale are split pro rata (see para.13–97). Two reasons have been suggested for this difference of approach: (1) "the influence of property concepts . . . [has] been too strong" for the courts to restrict fiduciaries to the value of their initial input in the latter type of case: D. Friedmann, "Restitution for Wrongs: The Measure of Recovery" (2001) 79 Texas L.R. 1879, p.1899; (2) as a necessary evidential preliminary to claiming an ownership share in assets acquired with the principal's property and the fiduciary's labour, the fiduciary must trace the value of his labour into the value inherent in the asset, but his labour "does not deliver a 'physical exchange', and so . . . delivers no traceable substitute" under the tracing rules as they are generally understood: T. Akkouh and S. Worthington *"Re Diplock"* in C. Mitchell and P. Mitchell (eds), *Landmark Cases in the Law of Restitution* (2006) p.312.

202 *Guinness Plc v Saunders* [1990] 2 A.C. 663 at 701, followed in e.g. *Quarter Master UK Ltd (in liq.) v Pyke* [2005] 1 B.C.L.C. 245 at [76]–[77], though cf. *Nottingham University v Fishel* [2000] I.C.R. 1462 at 1499–1500. See too *Imageview Management Ltd v Jack* [2009] Bus. L.R. 1034 at [54]–[60]; and cf. para.8–58.

203 [2005] W.T.L.R. 1573 at [82], per Arden L.J. For concurring dicta, see [121] per Jonathan Parker L.J. and [156]–[158] per Clarke L.J. The same point was previously made in *Holder v Holder* [1968] Ch. 353 at 398.

204 *Chan v Zachariah* (1984) 154 C.L.R. 178 at 199 where all the citations in this paragraph are to be found.

205 *Phipps v Boardman* [1967] 2 A.C. 46 at 130.

206 *Nanus Asia Co Inc v Standard Chartered Bank* [1990] Hong Kong L.R. 396.

207 *Att.-Gen. for Hong Kong v Reid* [1994] 1 A.C. 324.

208 *Maguire v Makaronis* (1997) 188 C.L.R. 449 at 468: there is "a need to specify criteria for a sufficient connection (or 'causation') between breach of duty and the profit derived." See too *Swain v Law Society* [1982] 1 W.L.R. 17 at 37; *Estate Realties Ltd v Wignall* [1992] 2 N.Z.L.R. 615 at 631; *Button v Phelps* [2006] EWHC 53 (Ch) at [66].

209 *Murad v Al-Saraj* [2005] W.T.L.R. 1573 at [62], per Arden L.J. See too *3464920 Canada Inc v Strother* (2005) 7 I.T.E.L.R. 748 at [47].

to determine whether a fiduciary's gain has been caused by a breach of fiduciary duty is a simple one. The breach must have been one cause of the gain. It need not have been the only cause, nor need it have been the predominant cause, for "in this sort of case the court 'does not allow an examination into the relative importance of contributory causes' ".[210] Nor can the fiduciary escape liability by proving that he would have made the gain even if he had not breached his duty: "the question whether or not the benefit would have been obtained but for the breach of trust has always been treated as irrelevant."[211] Furthermore, "the court lays the burden on the defaulting fiduciary to show that the profit is not one for which he should account".[212] In effect, therefore, he must prove that his breach of duty had no causative effect whatsoever, by showing that the gain came into his hands exclusively as a result of activities legitimately undertaken in his own interest.

These rules were applied in *Murad v Al-Saraj*,[213] where the claimants agreed to participate in a property development deal with the defendant who owed them fiduciary duties of fidelity and loyalty. The claimants put up £1 million in cash in the belief that he would also contribute cash towards the purchase price, but in fact he never paid any cash to the vendor who instead released him from a legally unenforceable liability arising out of their prior personal dealings. Had the claimants been aware of this fact, they would have gone ahead with the deal but rather than agreeing to a half and half capital profit split on resale of the hotel, they would have insisted on a higher profit share for themselves. After the hotel was sold, the facts came to light, and the claimants asserted that the defendant's share of the profits were all held on constructive trust for them, as the proceeds of his breach of fiduciary duty. He claimed to keep that portion of the profits which they would have let him take even if he had made full disclosure, i.e. he argued that a "but-for" causation test should be used to identify the gains for which he should account. This was roundly rejected by Arden and Jonathan Parker L.JJ., in whose view "the courts decline to investigate hypothetical situations as to what would have happened if the fiduciary had performed his duty",[214] and "it is no defence for a fiduciary to say that he would have made the profit even if there had been no breach of duty."[215] **15–85**

D. *Proprietary and/or Personal Liability*

If there is a proprietary liability because a fiduciary F holds specific property as constructive trustee then there is a co-extensive personal liability to account and if F is wealthy enough the claimants will usually be happy enough to rely on F's personal liability and take the cash profits from him (rather than take the property upon paying F sufficient for his lien on the property for its cost to him). Thus, a House of Lords case like *Regal Hastings Ltd v Gulliver*[216] was pleaded only as a personal claim to account and in *Phipps v Boardman*[217] counsel and judges concentrated upon making the wealthy Boardman personally liable to **15–86**

[210] *Fexuto Pty Ltd v Bosnjak Holdings Pty Ltd (No.2)* (1998) 29 A.C.S.R. 290 at 297, per Young J., quoting from *Barton v Armstrong* [1976] A.C. 104 at 118. *Barton* was a claim to set aside a contract on the ground of duress to the person where the defendant had put a gun to the claimant's head. It is a measure of the strength of Young J.'s deterrent impulse that he thought it appropriate to analogise between *Barton* and a claim to strip a fiduciary of unauthorised gains.

[211] *Brickenden v London Loan & Savings Co* [1934] 3 D.L.R. 465 at 469; *Industrial Development Consultants Ltd v Cooley* [1972] 1 W.L.R. 443 at 453; *Beach Petroleum NL v Kennedy* (1999) 48 N.S.W.L.R. 1 at [440]; *Gwembe Valley Development Co Ltd (in rec.) v Koshy (No.3)* [2004] 1 B.C.L.C. 131 at [145]–[146].

[212] *Murad* at [77], per Arden L.J.

[213] [2005] W.T.L.R. 1573. See too *Manley v Santori* [1927] 1 Ch. 157, approved in *Murad* at [77]; *Gray v New Augarita Porcupine Mines Ltd* [1952] 3 D.L.R. 1 at 15.

[214] *Murad* at [76].

[215] *Murad* at [67].

[216] [1967] 2 A.C. 134.

[217] [1967] 2 A.C. 46.

account. In *Phipps v Boardman*, which is reproduced below,[218] the claimant with a 5/18 interest under a trust claimed (i) a declaration that the defendants held 5/18 of the shareholding obtained by them through using information acquired by them when representing the trust as constructive trustees for him, (ii) an account of the profits made by the defendants, and (iii) an order that they should transfer to him the shares held by them as constructive trustees and should pay him 5/18 of profits found to be due upon taking the account. Wilberforce J. gave the claimant the relief requested under (i) and (ii) but adjourned (iii) having ordered an inquiry as to a liberal allowance for the defendant's work. Presumably, this was to allow the taking of accounts of profits made on sale of some of the shares and the inquiry as to the proper payment to be allowed to the defendants for their skilful efforts, whereupon the balance would be due to the claimant, who could then consider whether to call for the remaining shares subject to reimbursing the defendants for their costs in purchasing the shares. No doubt, at the end of the day the claimant preferred to receive all cash rather than cash plus shares, and the defendants agreed to this.

15–87 The Court of Appeal and the House of Lords, due to counsels' concentration on personal accountability, held that the defendants were constructive trustees who were liable to account for their profits but they confirmed Wilberforce J.'s order which included a proprietary declaration of constructive trust.[219] Where the gain emanates from property entrusted to the fiduciary it is clear that the gain should be held on a proprietary constructive trust, but three[220] of the five Law Lords held that the defendants' information obtained qua fiduciaries was not trust property so that the shares purchased as a result of using such information did not thereby constructively become trust property. Two Law Lords[221] thought that there was no sensible possibility of conflict of duty and interest. However, the majority[222] thought that there was: the defendant as solicitor to the trustees was not in a position to give disinterested impartial advice at the stage when he was almost about to make large profits for himself and yet when he ought, if consulted, to have been advising the trustees to obtain wider investment powers from the court so as to enable the trust (and not himself) to make large profits. Thus, the defendants had to account for their profits on the shares because they had acquired the knowledge and the opportunity to purchase the shares while purporting to represent the trust.

15–88 The Lords did not openly consider the question of a proprietary constructive trust but the court order accepts the existence of such a trust, so that the use of position as opposed to the use of trust property seemed capable of generating a proprietary constructive trust of the profit made in breach of the duty to avoid conflicts of interest. This was despite an earlier contrary Court of Appeal decision, *Lister v Stubbs*,[223] rejecting any constructive trust of a bribe obtained by a fiduciary abusing his position, so that the dishonest fiduciary was only personally accountable for the bribe and his employer could not trace the bribe into assets purchased therewith. Subsequently Lord Templeman, delivering the advice of the Privy Council in *Att.-Gen. for Hong Kong v Reid*,[224] reproduced below,[225] rejected that decision and explained that *Phipps v Boardman:*

> "demonstrates the strictness with which equity regards the conduct of a fiduciary and the extent to which equity is willing to impose a constructive trust on property obtained by a fiduciary by virtue of his office . . . the solicitor was held to be a constructive trustee . . . because the solicitor obtained the information . . . and the opportunity of acquiring the shares as a result of acting for

---

218 At paras 15–98 ff.
219 See [1964] 2 All E.R. 187 at 208; [1965] Ch. 992 at 1006, 1021; [1967] 2 A.C. 46 at 99, 112.
220 Lords Cohen and Upjohn and Viscount Dilhorne.
221 Viscount Dilhorne and Lord Upjohn.
222 Lords Hodson, Guest and Cohen; see at paras 6–53 et seq.
223 (1890) 45 Ch.D. 1.
224 [1994] 1 A.C. 324. See too *Daraydan Holdings Ltd v Solland International Ltd* [2005] Ch. 119.
225 At paras 15–129 ff.

> certain purposes on behalf of the trustees. If a fiduciary acting honestly in good faith and making a profit which his principal could not make for himself becomes a constructive trustee of that profit, then a fiduciary acting dishonestly who accepts a bribe must also be a constructive trustee."

Thus, the Attorney General could enter a caveat against three New Zealand properties purchased with bribes received by Reid as public prosecutor to drop prosecutions, such properties being held on constructive trust for the Crown.

It seems easier to support a proprietary constructive trust in *Lister* and *Reid* than in *Boardman*. In a bribe case is there not an incontrovertible assumption that the victim has lost property of a value at least equal to the bribe, so that the bribe may justifiably be regarded as representing the victim's property? As between the victim and the fiduciary surely the victim has a better claim not only to the bribe but to the fruits thereof: the fiduciary would certainly be unjustly enriched if allowed to retain the bribe and its fruits. If he himself should not benefit from his dishonest wrongdoing why should his creditors be better off and receive a windfall if he is insolvent? **15–89**

In *Boardman* the case for a proprietary constructive trust for profits gained by use of position seems weaker. The profit, literally speaking, was not made at the expense of the beneficiaries, though it was made at the expense of the fiduciary not being able to give disinterested advice to the beneficiaries (if asked) and so at the risk of harming the beneficiaries' interests. Should the latter honest but wrongful breach of his duty to avoid a conflict make the fiduciary subject to a proprietary constructive trust of his profit as opposed to a mere personal liability to account? **15–90**

E. Defences

It will be a defence to show that the conduct generating the profit was authorised by the trust instrument expressly or by necessary implication,[226] or by the contract of agency,[227] or the deed of partnership, or the articles of a company,[228] or by the court.[229] A further defence is to show the informed consent of all the beneficiaries being each of full capacity and between them absolutely entitled to the trust property.[230] A partner will need the consent of the other partners; a director the consent of all the members of the company for it will be a fraud on the minority to expropriate property held on a constructive trust for the company.[231] It would seem that someone employed by trustees in a fiduciary position (e.g. a solicitor or accountant) or a beneficiary acquiring special information while purportedly representing the trust so as to be treated as a fiduciary, may have a defence if obtaining the informed consent of independent trustees.[232] **15–91**

---

226 *Re Llewellin* [1949] Ch. 225; *Sargeant v National Westminister Bank* (1990) 61 P. & C.R. 518; *Edge v Pensions Ombudsman* [1998] Ch. 512.

227 *Kelly v Cooper* [1993] A.C. 205.

228 *Movitex Ltd v Bulfield* [1988] B.C.L.C. 104; *Guinness Plc v Saunders* [1990] 2 A.C. 663.

229 e.g. Trustee Act s.42; CPR Pt 64.

230 *Phipps v Boardman* [1967] 2 A.C. 46.

231 *Cook v Deeks* [1916] 1 A.C. 554; *Borland's Trustees v Steel Bros Ltd* [1901] Ch. 279. In contrast a majority by resolution in general meeting may waive a director's personal liability to account if they consider he acted in the company's best interests: *Regal (Hastings) Ltd v Gulliver* [1967] 2 A.C. 134.

232 *Regal (Hastings) Ltd v Gulliver* [1967] 2 A.C. 134 (solicitor not liable though closely involved with the directors as emerges from *Luxor (Eastbourne) Ltd v Cooper* [1941] A.C. 108, especially [1939] 4 All E.R. 411 at 414–417); *Phipps v Boardman* [1967] 2 A.C. 46 at 93 and 117 and implicit in Lord Upjohn's speech 130–133; *Anson v Potter* (1879) 13 Ch.D. 141. The trustees should be independent just like company directors must be if disclosure to them is to protect a promoter: *Gluckstein v Barnes* [1900] A.C. 240. If to the fiduciary's knowledge a fund is distributable under a bare trust because the beneficiaries are each of full capacity and between them absolutely entitled to call for the capital then according to Lord Cohen in *Phipps v Boardman* [1967] 2 A.C. 46 at 104, the informed consent of the beneficiaries is required. Presumably, trustees can employ an agent to exploit information on terms he receives as fee a percentage of the profit.

15–92 Where a fiduciary in his professional capacity may have clients with differing interests he has to cope with his need not to have his fiduciary duty to one conflicting with his duty to another. He can take advantage of the principle that the scope of the fiduciary duties owed by him to his clients is to be defined by the express or implied terms of his contract with each of them.[233] Indeed, "it is the contractual foundation which is all-important. . . . The fiduciary relationship, if it is to exist at all, must accommodate itself to the terms of the contract so that it is consistent with, and conforms to, them."[234]

KEECH v SANDFORD

Lord Chancellor (1726) 2 Eq.Cas.Abr. 741; Sel.Cas.Ch. 61

15–93 A person being possessed of a lease of the profits of a market devised his estate to a trustee in trust for his infant. Before the expiration of the term the trustee applied to the lessor for a renewal, for the benefit of the infant, which he refused, since the lease being only of the profits of a market, there could be no distress, and its enforcement must rest in covenant, by which the infant could not be bound. The infant sought to have the lease assigned to him, and for an account of the profits, on the principle that wherever a lease is renewed by a trustee or executor it shall be for the benefit of the cestui que use, which principle was agreed on the other side, though endeavoured to be differenced on account of the express proof of refusal to renew to the infant.

15–94 LORD KING L.C.: I must consider this as a trust for the infant, for I very well see, if a trustee, on the refusal to renew, might have a lease to himself, few trust estates would be renewed to cestui que use. Though I do not say there is fraud in this case, yet he should rather have let it run out than to have had the lease to himself. This may seem hard, that the trustee is the only person of all mankind who might not have the lease; but it is very proper that the rule should be strictly pursued, and not in the least relaxed; for it is very obvious what would be the consequences of letting trustees have the lease on refusal to renew to cestui que use.

15–95 So decreed, that the lease should be assigned to the infant, and that the trustee should be indemnified from any covenants comprised in the lease, and an account of the profits made since the renewal.

15–96 The rule applies whether the trustee obtains a renewal by virtue of a provision in the lease to that effect or whether he obtains it by virtue of the advantage which his position as sitting tenant gives him.[235] The principle applies not only to trustees and tenants for life,[236] but also to mortgagees,[237] directors[238] and partners.[239] But unlike trustees and tenants for life the latter group of persons are not irrebuttably precluded from taking the renewal of a lease. In *Re Biss*,[240] a lease formed part of the personalty of an intestate, and after the lessor had refused to renew to the administratrix, one of her sons (helping her run the deceased's business at the premises) obtained a renewal for himself. It was held, however, to be unimpeachable, since he could show affirmatively that he acted bona fide and did not

---

233 *Kelly v Cooper* [1993] A.C. 205; *Clark Boyce v Mouat* [1994] 1 A.C. 428.

234 *Hospital Products Ltd v United States Surgical Corp* (1984) 156 C.L.R. 41 at 97 endorsed in *Kelly v Cooper*, above.

235 *Re Knowles' Will Trusts* [1948] 1 All E.R. 866.

236 *James v Dean* (1808) 15 Ves. 236; *Lloyd-Jones v Clark-Lloyd* [1919] 1 Ch. 424; ss. 16, 107 of the Settled Land Act 1925.

237 *Rushworth's Case* (1676) Freem.Ch. 13; *Leigh v Burnett* (1885) 29 Ch.D. 231.

238 *GE Smith Ltd v Smith* [1952] N.Z.L.R. 470; *Crittenden & Cowler Co v Cowler* 72 N.Y. 701 (1901).

239 *Featherstonhaugh v Fenwick* (1810) 17 Ves. 298; cf. *Piddock v Burt* [1894] 1 Ch. 343; *John Taylors (a firm) v Masons (a firm)* [2001] EWCA Civ 2106; *Lindsley v Woodfall* [2004] 2 B.C.L.C. 131.

240 [1903] 2 Ch. 40.

take advantage of the other persons interested. Romer L.J. said,[241] "where the person renewing the lease does not clearly occupy a fiduciary position" he "is only held to be a constructive trustee of the renewed lease if, in respect of the old lease, he occupied some special position and owed, by virtue of that position, a duty towards the other persons interested."

In *Protheroe v Protheroe*[242] the Court of Appeal in a one-page extempore judgment of Lord Denning held that under the *Keech v Sandford* principle there was "a long-established rule of equity" that a trustee purchasing the reversion upon a lease held by him automatically held the reversion upon the same trusts as the lease. This is unsound as till then such constructive trusts of the reversion were only imposed where the lease was renewable by custom or contract (the purchase thus cutting off the right of renewal) or where the trustee obtained the reversion by virtue of his position qua leaseholder (e.g. a landlord offering enfranchisement to all his leaseholders).[243] The reason for the distinction is that whereas in the case of a renewal the trustee is in effect buying a part of the trust property, in the case of a reversion this is not so; it is a separate item altogether. However, *Protheroe* can be justified because purchasers of a reversion fall foul of the strict principles illustrated by *Phipps v Boardman*, below, especially since the trustee would personally be the landlord of the trust tenancy. **15–97**

PHIPPS v BOARDMAN

House of Lords [1967] 2 A.C. 46; [1966] 3 All E.R. 721

The respondent, Mr J.A. Phipps, was one of the residuary legatees under the will of his father, Mr C.W. Phipps, who died in 1944. The residuary estate included 8,000 out of 30,000 issued shares in a private company, Lester & Harris Ltd. By his will the testator left an annuity to his widow and subject thereto 5/18 of his residuary estate to each of his three sons and 3/18 to his only daughter. At the end of 1955 the trustees of the will were the testator's widow (who was senile and took no part in the affairs of the trust), his only daughter, Mrs Noble, and an accountant, Mr W. Fox. The first appellant, Mr T.G. Boardman, was at all material times solicitor to the trustees and also to the children of the testator (other than the respondent). The second appellant, Mr T.E. Phipps, was the younger brother of the respondent and in the transactions which gave rise to this action he was associated with and represented by the first appellant, Mr Boardman. **15–98**

In 1956 Mr Boardman and Mr Fox decided that the recent accounts of Lester & Harris Ltd were unsatisfactory and with a view to improving the position the appellants attended the annual general meeting of the company in December 1956 with proxies obtained from two of the trustees, Mrs Noble and Mr Fox. They were not satisfied with the answers given at the meeting regarding the state of the company's affairs. Shortly after this meeting the appellants decided with the knowledge of Mrs Noble and Mr Fox to try to obtain control of Lester & Harris Ltd by themselves making an offer for all the outstanding shares in that company other than the 8,000 held by the trustees. The trustees had no power to invest in the shares of the company without the sanction of the court and Mr Fox said in evidence that he would not have considered seeking such sanction. The appellants originally offered £2 5s per share, which they later increased to £3, but by April 1957 they had received acceptances only in respect of 2,925 shares and it was clear that as things then stood they would not go through with their offer. This ended the first phase in the negotiations which ultimately led to the acquisition by the appellants of virtually all the outstanding shares in Lester & Harris Ltd. During this phase the appellants attended the annual general meeting as **15–99**

[241] ibid. at 61. See *Chan v Zachariah* (1984) 154 C.L.R. 178.
[242] [1968] 1 W.L.R. 519; followed in *Thompson's Trustee v Heaton* [1974] 1 W.L.R. 605.
[243] *Bevan v Webb* [1905] 1 Ch. 620; *Longton v Wilsby* (1887) 76 L.T. 770; *Randall v Russell* (1817) 3 Mer. 190; *Phillips v Phillips* (1884) 29 Ch.D. 673; *Brenner v Rose* [1973] 1 W.L.R. 443 at 448, but cf. *Thompson's Trustee v Heaton* [1974] 1 W.L.R. 605; *Popat v Shonchhatra* [1995] 4 All E.R. 646.

proxies of the two trustees and obtained information from the company as to the prices at which shares had recently changed hands; but they made the offer to purchase on their own behalf.

15–100 The second phase lasted from April 1957 to August 1958. Throughout this period Mr Boardman carried on negotiations with the chairman of Lester & Harris Ltd with a view to reaching agreement on the division of the assets of that company between the Harris family and the directors on the one hand and the Phipps family on the other. During this phase Mr Boardman obtained valuable information as to the value of the company's assets and throughout he purported to act on behalf of the trustees. These negotiations proved abortive.

15–101 The third phase began in August 1958 with the suggestion by Mr Boardman that he and Mr T.E. Phipps should acquire for themselves the outstanding shares in the company. The widow died in November 1958 and a conditional agreement for the sale of the shares was made on March 10, 1959. On May 26, 1959, the appellants gave notices making the agreements unconditional to buy 14,567 shares held by the chairman of the company and his associates at £4 10s per share. This, in addition to the earlier agreements to purchase 2,925 shares at £3 each and the purchase of a further 4,494 shares at £4 10s each, made the appellants holders of 21,986 shares.

15–102 Thereafter the business of the company was reorganised, part of its assets was sold off at considerable profit, and substantial sums of capital, amounting in the aggregate to £5 17s 6d per share, were returned to the shareholders, whose shares were still worth at least £2 each after the return of capital. The appellants acted honestly throughout.

15–103 The respondent, like the other members of the Phipps family, was asked by Mr Boardman whether he objected to the acquisition of control of the company by the appellants for themselves; but Mr Boardman did not give sufficient information as to the material facts to succeed in the defence of consent on the part of the respondent. At first the respondent expressed his satisfaction but later he became antagonistic and issued a writ claiming (i) that the appellants held 5/18 of the above-mentioned 21,986 shares as constructive trustees for him[244] and (ii) an account of the profits made by the appellants out of the said shares. Wilberforce J. granted this relief[245] and his decision was affirmed by the Court of Appeal,[246] and this decision was affirmed in turn by a majority of the House of Lords (Lords Cohen, Hodson and Guest; Viscount Dilhorne and Lord Upjohn dissenting).

15–104 LORD COHEN: . . . As Wilberforce J. said,[247] the mere use of any knowledge or opportunity which comes to the trustee or agent in the course of his trusteeship or agency does not necessarily make him liable to account. In the present case had the company been a public company and had the appellants bought the shares on the market, they would not, I think have been accountable. The company, however, is a private company and not only the information but also the opportunity to purchase these shares came to them through the introduction which Mr Fox gave them to the board of the company and, in the second phase, when the discussions related to the proposed split up of the company's undertaking, it was solely on behalf of the trustees that Mr Boardman was purporting to negotiate with the board of the company. The question is this: when in the third phase the negotiations turned to the purchase of the shares at £4 10s a share, were the appellant debarred by their fiduciary position from purchasing on their own behalf the 21,986 shares in the company without the informed consent of the trustees and the beneficiaries?

15–105 Wilberforce J.[248] and, in the Court of Appeal,[249] both Lord Denning M.R. and Pearson L.J. based their decision in favour of the respondent on the decision of your Lordships' House in *Regal (Hastings) Ltd v Gulliver*.[250] I turn, therefore, to consider that case. Counsel for the respondent relied on a number of passages in the judgments of the learned Lords who heard the appeal, in particular on (i) a passage in the speech of Lord Russell of Killowen where he said:[251]

---

244 The appellants would, of course, have a lien for their outlay on the purchase of the shares.
245 [1964] 1 W.L.R. 993.
246 [1965] Ch. 992 (Lord Denning M.R., Pearson and Russell L.JJ.).
247 [1964] 1 W.L.R. 993 at 1011.
248 ibid.
249 [1965] Ch. 992.
250 [1942] 1 All E.R. 378.
251 ibid. at 386.

> "The rule of equity which insists on those, who by use of a fiduciary position make a profit, being liable to account for that profit, in no way depends on fraud, or absence of bona fides; or upon such questions or considerations as whether the profit would or should otherwise have gone to the plaintiff, or whether the profiteer was under a duty to obtain the source of the profit for the plaintiff, or whether he took a risk or acted as he did for the benefit of the plaintiff, or whether the plaintiff has in fact been damaged or benefited by his action. The liability arises from the mere fact of a profit having, in the stated circumstances, been made"

(ii) a passage in the speech of Lord Wright where he says:[252]

> "That question can be briefly stated to be whether an agent, a director, a trustee or other person in an analogous fiduciary position, when a demand is made upon him by the person to whom he stands in the fiduciary relationship to account for profits acquired by him by reason of his fiduciary position, and by reason of the opportunity and the knowledge, or either, resulting from it, is entitled to defeat the claim upon any ground save that he made profits with the knowledge and assent of the other person. The most usual and typical case of this nature is that of principal and agent. The rule in such cases is compendiously expressed to be that an agent must account for net profits secretly (that is, without the knowledge of his principal) acquired by him in the course of his agency. The authorities show how manifold and various are the applications of the rule. It does not depend on fraud or corruption."

These paragraphs undoubtedly help the respondent but they must be considered in relation to the facts of that case. In that case the profit arose through the application by four of the directors of Regal for shares in a subsidiary company which it had been the original intention of the board should be subscribed for by Regal. Regal had not the requisite money available but there was no question of it being ultra vires Regal to subscribe for the shares. In the circumstances Lord Russell of Killowen said:[253] "I have no hesitation in coming to the conclusion, upon the facts of this case, that these shares, when acquired by the directors, were acquired by reason, and only by reason, of the fact that they were directors of Regal, and in the course of their execution of that office." He went on to consider whether the four directors were in a fiduciary relationship to Regal and concluded that they were. Accordingly, they were held accountable. Counsel for the appellants argued that the present case is distinguishable. He puts his argument thus. The question one asks is whether the information could have been used by the principal for the purpose for which it was used by his agents. If the answer to that question is no, the information was not used in the course of their duty as agents. In the present case the information could never have been used by the trustees for the purpose of purchasing shares in the company; therefore purchase of shares was outside the scope of the appellants' agency and they are not accountable.

This is an attractive argument, but it does not seem to me to give due weight to the fact that the appellants obtained both the information which satisfied them that the purchase of the shares would be a good investment and the opportunity of acquiring them as a result of acting for certain purposes on behalf of the trustees. Information is, of course, not property in the strict sense of that word and, as I have already stated, it does not necessarily follow that, because an agent acquired information and opportunity while acting in a fiduciary capacity, he is accountable to his principals for any profit that comes his way as the result of the use he makes of that information and opportunity. His liability to account must depend on the facts of the case. In the present case much of the information came the appellants' way when Mr Boardman was acting on behalf of the trustees on the instructions of Mr Fox, and the opportunity of bidding for the shares came because he purported for all purposes except for making the bid to be acting on behalf of the owners of the 8,000 shares in the company. In these circumstances it seems to me that the principle of the Regal case applies and that the courts below came to the right conclusion. **15–106**

That is enough to dispose of the case but I would add that an agent is, in my opinion, liable to account for profits which he makes out of the trust property if there is a possibility of conflict between his interest and his duty to his principal. Mr Boardman and Mr Tom Phipps were not general agents of the trustees, but they were their agents for certain limited purposes. The information which they had obtained and the **15–107**

[252] ibid. at 392.
[253] ibid. at 387.

opportunity to purchase the 21,986 shares afforded them by their relations with the directors of the company—an opportunity they got as the result of their introduction to the directors by Mr Fox—were not property in the strict sense but that information and that opportunity they owed to their representing themselves as agents for the holders of the 8,000 shares held by the trustees. In these circumstances they could not, I think, use that information and that opportunity to purchase the shares for themselves if there was any possibility that the trustees might wish to acquire them for the trust. Mr Boardman was the solicitor whom the trustees were in the habit of consulting if they wanted legal advice. Granted that he would not be bound to advise on any point unless he were consulted, he would still be the person they would consult if they wanted advice. He would clearly have advised them that they had no power to invest in shares of the company without the sanction of the court. In the first phase he would also have had to advise on the evidence then available that the court would be unlikely to give such sanction: but the appellants learnt much more during the second phase. It may well be that even in third phase the answer of the court would have been the same but, in my opinion, Mr Boardman would not have been able to give unprejudiced advice if he had been consulted by the trustees and was at the same time negotiating for the purchase of the shares on behalf of himself and Mr Tom Phipps. In other words, there was, in my opinion, at the crucial date (March 1959) a possibility of a conflict between his interest and his duty.

15–108 In making these observations I have referred to the fact that Mr Boardman was the solicitor to the trust. Mr Tom Phipps was only a beneficiary and was not as such debarred from bidding for the shares, but no attempt was made in the courts below to differentiate between them. Had such an attempt been made it would very likely have failed, as Mr Tom Phipps left the negotiations largely to Mr Boardman, and it might well be held that, if Mr Boardman was disqualified from bidding, Mr Tom Phipps could not be in a better position. Be that as it may, counsel for the appellants rightly did not seek at this stage to distinguish between the two. He did, it is true, say that Mr Tom Phipps as a beneficiary would be entitled to any information that the trustees obtained. This may be so, but nonetheless I find myself unable to distinguish between the two appellants. They were, I think, in March 1959, in a fiduciary position vis-à-vis the trust. That fiduciary position was of such a nature that (as the trust fund was distributable) the appellants could not purchase the shares on their own behalf without the informed consent of the beneficiaries: it is now admitted that they did not obtain that consent. They are therefore, in my opinion, accountable to the respondent for his share of the net profits which they derived from the transaction.

15–109 I desire to repeat that the integrity of the appellants is not in doubt. They acted with complete honesty throughout, and the respondent is a fortunate man in that the rigour of equity enables him to participate in the profits which have accrued as the result of the action taken by the appellants in March 1959 in purchasing the shares at their own risk. As the last paragraph of his judgment clearly shows, the trial judge evidently shared this view. He directed an inquiry as to what sum was proper to be allowed to the appellants or either of them in respect of their or his work and skill in obtaining the said shares and the profits in respect thereof. The trial judge concluded by expressing the opinion that payment should be on a liberal scale. With that observation I respectfully agree. . . .

15–110 LORD HODSON: . . . The proposition of law involved in this case is that no person standing in a fiduciary position, when a demand is made on him by the person to whom he stands in the fiduciary relationship to account for profits acquired by him by reason of his fiduciary position and by reason of the opportunity and the knowledge, or either, resulting from it, is entitled to defeat the claim on any ground save that he made profits with the knowledge and assent of the other person . . .

15–111 . . . it is said on behalf of the appellants that information as such is not necessarily property and it is only trust property which is relevant. I agree, but it is nothing to the point to say that in these times corporate trustees, e.g. the Public Trustee and others, necessarily acquire a mass of information in their capacity of trustees for a particular trust and cannot be held liable to account if knowledge so acquired enables them to operate to their own advantage, or to that of other trusts. Each case must depend on its own facts, and I dissent from the view that information is of its nature something which is not properly to be described as property. We are aware that what is called "know-how" in the commercial sense is property which may be very valuable as an asset. I agree with the learned judge[254] and with the Court of Appeal[255] that the

[254] [1964] 1 W.L.R. 993 at 1008–1011.
[255] [1965] Ch. 992.

confidential information acquired in this case, which was capable of being and was turned to account, can be properly regarded as the property of the trust. It was obtained by Mr Boardman by reason of the opportunity which he was given as solicitor acting for the trustees in the negotiations with the chairman of the company, as the correspondence demonstrates. The end result was that, out of the special position in which they were standing in the course of the negotiations, the appellants got the opportunity to make a profit and the knowledge that it was there to be made. . . .

Regal (Hastings) Ltd v Gulliver differs from this case mainly in that the directors took up shares and made a profit thereby, it having been originally intended that the company should buy these shares. Here there was no such intention on the part of the trustees. There is no indication that they either had the money or would have been ready to apply to the court for sanction enabling them to do so. On the contrary, Mr Fox, the active trustee and an accountant who concerned himself with the details of the trust property, was not prepared to agree to the trustees buying the shares and encouraged the appellants to make the purchase. This does not affect the position. As *Keech v Sandford* shows, the inability of the trust to purchase makes no difference to the liability of the appellants, if liability otherwise exists. The distinction on the facts as to intention to purchase shares between this case and *Regal (Hastings) Ltd v Gulliver* is not relevant. The company (Regal) had not the money to apply for the shares on which the profit was made. The directors took the opportunity which they had presented to them to buy the shares with their own money and were held accountable. Mr Fox's refusal as one of the trustees to take any part in the matter on behalf of the trust, so far as he was concerned, can make no difference. Nothing short of fully informed consent, which the learned judge found not to have been obtained, could enable the appellants in the position which they occupied, having taken the opportunity provided by that position, to make a profit for themselves. . . . **15–112**

The confidential information which the appellants obtained at a time when Mr Boardman was admittedly holding himself out as solicitor for the trustees was obtained by him as representing the trustees, the holders of 8,000 shares of Lester & Harris Ltd. As Russell L.J. put it:[256] "The substantial trust shareholding was an asset of which one aspect was its potential use as a means of acquiring knowledge of the company's affairs, or of negotiating allocations of the company's assets, or of inducing other shareholders to part with their shares." That aspect was part of the trust assets. Whether this aspect is properly to be regarded as part of the trust assets is, in my judgment, immaterial. The appellants obtained knowledge by reason of their fiduciary position, and they cannot escape liability by saying that they were acting for themselves and not as agents of the trustees. Whether or not the trust, or the beneficiaries in their stead, could have taken advantage of the information is immaterial, as the authorities clearly show. No doubt it was but a remote possibility that Mr Boardman would ever be asked by the trustees to advise on the desirability of an application to the court in order that the trustees might avail themselves of the information obtained. Nevertheless, whenever the possibility of conflict is present between personal interest and the fiduciary position the rule of equity must be applied . . . **15–113**

LORD GUEST: . . . I take the view that from first to last Mr Boardman was acting in a fiduciary capacity to the trustees. This fiduciary capacity arose in phase 1 and continued into phase 2, which glided into phase 3. In saying this I do not for one moment suggest that there was anything dishonest or underhand in what Mr Boardman did. He has obtained a clean certificate below and I do not wish to sully it; but the law has a strict regard for principle in ensuring that a person in a fiduciary capacity is not allowed to benefit from any transactions into which he has entered with trust property. If Mr Boardman was acting on behalf of the trust, then all the information that he obtained in phase 2 became trust property. The weapon which he used to obtain this information was the trust holding; and I see no reason why information and knowledge cannot be trust property. . . . **15–114**

LORD UPJOHN (dissenting): On the evidence there was never any suggestion at any subsequent stage [after 1956] that Mr Fox or any other trustee would ever have contemplated any purchase of further shares. . . . In *Aberdeen Railway Co v Blaikie Bros*[257] Lord Cranworth L.C. said, "and it is a rule of universal application that no-one having such duties to discharge shall be allowed to enter into engagements in which he has or can have a personal interest conflicting or which possibly may conflict with the interests of those whom he is bound to protect." The phrase "possibly may conflict" requires consideration. In my view it **15–115**

[256] [1965] Ch. 992 at 1031.
[257] [1843–1860] All E.R. Rep. 249 at 252.

means that the reasonable man would think that there was a real sensible possibility of conflict; not that you could imagine some situation arising which might, in some conceivable possibility in events not contemplated as real sensible possibilities by any reasonable person, result in a conflict . . . [*Regal (Hastings) Ltd v Gulliver* and *Keech v Sandford* bear no relation to this case].

15–116 This case, if I may emphasise it again, is one concerned not with trust property or with property of which the persons to whom the fiduciary duty was owed were contemplating a purchase but, in contrast to the facts in Regal, with property which was not trust property or property which was ever contemplated as the subject-matter of a possible purchase by the trust. . . .

15–117 This question whether the appellants were accountable requires a closer analysis than it has received in the lower courts. This analysis requires detailed consideration:

1. The facts and circumstances must be carefully examined to see whether in fact a purported agent and even a confidential agent is in a fiduciary relationship to his principal. It does not necessarily follow that he is in such a position.
2. Once it is established that there is such a relationship, that relationship must be examined to see what duties are thereby imposed on the agent, to see what is the scope and ambit of the duties charged on him.
3. Having defined the scope of those duties one must see whether he has committed some breach thereof by placing himself within the scope and ambit of those duties in a position where his duty and interest may possibly conflict. It is only at this stage that any question of accountability arises.
4. Finally, having established accountability it only goes so far as to render the agent accountable for profits made within the scope and ambit of his duty.

15–118 Before applying these principles to the facts, however, I shall refer to the judgment of Russell L.J. which proceeded on a rather different basis. He said:

> "The substantial trust shareholding was an asset of which one aspect was its potential use as a means of acquiring knowledge of the company's affairs, or of negotiating allocations of the company's assets, or of inducing other shareholders to part with their shares. That aspect was part of the trust assets."

My Lords, I regard that proposition as untenable.

15–119 In general, information is not property at all. It is normally open to all who have eyes to read and ears to hear. The true test is to determine in what circumstances the information has been acquired. If it has been acquired in such circumstances that it would be a breach of confidence to disclose it to another, then courts of equity will restrain the recipient from communicating it to another. In such cases such confidential information is often and for many years has been described as the property of the donor, the books of authority are full of such references; knowledge of secret processes, "know-how", confidential information as to the prospects of a company or of someone's intention or the expected results of some horse race based on stable or other confidential information. But in the end the real truth is that it is not property in any normal sense, but equity will restrain its transmission to another if in breach of some confidential relationship.

15–120 With all respect to the views of Russell L.J., I protest at the idea that information acquired by trustees in the course of their duties as such is necessarily part of the assets of trust property which cannot be used by the trustees except for the benefit of the trust. Russell L.J. referred to the fact that two out of three of the trustees could have no authority to turn over this aspect of trust property to the appellants except for the benefit of the trust; this I do not understand, for if such information is trust property not all the trustees acting together could do it for they cannot give away trust property.

15–121 We heard much argument on the impact of the fact that the testator's widow was at all material times incapable of acting in the trust owing to disability. Of course trustees must act all of them and unanimously in matters affecting trust affairs, but they never performed any relevant act on behalf of the trust at all; I quoted Mr Fox's answer earlier for this reason. At no time after going to the meeting in December 1956, did Mr Boardman or Tom rely on any express or implied authority or consent of the trustees in relation to trust property. They understood rightly that there was no question of the trustees acquiring any further trust property by purchasing further shares in the company, and it was only in the purchase of other shares that they were interested.

There is, in my view, and I know of no authority to the contrary, no general rule that information learnt by a trustee during the course of his duties is property of the trust and cannot be used by him. If that were to be the rule it would put the Public Trustee and other corporate trustees out of business and make it difficult for private trustees to be trustees of more than one trust. This would be the greatest possible pity for corporate trustees and others may have much information which they may initially acquire in connection with some particular trust but without prejudice to that trust can make it readily available to other trusts to the great advantage of those other trusts. **15–122**

The real rule is, in my view, that knowledge learnt by a trustee in the course of his duties as such is not in the least property of the trust and in general may be used by him for his own benefit or for the benefit of other trusts unless it is confidential information which is given to him (i) in circumstances which, regardless of his position as a trustee, would make it a breach of confidence for him to communicate to anyone, for it has been given to him expressly or impliedly as confidential; or (ii) in a fiduciary capacity, and its use would place him in a position where his duty and his interest might possibly conflict. Let me give one or two simple examples. A, as trustee of two settlements X and Y holding shares in the same small company, learns facts as trustee of X about the company which are encouraging. In the absence of special circumstances (such, for example, that X wants to buy more shares) I can see nothing whatever which would make it improper for him to tell his co-trustees of Y who feel inclined to sell that he has information that this would be a bad thing to do. Another example: A as trustee of X learns facts that make him and his co-trustees want to sell. Clearly he could not communicate this knowledge to his co-trustees of Y until at all events the holdings of X have been sold for there would be a plain conflict, reflected in the prices that might or might possibly be obtained. **15–123**

My Lords, I do not think for one moment that Lord Brougham in *Hamilton v Wright*,[258] quoted in the speech of my noble and learned friend, Lord Guest, was saying anything to the contrary; one has to look and see whether the knowledge acquired was capable of being used for his own benefit to injure the trust (my italics). That test can have no application to the present. There was no possibility of the information being used to injure the trust. The knowledge obtained was used not in connection with trust property but to enhance the value of the trust property by the purchase of other property in which the trustees were not interested. . . . **15–124**

As a result of the information the appellants acquired, admittedly by reason of the trust holding, they found it worthwhile to offer a good deal more for the shares than in phase 1 of chapter 2. I cannot see that in offering to purchase non-trust shares at a higher price they were in breach of any fiduciary relationship in using the information which they had acquired for this purpose. I cannot see that they have, from start to finish, in the circumstances of this case, placed themselves in a position where there was any possibility of a conflict between their duty and interest. **15–125**

I have dealt with the problems that arise in this case at considerable length but it could, in my opinion, be dealt with quite shortly. In *Barnes v Addy*,[259] Lord Selborne L.C., said: **15–126**

> "It is equally important to maintain the doctrine of trusts which is established in this court, and not to strain it by unreasonable construction beyond its due and proper limits. There would be no better mode of undermining the sound doctrines of equity than to make unreasonable and inequitable applications of them."

That, in my judgment, is applicable to this case.

The trustees were not willing to buy more shares in the company. The active trustees were very willing that the appellants should do so themselves for the benefit of their large minority holding. The trustees, so to speak, lent their name to the appellants in the course of prolonged and difficult negotiations and, of course, the appellants thereby learnt much which would have otherwise been denied to them. The negotiations were in the end brilliantly successful. How successful Tom was in his reorganisation of the company is apparent to all. They ought to be very grateful. **15–127**

[258] (1842) 9 Cl. & Fin. 111.
[259] (1874) 9 Ch. App. 244 at 251.

15–128 In the long run the appellants have bought for themselves with their own money shares which the trustees never contemplated buying and they did so in circumstances fully known and approved of by the trustees. To extend the doctrines of equity to make the appellants accountable in such circumstances is, in my judgment, to make unreasonable and inequitable applications of such doctrines.

ATT.-GEN. FOR HONG KONG v REID

Privy Council [1994] 1 A.C. 324 [1993] 3 W.L.R. 1143 [1994] 1 All E.R. 1

15–129 LORD TEMPLEMAN (with whom LORD GOFF, LORD LOWRY, LORD LLOYD and SIR THOMAS EICHELBAUM agreed): Bribery is an evil practice which threatens the foundations of any civilised society. In particular, bribery of policemen and prosecutors brings the administration of justice into disrepute. Where bribes are accepted by a trustee, servant, agent or other fiduciary, loss and damage are caused to the beneficiaries, master or principal whose interests have been betrayed. The amount of loss or damage resulting from the acceptance of a bribe may or may not be quantifiable. In the present case the amount of harm caused to the administration of justice in Hong Kong by Mr Reid in return for bribes cannot be quantified.

15–130 When a bribe is offered and accepted in money or in kind, the money or property constituting the bribe belongs in law to the recipient. Money paid to the false fiduciary belongs to him. The legal estate in freehold property conveyed to the false fiduciary by way of bribe vests in him. Equity however which acts in personam insists that it is unconscionable for a fiduciary to obtain and retain a benefit in breach of duty. The provider of a bribe cannot recover it because he committed a criminal offence when he paid the bribe. The false fiduciary who received the bribe in breach of duty must pay and account for the bribe to the person to whom that duty was owed. In the present case, as soon as Mr Reid received a bribe in breach of the duties he owed to the Government of Hong Kong, he became a debtor in equity to the Crown for the amount of that bribe. So much is admitted. But, if the bribe consists of property which increases in value or if a cash bribe is invested advantageously, the false fiduciary will receive a benefit from his breach of duty unless he is accountable not only for the original amount or value of the bribe but also for the increased value of the property representing the bribe. As soon as the bribe was received it should have been paid or transferred instanter to the person who suffered from the breach of duty. Equity considered as done that which ought to have been done. As soon as the bribe was received, whether in cash or in kind, the false fiduciary held the bribe on a constructive trust for the person injured. Two objections have been raised to this analysis. First it is said that, if the fiduciary is in equity a debtor to the person injured, he cannot also be a trustee of the bribe. But there is no reason why equity should not provide two remedies, so long as they do not result in double recovery. If the property representing the bribe exceeds the original bribe in value, the fiduciary cannot retain the benefit of the increase in value which he obtained solely as a result of his breach of duty. Secondly, it is said that if the false fiduciary holds property representing the bribe in trust for the person injured, and if the false fiduciary is or becomes insolvent, the unsecured creditors of the false fiduciary will be deprived of their right to share in the proceeds of that property. But the unsecured creditors cannot be in a better position than their debtor. The authorities show that property acquired by a trustee innocently but in breach of trust and the property from time to time representing the same belong in equity to the cestui que trust and not to the trustee personally whether he is solvent or insolvent. Property acquired by a trustee as a result of a criminal breach of trust and the property from time to time representing the same must also belong in equity to his cestui que trust and not to the trustee whether he is solvent or insolvent.

15–131 When a bribe is accepted by a fiduciary in breach of his duty then he holds that bribe in trust for the person to whom the duty was owed. If the property representing the bribe decreases in value the fiduciary must pay the difference between that value and the initial amount of the bribe because he should not have accepted the bribe or incurred the risk of loss. If the property increases in value, the fiduciary is not entitled to any surplus in excess of the initial value of the bribe because he is not allowed by any means to make a profit out of a breach of duty. . . .

8. Proceeds of Breach of Confidence

The equitable right of confidentiality "depends on the broad principle of equity that he who has received information in confidence shall not take unfair advantage of it. He must not make use of it to the prejudice of him who gave it without obtaining his consent".[260] Thus the information must have the necessary quality of confidentiality, must have been imparted in circumstances importing an obligation of confidence, and there must have been unauthorised use of the information.[261] If the circumstances are such that any reasonable man, standing in the shoes of the recipient of the information, would have realised upon reasonable grounds that the information was being given to him in confidence, then this should suffice to impose upon him the equitable obligation of confidence.[262] Indeed, Lord Goff has stated that:[263] **15–132**

> "a duty of confidence arises when confidential information comes to the knowledge of a person (the confidant) in circumstances where he has notice, or is held to have agreed, that the information is confidential, with the effect that it would be just in all the circumstances that he should be precluded from disclosing the information to others."

It will be a defence to show that disclosure was in the public interest[264] or that the obligation of confidentiality was at an end at the relevant time because the information was in the public domain available to all on reasonable inquiry.[265]

The equitable right of confidence can be protected by the grant of an injunction to prevent disclosure of the confidence, but if it is too late and the confidence has been disclosed then the confider may be entitled to an award of monetary compensation,[266] or to an account of the confidant's profits.[267] There are some indications in the case law that a constructive trust may also be imposed on these profits. In *LAC Minerals Ltd v International Corona Resources Ltd*[268] the Supreme Court of Canada held that LAC was constructive trustee of land that it had bought for itself, because it had been told in confidence by a potential joint venturer that the land could well contain gold deposits. In *Att.-Gen. v Guardian Newspapers Ltd (No.2)* Lord Goff considered obiter that if a confidant disclosed information in a book so that it lost its quality of confidentiality, and then sought to profit further from his wrongdoing by selling the film rights to the book "the copyright in the book, including the film rights, are held by him on constructive trust for the confider".[269] And in *United Pan-Europe Communications NV v Deutsche Bank* **15–133**

---

[260] *Seager v Copydex Ltd* [1967] 1 W.L.R. 923 at 931.

[261] *Coco v Clark (Engineers) Ltd* [1969] R.P.C. 41 at 47, endorsed by CA in *Murray v Yorkshire Fund Managers* [1998] 2 All E.R. 1015 at 1020; *Att.-Gen. v Jonathan Cape* [1975] 3 All E.R. 484 at 494; *Fraser v Thames Television* [1983] 2 All E.R. 101 at 116.

[262] *Coco v Clark (Engineers) Ltd* [1969] R.P.C. 41 at 48; *Att.-Gen. v Guardian Newspapers (No.2)* [1988] 3 All E.R. 545.

[263] *Att.-Gen. v Guardian Newspapers (No.2)* [1990] 1 A.C. 109 at 281.

[264] *Initial Services Ltd v Putterill* [1968] 1 Q.B. 396 at 405; *Lion Laboratories Ltd v Evans* [1984] 2 All E.R. 417; *Francome v Mirror Group Newspapers* [1984] 2 All E.R 408.

[265] *Peter Pan Manufacturing Co v Corsets Silhouette Ltd* [1964] 1 W.L.R. 96; *British Syphon Co v Homewood* [1956] 1 W.L.R. 1190; *Att.-Gen. v Guardian Newspapers (No.2)* [1990] 1 A.C. 109. *Att.-Gen. v Blake* [1998] Ch. 439.

[266] e.g. *Saltman Engineering Co Ltd v Campbell Engineering Co Ltd* (1948) 65 R.P.C. 203 at 219; *Seager v Copydex Ltd* [1967] 1 W.L.R. 923 at 932; and *Seager v Copydex (No.2)* [1969] 1 W.L.R. 809; *Indata Equipment Supplies Ltd v ACL Ltd* [1998] F.S.R. 248 at 259–262, 263 and 264; *Campbell v MGN Ltd* [2002] E.M.L.R. 617 at [75], affirmed [2004] 2 A.C. 457; *Douglas v Hello! Ltd (No.3)* [2006] Q.B. 125 at [120], [243]–[250] and [259]; *OBG Ltd v Allan* [2008] 1 A.C. 1 at [276].

[267] *Peter Pan Manufacturing Corp v Corsets Silhouette Ltd* [1964] 1 W.L.R. 96 at 106; *Att.-Gen. v Observer Ltd* [1990] 1 A.C. 109 at 255–256, 262 and 288; *OBG Ltd v Allan* [2008] 1 A.C. 1 at [276]; *Vestergaard Frandsen A/S v BestNet Europe Ltd* [2010] F.S.R. 2 at [93].

[268] (1989) 61 D.L.R. (4th) 14. See too *Minera Aquiline Argentina SA v IMA Exploration Inc* (2007) 10 W.W.R. 648.

[269] *Att.-Gen. v Guardian Newspapers (No.2)* [1990] 1 A.C. 109 at 288.

AG[270] the Court of Appeal held that in principle a constructive trust could be awarded for breach of confidence. However, there seems to be no English case to date in which this has actually been done, and some murky questions need to be resolved before the courts can confidently take this step[271] e.g. whether confidential information is property, whether relationships of confidence are fiduciary, whether breach of confidence should retain a discrete equitable identity or be subsumed within a privacy tort which gives effect to the right to privacy conferred by the European Convention on Human Rights,[272] and whether the law should operate a hierarchy of remedies in breach of confidence cases so that the claimants may be restricted to loss-based remedies in some circumstances.[273]

9. Proceeds of Crime

15–134 When Crippen murdered his wife her property did not on her intestacy pass to him via his will to Miss Le Neve, but passed to his wife's blood relatives.[274] Likewise, where R murdered both his parents (Mr and Mrs S) who died intestate, R could not inherit their property, and neither could his son, T, so that Mr S's sister inherited his estate and Mrs S's sister's children inherited her estate.[275] If the property is not intercepted before passing to the killer it seems that he will hold it on constructive trust for those who are entitled to it by operation of the forfeiture rule.[276] Their claims will have priority if he becomes bankrupt while still owning the property, and they can also follow the property into the hands of anyone other than a bona fide purchaser of the legal estate for value without notice, and assert a proprietary claim against him.

15–135 If one joint tenant murders another he should hold the property on constructive trust for himself and his victim in equal shares.[277] If a remainderman murders the life tenant then the victim should be deemed to live his actuarial life-span (except for a death-bed mercy killing), so that for the period of this notional life-span the victim's interest should be held on constructive trust for his estate; thereafter, devolution should occur normally.[278] Murder and manslaughter including manslaughter by reason of diminished responsibility invoke the principle, but it does not apply to a killer who is found not guilty by reason of insanity.[279] The Forfeiture Act 1982 now enables the court to modify the effect of the forfeiture rule where the justice of the case requires it, if the killer brings proceedings within three months of conviction.[280]

---

270 [2000] 2 B.C.L.C. 461.

271 For discussion of these and other relevant questions, see M. Conaglen, "Thinking about Proprietary Remedies for Breach of Confidence" [2008] I.P.Q. 82; N. Witzleb, "Justifying Gain-Based Remedies for Invasions of Privacy" (2009) 29 O.J.L.S. 325.

272 As to which, see *Campbell v Mirror Group Newspapers Ltd* [2004] 2 A.C. 457; *Douglas v Hello! (No.3)* [2006] Q.B. 125; *Mosley v News Group Newspapers* [2008] E.M.L.R. 20.

273 As mooted by Sales J. in *Vercoe v Rutland Fund Management Ltd* [2010] EWHC 424 (Ch) at [332].

274 *Re Crippen* [1911] P. 108. See too *Re Sigsworth* [1935] Ch. 89.

275 *Re DWS, deceased* [2001] Ch. 568. The reason was the intestacy rule that a child can only inherit property that would otherwise pass to his parent if the parent predeceases the intestate. The outcome of this case is regarded as unsatisfactory, and recommendations are made to reform the law by introducing a "deemed predecease" rule, in Law Commission, *The Forfeiture Rule and the Law of Succession* (Law Com. No.295, 2005).

276 *Schobelt v Barber* (1966) 60 D.L.R. (2nd) 519; *Re Pechar* [1969] N.Z.L.R. 574; *Rasmanis v Jurewitsch* [1970] N.S.W.L.R. 650; *Beresford v Royal Insurance Co Ltd* [1938] A.C. 586 at 600. See further G. Virgo, *The Principles of the Law of Restitution* (1999), pp.570–588; G. Jones, "Stripping a Criminal of the Profits of Crime" (2000) 1 Theoretical Inquiries in Law 59.

277 *Rasmanis v Jurewitsch* [1970] N.S.W.L.R. 650; *Re K* [1985] 1 All E.R. 403 (if A's murder of B severs their joint tenancy then A holds legal title on constructive trust for A and B's estate equally). If X, Y, and Z are joint tenants and X kills Y then X should become tenant in common of one-third and Z of two-thirds. For the destination of surplus endowment assurance moneys on the death of the murder's co-owner, see *Davitt v Titcumb* [1990] 1 Ch. 110.

278 (1973) 89 L.Q.R. 231, pp. 250–251 (T.G. Youdan).

279 *Re Giles* [1972] Ch. 544; *Re Pitts* [1931] 1 Ch. 546; *Re Plaister* (1934) S.R. (N.S.W.) 547; *Permanent Trustee Co v Gillett* (2004) 6 I.T.E.L.R. 1063 at [36] ff.

280 See, e.g. *Re K* [1986] Ch. 180; *Re H* [1990] 1 F.L.R. 441; *Jones v Roberts* [1995] 2 F.L.R. 422; *Dunbar v Plant* [1998] Ch. 412; *Dalton v Latham* [2003] W.T.L.R. 687.

10. Vitiated Transfers

15–136 In *Chase Manhattan Bank v Israel-British Bank (London) Ltd*[281] Goulding J. held that money paid by mistake should be held on constructive trust for the payor by the recipient.[282] Constructive trusts have also been imposed on property stolen from a claimant or obtained from him by fraud,[283] on property transferred by a claimant who has been unduly influenced by the recipient,[284] or whose ability to make decisions has otherwise been compromised by his relationship with the recipient,[285] and even on property that has been transferred to a defendant for a consideration that fails.[286] These cases are discussed further below, when we consider the argument that constructive trusts can be imposed to reverse unjust enrichment.

11. Why Are Constructive Trusts Imposed?

15–137 It can be seen from the foregoing discussion that constructive trusts are imposed in a wide variety of situations. This makes it very difficult to find a single unifying principle to explain why they are imposed, and it seems more likely that they are imposed for different reasons in different situations. Some of the possible explanations are considered in this final section.

A. Intention

15–138 It has been said that constructive trusts do not give effect to intention, but are, on the contrary, imposed "against the intentions of the trustee".[287] Nevertheless it can be argued that in all of the cases discussed in sections 2–6, as well as the cases on *Re Rose*, mutual wills, and secret trusts, that are discussed elsewhere in the book, constructive trusts were imposed in order to give effect to an intention that beneficial ownership of property should pass from one party to another.[288] Arguably, the cases on unauthorised fiduciary gains (discussed in section 7) can also be explained on this basis because those who voluntarily assume office as trustees or other fiduciaries cannot deny that they intend to act in their principals' best interests.[289]

---

281 [1981] Ch. 105.

282 *Chase Manhattan* remains good law in England, although its status has been diminished by Lord Browne-Wilkinson's gloss on the case in *Westdeutsche Landesbank Girozentrale v Islington LBC* [1996] A.C. 669, and by judicial reactions to this gloss in *Barclays Bank Plc v Box* [1998] Lloyd's Rep. Bank. 185 at 200–201; *Papamichael v National Westminster Bank Plc* [2003] 1 Lloyd's Rep. 341 at [232]–[242]; and *Shalson v Russo* [2005] Ch. 281 at [108]–[127].

283 *Westdeutsche Landesbank Girozentrale v Islington LBC* [1996] A.C. 669 at 715–716, per Lord Browne-Wilkinson, followed in *Niru Battery Manufacturing Co v Milestone Trading Ltd (No.1)* [2002] 2 All E.R. (Comm.) 705 at [55]–[56]. See too *Black v S Freedman & Co* (1910) 12 C.L.R. 105 at 109; *Creak v James Moore & Sons Pty Ltd* (1912) 15 C.L.R. 426 at 432; *Australian Postal Corp v Lutak* (1991) 12 N.S.W.L.R. 584 at 589; *Zobory v Commissioner of Taxation* (1995) 64 F.C.R. 86 at 90–93; *Evans v European Bank Ltd* (2004) 7 I.T.E.L.R. 19 at [111].

284 *Janz v McIntosh* (1999) 182 Sask. R. 197.

285 *Louth v Diprose* (1992) 175 C.L.R. 621; *McCulloch v Fern* [2001] NSWSC 406; *Smith v Smith* [2004] NSWSC 663. On the Australian law governing unconscionable transactions and the law of unjust enrichment, see M. Bryan "Unjust Enrichment and Unconscionability in Australia: A False Dichotomy?" in J. W. Neyers et al. (eds), *Understanding Unjust Enrichment* (2004).

286 *Neste Oy v Lloyd's Bank Plc* [1983] 2 Lloyds Rep. 658; *Re Farepak Food and Gifts Ltd* [2007] 2 B.C.L.C. 1; subsequent proceedings [2009] EWHC 2580 (Ch). For discussion, see paras 4–44 ff.

287 *Westdeutsche Landesbank Girozentrale v Islington LBC* [1996] A.C. 669 at 708, per Lord Browne-Wilkinson. See too *Rathwell v Rathwell* [1978] 2 S.C.R. 436 at 454, per Dickson J.; *Air Jamaica Ltd v Charlton* [1999] 1 W.L.R. 1399 at 1412, per Lord Millett.

288 R. Chambers, "Constructive Trusts in Canada" (1999) 37 Alberta L.R. 173, reprinted in (2001) 15 Tru L.I. 214 and (2002) 16 Tru. L.I. 2. A similar line is taken in the chapters on constructive trusts in *Oosterhoff on Trusts: Text, Commentary and Materials* 6th edn (2004), of which Chambers is an editor. See too S. Gardner, *Introduction to the Law of Trusts* 2nd edn (2003), p.159 ff.

289 See paras 9–15 to 9–16.

15–139 Obviously constructive trusts are not needed in cases where a property-owner intends to transfer beneficial ownership to another party unless this intention is thwarted for some reason: by a failure to comply with applicable formality rules, for example, or by the property-owner's change of heart. In cases of the latter sort we could say that the constructive trust is imposed against the current wishes of the property-owner, and that it responds to his "wrongdoing" in denying the claimant's beneficial interest.[290] But if we focus instead on his original intention, then we can say that in these cases, just as in the cases where an intended transfer has failed for non-compliance with some formality rule, the function of the constructive trust is "perfectionary": it perfects the property-owner's intention that beneficial ownership should be transferred.[291]

15–140 Authorities supporting this analysis include the statement by the High Court of Australia in *Bathurst CC v PWC Properties Pty Ltd* that:[292]

> "One species of constructive trust is concerned with cases where the intent of a settlor or testator in transferring or devising property otherwise would fail for want of compliance with the formalities for creation of express trusts inter vivos or by will. The necessary elements are on which the question turns in many cases are 'intention, communication, and acquiescence'."[293]

Millett L.J. also held in *Paragon Finance Plc v DB Thakerar & Co (a firm)* that some constructive trusts arise where the trustee receives the trust property:[294]

> "by a transaction which both parties intend to create a trust from the outset and which is not impugned by the plaintiff. [The defendant's] possession of the property is coloured from the first by the trust and confidence by means of which he obtained it, and his subsequent appropriation to his own use is a breach of that trust. Well known examples of such a constructive trust are *McCormick v Grogan*[295] (a case of secret trust) and *Rochefoucauld v Boustead*[296] (where the defendant agreed to buy property for the plaintiff but the trust was improperly recorded). *Pallant v Morgan*[297] (where the defendant sought to keep for himself property which the plaintiff trusted him to buy for both parties) is another. In these cases the plaintiff does not impugn the transaction by which the defendant obtained control of the property. He alleges that the circumstances in which the defendant obtained control make it unconscionable for him thereafter to assert a beneficial interest in the property."

15–141 Against this it can be argued that in cases like *Rochefoucauld*, where statutory formality rules render an express trust unenforceable but the settlor is estopped from relying on the statute to deny the beneficiary's rights, the trust under which these rights arise is not a constructive trust at all, but the express trust that the settlor intended to create.[298] It might be objected that trust cannot be

---

[290] *Lonrho Plc v Fayed (No.2)* [1992] 1 W.L.R. 1 at 10, per Millett J.

[291] G. Elias, *Explaining Constructive Trusts* (1990), p.157.

[292] (1998) 195 C.L.R. 566 at [39], per curiam. See too *Allen v Snyder* [1977] 2 N.S.W.L.R. 685 at 693, per Glass J.A.; *Re Australian Elizabethan Theatre Trust* (1991) 30 F.C.R. 491 at 510, per Gummow J., considering *Le Compte v Public Trustee* [1983] 2 N.S.W.L.R. 109.

[293] Citing *Vosges v Monaghan* (1954) 94 C.L.R. 231 at 233, 235, and 237; *Blackwell v Blackwell* [1929] A.C. 318 at 334.

[294] [1999] 1 All E.R. 400 at 408–409.

[295] (1869) 4 App. Cas. 82.

[296] [1897] 1 Ch. 196.

[297] [1953] Ch. 43.

[298] See paras 3–60 ff. and also W. Swadling, "The Nature of the Trust in *Rochefoucauld v Boustead*" in C. Mitchell (ed.), *Constructive and Resulting Trusts* (2010).

express because the courts cannot simply override a statute which requires declarations of express trust to take a particular form. However, if that is correct then there is no reason to think that they can impose a constructive trust either: i.e. the court is neither more nor less entitled to enforce an express trust despite non-compliance with statutory formalities than it is to use constructive trust reasoning to achieve the same effect. Either course should be open to the court, or neither.[299]

If some constructive trusts are perfectionary then it is unclear what role is played by detriment.[300] Some cases hold that the claimant must have suffered detriment as this is the element which makes it unconscionable for the defendant to act in a manner contrary to the parties' original intentions, leading to the imposition of the constructive trust. For example, detriment is said to be necessary in many shared homes cases, and in cases invoking the rule in *Re Rose*. Yet it seems that detriment is not always needed, e.g. in cases concerning purchasers' undertakings, cases concerning the rule in *Pallant v Morgan*, and cases concerning unauthorised fiduciary gains. **15–142**

B. Detrimental Reliance

Another view of many of the same cases holds that intention is peripheral and that the constructive trust should be seen instead as a mechanism to reverse the detriment suffered by a party who, acting in reasonable reliance on another's undertaking, foregoes his opportunity to achieve the content of the undertaking in some other way.[301] So, for example, in a secret trusts case the relevant detriment is the testator's lost opportunity to provide for the beneficiary by some means other than his arrangement with the trustee; and in a *Pallant v Morgan* case it is the claimant's lost chance to acquire the property that has been acquired by the defendant. This analysis runs into the same objection as the previous analysis, that the trust imposed in some of the cases, e.g. *Rochefoucauld*, was not constructive but express. It can also be objected that a very broad characterisation of the claimant's "opportunity loss" is needed to make some of the cases fit with the analysis, e.g. various shared homes cases and *Pallant v Morgan* cases, where the interest acquired by the claimant under the trust is greater than any interest which he had the opportunity to acquire by other means. **15–143**

C. Wrongs

Constructive trusts to capture the profits of a breach of confidence, and the proceeds of crime, respectively discussed in sections 8 and 9, can clearly be analysed as wrong-based. A more controversial question is whether constructive trusts to capture unauthorised fiduciary gains (discussed in section 7) should be analysed in the same way, or whether these should be seen as responding to the fiduciary's original intention to act in his principal's best interests, from which he cannot subsequently resile. This question has been discussed already in Chapter 9.[302] **15–144**

---

[299] cf. *Re Australian Elizabethan Theatre Trust* (1991) 30 F.C.R. 491 at 508, per Gummow J.: "constructive trusts should not readily be imposed in favour of parties which have failed in their attempts to show the necessary facts for a consensual arrangement by way of express trust." But in the particular case of non-compliance with the LPA 1925 s.53(1)(b) and (c), note the words of s.53(2).

[300] For discussion of this and other issues arising out of the cases, see: T. Youdan, "Formalities for Trusts of Land and the Doctrine in *Rochefoucauld v Boustead*" (1984) 43 C.L.J. 306; N. Hopkins "Acquiring Property Rights from Uncompleted Sales of Land" (1998) 61 M.L.R. 486; P. Critchley, "Instruments of Fraud, Testamentary Dispositions, and the Doctrine of Secret Trusts" (1999) 115 L.Q.R. 631; N. Hopkins "The *Pallant v Morgan* 'Equity'?" [2002] Conv. 35; J. Cartwright, "Formality and Informality in Property and Contract" in J. Getzler (ed.) *Rationalizing Property, Equity and Trusts* (2003) 36; B. Macfarlane, "Constructive Trusts Arising on a Receipt of Property *Sub Conditione*" (2004) 120 L.Q.R. 667; B. Macfarlane, "The Enforcement of Non-Contractual Agreements to Dispose of Interests in Land" (2005) 16 K.C.L.J.

[301] S. Gardner, "Reliance-Based Constructive Trusts" in C. Mitchell (ed.), *Constructive and Resulting Trusts* (2010).

[302] See paras 9–15 to 9–16.

D. *Unjust Enrichment*

15–145 Claims in unjust enrichment arise under English law when a defendant is enriched at the expense of a claimant in circumstances which make his enrichment unjust.[303] Under Canadian law it was formerly held that all constructive trusts respond to unjust enrichment,[304] but it has now been recognised that some do not.[305] In contrast, the English and Australian courts have never subscribed to the view that all constructive trusts respond to unjust enrichment, but they have held that some do, as previously noted in section 10.

15–146 These authorities are controversial for a number of reasons. Many of the Canadian cases concern shared family homes, and in their wish to do justice between the parties, the courts have made awards designed to fulfil the claimant's expectations rather than to reverse a transfer of value to the defendant, riding roughshod over the requirement that a claimant in unjust enrichment must prove that the defendant's enrichment has been acquired at his expense, and taking a very loose approach to the identification of benefit, and to the question whether the claimant should be entitled to a personal or a proprietary remedy.[306] More generally, some difficult questions arise, once it is accepted that at least some claimants in unjust enrichment are entitled to a proprietary rather than a personal restitutionary remedy.

15–147 First, should all claimants in unjust enrichment be entitled to a proprietary remedy, and if not, then how should the law distinguish those who are from those who are not? Different writers offer different answers to this question, many of them focussing on the question whether the claimant has taken the risk of the defendant's insolvency,[307] others focusing on the question whether the basis of the claimant's transfer to the defendant has immediately failed at the moment of receipt.[308] In *Westdeutsche Landesbank Girozentrale v Islington LBC*,[309] Lord Browne-Wilkinson took another approach, suggesting that a claimant in unjust enrichment should be entitled to a proprietary remedy against a defendant only if his conscience is affected by knowledge of the circumstances making his enrichment unjust, at a time when the property he has received from the claimant is still identifiable in his hands. However, it is hard to see why the claimant's position relative to the defendant's other creditors should be improved by a change in the defendant's state of mind at some time between the date of receipt and the date of his insolvency.[310]

15–148 Second, if a trust is to be imposed on assets in a defendant's hands in order to reverse his enrichment at a claimant's expense, then is this trust a resulting trust or a constructive trust? Given that

---

303 *Banque Financière de la Cité v Parc (Battersea) Ltd* [1999] 1 A.C. 221 at 227 and 234; *Kleinwort Benson Ltd v Lincoln CC* [1999] 2 A.C. 349 at 373, and 407–408; *Deutsche Morgan Grenfell Plc v IRC* [2007] 1 A.C. 558 at [21]; *Sempra Ltd v IRC* [2008] 1 A.C. 561 at [23]–[25].

304 *Deglman v Guaranty Trust Co* [1954] S.C.R. 725; *Pettkus v Becker* [1980] 2 S.C.R. 834; *Sorochan v Sorochan* [1986] 2 S.C.R 38; *Peter v Beblow* [1993] 1 S.C.R. 980.

305 *Korkontzilas v Soulos* [1997] 2 S.C.R. 217.

306 For critical comment, see J. Mee, *The Property Rights of Cohabitees* (1999) esp. pp. 219–222 and 224; M. McInnes, "Reflections on the Canadian Law of Unjust Enrichment: Lessons From Abroad" (1999) 78 Can. Bar. Rev 416; M. McInnes, "The Measure of Restitution" (2002) 52 University of Toronto L.J. 163; J. McCamus, "Restitution on Dissolution of Marital or Other Intimate Relationships: Constructive Trust or *Quantum Meruit*?" in J. W. Neyers et al. (eds), *Understanding Unjust Enrichment* (2004) esp. pp.372–375.

307 e.g. C. Rotherham, *Proprietary Interests in Context* (2002), Chs 4, 6, 9, 11 and 12; A. Burrows, *The Law of Restitution* 2nd edn (2002), pp.69–73.

308 e.g. P. Birks, *Unjust Enrichment* (2003), pp.162–178; P. Birks, "Retrieving Tied Money" in W. Swadling (ed.), *The Quistclose Trust: Critical Essays* (2004) 121, pp.130–138.

309 [1996] A.C. 669.

310 cf. Lord Millett, "Restitution and Constructive Trusts" (1998) 114 L.Q.R. 399, p.413: "By itself notice of the existence of a ground of restitution is obviously insufficient to found a proprietary remedy; it is merely notice of a personal right to an account and payment."

resulting trusts are always restitutionary in pattern and constructive trusts are not, then it might make sense to say that trusts imposed to reverse unjust enrichment are always resulting trusts.[311] Developing the law in this way would make it easier to understand why trusts are imposed by law, and how resulting and constructive trusts differ from one another. It would enable us to say that resulting trusts align with unjust enrichment, and that constructive trusts align with wrongdoing, intention, and other causative events.

Third, should the law distinguish between transfers pursuant to voidable contracts and transfers between parties who have never had a contract? In *Twinsectra Ltd v Yardley*, Potter L.J. gave a positive answer to this question, holding that in cases where a defendant has acquired a claimant's money by fraudulent means:[312] **15–149**

> "the distinction of importance . . . is that between non-consensual transfers and transfers pursuant to contracts which are voidable for misrepresentation. In the latter case, the transferor may elect whether to avoid or affirm the transaction and, until he elects to avoid it, there is no constructive (resulting) trust;[313] in the former case the constructive trust arises from the moment of transfer. The result, so far as third parties are concerned, is that, before rescission, the owner has no proprietary interest in the original property; all he has is the 'mere equity' of his right to set aside the voidable contract."

Hence, where a claimant, C, enters a contract with a defendant, D, under which he transfers legal and beneficial[314] ownership in particular assets to D, and his intention to benefit D is vitiated by a factor such as undue influence or induced mistake, C can rescind the transaction and ask the court to exercise its discretion to restore the assets.[315] Until C elects to rescind, it cannot be said that he has a proprietary interest in the assets, but once he does so,[316] the court can treat equitable title as retrospectively vesting in C for the purpose of allowing C to trace what happened to his assets in D's hands.[317] Since D, his trustee in bankruptcy, and his personal representatives are all bound to retransfer the original assets to C from the time when he elects to rescind and demands the return of the assets, it can be said that C enjoys a proprietary interest in the assets from that time.[318] This interest can be devised[319] or assigned,[320] but it is a mere equity rather than an equitable interest: i.e. it will bind **15–150**

---

[311] As mooted in *El Ajou v Dollar Land Holdings Plc* [1993] 3 All E.R. 717 at 734, per Millett J.; *Evans v European Bank Ltd* (2004) 7 I.T.E.L.R. 19 at [112], per Spigelman C.J.; P.J. Millett, "Tracing the Proceeds of Fraud"' (1991) 107 L.Q.R. 71, p.81; *Oosterhoff on Trusts* 6th edn (2004), p.695; and cf. the discussion in paras 14–162 ff.

[312] [1999] Lloyd's Rep. Bank. 438 at [99], considered in *Halley v Law Society* (2003) 6 I.T.E.L.R. 40 at [46]–[48]. See too Brennan J.'s judgment in *Daly v Sydney Stock Exchange* (1986) 160 C.L.R. 371.

[313] It is unclear what his Lordship meant by "constructive (resulting) trust", but conceivably he meant to indicate that trusts imposed to reverse unjust enrichment are resulting trusts.

[314] A case of undue influence "assumes a transfer of the beneficial interest but in circumstances which entitle the transferor to recall it": *Hodgson v Marks* [1971] Ch. 892 at 929. So does a case of fraudulent misrepresentation: *Shalson v Russo* [2005] Ch. 281 at [119].

[315] *Lonrho Plc v Fayed (No.2)* [1992] 1 W.L.R. 1 at 9; *Re Goldcorp Exchange Ltd* [1995] 1 A.C. 74 at 103, per Lord Mustill; *Cheese v Thomas* [1994] 1 All E.R. 35 at 42; *London Allied Holdings Ltd v Lee* [2007] EWHC 2061 (Ch) at [275] ff.

[316] A claimant's action in issuing proceedings can amount to an implied election to rescind in itself: *Shalson v Russo* [2005] Ch. 281 at [120], citing *Banque Belge pour l'Etranger v Hambrouck* [1921] 1 K.B. 321 at 332.

[317] *O'Sullivan v Management Agency & Music Ltd* [1985] Q.B. 428 at 475; *El Ajou v Dollar Land Holdings Plc* [1993] 3 All E.R. 717 at 734; *Bristol & West BS v Mothew* [1996] 4 All E.R. 698 at 716.

[318] *Load v Green* (1846) 15 M. & W. 216; *Re Eastgate* [1905] 1 K.B. 465; *Tilley v Bowman* [1910] 1 K.B. 745 at 750; *Banque Belge pour l'Etranger v Hambrouck* [1921] 1 K.B. 321 at 332; *Shalson v Russo* [2005] Ch. 281 at [122]–[126]. See generally S. Worthington, "The Proprietary Consequences of Rescission" [2002] R.L.R. 28.

[319] *Stump v Gaby* (1852) 2 De G. M. & G. 623.

[320] *Dickinson v Burrell* (1866) L.R. 1 Eq. 337; *Bruty v Edmundson* (1915) 85 L.J. Ch. 568.

a third party who is a volunteer or a purchaser with notice, but it will not bind a bona fide purchaser without notice of a legal or equitable interest in the assets.[321]

15–151 Fourth, and finally, it is arguable that this "power model" should be generalised to all cases where a transferor's intention to benefit a transferee is vitiated by mistake or for some other reason, i.e. that the power model should extend beyond cases where the relevant benefit is transferred under a (voidable) contract, to take in cases where there is no contract between the parties. This model of proprietary restitutionary liability can be contrasted with an "immediate interest model" under which the transferee holds property on trust from the moment of receipt. Under the power model, if D receives £10,000 from C, buys a painting with that money, and exchanges the painting for a car, then even if the money came to D in circumstances in which C acquired, or retained, an immediate interest in the money, C would still have only a power to crystallize a similar interest in first the painting, then the car. The applicability of the power model here is controversial,[322] but the immediate interest model leads to grave practical difficulties.[323] Generalising the power model would also facilitate the operation of the change of position defence and enable the bona fide purchase of equitable interests by innocent third parties.[324]

Questions

15–152 1. "*Stack v Dowden* and *Abbott v Abbott* have not made the law on shared homes any clearer, but they have made it fairer." **Discuss.**

15–153 2. "[The circumstances] which give rise to a common intention constructive trust and the circumstances where a proprietary estoppel arises [are similar, but] the remedies available to the court may differ between the two kinds of case. If the court finds that . . . a proprietary estoppel arises, the court has a [wide] power to craft and impose whatever remedy it considers to be equitable in the circumstances. That remedy may take the form of declaring that the claimant shall become the beneficial owner of the property or of a share in it (thus having the same effect as a finding that there is a constructive trust), but it may take other forms." (Park J. in *Lalani v Crump Holdings Ltd* (2007).) **Discuss.**

15–154 3. David, Eric and Ferdinand are trustees of a fund whose portfolio of investments includes some 10,000 shares out of an issued 30,000 shares in a private company. The Fund is held upon protective trusts for Ferdinand during his life and after his death for George and Harry equally. Ian, who is the trustees' solicitor, discussed with them the possibility of them acquiring a sufficient number of shares in the company to give them a majority holding. The trustees refused for though they had power to retain their existing shares they had no power to invest in further shares in any private companies. Ian told them that they had a chance of applying successfully to the court for such a power but the trustees considered that it would not be worth it. In consideration of Ian

321 *Phillips v Phillips* (1861) 4 De G.F. & J. 208 at 218 and 221–223; *Lancashire Loans Ltd v Black* [1934] 1 K.B. 380; *Latec Investments Pty Ltd v Terrigal Pty Ltd* (1965) 113 C.L.R. 265; *Blacklocks v JB Developments Ltd* [1981] 3 All E.R. 392 at 400. See too Lord Millett, "Restitution and Constructive Trusts" (1998) 114 L.Q.R. 399, p.416.

322 In *Cave v Cave* (1880) 15 Ch.D. 639, Fry J. favoured the immediate interest model, a view preferred in L.D. Smith, *The Law of Trading* (1997) pp.358–361. However *Cave* was criticised in *Re Ffrench's Estate* (1887) 21 L.R. Ir. 83 and may be incompatible with *Re Leslie (Engineers) Ltd* [1976] 1 W.L.R. 292. Also, it would be undesirable for different models to be used at common law and in equity, and the House of Lords clearly applied the power model in *Lipkin Gorman v Karpnale Ltd* [1991] 2 A.C. 548.

323 Illustrated by the facts of *Trustee of FC Jones & Son (a firm) v Jones* [1997] Ch. 159, as noted in P. Birks, "On Taking Seriously the Difference between Tracing and Claiming" (1997) 11 Tru. L.I. 2.

324 B. Häcker, "Proprietary Restitution after Impaired Consent: A Generalised Power Model" (2009) 68 C.L.J. 324.

agreeing not to charge legal fees for his unbilled work for the preceding year they told Ian that if he wished he could personally go ahead and try to obtain control for himself for as far as they could see this could only enhance the value of the trust's shareholding.

Ian then acquired all the remaining shares in the company, disposed of some of its assets, reorganised the business and increased the value of the shares from £1 each to £4 each. In the meantime, Ferdinand had become bankrupt and David and Eric removed him from his trusteeship on the ground of his unfitness to act (without replacing him) and refused to apply any income for his benefit.

How far is Ian entitled to keep the profit on these transactions; and how far is the conduct of David and Eric legally justified? Can Ferdinand call for the correspondence which passed between David and Eric, on the one hand, and Ian, on the other, relating to his removal from office and to the decision not to pay him any money?

4. Tom and Trevor, holding a lease with two years unexpired on trust for Brian for life, remainder for Brian's children equally, were trying to sell the lease as they were likely to receive a heavy dilapidations schedule for remedying at the expiry of the lease. They had tried to purchase the freehold reversion for the trust but the landlord had refused. Tom's friend Joe, hearing of their predicament, had relieved the trust of the lease at the proper, but low, market price. Joe happened to play golf regularly with the landlord and after persisting for four months was able to contract to purchase the freehold. Joe, only having half the purchase price, went to see Tom and suggested that Tom put up the other half for he had been a good friend and without him Joe would never have heard of the property and obtained the opportunity to buy the freehold. Tom was only too happy to put up half the purchase price, delighted that Joe was letting him in on the deal rather than merely borrow the money from Tom or a bank. Shortly afterwards Joe and Tom sold the property with vacant possession making £25,000 profit each. **Advise Brian.** **15–155**

PART VII

TRUSTS AND THE CONFLICT OF LAWS

16 TRUSTS AND THE CONFLICT OF LAWS

1. Introduction

A. Background

16–01 The conflict of laws is that part of the private law of the English and Welsh system of law which deals with issues which concern elements connected with other legal systems, e.g. of Scotland, Northern Ireland, the Republic of Ireland, Jersey, the Isle of Man, each of the American and Australian states, each of the Canadian or Spanish provinces. A settlor of British nationality domiciled[1] in California may create a trust of assets, half of which are in Bermuda and half in Ontario, and appoint four trustees, one habitually resident in Bermuda, one habitually resident in Ontario and two old friends habitually resident in England. One-third of the beneficiaries may be habitually resident in California, one-third in England, and one-third in Jersey. The trust instrument may specify Californian law as governing the validity of the trust, and Bermudian law as governing administration of trust assets there, and Ontario law as governing administration of the assets there. It may also confer express powers on the trustees to change the law governing the validity of the trust and to change the place of administration and the law governing administration. An alleged breach of trust may lead the beneficiaries to bring an action against the trustees before the Chancery Division of the English High Court.

16–02 The two questions that arise are (1) does the English court have jurisdiction to hear the case, and, if so, (2) what system of law shall apply to each point in issue? Sometimes, the case may be an exceptional one where, though the English court technically has jurisdiction, it will stay or strike out the proceedings on the ground of *forum non conveniens*, because the defendant shows that there is another forum to whose jurisdiction he is amenable, in which justice can be done at substantially less inconvenience and expense, and where the claimant will not be deprived of a legitimate personal or juridical advantage which would be available to him under the English jurisdiction.[2] Sometimes, the question arises whether the English court will recognise or enforce a foreign judgment purporting to determine an issue that relates to the action before the court. In the absence of special legislation for the reciprocal recognition and enforcement of foreign judgments, the successful claimant in foreign proceedings will need to bring English proceedings for summary judgment based on the res judicata established

[1] Domicile is a technical concept: it does not mean habitual residence. No one can be without a domicile since it is this that connects him with some legal system for many conflict of laws purposes. A person has a domicile of origin at birth (being his father's domicile or if a non-marital child, his mother's domicile) a domicile of dependency when the minor's parents change domicile and may acquire a domicile of choice by the factum of permanent residence with the animus of residing there permanently or indefinitely. Upon giving up a domicile of choice the domicile of origin applies until acquisition of a new domicile of choice. However, for the purposes of the Civil Jurisdiction and Judgments Act 1982 by s.41 an individual's domicile simply requires residence in, and a substantial connection with, a territorial unit having its own system of law.

[2] *Spiliada Maritime Corp v Cansulex Ltd* [1987] A.C. 460 and *Chellaram v Chellaram (No.2)* [2002] 3 All E.R. 17, but in EU and EFTA countries jurisdiction under the EC Council Regulation 44/2001 and the Lugano Convention arts 23 and 27 is on a first come (or "first seised") basis.

between the parties by the foreign court, assuming it had jurisdiction according to English law and there was no fraud or absence of natural or substantial justice.[3]

16–03 Detailed matters relating to questions of jurisdiction, of *forum non conveniens*, and of recognition or enforcement of foreign judgments are best left to the major works on conflict of laws,[4] though the EC Council Regulation on Jurisdiction and the Recognition and Enforcement of Judgments Regulation 44/2001 (known as the Brussels 1 Regulation) and the Revised Lugano EFTA Convention on Civil Jurisdiction and the Enforcement of Judgments that are in force in the United Kingdom will be considered in outline at the end of the chapter. For the moment, it is the choice of law issue—determining the law applicable to the matter in question—that will be examined. However, as will be seen, there are some situations where if the English court has jurisdiction it will apply English domestic law. One is used to this in family matters relating to divorce, separation and maintenance, and guardianship, custody and adoption of children, but in *Chellaram v Chellaram*[5] Scott J. held that the machinery for the enforcement of beneficiaries' rights determined under the proper law, particularly the removal of trustees and the appointment of new ones, is a matter to be governed by English law where the English court has jurisdiction to hear the case,[6] even though the proper law governing the validity of the trust may not be English but Indian and regardless of whether the law governing administration may be English or Indian.[7] He was strongly influenced by the maxim "Equity acts in personam" enabling the court to make orders effective against trustees within the jurisdiction of the court.

B. Antecedent Matters and "Characterisation"

16–04 A distinction needs to be made between the testator's will or the settlor's trust document, which may be considered as the "rocket-launcher" on the one hand, and the trust itself—the "rocket"—on the other hand.[8] The law that governs whether or not the property of the testator or settlor has been effectively vested under a valid will or other instrument in personal representatives or trustees, free or not from third-party rights (e.g. under forced heirship regimes,[9] matrimonial property regimes[10] or bankruptcy or defranding creditor[11] laws) may well be different from the law that governs the trust

[3] *Reid v Reid* [2000] C.C.J. 8; *Adams v Cape Industries Plc* [1990] Ch. 433.

[4] *Dicey and Morris on Conflict of Laws; Cheshire & North on Private International Law*. On trusts and conflict of laws there is a very useful chapter in J. Glasson (ed.), *International Trust Laws* and in Underhill & Hayton, *Law of Trusts and Trustees*, 17th edn (2007).

[5] [1985] Ch. 409.

[6] The English Court (ignoring the EU and EFTA Brussels 1 Regulation and the revised Lugano Convention) has jurisdiction against persons served with proceedings in England, those voluntarily submitting to the jurisdiction, and those served abroad with the court's leave if a necessary or proper party to a claim against a duly served person or if a trustee of a trust governed by English law or if the subject-matter is located within England: Civil Procedure Rule 6.36 as supplemented by Practice Direction B to Part 6.

[7] Essentially, Scott J. seems to be regarding the enforcement of beneficiaries' rights as a matter of procedure and so governed by the *lex fori: Chellaram v Chellaram (No.2)* [2002] 3 All E.R. 17 at [42]. Also see *Stirling-Maxwell v Cartwright* (1879) 11 Ch.D. 5 at 22; *Re Lord Cable* [1976] 3 All E.R. 417 at 431–432.

[8] *Re Lord Cable* [1976] 3 All E.R. 417 at 431; *Att.-Gen. v Campbell* (1872) L.R. 5 H.L. 524; art.4 of Hague Convention.

[9] e.g. under French law a deceased's children have rights to part of his estate so that if he has three children he may only freely dispose of, say, one-quarter of his estate: *Re Annesley* [1926] Ch. 692; *Re Adams* [1967] I.R. 424. In ascertaining the size of his estate, gifts of capital in his lifetime are notionally added back to the value of his estate and if the actual estate at death is insufficient to satisfy the heirs' claims they have personal claims to make up the amount of their fixed or forced shares from donees, starting with the most recent donee. Gifts are safe if made over 30 or 20 or 10 or 5 or 2 years before the donor's death, depending on the relevant state's law.

[10] e.g. a husband cannot dispose of property within the matrimonial regime without his wife's participation: cf. the position under *Pullan v Koe* [1913] 1 Ch. 9, discussed in Chapter 2.

[11] Insolvency Act 1986 ss. 339–342, 423–425.

provisions once the intended trust property has wholly or partly survived the application of the law, or laws, relating to the preliminary issues.

16–05 Clearly, the formal requirements of the *lex situs* (the law of the jurisdiction of the location of the assets) need to be satisfied for transferring assets or declaring trusts thereof. If H wrongfully transfers to trustees property subject to a matrimonial property regime without W's written consent it may be that she will have a personal claim in tort or unjust enrichment against the trustees or a proprietary half share in the transferred assets and their traceable product. It is up to the *lex fori* (the law of the jurisdiction whose court is hearing the case) to characterise the issue which arises[12] and then give effect to a personal or a proprietary claim as the case may be.

16–06 This raises difficult problems where a forced heirship claim arises[13] because the deceased died domiciled in Civilopia which requires three quarters of his estate to pass to his three children absolutely, such estate being notionally increased for this purpose by earlier lifetime gifts of capital made by the deceased. Let us assume, the deceased, D, a widower, left an actual estate worth £6 million, but nine years before death transferred English assets worth £18 million to English trustees of a trust governed by English law. Thus, the three children sue the trustees for £12 million to make up their £18 million forced heirship claim in the notional £24 million.[14] Civilopia[15] characterises their claims as succession claims governed by the Civilopian *lex successionis* as the jurisdiction of D's last habitual residence, which as D's last domicile is also regarded by the English court as the *lex successionis*.

16–07 The heirs' "clawback" claims[16] would not, of course, have arisen but for D's death, but the central issue is how to treat the lifetime gift when, of course, no-one could know what would ultimately be D's *lex successionis* and whether he would die with sufficient actual estate to satisfy his heirs' claims or whether he would even be survived by any descendants. It would appear that the English *lex fori* would characterise the £18 million gift as a lifetime transfer valid by the English *lex situs*,[17] although potentially impeachable by the Insolvency Act 1986 or if he died domiciled in England within six years, having intended to defeat claims of his children to reasonable maintenance, by the Inheritance (Provision for Family and Dependants) Act 1975 when s.13 thereof protects trustees against being liable beyond the value of the property in their hands. No such potential having materialised, the lifetime transfer is unimpeachable and so falls outside D's estate[18] to which the Civilopian *lex successionis* applies. Such conclusion is reinforced when considering art.15(1)(d) and (f) of the Hague Trust

---

12 *Macmillan Inc v Bishopsgate Investment Trust (No.3)* [1996] 1 All E.R. 585; *RZB v Five Star LLC* [2001] 3 All E.R. 257.

13 See D. J. Hayton (ed.), *European Succession Laws*, 2nd edn (2002), for the mainland European forced heirship rules. The issue is not one of capacity (like infancy or a mental deficiency). It is because the lifetime gift was effective that the forced heirship claim arises.

14 This could even occur if the trustees had transferred the assets on to trustees of a Cayman or Bermudan trust where legislation ousts forced heirship claims so no such claims could be brought there.

15 Thus, assets found to be located in civil law jurisdictions can be frozen by the forced heirs in pursuing their claims.

16 See Prof. Paisley's survey of these in Annexe 1 of Ministry of Justice, *European Commission Proposal on Succession and Wills* (C.P. 41/09) published online at *www.justice.gov.uk/consultations/ec-succession-wills.htm*.

17 D.J. Hayton (ed.), *European Succession Laws*, 2nd edn (2002), paras 1–67 to 1–69; *Lewin on Trusts* (17th edn) paras 11–59 to 11–60; P. Matthews (2001) 5 Chase Journal 15.

18 If the settlement were revocable or subject to the settlor's general power of appointment, there is a plausible case for permitting the trustees thereof to be subject (by analogy) to the forced heirship claims of heirs under the Civilopian mandatory family protection rules since the trust fund would automatically be regarded as part of the deceased's net estate subject to children's family provision claims under English family protection rules if the settlor had died domiciled in England: see Inheritance (Provision for Family and Dependants) Act 1975 s.25(1) "net estate" definition. The s.10 position is very different: it only applies if D died within 6 years, had the requisite intent to defeat his children's claims and had not by virtue of lifetime and testamentary provisions (including trusts) made reasonable provision for them, in which circumstances the court may invade the trust to the extent necessary to make reasonable provision, but the trustees under s.13 cannot be liable beyond the trust assets then in their hands. Any analogy between this specific narrow provision and general forced heirship rules would be false.

Convention (made English law by the Recognition of Trusts Act 1987) which require the application of the mandatory provisions of the *lex situs* designated by the English forum's choice of law rules concerning "the transfer of title to property" and "the protection, in other respects, of third parties acting in good faith", whether the trustees or the beneficiaries are regarded as "third parties".

16–08 Characterisation of a transaction as testamentary and so governed by the *lex successionis*, or as a lifetime disposition (governed by the *lex situs*) is crucial from the perspective of formalities and forced heirship claims where the deceased opened a joint account with X some years before death. The North American,[19] English[20] and Irish[21] approach is to treat property passing on death by virtue of being surviving joint tenant as being by virtue of an earlier lifetime disposition and not a testamentary disposition.

16–09 Once the court of the forum has held that, under the applicable *lex situs*, the owner of assets has effectively vested them in a person as trustee (including settlor-trustee), it seems it should be the applicable (or proper) law governing the trust that determines what interests have then arisen in favour of intended beneficiaries.[22] Capacity to alienate property and capacity to create a trust must thus be considered separately.

16–10 In the case of English immovables the *lex situs* has particular significance, especially in governing succession on the death of the owner thereof, while succession to movables is governed by the law of the deceased's last domicile according to the law of England and other common law countries—some civil law countries applying the law of the deceased's last habitual residence, some the law of the last nationality, some the law of the deceased's nationality (or, even, habitual residence) as chosen at the date of, and in, the deceased's will, and some applying such *lex successionis* to immovables as well as movables.[23] In October 2009 the Commission of the European Communities issued a Proposed EU Regulation to cover jurisdiction, applicable law and enforcement in matters of succession (excluded from Reg.44/2001). The Regulation will allow a testator to choose his nationality law as his *lex successionis* for the whole of his estate, movable and immovable, with the law of his habitual residence at death applying in the absence of such choice. The UK is unlikely to opt in to this since it permits "clawback" claims in respect of gifted UK property and does not define "habitual residence", so creating problems for persons who die while on a lengthy secondment abroad.

16–11 This distinction between movables and immovables is not the same as that between real property and personal property. Leasehold interests in land, though personal property, are immovables.[24] Where Settled Land Act 1925 capital moneys have been invested in stocks and shares but by s.75(5) such capital moneys and investments therewith are regarded as "land", then the stocks and shares are immovables.[25]

16–12 General equitable principles of the Court of Chancery have a significant role, especially the maxim "Equity acts in personam".[26] Other maxims that may be applicable are, for example, "equity will do nothing in vain" and "equity will not require persons to do acts illegal by the law of the place where the acts are to be performed", e.g. where foreign exchange laws or cultural

---

19 *Hutchinson v Ross* 211 N.E. 2d 637 (1965); *Sanchez v Sanchez* 547 So. 2d 945 (1989); *Re Reid* (1921) 64 D.L.R. 598; *Edwards v Bradley* [1956] O.R. 225.
20 *Young v Sealey* [1949] Ch. 278; *Re Figgis* [1969] 1 Ch. 123 at 149.
21 *Lynch v Burke* [1995] 1 I.R. 159.
22 Further see J. Harris, *The Hague Trusts Convention* (2003), pp.7–20.
23 Generally see D.J. Hayton (ed.), *European Succession Laws*, 2nd edn (2002).
24 *Freke v Carberry* (1873) L.R. 16 Eq. 461.
25 *Re Cutcliffe's WT* [1940] Ch. 565.
26 See e.g. *Cook Industries Ltd v Galliher* [1979] Ch. 439; *Derby & Co Ltd v Weldon (No.2)* [1989] 1 All E.R. 1002; *Webb v Webb* [1991] 1 W.L.R. 1410 (Ch.D.); [1994] Q.B. 696 (E.C.J.).

heritage laws prevent trustees from getting money or archeological artefacts out of the country for the beneficiaries.[27]

2. Choice of Applicable Law

A. Settlor's Choice of Law or Close Connection with Trust

After art.4 of The Hague Convention on the Law Applicable to Trusts and on their Recognition has excluded from its scope "preliminary issues relating to the validity of wills or of other acts by virtue of which assets are transferred to the trustee", arts 6 and 7 of the Convention, implemented by the Recognition of Trusts Act 1987, provide that a trust is governed by the law expressly or impliedly chosen by the settlor, or in the absence of such choice, by the law with which the trust is most closely connected. **16–13**

It is easy to assume that there can be only one applicable law governing the trust except where the trust assets are physically situated in two or more countries where different applicable laws may be chosen to cover the assets situate in different countries. Upon a little reflection it can be seen that there may well be one law governing the validity of the trust provisions, often referred to as the "proper" law, and one law governing the administration of the trust. Upon further reflection, quite apart from preliminary issues concerning form or capacity with respect to the instrument creating the trust, there may be questions relating to formal validity of the trust itself[28] or capacity to act as trustee,[29] as well as questions relating to the substantive (or essential) validity of the trust provisions or questions affecting the interpretation (or construction) of such provisions. A settlor in a most exceptional case might thus state that his trust is to be governed by English law except that Scots law is to govern matters of interpretation[30] and Cayman Isles law is to govern matters of administration. **16–14**

Where there is an express choice[31] the position is clear enough, except for the finer points of the distinction between matters of validity and matters of administration and except for any rule of public policy that might invalidate such choice. Leaving these aside for the moment, a settlor may expressly[32] go further and empower his trustees to change the law governing the validity of the trust (with the proviso that it does not invalidate the rights of the beneficiaries under the original law governing validity or that, if it would if the trustees did not amend the trust, the trustees must previously amend the trust so as to preserve its validity after the change) and to change the law governing the administration of the trust, with or without changing the principal place of administration of the trust. It would seem that the law governing validity at the time of the disputed issue should determine **16–15**

---

[27] *Re Lord Cable* [1976] 3 All E.R. 417, for analogous contracts, see *Kahler v Midland Bank Ltd* [1950] A.C. 24. See arts 15 and 16, Hague Convention.

[28] e.g. if the proper law applicable to the transfer of property allowed it to be done by conduct or by writing, while the proper law applicable to the creation of a trust of such property required use of a deed.

[29] e.g. if the proper law applicable to the transfer of property allowed transfer to any person of full capacity but the proper law applicable to the creation of a trust requires a trustee to be an official trust corporation or a person over 35 years of age.

[30] At first sight a Chancery lawyer might wonder how substantive validity and interpretation can be governed by different laws: validity almost inevitably depends on interpretation or construction. However, a trust provision may be valid whatever the interpretation, e.g. if "children" covers marital (or legitimate) children or children whether marital or non-marital (or illegitimate). Even if a trust provision would have been void under the old rule against remoteness if "issue" meant "descendants" and not just "children" the meaning of "issue" may be determined by the law expressly chosen by the testator even if different from the law governing validity. A testator may create his own dictionary of meanings whether by using specific foreign legal phrases or, generally incorporating a foreign law to govern interpretation: *Studd v Cook* (1883) 8 App.Cas. 577.

[31] For split laws in a contractual context see *Forsikrings Vesta v Butcher* [1986] 2 All E.R. 488 at 504–505; *Libyan Arab Bank v Bankers Trust Co* [1989] 3 All E.R. 252 at 267, and the Contracts (Applicable Law) Act 1990 implementing the 1980 Rome Convention, especially arts 3 and 4.

[32] *Chellaram v Chellaram (No.2)* [2002] 3 All E.R. 17 at [146] and [160]–[161].

whether that issue was a matter for the law governing validity or for the law governing administration and should, indeed, determine whether or not and by what formal methods the law governing administration may be replaced by another law.[33] This last point is particularly significant where there is no express power to change the law governing administration.

16–16 This leads one to implied choice of law for matters of validity or matters of administration and to implied powers to change the law governing administration. If the addresses of the settlor and the trustees are English and the trust instrument refers to the English Trustee Act 1925 (e.g. in extending the powers in ss. 31 and 32 thereof) then there will be an implied choice of English law as the applicable law governing the trust in all its aspects. At some stage implied subjective intent shades off into an imputed objective intent that the trust shall be governed by the law with which it is most closely connected at the time of its creation.[34] In ascertaining such objective law various factors are taken into account, with the weight to be attached to each factor varying according to the particular circumstances. In a testamentary trust the domicile of the testator at his death traditionally had much significance.[35] It still should have significance[36] under art.7 (which enumerates four indicators "in particular" for ascertaining the law with which a trust is most closely connected) as will obviously be the case where the home trust jurisdiction considers the matter as will normally be the position for matters concerning the internal trustee–beneficiary relationship. In the case of an inter vivos trust the domicile or habitual residence of the settlor at the time he created the trust has some significance as well as the place of execution of the trust instrument. Regard will also be had to the trustee's place of residence or business,[37] though it must not be overlooked that trustees (other than professional corporate trustees) are often chosen for their personal qualities irrespective of where they live or work. Thus, if the testator or settlor expressly designates where the trust is to be administered this will be a more significant factor. Account will also be taken of the situs of the trust assets and the objects of the trust and the places where they are to be fulfilled.[38] The fact that the greater balance of objective factors leads to some applicable law that would not uphold the trust should not lead the court to treat this of itself as a factor that with others points the way to an applicable law that would uphold the trust.[39]

16–17 It seems there will be a presumption in favour of one implied or imputed applicable law governing all aspects of the trust,[40] the onus being upon he who alleges that one law governs validity and another law governs administration. If the original trustees appointed to administer the trust are foreign there will usually be other foreign elements and rarely will there be no express choice of the applicable law—in such rare case if there is a preponderant connection with one foreign system of law it is very likely that such law will govern both validity and administration and not just administration. If the trust instrument authorises the trustees to retire in favour of foreign trustees and to transfer the

---

33 In England we consider the law governing validity as the "mother" law to which the law governing administration is attached by an umbilical cord: cf. *Marlborough v Att.-Gen.* [1945] Ch. 78 at 85; *Iveagh v IRC* [1954] Ch. 364 at 370; *Fattorini v Johannesburg Trust* (1948) 4 S.A.L.R. 806 at 812. The original settlement's perpetuity period applies to property transferred thereout to a separate settlement: *West v Trennery* [2005] 1 All E.R. 827 at [41]. See art.10, Hague Convention.

34 *Iveagh v IRC* [1954] Ch. 364.

35 *Re Lord Cable* [1976] 3 All E.R. 417 at 431. Older cases tended to assume that the law of the testator's domicile because it governed the validity of the will must govern trust dispositions in that will: this may happen to be the case but such does not necessarily follow: *Chellaram v Chellaram (No.2)*, above.

36 But will not necessarily be determinative: see *Tod v Barton* (2002) 4 I.T.E.L.R. 715.

37 As in *Chellaram (No.2)* [2002] 3 All E.R. 17 above where the judge considered that there was not any significant difference between art.7 and the common law, but held the trust to have an Indian proper law despite the majority of trustees being resident in England.

38 *Fordyce v Bridges* (1848) 2 Ph. 497; *Re Mitchner* [1922] St.R.Qd. 252. See art.7, Hague Convention.

39 *Re CIS 213/2004* [2008] W.T.L.R. 189.

40 *Chellaram v Chellaram* [1985] Ch. 409.

assets to such foreign trustees it seems likely that this power to change the place of administration impliedly carries with it the power to change the law governing administration to the law with which those foreign trustees are familiar, so far as this will be the law of a state that has its own internal law of trusts. For the law governing validity to be changed as well, the authority to transfer assets to foreign trustees will need to state that this is so,[41] so that such assets shall thereafter be exclusively governed by such foreign law so far as not contravening mandatory rules of the original "mother" law. As Lord Walker remarked in *West v Trennery*,[42] the second settlement serves "as a vehicle to receive and continue the act of bounty effected by the first settlement, with the rule against perpetuities acting as a sort of umbilical cord between the two settlements". Declaring the trust to be governed henceforth by the law of Suntrustopia so far as not invalidating any beneficial interests under the original English trust will have Suntrustopian law operating under the continuing umbrella of English law whether the Suntrustopian trust is a sub-trust or a new separate settlement for capital gain tax purposes.

B. Matters of Validity Contrasted with Matters of Administration

Where there is an express power to replace the law governing administration a wise settlor will specify what are matters of administration since there is precious little case law guidance on what amounts to matters of administration as opposed to matters of validity. **16–18**

Some guidance may be found in *Pearson v IRC*,[43] which was concerned with "dispositive" (or distributive) powers of trustees that prevent a beneficiary having an interest in possession and "administrative" powers that do not. After all, dispositive (or distributive) powers affect the nature or quantum of a beneficiary's beneficial interest and so would appear not to be matters of administration. From obiter dicta in *Chellaram v Chellaram*,[44] it appears that the rights of the beneficiaries are matters of validity so that the corresponding duties of the trustees must also be matters of validity. This is obviously true where the beneficial interests are concerned but not as concerns the beneficiaries' rights and the trustees' duties relating to investments authorised only under the Trustee Act 2000. Matters of investment are clearly matters of administration. If the law governing administration changes from one jurisdiction to another which permits investment in "x" then beneficiaries have no right to object to investment in "x" if the trustees exhibit the requisite standard of care—even if this be of a lower standard than that required by the previous jurisdiction's law.[45] **16–19**

Matters of administration, it seems, must include the powers of trustees to administer and dispose and acquire trust assets, their powers of investment, their powers of delegation, their powers to pay debts and expenses and compromise claims, their rights to remuneration, their rights to contribution and indemnity between themselves, the appointment, retirement and removal of trustees and the devolution of trusteeship, the powers of the court to give advice and to confer powers upon trustees. **16–20**

Powers of maintenance and advancement can affect the nature and extent of beneficiaries' interests, e.g. if the law of administration is changed to a foreign law which allows up to three-quarters of **16–21**

---

41 *Chellaram v Chellaram (No.2)* [2002] 3 All E.R. 17.

42 [2005] 1 All E.R. 827 at [41].

43 [1981] A.C. 753. A dispositive power prevents any beneficiary having an interest in possession because it enables net income to be diverted away from him after it has arisen.

44 [1985] Ch. 409 at 432.

45 It would be a fraud on the power if trustees exercised their power to change the law governing administration—or validity—for the purpose of benefiting themselves by reducing their duties of care or increasing the scope of exemption from liability for breach of trust.

a beneficiary's contingent share to be advanced to him or gives no right to income at the age of 18 years to a beneficiary whose interest in capital is contingent on acquiring a greater age such as 30 years.[46] Thus ss.31 and 32 of the English Trustee Act 1925 should continue to apply even if the place and law of administration are changed to a different system of law, unless the clause that empowers such change can be broadly construed as authorising the foreign state's Trustee Act to apply to the exclusion of the English Act.

16–22 Matters pertaining to the validity of the trust provisions (e.g. the rules against remoteness, accumulations and inalienability and prohibiting purpose trusts unless charitable trusts) are for the law governing validity. However, if an English testator in his will directs his executors to transfer some Scottish property, whether movable or immovable, that he himself had earlier inherited to two Scottish trustees on public but non-charitable trusts (valid according to Scots law but not English law) then although the law governing the testator's will and other trust dispositions in it may be English it should be Scots law that governs and upholds the validity of the public trusts.[47] The position should be similar if the English domiciled testator had directed his executors to transfer his shares in a Jersey company to a Jersey trustee for furthering the purposes of a particular Jersey political party to be enforceable by its leader from time to time.

C. *The Variation of Trusts Act 1958 and the Matrimonial Causes Act 1973*

16–23 The Variation of Trusts Act position is special. Most jurisdictions have such Acts. Since the legislation can drastically alter the nature and extent of beneficiaries' interests one might have expected that the court's jurisdiction should be restricted to those trusts whose validity is governed by the *lex fori*. Nevertheless, the English courts have arrogated to themselves unlimited jurisdiction in the absence of restricting words in the Variation of Trusts Act 1958.[48]

> "However, where there are substantial foreign elements in the case, the court must consider carefully whether it is proper to exercise the jurisdiction. If, for example, the court were asked to vary a settlement which was plainly a Scottish settlement, it might well hesitate to exercise its jurisdiction to vary the trusts simply because some of, or even all, the trustees and beneficiaries were in this country. It may well be that the judge would say that the Court of Session was the appropriate tribunal to deal with the case."[49]

In the light of art.8(2)(h) of the Hague Convention it is very likely that an English court will decline jurisdiction for trusts governed by a foreign law (unless legislation thereof specifically authorised the English court). One must remember that all the parties before the court will be anxious for the jurisdiction to be exercised for family or for taxation reasons and that the interests of infant or unborn beneficiaries will hardly ever[50] be prejudiced by any variation. However, the taxation authorities in a

---

[46] He will only be entitled to income on attaining the specified age in some jurisdictions. Some jurisdictions, indeed, exclude a beneficiary's rights under *Saunders v Vautier* either altogether or only with the court's leave. The distinction between capital and income is probably a matter of validity because it affects beneficiaries' entitlements.

[47] cf. *Jewish National Fund v Royal Trust Co* (1965) 53 D.L.R. (2d) 577. The courts tend, where possible, to choose as the impliedly chosen applicable law one which will sustain the validity of the trust: *Augustus v Permanent Trustee Co (Canberra) Ltd* (1971) 124 C.L.R. 245.

[48] *Re Ker's Settlement* [1963] Ch. 553; *Re Paget's Settlement* [1965] 1 W.L.R. 1046. The same has happened in Western Australia: *Faye v Faye* [1973] W.A.R. 66.

[49] *Re Paget's Settlement* [1965] 1 W.L.R. 1046 at 1050, per Cross J.

[50] See *Re Remnant's WT* [1970] 1 Ch. 560.

particular country may take the point that the variation is ineffective except to the extent that adult beneficiaries are estopped from reverting to the pre-variation position.

Court orders varying nuptial settlements[51] under the Matrimonial Causes Act 1973 s.24(1)(c) and (d) can, however, be made even in respect of foreign trusts of foreign property held by foreign trustees[52] but will not be made if they would be likely to be ineffective in the relevant foreign country.[53] One can invoke art.15 generally or 15(1)(b) specifically to justify such English jurisdiction so that there can be a proper determination of all matters arising out of the divorce, application of the Act being an effect of the marriage. The Variation of Trusts Act jurisdiction is different in requiring the consent of all adult beneficiaries coupled with the court's consent, while the trustees have a non-partisan co-operative function. The Jersey Royal Court cannot give effect to a foreign variation of a Jersey trust,[54] so only if it itself can vary the trust to similar effect, e.g. so as to restore the spouse to membership of a class of beneficiaries, will the divorced spouse benefit.[55] Where, however, taking account of resources available to a husband[56] under a Jersey trust under which he can benefit as a discretionary object, the English divorce court makes a financial order against the husband, leaving him in need of seeking financial support from the Jersey trustees, the trustees can and normally should seek the court's acceptance that a proposed payment to the husband is a proper intra vires exercise of the trustees' discretionary powers.[57] **16–24**

D. Limitations upon Free Choice of Law

Obvious problems exist where immovables are concerned but under the Trusts Convention the *lex situs* does not need to govern the validity of trusts of immovables. Take land in Spain (which does not have the trust concept within its code of law) or in Jersey (which allows trusts so long as they are not of land in Jersey). There are practical problems if recourse has to be had to Spanish or Jersey courts and so far as title to the land is concerned the trustees would appear as ordinary private beneficial owners. However, if the land comprised say $^1/_{20}$ of the aggregate of property subjected to trusts with an English proper law why should the English trustees not be under valid in personam trusteeship obligations to the English beneficiaries in respect of the land, e.g. to pay rents over to the beneficiaries and to keep the premises in reasonable repair or to sell the land and buy property within a common law trust jurisdiction?[58] **16–25**

---

[51] *Brooks v Brooks* [1995] 3 All E.R. 257 at 263.

[52] *E v E* [1990] F.L.R. 233, 242; *T v T* [1996] 2 F.L.R. 357 at 363; *Charalambous v Charalambous* [2004] 2 F.L.R. 1093, though local foreign proceedings to recognise the English court order will also be necessary to protect the trustees giving effect to such order, e.g. *Compas Trustees v McBarnett* [2002] Jersey L.R. 321, where the court accepted this as a matter of comity, though this is an inadequate basis, an intra vires legal obligation as res judicata being required: *Mubarak v Mubarak* [2009] 1 F.L.R. 644 at [61] and [68].

[53] *Goff v Goff* [1934] P. 107 at 113.

[54] Article 9 of the Trusts (Jersey) Law as amended in October 2006.

[55] As in *Mubarak v Mubarak* [2009] 1 F.L.R. 664, affirmed [2009] W.T.L.R. 1543.

[56] See *A v A* [2007] 2 F.L.R. 467 at [92]–[100]; *Charman v Charman* [2007] 1 FLR 1246 at [48] and [57].

[57] See *Mubarak v Mubarak* [2009] 1 F.L.R. 664 at [73]–[74] .

[58] cf. *Re Fitzgerald* [1904] 1 Ch. 573; *Webb v Webb* [1994] 3 All E.R. 911. Sufficient scope is afforded to the *lex situs* to govern preliminary or policy issues, e.g. *Re Ross* [1930] 1 Ch. 377 (*legitima portio*); *Re Hoyles* [1911] 1 Ch. 179; *Duncan v Lawson* (1889) 41 Ch.D. 394 (Mortmain Acts); *Freke v Carberry* (1873) L.R. 16 Eq. 461 (perpetuities and accumulations); *Re Pearse's Settlement* [1909] 1 Ch. 304 (Jersey land could not be conveyed by a married woman to someone except for adequate pecuniary compensation so that her after-acquired property covenant in an English settlement was construed as not intended to include after-acquired Jersey land within the scope of the covenant).

16–26 A settlor has total freedom of choice of law unless such choice is manifestly incompatible with public policy.[59] Article 13 of the Hague Convention affords a discretion to refuse to recognise a trust or a category of trust if its significant elements, except for the choice of law, the place of administration and the habitual residence of the trustee, are more closely connected with a non-trust-State. The United Kingdom considered it unhelpful for its courts to have such a discretion and so the Recognition of Trusts Act 1987 deliberately omits the uncertainties of art.13.

16–27 If, in what would otherwise be a trust governed by English law, an Englishman purports to create a trust of English land but expressly chooses a foreign law with the intent of enabling the land to be held for ever on valid non-charitable purpose trusts it is clear that the land will not be so held. The English court will have to give effect to the English policy rules as to the administration of land within the jurisdiction. Indeed, the policy rules recognising the unenforceability of purpose trusts, where no one has locus standi to apply to the court to have the purposes positively carried out, would prevent the trust being effective even if the property was not land.

16–28 If, however, it was movable or immovable property in Scotland subjected to public non-charitable purpose trusts expressed to be subject to Scots law (and valid by Scots law) then there seems no policy reason for the English court to invalidate such trusts of an English testator in his English will. Indeed, if the trusts were private non-charitable purpose trusts of movables in the Isle of Man, Jersey, Bermuda or Cayman valid under special legislation owing to the trust instrument having expressly designated an enforcer with standing to enforce the trust, the English court should not invalidate them, nor should it if such trusts purchase English assets as investments or even if such assets are directly transferred to the trustees to become original settled assets.[60] However, the purposes must not amount to a mere investment clause[61] or to a device purporting to put beneficial ownership in suspense protected from claims of creditors and tax inspectors.[62]

16–29 One should note that a choice of law (e.g. English law) to govern a trust makes that law govern the relationship between the trustees and the beneficiaries: that law governs the "internal" aspects of the trust. As far as the trustees' "external" relations with third parties are concerned, e.g. in contracting with them or transferring property to them one has to apply the conflict of laws rules applicable to contracts or to the transfer of property. Thus, a trustee of a trust governed by the law of Jersey may rely when contracting in Jersey on art.32(1) of the Trusts (Jersey) Law 1984, "Where in any transaction or matter affecting a trust a trustee informs a third party that he is acting as trustee a claim by such third party in relation thereto shall extend only to the trust property." If the trustee contracts in

---

[59] See arts 6 and 18 but note the safeguards in arts 15 and 16 of the Hague Convention. English courts are likely to invoke public policy where a settlor uses Belize or Cook Islands law to settle his own property on protective trusts for himself for life (see *Re Lawrence* (2003) 5 I.T.E.L.R. 1) or creates a Cook Islands asset protection trust which can only be upset if the creditor intended to be defrauded brings an action within one year of the property being transferred to the trustees and proves his case beyond reasonable doubt.

[60] See D.J. Hayton, "Developing the Obligation Characteristic of the Trust" (2001) 117 L.Q.R. 96. Further on offshore developments see D.J. Hayton (ed.) *Modern International Developments in Trust Law* (1999) Chapters 1 and 15; A.G.D. Duckworth, "The Role of Offshore Jurisdictions in the Development of the International Trust" (1999) 32 Vanderbilt Jo. Transnational Law 879; A.G.D. Duckworth "Trust Law in the New Millennium: Fundamentals" [2001] Trusts & Trustees 9; and D.J. Hayton (ed.), *Extending the Boundaries of Trusts and Similar Ring-Fenced Funds* (2002), chapter by D. Waters, "Reaching for the Skies".

[61] e.g. a trust for the purpose of developing the income yield and capital growth of the trust fund, so in default of any disposal of the beneficial interest there will be a resulting trust for the settlor.

[62] e.g. a trust to develop the business of X Co Ltd where X Co or its owner should be regarded as beneficiary or a trust to maintain a collection of paintings together as a private collection when the settlor should be regarded as beneficiary under a resulting trust. Under the Cayman Special Trusts Alternative Regime Law 1997 s.7 "beneficiaries" have no interests whatsoever in the trust property and have no rights to sue the trustees or the expressly appointed "enforcer", so unless a "beneficiary" has been appointed an enforcer the English court seems likely to treat "beneficiaries" as objects of a power, leaving a resulting trust for the settlor: cf. *Armitage v Nurse* [1998] Ch. 241 at 253.

England under English law (not expressly choosing Jersey law to govern the contract) he will be personally liable since any person contracting under English law is personally liable except to the extent he expressly restricts liability, for example to trust property to which he has a right of recourse for paying trust expenses.

3. The Recognition of Trusts Act 1987 and the Limited Scope of the Hague Trusts Convention

Since August 1, 1987, arts 1 to 18 (except 13 and 16 para.2) and 22 of the Hague Trusts Convention, have been in force in the United Kingdom in respect of trusts whenever created, but this does not affect the law to be applied to anything done or omitted before August 1, 1987.[63] Section 1(2) extends the Convention's provisions to any other trusts of property arising (e.g. orally or by statute) under the law of any part of the United Kingdom or by virtue of a judicial decision in the United Kingdom or elsewhere. This is because art.3 restricts the Convention to trusts created voluntarily and evidenced in writing.[64] Despite the superficial width of art.2 the Convention does not extend beyond trusts to agency or mandate as earlier explained.[65] **16–30**

A. Limited Scope of Hague Trusts Convention

This (private international law) Convention does not introduce the trust into the internal private law of States that do not have the concept of the trust; it simply makes foreign States recognise trusts of property as a matter of private international law, although, for recognition to mean something, the internal private law needs to recognise that the trust fund is separate from the owner's private patrimony, so as to be immune from claims of the owner's creditors heirs and spouse.[66] **16–31**

This (private international law) Convention does not affect the internal private law of States that have the trust concept: the extent to which the applicable law can be expressly or impliedly changed and the distinction between matters of validity and matters of administration may vary according to the appropriate applicable law because State A's internal trust rules may differ from such rules of State B. **16–32**

Non-trust states expect the home jurisdiction to resolve matters concerning the internal trustee–beneficiary relationship, so the Trusts Convention will help them where the external relationship of the trustees with third parties is concerned. **16–33**

The Convention applies only to a trust ("the rocket") and not to the instrument launching the trust ("the rocket-launcher"). Antecedent preliminary issues that may affect the validity of wills, deeds or other acts by which property is allegedly subjected to a trust fall outside the Convention: art.4. The Convention only applies if whatever is the applicable law governing capacity or formal or substantive validity of wills or inter vivos declarations of trust by the settlor or transfers of property to trustees has not operated to prevent the relevant property being available to be subjected to trusts. **16–34**

---

[63] S.I. 1987/1177. The Convention is regarded as clarifying the common law position (on which see Wallace (1987) 36 I.C.L.Q. 454) but the non-retrospective provision was inserted in s.1(5) of the 1987 Act *ex abundante cautela*.

[64] The French text is *"et dont la preuve est apportée par écrit"* which appears to need dilution to reflect "evidenced" in writing and so to cover most trusts which are first established in respect of a nominal sum, with substantial assets being added subsequently and with written evidence subsequently arising, whether produced by the settlor or the trustees, e.g. in their accounts.

[65] A settlor's declaration of himself as trustee of assets now controlled by him as trustee should be within art.2, but, in any event, if valid by its own governing law should be recognised under arts 11 et seq.

[66] The Dutch implementing legislation provides for this: D.J. Hayton (1996) 5 J. Int. P. 127.

16–35 While the Convention recognises the equitable proprietary right of beneficiaries in trust property and its traceable product in States that have such equitable concept, it does not introduce such proprietary right into States that have no concept of equitable proprietary interest in their fixed scheme of property interests. If trust property is transferred in such a State to X the *lex situs* will govern the effect of such transfer and deny the existence of any equitable proprietary interest, though any actual knowledge by X of a breach of trust may make it possible to take advantage of any *lex situs* rules on fraud: see the last sentence of art.11 para.3(d) and also art.15(d)(f) and para.113 of the Von Overbeck *Official Report on the Trusts Convention*.[67] However, in *El Ajou v Dollar Land Holdings Plc*[68] the equitable tracing process was held not to be defeated if traceable assets passed from a common law jurisdiction through various civil law jurisdictions so as to end up in a common law jurisdiction.

16–36 Although civil law States do not have equitable proprietary interests, virtually all have some concept of a ring-fenced fund as a separate pool of assets from its owner's private patrimony where there is a fund dedicated for achieving a particular purpose and property substituted for dedicated property is dedicated to the same purpose as that property.[69] Article 2 para.2(a) and the second sentence of art.11 make it clear that the trust assets constitute a separate fiduciary fund and are not treated as part of the owner's private patrimony available for his personal creditors and his heirs, while under para.(d) of the third sentence of art.11, recognition implies "that the trust assets may be recovered when the trustee, in breach of trust, has mingled trust assets with his own property or has alienated trust assets." These are essential elements of a trust "without which its recognition would have no meaning", as accepted in para.108 of the von Overbeck *Report*. The ring-fenced protection of a fiduciary patrimony against the trustee-owner's creditors and heirs would be wholly undermined if it were to be lost as soon as the trustee-owner mingled the trust assets with his own assets or sold trust assets to purchase an asset intended by him to be part of his private patrimony. Thus the beneficiaries can claim against the trustee and his creditors and heirs that the relevant fraction of the mingled assets and the purchased substituted asset are held as a fiduciary patrimony for their exclusive benefit. If, however, the trustee-owner had not sold a trust asset but had simply given it away to X, then X would take free from any claims of the beneficiaries upon obtaining a good title under the *lex situs* as mentioned in the preceding paragraph.

16–37 Article 15 detracts significantly from art.11 in order to deal with the interface between trust law and other laws. It ensures the application of the internal mandatory rules of a State whose law is applicable according to the conflicts rules of the forum, irrespective of the law applicable to the trust. A forum will have choice of law rules in areas such as succession, property, bankruptcy, divorce and matrimonial property regimes. While it seems that the Convention requires recognition of a fiduciary patrimony separate from a private patrimony which alone is subject to art.15, the Dutch, out of an abundance of caution when implementing the Convention in 1995, ousted the application of paras (d) and (e) of art.15 in case it might be thought that those paragraphs took away the protection intended to be afforded to beneficiaries against the trustee's creditors and heirs. Mandatory succession rules (*réserve héréditaire, legitima portio, pflichtteil*) have special significance, especially if a settlor's trust assets are found in the civil law forum of

---

67 The Report is reproduced in J. Glasson (ed.), *International Trust Laws* and in J. Harris, *The Hague Trust Convention*. It will be taken account of by the court in construing the Convention as implemented by the 1987 Recognition of Trusts Act: e.g. *Three Rivers DC v Bank of England (No.2)* [1996] 2 All E.R. 363.

68 [1993] 3 All E.R. 717 at 736–737; [1995] 2 All E.R. 213 at 221, in respect of a personal claim but the position should be the same for a proprietary remedy despite the continuing interest in property vindication approach in *Foskett v McKeown* [2001] 1 A.C. 102: the life of the law has not always been logical.

69 e.g. property subject to a matrimonial property regime or a commercial partnership regime or a deceased's estate vested in his heir or a sinking fund for major repairs to a block of flats or an asset held by an agent for an undisclosed principal or a *fondo patrimoniale* for an Italian's children's upbringing.

a forced heir who seeks such assets.[70] Choice of law rules may lead to the *lex successionis, lex situs* or *lex fori* being invoked so as wholly or partly to undo the effects of a trust. While an English court should characterise a Frenchman's transfer of assets in England to English trustees as a straightforward inter vivos transfer of property governed by the English *lex situs*, protected by art.15(d) of the Convention, and then by the English applicable law of the trust, a French court will characterise such transfer as pertaining to the French *lex successionis* so far as it affects property subject to *réserve héréditaire*. So long as the trust property remains in England (or another common law country) it should remain intact but if the property is found in France (or a sympathetic civil law country) then the heirs may claim it in satisfaction of their *réserves héréditaires*.

16–38 Under the first paragraph of art.16 the *lex fori* court must of course apply its own international mandatory rules, e.g. if a beneficiary is suing the trustee for failure to export to the beneficiary some heritage object whose export is prohibited by the *lex fori*.

16–39 Under the second paragraph the *lex fori* court has a discretion, to be exercised only in the most exceptional case, to apply the international mandatory rules of some other State with a sufficiently close connection with the case, where the State's law is neither the *lex fori* nor the law applicable to the trust as such.

16–40 Trust States find it difficult to appreciate the need for such a provision since a Court of Equity will do nothing in vain (i.e. will not make orders which cannot be carried out as where foreign immovables are concerned) and will not require a person to do an act that is illegal in the place where it is to be done.[71] Thus, if the law of the trust is that of State A, the law of the forum that of State B, and the law of State C makes it illegal to take certain sorts of assets out of State C, any action by a beneficiary against the trustees for not getting such assets out to the beneficiary will fail, regardless of the second paragraph. The uncertain ambit of the paragraph is also unsatisfactory for lawyers and for courts. The United Kingdom government therefore made the reservation allowed by the third paragraph.

16–41 By art.13 a court in a trust or non-trust State has a discretionary power to refuse to recognise a trust or a category (e.g. non-charitable purpose trusts) if the significant elements of the trust (e.g. situs of assets, settlor's and beneficiaries' habitual residence) are more closely connected with non-trust, than with trust, States, except for the choice of the applicable law, the place of administration and the habitual residence of the trustee. It seems that it is up to the court to decide in a particular case what are the significant elements which connect the trust closely to a non-trust State. The relevant time for these significant elements to be so connected seems to be the time of the events occasioning the claim for recognition and not the time of creation of the trust. The United Kingdom Recognition of Trusts Act 1987 deliberately omitted art.13 because it was considered unnecessary for such a discretion to be available.

16–42 The Convention is only concerned with trusts of property created voluntarily and evidenced in writing[72] and not with the imposition of constructive trusteeship upon a defendant so that he is personally liable to account as a constructive trustee, e.g. if he dishonestly assisted in a breach of trust, whether or not any trust property was ever in his hands. Where a defendant cannot be made personally liable in tort or contract but has acted with want of probity equity constructively treats him as if he had been a trustee as a formula for an equitable personal (as opposed to proprietary) remedy, which will be of no assistance if the defendant is deeply insolvent. A defendant in a State not having the trust and any equitable jurisdiction can never be liable in such fashion in that State. Where a

---

[70] *Holzberg v Sasson* 1986 Rev. crit. de dr. int. pr. 685.

[71] *Re Lord Cable* [1976] 3 All E.R. 417 at 435.

[72] Seemingly of the settlor or the trustees in signing trust accounts, e.g. in relation to property subsequently added to trusts of nominal sums.

trustee of a trust expressly created voluntarily and evidenced in writing acts in breach of trust so as to purport to make a profit for his private patrimony or to place within his private patrimony assets purchased with trust money, such profit or assets from the date of their acquisition are held subject to the express trusts[73] as protected under the Convention. The crucial ring-fenced protection of beneficiaries' core interests would be wholly illusory if the trustee at will could benefit himself (and thus his creditors and heirs) at the expense of the beneficiaries' interests that he has exclusively agreed to protect and advance. Where a trust of property created voluntarily and evidenced in writing fails to deal completely with the beneficial interests created thereunder, the law governing such trust determines the resulting trust that arises on such failure.

16–43 The position as to purchase-money resulting trusts is not so clear. Assume that S and T together in equal shares purchase an English house of which T is registered as proprietor, so T holds it on resulting trust for S and T in equal shares without there being any written evidence of this. T sells the house when S is in Australia caring for her terminally ill mother. T uses the proceeds of sale to buy a house for himself in Civilopia (an EU State that has implemented the Convention on Trusts). If T is "domiciled" (resident with a substantial connection[74]) in England S can obtain an English in personam judgment against him[75] which can then be recognised and enforced in Civilopia under the Brussels 1 Regulation. If, however, T had become "domiciled" in his Civilopian home, he could only be sued in England as the State whose law governs the trust[76] if he was "settlor, trustee or beneficiary of a trust created by the operation of a statute or by a written instrument or created orally and evidenced in writing".[77] The resulting trust for S and T, however, was created not by operation of a statute but by the operation of Equity on the conduct of S and T, albeit that the Trusts of Land and Appointment of Trustees Act 1996 then imposed a regulatory regime on the trust so created. Thus the English court has no jurisdiction to hear the case and in its judgment produce the necessary written evidence. If T is sued in his Civilopian domicile the Civilopian court only has to apply the Trusts Convention if the English trust was created voluntarily and evidenced in writing. Such evidence is lacking even if S and T of their own volition are presumed obviously to have intended that the house should be held for themselves in shares proportionate to their contributions to its purchase. Query if the Civilopian court might be able to prevent the unjust enrichment of T by applying some of its own laws. The position is similar for the situation where T created a common intention constructive trust of his English house for himself and S before selling it and purchasing a Civilopian house for himself with the proceeds.

4. Civil Jurisdiction and Judgments Acts 1982 and 1991 and Brussels 1 Regulation

16–44 These Acts make special provision for EU and EFTA countries as required by the Brussels 1968 Convention on Jurisdiction and Recognition and Enforcement of Judgments in Civil and Commercial Matters and the parallel Lugano Convention of 1988 for EFTA countries (Switzerland, Norway and Iceland). For EU countries the Brussels Convention has been replaced by Brussels 1 (Council

[73] See *Foskett v McKeown* [2001] 1 A.C. 102 at 110 and 127 and Lord Millett's paper on "Proprietary Restitution" in S. Degeling and J. Edelman (eds) *Equity in Commercial Law* (2005), pp. 315–316, though traditionally judges have often referred to property that the trustee wrongfully denies to be trust property to be held on constructive trust for the beneficiaries on the same terms as the express trusts for the beneficiaries eg *Att.-Gen. for Hong Kong v Reid* [1994] 1 A.C. 324.

[74] Civil Jurisdiction and Judgments Act 1982 s.41(2) and Civil Jurisdiction and Judgments Order 2001 Sch.1 para.9.

[75] *Webb v Webb* [1994] Q.B. 696.

[76] Civil Jurisdiction and Judgments Act 1982 s.45 and Civil Jurisdiction and Judgments Order 2001 Sch.1 para.12.

[77] Article 5(6), Brussels 1.

Regulation 44/2001),[78] while the Lugano Convention has been revised in 2007 to bring it into line with the Regulation. The basic principle is that jurisdiction is conferred on the courts of the "domicile" of the defendant, which requires him to reside in and have a substantial connection with the jurisdiction alleged to be that of his domicile.[79] Exceptionally, in the case of a "trust created by operation of a statute, or by a written instrument, or created orally and evidenced in writing" a person may, instead, be sued as settlor, trustee[80] or beneficiary in the courts of the Member State in which the trust is "domiciled".[81] A trust is domiciled in the state having the system of law with which the trust has its closest and most real connection,[82] which seems to be the system that provides the applicable (or governing) law of the trust, so giving birth to the trust.[83] The court first "seised" of the action hears it,[84] even if a trust instrument confers jurisdiction on a another system of law to have exclusive jurisdiction in any proceedings brought against a settlor, trustee or beneficiary if relations between these persons or their rights or obligations under the trust are involved.[85] However, such first court in its discretion may refer the matter to the courts in the designated exclusive jurisdiction. Where the proceedings have as their object rights in rem in immovable property or tenancies of immovable property, then the courts of the state in which such property is situated have exclusive jurisdiction.[86] If a father claims that French immovable property vested in his son is held on a resulting trust for the father this is regarded as a personal matter between them so that the French court does not have exclusive jursidiction: English Equity acts in personam and the English court has jurisdiction if the son is resident in England or the trust is an English trust.[87] Where the defendant is "domiciled" in a Regulation or Lugano Convention State proceedings may be served out of the English jurisdiction without the permission of the English court.[88]

16–45 The Conventions and then Brussels 1 and the revised Lugano Convention do not apply to rights in property arising out of a matrimonial relationship, wills or succession or bankruptcy or insolvency,[89] thus excluding ante-nuptial marriage settlements. However, once under the relevant law governing wills and succession a testamentary trust has been permitted to arise, any subsequent breach of trust dispute (e.g. arising 20 or 30 years later) should fall within the Conventions and Brussels 1 and the revised Lugano Convention, just as in the case of a dispute arising under a trust set up in the settlor's lifetime. Once the right in property has been established as vested in a trustee, T, or an absolute

---

78 See Civil Jurisdiction and Judgments Order 2001 (SI 2001/3929) and Civil Jurisdiction and Judgments Regulations 2007 (SI 2007/1655) (bringing in Denmark).

79 Civil Jurisdiction and Judgments Act 1982 s.41(2), and Civil Jurisdiction and Judgments Order 2001 art.3 and Sch.1 para.9.

80 This has been narrowly interpreted to cover just the trustee owner-manager of the trust fund so as not to extend to persons who as protectors or as holders of powers of appointment are an integral part of the internal relationships within the settlor's trust structure: *Gomez v Gomez-Monche* [2009] Ch. 245, discussed by Hayton J. in "Trust Disputes within Article 5(6) of Brussels 1" (2009) 23 Tru. L.I. 3; Prof. Schlosser in para.114 of his official Report in (1979) O.J.C. 59/71 reveals that art.5(6) was intended to deal with these internal relationships, the art.2 "domicile" of the defendant being apt for external relationships with third parties e.g. under contracts.

81 Article 5(6).

82 Section 45 of the 1982 Act.

83 *Gomez v Gomez-Monche Vives* [2009] Ch. 245 at [58]–[64].

84 Articles 21 and 23 respectively of the Brussels and Lugano Conventions; art.27 of Regulation 44/2001.

85 Article 17 (now art.23 of Regulation) as restricted by *Erich Gasser GmbH v Misat* [2005] Q.B. 1 (E.C.J.).

86 Article 16(1) of Convention and art.22 of Regulation 44/2001.

87 *Webb v Webb* [1994] Q.B. 696; applied by CA in *Pollard v Ashurst* [2001] 2 All E.R. 75, upholding judge's order on behalf of husband's trustee in bankruptcy that husband and wife should sell their jointly owned Portuguese villa to enable the trustee to obtain the husband's share of the proceeds.

88 Civil Procedure Rules Pt 6 r.6.33. In non-EU or non-EFTA cases, permission needs to be sought but only if certain requirements are satisfied eg the trusts are governed by English law and the person to be served is a trustee when it is also possible to get leave for service on a party who is a necessary or proper party to the claim: CPR Pt 6 r.6.36 and para.3.1 of Practice Direction B to Pt 6.

89 Article 1 of the Convention and Regulation.

owner, O, then matters arising years later concerning breaches of trust or contract or delicts affecting T or O surely cannot be matters of succession.[90] In October 2009 the EU Commission produced a draft Regulation to establish harmonised rules on the law governing succession in EU States and to provide for jurisdiction and recognition and enforcement of succession judgments. It seems, however, most unlikely that the UK government will opt in to this Regulation because, for example, it allows a foreign *lex successionis* by its "claw-back" rules to undermine lifetime gifts of English property made by the deceased and currently regarded as unimpeachable.

16–46 Judgments on trusts and other matters given in a Member State are to be recognised and enforced in the other Member States by a straightforward registration or declaration process.[91] However, a judgment will not be recognised:[92]

- if such recognition is manifestly contrary to public policy in the State in which recognition is sought;
- where it was given in default of appearance if the defendant was not duly served with the relevant proceedings in sufficient time to enable him to arrange for his defence, unless the defendant failed to commence proceedings to challenge the judgment when it was possible to do so;
- if the judgment is irreconcilable with a judgment in a dispute between the same parties in the State in which recognition is sought;
- if the judgment is irreconcilable with an earlier judgment given in another Member State or in a third State involving the same cause of action and between the same parties, provided that the earlier judgment fulfils the conditions necessary for its recognition in the Member State addressed; or
- the judgment was given by a court other than that having exclusive jurisdiction under art.22 where proceedings have as their object rights in rem to immovable property or tenancies of immovable property.

HAGUE CONVENTION ON THE LAW APPLICABLE TO TRUSTS AND ON THEIR RECOGNITION[93]

16–47 The States signatory to the present Convention,

Considering that the trust, as developed in courts of equity in common law jurisdictions and adopted with some modifications in other jurisdictions, is a unique legal institution,

---

[90] Further on this and what are "trusts" within the Conventions and the Regulation see D.J. Hayton, "The Trust in European Commercial Life" in J. Lowry and L. Mistelis (eds), *Commercial Law: Perspectives and Practice* (2005).

[91] Articles 33 and 38 of Regulation 44/2001.

[92] Article 34 of the Regulation.

[93] Generally see J. Harris, *The Hague Trusts Convention* (2003); *Explanatory Report* by A.E. von Overbeck published by Permanent Bureau of The Hague Conference in *Acts and Documents of the 15th Session of the Hague Conference* pp.370 ff. (reprinted in Harris op. cit.); D.J. Hayton (1987) 36 I.C.L.Q. 260; *Underhill & Hayton* (17th edn) Chapter 25; *Lewin on Trusts* (18th edn) Ch.11; O'Sullivan [1993] 2 J.Int. P. 85; Albisini & Gambino [1993] 2 J.Int. P. 73; Schoenblum [1994] 1 J.Int. P. 5; Hayton [1994] J.Int. P. 23; *Dicey & Morris*, Ch.29; Hayton in Borras (ed.) *Liber Amicorum Georges Droz* (1996). The Convention has been implemented by Italy, Switzerland, Liechtenstein, Malta, Monaco, San Marino, Australia, Netherlands, Luxembourg, Canada (for Alberta, New Brunswick, British Columbia, Newfoundland, Prince Edward Island, Manitoba, Saskatchewan) and the United Kingdom (including Isle of Man, Jersey, Guernsey, Gibraltar, Bermuda, Hong Kong, British Virgin Islands, Turks and Caicos, Montserrat, but not Cayman Islands).

Desiring to establish common provisions on the law applicable to trusts and to deal with the most important issues concerning the recognition of trusts,

Have resolved to conclude a Convention to this effect, and have agreed upon the following provisions—

Chapter I. Scope

Article 1

This Convention specifies the law applicable to trusts and governs their recognition. **16–48**

Article 2

For the purposes of this Convention, the term "trust" refers to the legal relationships created—inter vivos or on death—by a person, the settlor, when assets have been placed under the control of a trustee for the benefit of a beneficiary or for a specified purpose. **16–49**

A trust has the following characteristics—

(a) the assets constitute a separate fund and are not a part of the trustee's own estate;

(b) title to the trust assets stands in the name of the trustee or in the name of another person on behalf of the trustee;

(c) the trustee has the power and the duty, in respect of which he is accountable, to manage, employ or dispose of the assets in accordance with the terms of the trust and the special duties imposed upon him by law.

The reservation by the settlor of certain rights and powers and the fact that the trustee may himself have rights as a beneficiary, are not necessarily inconsistent with the existence of a trust.

Article 3

The Convention applies only to trusts created voluntarily and evidenced in writing. **16–50**

Article 4

The Convention does not apply to preliminary issues relating to the validity of wills or of other acts by virtue of which assets are transferred to the trustee. **16–51**

Article 5

The Convention does not apply to the extent that the law specified by Chapter II does not provide for trusts or the category of trusts involved. **16–52**

Chapter II. Applicable Law

Article 6

A trust shall be governed by the law chosen by the settlor. The choice must be express or be implied in the terms of the instrument creating or the writing evidencing the trust, interpreted, if necessary, in the light of circumstances of the case. **16–53**

Where the law chosen under the previous paragraph does not provide for trusts or the category of trust involved, the choice shall not be effective and the law specified in Art.7 shall apply.

Article 7

Where no applicable law has been chosen, a trust shall be governed by the law with which it is most closely connected. **16–54**

In ascertaining the law with which a trust is most closely connected reference shall be made in particular to—

(a) the place of administration of the trust designated by the settlor;

(b) the situs of the assets of the trust;

(c) the place of residence or business of the trustee;

(d) the objects of the trust and the places where they are to be fulfilled.

Article 8

16–55 The law specified by Art. 6 or 7 shall govern the validity of the trust, its construction, its effects, and the administration of the trust. In particular that law shall govern—

(a) the appointment, resignation and removal of trustees, the capacity to act as a trustee, and the devolution of the office or trustee;

(b) the rights and duties of trustees among themselves;

(c) the right of trustees to delegate in whole or in part the discharge of their duties or the exercise of their powers;

(d) the power of trustees to administer or to dispose of trust assets, to create security interests in the trust assets, or to acquire new assets;

(e) the powers of investment of trustees;

(f) restrictions upon the duration of the trust, and upon the power to accumulate the income of the trust;

(g) the relationships between the trustees and the beneficiaries including the personal liability of the trustees to the beneficiaries;

(h) the variation or termination of the trust;

(i) the distribution of the trust assets;

(j) the duty of trustees to account for their administration.

Article 9

16–56 In applying this Chapter a severable aspect of the trust, particularly matters of administration, may be governed by a different law.

Article 10

16–57 The law applicable to the validity of the trust shall determine whether that law or the law governing the severable aspect of the trust may be replaced by another law.

Chapter III. Recognition

Article 11

16–58 A trust created in accordance with the law specified by the preceding Chapter shall be recognized as a trust. Such recognition shall imply, as a minimum, that the trust property constitutes a separate fund, that the trustee may sue and be sued in his capacity as trustee, and that he may appear or act in this capacity before a notary or any person acting in an official capacity.

In so far as the law applicable to a trust requires or provides, such recognition shall imply, in particular—

(a) that personal creditors of the trustee shall have no recourse against the trust assets;

(b) that the trust assets shall not form part of the trustee's estate upon his insolvency or bankruptcy;

(c) that the trust assets shall not form part of the matrimonial property of the trustee or his spouse nor part of the trustee's estate upon his death;

(d) that the trust assets may be recovered when the trustee, in breach of trust, has mingled trust assets with his own property or has alienated trust assets. However, the rights and obligations of any third party holder of the assets shall remain subject to the law determined by the choice of law rules of the forum.

Article 12

16–59 Where the trustee desires to register assets, movable or immovable, or documents of title to them, he shall be entitled, in so far as this is not prohibited by or inconsistent with the law of the State where registration is sought, to do so in his capacity as trustee or in such other way that the existence of the trust is disclosed.

Article 13

No State shall be bound to recognise a trust the significant elements of which, except for the choice of the applicable law, the place of administration and the habitual residence of the trustee, are more closely connected with States which do not have the institution of the trust or the category of trust involved. **16–60**

Article 14

The Convention shall not prevent the application of rules of law more favourable to the recognition of trusts. **16–61**

Chapter IV. General Clauses

Article 15

The Convention does not prevent the application of provisions of the law designated by the conflicts rules of the forum, in so far as those provisions cannot be derogated from by voluntary act, relating in particular to the following matters— **16–62**

(a) the protection of minors and incapable parties;

(b) the personal and proprietary effects of marriage;

(c) succession rights, testate and intestate, especially the indefeasible shares of spouses and relatives;

(d) the transfer of title to property and security interests in property;

(e) the protection of creditors in matters of insolvency;

(f) the protection, in other respects, of third parties acting in good faith.

If recognition of a trust is prevented by application of the preceding paragraph, the court shall try to give effect to the objects of the trust by other means.

Article 16

The Convention does not prevent the application of those provisions of the law of the forum which must be applied even to international situations, irrespective of rules of conflict of laws. **16–63**

If another State has a sufficiently close connection with a case then, in exceptional circumstances, effect may also be given to rules of that State which have the same character as mentioned in the preceding paragraph.

Any Contracting State may, by way of reservation, declare that it will not apply the second paragraph of this article.

Article 17

In the Convention the word "law" means the rules of law in force in a State other than its rules of conflict of laws. **16–64**

Article 18

The provisions of the Convention may be disregarded when their application would be manifestly incompatible with public policy (*ordre public*). **16–65**

Article 19

Nothing in the Convention shall prejudice the powers of States in fiscal matters. **16–66**

Article 20

Any Contracting State may, at any time, declare that the provisions of the Convention will be extended to trusts declared by judicial decisions. **16–67**

This declaration shall be notified to the Ministry of Foreign Affairs of the Kingdom of the Netherlands and will come into effect on the day when this notification is received.

Article 31 is applicable to the withdrawal of this declaration in the same way as it applies to a denunciation of the Convention.

Article 21

Any Contracting State may reserve the right to apply the provisions of Chapter III only to trusts the validity of which is governed by the law of a Contracting State. **16–68**

Article 22

16–69 The Convention applies to trusts regardless of the date on which they were created.

However, a Contracting State may reserve the right not to apply the Convention to trusts created before the date on which, in relation to that State, the Convention enters into force.

Article 23

16–70 For the purpose of identifying the law applicable under the Convention, where a State comprises several territorial units each of which has its own rules of law in respect of trusts, any reference to the law of that State is to be construed as referring to the law in force in the territorial unit in question.

Questions

16–71 1. Major Major desires to create a trust to further the purposes of the Conservative Party for as long as it exists and for it to be enforceable by the Leader from time to time of the Conservative Party. He wants to settle either English company shares worth £15million or £15million and will be happy if the trustees buy London premises for the Party in due course, whether holding title directly or through an underlying company owned by the trust. He knows that under arts 12 and 15 of the Trusts (Jersey) Law 1984 (as amended in 1996 and 2006) a non-charitable purpose trust for ever will be valid. Advise him, considering whether a small initial settlement might be set up with Jersey trustees of Jersey assets of a trust governed by Jersey law and to which assets could later be added or whether to create the trust by transferring the whole trust fund to trustees in England of a trust governed by Jersey law.

16–72 2. "In the light of *Pullan v Koe* [1913] 1 Ch. 9 and *RZB v Five Star LLC* [2001] 3 All E.R. 257, trustees need to check whether property about to be transferred to them is not subject to a foreign matrimonial community of property regime because the settlor's spouse (if not a party to such transfer) may well have a proprietary interest in such property." **Discuss.**

16–73 3. W who was living with M inherited £200,000. They sold his flat for £300,000 and bought a flat with their joint £500,000. She was in Australia looking after her terminally ill mother at the time for completion of the purchase so M became sole registered proprietor. It took W's mother ten months to die in which time M became infatuated with F. He sold the flat to a person who had been interested in buying the flat when M bought it. He used the £500,000 proceeds of sale to buy in his name a villa in Italy where he lived with F. W has just discovered this, a year after finding the flat belonged to a stranger. **Advise her. Would your advice differ if the M–F relationship had broken down and M had obtained a job in London and was now living in his mother's house?**

16–74 4. H and his Dutch wife lived in England until he died after 40 years of marriage, leaving his estate (including the marital home) to her as executrix and trustee on trust for herself for life remainder to their two children. She sold the marital home and moved to The Netherlands and used the trust fund to buy a house there. She opened a trust account with a Dutch bank separate from her private account but a week before she died she sold shares owned as trustee and paid the €100,000 proceeds into her private account. Dutch creditors seek to make the house and the €100,000 available to satisfy their claims. **Advise the two children.**

PART VIII

EQUITABLE REMEDIES

17 EQUITABLE REMEDIES

1. Equitable and Common Law Remedies

17–01 The following equitable remedies are discussed in this chapter: injunctions; specific performance; damages awarded in addition to, or in lieu of, injunctions and specific performance; rescission; and rectification.[1]

17–02 Equitable remedies are those which, historically, were granted by the courts exercising an exclusive equitable jurisdiction prior to the fusion of the courts by the Judicature Acts 1873–1875. It is a controversial issue whether it desirable to fence equitable remedies off and treat them separately from common law remedies, retaining and emphasising the differences which existed between them prior to 1873. On one view,[2] this is desirable because equitable remedies possess unique characteristics, most notably that they are discretionary, and are subject to discretionary defences. In this, they are said to differ from common law remedies which may be claimed as of right on proof of a legal wrong (with or without proof of consequent loss, depending on the cause of action). Equitable remedies are also said to possess the distinctive feature that their effect is to force a defendant, through the threat of punishment or otherwise, to comply with his legal obligations in kind.[3] So, for example, a defendant who is made the subject of injunctive relief or a decree of specific performance may not leave his "primary" contractual or tortious obligations unfulfilled, and may not choose instead to fulfil the "secondary" obligation to pay damages which arises on breach of a primary duty of performance, as he can at common law. In equity he must, on pain of punishment, act or refrain from acting in the manner specified in the court order. Indeed, even if he chooses to take the punishment rather than act as he should, the court may simply by-pass him and in an appropriate case empower someone else to do the act instead.[4] On this view of the law, it makes sense to consider equitable remedies alongside one another, because this enables us to gain a better understanding of their common features.

17–03 On another view,[5] it is misleading to distinguish equitable and common law remedies on the ground that the former are discretionary and the latter are not, given that both are granted and withheld in line with clearly established rules and principles. Granted that some of these principles allow the courts a wide discretion when exercising their equitable jurisdiction, the same can also be said of certain common law principles (e.g. the rules limiting the award of compensatory damages, and the rules authorising the award of punitive damages). Moreover, it is untrue that the common law lacks the means to compel the performance of primary obligations, for this is the function of the award of an agreed sum in contract cases.

---

1 Others are declarations; appointment of receivers; cancellation and delivery up of documents; and disclosure (formerly termed discovery), being the process whereby a party to a suit is obliged to divulge the existence of documentation relevant to the issues in the claim.

2 Meagher, Gummow and Lehane's *Equity: Doctrines and Remedies*, 4th edn (2002) paras [2–270]–[2–320].

3 "*In specie*" in Latin, from which root the term "specific performance" derived.

4 For example, it is possible for the court to order that a conveyance or transfer of the defendant's land which he has promised to convey to the claimant be executed by someone other than the defendant if he will not execute it himself.

5 A. Burrows, *Fusing Common Law and Equity: Remedies, Restitution and Reform* (Hochelaga Lecture, 2002) at pp.1–26; A. Burrows, "We Do This at Common Law But That in Equity" (2002) 22 O.J.L.S. 1. Cf. S. Worthington, *Equity* 2nd edn (2006), Ch.2.

17–04 More profoundly, it is said to diminish our understanding of the law to consider equitable and common law remedies separately, because this obscures the full range of the courts' remedial armoury in the law of obligations, and disguises the similarities which exist between some equitable and common law remedies, e.g. an account of profits in equity and an order that the defendant account for and pay over a sum of money made pursuant to an action for unjust enrichment at common law. Granted that there are some differences between equitable and common law remedies (e.g. common law damages, in contrast to equitable damages awarded in lieu of an injunction, cannot be awarded in response to an anticipated wrong[6]), "nothing would be lost, and some simplicity and rationality would be gained, if one took the small steps necessary to move to a fully-fused system of remedies where it would be unnecessary to use the labels common law and equitable."[7] On this second view of the law, the discussion which follows in this chapter would serve a better purpose if it appeared alongside a discussion of common law remedies in books on contract, tort, unjust enrichment, and remedies.

2. Injunctions

A. Definition and Classification

17–05 An injunction is an order of the court forbidding the initiation or the continuance of some act or state of affairs or commanding that an act be done.[8] An injunction may therefore be prohibitory or mandatory and the distinction, as in the case of positive and negative covenants in regard to land, is one of substance not form:[9] while an order of the court requiring the demolition of a house wrongfully erected could be framed as an order not to leave it standing, the order would nonetheless be mandatory. A tell-tale sign is that mandatory injunctions normally require some expenditure on the part of the defendant. In addition, whereas the execution of prohibitory injunctions generally needs no supervision (the defendant simply has to refrain from committing the prohibited act), the execution of a mandatory order may do so e.g. in the case of an order to demolish a house in a particular manner.

B. Distinguished from Specific Performance

17–06 Positive contractual obligations of certain kinds are normally enforced, in equity, by orders for specific performance rather than mandatory injunctions.[10] What is the point of insisting on this difference? Does it matter to a claimant or defendant whether the claimant obtains a mandatory injunction or a decree of specific performance? In terms of enforcement, it could not seriously matter for both remedies are enforced in the same way: in the case of an individual defendant, by imprisonment,[11] fine or sequestration of assets (or any combination of these) and in the case of a corporation (whose officers may, additionally, be punished in their individual capacities), by fine or sequestration of assets or

[6] But cf. *Dennis v Ministry of Defence* [2003] 2 E.G.L.R. 121, where Buckley J. awarded common law damages for nuisance which included the loss of capital value that would be sustained by the claimant if he sold his house during the currency of the defendant's continuing nuisance; and *Transco Plc v Stockport MBC* T.C.C. May 7, 1999, where His Honour Judge Howarth awarded common law damages for negligence, and under the rule in *Rylands v Fletcher* (1868) L.R. 3 H.L. 330, to compensate the claimant for the cost of remedial works to prevent damage occurring (reversed on liability: [2001] Env. L.R. 44; [2004] 2 A.C. 1).

[7] A. Burrows, *Remedies for Torts and Breach of Contract* 3rd edn (2004) pp.11–12.

[8] An exception to this definition appears to be the order of prohibition in judicial review proceedings.

[9] *Truckell v Stock* [1957] 1 W.L.R. 161.

[10] See Section 3 below.

[11] Contempt of Court Act 1981 s.14(1) considered by Laddie J. in *Re Swaptronics Ltd*, *The Times*, August 17, 1998, and by Thorpe L.J. in *Harris v Harris (No.2)* [2002] 1 F.L.R. 248.

both.[12] Yet, it does matter which a claimant is required to apply for because, as will be seen, the number of grounds on which a decree for specific performance may be refused is considerably greater than the number of grounds on which a final injunction may be refused. And this appears to be for a justifiable reason: by contract an individual may either, by negative stipulation, put himself under disabilities that he does not have under the general law or, by positive stipulation, impose on himself obligations which he does not have under the general law (apart from the contract). In the former case, he is merely restricting his freedom to act, which restriction can be enforced by a prohibitory injunction without imposing burdens on him over and above those which the general law imposes. But in the latter case, where the defendant has agreed to do something which the general law does not require him to do, the court will be astute to enquire into the justice of making him perform his promise in kind. It will want to be certain that, for example, the claimant is ready, willing and able to perform his own contractual obligations, that there is "mutuality" between the parties,[13] and so on.

Moreover, it is often said that, unlike the case with mandatory injunctions, no decree of specific performance will lie on an interim (formerly referred to as "interlocutory") basis (i.e. pending trial). If true, it would matter very much whether a claimant's claim were for a mandatory injunction or a decree of specific performance for, in the first case he might obtain interim relief but in the second could not. The case of *Sky Petroleum Ltd v VIP Petroleum Ltd*,[14] however, tends to blur the distinction and, moreover, suggests that it is not true that specific performance will not lie on an interim basis. There, the claimant applied for an interim prohibitory injunction restraining the defendant from failing to supply it with petrol, which failure was allegedly in breach of contract. Goulding J. treated the motion as one for an interlocutory decree of specific performance, looking at the substance rather than the form, and granted it. **17–07**

Another case in point is *Capita Trust Co (Channel Islands) Ltd v Chatham Maritime J3 Developments Ltd*,[15] which concerned a lease of a shopping centre. The tenant covenanted to use all reasonable endeavours to keep units continuously underlet and to manage the premises in accordance with principles of good estate management. The claimant landlord won an interim mandatory injunction ordering the defendant to perform this term by granting an under-lease to Marks and Spencer Plc, a "magnet tenant" found by the landlord whose presence in the centre would encourage other retail companies to lease premises there. The defendant's refusal to grant the under-lease was a clear breach of contract, and granting the injunction did not amount to ordering specific performance of the covenant, contrary to the House of Lords' finding in *Co-operative Insurance Society Ltd v Argyll Stores (Holdings) Ltd*,[16] that terms of this kind are not specifically enforceable (because they require the court's constant supervision). In Pumfrey J.'s view, "If one can point to an order which achieves a single result which prevents a breach of covenant, it really does not matter if the covenant itself cannot be enforced by specific performance process across its full width because such a covenant involves an activity or process lasting over a period of time and involving much judgment."[17] **17–08**

[12] Rules of the Supreme Court, Orders 45 and 52, as incorporated into the Civil Procedure Rules 1998. On the court's inherent power, see *Webster v Southwark LBC* [1983] Q.B. 698.
[13] See below, para.17–109.
[14] [1974] 1 W.L.R. 576.
[15] [2007] L. & T.R. 2.
[16] [1998] A.C. 1; discussed below at paras 17–112 to 17–113, and reproduced at paras 17–184 ff.
[17] *Capita* at [29].

C. *Interim or Perpetual*

17–09 All injunctions may be classified as interim (formerly termed "interlocutory") or perpetual (also termed "permanent" and "final").[18] Interim injunctions are those granted pending the final resolution of an issue between the parties or some earlier specified event[19] and the courts have developed a special approach to the granting of them, quite different from those applicable to perpetual injunctions.[20] It will be convenient to consider the principles on which perpetual injunctions are granted first. Before doing so, however, three other general points may usefully be made about the jurisdiction to grant injunctions.

D. *The Statutory Basis of the Modern Jurisdiction*

17–10 The equitable and therefore discretionary nature of the jurisdiction to grant injunctions does not absolve a claimant from the requirement to show some legal or equitable cause of action, despite the wording of the Senior Courts Act 1981 s.37(1), which provides:

> "The High Court[21] may by order (whether interlocutory or final) grant an injunction . . . in all cases in which it appears to the court to be just and convenient to do so."

The case of *Normid Housing Association Ltd v Ralphs*[22] illustrates this point. There, an injunction was refused to the claimants who were suing their architects, the defendants, for negligence. The defendants, as would be expected, had professional insurance. The insurers, however, were desirous of settling whatever claim the defendants might have against them. The sum which the insurers offered the defendants was less than the sum claimed by the claimants from the defendants. When the claimants discovered this, they sought an injunction preventing the defendants from accepting the insurers' offer. They failed because the defendants owed no legal duty to the claimants to insure at all, let alone for any particular sum.

E. *The Quia Timet Jurisdiction*

17–11 Second, the foregoing principle has not prevented the issuing of injunctions *quia timet*.[23] Equity, achieving more perfect justice than the common law (which was limited to the award of damages to make good injury which had already occurred), acted to restrain future wrongs. Indeed, all (perpetual) prohibitory injunctions achieve as much, in that, although normally sought only where there has been an actual wrong done, they ensure, so far as any court order can, that the wrong will not be repeated, thus rendering

---

[18] Although "perpetual" is the preferred terminology under the Civil Procedure Rules, it is potentially misleading in that the injunction might not, on its terms, be intended to have perpetual effect at all. Indeed, all that is meant is that the injunction granted is finally decisive of the issue between the parties. The actual order granted, for example, in the case of a one-year restrictive covenant being enforced against a former employee, will endure only for one year.

[19] Such as the disposal of an appeal against the dismissal of a motion seeking interim relief pending trial. The grant of an injunction in such case is purely so that, should the appeal against the substantive refusal succeed, an order made on appeal will not be in vain.

[20] See below, paras 17–25 ff.

[21] By the County Courts Act 1984 s.38, the County Court may make any order within its jurisdiction that could be made by the High Court except those of a "prescribed kind", i.e. specified under regulations made by the Lord Chancellor. To date, such regulations have been made in the County Court Remedies Regulations 1991 where, by reg.2, *Anton Piller* (now called "search") orders and *Mareva* (now called "freezing") injunctions are prescribed except in (i) family proceedings, (ii) for the purpose of preserving property forming the subject matter of proceedings or (iii) in aid of execution of county court orders or judgments for the purpose of preserving assets until execution.

[22] [1989] 1 Lloyd's Rep. 265. See also *Day v Brownrigg* (1878) 10 Ch.D. 294.

[23] Literally, "because (the claimant) fears".

unnecessary a multiplicity of suits. It was only one step from that to hold that a threatened future wrong should be restrained before it had occurred. However, "mere vague apprehension is not sufficient to support an action for a *quia timet* injunction. There must be an immediate threat to do something".[24]

F. *In Personam or In Rem*

17–12 The fact that the jurisdiction is equitable means that, in theory, the order of the court operates in personam rather than in rem. These Latin tags refer to a traditional distinction between rights against particular persons (such as arise under contracts) and rights against persons generally (such as arise in ownership). Historically, the Chancellor acted to perfect the injustices of the operation of the common law, administered in the King's courts, not by changing any substantive rule of law but, rather, by requiring a legal right-holder not to enforce his right. The Chancellor's method of securing compliance was to threaten imprisonment. The jurisdiction, therefore, was said to be solely in personam: directed against particular persons. However the modern trust, which is descended from the practice of the Chancellors who would regularly require a legal owner to hold property for the benefit and enjoyment of another, is a good example of how blurred the distinction between personal and property rights can become: few people would now argue that a beneficiary's rights under a trust are merely personal rights.[25] The reason that a beneficiary's rights prevail over the rights of a trustee's creditors where the trustee becomes insolvent is precisely that the beneficiary's rights in the trust property are rights of ownership. Hence, statements that the equitable jurisdiction is purely personal must be treated with caution.[26]

17–13 In relation to the equitable jurisdiction to issue injunctions a similar blurring of the traditional distinction may also be seen. In practice, injunctions may operate against people to whom they are not immediately directed, as in *Att.-Gen. v Times Newspapers Ltd*, for example, where it was said by Lord Brandon that:[27]

> "if C's conduct, in knowingly doing acts which would, if done by B, be a breach of the injunction against [B], results in impedance to or interference with the administration of justice by the court in the action between A and B, then, so far as the question of C's conduct being a contempt of court is concerned, it cannot make any difference whether such conduct takes the form of aiding and abetting B on the one hand or acting solely of his own volition on the other."

G. *General Equitable Principles Governing the Grant of Final Injunctions*

i. Adequacy of Common Law Remedies

17–14 Equity had no cause to supplement an existing legal remedy which was adequate and it came to be a requirement of the first order that before any equitable remedy would lie, the legal remedy be

---

[24] *Graigola Merthyr Co Ltd v Swansea Corporation* [1929] A.C. 344 at 353, per Lord Buckmaster. See too *Morris v Redland Bricks Ltd* [1970] A.C. 652; *Hooper v Rogers* [1975] Ch. 43; *British Telecommunications Plc v One In A Million Ltd* [1999] 1 W.L.R. 903 (where D was said to have equipped himself with "the instruments of fraud" by registering internet domain names).

[25] But see B. Macfarlane, *The Structure of Property Law* (2008), who argues that there is no such thing as an equitable property right and that trust beneficiaries merely have personal rights to insist that trustees and others in whom legal rights to trust property become vested should exercise these legal rights in the beneficiaries' favour.

[26] Personal accountability of the trustee to the beneficiary is the hallmark of the trust and part of the "irreducible core content" of trusteeship: *Armitage v Nurse* [1998] Ch. 241. But this does not preclude the idea that as against the trustee and the rest of the world, the beneficiary's rights are also in rem. For further discussion, see P. Matthews, "From Obligation to Property, and Back Again?" in D.J. Hayton (ed.) *Extending the Boundaries of Trusts and Similar Ring-Fenced Funds* (2002) and other references collected at para.1–47, n.43.

[27] [1992] 1 A.C. 191 at 206. See also *Jockey Club v Buffham* [2003] 2 W.L.R. 178; *Att.-Gen. v Punch Ltd* [2003] 1 A.C. 1046. And for general discussion, see P. Devonshire, "Freezing Orders, Disappearing Assets and the Problem of Enjoining Non-Parties" (2002) 118 L.Q.R. 124.

shown to be inadequate—a matter to be determined having regard to the nature of the injury (whether it is assessable in monetary terms), the prospect of its being repeated (when, otherwise, a multiplicity of suits would be necessary) and, to a lesser extent, the ability of a defendant to satisfy an award of damages. Damages are very often found to be an inadequate remedy, and injunctions are very often awarded, for the torts of trespass to land and nuisance, reflecting the strong protection afforded by the law to a landowner's right to the quiet enjoyment of his property.[28] But injunctions can be awarded to restrain other torts, too,[29] and equitable wrongs,[30] and breaches of contract, of which Sachs L.J. observed in *Evans Marshall & Co Ltd v Bertola SA* that:[31]

> "The courts have repeatedly recognised there can be claims under contracts in which, as here, it is unjust to confine a plaintiff to his damages for their breach. Great difficulty in estimating these damages is one factor that can be and has been taken into account. Another factor is the creation of certain areas of damage which cannot be taken into monetary account in a common law action for breach of contract. Loss of goodwill and trade reputation are examples. Generally, indeed, the grant of injunctions in contract cases stems from such factors."

ii. Equity Will not Act in Vain

17–15 This principle (or "maxim" of equity), like the last, is common to specific performance.[32] The idea is that if issuing an injunction would be futile, no injunction will be issued. In *Wookey v Wookey*,[33] a family case, it was said that where there was evidence that an order would not be complied with and that nothing would be done about the non-compliance in judicial terms (because the subject of the order would, on account of youth, not be imprisoned and, on account of impecuniosity, not be fined) then the order should not be made. This is perhaps an extreme application of the principle but it can be defended. More regular applications of the principle are to be found in cases where it would be impossible for the defendant to comply with the order (because, for example, in a case where a mandatory injunction was sought requiring him to tear down a building, he no longer owned the land and had no right to tear down any building upon it). Another illustration of the principle is provided by the *Spycatcher* case,[34] where a final injunction was refused against a newspaper preventing it from publishing certain information. Although that information had been confidential it had already been published in a book that had become widely available in the United Kingdom by the time of the litigation.

iii. Delay and Acquiescence

17–16 The requirement that one who seeks equitable relief must do so without delay, even within the statutory limitation period (the doctrine of "laches") is often factually indistinguishable from the doctrine of acquiescence whereby knowing failure to object to a wrong may give rise to an inability to resurrect an objection to it at a later date. The cases on delay diverge on the question whether mere delay (i.e. unac-

---

[28] e.g. *Hodgson v Duce* (1856) 2 Jur. N.S. 1014; *Eardley v Granville* (1876) 3 Ch.D. 826; *Litchfield-Speer v Queen Anne's Gate Syndicate (No.2) Ltd* [1919] 1 Ch. 407; *Anchor Brewhouse Developments Ltd v Berkley House (Docklands Developments) Ltd* (1987) 38 B.L.R. 82; *Harrow LBC v Donohue* [1995] 1 E.G.L.R. 257 (distinguishing acts of mere trespass—where damages might be substituted for an injunction—and dispossession—where a claimant is entitled as a matter of right to the protection of an injunction).

[29] As noted in J. Murphy, "Rethinking Injunctions in Tort Law" (2007) 27 O.J.L.S. 509, arguing that the law attaches just as much importance to, and so should be just as willing to award injunctions to protect, other interests besides proprietary interests, e.g. bodily integrity.

[30] See e.g. *Fox v Fox* (1870) L.R. 11 Eq. 142; *Buttle v Saunders* [1950] 2 All E.R. 193.

[31] [1973] 1 W.L.R. 349 at 380. See too *Manning v AIG Europe UK Ltd* [2005] 1 B.C.L.C. 1 (breach of subordinated debt agreement); *Sheffield United Football Club Ltd v West Ham United Football Club Plc* [2009] 1 Lloyd's Rep. 167 (breach of arbitration clause).

[32] See paras 17–100 to 17–107.

[33] [1991] Fam. 121.

[34] *Att.-Gen. v Observer Ltd* [1990] 1 A.C. 109.

companied by acquiescence) will bar the grant of relief,[35] but the position now seems to be that if detriment is present, this will usually lead the court to conclude that it would be unconscionable for the claimant to seek to enforce his rights, "but, absent detriment, the court would need to find some other factor which made it unconscionable for the party having the benefit of the rights to change his mind."[36] As to acquiescence, the test is whether the plaintiff represented that he would no longer enforce his rights.[37]

An example of how acquiescence may operate to bar not just equitable but any relief is to be found in *Gafford v Graham*.[38] The defendant was in breach of a restrictive covenant which prevented him from converting his bungalow or extending his barn without the claimant's consent. He breached the covenant in 1986 but, as the Court of Appeal said, "the [claimant] made no complaint until his solicitor wrote to the defendant about three years after the acts complained of", despite full knowledge of the breaches. At first instance, the judge had awarded the claimant damages in respect of the conversion and extension. The Court of Appeal, however, held that his acquiescence was a bar not just to equitable relief but all relief and discharged the order for damages. It held that, in all the circumstances, it would be unconscionable for the claimant to enforce the (legal) rights which he undoubtedly had in 1986. This, notwithstanding that the claimant's action was begun well within the limitation period. The case is an example (closely related to proprietary estoppel) of how equity can operate to extinguish accrued legal rights. Not all cases in which equitable relief is refused, however, are so draconian: normally, a claimant's delay will, if it has any effect, merely serve to deprive him of his (presumably more adequate) equitable remedy. His legal rights and remedies for breach (i.e. his right to damages) will remain intact in the absence of something like an estoppel. **17–17**

But even a claimant who, knowing of a threatened or incipient wrong, begins proceedings for an injunction in good time must think carefully when deciding whether to seek interim injunctive relief at an early stage of the action. *Jaggard v Sawyer*,[39] reproduced below,[40] shows how the very possibility of obtaining perpetual injunctive relief may turn on that decision (the court awarded damages in lieu), although it may be contrasted with *Mortimer v Bailey*[41] where the claimants' delay in seeking an interim injunction did not prevent them from obtaining a perpetual injunction, given the speed with which they had begun their proceedings. **17–18**

iv. Clean Hands

A claimant who has behaved improperly may be denied equitable relief, although the "clean hands" principle will not be triggered where the claimant's conduct is morally shabby but legally unimpeachable.[42] There must also exist a close connection between the impropriety of the claimant's behaviour and the relief which he seeks: "Equity does not demand that its suitors shall have led blameless lives",[43] and mere general depravity is not enough in itself to deny a claimant relief.[44] Thus, in *Grobelaar v News Group Newspapers Ltd*[45] the House of Lords granted the claimant footballer an injunction restraining **17–19**

---

[35] *Fullwood v Fullwood* (1878) 9 Ch.D. 176, per Fry J., no.; *HP Bulmer Ltd & Showerings Ltd v J Bollinger SA* [1977] 2 C.M.L.R. 625: only if "inordinate", per Goff L.J.
[36] *Harris v Williams-Wynne* [2006] 2 P. & C.R. 595 at [39], per Chadwick L.J. cf. *Fisher v Brooker* [2009] 1 W.L.R. 1764 at [64].
[37] *Allen v Veranne Builders Ltd* [1988] E.G.C.S. 2.
[38] [1995] 3 E.G.L.R. 75.
[39] [1995] 1 W.L.R. 269.
[40] See paras 17–221 ff.
[41] [2005] 2 E.G. 102.
[42] *Dering v Earl of Winchelsea* (1787) 1 Cox Eq. Cas. 318; *Loosley v NUT* [1988] I.R.L.R. 157; *Lonhro Plc v Fayed (No.5)* [1993] 1 W.L.R. 1489; *Ministry of Justice v Prison Officers Association* [2008] I.C.R. 702.
[43] *Loughran v Loughran* (1934) 292 U.S. 216 at 292, per Brandeis J.
[44] *Meyers v Casey* (1913) 17 C.L.R. 90: *Att.-Gen. v Equiticorp Industries Group Ltd* [1996] 1 N.Z.L.R. 528.
[45] [2002] 1 W.L.R. 3024.

the defendant newspaper from repeating its unproven allegation that he had thrown football matches, although he had been proven to have taken bribes, to have told his co-conspirator that he had thrown matches in exchange for the bribe money, and to have lied about this in court.

17–20 Further discussion of this requirement, also common to specific performance, is to be found in Section 3.[46] It is accepted that a claimant who has himself defaulted on a contract cannot obtain injunctive relief to enforce any of its terms.[47] That is an application, in the field of contract, of the clean hands maxim. It is, however, a different requirement from the similar doctrine that he who comes to equity must do equity, which looks not to whether the claimant's hands are already soiled by wrongdoing, but rather to the future question whether the claimant is prepared to fulfil his outstanding obligations.[48] In applications for specific performance, this translates into a requirement that the claimant demonstrate that he is "ready, willing and able" to perform his side of the bargain. Both requirements are morally defensible in that, by seeking an equitable remedy over and above the legal one to which he is entitled, a claimant must appeal to a court of conscience. He cannot do so if his is not clear.

v. No Undue Hardship

17–21 Interim and mandatory injunctions in particular provide scope for an argument that an injunction ought to be refused as a matter of discretion on the ground of hardship to the defendant. In the former case, this is so because, by definition, the claimant has not yet established his right to any relief (because there has not yet been a trial) and in the latter because often, as was suggested above, what is distinctive of a mandatory injunction is that compliance will involve the defendant in expenditure which may be out of all proportion to the benefit which the claimant will derive from the grant of an injunction.

17–22 Some cases which sought to circumvent hardship to the defendant by granting an injunction but suspending its operation for a period[49] are now suspect in light of the decision in *Jaggard v Sawyer*,[50] reproduced below,[51] where that practice was specifically disapproved. The jurisdiction to award damages in lieu of an injunction, now contained in the Senior Courts Act 1981 s.50 (which jurisdiction was analysed closely in that case), is a statutory recognition of the fact that sometimes the award of an injunction can be oppressive to a defendant (particularly a mandatory one requiring, for example, the demolition of a building). By giving courts of equity the power to award damages in lieu, Parliament made it easier to justify declining to grant injunctions in such cases. But the practice of doing so existed prior to the statutory provision where undue hardship would have resulted. A claimant would, in those circumstances, be confined to his legal remedy of damages. The innovation of the provision (first introduced by Lord Cairns in 1858) was that where the injunction had been sought to restrain future wrongs, for which common law damages could not be awarded, a plaintiff would not be put out of court without any remedy: he might be given damages instead.

vi. The Public Interest

17–23 Although in specific performance cases the notion has long been accepted that public interest considerations might affect the availability of equitable remedies in contract[52] (in which branch of the law, more generally, it is well accepted that private individuals cannot create rights and duties for

---

[46] See para.17–115.

[47] *Measures Bros Ltd v Measures* [1910] 2 Ch. 248.

[48] Although Lord Denning M.R. appears to have confused the doctrines in *Shell (UK) Ltd v Lostock Garage Ltd* [1976] 1 W.L.R. 1187.

[49] e.g. *Woollerton and Wilson Ltd v Richard Costain Ltd* [1970] 1 W.L.R. 411. See also Lane L.J.'s proposed solution to the problem raised in *Miller v Jackson* [1977] Q.B. 966.

[50] [1995] 1 W.L.R. 269.

[51] See paras 17–221 ff.

[52] See para.17–108.

each other which contravene public policy), the matter is more controversial as regards those torts which create a perimeter of inviolability around the notion of private ownership of land. In *Miller v Jackson*[53] Lord Denning M.R. opined obiter that if the defendants in that case had committed the tort of nuisance (he held to the contrary), then an injunction should have been refused on the ground that the public interest in (i) protecting the environment achieved by the preservation of playing fields and (ii) enabling youth to enjoy the benefits of outdoor games prevailed over the private interest in securing the privacy of home and garden without the intrusion or interference caused by cricket balls hit out of the defendants' neighbouring cricket ground. That aspect of the decision was disavowed by a later Court of Appeal in *Kennaway v Thompson*,[54] which held that the public interest in motor-boat racing could not prevail over the private right of quiet enjoyment of the home.

More recently, in *Dennis v Ministry of Defence*,[55] Buckley J. declined to hold that the public importance of the defendant's activities in training fighter jet pilots prevented the claimant from suing in private nuisance in respect of the noise made by the jets flying over his house. However, the judge also held that the public interest did affect the question of remedy, and concluded that it would not be in the public interest to grant the claimant an injunction, although he would be entitled to damages. This was consistent with the result, if not with the reasoning, in *Kennaway*, where the Court of Appeal did not order the claimant to desist from his activities altogether, but instead struck a balance between the parties by specifying the number of events that would henceforth be allowed, the number of boats which would be allowed to race, and the timing of the events.[56] **17–24**

H. *Interim Injunctions*

i. General Principles

Unlike perpetual injunctions, where the lawyer finds himself considering principles of equity, interim injunctions are granted or refused on grounds which have nothing to do, either historically or logically, with the maxims of equity. The principles on which the court acts, or has acted up to the introduction of the Civil Procedure Rules at least, are designed to achieve justice between the parties under circumstances of ignorance or uncertainty (i.e. when it is not known whether the claimant's claim is well founded). It must be cautioned at this stage, however, that both the Civil Procedure Rules and the Human Rights Act 1998 have an effect on the substance of these principles and it will be necessary to qualify what follows.[57] **17–25**

In order to circumvent the necessity, at an early stage of an action, of deciding disputed questions of fact or determining points of law with insufficient argument, the House of Lords laid down guidelines for the exercise of judicial discretion whether to grant an interim injunction in *American Cyanamid Co. v Ethicon Ltd*,[58] reproduced below.[59] The House had previously held in *JT Stratford & Son Ltd v Lindley*[60] that a claimant had to show a prima facie case that he would succeed at trial in obtaining injunctive relief. The decision in *Cyanamid* is to the effect that a claimant need only show **17–26**

---

[53] [1977] Q.B. 966.
[54] [1981] Q.B. 88.
[55] [2003] 2 E.G.L.R. 121.
[56] See too *Watson v Croft Promo-Sport Ltd* [2009] 3 All E.R. 249, where the CA granted an injunction restricting the defendant's use of land as a motor-racing circuit to the level which was the threshold for the tort of nuisance (by noise) against the claimants.
[57] See paras 17–36 to 17–38.
[58] [1975] A.C. 396.
[59] At paras 17–49 ff.
[60] [1965] A.C. 269. *Cyanamid* has been said to be irreconcilable with this decision but as *Cyanamid* was the later case, that is the one the Court of Appeal should follow: *Hubbard v Pitt* [1976] Q.B. 142.

that he has a case that is not frivolous or vexatious and that there is a serious question to be tried. Once that is established, the question whether an injunction should be granted turns on the balance of convenience, a much used shorthand phrase to describe the balancing exercise in which the court engages in order to minimise the risk of doing injustice.

17–27 That balancing exercise is undertaken as follows: once a serious question for trial is raised, unless there is no arguable defence to the claim (in which case an injunction should be granted until trial[61]), the court considers whether damages would be an adequate remedy for loss caused to the claimant by not granting an injunction pending trial. If so, and the defendant can afford to pay, then the balance favours no injunction. If the loss likely to be caused is not remediable in damages (either as a matter of legal principle or practice, i.e. the defendant could not pay them) then the court considers to what extent the claimant would be able to compensate the defendant for any loss caused to him by granting an injunction pending trial. (Thus making the claimant's relief conditional on the provision of what is called a cross-undertaking in damages.[62]) This has the result that if damages would not be an adequate remedy for the claimant (either as a matter of principle or practice) then if the defendant's potential loss is compensable, the balance favours an injunction. Where damages would be inadequate for both parties, however, (either as a matter of principle or practice) then injustice is best avoided by maintaining the status quo.[63] "Special factors" might properly be taken into account, but only as a last resort can the merits be examined and, even then, only if the strength of one case is disproportionate to the other.

17–28 Much judicial ink has been spilled over the relationship of these guidelines to instant cases, and in particular, on the question whether apparent exceptions to the *Cyanamid* approach are truly exceptions or merely different ways of striking the balance of convenience in instant cases.[64] An instance of judicial divergence on that (rather semantic) issue is to be found in *Cambridge Nutrition Ltd v BBC*.[65] There certainly appear to be categories of cases (whether *Cyanamid* "exceptions" or not) where the claimant has to show more than that his case is not frivolous or vexatious, raising merely a serious question to be tried. They are as follows.

Trade Disputes

17–29 The Trade Union and Labour Relations (Consolidation) Act 1992 s.221(2) provides that, on an application for an interlocutory injunction, where the defendant claims that he acted in contemplation or furtherance of a trade dispute, the court is to have regard to the likelihood of the defendant's establishing at the trial any of the matters which, under the Act, confer immunity from tortious liability.

Trial of Action Unlikely or Delayed

17–30 In *Cambridge Nutrition*,[66] the claimants sought an injunction preventing the defendant from broadcasting a programme (in the making of which they had participated) until after the imminent publication

---

[61] Unless, with the defendant's consent, the hearing of the motion is treated as the trial of the action in which case a perpetual injunction will lie.

[62] This undertaking is extracted, if the injunction is granted, as a matter of course. Not, however, from the Crown when it is seeking to enforce the law (as opposed to its own proprietary or contractual rights): *Hoffman-La Roche (F) & Co v Secretary of State for Trade and Industry* [1975] A.C. 295. The same is true of (i) relator actions where an undertaking will be required of the relator but not of the Attorney-General and (ii) local authorities enforcing the law: *Kirkless BC v Wickes Building Supplies Ltd* [1992] 3 W.L.R 170.

[63] Which, in effect, means letting any alleged wrong already initiated continue and, in the case of *quia timet* relief, prohibiting the occurrence of any alleged future wrong. See Lord Diplock in *Garden Cottage Foods Ltd v Milk Marketing Board* [1984] A.C. 130 at 140.

[64] For further discussion, see A. Keay "Whither *American Cyanamid*?: Interim Injunctions in the 21st Century" (2004) 23 C.J.Q. 132, arguing that the precision which *Cyanamid* sought to bring is illusory, because (i) apart from a few cases which are resolved by Lord Diplock's preliminary considerations, the courts are required to move on to a vague balancing act, and (ii) when it has suited them, the courts have simply declined to apply the guidelines at all.

[65] [1990] 3 All E.R. 523.

[66] See also *Cayne v Global Natural Resources Plc* [1984] 1 All E.R. 225.

of a government report on the claimant low calorie diet, the subject matter also of the programme. The programme, however, would have had no impact if broadcast after the publication of the report and, if an injunction were granted to trial, it would effectively prevent the broadcast for good. Clearly, if the *Cyanamid* principles are designed to achieve a fair resolution pending trial, others must be used to achieve such resolution where there is likely to be no trial. The court therefore looked at the merits of the claim and, finding the basis of it to be implausible (an oral agreement not to broadcast until after publication of the report—for which there was remarkably little evidence) declined to grant an injunction.

No Arguable Defence

This has already been mentioned in the discussion above of *Cyanamid*. **17–31**

Injunctions to Restrain the Presentation of Winding-Up Petitions

It has been held since *Cyanamid* that the guidelines do not apply to an interlocutory injunction to restrain the bringing of other proceedings on the ground that these latter would be an abuse of the court's process: the grant of such injunction finally determines the matter.[67] So a claimant would fail unless he demonstrated not merely a serious issue whether the defendant's proceedings would be an abuse but, over and above that, that the defendant was bound to fail in those proceedings. In *Ward v Coulson Sanderson and Ward Ltd*[68] the Court of Appeal followed that reasoning to hold that *Cyanamid* did not apply to injunctions to restrain the presentation of a winding-up petition by a creditor. **17–32**

Mandatory Interlocutory Injunctions

For the grant of a mandatory injunction on an interlocutory basis there must be a "high degree of assurance" that it will appear at trial that the injunction was rightly granted.[69] **17–33**

In cases where the nature of the interlocutory relief sought requires that the defendant be taken by surprise, or where the relief sought is urgent, in that it must be granted right away, if it is to be granted at all, interim injunctions may be applied for without notice (formerly termed ex parte): i.e. in the absence of the party against whom the order is sought. An order can then be made, normally effective only over a short period, which will be reviewed at a hearing with notice to the other side at the end of that period (or at an earlier time if the defendant applies before the end of the period to have the order discharged). On applications without notice, applicants must fully and frankly disclose all the facts in their knowledge which are relevant to the exercise of the court's discretion, and this extends to disclosing possible defences which the defendant may have. Breach of this duty is a serious matter that will entitle (though not oblige) the court to discharge the injunction without more, and leave the applicant to apply again.[70] **17–34**

The court's power to grant interim injunctions is not limited to forbidding actions which are inherently unlawful. Freezing orders[71] are often made to restrain defendants from actions which are lawful **17–35**

---

[67] *Bryanston Finance v De Vries (No.2)* [1976] Ch. 63, per Stephenson L.J. and Sir John Pennycuick. Buckley L.J. concurred in refusing the injunction but purported to follow *Cyanamid*.

[68] [1986] P.C.C. 57.

[69] *Shepherd Homes Ltd v Sandham* [1971] Ch. 340; *Locabail International Finance Ltd v Agroexport* [1986] 1 W.L.R. 657. Note, however, Hoffmann J. in *Films Rover International Ltd v Cannon Film Sales Ltd* [1987] 1 W.L.R. 670, observing that in exceptional cases where the risk of injustice was greater in not granting an injunction, the *Shepherd Homes* test need not be met.

[70] *Lloyd's Bowmaker Ltd v Britannia Arrow Holdings Plc* [1988] 1 W.L.R. 1337 at 1343–1344; *Memory Corporation Plc v Sidhu (No.2)* [2000] 1 W.L.R. 1443 at 1459; *Network Telecom (Europe) Ltd v Telephone Systems International Inc* [2004] 1 All E.R. (Comm.) 418. cf. *Dadourian Group International Inc v Simms* [2009] 1 Lloyd's Rep. 601 at [196]–[210].

[71] See paras 17–40 ff.

in themselves (e.g. withdrawing money from a bank account); and in harassment cases, the courts have granted interim injunctions forbidding defendants to enter specified "exclusion zones", even though they have the same basic right as any other member of the public to use the public highway running through these zones.[72]

ii. The Effect of the Civil Procedure Rules ("CPR")

17–36 By virtue of s.2 of the Civil Procedure Act 1997 and the Civil Procedure Rules 1998,[73] all civil claims brought after April 25, 1999 have fallen to be dealt with according to the CPR. Based on a review of Civil Justice by Lord Woolf, the then Master of the Rolls, these were intended to effect a fundamental change in the administration of civil justice. For present purposes, it is pertinent to note that the principles according to which the courts have, since *Cyanamid*, awarded interim relief, must now be read subject to the "overriding objective" of allowing the court (through, among other things, active "case management") to deal with cases justly. This may include taking steps to ensure that the parties are on an equal footing, saving expense, and dealing with a case in ways which are appropriate to the amount involved, the importance of the case, the complexity of the case and the financial situation of the parties. Some or all of these might well militate in favour of the approach boldly (and, it is suggested, sensibly) advocated by Laddie J. in *Series 5 Software v Clark Ltd*,[74] reproduced below,[75] which cannot be interpreted as anything other than a first instance rejection of the *Cyanamid* approach.

iii. The Effect of the Human Rights Act 1998

17–37 The Human Rights Act 1998 most obviously affects the award of interim injunctions through s.12(3), which imposes a special threshold test which must be satisfied before a court may grant an interim injunction which might affect the exercise of a defendant's right to freedom of expression under art.10 of the European Convention. The section sets a higher threshold for the grant of interim injunctions against the news media than the *Cyanamid* guideline of a "serious question to be tried" or a "real prospect of success" at the trial, as it provides that interim injunctions should not be granted "so as to restrain publication before trial unless the court is satisfied that the applicant is likely to establish that publication should not be allowed." In *Cream Holdings Ltd v Banerjee*[76] the House of Lords held that the word "likely" in s.12(3) will generally mean "more likely than not", although there are some cases where a lesser degree of likelihood may suffice: for example, "where the potential adverse consequences of the disclosure are particularly grave".[77] Applying this test, their Lordships concluded that the applicants were not entitled to an interim injunction preventing the disclosure of confidential information because the matters which the defendant newspaper wished to publish were of serious public interest, suggesting that the applicants' prospects of success at trial were insufficiently strong to justify an interim injunction.

17–38 In *Greene v Associated Newspapers Ltd*[78] the question arose whether the *Cream Holdings* test also applies where an applicant seeks an interim injunction restraining the publication of material which is alleged to be defamatory. The Court of Appeal held that it does not, reasoning that defamation

---

[72] e.g. *Burris v Azadani* [1995] 1 W.L.R. 1372: *Dailchi Pharmaceuticals UK Ltd v SHAC* [2004] 1 W.L.R. 1503.
[73] SI 3132/1998.
[74] [1996] All E.R. 853.
[75] At paras 17–75 ff.
[76] [2005] 1 A.C. 253, followed in e.g. *Douglas v Hello! Ltd (No.3)* [2006] Q.B. 135; *Browne v Associated Newspapers Ltd* [2008] Q.B. 103.
[77] *Cream Holdings* at [22], per Lord Nicholls.
[78] [2005] Q.B. 972.

cases raise different issues from cases concerned with breach of confidence and breach of privacy:[79] confidentiality and privacy, once lost, are lost forever, unlike reputations which can be rebuilt. Defamation cases therefore continue to be governed by the rule in *Bonnard v Perryman*:[80] if a defendant in a libel action makes a statement verified as true in which he maintains that he can and will justify his alleged libel, then the claimant cannot have an interim injunction to restrain the publication of an allegedly defamatory statement unless it is plain that the plea of justification is bound to fail. However, the defamation rule does not apply, and the *Cream Holdings* test is used, in comparative advertising cases concerned with trade mark infringements.[81] It is also used where publication of information would allegedly create a substantial risk that the course of justice in an ongoing criminal trial will be seriously impeded or prejudiced, contrary to the Contempt of Court Act 1981.[82]

I. Two Special Types of Interim Injunction

Both *Mareva* (now "freezing") injunctions and *Anton Piller* (now "search") orders are interim orders. As **17–39** Lord Donaldson M.R. made plain in *Polly Peck International v Nadir (No.2)*,[83] there is no question of *Cyanamid* applying to *Mareva* injunctions, "which proceed on principles quite different from those applicable to other interlocutory injunctions." The same is true of *Anton Piller* or search orders. Together they have been described by the same judge as the law's "nuclear weapons".[84]

i. Freezing Injunctions

Section 37 of the Senior Courts Act 1981 provides that: **17–40**

> "(1) The High Court may by order (whether interlocutory or final) grant an injunction or appoint a receiver in all cases in which it appears to the court to be just and convenient to do so . . .
>
> "(3) The power of the High Court under subsection (1) to grant an interlocutory injunction restraining a party to any proceedings from removing from the jurisdiction of the High Court, or otherwise dealing with, assets located within that jurisdiction shall be exercisable in cases where that party is, as well as in cases where he is not, domiciled, resident or present within that jurisdiction."

This provision is now the statutory basis for the injunction that was first granted in *Nippon Yusen* **17–41** *Kaisha v Karageorgis*[85] but which took its name from the second case of its grant, *Mareva Compania Naveira SA v International Bulkcarriers SA*.[86] The criteria for obtaining a freezing injunction are: (1) a good arguable case;[87] (2) that there is a real risk that any judgment will go unsatisfied by reason of the disposal by the defendant of his assets, unless he is restrained by court order from disposing of them; and (3) it would be just and convenient in all the circumstances of the case to grant the relief sought.

On (1), it has been said that this amounts to a case "which is more than barely capable of serious **17–42** argument, but not necessarily one which the judge considers would have a better than 50 per cent chance of success".[88] The requirement in (2) is not that of "nefarious intent" (i.e. that the defendant

---

[79] cf. *Campbell v MGN Ltd* [2004] A.C. 457: *Re S (a child)* [2005] 1 F.L.R. 591.
[80] [1891] 2 Ch. 269.
[81] *Boehringer Ingelheim Ltd v Vetplus Ltd* [2007] Bus. L.R. 1456.
[82] *Att.-Gen. v Random House Group Ltd* [2010] E.M.L.R. 9.
[83] [1992] 2 Lloyd's Rep. 238 at 249.
[84] *Bank Mellat v Nikpour* [1985] F.S.R. 87 at 91–92.
[85] [1975] 1 W.L.R. 1093.
[86] [1975] 2 Lloyd's Rep. 509.
[87] The court is bound therefore to consider the merits of the case.
[88] *Ninemia Corporation v Trave Schiffahrtsgesellschaft GmbH (The "Niedersachsen")* [1983] 2 Lloyd's Rep. 600 at 605, per Mustill J.

will dissipate assets so that a judgment will be unsatisfied) but, rather an objective risk that there will be dissipation making it likely that the result of his dissipation will be that the judgment goes unsatisfied.[89] The requirement in (3) is no mere formula: it may be regarded as justifying the approach taken in *Polly Peck International v Nadir (No.2)*[90] with regard to banks whose business, depending on the confidence of their investors, might be destroyed at a stroke: the claimant's cross-undertaking in damages would be of little consolation or utility.

17–43 It is important for third parties to know just what acts are prohibited by the order, since they can commit a contempt of court if they have notice of the terms of an injunction with which they act inconsistently, as we have seen.[91] In *Customs & Excise Commissioners v Barclays Bank Plc*,[92] however, the House of Lords held that third parties such as banks owe no duty of care, and so cannot be liable for the tort of negligence, if they break the terms of a freezing order, e.g. by allowing withdrawals from a frozen bank account.

17–44 The injunction is available both before and after judgment and may restrict dealings with all assets of the defendant or merely assets up to a certain value (i.e. the value of the claimant's claim plus costs). However, it gives the claimant no right in rem or security or priority over the defendant's creditors (of which the claimant has not yet shown himself to be one).

17–45 Prior to the enactment of the Civil Jurisdiction and Judgments Act 1982, there was no power in the High Court to grant a freezing injunction against a defendant who had assets in the jurisdiction but against whom there was no substantive claim subject to the jurisdiction, the claimant asserting no proprietary interest in the assets.[93] The Act, which gives effect to the Convention on Jurisdiction and the Enforcement of Judgments in Civil and Commercial Matters, has been interpreted by the Court of Appeal[94] to provide that such an injunction can be obtained in England before trial or after judgment even though the claimant has no cause of action, in England, against the defendant: so long as a court in another contracting state has jurisdiction, it suffices.

ii. Search Orders

17–46 In *Anton Piller KG v Manufacturing Process*[95] the Court of Appeal approved the making of an order, in substance an interim mandatory injunction, requiring the defendants to allow the claimant's solicitors to enter the defendants' premises to inspect documents and remove them to the claimant's solicitors' custody. The jurisdiction to make such orders was subsequently placed on a statutory footing by the Civil Procedure Act 1997 s.7. Failure to comply with the order is a contempt by the defendant and so, even though the order does not entitle the claimant to enter as if he had a search warrant, the defendant has good reason to allow him so to do. The order is made so as to safeguard vital evidence which is needed to prove the claim although it may be granted simply to obtain information necessary to safeguard the claimant's rights, to locate assets against which a judgment might be enforced, and to preserve property which might otherwise be dissipated or destroyed.

---

[89] In *Derby & Co Ltd v Weldon* [1990] Ch. 48, the Court of Appeal rejected the subjective interpretation of the requirement even in the case of the wide ("draconian", per May L.J.) relief granted there. A fortiori, then, in a standard case.

[90] [1992] 2 Lloyd's Rep. 238.

[91] At para.17–13. In the particular case of freezing injunctions, note Eveleigh L.J.'s comments in *Z Ltd v A-Z and AA-LL* [1982] Q.B. 558 at 583, but cf. *Z Bank v D* [1994] 1 Lloyd's Rep. 656.

[92] [2007] 1 A.C. 181.

[93] *Siskina (Owners of Cargo Lately Laden on Board) v Distos Compania Naveira SA* [1979] A.C. 210, although in his dissenting speech in *Mercedes-Benz AG v Leiduck* [1996] A.C. 284, Lord Nicholls considered the law should move on to allow "free-standing" freezing injunctions auxiliary to foreign proceedings and in 1999 the Privy Council gave leave for an appeal from the Bahamas to raise the point, but the appeal ultimately was not proceeded with.

[94] *Babanaft International Co SA v Bassatne* [1990] Ch. 13. See also *Republic of Haiti v Duvalier* [1990] Q.B. 202; *Baltic Shipping Co v Translink Shipping Ltd* [1995] 1 Lloyd's Rep. 673; *Bank of China v NBM LLC* [2002] 1 W.L.R. 864.

[95] [1976] Ch. 55. The first reported case of such order was *EMI v Pandit* [1975] 1 W.L.R. 302.

17–47 Because of the truly draconian effect of an order of this sort which, to a greater extent than the freezing injunction, involves serious inroads into basic civil liberties,[96] it is now accepted that they are to be granted sparingly.[97] The three essential requirements (according to Ormrod L.J in the *Anton Piller* case[98]) are (1) an extremely strong prima facie case; (2) the potential or actual damage to the claimant (if an order is not made) must be very serious; and (3) there must be clear evidence that the defendant has in his possession incriminating documents or things and that there is a real possibility that he may destroy such material before any application with notice can be made.[99] Even if all the conditions are met, the court still has to be satisfied that the need for the order outweighs the injustice of making an order against a defendant without his having been heard.[100] This has the effect that an order will not be made against persons of good standing who are likely to obey an order of the court to deliver up.[101]

17–48 There is a common law principle enshrined in the Civil Evidence Act 1968 s.14(1), that no person may be obliged in civil proceedings to produce any document or thing which may incriminate him (or his spouse).[102] *Emmanuel v Emmanuel*[103] clarifies, however, that an order may be made if the risk of incrimination extends only to a charge of perjury in the proceedings in the context of which the order is sought. In *C Plc v P*,[104] child pornography was found on a computer that the defendant had handed over pursuant to a search order made in connection with an action for breach of confidence and copyright infringement. The defendant had only permitted the examination of his computer to take place after asserting his privilege against self-incrimination. Nevertheless, the Court of Appeal upheld the trial judge's direction that the computer should be passed to the police, because the privilege against self-incrimination did not apply to material constituting freestanding evidence which was not produced under compulsion.

AMERICAN CYANAMID CO v ETHICON LTD

House of Lords [1975] A.C. 396, [1975] 2 W.L.R. 316, [1975] 1 All E.R. 504

17–49 LORD DIPLOCK (with whom VISCOUNT DILHORNE, LORD CROSS, LORD SALMON and LORD EDMUND-DAVIES agreed): . . . In my view the grant of interlocutory injunctions in actions for infringement of patents is governed by the same principles as in other actions. I turn to consider what those principles are.

---

96 i.e. the right to be heard before the making of an order against one (a feature which, in virtue of its essential ex parte nature, it shares with the freezing injunction), the right to be free from arbitrary search and seizure, and the right to privacy in one's own home (orders were commonly made against defendants to be executed at their places of residence).

97 The frequency with which orders came to be granted (see Oliver L.J.'s reference to them as "very, very commonly employed" and "almost commonplace" in *Dunlop Holdings Ltd v Staravia Ltd* [1982] Com. L.R. 3) led to the expression of judicial concern in a number of cases about claimants' failures to demonstrate, and judicial failure to insist on demonstration, of the necessity of making an order (e.g. Hoffmann J. in *Lock International Plc v Beswick* [1989] 1 W.L.R. 1268) and led to the establishment of a committee under Staughton L.J. which made recommendations (largely followed in the model orders which preceded the current model orders contained in CPR) on future practice.

98 [1976] Ch. 55 at 62.

99 The Staughton Committee added a fourth requirement that the harm likely to be caused by the execution of the order to the defendant and his business affairs must not be excessive or out of proportion to the legitimate object of the order.

100 This is no mere formula and is a more important element in the judicial balancing exercise in search order cases than in freezing injunction or other cases of applications without notice. This is for the reason that although interlocutory, once executed the order cannot be "unexecuted". There is often no sense in a defendant's bothering to discharge a search order at a hearing with notice to the other side once it has been executed.

101 e.g. barristers and their clerks: *Randolph M Fields v Watts* (1985) 129 Sol. Jo. 67.

102 Subject to the exceptions contained in the Theft Act 1968 s.31, and the Senior Courts Act 1981 s.72.

103 [1982] 1 W.L.R. 669.

104 [2008] Ch. 1.

17–50 My Lords, when an application for an interlocutory injunction to restrain a defendant from doing acts alleged to be in violation of the plaintiff's legal right is made upon contested facts, the decision whether or not to grant an interlocutory injunction has to be taken at a time when *ex hypothesi* the existence of the right or the violation of it, or both, is uncertain and will remain uncertain until final judgment is given in the action. It was to mitigate the risk of injustice to the plaintiff during the period before that uncertainty could be resolved that the practice arose of granting him relief by way of interlocutory injunction; but since the middle of the 19th century this has been made subject to his undertaking to pay damages to the defendant for any loss sustained by reason of the injunction if it should be held at the trial that the plaintiff had not been entitled to restrain the defendant from doing what he was threatening to do. The object of the interlocutory injunction is to protect the plaintiff against injury by violation of his right for which he could not be adequately compensated in damages recoverable in the action if the uncertainty were resolved in his favour at the trial; but the plaintiff's need for such protection must be weighed against the corresponding need of the defendant to be protected against injury resulting from his having been prevented from exercising his own legal rights for which he could not be adequately compensated under the plaintiff's undertaking in damages if the uncertainty were resolved in the defendant's favour at the trial. The court must weigh one need against another and determine where "the balance of convenience" lies.

17–51 In those cases where the legal rights of the parties depend upon facts that are in dispute between them, the evidence available to the court at the hearing of the application for an interlocutory injunction is incomplete. It is given on affidavit and has not been tested by oral cross-examination. The purpose sought to be achieved by giving to the court discretion to grant such injunctions would be stultified if the discretion were clogged by a technical rule forbidding its exercise if upon that incomplete untested evidence the court evaluated the chances of the plaintiff's ultimate success in the action at 50 per cent or less, but permitting its exercise if the court evaluated his chances at more than 50 per cent.

17–52 The notion that it is incumbent upon the court to undertake what is in effect a preliminary trial of the action upon evidential material different from that upon which the actual trial will be conducted, is, I think, of comparatively recent origin, though it can be supported by references in earlier cases to the need to show "a probability that the plaintiffs are entitled to relief"[105] or "a strong prima facie case that the right which he seeks to protect in fact exists".[106] These are to be contrasted with expressions in other cases indicating a much less onerous criterion, such as the need to show that there is "certainly a case to be tried"[107] which corresponds more closely with what judges generally treated as sufficient to justify their considering the balance of convenience upon applications for interlocutory injunctions, at any rate up to the time when I became a member of your Lordships' House. . . .

17–53 *Hubbard v Vosper*[108] was treated by Graham J. and the Court of Appeal in the instant appeal as leaving intact the supposed rule that the court is not entitled to take any account of the balance of convenience unless it has first been satisfied that if the case went to trial upon no other evidence than is before the court at the hearing of the application the plaintiff would be entitled to judgment for a permanent injunction in the same terms as the interlocutory injunction sought.

17–54 Your Lordships should in my view take this opportunity of declaring that there is no such rule. The use of such expressions as "a probability", "a prima facie case", or "a strong prima facie case" in the context of the exercise of a discretionary power to grant an interlocutory injunction leads to confusion as to the object sought to be achieved by this form of temporary relief. The court no doubt must be satisfied that the claim is not frivolous or vexatious; in other words, that there is a serious question to be tried.

17–55 It is no part of the court's function at this stage of the litigation to try to resolve conflicts of evidence on affidavit as to facts on which the claims of either party may ultimately depend nor to decide difficult questions of law which call for detailed argument and mature considerations. These are matters to be dealt with at the trial. One of the reasons for the introduction of the practice of requiring an undertaking as to damages upon the grant of an interlocutory injunction was that "it aided the court in doing that which was its great object, viz. abstaining from expressing any opinion upon the merits of the case until the

---

[105] *Preston v Luck* (1884) 27 Ch.D. 497 at 506, per Cotton L.J.
[106] *Smith v Grigg Ltd* [1924] 1 K.B. 655 at 659, per Atkin L.J.
[107] *Jones v Pacaya Rubber and Produce Co Ltd* [1911] 1 K.B. 455 at 457, per Buckley L.J.
[108] [1972] 2 Q.B. 84.

hearing".[109] So unless the material available to the court at the hearing of the application for an interlocutory injunction fails to disclose that the plaintiff has any real prospect of succeeding in his claim for a permanent injunction at the trial, the court should go on to consider whether the balance of convenience lies in favour of granting or refusing the interlocutory relief that is sought.

As to that, the governing principle is that the court should first consider whether, if the plaintiff were to **17–56** succeed at the trial in establishing his right to a permanent injunction, he would be adequately compensated by an award of damages for the loss he would have sustained as a result of the defendant's continuing to do what was sought to be enjoined between the time of the application and the time of the trial. If damages in the measure recoverable at common law would be adequate remedy and the defendant would be in a financial position to pay them, no interlocutory injunction should normally be granted, however strong the plaintiff's claim appeared to be at that stage. If, on the other hand, damages would not provide an adequate remedy for the plaintiff in the event of his succeeding at the trial, the court should then consider whether, on the contrary hypothesis that the defendant were to succeed at the trial in establishing his right to do that which was sought to be enjoined, he would be adequately compensated under the plaintiff's undertaking as to damages for the loss he would have sustained by being prevented from doing so between the time of the application and the time of the trial. If damages in the measure recoverable under such an undertaking would be an adequate remedy and the plaintiff would be in a financial position to pay them, there would be no reason upon this ground to refuse an interlocutory injunction.

It is where there is doubt as to the adequacy of the respective remedies in damages available to **17–57** either party or to both, that the question of balance of convenience arises. It would be unwise to attempt even to list all the various matters which may need to be taken into consideration in deciding where the balance lies, let alone to suggest the relative weight to be attached to them. These will vary from case to case.

Where other factors appear to be evenly balanced it is a counsel of prudence to take such measures as **17–58** are calculated to preserve the status quo. If the defendant is enjoined temporarily from doing something that he has not done before, the only effect of the interlocutory injunction in the event of his succeeding at the trial is to postpone the date at which he is able to embark upon a course of action which he has not previously found it necessary to undertake; whereas to interrupt him in the conduct of an established enterprise would cause much greater inconvenience to him since he would have to start again to establish it in the event of his succeeding at the trial.

Save in the simplest cases, the decision to grant or to refuse an interlocutory injunction will cause to **17–59** whichever party is unsuccessful on the application some disadvantages which his ultimate success at the trial may show he ought to have been spared and the disadvantages may be such that the recovery of damages to which he would then be entitled either in the action or under the plaintiff's undertaking would not be sufficient to compensate him fully for all of them. The extent to which the disadvantages to each party would be incapable of being compensated in damages in the event of his succeeding at the trial is always a significant factor in assessing where the balance of convenience lies; and if the extent of the uncompensatable disadvantage to each party would not differ widely, it may not be improper to take into account in tipping the balance the relative strength of each party's case as revealed by the affidavit evidence adduced on the hearing of the application. This, however, should be done only where it is apparent upon the facts disclosed by evidence as to which there is no credible dispute that the strength of one party's case is disproportionate to that of the other party. The court is not justified in embarking upon anything resembling a trial of the action upon conflicting affidavits in order to evaluate the strength of either party's case.

I would reiterate that, in addition to those to which I have referred, there may be many other special fac- **17–60** tors to be taken into consideration in the particular circumstances of individual cases. The instant appeal affords one example of this.

[109] *Walkefield v Duke of Buccleugh* (1865) 12 L.T. 628 at 629.

CAMBRIDGE NUTRITION LTD v BRITISH BROADCASTING CORPORATION

Court of Appeal [1990] 3 All E.R 523

17–61 The claimants were manufacturers of a widely used low-calorie diet and agreed to participate in the making of a programme about this diet by the defendants. The claimants contended and the defendants denied that it was a contractual term of their agreement that the programme would not be broadcast until after the publication of a government report on the medical aspects of diets such as the claimants'. Having become increasingly concerned about the tone of the proposed programme, the claimants applied for injunctive relief preventing broadcast until after publication of the government report and they sought an interlocutory injunction pending trial. The nature of the programme as proposed was such that it was only appropriate for transmission before publication of the government report. The judge granted an injunction but on appeal his decision was reversed and the injunction lifted.

17–62 KERR L.J.: I would unhesitatingly refuse such an injunction in this case, and I summarise my reasons as briefly as I can.

17–63 First, I do not consider that the question whether or not an injunction should be granted should in this case be tested simply by reference to the guidelines laid down in the *American Cyanamid* case. I accept that the judge was entitled to conclude that he should be guided by that case, but in my view it is not suitable for that purpose. Although *Cayne v Global Natural Resources Plc*[110] was clearly an exceptional case, I would reiterate without repeating what I then said[111] and I refer equally to the tenor of the judgments of Eveleigh and May L.JJ. in that case, which are much to the same effect. It is important to bear in mind that the *American Cyanamid* case contains no principle of universal application. The only such principle is the statutory power of the court to grant injunctions when it is just and convenient to do so. The *American Cyanamid* case is no more than a set of useful guidelines which apply in many cases. It must never be used as a rule of thumb, let alone as a strait-jacket. Admittedly, the present case is miles away on its facts from the *Global Natural Resources* case, and it is also much weaker than *NWL Ltd v Woods*[112] where Lord Diplock himself recognised the limitations of the *Cyanamid* guidelines. But nevertheless, I do not consider that it is an appropriate case for the *Cyanamid* guidelines because the crucial issues between the parties do not depend on a trial, but solely or mainly on the grant or refusal of the interlocutory relief. The *American Cyanamid* case provides an authoritative and most helpful approach to cases where the function of the court in relation to the grant or refusal of interlocutory injunctions is to hold the balance as justly as possible in situations where the substantial issues between the parties can only be resolved by a trial. In my view, for reasons which require no further elaboration, the present case is not in that category. Neither side is interested in monetary compensation, and once the interlocutory decision has been given, little, if anything, will remain in practice.

17–64 But for present purposes the point can be put more narrowly. It seems to me that cases in which the subject matter concerns the right to publish an article, or to transmit a broadcast, whose importance may be transitory but whose impact depends on timing, news value and topicality, do not lend themselves easily to the application of the *Cyanamid* guidelines. Longer term publications, such as films or books, may not be in the same category. I think that it would be an inappropriate test for the grant or refusal of interlocutory injunctions in such cases if the transmission of a broadcast, or the publication of an article, whose value and impact depended on their timing, could be prevented merely by the plausible, or not implausible, allegation of a term alleged to have been agreed orally in an informal conversation. In such cases it should matter whether the chances of success in establishing some binding agreement are 90 per cent or 20 per cent. I use that phraseology because counsel for the plaintiffs referred us to the decision of this court in *Alfred Dunhill Ltd v Sunoptic SA*,[113] where Megaw L.J. said that in the application of the *Cyanamid* test it did not matter whether the chances of success in establishing liability were 90 per cent or

---

110 [1984] 1 All E.R. 225.
111 At 234–235.
112 [1979] 1 W.L.R. 1294.
113 [1979] F.S.R. 337 at 373.

20 per cent. The *Dunhill* case, like *Cyanamid* itself, was a typical case in which the *Cyanamid* guidelines are of great value, because everything depended on the trial and the long-term rights of the parties. The present type of case is not in the same category.

Accordingly, since I would not follow the structured approach of the *American Cyanamid* case in the present case, in carrying out the necessary balancing exercise I would have some regard to the relative weakness of the plaintiffs' case in establishing the contract on which they rely. Counsel for the plaintiffs conceded that clearly no contract of any kind had been made in the telephone conversations themselves. It is obvious that neither party was bound to anything at that stage. The conversations were no more than preliminary discussions. At most, as suggested by counsel for the plaintiffs, they resulted in a statement of terms which would apply if the BBC went ahead with the programme and the plaintiffs cooperated in making it. Even then, either side could no doubt have resiled from the project; for some time at least. The whole situation was by its nature undefined, and not easily definable in legal terms. Moreover, the alleged conditions were to be confirmed in writing, but never were. The second alleged condition, concerning the featuring of users of the diet "before and after" was never pursued. And no reference to the existence of any condition was made for five months or so, despite all that intervened. **17–65**

In my view it would be highly undesirable if, on evidence of that nature, which the judge rightly characterised as being no more than "plausible" in support of the alleged condition, the court were driven to grant an injunction because of the application of the *Cyanamid* guidelines. In situations of this kind, quite apart from the alleged express reference to a written confirmation in the original telephone calls, it is essential that there should indeed be written confirmation of any fetter on transmission or other publication. In the absence of clear evidence of a contract having been made, I consider that the court should be extremely slow to grant an interlocutory injunction in such situations. And if the application of the *Cyanamid* test were to lead to a different conclusion, then that would demonstrate that it is not appropriate in these situations. **17–66**

However, in the same way as the judge, I do not think that it makes any difference whether this case is decided in accordance with the *Cyanamid* test or not. On either basis the answer is the same. The judge and I agree about that, even though our answers are different. That in itself serves to demonstrate that one must be careful not to lose sight of the real demands of justice in any given case by attaching too much importance to the *Cyanamid* guidelines. The only real difference of substance in the court's approach concerns the extent to which it is permissible or otherwise to have some regard to the relative strength of the parties' contentions on the merits. But in that connection it should also be remembered that the speech of Lord Diplock in the *American Cyanamid* case itself contains a later passage where he appears himself to qualify to some extent the earlier passage on this aspect.[114] I can summarise the position by saying that in a context such as the present a doubtful contract should never prevail over the right of free speech, all other things being even. **17–67**

In these circumstances it seems to me to be obviously contrary to the public interest that the plaintiffs should be entitled to an order which has the effect of suppressing similar discussion of this topic by the BBC in a programme made with the plaintiffs' full co-operation, merely on the basis of a shadowy claim of an oral agreement concerning the timing of this programme alleged to have been made on the telephone some eight months ago. **17–68**

RALPH GIBSON L.J. (with whose approach EASTHAM J. agreed): It is necessary to go back to the *Cyanamid* principles as set out by Lord Diplock. The judge had reached the point that the plaintiffs had a good arguable case for the injunction sought, and that the plaintiffs would not be adequately compensated by an award of damages at trial. The finding that the BBC would be adequately compensated by an award of damages, which the plaintiffs could pay, could have been regarded by the judge as sufficient to establish that, in the absence of any other relevant factor, there could be no reason to refuse an interlocutory injunction.[115] The judge in fact went on to consider the balance of justice or convenience, as I have said, and it is important to note that in my view it was essential that that balance be considered, because on the evidence, contrary to the judge's view, the remedy in damages was not adequate to compensate for the loss which would be suffered by either party if the injunction was wrongly granted or wrongly withheld. **17–69**

---

114 [1975] A.C. 396 at 409.

115 See the *American Cyanamid* case [1975] A.C. 396 at 408 per Lord Diplock.

17–70 Since neither party would be adequately compensated by an award of damages, the guidance offered in the following paragraph in Lord Diplock's speech was of crucial importance:[116]

> "Save in the simplest cases, the decision to grant or to refuse an interlocutory injunction will cause to whichever party is unsuccessful on the application some disadvantages which his ultimate success at the trial may show he ought to have been spared and the disadvantages may be such that the recovery of damages to which he would then be entitled either in the action or under the plaintiff's undertaking would not be sufficient to compensate him fully for all of them. The extent to which the disadvantages to each party would be incapable of being compensated in damages in the event of his succeeding at the trial is always a significant factor in assessing where the balance of convenience lies; and if the extent of the uncompensatable disadvantage to each party would not differ widely, it may not be improper to take into account in tipping the balance the relative strength of each party's case as revealed by the affidavit evidence adduced on the hearing of the application. This, however, should be done only where it is apparent on the facts disclosed by evidence as to which there is no credible dispute that the strength of one party's case is disproportionate to that of the other party. The court is not justified in embarking on anything resembling a trial of the action on conflicting affidavits in order to evaluate the strength of either party's case."

17–71 It is clear that what is there said is the setting out of guidelines for the assistance of the judges. I quote this passage again:

> ". . . if the extent of the uncompensatable disadvantage to each party would not differ widely, it may not be improper to take into account in tipping the balance the relative strength of each party's case . . .".

17–72 For my part, I would hold that on the evidence before the judge this case was at best for the plaintiffs clearly within that principle. The uncompensatable disadvantage of each party in this case is difficult to assess separately for this purpose, and therefore even more difficult to compare with any confidence that one is more grave than the other.

17–73 This is a case, therefore, in which I think that the relative strength of the parties' cases should be taken into account, and this can be done by reference to the undisputed evidence on the affidavits and documents. . . .

17–74 There is one further matter to be taken into account on the balance of justice. Since I am following the judge through the principles stated in the *American Cyanamid* case, I should point out that it comes under the heading: ". . . many other special factors to be taken into consideration in the particular circumstances of individual cases".[117] I refer to the public interest in the exercise by the BBC of their rights and duties in communication to the people of this country. . . .

SERIES 5 SOFTWARE LTD v CLARKE

Chancery Division [1996] 1 All E.R. 853

17–75 LADDIE J.: It is, of course, comparatively rare for applications for interlocutory relief to reach the House of Lords. However, 1975 was an exception. In that year two cases, both of which involved an analysis of the courts' power to grant interlocutory injunctions, were heard more or less one after the other. The first was *F Hoffmann-La Roche & Co AG v Secretary of State for Trade and Industry*.[118] . . . In the course of that case their Lordships considered the circumstances in which interlocutory injunctions were granted and the conditions to which their grant could be subject. In particular Lord Diplock said:[119]

---

116 [1975] A.C. 396 at 408–409.
117 [1975] A.C. 396 at 409.
118 [1973] A.C. 295.
119 At 360–361.

"An interim injunction is a temporary and exceptional remedy which is available before the rights of the parties have been finally determined and, in the case of an ex parte injunction, even before the court had been apprised of the nature of the defendant's case. *To justify the grant of such a remedy the plaintiff must satisfy the court first that there is a strong prima facie case that he will be entitled to a final order restraining the defendant from doing what he is threatening to do*, and secondly that he will suffer irreparable injury which cannot be compensated by a subsequent award of damages in the action if the defendant is not prevented from doing it between the date of the application for the interim injunction and the date of the final order made on trial of the action. Nevertheless, at the time of the application it is not possible for the court to be absolutely certain that the plaintiff will succeed at the trial in establishing his legal right to restrain the defendant from doing what he is threatening to do. If he should fail to do so the defendant may have suffered loss as a result of having been prevented from doing it while the interim injunction was in force; and any loss is likely to be *damnum absque injuria* for which he could not recover damages from the plaintiff at common law. So unless some other means is provided in this event for compensating the defendant for his loss there is a risk that injustice may be done." (Emphasis added.)

Then, having explained that the imposition of the cross-undertaking is designed to mitigate the risk to the defendant, Lord Diplock proceeded:[120] **17–76**

"Beside mitigating the risk of injustice to the defendant the practice of exacting an undertaking as to damages facilitates the conduct of the business of the courts. It relieves the court of the necessity to embark at an interlocutory stage upon an enquiry as to the likelihood of the defendant's being able to establish facts to destroy *the strong prima facie case which ex hypothesi will have been made out by the plaintiff*. The procedure on motion is unsuited to inquiries into disputed facts. This is best left to the trial of the action . . ." (Emphasis added.)

This was consistent with the approach which was followed in many, but not all, cases before *American Cyanamid*. The court had to pay regard to the strength or otherwise of the plaintiff's case as revealed by a consideration of all the affidavit evidence. **17–77**

Judgment in *Hoffmann-La Roche* was given just before the long vacation on July 3, 1974 **17–78**

That brings me to *American Cyanamid*, the hearing for which commenced after the long vacation on November 12, 1974. It can be assumed that the panel read the parties' briefs before that date. The panel consisted of Lord Diplock, Viscount Dilhorne, Lord Cross, Lord Salmon and Lord Edmund-Davies—that is, it included two members of the panel which decided *Hoffmann-La Roche*. If the House of Lords intended to say that it was inappropriate on an application for interlocutory relief, save in rare cases, to take into account the apparent strength of the plaintiff's case, it would mean that Lord Diplock performed a *volte face* on this issue in a matter of four months. In my view it is inconceivable that Lord Diplock and Lord Cross could have forgotten what was said in the *Hoffmann-La Roche* judgment a few months earlier. Therefore, if they were saying the opposite of what was said in *Hoffmann-La Roche*, they must have been aware that they were doing so but chose not to mention that fact or explain it in *American Cyanamid*. That is a proposition I find difficult to accept. It seems to me that it is therefore appropriate to consider whether what Lord Diplock said in *Hoffmann-La Roche* is incompatible with what he said in *American Cyanamid* only a few months later. For this it is necessary to consider the *American Cyanamid* decision with some care. **17–79**

The *American Cyanamid* case was concerned with the alleged infringement of the main claim in the plaintiff's patent for absorbable surgical sutures. In response to the allegation of infringement, Ethicon presented a classic squeeze argument beloved of patent lawyers. It said that its sutures did not fall within the monopoly defined by the claim—that is it did not infringe, or, in the alternative, if the claim was construed widely enough to include its product, the patent was invalid on a number of grounds under the Patents Act 1949. **17–80**

In the House of Lords, as in the High Court and the Court of Appeal, both parties had addressed the question of whether the plaintiff had demonstrated a strong prima facie case. In the course of his judgment, Lord Diplock said:[121] **17–81**

[120] At 361.
[121] [1975] A.C. 396 at 407.

> "Your Lordships should in my view take this opportunity of declaring that there is no such rule. The use of such expressions as 'a probability', 'a prima facie case', or 'a strong prima facie case' in the context of the exercise of a discretionary power to grant an interlocutory injunction leads to confusion as to the object sought to be achieved by this form of temporary relief. The court no doubt must be satisfied that the claim is not frivolous or vexatious; in other words, that there is a serious question to be tried."

17–82 The first question to be answered is precisely what was "such rule" the existence of which the House of Lords disapproved. This can be found in the early part of Lord Diplock's judgment. In the High Court, Graham J. had held that the plaintiff had made out a strong prima facie case and went on to say that the balance of convenience favoured the grant of interlocutory relief. The way in which the Court of Appeal dealt with the application was set out in the following passage in Lord Diplock's judgment:[122]

> "As Russell L.J. put it in the concluding paragraph of his reasons for judgment with which the other members of the court agreed—'. . . if there be no prima facie case on the point essential to entitle the plaintiff to complain of the defendant's proposed activities, that is the end of the claim to interlocutory relief.' 'Prima facie case' may in some contexts be an elusive concept, but the sense in which it was being used by Russell L.J. is apparent from an earlier passage in his judgment. After a detailed analysis of the more conflicting expert testimony he said: 'I am not satisfied on the present evidence that on the proper construction of this specification, addressed as it is to persons skilled in the relevant art or science, the claim extends to sterile surgical sutures produced not only from a homopolymer of glycolide but also from a copolymer of glycolide and up to 15 per cent of lactide. That is to say that I do not consider that a prima facie case of infringement is established.' In effect what the Court of Appeal was doing was trying the issue of infringement on the conflicting affidavit evidence as it stood, without the benefit of oral testimony or cross-examination. They were saying: 'If we had to give judgment in the action now without any further evidence we should hold that Cyanamid had not satisfied the onus of proving that their patent would be infringed by Ethicon's selling sutures made of XLG.' The Court of Appeal accordingly did not find it necessary to go into the questions raised by Ethicon as to the validity of the patent or to consider where the balance of convenience lay."

17–83 As Lord Diplock put it:[123]

> "[The Court of Appeal] considered that there was *a rule of practice so well established as to constitute a rule of law* that precluded them from granting any interim injunction unless on the evidence adduced by both the parties on the hearing of the application the applicant had satisfied the court that on the balance of probabilities the acts of the other party sought to be enjoined would, if committed, violate the applicant's legal rights." (Emphasis added.)

Lord Diplock then made it clear that it was in order to enable the existence of that rule of law to be considered that leave to appeal had been granted.

17–84 The result of applying that "rule of law" was that in the Court of Appeal the motion lasted for two working weeks while the parties argued questions of polymer chemistry, infringement and validity. In the House of Lords the defendant tried to do the same thing. The note of argument there shows that sophisticated arguments of patent ambiguity, construction, inutility, false suggestion, insufficiency and unfair basis were advanced. In effect, the Court of Appeal had abandoned any attempt to evaluate the pros and cons of granting an interlocutory injunction and had said that there was a mandatory initial hurdle at which the plaintiff had fallen. The flexibility and absence of strict rules which had been advocated by the Court of Appeal in *Hubbard v Vosper* was ignored. If such a rule of law as envisaged by the Court of Appeal in *American Cyanamid* did exist, it would inevitably force the parties to engage in trying to prove at the interlocutory stage all those issues which were for determination at the trial. In a case as complicated as

---

122 [1975] A.C. 396 at 404–405.
123 [1975] A.C. 396 at 405.

American Cyanamid it was likely to be impossible to show a strong prima facie case of infringement and validity and any attempt to do so would force the parties to expound at length on complicated technical and legal issues. But those were issues which at an interlocutory stage the court could not hope to resolve. It would have followed that if such a rule of law existed, interlocutory injunctions in patent cases, or in any other complicated case, would become a thing of the past no matter how severe was the damage to be suffered by the plaintiff in the interim.

When Lord Diplock said that there was no such rule, he was referring to the so-called rule of law which the Court of Appeal had followed. In dismissing this approach, the House of Lords approved of the decision in *Hubbard v Vosper* and in particular that part of the decision in which the Court of Appeal deprecated any attempt to fetter the discretion of the court by laying down any rules which would have the effect of limiting the flexibiity of the remedy.[124] **17–85**

Once it had disposed of the inflexible rule as applied by the Court of Appeal in the instant case, the House of Lords went on to consider what principles a court should bear in mind when deciding whether to grant interlocutory relief. First, it said:[125] **17–86**

> ". . . [the court should] consider whether if the plaintiff were to succeed at the trial in establishing his right to a permanent injunction he would be adequately compensated by an award of damages for the loss he would have sustained as a result of the defendant's continuing to do what was sought to be enjoined between the time of the application and the time of the trial. If damages in the measure recoverable at common law would be adequate remedy and the defendant would be in a financial position to pay them, no interlocutory injunction should *normally* be granted, *however strong the plaintiff's claim appeared to be at that stage*." (Emphasis added.)

It should be noticed from the emphasised words in that passage that this approach was not said to be invariably the correct one and furthermore the words used suggest that where damages for the plaintiff was not an adequate remedy the apparent strength of the plaintiff's claim might well be a relevant consideration.

Having considered the issue of adequacy of damages, Lord Diplock proceeded as follows:[126] **17–87**

> "It is where there is doubt as to the adequacy of the respective remedies in damages available to either party or to both, that the question of balance of convenience arises. It would be unwise to attempt even to list all the various matters which may need to be taken into consideration in deciding where the balance lies, let alone to suggest the relative weight to be attached to them. These will vary from case to case."

The reality is that the balance of convenience issue will need to be considered in most cases because evidence relating to the adequacy of damages normally will be contradictory and there will be no possibility of resolving the differences by cross-examination. In the result, normally there will be doubt as to the adequacy of damages. It follows that in most cases it will be the exercise of taking into account all the issues relevant to the balance of convenience which will be the major task of the court faced with an application for interlocutory relief. As Lord Diplock went on to point out:[127] **17–88**

> "Save in the simplest cases, the decision to grant or to refuse an interlocutory injunction will cause to whichever party is unsuccessful on the application some disadvantages which his ultimate success at the trial may show he ought to have been spared and the disadvantages may be such that the recovery of damages to which he would then be entitled either in the action or under the plaintiff's undertaking would not be sufficient to compensate him fully for all of them. The extent to which the disadvantages to each party would be incapable of being compensated in damages in the event of his succeeding at the trial is always a significant factor in assessing where the balance of convenience lies . . .".

124 See [1975] A.C. 396 at 407.
125 [1975] A.C. 396 at 408.
126 [1975] A.C. 396 at 408.
127 [1975] A.C. 396 at 408–409.

17–89 In many cases before *American Cyanamid* the prospect of success was one of the important factors taken into account in assessing the balance of convenience. The courts would be less willing to subject the plaintiff to the risk of irrecoverable loss which would befall him if an interlocutory injunction was refused in those cases where it thought he was likely to win at the trial than in those cases where it thought he was likely to lose. The assessment of the prospects of success therefore was an important factor in deciding whether the court should exercise its discretion to grant interlocutory relief. It is this consideration which *American Cyanamid* is said to have prohibited in all but the most exceptional case, so it is necessary to consider with some care what was said in the House of Lords on this issue.

17–90 Lord Diplock said:[128]

> ". . . if the extent of the uncompensatable disadvantage to each party would not differ widely, it may not be improper to take into account in tipping the balance the relative strength of each party's case as revealed by the affidavit evidence adduced on the hearing of the application. . . . The court is not justified in embarking on anything resembling a trial of the aciton on conflicting affidavits in order to evaluate the strength of either party's case."

17–91 It appears to me that there is nothing in this which is inconsistent with the old practice. Although couched in terms "it may not be improper", this means that it is legitimate for the court to look at the relative strength of the parties' case as disclosed by the affidavits. The warning contained in the second of the quoted sentences is to avoid courts at the interlocutory stage engaging in mini-trials, which is what happened, at least in the Court of Appeal, in *American Cyanamid* itself. Interlocutory applications are meant to come on quickly and to be disposed of quickly.

17–92 The supposed problem with *American Cyanamid* centres on the following statement by Lord Diplock:[129]

> "[Assessing the relative strength of the parties' case], however, should be done only where it is apparent upon the facts disclosed by evidence as to which there is no credible dispute that the strength of one party's case is disproportionate to that of the other party."

If this means that the court cannot take into account its view of the strength of each party's case if there is any dispute on the evidence, as suggested by the use of the words "only" and "no credible dispute", then a new inflexible rule has been introduced to replace that applied by the Court of Appeal. For example, all a defendant would have to do is raise a non-demurrable dispute as to relevant facts in his affidavit evidence and then he could invite the court to ignore the apparent strength of the plaintiff's case. This would be inconsistent with the flexible approach suggested in *Hubbard v Vosper*[130] which was cited with approval earlier in *American Cyanamid*.[131] Furthermore, it would be somewhat strange, since *American Cyanamid* directs courts to assess the adequacy of damages and the balance of convenience, yet these too are topics which will almost always be the subject of unresolved conflicts in the affidavit evidence.

17–93 In my view Lord Diplock did not intend by the last-quoted passage to exclude consideration of the strength of the cases in most applications for interlocutory relief. It appears to me that what is intended is that the court should not attempt to resolve difficult issues of fact or law on an application for interlocutory relief. If, on the other hand, the court is able to come to a view as to the strength of the parties' case on the credible evidence, then it can do so. In fact, as any lawyer who has experience of interlocutory proceedings will know, it is frequently the case that it is easy to determine who is most likely to win the trial on the basis of the affidavit evidence and any exhibited contemporaneous documents. If it is apparent from that material that one party's case is much stronger than the other's then that is a matter the court should not ignore. To suggest otherwise would be to exclude from consideration an important factor and such exclusion would fly in the face of the flexibility advocated earlier in *American Cyanamid*. As Lord

[128] [1975] A.C. 396 at 409.
[129] [1975] A.C. 396 at 409.
[130] [1972] 2 Q.B. 84.
[131] [1975] A.C. 396 at 407.

Diplock pointed out in *Hoffmann-La Roche*, one of the purposes of the cross-undertaking in damages is to safeguard the defendant if this preliminary view of the strength of the plaintiff's case proves to be wrong.

Accordingly, it appears to me that in deciding whether to grant interlocutory relief, the court should bear the following matters in mind. **17–94**

(1) The grant of an interlocutory injunction is a matter of discretion and depends on all the facts of the case.

(2) There are no fixed rules as to when an injunction should or should not be granted. The relief must be kept flexible.

(3) Because of the practice adopted on the hearing of applications for interlocutory relief, the court should rarely attempt to resolve complex issues of disputed fact or law.

(4) Major factors the court can bear in mind are

  (a) the extent to which damages are likely to be an adequate remedy for each party and the ability of the other party to pay,
  (b) the balance of convenience,
  (c) the maintenance of the status quo, and
  (d) any clear view the court may reach as to the relative strength of the parties' cases.

In coming to this conclusion I am encouraged by the following considerations. **17–95**

(1) The House of Lords in *American Cyanamid* did not suggest that it was changing the basis upon which most courts had approached the exercise of discretion in this important area.

(2) The only issue which it was expressly addressing was the existence of the inflexible rule of law which had been applied as a mandatory condition by the Court of Appeal.

(3) It would mean that there was no significant inconsistency between the *Hoffmann-La Roche* and *American Cyanamid* decisions.

(4) It would be consistent with the approval given by the House of Lords to the decision in *Hubbard v Vosper* and, implicitly, the decision to the same effect in *Evans Marshall & Co Ltd v Bertola SA*[132] (a decision of Lord Edmund-Davies when in the Court of Appeal).

(5) It would preserve what is one of the great values of interlocutory proceedings, namely an early, though non-binding, view of the merits from a judge. Before *American Cyanamid* a decision at the interlocutory stage would be a major ingredient leading to the parties resolving their differences without the need for a trial. There is nothing inherently unsatisfactory in this. Most clients ask for and receive advice on prospects from their lawyers well before there has been cross-examination. In most cases the lawyers have little difficulty giving such advice. It should also be remembered that in many jurisdictions on the continent trials are conducted without discovery or cross-examination. There is nothing inherently unfair in a court here expressing at least a preliminary view based on written evidence. After all, it is what the courts managed to do for a century and a half.

(6) Allowing parties to come to an earlier view on prospects would assist in reducing the costs of litigation. This is an issue to which much attention is being given at the moment.

(7) It would mean that the approach of the courts in England and Wales to the grant of interlocutory relief would be the same as that followed in Scotland. . . .

---

[132] [1973] 1 W.L.R. 349.

3. Specific Performance

17–96 A decree of specific[133] performance is an order[134] of the court[135] compelling the defendant[136] personally to do what he has promised to do.[137] While the common law allows a defendant to be a "bad man" and break his contractual obligations and pay damages for the privilege, where equity intervenes it will compel a defendant to be a "good man" and fulfil his obligations.[138] Compulsion may take various forms, e.g. empowering a person other than the defendant to execute a conveyance which the latter has promised but refused to execute,[139] or, more generally, committing the defendant to prison on account of his contempt[140] (i.e. disobedience to the order of the court) until he complies with the court order and purges his contempt.

17–97 In *Johnson v Agnew*,[141] which is reproduced below,[142] Lord Wilberforce held that if a decree is granted, the contract continues "under control of the court",[143] so that a further court order is needed to dissolve the decree before either party can terminate the contract for breach and ask for damages. He also held that the court can refuse to dissolve the decree "if to do so would be unjust".[144] The advantage of this is that it enables the court to prevent a claimant who has won an order for specific performance from changing his mind and asserting a right to damages after the defendant has detrimentally relied on the court's original order. However, it also means that whenever an order for specific performance is made, the parties' original rights under the contract are replaced by a set of new equitable rights which replicate the parties' original rights, including the right to terminate the contract for breach, but which are subject to equitable principles that would not have affected the parties' original rights at common law. This model of the law is complex, and it is also inconsistent with Lord Wilberforce's own statement that "if an order for specific performance is sought and is made, the contract remains in effect and is not merged in the judgment for specific performance".[145] Hence there is much to be said for the

---

133 Referring to the performance in kind (in Latin, *in specie*) of a contractual (or primary) obligation rather than the performance of the secondary obligation to pay damages for loss caused by breach of a primary obligation. Meagher, Gummow and Lehane's *Equity, Doctrines and Remedies* 4th edn (2002) observes the technical distinction between specific performance proper (which applies only to executory contracts requiring something to be done such as the execution of a deed or conveyance) and specific performance of executed agreements (whereby the performance of any contractual obligation may be decreed): the principles applying to both are the same, but the distinction makes it easier to understand decisions such as *CH Giles & Co Ltd v Morris* [1972] 1 W.L.R. 307 and *Posner v Scott-Lewis* [1987] Ch. 25.

134 i.e. a final order. An interim decree is not possible but see *Hill v CA Parsons & Co Ltd* [1972] Ch. 305 and *Sky Petroleum Ltd v VIP Petroleum Ltd* [1974] 1 W.L.R. 576, cases where injunctions amounting in substance to the specific performance of obligations were granted on an interlocutory (now "interim") basis.

135 Both the High Court and the County Court have jurisdiction to grant specific performance and, whereas the County Court jurisdiction is limited in the case of contracts to sell or lease land to cases where the purchase price (or, in the case of leases, the value of the property) does not exceed the County Court limit, the County Court must give effect to every defence or counterclaim to which effect would be given in the High Court: County Courts Act 1984 s.38. Even where a case falls outside the County Court's jurisdiction to decree specific performance, that court might still declare that a party would be entitled to such decree: *Rushton v Smith* [1976] Q.B. 480.

136 Specific performance cannot be ordered against the Crown (Crown Proceedings Act 1947 s.21(1)(a)) but a declaration may be made as to the Crown's position.

137 It is only available to enforce positive obligations. Negative ones must be enforced by injunction.

138 See Sir Peter Millett in 1993 Restitution L.R. 7 at pp. 19–20, developing the celebrated view of O.W. Holmes in *The Common Law* (1881) and in "The Path of the Law" (1897) 10 Harv. L.R. 457.

139 Senior Courts Act 1981 s.39.

140 Sequestration of assets until compliance is also available against both individuals and corporations and is the only way of proceeding against corporations for contempt, although their directors may, of course, be imprisoned. Fines may also be imposed.

141 [1980] A.C. 367.

142 At paras 17–155 ff.

143 *Johnson* at 398. See too Megarry V.C.'s comments in *Singh (Sudagar) v Nazeer* [1979] Ch. 474 at 480–481.

144 *Johnson* at 399.

145 *Johnson* at 393, citing *Austins of East Ham Ltd v Macey* [1941] Ch. 338 at 341, where Sir Wilfrid Greene M.R. stressed that after an order for specific performance has been made "the contract is still there". See too *John Barker & Co Ltd v Littman* [1941] Ch. 405 at 412.

different view that even after an order for specific performance has been made, both parties' common law rights under the contract subsist, including the right to terminate for breach and sue for damages, and that either party can exercise these rights without complying with equitable requirements such as the rule that a claimant must come into court with clean hands.[146]

Not all positive contractual stipulations or promises will be specifically enforced, and in the rest of this section we shall examine the principles upon which the court's discretion to order specific performance will be exercised. It is nowadays refused only according to reasonably settled principles, the most important of which are: (a) lack of consideration; (b) adequacy of common law remedies, (c) equity will not act in vain, (d) illegality or public policy, (e) lack of mutuality of a sort irremediable by imposition of terms, (f) that the contract is incapable of being enforced in its entirety, (g) that the order could not be enforced without the constant supervision of the court, (h) delay, (i) lack of clean hands, (j) undue hardship, (k) performance would involve the defendant in a breach of contract (or trust), (l) set-off, (m) mistake and misrepresentation, and (n) misdescription of subject-matter. Each of these will be looked at in turn. **17–98**

A. *Lack of Consideration*

Lack of consideration in fact prevents there being a contract at all so that there is nothing to perform, *in specie* or otherwise.[147] The consideration provided by a deed, although sufficient for the courts to discover a binding contract at law, is insufficient for the courts to hold that this contract is specifically enforceable in equity.[148] Nor will past consideration support a suit in equity.[149] However, there is no equitable test of adequacy of consideration (it follows the law in that respect) and the provision of money or money's worth, however small the sum, will suffice.[150] **17–99**

B. *Inadequacy of Damages*

The best way of illustrating how this principle operates in relation to the enforcement of positive contractual stipulations is to examine different categories of contracts. First, some that have been held to be specifically enforceable and then some that have been held not to be. **17–100**

i. Contracts for the Disposition of an Interest in Land

Each piece of real estate is regarded as unique and, therefore, damages will be an inadequate remedy for a purchaser in the sense that damages will not enable him to buy a replacement in the market, as held in *Adderley v Dixon*,[151] which is reproduced below.[152] Although damages will, clearly, be an **17–101**

---

146 M. Hetherington, "Keeping the Plaintiff out of his Contractual Remedies: The Heresies That Survive *Johnson v Agnew*" (1980) 96 L.Q.R. 403; Meagher, Gummow and Lehane's *Equity: Doctrines and Remedies* 4th edn (2002), para.20–265.

147 A similar consideration requires that, for example, contracts for the sale or disposition of interests in land must comply with s.2 of the Law of Property (Miscellaneous Provisions) Act 1989 before specific performance may be ordered. Likewise contracts void at law for other reasons, e.g. mistake, illegality and uncertainty.

148 *Re Pryce* [1917] 1 Ch. 234 at 241, per Eve J. Mere covenantees are therefore volunteers in equity and can only enforce the covenant at law: *Cannon v Hartley* [1949] Ch. 213. In marriage settlement cases, however, children of a marriage may obtain specific performance, as they are treated in equity as having provided consideration: *Re Pryce; Re Kay's Settlement* [1939] Ch. 329.

149 *Robertson v St John* (1786) 2 Bro. C.C. 140

150 *Mountford v Scott* [1975] Ch. 258. But cf. *Milroy v Lord* (1862) 4 De G.F. & J. 264 and *Peffer v Rigg* [1977] 1 W.L.R. 285.

151 (1824) 1 Sim. & St. 607. See too *Hall v Warren* (1804) 9 Ves. 605. In *Verrall v Great Yarmouth Borough Council* [1981] 1 Q.B. 202, the Court of Appeal affirmed the grant of specific performance to enforce a contractual licence to occupy premises. As no other premises could be found damages would have been an inadequate remedy (the promisee being unable to hire any premises with any damages awarded).

152 At paras 17–122 ff.

adequate remedy for a vendor (who wants only money), a decree will lie against a purchaser on grounds of mutuality.[153] "A contract to mortgage property, real or personal, will, normally at least, be specifically enforceable, for a mere claim to damages or repayment is obviously less valuable than a security in the event of the debtor's insolvency".[154]

ii. Chattels of Especial Value

17–102 The Court of Chancery had always claimed jurisdiction to order the return of a specific chattel wrongly retained by another[155] (not properly a contractual claim) but, as rationalised by Lord Eldon,[156] its justification for so doing was that such chattels possessed a *pretium affectionis*[157] which could not be estimated in damages.[158] Extending that reasoning by one step in *Sky Petroleum Ltd v VIP Petroleum Ltd*,[159] part of which is reproduced below,[160] Goulding J. held that the court had jurisdiction to order specific performance of a contract to sell non-specific chattels in a case where the remedy of damages would be inadequate.

iii. Shares in a Private Limited Company

17–103 There being no readily available market in such shares, in light of the restriction on the transferability of shares in private companies and of the criminal prohibition in s.755 of the Companies Act 2006,[161] damages will normally be an inadequate remedy.[162]

iv. Contracts for Sale of Personal Property not within (ii) or (iii) above

17–104 Such contracts are not specifically enforceable so that, for example, contracts for the sale of shares in which there is a ready market, i.e. those of a quoted public company, and, indeed, any other contract[163] for the disposition of personal property, tangible or intangible, will not be specifically enforced unless it can be shown in the instant case that damages would not be an adequate remedy.[164] A

---

153 As in e.g. *Alchemy Estates Ltd v Astor* [2008] 3 E.G.L.R. 143. It follows that the vendor can "thrust the property down the purchaser's throat", per Lindley L.J. in *Hope v Walter* [1900] 1 Ch. 257 at 258. But, on mutuality, see below, para.17–109.

154 *Swiss Bank Corp v Lloyd's Bank Ltd* [1980] 2 All E.R. 419 at 425, per Buckley L.J.

155 *Pusey v Pusey* (1684) 1 Vern. 273 (an ancient horn, reputedly a gift of Canute).

156 *Nutbrown v Thornton* (1804) 10 Ves. 160 at 163.

157 Roughly, a "sentimental value".

158 *Falcke v Gray* (1859) 4 Dr. 651; *Thorn v Commissioners of Public Works* (1863) 32 Beav. 490 (stones from Old Westminster Bridge); *Phillips v Lamdin* [1949] 2 K.B. 33 (ornate Adam door). Damages would clearly be an inadequate remedy if an award would not enable the promisee to go into the market place and purchase a similar chattel. By definition it could not do so in cases of this sort. Note also that s.52 of the Sale of Goods Act 1979 enables the court, additionally, to decree specific performance of contracts for the sale of "specific or ascertained goods", i.e. identified and agreed upon when the contract is made. Neither under the statutory nor under the equitable jurisdictions (both being discretionary) will specific performance be decreed of contracts for the sale of "ordinary articles of commerce", even though specific or ascertained goods within the Act, as damages would be an adequate remedy: *Cohen v Roche* [1927] 1 K.B. 169 (set of Hepplewhite chairs); *Whiteley Ltd v Hilt* [1918] 2 K.B. 808, at 819. Inadequacy of damages seems, therefore, to be the touchstone.

159 [1974] 1 W.L.R. 576 (enforcement of obligation to supply petrol during petrol shortage, no alternative source available).

160 At paras 17–127 ff.

161 Prohibiting a private company (other than a company limited by guarantee and not having a share capital) from offering its securities to the public directly or indirectly.

162 See e.g. *Pena v Dale* [2004] 2 B.C.L.C. 508; *Gaetano Ltd v Obertor Ltd* [2009] EWHC 2653 (Ch) at [48].

163 Note, however, that in the case of contracts to assign choses in action there is no need (save for the purpose of perfecting legal title) to obtain specific performance at all, since an assignment for value operates without more as an assignment in equity on the principle that equity considers that done which ought to be done: per Lord Macnaghten in *Tailby v Official Receiver* (1888) App. Cas. 523 at 547–548. The operation of this principle does not depend on the specific enforceability of the contract to assign.

164 Additionally, a contract for the transfer of the goodwill of a business is too uncertain to enforce *in specie: Darbey v Whitaker* (1857) 4 Drew. 134 (unless premises or other business assets are contracted to be transferred with it). This appears to be an example of a contract sufficiently certain at law but not specifically enforceable for lack of certainty, an odd conclusion save that, for specific performance to lie, the court must be able to supervise the exact performance of the contract (per Lord Hardwicke L.C. in *Buxton v Lister* (1746) 3 Atk. 383 at 386). As imprisonment may result from non-compliance, this requirement is understandable.

contract to leave personal or real property by will is not enforceable directly (which would interfere with freedom of testamentary power) but a legatee who receives it in breach will be ordered to yield it up[165] and, before death of the testator, the promisee can obtain a declaration of right and an injunction restraining any inconsistent disposition.[166]

v. Contracts for Personal Services

17–105 Contracts of employment, by statute,[167] are not specifically enforceable. The equitable approach is illustrated by Fry L.J.'s comment in *De Francesco v Barnum*:[168] "The courts are bound to be jealous lest they should turn contracts of service into contracts of slavery". This approach applies to contracts of service not covered by the statute and any contract for personal services, but there seems to be no hard and fast rule.[169]

vi. Contracts to Pay Money

17–106 In *South African Territories Ltd v Wallington*,[170] a contract to make a loan was not specifically enforced because damages would be an adequate remedy. In *Beswick v Beswick,*[171] reproduced below,[172] the contract was to pay an annuity to a third party. It was enforced because damages would have been an inadequate remedy in the sense that either (i) damages awarded to the promisee would have been nominal or (ii) a multiplicity of suits might need to be brought if there were future breaches or (iii) the worth of an annuity, depending on the longevity of the annuitant, might be too conjectural to quantify.[173] It remains doubtful whether a promisee could obtain specific performance of a promise to pay a lump sum to a third party: if he could, it would require an English court to uphold (i) as a sufficient reason for enforcing a promise *in specie* and, moreover, one which the promisee could not have enforced for his own benefit.[174]

C. *Equity never Acts in Vain*

17–107 Equity never acts in vain and, therefore, it will not decree performance of the impossible or the futile. Therefore, a vendor of land who has wrongfully conveyed away the property will not be ordered to convey to a purchaser what he no longer has unless the transferee is, for example, a company controlled by the vendor and used as a crude device or sham to avoid specific performance.[175] Likewise,

---

165 *Synge v Synge* [1894] 1 Q.B. 466 (on the ground that he is a volunteer and takes subject to the equity).
166 *Schaefer v Schumann* [1972] A.C. 572 (Privy Council).
167 Trade Union and Labour Relations (Consolidation) Act 1992 s.236: "no court shall . . . by way of an order of specific performance . . . compel an employee to do any work or to attend at any place for the doing of any work."
168 (1890) 45 Ch.D. 430.
169 In *Giles (CH) & Co Ltd v Morris* [1972] 1 W.L.R. 307, Megarry J. denied that there was a rule preventing enforcement: it was, rather, a question of looking at the particular obligations in question. In *Hill v CA Parsons & Co Ltd* [1972] Ch. 305 the Court of Appeal by a majority enforced a contract for personal services in what were described as exceptional circumstances. See also *Lumley v Wagner* (1852) 1 De G.M. & G. 604, where a singer was prevented by injunction from breaching her promise to sing only at the plaintiff's theatre, effectively thereby being forced to sing for the plaintiff. This and other cases were reviewed in the Court of Appeal by Mance L.J in *Lady Navigation Inc v Lauritzencool AB* [2005] 2 All E.R. (Comm.) 183, where he concluded that there is no general rule that injunctive relief will be withheld if the practical effect would be to compel performance of a contract for personal services.
170 [1898] A.C. 309.
171 [1968] A.C. 58.
172 At paras 17–129.
173 But query: actuaries and judges in personal injury cases do it routinely.
174 Because in that case, damages clearly would be adequate. Note that it is not to be thought that the question whether such promise be specifically enforceable is an academic one. A defendant is at risk of imprisonment for failure to comply with a decree of specific performance but cannot nowadays (since abolition of debtors' prison) be gaoled for inability to pay a civil debt.
175 *Jones v Lipman* [1962] 1 W.L.R. 832.

an agreement for a lease which has already expired will not be enforced,[176] nor an agreement for a partnership not being of fixed duration,[177] nor an agreement to purchase property when the claimant has no funds to pay the purchase price.[178]

D. Illegality and Public Policy

17–108 A contract which is illegal is void and there is nothing to enforce, specifically or otherwise. A contract which is valid but which, if executed, might achieve some goal contrary to public policy might not be enforced specifically. *Wroth v Tyler*[179] provides a good example of this. In that case, a husband contracted to sell his property. After conclusion of the contract, his wife registered a charge against the property under the Matrimonial Homes Act 1967, which gave her the right (but no more than the right) not to be evicted. The purchasers sought either specific performance or damages in lieu. Specific performance was refused on the ground that if it were ordered, the purchasers would have to take the property subject to the wife's occupation. But they would be able to evict the husband and other members of the family. The splitting up of a family in that way would be an end contrary to public policy and so it was preferable for the purchasers to be awarded damages in lieu.

E. Mutuality

17–109 It used to be said that specific performance will not be granted to a promisee who could not himself be the subject of a decree,[180] i.e. all the obligations imposed by the contract upon the claimant promisee must themselves be specifically enforceable. This is the traditional statement of the requirement of mutuality. Fry's statement of it, which required mutuality at the time of entering into the contract (rather than it sufficing at the date of the hearing) was rejected in *Price v Strange*.[181] There Goff L.J. stated that "want of mutuality raises a question of the court's discretion to be exercised according to everything that has happened up to the decree" so that, "the court will grant specific performance if it can be done without injustice or unfairness to the defendant".[182] This might involve some payment to the defendant as in *Price*.[183] Where injustice can be avoided by the imposition of terms on the claimant or an award of damages to the defendant, a decree may be made. Indeed, since the decision in *Price*, there has been a steady academic and judicial retreat from the doctrine of mutuality as a coherent explanation for the outcome of older, decided cases or, indeed, as a sound objection as a matter of moral principle. This is to be welcomed, for it seems at times to have been used as a principle to justify the specific enforcement of

---

176 *Turner v Clowes* (1869) 20 L.T. 214 It might be otherwise if the lessee would derive some benefit by being granted legal rights under the lease: *Walters v Northern Coal Mining Board Co* (1855) 5 De G.M. & G. 629.

177 *Henry v Birch* (1804) 9 Ves. 357: either partner might dissolve it at will.

178 *Wilkie v Redsell* [2003] EWCA Civ 926.

179 [1974] Ch. 30.

180 *Flight v Bolland* (1828) 4 Russ. 298 (minor failing to obtain decree because, qua minor, suit could not be maintained against him).

181 [1978] 1 Ch. 337.

182 *Price* at 354. At 368–369 Buckley L.J. stated: "The court will not compel a defendant to perform his obligations specifically if it cannot at the same time ensure that any unperformed obligations of the plaintiff will be specifically performed unless, perhaps, damages would be an adequate remedy to the defendant for any default on the plaintiff's part." There is some tension between this finding and the HL's decision in *White & Carter (Councils) Ltd v McGregor* [1962] A.C. 413, that the court has no general equitable discretion to prevent the innocent party to a contract from forcing performance on to the other party and claiming payment. For discussion, see *Ministry of Sound (Ireland) Ltd v World Online Ltd* [2003] 2 All E.R. (Comm.) 823 at [67]–[72].

183 *Price* at 357.

certain types of contract (such as those for the disposition of land when, quite plainly, damages would be an adequate remedy for a vendor) and, capriciously, to deny the specific enforceability of others. In other words, it was serving a dual role in the case law. The judicial retreat from it must now be almost complete in light of the High Court's decision in *Rainbow Estates v Tokenhold Ltd*.[184]

A word of background explanation about this decision is necessary. A landlord's repairing covenant is enforceable by statute notwithstanding any equitable rule restricting the tenant's remedy "whether based on mutuality or otherwise".[185] This provision was enacted precisely because it was thought that repairing covenants were not specifically enforceable either because, the tenant's covenants not being so enforceable, the landlord's covenants could not be so for want of mutuality, or, alternatively, because of the need for constant supervision. The court in this case, however, decided that neither of these reasons had been the ratio of any decided case and, there being no reason in principle why a tenant's repairing covenant should not be specifically enforced (so long as oppression was avoided and the work required to be done was sufficiently defined[186]), the court in an appropriate case would order specific performance of a tenant's repairing covenant. The qualifications in parentheses would mean, however, that appropriate cases were rare. **17–110**

F. Entire Contracts Only

That the contract sought to be enforced *in specie* should be capable of being enforced in its entirety[187] is an old rule[188] but one which may now be more flexible. In *CH Giles & Co Ltd v Morris*,[189] a case where specific performance was sought of a contract for the sale of shares, one of the terms of which required the vendors to procure the appointment of a particular individual as managing director of the company, Megarry J. said "the court may refuse to let the disadvantages and difficulties of specifically enforcing the obligation to perform personal services outweigh the suitability of the rest of the contract for specific performance . . .".[190] Where the contract can properly be construed as two distinct contracts, specific performance may be obtained to enforce one of them.[191] **17–111**

G. The Need for Constant Supervision

Ryan v Mutual Tontine Westminster Chambers Association[192] holds that breach of a contract which would need constant supervision by the court if it were to be performed *in specie* will only sound in **17–112**

---

184 [1999] Ch. 64. See too *Bolkiah v Brunei Darussalam* [2007] UKPC 63 at [42] where Lord Scott laid particular stress on Buckley L.J.'s statement in *Price* at 369 that "considerations of mutuality go to discretion, not to jurisdiction".

185 Landlord and Tenant Act 1985 s.17.

186 On this last requirement see para.17–113.

187 Distinguish this requirement, which stresses the need for all of the defendant's obligations to be enforceable from the requirement of mutuality, which focuses on the (alleged) need for all the claimant's obligations to be enforceable against him.

188 *Ogden v Fossick* (1862) 4 De G.F. & J. 426.

189 [1972] 1 W.L.R. 307. See too *Rainbow Estates Ltd v Tokenhold Ltd* [1997] Ch. 64 at 73; *Internet Trading Clubs Ltd v Freeserve (Investments) Ltd* [2001] E.B.L.R. 142 at [30] per Tomkinson J., considering *Odessa Tramways Co v Mendel* (1878) 8 Ch.D. 235.

190 *Giles* at 317–318.

191 e.g. *Lewin v Guest* (1826) 1 Russ. 325 (Separate contracts to purchase two plots; purchaser obliged to take one plot even though vendor could not show title to other). It would be otherwise where, e.g., a vendor knew that from purchaser's point of view the purchases were interdependent: *Poole v Shergold* (1786) 1 Cox Eq. Cas. 273.

192 [1893] 1 Ch. 116 (lessor's covenant to provide resident porter who would always be in attendance at block of flats). See also *Dowty Boulton Paul Ltd v Wolverhampton Corporation* [1971] 2 All E.R. 277 (mandatory injunction refused to enforce covenant to maintain aerodrome for period of over 60 years: same principle applied).

damages. In *Posner v Scott-Lewis*,[193] however, Mervyn Davies J. at a tenant's request, and on facts difficult to distinguish from *Ryan*, made an order against the landlord for the appointment of a resident porter whom the landlord had covenanted to employ for the purpose of carrying out certain duties at a block of flats: he found that there was a sufficient definition of what had to be done in order to comply with the order of the court. The more recent and important case of *Co-operative Insurance Society Ltd v Argyll Stores (Holdings) Ltd*,[194] which is reproduced below,[195] provided the House of Lords with the opportunity to review and reconcile the authorities clustered around this principle. In that case the tenant (owners of Safeway supermarkets) had given a covenant to keep the demised premises open for retail trade during normal business hours. The tenant was the anchor-tenant in a new shopping mall in Hillsborough but had made a decision, based on national performance, to close all of its loss-making stores of which the demised premises were one. The tenant was content to pay damages for breach but resisted an order for specific performance. The Court of Appeal, by a majority,[196] granted a decree which the House of Lords discharged.

17–113 Lord Hoffmann, speaking for the whole court, approved a long line of authority to the effect that the court will not order anyone to run a business. He examined the normal reason for this: the need for constant supervision. In *CH Giles & Co v Morris* Megarry J.[197] had suggested that difficulties of supervision were "a narrow consideration": performance would normally be secured by the defendant's realisation that he is liable to contempt for failure to obey the order and, therefore, there would in practice be little need for the court to "supervise". This kind of consideration had been relied on by the Court of Appeal to justify its order. The House, however, distinguished between orders to carry on an activity, such as running a business over time, and orders requiring a defendant merely to achieve a result. In the former case, the risk of repeated, expensive and cumbersome applications to the court for guidance is much higher than in the latter: even if the result which the court has ordained that the defendant shall bring about is a complex thing (such as erecting a building in accordance with complex plans) the court will still only have to rule once, after the fact, to say whether or not there has been compliance. If a defendant, on the other hand, were ordered to run a retail grocery business during ordinary business hours, there might be innumerable applications. It was with this distinction in mind, said Lord Hoffmann, that courts had in the past ordered the specific performance of repairing covenants and building contracts. What the courts had been prepared to do in those cases (of orders to achieve a result) was not to be confused with the approach to orders to carry on an activity. That was where the majority in the Court of Appeal had fallen into error.[198]

H. Delay or Laches

17–114 There being no statutory limit on the time after which a claim for specific performance may be brought[199] equitable considerations govern and may deprive a claimant of the right to performance *in*

193 [1987] Ch. 25.
194 [1998] A.C. 1.
195 At paras 17–184 ff.
196 [1996] Ch. 286 (Millett L.J. forcefully dissenting).
197 [1972] 1 W.L.R. 307.
198 In a Scottish case with essentially identical facts, *Highland & Universal Properties Ltd v Safeway Properties Ltd* [2000] 3 E.G.L.R. 110, the Inner House granted specific implement of the defender's obligation to keep its premises open, noting that Scots law differs from English law in this area, but suggesting that in *Argyll Stores* Lord Hoffmann overstated the difficulties of superintending orders to carry on an activity in cases of this kind.
199 Limitation Act 1980 s.36. Nor do the Limitation Acts apply by analogy: *Talmash v Mugleston* (1826) 4 L.J.O.S. Ch. 200.

specie where there is delay either sufficient to be evidence of the plaintiff's abandonment of the contract,[200] or coupled with circumstances which make it unjust to order specific performance.[201]

I. Lack of Clean Hands

If the claimant is guilty of some impropriety connected to the contract[202] he may be disentitled to an equitable remedy. The jurisdiction of the court to consider this matter cannot be ousted by agreement.[203] However, this last point was decided in a case where a clause in a sale agreement, which provided that the consideration was to be paid in cash "free from any equity cross-claim set-off or other deduction whatsoever", was held not to prevent the purchaser from raising an unclean hands defence. This was for the reason that the wording was not apt to exclude such a claim but alternatively for the reason that, even if it had been apt, "it could not have the effect of fettering the discretion of the court. Once the court is asked for the equitable remedy of specific performance, its discretion cannot be fettered".[204] Although defensible on its own, this decision does not sit easily with the long-established practice[205] of parties contracting that a particular obligation, if breached, shall "sound only in damages". This is just as much an attempt to oust the discretionary jurisdiction of the court to award a specific remedy. Perhaps all that can be said about it is that it is not, all other things being equal, an objectionable one. **17–115**

J. Undue Hardship

Specific performance may be refused if hardship will be caused to either of the parties or a third party.[206] The decisions in individual cases tend to turn on the facts (see, for an example, *Wroth v Tyler*,[207] which is reproduced below[208]). Although there is Commonwealth authority requiring the hardship to have existed at the date of contract,[209] in England it has been held that specific performance could be refused on the ground of hardship arising after contract.[210] **17–116**

---

200 *Parkin v Thorold* (1852) 16 Beav. 59 at 73. The claimant will still have his legal remedy.

201 *Lindsay Petroleum Co v Hurd* (1874) L.R. 5 P.C. 221. Where the plaintiff took possession and waited 10 years before seeking a decree to have the legal title vested in him, mere delay with no injustice to the defendant was no bar: *Williams v Greatrex* [1957] 1 W.L.R. 31. See too *Ridgeway Motors (Isleworth) Ltd v Michael* Ch.D. June 13, 1996 (claim for SP after 17 years struck out for laches); *Yewbelle Ltd v London Green Developments Ltd* [2007] 1 E.G.L.R. 137 at [92], where Lewison J. held that "In cases where the contract in question concerns land to be exploited for commercial purposes, the period of delay that can lead to the refusal of specific performance may be comparatively short."

202 *Moody v Cox* [1917] 2 Ch. 71 at 87–88; *van Gestel v Cann, The Times*, August 7, 1987 (claim that plaintiff guilty of fraud unconnected with contract of no assistance to defendant).

203 *Quadrant Visual Communications Ltd v Hutchison Telephone (UK) Ltd* [1993] B.C.L.C. 442.

204 [1993] B.C.L.C. 442 at 451.

205 Endorsed by the Court of Appeal in *Co-operative Insurance Society Ltd v Argyll Stores (Holdings) Ltd*, above and not criticised on this point by the House of Lords.

206 *Thomas v Dering* (1837) 1 Keen 729 at 747–748.

207 [1974] Ch. 30. Other situations include: trustee vendors, contractually obliged to discharge personally incumbrances on property, relieved from so doing as purchase price insufficient to cover secured amounts (*Wedgwood v Adams* (1843) 6 Beav. 600); purchaser not obliged to take property which had no right of access, so no possibility of enjoyment (*Denne v Light* (1857) 8 De G.M. & G. 774).

208 At paras 17–142 ff.

209 e.g. *Nicholas v Ingram* [1958] N.Z.L.R. 972.

210 *Patel v Ali* [1984] Ch. 283 at 288 (husband and wife vendors; husband bankrupted, causing delay; wife seriously ill; young children; wife dependent on proximity of relatives so moving difficult).

K. *Breach of Contract*

17–117 It is a well-established principle that the court will not grant a decree if compliance with it would involve the defendant in breach of a prior contract (or, indeed, trust).[211]

L. *Set-Off*

17–118 In *BICC Plc v Burndy Corp*[212] the Court of Appeal accepted by a majority that a right of equitable set-off (where a defendant seeks to defend a claim on the basis that the plaintiff is liable, under a related cross-claim, to him in a sum equal to or greater than the claim made by the plaintiff) could stand as a complete defence to a claim by a plaintiff not merely for a debt but also for specific performance.

M. *Mistake and Misrepresentation*

17–119 A contract which is not avoidable in equity for mistake or misrepresentation might sound only in damages if, owing to misrepresentation or (even unilateral) mistake, performance *in specie* would involve real hardship for the defendant amounting to injustice.[213]

N. *Misdescription of Subject-Matter*

17–120 Although the authorities on this relate to sales of land the principles ought to apply to contracts for the disposition of personalty which are otherwise specifically enforceable. A misdescription in the contract will amount to a breach because the vendor cannot then convey what he has contracted to convey. Quite apart from the common law rules determining the rights of an innocent party equity developed the following rules[214] to deal specifically with this kind of breach when a question arose, assuming the contract was not discharged at law, whether it should be performed *in specie*.

17–121 If the misdesription is substantial so that the purchaser does not get what he wanted, i.e. but for the misdescription he would never have contracted at all, then the vendor cannot enforce either at law or in equity even with abatement of price.[215] If insubstantial, the vendor can enforce though with abatement of price by way of compensation.[216] Whether substantial or not, the purchaser can enforce and take whatever the vendor has and secure an abatement.[217]

---

211 *Harvela Investments Ltd v Royal Trust Co of Canada Ltd* [1985] Ch. 103 at 122.

212 [1985] Ch. 232.

213 *Tamplin v James* (1880) 15 Ch.D. 215 (land correctly described in plans, not consulted by purchaser; purchaser obliged to buy despite unilateral error in thinking adjacent land included. No injustice.) cf. *Denny v Hancock* (1870) 6 Ch. App. 1 (similar error was caused by vendor's unsatisfactory plans: no decree). See also *Riverlate Properties v Paul* [1975] Ch. 133; *Geest Plc v Fyffes Plc* Q.B.D. (Comm. Ct.) March 23, 1998.

214 Applicable to open contracts. In practice, parties to contracts for the sale of land use Standard Conditions which moderate the position. These, however, are subject to the Unfair Contract Terms Act 1977 and to a judicial reluctance to allow parties to escape their equitable duties, e.g. *Rignall Developments Ltd v Halil* [1988] Ch. 190.

215 *Flight v Booth* (1834) 1 Bing. N.C. 370; *Walker v Boyle* [1982] 1 W.L.R. 495

216 *Jacobs v Revell* [1900] 2 Ch. 858; *Bechal v Kitsford Holdings Ltd* [1989] 1 W.L.R. 105.

217 *Rutherford v Acton-Adams* [1915] A.C. 866 at 870.

ADDERLEY v DIXON

High Court of Chancery (1824) 1 Sim. & St. 607

The claimants took assignments of certain debts which had been proven in the estates of two bankrupts. This entitled them to whatever dividend might be declared on the debts in the bankruptcy. The claimants then contracted to sell their rights under the assignments for 2 shillings and sixpence in the pound to the defendant. The claimants sought specific performance of the purchaser's obligation to pay the price. **17–122**

SIR JOHN LEACH V.C.: Courts of Equity decree the specific performance of contracts not upon any distinction between realty and personalty, but because damages at law may not in the particular case, afford a complete remedy. Thus a Court of Equity decrees performance of a contract for land, not because of the real nature of the land, but because damages at law, which must be calculated upon the general money value of land, may not be a complete remedy to the purchaser, to whom the land may have a peculiar and special value. So a Court of Equity will not, generally, decree performance of a contract for the sale of stock or goods, not because of their personal nature, but because damages at law, calculated upon the market price of the stock or goods, are as complete a remedy to the purchaser as the delivery of the stock or goods contracted for; inasmuch as, with the damages, he may purchase the same quantity of the like stock or goods. **17–123**

In *Taylor v Neville*, cited in *Buxton v Lister*,[218] specific performance was decreed of a contract for sale of 800 tons of iron, to be delivered and paid for in a certain number of years and by instalments; and the reason given by Lord Hardwicke is that such sort of contracts differ from those that are immediately to be executed and they do differ in this respect, that the profit upon the contract, being to depend upon future events, cannot be correctly estimated in damages where the calculation must proceed upon conjecture. In such a case, to compel a party to accept damages for the non-performance of his contract, is to compel him to sell the actual profit which may arise from it, at a conjectural price. In *Ball v Coggs*,[219] specific performance was decreed in the House of Lords of a contract to pay the plaintiff a certain annual sum for his life, and also a certain other sum for every hundred weight of brass wire manufactured by the defendant during the life of the plaintiff. The same principle is to be applied to this case. Damages might be no complete remedy, being to be calculated merely by conjecture; and to compel the plaintiff in such a case to take damages would be to compel him to sell the annual provision during his life for which he had contracted at a conjectural price. In *Buxton v Lister* Lord Hardwicke puts the case of a ship carpenter purchasing timber which was peculiarly convenient to him by reason of its vicinity; and also the case of an owner of land covered with timber contracting to sell his timber in order to clear his land; and assumes that as, in both those cases, damages would not, by reason of the special circumstances, be a complete remedy, equity would decree specific performance. **17–124**

The present case being a contract for the sale of the uncertain dividends which may become payable from the estates of the two bankrupts, it appears to me that, upon the principle established by the cases of *Ball v Coggs* and *Taylor v Neville*, a Court of Equity will decree specific performance, because damages at law cannot accurately represent the value of the future dividends; and to compel this purchaser to take such damages would be to compel him to sell these dividends at a conjectural price. **17–125**

It is true that the present bill is not filed by the purchaser, but by the vendor, who seeks, not the uncertain dividends, but the certain sum to be paid for them. It has, however, been settled, by repeated decision, that the remedy in equity must be mutual; and that, where a bill will lie for the purchaser, it will also lie for the vendor. **17–126**

---

218 (1746) 3 Atk. 383 at 384.

219 (1710) 1 Bro. P.C. 140.

SKY PETROLEUM LTD v VIP PETROLEUM LTD

Chancery Division [1974] 1 W.L.R. 576, [1974] 1 All E.R. 954

17–127 The claimants had contracted to purchase all their petrol, at fixed prices, from the defendants. During a petrol shortage the defendants purported to terminate the contract on the ground of breach of certain credit provisions therein by the claimants. Pending trial of that issue, the claimants sought an injunction to restrain the defendants from withholding supplies.

17–128 GOULDING J.: What I have to decide is whether any injunction should be granted to protect the plaintiffs in the meantime. There is trade evidence that the plaintiffs have no great prospect of finding any alternative source of supply for the filling stations which constitute their business. The defendants have indicated their willingness to continue to supply the plaintiffs, but only at prices which, according to the plaintiffs' evidence, would not be serious prices from a commercial point of view. There is, in my judgment, so far as I can make out on the evidence before me, a serious danger that unless the court interferes at this stage the plaintiffs will be forced out of business. In those circumstances, unless there is some specific reason which debars me from doing so, I should be disposed to grant an injunction to restore the former position under the contract until the rights and wrongs of the parties can be fully tried out. The most serious hurdle in the way of the plaintiffs is the well known doctrine that the court refuses specific performance of a contract to sell and purchase chattels not specific or ascertained. That is a well-established and salutary rule, and I am entirely unconvinced by Mr Christie, for the plaintiffs, when he tells me that an injunction in the form sought by him would not be specific enforcement at all. The matter is one of substance and not of form, and it is, in my judgment quite plain that I am, for the time being, specifically enforcing the contract if I grant an injunction. However, the ratio behind the rule is, as I believe, that under the ordinary contract for the sale of non-specific goods, damages are a sufficient remedy. That, to my mind, is lacking in the circumstances of the present case. The evidence suggests, and indeed it is common knowledge that the petroleum market is in an unusual state in which a would-be buyer cannot go out into the market and contract with another seller, possibly at some sacrifice as to price. Here, the defendants appear for practical purposes to be the plaintiffs' sole means of keeping their business going, and I am prepared so far to depart from the general rule as to try to preserve the position under the contract until a later date. I therefore propose to grant an injunction.

BESWICK v BESWICK

House of Lords [1968] A.C. 58, [1967] 3 W.L.R. 932, [1967] 2 All E.R. 1197

17–129 Peter Beswick agreed with his nephew to transfer to him his business in consideration of the nephew's (a) employing Peter as a consultant for life and (b) paying thereafter to Peter's widow an annuity at the rate of £5 per week for life. Peter died and the nephew refused to make any payments to the widow but the first. She sued for specific performance in her capacity as administratix of Peter's estate and in her personal capacity. The House unanimously rejected her personal claim as a *ius quaesitum tertio* but allowed her representative claim.

17–130 LORD UPJOHN (with whom LORD PEARCE, LORD REID, LORD HODSON and LORD GUEST concurred): As it is necessary to keep clear and distinct the right of the widow as administratix of her husband and personally, I think it will be convenient to use letters: letter A represents the deceased and A1 the widow, as personal representative. B the widow in her personal capacity and C the appellant. And in other examples I shall give, these letters will serve the same purpose.

17–131 Much is common ground between the parties: (1) B was not a party to the agreement: (2) A did not enter into the agreement as trustee for B in relation to the annuity to be paid to her; (3) A1 stands for all relevant purposes in the shoes of A and is entitled to sue C for breach of his admitted repudiation of the agreement (see paragraph 5 of the defence), but the parties differ fundamentally as to the remedy to which A1 is entitled in such an action. . . .

Leaving section 56 out of account, there was no real dispute between the parties as to their respective rights (as distinct from remedies) under the agreement. (a) B has no rights thereunder. But it was clear from the whole tenor of the agreement that the annuity was to be paid to her for her own beneficial enjoyment, so if C paid it to her she could keep it and did not hold it as a constructive trustee for A1; (b) C would completely perform his obligation under the contract by continuing to pay the annuity to B during her life. Neither A nor A1 could compel C to pay it to A or A1, but (c) A or A1 and C could, if they pleased, agree to modify, compromise or even discharge further performance of the contract by C, and B would have no right to complain. If authority be wanted for these fundamental propositions, it is to be found in *Re Schebsman*[220] and *Re Stapleton-Bretherton*.[221] **17–132**

But when A dies and his rights pass to A1, it is said that the remedy of specific performance is no longer appropriate against C. The argument was first that the estate of A suffered no damage by reason of C's failure to pay B, so A1 is entitled to nominal damages but as she is not otherwise interested in the agreement as such it would be wrong to grant specific performance; for that remedy is available only where damages will be an inadequate remedy. Here nominal damages are adequate. Further, it was argued, to do so would really be to confer upon B a right which she does not have in law or equity to receive the annuity. Then, secondly, it was said that if the remedy of specific performance is granted it might prejudice creditors of A so that the parties ought to be left to their strict rights at law. Thirdly, it is said that there are procedural difficulties in the way of enforcing an order for specific performance in favour of a third party. I will deal with these points, though in reverse order. **17–133**

As to procedural difficulties, I fear I do not understand the argument. The point if valid applies to an action for specific performance by A just as much as by A1 yet in the authorities I have quoted no such point was ever taken; in *Drimmie v Davies*[222] indeed the action was by executors. Further, it seems to me that if C fails to obey a four-day order obtained by A1, B could enforce it under the clear and express provisions of RSC Ord.45 r.9 (formerly Ord.42 r.26). Alternatively A1 could move for and obtain the appointment of a receiver of the business upon which the annuity is charged and the receiver would then be directed by the Court to pay the annuity to B out of the profits of the business. Finally, A1 could issue a writ of fi. fa. under Ord.45 r.1, but as A1 would then be enforcing the contract and not modifying or compromising it the court would obviously in executing its order compel her to carry out the contract *in toto* and hand the proceeds of execution to B. This point is entirely without substance. **17–134**

Then as to the second point. Let me assume (contrary to the fact) that A died with substantial assets but also many creditors. The legal position is that prima facie the duty of A1 is to carry out her intestate's contracts and compel C to pay B; but the creditors may be pressing and the agreement may be considered onerous; so it may be her duty to try and compromise the agreement with C and save something for the estate even at the expense of B.[223] So be it, but how can C conceivably rely upon this circumstance as a defence by him to an action for specific performance by A1? Of course not; he, C, has no interest in the estate; he cannot plead a possible jus tertii which is no concern of his. It is his duty to fulfil his contract by paying C. A1 alone is concerned with the creditors, beneficiaries or next of kin of A and this point therefore can never be a defence by C if A1 in fact chooses to sue for specific performance rather than to attempt a compromise in the interest of the estate. This point seems to me misconceived. In any event, on the facts of this case there is no suggestion that there are any unpaid creditors and B is sole next of kin, so the point is academic. **17–135**

Then, as to the first point. On this question we were referred to the well-known dictum of Lush L.J. in *Lloyd's v Harper*:[224] **17–136**

> "I consider it to be an established rule of law that where a contract is made with A for the benefit of B, A can sue on the contract for the benefit of B and recover all that B could have recovered if the contract had been made with B himself."

While in the circumstances it is not necessary to express any concluded opinion thereon, if the learned Lord Justice was expressing a view on the purely common law remedy of damages, I have some difficulty

---

[220] [1944] Ch. 83.
[221] [1941] Ch. 482.
[222] [1899] 1 Ir. R. 176.
[223] See *Ahmed Angullia v Estate & Trust Agencies (1927) Ltd* [1938] A.C. 624 at 632, per Lord Romer.
[224] (1880) 16 Ch.D. 290 at 321.

in going all the way with him. If A sues for damages for breach of contract by reason of the failure to pay B he must prove his loss; that may be great or nominal according to circumstances.

17–137 I do not see how A can, in conformity with clearly settled principle in assessing damages for breach of contract, rely at common law on B's loss. I agree with the observations of Windeyer J, in . . . *Coulls v Bagot's Executor and Trustee Co Ltd*[225] in the High Court of Australia. But I note, however, that in *Lloyd's v Harper*[226] James and Cotton L.JJ. treated A as trustee for B and I doubt whether Lush L.J. thought otherwise.

17–138 However, I incline to the view that on the facts of this case damages are nominal for it appears that A died without any assets save and except the agreement which he hoped would keep him and then his widow for their lives. At all events let me assume that damages are nominal. So it is said nominal damages are adequate and the remedy of specific performance ought not to be granted. That is, with all respect, wholly to misunderstand that principle. Equity will grant specific performance when damages are inadequate to meet the justice of the case.

17–139 But in any event quantum of damages seldom affects the right to specific performance. If X contracts with Y to buy Blackacre or a rare chattel for a fancy price because the property or chattel has caught his fancy he is entitled to enforce his bargain and it matters not that he could not prove any damage.

17–140 In this case the court ought to grant a specific performance order all the more because damages are nominal. C has received all the property: justice demands that he pay the price and this can only be done in the circumstances by equitable relief. It is a fallacy to suppose that B is thereby obtaining additional rights: A1 is entitled to compel C to carry out the terms of the agreement. The observations of Holmes L.J. already quoted are very much in point.

17–141 My Lords, in my opinion the Court of Appeal were clearly right to grant a decree of specific performance. . . .

WROTH v TYLER

Chancery Division [1974] Ch. 30, [1973] 2 W.L.R. 405

17–142 The defendant contracted to sell his property to the claimants for £6,000. The next day, the defendant's wife registered a charge against the property under the Matrimonial Homes Act 1967 which gave her the right not to be evicted or excluded from the property. She refused to remove the charge and the defendant told the claimants he could not complete. The claimants sought specific performance or damages in lieu. The property was worth £7,500 at the date fixed for completion and £11,500 at the date of the hearing.

17–143 MEGARRY J.: The issues before me may be summarised as follows. (1) Delay apart, are the plaintiffs entitled to specific performance of the contract with vacant possession? If they are, a form of order is sought that will require the defendant to make an application to the court for an order against his wife terminating her rights of occupation under the Matrimonial Homes Act 1967 in accordance with section 1(2). (2) Delay apart, are the plaintiffs, as an alternative, entitled to specific performance of the contract subject to the rights of occupation of the defendant's wife, with damages or an abatement of the purchase price in respect thereof? If they are, they will be able to make the application to the court under the Act of 1967, by virtue of section 1(2) and section 2(3). (3) If, apart from delay, the plaintiffs would be entitled to an order for specific performance under either of these two heads, is their right to it barred by delay? (4) If the plaintiffs have no right to specific performance, then it is common ground that they are entitled to damages. There is, however, an acute conflict as to the measure of damages. . . .

17–144 The defendant says that the damages must be assessed as at the date of the breach, in accordance with the normal rule: the plaintiffs says that this is a case where damages must be assessed as at the date of assessment, that is, today, if I assess the damages. . . . Damages assessed as at the date of breach would be £1,500, but as at the date of the hearing would be £5,500. At which figure should damages for the loss of the bargain be assessed? The defendant says that the former figure applies, in accordance with the

[225] (1967) 40 A.L.J.R. 471.
[226] (1880) 16 Ch.D. 290 at 315, 317.

general rule, but the plaintiffs say that the latter figure applies, for unless it does, they will be unable to acquire an equivalent house at today's prices. . . .

I may summarise my conclusions as to the essentials of the right given by the Act to an occupying 17–145
spouse as follows. The right is in essence a personal and non-assignable statutory right not to be evicted from the matrimonial home in question during marriage or until the court otherwise orders; and this right constitutes a charge on the estate or interest of the owning spouse which requires protection against third parties by registration. For various reasons, the right may be said to be one which readily fits into no category known to conveyancers before 1967; the phrase sui generis seems apt, but of little help.

With that in mind, I turn to the first question before me. Delay apart, are the plaintiffs entitled to spe- 17–146
cific performance of the contract with vacant possession? If they are, the form of order sought will require the defendant to make an application to the court under section 1(2) to terminate his wife's rights of occupation which arose and became a charge on the defendant's estate on January 1, 1968, and were protected by registration on May 28, 1971. . . .

It seems to me that where a third party has some rights over the property to be sold, there are at least 17–147
three categories of cases. First, there are those cases where the vendor is entitled as of right to put an end to the rights of the third party, or compel his concurrence or co-operation in the sale. Second, and at the other extreme, there are cases where the vendor has no right to put an end to the third party's rights, or compel his concurrence or co-operation in the sale, and can do no more than to try to persuade him to release his rights or to concur in the sale.

A vendor must do his best to obtain any necessary consent to the sale; if he has sold with vacant possession 17–148
he must, if necessary, take proceedings to obtain possession from any person in possession who has no right to be there or whose right is determinable by the vendor, at all events if the vendor's right to possession is reasonably clear; but I do not think that the vendor will usually be required to embark upon difficult or uncertain litigation in order to secure any requisite consent or obtain vacant possession. Where the outcome of any litigation depends upon disputed facts, difficult questions of law, or the exercise of a discretionary jurisdiction, then I think the court would be slow to make a decree of specific performance against the vendor which would require him to undertake such litigation. In such a case, the vendor cannot know where the litigation will end. If he succeeds at first instance, the defendant may carry him to appeal; if he fails at first instance, the purchaser may say that there ought to be an appeal. No doubt the line between simple and difficult cases will sometimes be hard to draw; and it may be that specific performance will be readily decreed only where it is plain that the requisite consent is obtainable without difficulty. The form of decree appropriate to such cases might specifically require the defendant to undertake such litigation; the court moulds the decree as need be. But it may be that the court will do no more than direct the defendant to procure the requisite consent.[227]

In the present case the defendant has endeavoured to persuade his wife to concur in the sale, but has 17–149
failed. It is true that after the failure of his initial attempt on the Friday night he then instructed his solicitors to withdraw from both the sale and his Norfolk purchase; but he again tried to persuade his wife on the Sunday, and there is some evidence of later attempts. As the evidence stands, I think that the defendant has sufficiently attempted to obtain her consent, short of litigation. The mere fact that he sought to withdraw from the contract before he had made all his attempts does not seem to me to make much difference; if a later attempt had succeeded, he could still have completed at the date fixed for completion.

Persuasion having failed, I think that the court should be slow to grant a decree of specific performance 17–150
that would require an unwilling husband to make an application to the court under section 1(2) of the Act of 1967, particularly as the decision of the court depends upon the application of phrases such as "just and reasonable" under section 1(3). In any case, the court would be reluctant to make an order which requires a husband to take legal proceedings against his wife, especially while they are still living together. Accordingly, although this is a contract of a type which the court is normally ready to enforce by a decree of specific performance, in my judgment it would, in Lord Redesdale L.C.'s phrase, be "highly unreasonable" to make such a decree if there is any other form of order that could do justice; and that I must consider in due course. Let me add that I would certainly not regard proceedings under the Act by the defendant against his wife as being without prospect of success. As the evidence stands (and of course I have not heard the defendant's wife) there is at least a real prospect of success for the defendant. He does not in any way seek to deprive his wife

[227] See *Long v Bowring* (1864) 33 Beav. 585; *Seton's Judgments and Orders*, 7th edn (1912), p.2204.

of a home; the difference between them is a difference as to where the matrimonial home is to be. In that, the conduct of the wife towards the plaintiffs and the defendant must play a substantial part.

17–151 In turn to the second main question, that of Mr Blackburne's alternative claim to specific performance for which he contended if he failed in his main claim to specific performance, and if he also was limited to damages assessed as at the date of the breach. This alternative claim was for specific performance of the contract, but with the plaintiffs taking subject to the charge in favour of the defendant's wife, and receiving damages or an abatement of the purchase money. By virtue of section 2(3) of the Act of 1967, section 1(2) to (5) would apply to the plaintiffs as they apply to the defendant, in that the plaintiffs would be persons deriving title under the defendant, and affected by the charge. If the plaintiffs took subject to the charge in favour of the defendant's wife, the result would be remarkable, for reasons which I have already indicated. The defendant has no rights of occupation under the Act, for his right of occupation stems from his estate in the land, and so section 1(1) of the Act gives him no statutory rights of occupation. The defendant's daughter has no rights of occupation under the Act, for the Act does not purport to confer such rights on anyone except a spouse. The defendant's wife alone has statutory rights of occupation, and on the facts of this case, these are expressed as being no more than "a right not to be evicted or excluded from the dwelling house or any part thereof". It has not been contended that this language is wide enough to empower the wife to authorise others to occupy the house with her, so that on that footing the plaintiffs, after completion, would be unable to evict the wife without an order of the court made under the Act, whereas the defendant and the daughter would have no defence to proceedings to evict them.

17–152 There seems to be considerable force in the contention that this would be the result. Neither the defendant nor the daughter would have any rights of their own to remain in the house, and what the statute gives the wife is not a positive right of occupation, whether a licence or otherwise, but a mere negative right not to be evicted or excluded. A person who is given a positive right of occupation might be envisaged as having been given the right to permit others to occupy with him or her: but a mere negative right not to be evicted or excluded cannot so readily be construed in this sense. . . .

17–153 If one leaves the position of the children on one side as being debatable, there remains the position of the defendant vis-à-vis the plaintiffs. Even if the wife not only is protected against eviction or exclusion, but also has the right to permit others to occupy the dwelling with her, the defendant has contracted to give vacant possession to the plaintiffs. Could he, then, in breach of his contract, remain in occupation under cover of his wife's statutory right not to be evicted or excluded? Would a decree of specific performance of the contract subject only to his wife's statutory rights in effect be nugatory as to his contractual obligation not himself to remain in occupation but to give vacant possession? The Act seems to me to have created much doubt and uncertainty in this sphere, but there is at least a real possibility that a decree of specific performance subject to the wife's right not to be evicted or excluded would enable the plaintiffs, by taking suitable proceedings, to evict the defendant and perhaps the daughter, and thus split up the family. These circumstances seem to me to make the case one in which the court should be slow to decree specific performance if any reasonable alternative exists. I shall accordingly turn to the question of damages to see whether they would provide the plaintiffs with an adequate remedy. . . .

17–154 [He then held that the measure of damages perhaps at common law but certainly in lieu of specific performance was to be assessed at the date of judgments and so awarded £5,500 damages; *Johnson v Agnew*, which is reproduced immediately below, now makes it clear that in many cases common law and equitable damages have the same measure (but note the discussion at paras 17–213 below).]

JOHNSON v AGNEW

House of Lords [1980] A.C. 367, [1979] 2 W.L.R. 487

17–155 The claimants, in arrears of mortgage, contracted to sell their properties to the defendant at a price in excess of the amount owing on mortgage and sufficient to allow them to purchase another property. The defendant failed to complete and an order for specific performance was made. Before it was carried out the claimants' mortgagees enforced their securities so that (a) the claimants could no longer convey the properties and (b) there was insufficient even to pay off the mortgages, let alone purchase another property with the proceeds. The claimants therefore sought an order that the defendant should pay the purchase price, less the moneys received on the mortgagees' sales, and an inquiry as to damages.

LORD WILBERFORCE (with whom LORD SALMON, LORD FRASER, LORD KEITH and LORD SCARMAN agreed): My Lords, this appeal arises in a vendors' action for specific performance of a contract for the sale of land, the appellant being the purchaser and the vendors respondents. The factual situation is commonplace, indeed routine. An owner of land contracts to sell it to a purchaser; the purchaser fails to complete the contract; the vendor goes to the court and obtains an order that the contract be specifically performed; the purchaser still does not complete; the vendor goes back to the court and asks for the order for specific performance to be dissolved, for the contract to be terminated or "rescinded", and for an order for damages. One would think that the law as to so typical a set of facts would be both simple and clear. It is no credit to our law that it is neither. . . . **17–156**

By April 3, 1975, specific performance of the contract for sale had become impossible. The vendors took no action upon the order for specific performance [entered on November 26, 1974] until November 5, 1976, when they issued a notice of motion seeking (a) an order that the purchaser should pay the balance of the purchase price and an inquiry as to damages or (b) alternatively a declaration that they were entitled to treat the contract as repudiated by the purchaser and to forfeit the deposit and an inquiry as to damages. **17–157**

On February 25, 1977, Megarry V.C. dismissed the motion. He rejected the first claim on the ground that, as specific performance was no longer possible, it would be unjust to order payment of the full purchase price. The second claim was not pressed, on the ground that it was precluded by authority: *Capital and Suburban Properties Ltd v Swycher*.[228] **17–158**

The vendors appealed to the Court of Appeal who again rejected each alternative: they followed the previous decision in *Swycher's case*. However they held that the vendors could recover damages under the Chancery Amendment Act 1858 (Lord Cairns' Act), which enables the court to award damages in addition to or in substitution for specific performance. They accordingly made an order discharging the order for specific performance and an order for an inquiry as to damages. They fixed the date on which damages should be assessed as November 26, 1974, being the date of entry of the order for specific performance. The purchaser is now appealing against this order. **17–159**

In this situation it is possible to state at least some uncontroversial propositions of law. **17–160**

First, in a contract for the sale of land, after time has been made, or has become, of the essence of the contract, if the purchaser fails to complete, the vendor can either treat the purchaser as having repudiated the contract, accept the repudiation, and proceed to claim damages for breach of the contract, both parties being discharged from further performance of the contract; or he may seek from the court an order for specific performance with damages for any loss arising from delay in performance. (Similar remedies are of course available of purchasers against vendors.) This is simply the ordinary law of contract applied to contracts capable of specific performance. **17–161**

Secondly, the vendor may proceed by action for the above remedies (viz., specific performance or damages) in the alternative. At the trial he will however have to elect which remedy to pursue. **17–162**

Thirdly, if the vendor treats the purchaser as having repudiated the contract and accepts the repudiation, he cannot thereafter seek specific performance. This follows from the fact that, the purchaser having repudiated the contract and his repudiation having been accepted, both parties are discharged from further performance. **17–163**

At this point it is important to dissipate a fertile source of confusion and to make clear that although the vendor is sometimes referred to in the above situation as "rescinding" the contract, this so-called "rescission" is quite different from rescission ab initio, such as may arise for example in cases of mistake, fraud or lack of consent. In those cases, the contract is treated in law as never having come into existence. (Cases of a contractual right to rescind may fall under this principle but are not relevant to the present discussion.) In the case of an accepted repudiatory breach the contract has come into existence but has been put an end to or discharged. Whatever contrary indications may be disintered from old authorities, it is now quite clear, under the general law of contract, that acceptance of a repudiatory breach does not bring about "rescission ab initio". **17–164**

[228] [1976] Ch. 319.

17–165 Fourthly, if an order for specific performance is sought and is made, the contract remains in effect and is not merged in the judgment for specific performance. This is clear law, best illustrated by the judgment of Sir Wilfrid Greene M.R. in *Austins of East Ham Ltd v Macey*[229] in a passage which deals both with this point and with that next following. It repays quotation in full.

> "The contract is still there. Until it is got rid of, it remains as a blot on the title, and the position of the vendor, where the purchaser has made default, is that he is entitled, not to annul the contract by the aid of the court, but to obtain the normal remedy of a party to a contract which the other party has repudiated. He cannot, in the circumstances, treat it as repudiated except by order of the court and the effect of obtaining such an order is that the contract, which until then existed, is brought to an end. The real position, in my judgment, is that, so far from proceeding to the enforcement of an order for specific performance, the vendor, in such circumstances is choosing a remedy which is alternative to the remedy of proceeding under the order for specific performance. He could attempt to enforce that order and could levy an execution which might prove completely fruitless. Instead of doing that, he elects to ask the court to put an end to the contract, and that is an alternative to an order for enforcing specific performance."

17–166 Fifthly, if the order for specific performance is not complied with by the purchaser, the vendor may either apply to the court for enforcement of the order, or may apply to the court to dissolve the order and ask the court to put an end to the contract. This proposition is as stated in *Austins of East Ham Ltd v Macey*[230] (and see *Singh (Sudagar) v Nazeer*[231]) and is in my opinion undoubted law, both on principle and authority. It follows, indeed, automatically from the facts that the contract remains in force after the order for specific performance and that the purchaser has committed a breach of it of a repudiatory character which he has not remedied, or as Megarry V.C. puts it,[232] that he is refusing to complete.

17–167 These propositions being, as I think they are, uncontrovertible, there only remains the question whether, if the vendor takes the latter course, i.e., of applying to the court to put an end to the contract, he is entitled to recover damages for breach of the contract. On principle one may ask "Why ever not?" If, as is clear, the vendor is entitled, after, and notwithstanding that an order for specific performance has been made, if the purchaser still does not complete the contract, to ask the court to permit him to accept the purchaser's repudiation and to declare the contract to be terminated, why, if the court accedes to this, should there not follow the ordinary consequences, undoubted under the general law of contract, that on such acceptance and termination the vendor may recover damages for breach of contract?

17–168 I now consider the arguments which are said to support the negative answer.

17–169 The principal authority lies in the case of *Henty v Schröder*,[233] in which Sir George Jessel M.R. is briefly reported as having laid down that a vendor "could not at the same time obtain an order to have the agreement rescinded and claim damages against the defendant for breach of the agreement."

17–170 At first instance, if has been followed usually uncritically . . . [and it was also] endorsed by the Court of Appeal in *Capital and Suburban Properties Ltd v Swycher* ("*Swycher's case*"),[234] but on a new basis which I shall shortly consider, and in the present case.

17–171 This is however the first time that this House has had to consider the right of an innocent party to a contract for the sale of land to damages on the contract being put an end to by accepted repudiation, and I think that we have the duty to take a fresh look. I should certainly be reluctant to invite your Lordships to endorse a line of authority so weak and unconvincing in principle. Fortunately there is support for a more attractive and logical approach from another bastion of the common law whose courts have adopted a more robust attitude. . . .

17–172 [He then considered *McDonald v Dennys Lascelles Ltd*,[235] *Holland v Wiltshire*,[236] and *Mckenna v Richey*.[237]]

---

[229] [1941] Ch. 338 at 341.
[230] [1941] Ch. 338.
[231] [1979] Ch. 474 at 480, per Megarry V.C.
[232] [1979] Ch. 474 at 480.
[233] (1879) 12 Ch.D. 666 at 667.
[234] [1976] Ch. 319.
[235] (1933) 43 C.L.R. 457.
[236] (1954) 90 C.L.R. 409.
[237] [1950] V.L.R. 360.

My Lords, I am happy to follow the latter case. In my opinion *Henty v Schröder* cannot stand against the powerful tide of logical objection and judicial reasoning. It should no longer be regarded as of authority: the cases following it should be overruled. . . . **17–173**

The second basis for denying damages in such cases as the present is that which underlines the judgment of the Court of Appeal in *Swycher's case*. This is really a rationalisation of *Henty v Schröder*, the weakness of which case the court well perceived. The main argument there accepted was that by deciding to seek the remedy of specific performance the vendor (or purchaser) has made an election which either is irrevocable or which becomes so when the order for specific performance is made. A second limb of this argument (but in reality a different argument) is that the vendor (or purchaser) has adequate remedies under the order for specific performance so that there is no need, or equitable ground, for allowing him to change his ground and ask for damages. **17–174**

In my opinion, the argument based on irrevocable election, strongly pressed by the appellant's counsel in the present appeal, is unsound. Election, though the subject of much learning and refinement, is in the end a doctrine based on simple considerations of common sense and equity. It is easy to see that a party who has chosen to put an end a contract by accepting the other party's repudiation cannot afterwards seek specific performance. This is simply because the contract has gone—what is dead is dead. But it is no more difficult to agree that a party, who has chosen to seek specific performance, may quite well thereafter, if specific performance fails to be realised, say, "Very well, then, the contract should be regarded as terminated." It is quite consistent with a decision provisionally to keep alive, to say, "Well, this is no use—let us now end the contract's life." A vendor who seeks (and gets) specific performance is merely electing for a course which may or may not lead to implementation of the contract—what he elects for is not eternal and unconditional affirmation, but a continuance of the contract under control of the court which control involves the power, in certain events, to terminate it. If he makes an election at all, he does so when he decides not to proceed under the order for specific performance, but to ask the court to terminate the contract: see the judgment of Sir Wilfrid Greene M.R. in *Austins of East Ham Ltd v Macey*[238] quoted above. The fact is that the election argument proves too much. If it were correct it would deny the vendor not just the right to damages, but the right to "rescind" the contract, but there is no doubt that this right exists: what is in question is only the right on "rescission", to claim damages. **17–175**

In my respectful opinion therefore *Swycher's case*, whether it should be regarded as resting upon *Henty v Schröder*, or upon an independent argument based on election was wrongly decided in so far as it denied a right to contractual damages and should so far be overruled. The vendors should have been entitled, upon discharge of the contract, on grounds of normal and accepted principle, to damages appropriate for a breach of contract. **17–176**

There is one final point, on this part of the case, on which I should make a brief observation. Once the matter has been placed in the hands of a court of equity, or one exercising equity jurisdiction, the subsequent control of the matter will be exercised according to equitable principles. The court would not make an order dissolving the decree of specific performance and terminating the contract (with recovery of damages) if to do so would be unjust, in the circumstances then existing, to the other party, in this case to the purchaser. This is why there was, in the Court of Appeal, rightly, a relevant and substantial argument, repeated in this House, that the non-completion of the contract was due to the default of the vendors: if this had been made good, the court could properly have refused them the relief sought. But the Court of Appeal came to the conclusion that this non-completion, and the ultimate impossibility of completion, was the fault of the purchaser. I agree with their conclusion and their reasons on this point and shall not repeat or add to them. **17–177**

It is now necessary to deal with questions relating to the measure of damages. The Court of Appeal, while denying the vendors' right to damages at common law, granted damages under Lord Cairns' Act. Since, on the view which I take, damages can be recovered at common law, two relevant questions now arise. (1) Whether Lord Cairns' Act provides a different measure of damages from the common law; if so, the respondents would be in a position to claim the more favourable basis to them. (2) If the measure of damages is the same, on what basis they should be calculated. **17–178**

Since the decision of this House, by majority, in *Leeds Industrial Co-operative Society Ltd v Slack*[239] it is clear that the jurisdiction to award damages in accordance with section 2 of Lord Cairns' Act (accepted by the House as surviving the repeal of the Act) may arise in some cases in which damages could not be recovered **17–179**

---

[238] [1941] Ch. 338.
[239] [1924] A.C. 851.

at common law; examples of this would be damages in lieu of a *quia timet* injunction and damages for breach of a restrictive covenant to which the plaintiff was not a party. To this extent the Act created a power to award damages which did not exist before at common law. But apart from these, and similar cases where damages could not be claimed at all at common law there is sound authority for the proposition that the Act does not provide for the assessment of damages on any new basis. The wording of section 2 "may be assessed in such manner as the court shall direct" does not so suggest, but clearly refers only to procedure. . . .

17–180 [He examined various cases and continued:] On the balance of these authorities and also on principle, I find in the Act no warrant for the court awarding damages differently from common law damages, but the question is left open on what date such damages, however awarded, ought to be assessed.

17–181 The general principle for the assessment of damages is compensatory, i.e., that the innocent party is to be placed, so far as money can do so, in the same position as if the contract had been performed. Where the contract is one of sale, this principle normally leads to assessment of damages as at the date of the breach—a principle recognised and embodied in section 51 of the Sale of Goods Act 1893. But this is not an absolute rule: if to follow it would give rise to injustice, the court has power to fix such other date as may be appropriate in the circumstances.

17–182 In cases where a breach of a contract for sale has occurred, and the innocent party reasonably continues to try to have the contract completed, it would to me appear more logical and just rather than tie him to the date of the original breach, to assess damages as at the date when (otherwise than by his default) the contract is lost. Support for this approach is to be found in the cases. In *Ogle v Earl Vane*[240] the date was fixed by reference to the time when the innocent party, acting reasonably, went into the market; in *Hickman v Haynes*[241] at a reasonable time after the last request of the defendants (buyers) to withhold delivery. In *Radford v De Froberville*,[242] where the defendant had convenanted to build a wall, damages were held measurable as at the date of the bearing rather than at the date of the defendant's breach, unless the plaintiff ought reasonably to have mitigated the breach at an earlier date.

17–183 In the present case if it is accepted, as I would accept, that the vendors acted reasonably in pursuing the remedy of specific performance, the date on which that remedy became aborted (not by the vendor's fault) should logically be fixed as the date on which damages should be assessed. Choice of this date would be in accordance both with common law principle, as indicated in the authorities I have mentioned, and with the wording of the Act "in substitution for . . . specific performance". The date which emerges from this is April 3, 1975—the first date on which mortgages contracted to sell a portion of the property. I would vary the order of the Court of Appeal by substituting this date for that fixed by them—viz. November 26, 1974. The same date (April 3, 1975) should be used for the purpose of limiting the respondents' right to interest on damages. Subject to these modifications I would dismiss the appeal.

CO-OPERATIVE INSURANCE SOCIETY LTD & ARGYLL STORES (HOLDINGS) LTD

House of Lords [1998] A.C. 1

17–184 LORD HOFFMANN (with whom LORD BROWNE-WILKINSON, LORD SLYNN, LORD HOPE and LORD CLYDE agreed):

The Issue

17–185 In 1955 Lord Goddard C.J. said:[243]

> "No authority has been quoted to show that an injunction will be granted enjoining a person to carry on a business, nor can I think that one ever would be, certainly not where the business is a losing concern."

240 (1867) L.R. 2 Q.B. 275; L.R. 3 Q.B. 272.
241 (1875) L.R. 10 C.P. 598.
242 [1977] 1 W.L.R. 1262.
243 *Att.-Gen. v Colchester Corporation* [1955] 2 Q.B. 207 at 217.

In this case his prediction has been falsified. The appellant defendants, Argyll Stores (Holdings) Ltd ("Argyll"), decided in May 1995 to close their Safeway supermarket in the Hillsborough Shopping Centre in Sheffield because it was losing money. This was a breach of a covenant in their lease, which contained in clause 4(19) a positive obligation to keep the premises open for retail trade during the usual hours of business. Argyll admitted the breach and, in an action by the landlord. Co-operative Insurance Society Ltd ("CIS") consented to an order for damages to be assessed. But the Court of Appeal,[244] reversing the trial judge, ordered that the covenant be specifically performed. It made a final injunction ordering Argyll to trade on the premises during the remainder of the term (which will expire on 3 August 2014) or until an earlier subletting or assignment. The Court of Appeal suspended its order for three months to allow time for Argyll to complete an assignment which by that time had been agreed. After a short agreed extension, the lease was assigned with the landlord's consent. In fact, therefore, the injunction never took effect. The appeal to your Lordships is substantially about costs. But the issue remains of great importance to landlords and tenants under other commercial leases. . . .

17–186 The judge refused to order specific performance. He said that there was on the authorities a settled practice that orders which would require a defendant to run a business would not be made. He was not content, however, merely to follow authority. He gave reasons why he thought that specific performance would be inappropriate. Two such reasons were by way of justification for the general practice. An order to carry on a business, as opposed to an order to perform a "single and well-defined act", was difficult to enforce by the sanction of committal. And where a business was being run at a loss, specific relief would be "too far-reaching and beyond the scope of control which the court should seek to impose." The other two related to the particular case. A resumption of business would be expensive (refitting the shop was estimated to cost over £1m) and although Argyll had knowingly acted in breach of covenant, it had done so "in the light of the settled practice of the court to award damages." Finally, while the assessment of damages might be difficult, it was the kind of exercise which the courts had done in the past.

The Settled Practice

17–187 There is no dispute about the existence of the settled practice to which the judge referred. It sufficient for this purpose to refer to *Braddon Towers Ltd v International Stores Ltd* where Slade J. said:[245]

> "Whether or not this may be properly described as a rule of law. I do not doubt that for many years practitioners have advised their clients that it is the settled and invariable practice of this court never to grant mandatory injunctions requiring persons to carry on business."

But the practice has never, so far as I know, been examined by this House and it is open to CIS to say that it rests upon inadequate grounds or that it has been too inflexibly applied.

17–188 Specific performance is traditionally regarded in English law as an exceptional remedy, as opposed to the common law damages to which a successful plaintiff is entitled as of right. There may have been some element of later rationalisation of an untidier history, but by the 19th century it was orthodox doctrine that the power to decree specific performance was part of the discretionary jurisdiction of the Court of Chancery to do justice in cases in which the remedies available at common law were inadequate. This is the basis of the general principle that specific performance will not be ordered when damages are an adequate remedy. By contrast, in countries with legal systems based on civil law, such as France, Germany and Scotland, the plaintiff is prima facie entitled to specific performance. The cases in which he is confined to a claim for damages are regarded as the exceptions. In practice, however, there is less difference between common law and civilian systems than these general statements might lead one to suppose. The principles upon which English judges exercise the discretion to grant specific performance are reasonably well settled and depend upon a number of considerations, mostly of a practical nature, which are of very general application. I have made no investigation of civilian systems, but a priori I would expect that judges take much the same matters into account in deciding whether specific performance would be inappropriate in a particular case.

17–189 The practice of not ordering a defendant to carry on a business is not entirely dependent upon damages being an adequate remedy. In *Dowty Boulton Paul Ltd v Wolverhampton Corporation*[246] Sir John Pennycuick

[244] [1996] Ch. 286.
[245] [1987] 1 E.G.L.R. 209 at 213.
[246] [1971] 1 W.L.R. 204.

V.C. refused to order the corporation to maintain an airfield as a going concern because: "It is very well established that the court will not order specific performance of an obligation to carry on a business."[247] He added: "It is unnecessary in the circumstances to discuss whether damages would be an adequate remedy to the company."[248] Thus the reasons which underlie the established practice may justify a refusal of specific performance even when damages are not an adequate remedy.

17–190 The most frequent reason given in the cases for declining to order someone to carry on a business is that it would require constant supervision by the court. In *JC Williamson Ltd v Lukey and Mulholland*[249] Dixon J. said flatly: "Specific performance is inapplicable when the continued supervision of the court is necessary in order to ensure the fulfillment of the contract."

17–191 There has, I think, been some misunderstanding about what is meant by continued superintendence. It may at first sight suggest that the judge (or some other officer of the court) would literally have to supervise the execution of the order. In *CH Giles & Co Ltd v Morris*[250] Megarry J. said that "difficulties of constant superintendence" were a "narrow consideration" because:

> "there is normally no question of the court having to send its officers to supervise the performance of the order. . . . Performance . . . is normally secured by the realisation of the person enjoined that he is liable to be punished for contempt if evidence of his disobedience to the order is put before the court . . .".

This is, of course, true but does not really meet the point. The judges who have said that the need for constant supervision was an objection to such orders were no doubt well aware that supervision would in practice take the form of rulings by the court, on applications made by the parties, as to whether there had been a breach of the order. It is the possibility of the court having to give an indefinite series of such rulings in order to ensure the execution of the order which has been regarded as undesirable.

17–192 Why should this be so? A principal reason is that, as Megarry J. pointed out in the passage to which I have referred, the only means available to the court to enforce its order is the quasi-criminal procedure of punishment for contempt. This is powerful weapon: so powerful, in fact, as often to be unsuitable as an instrument for adjudicating upon the disputes which may arise over whether a business is being run in accordance with the terms of the court's order. The heavy-handed nature of the enforcement mechanism is a consideration which may go to the exercise of the court's discretion in other cases as well, but its use to compel the running of a business is perhaps the paradigm case of its disadvantages and it is in this context that I shall discuss them.

17–193 The prospect of committal or even a fine, with the damage to commercial reputation which will be caused by a finding of contempt of court, is likely to have at least two undesirable consequences. First, the defendant, who *ex hypothesi* did not think that it was in his economic interest to run the business at all, now has to make decisions under a sword of Damocles which may descend if the way the business is run does not conform to the terms of the order. This is, as one might say, no way to run a business. In this case the Court of Appeal made light of the point because it assumed that, once the defendant had been ordered to run the business, self-interest and compliance with the order would thereafter go hand in hand. But, as I shall explain, this is not necessarily true.

17–194 Secondly, the seriousness of a finding of contempt for the defendant means that any application to enforce the order is likely to be a heavy and expensive piece of litigation. The possibility of repeated applications over a period of time means that, in comparison with a once-and-for-all inquiry as to damages, the enforcement of the remedy is likely to be expensive in terms of cost to the parties and the resources of the judicial system.

17–195 This is a convenient point at which to distinguish between orders which require a defendant to carry on an activity, such as running a business over or more or less extended period of time, and orders which require him to achieve a result. The possibility of repeated applications for rulings on compliance with the order which arises in the former case does not exist to anything like the same extent in the latter. Even if the achievement of the result is a complicated matter which will take some time, the court, if called upon to rule, only has to examine the finished work and say whether it complies with the order. This point was

[247] At 211.
[248] At 212.
[249] (1931) 45 C.L.R. 282 at 297–298.
[250] [1972] 1 W.L.R. 307 at 318.

made in the context of relief against forfeiture in *Shiloh Spinners Ltd v Harding*.[251] If it is a condition of relief that the tenant should have complied with a repairing covenant, difficulty of supervision need not be an objection. As Lord Wilberforce said:[252]

> "what the court has to do is to satisfy itself, ex post facto, that the covenanted work has been done, and it has ample machinery, through certificates, or by inquiry, to do precisely this."

This distinction between orders to carry on activities and orders to achieve results explains why the courts have in appropriate circumstances ordered specific performance of building contracts and repairing covenants: see *Wolverhampton Corporation v Emmons*[253] (building contract) and *Jeune v Queens Cross Properties Ltd*[254] (repairing covenant). It by no means follows, however, that even obligations to achieve a result will always be enforced by specific performance. There may be other objections, to some of which I now turn.

One such objection, which applies to orders to achieve a result and a fortiori to orders to carry on an activity, is imprecision in the terms of the order. If the terms of the court's order, reflecting the terms of the obligation, cannot be precisely drawn, the possibility of wasteful litigation over compliance is increased. So is the oppression caused by the defendant having to do things under threat of proceedings for contempt. The less precise the order, the fewer the signposts to the forensic minefield which he has to traverse. The fact that the terms of a contractual obligation are sufficiently definite to escape being void for uncertainty, or to found a claim for damages, or to permit compliance to be made a condition of relief against forfeiture, does not necessarily mean that they will be sufficiently precise to be capable of being specifically enforced. So in *Wolverhampton Corporation v Emmons*, Romer L.J. said that the first condition for specific enforcement of a building contract was that:[255] **17–196**

> "the particulars of the work are so far definitely ascertained that the court can sufficiently see what is the exact nature of the work of which it is asked to order the performance."

Similarly in *Morris v Redland Bricks Ltd*,[256] Lord Upjohn stated the following general principle for the grant of mandatory injunctions to carry out building works: **17–197**

> "the court must be careful to see that the defendant knows exactly in fact what he has to do and this means not as a matter of law but as a matter of fact, so that in carrying out an order he can give his contractors the proper instructions."

Precision is of course a question of degree and the courts have shown themselves willing to cope with a certain degree of imprecision in cases of orders requiring the achievement of a result in which the plaintiffs' merits appeared strong; like all the reasons which I have been discussing, it is, taken alone, merely a discretionary matter to be taken into account.[257] It is, however, a very important one.

I should at this point draw attention to what seems to me to have been a misreading of certain remarks of Lord Wilberforce in *Shiloh Spinners Ltd v Harding*.[258] He pointed out, as I have said, that to grant relief against forfeiture subject to compliance with a repairing covenant involves the court in no more than the possibility of a retrospective assessment of whether the covenanted work has been done. For this reason, he said: **17–198**

> "Where it is necessary, and, in my opinion, right, to move away from some 19th century authorities, is to reject as a reason against granting relief, the impossibility for the courts to supervise the doing of work."

---

[251] [1973] A.C. 691.
[252] At 724.
[253] [1901] 1 K.B. 515.
[254] [1974] Ch. 97.
[255] At 525.
[256] [1970] A.C. 652 at 666.
[257] See Spry, *Equitable Remedies*, 4th edn (1990). p.112.
[258] At p.724.

This is plainly a remark about cases involving the achievement of a result such as doing repairs, and, within that class, about making compliance a condition of relief against forfeiture. But in *Tito v Waddell (No.2)*[259] Sir Robert Megarry V.C. took it to be a generalisation about specific performance and, in particular, a rejection of difficulty of supervision as an objection, even in cases of orders to carry on an activity. Sir Robert Megarry V.C. regarded it as an adoption of his own views (based, as I have said, on incomplete analysis of what was meant by difficulty of supervision) in *CH Giles & Co Ltd v Morris*.[260] In the present case[261] Leggatt L.J. took this claim at face value. In fact, Lord Wilberforce went on to say that impossibility of supervision "is a reality, no doubt, and explains why specific performance cannot be granted of agreements to this effect . . .". Lord Wilberforce was in my view drawing attention to the fact that the collection of reasons which the courts have in mind when they speak of difficulty of supervision apply with much greater force to orders for specific performance, giving rise to the possibility of committal for contempt, than they do to conditions for relief against forfeiture. While the paradigm case to which such objections apply is the order to carry on an activity, they can also apply to an order requiring the achievement of a result.

17–199 There is a further objection to an order requiring the defendant to carry on a business, which was emphasised by Millett L.J. in the Court of Appeal. This is that it may cause injustice by allowing the plaintiff to enrich himself at the defendant's expense. The loss which the defendant may suffer through having to comply with the order (for example, by running a business at a loss for an indefinite period) may be far greater than the plaintiff would suffer from the contract being broken. As Professor R.J. Sharpe explains:[262]

> "In such circumstances, a specific decree in favour of the plaintiff will put him in a bargaining position vis-à-vis the defendant whereby the measure of what he will receive will be the value to the defendant of being released from performance. If the plaintiff bargains effectively, the amount he will set will exceed the value to him of performance and will approach the cost to the defendant to complete."

17–200 This was the reason given by Lord Westbury L.C. in *Isenberg v East India House Estate Co Ltd*[263] for refusing a mandatory injunction to compel the defendant to pull down part of a new building which interfered with the plaintiff's light and exercising instead the Court of Chancery's recently-acquired jurisdiction under Lord Cairns's Act 1858 to order payment of damages:

> ". . . I hold it . . . to be the duty of the court in such a case as the present not, by granting a mandatory injunction, to deliver over the defendants to the plaintiff bound hand and foot, in order to be made subject to any extortionate demand that he may by possibility make, but to substitute for such mandatory injunction an inquiry before itself, in order to ascertain the measure of damage that has been actually sustained."

17–201 It is true that the defendant has, by his own breach of contract, put himself in such an unfortunate position. But the purpose of the law of contract is not to punish wrongdoing but to satisfy the expectations of the party entitled to performance. A remedy which enables him to secure, in money terms, more than the performance due to him is unjust. From a wider perspective, it cannot be in the public interest for the courts to require someone to carry on business at a loss if there is any plausible alternative by which the other party can be given compensation. It is not only a waste of resources but yokes the parties together in a continuing hostile relationship. The order for specific performance prolongs the battle. If the defendant is ordered to run a business, its conduct becomes the subject of a flow of complaints, solicitors' letters and affidavits. This is wasteful for both parties and the legal system. An award of damages, on the other hand, brings the litigation to an end. The defendant pays damages, the forensic link between them is severed, they go their separate ways and the wounds of conflict can heal.

17–202 The cumulative effect of these various reasons, none of which would necessarily be sufficient on its own, seems to me to show that the settled practice is based upon sound sense. Of course the grant or refusal of specific performance remains a matter for the judge's discretion. There are no binding rules, but this

---

259 [1977] Ch. 106 at 322.
260 [1972] 1 W.L.R. 307 at 318.
261 [1996] Ch. 286 at 292–293.
262 In "Specific Relief for Contract Breach", Ch.5 of *Studies in Contract Law* (1980), edited by Reiter and Swan p.129.
263 (1863) 3 De G.J. & S. 263 at 273.

does not mean that there cannot be settled principles, founded upon practical considerations of the kind which I have discussed, which do not have to be re-examined in every case, but which the courts will apply in all but exceptional circumstances. As Slade J. said, in the passage which I have quoted from *Braddon Towers Ltd v International Stores Ltd*,[264] lawyers have no doubt for many years advised their clients on this basis. In the present case. Leggatt L.J.[265] remarked that there was no evidence that such advice had been given. In my view, if the law or practice on a point is settled, it should be assumed that persons entering into legal transactions will have been advised accordingly. I am sure that Leggatt L.J. would not wish to encourage litigants to adduce evidence of the particular advice which they received. Indeed, I doubt whether such evidence would be admissible.

The Decision of the Court of Appeal

17–203 I must now examine the grounds upon which the majority of the Court of Appeal[266] thought it right to reverse the judge. In the first place, they regarded the practice which he followed as outmoded and treated Lord Wilberforce's remarks about relief against forfeiture in *Shiloh Spinners Ltd v Harding*[267] as justifying a rejection of the arguments based on the need for constant supervision. Even Millett L.J., who dissented on other grounds, said that such objections had little force today.[268] I do not agree. As I have already said, I think that Lord Wilberforce's remarks do not support this proposition in relation to specific performance of an obligation to carry on an activity and that the arguments based on difficulty of supervision remain powerful.

17–204 The Court of Appeal said that it was enough if the contract defined the tenant's obligation with sufficient precision to enable him to know what was necessary to comply with the order. Even assuming that this to be right, I do not think that the obligation in clause 4(19) can possibly be regarded as sufficiently precise to be capable of specific performance. It is to "keep the demised premises open for retail trade." It says nothing about the level of trade, the area of the premises within which trade is to be conducted, or even the kind of trade, although no doubt the tenant's choice would be restricted by the need to comply with the negative covenant in clause 4(12)(a) not to use the premises "other than as a retail store for the sale of food groceries provisions and goods normally sold from time to time by a retail grocer food supermarkets and food superstores . . .". This language seems to me to provide ample room for argument over whether the tenant is doing enough to comply with the covenant.

17–205 The Court of Appeal thought that once Argyll had been ordered to comply with the covenant, it was, as Roch L.J. said,[269] "inconceivable that they would not operate the business efficiently." Leggatt L.J. said,[270] that the requirement

> "was quite intelligible to the defendants, while they were carrying on business there. . . . If the premises are to be run as a business, it cannot be in the defendants' interest to run it half-heartedly or inefficiently . . .".

This treats the way the tenant previously conducted business as measuring the extent of his obligation to do so. In my view this is a non sequitur: the obligation depends upon the language of the covenant and not upon what the tenant has previously chosen to do. No doubt it is true that it would not be in the interests of the tenant to run the business inefficiently. But running the business efficiently does not necessarily mean running it in the way it was run before. Argyll had decided that, from its point of view, the most efficient thing to do was to close the business altogether and concentrate its resources on achieving better returns elsewhere. If ordered to keep the business open, it might well decide that the next best strategy was to reduce its costs as far as was consistent with compliance with its obligations, in the expectation that a lower level of return would be more than compensated by higher returns from additional expenditure on more profitable shops. It is in my view wrong for the courts to speculate about whether Argyll might voluntarily carry on business in a way which would relieve the court from having to construe

[264] [1987] 1 E.G.L.R. 209 at 213.
[265] [1996] Ch. 286 at 294.
[266] [1996] Ch. 286.
[267] [1973] A.C. 691 at 724.
[268] At 303.
[269] At 298.
[270] At 292.

its order. The question of certainty must be decided on the assumption that the court might have to enforce the order according to its terms.

17–206 CIS argued that the court should not be concerned about future difficulties which might arise in connection with the enforcement of the order. It should simply make the order and see what happened. In practice Argyll would be likely to find a suitable assignee (as it in fact did) or conduct the business so as to keep well clear of any possible enforcement proceedings or otherwise come to terms with CIS. This may well be true, but the likelihood of Argyll having to perform beyond the requirements of its covenant or buy its way out of its obligation to incur losses seems to me to be in principle an objection to such an order rather than to recommend it. I think that it is normally undesirable for judges to make orders in terrorem, carrying a threat of imprisonment, which work only if no one inquires too closely into what they mean.

17–207 The likelihood that the order would be effective only for a short time until an assignment is an equivocal argument. It would be burdensome to make Argyll resume business only to stop again after a short while if a short stoppage would not cause any substantial damage to the business of the shopping centre. On the other hand, what would happen if a suitable assignee could not be found? Would Argyll then have to carry on business until 2014? Mr Smith, who appeared for CIS, said that if the order became oppressive (for example, because Argyll were being driven into bankruptcy) or difficult to enforce, they could apply for it to be varied or discharged. But the order would be a final order and there is no case in this jurisdiction in which such an order has been varied or discharged, except when the injuncted activity has been legalised by statute. Even assuming that there was such a jurisdiction if circumstances were radically changed. I find it difficult to see how this could be made to apply. Difficulties of enforcement would not be a change of circumstances. They would have been entirely predictable when the order was made. And so would the fact that Argyll would suffer unquantifiable loss if it was obliged to continue trading. I do not think that such expedients are an answer to the difficulties on which the objections to such orders are based.

17–208 Finally, all three judges in the Court of Appeal took a very poor view of Argyll's conduct. Leggatt L.J. said that they had acted "with gross commercial cynicism";[271] Roch L.J. began his judgment by saying that they had "behaved very badly" and Millett L.J. said that they had no merits.[272] The principles of equity have always had a strong ethical content and nothing which I say is intended to diminish the influence of moral values in their application. I can envisage cases of gross breach of personal faith, or attempts to use the threat of non-performance as blackmail, in which the needs of justice will override all the considerations which support the settled practice. But although any breach of covenant is regrettable, the exercise of the discretion as to whether or not to grant specific performance starts from the fact that the covenant has been broken. Both landlord and tenant in this case are large sophisticated commercial organisations and I have no doubt that both were perfectly aware that the remedy for breach of the covenant was likely to be limited to an award of damages. The interests of both were purely financial: there was no element of personal breach of faith, as in the Victorian cases of railway companies which refused to honour obligations to build stations for landowners whose property they had taken: compare *Greene v West Cheshire Railway Co.*[273] No doubt there was an effect on the businesses of other traders in the Centre, but Argyll had made no promises to them and it is not suggested that CIS warranted to other tenants that Argyll would remain. Their departure, with or without the consent of CIS, was a commercial risk which the tenants were able to deploy in negotiations for the next rent review. On the scale of broken promises, I can think of worse cases, but the language of the Court of Appeal left them with few adjectives to spare.

17–209 It was no doubt discourteous not to have answered Mr Wightman's letter. But to say, as Roch L.J. did,[274] that they had acted "wantonly and quite unreasonably" by removing their fixtures seems to me an exaggeration. There was no question of stealing a march, or attempting to present CIS with a fait accompli, because Argyll had no reason to believe that CIS would have been able to obtain a mandatory injunction whether the fixtures had been removed or not. They had made it perfectly clear that they were closing the shop and given CIS ample time to apply for such an injunction if so advised.

---

[271] [1996] Ch. 286 at 295.
[272] At 301.
[273] (1871) L.R. 13 Eq. 44.
[274] At 299.

Conclusion

I think that no criticism can be made of the way in which Judge Maddocks exercised his discretion. All the reasons which he gave were proper matters for him to take into account. In my view the Court of Appeal should not have interfered and I would allow the appeal and restore the order which he made. **17–210**

4. Damages in Addition to or in Lieu of Injunctions and Specific Performance

Section 50 of the Senior Courts Act 1981 provides: **17–211**

> "Where the Court of Appeal or the High Court has jurisdiction to entertain an application for an injunction or specific performance, it may award damages in addition to, or in substitution for, an injunction or specific performance."

This provision embodies and confers upon the named courts the jurisdiction that was conferred upon the Court of Chancery by s.2 of the Chancery Amendment Act 1858 (Lord Cairns' Act) which was later repealed.[275] *Jaggard v Sawyer*,[276] reproduced below,[277] is now the leading case on the jurisdiction so far as it relates to damages in lieu of injunctions, and the Court's findings also affect the question of how the section might apply to awards of damages in substitution for specific performance. It is convenient, however, to take injunctions first.

17–212 Lord Cairns' Act enabled the Court of Chancery (i) to award damages (previously only awardable in common law courts) for past unlawful conduct "in addition to" awarding injunctions to restrain future unlawful conduct and (ii) to award damages "in substitution for" the grant of an injunction to restrain future unlawful conduct. Authoritative guidance on the exercise of the discretion in (ii) was given by A.L. Smith L.J. in *Shelfer v City of London Electric Lighting Co*[278] in the form of four conditions that required, as a working rule, to be met: the injury to the claimant's rights had to be small, capable of being estimated in money, and adequately compensable by a small sum; it must also be oppressive to the defendant to grant the injunction.[279] Despite judicial zeal not to allow a wrong doer merely to purchase the right to engage in wrongful activity, the net effect of an award of damages under (ii) is to allow a wrong doer to engage lawfully in conduct that infringed a claimant's legal or other right. This is because, per Sir Thomas Bingham M.R., "a succession of future actions based on that conduct would, if brought, be dismissed or struck out, since a plaintiff could not complain of that for which he had already been compensated"[280] or, per Millett L.J., "the doctrine of res judicata operates to prevent the plaintiff and his successors from bringing proceedings thereafter to recover even nominal damages in respect of further wrongs for which the plaintiff has already been fully compensated." In addition, damages are awardable under (ii) if injunctive relief is refused on the grounds of delay, acquiescence, etc.

---

275 J.A. Jolowicz, "Damages in Equity—A Study of Lord Cairns' Act" [1975] C.L.J. 224; P.M. McDermott, *Equitable Damages* (1994) Ch.3; and for judicial statements that the courts' former jurisdiction under Lord Cairns' Act is now embodied by s.50, see e.g. *Jaggard v Sawyer* [1995] 1 W.L.R. 269 at 284, per Millett L.J.; *Regan v Paul Properties DPF No.1 Ltd* [2007] Ch. 135 at [24], per Mummery L.J.

276 [1995] 1 W.L.R. 269. See too *Deakins v Hoskings* [1994] 1 E.G.L.R. 190; *Gafford v Graham* [1995] 3 E.G.L.R. 75; *Daniells v Mendonca* [1999] 78 P. & C.R. 401; *Marcic v Thames Water Utilities Ltd (No.2)* [2002] Q.B. 1003, overtaken by the HL's findings on liability in *Marcic (No.1)* [2004] 2 A.C. 42; *Midtown Ltd v City of London Real Property Co Ltd* [2005] 1 E.G.L.R. 65 at [66]–[77]; *Regan v Paul Properties DPF No.1 Ltd* [2007] Ch. 135.

277 At paras 17–221 ff.

278 [1895] 1 Ch. 287 at 322–323.

279 [1995] 1 W.L.R. 269 at 280–281.

280 *Jaggard* at 286.

A.L. Smith L.J.'s "working rule" was, after all, no more than a crystallisation of the perceived practice of the courts of equity which, in the last analysis, awarded remedies according to the justice of the case.

17–213 On the measure of damages to be awarded in lieu, despite the dicta of Lord Wilberforce in *Johnson v Agnew*[281] to the effect that there could be no difference between the bases of assessment at common law and in equity, *Jaggard v Sawyer* makes clear that as regards injunctions, Lord Wilberforce cannot be taken to have intended to deny that some awards of damages under Lord Cairns' Act compensate for future wrongs—wrongs, therefore, which are not compensable at law. In Millett L.J.'s words, "Lord Wilberforce's statement . . . must be taken to be limited to the case where [the damages] are recoverable in respect of the same cause of action".[282] This may have consequences even for contractual cases where the duty breached, as in *Beswick v Beswick*,[283] is an on-going one so that, should specific performance be refused on some discretionary ground, an award of damages in lieu could properly be assessed, indeed, would require to be assessed, on a basis other than that adopted by courts of common law. This is a convenient moment at which to turn to damages in lieu of specific performance.

17–214 The extent of the jurisdiction, preserved by the Senior Courts Act 1981 s.50, is a matter of some doubt. It is clear that, in order for there to arise a power to award damages in lieu of specific performance, there must have been jurisdiction to order specific performance (even if, as a matter of discretion it was likely to be refused) as at the date of the writ.[284] But which of the grounds for refusing a decree go to jurisdiction and which to discretion? Ultimately the matter is one of statutory construction. It is here suggested that the first seven grounds covered in the preceding section ought to be seen as going to jurisdiction, but the remainder only to discretion. This suggestion is put forward without any appeal to authority but principle enough can be advanced to defend it: it is impossible to enforce a promise made without consideration, unnecessary to grant a remedy where the common law remedy is adequate, pointless or impossible to act in vain, obnoxious to act contrary to public policy (and so on). Matters such as delay, hardship, mistake (and so on) can fairly be characterised as grounds on which, if appropriate, to exercise some grace but nothing more.

17–215 There is authority for the view that no damages can be awarded unless specific performance is claimed[285] but that must be read subject to the dicta of Millett L.J. in *Jaggard v Sawyer*[286] which, in relation to injunctions, dissent from that view: if a claimant omitted to claim an injunction because, realistically, it would not be granted, the jurisdiction to award damages in lieu still existed. As a matter of principle, that ought to apply to specific performance as well.

17–216 Note that the jurisdiction also allows damages in addition to specific performance. The purpose of this provision in relation to injunctions has already been explained[287] but in the present context, they might be awarded where, exceptionally, only part of a contract is specifically enforced the claimant being awarded damages for the defendant's failure to perform the rest.[288]

17–217 As to the measure of damages, Lord Wilberforce in *Johnson v Agnew*[289] rejected the view that damages could be assessed on different bases under the Act and at common law. Megarry J. had said in *Wroth v Tyler*[290] that the purpose of an award was to offer a true substitute for specific performance—

---

[281] [1980] A.C. 367 at 400.
[282] [1995] 1 W.L.R. 269 at 291.
[283] [1968] A.C. 58.
[284] *Jaggard v Sawyer* [1995] 1 W.L.R. 269 at 284–285.
[285] *Horsler v Zorro* [1975] Ch. 302.
[286] *Jaggard* at 289–290.
[287] See para.17–212 and *Jaggard* at 284.
[288] e.g. *Soames v Edge* (1860) John 669 (agreement to build house and lease to plaintiff: damages for failure to build, decree that lease of land be executed).
[289] [1980] A.C. 367.
[290] [1974] Ch. 30.

which could only be refused at trial. Hence the date of trial, rather than the date of breach, might be the relevant one in assessing compensation. This view is, with respect, clearly right, and is reconcilable with Lord Wilberforce's view. The common law rule did not invariably select the date of breach as the relevant one in determining loss: that was merely the normal rule in commercial contracts. But as it is always reasonable to seek specific performance of a contract for the sale of land[291] any increase in loss caused by denial of the relief at trial (so late in the day) ought, as a matter of justice, to be taken into account because "if to follow [the normal rule] would give rise to injustice, the court has power to fix such other date as may be appropriate in the circumstances."[292]

Various Commonwealth cases have adopted Megarry J.'s reasoning in *Wroth* to develop special principles of assessment for equitable damages in cases where common law damages could alternatively have been awarded. The most significant of these is *Semelhago v Paramadevan*.[293] The parties entered a contract for the sale of a house for $205,000 with a closing date at the end of October 1986. The purchaser had $75,000 in cash, and he planned to mortgage his existing house to secure a loan for the remaining $130,000. To this end he negotiated a six-month open mortgage, intending to sell his existing house over the next six months and repay the loan with the proceeds. However the vendor reneged on the deal and transferred title to a third party in December 1986. The purchaser therefore issued a writ for specific performance or damages in lieu, and stayed in his existing house. This was worth $190,000 in the autumn of 1986, but had risen in value to $300,000 by the time of trial. By then the new house which he had planned to buy from the vendor had also risen in value, to $325,000. **17–218**

At trial the purchaser elected to take damages rather than specific performance, and in line with *Wroth* the trial judge assessed these at $120,000, representing the difference between the purchase price and the value of the new house at the time of trial. The Ontario Court of Appeal reduced this to $81,000, accepting the vendor's argument that certain items should be deducted, namely the interest which the purchaser had avoided paying on the $130,000 loan which would have been needed to finance the purchase, the interest earned on the $75,000 that he would have used for the down payment, and the legal fees which he would have incurred. The vendor appealed, arguing that a deduction should also be made to reflect the fact that the purchaser's existing house had risen in value, a gain which he would not have made if he had sold it as planned. The Supreme Court of Canada rejected this, Sopinka J. stating that:[294] **17–219**

> "If the respondent had received a decree of specific performance, he would have had the property contracted for and retained the amount of the rise in value of his own property. Damages are to be substituted for the decree of specific performance. I see no basis for deductions that are not related to the value of the property which was the subject of the contract. To make such deductions would depart from the principle that damages are to be a true equivalent of specific performance."

This result seems to overcompensate by the claimant by overriding the normal rule that a claimant must mitigate his loss between the date of breach and the date of judgment. However, *Semelhago* is a **17–220**

---

[291] Except, perhaps, if one knows or ought to know that one's own hands are unclean.

[292] Per Lord Wilberforce at 401. Note also Millett L.J.'s explanation, in *Jaggard* at 290–291, of Lord Wilberforce's view as it affects injunction cases concerned with the prevention of future wrongs.

[293] [1996] 2 SCR 415. See too *Souster v Epsom Plumbing Contractors Ltd* [1974] 2 N.Z.L.R. 515; *Metropolitan Trust Co of Canada v Pressure Concrete Services Ltd* (1975) 60 D.L.R. (3d) 431; *Kopec v Pyret* (1987) 36 D.L.R. (4th) 1; *Mills v Ruthol Pty Ltd* (2004) 61 N.S.W.L.R. 1. In *Semelhago* at [22] Sopinka J. also held that contracts for the sale of land are not routinely specifically enforceable, and that claimants must produce evidence that the property is "unique to the extent that its substitute is not readily available". For critical comment on this aspect of the case, see R. Chambers, "The Importance of Specific Performance" in S. Degeling and J. Edelman (eds), *Equity in Commercial Law* (2005).

[294] *Semelhago* at [19].

perfectly logical extension of the *Wroth* principle that equitable damages under Lord Cairns' Act are a monetised substitute for specific performance. As Professor Lionel Smith has observed,[295] the purpose of an order for specific performance is not to compensate the claimant for the loss of his performance interest under the contract, but to vindicate his performance right by compelling the defendant to perform his promise. If equitable damages in lieu of specific performance are awarded with the same goal in mind, then the duty to mitigate has no application for the same reasons that it has no application to a claim for specific performance: since neither remedy is designed to compensate the claimant for his loss, complaints that the claimant has been "overcompensated" miss the point.

JAGGARD v SAWYER

Court of Appeal [1995] 1 W.L.R. 269; [1995] 2 All E.R. 189

17–221 In a cul-de-sac residential development consisting of ten plots, the claimant and defendants each owned one, together with part of the private road immediately fronting each. Each plot was bound by a restrictive covenant preventing the user of any part of any plot not built upon from being used other than as a private garden. The defendants purchased land adjacent to their plot but inaccessible from the private road other than through their plot. They obtained, in 1988, planning permission to build on the adjacent land and (wrongly believing the road to be a public one) to construct a driveway leading to it, over their garden, from the road. The claimant threatened injunctive proceedings on the ground of (i) breach of covenant and (ii) trespass over her portion of the road but did not act on the threat. On 14 June 1989 the defendants began building and on 10 August 1989, the building at an advanced stage, the claimant began proceedings for an injunction. No interlocutory relief was sought and the building was completed thereafter. At trial it was common ground that the road was private but was the only means of access to the plot. The judge held that although the defendants were in breach of covenant, had committed trespass and would by using the road in future, continue to commit trespass, it would, in the circumstances, have been oppressive to grant an injunction and that damages should be awarded in lieu. The award would be £694.44, one ninth share of £6,250, the sum which the nine plot-owners might reasonably have demanded from the defendants as the price of release from the covenant and for the grant of a right of way. The claimant appealed.

17–222 SIR THOMAS BINGHAM M.R. (with whom KENNEDY L.J. agreed): The judge recognised that a plaintiff who can show that his legal right will be violated by the defendant's conduct is prima facie entitled to the grant of an injunction. He accepted that the court will only rarely and reluctantly permit such violation to occur or continue. But he held that this case fulfilled the four tests laid down by A.L. Smith L.J. in *Shelfer's case* to bring this case within the exception. The real question in this appeal is whether that judgment is sustainable.

17–223 (1) He regarded the injury to the plaintiff's right as small. This is in my view so. It is not suggested that the increase in traffic attributable to the existence of No.5A will be other than minimal, or that the cost of keeping up the road will be significantly increased. The defendants have in any event offered throughout to contribute to the cost of upkeep and are willing, if a draft is tendered to them, to execute a deed binding themselves by the same covenants as other residents of the Avenue. It is not suggested that the driveway to No.5A impairs the visual amenity of the plaintiff's house or affects its value. There is of course a violation of the plaintiff's strict legal right, but that will be so in any case of this kind.

[295] L.D. Smith, "Understanding Specific Performance" in N. Cohen and E. McKendrick (eds), *Comparative Remedies for Breach of Contract* (2005). See too C. Webb, "Performance and Compensation: An Analysis of Contract Damages and Contractual Obligation" (2006) 26 O.J.L.S. 41, developing ideas in D. Friedmann, "The Performance Interest in Contract Damages" (1995) 111 L.Q.R. 628.

(2) The judge considered the value of the injury to the plaintiff's right as capable of being estimated in money. He based himself on the Wrotham Park approach. In my view he was justified. He valued the right at what a reasonable seller would sell it for. In situations of this kind a plaintiff should not be treated as eager to sell, which he very probably is not. But the court will not value the right at the ransom price which a very reluctant plaintiff might put on it. I see no error in the judge's approach to this aspect. **17–224**

(3) The judge held that the injury to the plaintiff's legal right was one which could be adequately compensated by a small money payment. I agree, and I do not think this conclusion can be faulted. **17–225**

(4) The judge concluded that in all the circumstances it would be oppressive to the defendants to grant the injunctions sought. Most of the argument turned on this condition, and in particular on the significance which the judge attached to the plaintiff's failure to seek interlocutory relief. **17–226**

It is important to bear in mind that the test is one of oppression, and the court should not slide into application of a general balance of convenience test. But oppression must be judged as at the date the court is asked to grant an injunction, and (as Brightman J. recognised in the *Wrotham Park* case) the court cannot ignore the reality with which it is then confronted. It is relevant that the plaintiff could at an early stage have sought interlocutory relief, which she would seem very likely to have obtained; but it is also relevant that the defendants could have sought a declaration of right. These considerations are not decisive. It would weigh against a finding of oppression if the defendants had acted in blatant and calculated disregard of the plaintiff's rights, of which they were aware, but the judge held that this was not so, and the plaintiff's solicitors may be thought to have indicated that damages would be an acceptable remedy. . . . The judge was in my view entitled to hold on all the facts before the court at trial that the grant of an injunction would be oppressive to the defendants, and I share that view. **17–227**

I am of the clear opinion that the appeal must be dismissed. **17–228**

MILLETT L.J.: This appeal raises yet again the question: what approach should the court adopt when invited to exercise its statutory jurisdiction to award damages instead of granting an injunction to restrain a threatened or continuing trespass or breach of a restrictive covenant? And if the court accedes to the invitation on what basis should damages be assessed? **17–229**

Before considering these questions, it is desirable to state some general propositions which are established by the authorities and which are, or at least ought to be, uncontroversial. **17–230**

(1) The jurisdiction was originally conferred by section 2 of the Chancery Amendment Act 1858, commonly known as Lord Cairns's Act. It is now to be found in section 50 of the Supreme Court Act 1981.[296] It is a jurisdiction to award damages "in addition to or in substitution for such injunction or specific performance". **17–231**

(2) The principal object of Lord Cairns's Act is well known. It was described by Turner L.J. in *Ferguson v Wilson*.[297] It was to enable the Court of Chancery, when declining to grant equitable relief and leaving the plaintiff to his remedy at law, to award the plaintiff damages itself instead of sending him to the common law courts to obtain them. From the very first, however, it was recognised that the Act did more than this. The jurisdiction of the Court of Chancery was wider than that of the common law courts, for it could give relief where there was no cause of action at law. As early as 1863, Turner L.J. himself had recognised the potential effect of Lord Cairns's Act. In *Eastwood v Lever*,[298] he pointed out that the Act had empowered the courts of equity to award damages in cases where the common law courts could not. The Act, he said, was not "confined to cases in which the plaintiffs could recover damages at law." Damages at common law are recoverable only in respect of causes of action which are complete at the date of the writ; damages for future or repeated wrongs must be made **17–232**

[296] [Editor's note: Now known as the Senior Courts Act 1981.]
[297] (1866) L.R. 2 Ch. App. 77 at 88.
[298] (1863) 4 De G.J. & S. 114 at 128.

the subject of fresh proceedings. Damages in substitution for an injunction, however, relate to the future, not the past. They inevitably extend beyond the damages to which the plaintiff may be entitled at law. In *Leeds Industrial Co-operative Society Ltd v Slack*[299] the House of Lords confirmed the jurisdiction of the courts to award damages under the Act in respect of an injury which was threatened but had not yet occurred. No such damages could have been awarded at common law.

17–233 (3) The nature of the cause of action is immaterial; it may be in contract or tort. Lord Cairns's Act referred in terms to "a breach of any covenant, contract, or agreement, or against the commission or continuance of any wrongful act." The jurisdiction to award damages in substitution for an injunction has most commonly been exercised in cases where the defendant's building has infringed the plaintiff's right to light or where it has been erected in breach of a restrictive covenant. Despite dicta to the contrary in *Woollerton and Wilson Ltd v Richard Costain Ltd*[300] there is in my opinion no justification for excluding cases of threatened or continuing trespass on the ground that trespass is actionable at law without proof of actual damage. Equitable relief, whether by way of injunction or damages under Lord Cairns's Act, is available because the common law remedy is inadequate; but the common law remedy of damages in cases of continuing trespass is inadequate not because the damages are likely to be small or nominal but because they cover the past only and not the future.

17–234 (4) The power to award damages under Lord Cairns's Act arises whenever the court "has jurisdiction to entertain an application" for an injunction or specific performance. This question must be determined as at the date of the writ. If the court would then have had jurisdiction to grant an injunction, it has jurisdiction to award damages instead. When the court comes to consider whether to grant an injunction or award damages instead, of course, it must do so by reference to the circumstances as they exist at the date of the hearing.

17–235 (5) The former question is effectively one of jurisdiction. The question is whether, at the date of the writ, the court could have granted an injunction, not whether it would have done: *City of London Brewery Co v Tennant*.[301] Russell L.J. put it neatly in *Hooper v Rogers*[302] when he said that the question was "whether . . . the judge could have (however unwisely . . .) made a mandatory order." There have been numerous cases where damages under Lord Cairns's Act were refused because at the date of the writ it was impossible to grant an injunction or specific performance: for one well known example, see *Lavery v Pursell*.[303] The recent case of *Surrey County Council v Bredero Homes Ltd*[304] appears to have been a case of this character.

17–236 (6) It is not necessary for the plaintiff to include a claim for damages in his writ. As long ago as 1868 Lord Chelmsford L.C. held that damages may be awarded under Lord Cairns's Act:[305]

"though not specifically prayed for by the bill, the statute having vested a discretion in the judge, which he may exercise when he thinks the case fitting without the prayer of the party."

It would be absurd as well as misleading to insist on the plaintiff including a claim for damages in his writ when he is insisting on his right to an injunction and opposing the defendant's claim that he should be content to receive damages instead. By a parity of reasoning it is not in my opinion necessary for a plaintiff to include a claim for an injunction in order to found a claim for damages under the Act. It would be absurd to require him to include a claim for an injunction if he is sufficiently realistic to recognise that in the circumstances he is unlikely to obtain one and intends from

299 [1924] A.C. 851.
300 [1970] 1 W.L.R. 411.
301 (1873) L.R. 9 Ch. App. 212.
302 [1975] Ch. 43 at 48.
303 (1888) 39 Ch.D. 508.
304 [1993] 1 W.L.R. 1361.
305 *Betts v Neilson* (1868) L.R. 3 Ch. App. 429 at 411.

the first to ask the court for damages instead. But he ought to make it clear whether he is claiming damages for past injury at common law or under the Act in substitution for an injunction.

(7) In *Anchor Brewhouse Developments Ltd v Berkley House (Docklands Developments) Ltd*[306] Scott J. granted an injunction to restrain a continuing trespass. In the course of his judgment, however, he cast doubt on the power of the court to award damages for future trespasses by means of what he described as a "once and for all payment". This was because, as he put it, the court could not by an award of damages put the defendant in the position of a person entitled to an easement; whether or not an injunction were granted, the defendant's conduct would still constitute a trespass; and a succession of further actions for damages could accordingly still be brought. This reasoning strikes at the very heart of the statutory jurisdiction; it is in marked contrast to the attitude of the many judges who from the very first have recognised that, while the Act does not enable the court to license future wrongs, this may be the practical result of withholding injunctive relief; and it is inconsistent with the existence of the jurisdiction, confirmed in *Leeds Industrial Co-operative Society Ltd v Slack*,[307] to award damages under the Act in a *quia timet* action. It is in my view fallacious because it is not the award of damages which has the practical effect of licensing the defendant to commit the wrong, but the refusal of injunctive relief. Thereafter the defendant may have no right to act in the manner complained of, but he cannot be prevented from doing so. The court can in my judgment properly award damages "once and for all" in respect of future wrongs because it awards them in substitution for an injunction and to compensate for those future wrongs which an injunction would have prevented. The doctrine of res judicata operates to prevent the plaintiff and his successors in title from bringing proceedings thereafter to recover even nominal damages in respect of further wrongs for which the plaintiff has been fully compensated. . . . **17–237**

When the plaintiff claims an injunction and the defendant asks the court to award damages instead, the proper approach for the court to adopt cannot be in doubt. Clearly the plaintiff must first establish a case for equitable relief, not only by proving his legal right and an actual or threatened infringement by the defendant, but also by overcoming all equitable defences such as laches, acquiescence or estoppel. If he succeeds in doing this, he is prima facie entitled to an injunction. The court may nevertheless in its discretion withhold injunctive relief and award damages instead. How is this discretion to be exercised? In a well known passage in *Shelfer v City of London Electric Lighting Co*,[308] A.L. Smith L.J. set out what he described as "a good working rule" that **17–238**

"(1) If the injury to the plaintiff's legal right is small, (2) And is one which is capable of being estimated in money, (3) And is one which can be adequately compensated by a small money payment, (4) And the case is one in which it would be oppressive to the defendant to grant an injunction–then damages in substitution for an injunction may be given."

Laid down just 100 years ago, A.L. Smith L.J.'s check-list has stood the test of time; but it needs to be remembered that it is only a working rule and does not purport to be an exhaustive statement of the circumstances in which damages may be awarded instead of an injunction.

Reported cases are merely illustrations of circumstances in which particular judges have exercised their discretion, in some cases by granting an injunction, and in others by awarding damages instead. Since they are all cases on the exercise of a discretion, none of them is a binding authority on how the discretion should be exercised. The most that any of them can demonstrate is that in similar circumstances it would not be wrong to exercise the discretion in the same way. But it does not follow that it would be wrong to exercise it differently. **17–239**

The outcome of any particular case usually turns on the question: would it in all the circumstances be oppressive to the defendant to grant the injunction to which the plaintiff is prima facie entitled? Most of **17–240**

306 (1987) 38 B.L.R. 87.
307 [1924] A.C. 851
308 [1895] 1 Ch. 287 at 322–323.

the cases in which the injunction has been refused are cases where the plaintiff has sought a mandatory injunction to pull down a building which infringes his right to light or which has been built in breach of a restrictive covenant. In such cases the court is faced with a fait accompli. The jurisdiction to grant a mandatory injunction in those circumstances cannot be doubted, but to grant it would subject the defendant to a loss out of all proportion to that which would be suffered by the plaintiff if it were refused, and would indeed deliver him to the plaintiff bound hand and foot to be subjected to any extortionate demands the plaintiff might make. In the present case, as in the closely similar case of *Bracewell v Appleby*,[309] the plaintiff sought a prohibitory injunction to restrain the use of a road giving access to the defendants' house. The result of granting the injunction would be much the same; the house would not have to be pulled down, but it would be rendered landlocked and incapable of beneficial enjoyment. . . .

17–241 In considering whether the grant of an injunction would be oppressive to the defendant, all the circumstances of the case have to be considered. At one extreme, the defendant may have acted openly and in good faith and in ignorance of the plaintiff's rights, and thereby inadvertently placed himself in a position where the grant of an injunction would either force him to yield to the plaintiff's extortionate demands or expose him to substantial loss. At the other extreme, the defendant may have acted with his eyes open and in full knowledge that he was invading the plaintiff's rights, and hurried on his work in the hope that by presenting the court with a fait accompli he could compel the plaintiff to accept monetary compensation. Most cases, like the present, fall somewhere in between.

17–242 In the present case, the defendants acted openly and in good faith and in the not unreasonable belief that they were entitled to make use of Ashleigh Avenue for access to the house that they were building. At the same time, they had been warned by the plaintiff and her solicitors that Ashleigh Avenue was a private road, that they were not entitled to use it for access to the new house, and that it would be a breach of covenant for them to use the garden of No.5 to gain access to No.5A. They went ahead, not with their eyes open, but at their own risk. On the other hand, the plaintiff did not seek interlocutory relief at a time when she would almost certainly have obtained it. She should not be criticised for that, but it follows that she also took a risk, namely, that by the time her case came on for trial the court would be presented with a fait accompli. The case was a difficult one, but in an exemplary judgment the judge took into account all the relevant considerations, both those which told in favour of granting an injunction and those which told against, and in the exercise of his discretion he decided to refuse it. In my judgment his conclusion cannot be faulted.

17–243 Having decided to refuse an injunction and to award the plaintiff damages instead, the judge had to consider the measure of damages. He based them on her share of the amount which, in his opinion, the plaintiff and the other residents of Ashleigh Avenue could reasonably have demanded as the price of waiving their rights. In this he applied the measure of damages which had been adopted by Brightman J. in *Wrotham Park Estate Co Ltd v Parkside Homes Ltd*,[310] a case which has frequently been followed. It would not be necessary to consider this matter further but for the fact that in the recent case in this court of *Surrey County Council v Bredero Homes Ltd*[311] doubts were expressed as to the basis on which this measure of damages could be justified and whether it was consistent with the reasoning of Lord Wilberforce in *Johnson v Agnew*.[312] It is, therefore, necessary to examine those cases further.

17–244 In *Surrey County Council v Bredero Homes Ltd* the plaintiffs claimed damages from the original covenantor, a developer, for breach of a restrictive covenant against building more than 72 houses, and sought to measure the damages by reference to the additional profit which the defendant had made by building the extra houses. Their claim to substantial damages failed. The case is not authority on the proper measure of damages under Lords Cairns's Act, since (as Dillon L.J. made clear[313]) the plaintiffs' claim was for damages at common law and not under the Act. . . .

17–245 Examination of the facts stated in the headnote reveals that the defendant had disposed of all the houses on the estate before the plaintiffs commenced proceedings, and that the purchasers were not joined as parties. Any claim to damages under Lord Cairns's Act must have failed; at the date of the writ

309 [1975] Ch. 408.
310 [1974] 1 W.L.R. 798.
311 [1993] 1 W.L.R. 1361.
312 [1980] A.C. 367.
313 At 1367.

the court could not have ordered the defendant to pull down the houses, since this was no longer something which was within its power to do.

17–246 Unfortunately, however, Dillon L.J. cast doubt on the correctness of the measure of damages which had been adopted by Brightman J. in *Wrotham Park Estate Co Ltd v Parkside Homes Ltd* a case which was decided under Lord Cairns's Act. He said:[314]

> "The difficulty about the decision in the *Wrotham Park* case is that in *Johnson v Agnew*[315] Lord Wilberforce, after citing certain decisions on the scope and basis of Lord Cairns's Act which were not cited to Brightman J., stated in the clearest terms that on the balance of those authorities and on principle he found in the Act no warrant for the court awarding damages differently from common law damages."

17–247 This statement must not be taken out of context. Earlier in his speech Lord Wilberforce had clearly recognised that damages could be awarded under Lord Cairns's Act where there was no cause of action at law, and he cannot have been insensible to the fact that, when the court awards damages in substitution for an injunction, it seeks to compensate the plaintiff for loss arising from future wrongs, that is to say, loss for which the common law does not provide a remedy. Neither *Wroth v Tyler* nor *Johnson v Agnew* was a case of this kind. In each of those cases the plaintiff claimed damages for loss occasioned by a single, once and for all, past breach of contract on the part of the defendant. In neither case was the breach a continuing one capable of generating further losses. In my view Lord Wilberforce's statement that the measure of damages is the same whether damages are recoverable at common law or under the Act must be taken to be limited to the case where they are recoverable in respect of the same cause of action. It cannot sensibly have any application where the claim at common law is in respect of a past trespass or breach of covenant and that under the Act is in respect of future trespasses or continuing breaches of covenant.

17–248 Accordingly I am of opinion that the judge was not precluded by the decision of the House of Lords in *Johnson v Agnew* from adopting the measure of damages which he did. It is, however, necessary to notice the observations of Steyn L.J. in *Surrey County Council v Bredero Homes Ltd*:[316]

> "In my view *Wrotham Park Estate Co Ltd v Parkside Homes Ltd* is only defensible on the basis of the third or restitutionary principle. . . . The plaintiffs' argument that the *Wrotham Park* case can be justified on the basis of a loss of bargaining opportunity is a fiction."

I find these remarks puzzling. It is plain from his judgment in the *Wrotham Park* case that Brightman J.'s approach was compensatory, not restitutionary. He sought to measure the damages by reference to what the plaintiff had lost, not by reference to what the defendant had gained. He did not award the plaintiff the profit which the defendant had made by the breach, but the amount which he judged the plaintiff might have obtained as the price of giving its consent. The amount of the profit which the defendant expected to make was a relevant factor in that assessment, but that was all.

17–249 Both the *Wrotham Park* and *Bredero Homes* cases (unlike the present) were concerned with a single past breach of covenant, so that the measure of damages at common law and under the Act was the same. Prima facie the measure of damages in either case for breach of a covenant not to build a house on neighbouring land is the diminution in the value of the plaintiff's land occasioned by the breach. One element in the value of the plaintiff's land immediately before the breach is attributable to his ability to obtain an injunction to prevent the building. Clearly a defendant who wished to build would pay for the release of the covenant, but only so long as the court could still protect it by the grant of an injunction. The proviso is important. It is the ability to claim an injunction which gives the benefit of the covenant much of its value. If the plaintiff delays proceedings until it is no longer possible for him to obtain an injunction, he destroys his own bargaining position and devalues his right. The unavailability of the remedy of injunction at one and the same time deprives the court of jurisdiction to award damages under the Act and removes the basis for awarding substantial damages at common law. For this reason, I take the view that damages

[314] At 1366.
[315] [1980] A.C. 367 at 400.
[316] [1993] 1 W.L.R. 1361 at 1369.

can be awarded at common law in accordance with the approach adopted in the Wrotham Park case, but in practice only in the circumstances in which they could also be awarded under the Act.

17–250 This may be what Steyn L.J. had in mind when he said that the loss of bargaining opportunity was a fiction. If he meant it generally or in relation to the facts which obtained in the *Wrotham Park* case, then I respectfully disagree. But it was true in the circumstances of the case before him, and not merely for the reason given by Rose L.J. (that the plaintiffs did not object to the extra houses and would have waived the breach for a nominal sum). The plaintiffs did not bring the proceedings until after the defendant had sold the houses and was no longer susceptible to an injunction. The plaintiffs had thereby deprived themselves of any bargaining position. Unable to obtain an injunction, they were equally unable to invoke the jurisdiction to award damages under Lord Cairns's Act. No longer exposed to the risk of an injunction, and having successfully disposed of the houses, the defendant had no reason to pay anything for the release of the covenant. Unless they were able to recover damages in accordance with restitutionary principles, neither at common law nor in equity could the plaintiffs recover more than nominal damages.

17–251 In the present case the plaintiff brought proceedings at a time when her rights were still capable of being protected by injunction. She has accordingly been able to invoke the court's jurisdiction to award in substitution for an injunction damages which take account of the future as well as the past. In my view there is no reason why compensatory damages for future trespasses and continuing breaches of covenant should not reflect the value of the rights which she has lost, or why such damages should not be measured by the amount which she could reasonably have expected to receive for their release.

17–252 In my judgment the judge's approach to the assessment of damages was correct on the facts and in accordance with principle. I would dismiss the appeal.

5. Rescission

17–253 The equitable right to rescind[317] is the right of a party to a transaction to set it aside and so to be restored to his former position. It must be distinguished as a voidable transaction from a transaction that is void ab initio (e.g. a contract void for illegality or a very fundamental mistake). It must also be distinguished from the case where a contract with no inherent invalidity is said to be rescinded for the future when the innocent party accepts the wrongdoer's repudiatory breach of contract as terminating the contract, but leaving the innocent party free to sue the wrongdoer for his past breaches of a valid contract.[318]

17–254 Equity can set aside a transaction in circumstances where the common law would not and is more flexible in its view of the requirement that the claimant make counter restitution e.g. taking accounts and making an allowance for services rendered or for deterioration of property.[319] Moreover, equity by applying the maxim "he who comes to equity must do equity" can grant relief on terms, e.g. so that a contract is set aside so long as the vendor offers the property in question to the purchaser at a proper price.[320]

---

317 The differences between recission in equity and at common law are rehearsed in *Alati v Kruger* (1955) 94 C.L.R. 216 at 223–224, endorsed by Dunn L.J. in *O'Sullivan v Management Agency & Music Ltd* [1985] Q.B. 428 at 457. Whether these should be perpetuated is a controversial topic. Some would argue that the current distinctions between the bars to rescission in law and equity are indefensible, and that it is confusing and unnecessary for the law to operate more than one version of the remedy. This outlook informs e.g. Carnwath L.J.'s comments in *Halpern v Halpern (Nos 1 and 2)* [2008] Q.B. 195 at [70] ff. Others would argue that it is desirable to maintain a common law right of election as a self-help remedy, available automatically on strong facts, and an equitable remedy that is available at the discretion of the court on weaker facts where a more sensitive balancing of interests is required. For the latter view, see e.g. D. O'Sullivan, S. Elliott and R. Zakrzewski, *The Law of Rescission* (2008) Ch.10.

318 *Johnson v Agnew* [1980] A.C. 367 at 396–398; *Photo Production Ltd v Securicor Transport Ltd* [1980] A.C. 827 at 844.

319 See *Alati* and *O'Sullivan*, above.

320 *Grist v Bailey* [1967] Ch. 532; *Magee v Pennine Insurance Co Ltd* [1969] 2 Q.B. 507.

Rescission has been awarded in cases:[321] **17–255**

(a) where a party was induced to enter into a contract by a fraudulent misrepresentation–or even an innocent misrepresentation, but the court now has a discretion to award damages in lieu of rescission if it would be equitable to do so;[322]

(b) where a party entered into a transaction as a result of another's undue influence;[323]

(c) where a poor ignorant person entered into a disadvantageous transaction (e.g. at an undervalue) without any independent legal advice;[324]

(d) where the other party to a contract uberrimae fidei (e.g. a contract of insurance) breached his duty of full disclosure;[325]

(e) where the other party to a transaction breached his fiduciary duty of full disclosure;[326]

(f) where a donor made a gift by reason of another's misrepresentation or undue influence;[327] and

(g) where a donor made a gift under a unilateral mistake as to present facts (but not a misprediction), as in *Re Griffiths (deceased)*,[328] which is reproduced below.[329]

In *TSB Bank Plc v Camfield*[330] the Court of Appeal held that if a claimant can set aside a transaction for misrepresentation (or undue influence) then it must be set aside entirely rather than partially. So, a claimant who has agreed to mortgage her house for £30,000 can escape liability for the entire sum, although she would have agreed to liability for £15,000 irrespective of the misrepresentation (or undue influence). Note, however, that she must return any benefit she has personally received under the contract before it can be set aside.[331] **17–256**

The Court of Appeal's reasoning in *Camfield* was repudiated, and the opposite result reached, in *Vadasz v Pioneer Concrete SA*[332] where the High Court of Australia held that the court should be concerned to achieve a practically just result when putting the claimant on terms, and should seek to put the claimant in the position which he would have occupied if the misconduct had not occurred. **17–257**

---

321 There is no equitable jurisdiction to grant rescission of a contract on the ground of common mistake where the contract is valid at common law: *Great Peace Shipping Ltd v Tsavlisis Salvage (International) Ltd* [2003] Q.B. 679, disapproving *Solle v Butcher* [1950] 1 K.B. 671. Nor is there an equitable jurisdiction to grant rescission of a contract where one party has made a unilateral mistake as to a fact or state of affairs which is the basis upon which the terms of the contract are agreed, but that assumption does not become a term of the contract: *Statoil ASA v Louis Dreyfus Energy Services LP* [2008] 2 Lloyd's Rep. 685 at [98]–[105], rejecting *Huyton SA v Distribuidora Internacional De Productos Agricolas SA de CV* [2003] 2 Lloyd's Rep. 780 at [455].

322 Misrepresentation Act 1967 s.2(2). Indeed, s.2(1) allows damages of a tortious measure to be awarded for a negligent misrepresentation: *Royscot Trust Ltd v Rogerson* [1991] 2 Q.B. 297; *Witter Ltd v TBP Industries Ltd* [1996] 2 All E.R. 573.

323 *Barclays Bank Plc v O'Brien* [1994] 1 A.C. 180; *CIBC Mortgages Plc v Pitt* [1994] 1 A.C. 200.

324 *Cresswell v Potter* [1978] 1 W.L.R. 255; *Crédit Lyonnais Nederland NV v Burch* [1997] 1 All E.R. 144; *Portman BS v Dusangh* [2001] W.T.L.R 117.

325 *Pan Atlantic Insurance Co Ltd v Pine Top Insurance Co Ltd* [1995] 1 A.C. 501; *Manifest Shipping Co Ltd v Uni-Polaris Insurance Co Ltd* [2003] 1 A.C. 469.

326 *Daly v Sidney Stock Exchange* (1986) 160 C.L.R. 371; *Guinness Plc v Saunders* [1990] 2 A.C. 663; *Ross River Ltd v Cambridge City Football Club Ltd* [2008] 1 All E.R. 100.

327 *Re Glubb* [1900] 1 Ch. 354.

328 [2009] Ch. 162. See too *Hood (Lady) of Avalon v Mackinnon* [1909] 1 Ch. 476; *Gibbon v Mitchell* [1990] 1 W.L.R. 1304; *Bhatt v Bhatt* [2009] W.T.L.R. 1139.

329 At paras 17–259 ff.

330 [1995] 1 W.L.R. 430.

331 *Camfield* at 432 and 437; *Dunbar Bank Plc v Nadeem* [1998] 3 All E.R. 876 at 883.

332 (1995) 184 C.L.R. 102.

This approach has a strong intuitive appeal, and it was also taken by the New Zealand Court of Appeal in *Scales Trading Co Ltd v Far Eastern Shipping Co Public Ltd*.[333] However, it seems to treat rescission as though it were a compensatory remedy when the point of the remedy is rather to require the parties to return whatever benefits they may have received under the contract. The *Vadasz* approach also means that a claimant who would have contracted on precisely the same terms irrespective of the defendant's misconduct cannot rescind at all, a proposition that is contradicted by many authorities, including the High Court of Australia's decision a year after *Vadasz* in *Maguire v Makaronis*,[334] where the court was forced to side-step the problem by holding that *Vadasz* does not apply in cases involving fiduciaries.

17–258 The equitable right to rescind is lost if: (a) the party entitled to rescind affirms the transaction;[335] (b) restitutio in integrum is not substantially possible, taking account of services rendered or for property deterioration;[336] or (c) the right is not exercised within a reasonable time.[337] It is often said by writers that the intervention of third party rights also constitutes a bar to rescission in equity, but in fact Equity has always managed to protect third party purchasers without barring rescission,[338] for example by letting third parties keep the relevant asset but requiring the defendant to hand over the proceeds of sale[339] or exchange products.[340]

RE GRIFFITHS (DECEASED)

Chancery Division [2009] Ch. 162, [2009] 2 W.L.R. 394, [2008] 2 All E.R. 655

17–259 To mitigate the effect of inheritance tax on his death, Griffiths executed three potentially exempt transfers by which property was transferred into various trusts. A year later he was diagnosed with lung cancer and six months after that he died. Since he had not survived for more than three years since the transfers were made, all three transfers were chargeable for inheritance tax purposes. Had he not made the transfers, inheritance tax would not have been payable immediately. The executors of Griffiths' estate successfully applied to set aside the transfers on the ground that they had been made under a mistake of fact.

17–260 LEWISON J. (after stating the facts): The executors rely on a broad equitable jurisdiction to set aside a voluntary transaction on the ground of mistake. The nature of the jurisdiction was described by Lindley L.J. in *Ogilvie v Littleboy*:[341]

> "Gifts cannot be revoked, nor can deeds of gift be set aside, simply because the donors wish they had not made them and would like to have back the property given. Where there is no fraud, no undue influence, no fiduciary relationship between donor and donee, no mistake induced by those who derive any benefit by it, a gift, whether by mere delivery or by deed, is binding on the donor. . . . In the absence of all such circumstances of suspicion a donor can only obtain back property which he has given away by showing that he was under some mistake of so serious a character as to render it unjust on the part of the donee to retain the property given to him."

---

333 [1999] 3 N.Z.L.R. 26.
334 (1996) 188 C.L.R. 449.
335 *Mitchell v Homfray* (1881) 8 Q.B.D. 587; *Leaf v International Galleries Ltd* [1950] 2 K.B. 86; *Peyman v Lanjani* [1985] Ch. 457; *Insurance Corp of the Channel Islands v Royal Hotel Ltd* [1998] Lloyd's Rep. I.R. 151.
336 *Erlanger v New Sombrero Phosphate Co* (1873) 3 App. Cas. 1218; *Spence v Crawford* [1939] 3 All E.R. 271; *O'Sullivan v Management Agency & Music Ltd* [1985] Q.B. 428.
337 *Lindsay Petroleum Co v Hurd* (1874) L.R. 5 P.C. 221 at 239–240; *Erlanger v New Sombrero Phosphate Co* (1878) 3 App. Cas. 1218 at 1279–1280 and 1230–1231; *Leaf v International Galleries Ltd* [1950] 2 K.B. 86.
338 A point well made in D. O'Sullivan S. Elliott and R. Zakrzewski, *The Law of Rescission* (2008) paras 20.23 ff.
339 *Fox v Mackreth* (1788) 2 Bro. C.C. 44; *Lagunas Nitrate Co v Lagunas Syndicate* [1899] 2 Ch. 392 at 434.
340 *Small v Attwood* (1832) You. 407 at 535–538; *Shalson v Russo* [1995] Ch. 281 at 320–322.
341 (1897) 13 T.L.R. 399 at 400.

An appeal to the House of Lords reported as *Ogilvie v Allen*[342] was dismissed. Lord Halsbury L.C. said that he agreed with the judgment of Lindley L.J., but he contemplated that there might be "circumstances when misunderstanding on both sides may render it unjust to the giver that the gift should be retained". Lord Macnaghten and Lord Morris agreed. **17–261**

In *Sieff v Fox*[343] Lloyd L.J. said that this case established a broad principle of injustice as the test for setting aside a voluntary disposition, in the absence of any circumstances of suspicion. He added that because this case had not been reported in the Law Reports it does not appear to have been cited in any of the later cases that considered the ambit of the jurisdiction. **17–262**

One of the areas of debate has been the nature of the operative mistake which brings the jurisdiction into play. In *Gibbon v Mitchell* Millett J. expressed the principle as follows:[344] **17–263**

> "In my judgment, these cases show that, wherever there is a voluntary transaction by which one party intends to confer a bounty on another, the deed will be set aside if the court is satisfied that the disponor did not intend the transaction to have the effect which it did. It will be set aside for mistake whether the mistake is a mistake of law or of fact, so long as the mistake is as to the effect of the transaction itself and not merely as to its consequences or the advantages to be gained by entering into it. The proposition that equity will never relieve against mistakes of law is clearly too widely stated."

His Lordship's distinction between the effect of the transaction and its consequences or advantages has proved a difficult one to grasp. Davis J. in *Anker-Petersen v Christensen*,[345] Lloyd L.J. in *Sieff v Fox*[346] and Mann J. in *Wolff v Wolff*[347] have all expressed that difficulty. The principal debate has been whether a mistake by an individual (as opposed to a trustee) about the fiscal consequences of entering into a transaction counts as a mistake about the effect of the transaction or a mistake about its consequences or advantages. I do not need to resolve this debate. Mr Grierson said that a mistake about the fiscal consequences of entering into a transaction was enough to bring the jurisdiction into play even in a case involving an individual rather than trustees. But even if he is right, I do not think that this helps him on the facts of this case. The initial transfer of the shares into the discretionary trust was a chargeable transfer for the purposes of inheritance tax and was intended to be a chargeable transfer. So there was no mistake about its fiscal consequences. The grant of the deferred lease was intended to be a potentially exempt transfer. That is precisely what it was. There was no mistake about the immediate tax consequences of the grant. Similarly the intended effect of the transaction consisting of the transfer of Mr Griffiths's reversionary interest in the shares was intended to be a potentially exempt transfer for the purposes of inheritance tax. Again that is precisely what it was. There was no mistake about the immediate tax consequences of that transfer either. What was unexpected was Mr Griffiths's subsequent death just over a year later. Mr Grierson accepted, as I understood it, that if Mr Griffiths had been a hale and hearty young man and had entered into all the relevant transactions but fallen under a bus the following week, his executors would not have been able to ask the court to set aside the transactions on the ground of a mistake. I think that is right. The operative mistake must, in my judgment, be a mistake which existed at the time when the transaction was entered into. The mere falsification of expectations entertained at the date of the transaction is not, in my judgment, enough. **17–264**

However, the claimants' alternative argument is that there was an operative mistake of fact which Mr Griffiths made at the time of the transactions. The relevant mistake was a mistake about Mr Griffiths's state of health. That was a mistake about a fact existing at the time of the transaction, not a mistake about the effect of the transaction. I do not read the formulation by Millett J. as limiting the overall scope of the equitable jurisdiction to relieve against the consequences of a mistake. He said that a voluntary deed will be set aside if the court is satisfied that the disponor did not intend the transaction to have the effect which it did. He did not say that a voluntary deed will only be set aside if the court is satisfied that the disponor **17–265**

---

[342] (1899) 15 T.L.R. 294.
[343] [2005] 1 W.L.R. 3811 at 3843.
[344] [1990] 1 WLR 1304 at 1309.
[345] [2002] W.T.L.R. 313.
[346] [2005] 1 W.L.R. 3811.
[347] [2004] S.T.C. 1633.

did not intend the transaction to have the effect which it did. The formulation of principle by Lindley L.J. and approved by the House of Lords is not so limited. In *Lady Hood of Avalon v Mackinnon*[348] Lady Hood appointed sums of money to her daughters. She had intended to achieve equality between them but had forgotten that some years earlier she had already made appointments to her elder daughter. Eve J. discussed at length whether forgetting an existing fact could amount to a mistake. He concluded that it could and said:[349]

> "I think she executed the deed under a mistake with regard to the existing facts, and I cannot myself see that it is material whether that mistake arose from her being misinformed as to the true state of things, or from her state of mind being such that she had not, at that moment, knowledge of the true state of things. The absence of knowledge arose from her not bearing in mind, or not appreciating, that she had already appointed to the elder daughter a moiety of the fund, and in these circumstances I feel bound to hold, and, having regard to the evidence, I am glad to be able to hold, that this deed which it is sought to rescind was executed by Lady Hood under a mistake brought about by such circumstances as entitle her to the relief she seeks."

17–266 It is plain in my judgment that a mistake of fact is capable of bringing the equitable jurisdiction into play. All that is required is a mistake of a sufficiently serious nature. In my judgment a mistake about an existing or pre-existing fact if sufficiently serious is enough to bring the jurisdiction into play. If and to the extent that Millett J. intended to restrict the scope of the equitable jurisdiction to a mistake about the effect of a transaction, I respectfully disagree.

17–267 The next question I must consider is what needs to be shown as the consequence of the mistake. In *Sieff v Fox*[350] Lloyd L.J., as well as considering the circumstances in which a voluntary transaction may be set aside for mistake also considered the rule in *Re Hastings-Bass, decd*.[351] In his discussion of the latter rule he considered whether having shown that trustees failed to take into account relevant considerations, it was necessary to show that had they taken all relevant considerations into account they "would have" acted differently or merely that they "might have" acted differently. He distinguished between a case in which trustees were under a duty to act and cases in which they had a discretion whether to act or not. In the former case it was sufficient to show that they might have acted differently, whereas in the latter case it was necessary to show that they would have acted differently. He said:[352]

> "It seems to me that, for the purposes of a case where the trustees are not under a duty to act, the relevant test is still that stated in *Re Hastings-Bass*,[353] namely whether, if they had not misunderstood the effect that their actual exercise of the discretionary power would have, they would have acted differently. In my judgment that is correct both on authority, starting with *Re Hastings-Bass* itself, and on principle. Only in a case where the beneficiary is entitled to require the trustees to act, such as *Kerr's case*[354] or *Stannard's case*,[355] should it suffice to vitiate the trustees' decision to show that they might have acted differently. The word 'might' has been used, as matter of decision, only in those two cases. In two cases it has been said (not as a matter of decision) that the 'might' test applies to a voluntary exercise of a power: *AMP (UK) Plc v Barker*[356] and *Hearn v Younger*.[357] I respectfully disagree with those observations, having had the benefit of what may have been fuller, and were no doubt different, submissions on the point. If an act by trustees is set aside, where the trustees have acted under an obligation, then the

348 [1909] 1 Ch. 476.
349 At 484.
350 [2005] 1 W.L.R. 3811; see paras 000.
351 [1975] Ch. 25.
352 At [77].
353 [1975] Ch. 25.
354 [2001] W.T.L.R. 1071.
355 [1991] P.L.R. 225.
356 [2001] P.L.R. 77.
357 [2002] W.T.L.R. 1317.

beneficiaries can require the trustees to start again, on the correct basis. It seems to me that the lower test of 'might' is appropriate in such cases. . . . If the trustees' act was voluntary, so that they cannot be compelled to act again if the act is set aside, the more demanding test of 'would' is justified in order to decide whether the trustees' act can be set aside."

In a case where it is an individual disposing of his own property, it seems to me that the higher test applies. Thus the claimants must show that if Mr Griffiths had been aware of the true facts he would not have acted as he did. I should add that I do not consider that it is necessary for the claimants to show what Mr Griffiths would have done if he had not made the mistake. It is sufficient for them to show that he would not have done what he in fact did. I say this because the evidence suggests that Mr Griffiths would have done nothing and simply left his widow to inherit under his will. But that course of action would only have been effective if (as actually turned out) Mrs Griffiths survived her husband. In the course of argument Mr Grierson preferred the suggestion that Mr Griffiths would have made lifetime gifts to his wife leaving it to her to enter into the transactions recommended by the tax consultants. The difficulty with this suggestion was that there was no evidence to support it. But it shows that there were at least two possibilities available to Mr Griffiths had he not entered into the transactions into which he did in fact enter. **17–268**

I turn at last to the three transactions themselves. The first two took place in April 2003 at a time when Mr Griffiths did not have lung cancer. It is true that he had rheumatoid arthritis which was being controlled by drugs, but he knew that. So he made no mistake about his state of health. It is said that he made a mistake about his life expectancy, not being aware that the drugs had reduced his life expectancy by three to five years. However, there is no evidence to support that at all, and he must have known that although his parents lived into their 90s, his sister had died of rheumatoid arthritis in her 60s. Even if he had been aware of a reduced life expectancy he might well have taken the view that there was a reasonable chance that he would survive for seven years, or at least that he would survive long enough for the reduced rates of inheritance tax to be available. I am not satisfied that it has been shown either that Mr Griffiths made any relevant mistake in April 2003 or that, if he did, it has been shown that he would have acted differently. **17–269**

In the case of the deferred lease there is another problem. The deferred lease was a joint grant by Mr and Mrs Griffiths. Mrs Griffiths has not applied for the grant to be set aside. Mr Grierson said that she would be happy to make such an application. But the fact is that she has not; and even if she had it would have been necessary to show that she too made a relevant mistake. There is no evidence to that effect. I decline therefore to set aside either of the transactions entered into in April 2003. **17–270**

The assignment of the reversionary interest in February 2004 is a different matter. By that time Mr Griffiths was suffering from lung cancer about which he was unaware. He did therefore make a mistake about his state of health. Had he known in February 2004 that he was suffering from lung cancer he would also have known that his chance of surviving for three years, let alone for seven years, was remote. In those circumstances I am persuaded that he would not have acted as he did by transferring his reversionary interest in the shares to trustees. He would either have transferred them to his wife in his remaining lifetime or he would have allowed her to inherit under his will. I do not need to decide which of these courses of action he would have adopted. **17–271**

I am therefore satisfied that the conditions allowing the equitable jurisdiction to be exercised have been established in relation to the assignment of the reversionary interest in the shares. I need also to consider whether the satisfaction of these conditions means that the assignment of that interest is void or merely voidable. It makes a difference in this case because the executors have paid inheritance tax on a provisional basis. If the assignment is void they are entitled to interest on the overpaid tax as from the date on which they made the payments (section 235 of the Inheritance Tax Act 1984), whereas if it is voidable then interest is only payable from the date when a claim to repayment is made (section 150 and section 236(3) of the 1984 Act). This equitable jurisdiction has always been described as a jurisdiction to relieve against the consequence of a mistake or as a jurisdiction to set aside unilateral transactions entered into under a mistake. This description of the jurisdiction suggests strongly that unless and until the transaction is set aside (or relief is given) it did have some legal effect. In other words the transaction is voidable rather than void ab initio. In this respect the position differs from the effect of mistake at common law on what appears **17–272** to be a contract. But that is not surprising since the equitable jurisdiction is wider than the common law principle. In *Abacus Trust Co (Isle of Man) v Barr*[358] Lightman J. considered the question whether an exercise of discretion by trustees, which was vitiated by the principle in *Re Hastings-Bass, decd.*, was void or voidable. He described resolution of that issue as of "critical significance" in the case before him. He decided that the exercise was voidable rather than void. The question was discussed by Lloyd L.J. in *Sieff v Fox*, but as he recognised, nothing turned on the distinction in that case. He said that Lightman J.'s view was "open to doubt" although he also expressed the view that to hold that an appointment was voidable rather than void was attractive. He was of course discussing the *Hastings-Bass* principle rather than the wider equitable jurisdiction to relieve against the consequences of a mistake.

17–273 In *Barrow v Isaacs & Son*[359] the tenant of a warehouse in the City of London sublet it. The head lease contained a covenant against subletting without the landlord's consent such consent not to be unreasonably withheld. However, the tenant forgot to ask the landlord for consent and the landlord claimed to forfeit the lease. The majority judgment of the Court of Appeal was delivered by Kay L.J. He held that forgetting to ask for consent could properly be described as making a mistake. It was this part of the judgment that Eve J. relied on in *Lady Hood of Avalon v Mackinnon*.[360] However, although a relevant mistake was made, the court nevertheless refused relief. In describing the issues Kay L.J. said:[361]

> "But of course this left unaffected the undoubted jurisdiction to relieve in case of breach occasioned by fraud, accident, surprise, or mistake. At present the only one of these we have to deal with is mistake; and the questions are, (1) whether the facts I have described amount to mistake; and, if so, (2) whether in its discretion the court will relieve."

17–274 Having held that there was a relevant mistake Kay L.J. went on to say:[362]

> "It is an entirely different question whether on the ground of such a mistake equity, in the exercise of its discretionary jurisdiction, would relieve a man from a forfeiture incurred by his own gross carelessness."

17–275 Relief was refused. If the exercise of the jurisdiction is discretionary (as Kay L.J. undoubtedly said it was) it must follow that if as a matter of discretion relief is refused the impugned transaction will stand. If it stands it will have the effect it purports to have. I do not see how such a result is possible unless the impugned transaction is voidable rather than void ab initio.

17–276 I hold therefore that the assignment of the reversionary interest in the shares made on 3 February 2004 is voidable. It is unjust for the donees to retain the gift in circumstances which impose upon the donor an unintended liability to a very substantial amount of inheritance tax. There is no reason why I should refrain from exercising my discretion to set it aside; and I do so.

6. RECTIFICATION

17–277 Rectification is a discretionary remedy to rectify a document so that it accords correctly with what the parties agreed,[363] or in the case of a settlement with what the settlor intended.[364] For this purpose there is an exception to the "parole evidence rule" so that oral evidence may be given

---

358 [2003] Ch. 409.
359 [1891] 1 Q.B. 417.
360 [1909] 1 Ch. 476.
361 At 425.
362 At 426.
363 *Joscelyne v Nissen* [1970] 2 Q.B. 86; *Racal Group Services Ltd v Ashmore* [1994] S.T.C. 416.
364 *Re Butlin's ST* [1976] Ch. 251; *Lake v Lake* [1989] S.T.C. 865.

to establish the error with the "convincing proof"[365] that is required. When rectification occurs it is retrospective.[366]

In bilateral transactions where there was a unilateral mistake, rectification will only exceptionally be available, where the party who was not mistaken is fraudulent or estopped from resisting rectification by virtue of his unconscionable conduct.[367] Otherwise, the mistake must be common to both parties so that the document fails to record what they agreed.[368] Often it is possible to apply rules of construction to rescue parties in this situation, as in *Chartbrook Ltd v Persimmon Homes Ltd*,[369] part of which is reproduced below.[370] Whether or not that route can be taken, however, the House of Lords also held there that rectification will be ordered, provided that it can be said with certainty what the parties' contract was, and that it was wrongly expressed in the document, after comparing the document with what they said or wrote to one another in the course of reaching their agreement. **17–278**

Rectification of a voluntary deed, like a settlement, can be obtained if the donor's real intention was not accurately reflected in the deed.[371] Rectification is available whether the mistake relates to the contents of the deed, e.g. because the draftsman has accidentally departed from his client's instructions,[372] or to the legal effects of the deed, e.g. because it does not produce an intended fiscal advantage, as in *Wolff v Wolff*,[373] reproduced below. **17–279**

The law relating to rectification as it applies to pension schemes has been developed in a series of decisions since 2000, culminating in *Scania v Wager* where the Chancellor summarised the relevant principles as follows:[374] **17–280**

> "First that documents relating to pension schemes, be they trust deeds, rules or amendments to either, are as amenable to rectification as any other document with a legal effect. Second, it is necessary to show that the relevant employer or employers and the trustees shared the same intention, whether or not an outward expression of accord is required, down to the execution of the deed in question. Third rectification will only be granted if there is convincing proof on the balance of probabilities, that the employer and the trustees held the requisite common intention as to the meaning or effect of the relevant documents."

---

365 *Joscelyne v Nissen* [1970] 2 Q.B. 86; *Thor Navigation Inc v Ingosstrakh Insurance Co Ltd* [2005] 1 Lloyd's Rep. 547 at [51], per Gloster J. Note that "subsequent conduct [by the parties to an instrument] is both relevant and highly persuasive as to what a party's intention was at and leading up to the execution of the instrument in question": *Westland Savings Bank v Hancock* [1987] 2 N.Z.L.R. 21 at 31 per Tipping J.; see too *Gallaher Ltd v Gallaher Pensions Ltd* [2005] Pens. L.R. 43 at [141].

366 *Lake v Lake* [1989] S.T.C. 865.

367 *Thomas Bates & Son Ltd v Wyndham's (Lingerie) Ltd* [1981] 1 All E.R. 1077 at 1086; *Commission for New Towns v Cooper (GB) Ltd* [1995] Ch. 259; *Thor Navigation Inc v Ingosstrakh Insurance Co Ltd* [2005] 1 Lloyd's Rep. 547 at [57]–[62] per Gloster J. A person is not necessarily dishonest for the purposes of this rule simply because he has Nelsonian or naughty knowledge of the other party's mistake: *George Wimpey UK Ltd v VI Construction Ltd* [2005] B.L.R. 135.

368 *The Nai Genova* [1984] 1 Lloyd's Rep. 353 at 359, per Slade L.J.; *KPMG v Network Rail Infrastructure Ltd* [2007] Bus. L.R. 1336. It is not enough that the parties can be shown to have made a common mistake as to the effect of their transaction: it must be shown that they commonly intended to include or exclude something in their document which was not included or excluded: *Frederick Rose (London) Ltd v William Pimm Jr Co Ltd* [1953] 2 Q.B. 450; *Lloyd v Stanbury* [1971] 1 W.L.R. 535 at 543; *James Hay Pension Trustees Ltd v Hird* [2005] EWHC 1093 (Ch) at [113].

369 [2009] 1 A.C. 1101.

370 At paras 17–293 ff.

371 *Re Butlin's ST* [1976] Ch. 251.

372 *Tankel v Tankel* [1999] 1 F.L.R. 676; *Re Smouha Family Trust* [2000] W.T.L.R. 133.

373 [2004] W.T.L.R. 1349.

374 (2007) 50 P.B.L.R. 12 at [17].

17–281 Rectification will not be granted where a bona fide purchaser for value without notice has acquired a proprietary interest under the document.[375] Laches or acquiescence will also bar the claim.[376] In the case of a voluntary settlement the court may refuse to rectify if a trustee, who took office in ignorance of the mistake, has a reasonable objection to rectification.[377]

17–282 Section 20 of the Administration of Justice Act 1982 allows a will to be rectified if the court is satisfied that it fails to carry out the testator's intentions in consequence of a clerical error or a failure to understand his instructions.[378]

WOLFF v WOLFF

Chancery Division [2004] W.T.L.R. 1349, [2004] S.T.C. 1633

17–283 The claimants intended to enter into an inheritance tax saving scheme with the assistance of a solicitor who was not clear as to what he was doing. On June 4, 1997 he had them execute a reversionary lease of their home in favour of their two daughters for 125 years commencing June 4, 2017 at a peppercorn rent. The same day the claimants as settlors by deed purported to assign to trustees the lease (held by their daughters) and £1,000, and declared trusts giving a life interest to their daughters, and the capital to such of the daughters' children as attained 18 in such proportions as the trustee might appoint, but otherwise in equal shares, while then declaring that after 80 years the trust property should be held for the daughters in equal shares (with substitutionary gifts in favour of the daughters' issue then living); there was no power to advance or appoint capital to the daughters. The claimants intended to make a gift of their home to their daughters but only on the basis it did not deprive them of their right to live there free of charge, while the lease did so deprive them from June 2017; and they intended their daughters to have capital or access to it, which was not the case under the trust in any meaningful way (as they were unlikely to survive for 80 years with their children all having died before 18).

17–284 MANN J.: So far as the lease and trust deed are concerned Mr Brownbill, on behalf of the Wolffs, relies on each of what he says is two lines of cases. The first line is said to show that a voluntary settlor can claim to have a settlement set aside if he made it under a mistake as to its effect. That, says Mr Brownbill, applies in this case because the Wolffs made such a mistake in believing, wrongly, that the lease did not affect their right to live in the property for as long as they wished. They also made a relevant mistake in relation to the trust deed, believing that it gave the daughters an interest in capital. The second line of cases is said to entitle a voluntary settlor to have a settlement set aside where there has been an inadequate explanation of the transaction and a lack of understanding of it—it will be set aside unless there is a sufficient level of understanding which brings home its effect, particularly where it is so improvident as to expose the settler to the risk of destitution or something close to it. The Wolffs did not have that understanding or explanation in relation to the effects of the lease on their rights of occupation (and indeed their lack of understanding went further), and in relation to the effect of the trust deed. Although these lines of cases might sound as though they were so close as to be aspects of the same thing, Mr Brownbill submitted they were different and distinct.

17–285 The law on the first line of cases was considered by Millett J. in *Gibbon v Mitchell*.[379] In that case a protected life interest was surrendered by the life tenant, who thereby intended to accelerate the absolute interest of the remainderman. He had not appreciated that the effect of the surrender was in fact to forfeit his life interest and bring into operation the discretionary trusts which followed it. Millett J. set aside the deed under the

[375] *Smith v Jones* [1954] 1 W.L.R. 1089, or nowadays, presumably if an innocent volunteer has changed his position.
[376] *Beale v Kyte* [1907] 1 Ch. 564.
[377] *Re Butlin's ST* [1976] Ch. 251.
[378] *Wordingham v Royal Exchange Trust Co* [1992] Ch. 412; *Pengelly v Pengelly* [2008] Ch. 375.
[379] [1990] 1 W.L.R. 1304.

"much wider equitable jurisdiction to relieve from the consequences of a mistake".[380] Having considered a number of cases (all of which have been shown to me by Mr Brownbill) he concluded:[381]

> "In my judgment, these cases show that, wherever there is a voluntary transaction by which one party intends to confer a bounty on another, the deed will be set aside if the court is satisfied that the disponor did not intend the transaction to have the effect which it did. It will be set aside for mistake whether the mistake is a mistake of law or of fact, so long as the mistake is as to the effect of the transaction itself and not merely as to its consequences or the advantages to be gained by entering into it."

Mr Brownbill seeks to deploy that principle. He says that the Wolffs made a mistake, and it was not merely as to the consequences of the transaction—it was a mistake as to its nature and what it had achieved and therefore as to its effect. They intended a transaction with a lease which left them with a right of occupation, and they got a transaction which was a lease which deprived them of a right of occupation. **17–286**

I confess that originally I had thought that the mistake of the Wolffs (which I have found they made as a matter of fact) was more as to the consequences of their transaction than as to its effect (though that distinction is not always easy to grasp). They intended a lease to their daughters, and they knew that that would give their daughters an interest. The fact that the lease deprived them of their right of possession seemed to me to be more of a "consequence", the words of Millett J. On the facts, depriving them of their actual occupation was not even clearly a necessary consequence, because there is no suggestion that the daughters would evict them or even charge them rent. Were that to happen there would be tax consequences, but that is clearly a "consequence" in Millett J.'s terminology. **17–287**

However, I have been persuaded that my initial reaction was wrong. The Wolffs intended to give away an interest to their daughters, but there were limits to that gift. It was to take effect in the future, but even then it was not to deprive them of the rights of occupation free of charge that they had enjoyed hitherto. In fact and in law the lease deprives them of that right from June 2017. That seems to me to be an effect of the transaction—they have given away more than they intended. The matter can be tested in this way. Suppose that the lease took effect one day after its execution rather than 20 years, but the Wolffs still had the belief that they could continue to live in the property. Those stark facts show more clearly that their mistake was as to the effect of the transaction. In *AMP (UK) Plc v Barker*[382] Lawrence Collins J. observed, in relation to Millett J.'s distinction between effects and consequences: **17–288**

> "If anything, it is simply a formula designed to ensure that the policy involved in equitable relief is effectuated to keep it within reasonable bounds and to ensure that it is not used simply when parties are mistaken about the commercial effects of their transactions or have second thoughts about them. The cases certainly establish that relief may be available if there is a mistake as to law or the legal consequences of an agreement or settlement . . .".

If that is indeed the significance of the distinction, then the mistake of the Wolffs in this case falls on the right side of the line (so far as they are concerned). They made a mistake as to the legal effects of the transaction, and it was a significant one. It is certainly serious enough to give rise to the equity of setting it aside.

In those circumstances the lease falls to be set aside. **17–289**

That conclusion renders a decision on the other points academic. However, I make the following observations on them. **17–290**

So far as Mr Brownbill's alternative line of cases is concerned, I rather doubt if it can now be taken to exist. The jurisdiction seems to me to be based on mistake. One of the high water marks of this alternative line, so far as Mr Brownbill was concerned, was *Philippson v Kerry*,[383] where an elderly lady gave away a material part of her wealth believing that the donee would give her the dividends for the rest of her life. She received no explanation of the consequences of the transaction. On analysis I think that this can be **17–291**

---

[380] At 1307.
[381] At 1309.
[382] [2001] P.L.R. 77 at [70].
[383] (1863) 32 Beav. 628.

treated as a mistake case, and Millett J. certainly treated it as one.[384] Mr Brownbill did cite other cases on the point, but I do not need to deal with them.

17–292 Had it been necessary for me to do so, I would have held that the trust deed fell to be set aside for the same reason as the lease. The Wolffs clearly intended their daughters to have capital or access to it, and the trust deed, whatever else it might did not do that (or at least not in any meaningful way—they might have had capital if they survived for 80 years). However, I do not need to consider this further since the setting aside of the lease will mean that there is no asset in the trust.

CHARTBROOK LTD v PERSIMMON HOMES LTD

House of Lords [2009] 1 A.C. 1101, [2009] Bus. L.R. 1200, [2009] 3 W.L.R. 267, [2010] 1 All E.R. (Comm.) 365

17–293 The claimant landowner and defendant developer entered a contract to develop the claimant's land, under which the defendant agreed to obtain planning permission, construct a mixed residential and commercial development, and sell the properties on long leases. The price payable by the defendant included an "Additional Residential Payment" (ARP) which was defined by a term of the contract, the proper interpretation of which was later disputed by the parties. According to the defendant's interpretation, the term required the defendant to pay around £900,000, but according to the claimant the sum due was around £4,500,000. The claim succeeded at first instance and in Court of Appeal, but on appeal the House of Lords found for the defendant, holding that the defendant's interpretation of the term was the right one, that the lower courts had been wrong to exclude evidence of the parties' pre-contractual negotiations, and that even if the claimant's interpretation of the term had been correct, the defendant would have been entitled to rectification. The portion of Lord Hoffmann's speech that concerns this final point is reproduced below.

17–294 LORD HOFFMANN (with whom LORD HOPE, LORD RODGER, LORD WALKER and BARONESS HALE agreed): The last point is whether, if Chartbrook's interpretation of the agreement had been correct, it should have been rectified to accord with Persimmon's interpretation. The requirements for rectification were succinctly summarized by Peter Gibson L.J. in *Swainland Builders Ltd v Freehold Properties Ltd*:[385]

> "The party seeking rectification must show that: (1) the parties had a common continuing intention, whether or not amounting to an agreement, in respect of a particular matter in the instrument to be rectified; (2) there was an outward expression of accord; (3) the intention continued at the time of the execution of the instrument sought to be rectified; (4) by mistake, the instrument did not reflect that common intention."

17–295 To explain how the claim for rectification arose, I must summarise the relevant pre-contractual exchanges between the parties. They began by discussing a proposal for an outright sale of the land by Chartbrook to Persimmon at a price calculated by reference to such planning permission as Chartbrook might obtain. In early 2001 this structure was abandoned and Persimmon in a letter dated 1 February 2001 proposed the building licence arrangement eventually agreed. The letter included the following passages:

> ". . . we would be prepared to pay you 29.8% of the net sales proceeds generated from the private sale residential element of the scheme and a further 45% of the net sales revenue generated from the disposal of the commercial element of the site. We would pay you this proportion of the income regardless of the development costs incurred by my company and the quantum of accommodation that we ultimately obtain planning permission for. . . . By tying your land value to a percentage of the income, you will also automatically share in any sales uplift that we experience."

[384] See his rationale of it at 1309.
[385] [2002] 2 E.G.L.R. 71 at 74.

This offer of a straightforward sharing of the proceeds was modified in a letter dated 6 February 2001 by the addition of what were described as "guaranteed backstop dates and minimum payments": **17–296**

> "Upon receipt of the purchase monies, the revenue will be apportioned to Chartbrook on the basis of 29.8% of the net revenue achieved from the disposal of the private sale residential units and 45% of the net revenue from the disposal of the commercial units. In addition, we are prepared to provide you with guaranteed backstop dates and minimum payments that will be made regardless of the actual performance of the project both in terms of timescales and costs. I set out on the attached schedule our proposals concerning this element of the deal. Based on the current scheme for 80 units, and 9,020 sq ft of commercial floor space, the minimum land value we are prepared to pay to Chartbrook on the disposal of each residential unit is £67,000, together with a further minimum payment of £400,000 on the disposal of the commercial unit. If as a result of improvements in the market, Chartbrook are entitled to more than the minimum payments I suggest an equalisation calculation takes place following the disposal of the last unit. . . . Within the contract, I . . . suggest that a formula is included whereby the land value is calculated using the following inputs: private sale residential accommodation . . . 94.96/sq ft . . . Once the total land value has been calculated, a simple formula can then be applied to divide the land values by the number of units, in order for us to calculate the guaranteed payments that you will receive on the sale of each plot . . .".

On 12 February there was a further modification to make separate provision for the sales of car parking spaces, but the overall offer for land value remained the same. The judge found[386] that Chartbrook accepted this offer in principle and Persimmon's solicitors were instructed to draft an agreement. Their draft was attached to an email dated 1 March 2001 and contained essentially the same formulae for calculating the price as those in the final agreement. The definition of "additional residential payment" was (save for the percentage figure) in precisely the same words as those of the final agreement. **17–297**

Between March and May Chartbrook acquired some additional adjoining land and Persimmon revised its cost estimates. The result was a change in the figures but not in the formulae. In a letter dated 24 May 2001 Persimmon offered a new total land value of £7,191,947. The letter contained a table setting out: **17–298**

> ". . . the minimum guaranteed land values that you will receive for the respective elements of the scheme, together with the percentage of sales revenue that you will also be entitled to if the project performs better than is currently anticipated."

The figures in the table were 23.4 per cent for "percentage of sales revenue" and £53,333 for "minimum value per plot". The judge found that this offer was also accepted in principle and the new figures were inserted into the final contract. The words of the definition of ARP in the final draft remained (subject to the change in the percentage figure) exactly the same as in the first draft. **17–299**

It is I think clear that a reasonable person who read the February and May letters in the light of the background known to the parties would have taken them to have been intending that Chartbrook should receive an ARP if, but only if, "the project performs better than is currently anticipated". **17–300**

Persimmon's case on rectification at the trial was that the letter of 24 May 2001 was an outward expression of the common and continuing intention of the parties and (if Chartbrook was right about its true construction) the definition had been drafted in the mistaken belief that it gave effect to that common intention. On the other hand, the evidence of the two principals of Chartbrook, Mr Vantreen and Mr Reeve, was that they had made no mistake. The definition accorded exactly with what they had thought they were being offered in the letters of February and May 2001. Indeed, they said they would not have done the deal for any less. It was put to them in cross-examination that no rational person could have understood the letters in the sense which they claimed and Mr Vantreen was caused some little difficulty by the fact that, on his copy of the May 2001 letter, he had calculated the amount which (on Persimmon's construction of the definition) the sale price of a 700 sq ft flat would have to exceed before any ARP became payable (£228,000). This calculation would have been irrelevant on his own construction of the definition and he was unable to explain why he had made it. Nevertheless the judge accepted the evidence of Mr Reeve and Mr Vantreen that they had honestly believed that the definition (as they claimed to have understood it) was **17–301**

[386] [2007] 1 All E.R. (Comm.) 1083 at [110].

what had been agreed and they were not been mistaken. The judge therefore held that the mistake was not common to both parties and dismissed the claim for rectification.

17–302 The case was argued at trial on the assumption that rectification required both parties to be mistaken about whether the written agreement reflected what they believed their prior consensus to have been. In the Court of Appeal, Persimmon challenged the finding of fact about what Mr Reeve and Mr Vantreen had believed, but not the underlying proposition of law. The Court of Appeal unanimously dismissed this part of the appeal on the ground that it could not disturb the findings of fact. There are accordingly concurrent findings of fact about the states of mind of Mr Reeve and Mr Vantreen. Your Lordships indicated at the hearing that in accordance with the usual practice, you would not re-examine them.[387]

17–303 In the printed case, however, Persimmon (encouraged by articles in the Law Quarterly Review by Marcus Smith[388] and Professor McLauchlan[389] asked for leave to challenge, for first time, the proposition of law. Mr Nugee submitted that the judge and the Court of Appeal had been wrong in their assumption about what a party had to be mistaken about. Rectification required a mistake about whether the written instrument correctly reflected the prior consensus, not whether it accorded with what the party in question believed that consensus to have been. In accordance with the general approach of English law, the terms of the prior consensus were what a reasonable observer would have understood them to be and not what one or even both of the parties believed them to be. In the present case, submitted Mr Nugee, the prior consensus was contained in the May letter, which made it clear that the terms were to be as contended for by Persimmon. If the definition in the final agreement did not have that meaning, it was not in accordance with the prior consensus and if Mr Reeve and Mr Vantreen believed that it was, then they, like the representatives of Persimmon, were mistaken.

17–304 Mr Robert Miles QC, for Chartbrook, objected to Persimmon being given leave to advance this argument. He said that if the point had been taken at the trial, the evidence might have taken a different shape. I rather doubt this, but as I understand that the Committee shares my view that Persimmon is entitled to succeed without rectification, the question is academic. Nevertheless, as it has been very well and fully argued, I propose to express an opinion about it.

17–305 Until the decision of the Court of Appeal in *Joscelyne v Nissen*[390] there was a view, based upon dicta in 19th and early 20th century cases, that rectification was available only if there had been a concluded antecedent contract with which the instrument did not conform. In *Lovell & Christmas Ltd v Wall*[391] Cozens-Hardy M.R. said that rectification "may be regarded as a branch of the doctrine of specific performance". It presupposed a prior contract and required proof that, by a common mistake, the final completed agreement as executed failed to give proper effect to the prior contract. In *Joscelyne's case* the Court of Appeal declared itself puzzled by the reference to specific performance, but I think it is clear enough that Cozens-Hardy M.R. had in mind a contractual obligation to execute a lease, conveyance, settlement or similar instrument, giving rise to a specifically enforceable obligation to do so. A failure to execute a document giving effect to the terms of the agreement would be a breach of that obligation and the court, in rectifying the instrument, would be specifically performing the agreement. Since the decision in *Joscelyne's case* extended the availability of rectification to cases in which there had been no enforceable prior agreement, specific performance is plainly an inadequate explanation of the doctrine. But for present purposes the significance of cases like *Lovell & Christmas Ltd v Wall* is that the terms of the contract to which the subsequent instrument must conform must be objectively determined in the same way as any other contract. Thus the common mistake must necessarily be as to whether the instrument conformed to those terms and not to what one or other of the parties believed those terms to have been.

17–306 Now that it has been established that rectification is also available when there was no binding antecedent agreement but the parties had a common continuing intention in respect of a particular matter in the instrument to be rectified, it would be anomalous if the "common continuing intention" were to be an objective fact if it amounted to an enforceable contract but a subjective belief if it did not. On the contrary, the authorities

---

387 See *Smith New Court Securities Ltd v Scrimgeour Vickers (Asset Management) Ltd* [1997] A.C. 254 at 274–275.

388 "Rectification of Contracts for Common Mistake, *Joscelyne v Nissen* and Subjective States of Mind" (2007) 123 L.Q.R. 116.

389 "The 'Drastic' Remedy of Rectification for Unilateral Mistake" (2008) 124 L.Q.R. 608.

390 [1970] 2 Q.B. 86.

391 (1911) 104 L.T. 85 at 88.

suggest that in both cases the question is what an objective observer would have thought the intentions of the parties to be. Perhaps the clearest statement is by Denning L.J. in *Frederick E Rose (London) Ltd v William H Pim Jnr & Co Ltd*:[392]

> "Rectification is concerned with contracts and documents, not with intentions. In order to get rectification it is necessary to show that the parties were in complete agreement on the terms of their contract, but by an error wrote them down wrongly; and in this regard, in order to ascertain the terms of their contract, you do not look into the inner minds of the parties—into their intentions—any more than you do in the formation of any other contract. You look at their outward acts, that is, at what they said or wrote to one another in coming to their agreement, and then compare it with the document which they have signed. If you can predicate with certainty what their contract was, and that it is, by a common mistake, wrongly expressed in the document, then you rectify the document; but nothing less will suffice."

Likewise in *Etablissements Georges et Paul Levy v Adderley Navigation Co Panama SA* Mustill J said:[393] **17–307**

> "The prior transaction may consist either of a concluded agreement or of a continuing common intention. In the latter event, the intention must have been objectively manifested. It is the words and acts of the parties demonstrating their intention, not the inward thoughts of the parties, which matter."

An example of the application of this objective ascertainment of the terms of the prior transaction is **17–308** *George Cohen Sons & Co Ltd v Docks and Inland Waterways Executive*[394] in which a landlord negotiating a new lease proposed to the tenant that "the terms and conditions contained in the present lease to be embodied in the new lease where applicable". The tenant accepted this offer, but the new lease as executed made the tenant liable for repairs which under the old lease had been the responsibility of the landlord. In answer to a claim for rectification, the landlord said that the new lease was in accordance with what he had understood to be the effect of his offer. The Court of Appeal said that this was irrelevant. What mattered was the objective meaning of what the landlord had written. Evershed M.R. said:[395]

> "If the defendants . . . did misconstrue [the letter] that is unfortunate for them, but at least they cannot be heard to say that their letter was intended to mean anything other than that which the words convey to the reader as a piece of ordinary English."

As against these authorities, there are two cases upon which Mr Miles relied. The first is *Britoil Plc v Hunt* **17–309** *Overseas Oil Inc*,[396] in which the Court of Appeal by a majority (Glidewell L.J. and Hobhouse L.J., Hoffmann L.J. dissenting) refused to rectify an agreement which was alleged not to be in accordance with what had previously been agreed in summary heads of agreement. Hobhouse L.J., who gave the majority judgment, affirmed the decision of Saville J., who said that the defendants had failed to establish that there was a prior common agreement or intention in terms that the court could ascertain or (which is probably another way of saying the same thing) that the definitive agreement failed to reflect that prior agreement. In other words, the language of the heads of agreement was too uncertain to satisfy the requirement stated by Denning L.J. in *Rose's case*[397] that one should be able to "predicate with certainty what their contract was". Hobhouse L.J. noted[398] that Saville J. "did not base himself upon any consideration of the evidence as to the actual state of mind of the parties" and in my opinion the case lends no support to the view that a party must be mistaken as to whether the document reflects what he subjectively believes the agreement to have been.

---

392 [1953] 2 Q.B. 450 at 461.
393 [1980] 2 Lloyd's Rep 67 at 72.
394 (1950) 84 Ll. L. Rep 97.
395 At 107.
396 [1994] C.L.C. 561.
397 [1953] 2 Q.B. 450 at 461.
398 At 571.

17–310 The other case is the decision of Laddie J. in *Cambridge Antibody Technology Ltd v Abbott Biotechnology Ltd*,[399] in which he rejected a submission that evidence of the subjective state of mind of one of the parties contained in statements which had not been communicated to the other party ("crossed the line") was inadmissible. In my opinion, Laddie J. was quite right not to exclude such evidence, but that is not inconsistent with an objective approach to what the terms of the prior consensus were. Unless itself a binding contract, the prior consensus is, by definition, not contained in a document which the parties have agreed is to be the sole memorial of their agreement. It may be oral or in writing and, even if the latter, subject to later variation. In such a case, if I may quote what I said in *Carmichael v National Power Plc*:[400]

> "The evidence of a party as to what terms he understood to have been agreed is some evidence tending to show that those terms, in an objective sense, were agreed. Of course the tribunal may reject such evidence and conclude that the party misunderstood the effect of what was being said and done."

17–311 In a case in which the prior consensus was based wholly or in part on oral exchanges or conduct, such evidence may be significant. A party may have had a clear understanding of what was agreed without necessarily being able to remember the precise conversation or action which gave rise to that belief. Evidence of subsequent conduct may also have some evidential value. On the other hand, where the prior consensus is expressed entirely in writing (as in *George Cohen Sons & Co Ltd v Docks and Inland Waterways Executive*) such evidence is likely to carry very little weight. But I do not think that it is inadmissible.

17–312 In this case there was no suggestion that the prior consensus was based on anything other than the May letter. It is agreed that the terms of that letter were accepted by Chartbrook and no one gave evidence of any subsequent discussions which might have suggested an intention to depart from them. It follows that (on the assumption that the judge was right in his construction of the ARP definition) both parties were mistaken in thinking that it reflected their prior consensus and Persimmon was entitled to rectification.

Questions

17–313 1. To what extent do general principles and discretionary factors govern the award of equitable remedies?

17–314 2. Given that the general objective of tort damages is to restore the claimant to his ex ante position, why should it matter whether tortious harm is prevented by way of injunction or compensated by way of damages?

17–315 3. (a) Should specific performance be confined to a secondary remedy available only after damages have been assessed as "inadequate"?
(b) When are damages an "*inadequate* remedy"? Do you agree with the decisions on this point in *Sky Petroleum v VIP* and *Beswick v Beswick*?

17–316 4. Is the decision in *Argyll Stores* best explained as being based upon the objection of "constant supervision", or "severe hardship"?

17–317 5. When might a court refuse to award specific performance or an injunction in an action for tort or breach of contract and instead award equitable damages in lieu? Can equitable damages be awarded to a claimant who has no cause of action at common law?

[399] [2005] F.S.R. 590.
[400] [1999] 1 W.L.R. 2042 at 2050–2051.

INDEX

LEGAL TAXONOMY
FROM SWEET & MAXWELL

This index has been prepared using Sweet and Maxwell's Legal Taxonomy. Main index entries conform to keywords provided by the Legal Taxonomy except where references to specific documents or non-standard terms (denoted by quotation marks) have been included. These keywords provide a means of identifying similar concepts in other Sweet & Maxwell publications and online services to which keywords from the Legal Taxonomy have been applied. Readers may find some minor differences between terms used in the text and those which appear in the index. Suggestions to: sweetandmaxwell.taxonomy@thomson.com